California

Sara Benson

Alexis Averbuck, Amy C Balfour, Andrew Bender,

Alison Bing, Nate Cavalieri, Beth Kohn, John A Vlahides

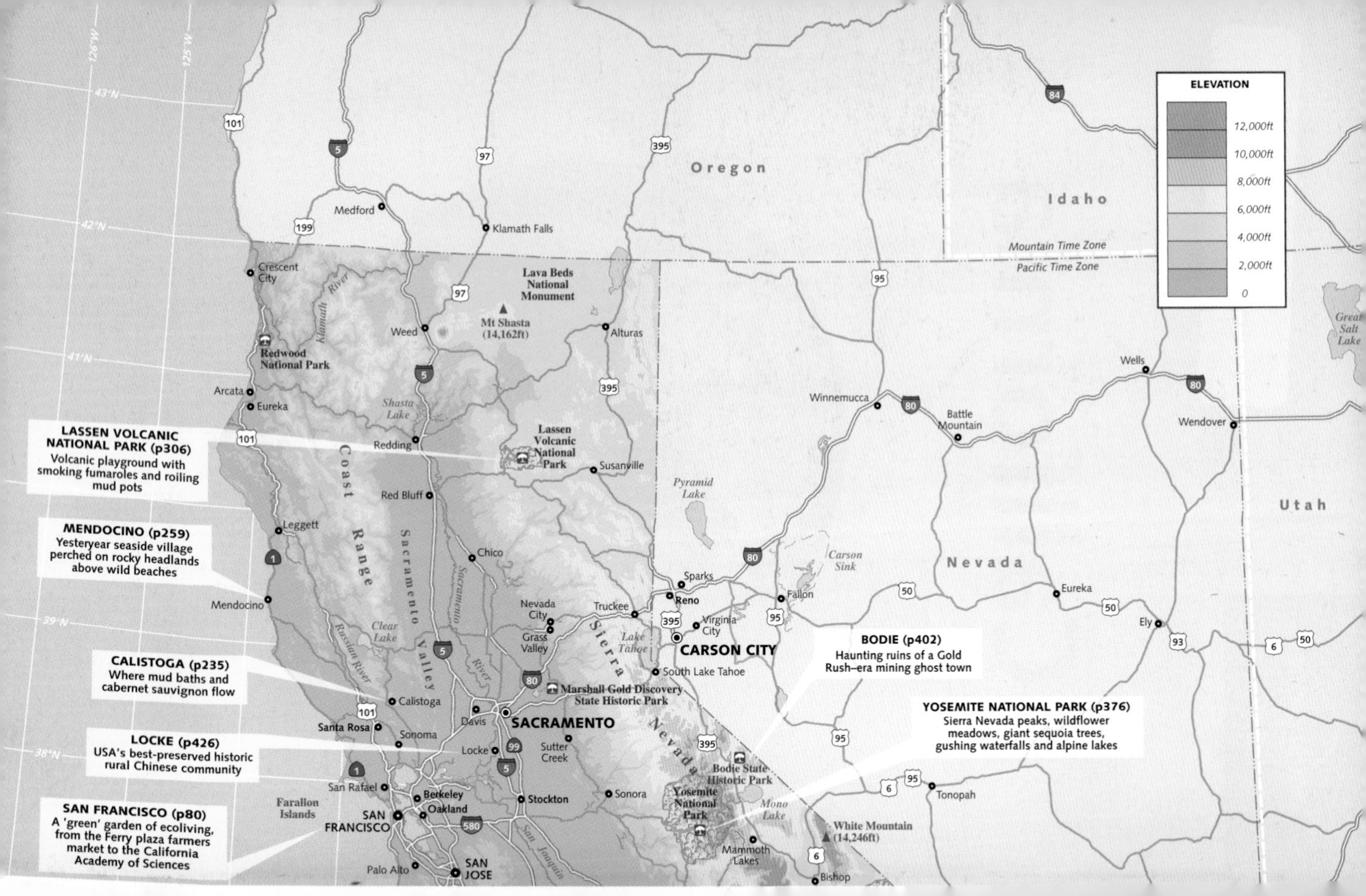

LASSEN VOLCANIC NATIONAL PARK (p306)
Volcanic playground with smoking fumaroles and roiling mud pots
MENDOCINO (p259)
Yesteryear seaside village perched on rocky headlands above wild beaches
CALISTOGA (p235)
Where mud baths and cabernet sauvignon flow
LOCKE (p426)
USA's best-preserved historic rural Chinese community
SAN FRANCISCO (p80)
A 'green' garden of ecoliving, from the Ferry plaza farmers market to the California Academy of Sciences
BODIE (p402)
Haunting ruins of a Gold Rush–era mining ghost town
YOSEMITE NATIONAL PARK (p376)
Sierra Nevada peaks, wildflower meadows, giant sequoia trees, gushing waterfalls and alpine lakes
ELEVATION
12,000ft
10,000ft
8,000ft
6,000ft
4,000ft
2,000ft
0
Oregon
Idaho
Nevada
Utah
Mountain Time Zone
Pacific Time Zone
Great Salt Lake
126°W
125°W
43°N
42°N
41°N
39°N
38°N
Medford
Klamath Falls
Crescent City
Lava Beds National Monument
Mt Shasta (14,162ft)
Weed
Alturas
Redwood National Park
Klamath River
Arcata
Eureka
Shasta Lake
Redding
Lassen Volcanic National Park
Susanville
Coast Range
Red Bluff
Sacramento Valley
Leggett
Chico
Sacramento River
Mendocino
Clear Lake
Russian River
Nevada City
Grass Valley
Truckee
Sierra Nevada
Lake Tahoe
Sparks
Reno
Virginia City
CARSON CITY
South Lake Tahoe
Marshall Gold Discovery State Historic Park
Calistoga
Davis
SACRAMENTO
Santa Rosa
Sonoma
Locke
Sutter Creek
San Rafael
Berkeley
Oakland
Stockton
Sonora
Farallon Islands
SAN FRANCISCO
San Joaquin
Palo Alto
SAN JOSE
Bodie State Historic Park
Yosemite National Park
Mono Lake
Mammoth Lakes
White Mountain (14,246ft)
Bishop
Tonopah
Pyramid Lake
Carson Sink
Fallon
Winnemucca
Battle Mountain
Wells
Wendover
Eureka
Ely
101
5
97
395
199
1
99
580
80
95
50
93
6
84

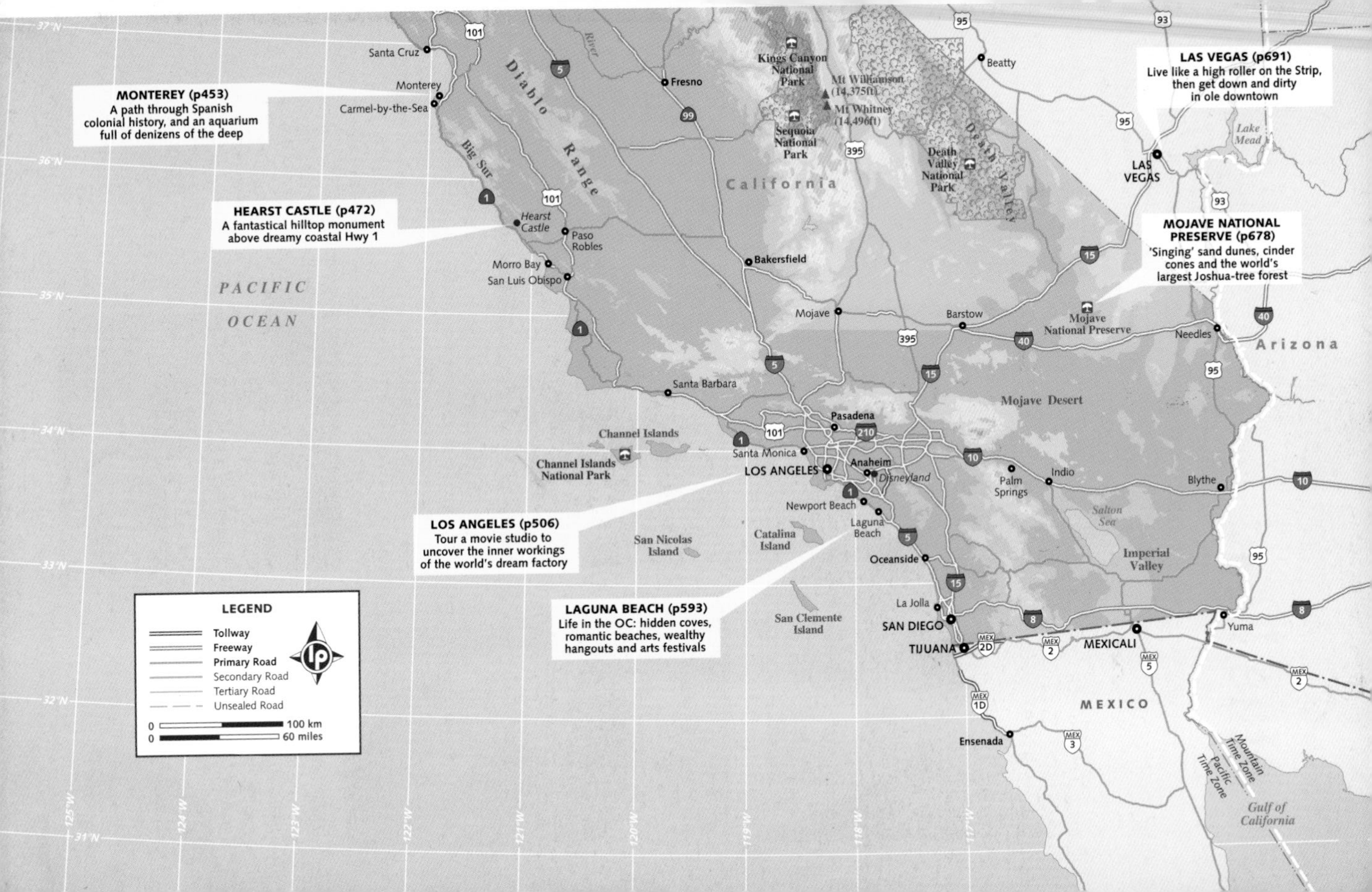
MONTEREY (p453)
A path through Spanish colonial history, and an aquarium full of denizens of the deep
HEARST CASTLE (p472)
A fantastical hilltop monument above dreamy coastal Hwy 1
LOS ANGELES (p506)
Tour a movie studio to uncover the inner workings of the world's dream factory
LAGUNA BEACH (p593)
Life in the OC: hidden coves, romantic beaches, wealthy hangouts and arts festivals
LAS VEGAS (p691)
Live like a high roller on the Strip, then get down and dirty in ole downtown
MOJAVE NATIONAL PRESERVE (p678)
'Singing' sand dunes, cinder cones and the world's largest Joshua-tree forest
LEGEND
Tollway
Freeway
Primary Road
Secondary Road
Tertiary Road
Unsealed Road
0 100 km
0 60 miles
PACIFIC OCEAN
California
Arizona
MEXICO
Santa Cruz
Monterey
Carmel-by-the-Sea
Big Sur
Diablo Range
Hearst Castle
Paso Robles
Morro Bay
San Luis Obispo
Fresno
Bakersfield
Kings Canyon National Park
Sequoia National Park
Mt Williamson (14,375ft)
Mt Whitney (14,496ft)
Death Valley National Park
Death Valley
Beatty
LAS VEGAS
Lake Mead
Mojave
Barstow
Mojave National Preserve
Needles
Mojave Desert
Santa Barbara
Pasadena
Santa Monica
LOS ANGELES
Anaheim
Disneyland
Newport Beach
Laguna Beach
Oceanside
La Jolla
SAN DIEGO
TIJUANA
Palm Springs
Indio
Blythe
Salton Sea
Imperial Valley
MEXICALI
Yuma
Ensenada
Channel Islands
Channel Islands National Park
San Nicolas Island
Catalina Island
San Clemente Island
Mountain Time Zone
Pacific Time Zone
Gulf of California
River
37°N
36°N
35°N
34°N
33°N
32°N
31°N
125°W
124°W
123°W
122°W
121°W
120°W
119°W
118°W
117°W

On the Road

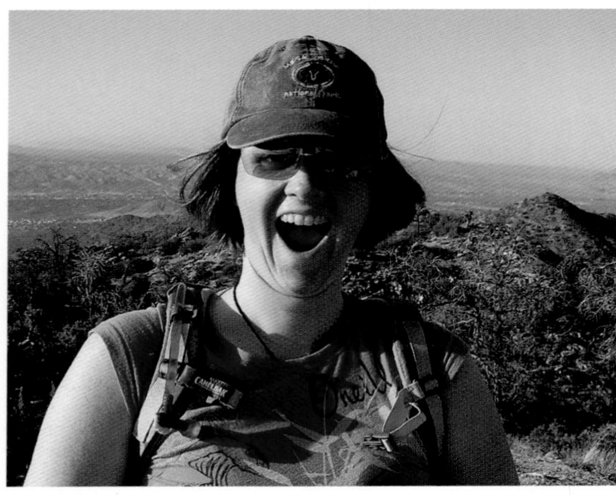

SARA BENSON
Coordinating Author
No matter how many times I head down to the Mojave Desert (p678), there's always another California fan palm oasis to track down, another sandy wash to hike, another Old West mine to explore or, in this case, another rugged, off-the-beaten-path mountain with a summit register to scribble in.

ALEXIS AVERBUCK For me, there's nothing quite like the serenity and power of a redwood forest. The moist carpet of ferns and needles soaks up all the sound and puts off a rich, loamy aroma. Walking in an ancient grove like the Rockefeller Forest (p278), pictured here, always reinforces my appreciation for life.

AMY C BALFOUR Right about now I'm hoping there's not an earthquake. I'm standing in front of an African lion at the Lion Camp at San Diego Zoo Wild Animal Park (p613). From here you can easily hop the Journey into Africa tram or take a safari walk past more big cats.

ANDREW BENDER Keep your eyes peeled in LA and you'll see so much more than Hollywood. Lunch in Thai Town (p554) brings an opportunity to browse bakeries, acupuncturists and dozens of restaurants. I'm amazed that I make new discoveries pretty much whenever I step outside, some in places I've been driving past for years.

Author Tip

Many mountain roads are marked on maps as 'closed in winter', but what that usually means is 'open only in summer'. For example, Tioga Rd in Yosemite National Park usually closes after the first heavy snowfall in October and doesn't reopen until June.

❶ Yosemite National Park

Explore what naturalist John Muir called his 'high pleasure-ground' (p376). Meander through wildflower-strewn meadows and glacier-carved valleys; iconic granite domes beckon to rock climbers. Glacier Point is sublime on full-moon nights.

❷ Sequoia & Kings Canyon National Parks

These twin parks (p391) encapsulate the very best of the Sierra Nevada: granite peaks, alpine meadows and lakes, North America's deepest canyons and shaggy forests of giant sequoias, the biggest trees on earth.

❸ Mammoth Lakes

Head over to the east side of the Sierra Nevada. Join the throngs of winter skiers worshipping Mammoth Mountain (p406), which turns to single-track mountain-biking in summer, or backpack out to blissful wilderness lakes and hot springs.

❹ Mt Whitney

At an elevation of 14,496ft, the highest mountain in the USA outside of Alaska issues a siren's call to climbers and backpackers, making this California's most sought-after peak. Enter the permit lottery (p415), then cross your fingers.

❺ Lassen Volcanic National Park

In the shadow of the Sierra Nevada, this park (p306) anchors the southern end of the Cascades with an alien lavascape of roiling mud pots, noxious sulfur vents, steamy fumaroles, colorful cinder cones and reflective crater lakes.

❻ Mt Shasta

Nowhere in California will you find a mountain as sacred as this almost symmetrical volcanic peak (p313), which, over the centuries since it last erupted, has brought together Native Americans, new-agey spiritualists, accomplished alpinists, poets and painters.

Wine Countries

No matter where you go in California, vineyards never seem far away. World-beating wines are waiting to be tasted, alongside all the other sundry regional pleasures, such as an afternoon cycling country roads, past biodynamic farms and ranches that supply risk-taking restaurants.

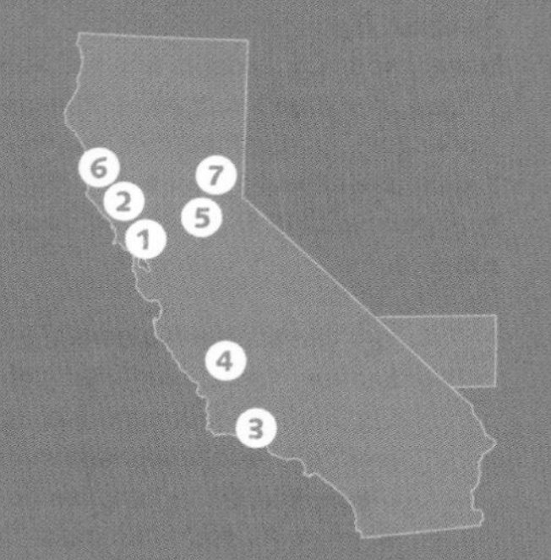

Author Tip

Call ahead to visit smaller, family-run wineries, whose tasting rooms are open by appointment only. No expertise is required – just bring an open mind, a whetted palate and lots of questions to ask once you've shaken the winemaker's hand.

1 Napa & Sonoma Valleys

California's premier wine-growing region (p194) may have grown too big for its britches, but you can still unearth the uniqueness of *terroir*, where sun-dappled vineyards are surrounded by pastoral ranchlands.

2 Russian River Valley

Amid the apple orchards of western Sonoma County, this tranquil valley (p208) with its cool coastal fog is famed for delicate pinot noir. Go antiquing in Sebastopol (p211), then paddle a canoe along the river near Guerneville (p216).

3 Santa Ynez & Santa Maria Valleys

In the limelight since the 2004 movie *Sideways*, Santa Barbara's wine country (p492) has hit the big time. Rural routes like the Foxen Canyon Wine Trail connect small wineries for connoisseurs and novices alike.

4 Paso Robles

Almost every back road off Hwy 46 in Paso Robles (p482), an unsung hero of California winemaking, hides family-run estate vineyards bottling cabernet sauvignon, zinfandel and syrah. Farther south, the Edna Valley crafts exquisite chardonnay.

5 Lodi

Sacramento River delta breezes cool the hot-as-hell vineyards of Lodi (p434), where more zinfandel grapes are grown than anywhere else in the world. Characterful old vines have often been tended by the same family for over a century.

6 Mendocino County

It's a memorably winding drive into the Anderson Valley (p270), which is known for its delicate Alsatian-style whites, sparkling wines and pinot noir, thanks to sun-drenched days and coastal fog that drifts over the vineyards at night.

7 Amador County

Sip without a whiff of pretension in the heart of California's Gold Country (p341), where the old-vine zins have a lot in common with the hypnotic landscape – bold and richly colored, earthy and surprising.

The Cities

A mosaic of Old and New Worlds, California's cities altogether have more flavors than a jar of jellybeans. Start from San Francisco, equal parts earth mother and geek chic, or Los Angeles, where nearly 90 independent cities are all rolled into one, then drift down to SoCal's blond, botoxed enclaves or across the San Francisco Bay to radical, hippie-dippie Berkeley.

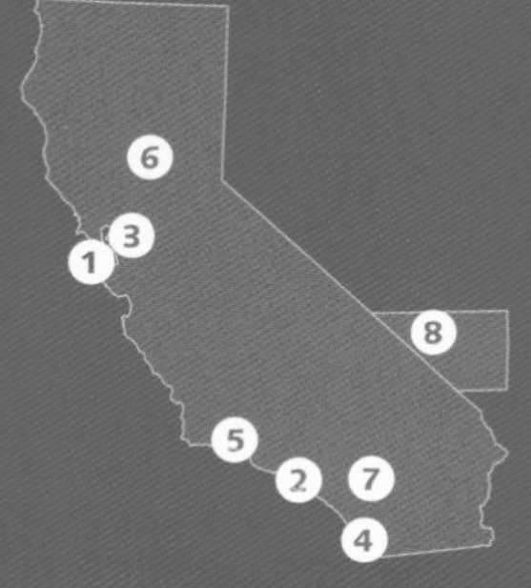

Author Tip

California's biggest cities are not as public-transportation friendly as they could be, but you can reach almost all of them via train. Amtrak's *Coast Starlight* and *Pacific Surfliner* are stunningly beautiful coastal routes, sometimes passing through scenic spots that are otherwise off-limits to the public.

❶ San Francisco
Uncover what makes California so characterful in Fog City (p80), where DIY self-expression and hedonism don't require any sacrifice from the ecoconscious. There's a fertile garden of green tourism experiences here, especially for outdoors lovers and foodies.

❷ Los Angeles
There's more to life in La La Land (p506) than just sunny beaches and air-kissing celebs. Get a dose of culture downtown, then dive into LA's diverse neighborhoods, from historic Little Tokyo to nouveau-hipster haunts in a recently revitalized Hollywood.

❸ Berkeley
Think all the California hippies have died and gone to...well, nirvana? Guess again. Berkeley's radical 1960s roots are evident wherever you look (p169), with progressive politics, social justice and locavorian food for all.

❹ San Diego
Thanks to the nearly perfect year-round climate of San Diego (p600), residents of this southernmost city always seem to take it easy – and who can blame them? Take a permanent vacation in San Diego's laid-back beach towns.

❺ Santa Barbara
Nicknamed the 'American Riviera', this posh Mediterranean-styled city (p495) has a distinctive white-stucco, red-tile-roofed downtown district (rebuilt after a 1925 earthquake), where a promenade of shops and restaurants leads down to a maritime wharf.

❻ Sacramento
California's state capital (p418) doesn't excite like the coastal cities do, but it's an unbeatable place to start digging up California's roots, from pioneer-era gold mines to farming communities spread out across the river delta and the central valleys.

❼ Palm Springs
More of a desert resort playground than a city, this Mid-Century Modern architectural mecca (p649) has seen a rebirth of Rat Pack–era cool. Down swinging '60s cocktails while lounging poolside outside your own private deluxe bungalow. Ah, heaven.

❽ Las Vegas, NV
So many Californians head to Sin City (p692) for long (and often dirty) weekends that it almost feels like a suburb of LA. Doll up for the glitz and glamour of the Strip, then roll downtown into vintage Vegas.

Road Trips

California is the third-largest state in the USA, and you could easily spend weeks navigating its blue highways and rural byways, safely distant from the nerve-jangling, always-jammed interstate system. These classic road-tripping routes are soaked in enough epic scenery to make each deliciously slow, winding mile of your detour worthwhile.

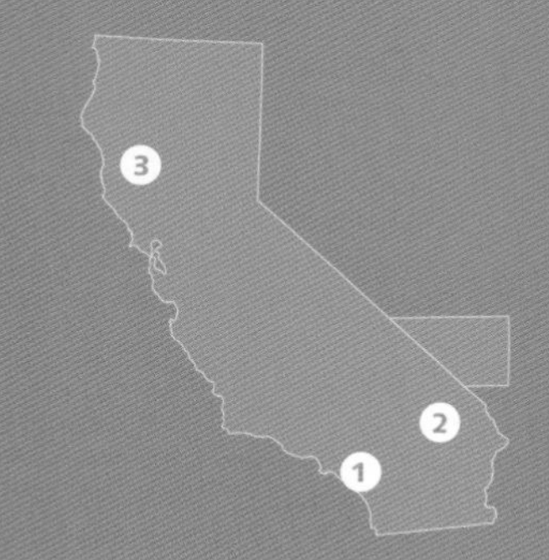

Author Tip

An essential road-trip companion is the *California Road & Recreation Atlas* (Benchmark Press), which answers the perennial question, 'What's over there?'. With a 4WD vehicle, it'll take you off-road and help you get unstuck from highway traffic jams courtesy of locals-only back roads.

❶ Pacific Coast Highway

Although CA Hwy 1 runs almost the entire length of the state, it's the official 'PCH' stretch from Orange County (p587) north into LA past Santa Monica and Malibu that gets raves for its oceanfront views.

❷ Route 66

Get your kicks on America's 'Mother Road' (p675), which brought Dust Bowl refugees, Hollywood starlets and hippies to California. Pull up alongside retro relics, sleep at vintage motor lodges and stuff yourself silly at mom-and-pop diners.

❸ Avenue of the Giants

Even before Hwy 101 reaches the Redwood Coast proper, this 32-mile, two-lane byway (p278) passes right by some of the tallest trees on earth. Go in the morning, when sunlight glints off dew-laden ferns.

Contents

Regional Map Contents

NORTHERN MOUNTAINS (p301)
NORTH COAST (p251)
WINE COUNTRY (p196)
GOLD COUNTRY (p331)
SAN FRANCISCO (pp86-7)
SIERRA NEVADA (p352)
SAN FRANCISCO BAY AREA (p145)
CENTRAL VALLEY (p419)
LAS VEGAS (p709)
CENTRAL COAST (p445)
THE DESERTS (p650)
ORANGE COUNTY (p578)
LOS ANGELES (pp510-11)
SAN DIEGO AREA (p600)

Destination California

The moment you arrive in the Golden State, you may suspect you've been cast as the ingenue in a road-trip movie. Everything seems staged for a script riddled with exclamation points: no way are they going to surf those skyscraper-sized waves at Mavericks! That can't be the Terminator in the governor's mansion – *in his second term*! Brrrrrrr...don't all those naked people ever get cold?!

The dialogue is all improvised, though you'll note some recurring themes. Recently the hot topic has been same-sex marriage, and the proposed constitutional amendment to ban it and annul the marriages legally performed in California since June 2008. Medical marijuana is old news for Californians, who approved a state proposition allowing its use back in 1996 – though the proliferation of marijuana clubs in urban areas and rumors of mafia intervention have raised even California eyebrows lately.

Even if you've seen it on TV, California still comes as a shock to the system. The Venice Beach skateboarders, San Francisco same-sex-wedding planners, Santa Cruz wild-mushroom hunters, Rodeo Dr–pillaging trophy wives and cheerful San Diego doomsday cult members aren't on different channels. They live here.

To strike up conversation with a local, skip the weather and start in on the food. If you say, 'Nice weather we've been having,' you'll get a puzzled look: of course it's nice, it's *California*. But ask, 'So where's a good place for a taco around here?' and now you're talking. Mulling over menus means taking a stand on issues close to many California hearts: organics, veganism, grass-fed versus grain-fed, biodynamics, fair-trade coffee, and the importance of buying local food (the *New Oxford American Dictionary*–approved term 'locavore,' meaning people who eat food grown nearby, was invented here). Californians will listen with interest to your perspective, even if they do tend to proselytize about their own – but once you try the food, you'll understand the obsession.

Unless you want to stir up old NorCal/SoCal rivalries dating from the 19th century – a diverting local pastime when played with good sports – don't get Californians started about water. NorCal scolds SoCal for watering its lawns and filling its pools with water piped in from the Sierras, while SoCal points out that NorCal shouldn't talk with its mouth full of organic veggies grown in the Sierras-irrigated Central Valley.

You might not get a word in edgewise when it comes to technology or the environment – but listen up, because those wild California ideas might become the next big thing. California's technological innovations need no introduction: perhaps you've heard of PCs, iPods, Google and the internet?

European and Japanese visitors may find it a bit rich to hear Americans holding forth on global warming and the need for emissions reductions, since the US is a holdout on international conventions on these issues. To be fair, Californians helped start the conservation movement in the midst of the 19th-century industrial revolution, with environmental action groups, laws curbing industrial dumping, swaths of prime real estate set aside as urban green space, and pristine wilderness preserved as national and state parks. While California's culture of conspicuous consumption (à la *Lifestyles of the Rich and Famous*) is exported via TV and movies, California's environmentalists have diligently chipped away at the glossy varnish Stateside. Since the 1960s, Californians have trailblazed with sustainable

FAST FACTS

Population: 36.5 million (the largest of any US state)

Highest point: Mt Whitney (14,497ft)

Lowest point: Death Valley (-282ft)

Area of national and state parks: 5.4 million acres

Tallest waves ever surfed in California: 100ft, at Mavericks, 2003

Miles of shoreline with guaranteed public access: 1100

Number of nude and clothing-optional beaches: 50

Annual tax earned from medical marijuana sales: $100 million

Proportion of US GDP contributed by California: 67% ($1.7 trillion)

foods and low-impact lifestyles, pushed for the establishment of the Environmental Protection Agency, preserved old-growth forests with tree-sitting activism, and established the US market for hybrid vehicles (no small thing here in the USA's quintessential car culture).

Once you get the hang of California's improvised lifestyle, you'll notice that plot devices aren't necessary to get Californians to act out. On the contrary, movies can't begin to capture how Californians behave when there are no cameras on. The Sierra Nevada Gold Rush, San Francisco's Summer of Love, the LA punk scene, Silicon Valley high-tech booms: no screenwriter could make this stuff up, no matter how talented. Like any Hollywood blockbuster based on a great work of fiction, movies about California can't compare to the original. But don't just sit back and enjoy the show – California is the place to take part and make a scene. Other places on the planet have their wow factor, but there's only one region that so consistently merits the delighted disbelief of a long, drawn-out 'Duuuuuuuuuuuuuuude!'

Getting Started

California is huge – in the USA, only Texas and Alaska are bigger states – and it takes time to get around. You can ride trains or buses between major cities and certain towns, but you'll need a car to reach more remote areas, including many state and national parks. Reservations are essential during peak travel seasons, especially during the summer months and around major holidays. But don't let a lack of advance planning stop you from hitting the road any time, because spontaneity and an anything-goes casual lifestyle are what California is really all about.

WHEN TO GO

Any time of year is a fantastic time to be traveling somewhere in California, but the ideal time for you to visit depends on where you're going and what you want to do.

See Climate Charts (p714) for more information.

Most travelers arrive in summer, between Memorial Day in late May and Labor Day in early September, crowding major tourist attractions and causing room rates to spike, even at motels. Summer is prime time for hitting the beaches and also the best time of year to visit the mountains for camping, hiking and mountain-biking. From June to August, festivals happen statewide. If you decide to visit California in summer, try to travel midweek, when crowds are thinnest and rates cheaper. The shoulder seasons (March to May, September and October) bring smaller crowds and lower prices.

Along the coast, expect summer fog and chilly weather anywhere north of Los Angeles. In spring and fall, that persistent 'June gloom' clears along much of the coast, revealing the panoramic ocean vistas you've seen in Hollywood movies. In fall it can be warm enough to swim in the Pacific Ocean, at least in Southern California (SoCal).

Unless you're planning a beach vacation, winter (November to February) is an interesting time to visit. The mountains turn into a winter wonderland, drawing skiers and snowboarders to the slopes, and whale-watching is fantastic. Chances of rain are greatest in the winter months, but they're still pretty slim unless you're traveling in Northern California (NorCal).

In spring (from February to April), SoCal deserts are carpeted with wildflowers – if recent rains have been plentiful. Fall is another beautifully temperate time for desert travel. In winter, overnight lows can dip below freezing and snow-covered Joshua trees are not unheard of. Summer is not ideal for venturing into the deserts, where the mercury can soar above 120°F, although low lodging prices and sparse crowds are enticing, mostly to heat-seeking masochists.

For year-round festivals and special events, see p717. For holidays, see p718.

COSTS & MONEY

California is not a bargain travel destination. The easiest way to get around is by car. Rental-car rates start at $125 per week; insurance costs extra. Gasoline (under $3 per gallon at press time) is even more expensive during summer, from Memorial Day to Labor Day, and in remote places such as Big Sur and the SoCal deserts – as much as a dollar more per gallon than in metropolitan areas. For more advice on getting around, including via public transportation, see p731.

Like fuel, lodging costs peak between late May and early September. Cheap motel rooms start at $50, while midrange hotels and B&Bs charge from $125 to $225 per room. The sky's the limit at top-end resorts, where 'basic' rooms can start at over $400. Throughout this book, we've quoted peak-season prices for accommodations; you can expect discounts of up to 50% during the low season. To save more money, avoid the coast and stay near major freeways. See p711 for information about lodgings.

You can lower your budget by buying take-out food instead of sitting down to eat. For more substantial restaurant meals, lunch is always cheaper than dinner. A two-course meal without drinks in an average restaurant costs between $20 and $30, plus tax and a tip (see p717). For more tipping and sales tax advice, see p721.

HOW MUCH?

Local phone call 35-50¢

Iced latte with soy milk $3.50

Pack of cigarettes $5

Movie ticket $11

One-star motel room $50-125

For mere survival, you probably won't be able to spend less than $75 per day – this means sleeping in hostels, riding buses, preparing your own meals or eating snacks and takeout, and limiting your entertainment. Renting a car, staying at motels and hotels, eating out twice a day, spending money on sightseeing and activities, and going to bars or clubs will cost at least $150 per day, if you split costs with a travel partner.

Families can save by booking accommodations that don't charge extra for children staying in the same room as their parents, by asking for children's menus at restaurants and by taking advantage of discounts for children at museums, theme parks and other sights. For more on traveling with children, see p714. For discount cards that everyone can use, see p716.

For more everyday prices, see the Index inside the front cover.

INTERNET RESOURCES

California State Parks (www.parks.ca.gov) Indispensable site for history, descriptions and outdoor activity information for all state parks.

California Tourism (www.visitcalifornia.com) Links to all visitors centers throughout the state and free travel e-guides in nine languages.

Caltrans (www.dot.ca.gov) Packed with highway information, route planning, map assistance, and highway and weather conditions.

Lonelyplanet.com (www.lonelyplanet.com) Travel news and summaries, the Thorn Tree travel forum and links to other web resources.

Los Angeles Times (http://travel.latimes.com) This newspaper travel site is 'taking Southern California on vacation' – and often the rest of the state, too.

Theme Park Insider (www.themeparkinsider.com) Breaking news and user reviews of rides and attractions at major theme parks in California.

DON'T LEAVE HOME WITHOUT...

- checking the latest passport and visa requirements (p719)
- valid travel and health insurance (p719)
- up-to-date vaccinations (p739)
- hotel, motel, B&B, hostel and camping reservations, especially in summer (p711)
- nerves of steel for driving on the freeways, especially around San Diego, LA and the San Francisco Bay Area (p736)
- reservations for child safety seats in rental cars (p714)
- spare batteries and memory cards for your digital camera (p723)
- a waterproof layer (lightweight Gore-Tex jacket, rain pants, water-resistant shoes) for all-weather outdoor adventures
- chic clothes and fashionable shoes (not sneakers) for hitting big-city clubs, shows and hot chefs' restaurants

LOOK MA, NO WIRES

These websites provide wi-fi hotspot lists (both free and for a fee) in California, and also provide helpful advice and links to gear:

www.hotspot-locations.com
www.wi-fi.com Run by the nonprofit Wi-Fi Alliance.
www.wififreespot.com
www.wi-fihotspotlist.com

TRAVELING RESPONSIBLY

Water has always been at the heart of the conflict between agricultural, urban and environmental interests in California, which is no stranger to drought. Tourism development contributes to perennial water shortages, but some hotels have taken steps to reduce water waste, including installing low-flush toilets and encouraging guests to request that their bedsheets and towels are not changed daily. A few hotels have done away with toiletries in plastic bottles, hanging bulk dispensers in bathrooms instead.

For more-sustainable travel options, including ecofriendly hotels, lodges and inns, see our GreenDex (p766), which lists environmentally, socially and culturally responsible places that travelers can support. Our GreenDex also includes restaurants that serve seasonal, organic produce and are committed to sourcing their food from local vendors, a trend that has caught on across the state. If you're cooking for yourself, there are farmers markets in many cities and even rural towns.

Another way that you can reduce your carbon footprint while you travel, and at the same time help fight California's air pollution problems, is to use public transportation to get around the state, rather than driving or flying everywhere. Amtrak's *Coast Starlight* and *Pacific Surfliner* routes (p738) reward carbon-conscious travelers with epic scenery. Although riding Greyhound buses (p732) lacks the romance of the rails, you'll definitely meet a diverse cross-section of Californians who will give you insight into the real 'state of the state,' something drivers cocooned inside their cars don't get. Cities sometimes offer car-free tourism incentives, as in Santa Barbara (go to www.santabarbaracarfree.org).

While hitchhiking (p737) is risky, ride-sharing using online bulletin boards like **Craigslist** (www.craigslist.org) is not uncommon. Craigslist also has listings for vacation rentals and housing sublets, short-term jobs, community activities and fee-free classified ads for anything you might want to buy, sell or barter during your trip, whether that's a surfboard, a pair of skis or a used car.

For volunteering opportunities, see p724.

TRAVEL LITERATURE

The passionate writings of naturalist John Muir (1838–1914) provide reading material for half a lifetime. Dip into his canon with *The Wild Muir: 22 of John Muir's Greatest Adventures*, compiled by Lee Stetson, with rustic woodcut illustrations by Fiona King.

In *Where I Was From*, Joan Didion's ruminations on California shatter palm-fringed fantasies as she skewers the rancidly rich, their violence and shallowness while describing her pioneering family's history on this warped shore.

Bill Barich's *Big Dreams: Into the Heart of California* amusingly narrates an ultimately heartbreaking trip from the Oregon border down Mexico way, searching for the elusive American Dream that so many California immigrants fail to find.

TOP 10

San Francisco
CALIFORNIA
Los Angeles

BIG ADVENTURES

For more outdoor adventures, see p67.

1. Hang with the dawn patrol at Malibu's Surfrider Beach (p544)
2. Battle thin air on your way to the rooftop of Mt Whitney (p415)
3. Scream your head off while rafting the ferocious American River (p338)
4. Dangle in the rock-climbing mecca of Joshua Tree National Park (p665)
5. Go spelunking inside the mysterious lava-tube caves of Lava Beds National Monument (p322)
6. Scale the heart-stopping cables up Yosemite's Half Dome (p383)
7. Paddle a kayak into 'The Big Blue' at Lake Tahoe (p351)
8. Party like a rock star and put your paycheck on the poker table in Las Vegas (p691)
9. Get your retro Americana kicks on Route 66 (p675)
10. Brave the sensory onslaught (and potent margaritas) on Avenida Revolución in Tijuana (p641)

FAMILY FUN

For more tips on traveling with kids, see p714.

1. Crawl through the pitch-dark Tactile Dome at San Francisco's fun science-minded Exploratorium (p105)
2. Meet denizens of the deep and touch tide-pool critters at Monterey Bay Aquarium (p455)
3. Take a spin on a 1908 carousel or solar-powered Ferris wheel at Santa Monica Pier (p537)
4. Devour funnel cake and pet livestock at the California State Fair (p422)
5. Hold tight during a virtual earthquake at the OC's Discovery Science Center (p586)
6. Ride a giant wooden rollercoaster and a narrow-gauge steam train through the redwoods around Santa Cruz (p444)
7. Play croquet and chase chickens and cats around the barnyard at Frog's Leap winery (p227)
8. Earn a junior ranger badge in Sequoia National Park's Giant Forest at the Beetle Rock Education Center (p396)
9. Gaze into the heavens at Oakland's Chabot Space & Science Center (p165)
10. Relive the Old West at Drakesbad Guest Ranch (p308)

ESCAPING CROWDS

Save your sanity, even during peak travel times, at these often overlooked spots. For more advice on when to visit California, see p23.

1. Channel Islands National Park (p504)
2. Tall Trees Grove (Redwood National Park, p294)
3. Mineral King (Sequoia National Park, p397)
4. Glen Ellen (Wine Country, p206)
5. Panamint Springs (Death Valley National Park, p684)
6. Angel Island (San Francisco Bay Area, p152)
7. Seal Beach (Orange County, p587)
8. Sacramento River Delta (p426)
9. Medicine Lake and Little Glass Mountain (Modoc National Forest, p324)
10. Mojave National Preserve (p678)

Another Beat Generation rabble-rouser, Gary Snyder paid tribute to the same glorious mountains in his collection *Riprap and Cold Mountain Poems*, written after he spent a summer building trails in Yosemite National Park.

John Steinbeck's *East of Eden* is a mid-20th-century novel about the triumphs and tragedies of immigrant families in the Salinas Valley of central California. The landscape he describes in this epic intergenerational tale is instantly recognizable today.

By the author of the Pulitzer Prize–winning *Cadillac Desert: The American West and Its Disappearing Water,* Marc Reisner's *A Dangerous Place: California's Unsettling Fate* is a fictionalized nightmare vision of California's impending 'big one' (earthquake).

The White Heart of Mojave: An Adventure with the Outdoors of the Desert, by Edna Brush Perkins, is a timeless travelogue of two adventurous suffragettes' life-changing journey into Death Valley in the 1920s.

Itineraries

CLASSIC ROUTES

THE GRAND TOUR — Three to Four Weeks/Los Angeles to Santa Barbara

Kick off your adventure in **Los Angeles** (p506), with its legendary beaches, incredibly diverse neighborhoods and a hot cuisine scene. Pound the pavement in a vibrantly revitalized Hollywood; go museum-hopping downtown, in the Mid-City or suburban Pasadena; then kick back in chic Santa Monica, crazy-funky Venice or the surfer-friendly South Bay beach towns.

Following a couple of metro-intense days, exchange LA's concrete jungle for **Sequoia and Kings Canyon National Parks** (p391) to gaze in awe up at the world's biggest trees and down at a gorge deeper than the Grand Canyon. Nothing can prepare you for off-the-charts **Yosemite National Park** (p376) either: thunderous waterfalls, eroded granite monoliths, alpine lakes and wildflower meadows.

Head west on Hwy 120, then wind north along Hwy 49 through the heart of the mother lode, where the spirit of the Gold Rush still pervades Old West mining towns like **Sonora** (p347), **Placerville** (p347) and **Nevada City** (p333). A short drive east is **Lake Tahoe** (p351), a deep-blue jewel cradled by jutting peaks crisscrossed with rugged hiking trails and the slopes of world-famous ski resorts. Veer north on US Hwy 395, stopping in **Reno** (p371) for a little

Passing right alongside the spirit-lifting coast, vivacious cities, awe-inspiring mountains and ancient forests, this epic 2050-mile loop route can be done in three weeks. Add one (or even two) more weeks for a more satisfying five-senses immersion in the Golden State.

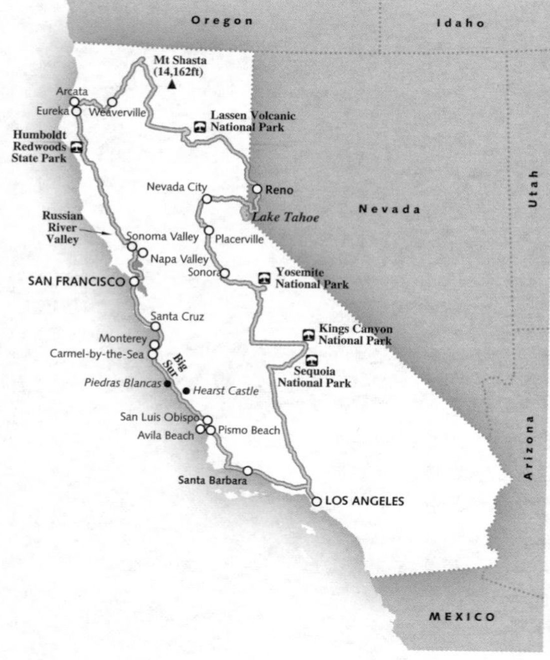

casino gambling, then cut west to unearthly **Lassen Volcanic National Park** (p306), a hellishly beautiful world of odiferous fumaroles and steamy mud pots.

Head north on I-5 to **Mt Shasta** (p313), which you'll spot piercing the sky from afar. Pay your respects to this majestic mountain, then detour onto Hwy 3 for the long but supremely scenic journey south through the lake-studded Trinity Alps to Gold Rush–era **Weaverville** (p325), with its famous Chinese temple. Continue west on Hwy 299 toward the Pacific Ocean, where harborfront **Eureka** (p284), with its candy-colored Victorian buildings, and its more funky, radical northern neighbor, **Arcata** (p287), unlock the secrets of the Redwood Coast.

Work your way south through fragrant **Humboldt Redwoods State Park** (p278) to encounter the tallest trees on earth while hiking fern-fringed trails or driving along the 'Avenue of the Giants.' Follow Hwy 101 south to California's best-known wine country. The most famous grapes grow in the **Russian River Valley** (p207), **Sonoma Valley** (p197) and **Napa Valley** (p224).

After all this rural meandering, get a dose of big-city culture by crossing the Golden Gate Bridge into **San Francisco** (p80), sitting proudly on its often foggy bay. Peek into the mural-filled alleyways of Chinatown and the Mission District, bite into inspiring nouveau California cuisine at the waterfront Ferry Building, then hop on a boat over to infamous Alcatraz prison, aka 'the Rock.'

South of San Francisco, Hwy 1 traces a beautiful stretch of coast. Stop at wacky **Santa Cruz** (p444) and historic **Monterey** (p453) before reaching pint-sized **Carmel-by-the-Sea** (p462), the gateway to beguiling **Big Sur** (p465), whose timeless charms have inspired generations of poets and painters. Take your sweet time driving south, stopping to meet the elephant-seal colony at **Piedras Blancas** (p471) and tour hilltop **Hearst Castle** (p472). Then stroll the streets of laid-back, student-friendly **San Luis Obispo** (p484) and the old-fashioned piers of **Avila Beach** (p488) and **Pismo Beach** (p490), where you can feast on fresh seafood.

Posh **Santa Barbara** (p495), with its symphony of red-tile roofs, is your final stop before arriving back in LA.

PACIFIC COASTIN'

Two Weeks/ San Diego to Del Norte Coast Redwoods State Park

Start your easy, breezy coastal tour in **San Diego** (p599), where the views from Coronado Island and Point Loma will capture your attention. Heading north, detour briefly inland to **Mission San Juan Capistrano** (p597) before cruising through arty **Laguna Beach** (p593) and **Huntington Beach** (p587), aka 'Surf City USA.' Swoop down on **Los Angeles** (p506) for a spot of stargazing and cosmopolitan style.

North of LA, **Ventura** (p505) is a jumping-off point for adventures in **Channel Islands National Park** (p504), while **Santa Barbara** (p495) is the gateway to the Santa Ynez and Santa Maria Valleys' wine country. North of retro **Pismo Beach** (p490) and the college town of **San Luis Obispo** (p484), pick up Hwy 1, passing laid-back little beach towns like **Morro Bay** (p477) and **Cayucos** (p475), as well as **Hearst Castle** (p472), on the way up to soul-stirring **Big Sur** (p465). Further north is bohemian and countercultural **San Francisco** (p80).

North of the Golden Gate Bridge, the Pacific coast turns increasingly raw and untamed as Hwy 1 skirts rocky shores, secluded coves and wind-tossed beaches. The lonely stretch between **Jenner** (p254) and Victorian-era **Mendocino** (p259) is especially scenic; don't miss climbing to the top of the **Point Arena Lighthouse** (p256). **Fort Bragg** (p263) is worth a stop for a ride on the vintage Skunk Train.

Hwy 1 then hooks inland, merging in Leggett with Hwy 101, which passes by turnoffs for the remote **Lost Coast** (p280). Welcome to the Redwood Coast, protected by a string of state and national parks, including **Humboldt Redwoods State Park** (p278), **Redwood National Park** (p292), **Prairie Creek Redwoods State Park** (p294) and **Del Norte Coast Redwoods State Park** (p295), almost up to the Oregon border.

A ride along California's coast reveals eye candy at every bend in the road. Take your time as you travel along this 1000-mile roller coaster of urban and natural delights – its true charms are better savored.

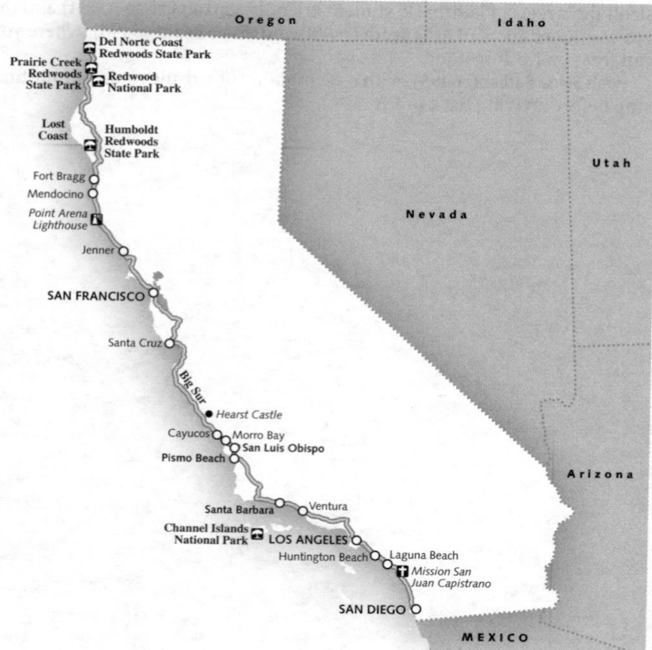

DESERT DAYS & NIGHTS

One Week to 10 Days/ Palm Springs to Death Valley National Park

Start your desert road trip in chic-again **Palm Springs** (p649), the retro-hip celeb hangout where the Rat Pack, Elvis and Marilyn Monroe once frolicked. It's a masterpiece of Mid-Century Modern architecture. Sip mojitos poolside, hike to palm-studded canyons, then ride a revolving tram up into the cool pine-scented mountains, all in one day.

When you've tired of the scene, dahling, drive through the Coachella Valley past the date farms of **Indio** (p659), along the shores of the miragelike **Salton Sea** (p668), then turn west into wild **Anza-Borrego Desert State Park** (p669), the largest US state park outside of Alaska. Observe bighorn sheep at spring-fed watering holes, then follow dirt roads past elephant trees, wind-sculpted caves, Native American pictographs and Old West stagecoach stops.

North of Palm Springs, mystical **Joshua Tree National Park** (p662), with its piles of giant boulders and twisted namesake trees, has inspired artists, most famously the rock band U2. Take time to absorb the stark beauty of the landscape, then continue north into the **Mojave National Preserve** (p678), a vast land of 'singing' sand dunes, volcanic cinder cones and the world's largest Joshua-tree forest. Don't miss the restored Kelso railway depot.

Ready for a change of pace? Drive straight to **Las Vegas** (p691), baby. Sin City is seductive, sophisticated and a daredevil's fantasyland. Before you gamble away your life savings, hop back in the car for the drive west to **Death Valley National Park** (p680), where the desert puts on a spectacular show: mysteriously moving boulders, otherworldly salt flats, saw-toothed mountains and mosaic-marbled canyons are just a few of the amazing attractions.

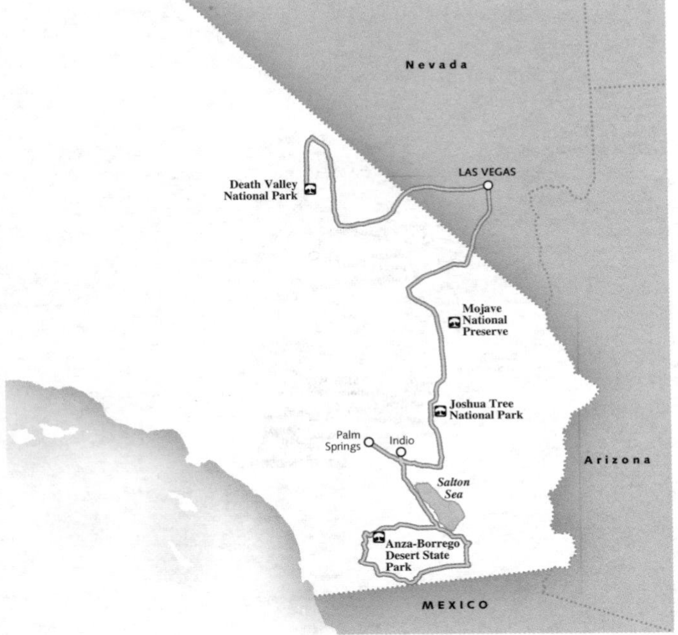

Open roads, big skies and surreal scenery await you on this 550-mile magical mystery tour through California's desert outback, with plenty of time for stops in fabulously retro Palm Springs and the rejuvenating neon oasis of Las Vegas, where hedonism happens 24/7/365.

SAN FRANCISCO, MARIN COUNTY & WINE COUNTRY

Five Days to One Week/San Francisco to Calistoga

Nicknamed 'the Paris of the West' more than a century ago, **San Francisco** (p80) still has as much romance, sophistication and gaiety as the French capital. Steal away with your honey for a long weekend, starting with classic cocktails at the **Top of the Mark** (p132). Uncover the alleyways of **Chinatown** (p100) and wander the mural-adorned **Mission District** (p108), then take our **literary walking tour** (p113) through Italian-flavored North Beach and Russian Hill. Brave the fog on a cruise over to **Alcatraz** (p85) or lose yourself on a sunny day in **Golden Gate Park** (p110), stopping to smell the flowers where hippies danced in the 'Summer of Love.'

Escape the city's 7-sq-mile peninsula via the landmark **Golden Gate Bridge** (p85) to hike across the **Marin Headlands** (p144) or take the ferry from **Tiburon** (p151) over to **Angel Island** (p152) and go kayaking, hiking and mountain-biking. Then meander along the coast, passing the tall redwood trees of **Muir Woods National Monument** (p156), idyllic **Stinson Beach** (p157) and the turnoff to quirky **Bolinas** (p158) on your way north to wildly beautiful **Point Reyes National Seashore** (p160).

Past **Bodega Bay** (p250), take country back roads through **Occidental** (p214) into the **Russian River Valley** (p207), where wineries are nestled between redwood groves. Truck east across Hwy 101, then turn south through **Glen Ellen** (p206) into the heart of California's most famous **Wine Country** (p194), orbiting stylish **Napa** (p229) and its countrified but still chic cousin **Sonoma** (p201). In Napa, tipple and nibble your fill at landmark **Copia** (p229), next to the **Oxbow Public Market** (p229), then soak your road-weary bones in a mud bath in **Calistoga** (p235) before looping back to San Francisco.

On this 300-mile ramble, indulge in the secret delights of hilly San Francisco, then strike out across the Golden Gate Bridge into fun-lovin', outdoorsy Marin County, skipping alongside Pacific beaches before entering the lotusland of California's premier wine country.

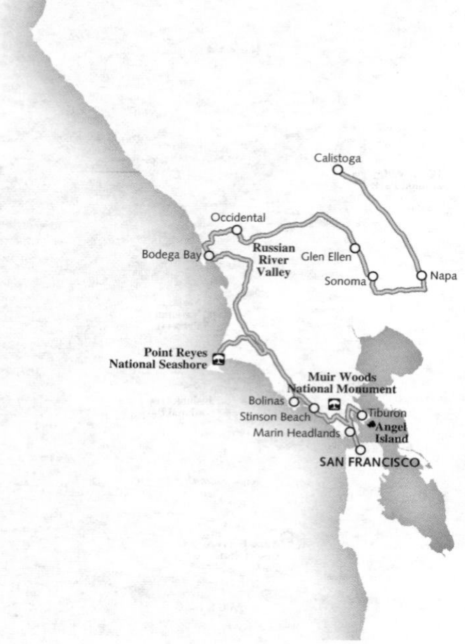

SOCAL WITH KIDS

One Week to 10 Days/Los Angeles to San Diego

LA's **Universal Studios Hollywood** (p539) is one of the world's largest film studios; its cinematic theme park packs an entertaining mix of tame rides, live-action and audience-participation shows, plus a studio-backlot tram tour peppered with special effects. North of LA in Valencia at **Six Flags Magic Mountain** and **Hurricane Harbor** (p572), hair-raising roller coasters should scare the bejeezus out of even speed-crazed teens.

Topping everyone's must-do family fun list is the perfectly 'imagineered' **Disneyland** (p579), where you can wave at Mickey and Minnie, scream at the top of your lungs on thrill rides, then (in summer) watch a spectacular fireworks show. Next door, **Disney's California Adventure** (p582) celebrates the glories of the Golden State and has some amusing rides. Both Disney parks are in Anaheim, not far from **Knott's Berry Farm** (p585), which has an Old West theme, frighteningly fun rides and the spookiest Halloween party around.

A short drive south in Santa Ana at the **Discovery Science Center** (p586), experience a simulated 6.9 magnitude earthquake inside the 'Shake Shack.' Further south along the coast in Carlsbad you'll find the rainbow-colored fantasyland of **Legoland California** (p645), where tots ride the 'Coastersaurus,' pilot helicopters and do stacks of other fun stuff.

San Diego is all about the wild kingdom. The **San Diego Zoo** (p612) has an entire Noah's Ark worth of critters, plus the conservation-minded 'Monkey Trails and Forest Tales' exhibit. **SeaWorld** (p617) is an aquatic zoo where millions have been entertained by the antics of Shamu the Killer Whale and his finned friends. At the safari-style drive-through **San Diego Wild Animal Park** (p613) giraffes, lions and zebras roam 'freely' in open-range enclosures.

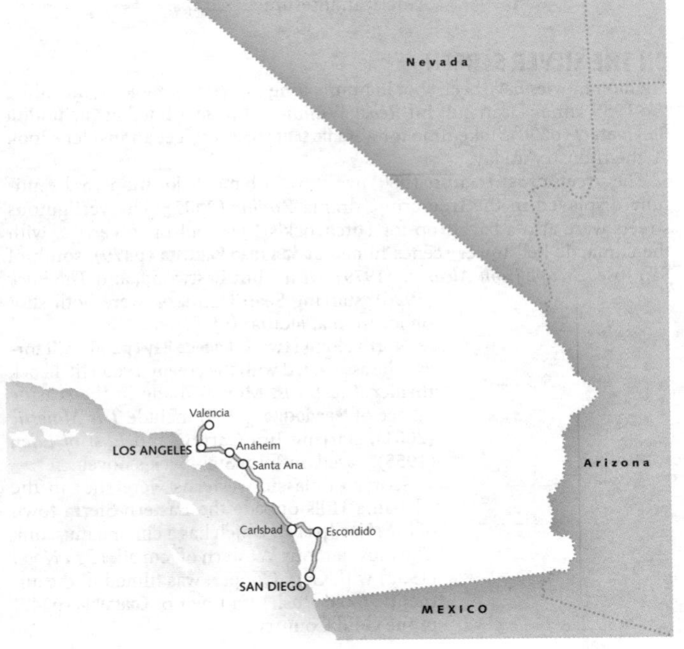

It's no secret: kids love sunny Southern California for its beaches, theme parks and cool museums. This 300-mile family-vacation road trip revolves around Los Angeles and San Diego, so consider setting up base camp for your minivan entourage in either city.

TAILORED TRIPS

FOOTSTEPS OF HISTORY

Spanish conquistador Gaspar de Portolá and Franciscan friar Junípero Serra paved the way for the European settlement of California by building *presidios* (forts) and Catholic missions, starting in San Diego.

Catch a glimpse of the past at Presidio Hill, overlooking the streets of **Old Town** (p614). Later missions in **San Juan Capistrano** (p597) and at **La Purísima** (p492) are even more impressive.

After Alta California came under Mexican control in 1821, the international port of Monterey swelled. Today, California's best-preserved collection of 19th-century adobe buildings awaits at **Monterey State Historic Park** (p455). Delve further into California's multicultural past – Native American, Spanish and Mexican – at **El Pueblo de Los Angeles** (p523) in LA.

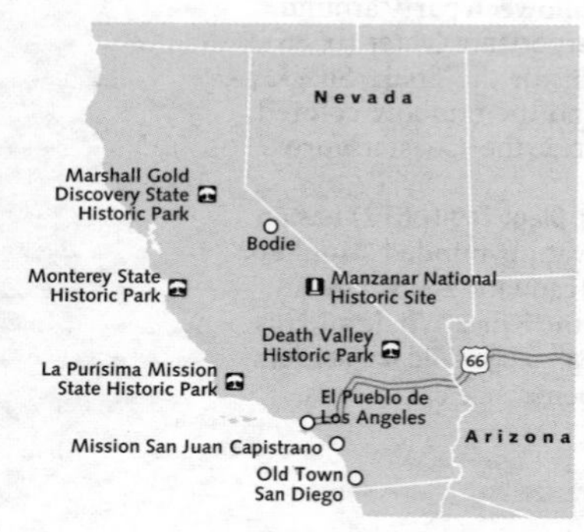

The discovery of gold at Sutter's Mill, now part of **Marshall Gold Discovery State Historic Park** (p338), sparked the Gold Rush of 1849. A few pioneers struck it rich, while the unlucky ones included the Death Valley '49ers (p684). Relive the rough-and-tumble Gold Rush era in the ghost town of **Bodie** (p402), sitting in a state of arrested decay on a wind-battered plain in the Eastern Sierra. Not far away, **Manzanar National Historic Site** (p414) takes a heartrending look at WWII-era Japanese American internment camps.

ON THE SILVER SCREEN

A zillion movies have been shot in filmmaking capital Los Angeles, including the 1955 James Dean cult hit *Rebel Without a Cause,* filmed at the **Griffith Observatory** (p530). Take time for a **studio tour** (p529) to get an insider's look at 'the Industry' today.

The streets of **San Francisco** (p80) overflow with movie locations, as beautifully displayed in the true-crime drama *Zodiac* (2007). The vertiginous streets were also a backdrop for Hitchcock's 1958 nail-biter *Vertigo,* with the climactic bell-tower scenes filmed at **San Juan Bautista** (p479), south of San Jose. *Escape from Alcatraz* (1979), with Clint Eastwood, and *The Rock* (1996), starring Sean Connery, were both shot on location at **Alcatraz** (p85).

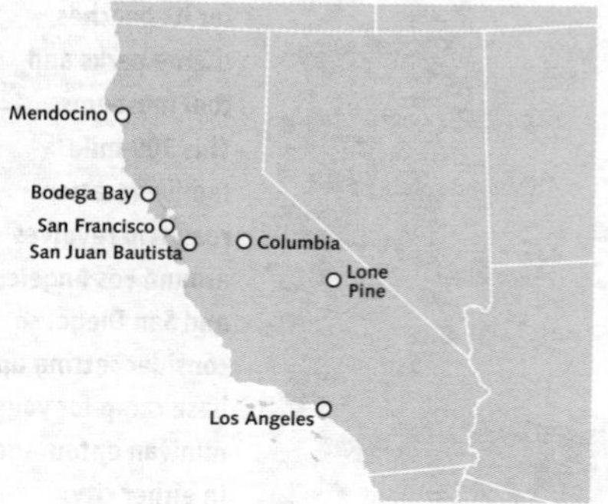

North along Hwy 1, **Bodega Bay** (p250) will forever be associated with the creepy 1963 Hitchcock thriller *The Birds.* Movies made in the seaside village of **Mendocino** (p259) include *The Majestic* (2001), starring Jim Carrey, and *East of Eden* (1955), based on John Steinbeck's novel.

Scores of classic westerns were shot in the Alabama Hills outside the Eastern Sierra town of **Lone Pine** (p414), which has a cinema museum. The most famous Western of 'em all, *High Noon* (1952) with Gary Cooper, was filmed in the authentic Gold Rush–era town of **Columbia** (p347) in the Gold Country.

CALIFORNIA QUIRKS

Fans of fabulous kitsch, wacky fun and weirdness are in luck in California.

Families flock to old-timey tourist traps like the **Mystery Spot** (p446) in Santa Cruz and the **Trees of Mystery** (p295) in Klamath. Check out the *X-Files*-worthy evidence of Bigfoot in **Willow Creek** (p328), conveniently at the start of the Bigfoot Scenic Byway. In SoCal, you'll find the **World's Biggest Dinosaurs** (p662) outside Palm Springs.

The Mojave Desert is littered with quirky roadside attractions built by eccentrics following artistic, heavenly or UFO-inspired visions. Visit **Salvation Mountain** (p669) near the bizarre **Salton Sea** (p668), the **Integratron** (p666) near Joshua Tree or the ghostly **Amargosa Opera House** (p688) and even creepier **Goldwell Open-Air Museum** (p688) near Death Valley.

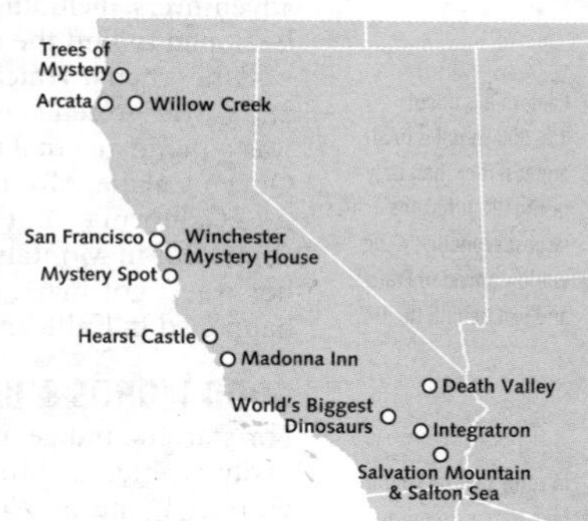

California's oddball monuments to megalomaniacal obsession include **Hearst Castle** (p472) on the Central Coast and the allegedly haunted **Winchester Mystery House** (p186) in San Jose. The latter, a sprawling Victorian mansion, is slightly reminiscent of San Luis Obispo's own **Madonna Inn** (p486), a shrine to outrageous kitsch.

Feeling festive? Attend the **Kinetic Sculpture Race** (p283) from Arcata to Ferndale over Memorial Day Weekend or join San Francisco's own **Bay to Breakers** (p116) race. Founded to lift the city's spirits after the 1906 earthquake, the latter is a carnival of costumed (and naked!) runners in late May.

GO GREEN

Never mind 'greenwashing' – California abounds with opportunities for *real* ecoconscious travel.

In San Francisco, organic seasonal produce from **Ferry Plaza farmers market** (p85) is just the tip of the iceberg lettuce. The Bay area's original 'green' chef is Alice Waters, whose **Chez Panisse** (p175) is a Berkeley landmark; **farmerbrown** (p123) in San Francisco buys from African American farmers. In Marin County, organic **Cowgirl Creamery** (p159) offers tours. It's not far from Zen Buddhist–run **Green Gulch Farm** (p157), which supplies San Francisco's bayside restaurant **Greens** (p126). In the nearby **Wine Country** (p194), organic and biodynamic vineyards are becoming widespread. Afterward, spend the night at **Cavallo Point** (p150), an ecolodge just north of the Golden Gate Bridge.

Or leave your car behind and hop aboard Amtrak's *Coast Starlight,* California's most spectacular railway journey (p738). Stop off in **San Luis Obispo** (p484) and visit its farmers market. SLO is also a gateway to all-natural outdoor adventures like cycling Hwy 1 north to **Big Sur** (p465) or kayaking **Morro Bay** (p477), where endangered species persist. Further south, beach-laden **Santa Barbara** (p495) offers all kinds of discounts and incentives for car-free travel (p503).

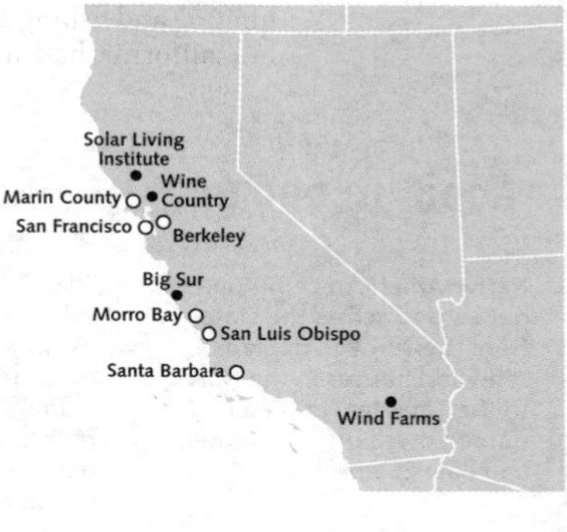

In NorCal, Hopland's **Solar Living Institute** (p268) has been spreading the renewable-energy message almost as long as Al Gore has. Down in the Mojave Desert, you can tour the quixotic-looking **wind farms** (p657) outside Palm Springs.

History

STRANGER THAN FICTION

Gold is the usual reason given for the madcap course of Californian history, but it all actually started with a dazzling pack of lies. Have you heard the one about the sunny island of Amazon women armed with gold weapons, who flew griffins fed with their own sons? No, this isn't a twisted Hollywood *Wonder Woman* remake. It's the plot of a 16th-century Spanish novel by Garcí Ordóñez de Montalvo that became wildly popular among Spanish adventurers, including Hernán Cortés, who said in a 1524 letter from Mexico he hoped to find the island a couple of days' sail to the northwest.

Other than mythical bird-beasts and filicidal Wonder Women, Montalvo and Cortés weren't entirely wrong. Across the water from mainland Mexico was a peninsula that Spanish colonists called Baja (lower) California, after Queen Calafía, Montalvo's legendary queen of the Amazons. Above it was Alta California – not exactly an island, but still a land rich in gold and sunshine. But in Montalvo's tale, the warrior Queen Calafía willingly changed her ways, got married and converted to Christianity – not quite how it happened in California.

California is about 156,000 sq miles in area and is larger than Italy or the UK. It has the 7th-largest economy in the world – ahead of France, and just behind the UK.

GOOD WORDS & BAD DREAMS

For starters, indigenous Californians were not a small group of people as easily typified as Montalvo's Amazons. Settlers first arrived some 15,000 years ago, and by AD 1500, more than 300,000 Native Americans in the California area spoke some 100 distinct languages. Most political leaders were men but shamans were typically women, who summoned dreamworld powers to cure illness, control the weather and bring victories in hunting and war. Communal central-coast fishing communities such as the Ohlone, Miwok and Pomo built subterranean roundhouses and saunas, where they also held ceremonies, told stories and gambled for fun. Northwest hunting communities such as the Hupa, Karok and Wiyot had strong heads of family and constructed big houses and redwood dugout canoes. Southwest Californian groups such as the Yuma and Mojave made sophisticated pottery and developed irrigation systems to farm corn and beans in the desert.

In some Central Californian Native American communities, mothers-in-law were traditionally so revered that you dared not speak to yours, and obeyed her without question.

Unlike Montalvo's Amazons, Native Americans did not hoard gold or attack offensively. While some village leaders had more power than others, none had a warrior class, wealth was distributed relatively evenly and gold had no particular value. Native territories, however, were often clearly delineated, and children were raised on didactic songs that defined allowable hunting and fishing areas and proper harvesting methods. Native Americans in California had no written language but observed oral contracts and

TIMELINE

6000–10,000 BC

Native American communities get settled across the state, from the Yurok in gabled redwood houses in the North to the Tipai-Ipai in thatched domed dwellings in Southern and Baja California.

AD 1542–43

Juan Rodríguez Cabrillo becomes the first European explorer to navigate the coast of California. However, after stumbling against a jagged rock, his journey ends with a gangrenous wound and his eventual death.

1769

Padre Junípero Serra and Captain Gaspar de Portolá lead a Spanish expedition to establish missions, rounding up Native Americans as converts and conscripted labor.

zoning laws, and expected that newcomers would likewise make good on their word. So the arrival of Juan Rodríguez Cabrillo's Spanish exploratory mission to Alta California in 1542 did not immediately spark a war, despite one skirmish and understandable wariness at the uninvited guests. After English pirate Sir Francis Drake looted silver-laden Spanish galleons en route to the Philippines in 1579, he harbored briefly on Miwok land north of San Francisco. The English were taken to be the dead returned from the afterworld, and shamans saw the arrival as a warning of apocalypse. But this did not immediately come to pass, and story and gift exchanges eased tensions between Native Americans and Spanish and English adventurers.

Traces of a sophisticated Native American culture dating from 5000-3000 BC remain at Chumash Painted Cave State Historic Park (p497), which features the most elaborate Native rock designs in North America.

The centuries between the first European explorations of the Californian coast and the arrival of Spanish colonists in 1769 turned out to be a grace period for Native Americans. Within a century of colonization, a population of as many as 325,000 indigenous peoples would be decimated to 20,000 by the arrival of European diseases, conscripted labor regimes and famine. Yet Californian Native shamans are still alive and dreaming today, echoing spirit-world cautions about the need to protect this fragile land first voiced centuries ago.

California may produce almost 20 million gallons of wine a year, but tomatoes bring in the most revenue.

SPAIN'S MISSION IMPOSSIBLE

When 18th-century Russian and English trappers began trading sought-after otter pelts from Alta California, Spain quickly concocted a plan for colonization. For the glory of God and the tax coffers of Spain, missions would be built across the state, and within 10 years these would be going concerns run by devoted local converts. This 'Sacred Expedition' was approved by Spain's quixotic Visitor-General José de Gálvez of Mexico, also known for his scheme to control Sonora province with a trained army of apes.

Almost immediately after Spain's missionizing plan was approved in 1769, it began to fail. When Franciscan Padre Junípero Serra and Captain Gaspar de Portolá made the overland journey to establish Mission San Diego de Alcalá (p613), only half the sailors on their supply ships survived the ocean journey. Portolá's exploratory party pressed on, but they arrived in a Los Angeles rattled by earthquakes. Portolá had heard of a fabled cove to the north, but failing to recognize Monterey Bay in the fog, he gave up and turned back.

Fresno is the self-proclaimed raisin capital of the world, but other Californian towns also have claims to foodie fame: Gilroy and garlic, Castroville and artichokes, and Half Moon Bay and pumpkins.

Portolá reported to Gálvez that if the Russians or English wanted the thankless territory of California, they'd be welcome to it, but Padre Serra wouldn't give up, and secured more military support for Californian mission-building. Presidios (military posts) were set up alongside missions in 1775 in Monterey (p455), in 1776 in San Francisco (p108) and in 1782 in Santa Barbara (p496). But soldiers weren't paid regularly, and they looted and pillaged local communities. Soldiers convicted of murdering and raping locals were condemned to exile in California, which didn't exactly solve the

1821

Mexican independence ends the Spanish colonization of California, and Mexico inherits 21 missions in various states of disrepair, along with unruly Californio cowboys and a decimated Native population.

1826–32

Teenager Kit Carson helps blaze the Santa Fe Trail, which eventually leads to Los Angeles through 900 miles of rattlesnake-filled high desert, and plains vigilantly guarded by the Apache and Comanche.

1835

An emissary of President Andrew Jackson makes a formal offer of $500,000 to buy Northern California, but Mexico testily refuses, and tries to sell California as a package deal to England.

problem. Clergy objected to this treatment of potential Native converts, but relied on the soldiers to round up conscripts to build missions. In exchange for their labor, Native Americans were allowed one meager meal a day (when available) and a place in God's kingdom – which came much sooner than expected, due to the smallpox the Spanish brought with them.

Native Americans often rebelled against the 21 Spanish missions. Only a month after the mission was established in San Diego, escaped converts attacked it. One of the most organized and effective rebellions was in 1781, after Yuma villagers found soldiers' cattle munching through their winter bean supply. They launched a surprise attack, killing 30 soldiers and four priests and holding others for ransom. Spain wasn't prepared to handle losses on an already unprofitable venture, and after Padre Serra passed away in 1784, left only a handful of skittish soldiers manning the presidios.

SOAP OPERAS DOWN ON THE RANCH

When the 1810–21 Mexican war for independence from Spain broke out, supplies from Mexico were cut off completely. Handing over the troublesome colony to Mexico, Spain's attitude echoed Portolá's: good luck and good riddance. But where Spain saw disaster in failing missions, crafty rancheros (ranchers) saw opportunity. As long as missions had the best grazing land plus unpaid Native labor, rancheros couldn't compete in the growing market for cowhides and tallow (for use in soap). Spanish, Mexican and American settlers who had intermarried with Native Americans were now a sizable constituency, and together these Californios convinced Mexico to secularize the missions in 1834.

The Oscar-winning *There Will Be Blood* (2007), adapted from Upton Sinclair's book *Oil!*, depicts a Californian oil magnate and was based on real-life SoCal tycoon Edward Doheny.

Californios quickly snapped up deeds to privatized mission property. Only a few dozen Californios were literate in the entire state, so boundary disputes that arose were typically settled with muscle, not paper. By law, half the lands were supposed to go to Native Americans who worked at the missions, but few Native mission workers actually received their entitlements. The average rancho soon expanded to 16,000 acres in size, and was staffed by 20 to 200 of the same Native laborers who had worked at the missions.

Ranchero life was transformed from hardscrabble living on leather cots in cramped two-room shanties to grand fiestas in haciendas where women were confined to quarters at night. But ranchera women were no hothouse flowers: women owned 13% of Californian ranches, rode horses as deftly as men, and despite elaborate precautions, caused romantic scandals worthy of telenovelas (soap operas). But through marriage and other mergers, most of the land and wealth in California was held by just 46 ranchero families by 1846.

THE GOLDEN BEAR

While rancheros were occupied with leather, soap and juicy scandal, Americans began arriving in the trading post of Los Angeles via the Santa

1846

Sierra Nevada blizzards cause the Donner Party of settlers to eat their own, but thanks to five women and two men who snowshoe 100 miles for help, just over half the party of 87 survives.

1848

Gold is discovered near present-day Placerville by mill employees. Sometime San Francisco newspaper publisher and full-time bigmouth Sam Brannan lets word out, and the Gold Rush is on.

1850

With hopes of solid-gold tax revenues, the US hastily dubs California the 31st state. But when miners find gold and tax loopholes, SoCal ranchers are left carrying the tax burden, creating early north–south rivalries.

Fe Trail. The northern passes through the Sierras were trickier, as the Donner Party (see p367) tragically discovered in 1846 – stranded in a desolate mountain pass, they resorted to cannibalism. The US saw potential in California, but when US President Andrew Jackson offered the financially strapped Mexican government $500,000 for the territory, the offer was tersely rejected – an insult aggravated by rumors that Mexico was entertaining a British buyout offer. When the USA annexed the Mexican territory of Texas in 1845, Mexico broke off diplomatic relations and ordered all foreigners without proper papers to be deported from California.

News was slow to arrive in California from Washington DC and Mexico City, and locals were spoiling for a fight. United States Commodore Thomas Catesby Jones actually invaded Monterey, on the assumption that Mexico and the US were at war; two days later he realized his mistake, hastily apologized, and returned to his ships. Then in June 1846 some American settlers, tanked up on liquid courage, declared independence in the town of Sonoma. Not a shot was fired – instead, they captured the nearest Mexican official and hoisted a hastily made flag. Locals awoke to discover they were living in the independent 'Bear Republic,' under a flag with a grizzly that looked like a drunken dog (p202). The Bear Flag Republic lasted an entire month before US orders arrived to stand down.

The fierce grizzly turned out to be more of a teddy bear when the Mexican–American War was declared in 1846, which lasted two years with very little fighting in California. The hostilities formally ended with the Treaty of Guadalupe Hidalgo, ceding California and the present-day southwest to the USA. Mexico could not have had worse timing: within days of signing away California, gold was discovered.

THE EUREKA YEARS

The Gold Rush began with another bluff. Real estate speculator, lapsed Mormon and tabloid publisher Sam Brannan was looking to unload some California swampland in 1848 when he heard rumors of gold flakes found near Sutter's Mill, 120 miles from San Francisco. Figuring that this news should sell some newspapers and raise the value of local real estate, Brannan published the rumor as fact. Initially the story didn't generate much excitement – modest finds of gold flake had occurred in southern California as far back as 1775. So Brannan ran another story, this time with a leak from Mormon employees at Sutter's Mill who had sworn him to a sacred oath of secrecy. Brannan reportedly kept his word by running through the San Francisco streets, brandishing a vial of gold flakes entrusted to him as tithes for the Mormon church, shouting, 'Gold on the American River!'

Other newspapers around the world weren't scrupulous about getting their facts straight either, and hastily published stories of 'gold mountains' near San Francisco. By 1850, the year California was fast-tracked for admission as the

The Hollywood Walk of Fame celebrates top talent with more than 2000 stars embedded in the sidewalk. In a controversial 2008 move, corporate sponsor Absolut Vodka will also get the star treatment.

1851

The discovery of gold in Australia means cheering in the streets of Melbourne and panic in the streets of San Francisco, as the price for California gold plummets.

May 10, 1869

The Golden Spike is nailed in place, completing the first transcontinental railroad linking California to the East Coast. The event is reported blow by blow using a new invention, the telegraph, in the world's first real-time communication.

1882

The US Chinese Exclusion Act suspends new immigration from China, denies citizenship to those already in the country and sanctions racially targeted laws that stay on the books until 1943.

31st state, California's non-native population had ballooned from 15,000 to 93,000. Most of the arrivals weren't Americans, but Peruvians, Australians, Chileans and Mexicans, with some Chinese, Irish, native Hawaiian and French prospectors.

In her bestselling *The Joy Luck Club*, Amy Tan weaves the stories of four Chinese-born women and their American-born daughters into a textured history of immigration and aspiration in San Francisco's Chinatown.

For a couple of flush years, these early arrivals panned for gold side by side, slept in close quarters, drank firewater with Chinese takeout and splurged on French food and Australian wines. But with each wave of new arrivals, profits per person dropped and gold became harder to find. In 1848 each prospector earned an average of about $300,000 in today's terms; by 1849 that number was $95,000 to $145,000; by 1865 the number dipped to $35,000. When surface gold became harder to find, miners picked, shoveled and dynamited their way through mountains. The work was grueling and dangerous, and with few doctors to tend ailments, injuries often proved lethal. The cost of living in muddy, cold, stinky camps was sky-high: in 1849 a cot in a drafty miners' flophouse among men who rarely washed could run $10 (about $250 in today's terms), and meals featuring such abominations as a jelly omelette cost $2 (about $50 today). With one woman per 400 men in some camps, many turned to paid company, drink and opium for consolation.

VIGILANTES, ROBBER BARONS & THE RAILROAD

Prospectors who did best arrived early and got out quick; those who stayed too long either lost fortunes searching for the next nugget or became targets of resentment. Successful Peruvians and Chileans were harassed and denied renewals to their mining claims, and most left California by 1855. Native American laborers who had helped the '49ers strike it rich were also denied the right to hold claims. Any wrongdoing was hastily pinned on Australians – from 1851–56, San Francisco's self-appointed Vigilante Committee tried, convicted and hung 'Sydney Ducks' in hour-long proceedings that came to be known as 'kangaroo trials.' Australian boarding houses were torched six times by arsonists from 1849–51, so when gold was found in Australia in 1851, many were ready to head home. Australians who stayed were promptly blamed for the ensuing California gold panic. Also at the receiving end of nativist hostility were the Chinese, the most populous group in California by 1860. Frozen out of mining claims, many Chinese instead opened service-based businesses that survived when all-or-nothing mining ventures went bust – incurring further resentment among miners.

But rivalries among miners only obscured the real competitive threat. Increasingly, fortunes weren't earned by claim-holders or service workers, but by those who controlled the means of production: the Californian robber barons. These Californian speculators hoarded the capital and industrial machinery necessary for deep-mining operations at the Comstock silver lode, discovered in 1860 in the neighboring Nevada territory. As mining became industrialized, fewer miners were needed, and jobless prospectors

1906

A massive earthquake levels entire blocks of San Francisco in 47 seconds flat, setting off fires that rage for three days without adequate water supply or fire breaks. Survivors start rebuilding immediately.

1927

After a year of tinkering, 21-year-old San Francisco inventor Philo Farnsworth transmits the first successful TV broadcast of...a straight line. California spends the next 82 years producing marginally better televised entertainment.

1928

The Jazz Singer, about a Jewish singer who rebels against his father and performs in blackface, is released as the first feature-length 'talkie' movie. The worldwide demand for films brings a boom to Hollywood.

focused their resentments on a convenient target: Chinese dockworkers. Discriminatory Californian laws restricting housing and employment for anyone born in China were reinforced nationwide in the 1882 US Chinese Exclusion Act, which also excluded Chinese from citizenship until it was repealed in 1943. Chinese arrivals were increasingly denied property rights and mining claims starting in the 1860s, which served the needs of mining magnates in need of cheap labor to build railroads to their claims.

For Chinese laborers looking for work outside the goldfields, rail offered a new prospect in the 1860s. A cross-country railroad would shorten the trip from New York to San Francisco from two months to five days, and open up markets on both coasts. Tracks were laid simultaneously from Omaha in the east and Sacramento in the west, but there was one seemingly insurmountable problem: the Sierra Nevada. The mountains were too high to go over, so tunnels would have to be gouged through them. This job description involved workers being lowered down a sheer mountain face in wicker baskets, planting sticks of dynamite in rock crevices, lighting them, and praying to be hoisted out of harm's way before the blast detonated. Those who survived the day's work were confined to bunkhouses under armed guard in cold, remote mountain regions. With little other choice of legitimate employment, an estimated 12,000 Chinese laborers blasted through the Sierra Nevada, meeting the westbound end of the railroad in 1869.

THE GREAT WATER FIGHT

Though not everyone saw the upside of California's first boom years, there was one noticeable improvement: the food. During the American Civil War (1861–65), California couldn't count on food shipments from the East Coast and started growing its own. Ever ready with a good slogan, California enjoyed swift success marketing its oranges on the East Coast and selling Midwestern homesteaders on farming the Central Valley. 'Acres of Untaken Government Land for a Million Farmers Without Cyclones or Blizzards,' trumpeted one California-boosting poster – no mention of earthquakes or ongoing land disputes with rancheros and Native groups. With romantic notions of sun-drenched farms overlooking the sparkling Pacific, more than 120,000 homesteaders came to California in the 1870s and '80s.

Chinatown (1974) is the fictionalized yet surprisingly accurate account of the brutal water wars that were waged to build both Los Angeles and San Francisco.

Homesteaders soon discovered that California's golden years had left much of the state badly tarnished. After years of industrialized and hydraulic mining, hills were stripped bare, erosion had wiped out vegetation, streams had silted up and mercury washed into water supplies. Cholera, spread through the open sewers of poorly drained camps, had claimed many lives, and the Native American population was further decimated by new diseases to which they had no resistance. Smaller finds in the mountains of southern California diverted streams essential to the dry valleys below. Because mining claims leased by the US government were granted significant tax

1934

A West Coast longshoremen's strike ends with 34 San Francisco strikers and sympathizers shot and 40 beaten by police. A mass funeral procession and citywide strike follow, and shipping magnates meet union demands.

February 1942

During WWII, Executive Order 9066 sends 120,000 Japanese Americans to internment camps. California's Japanese American Citizens' League demands civil rights in court, providing legal support for the 1964 Civil Rights Act.

1957

City Lights wins a landmark ruling against book banning over the publication of Allen Ginsberg's *Howl*, and free speech and free spirits enjoy a reprieve from McCarthyism.

exemptions, there were insufficient public funds for clean-up programs or public water works.

Frustrated Californian farmers south of San Luis Obispo voted to secede from California in 1859, but appeals for secession were shelved during the Civil War. In 1884 Southern Californians passed a pioneering law preventing dumping into Californian rivers and, with the support of budding agribusiness and real-estate concerns, passed bond measures to build aqueducts and dams that made large-scale farming and real-estate development possible. By the 20th century, the lower one-third of the state took two-thirds of available water supplies, inspiring Northern Californian calls for secession.

While bucolic Southern California was pushing for urbanization, urban Northern Californians who had witnessed devastation from mining and logging firsthand were forming the nation's first conservation movement. Naturalist John Muir founded the Sierra Club in 1892 and campaigned for the federal government to establish the first national park in Yosemite (p376). Though Muir succeeded in establishing the National Park Service in 1916, dams and pipelines to support communities in SoCal deserts and coastal cities were built over his objections – including the enormous Hetch Hetchy reservoir in Yosemite, which supplies most water to the Bay Area today. But water remains a hot topic in drought-prone California, with tensions regularly coming to a boil between developers and conservationists, NorCal water hoarders who'd prefer to keep Hetch Hetchy's pure mountain drinking water all to themselves, and SoCal water splurgers who keep their lawn sprinklers on come rain or shine.

SHAKING UP THE WILD WEST

Marc Reisner's *Cadillac Desert: The American West and Its Disappearing Water* is an examination of how the western states have exploited and argued over every drop of available water.

On April 18, 1906, a quake estimated at a terrifying 7.8 to 8.3 on today's Richter scale struck the city of San Francisco. Gas mains ruptured and survivors watched helplessly as their city was engulfed in flames for three days. With public funds for citywide water mains and fire hydrants siphoned off by corrupt bosses, there was only one functioning water source in the city. When the smoke lifted, one thing was clear: it was time for the Wild West to clean up its act.

While San Francisco was rebuilt at a rate of 15 buildings a day, California's reformers set to work on city, state and national politics, one plank at a time. Californians concerned about public health and trafficking in women pushed for regulation of prostitution across the state, resulting in the indictment of San Francisco 'pimp mayor' Eugene Schmitz for extorting money from brothels, and the 1914 statewide Red Light Abatement Act.

Mexico's revolution from 1910 to 1921 brought a new wave of migrants and revolutionary ideas, including ethnic pride movements that countered California's prevailing local sentiments. As California's ports grew, longshoremen's unions coordinated a historic 83-day strike in 1934 along the

1966

Ronald Reagan is elected governor, setting a career precedent for fading film stars. He served until 1975 and in 1981 became the 40th president of the United States.

January 14, 1967

The Summer of Love kicks off at the Human Be-In in Golden Gate Park with the blowing of conch shells and minds, and the lighting of draft cards used as rolling papers.

June 5, 1968

Presidential candidate, former US Attorney General, civil-rights ally and antipoverty campaigner Robert Kennedy is fatally shot moments after winning the critical California primary.

entire West Coast that forced concessions for safer working conditions and fair pay. When Japanese Americans along the West Coast were ordered into internment camps by President Roosevelt, they didn't go quietly, but immediately filed suits that became groundbreaking civil rights cases.

Then at the height of the Depression in 1935, some 200,000 farming families fleeing the drought-struck Dust Bowl in Texas and Oklahoma arrived in California. Migrants arriving with dreams of the Golden West found scant pay and deplorable working and living conditions at major farming concerns. California's artists alerted middle America to the migrants' plight, and the nation rallied around Dorothea Lange's haunting documentary photos of famine-struck families and John Steinbeck's harrowing fictionalized account of 'the Great Migration' in his 1939 novel *The Grapes of Wrath*. Initially the book was widely banned, and the 1940 movie version, its star Henry Fonda, and Steinbeck himself were accused of harboring Communist sympathies – but Steinbeck won both the Pulitzer and Nobel Prizes for his masterwork, and the public sympathy he generated for farm workers helped launch the United Farm Workers' union.

At the same time, industry was transformed by tapping the Golden State's other natural resources: sunshine, coastal waters and cultural diversity. California provided dry docks and launching pads to build ships and airplanes during WWII and women and African Americans found unprecedented economic opportunity in the shipbuilding and aviation boom. Contracts in military communications and aviation attracted engineers who launched California's high-tech industry. The state that had strictly limited the influx and impact of international arrivals began encouraging international investment, attracting top talent through universities and pioneering merit-based hiring practices, and parlaying Pacific Rim ties into import/export business.

But perhaps California's greatest export was the sunny, wholesome image it projected to the world through its homegrown film and television industry. In 1908 California became a convenient movie location for its consistent sunlight and versatile locations, although its role was limited to doubling for more exotic locales and to period-piece productions like Charlie Chaplin's *Gold Rush*. Then Hollywood studios discovered its star potential and California landed feature roles in movies and iconic TV shows (see p51). Through the power of its media, California tamed its Wild West image and adopted a more marketable image of beach boys and bikini-clad blondes.

COUNTERCULTURE HITS THE MAINSTREAM

Not all Californians saw themselves as extras in *Beach Blanket Bingo*, however. WWII sailors discharged for insubordination and homosexuality in San Francisco found themselves at home among the bebop jazz clubs, Bohemian coffeehouses and anarchic alleys of North Beach. San Francisco became the

Oscar-winning film *LA Confidential* (1997) traces three cops' search for the truth amid the Hollywood deception and police corruption of postwar Los Angeles.

Former child-actor Kenneth Anger took the ultimate Tinseltown revenge with his 1965 bestseller *Hollywood Babylon* - a tell-all that alleged movie-star drug addictions, mental breakdowns, crime cover-ups and blacklist backstabbings.

Erin Brockovich (2000) is based on the true story of a Southern Californian mom who discovered a small town being poisoned by industrial waste and won a class-action lawsuit that raised the standard for corporate accountability.

1969

UCLA links to Stanford Research Institute via ARPANET, a precursor to the internet. Within a few years an unsolicited group message about politics is sent across the network and spam is born.

1977

San Francisco Supervisor Harvey Milk becomes the first openly gay man to be elected to US public office. Milk sponsors a gay-rights bill and trendsetting 'pooper-scooper' ordinance before his murder by political opponent Dan White.

October 17, 1989

The Loma Prieta Earthquake hits 6.9 on the Richter scale near Santa Cruz, destroying a two-level section of the Interstate 880 and resulting in 63 deaths and thousands of injuries.

Dogtown and Z-Boys (2001) is the counterculture classic documentary tracking the Santa Monica teens who inveunted freestyle skateboarding when they skated in dry LA pools during the late-1970s drought.

In 2004, San Francisco Mayor Gavin Newsom granted 4000 marriage licenses to same-sex couples in accordance with California's 'equal protection' clause. The marriages were annulled, then California's same-sex marriage ban was lifted in 2008. A proposition to ban same-sex marriage was passed in November 2008.

The ultimate Californian period movie is *Valley Girl* (1983), which unleashed excess pastels, 'Bitchin'!' and the indiscriminate use of the word 'like' onto an unsuspecting American public. Brace yourselves: a stage musical is in the works.

home of free speech and free spirits, and soon everyone who was anyone was getting arrested: Beat poet Lawrence Ferlinghetti for publishing Allen Ginsberg's epic poem *Howl*, comedian Lenny Bruce for uttering the F word onstage and Carol Doda for going topless.

When the CIA made the mistake of using writer and willing test subject Ken Kesey to test psychoactive drugs intended to create the ultimate soldier, it inadvertently kicked off the psychedelic era. At the January 14, 1967 Human Be-In in Golden Gate Park, trip-master Timothy Leary urged a crowd of 20,000 hippies to dream a new American dream and 'turn on, tune in, drop out.' For the duration of the Summer of Love – weeks, months, even a year, depending on who you talk to and how stoned they were at the time – San Francisco was the place where it seemed possible to make love, not war. When Flower Power faded, other Bay Area rebellions grew in its place: Black Power, Gay Pride and medical marijuana clubs.

But while San Francisco had the more attention-grabbing counterculture in the 1940s to '60s, nonconformity in sunny Southern California shook America to the core. In 1947 when Senator Joseph McCarthy attempted to root out suspected Communists in the movie industry, 10 writers and directors who refused to admit Communist alliances or to name names were charged with contempt of Congress and barred from working in Hollywood. The Hollywood Ten's impassioned defenses of the Constitution were heard nationwide, and Hollywood players with everything to lose increasingly voiced dissent and hired blacklisted talent until Californian lawsuits put a legal end to McCarthyism in 1962. That same year farmworker and labor leader César Chávez formed United Farm Workers. While civil rights leaders marched on Washington, Chávez and Californian grape pickers marched on Sacramento, bringing the issue of fair wages and the health risks of pesticides to the nation's attention. When Bobby Kennedy was sent to investigate, he sided with Chávez, bringing Latinos into the political fold. Protests by Santa Barbara beachcombers spurred the establishment of the Environmental Protection Agency after an oil rig dumped 200,000 gallons of oil into Santa Barbara Channel on January 28, 1969, killing dolphins, seals and some 3600 shore birds.

TECHNO-TRENDS

For better and occasionally worse, California's innovations have tended to catch on. Falling into the regrettable column are aerobics headbands as fashion statements, Valspeak entering the vernacular with 'for sure' and 'totally,' and suicide cults like Heaven's Gate and Jim Jones' People's Temple. But consider the plus side: skateboarding and snowboarding, organic farming, personal computers and the internet.

California's techno-trendiness began when Silicon Valley introduced the first personal computer in 1968. Advertisements breathlessly gushed that

1992

Charged with the 1991 beating of African American Rodney King, three of the four white police officers involved are acquitted by a predominantly white jury. Following the trial, Los Angeles endures six days of riots.

March 10, 2000

The Nasdaq crashes, ending the dot-com era. Traditional industry wonks gloat over the burst bubble, until knock-on effects lead to a devalued dollar and a NYSE slide beginning in 2002.

2003

Republican Arnold Schwarzenegger (aka The Governator) is elected governor of California. Schwarzenegger breaks party ranks on environmental issues and wins 2007 reelection.

Hewlett-Packard's 'light' (40lb) machine could 'take on roots of a fifth-degree polynomial, Bessel functions, elliptic integrals and regression analysis' – all for the low, low price of $4900 (about $29,000 today). Consumers didn't quite know what to do with personal computers, until another CIA LSD tester named Stewart Brand explained their potential in simple terms. In his 1969 *Whole Earth Catalog*, Brand reasoned that the technology governments used to run countries could empower ordinary people. That same year UCLA professor Len Kleinrock proved Brand right, sending a message from a computer in Los Angeles to another at Stanford. The message he typed was 'L' then 'O' then 'G' – at which point the computer crashed.

To read more about the garage-workshop culture of Silicon Valley go to www.folklore.org, which covers the crashes and personality clashes that made geek history.

The next wave of Californian techies was determined to create a personal computer that could compute and communicate without crashing. When 21-year-old Steve Jobs and Steve Wozniak introduced the Apple II at the first West Coast Computer Faire in 1977, techies were abuzz about the memory (4KB of RAM!), the microprocessor speed (1MHz!) and a function straight out of science fiction: the ability to communicate directly with other computers, without a person in between.

Not until the 1990s would Silicon Valley engineers finally give computers something to talk about. Start-up ventures rushed to be the first to grab users' attention along the new 'information superhighway,' and suddenly people were getting their mail, news, politics, pet food and, yes, sex online. But venture funding dried up and the paper fortunes of the dot-com boom disappeared on one nasty Nasdaq-plummeting day…or did it? Today San Francisco's lofts are filling with consumer-centric Web 2.0 companies, alongside a shiny new Mission Bay development earmarked for the next boom: biotech.

California accounts for a quarter of all US high-tech companies, jobs and R&D, plus 43% of biotech employment, 48% of biotech R&D and 53% of biotech revenues.

Biotech has been all the talk in California since 1976, when Genentech was formed at a San Francisco bar. The company has since cloned human insulin, introduced the hepatitis B vaccine and developed breast cancer–fighting drugs. But instead of waiting for the next eureka moment from the private sector, Californian voters approved a 2004 bond measure committing $3 billion to stem cell research – a contrary move as federal funds were being cut for research involving embryo-derived stem cells. As of 2008 the state of California is the biggest funder of stem cell research, and Nasdaq has launched its boom-monitoring Biotech Index. Now all that's missing is the actual boom, but if history is any indication, California will make good on its talk, no matter how outlandish.

February 12, 2004

Defying California's same-sex marriage ban, SF Mayor Gavin Newsom officiates at the wedding of Phyllis Lyon and Del Martin. Courts declare the marriage void, but the ban unconstitutional.

October 2007

Wildfires sweep across drought-stricken Southern California as 900,000 people evacuate homes. FEMA rescues its damaged reputation and local migrant workers, state prisoners and Tijuana firefighters volunteer to curb blazes.

2008

Not to be outdone by SoCal, Northern and Central California endure more than 2000 wildfires that threaten farming land and forests. Years of below-average rainfall are to blame.

The Culture

California is not just a place on the map, but also a recurring dream that occasionally touches on reality. To really understand it, let's take a look at a familiar fantasy of a day in this Golden State of mind, then compare it to how Californians actually live.

In the dream-world California, you wake up, have your shot of wheatgrass, and roll down to the beach while the surf's up. Lifeguards wave to you as they go jogging by in their bikinis, and you take a moment to help some kids finish a Frank Gehry sand castle and kick a ball around with David Beckham. You skateboard down the boardwalk with Tony Alva to your yoga class, where Madonna admires your downward dog. A taco truck pulls up with your favorite: low-carb sustainable line-caught tilapia fish tacos with sugar-free organic mango chipotle salsa.

Talk about nature lovers: over 60% of Californians admit to having hugged a tree.

Napping on the beach afterward, you awake to find a casting agent hovering over you, blocking your sunlight, imploring you to star in a movie based on a best-selling comic book. You say you'll have your lawyer look over the papers, and by your lawyer you mean your roommate who plays one on TV. The conversation is cut short when you get a text to meet up with some friends at a bar. That casting agent was a stress case – she wanted an answer in, like, a month – so you swing by your medical pot dispensary and a tattoo parlor to get 'Peace' inscribed on your bicep in five languages as a reminder to yourself to stay chill. At the bar, the bouncer ushers you into the VIP room, where all the Scientologists wave 'hi' and top chefs ply you with hors d'oeuvres. You're called onstage to play a set with the band, and afterward you tell the drummer how the casting agent harshed your mellow. She recommends a Wine Country Zen getaway, but you're already doing that Big Sur primal scream colon-cleansing retreat this weekend.

You head back to your beach house to update your status on your social-networking profile, alerting your million online friends to the major events of the day: 'Killer taco, solid downward dog, third peace tattoo, movie offer.' Then you repeat your nightly self-affirmations: 'I am a child of the universe... I am blessed, or at least not a New Yorker...tomorrow will bring sunshine and possibility...om.'

REGIONAL IDENTITY

California Indians: A Source Book, edited by Robert Fleming Heizer, is a wide-ranging introduction to the state's network of West Coast tribes, with essays on ecology, linguistics, history and ghost dances.

Now for the reality check: any Northern Californian hearing your California dream is bound to get huffy. What, big-wave surfing, political protests and open-source software inventions don't factor in your dreams? Huh, typical SoCal slacker. But Southern Californians will also roll their eyes at the stereotypes: they didn't create NASA's Jet Propulsion Lab, MySpace, almost half the world's movies and all that porn by slacking off.

But there is some truth to your California dreamscape. Some 80% of Californians live near the coast rather than inland, even though California beaches aren't always sunny or swimmable. Self-help, fitness and body modification are major industries here, successfully marketed since the 1970s as 'lite' versions of religious experience – all the agony and ecstasy of the major religious brands, without all those heavy commandments. Californian cuisine is fresh and creative, and the sound of the taco truck attracts more Californians than church bells, minarets and gongs combined. The exercise and good food help keep Californians the fittest in the nation, with the lowest body-mass index nationwide. Yet 250,000 Californians are apparently ill enough to merit prescriptions for medical marijuana. Northern and Southern Californians do have one thing in common: they are baffled by New Yorkers' delusion that the world revolves around the Big Apple, when everyone knows it revolves around California.

Not all Californians are slackers. California-based MoveOn.org (www.moveon.org) has mobilized thousands of netizens to vote, blog, donate and send endlessly recirculated spam about 'left coast' causes.

LIFESTYLE

The charmed existence you dreamed about is a stretch, even in California. Few Californians can afford to spend entire days tanning and incidentally networking, what with UVB rays and the rent to consider. But according to a recent Cambridge University study, mellowness is a defining characteristic of Californians, who rank lower in a 'neuroticism' index than inhabitants of other states.

Most Californians rent rather than own, and few could afford a beach dream-home, even on a median household income of $53,629 per year. Eight of the 10 most expensive US housing markets are in California, and in the number-one most expensive area, suburban La Jolla, the average house price is $1.8 million. Almost half of all Californians reside in cities, but the other half live in the suburbs, where the cost of living is just as high, if not higher: Marin County outside San Francisco is currently the most costly place to live in America. Yet Californian cities (especially San Francisco and San Diego) consistently top national quality-of-life indexes, and the state is growing by about half a million people per year.

If you're like most Californians, you actually live in your car, not your house. Californians commute an average of 30 minutes each way to work, and spend at least $1 out of every $5 earned on car-related expenses. But Californians have zoomed ahead of the national energy-use curve in their smog-checked cars, buying more hybrid and fuel-efficient cars than any other state. Despite California's reputation for smog, seven of the 25 US cities with the cleanest air are in California.

The richest town in America is just south of San Francisco. In Hillsborough, CA, the median household income is $263,456 and the median home price is $2,606,764.

As for those roommates you dreamed about: if you're a Californian aged 24 to 29, there's a one in three possibility your roomies are your parents. Among adult Californians, one in four live alone, and almost 50% are unmarried. Of those who are currently married, 53% won't be in 10 years. Increasingly, Californians are shacking up: the number of unmarried cohabiting couples has increased 40% since 1990.

ECONOMY

Not all Californians spend their days swanning about on set as stars of major motion pictures. More than one third of LA area residents are employed in the entertainment industry, but most hold nebulous-sounding jobs like prop stylist and key grip. Over one million entertainment jobs in the LA/Orange County area generate $140 billion in sales, not including the money earned

THE GOLDEN STATE AT THE END OF THE RAINBOW

In California, you might notice a new version of the state flag, designed to celebrate gay marriage: California's iconic grizzly walking along a rainbow. Forty thousand Californians were already registered as domestic partners when, in 2004, San Francisco Mayor Gavin Newsom issued marriage licenses to same-sex couples in defiance of a California same-sex marriage ban. Four thousand same-sex couples promptly got hitched. The state ban was nixed by California courts in June 2008, but then a proposition passed in November 2008 to amend the state's constitution to prohibit same-sex marriage. Civil-rights activists are challenging the constitutionality of the proposition, but meanwhile California's reputation as a global hub of GLBT (gay/lesbian/bisexual/transgender) is lagging behind some regions in the American South, where the number of same-sex couples has more than quadrupled since 1990.

annually in related areas: $14 billion in video-game production, $8 billion in advertising and $20 billion in performing arts. During the Hollywood writers' strike of 2007–08, when writers fought for a greater share of the profits, the studios lost revenues totaling $2.7 billion due to the standstill.

Since 1990, California's prison population has increased by 73%, mostly for drug-related crimes. Six out of every 1000 Californians are currently in jail.

The home of Silicon Valley and the burgeoning biotech industry, Northern California is giving Southern California a run for its money as the state's main economic engine. SoCal may have invented strapless bras, Hula-hoops and autograph books, but NorCal has produced spiffy high-tech products including personal computers, the iPod and Facebook. All this innovation is driven by research at California's 11 top-tier universities, and a $60 billion annual investment in R&D – that's four to six times the amount of any other competitive state, including Massachusetts and Texas.

Only 5% of Californians live in rural areas, yet they're responsible for a couple of major industries: agriculture and gambling. Despite encroachment from real-estate developers, the Central Valley still produces almost 50% of all fruit in the US. Though Native American tribal reservations account for just 0.6% of the total land in the state, voter-approved 1998 state Proposition 5, allowing gambling on reservations, has generated $5 billion annually.

Although California has the world's seventh-largest economy, not every one rakes in big bucks. Women earn just 80¢ for every dollar earned by men. The richest counties (Marin, San Francisco and San Mateo) are all in the Bay Area, though some of America's richest individuals live in SoCal – in places like Malibu, Bel Air and, of course, Beverly Hills. The state's poorest towns are in inland valleys, southern deserts and northern mountains. Employment is 'at will' in California, which means anyone can be laid off at any time without being given a reason, and it's unusual to meet someone in Silicon Valley who hasn't been unemployed during a tech slump.

Most immigrants to California come to join family members who already live here; 72% of immigration is family-sponsored.

Homelessness is not part of the California dream, but it's a reality for more than 350,000 Californians. Some are teens who have run away or been locked out by their parents, but the largest contingent of homeless Californians are US war veterans – 49,000 in all. What's more, in the 1970s mental health programs were cut, and state-funded drug treatment programs were dropped in the 1980s, leaving many Californians with mental illnesses and substance abuse problems no place to go. Also standing in line at homeless shelters are the working poor, unable to cover medical care and high rent on minimum-wage salaries. San Francisco is pioneering efforts to provide universal health-care citywide and set a realistic living wage, but no one city can carry the burden for the statewide crisis. Rather than addressing the underlying causes of homelessness, some California cities have criminalized loitering, panhandling, even sitting on sidewalks. But since empathy has not yet been outlawed, you are free to give to local charities doing their part to keep California alive and dreaming.

POPULATION & MULTICULTURALISM

In your California dream, did you picture yourself as a blond surfer? If so, you probably dyed your hair that way, like 40% of American women. As for the surfing skills: most Californians can wear board shorts even in chilly weather, but only one in four have actually surfed.

Over 200 different languages are spoken in California, with Tagalog, Japanese and Persian in the top 10.

If you were the average Californian, you'd be statistically likely to be Latina, aged about 30, live in densely populated LA, Orange or San Diego Counties, and speak more than one language. There's a one in four chance you were born outside the US, and if you were born in the US, the odds are 50/50 you moved here recently from another state. One of every four immigrants to the USA lands in California, with the largest segment coming from Mexico. In addition, an estimated two million undocumented immigrants

ANCIENT ART IN THE AMERICAN WEST

The earliest California artists were Native Americans who used pigment to make pictographs on rocks and caves, often as part of shamanistic rituals intended to ensure successful hunts. The Chumash created emblematic designs in bright colors that are considered the most accomplished Native American pictograms in the US. In LA, the Autry National Center's Southwest Museum of the American Indian (p531) and the Museum of the American West (p531) have important collections of contemporary and traditional works by local Native American tribal artists including baskets, carvings, pottery and painting.

currently live in California. But this is not a radical new development: before California became a US state in 1850, it was a territory of Mexico and Spain, and historically most of the state's growth has come from immigration, legal or otherwise.

Most Californians see their state as an easygoing multicultural society that gives everyone a chance to live the American dream. No one is expected to give up their cultural or personal identity to become Californian: Chicano pride, gay pride and black power all began here. But historically, California's Chinatowns, Japantowns and other ethnic enclaves were often created by segregationist sentiment, not by choice. While equal opportunity may be a shared goal, in practice it's very much a work in progress. Even racially integrated areas can be quite segregated in terms of income, language, education and internet access – even in the state that invented the internet.

For a history of multiculturalism in the Central Valley, from early settlers to 20th-century Mexican and Asian immigrant farmers, check out *Highway 99: A Literary Journey Through California's Central Valley*.

Californian culture reflects the composite identity of the state. California's Hispanic and Asian populations are steadily increasing – 40% of the Asian American population currently lives in California – while a net one million non-Hispanic whites left the state during the 1990s. Despite being just 7% of the population and relatively late arrivals with the WWII shipping boom, African Americans have also defined West Coast popular culture in jazz, hip-hop and fashion. Latino culture is deeply enmeshed with Californian culture, from J.Lo and Tejano pop to burritos and margaritas and Governor Schwarzenegger's drawled 1991 catchphrase in *Terminator II*: 'Hasta la vista, baby.' But the bond holding the Golden State together isn't a shared ethnic background, common language, ubiquitous cocktail or signature catchphrase: it's choosing to be Californian.

California is the most populous US state: one in every eight Americans lives here.

SPORTS

Your California dream was mellow, probably because there wasn't a hometown game on TV. California has more professional sports teams than any other state, and loyalties to local NFL football, NBA basketball and major-league baseball teams run deep. For proof that Californians do get excited, buy tickets for a pro game before they sell out – especially Oakland Raiders and San Diego Chargers football, San Francisco Giants baseball and 49ers football, and LA Lakers basketball and Kings hockey matches. To see small but dedicated crowds of hometown fans in action, check out pro men's or women's (WNBA) basketball in Sacramento, pro hockey in Anaheim and San Jose, or pro soccer and arena football action in San Jose or LA. Except for championship play-offs, the regular season for major-league baseball runs from April to September, soccer from April to mid-October, WNBA basketball from late May to August, NFL football from September to early January, NHL ice hockey from October to March and NBA basketball from November to April.

According to a recent study, Californians are less likely to be couch potatoes than other Americans – but when one Californian team plays another,

CALLING ALL NONSPORTS FANS

Even if you're not typically a sports buff, you may find a sport that captivates you in California:

- Professional beach volleyball – the **Association of Volleyball Professionals** (www.avp.com) holds major tournaments every summer at Hermosa and Manhattan Beaches near LA.
- Motor sports are an obsession, especially inland at Bakersfield.
- Surfing is the coastal spectator sport of choice, with waves reaching 100ft at the annual Mavericks competition near Half Moon Bay.

the streets are deserted and all eyes glued to the tube. The biggest grudge matches in the state are when San Francisco 49ers play the Oakland Raiders, LA Lakers play the LA Clippers, San Francisco Giants play the LA Dodgers, or baseball's Oakland A's take on Anaheim's Angels. California college sports rivalries are even fiercer, especially between UC Berkeley's Cal Bears and Stanford Cardinals, and USC Trojans versus the UCLA Bruins.

RELIGION

LA has thousands of believers in Santeria, a fusion of Catholicism and Yoruba beliefs practiced by West African slaves in the Caribbean and South America. Drop by a *botànica* (herbal cure) shop for charms and candles.

Just as Scientology and Zen made cameo appearances in your California dream, religion tends to play a supporting role in Californian culture. Californians are less churchgoing than the American mainstream, and one in five Californians professes no religion at all. Two-thirds of the population are Protestant or Catholic. In 1920s Los Angeles, Aimee Semple McPherson founded one of the first Christian Pentecostal sects, the International Church of the Foursquare Gospel, with over 3.5 million adherents in the world today – though the founder was discredited when she was caught on vacation after claiming to have been abducted. Californian televangelists with international fundraising reach built Orange County's mall-sized house of worship, the Crystal Cathedral. But there are also one million Muslims statewide, and LA has the second-largest Jewish community in North America. California also has the largest number of Buddhists anywhere outside Asia, plus historic Hindu, Sikh and Baha'i communities.

Despite their proportionately small numbers, California's newer religions and utopian communities dominate the popular imagination, from satanic churches to new-age healers. 'Cultifornia' made national headlines in the 1960s with gurus and Charles Manson, in the 1970s with Jim Jones' People's Temple and Erhard Seminars Training, and in the 1990s with Heaven's Gate doomsday cult and Landmark Forum. Though it's been around since the 1950s, the Church of Scientology is still seeking acceptance as a mainstream religion – a cause not advanced by an incoherent Tom Cruise video widely circulated online. Occult and pagan traditions have been practiced in California since the turn of the 20th century, and California has helped popularize Wicca as one of the fastest-growing religions in the US.

Mind-control cult, community of faith or just another California fad? You be the judge after getting the background from cult-monitoring site FACTNet (www.factnet.org).

ARTS

When Californians thank their lucky stars, or good karma, or the goddess, that they don't live in New York, they're not just talking about beach weather: California supports a homegrown arts scene that isn't afraid to be completely outlandish. The movies may still be prone to predictable Hollywood endings, but California's historic literature and poetry scene is still wide open to ideas and interpretation, and the visual and performing arts revolve around the big risk more than the big sale. Even Californians acknowledge that their music is eclectic and frequently weird, ranging from acclaimed, pitch-perfect opera to acclaimed, off-key punk. Critics have tried and failed to find any consistency whatsoever to the styles and schools of thought that have flourished here – but in a Californian context, somehow that makes perfect sense.

Cinema & Television

Shakespeare claimed that 'all the world's a stage,' but in California, it's actually more of a film set. Every palm-lined boulevard and Victorian gabled roofline you see in California seems to come with its own IMDB filming résumé, and no wonder: in any given year some 40 television shows and dozens of movies use Californian locations, not including those shot on SoCal studio backlots. California has proved its versatility as a backdrop in iconic sitcoms, cop shows, prime-time soaps, reality TV and other classic shows: *The Brady Bunch, The Streets of San Francisco, Baywatch, Beverly Hills 90210, Melrose Place, Six Feet Under, The OC, Laguna Beach, The Hills*. You can watch any TV program you want at LA's Paley Center for Media (p534) or get a sneak preview of next season by joining a live studio audience (p534).

During the 1940s and '50s, F Scott Fitzgerald, Dorothy Parker, Truman Capote, Ernest Hemingway and Tennessee Williams all did stints as Hollywood screenwriters.

'The Industry' has been based in California ever since *The Jazz Singer* premiered in downtown LA in 1927, ushering in the era of 'talkies' and Hollywood's Golden Age. In movies California has also played against type, diverging from kooky, sunny backdrop in Steve Martin's *LA Story* to brooding main character in such acclaimed noirs as *LA Confidential*, *Chinatown* and *Blade Runner*. Today, the high cost of filming in Los Angeles has sent location scouts beyond the studio-packed San Fernando Valley to Canada. With a few bikinis and fake palms Vancouver, Toronto and Montréal double as iconic Southern Californian locations.

Some production companies have long been based in San Francisco, including *Godfather* auteur Francis Ford Coppola's American Zoetrope and George Lucas' Industrial Light & Magic, the team of special effects wizards who brought you the *Star Wars* and *Raiders of the Lost Ark* series. San

TOP 10 FILMS ABOUT CALIFORNIA

- *The Maltese Falcon* (1941) John Huston directs Humphrey Bogart as Sam Spade, the classic San Francisco private eye.
- *Sunset Boulevard* (1950) Billy Wilder's classic stars Gloria Swanson and William Holden in a bonfire of Hollywood vanities.
- *Vertigo* (1958) The Golden Gate Bridge dazzles and dizzies in Alfred Hitchcock's thriller starring Jimmy Stewart and Kim Novak.
- *The Graduate* (1967) Dustin Hoffman flees status-obsessed California suburbia to search for meaning, heading across the Bay Bridge to Berkeley (in the wrong direction).
- *Harold and Maude* (1971) The ultimate May to December romance features the eternal spring of the Conservatory of Flowers and the fabulous ruins of the Sutro Baths.
- *Chinatown* (1974) Roman Polanski's gripping version of the early-20th-century water wars that made and nearly broke LA.
- *Blade Runner* (1982) Ridley Scott's sci-fi cyberpunk thriller projects LA into the 21st century, with high-rise corporate fortresses and chaotic streets.
- *The Player* (1992) Directed by Robert Altman and starring Tim Robbins, this satire on the Industry features dozens of cameos by actors spoofing themselves.
- *The Big Lebowski* (1998) The Coen brothers' madcap film of The Dude's SoCal misadventures spawned San Francisco's annual **Lebowski Fest** (http://lebowskifest.com).
- *Sideways* (2004) An Oscar-winning bachelors' romp through the Santa Barbara Wine Country maligns merlot and scores points for pinot.

Francisco remains a hub for documentary and independent filmmakers, while local ethnic media programs are produced statewide in dozens of languages from Persian to Portuguese. With Silicon Valley providing more of the effects for movies, Pixar Animation Studios fit right in among the dot-coms and interactive toy companies of San Francisco's East Bay, and have produced a string of hits from *Toy Story* to *Wall-E*.

California Babylon: A Guide to Sites of Scandal, Mayhem, and Celluloid in the Golden State by Kristan Lawson and Anneli Rufus is a bizarre guide to infamous locations throughout the state.

Literature

Californians read more than movie scripts: they make up the largest market for books in the US, and read more than the national average. Skewing the curve is bookish San Francisco, with more writers, playwrights and book purchases per capita than any other US city.

You've probably already read books by Californians without knowing it, since some of the best-known books by resident authors aren't set in their home state. Take for example Ray Bradbury's 1950s dystopian classic *Fahrenheit 451;* Alice Walker's Pulitzer Prize–winning *The Color Purple*; Ken Kesey's quintessential '60s novel *One Flew Over the Cuckoo's Nest*; Isabel Allende's best-selling *House of the Spirits*; and Michael Chabon's Pulitzer Prize–winning *The Amazing Adventures of Kavalier and Clay*. For a memorable romp through California with contemporary authors from Pico Iyer to Michael Chabon, check out *My California: Journeys by Great Writers* (2004) – proceeds support the California Arts Council.

Music

In your California dream, you jammed with a band – so what kind of music did you play? Beach Boys covers, rap, bluegrass, chamber music, hardcore, swing, classic soul, hard bop, heavy-metal riffs on opera or DJ mashups of all of the above? All of these homegrown styles makes sense in California, where a walk down the street sounds like the world's most eclectic iPod set to shuffle.

Chronologically speaking, Mexican folk music arrived in California before the Gold Rush introduced Western bluegrass, bawdy dancehall ragtime and Chinese classical music – but opera soon became California's favorite music. The city had 20 concert and opera halls before the 1906 San Francisco earthquake literally brought down the houses, but talented opera performers converged on the shattered city for free public performances that turned arias into anthems for the city's rebirth. Among San Francisco's first public buildings to be completed was the War Memorial Opera House (p137), now home to the second-largest US opera company after New York's Metropolitan. Walt Disney Concert Hall (p524) was inaugurated in 2003, but the venue remains better known for Frank Gehry's splashy design and the Los Angeles Philharmonic than opera.

Spot the next big writer or artist in California's influential indie arts journal *Zyzzyva* (www.zyzzyva.org)

Swing was the next big thing to hit California, in the 1930s and '40s, as big bands sparked a lindy-hopping craze in LA and sailors on shore leave hit San Francisco's underground, integrated jazz clubs. With Beat poets riffing over improvised bass-lines and audiences finger-snapping their approval, the cool, 1950s West Coast jazz of Chet Baker and Dave Brubeck emerged from San Francisco's North Beach. In the African American cultural hub along LA's Central Ave, the hard bop of Charlie Parker and Charlie Mingus kept the SoCal scene alive and swinging.

In 1950s and '60s California, doo-wop, rhythm and blues, and soul music were all in steady rotation at nightclubs in South Central LA, considered the 'Harlem of the West.' In the 1960s, hitmaker Sam Cooke ran his own record label, attracting soul and gospel talent to Los Angeles. Meanwhile, the hard-edged, honky-tonk Bakersfield Sound had already emerged inland.

READING CALIFORNIA, NORTH TO SOUTH

Here's what to read where in California's most literary locations:

North Coast & Sierras

- *Time and Materials* (Robert Hass) The winner of the 2008 Pulitzer Prize for Literature, this book is as palpably timeless as the cliffs of Point Reyes.
- *Roughing It* (Mark Twain) The master of sardonic observation tells of earthquakes, silver booms and busts, and getting by for a month on a dime in the Wild West.
- *Riprap and Cold Mountain Poems* (Gary Snyder) Beat poet and deep ecologist Snyder captures the daunting openness of the Yosemite landscape and California mindscape.
- *Already Dead: A California Gothic* (Denis Johnson) The chill sets in on the summer of love in this tale of paranoid, double-crossing pot farmers in Mendocino.

San Francisco Bay Area

- *On the Road* (Jack Kerouac) The book Kerouac banged out on one long scroll of paper in a San Francisco attic over a couple sleepless months in 1951 woke up America.
- *Tales of the City* (Armistead Maupin) This 1976 romp follows San Francisco characters: pot-growing landladies, ever-hopeful Castro club-goers, and titillated Midwestern arrivals.
- *Woman Warrior: Memoirs of a Girlhood Among Ghosts* (Maxine Hong Kingston) A memoir of growing up Chinese American in Stockton, reflecting the shattered mirror of Californian identity.
- *Slouching Towards Bethlehem* (Joan Didion) These 1968 essays burn through the hippie haze to reveal glassy-eyed teenage revolutionaries adrift in the summer of love.
- *The Electric Kool-Aid Acid Test* (Tom Wolfe) Follow Ken Kesey, the Merry Pranksters, the Grateful Dead and Hell's Angels as they tune in, turn on and drop out.
- *The Man in the High Castle* (Philip K Dick) The bestselling Berkeley sci-fi writer presents the ultimate what-if scenario: imagine San Francisco circa 1962 if Japan and Nazi Germany had won WWII.
- *Martin Eden* (Jack London) Semiautobiographical account of San Francisco's first literary star, who got by on his wits in the illicit oyster trade.

Central California

- *The Grapes of Wrath* (John Steinbeck) Salinas-born Steinbeck brought the plight of Central Valley migrant farmworkers home to readers across the world in this Pulitzer Prize–winning 1940 novel.
- *Fast Food Nation* (Eric Schlosser) Dossier of stomach-churning industry secrets, from Central Valley feedlots to drive-through windows, that changed the eating habits of some Americans.
- *Selected Poetry of Robinson Jeffers* In the looming, windswept pines surrounding Tor House (p464), Jeffers found inspiration for staggering, twisted poems.

Los Angeles

- *The Big Sleep* (Raymond Chandler) Iconic detective Philip Marlowe investigates the gritty underside of silver-screen-era 1930s Los Angeles.
- *LA Confidential* (James Ellroy) His streetwise staccato and sharp eye cut right through the soft-focus flim-flammery of LA, but Ellroy's detective wants to believe just the same.
- *Post Office* (Charles Bukowski) Arguably a better novelist than poet and the most cogent drunk ever, Bukowski captures LA's underbelly in this semiautobiographical novel.
- *Chicano* (Richard Vasquez) Cultures clash and dramas erupt in LA's barrio in this 1970 tale of a Chicano family divided over a daughter's romance with an Anglo.

PUNK'S NOT DEAD IN CALIFORNIA

In the 1970s, American airwaves were jammed with commercial arena rock that record companies paid DJs to shill like laundry soap, much to the articulate ire of California rock critics Lester Bangs and Greil Marcus. California teens bored with prepackaged anthems started making their own with secondhand guitars, three chords and crappy amps that added a loud buzz to their unleashed fury.

LA punk paralleled the scrappy local skate scene with the hardcore grind of Black Flag and the Germs. LA band X bridged punk and new wave from 1977 to 1986 with John Doe's rockabilly guitar, Exene Cervenka's angsty wail, and disappointed-romantic lyrics inspired by Charles Bukowski and Raymond Chandler. Local LA radio station KROQ rebelled against the tyranny of playlists, putting local punk on the airwaves and launching punk-funk sensation Red Hot Chili Peppers.

San Francisco's punk scene was arty and absurdist, in rare form with Dead Kennedys singer (and future San Francisco mayoral candidate) Jello Biafra howling 'Holiday in Cambodia.' The Avengers opened for the Sex Pistols' 1978 San Francisco show, which Sid Vicious celebrated with an OD in the Haight that broke up the band. Berkeley revived punk in the 1990s with ska-punk Rancid and Grammy Award–winning Green Day.

California's African American community grew with the 'Great Migration' during the WWII shipping boom, and from this thriving scene emerged the West Oakland blues sound.

California was where folk met rock, starting in the '50s with Ritchie Valens' 'La Bamba,' a rockified Mexican folk song. After Joan Baez and Bob Dylan had their Northern California fling in the early 1960s, Dylan plugged in his guitar and played folk rock. When Janis Joplin and Big Brother & the Holding Company applied their shambling musical stylings to 'Me & Bobby McGee,' folk rock splintered into psychedelia. Jimi Hendrix turned the American anthem into a tune suitable for an acid trip, and Jefferson Airplane turned Lewis Carroll's children's classic *Alice's Adventures in Wonderland* into the psychedelic hit 'White Rabbit.' Jim Morrison and The Doors blew minds from the Sunset Strip to San Francisco. Sooner or later, most of these Fillmore auditorium (p135) headliners wound up ODing in San Francisco's Haight district, and those that survived eventually cleaned up and cashed out – though for original jam-band the Grateful Dead, the song remained the same until guitarist Jerry Garcia's passing in rehab in 1995.

Waiting for the Sun: Strange Days, Weird Scenes and the Sound of Los Angeles, by British rock historian Barney Hoskyns, follows the twists and turns of the late-20th-century SoCal music scene.

While soul and hip-hop went pop in the 1980s and 1990s, California maintained a grassroots scene closer to the streets in LA and the heart of the black power movement in Oakland. Eazy E, Ice Cube and Dr Dre defined West Coast rap with 1989's *Straight Outta Compton*, and Dre's Death Row Records launched megawatt rap talents including Long Beach bad-boy Snoop Dog and Tupac Shakur, raised in Oakland and fatally shot in 1996 in a suspected East Coast/West Coast rap feud. Feuds continue to checker the musical and legal career of LA rapper The Game and his 2008 album *LAX*, while in Oakland Michael Franti blends rap with reggae stylings into messages for Middle East peace in 2008's *All Rebel Rockers*.

Architecture

There's more to California than beach houses and boardwalks. Californians have adapted imported styles to the climate and available materials, building cool, adobe-inspired houses in San Diego and fog-resistant redwood-shingle houses in Mendocino. But after a century and a half of Californians grafting on inspired influences and eccentric details as the mood strikes them, the element of the unexpected is everywhere: tiled Maya deco facades in Oakland, Shinto-inspired archways in LA, English thatched roofs in Carmel,

Chinoiserie streetlamps in San Francisco. California's architecture was postmodern before the word even existed.

The earliest standing structures in California are Spanish missions, and it's a testament to local Native American building techniques in adobe, limestone and grass that so many of the original 21 mission courtyard structures are still standing. Early Californian settlers adapted the original Spanish Mission style to create the rancho adobe style seen at El Pueblo de Los Angeles (p523) and in San Diego's Old Town (p614).

During the Gold Rush, California's nouveau riche imported materials to construct grand mansions that matched Continental fashions, and raised the stakes with ornamental excess. Some Victorian architecture in California is restrained, but many Gold Rush millionaires loved the Queen Anne style swagged with gilded ornaments, fishtail shingles and stucco garlands. Outrageous Victorian architecture that would surely make namesake Queen Victoria blush can be found in Northern California towns such as San Francisco, Ferndale and Eureka, and San Diego's Hotel del Coronado (p616).

Californian architecture has always had its contrarian streak, and many architects rejected frilly Victorian styles in favor of the simple, classical lines of Spanish colonial architecture. Mission revival details are restrained and functional: arched doors and windows, long covered porches, fountains, courtyards, solid walls and red tiled roofs. LA and San Diego train depots showcase this style, as do some buildings in San Diego's Balboa Park (p607).

Simplicity was also the hallmark of California's Arts and Crafts style, with woodwork and handmade touches marking deliberate departures from the Industrial Revolution, influenced by Japanese design principles and England's Arts and Crafts movement. Architects Charles and Henry Greene in Southern California and Bernard Maybeck in Northern California popularized the versatile one-story bungalow, epitomized by Pasadena's Gamble House (p542). Bungalows became trendy at the turn of the 20th century, and you'll spot them throughout Southern California and Berkeley with overhanging eaves, terraces and sleeping porches harmonizing indoors and outdoors.

California was cosmopolitan from the start, and couldn't be limited to any one set of international influences. William Randolph Hearst commissioned California's first licensed female architect Julia Morgan to build his Hearst Castle (p472) – a mixed blessing, since the commission would take Morgan decades, careful diplomacy through constant changes, and a delicate balancing act among Hearst's preferred Spanish, Gothic and Greek styles. In

Acclaimed writers from John Muir to Gary Snyder bring California landscapes to life in two outstanding anthologies, *Natural State: A Literary Anthology of California Nature Writing* and *Unfolding Beauty: Celebrating California's Landscapes.*

Jim Heimann's *California Crazy & Beyond: Roadside Vernacular Architecture* is a romp through the zany, whimsical world of California, where lemonade stands look like giant lemons and motels are shaped like tipis.

CALIFORNIA'S NAKED ARCHITECTURE

Clothing-optional California has never been shy about showcasing its assets, and embraced the stripped-down, glass-wall aesthetics of the International Style championed by Bauhaus architects Walter Gropius and Ludwig Mies van der Rohe, and Le Corbusier. Open floor-plans and floor-to-ceiling windows were especially suited to the see-and-be-seen culture of Southern California, in a residential style adapted by Austrian-born Rudolph Schindler and Richard Neutra that can be spotted today in LA and Palm Springs. Neutra and Schindler were influenced by Frank Lloyd Wright, who designed LA's Hollyhock House (p530) in a style he dubbed 'California Romanza.' Neutra also contributed with Charles and Ray Eames to the experimental open-plan Case Study Houses, several of which jut out of the landscape in Pacific Palisades, Beverly Hills and Pasadena.

But while Case Study houses are still used as the quintessential LA locations for films ranging from *Nurse Betty* to *LA Confidential*, Joseph Eichler's open-concept homes set the tone for the swinging '60s across California, with some 10,000 homes in the Bay Area and 900 in Southern California. Eichler homeowners had enough unstructured space to organize sit-ins and plenty of windows to let it all hang out.

SAN FRANCISCO'S LEAN, GREEN LANDMARKS

San Francisco has lately championed a brand of postmodernism by Pritzker Prize–winning architects that magnifies and mimics California's great outdoors. LA architect Thom Mayne incorporated solar panels and breathable mesh walls into his landmark green Federal Building (p100), and Swiss architects Herzog & de Meuron clad the MH de Young Memorial Museum (p110) in copper, which rapidly oxidized green to match its Golden Gate Park setting. Renzo Piano literally raised the roof on green design with his 2008 wildflower-capped California Academy of Sciences (p110).

the early 1920s, the art deco style took elements from the ancient world – Maya glyphs, Egyptian pillars, Babylonian ziggurats – and flattened them into modern motifs to cap stark facades and outline streamlined skyscrapers, notably in downtown Oakland. Streamline moderne kept decoration to a minimum and mimicked the aerodynamic look of ocean liners and airplanes, as at Orange County's John Wayne Airport (p577).

In the 1980s *Love & Rockets* started Californians reading comics again, with authors Jaime and Gilbert Hernandez drawing inspiration from LA's Chicano punk scene and Gabriel García Márquez' magic-realist plotlines.

But true to its mythic nature, California couldn't help wanting to embellish the facts a little, veering away from strict high modernism to add unlikely postmodern shapes to the local landscape. Richard Meier made his mark on West LA with the Getty Center (p536), a cresting white wave of a building atop a sunburned hilltop. Canadian-born Frank Gehry relocated to Santa Monica, and his billowing, sculptural style for LA's Walt Disney Concert Hall (p524) winks cheekily at shipshape Californian streamline moderne. Renzo Piano's signature inside-out industrial style can be glimpsed in the sawtooth roof and red-steel veins on the new Broad Contemporary Art Museum extension of LACMA (p533).

Visual Arts

Although the earliest European artists were trained cartographers accompanying Spanish explorers, their images of California as an island show more imagination than scientific rigor. This mythologizing tendency continued throughout the Gold Rush and through the 1880s, as Western artists alternated between caricatures of Wild West debauchery and manifest-destiny propaganda urging pioneers to settle the golden west. The completion of the Transcontinental Railroad in 1869 brought an influx of romantic painters, who produced the classic California landscapes seen at the Oakland Museum (p163) and Long Beach Museum of Art (p539).

But with the invention of photography, the improbable truth of California's landscape and its inhabitants was revealed. Pirkel Jones saw expressive potential in California landscape photography in the 19th century, and San Francisco native Ansel Adams' sublime 1940s photographs finally did justice to Yosemite. Adams founded Group f/64 with Seattle-based Imogen Cunningham and Edward Weston from Carmel. Dorothea Lange turned her unflinching lens on the plight of Californian migrant workers in the Great Depression and Japanese Americans forced to enter internment camps in WWII, producing poignant photographs seen at the Oakland Museum (p163). Photography buffs plan California vacations around two of the world's finest photography collections: the SFMOMA (p106), whose superb collection runs from early Western daguerreotypes to experimental postwar Japanese photography, and the Getty Center (p536), which has become the Louvre of photography with over 31,000 photographs in a newly expanded wing.

Timeless, rare Ansel Adams photographs are paired with excerpts from canonical Californian writers such as Jack Kerouac and Joan Didion in *California: With Classic California Writings*, edited by Andrea G Stillman.

As the postwar golden west became crisscrossed with freeways and divided into planned communities, Californian painters captured the abstract forms of manufactured landscapes on canvas. In San Francisco Richard

Diebenkorn, Clyfford Still and David Park became leading proponents of Bay Area Figurative Art, while San Francisco sculptor Richard Serra captured port-town aesthetics in massive, rusting monoliths resembling ship prows and industrial Stonehenges. Meanwhile, pop artists captured the ethos of conspicuous consumerism, through Wayne Thiebaud's bubblegum machines, British émigré David Hockney's LA pools, and above all, Ed Ruscha's studies of Standard Oil signs and SoCal mini-malls. San Diego's Museum of Contemporary Art (p621) specializes in post-1950s pop and conceptual art, and Ruscha's best work can be seen at LACMA (p533).

Due to cuts in the 2003 California Arts Council budget, Californians now invest less than 3¢ per capita in the arts - a minuscule amount compared to Canadians, who contribute $145 annually toward the arts.

Pristine, poolside SoCal aesthetics competed with San Francisco's love of rough-and-readymade 1950s Beat collage, 1960s psychedelic Fillmore posters, earthy '70s funk and beautiful-mess punk, and '80s graffiti and skate culture. Today's California contemporary art scene brings all these influences together with muralist-led social commentary, California's cutting-edge technology, and an obsessive dedication to craft. From this new-media milieu emerged San Francisco–raised Matthew Barney, who debuted his Cremaster Cycle videos at SFMOMA (p106). In LA, the Museum of Contemporary Art (p524) puts on provocative and avant-garde shows. To see Californian art at its most exciting and experimental, don't miss the alternative gallery scene in Culver City and converted warehouses of LA's Chinatown, and check out the indie art spaces in San Francisco's Mission District and laboratory-like galleries and museums in Yerba Buena Arts District (p106).

Theater

In your California dream you were discovered by a movie talent scout, but most Californian actors get their start in theater. Home to about 25% of the nation's professional actors, LA is the second-most influential city in America for theater, and San Francisco has been the US hub for experimental theater since the 1960s. Spaces to watch in LA include the Geffen Playhouse close to UCLA, the Mark Taper Forum (p564) and the Actors' Gang Theatre (p565), cofounded by actor Tim Robbins. Small theaters flourish in West Hollywood (WeHo) and North Hollywood (NoHo), West Coast's answers to off- and off-off-Broadway. Influential multicultural theaters include Little Tokyo's East West Players (p565), while critically acclaimed outlying companies include the innovative Long Beach Opera and Costa Mesa's South Coast Repertory.

When the 1906 earthquake hit San Francisco, the visiting Metropolitan opera lost all its costumes and tenor Enrico Caruso was thrown from his bed. Caruso never returned, but the Met played free shows in the rubble-choked streets.

San Francisco's priorities have been obvious since the great earthquake of 1906, when survivors were entertained in tents set up amid the smoldering ruins, and its famous theaters were rebuilt well before City Hall. Major productions destined for the lights of Broadway and London premiere at the American Conservatory Theater (p136), and San Francisco's answer to

TAKING IT TO THE STREETS

Beginning in the 1930s, when the federal Works Progress Administration sponsored schemes to uplift and beautify California cities, murals defined California cityscapes. Mexican muralists Diego Rivera, David Alfaro Siqueiros and Jose Clemente Orozco sparked an outpouring of murals across LA that today number in the thousands. Rivera was also brought to San Francisco for murals at the San Francisco Art Institute (p104), and his influence is reflected in the interior of San Francisco's Coit Tower (p103) and some 250 murals lining the Mission District preserved and expanded by Precita Eyes (p105). Murals gave voice to Chicano pride and protests over US Central American policies in the 1970s, notably in San Diego's Chicano Park and East Los Angeles murals by collectives such as East Los Streetscapers. Contemporary California street art maintains deep roots in Latin American traditions, which can be traced at the Long Beach's Museum of Latin American Art (p539).

Edinburgh is the annual Fringe Theater Fest at the Exit Theatre (p137). Magic Theatre (p136) gained a national reputation in the 1970s, when Sam Shepard was the theater's resident playwright, and Berkeley Repertory Theatre (p177) has launched acclaimed productions based on such unlikely subjects as the rise and fall of Jim Jones' People's Temple.

Dance

For coverage of art museums, galleries, fine-art exhibition spaces and upcoming shows throughout California, check out *Artweek* (www.artweek.com), the leading West Coast art magazine.

In LA and San Francisco, dance has always leaned toward the experimental and the avant-garde, with Martha Graham, Alvin Ailey and Bella Lewitzky pioneering new movements in Los Angeles. LA's American Repertory Dance Company is dedicated to keeping alive the legacy of early-20th-century modern dances, including those by San Francisco dance pioneer Isadora Duncan. Founded in 1933, internationally renowned San Francisco Ballet (p137) is America's oldest resident professional ballet company and still draws dancers and commissions works from all over the globe. LA's dance companies are highly eclectic: Lula Washington Dance Theatre is one of the premier African American dance companies in the west; Loretta Livingston & Dancers shows Lewitzky's influence; and Diavolo Dance Theater practices surreal 'hyper-dance' in custom-built spaces. San Francisco's modern dance troupes, including ODC/San Francisco, Alonzo King's Lines Ballet and Liss Fain Dance, are known for combining raw Western physicality with Californian ingenuity.

Environment

From soaring snowcapped peaks, to scorching deserts and dense forests, California is home to a bewildering variety of ecosystems and animals. In fact the state not only has the highest biodiversity in North America, it has more types of climate and more types of soils than nearly any location in the world. California is one of few places in the world with a Mediterranean climate, a climate characterized by dry summers and mild wet winters favored by unique plants and animals. At the same time, California has the largest human population of any state and the highest projected growth rate in the nation, putting a tremendous strain on California's many precious resources.

For information on traveling responsibly in the state see p25.

THE LAND

The third-largest state after Alaska and Texas, California covers more than 160,000 sq miles and is larger than the UK. It is bordered to the north by Oregon, to the south by Mexico, with Nevada and Arizona on its eastern border, and 840 miles of glorious Pacific shoreline on the west. Its cool northern border stands at the same latitude as Rome, while the arid southern border is at the same latitude as Tel Aviv.

California is larger than 85 of the smallest nations in the world.

Geology & Earthquakes

California is an exceedingly complex geologic landscape formed from fragments of rock and earth crust scraped together as the North American continent drifted westward over hundreds of millions of years. Crumpled coast ranges, the downward-bowing Central Valley and the still-rising Sierra Nevada all provide evidence of gigantic forces exerted as the continental and ocean plates crushed together. This changed about 25 million years ago, when the plates stopped colliding and started sliding against each other, creating the San Andreas Fault. Because this contact zone doesn't slide smoothly, but catches and slips irregularly, it rattles California with an ongoing succession of tremors and earthquakes.

The state's most famous earthquake was one in 1906 that measured 7.8 on the Richter scale and demolished San Francisco, leaving more than 3000 people dead. The Bay Area made headlines again in 1989 when the Loma Prieta earthquake (7.1) caused a section of the Bay Bridge to collapse. Los Angeles' last 'big one' was in 1994, when the Northridge quake (6.7) caused parts of the Santa Monica Fwy to fall down, making it the most costly quake in US history – so far.

One of the most fascinating aspects of the sliding San Andreas Fault is that all the lands west of the fault, including San Diego, Los Angeles and San Francisco, are sailing toward Alaska at a rate of 1.9in a year. Because they live on a separate plate, some residents jokingly brag that they don't belong to the rest of North America.

Curious about all the rumbling along the San Andreas Fault? Check out *A Land in Motion* by Michael Collier for a lively overview of the subject.

Mountains & Valleys

Much of the California coast is fronted by rugged, little-explored coastal mountains that capture winter's water-laden storms. Over 120in of rain a year fall in the northernmost reaches of the Coast Ranges and, in places, persistent summer fog contributes another 12in of precipitation. Nutrient-rich soils and abundant moisture foster forests of giant trees (where they haven't been cut), including stands of towering redwoods in numerous areas north of Monterey. South of Santa Barbara, the mountains begin to diminish and habitats become increasingly desertlike. San Francisco divides the Coast Ranges roughly in half: the foggy North Coast remains sparsely populated, while the Central and South Coasts have a balmy climate, sandy beaches and lots of people.

Take a virtual field trip courtesy of the myriad links put together by the California Geological Survey at www.conservation.ca.gov/cgs/geotour.

On their eastern flanks, the Coast Ranges subside into gently rolling hills that give way to the sprawling Central Valley. Once an inland sea, this flat inland basin is now an agricultural powerhouse producing about half of America's fruits, nuts and vegetables with a value of over $14 billion a year. Stretching approximately 500 miles long and 40 miles wide, the Central Valley gets about as much rainfall as a desert, but receives huge volumes of water running off the Sierra Nevada. Before the arrival of Europeans the valley was a natural wonderland – a region of vast marshes and flocks of geese that blackened the sky, not to mention grasslands carpeted with countless flowers and grazed by millions of antelopes, elk and grizzly bears. Virtually this entire landscape has been plowed under and replaced with alien weeds (including agricultural crops) and livestock.

According to the US Geological Survey, the odds of a magnitude 6.7 or greater earthquake hitting California in the next 30 years is 99.7%.

Bordering the Central Valley on its eastern side looms California's most prominent topographic feature, the world-famous Sierra Nevada. At 400 miles long and 50 miles wide, this is not only one of the largest mountain ranges in the world but it is also the home of vast wilderness areas and 13 peaks over 14,000ft. In fact, the entire 150-mile region from Sonora Pass south to Mt Whitney lies mostly above 9000ft and is known as the High Sierra; this is a stunning landscape of glaciers, sculpted granite peaks and remote canyons, beautiful to look at but difficult to access, and one of the greatest challenges for settlers attempting to reach California in the 1800s.

The soaring Sierra Nevada captures storm systems and drains them of their water, with most of the precipitation over 3000ft falling as snow. Snowfalls average 38ft at midelevations on the west slope, with a record of 73.5ft at one location, making this a premier skiing and winter sports destination. These waters eventually flow into 11 major river systems on the west slope and several on the east slope, providing the vast majority of water for agriculture in the Central Valley and meeting the needs of major metropolitan areas from San Francisco to Los Angeles.

Most of the Sierra Nevada is cloaked in dense conifer forests with stands of oaks taking over in the western foothills and in dry canyons. Twenty-three species of conifer occur in the Sierra Nevada, ranging from the scraggly twisting gray pines of the western foothills to tiny wind-sculpted whitebark pines at 12,000ft. In between, midelevation forests are home to massive Douglas firs, ponderosa pines and, biggest of all, the giant sequoia.

A Natural History of California, by Allan A Schoenherr, is a comprehensive, readable explanation of the geologic and environmental forces that have shaped every region of the state.

At its northern end the Sierra Nevada merges imperceptibly into the southern tip of the volcanic Cascade Mountains that continue north into Oregon and Washington. This wet mountainous region extends westward to the coast through a tangle of ancient and geologically complex ranges that are sparsely populated and also heavily cloaked with conifer forests.

Deserts

With the west slope of the Sierra Nevada capturing the lion's share of water, all lands east of the Sierra crest are dry and desertlike, receiving less than 10in of rain a year. Areas in the northern half of the state, especially on the elevated Modoc Plateau of northeastern California, are a cold desert (known as the Great Basin desert) blanketed with hardy sagebrush shrubs and pockets of juniper trees. Temperatures increase as you head south, with a prominent transition occurring when you descend from Mono Lake and Mammoth into Bishop and the Owens Valley. This hot desert (the Mojave Desert) includes Death Valley, one of the hottest places on earth. Surprisingly, some of the

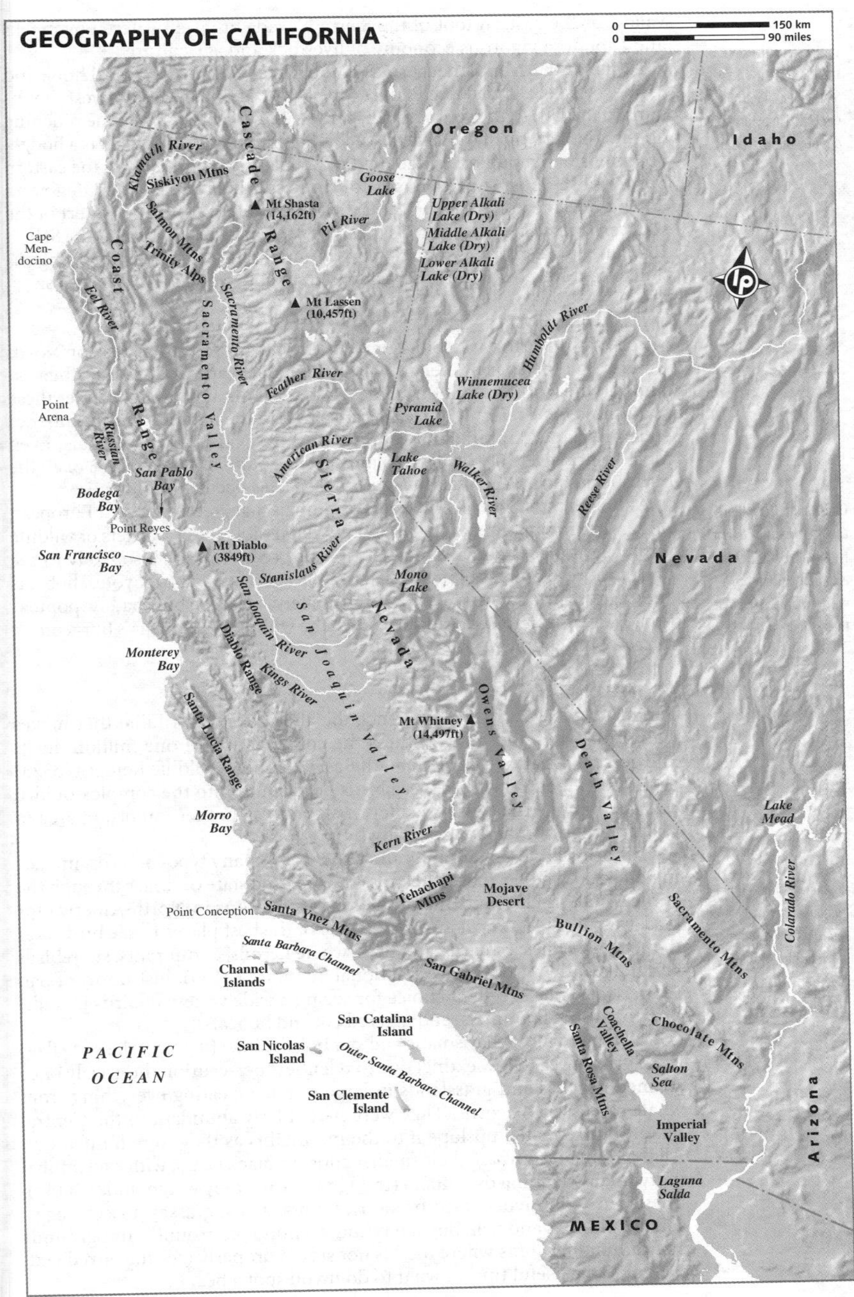
GEOGRAPHY OF CALIFORNIA
0 150 km
0 90 miles
Oregon
Idaho
Nevada
Arizona
MEXICO
PACIFIC OCEAN
Cascade Range
Klamath River
Siskiyou Mtns
Goose Lake
Mt Shasta (14,162ft)
Pit River
Upper Alkali Lake (Dry)
Middle Alkali Lake (Dry)
Lower Alkali Lake (Dry)
Salmon Mtns
Trinity Alps
Cape Mendocino
Coast Range
Eel River
Sacramento River
Sacramento Valley
Mt Lassen (10,457ft)
Humboldt River
Feather River
Winnemucea Lake (Dry)
Point Arena
Russian River
Pyramid Lake
American River
Lake Tahoe
Walker River
Reese River
San Pablo Bay
Bodega Bay
Point Reyes
Sierra Nevada
Mt Diablo (3849ft)
San Francisco Bay
Stanislaus River
Mono Lake
San Joaquin River
San Joaquin Valley
Diablo Range
Monterey Bay
Kings River
Santa Lucia Range
Mt Whitney (14,497ft)
Owens Valley
Death Valley
Morro Bay
Kern River
Lake Mead
Colarado River
Tehachapi Mtns
Mojave Desert
Point Conception
Santa Ynez Mtns
Santa Barbara Channel
Channel Islands
Bullion Mtns
Sacramento Mtns
San Gabriel Mtns
San Catalina Island
San Nicolas Island
Outer Santa Barbara Channel
San Clemente Island
Coachella Valley
Santa Rosa Mtns
Chocolate Mtns
Salton Sea
Imperial Valley
Laguna Salda

During and after WWII, the US Army used the Salton Sea (p668) for target practice by dropping dummy bombs into it.

valleys at the eastern foot of the Sierra Nevada are well-watered by creeks and support a vigorous economy of livestock and agriculture.

At its southern end, the Sierra Nevada makes a funny westward hook and connects via the Transverse Ranges (one of few examples of east–west mountains in the US) to the southern Coast Ranges, and at the same time pinching off the southern tip of the Central Valley. Southern California itself is a hodgepodge of small mountain ranges and desert basins. Mountains on the eastern border of the Los Angeles Basin continue southward past San Diego and down the spine of northern Baja California, while the Mojave Desert of the southern Sierra Nevada morphs into the Colorado Desert around the Salton Sea. This entire region is remarkably dry and rocky, mostly devoid of vegetation except for pockets of desert-adapted shrubs, cacti and Joshua trees.

WILDLIFE

Much of California is a biological island cut off from the rest of North America by the soaring heights of the Sierra Nevada and, as on other 'islands' in the world, evolution creates unique plants and animals under these conditions. As a result, California ranks first in the nation for its number of endemic plants, amphibians, reptiles, freshwater fish and mammals. Even more impressive, 30% of all the plant species found in the US, 50% of all the bird species and 50% of all the mammal species occur in California.

One way to fully appreciate the size of a condor is to realize it can take a condor chick up to a week to break free of its thick-shelled egg.

Although the staggering numbers of animals that greeted the first European settlers are now a thing of the past, it is still possible to see pockets of wildlife in the right places and at the right times of year. You are also likely to see one or more examples of many charismatic species, such as coyotes, bobcats and eagles, during your travels. Unfortunately, these are but shadow populations, hovering at the edge of survival at the whim of California's burgeoning human population.

Animals

Perhaps the best way to experience the abundance of wildlife that makes California so famous is to witness the congregation of one million ducks and geese that gather at the Klamath Basin National Wildlife Refuges (p323) each November. By winter these birds head south into the complex of bird refuges that line the Central Valley, making this another important area to observe huge numbers of waterfowl.

Take along John Kemper's *Birding Northern California* for tips on planning your bird-watching expedition.

California lies on major migratory routes for many types of birds, including ducks and geese, that either pass through the state or linger through the winter, making the state one of the top destinations in North America for bird-watchers. At almost any season one of the best places to see birds is at the state's beaches, estuaries and bays, where herons, cormorants, shorebirds and gulls gather. Point Reyes National Seashore (p160), just north of San Francisco, is one excellent choice for seeing a wide variety of birds in addition to marine mammals, endangered elk and bobcats.

California's most charismatic and symbolic animal (it graces the state flag) is the grizzly bear. Now extinct due to relentless persecution the grizzly once roamed beaches and grasslands in large numbers, eating everything from whale carcasses to acorns. They were particularly abundant in the Central Valley, but retreated upslope into the mountains as they were hunted out. All that remains now are their smaller cousins, black bears, with exceptional individuals weighing over 400lb (though typically they weigh under 300lb). These burly omnivores feed on berries, nuts, roots, grasses, insects, eggs, small mammals and fish, but can become a nuisance around campgrounds and mountain cabins where food is not stored properly (see the boxed text, p70 for some useful tips on what to do if you spot a bear).

Other large mammals fared poorly as European settlers moved into the state in the 1800s. Immense herds of tule elk and antelope in the Central Valley were particularly hard hit, with antelope retreating in small numbers to the northeastern corner of the state, and elk hunted into near-extinction (a small remnant herd was moved to Point Reyes where it has thrived).

In Pacific Grove, near Monterey, you can be fined $500 for molesting one of their treasured monarch butterflies.

Some smaller animals have done well around the edges of towns. Bobcats, coyotes and foxes are prolific enough that you are almost guaranteed a sighting of these creatures when you travel through the wilder areas of the state (keep an eye out for them while looking for elk at Point Reyes). Sharp-eyed visitors may even spot a weasel, a badger, a beaver, or one of the truly rare animals like a marten or a fisher. Purchasing a local wildlife guide will help direct you to viewing locations for any of these creatures.

The coast of California is blessed with a fantastic assortment of marine mammals, including one of the few whale migrations in the world that can be easily viewed from land or nearshore boats. Once threatened by extinction, gray whales now migrate in decent numbers along the Pacific coast. In November and December they head south toward their breeding grounds in Baja California, and numerous coastal communities and sightseeing boats offer premier viewing opportunities. Adult whales are longer than a city bus and weigh at least 16 tons, making quite a splash when they lunge or leap out of the water (see the boxed text, p161).

The coast also offers many chances to see seals and sea lions. Año Nuevo State Reserve (p193) is the world's biggest breeding ground for 3000lb elephant seals (the largest one on record weighed 11,000lb!) that haul out of the ocean in November and December and engage in ferocious bloody battles for the rights to mate with females (see the boxed text, p193). A smaller rookery has been established at Chimney Rock at Point Reyes (p161). There is a larger colony at Piedras Blancas near Hearst Castle, just south of Big Sur. Wander up the Big Sur coastline to see free-flying examples of highly endangered California condors (p467).

Those lovely sea otters you see in Monterey Bay spend five to six hours a day grooming their silky hair.

Since the 1989 earthquake, loudly barking sea lions have been piling up on San Francisco's Pier 39, much to the delight of ogling tourists. Other locations for sea lion viewing include Point Lobos State Reserve near Carmel (p464), San Simeon's Piedras Blancas (p471) and some of the Channel Islands off Santa Barbara (see p504).

Plants

California's 6000 species of plants are both flamboyant and subtle. Many species are so obscure and similar that only a dedicated botanist could tell them apart, but add them all together in the spring and you end up with riotous carpets of wildflowers that can take your breath away.

Get daily reports from professional photographers seeking the premier wildflower displays in the spring, and the top autumn colors in the fall, at www.calphoto.com.

California is a land of superlatives: the tallest (coastal redwoods approaching 380ft), the largest (giant sequoias of the Sierra Nevada 38ft across at the base), the oldest (bristlecone pines of the White Mountains that are almost 5000 years old; see p413) and the smallest (a pond-dwelling plant that measures a fraction of a tenth of an inch).

Water is an overriding issue for many of California's plants because there is almost no rain during the prime growing season. Plants have adapted by growing prolifically during the state's mild wet winters, springing to life with the first rains of autumn and blooming as early as February. Desert areas begin their peak blooming in March, with other lowland areas of the state producing abundant wildflowers in April. Check out Anza-Borrego Desert State Park (p669), Death Valley National Park (p680) and the Carrizo Plain National Monument (see the boxed text, p488) for some of the most spectacular and predictable wildflower displays in the state.

Both experts and enthusiasts will treasure www.calflora.org, a massive project with mapped locations and photos of every plant species in California.

The famous 'golden hills' of California are the result of many plants drying up in preparation for the long dry summer, but a closer inspection reveals that some plants tough out the heat with a variety of special adaptations. These include small waxy leaves and dense silvery hairs. Except for oaks, broad-leaved trees do poorly under these dry conditions, but conifers do exceptionally well because they keep their leaves year-round and can patiently wait to slake their thirst in the winter.

Coastal plants are able to squeeze droplets of water out of the persistent summer fog, which adds up to 12in of precipitation a year in some areas. Redwoods on the northern coast are particularly effective at sweeping water from wisps of drifting fog, capturing so much water that the trees drip water onto the forest floor and help keep other plants alive.

Browse through stunning photos of every inch of California's coast at www.californiacoastline.org.

Meanwhile, the Sierra Nevada has three distinct ecozones: the dry western foothills covered with oak and chaparral, conifer forests starting from about 2000ft and an alpine zone above 8000ft. The giant sequoia, which is unique to California, stands in isolated groves scattered in and near Yosemite and Sequoia National Parks. Although sequoias were once widespread in the American West, only a handful survived on the west slope of the Sierra Nevada after the mountains rose to their current height and frigid winter storms killed off the species elsewhere.

Deciduous trees of the Sierra Nevada include the delightful quaking aspen, a white-trunked tree whose shimmering leaves brighten many mountain meadow edges. Its large rounded leaves turn butter-yellow to orange in the fall, creating some of the most spectacular scenery you'll see in California. Check out the autumn colors around June Lake (p405) for a breathtaking combination of aspens, black jagged peaks and lingering snowfields.

NATIONAL & STATE PARKS

The majority of Californians rank outdoor recreation as vital to their quality of life, and the amount of preserved lands has grown due to several important pieces of legislation passed since the 1960s, including the landmark 1976 California Coastal Act, which saved the coastline from further development, and the controversial 1994 California Desert Protection Act, which angered many ranchers, miners and off-roaders. It's in the state's economic best interests to protect wilderness, as recreational tourism is outpacing competing 'resource extraction' industries such as mining.

California claims both the highest point in continental USA (Mt Whitney, 14,497ft) and the lowest elevation in the western hemisphere (Badwater, Death Valley, 282ft below sea level) - plus they're only 90 miles apart, as the condor flies.

Unfortunately, many of California's national parks are being loved to death. Overcrowding severely impacts the environment, and it's increasingly difficult to balance public access with the natural state of parks. Try visiting in the shoulder seasons (ie not summer) and flee the paved roads and parking lots for rugged backcountry. Lesser-known parks, especially in the northern mountains and southern California deserts, may go relatively untouched most of the year, which means you won't have to reserve permits, campsites or accommodations months in advance.

At national park entrance stations, get ready to fork over some cash (credit cards are often not accepted). Entrance fees vary from free to $25 per vehicle for a seven-day pass. Federal budget shortfalls and chronic underfunding have been partly responsible for regular rises in parks fees. This makes the 'America the Beautiful' annual pass ($80) a deal. It admits four adults and their children under 16 years old for free to all national parks and federal recreational lands for one year and can be purchased at any national park entrance station. US citizens and permanent residents 62 years and older are eligible for a lifetime pass ($10); these are free for people with disabilities. State park entry fees range from $2 to $14, while the fee for a year-round pass is $125 and probably not worth it unless you live in California.

CALIFORNIA'S TOP NATIONAL & STATE PARKS

Park	Features	Activities	Best time to visit
Anza-Borrego Desert State Park (p669)	badlands, canyons, fan-palm oases, caves, hot springs, bighorn sheep, birds	hiking, 4WD roads, stargazing, horseback riding	Nov-Mar
Calaveras Big Trees State Park (p345)	grove of giant sequoias in the mid-Sierra	hiking, bird-watching, cross-country skiing	May-Oct
Carrizo Plain National Monument (p488)	pristine valley grasslands, endangered wildlife, flowers, remote landscapes	hiking, stargazing, wildflower viewing	Feb-Apr
Channel Islands National Park (p504)	rocky islands with steep cliffs, elephant seals, sea lions, otters, foxes	snorkeling, diving, kayaking, hiking, bird-watching	year-round
Death Valley National Park (p680)	unique geology, sand dunes, canyons, volcanic craters, ghost towns, wild horses	hiking, 4WD roads, horseback riding	Oct-Apr
Henry Coe State Park (p186)	coastal wilderness, oak woodlands, grasslands, flowers	backpacking, horseback riding, mountain biking	Oct-Apr
Joshua Tree National Park (p662)	rocky desert, fan-palm oases, spiky Joshua trees, cactus gardens, golden eagles	rock climbing, hiking, 4WD roads, mountain biking, bird-watching	Sep-May
Lassen Volcanic National Park (p306)	volcanic peak and terrain, geothermal activity	hiking, snowshoeing	Jun-Sep
Lava Beds National Monument (p322)	lava tube caves, pit craters, cinder cones, petroglyphs, antelope, bobcats, bald eagles	spelunking, hiking, bird-watching	May-Sep
Mendocino Headlands State Park (p260)	jutting coastal bluffs, rugged beaches, wildflowers, migrating whales	nature walks, hiking, beachcombing, surfing	year-round
Mojave National Preserve (p678)	volcanic cinder cones, sand dunes, cliffside canyons, caverns, Joshua trees, desert tortoises	hiking, 4WD roads	Oct-Apr
Morro Bay State Park (p477)	saltwater marshes, lagoons, coastal dunes, volcanic rock, peregrine falcons, migratory birds	sailing, surfing, hiking, bird-watching	year-round
Muir Woods National Monument (p156)	towering stands of old-growth redwood trees, banana slugs, northern spotted owls	nature walks, hiking	Apr-Nov
Point Reyes National Seashore (p160)	windswept beaches, lagoons, forested cliffs, tule elk, northern elephant seals, migrating whales	hiking, bird-watching	Apr-Nov
Redwood National & State Parks (p292)	virgin redwood groves, fern forests, pristine beaches, Roosevelt elk, great blue herons	hiking, scenic drives, kayaking	May-Sep
Sequoia & Kings Canyon National Parks (p391)	giant sequoias, deep canyons, montane forests, high-alpine wilderness, black bears	hiking	Jun-Oct
Yosemite National Park (p376)	sheer granite-walled valley, waterfalls, alpine meadows, black bears, mule deer, bighorn sheep	hiking, backpacking, rock climbing, rafting, skiing, snowshoeing	Jun-Sep

There are 18 national forests in California run by the **US Forest Service** (USFS; ☎ 707-562-8737; www.fs.fed.us/r5/), including lands around Mt Whitney, Mt Shasta and Big Bear Lake, and many other areas worth exploring. National wildlife refuges (NWR), favored by bird-watchers, are managed by the **US Fish & Wildlife Service** (USFWS; ☎ 916-414-6464; www.fws.gov/refuges), and wilderness tracts are overseen by the **Bureau of Land Management** (BLM; ☎ 916-978-4401; www.blm.gov/c a/st/en.html).

The challenge of water management in California is graphically explained in David Carle's *Introduction to Water in California*.

ENVIRONMENTAL ISSUES

Although California is in many ways a success story, development and growth have come at great environmental cost. Starting in 1849, Gold Rush miners tore apart the land in their frenzied quest for the 'big strike,' ultimately sending more than 1.5 billion tons of debris, and uncalculated amounts of poisonous mercury, downstream into the Central Valley where streams became so clogged that the California Supreme Court ruled in 1884 against then-common mining practices.

Water, or the lack thereof, has always been at the heart of California's epic environmental struggles and catastrophes. Damming of the Tuolumne River at Hetch Hetchy (inside the supposedly protected Yosemite National Park) so that San Francisco could have drinking water was reputed to have caused California's greatest environmental champion, , to die of grief. Likewise, the diversion of water to the Los Angeles area has contributed to the destruction of Owens Lake and its fertile wetlands, and the degradation of Mono Lake. For more information about this water diversion and its impact on the Owens Valley, see the boxed text, p404.

The University of California Press has a growing series of popular guides that introduce readers to nearly every aspect of California natural history (www.californianatural history.com).

The damming of rivers and capture of water for houses and farms has also destroyed salmon runs once numbering in the millions and drained marshlands where millions of ducks and waterbirds formerly nested. The once-vibrant Central Valley, for example, today more closely resembles a dust bowl, and its underground aquifer is in poor shape.

Altered and compromised habitats, both on land and water, are easy targets for invasive species, and California exemplifies one of the worst-case scenarios in the nation. Over 1500 species of weedy plants have made the state their new home, including some highly aggressive species that wreak havoc on the state's economy and ecosystems. In San Francisco Bay alone, one of the most important estuaries in the world, there are now nearly 250 alien species choking the aquatic ecosystem and in some areas they comprise as much as 99% of the total biomass.

Although air quality in California has improved markedly over the past two decades, it's still the worst in the country. In 2007 the American Lung Association rated Los Angeles air quality as the worst of any city in the nation and 26 California counties failed their clean air test. Auto exhaust and fine particulates generated by the unending turning of vehicle tires, along with industrial emissions, are the chief culprits. An even greater health hazard is ozone, the principal ingredient in smog, which makes sunny days in Los Angeles and the Central Valley look hazy. But there's hope: low-emission vehicles are rapidly becoming one of the most sought-after types of car in the state, and high gas costs are keeping many of the larger gas-guzzling vehicles off the road.

California Camping & Outdoors

California may have an obsession with cars, and it's where mall culture was born, but the smartest of those who count themselves lucky to live here know that it's really all about getting outdoors – and back to nature. They take every chance they can get to hit the trails, play in the surf, hop into the saddle or grab a paddle. The Golden State is an all-seasons outdoor playground. Here you can go hiking among desert wildflowers in spring, swimming in the Pacific kissed by the summer sun, mountain-biking among a kaleidoscope of fall foliage or celebrate winter by schussing through deep powder. For bigger thrills, launch a glider off Pacific bluffs, climb granite big walls and go bouldering in a wonderland of rocks, or hook a kite onto a surfboard and launch yourself over foamy ocean waves. Whatever your adrenaline fix, you'll find it here.

The *Backpacker* magazine website (http://backpacker.com) has a searchable online archive with thousands of campstove cooking recipes, from wild blueberry crepes to 'portable pub grub.'

CAMPING

All across California, campers are absolutely spoiled for choice. Pitch a tent beside alpine lakes and streams with views of snaggle-toothed Sierra Nevada peaks, along gorgeous strands of Southern California sand or on the wilder, windswept beaches of the North Coast. Take shelter underneath redwoods, the tallest trees on earth, from south of San Francisco north to the Oregon border. Inland, deserts are magical places to camp, especially next to sand dunes on full-moon nights. If you didn't bring camping gear with you, don't worry: camping supply and rental shops are listed throughout this book.

'Primitive' campsites usually have fire pits, picnic tables and access to drinking water and pit or vault toilets. These are most common in national forests managed by the USDA Forest Service (USFS) and on Bureau of Land Management (BLM) land. 'Developed' campgrounds in state and national parks have more amenities, including flush toilets, barbecue grills and occasionally hot showers and coin-op laundry. RV (recreational vehicle) hookups and dump stations are available at select campgrounds in state parks and national forests, but almost never in national parks. A few campgrounds offer walk-in 'environmental' sites; these may be reserved for long-distance hikers and cyclists, but often are also open to any tent campers willing to hump their gear a half-mile or less into the woods to be rewarded with peace and privacy. Many campgrounds, especially in the mountains and in Northern California, are closed from late fall through spring. Actual opening and closing dates vary each year, depending on weather conditions.

The California State Parks website (www.parks.ca.gov) has full-color details of all 278 state parks, along with travel ideas and downloadable maps, brochures and trail guides.

Private campgrounds are often open year-round, especially those that are closest to cities, beaches and major highways. They tend to cater more to families and the RV crowd; tent sites may be few and lack character. Standard amenities include hot showers, flush toilets, swimming pools and, increasingly, wireless internet access (wi-fi). Bonus perks include convenience stores, children's playgrounds and equipment for outdoor activities; for example, rental bicycles or canoes. Some private campgrounds offer camping cabins, which range from canvas-sided wooden platforms and yurts to log-frame structures with real beds, private bathrooms and heating. **Kampgrounds of America** (KOA; http://koa.com) is a national chain of private campgrounds with full facilities; they're not cheap, but they are reliable.

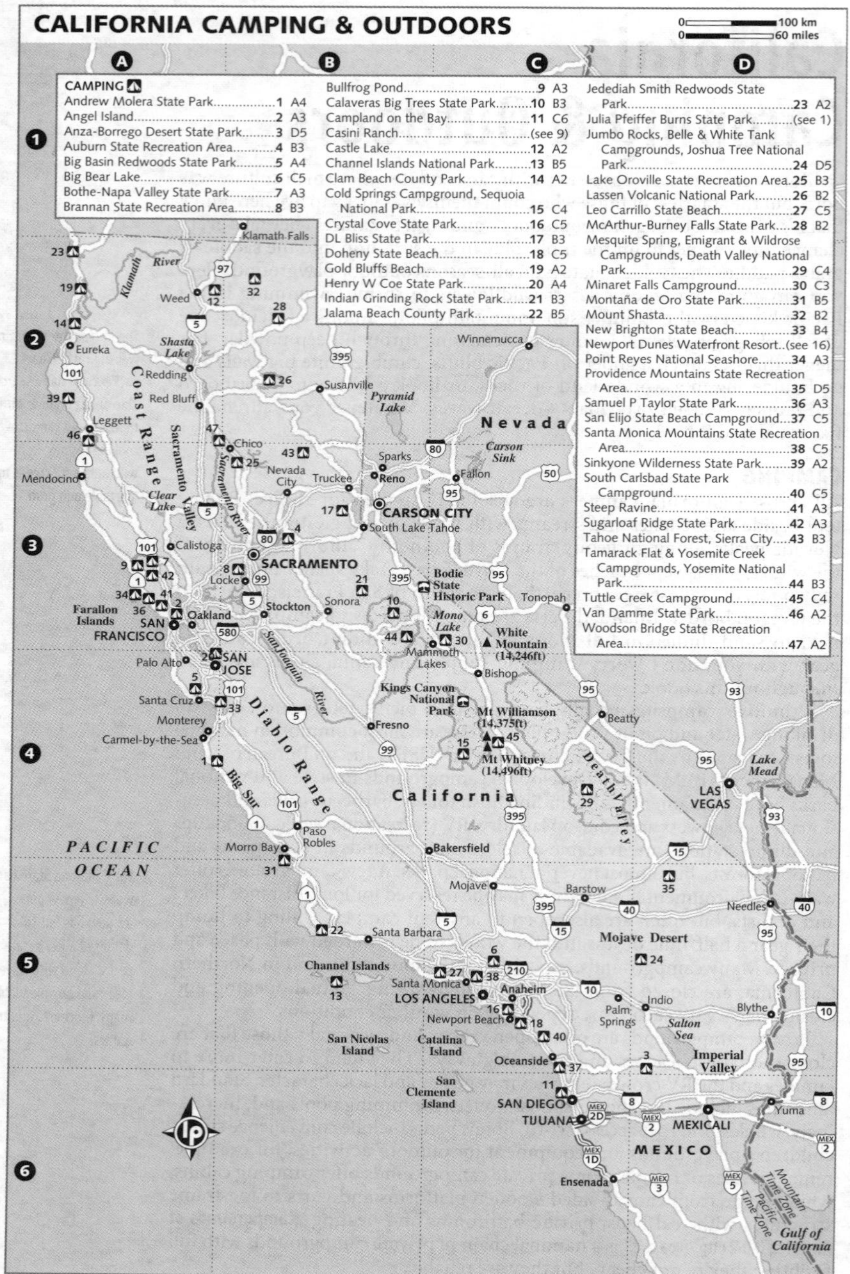
CALIFORNIA CAMPING & OUTDOORS
0 100 km
0 60 miles
A
B
C
D
1
2
3
4
5
6
CAMPING
Andrew Molera State Park 1 A4
Angel Island 2 A3
Anza-Borrego Desert State Park 3 D5
Auburn State Recreation Area 4 B3
Big Basin Redwoods State Park 5 A4
Big Bear Lake 6 C5
Bothe-Napa Valley State Park 7 A3
Brannan State Recreation Area 8 B3
Bullfrog Pond 9 A3
Calaveras Big Trees State Park 10 B3
Campland on the Bay 11 C6
Casini Ranch (see 9)
Castle Lake 12 A2
Channel Islands National Park 13 B5
Clam Beach County Park 14 A2
Cold Springs Campground, Sequoia National Park 15 C4
Crystal Cove State Park 16 C5
DL Bliss State Park 17 B3
Doheny State Beach 18 C5
Gold Bluffs Beach 19 A2
Henry W Coe State Park 20 A4
Indian Grinding Rock State Park 21 B3
Jalama Beach County Park 22 B5
Jedediah Smith Redwoods State Park 23 A2
Julia Pfeiffer Burns State Park (see 1)
Jumbo Rocks, Belle & White Tank Campgrounds, Joshua Tree National Park 24 D5
Lake Oroville State Recreation Area 25 B3
Lassen Volcanic National Park 26 B2
Leo Carrillo State Beach 27 C5
McArthur-Burney Falls State Park 28 B2
Mesquite Spring, Emigrant & Wildrose Campgrounds, Death Valley National Park 29 C4
Minaret Falls Campground 30 C3
Montaña de Oro State Park 31 B5
Mount Shasta 32 B2
New Brighton State Beach 33 B4
Newport Dunes Waterfront Resort (see 16)
Point Reyes National Seashore 34 A3
Providence Mountains State Recreation Area 35 D5
Samuel P Taylor State Park 36 A3
San Elijo State Beach Campground 37 C5
Santa Monica Mountains State Recreation Area 38 C5
Sinkyone Wilderness State Park 39 A2
South Carlsbad State Park Campground 40 C5
Steep Ravine 41 A3
Sugarloaf Ridge State Park 42 A3
Tahoe National Forest, Sierra City 43 B3
Tamarack Flat & Yosemite Creek Campgrounds, Yosemite National Park 44 B3
Tuttle Creek Campground 45 C4
Van Damme State Park 46 A2
Woodson Bridge State Recreation Area 47 A2
Klamath Falls
Klamath River
Weed
Eureka
Shasta Lake
Redding
Red Bluff
Coast Range
Sacramento Valley
Sacramento River
Leggett
Chico
Mendocino
Nevada City
Truckee
Sparks
Reno
Clear Lake
Calistoga
CARSON CITY
South Lake Tahoe
SACRAMENTO
Locke
Stockton
Sonora
Farallon Islands
SAN FRANCISCO
Oakland
Palo Alto
SAN JOSE
Santa Cruz
Monterey
Carmel-by-the-Sea
Diablo Range
San Joaquin River
Big Sur
Fresno
Paso Robles
Morro Bay
PACIFIC OCEAN
Susanville
Pyramid Lake
Winnemucca
Nevada
Carson Sink
Fallon
Bodie State Historic Park
Mono Lake
Tonopah
White Mountain (14,246ft)
Mammoth Lakes
Bishop
Kings Canyon National Park
Mt Williamson (14,375ft)
Mt Whitney (14,496ft)
Beatty
Death Valley
California
Lake Mead
LAS VEGAS
Bakersfield
Mojave
Barstow
Needles
Santa Barbara
Mojave Desert
Channel Islands
Santa Monica
LOS ANGELES
Anaheim
Newport Beach
Palm Springs
Indio
Salton Sea
Blythe
San Nicolas Island
Catalina Island
Oceanside
Imperial Valley
San Clemente Island
SAN DIEGO
TIJUANA
MEXICALI
Yuma
MEXICO
Ensenada
Mountain Time Zone
Pacific Time Zone
Gulf of California

Many public and private campgrounds accept reservations for all or some of their sites, while a few are strictly first-come, first-served. Overnight rates range from free for the most basic remote sites, between $10 and $20 at most state and national park campgrounds, to $45 or more for RV sites with full hookups at private campgrounds. Throughout this book, campsite prices are given for basic tent and RV sites without hookups, unless otherwise specified. Many campgrounds allow dogs; however, they must be leashed at all times and cannot be left tied up while you are away from your campsite. Since dogs are usually not allowed on state or national park trails and beaches, consider leaving your canine at home if you're planning an extended, parks-oriented trip. For details about backcountry camping and wilderness permits, see p73.

The National Park Service website (www.nps.gov/state/ca) has a clickable map for exploring California, from remote Lava Beds National Monument to offshore Channel Islands National Park.

The following reservations agencies let you search for campground locations and amenities, check availability, book a site, view maps and get driving directions online:

Recreation.gov (☎ 518-885-3639, 877-444-6777; www.recreation.gov) No-fee camping, cabin and lookout reservations accepted up to six months in advance for most federal lands, including national parks, national forests, BLM land etc.

ReserveAmerica (☎ 916-638-5883, 800-444-7275; www.reserveamerica.com) Reservations for campsites in California state parks, East Bay regional parks and private campgrounds statewide typically accepted up to six months in advance (fee per reservation $10).

If you can't get a reservation, plan to show up at the campground between 10am and noon, when some of last night's campers may be checking out. Don't be too choosy, or you may end up with no site at all, especially at the most popular parks along the coast and in the mountains. In peak summer months, especially on weekends and over the Memorial Day, July 4th and Labor Day holidays (p718), many campgrounds fill by Friday morning. In the SoCal deserts, spaces are scarce when wildflowers bloom, usually from late February through mid-April. Park rangers, visitors centers and campground hosts can usually tell you where spaces are still available, if there are any. During extremely busy times, overflow camping areas may open.

The often hilarious, yet informative *How to Shit in the Woods: An Environmentally Sound Approach to a Lost Art* by Kathleen Meyer is still the 'bible' on the subject of hiking, and a must-read for backcountry novices.

A few National Park Service (NPS) areas, many national forests and almost all BLM public lands allow dispersed camping on designated dirt roads wherever you can pull off without blocking other traffic. Many of these sites, away from ever more-crowded developed campgrounds, afford a more secluded camping experience for self-sufficient types who don't mind digging catholes and can remember to bring enough water. For advice about campfires – a serious potential hazard in this wildfire-prone state – and picking a minimal-impact campsite, see the boxed text, p73.

CYCLING & MOUNTAIN-BIKING

Top up those tires and strap on that helmet. California is outstanding cycling territory, whether you're off for a leisurely spin along the beach, an adrenaline-fueled mountain ride or a multiday cycling tour. The season runs pretty much year-round in the coastal areas, especially in Southern California. Avoid the mountains in winter and the desert in summer. For road rules, rental rates, purchase information and tips for taking bikes on public transportation, see p732.

Check out www.mtbr.com or www.dirtworld.com for free online reviews of hundreds of mountain-biking trails in California.

California's cities are not terribly bike-friendly, although there are exceptions (see p737). Even heavily trafficked urban areas may have some good cycling turf; for example, LA's oceanfront South Bay Trail (p543). In bike-friendly San Francisco (p111), you can cruise through Golden Gate Park and over the Golden Gate Bridge (p147), then hop the ferry back across the bay. Along the Central Coast, the waterfront Monterey

BEAR NECESSITIES

California's forests are home to an estimated 25,000 to 35,000 black bears, whose fur ranges in color from black to dark brown, cinnamon or even blond. They grow over 3ft tall (standing on all four feet). Adult females (called sows) average 200lb, while males typically weigh twice that much. Their main turf is below 8000ft in the forest and foothills of Northern California and the Sierra Nevada, but some also roam woodland coastal areas from Santa Cruz to San Diego. Observing a black bear can be a thrilling experience that'll remain etched in your memory forever. However, there are a few basic rules for ensuring a safe encounter.

In the Wild

If you spot a bear foraging in the woods…

- Don't panic! It's a lucky day when you get to observe a wild bear behaving naturally.
- Stay together and keep small children right next to you, picking up little ones.
- Stand still and watch (taking nonflash photos is OK) but don't linger too long.
- Don't get too near the animal(s); at least 100yd is a good distance. If a bear starts to chuff (ie huff and puff) and stamp its feet while pawing the ground, you are too close.
- Never, ever get between a sow and her cubs. If you spot a lone cub, its mother and siblings are probably nearby.
- Avoid surprising a bear by talking, singing, clapping or otherwise making noise to alert it that you're coming.
- If a bear starts walking toward you, move well off-trail to let it pass by, being careful not to block any of the animal's escape routes.

In Developed Areas

Black bears are curious, intelligent opportunists. They are often attracted to campgrounds, where they sniff out and steal food or any other scented items carelessly left out on picnic tables or stashed inside tents (which are easily ripped open by bear claws) and locked cars (ditto). Once a bear associates humans and food, it becomes bolder and more aggressive. Habituated bears

Peninsula Recreational Trail (p458) entices recreational cyclists, while hard-core road cyclists mount the famously scenic 17-Mile Drive (p462). Further south, Santa Barbara has a gorgeous beachfront recreational path (p498), while up north Redding (p302) has a paved bikeway along the Sacramento River. The Wine Country (p196) and Central Valley (p418) have some beautiful stretches for bike touring, although nothing surpasses coastal Hwy 1, especially the dizzying stretch through Big Sur (p465).

The Adventure Cycling Association website (www.adventurecycling.org) has useful trip-planning resources, including the *Cyclist's Yellow Pages*, plus an online store for maps and gear.

Mountain-biking erupted onto the scene in the 1970s in Marin County, where Mt Tamalpais (p156) lays claim to being the sport's birthplace. Just north of San Francisco, the Marin Headlands (p146) offers a bonanza of trails for fat-tire fans. Top-rated single-track rides in Sierra Nevada include Mr Toad's Wild Ride (p357) and the Flume Trail (p371). In the Gold Country, the Downieville Downhill (p332) offers an enormous vertical rush. Speed freaks also sing the praises of Mammoth Mountain (p408), whose biking park beckons with a slalom course, an obstacle area and a 100-mile network of dirt single-track, include kick-ass downhill stretches. Other ski areas that open trails and chairlifts to mountain-bikers in summer include Big Bear Lake (p573) and Mt Shasta (p314), where you can plan a more relaxing ride along the Bizz Johnson Trail (p309), east of Lassen Volcanic National Park.

Bikes are usually not allowed in designated wilderness areas. In national parks, bikes are usually allowed only on paved or unpaved roads that are also open to cars, never on trails. Yosemite National Park (p384) has must be 'hazed' by park rangers, and sometimes even killed. Remember: a fed bear is (potentially) a dead bear.

- Store all food products, toiletries, trash and any other scented items in bear-resistant lockers provided at campsites in bear country. Keep your campground clean and tidy.
- When staying in cabins or motels in high-impact areas (such as Yosemite Valley), remove all food and scented items from your vehicle. This includes coolers (full or empty), beverage containers, cosmetics and candy wrappers. Some trailhead parking lots also have bear boxes; use them, or else at least lock everything out of sight in the trunk.
- On many backcountry hikes, storing your food in bear-resistant canisters (widely available for rent) is mandatory. Hanging your food in a tree (the counter-balancing method) no longer works, as too many black bears figured out that trick years ago.
- If a bear wanders into your campground, don't approach it. Get everyone together and yell, clap your hands, bang pots and try looking big and more intimidating. Do *not* throw rocks, which can easily kill a black bear.

If Attacked

Black bears are naturally afraid of humans, but habituated or very hungry bears can become aggressive. In the extremely unlikely event that you are attacked by a bear:

- Never run from a bear, as this only triggers its instinct to chase, and you cannot outrun a bear, which can reach speeds of 35mph.
- Sometimes a bear will 'bluff charge' to test your dominance. Stand your ground by making yourself look as big as possible (eg waving your arms above your head) and shouting menacingly.
- If that fails to stop an attack, drop to the ground, crouch face down in a ball and play dead, covering the back of your neck with your hands, and your chest and stomach with your knees. As scary as it is, try not to resist the bear's inquisitive pawing – it may get bored and go away.
- If the attack persists, fight back by any means available.

Learn more about California's beautiful black bears at www.sierrawildbear.gov or www.tahoewildbears.org.

paved recreational paths through its waterfall-strewn valley, while Joshua Tree National Park (p666) has miles of backcountry roads for mountain-bikers. State parks can be more relaxed, although do check the regulations with rangers at the visitors center. Up north at Humboldt Redwoods State Park (p278), you'll be riding among the world's tallest trees. Other popular mountain-biking destinations include Prairie Creek Redwoods State Park (p294) on the North Coast, Montaña de Oro State Park (p478) on the Central Coast and Anza-Borrego Desert State Park (p673), east of San Diego. Many national forests and BLM lands are open to mountain-bikers. Just be sure to stay on established tracks at all times.

A guide to bicycle touring in California and links to free downloadable maps are available on the California Association of Bicycling Organizations website (www.cabobike.org).

Most towns have at least one bike-rental place, many of which are listed throughout this book. Prices range from around $10 per day for beach cruisers to $45 or more for high-tech mountain bikes, depending on the location. To get the inside scoop on the local scene, folks at bicycle shops can supply you with ideas, maps and advice. For the activists among you, **Critical Mass** (http://critical-mass.info) stages monthly rides in nearly 30 California cities, perfect for meeting up with die-hard local cyclists.

HIKING

California is perfect for exploring on foot, whether you've got your heart set on peak-bagging in the Sierra Nevada, trekking to desert palm-tree oases, rambling among the world's tallest, largest or most ancient trees, or simply heading for a coastal walk accompanied by booming surf. The best trails are generally found among the jaw-dropping scenery in national and state parks, national forests and wilderness areas. You can choose from an infinite variety of routes, from easy, interpretive nature walks negotiable by wheelchairs and baby strollers to multiday backpacking routes through rugged wilderness. Parks and forests almost always have a visitors center or ranger station with clued-in staff to offer route suggestions, trail-specific tips and weather forecasts. The most popular trails may be subject to daily quotas and require wilderness permits (see opposite).

Foghorn Outdoors' *California Hiking: The Complete Guide to More Than 1000 of the Best Hikes* (Avalon Travel Publishing, 2003) by Tom Stienstra and Ann Marie Brown is an invaluable compendium of famous and hidden hikes.

For short, well-established hikes in national or state parks, the free and basic maps handed out at ranger stations and visitors centers are usually sufficient. If you're headed into the rugged backcountry, especially on multiday trips, don't venture out on the trail without a good topographic map, often sold at visitors centers' bookstores, wilderness permit-issuing stations and commercial outdoor supply stores. The most detailed topographical maps are published by the **US Geological Survey** (USGS; ☎ 877-275-8747; http://store.usgs.gov), which offers online downloads and orders. Occasionally outdoor outfitters, such as **REI** (☎ 800-426-4840; www.rei.com), have in-store National Geographic map-machine kiosks where you can design a custom digital topo map and print it out on water-resistant, tearproof paper for around $10.

Carry a cell phone, but don't rely on it: service is spotty or nonexistent in many wilderness areas. Weather can be unpredictable, so always come prepared for windy, wet or cold conditions; afternoon summer thunderstorms, for instance, are common in the Sierra Nevada. For desert survival tips, see the boxed text, p671. Mosquito bites can potentially – though very rarely – transmit West Nile virus (p740). Tick bites can also become dangerously infected; for example, with Lyme disease (p741). For safe travels in bear country, see the boxed text, p70. Other wild animals, including mountain lions, rattlesnakes and spiders, are briefly discussed on p716.

With a database that's searchable by destination or activity, www.away.com has ideas for scores of active adventures in California and features content from *Outside* magazine.

Trails

No matter where you find yourself in California, you're never far from a trail, even in busy metropolitan areas. The Marin Headlands (p144), Muir Woods (p157), Mt Tamalpais (p155), Point Reyes National Seashore (p160) and Big Basin Redwoods State Park (p452), all within a 90-minute drive of San Francisco, are crisscrossed by dozens of superb trails. Further south of the Bay Area, hikers can spot rare California condors soaring over the eroded rock formations of Pinnacles National Monument (p481).

Even in LA, you can ditch the car and head for the outdoors in the Santa Monica Mountains National Recreation Area (p543), where many movies and TV shows have been filmed, or head out to Big Bear Lake (p573) in the San Bernardino National Forest or Mt San Jacinto State Park (p651), reached via either the Palm Springs Aerial Tramway or the scenic Palms to Pines Hwy (p663). In San Diego, you're only two hours from Anza-Borrego Desert State Park (p672) for rough-and-ready hikes to palm-canyon oases and historical ruins.

Watch out! Hikers can break out in a rash after being exposed to the urushiol oil in poison oak, even when the plant's distinctive tripartite leaves are missing.

Hiking is, of course, awesome in California's national parks, though trails do get crowded. In Yosemite National Park (p383) you can steer toward waterfalls and wildflower meadows or tackle mighty Half Dome. Sequoia & Kings Canyon National Parks (p391) will wow you with the world's biggest trees – giant sequoias – while Lassen Volcanic National Park (p307) welcomes you into a bizarre world of hissing fumaroles, cinder cones and craters. On the North Coast, Redwood National Park (p294) offers misty walks through groves of old-growth redwood; so do a half

LEAVE NO TRACE

Many of California's landscapes are being loved to death. While you're off having an outdoor adventure, remember that one thoughtless gesture – hiking off-trail through fragile cryptobiotic soil in the desert or building an illegal fire in the mountains – can cause damage that takes years for nature to repair. You know the drill: take only pictures, leave only footprints.

Once in the wild, do everything possible to minimize your impact. Stick to established trails and campsites. Be particularly sensitive to watershed areas: don't wash yourself or your dishes in lakes, streams or rivers, and camp and bury all human waste at least 200ft from water. Use a stove for cooking, or make fires using downed wood only when they are fully contained by established fire rings. When you leave, take out everything you packed in (yes, that means trash and toilet paper too).

Observe wildlife from a distance, but do not approach or feed it. If you find cultural or historic artifacts, leave them untouched. Finally, be aware and respectful of other visitors. Human noise travels far and is the fastest way to spoil a whole valley's worth of solitude.

For a big bag of tricks for minimizing your environmental impact while traipsing through the wilderness, browse the Leave No Trace Center for Outdoor Ethics website (www.lnt.org).

dozen nearby state parks, including along the aptly named Avenue of the Giants (p278). Up for more of a challenge? Tackle the truly wild beaches of the multiday Lost Coast Trail (p282). On the Central Coast, there's also amazing hiking in Big Sur (p466), where the Ventana Wilderness (p469) combines redwood forests, hidden waterfalls and hot springs with cool ocean views.

Coastwalk (www.coastwalk.org) is helping to build a coastal trail along California's 1100-plus miles of shoreline. Take a guided hike, or join a beach cleanup or trail maintenance day.

Hiking in the SoCal deserts is most tempting when spring wildflowers are in bloom or during winter, when other regions of the state may be too cold or wet. In Joshua Tree National Park (p665), you can dive into canyon oases or scramble between boulders. The Mojave National Preserve (p678) offers some surprisingly challenging clambers up sand dunes and cinder cones. Death Valley National Park (p684) has an unmatched variety of environments, from salt flats, natural bridges and volcanic craters to snowy mountains, plus mining ghost towns to explore.

Altitude junkies will feel the magnetic pull of Mt Whitney (p415), the tallest mountain in the contiguous US, and the equally breathtaking, if slightly shorter, Mt Shasta (p314). Standing on the summit of either is a truly uplifting experience, but getting there is a serious challenge requiring top form and good prep work.

Famous long-distance trails that wind through California include the 2650-mile **Pacific Crest Trail** (PCT; www.pcta.org) that will take you from Mexico to Canada. Mostly running along the PCT, the 211-mile **John Muir Trail** links Yosemite Valley and Mt Whitney along the backbone of the Sierra Nevada. Hikers, equestrians and – in some sections – mountain-bikers can enjoy inspirational views of the mountains and Lake Tahoe while tracing the footsteps of early pioneers, Basque shepherds and Washoe tribespeople along the 150-mile **Tahoe Rim Trail** (www.tahoerimtrail.org).

Scottish-born John Muir (1838-1914), one of California's earliest and most influential conservationists, lobbied to establish Yosemite National Park, which Congress did in 1892.

Wilderness Permits & Fees

To prevent them from being trampled to death, the most popular trails are subject to a quota system that limits the number of hikers and/or backpackers who start out daily from each trailhead. This system prevents overcrowding and reduces the environmental impact of thousands of hiking boots crunching along the trail each year. Quotas are only in effect during peak periods, usually from late spring to early fall. Most national parks and some national forests and wilderness areas require overnight

LOCAL ADVICE ON THE BEST HIKES

State Park Interpreter Michael Connolly, Jr shares with us his all-time favorite day hikes in California:

- Lower Paradise Valley (Kings Canyon National Park, p393) – see a mighty canyon, gushing rivers and Mist Falls shooting spray onto the trail
- Fern Canyon & James Irvine Trails (Prairie Creek Redwoods State Park, p294) – where lushly carpeted canyon walls lead deep into old-growth redwood forests
- Blair Valley (Anza-Borrego Desert State Park, p672) – past Native American pictographs, a narrow canyon funnels down to a dry waterfall with sweeping views
- Stateline Lookout (Lake Tahoe, p370) – so much scenery on such a short climb to 360-degree views of snowy mountains reflected on an emerald-blue lake, best at sunset; starts off at Forest Service Rd 1601, near Crystal Bay
- Bluff Trail (Montaña de Oro State Park, p478) – a four-seasons hike with oceanside cliffs, surf and whale-and bird-watching against the backdrop of the Irish Hills

backpackers and occasionally day hikers to carry wilderness permits, which are typically issued at ranger stations and sometimes visitors centers. A certain percentage of permits may be reserved ahead of time – the most popular trailheads fill up several months in advance and/or are subject to a special lottery – while the rest are issued on a first-come, first-serve basis. Permits and reservation fees range from absolutely nothing up to $15. Some less-impacted trails have self-issuing permits available at the trailhead or outside ranger stations. National forests often require backcountry campers and hikers to pick up free campfire permits, which are unlimited. More details about how to obtain wilderness permits for specific backcountry areas are provided throughout this book. For state and national park entry fees and passes, see p64.

SuperTopo (www.supertopo.com) is a one-stop shop for rock-climbing guidebooks, free topo maps and route descriptions across California, from Sierra Nevada big walls to desert towers.

ROCK CLIMBING

Rock hounds can test their mettle on world-class climbs on the big walls and granite domes of Yosemite National Park (p383), where the climbing season runs from April to October. In the warmest summer months, climbers move camp from the Yosemite Valley to Tuolumne Meadows, off Tioga Rd, which also has good bouldering. In SoCal, Joshua Tree National Park (p665) is another climbing mecca, with over 8000 established routes ranging from boulders and cracks to multipitch faces; the climbing season runs year-round, but beware of blistering summer heat. Both of these national parks are excellent places to try the sport for the first time; outdoor outfitters offer guided climbs and instruction, costing from $120 per day. Other prime spots for bouldering and rock climbing include Bishop (p412) in the Eastern Sierra; Sequoia & Kings Canyon National Parks (p391), south of Yosemite; and outside Truckee (p368), near Lake Tahoe.

The website www.trails.com has downloadable topo maps, guidebook excerpts and user reviews for hundreds of trails in California designed for two dozen outdoor sports.

SCUBA DIVING, SNORKELING & SEA KAYAKING

All along the coast, rock reefs, shipwrecks and kelp beds teem with sea creatures ready for their close-up, especially in the warmer waters of Southern California, where the San Diego-La Jolla Underwater Park Ecological Reserve (p625), Catalina Island (p571) and Channel Islands National Park (p504) are major diving and snorkeling destinations. Thanks to the national marine sanctuary, Monterey Bay (p458) offers year-round, world-renowned diving and snorkeling, although you'll need to don a wet suit. Further south, Point Lobos State Reserve (p464) is another gem for scuba divers (snorkeling prohibited), but you'll need a permit reservation. North of San Francisco, dive boats depart from Bodega Bay (p252).

If you've already got your PADI certification, you can rent one-tank dive outfits for $65 to $100 – it's wise to reserve them at least a day in advance. The website http://ladiver.com maintains exhaustive listings of dive sites and shops, certification programs, safety resources and weather conditions for the LA area, with links to sister sites for San Diego and Santa Barbara, along the Central Coast and in Northern California. Snorkeling kits can be rented from most dive shops for around $15 to $40 per day. If you're going to be taking the plunge more than once or twice, it's probably worth buying your own mask and set of fins. Remember not to touch anything while you're out snorkeling, don't snorkel alone and always put sunblock on your back!

Kayak Online (http://kayakonline.com/california.html) has helpful links to kayaking outfitters, schools and organizations, plus helpful information resources for beginning and expert paddlers alike.

Sea kayaking is a more accessible, family-friendly activity, as prior experience is rarely necessary. It's popular around Catalina Island and in Channel Islands National Park, as well as off such Central Coast cities and towns as Santa Barbara (p498), Morro Bay (p477), San Simeon (p473), Monterey (p458) and Santa Cruz (p446). In the San Francisco Bay Area, you can paddle around Angel Island (p152), Tomales Bay (p159) or Bodega Bay (p252). The chillier North Coast has opportunities for challenging ocean kayaking, including from such tiny towns as Gualala (p256), Elk (p258) and Trinidad (p291), or you can take a spin around Humboldt Bay, launching from Eureka (p285) or Arcata (p288).

Most rental shops offer a choice between sit-upon (open or ocean) or sit-in (closed-hull) kayaks, the latter usually requiring some training before you head out. Single/tandem rental kayaks typically cost $30 to $45 per day. A reputable outfitter will make sure you're aware of the tide schedule and wind conditions of your proposed route. Many also offer lessons and guided tours (per half/full day from $55/110), including full-moon paddles and hike-and-kayak combos. The best trips take small groups and have guides with a background in natural history or marine biology.

Surfline (www.surfline.com) has an atlas of California surf spots with detailed descriptions, weather reports and live surf cams, plus surfing news, tips and women-only features.

SURFING

Surf's up! Even if you never set foot on a board – and we, like, totally recommend that you do – there's no denying the influence of surfing on every aspect of California beach life. Invented by Pacific Islanders, surfing first washed ashore here in 1907 when railroad and real-estate tycoon Henry Huntington invited Irish-Hawaiian surfer George Freeth to give surfing demonstrations in LA. The state has just never been the same since.

BEYOND THE BOARD

Surfing was the ancient sport of Hawaiian royalty, who called it 'wave sliding,' but for modern-day Californians, sometimes just riding a surfboard isn't enough.

Windsurfing, using a modified board with a triangular sail, emerged in SoCal in the late 1960s. Today you can watch expert windsurfers freestylin' almost anywhere along the coast. Beginners can learn to skim on San Francisco Bay (p112), at Bodega Bay (p252), around Lake Tahoe and at several spots along the coast from LA south to San Diego.

Kitesurfing and kiteboarding are more extreme sports, using wind power to propel riders across the waves and even launch them into the air. Developed in France and the US, kitesurfing took off in the late 1990s when international surfing superstar Laird Hamilton became an early adopter. The sport has exploded in popularity in California. You can find out how to do all of those gnarly aerial stunts yourself in several places, including San Francisco (p112) and at Seal Beach (p587) in the OC. The **US Kitesurfing Association** (www.uskite.org) and www.ikiteboarding.com have links to dozens of kitesurfing schools in California.

SKIING, SNOWBOARDING & SNOWSHOEING

High-speed modern lifts, mountains of fresh powder, a cornucopia of trails from easy-peasy 'Sesame Street' to black-diamond 'Death Wish,' skyscraping alpine scenery, luxury mountain cabins, steaming mulled wine, hearty dinners by a crackling fireplace – they're all hallmarks of a California vacation in the snow.

Ski season runs from late November or early December until late March or early April, although this of course depends on specific elevations and weather conditions. Efficient snowmaking equipment ensures you can swoosh down the slopes even in years when nature doesn't play along. All resorts have ski schools and equipment-rental facilities, as well as plenty of lodgings, restaurants, shops, bars and nightlife. A variety of lift tickets are available, including half-day, all-day and multiday versions. Prices vary tremendously and can be as low as $25 or as high as $80 for adults; discounts for children, teens, students and seniors are always available. 'Ski & stay' lodging packages may offer the best value.

Sierra Nevada offers the best slopes and trails, not to mention the most reliable conditions. For sheer variety, the over a dozen downhill skiing and snowboarding resorts ringing **Lake Tahoe** (p351) are unbeatable. Alongside such world-famous places as Squaw Valley USA, host of the 1960 Winter Olympic Games, and Heavenly, you'll find scores of smaller operations, many of them with lower ticket prices, smaller crowds and great runs for beginners and families. Royal Gorge, near Truckee west of Lake Tahoe, is North America's largest cross-country ski resort.

About a three-hour drive south along US Hwy 395, in the Eastern Sierra, **Mammoth Mountain** (p408) is another darling of downhill devotees and usually has the longest season, often running

California comes fully loaded with easily accessible world-class surf spots, the lion's share of which are in SoCal. You won't find many killer waves north of San Francisco (p112), but if your travels take you there, check out www.northerncaliforniasurfing.com. From Santa Cruz south to San Diego, crowds can be a problem in many places. Local surfers can be aggressively (even violently) territorial, most infamously at San Diego's Windansea Beach (p625) near La Jolla, Huntington Beach (p588) in Orange County and Malibu (p544), north of LA. You'd better befriend a local surfer for an introduction before catching any waves.

Other famous surf spots include Santa Cruz's Steamers Lane (p446); Mavericks (p191), near Half Moon Bay; Rincon Point (p498), south of Santa Barbara; and Trestles (p598), south of San Clemente in Orange County. All are clean, glassy point breaks (where swells peak into steep waves as they encounter a shelf-like point). Mavericks is one of the world's most famous destinations for big-wave surfing, with breakers that can top out over 50ft when the most powerful winter swells arrive. In early summer, waves are generally the flattest up and down the coast, although Trestles still goes off then.

The mind-bogglingly detailed *California Coastal Access Guide* (California Coastal Commission, 2003) gives comprehensive driving directions and maps to every public beach, reef, harbor, overlook and coastal campground in the state.

You'll find surfboard rental stands on just about every patch of sand where surfing is possible in California. Expect to pay about $15 per half-day for a board. Just don't be fooled by all those images you've seen of hot blonds surfing in bikinis or swim trunks. You'll likely freeze your ass off in the water anywhere but SoCal in summer; bring a wet suit or rent one for about $10 per day.

The best places to learn to surf are at beach breaks or long, shallow bays where waves are small and rolling: try Mission Beach, Pacific Beach and Tourmaline (p625), all in San Diego, for good beginner spots; Seal Beach (p587) and Doheny State Beach (p598) in the OC; and Cowell Beach (p448) in Santa Cruz, Cayucos (p475) and around Santa Barbara (p498) on the Central Coast. Wherever you go, two-hour group lessons start at around $85 per person, more for private instruction. If you're ready to dive into

into June. There are enough runs to keep you busy for a week, and not one, not two but three constantly evolving terrain parks for snowboarders. It's infamous for its rollicking après-ski scene where people party as hard as they ski. Beginning and intermediate skiers hit the slopes of Mammoth's quieter neighbor, June Mountain (p406).

In the glacier-carved winter wonderland of Yosemite National Park, on the western side of the Sierra Nevada, **Badger Pass** (p384) is a low-key place that's ideal for beginners and families. One of California's oldest ski resorts, it still boasts a fun-for-all, old-fashioned atmosphere. Generations of families have learned to ski here, and it's also a launching pad for cross-country skiing and snowshoe walks into the wilderness. Free shuttle buses connect the ski area and Yosemite Valley, where you can do some more snowshoeing or take a spin around the Curry Village ice rink before toasting s'mores at the Yosemite Lodge at the Falls. In the southern Sierra Nevada at **Sequoia and Kings Canyon National Parks** (p397), you can glissade, tramp or even cross-country ski among giant sequoia trees.

In Northern California, **Mt Shasta Board & Ski Park** (p314) is the most popular ski area, with an enormously cool night-skiing operation. Even sunny Southern California gets in on the snow action with two ski mountains in **Big Bear Lake** (p574). Though they can't compete in size and variety with the Sierra Nevada resorts, they're only a 2½-hour drive from Los Angeles. Theoretically, you could ski in the morning and surf in the afternoon! And don't overlook the **Palm Springs Aerial Tramway** (p651), about two hours' drive east of LA, which will zip you from the desert floor into the pine-forested San Jacinto Mountains in under 15 minutes. From the top of the tramway, the whole family can rent snowshoes and cross-country skis in winter.

the deep end, many surf schools offer weekend clinics (from $150) and week-long 'surfari' camps (from $350). Women can take lessons from San Diego's Surf Diva (p625).

Safety issues to watch out for include riptides (p716). Sharks do inhabit California waters but attacks are rare. Most take place in the so-called Red Triangle, or Shark Belt, between Monterey on the Central Coast, Tomales Bay north of San Francisco and the offshore Farallon Islands. Water quality varies from beach to beach, and day to day. For current conditions, check the statewide 'Beach Report Card' at www.healthebay.org. Enlightened surfers can also support the **Surfrider Foundation** (www.surfrider.org), a grassroots nonprofit organization founded in Malibu in 1984, which strives to protect coastal biodiversity and ecological integrity worldwide.

California Whitewater Rafting (www.c-w-r.com) is a free online information resource, covering all of California's prime river-running spots, with links to outfitters and river conservation groups.

WHITE-WATER RAFTING

California has scads of kick-ass rivers, and feeling their surging power is like taking a thrilling ride on nature's rollercoaster. Sure, there are serene floats suitable for picnics with grandma and the kiddies, but then there are others. White-water giants swelled by the snowmelt that rip through sheer canyons. Roaring cataracts that hurtle you through chutes where gushing water compresses through a 10ft gap between menacing boulders. Pour-overs, voracious hydraulics, endless Class III–IV standing waves wrenching at your shoulders as you scream and punch on through to the next onslaught. Your thoughts are reduced to two simple words: 'survive' and 'damn!' Too much for you? Between these two extremes run myriad others suited to the abilities of any wannabe river rat.

Commercial outfitters run a variety of trips, from short, inexpensive morning or afternoon floats to overnight outings and multiday expeditions. Expect to pay from $75 for a guided half-day trip or $135 for a full day, with higher rates on weekends. Reservations are recommended, especially for overnight trips. The main river-running season is from April to October, although the exact months depend on both the river and the spring snowmelt runoff from

WANT MORE?

If you've still got energy to burn after trying out every activity we've outlined in this chapter, rest assured there's plenty of other stuff going on outdoors in the Golden State:

Ballooning Almost anywhere you'll find vineyaurds in California, there are hot-air balloon flights taking off in the pre-dawn light, including above Napa (p232) and Temecula (p646). Ocean-view flights are a trademark of Del Mar (p640) in north San Diego County.

Bird-Watching Ideally positioned along the Pacific Flyway (p324), California offers an incredible diversity of habitats for bird-watchers to work on their life lists, especially at **National Wildlife Refuges** (NWRs; www.fws.gov/refuges) from Klamath Basin (p323) near the Oregon border south to the Salton Sea (p669), as well as at private sanctuaries managed by **Audubon California** (☎ 919-649-7600; www.audubon-ca.org). For bird-watching checklists, maps of hot spots and links to organizations and festivals statewide, click to www.birding.com.

Caving Spelunkers strap on headlamps in Lava Beds National Monument (p323) and Pinnacles National Monument (p481), while underground novices can take a guided tour of Crystal Cave (p396) in Sequoia National Park. For more underground cavern and mine tours, check out www.caverntours.com.

Fishing You'll find folks casting a line off just about every pier and booking sportfishing charter boats everywhere along the coast, starting from San Diego (p625) and heading north to Oregon. Rivers streaming down from California's mountain ranges can be prime fishing spots, especially throughout the Sierra Nevada (p350) and further north in Klamath (p295). For fishing licenses, regulations and location information, contact the **California Department of Fish & Game** (☎ 916-327-8840; www.dfg.ca.gov).

Golf You can tee off at more than 100 courses in Palm Springs and the Coachella Valley (p656) alone, or walk in Tiger Woods' footsteps at famed Pebble Beach (p462) and Torrey Pines (p623).

Hang Gliding & Paragliding Some of the very best vistas and hang-gliding schools are found at Torrey Pines Glider Port (p623), north of San Diego. Check the website www.catoudoors.com for more places to fly up and down the coast.

Horseback Riding California's Wild West days may be long gone, but you can still saddle up and canter along coastal beaches and high into the mountains, including at Yosemite National Park (p384) and at the wild horse sanctuary near Lassen Volcanic National Park (p308).

Whale-Watching Gray whales can be spotted off the California coast from December to April. Blue, humpback and sperm whales pass by in summer and fall. Just about every port town offers whale-watching boat excursions; expect to pay about $30 to $45 for a three-hour excursion. Bring binoculars!

the mountains. You'll be hurtling along either in large rafts for a dozen or more people, or smaller ones seating half a dozen; the latter tend to be more exhilarating because they can tackle rougher rapids and everyone participates in the paddling. Instruction is usually provided. Most outfitters also rent white-water kayaks and canoes, which require more skill and maneuvering.

Nearest to Sacramento are the awesome American and Stanislaus Rivers. If you're a rafting virgin, a good place to get your feet wet – and the rest of you soaked to the bone – is the South Fork American (p338; Class II–III, April to October), which is also ideal for families. The North Fork American (Class IV, April to May) and Middle Fork American (Class III–IV, April to October) are quite a bit more challenging as they carve through deep gorges in the Sierra foothills, including at Auburn State Recreation Area (p337). There's also rafting on the Truckee River (p368; Class II–III+, June to September), near Lake Tahoe, and along several rivers in the Northern Mountains, with outfitters located in Mt Shasta City (p316).

For information - and valuable coupons - for more unusual activities, from gondola cruises to hot-air ballooning, skydiving and hang gliding, click to www.caladventures.com.

Mighty rivers cascade down from Yosemite National Park (p384), where families can float lazily along the Merced River through the valley. Starting below El Portal outside Yosemite, the Merced River Canyon (p389; Class III–IV, April to July) run passes abandoned gold mines and water flumes, making it the Sierra's best one-day intermediate trip. Experienced paddlers might prefer the more ferocious Tuolumne River (p384; Class IV+, April to September). A run on 'the T,' a federally designated Wild and Scenic River, is often considered the best all-around white-water trip in California. Legendary

Cherry Creek (Class V, June to August), a dam-controlled stretch of the upper Tuolumne River, is for technical experts only. In the Gold Country, Sonora (p348) is another good put-in point for the Tuolumne River, as well as for the Stanislaus River (Class II–IV, April to October), which offers trips for novices to the more adventure-minded.

Friends of the River (www.friendsoftheriver.com) is dedicated to conserving all of California's rivers, streams and watersheds, offering members-only rafting trips from May to September.

From the highest reaches of the Kings-Kern Divide, also in Sierra Nevada, flows the Kern River (p441), which cuts a steep canyon through Sequoia National Park. Trips on the Lower Kern (Class II–IV, April to September) and the Upper Kern (Class III–V, April to July), both staged near Bakersfield, have the best white water in the southern Sierra. Steeply dropping through Sequoia National Park (p395), the fast, furious Kaweah River (Class IV+, April to July) is for experienced paddlers craving hair-raising white-water features with names like Suicide Falls. To the north lies the Kings River (Class III–IV, April to July), one of California's most powerful rivers, cutting a groove deeper than the Grand Canyon through Kings Canyon National Park (p391). Note that all of these trips start outside the national park boundaries.

White-water trips are not without danger, and it's not unusual for participants to fall out of the raft in rough conditions. Serious injuries, though, are rare and most trips are without incident. No prior experience is needed for guided trips up to Class III, but for Class IV you want to be healthy, active, in good shape and an excellent swimmer; ideally, you'll have some paddling experience too. Rafters must wear life jackets. All trips have at least one river guide trained in emergency lifesaving techniques.

Rivers and rapids are ranked on the international six-point scale:

Class I (easy) Flat water to occasional series of mild rapids.

Class II (medium) Frequent stretches of rapids with waves up to 3ft high and easy chutes, ledges and falls. The best route is easy to identify, the entire river can be run in open canoes and no great skill or maneuvering is required.

Class III (difficult) Numerous rapids with high, irregular waves and difficult chutes and falls that often require scouting. These rivers are for experienced paddlers who either use kayaks or rafts or have spray covers for their canoes.

Class IV (very difficult) Long stretches of high, irregular waves, powerful back eddies and even constricted canyons. Scouting is mandatory, and rescues can be difficult in many places. Rafts or white-water kayaks in which paddlers are equipped with helmets are suitable for these rivers.

Class V (extremely difficult) Continuous violent rapids, large drops, powerful rollers and high, extreme hydraulics and holes, unavoidable waves and haystacks. These rivers are only for professional rafters and white-water kayakers who are proficient at rolling.

Class VI (highest level of difficulty) Rarely run except by highly experienced kayakers under ideal conditions. The likelihood of serious injury or worse is high.

San Francisco

The streets are lined with gold, the skies are patrolled by Amazons riding winged monsters and fairy godmothers are standing by to grant your wishes…well, not exactly. Don't believe everything that's been said about this peculiar peninsula over the past 200 years – San Francisco shows more imagination than that. Instead of sticking with boring old gold, alleyways are splashed with hundreds of rainbow-colored murals, and the skies over North Beach are ruled by trash-talking wild parrots. And who waits for fairy godmothers anymore? Year-round parades are all the excuse you need to throw on some glitter and a boa, take over the streets with a gaggle of Glinda the Good Witches and make your own wildest dreams come true in San Francisco.

Ditch your car and your sightseeing itineraries, and let your mind and feet wander across this 7x7 mile stretch of the imagination. If you choose not to bike across the Golden Gate Bridge or take the ferry to Alcatraz, you won't be heckled by San Franciscans, because few have bothered to do it themselves, and they're counting on you to tell them what they're missing. But they will harangue you to visit their beloved Golden Gate Park and to try their favorite restaurant, and they'll point out the neighborhood characters that define the streets of San Francisco even more than its 43 giddy hills and whimsical Victorian rooflines. Say what you will about slacker San Franciscans, but they work hard to maintain their cutting-edge green scene, innovative California cuisine and exceptionally high freak factor. Step out of the ordinary, and into San Francisco.

HIGHLIGHTS

- **Most unforgettable Golden Gate Bridge vantage points** Sprawled on Crissy Field (p106), breathless atop Sterling Park (p102) or naked on Baker Beach (p106)
- **Best outdoor art galleries** The mural-filled alleyways of Chinatown (p100) and the Mission (p108)
- **Tastiest landmark** The Ferry Building (p139)
- **Most breathtaking vistas** Summiting San Francisco's scenic Telegraph, Russian and Nob Hills via hidden garden stairways and literary lanes (p113)
- **Creepiest vacation destination** Behind bars at Alcatraz (p85)

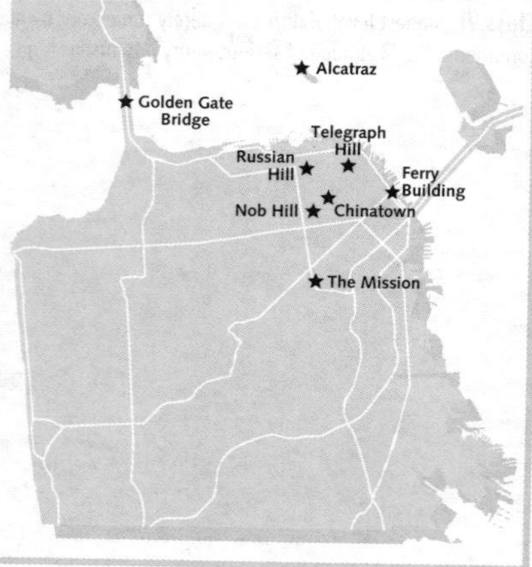

FAST FACTS

Population 801,400

Average temperature low/high Jan 46/58°F, Jul 54/68°F

Downtown San Francisco to Santa Cruz 70 miles, 1½ hours

San Francisco to Napa & Sonoma Valleys 45 to 55 miles, one to 1½ hours

San Francisco to Los Angeles 380 miles, six to seven hours

HISTORY

Before gold changed everything, San Francisco was a hapless Spanish mission, established in 1776. Without immunity to European diseases, many native Californians recruited to build the mission didn't even survive to see the end result – some 5000 Ohlone and northern Miwok are buried beside Mission Señora de los Dolores, 'Our Lady of the Sorrows.' Spain didn't especially mind losing the flea-infested colony to Mexico, which in turn surrendered the backwater in a war with the US in 1846.

But then godforsaken San Francisco turned golden. After nuggets were found in the American River, San Francisco ballooned from 800 to 100,000 prospectors from South America, China, Europe and Mexico between 1847 and 1849. Although California was fast-tracked for statehood in 1850, that didn't change the wild ways of the 'Barbary Coast' in 500 local saloons, where a buck would procure whiskey, opium, opera tickets and maybe a woman or two – though watching the latter cost $10.

When gold was discovered in Australia in 1854, panic ensued and irrational resentment turned on Australians and modest Chinese businesses that managed to survive. Ordinances restricted housing and employment for anyone born in China in 1870, and the 1882 US Chinese Exclusion Act barred Chinese from immigration and citizenship until 1943. New arrivals seeking their fortunes in San Francisco perceived long-established local Asian communities as stiff competition for scarce work in the rapidly consolidating mining, building and railroad industries, and anti-Asian sentiment grew. By 1900, 100 parallel ordinances limited citizenship, marriage, immigration and property rights for Japanese San Franciscans.

Comebacks and Setbacks

On April 18, 1906, a quake estimated at a terrifying 7.8 to 8.3 on today's Richter scale struck the city. For 47 seconds, the city emitted unholy groans as streets buckled, windows popped and brick buildings keeled over. Fire-fighters were unable to pass through the rubble-choked streets to put out blazes, and after three days an estimated 3000 people were dead and 100,000 homeless. Adding insult to injury, a city plan was concocted to relocate Chinatown to less desirable real estate outside the city – but those from the Chinese consulate, Waverly Place temples and several gun-toting merchants firmly refused.

The city redoubled its reconstruction efforts, and completed an astounding 15 buildings per day. Although all but one of San Francisco's 20 historic theaters were completely destroyed, theater tents were set up amid the rubble and opera singers performed for free to boost spirits. The ragged piers were built into a major port, though local longshoremen pulling long hours unloading heavy cargo for scant pay didn't see the upside of the shipping boom that brought SF back to life after the Great Quake. In 1934 a coordinated strike among 35,000 workers along the coast lasted 83 days, until police and the National Guard killed 34 strikers and wounded 40 sympathizers. Public sympathy forced concessions from shipping magnates, and 1930s murals by Diego Rivera and Works Project Administration (WPA) artists reflect the proworker sentiment that swept the city.

World War II brought a shipbuilding boom to town, with African Americans and women stepping into essential roles. But two months after the attack on Pearl Harbor, President Franklin Delano Roosevelt signed Executive Order 9066, ordering the relocation of 120,000 Japanese Americans to internment camps. The San Francisco–based Japanese American Citizens League challenged the measure, and after 40 years of lobbying won reparations and a formal letter of apology signed by President George HW Bush in 1989.

Free Speech & Free Spirits

During World War II, members of the Armed Services were dismissed from service for homosexuality and insubordinate behavior in San Francisco, building the city's notoriety for bohemian nonconformity. San Francisco became a proving ground for artistic freedom in 1957, when the City Lights Bookstore (opposite) won a landmark ruling against book banning over the publication of Allen Ginsberg's *Howl*. Meanwhile, jazz broke down barriers in desegregated clubs, burlesque dancer Carol Doda and comedian Lenny Bruce challenged obscenity laws, and drag empress José Sarria led gay bar patrons in nightly choruses of 'God Save Us Nelly Queens.'

Then, in what some might perceive to be a pronounced lapse in screening judgment, the CIA hired a local writer named Ken Kesey to test psychoactive drugs intended to create the ultimate soldier. Instead Kesey wrote the novel *One Flew Over the Cuckoo's Nest*, and turned on San Francisco to LSD and the Grateful Dead at the legendary Acid Tests.

By the time the civil rights movement arrived anything seemed possible, and it seemed the freaky force of free thinking would stop the unpopular Vietnam War. There were Be-Ins and draft-card-burning protests in Golden Gate Park and free food, love and music in the Haight from 1967 until 1969, when the assassinations of Bobby Kennedy and Martin Luther King, Jr brought a sudden chill to the 'Summer of Love.'

But just over the hill from the foggy-headed Haight, gay entrepreneurs like Harvey Milk were bringing a brighter outlook to the ramshackle Victorian neighborhood known as the Castro. Milk became the nation's first openly gay elected official, but eerily predicted his own assassination right before former supervisor Dan White shot Milk and then-mayor George Moscone in City Hall. White committed suicide a year after his 1984 release, but by then the city was preoccupied with a strange illness appearing in local hospitals. San Francisco healthcare providers and gay activists rallied to establish new standards for care and prevention of the pandemic now known as HIV/AIDS, and vital early interventions were made possible through local fundraisers. Another item still on the community's political agenda is same-sex marriage, authorized by San Francisco Mayor Newsom in time for Valentine's Day 2004. California courts voided those marriage contracts, but the civil rights challenges to differential treatment based on sexual orientation aren't over.

Geek Chic

Industry dwindled steadily in San Francisco after World War II, but the brains of military-industrial operations found work in the so-called Silicon Valley, a technology-centric area that runs south of San Francisco to San Jose. A company started in a South Bay garage called Hewlett-Packard introduced the forward-thinking 9100A 'computing genie' in 1968, and the ground-breaking Apple II was introduced at San Francisco's West Coast Computer Faire in 1977.

By the mid-1990s the tech boom had expanded to include internet sites that sold vegan dog food, art by the yard and extra socks – until venture capital funding dried up and multimillion dollar dot-coms shrank into online oblivion. Stock-option paper fortunes disappeared in 2000, leaving service-sector employees and 26-year-old former vice-presidents alike without job prospects.

Yet San Francisco somehow managed to retain its talent pool, with more entrepreneurs, musicians and patent-holders per capita than any other US city. It's a self-selecting community that can live with the risk of earthquakes and an economy tied to volatile technology and international markets, but there are more people living in San Francisco now than ever. Today there are new booms in the works: biotech in Mission Bay and Web 2.0 technology in former downtown dot-com headquarters.

ORIENTATION

San Francisco may loom large in the imagination, but it's just the tip of a 30-mile-long peninsula with the Pacific Ocean on one side and San Francisco Bay on the other. True to the spirit of the city, San Francisco's main Market St thoroughfare is a contrarian streak that runs diagonally across the otherwise tidy grid of east–west city streets. North of this dividing line past Van Ness Ave is Civic Center and the Tenderloin, Union Sq, the Financial District, Chinatown, North Beach, Nob Hill, Russian Hill and Fisherman's Wharf. SoMa (*So*uth of *Ma*rket) fades around Van Ness into the Mission, which blends into the Castro around Church St.

The scenery gets weirder and wilder north of Market from Van Ness on out to the Pacific Ocean. The landscape takes a turn for the surreal in Japantown and Pacific Heights with waving kitties and costumed pug parades, while the Haight's head shops, rehabs and community ventures are flashbacks to the Summer of Love. Hardcore surfers and gourmet adventurers hang out in the Richmond and Sunset, which frame Golden Gate Park, where the buffalo roam and the skies are cloudy most days.

Maps

Besides the maps included in this chapter, the best free map you'll find is the *San Francisco Street Map & Visitor Guide*, available at many of the city's hotels. If you're going to explore the city by public transportation, the MUNI (San Francisco Municipal Railway) *Street & Transit Map* is a wise $3 investment. Score your copy at the Visitors Information Center (p84), at any large bookstore, or online at www.sfm uni.com.

INFORMATION

Bookstores

San Francisco buys more books, hoards three times as many library books and has more writers per capita than any other US city. Not surprisingly, many city bookstores are open late and host excellent author-reading series.

A Different Light Bookstore (Map pp96-7; ☎ 415-431-0891; www.adlbooks.com; 489 Castro St) The city's largest gay and lesbian bookstore, with raucous author events that top the best Castro cocktail parties.

Babylon Falling (Map pp88-9; ☎ 415-345-1017; www.babylonfalling.com; 1017 Bush St; noon-7pm Tue-Sun) All the lit you could ever need to lead a revolution and inspire your next graphic novel. As the store boasts: '3000 titles, NO FILLER.'

City Lights Bookstore (Map pp92-3; ☎ 415-362-8193; www.citylights.com; 261 Columbus Ave; 10am-midnight) Ever since manager Shigeyoshi Murao and founder and Beat poet Lawrence Ferlinghetti successfully defended their right to 'willfully and lewdly print' Allen Ginsberg's magnificent *Howl and Other Poems* in 1957, this landmark bookstore has been a magnet for poets, free thinkers and omnivorous readers.

Get Lost (Map pp96-7; ☎ 415-437-0529; www.getlostbooks.com; 1825 Market St; 10am-7pm Mon-Fri, to 6pm Sat, 11am-5pm Sun) The travel lit, maps and magnetic backgammon games you wish you'd brought with you are here.

Green Apple Books (Map p91; ☎ 415-387-2272; www.greenapplebooks.com; 506 Clement St; 10am-10:30pm Sun-Thu, to 11:30pm Fri & Sat) If you can tear yourself away from the three-story selection of remainders and discounted books, there's also an annex for mags, used lit and CDs two doors down.

Emergency & Medical Services

Ambulance ☎ 911

American College of Traditional Chinese Medicine (off Map pp96-7; ☎ 415-282-9603; 450 Connecticut St; 8:30am-9pm Mon-Thu, 9am-5:30pm Fri & Sat) Acupuncture, herbal remedies and other traditional Chinese medical treatments.

Haight Ashbury Free Clinic (Map pp96-7; ☎ 415-746-1950; www.hafci.org; 558 Clayton St; 1-9pm Mon, 9am-9pm Tue-Thu, 1-5pm Fri) Since 1967 the Haight Ashbury Free Clinic has set national standards for considerate, free medical care. Advance appointments are required for a doctor or nurse-practitioner to treat whatever ails you, from a minor flu to chronic substance abuse.

Pharmaca (Map pp96-7; ☎ 415-661-1216; www.pharmaca.com; 925 Cole St; Mon-Fri 8am-8pm, Sat & Sun 9am-8pm) Pharmacy plus holistic and naturopathic remedies.

Planned Parenthood (Map pp88-9; ☎ 800-967-7526; www.ppgg.org; 815 Eddy St) Provides women's health care on a sliding scale based on your ability to pay.

San Francisco General Hospital (Map pp86-7; ☎ 415-206-8000; 1001 Potrero Ave; 24hr) Waits are long and fees *start* between $250 and $500 for an emergency-room visit, but this is still your best bet for reliable, low-cost urgent care.

St Luke's Women's Center (Map pp86-7; ☎ 415-285-7788; www.stlukes-sf.org; 1650 Valencia St) Women's and perinatal health care provided by highly rated women OBGYNs and nurse-midwives.

Walgreens (Map pp96-7; ☎ 415-861-6276; 498 Castro St; 24hr) Pharmacy and over-the-counter meds; dozens of locations citywide.

Internet Access

SF offers more than 370 free wi-fi hotspots. Most business-friendly hotels provide wi-fi access, and many cafés offer free wi-fi with your coffee purchase. If you don't have your own computer, try the terminals at these locations:

Apple Store (Map pp88-9; ☎ 415-392-0202; 1 Stockton St; 10am-9pm Mon-Sat, 11am-6pm Sun) Free wi-fi access and internet terminal usage.

Main Library (Map pp88-9; ☎ 415-557-4400; http://sfpl.lib.ca.us; 100 Larkin St; 10am-6pm Mon & Sat, 9am-8pm Tue-Thu, noon-6pm Fri, noon-5pm Sun) Six 'express' terminals on the 1st floor offer 15 minutes of free access on a first-come, first-served basis.

Internet Resources

This close to Silicon Valley, there's a plethora of websites that list only-in-SF events, entertainment and shopping, including:

http://sfbay.craigslist.org Events, activities, partners, freebies and dates.

http://sf.eater.com SF food, nightlife and bars.

www.dailycandy.com Trendy shops, new restaurants and clubs.

www.flavorpill.com Live music, lectures, art openings and movie premieres.

www.thrillist.com Bars, bands, shops, restaurants and events.

Laundry

Self-service laundries are easy to find in most residential neighborhoods. Typical costs are $1.75 for washing and 75¢ per 15-minute drying cycle. Clothing theft does happen, so keep an eye on your dryers.

Brain Wash (Map pp88-9; ☎ 415-255-4866; www.brainwash.com; 1122 Folsom St; per wash from $2; 🕑 7am-10pm Mon-Thu, to 11pm Fri & Sat, 8am-10pm Sun) Linger over laundry with breakfast served all day, cheap beer, pinball, free wi-fi, internet terminals (per 20 minutes $3) and often live music at night.

Media

For a worldly selection of newspapers and magazines, from Chinese *Vogue* to *Der Speigel*, check out **Café de la Presse** (Map pp88-9; ☎ 415-398-2680; www.aqua-sf.com/cdlp; 352 Grant Ave; 🕑 8am-10pm).

KALW 91.7 fm (www.kalw.org) Local National Public Radio (NPR) station.

KPFA 94.1 fm (www.kpfa.org) Alternative news and music.

KPOO 89.5 fm (www.kpoo.com) The West Coast's first African American–owned radio station, with jazz, R&B, blues and reggae.

KQED 88.5 fm (www.kqed.org) Local NPR station, affiliated with KALW.

San Francisco Bay Guardian (www.sfbg.com) Free weekly, published Wednesday; alternative news and entertainment listings.

San Francisco Chronicle (www.sfgate.com) Northern California's largest daily newspaper; news, entertainment and event listings on website (no registration required).

SF Weekly (www.sfweekly.com) Free weekly, also published Wednesday; local gossip and entertainment.

Money

Banks are ubiquitous in San Francisco and usually offer the best rates for currency exchange. At San Francisco International Airport, currency-exchange offices are run by **Travelex** (☎ 650-821-0900; 🕑 6:30am-10pm), but you'll get a better a rate using your bank card at an ATM to withdraw dollars.

Post

Civic Center post office (Map pp88-9; ☎ 415-563-7284, 800-725-2161; 101 Hyde St; 🕑 6am-5:30pm Mon, Wed & Fri, to 8:30pm Tue & Thu, to 3pm Sat) Mail can be sent to you here, c/o General Delivery, Civic Center Post Office, 101 Hyde St, San Francisco, CA 94142, USA.

Union Square post office (Map pp88-9; ☎ 415-956-0131; 170 O'Farrell St; 🕑 10am-5:30pm Mon-Sat, 11am-5pm Sun) In the basement of Macy's department store.

Telephone

When you can find one that works, public phones usually cost 50¢ for calls within San Francisco. For long-distance calls, your best bet is a discount phonecard available from most grocery and drug stores.

Area codes in the Bay Area

East Bay (including Berkeley and Oakland)	☎ 510
Marin County	☎ 415
Palo Alto	☎ 650
Peninsula	☎ 650
San Francisco	☎ 415
San Jose	☎ 408

Tourist Information

California Welcome Center (Map pp94-5; ☎ 415-981-1280; www.visitcwc.com; Pier 39, Bldg P, Suite 241b; 🕑 10am-5pm) Handy for travel information, brochures, maps and help booking accommodations.

San Francisco Visitors Information Center (Map pp88-9; ☎ 415-391-2000; www.onlyinsanfrancisco.com; Hallidie Plaza, 900 Market St; 🕑 8:30am-5pm Mon-Fri, 9am-3pm Sat & Sun) Just below the street level beside the Powell St BART station is this source for maps, guidebooks, brochures and phonecards.

DANGERS & ANNOYANCES

Keep your city smarts and wits about you, especially in the sketchier stretches of the Tenderloin, Mission, Western Addition, 6th and 7th Sts in SoMa, and Bayview-Hunters Point. Parks at night can get seedy, and if you should ever wind up somewhere you'd rather not be, head to the nearest store and call a taxi. Expect to be asked for spare change often, but don't feel obliged – donations stretch further at nonprofit **Haight Ashbury Food Program** (see p109). A nod of acknowledgement and a simple 'I'm sorry' is considered polite.

SIGHTS

The Bay & the Embarcadero

Twelve miles across, 60 miles long and at points only 6 feet deep at low tide, the silvery

THE UN-THANKSGIVING

Since ferrying guards and other necessities cost the state more than putting up prisoners at the Ritz, the state closed Alcatraz in 1963 – yet authorities refused a petition to establish a Native American study center on the abandoned island. On the eve of Thanksgiving in 1969, 79 Native American activists broke a Coast Guard blockade and took over Alcatraz in protest. Over the next 19 months, some 5600 Native Americans visited the occupied island, sparking Native American activism nationwide. Before the FBI seized the island, public support pressured President Richard Nixon to restore Native American territory and strengthen self-rule for Native American nations. Graffiti on the Alcatraz water tower is still legible: 'This is Indian Land.' Each Thanksgiving Day since 1975, an 'Un-Thanksgiving' ceremony has been held at dawn on Alcatraz, with Native American leaders and supporters symbolically renewing their determination to reverse the course of colonial history.

bay makes a grander entrance to San Francisco than any red carpet. But where today you can stroll the broad Embarcadero esplanade, during the Gold Rush this was once a mess of makeshift piers, abandoned ships and saloons prowled by pirates and pimps. The waterfront scene is much more genteel nowadays at swanky bayside restaurants in the Ferry Building and around Ghirardelli Sq – though the sea lions gleefully ignore all this dining etiquette and loudly digest their seafood feasts bellyflopped on Pier 39.

GOLDEN GATE BRIDGE

Brooklyn's suspension bridge may be bigger, but better? That's crazy talk to San Franciscans, who are only prepared to debate about the best vista of the 1937 **bridge** (Map pp86-7; ☎ 415-921-5858; www.goldengate.org; Fort Point Lookout, Marine Dr; southbound car $6, carpools free). Cinema buffs believe that Hitchcock had it right: seen from below at **Fort Point**, the bridge induces a thrilling case of *Vertigo*. Fog aficionados prefer the north-end lookout at Marin's **Vista Point**, to watch gusts billow through bridge cables like dry ice at a Kiss concert. Hard to believe that in 1933, the Navy almost nixed the signature art-deco design of architects Gertrude and Irving Murrow and engineer Joseph B Strauss in favor of a hulking concrete span painted with caution-yellow stripes.

To see both sides of the Golden Gate debate, hike or bike it yourself. MUNI buses 28 and 29 run to the toll plaza, and pedestrians can walk across the bridge on the east side, while bicyclists zoom along on the ocean side. Go during off-peak hours to minimize your exhaust inhalation, and bus it back via Golden Gate Transit if the 4-mile round-trip seems a bit much.

FERRY BUILDING

Slackers have the right idea at the **Ferry Building** (Map pp88-9; ☎ 415-693-0996; www.ferrybuildingmarketplace.com; Embarcadero), the transport hub turned gourmet emporium where no one's in a hurry to get anywhere. Boat traffic isn't what it was back when the grand hall and clock tower were built in 1898, and by the 1950s the building was literally overshadowed by a freeway overpass. But after the freeway collapsed in the 1989 Loma Prieta Earthquake, the city revived the Ferry Building as a tribute to San Francisco's monumental good taste. On weekends the **Ferry Plaza Farmers Market** (see p139) fans out around the south end of the building like a fabulous garnish. See p122 for restaurant suggestions and other foodie action.

ALCATRAZ

Almost 150 years before Guantanamo, a rocky island in the middle of San Francisco Bay became the nation's first military prison: **Alcatraz** (☎ 415-981-7625; www.nps.gov/alcatraz). Civil War deserters and those facing court-martial were kept in wooden pens along with Native American 'unfriendlies,' including 19 Hopis who refused to send their children to government boarding schools where speaking Hopi and practicing Hopi religion were punishable by beatings.

In 1934 the Federal Bureau of Prisons took over Alcatraz, determined to make a public example of bootleggers and other gangsters. 'The Rock' only averaged 264 inmates, but its roster included Chicago crime boss Al 'Scarface' Capone, Harlem mafioso and sometime poet 'Bumpy' Johnson, and Morton Sobell, found guilty of Soviet espionage along with Julius

(Continued on page 98)

SAN FRANCISCO

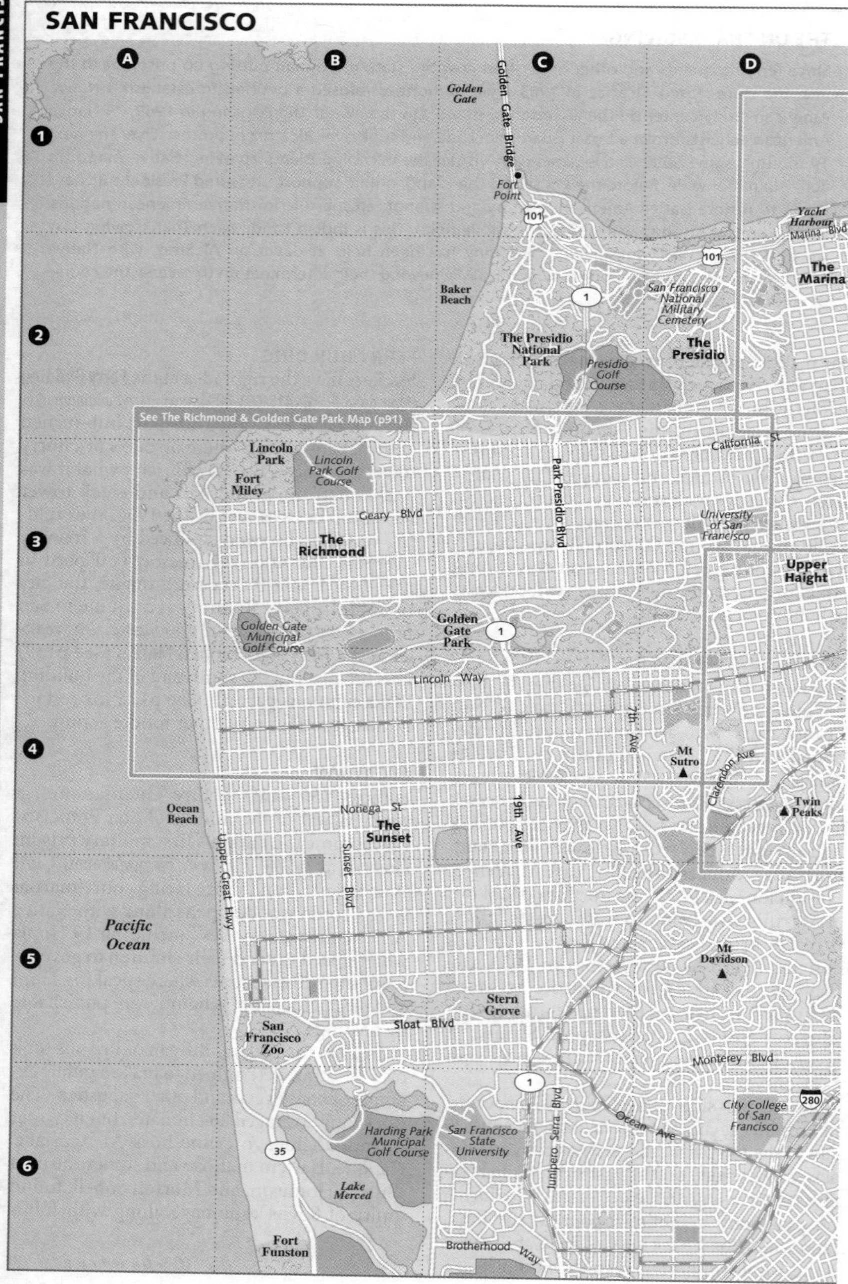

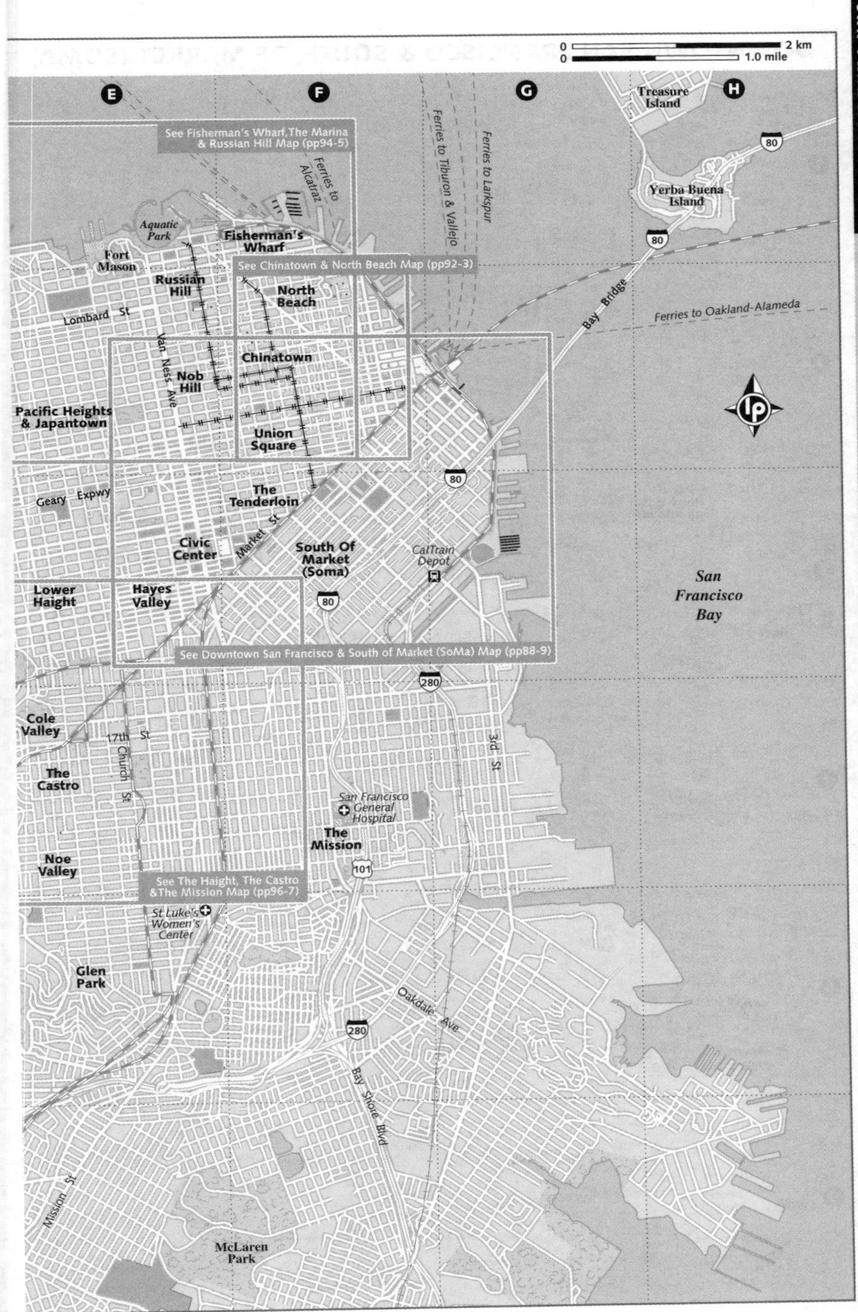

0 2 km
0 1.0 mile
E
F
G
H
Treasure Island
80
See Fisherman's Wharf, The Marina & Russian Hill Map (pp94-5)
Ferries to Alcatraz
Ferries to Tiburon & Vallejo
Ferries to Larkspur
Yerba Buena Island
Aquatic Park
Fisherman's Wharf
Fort Mason
See Chinatown & North Beach Map (pp92-3)
Russian Hill
North Beach
Bay Bridge
Ferries to Oakland-Alameda
Lombard St
Van Ness Ave
Chinatown
Nob Hill
Pacific Heights & Japantown
Union Square
The Tenderloin
Geary Expwy
Market St
Civic Center
South Of Market (Soma)
CalTrain Depot
San Francisco Bay
Lower Haight
Hayes Valley
See Downtown San Francisco & South of Market (SoMa) Map (pp88-9)
280
Cole Valley
17th St
Church St
3rd St
The Castro
San Francisco General Hospital
The Mission
101
Noe Valley
See The Haight, The Castro &The Mission Map (pp96-7)
St Luke's Women's Center
Glen Park
Oakdale Ave
Bay Shore Blvd
Mission St
McLaren Park

DOWNTOWN SAN FRANCISCO & SOUTH OF MARKET (SOMA)
Allyne Park
Green St
Vallejo St
Broadway
Pacific Ave
Jackson St
Clay St
Sacramento St
California St
Pine St
Sutter St
Geary Expwy
Lafayette Park
Pacific Heights & Japantown
Laguna St
Octavia St
Franklin St
Van Ness Ave
Polk St
Larkin St
Hyde St
Leavenworth St
Glover St
Broadway Tunnel
Powell-Hyde St Cable Car Line
Mini Park
Nob Hill
Washington St
Pleasant St
Huntington Park
California St Cable Car Line
California St Cable Car Turnaround
Austin St
Bush St
Fern St
Hemlock St
Post St
Cedar St
Geary St
Myrtle St
O'Farrell St
Olive St
Ellis St
Willow St
Eddy St
Larch St
Turk St
Elm St
Golden Gate Ave
Redwood St
McAllister St
Civic Center
Civic Center Plaza
United Nations Plaza
Civic Center BART & MUNI Station
Ash St
Fulton St
Grove St
Hayes St
Ivy St
Linden St
Fell St
Hickory St
Oak St
Lily St
Page St
Rose St
Haight St
Waller St
Hermann St
Hayes Valley
Lower Haight
The Castro
Buchanan St
Webster St
Gough St
Eddy St
Jefferson Sq
Turk Blvd
Hayward Playground
The Tenderloin
Shannon St
Taylor St
Jones St
Mason St
Powell St
Trenton St
Grant Ave
Waverly Pl
Clay St
Chinese Playground
Joice St
Powell-Mason & Powell-Hyde St Cable Car Lines
Stockton St
Cyril Magnin St
Hallidie Plaza
Powell St BART & MUNI Station
Union Square
Mission St
Mary St
Natoma St
Stevenson St
Jessie St
Market St
Minna St
8th St
6th St
Russ St
Moss St
Sherman St
7th St
Langton St
Rausch St
Sumner St
Harrison St
Ringold St
9th St
Sheridan St
10th St
Juniper St
Dore Al
Van Ness MUNI Station
11th St
Mission St
Grace St
Howard St
Lafayette St
Natoma St
Otis St
Kissling St
12th St
Norfolk St
Isis St
McCoppin St
Pearl St
Elgin Park
Valencia St
Stevenson St
13th St
Central Fwy
To Mighty (0.3mi)

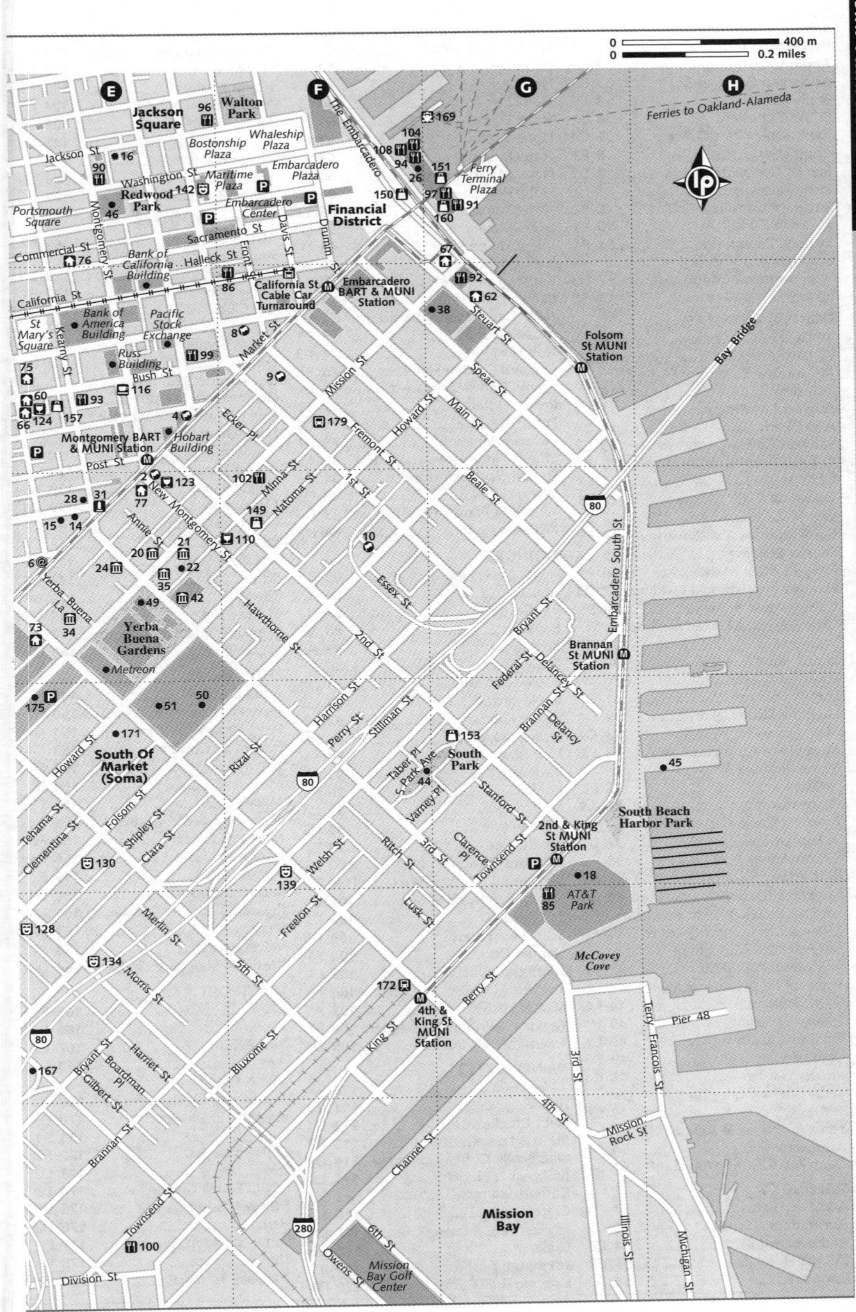
0 400 m
0 0.2 miles
E
F
G
H
Ferries to Oakland-Alameda
Jackson Square
Walton Park
Bostonship Plaza
Whaleship Plaza
Embarcadero Plaza
Maritime Plaza
Ferry Terminal Plaza
Redwood Park
Portsmouth Square
Embarcadero Center
Financial District
Bank of California Building
California St Cable Car Turnaround
Embarcadero BART & MUNI Station
St Mary's Square
Bank of America Building
Pacific Stock Exchange
Russ Building
Folsom St MUNI Station
Bay Bridge
Montgomery BART & MUNI Station
Hobart Building
Yerba Buena Gardens
Metreon
South Of Market (Soma)
South Park
Brannan St MUNI Station
South Beach Harbor Park
2nd & King St MUNI Station
AT&T Park
McCovey Cove
4th & King St MUNI Station
Pier 48
Mission Bay
Mission Bay Golf Center
Jackson St
Washington St
Commercial St
Sacramento St
Halleck St
California St
Bush St
Post St
Montgomery St
Kearny St
Front St
Davis St
Drumm St
The Embarcadero
Market St
Mission St
Steuart St
Spear St
Main St
Howard St
Fremont St
Beale St
1st St
Ecker Pl
Minna St
Natoma St
New Montgomery St
Annie St
Yerba Buena La
Essex St
Hawthorne St
2nd St
Bryant St
Federal St
Delancey St
Brannan St
Delancy St
Embarcadero South St
Harrison St
Perry St
Stillman St
Rizal St
Taber Pl
S Park Ave
Varney Pl
Stanford St
Townsend St
Clarence Pl
3rd St
Ritch St
Lusk St
Welsh St
Freelon St
Tehama St
Clementina St
Folsom St
Shipley St
Clara St
Merlin St
Morris St
5th St
Bluxome St
King St
Berry St
Terry Francois St
Mission Rock St
4th St
Channel St
Harriet St
Bryant St
Boardman Pl
Gilbert St
Brannan St
Townsend St
Division St
Owens St
6th St
Illinois St
Michigan St
80
280
16 90 96 46 142 76 86 108 104 94 26 151 169 150 97 91 160 67 92 62 38 8 99 9 75 60 66 124 157 93 116 4 179 2 123 77 28 31 15 14 102 149 110 10 21 20 22 6 24 35 42 49 34 73 175 51 50 171 153 44 45 18 85 130 139 128 134 172 167 100

INFORMATION

- Apple Store **1** D3
- Australian Consulate **2** E3
- Brain Wash **3** D5
- British Consulate **4** E2
- Civic Center Post Office **5** C4
- CompUSA **6** E3
- French Consulate **7** D2
- Irish Consulate **8** F2
- Japanese Consulate **9** F2
- Mexican Consulate **10** F3
- Planned Parenthood **11** B4
- San Francisco Visitors Information Center **12** D3
- Spanish Consulate **13** A3

SIGHTS & ACTIVITIES

- 49 Geary **14** E3
- 77 Geary **15** E3
- AP Hotaling Building (451-55 Jackson) **16** E1
- Asian Art Museum **17** C4
- AT&T Park **18** G4
- Babylon Falling **19** C2
- California Historical Society Museum **20** E3
- Cartoon Art Museum **21** E3
- Catharine Clark Gallery **22** E3
- City Hall **23** B4
- Contemporary Jewish Museum **24** E3
- Federal Building **25** C4
- Ferry Building Marketplace **26** F1
- Folk Art International Building **27** D3
- Gallery Paule Anglim **28** E3
- Glide Memorial United Methodist Church **29** D3
- James Flood Building **30** D3
- Looff Carousel (see 51)
- Lotta's Fountain **31** E3
- Luggage Store Gallery **32** D4
- Main Library **33** C4
- Museum of Craft and Folk Art **34** E3
- Museum of the African Diaspora **35** E3
- Peace Pagoda **36** A3
- Powell St Cable Car Turnaround **37** D3
- Rincon Annex Post Office **38** G2
- Ruth Asawa Fountains **39** A3
- San Francisco Bicycle Coalition **40** D4
- San Francisco Lesbian, Gay, Bisexual, Transgender Community Center **41** A6
- San Francisco Museum of Modern Art (SFMoma) **42** E3
- Sisters of Perpetual Indulgence **43** D3
- South Park **44** F4
- Spinnaker Sailing **45** H4
- Transamerica Pyramid **46** E1
- Union Square **47** D3
- Victory Garden **48** C4
- Yerba Buena Center for the Arts **49** E3
- Yerba Buena Ice Skating & Bowling Center **50** E4
- Zeum Art & Technology Center **51** E4

SLEEPING

- Adelaide Hostel **52** C3
- Amsterdam Hostel **53** C2
- Andrews Hotel **54** C3
- Dakota Hotel **55** C3
- Fairmont **56** D2
- Golden Gate Hotel **57** D2
- HI San Francisco City Center **58** C3
- Hotel Adagio **59** C3
- Hotel Des Arts **60** E2
- Hotel Frank **61** D3
- Hotel Griffon **62** G2
- Hotel Majestic **63** A3
- Hotel Metropolis **64** D4
- Hotel Rex **65** D2
- Hotel Triton **66** E2
- Hotel Vitale **67** G1
- Inn at Union Square **68** D3
- Kabuki Hotel **69** A3
- Kensington Park Hotel **70** D3
- Larkspur Hotel **71** D2
- Mark Hopkins InterContinental Hotel **72** D2
- Mosser Hotel **73** E3
- Nob Hill Hotel **74** C3
- Orchard Garden Hotel **75** E2
- Pacific Tradewinds Guest House **76** E1
- Palace Hotel **77** E3
- Petite Auberge **78** D2
- Phoenix Motel **79** B4
- Queen Anne Hotel **80** A3
- Sir Francis Drake Hotel **81** D3
- Warwick Regis **82** D3
- Westin St Francis Hotel **83** D3
- White Swan Inn **84** D2

EATING

- Acme Chop House **85** G5
- Aqua **86** F2
- Bar Crudo **87** D2
- Bar Jules **88** A5
- Benkyodo **89** A3
- Bocadillos **90** E1
- Boulette's Larder **91** G1
- Boulevard **92** G2
- Boxed Foods **93** E2
- farmerbrown (see 64)
- Hog Island Oysters **94** F1
- Jardinière **95** B5
- Kokkari **96** F1
- Mijita **97** G1
- Millennium **98** C3
- Mixt Greens **99** E2
- Patisserie Philippe **100** E6
- Restaurant Michael Mina (see 83)
- Saigon Sandwich Shop **101** C4
- Salt House **102** F3
- Sears Fine Foods **103** D3
- Slanted Door **104** F1
- Split Pea Seduction **105** D4
- Stacks **106** A5
- Suppenküche **107** A5
- Taylor's Automatic Refresher **108** F1
- Tu Lan **109** D4

DRINKING

- 111 Minna **110** F3
- AsiaSF **111** C5
- Aunt Charlie's Lounge **112** D4
- Bigfoot Lodge **113** B2
- Blue Bottle Coffee Company **114** D4
- Bourbon & Branch **115** C3
- Café de la Presse (see 66)
- Caffe Amici **116** E2
- City Beer Store & Tasting Room **117** D5
- Eagle **118** C6
- Edinburgh Castle **119** B3
- Emporio Rulli Caffè **120** D3
- Gold Dust Lounge **121** D3
- Hemlock Tavern **122** B3
- House of Shields **123** E3
- Irish Bank **124** E2
- John's Grill **125** D3
- Rye **126** C3
- Tonga Room (see 56)
- Top of the Mark (see 72)
- Tunnel Top Bar **127** D2

ENTERTAINMENT

- 1015 Folsom **128** E5
- American Conservatory Theater **129** D3
- Annie's Social Club **130** E4
- Cat Club **131** D5
- Curran Theatre **132** D3
- Davies Symphony Hall **133** B5
- EndUp **134** E5
- Exit Theatre **135** D3
- Golden Gate Theatre **136** D4
- Great American Music Hall **137** B3
- Harry Denton's Starlight Room (see 81)
- Herbst Theatre **138** B4
- Hotel Utah **139** F4
- Mezzanine **140** D4
- Orpheum Theatre **141** C4
- Punch Line **142** E1
- Rickshaw Stop **143** B5
- Slim's **144** C6
- The Stud **145** D6
- TIX Bay Area **146** D3
- War Memorial Opera House **147** B5
- Warfield **148** D4

SHOPPING

- Adolf Gasser **149** F3
- Ferry Plaza Farmers Market **150** F1
- Ferry Plaza Wine Merchant **151** G1
- Heart of the City Farmers' Market **152** C4
- Jeremy's **153** G4
- MAC **154** B5
- Macy's **155** D3
- Madame S & Mr. Leather **156** D5
- Margaret O'Leary **157** E2
- Nancy Boy **158** B5
- Polk-a-Dot **159** B2
- Recchiuti Chocolates **160** G1
- Residents Apparel Gallery **161** A5
- Studio **162** B2
- Velvet da Vinci **163** B1
- Westfield Shopping Center **164** D3

TRANSPORT

- AAA **165** B5
- Alamo **166** D2
- AutoReturn **167** E5
- Avis **168** C3
- Blue & Gold Fleet Alameda-Oakland Ferry **169** G1
- Budget **170** D3
- Budget **171** E4
- CalTrain Depot **172** F5
- Dollar **173** D3
- Ellis-O'Farrell Garage **174** D3
- Fifth & Mission Garage **175** E4
- Hertz **176** D3
- Sutter-Stockton Garage **177** D2
- Thrifty **178** D3
- Transbay Terminal **179** F2

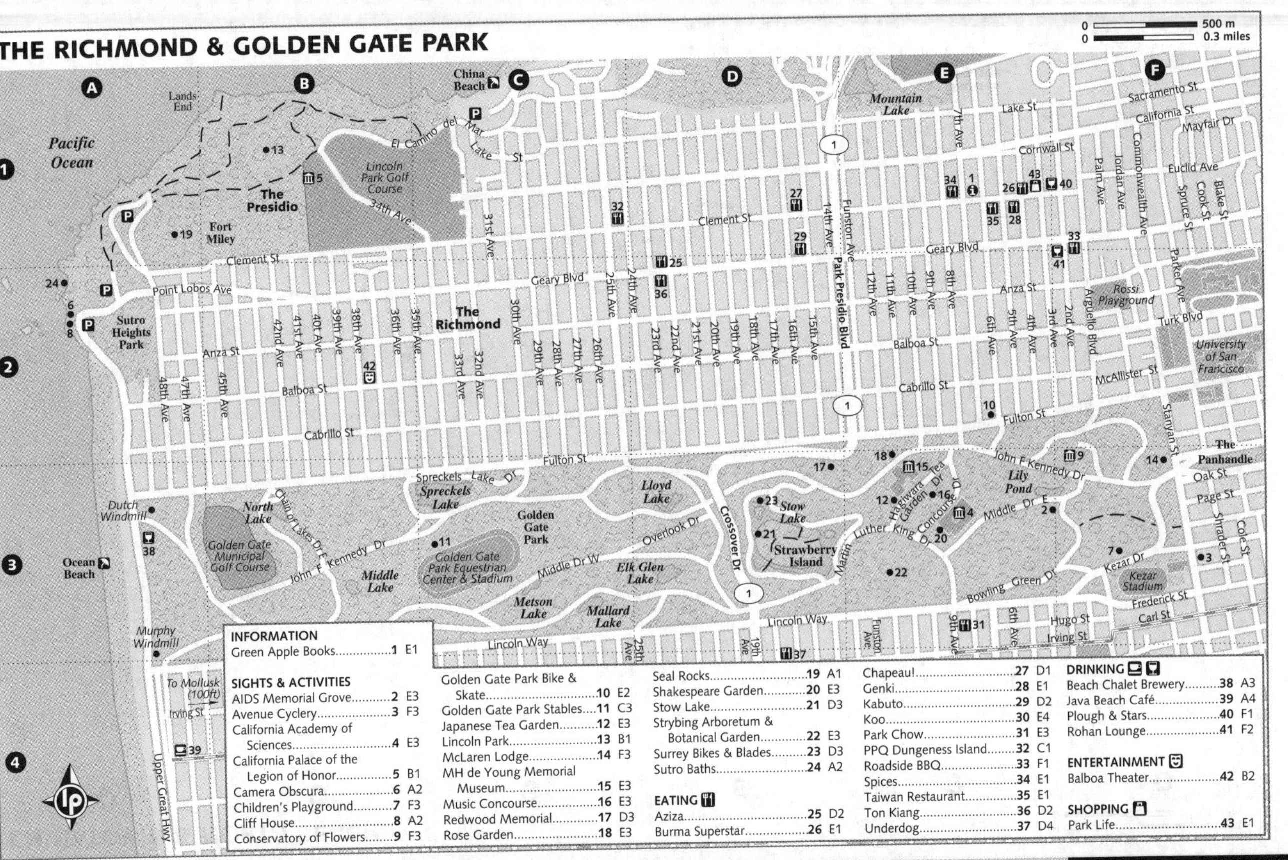
THE RICHMOND & GOLDEN GATE PARK
0 500 m
0 0.3 miles
INFORMATION
Green Apple Books....1 E1
SIGHTS & ACTIVITIES
AIDS Memorial Grove....2 E3
Avenue Cyclery....3 F3
California Academy of Sciences....4 E3
California Palace of the Legion of Honor....5 B1
Camera Obscura....6 A2
Children's Playground....7 F3
Cliff House....8 A2
Conservatory of Flowers....9 F3
Golden Gate Park Bike & Skate....10 E2
Golden Gate Park Stables....11 C3
Japanese Tea Garden....12 E3
Lincoln Park....13 B1
McLaren Lodge....14 F3
MH de Young Memorial Museum....15 E3
Music Concourse....16 E3
Redwood Memorial....17 D3
Rose Garden....18 E3
Seal Rocks....19 A1
Shakespeare Garden....20 E3
Stow Lake....21 D3
Strybing Arboretum & Botanical Garden....22 E3
Surrey Bikes & Blades....23 D3
Sutro Baths....24 A2
EATING
Aziza....25 D2
Burma Superstar....26 E1
Chapeau!....27 D1
Genki....28 E1
Kabuto....29 D2
Koo....30 E4
Park Chow....31 E3
PPQ Dungeness Island....32 C1
Roadside BBQ....33 F1
Spices....34 E1
Taiwan Restaurant....35 E1
Ton Kiang....36 D2
Underdog....37 D4
DRINKING
Beach Chalet Brewery....38 A3
Java Beach Café....39 A4
Plough & Stars....40 F1
Rohan Lounge....41 F2
ENTERTAINMENT
Balboa Theater....42 B2
SHOPPING
Park Life....43 E1
Pacific Ocean
Lands End
The Presidio
Fort Miley
Lincoln Park Golf Course
China Beach
The Richmond
Sutro Heights Park
Ocean Beach
Dutch Windmill
Murphy Windmill
Golden Gate Park
Golden Gate Park Equestrian Center & Stadium
Golden Gate Municipal Golf Course
Mountain Lake
Spreckels Lake
Middle Lake
North Lake
Lloyd Lake
Elk Glen Lake
Mallard Lake
Metson Lake
Stow Lake
Strawberry Island
Lily Pond
Kezar Stadium
The Panhandle
University of San Francisco
Rossi Playground
Upper Great Hwy
To Mollusk (100ft)
Park Presidio Blvd
Geary Blvd
Clement St
Fulton St
Lincoln Way
Crossover Dr
John F Kennedy Dr
Martin Luther King Dr
Middle Dr W
Middle Dr E
Bowling Green Dr
Chain of Lakes Dr E
Spreckels Lake Dr
Overlook Dr
Kezar Dr
Stanyan St
Arguello Blvd
Funston Ave

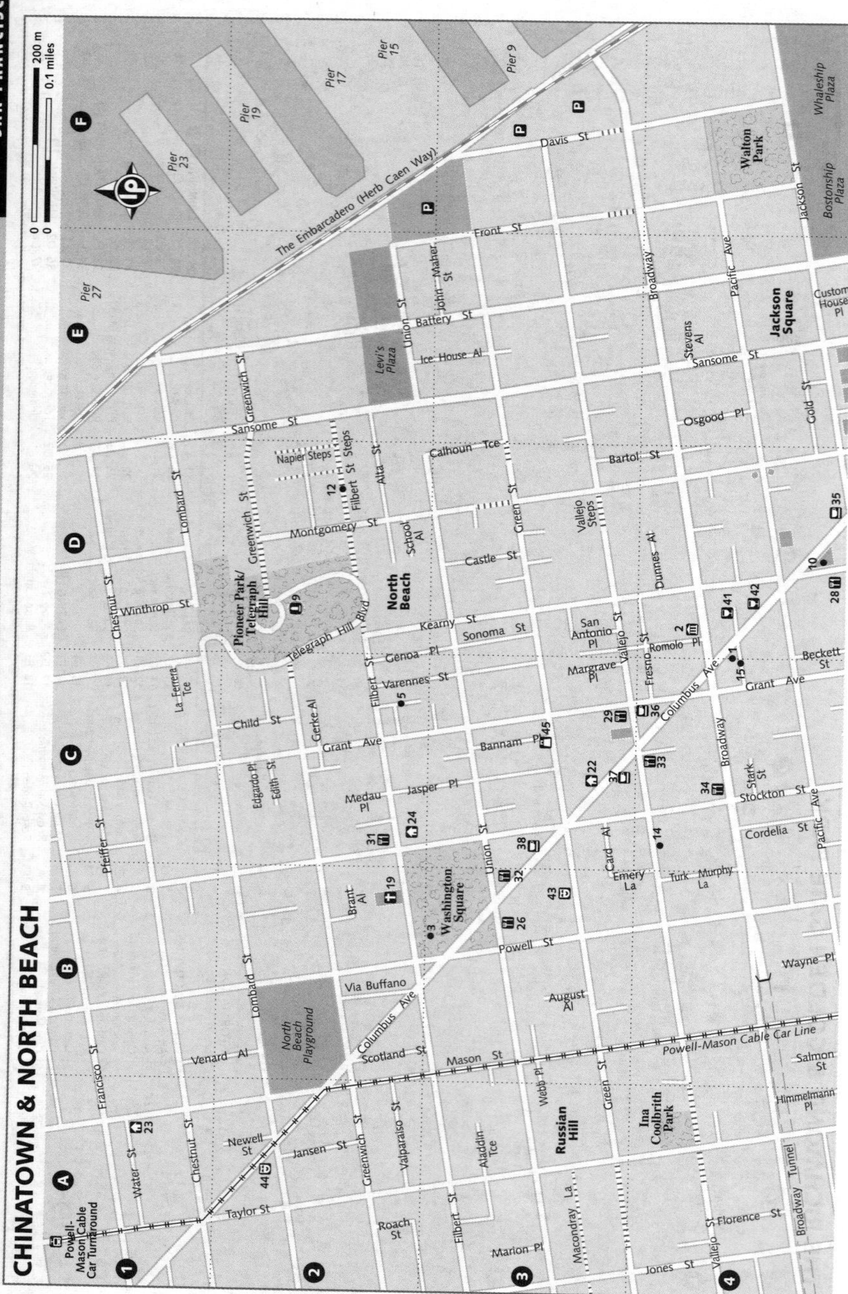
CHINATOWN & NORTH BEACH
0 200 m
0 0.1 miles
A
B
C
D
E
F
1
2
3
4
Pier 27
Pier 23
Pier 19
Pier 17
Pier 15
Pier 9
The Embarcadero (Herb Caen Way)
Levi's Plaza
Walton Park
Whaleship Plaza
Bostonship Plaza
Jackson Square
Custom House Pl
Pioneer Park/ Telegraph Hill
North Beach
Washington Square
North Beach Playground
Russian Hill
Ina Coolbrith Park
Powell-Mason Cable Car Turnaround
Powell-Mason Cable Car Line
Broadway Tunnel
Davis St
Front St
Battery St
John Maher St
Union St
Ice House Al
Sansome St
Greenwich St
Napier Steps
Filbert St Steps
Alta St
Calhoun Tce
Montgomery St
School Al
Castle St
Green St
Vallejo Steps
Bartol St
Osgood Pl
Stevens Al
Pacific Ave
Jackson St
Gold St
Broadway
Dunnes Al
Lombard St
Chestnut St
Winthrop St
Telegraph Hill Blvd
Kearny St
Sonoma St
San Antonio Pl
Vallejo St
Fresno St
Romolo Pl
Beckett St
Grant Ave
Columbus Ave
Margrave Pl
Genoa Pl
Varennes St
Filbert St
La Ferrera Tce
Child St
Gerke Al
Bannam Pl
Edgardo Pl
Edith St
Medau Pl
Jasper Pl
Stark St
Stockton St
Cordelia St
Card Al
Emery La
Turk Murphy La
Pfeiffer St
Brant Al
Powell St
Via Buffano
Wayne Pl
August Al
Venard Al
Scotland St
Mason St
Salmon St
Himmelmann Pl
Francisco St
Webb Pl
Water St
Newell St
Jansen St
Greenwich St
Valparaiso St
Aladdin Tce
Taylor St
Roach St
Macondray La
Florence St
Marion Pl
Jones St
Vallejo St

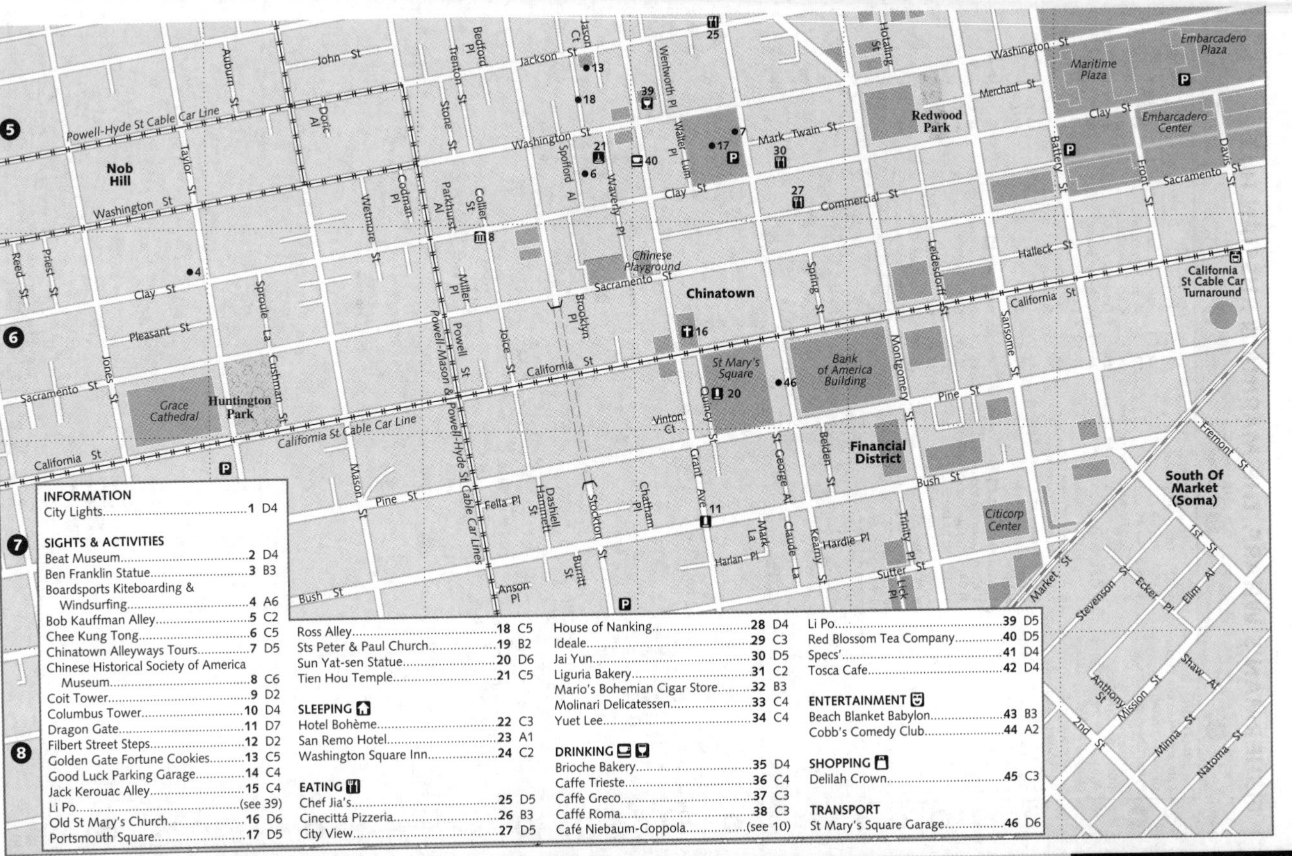
INFORMATION
City Lights....1 D4
SIGHTS & ACTIVITIES
Beat Museum....2 D4
Ben Franklin Statue....3 B3
Boardsports Kiteboarding & Windsurfing....4 A6
Bob Kauffman Alley....5 C2
Chee Kung Tong....6 C5
Chinatown Alleyways Tours....7 D5
Chinese Historical Society of America Museum....8 C6
Coit Tower....9 D2
Columbus Tower....10 D4
Dragon Gate....11 D7
Filbert Street Steps....12 D2
Golden Gate Fortune Cookies....13 C5
Good Luck Parking Garage....14 C4
Jack Kerouac Alley....15 C4
Li Po....(see 39)
Old St Mary's Church....16 D6
Portsmouth Square....17 D5
Ross Alley....18 C5
Sts Peter & Paul Church....19 B2
Sun Yat-sen Statue....20 D6
Tien Hou Temple....21 C5
SLEEPING
Hotel Bohème....22 C3
San Remo Hotel....23 A1
Washington Square Inn....24 C2
EATING
Chef Jia's....25 D5
Cinecittá Pizzeria....26 B3
City View....27 D5
House of Nanking....28 D4
Ideale....29 C3
Jai Yun....30 D5
Liguria Bakery....31 C2
Mario's Bohemian Cigar Store....32 B3
Molinari Delicatessen....33 C4
Yuet Lee....34 C4
DRINKING
Brioche Bakery....35 D4
Caffe Trieste....36 C4
Caffè Greco....37 C3
Caffé Roma....38 C3
Café Niebaum-Coppola....(see 10)
Li Po....39 D5
Red Blossom Tea Company....40 D5
Specs'....41 D4
Tosca Cafe....42 D4
ENTERTAINMENT
Beach Blanket Babylon....43 B3
Cobb's Comedy Club....44 A2
SHOPPING
Delilah Crown....45 C3
TRANSPORT
St Mary's Square Garage....46 D6
Nob Hill
Chinatown
Financial District
South Of Market (Soma)
Redwood Park
Huntington Park
Grace Cathedral
St Mary's Square
Bank of America Building
Chinese Playground
Maritime Plaza
Embarcadero Plaza
Embarcadero Center
Citicorp Center
California St Cable Car Turnaround
Powell-Hyde St Cable Car Line
Powell-Mason & Powell-Hyde St Cable Car Lines
California St Cable Car Line
Washington St
Jackson St
Clay St
Sacramento St
California St
Pine St
Bush St
Sutter St
Market St
Montgomery St
Kearny St
Grant Ave
Stockton St
Powell St
Mason St
Taylor St
Jones St
Sansome St
Battery St
Front St
Davis St
Commercial St
Merchant St
Halleck St
Leidesdorff St
Spring St
Belden St
Mark Twain St
Walter Lum Pl
Wentworth Pl
Waverly Pl
Spofford Al
Jason Ct
Brooklyn Pl
Quincy St
Vinton Ct
St George Al
Claude La
Mark La
Harlan Pl
Hardie Pl
Trinity Pl
Lick Pl
Hotaling St
Chatham Pl
Burritt St
Dashiell Hammett St
Fella Pl
Anson Pl
Joice St
Miller Pl
Collier St
Parkhurst Al
Codman Pl
Wetmore St
Stone St
Trenton St
Bedford Pl
John St
Doric Al
Auburn St
Sproule La
Cushman St
Pleasant St
Priest St
Reed St
Fremont St
1st St
2nd St
Elim Al
Ecker Pl
Stevenson St
Shaw Al
Mission St
Anthony St
Minna St
Natoma St

FISHERMAN'S WHARF, THE MARINA & RUSSIAN HILL

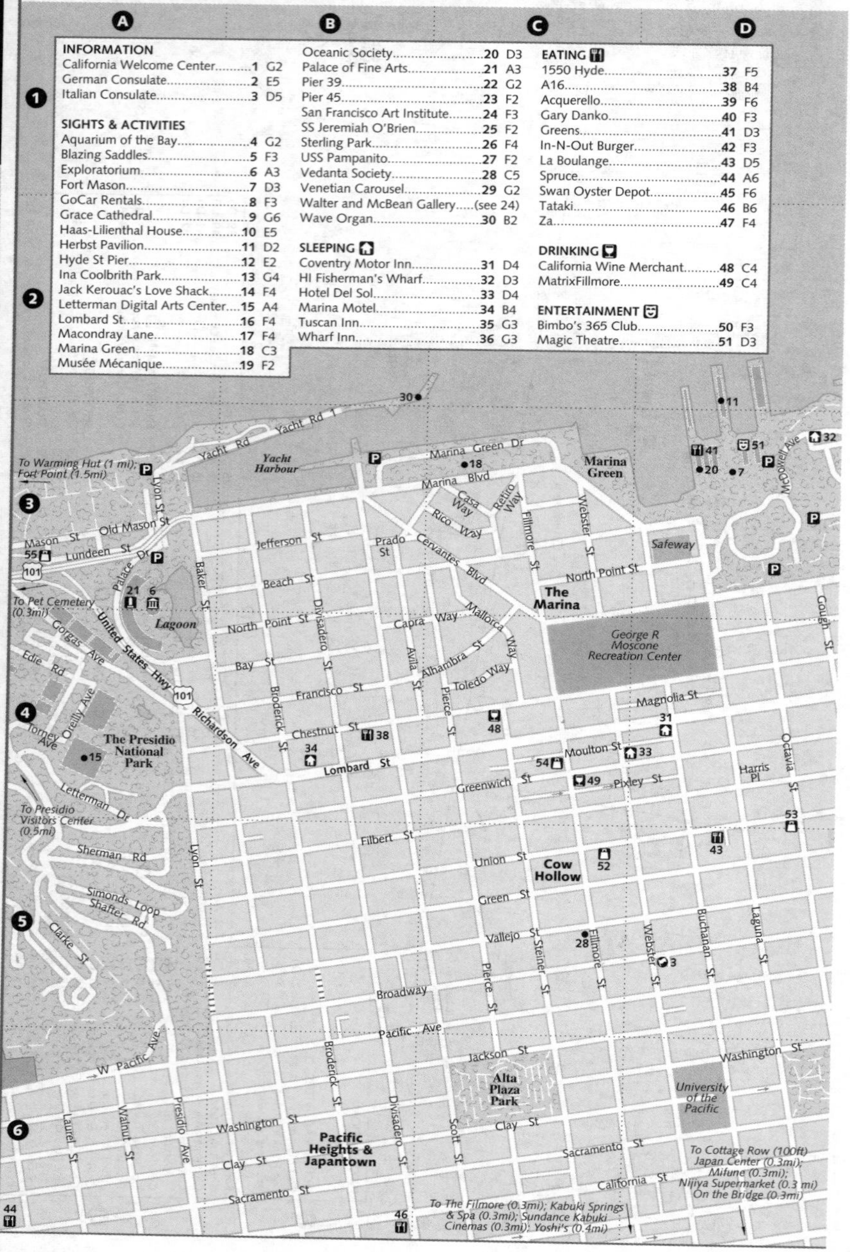

INFORMATION
- California Welcome Center.......... 1 G2
- German Consulate.......... 2 E5
- Italian Consulate.......... 3 D5

SIGHTS & ACTIVITIES
- Aquarium of the Bay.......... 4 G2
- Blazing Saddles.......... 5 F3
- Exploratorium.......... 6 A3
- Fort Mason.......... 7 D3
- GoCar Rentals.......... 8 F3
- Grace Cathedral.......... 9 G6
- Haas-Lilienthal House.......... 10 E5
- Herbst Pavilion.......... 11 D2
- Hyde St Pier.......... 12 E2
- Ina Coolbrith Park.......... 13 G4
- Jack Kerouac's Love Shack.......... 14 F4
- Letterman Digital Arts Center.......... 15 A4
- Lombard St.......... 16 F4
- Macondray Lane.......... 17 F4
- Marina Green.......... 18 C3
- Musée Mécanique.......... 19 F2
- Oceanic Society.......... 20 D3
- Palace of Fine Arts.......... 21 A3
- Pier 39.......... 22 G2
- Pier 45.......... 23 F2
- San Francisco Art Institute.......... 24 F3
- SS Jeremiah O'Brien.......... 25 F2
- Sterling Park.......... 26 F4
- USS Pampanito.......... 27 F2
- Vedanta Society.......... 28 C5
- Venetian Carousel.......... 29 G2
- Walter and McBean Gallery.....(see 24)
- Wave Organ.......... 30 B2

SLEEPING
- Coventry Motor Inn.......... 31 D4
- HI Fisherman's Wharf.......... 32 D3
- Hotel Del Sol.......... 33 D4
- Marina Motel.......... 34 B4
- Tuscan Inn.......... 35 G3
- Wharf Inn.......... 36 G3

EATING
- 1550 Hyde.......... 37 F5
- A16.......... 38 B4
- Acquerello.......... 39 F6
- Gary Danko.......... 40 F3
- Greens.......... 41 D3
- In-N-Out Burger.......... 42 F3
- La Boulange.......... 43 D5
- Spruce.......... 44 A6
- Swan Oyster Depot.......... 45 F6
- Tataki.......... 46 B6
- Za.......... 47 F4

DRINKING
- California Wine Merchant.......... 48 C4
- MatrixFillmore.......... 49 C4

ENTERTAINMENT
- Bimbo's 365 Club.......... 50 F3
- Magic Theatre.......... 51 D3

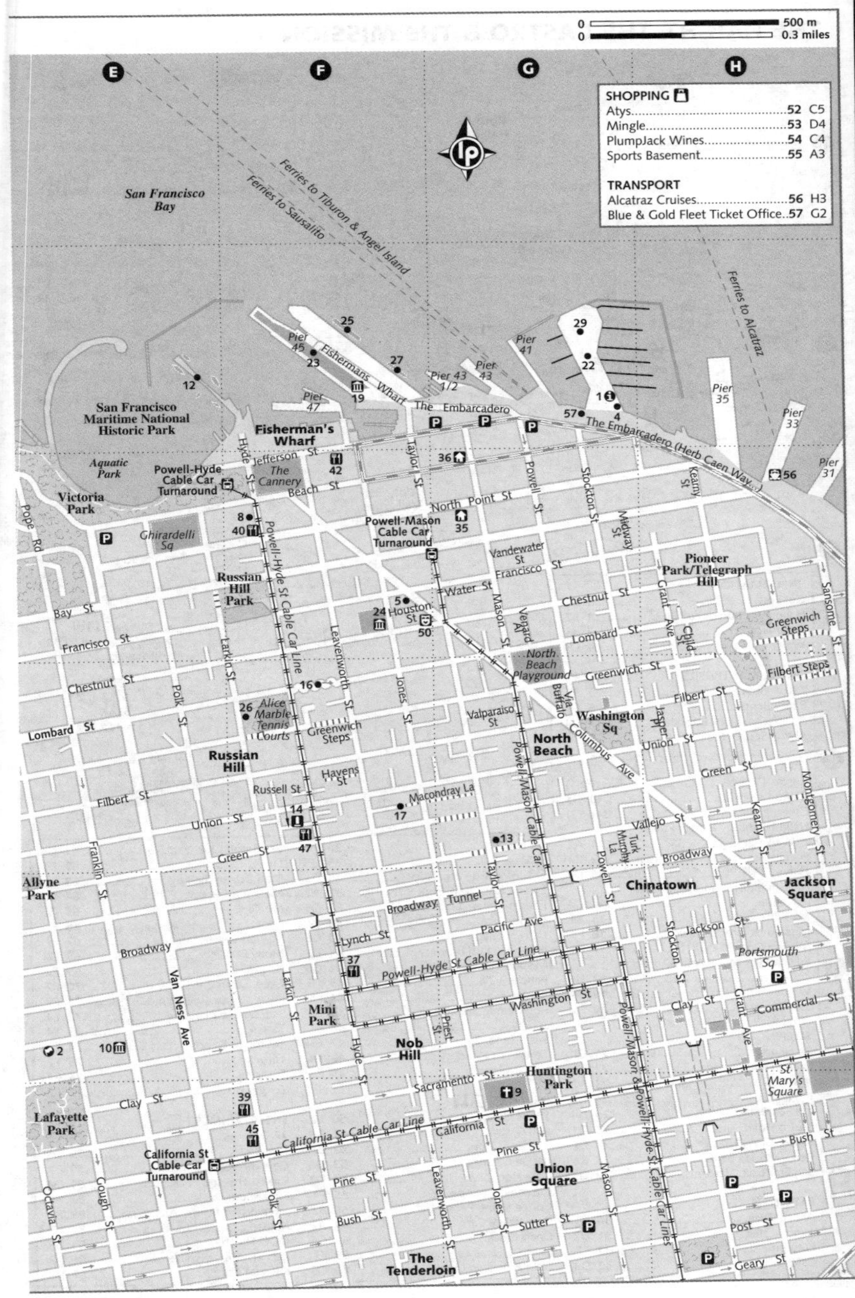
SHOPPING
Atys 52 C5
Mingle 53 D4
PlumpJack Wines 54 C4
Sports Basement 55 A3
TRANSPORT
Alcatraz Cruises 56 H3
Blue & Gold Fleet Ticket Office 57 G2
San Francisco Bay
Ferries to Tiburon & Angel Island
Ferries to Sausalito
Ferries to Alcatraz
San Francisco Maritime National Historic Park
Aquatic Park
Victoria Park
Fisherman's Wharf
The Cannery
Ghirardelli Sq
Powell-Hyde Cable Car Turnaround
Powell-Mason Cable Car Turnaround
Russian Hill Park
Russian Hill
Alice Marble Tennis Courts
Greenwich Steps
Pioneer Park/Telegraph Hill
North Beach Playground
Washington Sq
North Beach
Chinatown
Jackson Square
Allyne Park
Mini Park
Nob Hill
Huntington Park
Lafayette Park
California St Cable Car Turnaround
Union Square
The Tenderloin
St Mary's Square
Portsmouth Sq
The Embarcadero
The Embarcadero (Herb Caen Way...)
Powell-Hyde St Cable Car Line
Powell-Mason Cable Car
California St Cable Car Line
Powell-Mason & Powell-Hyde St Cable Car Lines
Columbus Ave
Broadway Tunnel
500 m
0.3 miles

THE HAIGHT, THE CASTRO & THE MISSION

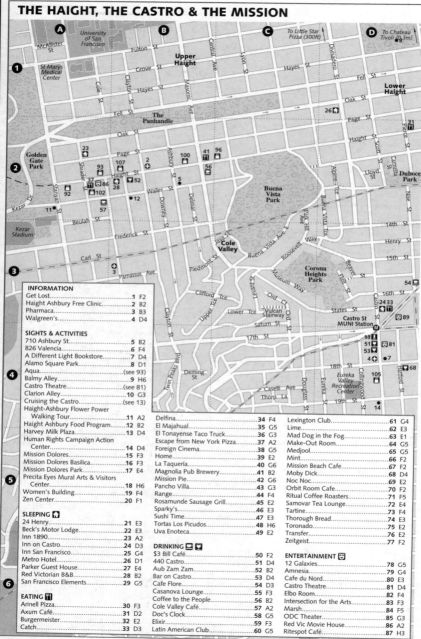

INFORMATION
Get Lost........................1 F2
Haight Ashbury Free Clinic........................2 B2
Pharmaca........................3 B3
Walgreen's........................4 D4

SIGHTS & ACTIVITIES
710 Ashbury St........................5 B2
826 Valencia........................6 F4
A Different Light Bookstore........................7 D4
Alamo Square Park........................8 D1
Aqua........................(see 93)
Balmy Alley........................9 H6
Castro Theatre........................(see 81)
Clarion Alley........................10 G3
Cruising the Castro........................(see 13)
Haight-Ashbury Flower Power Walking Tour........................11 A2
Haight Ashbury Food Program........................12 B2
Harvey Milk Plaza........................13 D4
Human Rights Campaign Action Center........................14 D4
Mission Dolores........................15 F3
Mission Dolores Basilica........................16 F3
Mission Dolores Park........................17 E4
Precita Eyes Mural Arts & Visitors Center........................18 H6
Women's Building........................19 F4
Zen Center........................20 F1

SLEEPING
24 Henry........................21 E3
Beck's Motor Lodge........................22 E3
Inn 1890........................23 A2
Inn on Castro........................24 D3
Inn San Francisco........................25 G4
Metro Hotel........................26 D1
Parker Guest House........................27 E4
Red Victorian B&B........................28 B2
San Francisco Elements........................29 G5

EATING
Arinell Pizza........................30 F3
Axum Café........................31 D2
Burgermeister........................32 E2
Catch........................33 D3
Delfina........................34 F4
El Majahual........................35 G5
El Tonayense Taco Truck........................36 G3
Escape from New York Pizza........................37 A2
Foreign Cinema........................38 G5
Home........................39 E2
La Taquería........................40 G6
Magnolia Pub Brewery........................41 B2
Mission Pie........................42 G6
Pancho Villa........................43 G3
Range........................44 F4
Rosamunde Sausage Grill........................45 E2
Sparky's........................46 E3
Sushi Time........................47 E3
Tortas Los Picudos........................48 H6
Uva Enoteca........................49 E2

DRINKING
$3 Bill Café........................50 F2
440 Castro........................51 D4
Aub Zam Zam........................52 B2
Bar on Castro........................53 D4
Cafe Flore........................54 D3
Casanova Lounge........................55 F3
Coffee to the People........................56 B2
Cole Valley Café........................57 A2
Doc's Clock........................58 G5
Elixir........................59 F3
Latin American Club........................60 G5
Lexington Club........................61 G4
Lime........................62 E3
Mad Dog in the Fog........................63 E1
Make-Out Room........................64 G5
Medjool........................65 G5
Mint........................66 F2
Mission Beach Cafe........................67 F2
Moby Dick........................68 D4
Noc Noc........................69 E2
Orbit Room Cafe........................70 F2
Ritual Coffee Roasters........................71 F5
Samovar Tea Lounge........................72 E4
Tartine........................73 F4
Thorough Bread........................74 E3
Toronado........................75 E2
Transfer........................76 E2
Zeitgeist........................77 F2

ENTERTAINMENT
12 Galaxies........................78 G5
Amnesia........................79 G4
Cafe du Nord........................80 E3
Castro Theatre........................81 D4
Elbo Room........................82 F4
Intersection for the Arts........................83 F3
Marsh........................84 F5
ODC Theater........................85 G3
Red Vic Movie House........................86 A2
Ritespot Café........................87 H3

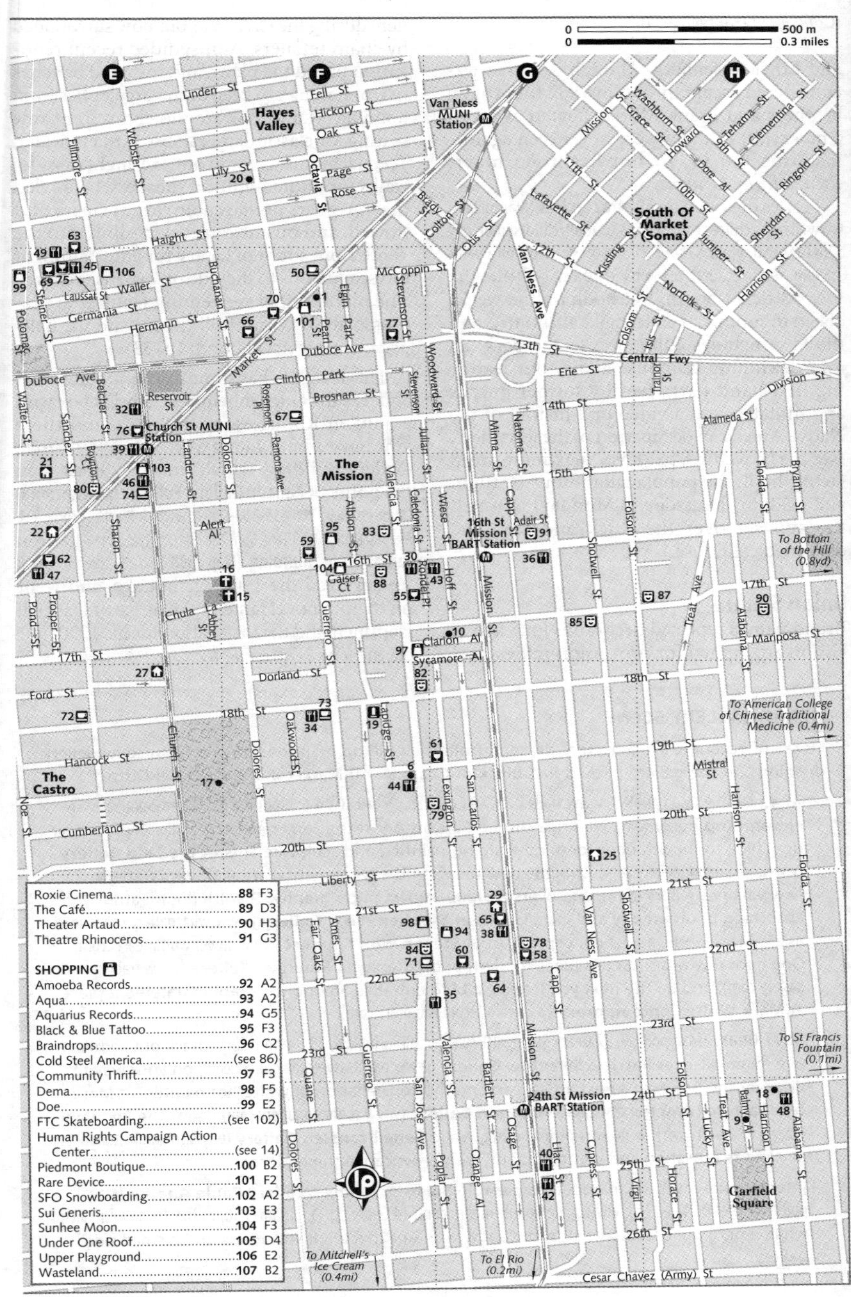

Roxie Cinema....................88 F3
The Café....................89 D3
Theater Artaud....................90 H3
Theatre Rhinoceros....................91 G3

SHOPPING

Amoeba Records....................92 A2
Aqua....................93 A2
Aquarius Records....................94 G5
Black & Blue Tattoo....................95 F3
Braindrops....................96 C2
Cold Steel America....................(see 86)
Community Thrift....................97 F3
Dema....................98 F5
Doe....................99 E2
FTC Skateboarding....................(see 102)
Human Rights Campaign Action Center....................(see 14)
Piedmont Boutique....................100 B2
Rare Device....................101 F2
SFO Snowboarding....................102 A2
Sui Generis....................103 E3
Sunhee Moon....................104 F3
Under One Roof....................105 D4
Upper Playground....................106 E2
Wasteland....................107 B2

(Continued from page 85)

and Ethel Rosenberg. Though Alcatraz was considered escape-proof, in 1962 the Anglin brothers and Frank Morris floated away on a makeshift raft and were never seen again – inspiring the 1979 Clint Eastwood movie *Escape from Alcatraz*.

Ferries operated by **Alcatraz Cruises** (Map pp94-5; www.alcatrazcruises.com; Pier 33; adult/child/senior day $26/16/24.50, night $33/19.50/30.50; departure 9am-3:55pm, return 9:20am-6:15pm) depart behind the Pier 33 ticket booth, but book online weeks ahead in summer. Ferries sail half-hourly, and the fare includes admission to the park, an award-winning cellhouse audio tour featuring first-hand narratives by former guards and inmates, and a video oral history of the Native American occupation of the ferry dock (see the boxed text, p85). For maximum creep factor, book the popular night tour (6:10pm and 6:50pm, Thursday to Monday) to watch the sun set over the Rock and tour the darkened cellhouse.

Union Square

Brand names replaced firebrands long ago at Union Sq, named for pro-union rallies held here during the Civil War but now surrounded by chain retailers. A misguided recent renovation paved the plaza, and installed benches narrow enough to keep even narcoleptics from nodding off. But look around: this is front-row seating for classic San Francisco street theater. Teen fashionistas camp out overnight on sidewalks for limited-edition sneakers, bejeweled theater-goers dodge cable cars at Geary and Powell, and business travelers slink into the Tenderloin south of Geary for entertainment too scandalous to include on expense reports. The plaza's other redeeming features are espresso at Emporio Rulli (p130) and the half-price theater ticket booth (p133).

This area also has some terrific architecture. Squeeze the Guggenheim into a brick box with a sunken Romanesque archway, and there you have Frank Lloyd Wright's 1949 Circle Gallery Building, which since 1979 has been the home of **Xanadu Gallery/Folk Art International** (Map pp88-9; 415-392-9999; www.folkartintl.com; 140 Maiden Lane; 10am-6pm Tue-Sat). The 1904 flatiron **James Flood Building** (Map pp88-9; cnr Market & Powell Sts) survived the 1906 earthquake, and went on to noir-novel fame as the office of Dashiell Hammett and the inspiration for his 1930 noir classic *The Maltese Falcon*.

GEARY GALLERY SCENE

Flocks of eccentric art collectors descend from their hilltop mansions for 'First Thursday' gallery openings on the gallery-packed first block of Geary St, off Market in the Financial District.

- At **49 Geary** (Map pp88-9; www.sfada.com; 49 Geary St; 10:30am-5:30pm Tue-Fri, 11am-5pm Sat), an elevator trip becomes a wild ride through art history at the San Francisco Art Dealers Association. Ride to the 5th floor for mind-warping painting and sculpture at **Gregory Lind Gallery** (www.gregorylindgallery.com), sublime new media and environmental art at **Haines Gallery** (www.hainesgallery.com), and oversize, high-impact photography. The 4th floor features absorbing photography and installations at **Stephen Wirtz Gallery** (www.wirtzgallery.com), and assemblage and Dadaist conceptual art at **Steven Wolf Fine Art** (www.stevenwolffinearts.com). One floor down is museum-piece modern photography at **Fraenkel Gallery** (www.fraenkelgallery.com), and on the next you'll make a bold entrance among the graphic statement pieces at **Mark Wolfe Contemporary** (www.wolfecontemporary.com).
- At **77 Geary** (Map pp88-9; 77 Geary St; 10:30am-5:30pm Tue-Fri, 11am-5pm Sat), check out seductive minimalism at **Patricia Sweetow Gallery** (www.patriciasweetowgallery.com) on your way to discover the Bay Area's next art star among the constellation of white-hot painters at **Marx & Zavattero** (www.marxzav.com). **Togonon Gallery** (www.togonongallery.com) keeps the 2nd floor down to earth with folk and political art, while **Rena Bransten Gallery** (www.renabranstengallery.com) adds sensation and contemplation with provocative think-pieces.
- International museum marquee names rule the front room at **Gallery Paule Anglim** (Map pp88-9; 415-433-2710; www.gallerypauleanglim.com; 14 Geary St; 10am-5:30pm Tue-Fri, to 5pm Sat), while emerging local artists steal the show with unexpected installations in the small side gallery.

GETTING LUCKY IN CHINATOWN

You'd be lucky to find parking anywhere near Chinatown, but a free space in the **Good Luck Parking Garage** (Map pp92-3; 735 Vallejo St) brings double happiness. Each parking spot comes with fortune-cookie wisdom stenciled onto the asphalt by artists Harrell Fletcher and Jon Rubin: 'You have already found your true love. Stop looking.' or 'You are not a has-been.'

You can see your fortune being made at **Golden Gate Fortune Cookie Company** (Map pp92-3; ☎ 415-781-3956; 56 Ross Alley; admission free; 🕑 9am-8pm), where cookies are stamped out on old-fashioned presses and folded while hot, just as they were in 1909 when they were invented in San Francisco for the Japanese Tea Garden (p109). But to really get lucky, pick up a bag of the risqué 'French' fortune cookies.

To shore up your luck, you shouldn't leave Chinatown without paying homage to the Golden Buddha at **Li Po** (Map pp92-3; ☎ 415-982-0072; 916 Grant Ave; 🕑 2pm-2am), which doesn't appear to have been dusted since the Beat crowd took up part-time residence in the vinyl booths here. According to local legend, if you toast the Buddha and make a wish, it's bound to come true – as long as your wish is for another beer.

Pause for a moment at Powell and Market at the **Powell St cable-car turnaround** (Map pp88–9) to notice operators leap out of a historic cable car, get a good grip on the trolley, and slooowly turn it around on a revolving wooden platform by hand. As technology goes, this seems pretty iffy. Cable cars can't go in reverse, they emit mechanical grunts on uphill climbs, and they require burly brakemen and bionic brakewomen to lean hard on the handbrake to keep from careening down Nob Hill. But for a city of risk-takers, this is the perfect joyride.

Financial District

Back in its Barbary Coast heyday, loose change would buy you time with loose women in what is today the Financial District. Now you'll be lucky to see a loose tie during happy hour, or anyone at all after 8pm. But the area still has redeeming quirks: a **redwood grove** has taken root in the remains of old whaling ships below the 1972 concrete rocketship that is the **Transamerica Pyramid** (Map pp88-9; 600 Montgomery St).

Besides the Geary St galleries (see the boxed text, opposite), the FiDi features three notable monuments to the power of drink. **Lotta's Fountain** (Map pp88-9; cnr Kearny & Market Sts) was named for its donor, diminutive opera diva Lotta Crabtree, who never forgot the audiences that paid for her trademark cigars. She commissioned this gilded, cast-metal pillar thrice her size with a spigot fountain as a present to the people of San Francisco – a handy gift during the 1906 fire, when it became the sole source of water downtown.

The opulent **Palace Hotel** (Map pp88-9; ☎ 415-512-1111; www.sfpalace.com; 2 New Montgomery St) was the swankiest hotel in town when it opened in 1875, but it drove its creator, William Ralston, to financial ruin and fatal heart palpitations. Consider this a cautionary tale, and take the edge off booms and busts alike at the Palace's plush Maxfield's bar.

The 1866 **AP Hotaling Building** (Map pp88-9; 451-455 Jackson St) is the whiskey warehouse that flummoxed believers in divine retribution for debauchery by improbably surviving the 1906 earthquake and fire. As the ditty that still graces the resilient Italianate building says: 'If, as they say, God spanked the town/For being over-frisky,/Why did He burn His churches down/And spare Hotaling's whiskey?'

Civic Center & The Tenderloin

Gilded Age grandeur with avant-garde art in the basement and protesters out front in the organic vegetable garden: yep, sounds like a perfectly San Franciscan **City Hall** (Map pp88-9; ☎ tours 415-554-6032, art exhibits 415-252-2568; www.ci.sf.ca.us/cityhall; 400 Van Ness Ave; 🕑 8am-8pm Mon-Fri; ♿). The city had begun building a new government center a respectable distance from waterfront fleshpots when the great quake hit in 1906, and grand plans were reduced to rubble. From the ashes rose a beaux-arts behemoth with a splendid **Rotunda**, which over the years since has seen it all: the first sit-in organized against McCarthy hearings in 1960, when singing protesters were hosed off the grand staircase; the murder of Harvey Milk, the nation's first openly gay elected official in 1978; 4037 jubilant same-sex newlyweds married here with the mayor's approval in 2004; and more same-sex couples queued up to get hitched in 2008, after the California Court of Appeals upheld same-sex marriage as consistent with state civil rights law. Downstairs are voter registration and visiting art exhibitions, which have featured works by visually impaired artists and photo-essays comparing Tehran and California.

But even fancy real estate couldn't alter San Francisco's red-light reputation. Where politicians went, prostitutes followed, and despite the 1911 Red Light Abatement measures, they set up shop alongside Civic Center in the Tenderloin. Recently the city has repackaged the 'Loin as **Little Saigon**, since the neighborhood has been home to a sizable Vietnamese community ever since refugees were resettled here during the Vietnam War. But though ancestor incense now covers unsavory smells and *banh mi* (sandwiches) lure the lunch trade, the back alleys are strictly rough trade.

The protesters out front of City Hall are another permanent presence, with a litany of causes – Tibet, healthcare, Iraq, education, Palestine, veteran's benefits – but the crop rotation here is new. For the time being, the bleak formal garden has been upgraded by an artists' collective with an edible, organic **Victory Garden** (Map pp88-9; www.sfvictorygardens.org), modeled after WWII initiatives to inspire communities to grow their own food. The garden is a fitting counterpart to the **Heart of the City Farmers Market** (see p139) on United Nations Plaza, which on other days is an obstacle course of skateboarders, Scientologists and raving self-talkers, plus a few crafts stalls.

Civic Center may be landlocked, but it has an unrivalled view of the Pacific thanks to the **Asian Art Museum** (Map pp88-9; ☎ 415-581-3500; www.asianart.org; 200 Larkin St; adult/child/student/senior $12/free/7/8; 🕑 10am-5pm Tue-Sun, to 9pm Thu; ♿). Cover 6000 years and thousands of miles here in under an hour, from racy ancient Rajasthan miniatures to futuristic Japanese manga (graphic novels) via priceless Ming vases and even a Bhutan collection. The Asian has worked diplomatic wonders with a rotating collection of 15,000 treasures that bring Taiwan, China and Tibet together, unite Pakistan and India, and strike a harmonious balance among Japan, Korea and China. Linger over bento box lunch at the downstairs **Café Asia**, and stick around for the thrill of the unexpected at educational events and First Thursday **MATCHA** nights from 5pm to 9pm, where soju cocktails flow, DJs spin Japanese hip-hop and guest acupuncturists assess visitors' tongues.

Next door, San Francisco's **Main Library** (Map pp88-9; ☎ 415-557-4400; http://sfpl.lib.ca.us; cnr Larkin & Grove Sts; 🕑 10am-6pm Mon, 9am-8pm Tue-Thu, noon-6pm Fri, 10am-6pm Sat, noon-5pm Sun; ♿) sheds light on favorite local subjects from cooking to civil rights, with the help of a splendid central lightwell and excellent lecture series. Special collections include the African American Center, Chinese Center, the James C Hormel Gay & Lesbian Center and the Center for San Francisco History. There are international newspapers in the news reading room and graphic novels galore in the Teen Zone.

Along the sad stretch of pawn shops, strip joints and urban blight between the Main Library and Powell St cable-car turnaround, there are three noticeable bright spots. For 20-plus years, nonprofit **Luggage Store Gallery** (Map pp88-9; ☎ 415-255-5971; www.luggagestoregallery.org; 1007 Market St; admission free; 🕑 noon-5pm Wed-Sat) has given streetwise art its due, and helped launch art-star street satirists Barry McGee, Clare Rojas and Rigo. You'll recognize the place by its graffitied door and the rooftop mural of a terrified kid holding a lit firecracker by Brazilian duo Osgemeos. Around the corner you'll see the tilted roof panels and breathable mesh walls of Thomas Mayne's green-minded **Federal Building** (Map pp88–9), designed for maximum energy savings with 90% of work stations enjoying direct sunlight, natural ventilation and window views (over the Tenderloin, but still).

On Sundays, some 1500 people traipse into the Tenderloin for the electrifying gospel services at GLBT-friendly (and just plain friendly) **Glide Memorial United Methodist Church** (Map pp88-9; ☎ 415-674-6090; www.glide.org; 330 Ellis St; 🕑 9am & 11am Sun). After the celebration ends in hearty handshakes and hugs, the radical Methodist congregation gets to work, providing one million free meals a year and homes for 52 formerly homeless families (56 more housing units are in the works).

Chinatown

Within a year of the 1849 Gold Rush, America's first Chinatown was built in San Francisco – but standing its ground would be no small feat. These 22 blocks are a tribute to a resilient community that has survived

SHIP-SHAPE SAN FRANCISCO

San Franciscans who give Fisherman's Wharf a wide berth are missing sneak peeks inside the berths of historic ships at **Hyde Street Pier** (Map pp94-5; ☎ 415-556-3002; www.maritime.org; Pier 45; adult/under 17yr $5/free; 9:30am-5pm Oct-May, to 5:30pm Jun-Sep;), including the elegant 1891 schooner **Alma**, the 1890 steamboat ferry **Eureka**, the toylike paddlewheel tugboat **Eppleton Hall** and the magnificent 19th-century triple-masted, iron-hulled **Balclutha**. You can explore two more historic boats at Pier 45: the **USS Pampanito** (Map pp94-5; ☎ 415-775-1943; Pier 45; adult/6-12yr/senior $9/4/5; 9am-8pm;), a WWII US Navy submarine that sank six Japanese ships (including two carrying British and Australian POWs); and the **SS Jeremiah O'Brien** (Map pp94-5; ☎ 415-544-0100; www.ssjeremiahobrien.org; Pier 45; adult/6-14yr/senior $8/4/5; 10am-4pm;), a 10,000-ton WWII Liberty ship turned out by San Francisco's women and men shipworkers in under eight weeks to deliver supplies to Allied forces on D-Day.

fire, prejudice and gun-battling bootleggers, and where many residents still get by on less than $10,000 per year in the most densely populated US urban area outside Manhattan. San Francisco passed its first law restricting housing and employment for anyone born in China in 1870, making it hard to earn an honest living in these increasingly cramped quarters. After the 1906 fire gutted Chinatown, officials planned to oust Chinese residents and develop this prime property. Instead, Chinatown businessmen headed by Look Tin Ely pooled funds to reinvent the area as the tourist attraction you see today, hiring architects to create a signature 'Chinatown Deco' look with pagoda-style roofs and dragon lanterns lining shopping streets.

Enter the **Dragon Gate** (Map pp92-3; at Bush St & Grant Ave), donated by Taiwan in 1970, and you'll find yourself on the once-notorious street known as Dupont in its red-light heyday. At California St is **Old St Mary's Church** (Map pp92-3; ☎ 415-288-3800; www.oldsaintmarys.org; 660 California St), where for decades after its 1854 construction the Catholic archdiocese valiantly tried to give this brothel district some religion. The 1906 fire destroyed one of the district's biggest bordellos directly across from the church, making room for St Mary's Sq where skateboarders stealthily ride handrails while Beniamino Bufano's 1929 **Sun Yat-sen statue** keeps a lookout.

To experience Chinatown behind the scenes, head off Grant St to Waverly Place and the historic **Tien Hou Temple** (Map pp92-3; 125 Waverly Pl; admission free but offering appreciated; Mon-Sun 10am-5pm;), dedicated in 1852 to the Buddhist Goddess of Heaven. It was a survivor of the 1906 earthquake and fire, with the charred altar to prove it. Waverly Place is lined with ground-floor barber shops, restaurants and laundries topped with neighborhood associations, and temples festooned with flags and lanterns.

Revolution is only a block away, left on Clay St and right on **Spofford Alley**, where Sun Yat-sen plotted the overthrow of China's last emperor at No 36. The 1920s brought bootleggers and gun battles to this alley, but Spofford has mellowed with age and in the evenings you'll hear the shuffling of mah-jong tiles and an *erhu* (two-stringed Chinese fiddle) warming up at local senior centers.

Jog right on Washington half a block and left onto **Ross Alley**, alternately known as Manila, Spanish and Mexico St after the women who worked this block until most perished behind locked doors in the 1906 fire. Ross Alley is occasionally pimped out for Hollywood productions, including *Karate Kid II* and *Indiana Jones and the Temple of Doom*.

Chinatown's living room is nearby **Portsmouth Square** (Map pp92-3; 733 Kearny St; night market 6-11pm Sat Jul-Oct;), where there's almost always chess, tai chi and a game of tag in progress. The square is named after John B Montgomery's sloop that docked nearby to stake the US claim on San Francisco in 1846, but the presiding deity at this people's park is the **Goddess of Democracy**, a bronze replica of the plaster statue made by Tiananmen Sq protesters in 1989. Historical markers dot the perimeter of the historic square, noting the site of San Francisco's first bookshop and newspaper, and the bawdy Jenny Lind Theater, which with a few modifications became San Francisco's first City Hall.

If you can't imagine what it must have been like to be Chinese during the Gold Rush, race riots, gangster battles or the Beat heyday, the

BOOKISH BEAUTIES

Atop Russian Hill are lanes with literary value and vistas that make the staunchly unromantic wax poetic:

- 29 Russell St is better known as **Jack Kerouac's love shack** (Map pp94–5), where he lived with Neal and Carolyn Cassady and their baby daughter while pounding out his 120ft-long scroll draft of *On the Road,* and at Neal's suggestion became lovers with Carolyn – until she kicked them both out.
- **Ina Coolbrith Park** (Map pp94-5; Vallejo St) is named for California's first Poet Laureate, who mentored Jack London, Isadora Duncan, George Sterling and Charlotte Perkins Gilman, and kept the fact that her uncle was Mormon prophet Joseph Smith a secret from her bohemian crowd. Staircases lead to hilltop gardens with plenty of her trademark full-bloom romance and vistas worthy of exclamation.
- With its cottage-lined stairway and leafy canopy, **Macondray Lane** (Map pp94–5), between Leavenworth and Taylor Sts, was the model for mysterious 'Barbary Lane' in Armistead Maupin's *Tales of the City*.
- **Sterling Park** (Map pp94-5), between Greenwich and Hyde Sts, is the hilltop park named for the 'King of Bohemia,' George Sterling, who loved poetry, women, men, nature, opium and San Francisco, though not necessarily in that order. Watch a sunset here, and you'll see what inspired him to gush: 'Homeward into the sunset/Still unwearied we go,/Till the northern hills are misty/With the amber of afterglow.'

Chinese Historical Society of America Museum (Map pp92-3; ☎ 415-391-1188; www.chsa.org; 965 Clay St; adult/child/student/senior $3/1/2/2, 1st Thu each month free; noon-5pm Tue-Fri, 11am-4pm Sat;) will help you picture it with vintage photos, mining tools, personal artifacts and fascinating documentation. Art shows are held across the courtyard in this graceful 1932 landmark building, built as Chinatown's YWCA by architect Julia Morgan of Hearst Castle fame.

North Beach

The Italian neighborhood where the US Navy dumped insubordinate sailors became a magnet for 1950s rebels: bebop jazz musicians, civil rights agitators, topless dancers and Beat poets. Boutiques outnumber bohemians on the street these days, but standing at the apex of the Filbert St Steps with wild parrots squawking overhead, you can still glimpse what Beat poets saw in North Beach: tough climbs and giddy vistas, a place with more sky than ground, an area that was civilized but never entirely tamed.

Bad luck, good reggae and *cannoli* worthy of a Corleone are the backstory of copper-topped **Columbus Tower** (Map pp92-3; 916 Kearny St). Shady political boss Abe Ruef had only just finished the building in 1905 when it was hit by the 1906 earthquake, and restored it right before he was convicted of bribery and bankrupted in 1907. The Kingston Trio bought the building in the 1960s, and recorded reggae and the Grateful Dead in the basement. Since 1970 the building has belonged to filmmaker Francis Ford Coppola, who leases the top floors to fellow filmmakers Sean Penn and Wayne Wang and offers mean desserts and his own-label Napa wine at the ground-level Café Niebaum-Coppola.

Just uphill after poetry-paved **Jack Kerouac Alley** (Map pp92–3), between Grant St & Columbus Ave, is the landmark **City Lights Bookstore** (Map pp92–3; p83), the beating heart of the Beat movement. Celebrate your freedom to read freely in the Poetry section upstairs, load up on 'zines on the mezzanine or entertain radical ideas downstairs in the Muckracking and Stolen Continents sections. For the complete Beat experience, stop by the **Beat Museum** (Map pp92-3; ☎ 1-800-537-6822; www.thebeatmuseum.org; 540 Broadway; admission $5; 10am-7pm Tue-Sun) and check out City Lights' banned edition of Allen Ginsberg's *Howl* (see p83), plus limited-edition poetry titles in the adjoining shop (entry is free).

From here, beat it up Grant St to Caffe Trieste (see p130), the legendary boho hangout with opera on the jukebox, poetry in the bathroom stalls and accordion jam sessions on weekends. Next, duck into **Bob Kauffman Alley** (Map pp92–3), off Grant

Ave near Filbert St, and enjoy a moment of profound silence courtesy of the Beat-bebop-jazz-poet-anarchist-voodoo-Jewish-biracial-African-all-American-street-corner-prophet who refused to speak for 12 years after the assassination of John F Kennedy. The day the Vietnam War ended, he broke his silence by walking into a café and reciting 'All Those Ships That Never Sailed': 'Today I bring them back/Huge and transitory/And let them sail/Forever.'

Wedding-cake cravings are to be expected upon sight of the 1924 **Saints Peter & Paul Church** (Map pp92-3; ☎ 415-421-0809; www.stspeterpaul.san-francisco.ca.us; 666 Filbert St), the frosting-white triple-decker cathedral where Joe Di Maggio and Marilyn Monroe famously posed for wedding photos (since they were both divorced, they were denied a church wedding here). The church overlooks Washington Sq, the North Beach park where nonagenarian *nonnas* (Italian grandmothers) feed wild parrots by the 1897 **Ben Franklin statue**.

A short but strenuous hike up Greenwich St to the top of **Telegraph Hill** will get you to the 210ft **Coit Tower** (Map pp92-3; ☎ 415-362-0808; 1 Telegraph Hill; adult/6-12yr/senior $4.50/2/3.50; 🕑 10am-5pm), a peculiar projectile monument to San Francisco firefighters financed by eccentric heiress Lillie Hitchcock Coit. Lillie could drink, smoke and play cards as well as any off-duty firefighter, rarely missed a fire or a firefighter's funeral, and even had the firehouse emblem embroidered on all her bedsheets. When her totem was completed in 1934, the worker-glorifying, Diego Rivera–style **WPA murals** lining the lobby were denounced as Communist, as were the 25 artists who worked on them. But the overall effect is spectacular, as are the panoramic views from the top of the tower.

Take the scenic way down Telegraph Hill via the **Filbert Street Steps** (Map pp92–3), stretching from Telegraph Hill Blvd to Sansome St, which lead down past Zen gardens and hidden cottages along Darrell Pl and Napier Lane to Levi's Plaza and the Embarcadero. If you need a few words of encouragement, the wild parrots in the trees have been known to spare a few choice words your gym trainer would probably get sued for using.

Fisherman's Wharf

Where once Italian fishermen in Genoese feluccas trapped unsuspecting crabs, San Francisco traps unwitting tourists at Fisherman's Wharf. Hapless hordes shiver in 'I ♥ San Francisco' fleece pullovers along blustery boardwalks, attempting to digest gloppy clam chowder served in sourdough bread bowls. A surgical strike is the best approach to Fisherman's Wharf, hitting specific attractions and keeping kids entertained, then sleeping and eating elsewhere if possible.

Sea mammal turf wars draw crowds to touristy **Pier 39** (Map pp94-5; ☎ 415-981-1280; www.pier39.com; at Beach St & Embarcadero; 🚸), where some 1300 sea lions chose to 'haul out' on the yacht docks in 1990 and have been belly-flopping here every January to July ever since (and whenever else they feel like it). Big bulls jostle for prime sunning location on the piers, while on the nearby boardwalk B-boyers compete for street-dance supremacy and kids wage battles of the will with parents over teddy bears sporting Alcatraz prison stripes. Pier 39's other worthwhile attraction is the **Aquarium of the Bay** (Map pp94-5; ☎ 415-623-5300; www.aquariumofthebay.com; Pier 39; adult/child/senior $14.95/8/8; 🕑 10am-6pm Mon-Thu, to 7pm Fri-Sun Sep-May, 9am-8pm Jun-Aug; 🚸), where conveyer belts guide you through glass tubes right into the bay as sharks circle, manta rays flutter and schools of fish flit overhead. Once you've seen the sea lion scene and hit the Aquarium, you're good to go – Pier 39 food is unpardonably bland and the simulated 1906-earthquake joyride is totally perverse.

For more-thrilling arcade games, head to the **Musée Mecanique** (Map pp94-5; ☎ 415-346-2000; www.museemecanique.org; Pier 45, Shed A; 🕑 11am-7pm Mon-Fri, 10am-8pm Sat & Sun; 🚸), where a few quarters let you start bar brawls in coin-operated Wild West saloons, peep at belly-dancers through a vintage Mutoscope, save the world from Space Invaders and get your fortune told by an eerily lifelike wooden swami.

Russian Hill & Nob Hill

Until Andrew Hallidie invented the cable car, Nob Hill was a windswept 338ft crag only hermits called home, and Russian Hill's sweeping views were mostly admired by hawks. Mansions soon mushroomed along Nob Hill, but without a windbreak between them, most were destroyed in the 1906 earthquake hit and the fire.

Grace Cathedral (Map pp94-5; ☎ 415-749-6300; www.gracecathedral.org; 1100 California St; 🕑 7am-6pm Sun-Fri, 8am-6pm Sat) has been rebuilt three times since the Gold Rush, and the progressive Episcopal church still continues to keep pace with the times. Additions include an AIDS Memorial Chapel, with a bronze altarpiece by the late artist and AIDS activist Keith Haring; stained-glass windows dedicated to Human Endeavor, including one of Albert Einstein uplifted in a swirl of nuclear particles; and a mystical stone labyrinth, meant to guide restless souls through the spiritual stages of releasing, receiving and returning.

Unlike in Nob Hill, more greenery was kept intact among Russian Hill's modest homes and switchback streets, including the zig-zag section of **Lombard St** (Map pp94–5), between Hyde and Leavenworth Sts. The recent clampdown on renegade skaters means that the Lombard St thrills featured in Tony Hawk's Pro Skater video game are strictly virtual.

Nearby are still more unexpected twists and turns at the **San Francisco Art Institute** (SFAI; Map pp94-5; ☎ 415-771-7020; www.sfai.edu; 800 Chestnut St; 🕑 11am-6pm Tue-Sat). Founded during the 1870s, SFAI was ground zero for the Bay Area's figurative art scene in the 1940s and '50s, turned to Bay Area Abstraction in the '60s and conceptual art in the '70s, and since the '90s has championed new media art in its **Walter and McBean Gallery** (Map pp94-5; ☎ 415-749-4563; www.waltermcbean.com; 800 Chestnut St; 🕑 11am-6pm Mon-Sat). Also on campus, the **Diego Rivera Gallery** features Rivera's 1931 mural *The Making of a Fresco Showing a Building of a City,* a fresco within a fresco showing the back of the artist himself as he pauses to admire his own work and the work in constant progress that is San Francisco. The school has a surprisingly good café in its 1970s concrete-bunker-style addition, with panoramic views of the bay.

Japantown & Pacific Heights

San Francisco's Japanese community dates back to at least the 1860s – older than the old money that dominates tony Pacific Heights just uphill. But while Pacific Heights seems to lead a charmed existence, with stately Victorians, hilltop parks and swanky boutiques along Fillmore St, just downhill trials and tribulations have faced the area known by 1900 as Nihonjinmachi, or 'Japanese people's town.'

During WWII, Japantown's approximately 7000 residents – including citizens and members of the US armed services – were ordered into government internment camps, bringing only what they could carry. After the war residents were resettled in makeshift Japantown apartments, sometimes not far from the family homes they'd once owned.

'Little Osaka' put on a brave face, and started rebuilding from the ground up. Celebrated modern sculptor and former WWII internee Ruth Asawa created the bronze origami dandelion **Ruth Asawa Fountains** (Map pp88-9; Buchanan Pedestrian St) that now grace pedestrianized Buchanan St. **Japan Center** (off Map pp94-5; www.sfjapantown.org; 1625 Post St; 🕑 10am-midnight) still looks much the way it did when it opened in 1968, with a fake-rock waterfall, indoor wooden pedestrian bridges and *maneki-neko* (waving cat) figurines beckoning from restaurant entryways. To complete the transformation, San Francisco's sister city of Osaka in Japan gifted Yoshiro Taniguchi's minimalist concrete **Peace Pagoda** (Map pp88-9; Peace Plaza) to the people of San Francisco in 1968.

Today's J-town may be cute as can be, but it's got tenacity and transformational powers worthy of the mighty Astro Boy. There's a new manga-themed hotel, creative new restaurants and boutiques, and the splashy new Sundance Kabuki Cinema (see p137), not to mention the ever-popular communal baths at Kabuki Springs & Spa (p112).

The transition between Japantown and Pacific Heights is marked by **Cottage Row** (Map pp94–5), off Bush St between Webster and Fillmore Sts, where 19th-century clapboard cottages hang back along a pedestrian promenade where plum trees and bonsai take center stage. Like most of the historic homes in Pacific Heights, these cottages are not open to the public. The exception is **Haas-Lilienthal House** (Map pp94-5; ☎ 415-441-3004; 2007 Franklin St; adult/child/senior $8/5/5; 🕑 noon-3pm Wed & Sat, 11am-4pm Sun), an 1882 Queen Anne with decor that looks like a murder-mystery setting, including a dark-wood ballroom, red-velvet parlor and spooky stairways. One-hour tours are led by volunteer docents whose devotion to Victoriana is almost cultish.

The Marina

Not many people wanted to be downwind from the Marina in its early days, when inland breezes carried its stench of dyspeptic cattle, moonshine stills, drying fish and most of Northern California's dirty laundry. Now the Marina is strictly top-shelf and dry-cleaned,

MISSION MURALS

Inspired by visiting artist Diego Rivera and the WPA murals, and outraged by US foreign policy in Central America, Mission *muralistas* set out in the 1970s to transform the political landscape, one alley at a time. Today murals are the defining physical feature of the Mission, and here's where to find the best of some 250 street artworks:

Balmy Alley (Map pp96-7; ☎ 415-285-2287; www.balmyalley.com; off 24th St) Between Treat Ave and Harrison St, historic early works transform garage doors into artistic and political statements, alongside new works like Tina Wolf's Hurricane Katrina-themed 'After the Storm.'

Clarion Alley (Map pp96-7; ☎ 415-285-2287) Only the strongest street art survives in Clarion, between 17th and 18th Sts off Valencia, where lesser works are peed on or painted over. Very few pieces have lasted years: a trompe l'oeil escalator, Andrew Schoultz's mural of gentrifying elephants displacing scraggly birds, and kung-fu-fighting women anarchists that make Charlie's Angels look like chumps.

Precita Eyes (Map pp96-7; ☎ 415-285-2287; www.precitaeyes.org; 2981 24th St; adult/child/12-17yr/student/senior $12/2/5/5/8; tours from 11am Sat-Sun) Restores historic murals, commissions new ones by rising San Francisco artists and has muralist-led tours that cover 75 Mission murals within an eight-block radius of its headquarters. The center sells postcards, books, art supplies and a mural walking-tour map ($4).

Women's Building (Map pp96-7; ☎ 415-431-1180; www.womensbuilding.org; 3543 18th St) San Francisco's biggest mural is the 1994 *MaestraPeace*, a show of female strength painted by 90 *muralistas* that wraps around the Women's Building, with icons of female strength from Mayan and Chinese goddesses to modern trailblazers including Rigoberta Menchú, Hanaan Ashrawi and Audre Lorde.

with chic Union St boutiques and 'breeder bars' where frat boys and sorority girls mingle post-college. But this being San Francisco, there's still a delightful oddity: the 1905 architectural conundrum of the **Vedanta Society** (Map pp94-5; ☎ 415-922-2323; www.sfvedanta.org; 2323 Vallejo St), with onion domes, red turrets and architectural styles representing world religions and the Hindu-inspired Society's theme of 'the oneness of existence.'

The Marina's transformation began when waterfront marshland was filled in (mainly with rubble created by the quake of 1906) to create the grounds for the 1915 Panama-Pacific International Exposition, celebrating the Panama Canal's completion and San Francisco's phoenixlike rebirth after the earthquake and fire. When the expo was over, SF couldn't bear to part with the Greco-Roman plaster **Palace of Fine Arts** (Map pp94-5; ☎ 415-567-6642; www.palaceoffinearts.org; 3301 Lyon St). California Arts and Crafts architect Bernard Maybeck's artificial ruin was recast in concrete, so that future generations could gaze up at the rotunda relief to glimpse Art under attack by Materialists, with Idealists leaping to her rescue.

Behind the ruin is the **Exploratorium** (Map pp94-5; ☎ 415-561-0360; www.exploratorium.edu; 3601 Lyon St; adult/4-12yr/student/senior $14/9/11/11; 10am-5pm Tue-Sun, extended hr in summer;), a hands-on museum that's been blowing minds since 1969 and answering the questions you always wanted to ask in science class: does gravity apply to skateboarding, do robots have feelings too and do toilets flush counterclockwise in Australia? One especially far-out exhibit is the **Tactile Dome** (admission $17), a pitch-black space that you can crawl, climb and slide through (advance reservations required).

Another intriguing Exploratorium project is the **Wave Organ** (Map pp94–5), a sound system of PVC tubes, concrete pipes and found marble from San Francisco's old cemetery, installed right into the Marina Boat Harbor jetty by artist Peter Richards in 1986. Depending on the waves, winds and tide, the tones emitted by the organ can sound like nervous humming, a gurgling baby or prank-call heavy breathing.

On the landlubber side of the harbor is the waterfront **Marina Green** (Map pp94–5), ideal for kite-flying, jogging and lounging as long as the weather holds. At the end of the green streak is **Fort Mason** (Map pp94-5; ☎ 415-441-3400; www.fortmason.org; cnr Bay & Franklin Sts), a US military outpost repurposed in the 1970s as a Golden Gate National Recreation Area. The cultural complex now defies all military discipline with leisurely organic vegetarian meals at Greens (see p126), cutting-edge theater at Magic Theater (p136) and outrageous art, food and crafts expos at dockside **Herbst Pavilion**.

The Presidio

San Francisco's official motto is still 'Oro in Paz, Fierro in Guerra' (Gold in Peace, Iron in War), but lately the Presidio has been more relaxed than iron-willed. The battle-hardened officers who once bunked here would probably have scoffed at camo-clad bird-watchers and nudists doing yoga headstands in their midst. But the only wars going on here are the interstellar ones in George Lucas' screening room in the **Letterman Digital Arts Center** (Map pp94–5), right by the Yoda statue.

Ordered by the Spanish as their first *presidio* (military post) and built by conscripted Ohlone in 1776, this outpost never saw much military action. Jerry Garcia began and ended his ignominious military career here by going AWOL nine times in eight months before getting court-martialed (twice) and co-founding the Grateful Dead. The **Presidio Visitors Center** (off Map pp94-5; ☎ 415-561-4323; www.nps.gov/prsf; cnr Montgomery St & Lincoln Blvd; 🕑 9am-5pm) has exhibits and information on the park's facilities, including the **Pet Cemetery** off Crissy Field Ave, where handmade tombstones commemorate military hamsters who've completed their final tour of duty.

The Presidio's military role ended in 1994, when the 1480-acre plot became part of the Golden Gate National Recreation Area. War is now officially for the birds at **Crissy Field**, a former military airstrip that's been restored as a tidal marsh and reclaimed by long-legged coastal birds. On blustery days, bird-watch from the shelter of **Crissy Field Center** (Map pp94-5; ☎ 415-561-7690; www.crissyfield.org; 603 Mason St; 🕑 9am-5pm Mon-Sun), which has a café counter facing the field with binoculars. Join joggers and puppies romping along beachside trails that were once oil-stained asphalt, and on foggy days stop by the certified green **Warming Hut** (Map pp94-5; ☎ 415-561-3040; www.parksconservancy.org; 983 Marine Dr; 🕑 9am-5pm) to thaw out with Fair Trade coffee, browse field guides and sample honey made by Presidio honeybees.

If you're up for a hike, forge onward to **Fort Point** (Map pp94-5; ☎ 415-556-1693; www.nps.gov/fopo; Marine Dr; 🕑 10am-5pm Thu-Mon) for a good look at the Golden Gate Bridge. Further along the ocean side of the peninsula is **Baker Beach** (Map pp86–7), the city's best beach with windswept pines uphill, craggy good looks along the cliffs and a whole lot of exposed goosebumps on the breezy, clothing-optional north end of the beach.

South of Market (SoMa)

Don't let the tony high-rises and poker-faced warehouses fool you: SoMa is scattered with outrageous art venues, adventurous dining and anything-goes after-hours clubs. The city is buzzing over the ever-expanding collection of museums and galleries around Yerba Buena Gardens and anchored by the **San Francisco Museum of Modern Art** (SFMOMA; Map pp88-9; ☎ 415-357-4000; www.sfmoma.org; 151 3rd St; adult/child/student/senior $12.50/free/7/8; 🕑 11am-5:45pm Mon, Tue & Fri-Sun, to 8:45pm Thu Sep-Apr, 10am-5:45pm Mon, Tue & Fri, to 9:45pm Thu, to 7:45pm Sat & Sun May-Aug). Swiss architect Mario Botta's light-filled brick box leans full-tilt toward the horizon, with curators similarly inclined to take early risks on Matthew Barney's poetic videos involving industrial quantities of Vaseline and Olafur Eliasson's outer-space light installations. SFMOMA has arguably the world's leading photography collection, with works by Ansel Adams, Daido Moriyama, Diane Arbus, Edward Weston, William Eggleston and Dorothea Lange, and since its 1995 grand reopening coincided with the tech boom, SFMOMA became an early champion of new media art. Free admission on the first Tuesday of the month means crowds and memorable people-watching, and half-price admission on Thursday evenings attracts a singles scene.

There are many other key museums and galleries in the Yerba Buena Arts District area, including the **Contemporary Jewish Museum** (Map pp88-9; ☎ 415-655-7800; www.jmsf.org; 736 Mission St; adult/child/student/senior $10/free/8/8; 🕑 11am-5:30pm Fri-Tue, 1-8:30pm Thu). The inside space and collections are most illuminating, from soundscapes based on the Hebrew alphabet by the likes of Lou Reed and Laurie Anderson to Marc Chagall's backdrops for 1920s Russian Jewish theater.

Comics fans need no introduction to the **Cartoon Art Museum** (Map pp88-9; ☎ 415-227-8666; www.cartoonart.org; 655 Mission St; adult/child/student/senior $6/2/4/4; 🕑 11am-5pm Tue-Sun; 👶), founded on a grant from Bay Area cartoon legend Charles M Schultz of *Peanuts* fame. International and noteworthy local talent includes long-time Haight resident R Crumb and East Bay graphic novelists Daniel Clowes *(Ghostworld)*, Gene Yang *(American Born Chinese)* and Adrian Tomine *(Optic Nerve)*. Lectures and openings are rare opportunities to mingle

GAY/LESBIAN/BI/TRANS SAN FRANCISCO

Singling out the best places to be queer in San Francisco (SF) is almost redundant. Though the Castro is a major gay center and the Mission is a magnet for lesbians, the entire city is known for being gay-friendly – hence the number of out elected representatives in City Hall at any given time. Nightlife is fabulous here. New York Marys may label SF the retirement home of the young – indeed, the sidewalks roll up early – but when it comes to sexual outlaws and underground weirdness, SF kicks New York's ass. Dancing queens and slutty boys head South of Market (SoMa), the location of most thump-thump clubs and sex venues. There was a time when bars would euphemistically designate Sunday afternoons as 'tea dances,' appealing to gay crowds to make money at an otherwise slow time. The tradition now makes Sundays one of the busiest times for SF's gay bars.

Of course it's all gay all day in the Castro, but here are some other GLBT faves:

AsiaSF (Map pp88-9; ☎ 415-255-2742; www.asiasf.com; 201 9th St; ⏲ dinner Sun-Thu, club 10pm-2am daily) This all-Asian tranny lounge has decent food. Respectable drinks are served by waitresses who'll make you look thrice and still you aren't sure.

Lexington Club (Map pp96-7; ☎ 415-863-2052; 3464 19th St) The odds are eerily high that you'll develop a crush on your ex-girlfriend's hot new girlfriend here over strong drink, pinball and tattoo comparisons – go on, live dangerously at SF's most famous/notorious full-time lesbian bar.

San Francisco Lesbian, Gay, Bisexual, Transgender Community Center (Map pp88-9; ☎ 415-865-5555; www.sfcenter.org; 1800 Market St) 'The Other City Hall' is home to nonprofits and hosts comedy nights, political rallies, drag showcases and other pursuits of happiness – it even provides childcare services to visiting proud parents.

Sisters of Perpetual Indulgence (Map pp88-9; ☎ 415-820-9697; www.thesisters.org) For guerrilla antics, see what the self-described 'leading-edge order of queer nuns' is up to. It's a charitable organization and a San Francisco institution.

Stud (Map pp88-9; ☎ 415-252-7883; www.studsf.com; 399 9th St; admission $5-8) Rocking the SF gay scene for 40-plus years yet brimming with youthful vigor, this is the bar equivalent of Viagra. Drag shows here draw San Franciscan crowds more varied than a UN delegation.

with comics legends, Pixar studio heads and obsessive collectors.

The **Museum of the African Diaspora** (MoAD; Map pp88-9; ☎ 415-358-7200; www.moadsf.org; 685 Mission St; adult/child/student/senior $10/free/5/5; ⏲ 11am-6pm Wed-Sat, noon-5pm Sun) has assembled a standout international cast of characters to tell the epic story of diaspora, with an emphasis on contemporary art. Highlights include a three-faced divinity by Ethiopian icon painter Qes Adamu Tesfaw, a stereotype in silhouette by American Kara Walker and a regal couple by British sensation Chris Ofili.

There's amazing handiwork with fascinating personal backstories on display at the **Museum of Craft and Folk Art** (Map pp88-9; ☎ 415-227-4888; www.mocfa.org; 51 Yerba Buena Lane; adult/under 18yr/senior $5/free/4; ⏲ 11am-6pm Tue-Fri, to 5pm Sat & Sun), from sublime Shaker women woodworking to contemporary Asian artists reinventing paper crafts traditions.

No material is too political or risqué at San Francisco's most cutting-edge gallery, **Catharine Clark Gallery** (Map pp88-9; ☎ 415-399-1439; www.cclarkgallery.com; 150 Minna St; ⏲ 10:30am-5:30pm Tue-Fri, 11am-5:30pm Sat). Witness Kara Maria's psychedelic candy-colored paintings combining Iraq war footage and porn, or Packard Jennings' instructional pamphlets for converting cities into wildlife refuges.

With more flashbacks than a hippie at a Dead show, the **California Historical Society Museum** (Map pp88-9; ☎ 415-357-1848; www.californiahistoricalsociety.org; 678 Mission St; adult/child/student/senior $3/free/1/1; ⏲ noon-4:30pm Wed-Sat) has wall-to-wall ephemera ranging from political campaign propaganda throughout California history to Gene Anthony's photographs of 1967 Be-Ins at Golden Gate Park.

At **Yerba Buena Center for the Arts** (Map pp88-9; ☎ 415-978-2787; www.ybca.org; 701 Mission St; adult/student/senior $7/5/5; ⏲ noon-5pm Tue-Sun, to 8pm Thu), lines of hipsters in faux fur stretch around the block for openings to ambitious shows of irreverent Nordic art, Vietnamese collage and especially the triennial Bay Area Now survey of emerging art stars.

The hands-on **Zeum Art & Technology Center** (Map pp88-9; ☎ 415-820-3320; www.zeum.org; 221 4th St; adult/3-18yr/senior $10/8/8; ⏲ 11am-5pm Tue-Sun summer, 1-5pm Wed-Fri, 11am-5pm Sat-Sun rest of year; 👶) encourages young people to create and produce their own works with audio, video, computer animation and more. Zeum also has a restored **Looff carousel** (two rides $2).

Outside the Yerba Buena hot zone, there are a few other notable landmarks. **Rincon Annex Post Office** (Map pp88-9; 101 Spear St) is lined with WPA murals of Northern California history that Russian-born painter Anton Refregier was commissioned to paint in 1941, only to be interrupted by WWII and political squabbles over differing versions of history. The murals were completed in 1948 after 92 changes, only to be denounced as 'Communist' by McCarthyists in 1953 – but now they're a National Landmark.

Further south is **South Park** (Map pp88–9), between 2nd and 3rd Sts, Bryant and Brannan. The picturesque oval of green was built in 1852 to mimic a London city square, and then largely neglected until it became the center of the dot-com phenom in 'Multimedia Gulch.' Nowadays it seems even the birds in the trees are atwitter with talk of the boom in nearby Mission Bay: biotech. Southeast of South Park is **AT&T Park**, home of the San Francisco Giants (see p138).

The Mission

If you don't like the weather or the scene downtown, head to the Mission, where it's always sunny and you can make your own scene with the local ensemble act of Latinos, lesbians, foodies, boozehounds, career activists, chichi designers, punks, prostitutes and suits. Tech money still mingles uneasily with gang activity and churchgoing devotion with nightly bar antics, but somehow it all makes sense – you just have to be here. Most of the action here is on Mission and Valencia Sts, with concentrations of bars, bookstores and restaurants along 16th, 18th and 22nd Sts. But the defining features of the neighborhood are hidden away in back alleys: the 250-plus Mission murals (see the boxed text, p105).

The Mission District is San Francisco's oldest enclave, and it takes its name from the oldest building in the city. **Mission Dolores** (Map pp96-7; ☎ 415-621-8203; www.missiondolores.org; cnr Dolores & 16th Sts; adult/child $3/2; 🕑 9am-4pm) was founded in 1776 and rebuilt in 1782 with conscripted native Ohlone labor in exchange for a meal a day. The distinguishing features of the original mission structure are its ceiling patterned after Native baskets and a recently discovered mural by Ohlone artisans of a stabbed sacred heart oozing blood. Some 5000 Ohlone who died in measles epidemics in 1814 and 1826 are said to be buried in the **graveyard** alongside early Mexican and European settlers.

Today the modest adobe mission is overshadowed by the adjoining **Mission Dolores Basilica** (Map pp96–7), built in 1913 with an ornate, fanciful *churrigueresque* design. To check out its splendid stained-glass windows of St Francis and California's 21 missions, enter through the small entryway shop, pass through the original mission structure and cross the courtyard. Two blocks south, **Mission Dolores Park** (Map pp96-7; cnr Dolores & 18th Sts) is the site of soccer games, street basketball, nonstop political protests, competitive tanning and other favorite local sports.

A mural by comic-artist Chris Ware marks **826 Valencia** (☎ 415-642-5905; www.826valencia.com; 826 Valencia St; 🕑 11am-6pm; 🚸), the nonprofit youth writing program and purveyor of essential pirate supplies: eye patches, tubs of lard and, of course, tall tales for long nights at sea published by partner McSweeney's across the street. Stop by the Fish Theater to see Otka the pufferfish immersed in Method acting. He's no Sean Penn, but as it says on the sign: 'Please don't judge the fish.' Check the website for monthly adult seminars on scripting video games and starting up magazines, taught by industry experts.

The Castro

Talk about a makeover. This frumpy Scandinavian-Irish neighborhood became a glamorous symbol of gay freedom when hippie house-hunters came looking for walk-in closets they weren't expected to live in. The Castro isn't San Francisco's only or first gay neighborhood – there were historic gay scenes in Polk Gulch near Civic Center and around Folsom St in SoMa by the 1950s – but the Castro was better organized. Within a few years of moving into the place, the Castro's gay community had established businesses, community services and even elected the nation's first gay official (see p81). **Harvey Milk Plaza** (Map pp96-7; cnr Market & Castro Sts) is dedicated to the Castro camera store owner and San Francisco supervisor who lifted San Francisco's spirits and prospects in the post-hippie era with the euphoria of gay liberation.

Today a huge rainbow flag flies high over the Castro, and the neighborhood gets down

GOLDEN GATE GREAT ESCAPES

Who says you need to leave town to enjoy the great outdoors? Explore these outdoor attractions right in the heart of the city, inside Golden Gate Park.

Japanese Tea Garden (Map p91; ☎ 415-752-1171; adult/child $2/1; 🕑 9am-6pm) Mellow out in the Zen Garden, sip toasted-rice green tea under a pagoda and admire doll-sized trees that are pushing 100. These bonsai are a credit to the dedicated gardeners of the Hagiwara family, who returned from WWII Japanese American internment camps to discover their bonsai had been sold. The Hagiwaras spent the next two decades tracking down the trees, and returned the bonsai grove to its rightful home.

Stow Lake (Map p91; ☎ 415-752-0347; boat rental per hr $13-18; 🕑 10am-4pm) A miniature resort in the heart of the park, with a picturesque island called **Strawberry Hill** for short but sweaty hikes, and pedal boats and row boats available at the boathouse. Boats must have at least one person aged 16 or older aboard, and dogs are allowed on rowboats.

Strybing Arboretum & Botanical Gardens (Map p91; ☎ 415-661-1316; www.sfbotanicalgarden.org; 9th Ave at Lincoln Way; 🕑 8am-4:30pm Mon-Fri, 10am-5pm Sat & Sun) There's always something blooming in these 70-acre gardens. The Garden of Fragrance is designed for the visually impaired, and the California native plant section explodes with color when the native wildflowers bloom in early spring, right off the redwood trail. Free arboretum tours take place daily; for details, stop by the bookstore inside the entrance.

to signing petitions for civil rights at the **Human Rights Campaign Action Center** (Map pp96-7; ☎ 415-431-2200; www.hrc.org; 600 Castro St), down to serious shopping in support of AIDS-related charities at nonprofit Under One Roof (see p139) and down to business on the dance floor at neighborhood bars (p133). The landmark that lets you know you've arrived at the center of it all is the magnificent Castro Theatre (see p137).

The Haight

The legendary intersection of Haight and Ashbury Sts was the place to be in the psychedelic '60s, and certain habits seem to have stuck – the clock overhead always reads 4:20, better known in herbal circles as International Bong Hit Time. But since then, the hedonist Haight has also built a serious rep for leftist politics, skateboarding, drug rehabs, potent coffee and retail therapy for rebels.

The Upper Haight west of Divisadero waxes nostalgic for its hippie days with head shops and vintage boutiques, and you can prove the Summer of Love isn't over yet by serving a meal or donating to job training programs at the historic **Haight Ashbury Food Program** (Map pp96-7; ☎ 415-566-0366; www.thefoodprogram.org; 1525 Waller St). Dedicated Deadheads may dimly recognize candy-colored **710 Ashbury St** (Map pp96–7), which back in the '60s was the free-form flophouse where the Grateful Dead blew minds, amps and brain cells.

Skaters and hipsters cruise downhill to the Lower Haight between Divis and Webster for regulation local-designer hoodies and edgy bars. You might catch a whiff of the neighborhood's many medical marijuana clubs, which require a prescription and a 30-day waiting period (sorry, dude). But you can enjoy a moment of Zen at the **Zen Center** (Map pp96-7; ☎ 415-863-3136; sfzc.org; 300 Page St), the largest Buddhist community outside Asia, headquartered in an elegant landmark building designed by Julia Morgan.

Another upside to the Lower Haight is **Alamo Square Park** (Map pp96–7), the hilltop park with downtown panoramas bordered by 'Painted Ladies' – the flamboyantly painted and outrageously ornamented Victorian homes that took San Franciscan liberties with the regal English style. The gingerbread houses of **Postcard Row** facing the park along Steiner have been disappointingly repainted in innocuous neutrals, but stroll around the square between Steiner and Scott and you'll spot Painted Ladies with drag-diva color palettes.

The Richmond

Cable cars and spiffy downtown restaurants are part of a diabolical ploy by San Franciscans to direct your attention away from the wild stretches and bargain eateries of the Richmond, which they like to keep to themselves. On the northern end are Presidio beaches, to the south is Golden Gate Park, and in between Arguello Blvd and the Pacific Ocean are long blocks of multiethnic mom-and-pop shops along Clement St and very tasty cheap eats along Geary, Balboa and Clement.

At the western end of Geary is the **Cliff House** (Map p91; ☎ 415-386-3330; www.cliffhouse.com; 1090 Point Lobos Ave), built by populist millionaire Adolph Sutro in 1863 as a workingman's escape from downtown crowds, and now in its fourth incarnation as an upscale (read: overpriced) restaurant with all the charm of a downtown fast-food restaurant. Sutro would not be pleased, though three of the area's popular attractions remain: wintertime views of sea lions blithely frolicking among the seagull guano on **Seal Rock**, the ruins of the public **Sutro Baths** and the **Camera Obscura** (Map p91; ☎ 415-750-0415; 1096 Point Lobos Ave; admission $2; 11am-sunset), a Victorian invention that projects the sea view outside onto a parabolic screen inside a small building.

Past the Sutro Baths, a walking path winds along a rugged stretch of coast with spectacular glimpses of the Golden Gate Bridge to **Lands End**, passing through the windswept pines of **Lincoln Park** (Map p91; ☎ 415-221-9911; Clement St; admission free; sunrise-sunset).

Inside the park off 34th Ave you'll find the **California Palace of the Legion of Honor** (Map p91; ☎ 415-863-3330; www.legionofhonor.org; adult/under 12yr/student $10/free/6, Tue free; 9:30am-5pm Tue-Sun), which was a gift to San Francisco from Alma de Bretteville Spreckels, a nude sculptor's model who married and spent very well indeed. The building houses a world-class collection spanning medieval to 20th-century European art, with highlights including the Achenbach Foundation for Graphic Arts, impressionist paintings and, in honor of 'Big Alma's' early career, a sizable collection of sculpture by Auguste Rodin and Henry Moore.

Golden Gate Park

When San Franciscans refer to 'the park,' there's only one that gets the definite article: Golden Gate Park. Everything that San Franciscans hold dear is here: free spirits, free music, redwoods, Frisbee, protests, fine art, bonsai and a balding penguin. An 1870 competition to design the park was won by 24-year-old William Hammond Hall, who spent the next two decades tenaciously fighting casino developers, theme-park boosters and slippery politicians to transform the 1017 acres of dunes into the largest developed park in the world.

Park information is available from **McLaren Lodge** (Map p91; ☎ 415-831-2700; cnr Fell & Stanyan Sts; 8am-5pm Mon-Fri), and free park walking tours are organized by **Friends of Recreation & Parks** (☎ 415-263-0991).

Capped with a 'living roof' of California wildflowers, the **California Academy of Sciences** (Map p91; ☎ 415-321-8000; www.calacademy.org; Concourse Dr;) showcases California's fascination with weird and wonderful wildlife in the Pritzker Prize–winning architect Renzo Piano's 2008 landmark green building, housing 38,000 animals in custom habitats: a white alligator stalks the swamp, butterflies flutter through the three-story rainforest dome and balding Pierre the Penguin paddles his massive new tank in a custom-made wet suit (shhh, don't mention the molting; he's sensitive).

At **MH de Young Memorial Museum** (Map p91; ☎ 415-750-3600; www.famsf.org/deyoung; 50 Hagiwara Tea Garden Dr; adult/child/student/senior $10/free/6/7; 9:30am-5:15pm Tue-Sun, to 8:45pm Fri) you'd think the art would be upstaged by the sleek building designed by Swiss architects Herzog & de Meuron (of London's Tate Modern fame), with its perforated copper cladding drawn from aerial photography of the park and cleverly treated to rapidly oxidize green to blend into the park. But the landmark collection of arts and fine crafts from around the world puts California's own artistic pursuits into global perspective and hides a surprise around every corner – don't miss 19th-century Oceanic ceremonial masks and stunning Central Asian rugs from the 11,000-plus textile collection. Blockbuster temporary shows range from Hiroshi Sugimoto's haunting time-lapse photographs of drive-in movies to Dale Chihuly's bombastic glass sculpture. Access to the tower viewing room is free, and worth the wait for the elevator.

Flower power is alive and well inside the grand Victorian **Conservatory of Flowers** (Map pp86-7; ☎ 415-666-7001; www.conservatoryofflowers.org; adult/5-11yr/12-17yr, student & senior $5/1.50/3/3/3; 9am-4:30pm Tue-Sun), where orchids sprawl out like Bohemian divas, lilies float contemplatively and carnivorous plants give off odors that smell exactly like insect belches. The original 1878 structure is newly restored, and the plants are thriving.

Sporty and not-so-sporty types will appreciate the park's range of outdoor activities, with 7.5 miles of bicycle trails, 12 miles of equestrian trails, an archery range, baseball

INSTANT SURFER STREET CRED

You don't have to surf the big waves at Mavericks (p191) to gain respect from SF's surfer crowd. Here's how it's done:

- Get skills: board and wet-suit rentals and lesson referrals are available at the friendly **Aqua** (Map pp96-7; ☎ 415-876-2782; www.aquasurfshop.com; 1742 Haight St; rental per day board/wet suit $25/15; 3-7pm Wed-Fri, 10am-6pm Sat & Sun)
- Gear up: boards by celebrity shapers and locally designed surfer style are sold at **Mollusk** (off Map p91; ☎ 415-564-6300; www.mollusksurfshop.com; 4500 Irving St; 9am-7pm)
- Chill out: compare session notes with the wet-suit crowd at **Java Beach Café** (p131) – to understand what they're actually saying, check out the surfer-slang decoder at www.riptionary.com
- Be righteous: to keep NorCal's beaches public and waves pristine, check out volunteering opportunities with the **Surfrider Foundation** (☎ 800-743-7873; www.sfsurfrider.org), SF's award-winning and generally rad environmental nonprofit

and softball diamonds, fly-casting pools, lawn bowling greens, four soccer fields and 21 tennis courts. To accommodate the masses that descend on weekends, John F Kennedy Dr is closed to motor vehicles on Sundays and Saturdays from June to October east of Crossover Dr, where the skateboarders, in-line skaters and unicyclists come out in force. There are places in and around the park to rent bicycles (see right) and skates (p112).

The Sunset & Twin Peaks

Surfer hangouts, sunset views over the velvety fog and a plethora of mouthwatering eateries make a wander south of Golden Gate Park worth your while. On the east end, the side-by-side 922ft and 904ft **Twin Peaks** (Map pp96–7), formerly known as El Pecho de la Chola (the Breasts of the Indian Girl), are ideal spots to watch the fog roll in from the ocean around sunset, and watch the Oakland Hills glitter with golden afternoon light across the bay. To drive to Twin Peaks, head southwest on Market St as it climbs steeply uphill (it becomes Portola Ave) and then turn right on Twin Peaks Blvd. The sleepy sweep of streets from Stanyan to the Pacific is known as **the Sunset**, with hopping foodie hubs along Irving St around 9th and 19th.

Take the N Judah all the way out to the Pacific, and you'll end up at surfer cafés where conversations revolve around sex wax (for your board, of course). At blustery **Ocean Beach** (Map pp86–7) the scene is dominated by wet-suited wave riders and Burning Man devotees keeping warm around ritual fires in new artist-designed tiled firepits. Be sure to follow park rules about fire maintenance and alcohol (not allowed) or you could get fined. On rare sunny days the waters may beckon, but only hardcore surfers and sea lions should brave these riptides.

One mile south, **Fort Funston** (Map pp86-7; ☎ 415-239-2366; Skyline Blvd; 6am-9pm) will double-dare you to hang-glide off cliffs and spelunk defunct Nike missile silos near the parking lot. If you're driving, bicycling or walking, follow the Great Hwy south and turn right on Skyline Blvd; the entrance to the park is past Lake Merced, on the right-hand side.

ACTIVITIES

Cycling

San Francisco hills and downtown traffic aren't for the faint of heart or calves, but there are easier rides here too. One classic cruise is along the Embarcadero past Fisherman's Wharf to the Marina, and onward to Crissy Field and across the Golden Gate Bridge if you're so inclined. Further afield, in Marin County, **Mount Tam** is the Bay Area's supreme mountain-biking challenge (see p156). Golden Gate Park and the Presidio are best explored on two wheels, but be sure to obey traffic signals or you may get ticketed. According to California law, riders under 18 must wear a helmet, and every cyclist must have a light when pedaling at night. Always carry a good lock too, since bike theft is common. The website for the **San Francisco Bicycle Coalition** (Map pp88-9; ☎ 415-431-2453; www.sfbike.org; 995 Market St; 10am-6pm Mon-Fri) contains all kinds of useful information about safe bicycling in San Francisco.

Avenue Cyclery (Map p91; ☎ 415-387-3155; www.avenuecyclery.com; 756 Stanyan St; per hr/day $8/30; ⏲ 10am-6pm) Just outside Golden Gate Park in the Upper Haight; bike rental includes a helmet.

Blazing Saddles (Map pp94-5; ☎ 415-202-8888; www.blazingsaddles.com; 1095 Columbus Ave; per hr $7-11, per day $20-48; ⏲ 8am-6pm) The main store is in North Beach, plus rental stands along Fisherman's Wharf. Get 10% off with online reservations, and ask about after-hours return locations.

Golf

Along with a bargain beauty of a nine-hole course where beginners can take lessons near the beach at **Golden Gate Park** (Map p91; ☎ 415-751-8987; www.goldengateparkgolf.com; cnr 47th Ave & Fulton St; greens fees Mon-Fri $14, Sat & Sun $18; ⏲ 6am-8pm), San Francisco has three 18-hole public golf courses.

Harding Park (Map pp86-7; ☎ 415-664-4690; www.harding-park.com; 99 Harding Rd; greens fees standard/twilight Mon-Thu $135/105, Fri-Sun $155/125; ⏲ 6:30am-7pm) Cypress-shaded course near Lake Merced, south of the Sunset.

Lincoln Park (Map p91; ☎ 415-221-9911; www.lincolnparkgc.com; cnr 34th Ave & Clement St; greens fees Mon-Thu $31, Fri-Sun $36; ⏲ sunrise-sunset) Scenic course bayside near the Presidio.

Presidio (Map pp86-7; ☎ 415-561-4653; www.presidiogolf.com; 300 Finley Rd; greens fees $65-95; ⏲ sunrise-sunset). The former officers' golf course; book online and save 15–30%.

Running & Skating

Marina Green has a 2.5-mile jogging track and fitness course, and you can tack on a run along Presidio trails to Baker Beach if you're feeling buff. For an easy, flat jog, head to Golden Gate Park. Skateboards can be bought or rented at skate shops along Haight St.

Golden Gate Park Bike & Skate (Map p91; ☎ 415-668-1117; www.goldengateparkbikeandskate.com; 3038 Fulton St; skate rental per hr/day $5/20; ⏲ 10am-6pm) Just outside the park. Rents out bikes (per hour/day $5/25) and blades, as well as some old-school roller skates and discs for Frisbee golf. During the week, call ahead to make sure they're not taking the day off – they live on Cali time.

Surrey Bikes & Blades (Map p91; ☎ 415-668-6699; 50 Stow Lake Dr; skate rental per hr/day $6/20) Rents skates and mountain bikes (per hour $6-8, per day $20-25) right in the heart of Golden Gate Park. Cheap cruiser bikes are also available for the same price as skate rental.

Sailing & Windsurfing

Boating and windsurfing on the bay look relaxing from the beach, but those riptides and gusty winds aren't exactly smooth sailing. Experienced sailors can rent boats from **Spinnaker Sailing** (Map pp88-9; ☎ 415-543-7333; www.spinnaker-sailing.com; Pier 40; half-day rental for up to 5 people from $115; ⏲ 10am-4pm), while landlubbers can hire a skippered boat, take private lessons ($75 an hour) or enrol in a two-day introductory (don't call it a crash) course ($375).

Experienced windsurfers take on the bay at the beach off Crissy Field, in the shadow of the Golden Gate Bridge. For kiteboarding and windsurfing rentals and lessons, check out **Boardsports Kiteboarding & Windsurfing** (Map pp92-3; ☎ 415-385-1224; www.boardsportsschool.com; 1200 Clay St; 2hr lessons $90-200; ⏲ rentals 3-7pm Thu-Fri, 10am-6pm Sat & Sun Mar-Sep). Most beginner classes are held east across the bay in Alameda, and include gear, a wet suit and an almost 1:1 instructor–student ratio.

Spas

Day spas can be found at upscale downtown hotels, and the Marina and Pacific Heights are also hot spots for the spa set. But for a truly relaxing cultural immersion experience, our top recommendation is Japantown's communal **Kabuki Springs & Spa** (off Map pp94-5; ☎ 415-922-6000; www.kabukisprings.com; 1750 Geary Blvd; spa $16-20; ⏲ 10am-9:45pm, women only Wed, Fri & Sun, men only Mon, Thu & Sat, coed Tue). Swimsuits required.

Surfing

Ocean Beach is no place for boogie boards and teensy bikinis, because rip tides and cold 12ft swells are powerful and chill-inducing, not to mention potentially denuding. There are no lifeguards; never surf alone or without at least a 3mm full-length wet suit. For a recorded message on the latest surfing conditions at Ocean Beach, telephone **Wise Surfboards** (☎ 415-273-1618) or **SF Surfshop** (☎ 415-437-6683), or check www.surfpulse.com.

Tennis

There are public tennis courts all over San Francisco, including free courts at **Mission Dolores Park** (Map pp96-7; cnr Dolores & 18th Sts) and courts named for SF tennis champ and anti-Nazi spy Alice Marble atop George Sterling Park (p102). The 21 courts in Golden Gate Park charge a fee.

Whale-Watching

Mid-October through December is peak season for whale-watching in the Bay Area, as gray whales make their annual migration south from the Bering Sea to Baja California. The **Oceanic Society** (Map pp94-5; ☎ 415-474-3385; www.oceanicsociety.org; Fort Mason Quarters 35; tours Fri/Sat $85/90; 🕒 9am-5pm Mon-Fri) leads whale-watching expeditions from the Yacht Harbor near Marina Green. Trips depart from Fort Mason and run about eight hours; reservations are required.

WALKING TOUR

Conquer one, two or three of San Francisco's three most famous hills – Telegraph, Russian and Nob – with this expandable itinerary. Along the way, you'll pass through revolutionary, cinematic and literary alleyways in Chinatown, savor the flavors of Italian North Beach, meet wild parrots in hidden hilltop parks and reward yourself with California cuisine and a stiff drink.

Enter **Dragon Gate** (**1**; p101) and walk up Grant Ave past dragon lamps and pagoda-topped

WALK FACTS

Start Dragon Gate
Finish Washington Square Park or Bar Crudo/Michael Minna
Distance 2.1 to 3.6 miles
Duration Three to 4½ hours

souvenir shops to Sacramento St, where you'll hang a left up half a block, then right onto **Waverly Place** (**2**; p100). Look up to admire prayer flags and red lanterns gracing painted temple balconies, then at Clay St jog left and right again onto **Spofford Alley (3)**. On this backstreet where Sun Yat-sen plotted revolution, mah-jong players now plot killer moves in senior centers. At the end of the block on Washington, take a right and then an immediate left onto **Ross Alley (4)**, where vivid murals hint at the colorful history of what was once San Francisco's bordello street – now more notorious as a location for regrettable Hollywood sequels like *Karate Kid II*.

Turn right down Jackson to Grant, turn left and follow the aroma of tea shops and roast duck to the right-hand turnoff for **Jack Kerouac Alley (5)**, where the pavement is embedded with a Kerouac ode to San Francisco: 'The air was soft, the stars so fine, and the promise of every cobbled alley so great…' At the mouth of the alley on Columbus is literary landmark **City Lights** (**6**; p102). Enter past the Dante-inspired sign warning 'Abandon All Despair, Ye Who Enter Here,' head upstairs to Poetry, open a book at random and read one poem. (If it's Allen Ginsberg's epic *Howl*, you could be here awhile.)

Now that you've got food for thought, it's time to address that growling belly. Head left up Columbus to the corner of Vallejo to **Molinari** (**7**; p124), where you can get your dream panini sandwich to go (house-cured salami highly recommended) and some *vino* for a picnic atop Telegraph Hill. To get there, you'll need to cross Columbus, veer right one block up Vallejo and fuel up with a shot of espresso at **Caffe Trieste** (**8**; p130) at the back table where Francis Ford Coppola drafted his script for *The Godfather*. When you're ready, walk up Vallejo and scale the steps to Montgomery St. Go left three blocks up, and turn left onto the **Greenwich Street Steps (9)** lined with cottages and terraced gardens to reach the top of Telegraph Hill. Choose your spot for a picnic in the company of wild parrots, and loll before you head inside **Coit Tower** (**10**; p103) to check out the once-controversial murals and an elevator ride for panoramic views of the bay.

If you choose to climb Coit Tower, your day pretty much ends with a downhill walk along Greenwich and a well-earned flop on a bench next to the parrot-feeding *nonne* (Italian grandmothers) at **Washington Square (11)**. Otherwise, you may still have enough stretch left in those legs to go from here left on Columbus, right on Vallejo, up three blocks and another picturesque stairway path to **Ina Coolbrith Park** (**12**; p102) atop Russian Hill. Any breath you have left will be taken away by these sweeping views from downtown to Alcatraz across the silvery Bay, and you'll be able to relate to Coolbrith's exclamation-pointed love poems to San Francisco.

Summit your last hill of the day the easy way, heading a block downhill to catch the **Mason-Powell Cable Car (13)**. Hop off at Bush St for Belgian beer and oysters at **Bar Crudo** (**14**; p123), or keep heading downhill in time for your dinner reservations for a well-earned feast at the wildly inventive **Restaurant Michael Mina** (**15**; p123).

SAN FRANCISCO FOR CHILDREN

Imaginations come alive in this storybook city, with wild parrots squawking indignantly at passersby on **Telegraph Hill** (p103), murals in hidden alleys awaiting discovery, and sunning sea lions nudging one another off the docks at **Pier 39** (p103) with a comical sploosh! San Francisco ditches the velvet ropes and takes a hands-on approach at major attractions, from DIY video games at **Zeum** (p107) and hair-raising static-electricity exhibits at the **Exploratorium** (p104) to walk-in cells at **Alcatraz** (p85) that put time-outs into perspective. The **California Academy of Sciences** (p110) makes little visitors positively giddy with the thrill of discovery, with penguins downstairs and an animal-packed rainforest spiraling up four floors to the wildflower-covered roof.

Throughout the city there's plenty of opportunity for heart-racing entertainment, starting with those rickety, seatbelt-free **cable cars** (p99). Pick up a kite in Chinatown souvenir shops and go fly that paper dragon or butterfly at **Crissy Field** (p106) – just be sure to bundle up for the wind. **Yerba Buena Ice Skating & Bowling Center** (Mapp88-9; ☎ 415-820-3532; www.skatebowl.com; 750 Folsom St; bowling per game $3.50-7, per hr $20-35, plus $3 shoe rental; 🕑 10am-10pm Sun-Thu, to midnight Fri & Sat; 👪) offers active family entertainment right in the heart of Yerba Buena Arts District, including bowling and skating (adult/child under 12/senior $8/6.25/5.50, plus $3 skate rental; check website for hours), amid museums galore and **SFMOMA** (p106) for young sophisticates.

San Franciscans have fewer kids per capita than anywhere else in the US, so your kids will never be starved for attention here, and most kiddie attractions are designed to appeal to adults too. The **Cartoon Art Museum** (p106) has original *Peanuts* strips and *Spiderman* cover drawings to entertain the whole family, plus the occasional show of political cartoons to spark discussions between parents and teenagers. At **Musée Mecanique** (p103), adults finally have a fighting chance at beating teen gamers at Foosball, air hockey, Ms Pacman and other vintage video games. The historic ships on **Hyde Street Pier** (p101) send active imaginations off sailing into the open sea, and the **USS Pampanito** (p101) submarine offers a fascinating underwater tour through control rooms and tunnels that are perfectly kid-scale (mind your head). When kids get tired of humoring adults and want to hang out with other kids for awhile, try **Golden Gate Park** (p110) and the playground at **Portsmouth Square** (p115).

QUIRKY SAN FRANCISCO

Wait, isn't that redundant? Other cities have the occasional kitschy toy store or oddball street character, but San Francisco has quirk to the core, right through to the seasonal organic veggie garden and perennial sign-waving politicos and sundry kooks on the front lawn of **City Hall** (p99). Still, the two top contenders for quirkiest neighborhood here in Quirk City are probably the Mission and the Haight.

The Mission defies all categorization, with pirate supplies at **826 Valencia** (p108), gender-ambiguous world-music club nights at **El Rio** (p134), riots of radical murals in quiet back alleys and the opportunity to French kiss your food on the run with tongue tacos from the **El Tonayense Taco Truck** (p127).

Then again, the Haight has a historic freak factor on its side, with hippie street murals, head shops and the themed flower-power rooms at the **Red Victorian B&B** (p121). But the Haight continues to cultivate quirks with a postapocalyptic bar at **Noc Noc** (p134), legs kicking out a Victorian Bay window above **Piedmont** (p138) drag supply shop and the cooperative **Red Vic Movie House** (p137), which shows the latest cult movies with popcorn sprinkled with brewer's yeast. And have you seen the sidewalk scene here? As one-time Haight resident Hunter S Thompson put it: 'When the going gets weird, the weird turn pro.'

TOURS

GoCar Tours

Cover more ground without the hassle of bus fare, parking or map-reading with a GPS-equipped, three-wheeled compact car from **GoCar Rentals** (Map pp94-5; ☎ 800-914-6227; www.gocartours.com; 2715 Hyde St; 1/2/3hr tours $46/82/108; 🕑 8am-5pm Mon-Thu, to 2pm Fri-Sun). The GPS-triggered audio tour comments on sights as you pass them so you don't miss a thing. Each GoCar seats two people and maxes out at 35mph to spare you the speeding tickets; drivers must be 18 years or older and have a valid driver's license.

Walking Tours

The **San Francisco Visitors Information Center** (Map pp88-9; ☎ 415-391-2000; www.onlyinsanfrancisco.com; lower level, Hallidie Plaza, 900 Market St; 🕑 8:30am-5pm Mon-Fri, 9am-3pm Sat & Sun) caters to adventurous pedestrians with an excellent line of walking-tour leaflets for Chinatown, Fisherman's Wharf, North Beach, Pacific Heights and Union Sq.

For specific interests and deeper historical insights, check out a guided tour:

Chinatown Alleyways Tours (Map pp92-3; ☎ 415-984-1478; www.chinatownalleywaytours.org/tourinfo; Portsmouth Sq; adult/under 5yr/6-9yr/10-17yr/student $18/free/5/12/12; 🕑 11am-1pm Sat) Teenage Chinatown residents guide you through alleys that have been here and done that: Sun Yat-sen plotting China's revolution, gold miners blowing fortunes on opium, monks standing their ground amid ashes of the 1906 earthquake. Tours leave from upper Portsmouth Sq and must be reserved at least five days in advance. Private tours for groups of at least six are also available.

Cruisin' the Castro (Map pp96-7; ☎ 415-255-1821; www.webcastro.com/castrotour; Harvey Milk Plaza; adult/child incl lunch $35/25; 🕑 10am-2pm Tue-Sat) Find out what it was like to be gay back in the day with this Castro walking tour covering SF GLBT history from the Gold Rush to today, followed by lunch at a popular restaurant. Reservations are required.

Haight-Ashbury Flower Power Walking Tour (Map pp96-7; ☎ 415-863-1621; www.haightashburytour.com; adult/under 9yr $20/free; 🕑 9:30am Tue & Sat, 2pm Thu, 11am Fri) Take a long strange trip through 12 blocks of hippie history, following in the steps of Jimi, Jerry and Janis – and if you have to ask for last names, you really need this tour, man. Tours meet at the corner of Stanyan and Waller Sts and last about two hours; reservations required.

Precita Eyes Mural Arts & Visitors Center (Map pp96-7; ☎ 415-285-2287; www.precitaeyes.org; 2981 24th St; adult/child/12-17yr/student/senior $12/2/5/5/8;

(⏲ tours from 11am Sat-Sun) Offers muralist-led weekend mural tours of the Mission on foot and by bike.

Victorian Home Walk (Map pp88-9; ☎ 415-252-9485; www.victorianwalk.com; Westin St Francis Hotel, cnr Powell & Post Sts; per person $20; ⏲ 11am) Learn to tell your Queen Annes from your Sticks with prime examples in Pacific Heights. Tours leave daily at 11am from the lobby of the St Francis Hotel in Union Sq and last about 2½ hours.

FESTIVALS & EVENTS

Every neighborhood hosts a street fair while the sun shines in San Francisco from May-August, and keep an eye out for small film fests from fall through spring.

February

Lunar New Year (☎ 415-986-1370; www.chineseparade.com) Firecrackers, legions of tiny-tot martial artists and a 200ft dancing dragon make this parade at the end of February the highlight of winter in San Francisco.

March, April & May

Asian American Film Festival (☎ 415-863-0814; www.asianamericanmedia.org) Pushing 30 and hotter than ever, with 200 directors and actors and 30,000 viewers converging on Sundance Kabuki Cinema headquarters (p137) in March for features, documentaries and shorts.

Cherry Blossom Festival (☎ 415-563-2313; www.nccbf.org) Celebrate spring in mid-April as nature intended, with scrumptious food-stall yakitori, raucous taiko drums and an origami flower kit from the street crafts fair.

San Francisco International Film Festival (☎ 925-866-9559; www.sfiff.org; adult/student/senior $12.50/11/11; ⏲ tickets 9am-4pm Mon-Fri) Pace yourself: the nation's longest-running film fest is a marathon event, with 325 films, 200 directors and sundry actors and producers over two weeks from late April. Key screenings are held at Sundance Kabuki Cinema headquarters (p137) and galas at the Castro Theatre (p137).

Bay to Breakers (☎ 415-359-2800; www.baytobreakers.com) On the third Sunday in May, 65,000 people jog costumed, naked and occasionally inebriated from Embarcadero to Ocean Beach – though a few runners dressed as salmon run upstream from the finish line to the beginning.

Carnaval (☎ 415-826-1401; www.carnavalsf.com) Shake your tail feathers in the Mission on the Memorial Day weekend in late May, and brave the inevitable fog – you might be surprised where it's possible to get goose bumps.

June

Other towns have a gay day, but SF goes all out for **Pride Month:**

Gay and Lesbian Film Festival (☎ 415-703-8650; www.frameline.org; No 300, 145 Ninth St) Here, queer and ready for a premiere for three decades. The oldest GLBT film fest anywhere launches new talents from 25-plus countries, with 200 film screenings over two weeks in the last half of June.

Dyke March & Pink Saturday (☎ 415-864-0831; www.sfpride.org) Around 50,000 lesbian, bisexual and transgender women converge in Dolores Park at 7:30pm and head to Castro St to show some coed Pride at the Pink Saturday street party on the last Saturday in June.

Lesbian, Gay, Bisexual and Transgender Pride Parade (☎ 415-864-0831 www.sfpride.org) No one does Pride like San Francisco on the last Sunday in June: 800,000 people, seven stages, tons of glitter, ounces of bikinis and more queens for the day than anyone can count.

September

SF Shakespeare Fest (☎ 415-558-0888; www.sfshakes.org; ⏲ plays begin 7:30pm) The play's the thing in the Presidio, outdoors and free of charge on sunny September weekends starting from the Labor Day weekend.

Folsom Street Fair (☎ 415-861-3247; www.folsomstreetfair.com) Enjoy public spankings for local charities on the last Sunday in September. To answer the obvious question in advance: yes, people do actually get pierced there, but it's probably best not to stare unless you're prepared to strip down and compare.

October & November

Jazz Festival (☎ 415-788-7353; www.sfjazz.org) Old schoolers and hot new talents jam around the city from mid-October to mid-November.

Litquake (☎ 415-750-1497; www.litquake.org) Authors spill true stories and trade secrets at events around the city in late September to early October and share more than they mean to at the legendary liquor-assisted Lit Crawl.

Hardly Strictly Bluegrass (www.strictlybluegrass.com; Golden Gate Park) In late September and early October San Francisco's historic, homegrown musical style gets its due with three days and three stages of bluegrass legends, all entirely free.

Dia de Los Muertos (Day of the Dead; www.dayofthedeadsf.org) Zombie brides, Aztec dancers and legions of toddler Frida Kahlos with drawn-on unibrows lead the parade honoring the dead down 24th St on November 2.

SLEEPING

Union Sq is convenient, near all public transportation and many major sights, but the area lacks color and abuts the Tenderloin on its southwest side, a neighborhood of panhandlers and junkies. Other districts, particularly the Marina, Castro and Mission, are less central, but provide a glimpse of local life.

On weekends, business hotel rates drop, tourist hotel rates go up. Most chains have airport hotels (15 miles from downtown), ideal before a 6am flight but inconvenient for longer stays. Book ahead, lest you arrive during a city-wide sellout and wind up at an airport hotel or across the bay in Oakland. The **Visitors Information Center** (☎ 415-391-2000, 800-637-5196; www.onlyinsanfrancisco.com) helps with reservations.

The following is a sampling of our favorite accommodations. For a list of author-reviewed properties, see the Hotels & Hostels pages of lonelyplanet.com. The rates we quote are for high season (summer) – you can sometimes do better, unless there's a convention in town.

TOP 5 HOTELS FOR A SHAG

- **Vitale** (p121) Hop from armless settee to low-slung bed, then roll over and gaze at the bay.
- **Adagio** (p118) Maximize the excessive floor space with *l'amour par terre.*
- **Mark Hopkins** (p119) Seduce with champagne and high heels at this romantic classic.
- **Kabuki** (p120) Steam up the traditional in-room Japanese baths.
- **Beck's Motor Lodge** (p121) Bang the headboard at the Castro's down-and-dirty gay motel.

Union Square

BUDGET

Amsterdam Hostel (Map pp88-9; ☎ 415-673-3277; www.hostelworld.com; 749 Taylor St; dm/r $30/80; 💻 wi-fi) This spiffy hostel attracts an international crowd. It features clean rooms, all of which have private baths.

Adelaide Hostel (Map pp88-9; ☎ 415-359-1915, 877-359-1915; www.adelaidehostel.com; 5 Isadora Duncan Lane; dm $31, r $55-90; 💻 wi-fi) The 18-room Adelaide sets the standard for SF hostels, with personal service, well-done decor and sparkling-clean bathrooms.

Dakota Hotel (Map pp88-9; ☎ 415-931-7475; www.hotelsanfrancisco.com; 606 Post St at Taylor St; r $55-99; 💻 wi-fi) Upgrade from hostel to hotel at this 42-room, vintage-1920s property with clean, basic rooms and clawfoot bathtubs. Alas, the elevator is temperamental.

MIDRANGE

Golden Gate Hotel (Map pp88-9; ☎ 415-392-3702, 800-835-1118; www.goldengatehotel.com; 775 Bush St; r without bath $95-105, with bath $150; 💻 wi-fi) Like an old-fashioned *pension*, the Golden Gate has kindly owners and simple rooms with mismatched furniture inside a 1913 Edwardian hotel safely up the hill from the Tenderloin.

our pick **Hotel Des Arts** (Map pp88-9; ☎ 415-956-3232, 800-956-4322; www.sfhoteldesarts.com; 447 Bush St; r without bath $99-149, with bath $139-199; wi-fi) Finally a budget hotel for art freaks. Specialty rooms are painted with jaw-dropping murals by underground street artists. The linens are thin and some sinks have separate hot and cold taps (ask when you book), but the art is incredible – it's like sleeping inside a painting. Standard rooms are less exciting, but clean and great value, with a few smart design touches.

Hotel Rex (Map pp88-9; ☎ 415-433-4434, 800-433-4434; www.jdvhospitality.com; 562 Sutter St; r $149-279; ❄ 💻 wi-fi) Designed with a nod to 1920s art salons, the Rex exudes a sexy broodiness with chocolate-brown and brick-red rooms, and top-notch mattresses with crisp linens and down pillows. Note: most rooms have limited natural light – good for late-sleepers, bad for sufferers of SAD. Great beds.

Larkspur Hotel (Map pp88-9; ☎ 415-421-2865, 800-919-9779; www.larkspurhotelunionsquare.com; 524 Sutter St; r $169-199; 💻 wi-fi) Built in 1915 and overhauled in 2008, the understatedly fancy Larkspur has a monochromatic, earth-tone color scheme and simple, clean lines. Baths are tiny but have fab rainfall showerheads.

White Swan Inn (Map pp88-9; ☎ 415-775-1755, 800-999-9570; www.jdvhospitality.com; 845 Bush St; r $169-199; 💻 wi-fi) In the tradition of English country inns, the romantic White Swan is styled with cabbage-rose wallpaper, red-plaid flannel bedspreads and polished colonial-style furniture. Hipsters may find it stifling, but if you love Tudor style, you'll feel right at home. Every room has a gas fireplace.

Hotel Triton (Map pp88-9; ☎ 415-394-0500, 800-433-6611; www.hoteltriton.com; 342 Grant Ave; r $169-239; ❄ 💻 wi-fi) The lobby of the Triton thumps with high-energy music and pops with color, like the pages of a comic book. Least-expensive rooms are tiny but all range from mod to ecologically friendly, with celeb suites named after Carlos Santana and Jerry Garcia.

Hotel Frank (Map pp88-9; ☎ 415-986-2000, 800-553-1900; www.hotelfranksf.com; 386 Geary St; r $169-299; ❄ 💻 wi-fi) Redone in 2008, the Frank has a snappy, vaguely *Austin Powers* black-and-white design aesthetic, with big houndstooth checks and faux-alligator headboards. The baths are tight, but extras like plasma-screen TVs compensate.

Orchard Garden Hotel (Map pp88-9; ☎ 415-399-9807, 888-717-2881; www.theorchardgardenhotel.com; 466 Bush St; r $179-249; wi-fi) San Francisco's first all-green-practices hotel opened in 2006, and uses sustainably grown wood, chemical-free cleaning products and recycled fabrics in its soothingly quiet rooms. Rooms have deluxe touches like flat-screen TVs and Egyptian-cotton sheets. The rooftop terrace is open to the public.

Also consider:

Andrews Hotel (Map pp88-9; ☎ 415-563-6877, 800-926-3739; www.andrewshotel.com; 624 Post St; r $109-149; wi-fi) Folksy character, great rates, good location.

Warwick Regis (Map pp88-9; ☎ 415-928-7900, 800-203-3232; www.warwicksf.com; 490 Geary St; r $115-219; wi-fi) Fancy midbudget substitute for the Ritz.

Petite Auberge (Map pp88-9; ☎ 415-928-6000, 800-365-3004; www.jdvhotels.com; 863 Bush St; r $169-219; wi-fi) French provincial charmer; some rooms have fireplaces.

Kensington Park Hotel (Map pp88-9; ☎ 415-788-6400, 800-553-1900; www.kensingtonparkhotel.com; 450 Post St; r $169-259; wi-fi) Stellar location for shopping trips; great beds, stylish rooms.

Inn at Union Square (Map pp88-9; ☎ 415-397-3510, 800-288-4346; www.unionsquare.com; 440 Post St; r $189-299; wi-fi) Conservative elegance just steps from Union Sq.

TOP END

Sir Francis Drake Hotel (Map pp88-9; ☎ 415-392-7755, 800-795-7129; www.sirfrancisdrake.com; 450 Powell St; r $219-279; wi-fi) The city's most famous doormen, clad like clownish Beefeaters, stand sentinel at this vintage-1920s classic. Rooms have less flair and their intentionally mismatched colors feel forced, but those on the 16th to 20th floors have expansive city views. Don't miss the top-floor Starlight Room (p135).

Hotel Adagio (Map pp88-9; ☎ 415-775-5000, 800-228-8830; www.thehoteladagio.com; 550 Geary St; r $219-339; wi-fi) Huge rooms and a supersnappy aesthetic set the Adagio apart. The hotel's designers placed a premium on style, blending chocolate-brown and off-white leather furnishings with bright-orange splashes. Beds are sumptuous, with Egyptian-cotton sheets and feather pillows, but bathrooms are disappointing. Still, it's a hot address for a reasonable-ish price.

Westin St Francis Hotel (Map pp88-9; ☎ 415-397-7000, 800-937-8461; www.westin.com; 335 Powell St; r $219-369 wi-fi) One of the city's most famous hotels, the St Francis lords over Union Sq. Tower rooms have stellar views, but feel generic; we prefer the original building's old-fashioned charm, with its high ceilings and crown moldings. The Westin's beds set the industry standard for comfort.

Financial District

Pacific Tradewinds Guest House (Map pp88-9; ☎ 415-433-7970, 888-734-6783; www.san-francisco-hostel.com; 680 Sacramento St; dm $28; wi-fi) San Francisco's smartest-looking all-dorm hostel has a blue-and-white nautical theme, fully equipped kitchen and spotless glass-brick showers. The nearest BART station is Embarcadero. Alas, you'll have to haul your bags up four flights.

Hotel Griffon (Map pp88-9; ☎ 415-495-2100, 800-321-2201; www.hotelgriffon.com; 155 Steuart St; r $199-299; wi-fi) Rooms have an exposed, 100-year-old brick wall, adding rich texture to the monochromatic color palette, but aesthetes bemoan the sink's placement in the bedroom. Pony up for a room overlooking the Bay Bridge – stunning at night. The hotel sells passes to the adjacent YMCA's excellent gym and swimming pool.

Palace Hotel (Map pp88-9; ☎ 415-512-1111, 888-627-7196; www.sfpalace.com; 2 New Montgomery St; r $199-329; wi-fi) The landmark Palace stands as a monument to turn-of-the-20th-century grandeur, aglow with century-old Austrian crystal chandeliers. The cushy (if staid) accommodations cater to expense-account travelers, but prices drop weekends. Even if you're not staying here drop into the opulent Garden Court, where you can sip tea in one of Northern California's most beautiful rooms.

Civic Center & The Tenderloin

Nicknamed the 'Trendyloin' for its happening bars, the 'Loin has a gritty inner-city vibe, best for intrepid travelers.

HI San Francisco City Center (Map pp88-9; ☎ 415-474-5721; www.sfhostels.com; 685 Ellis St; dm $24-29, r $82-100; wi-fi) A converted seven-story hotel, this better-than-average hostel sports 262 beds and 11 private rooms at the edge of the 'Loin, with cheap eats nearby. The opera, symphony and Asian Art Museum are a quick walk.

Hotel Metropolis (Map pp88-9; ☎ 415-775-4600, 800-553-1900; www.hotelmetropolis.com; 25 Mason St; r $89-125; wi-fi) Never mind the hookers outside, the Metropolis has fresh-looking rooms with standard-issue Ikea furniture, cushioned window sills and good bath amenities. If you're timid, you'll hate the neighborhood.

Phoenix Motel (Map pp88-9; ☎ 415-776-1380, 800-248-9466; www.jdvhospitality.com; 601 Eddy St; r $129-169; P wi-fi) The city's rocker crash pad draws minor celebs and Dionysian revelers to a vintage-1950s motor lodge with basic rooms dolled up with tropical decor. Check out the cool shrine to actor Vincent Gallo, opposite Room 43. The sometimes-happening Bambuddha Lounge occupies the former coffee shop. One complaint: noise. Bring earplugs.

North Beach

San Remo Hotel (Map pp92-3; ☎ 415-776-8688, 800-352-7366; www.sanremohotel.com; 2237 Mason St; r $55-85; wi-fi) One of the city's best values, the San Remo dates to 1906 and is long on old-fashioned charm. Rooms are simply done with mismatched turn-of-the-century furnishings, and all share bathrooms. Note: least-expensive rooms have windows onto the corridor, not the outdoors.

Hotel Bohème (Map pp92-3; ☎ 415-433-9111; www.hotelboheme.com; 444 Columbus Ave; r $174-214; wi-fi) Like a love letter to the jazz era, the Bohème has the moody orange, black and sage-green color schemes of the 1950s. Inverted Chinese umbrellas hang from the ceiling and photos from the Beat years decorate the walls. Rooms are smallish, and some front on noisy Columbus Ave, but the hotel is smack in the middle of North Beach's vibrant street scene. For quiet, book in back.

Washington Square Inn (Map pp92-3; ☎ 415-981-4220, 800-388-0220; www.wsisf.com; 1660 Stockton St; r $179-209) On a leafy, sun-dappled park, the inn looks decidedly European and caters to the over-40 set, with tasteful rooms and a few choice antiques, including carved-wooden armoires. The least expensive rooms are tiny. Wine and cheese each evening.

Fisherman's Wharf

HI Fisherman's Wharf (Map pp94-5; ☎ 415-771-7277; www.norcalhostels.org; Fort Mason, Bldg 240; dm $23-30, r $60-100; P wi-fi) This hostel trades downtown convenience for a lush, green, parklike setting. There's a kitchen and laundry facilities. Take MUNI bus 42 from the Transbay Terminal to Bay St and Van Ness Ave. Buses 30 and 47 also head here.

Wharf Inn (Map pp94-5; ☎ 415-673-7411, 800-548-9918; www.wharfinn.com; 2601 Mason St; r $159-195; P wi-fi) This standard-issue two-story motor lodge has exterior corridors and clean, simple rooms, good for kids who make a mess.

Tuscan Inn (Map pp94-5; ☎ 415-561-1100, 800-648-4626; www.tuscaninn.com; 425 North Point St; r $199-259; wi-fi) The Tuscan Inn has way more character than the Wharf's other tourist hotels, with bold colors and mixed patterns – who says stripes and checks don't match? Though under Best Western's banner, the hotel is managed by fashion-forward Kimpton Hotels. Pets welcome.

Nob Hill

Nob Hill Hotel (Map pp88-9; ☎ 415-885-2987; www.nobhillhotel.com; 835 Hyde St; r $139-155;) Rooms in this 1906 hotel have been dressed up in Victorian style, with brass beds and floral-print carpet. The look borders on grandma-lives-here, but it's definitely not cookie cutter. Rooms on Hyde St are loud; book in back. Friendly service. Wi-fi in lobby.

Mark Hopkins InterContinental Hotel (Map pp88-9; ☎ 415-392-3434, 800-327-0200; www.markhopkins.net; 999 California St; r $259-319; wi-fi) Glistening marble floors reflect glowing crystal chandeliers in the lobby of the 1926 Mark Hopkins, a San Francisco landmark. Detractors call it staid, but its timeless elegance is precisely why others love it. Rooms are done with tasteful furnishings and fabulous beds with Frette linens. The top-floor Top of the Mark (p132) lounge has knockout views and live jazz.

Fairmont (Map pp88-9; ☎ 415-772-5000, 800-441-1414; www.fairmont.com; 950 Mason St; r $259-439;) One of the city's most storied hotels, the Fairmont's enormous lobby is decked out with crystal chandeliers, marble floors and towering yellow-marble columns. Rooms sport traditional business-class furnishings, but lack the finer details of a top-end luxury hotel. For maximum character, book a room in the original 1906 building. Tower rooms have stupendous views, but look generic.

Japantown & Pacific Heights

Queen Anne Hotel (Map pp88-9; ☎ 415-441-2828, 800-227-3970; www.queenanne.com; 1590 Sutter St; r $109-239; wi-fi) The Queen Anne occupies a lovely

SEAFOOD TO SAVOR

Cravings for seafood come with the territory in San Francisco, where you're surrounded on three sides by water. But with Californian salmon fishing shut down in 2008 and over-fishing depleting sea life across the Pacific Rim, what's a conscientious foodie to do? Fret not: NorCal conservation groups and foodies are pioneering an approach to sustainable seafood that makes it possible to eat well *and* do good.

Monterey Bay Aquarium's **Seafood Watch** keeps tabs on what sea life is most at risk, along with better alternatives: for the West Coast, monkfish, Chilean seabass and farmed salmon currently fall in the 'Avoid' column, while 'Best Choices' include such SF delicacies as Dungeness crab, farmed sturgeon caviar and farmed shellfish, including albacore and oysters (hurrah!). To help you judge your menu options, download a wallet-sized card to carry in your wallet at www.mbayaq.org/cr/cr_seafoodwatch/download.asp, or a guide for your mobile phone at mobile.seafoodwatch.org.

You might also notice certain buzzwords cropping up on San Francisco fish menus: sustainable, wild-caught or diver-caught. These capture methods are generally less likely to damage Pacific aquaculture and deplete other sea life than industrial methods like trawling or trolling. When in doubt, ask where the seafood came from and how it was caught – any self-respecting SF restaurant should be able to answer. Notable seafood specialty restaurants like **Boulevard** (p126) and **Aqua** (p123) now prominently feature a sustainable seafood option on their menus.

Some San Francisco restaurants, including the following, have already taken the big leap and made a commitment to purchasing only sustainable seafood.

- Bar Jules (p124)
- Hog Island Oysters (p123)
- Jardinière (p124)
- Mijita (p122)
- Tataki (p125)

Enjoy, and be sure to compliment the chefs on their choice of seafood.

1890 Victorian building. While the decor borders on tacky (what's with the compact fluorescents in the chandeliers?), rooms are comfy and have a mishmash of antiques; some have romantic wood-burning fireplaces.

Hotel Majestic (Map pp88-9; ☎ 415-441-1100, 800-869-8966; www.thehotelmajestic.com; 1500 Sutter St; r $140-160, ste $200-260; wi-fi) The oh-so-civilized 1902 Hotel Majestic holds a torch for traditional elegance. Though a touch threadbare in spots, rooms are done in dusty rose and sage green, with Chinese porcelain lamps beside triple-sheeted beds. Standard rooms are small but better value than comparable Union Sq hotels. The clubby lobby bar is ideal for a clandestine meeting with your paramour.

Kabuki Hotel (Map pp88-9; ☎ 415-922-3200, 800-333-3333; www.radisson.com; 1625 Post St; r $189-249; wi-fi) The Kabuki nods to Japan with shoji (rice-paper) screens on the windows and bright-orange silk dust ruffles beneath platform beds. The boxy 1960s architecture is dull, but we love the deep Japanese soaking tubs and adjoining showers – perfect for a classic Nippon bathing ritual with your lover. Don't miss the lovely bonsai garden.

The Marina & Cow Hollow

San Francisco's motel row lies south of the Golden Gate along Lombard St (Hwy 101), a good place to troll for a room if you arrive without reservations. The neighboring streets are chock-a-block with shops, restaurants and the city's highest concentration of pick-up bars.

Marina Motel (Map pp94-5; ☎ 415-921-9406, 800-346-6118; www.marinamotel.com; 2576 Lombard St; r $105-145; P wi-fi) The vintage-1939 Marina has an inviting Spanish-Mediterranean look, with a quiet bougainvillea-lined courtyard. Rooms are homey, simple and well kept (never mind the occasional scuff mark); some have full kitchens (add $10 to the rate). Rooms on Lombard St are loud; request one in back.

Coventry Motor Inn (Map pp94-5; ☎ 415-567-1200; www.coventrymotorinn.com; 1901 Lombard St; r $135; wi-fi) Of the motels lining Lombard St, the generic Coventry has the highest overall quality-to-value ratio.

Hotel Del Sol (Map pp94-5; ☎ 415-921-5520, 877-433-5765; www.thehoteldelsol.com; 3100 Webster St; r $169-199; wi-fi) The kid-friendly Del Sol is a riot of color. A revamped 1950s motor lodge with a palm-lined central courtyard, it's also one of few San Francisco hotels with a heated outdoor pool. Family suites have bunks and board games.

South of Market (SoMa)

Mosser Hotel (Map pp88-9; ☎ 415-986-4400, 800-227-3804; www.themosser.com; 54 4th St; r without bath $75-109, with bath $149-179; wi-fi) A tourist-class hotel with stylish details, the Mosser has tiny rooms and tinier baths, but rates are a bargain. Service can be lackluster.

Hotel Vitale (Map pp88-9; ☎ 415-278-3700, 888-890-8688; www.jdvhotels.com; 8 Mission St; r $279-319; wi-fi) The ugly exterior disguises a fashion-forward shagadelic-chic hotel, with echoes of mid-century modern design enhanced by up-to-the-minute luxuries and a soothing spa theme. Beds are dressed with silky-soft 450-thread-count sheets. Suites have extras like waterfall showerheads, limestone baths, two-person soaking tubs and – best of all – semi-circular glass walls with stunning bay views.

The Mission

Considering the Mission's popularity, it's lacking in good cheap accommodations.

San Francisco Elements (Map pp96-7; ☎ 415-647-4100, 866-327-8407; www.elementssf.com; 2524 Mission St; dm/r $28/79; wi-fi) At the heart of the Mission nightlife scene, Elements has good-looking (if institutional) rooms with noise-blocking double-pane windows. Dorms are coed or segregated, and all have in-room baths. The rooftop bar is a happening weekend hangout.

Inn San Francisco (Map pp96-7; ☎ 415-641-0188, 800-359-0913; www.innsf.com; 943 S Van Ness Ave; r without bath $120-140, with bath $145-285; wi-fi) The Inn San Francisco occupies an elegant 1872 Italianate Victorian mansion, impeccably maintained and packed with period antiques. All rooms have fresh-cut flowers and sumptuous beds with fluffy featherbeds; some have Jacuzzi tubs. Outside there's an English garden and redwood hot tub open 24 hours. Full breakfast.

The Castro

All the following are geared toward gay travelers.

Inn on Castro (Map pp96-7; ☎ 415-861-0321; www.innoncastro.com; 321 Castro St; r without bath $95-105, with bath $115-165; wi-fi) A portal to the Castro's disco heyday, this Edwardian townhouse is decked out with top-end '70s mod furnishings. Rooms are likewise retro-cool, and spotlessly kept. Our fave: the patio suite with its flower-festooned private deck. Breakfasts are exceptional – the owner is a chef.

Beck's Motor Lodge (Map pp96-7; ☎ 415-621-8212, 800-227-4360; www.becksmotorlodgesf.com; 2222 Market St; r $95-135; wi-fi) If you meet a hot date in a Castro bar and have nowhere to get naked, head for Beck's. Book a rear-facing room for quiet, a room in front if you want to cruise with your blinds open.

24 Henry (Map pp96-7; ☎ 415-864-5686, 800-900-5686; www.24henry.com; 24 Henry St; r without bath $105-110, with bath $149; wi-fi) A converted Victorian on a quiet side street in the Castro, 24 Henry's rooms are simply decorated with cast-off antiques and utilitarian furniture. Great value for no-fuss gay travelers.

Parker Guest House (Map pp96-7; ☎ 415-621-3222; 888-520-7275; www.parkerguesthouse.com; 520 Church St; r without bath $139-159, with bath $179-249; wi-fi) The Castro's most stately gay digs occupy two side-by-side 100-year-old Edwardian mansions. Details are elegant and formal, but never froufrou or precious. Rooms feel more like a swanky hotel than a B&B, with super-comfortable beds with padded headboards and down comforters. Bathroom fixtures gleam. The garden is ideal for a lovers' tryst – as is the steam room.

The Haight

Metro Hotel (Map pp96-7; ☎ 415-861-5364; www.metrohotelsf.com; 319 Divisadero St; r $76-87; wi-fi) The off-the-beaten-path Metro's no-frills rooms are good value, if utilitarian. Plan to travel to reach anywhere noteworthy. Rooms in back are quietest.

Red Victorian B&B (Map pp96-7; ☎ 415-864-1978; www.redvic.com; 1665 Haight St; d $86-200) The '60s live on at the tripped-out Red Vic. Each individually decorated room pays tribute to peace, ecology and global friendship, with themes like sunshine, Flower Children and, of course, the Summer of Love. Only four of the 18 rooms have baths; all come with breakfast in the (naturally) organic café.

Inn 1890 (Map pp96-7; ☎ 415-386-0486; www.inn1890.com; 1890 Page St; r without bath $99-119, with bath $140-290; 💻) A block from Haight St's action, this stately 16-bedroom mansion has eclectically furnished rooms with no space-occupying froufrou to get in your way. Our favorites have wood-burning fireplaces. There's a big communal kitchen and in-room extras like robes, slippers and down comforters.

Chateau Tivoli (Map pp96-7; ☎ 415-776-5462; www.chateautivoli.com; 1057 Steiner St; r without bath $100-130, with bath $119-179; 💻) This glorious turreted chateau, on a side street near Alamo Sq, has faded since the days when Mark Twain and Isadora Duncan visited, but the place is full of soul, character and – rumor has it – the ghost of a Victorian opera diva. Rooms are modest, but what a house! Wi-fi in lobby.

EATING

Ready to be spoiled for choice? With one restaurant for every 28 people – that's almost 10 times more per capita than any other North American city – visits to this foodie city are reckoned not in days, but in meals. To plan yours accordingly, check out the recommendations below and local foodie sites like www.chowhound.com, http://sf.eater.com and www.slowfood.com. Look for foodie favorites in this chapter at every price level, from $2.50 gourmet sandwiches to $75 tasting menus, and scan the menus for sustainable seafood, pasture-raised meats and vegetarian options that aren't an afterthought.

The upside of this devilish selection is that reservations are almost always available even a day or two beforehand, and you may not have to wait to be seated as a walk-in. Calling ahead is advisable for reservations at the most famous top-end restaurants on Friday and Saturday nights, but last-minute reservations may be possible if you're flexible about eating early or late. Prices are also often more reasonable than you might expect for organic, sustainable fare, though you may notice some restaurants now tack on a 4% surcharge to cover city-mandated healthcare for SF food workers – a tacky way to pass along basic business costs, especially for upscale restaurants. Factor in 8.5% tax on top of your meal price, plus a tip ranging from 15% to 25%.

The Embarcadero

Mijita (Map pp88-9; ☎ 415-399-0814; www.mijitasf.com; No 44, 1 Ferry Bldg; small plates $2-7; 🕐 11am-7pm Mon-Wed, to 8pm Thu-Fri, 9am-8pm Sat, 10am-4pm Sun) *Agua fresca* (Mexican fruit punch) is made with fresh juice and sustainable fish tacos reign supreme at chef Traci des Jardins' thoughtful tribute to her Mexican grandmother's cooking, with bay views to be savored from your leather stool.

Boulette's Larder (Map pp88-9; ☎ 415-399-1155; www.bouletteslarder.com; 1 Ferry Bldg; breakfast $7.50-16.50, lunch $9-20, brunch $7-22; 🕐 breakfast Mon-Fri, lunch Mon-Sat, brunch Sun) Dinner theatre doesn't get better than brunch at Boulette's communal table, amid the swirl of chefs preparing for dinner service. Inspired by the truffled eggs and beignets? Get spices and mixes to go at the counter.

VEGETARIANS: TURNING THE TABLES IN SF

San Francisco offers far more than grilled cheese and veggie burgers for vegetarians and vegans.

- Vegan: San Francisco has vegetarian-oriented eateries in every neighborhood, but three organic vegan options rise above the pack for offerings that could convert even committed carnivores: **Millennium** (opposite), **Greens** (p126) and **Samovar Tea Lounge** (p131)
- Vegetarian prix-fixe: multicourse options featuring local, seasonal produce are offered at fancy restaurants like **Michael Minna** (opposite) and **Gary Danko** (p125), and are cheaper and often more intriguing than variations on the usual meat-and-starch theme
- Ethnic food: even omnivores veer to the vegetarian side of the menu to savor new ethnic flavors at specialty joints like Ethiopian **Axum** (p128) in the Haight, Mexican **Pancho Villa** (p127) in the Mission, and Moroccan-inspired **Aziza** (p129) and **Taiwan** (p129) in the Richmond
- Vegetarian power lunches: three organic salad joints downtown offer fresh perspectives on lunch, though vegans may have to ask them to hold the cheese: **Boxed Foods** (opposite), **Split Pea Seduction** (p126) and **Mixt Greens** (opposite)

Slanted Door (Map pp88-9; ☎ 415-861-8032; www.slanteddoor.com; No 3, 1 Ferry Bldg; lunch $9-19, dinner $15-27; lunch & dinner) California cuisine with a sparkling bay outlook, local produce and scintillating flavors from award-winning chef Charles Phan's native Vietnam. Reserve ahead or picnic on takeout from the Open Door stall.

Hog Island Oysters (Map pp88-9; ☎ 415-391-7117; www.hogislandoysters.com; 1 Ferry Bldg; oyster samplers $15-30; 11:30am-8pm Mon-Fri, 11am-6pm Sat & Sun) Decadence with a conscience: sustainably farmed, local Tomales Bay oysters served raw or cooked to perfection, with superb condiments and a glass of Sonoma bubbly. Better still: oysters are $1 from 5pm to 7pm on Mondays and Thursdays.

Union Square

Sears Fine Foods (Map pp88-9; ☎ 415-986-0700; www.searsfinefood.com; 439 Powell St; breakfast $8-12, lunch $7-10, dinner $14-29; breakfast, lunch & dinner;) Strike it rich at breakfast with silver dollar pancakes and thick ham slabs at this local institution beloved of foodies and weight-lifters, including California's own Governator, Arnold Schwarzenegger.

Bar Crudo (Map pp88-9; ☎ 415-956-0396; www.barcrudo.com; 603 Bush St; small plates $12-24; dinner Mon-Sat, to 11pm Fri & Sat) Start an international love affair here with Belgian beer and Pacific seafood served Italian-style as *crudi* (artfully composed raw fish dishes). Upstairs seating is limited and intimate, so go midweek or pray for a seat at the bar.

farmerbrown (Map pp88-9; ☎ 415-409-3276; www.farmerbrownsf.com; 25 Mason St; brunch buffet $15, dinner mains $14-19; 5pm-midnight daily, brunch Sun) Follow cool-cat crowds around a sketchy corner into this mellow repurposed tin-shack soul-food joint. Tingling, spicy mac and cheese and cayenne-rimmed margaritas are chef Jay Foster's down-home signatures, with ingredients sourced from local, organic and African American family farms.

Millennium (Map pp88-9; ☎ 415-345-3900; www.millenniumrestaurant.com; 580 Geary St; starters & small plates $5-10, mains $20-24; dinner; V) Three words you're not likely to hear together outside these doors sum up the menu: opulent vegan dining. GMO-free and proud of it, with wild mushrooms and organic fruit recurring features in sexy seasonal concoctions. Reserve ahead for monthly themed feasts.

Restaurant Michael Mina (Map pp88-9; ☎ 415-397-9222; www.michaelmina.net; 335 Powell St; 3-course dinner $100, bar menu mains $45; dinner) Wildly inventive trio dishes offering creative variations on an ingredient have been much copied – especially the tuna tartare triplet – but never replicated, even in Mina's own empire of 14 restaurants. To sample Mina's trios without a triple-figure bill, try the bar menu variations on Liberty Farms duck or Elysian Fields Farm lamb.

Financial District

Bocadillos (Map pp88-9; ☎ 415-982-2622; www.bocasf.com; 710 Montgomery St; small plates $4-10; breakfast & lunch Mon-Fri, dinner Mon-Sat) Just-right bites of juicy lamb-burger, crunchy BLT and, for the adventurous eater, savory braised tripe. Mix and match two or three small dishes for lunchtime fine dining that won't break the bank.

Boxed Foods (Map pp88-9; ☎ 415-981-9376; www.boxedfoodscompany.com; 245 Kearny St; mains $7-9; 8am-3pm Mon-Fri; V) The SF salad standard is set here daily, with organic greens topped by tart goat cheese, smoked bacon, wild strawberries and other local treats. Grab hidden seating in back, or get yours to go to the Transamerica Pyramid redwood grove.

Mixt Greens (Map pp88-9; ☎ 415-433-6498; www.mixtgreens.com; 120 Sansome St; mains $8-11; 10:30am-3pm Mon-Fri; V) No, they're not getting the Grateful Dead back together – that line of ponytailed stockbrokers is here for generous organic salads with mango and seared sushi-grade tuna. Grab a stool or get yours to go in a compostable corn container.

Kokkari (Map pp88-9; ☎ 415-981-0983; www.kokkari.com; 200 Jackson St; lunch $10-24, dinner $18-30; lunch Mon-Fri, dinner Mon-Sat, to 11pm Fri & Sat) This is one Greek restaurant where you'll want to lick your plate instead of break it, with starters like grilled lamb tongue souvlaki drizzled with mustard vinaigrette, and a lamb and eggplant moussaka rich as the Pacific Stock Exchange. Reserve ahead to avoid waits, or make a meal of appetizers at the bar.

Aqua (Map pp88-9; ☎ 415-956-9662; www.aqua-sf.com; 252 California St; lunch 3-7 courses $34-63, dinner 7 courses $95; lunch Mon-Fri, dinner daily) The prix-fixe business lunch is a sweet deal for three to seven distinct seasonal pleasures in chef Laurent Manrique's landmark to inventive seafood dining – a perky little tandoori hamachi with grapefruit, say, or the drool-inducing tombo tuna with bacon and truffle oil – but you may need a venture capitalist to finance dinner.

Civic Center & The Tenderloin

Saigon Sandwich Shop (Map pp88-9; ☎ 415-475-5698; 560 Larkin St; sandwiches $2.50-3; 6:30am-5:30pm) Might as well order two of those roast-pork *banh mi* (Vietnamese sandwiches) with housemade pickled vegetables now, so you don't have to wait in line on this sketchy stretch of sidewalk again – at $2.50 a pop, you can afford to get greedy.

Stacks (Map pp88-9; ☎ 415-241-9011; www.stacksrestaurant.com; 501 Hayes St; mains $8-15; breakfast & lunch;) Giant urns of artificial flowers just go to show how scrumptious the portobello-pesto crepe and wheat-germ blueberry pancakes are here, because only a truly memorable breakfast could convince trendy Hayes Valley shoppers to overlook the mortuary decor.

Suppenküche (Map pp88-9; ☎ 415-252-9289; www.suppenkuche.com; 525 Laguna St; mains $8-18.50; dinner daily, brunch Sun) German comfort-food cures for California hangovers, blissfully bucking small-plate trends with berry-studded inch-thick pancakes and farmers' omelets that deserve their own zip codes. Brunch is best, but anything involving sausages and pickles will surely satisfy.

Bar Jules (Map pp88-9; ☎ 415-621-5482; www.barjules.com; 609 Hayes St; lunch $9-13, dinner $9-26; lunch Wed-Sat, dinner Tue-Sat, brunch Sun) Small and succulent is the credo at this dinky bistro. The suitably short daily menu thinks big with flavor-rich, sustainably minded pairings like local duck breast with farro, an abbreviated but apt local wine selection and the dark, sinister 'chocolate nemesis.'

our pick **Jardinière** (Map pp88-9; ☎ 415-861-5555; www.jardiniere.com; 300 Grove St; mains $18-38; dinner) Opera arias can't compare to the high notes hit by multiple James Beard Award winner and onetime Iron Chef Traci des Jardins with succulent bites of diver-caught scallops, organic melon and Tsar Nicolai caviar, and anything chocolate on pastry chef Ellie Nelson's dessert menu is a tongue-caressing serotonin rush that will leave you fanning yourself like a diva. All ingredients are local, sustainable and seasonal, and cocktails and bar noshes in the new lounge downstairs make for delicious post-opera dish sessions.

Chinatown

City View (Map pp92-3; ☎ 415-398-2838; 662 Commercial St; small plates $3-8; lunch) Take your seat in a sunny dining room and your pick from carts loaded with delicate shrimp and leek dumplings, tangy pork spare ribs and other tantalizing, ultrafresh flavors that make dim sum seem like your brightest lunch idea yet.

Chef Jia's (Map pp92-3; ☎ 415-398-1626; 925 Kearny St; mains $5-10; 10am-10pm Sun-Thu, to 10:30pm Fri & Sat) Any meat, veg or seafood you order here comes in a brown sauce – vinegary Hunan-style, peppery black bean or savory-salty oyster sauce – but never mind how it looks, it's plenty tasty and there's more than enough to share.

House of Nanking (Map pp92-3; ☎ 415-421-1429; 919 Kearny St; starters $5-8, mains $6-12; lunch Mon-Sat, dinner daily) Bossy service with bravura cooking. Supply the vaguest outlines for your dinner – maybe seafood, nothing deep-fried, perhaps some greens – and within minutes you'll be devouring pan-seared scallops, minced squab lettuce cups and garlicky Chinese broccoli.

Yuet Lee (Map pp92-3; ☎ 415-982-6020; 1300 Stockton St; mains $8-18; lunch Wed-Mon) That brash fluorescent lighting isn't especially kind on first dates, but if you're willing to share Yuet Lee's legendary crispy salt and pepper crab or smoky-sweet tender roast duck with your booth mate, it must be love.

Jai Yun (Map pp92-3; ☎ 415-981-7438; www.menuscan.com/jaiyun; 680 Clay St; multicourse banquets from $45; dinner Fri-Wed) Don't expect a walk-in dinner or a menu from Chef Nei. By reservation only, he serves 12- to 16-course Shanghai-style, market-fresh feasts in his spiffy new mirrored bistro. Fingers crossed, your seasonal market menu includes tender abalone that drifts across the tongue like a San Francisco fog, or housemade rice noodles with cured pancetta. BYO wine – there's no corkage.

North Beach

Liguria Bakery (Map pp92-3; ☎ 415-421-3786; 1700 Stockton St; focaccia $3; breakfast & lunch) Bleary-eyed art students and Italian grandmothers are in line by 8am for the cinnamon-raisin focaccia, leaving 9am dawdlers a choice of tomato or classic rosemary, and 11am stragglers out of luck.

Molinari (Map pp92-3; ☎ 415-421-2337; 373 Columbus Ave; sandwiches $5-7; 8am-5:30pm Mon-Fri, 7:30am-5:30pm Sat) Grab a number and wait your turn ogling Italian wines and cheeses, and by the time you're called, the scent of house-cured salami dangling from the rafters and giant Parma prosciutto will have made your choice for you.

Mario's Bohemian Cigar Store (Map pp92-3; ☎ 415-362-0536; 566 Columbus Ave; dishes $7-12; 🕒 10am-midnight Mon-Sat, to 11pm Sun) The cigars are long gone, but Mario's is as bohemian as ever, with focaccia sandwiches, strong wine and rocket-fuel espresso served by paint-spattered Art Institute students.

Cinecittá (Map pp92-3; ☎ 415-291-8830; 663 Union St; pizza $8-14; 🕒 11am-10pm Sun-Thu, to midnight Fri & Sat) Squeeze in at the counter for your thin-crust pie and Anchor Steam on draft with a side order of sass from Roman owner Romina. Go with the two standouts: wild mushroom with sundried tomato for vegetarians, or the omnivore's delight with artichoke hearts, olives, prosciutto and egg.

Ideale (Map pp92-3; ☎ 415-391-4129; www.idealerestaurant.com; 1315 Grant Ave; mains $13-26; 🕒 dinner Tue-Sun) The most authentic Italian restaurant in SF. The Roman chef grills a mean fish and whips up a gorgeous truffled zucchini, but let him cook you anything with bacon or meat and the Tuscan staff recommend wine, and everyone goes home happy.

Fisherman's Wharf

In-N-Out Burger (Map pp94-5; ☎ 800-786-1000; www.in-n-out.com; 333 Jefferson St; burgers $3-5; 🕒 10:30am-1am Sun-Thu, to 1:30am Fri & Sat; 👶) Gourmet burgers have taken SF by storm, but In-N-Out has had a good thing going for 60 years: prime chuck beef processed in-house, plus fries and shakes made with ingredients you can pronounce, all served by employees paid a living wage.

Gary Danko (Map pp94-5; ☎ 415-749-2060; www.garydanko.com; 800 North Point St; 3/4/5 courses $66/83/98; 🕒 dinner) Apparently romance does come on a silver platter, served with casual flair in three to five decadent courses at this multiple-award-winning restaurant. Seafood and soufflés with bay views are the obvious aphrodisiacs, but the venison, duck and umami-laden cheese cart are lingering pleasures for the palate.

Russian Hill & Nob Hill

Za (Map pp94-5; ☎ 415-771-3100; 1919 Hyde St; slices from $3, pies from $15; 🕒 noon-10pm Mon-Wed, to 11pm Thu-Sun) Pizza lovers brave the uphill climb for cornmeal-dusted, thin-crust pizza by the slice piled with fresh ingredients, a pint of Anchor Steam and a cozy bar setting with highly flirtatious pizza-slingers – all for under 10 bucks.

Swan Oyster Depot (Map pp94-5; ☎ 415-673-1101; 1517 Polk St; seafood salad from $13.50, half-dozen oysters from $8; 🕒 8am-5:30pm Mon-Sat) Superior freshness without the superior attitude of most seafood restaurants. Order yours to go, browse nearby boutiques and breeze past the lines to pick up your picnic of crab salad and oysters with mignonette (wine and shallot) sauce.

1550 Hyde (Map pp94-5; ☎ 415-775-1550; www.1550hyde.com; 1550 Hyde St; mains $11-22; 🕒 dinner Tue-Sun) Low lights, bossa-nova mood music, succulent seasonal cuisine, charming views of passing cable cars – 1550 is putting all the San Francisco moves on you. Go Sunday to Thursday for the $29.95 three-course dinner and $15 wine flights, and be seduced.

Acquerello (Map pp94-5; ☎ 415-567-5432; www.acquerello.com; 1722 Sacramento St; 3/4/5 courses $60/72/82; 🕒 dinner Tue-Sat) A converted chapel makes a fitting setting for Suzette Gresham-Tognetti's sublime Cal-Italian concoctions, including sensational quail salads and lobster *panzerotti* (stuffed dough pockets) in a spicy lobster broth. Pair each course with a glass of a limited-production Italian vintage, and hear angels singing.

Japantown & Pacific Heights

BUDGET

Benkyodo (Map pp88-9; ☎ 415-922-1244; www.benkyodocompany.com; 1747 Buchanan St; sandwiches $2.25-3; 🕒 8am-5pm Mon-Sat) The perfect retro lunch counter cheerfully serves an old-school egg salad sandwich for a paltry $2.25 or pastrami for $2.50, plus chocolate-filled strawberry and green-tea mochi made in-house.

Nijiya Supermarket (off Map pp94-5; ☎ 415-563-1901; www.nijiya.com; 1737 Post St; bento boxes $5-12; 🕒 10am-8pm) Picnic by the Peace Pagoda with sushi or teriyaki bento boxes fresh from the deli counter and a swig of Berkeley-brewed Takara Sierra Cold sake from the drinks aisle – and save enough change from a $20 for mango ice-cream mochi or chocolate-filled panda cookies.

MIDRANGE

Tataki (Map pp94-5; ☎ 415-931-1182; www.tatakisushibar.com; 2815 California St; rolls $4-13; 🕒 lunch Mon-Fri, dinner Mon-Sat, to 11:30pm Fri & Sat) Sustainable sushi chefs are here to save the day for ecoconscious seafood fans, cleverly substituting buttery kampachi for hamachi and delicate arctic char for wild salmon, and serving local crabmeat salad with a scintillating sake gelee.

On the Bridge (off Map pp94-5; ☎ 415-563-1417; Japan Center Kintetsu Mall, 1825 Post St; mains $6-17; 🕒 noon-10pm daily) Curry favor with the chef by ordering the house specialty: Japanese-style curry made with fresh veggies and meats of your choice. Counter service is slow in this family-run place, but the collection of waving kitties behind the counter is hypnotizing.

Mifune (off Map pp94-5; ☎ 415-922-0337; www.mifune.com; Japan Center Kintetsu Mall, 1737 Post St; mains $7-17; lunch & dinner;) Slide into your high-backed booth and slurp your steaming pile of housemade soba (buckwheat) noodles like a pro. Sorry, only kids' meals come in the dish shaped like a bullet train.

Spruce (Map pp94-5; ☎ 415-931-5100; www.sprucesf.com; 3640 Sacramento St; lunch $10-13, dinner $15-25; lunch Mon-Fri, dinner Sat & Sun) It's VIP all the way, with studded ostrich-leather chairs, mahogany walls and your choice of 1000 wines. Expense-accounters dine on pork tenderloin with crispy pork belly, and lunch on lavish salads of warm duck confit, plums and greens grown on the restaurant's own organic farm.

The Marina & Cow Hollow

La Boulange (Map pp94-5; ☎ 415-440-4450; www.baybread.com; 1909 Union St; sandwiches $6-8; 7am-7pm) La Combo is a $7 lunchtime deal to justify your next Union St boutique purchase: half a *tartine* (open-faced sandwich) with soup or salad, plus all the Nutella and pickled cornichons you desire from the condiment bar.

Greens (Map pp94-5; ☎ 415-771-6222; www.greensrestaurant.com; Fort Mason, Bldg A; lunch $8-14, dinner $16-23; lunch Tue-Sat, dinner daily, brunch Sun; V) In a converted army barracks, ooh over the views and smoky-rich black bean chili with pickled jalapeños, plus peach crumble for dessert. All Greens' dishes are meat-free and organic, mostly raised on a Zen farm in Marin – sure beats army rations.

A16 (Map pp94-5; ☎ 415-771-2216; www.a16sf.com; 2355 Chestnut St; lunch $6-16, dinner $10-25; lunch Wed-Fri, dinner daily, to 11pm Fri & Sat) SF's James Beard Award–winning Neapolitan pizzeria requires reservations, then haughtily makes you wait in the foyer like a high-maintenance date. The housemade mozzarella burata and chewy-but-not-too-thick-crust pizza topped with kicky calamari makes it worth your while.

South of Market (SoMa)

BUDGET

Split Pea Seduction (Map pp88-9; ☎ 415-551-2223; www.splitpeaseduction.com; 138 6th St; breakfast $4-7, lunch $4-12; breakfast & lunch Mon-Fri; V) Right off Skid Row are unexpectedly healthy, homey $8.50 soup-and-sandwich gourmet combinations, including seasonal soups like potato with housemade pesto and a signature *crostata* (open-faced sandwich), such as cambozola cheese and nectarine drizzled with honey.

Patisserie Philippe (Map pp88-9; ☎ 415-558-8016; www.patisseriephilippe.com; 655 Townsend St; sandwiches $5-8; 8am-6pm Mon-Fri, to 5pm Sat) Come for the impeccable ham-and-cheese croissant or classic quiche Lorraine, but ignore that European glass counter or you'll skip straight to the tarte tatin loaded with sweet-tart apples or the bag of premium butter cookies for $1.

Tu Lan (Map pp88-9; ☎ 415-626-0927; 8 6th St; mains $5-9; 11am-9pm Mon-Sat) Suffering is a badge of honor among Tu Lan regulars, who endure grim waits outside on Skid Row, brusque service, five-alarm Vietnamese chilies and linoleum that was dingy 10 years ago for poached chicken cabbage salad with tangy dressing or spicy pan-fried prawns with roasted tomatoes and sweet onions.

MIDRANGE & TOP END

Salt House (Map pp88-9; ☎ 415-543-8900; www.salthousesf.com; 545 Mission St; lunch $13-22, dinner $23-28; 11:30am-11pm Mon-Thu, to midnight Fri, 5:30pm-midnight Sat, 5-10pm Sun) For a business lunch that feels more like a spa getaway, take your choice of light fare like duck confit or yellowfin tuna with beets. Service is leisurely, so order that ginger julep and carrot cake with cream-cheese ice cream now too.

Acme Chop House (Map pp88-9; ☎ 415-644-0240; www.acmechophouse.com; 24 Willie Mays Plaza; lunch $7-25, dinner $19-45; lunch Tue-Fri, dinner Tue-Sat) Envy your steak at Acme, because those pasture-raised beauties led a charmed existence in Marin until just before they landed on your plate. Chef Traci des Jardins built this ecoclubhouse next door to AT&T Park with recycled cork floors, certified sustainable mahogany tables and composting for table scraps – not that you'll have any.

Boulevard (Map pp88-9; ☎ 415-543-6084; www.boulevardrestaurant.com; 1 Mission St; lunch $17-25, dinner $29-39; lunch Mon-Fri, dinner daily) Pat Kuleto's belle epoque decor could have been a tad too precious in this 1889 building that once housed the Coast Seamen's Union, but chef Nancy Oakes has kept the menu honest with juicy pork chops, enough soft-shell crab to satisfy a sailor and crowd-pleasing desserts.

SLICES OF HEAVEN

When your palate hasn't felt the burn in awhile, toughen it up with pizza you can't help but eat while scorching:

- Spicy calamari pizza at **A16** (opposite)
- Deep-dish pie at **Little Star** (p128), with spinach, ricotta, feta, onion, mushroom and garlic
- Capricciosa topped with artichokes, prosciutto and an egg from **Cinecittá** (p124)
- Potato, pesto and roasted garlic slice at **Escape from New York** (p128)
- Plain cheese at **Arinell Pizza** (below) at 11:55pm on a Thursday

The Mission

BUDGET

El Tonayense Taco Truck (Map pp96-7; ☎ 415-550-9192; cnr 16th & South Van Ness; tacos $1.50-2; 🕑 9am-6pm) The best meal on wheels in SF. Burritos and quesadillas are generous to a fault, but the tacos are the ideal gourmet meal – especially the 'al pastor' (marinated roast pork) and *lengua* (beef tongue).

Mitchell's Ice Cream (off Map pp96-7; ☎ 415-648-2300; www.mitchellsicecream.com; 688 San Jose Ave; cones $2-4; 🕑 11am-11pm; 🚼) Grab a number by the door and join the masses deliberating among the not-too-sweet, perfectly creamy, tropical-inspired flavors: Kahlua mocha cream, no-fail mango, subtle macapuno (young coconut) or savory-rich purple yam.

El Majahual (Map pp96-7; ☎ 415-821-7514; 1142 Valencia St; papusas $2.50; 🕑 11am-9pm) *Papusas* are Salvadoran dough pockets stuffed with ground pork, green chili and *queso* (cheese) and fried, then loaded with pickled cabbage and salsa – but you can call it the most filling meal you've had for $2.50.

Arinell Pizza (Map pp96-7; ☎ 415-255-1303; 509 Valencia St; $2.50-3; 🕑 lunch & dinner daily, to midnight Thu-Sat) Slices as nature and New York intended, with the right amount of cheese, spicy tomato sauce and a few standard toppings – sausage, pepperoni, nothing fancy – slathered on a thin crust.

Mission Pie (Map pp96-7; ☎ 415-282-1500; www.pieranch.org; 2901 Mission St; slices from $3.50, pies from $18; 🕑 7am-9pm Mon-Thu, to 10pm Fri, 8am-10pm Sat, 8am-9pm Sun; 🚼) Pie with a purpose: from savory quiche to all-American apple, all purchases support a nonprofit sustainable farm where city kids find out where their food comes from, and learn about nutrition and cooking.

Pancho Villa (Map pp96-7; ☎ 415-864-8840; www.panchovillasf.com; 3071 16th St; burritos $4-6; 🕑 lunch & dinner) The hero of the downtrodden and burrito-deprived, delivering tinfoil-wrapped meals the girth of your forearm and a worthy condiments bar. The line moves fast going in, and as you leave the door is held open for you and your happily acquired Pancho's paunch.

La Taquería (Map pp96-7; ☎ 415-285-7117; 2889 Mission St; burritos $4-7; 🕑 11am-9pm) No debatable saffron rice, spinach tortilla or mango salsa here, just unadulterated burrito bliss: perfectly grilled meats, flavorful beans and classic tomatillo or mesquite salsa inside a flour tortilla, with optional housemade spicy pickled vegetables and *crema* (crème fraîche).

St Francis Fountain (off Map pp96-7; ☎ 415-826-4200; 2801 24th St; dishes $5-9; 🕑 breakfast & lunch; 🚼) Tender nostalgia and a mean griddle account for lines out the door for breakfast on weekends, but lunch and soda-fountain treats deliver a similar kick without the wait.

Tortas Los Picudos (Map pp96-7; ☎ 415-824-4199; 2969 24th St; tortas $6-8; 🕑 lunch) Mexico City's signature street food reinvented for San Francisco: sandwiches stuffed with farm-fresh veggies and healthy poached chicken, with optional pickled jalapeños. Wash it down with a strawberry smoothie or fresh-squeezed OJ, and you can skip dinner.

MIDRANGE & TOP END

Foreign Cinema (Map pp96-7; ☎ 415-648-7600; www.foreigncinema.com; 2534 Mission St; mains $16-30; 🕑 dinner daily, brunch Sat & Sun) Reliably tasty dishes like truffled swordfish are the main attraction, but Luis Buñuel and François Truffaut provide an entertaining backdrop, with movies screened in the courtyard and subtitles you can follow when the conversation lags.

Range (Map pp96-7; ☎ 415-282-8283; www.rangesf.com; 842 Valencia St; mains $18-26; 🕑 dinner daily, to 11pm Fri & Sat) Fine American dining is alive and well within Range. The menu is seasonal Californian, prices are reasonable and the style is repurposed industrial chic – think coffee-rubbed pork shoulder served with microbrewed beer from the blood-bank refrigerator.

Delfina (Map pp96-7; ☎ 415-552-4055; www.delfinasf.com; 3621 18th St; mains $18-28; 🕑 dinner daily, to 11pm Fri & Sat) Simple, sensational, seasonal California cuisine: steelhead trout graced with caramelized endive, roast chicken and mashed spuds trumped with royal trumpet mushrooms, and bucatini pasta with local sardines and chili. Reserve ahead and come prepared for a wait.

The Castro

Sparky's (Map pp96-7; ☎ 415-626-8666; 242 Church St; mains $7-10; 24hr) By day it's a family-friendly burger joint. But at around midnight Sparky's becomes the unofficial drunk tank of the Mission and the Castro. Its regulars come stumbling in, in their leather chaps (that single step at the door gets everyone); divas trailing boas demand home fries and omelets with plenty of Tabasco and grease. You might just catch the occasional impromptu sing-along.

Burgermeister (Map pp96-7; ☎ 415-437-2874; www.burgermeistersf.com; 138 Church St; burgers $8-10; 11am-11pm;) Skeptical Nebraskans and erstwhile vegetarians are among the regulars here ordering the slippery house special with free-range Niman Ranch beef, grilled onions, blue cheese and mesclun greens, best eaten two-handed.

Sushi Time (Map pp96-7; ☎ 415-552-2280; www.sushitime-sf.com; 2275 Market St; rolls $4-10; dinner Mon-Sat) Devour sashimi in the tiny glassed-in patio like a shark in an aquarium, or chew on Barbie, GI Joe and Hello Kitty rolls at this surreal sushi spot hidden below a bookstore and gym, Tokyo-style. Happy-hour specials run from 5pm to 6:30pm.

Home (Map pp96-7; ☎ 415-503-0333; www.home-sf.com; 2100 Market St; mains $8-18; 5pm-midnight daily, brunch Sat & Sun) Make yourself right at Home by the fire with a $3 happy-hour margarita in the company of gym-fresh men while you wait for your cayenne-spiked mac and cheese and rosemary roast chicken. Arrive before 6pm midweek for the Early Bird special, which includes a starter, a main and a glass of wine for $13.

Catch (Map pp96-7; ☎ 415-431-5000; www.catchsf.com; 2362 Market St; lunch $9-18, dinner $14-27; lunch Mon-Fri, dinner daily, to 11pm Fri & Sat, brunch Sat & Sun) Catch as in 'of the day' – monkfish, Dungeness crab, oysters – not necessarily a reference to that silver fox by the fireplace. Try the vat-sized cioppino, and maneuver away from the piano to hear the hot dish being served by fellow diners.

The Haight

BUDGET

Escape From New York Pizza (Map pp96-7; ☎ 415-668-5577; www.escapefromnewyorkpizza.com; 1737 Haight St; slices $3-4; 11:30am-midnight Sun-Thu, to 2am Fri & Sat) The Haight's obligatory midbender stop for a hot slice. Pesto with roasted garlic and potato will put you right to sleep, but the sundried tomato with goat cheese, artichoke hearts and spinach will recharge you to go another round.

Rosamunde Sausage Grill (Map pp96-7; ☎ 415-437-6851; 545 Haight St; sausages $4-6; lunch & dinner) Here's what they serve at baseball games in heaven. Divine duck, spicy lamb or wild boar sausages, fully loaded with your choice of roasted red peppers, grilled onions, mango chutney or wasabi mustard, devoured next door with Toronado's legendary selection of microbrews.

Axum Café (Map pp96-7; ☎ 415-252-7912; www.axumcafe.com; 698 Haight St; $7-14; dinner; V) When you've got a hot date with a vegan, the hunger of an athlete and/or the salary of an activist, Axum's vegetarian platter for two is your saving grace: lip-tingling red lentils, fiery mushrooms and mellow yellow chickpeas, scooped up with spongy *injera* bread.

MIDRANGE

Uva Enoteca (Map pp96-7; ☎ 415-829-2024; www.uvaenoteca.com; 568 Haight St; small plates $6-12; 5pm-midnight) 'Wine for hipsters' is the motto here. Boys with shags and girls with bangs discover the joys of bardolino and barbera by the tasting glass, inventive local veggies, cheese and charcuterie boards, and sassy tattooed wait staff.

Magnolia Pub Brewery (Map pp96-7; ☎ 415-864-7468; www.magnoliapub.com; 1398 Haight St; sandwiches $8-10, mains $9-15; lunch & dinner daily, to midnight Sun-Thu, to 1am Fri & Sat) Organic pub grub and homebrews with laid-back, Deadhead service in the hippie heart of the Haight. Join the communal table, work your way through the beer sampler and consult your neighbors on the all-local menu – bet they'll recommend the organic Prather Ranch burger.

Little Star Pizza (Map pp96-7; ☎ 415-441-1118; www.littlestarpizza.com; 846 Divisadero St; pizzas small $11-18, large $15-23; dinner Thu-Tue, to 11pm Fri & Sat) Midwest weather patterns reveal Chicago's thunder has been stolen by Little Star's deep-dish pie, with California additions of cornmeal crust, fresh veggies, just the right amount of cheese and a Chicago stockyard's worth of meat.

The Richmond

BUDGET

Genki (Map p91; ☎ 415-379-6414; www.genkicrepes.com; 330 Clement St; crepes $3-6; 2-10:30pm Mon, lunch & dinner Tue-Sun, to 11:30pm Fri & Sat;) A teen mob scene for French crepes by way of Tokyo with green tea ice cream and Nutella, and tropical fruit tapioca bubble tea. Attached to a Japanese convenience store where the snack/beauty supply aisle satisfies sudden Pocky/purple hair dye whims.

Spices (Map p91; ☎ 415-752-8884; www.eatspices.com; 294 8th Ave; mains $4-9; lunch & dinner) The menu reads like an oddly dubbed Hong Kong action flick, with dishes labeled 'explosive!!' and 'stinky!'. But the chefs can call zesty pickled Napa cabbage with chili oil, silky ma-po tofu and brain-curdling spicy chicken whatever they want – it's all sensational. Cash only.

Taiwan Restaurant (Map p91; ☎ 415-387-1789; 445 Clement St; mains $6-12; lunch & dinner;) The most lavish banquet for four you'll ever get for $28: smoky dry-braised green beans, grassy vegetable dumplings, feisty black bean squid and scrumptious housemade Shanghai sesame hot sauce noodles with pickled vegetables.

Roadside BBQ (Map p91; ☎ 415-221-7427; www.roadside-bbq.com; 3751 Geary Blvd; sandwiches $8, ribs $10; lunch & dinner, to 11pm Fri & Sat) Don't call it fast food: the pulled-pork sandwiches and racks of ribs are slow-cooked in a smoker, and the baked beans, sweet-potato fries and coleslaw 'roadsides' are made fresh from scratch.

MIDRANGE

Ton Kiang (Map p91; ☎ 415-752-4440; www.tonkiang.net; 5821 Geary Blvd; dim sum $4-12; 10am-9pm Mon-Fri, 9:30am-9pm Sat & Sun) Don't bother asking what's in those bamboo steamers: choose some on aroma alone and ask for the legendary *gao choy gat* (shrimp and chive dumplings), *dao miu gao* (pea tendril and shrimp dumplings) and *jin doy* (sesame balls) by name.

Burma Superstar (Map p91; ☎ 415-387-2147; 309 Clement St; mains $8-16; lunch & dinner) Rain or shine, there's always a line for aromatic catfish curries and green-tea-leaf salad tarted up with lima beans and dried shrimp. There are no reservations, so ask the host to call you at the café across the street, and enjoy a glass of wine while you wait.

Kabuto (Map p91; ☎ 415-752-5652; www.kabutosushi.com; 5121 Geary Blvd; sushi $2-7, mains $9-13; dinner Tue-Sun) There's a line out the door here to witness sushi chef Eric administer the sacrament of unagi (eel) with foie gras and chocolate sauce, ono (aka wahoo, the white-flesh cousin of mackerel) with grapefruit and crème fraîche, and the most religious experience of all: the 49er oyster with sea urchin, caviar, a quail's egg and gold leaf, chased with rare sake.

Chapeau! (Map p91; ☎ 415-750-9787; 1408 Clement St; mains $14-19; dinner Tue-Sun, brunch Sun) Like a scene from a French film, this little family-owned bistro is almost too charming to be real, with couples cooing over coq au vin, diners at adjoining tables making witty banter and a three-course prix-fixe meal for $39.

PPQ Dungeness Island (Map p91; ☎ 415-386-8266; www.ppqdungeness.com; 2332 Clement St; crab dishes $15-20; dinner Wed-Mon;) Dungeness crab season lasts most of the year in San Francisco, which means now is probably the right time to enjoy one whole atop garlic noodles, or dredged in peppercorn and flour and lightly fried. Ignore everything else on the menu and wear that bib with pride.

Aziza (Map p91; ☎ 415-752-2222; www.aziza-sf.com; 5800 Geary Blvd; mains $15-24; dinner Wed-Mon) The inspiration is Moroccan, the produce Californian and the flavors out of this world: *crostini* slathered with fava bean, ricotta and tender almonds, quail with huckleberry and cumin-orange glaze, and prawn tagine with Meyer lemons that's pure pizzazz in a pot.

The Sunset

Underdog (Map p91; ☎ 415-665-8881; 1634 Irving St; hot dogs $4-5; 11:30am-9pm;) For cheap, all-organic meals on the run in a bun, Underdog is a winner. The roasted garlic and Italian pork sausages are USDA certified organic, and the smoky veggie chipotle hot dog could win dedicated carnivores over to fake meat.

Park Chow (Map p91; ☎ 415-665-9912; www.chowfoodbar.com; 1240 9th Ave; mains $6-12; breakfast Mon-Fri, lunch & dinner daily, brunch Sat & Sun;) Cozy up by the fireplace downstairs or the patio heat lamps upstairs, and shake that fog-belt chill with California comfort food like mild curry Smiling Noodles, stalwart spaghetti with meatballs, and caramel gingerbread with pumpkin ice cream.

Koo (Map p91; ☎ 415-731-7077; www.sushikoo.com; 408 Irving St; rolls & small plates $6-15, minimum $20; dinner Tue-Sun, to 11pm Fri & Sat) Very smart, with mod decor, precision-cut sashimi and clever small plates instead of wacky rolls. You'll look like a genius for ordering the tuna with wild mushrooms and raspberry reduction, mint-miso spare ribs with potato noodles, and the aptly named Spoonful of Happiness: sea urchin and quail egg with truffle oil.

DRINKING

Cafés

San Francisco was a coffeehouse culture long before Seattle started banking on it, and sipped espresso back when New York was guzzling diner swill. Given SF's Chinese heritage, tea selections aren't limited to green or black, and self-respecting SF tea parlors and some cafés steep pots of exotic floral loose-leaf blends. Even at cafés, San Franciscans take their food seriously, and breakfast could easily turn into lunch once you get a whiff of the pastries and hot sandwiches on offer.

DOWNTOWN AREA

Blue Bottle Coffee Company (Map pp88-9; ☎ 510-653-3394; www.bluebottlecoffee.net; 66 Mint St; 7am-7pm Mon-Fri, 8am-6pm Sat, 8am-4pm Sun) The microroaster with the crazy-looking $20,000 coffee siphon for superior Fair Trade organic drip coffee, rivaled only by the bittersweet mochas and cappuccinos with ferns drawn in the foam. Expect a wait and a charge of $4 for your fix.

Caffe Amici (Map pp88-9; ☎ 415-391-3241; 155 Montgomery St; 7am-5pm Mon-Fri, to 4pm Sat; wi-fi) Did you leave your heart in San Francisco? Not to worry: there's another waiting for you at Amici, drawn in foam on your cappuccino and served in a hand-painted Italian cup.

Emporio Rulli Caffè (Map pp88-9; ☎ 415-923-6464; www.rulli.com; 333 Post St; 7:30am-7pm) Ideal people-watching atop Union Sq, with excellent espresso and a wide range of pastries to fuel you up for your next round of shopping, plus wine by the glass afterward.

CHINATOWN

Red Blossom Tea Company (Map pp92-3; ☎ 415-395-0868; www.redblossomtea.com; 831 Grant Ave; 10am-6:30pm Mon-Sat, to 6pm Sun) Think beyond the world of black and green teas to the universe of white teas, herbal infusions and, of course, the signature blossom teas that unfurl in your pot like time-lapse photography of a dahlia in August.

NORTH BEACH

our pick **Caffe Trieste** (Map pp92-3; ☎ 415-392-6739; www.caffetrieste.com; 601 Vallejo St; 6:30am-11pm Sun-Thu, 6:30am-midnight Fri & Sat) Look no further for inspiration: Francis Ford Coppola drafted *The Godfather* here under the mural of Sicily, and Poet Laureate Lawrence Ferlinghetti still swings by en route to City Lights. With sonnets on the bathroom walls, opera on the jukebox and accordion jam sessions on Sundays, this is North Beach at its best, since 1956.

Caffé Roma (Map pp92-3; ☎ 415-296-7942; www.cafferoma.com; 526 Columbus Ave) After mass on Sundays, North Beach regulars converge here for *vero* (real) espresso, possibly true gossip and unbelievable news from the old country.

Brioche Bakery (Map pp92-3; ☎ 415-765-0412; 210 Columbus Ave; 7am-6pm Mon-Fri, 8am-4pm Sat) A decadent start to the day with flaky cinnamon twists, not-too-sweet pain au chocolat and the buttery namesake brioches – plus brioche pizzas for later.

Caffè Greco (Map pp92-3; ☎ 415-397-6261; 423 Columbus Ave) Greco's friendly crew prepare fine espressos, but only divine intervention will secure a sidewalk table among cultishly devoted regulars on a sunny Saturday.

THE MISSION

Mission Beach Cafe (Map pp96-7; ☎ 415-861-0198; www.missionbeachcafesf.com; 198 Guerrero St; 7am-6pm Mon,

TOP SF COCKTAILS

Industrial quantities of margaritas and dozens of variations on the San Francisco–invented martini are served on any given night, but don't miss these standout alternatives:

- Old Cuban (rum, fresh mint, lime juice, Angostura bitters) at **Rye** (p132)
- Pretty Pepper (hibiscus-infused Square One organic vodka, habañero-infused Corralejo Reposado tequila, Cointreau, and lemon and lime juices) at **Elixir** (p133)
- Revolver (bourbon, Tia Maria coffee liqueur and orange bitters) at **Bourbon & Branch** (p132)
- Superfly (soju, blue curaçao and sweet and sour) at **Rohan Lounge** (p134)
- House Cappuccino (frothy, creamy coffee with brandy) at **Tosca** (p132)
- Custom-made seasonal fruit cocktails at **Orbit Room** (p134)

to 10pm Tue-Thu, to 11pm Fri & Sat, 9am-10pm Sun) Come for Blue Bottle coffee and housemade pie in the afternoon, and linger over a glass of small-production local wine. Brunches are not to be missed – chef Ryan Scott (of *Top Chef* fame) has a downright naughty way with eggs.

Tartine (Map pp96-7; ☎ 415-487-2600; www.tartinebakery.com; 600 Guerrero St; 🕒 8am-7pm Mon-Wed, to 8pm Thu-Sat, 9am-8pm Sun) Lines out the door for pumpkin tea bread, Valrhona chocolate cookies and open-face *croques monsieurs* (toasted ham-and-cheese sandwiches) – all so loaded with butter that you feel fatter and happier just looking at them.

Ritual Coffee Roasters (Map pp96-7; ☎ 415-641-1024; www.ritualroasters.com; 1026 Valencia St; 🕒 6am-11pm Mon-Fri, 7am-11pm Sat, 7am-9pm Sun; wi-fi) House-roasted brews with organic milk and free wi-fi make lines and hovering for a spot among legions of MacBook users worthwhile.

THE CASTRO

Cafe Flore (Map pp96-7; ☎ 415-621-8579; 2298 Market St) The see-and-be-seen, glassed-in corner café at the center of the gay universe. Eavesdrop on blind dates and post-gym dish sessions with a bracing cappuccino or knee-weakening absinthe.

Thorough Bread (Map pp96-7; ☎ 415-558-0690; www.thoroughbreadandpastry.com; 248 Church St; 🕒 7am-7pm Tue-Sat, to 3pm Sun) Pedigreed pastries and excellent breads from the San Francisco Baking Institute chefs – at $4 to $5 each, less than you'd pay for restaurant equivalents without such fine ingredients and airy textures.

Samovar Tea Lounge (Map pp96-7; ☎ 415-626-4700; 498 Sanchez St; pot of tea $6-8; 🕒 10am-11pm) This smart teahouse is popular for light breakfasts and iron pots of tea with scintillating side dishes, especially pumpkin dumplings, honeycomb with blue cheese, and chocolate brownies with green tea mousse.

THE HAIGHT

Cole Valley Café (Map pp96-7; ☎ 415-668-5282; www.colevalleycafe.com; 701 Cole St; 🕒 6:30am-8:30pm; wi-fi) Powerful coffee, free wi-fi, and hot gourmet sandwiches that are a bargain at any price, let alone $6 for lip-smacking thyme-marinated chicken with lemony avocado spread or the smoky roasted eggplant with goat cheese and sundried tomatoes.

Coffee to the People (Map pp96-7; ☎ 415-626-2435; www. coffeetothepeople.squarespace.com; 1206 Masonic Ave; 🕒 6-8pm Mon-Fri, 7am-9pm Sat & Sun; wi-fi) The people, united, will never be decaffeinated at this utopian coffee shop with free wireless, 5% pledged to coffee-growers' nonprofits, a radical reading library and enough Fair Trade coffee to revive the Sandinista movement.

THE SUNSET

Java Beach Cafe (Map pp96-7; ☎ 415-665-5282; www.javabeachcafe.com; 1396 La Playa St; 🕒 5:30am-11pm Mon-Fri, 6am-11pm Sat & Sun) The last stop on the N Judah and the first before you hit Ocean Beach, with plenty of outdoor seating for wet-suited surfers fueling up on coffee and carbs.

Bars

First came the Gold Rush, then came the rush on the bar…or was it the other way around? Back in SF's Barbary Coast days, unscrupulous sea captains hired 'crimps' to ply naive new arrivals with drugged drink and drag them to ships where they'd wake up a mile from land with a clear choice: swab the decks or swim.

Today the drink choices are less lethal and more complicated. Wines from nearby Napa and Sonoma appear on virtually every local menu, but San Francisco's microbrewed beer is not to be overlooked. The Bay Area makes its own standout spirits, including Hangar One vodka, 209 gin and Takara sake, and pours a mean cocktail – according to legend, martinis were invented in SF.

Neighborhoods where you'll never want for drink are North Beach, the Mission, SoMa, Union Sq and the Tenderloin, ranging from trendy to seedy, diva to dive. Smoking is banned inside all bars, clubs, coffeehouses and restaurants, though some bars have smoking patios.

UNION SQUARE

Irish Bank (Map pp88-9; ☎ 415-788-7152; www.theirishbank.com; 10 Mark Lane; 🕒 11:30am-2am) Perfectly pulled pints, thick-cut fries with malt vinegar and juicy sausages served in a hidden alleyway or church pews indoors. Say 'hi' to Irish owner Ronin, who bought the place from his boss, and is now every working stiff's close and personal friend.

Gold Dust Lounge (Map pp88-9; ☎ 415-397-1695; 247 Powell St; 🕒 7am-2am) Barbary Coast bordello decor, throwback prices on Irish coffee and drinks plus cheerfully inauthentic Dixieland jazz, all in the heart of downtown.

Tunnel Top Bar (Map pp88-9; ☎ 415-986-8900; www.tunneltop.com; 601 Bush St; 🕒 Mon-Sat) The rickety balcony of this attic bar always seems about ready to give, so patrons batting eyes at one another across this crowded room get the added thrill of flirting with disaster.

John's Grill (Map pp88-9; ☎ 415-986-0069; 63 Ellis St; ⏲ 11am-10pm Mon-Sat, noon-10pm Sun) Could be the martinis, the low lighting or the *Maltese Falcon* statuette upstairs, but noir novelist Dashiell Hammett's favorite bar lends itself to hardboiled tales of lost love and true crimes, confessed while chewing toothpicks.

CIVIC CENTER & THE TENDERLOIN

Hemlock Tavern (Map pp88-9; ☎ 415-923-0923; www.hemlocktavern.com; 1131 Polk St; ⏲ 4pm-2am) Cheap drink at the oval bar, pogo-worthy punk rock in the back room, a heated smoking area and free peanuts in the shell to eat and throw at literary events – though it may all seem potentially lethal first thing tomorrow morning.

Edinburgh Castle (Map pp88-9; ☎ 415-885-4074; www.castlenews.com; 950 Geary St) Photos of bagpipers, the *Trainspotting* soundtrack on the jukebox, dart boards and a service delivering vinegary fish and chips in newspaper are all the Scottish authenticity you could ask for, short of haggis.

Aunt Charlie's Lounge (Map pp88-9; ☎ 415-441-2922; www.auntcharlieslounge.com; 133 Turk St; ⏲ 9am-2pm) Strong cheap drinks and dim lights disguise five-o'clock shadows at Aunt Charlie's, where Wednesdays bring tranny diva extravaganzas and Thursdays pack the hallway-sized dance floor with art-school gays grooving on '80s techno.

Rye (Map pp88-9; ☎ 415-474-4448; 688 Geary St; ⏲ 5:30pm-2am Mon-Fri, 7pm-2am Sat & Sun) The type of place where the bartender is called a mixologist, and earns the title. Come early, drink something challenging involving dark rum or juniper gin, and leave before the smoking cage overflows.

Bourbon & Branch (Map pp88-9; ☎ 415-346-1735; www.bourbonandbranch.com; 501 Jones St; ⏲ Wed-Sat by reservation) 'Don't even think of asking for a cosmo' reads one of many House Rules at this revived speakeasy, complete with secret exits from its Prohibition-era heyday. For top-shelf gin and bourbon cocktails without reservations in the Library, use the buzzer and the password 'books.'

CHINATOWN

Li Po (Map pp92-3; ☎ 415-982-0072; 916 Grant Ave; ⏲ 2pm-2am) Enter the grotto doorway and get the once-over by the dusty Buddha as you slide into red vinyl booths beloved of Beats, surly philosophers and career alcoholics.

NORTH BEACH

Tosca Cafe (Map pp92-3; ☎ 415-391-1244; 242 Columbus Ave) Come early for your pick of opera on the jukebox and red circular booths, and stay late for Irish coffee nightcap crowds and chance sightings of Sean Penn, Bono or Robert De Niro.

Specs' (Map pp92-3; ☎ 415-421-4112; 12 William Saroyan Pl) A saloon that doubles as a museum of nautical memorabilia gives neighborhood characters license to drink like sailors, tell tall tales to gullible newcomers and plot mutinies against last call.

NOB HILL

Tonga Room (Map pp88-9; ☎ 415-772-5278; www.fairmont.com; Fairmont Hotel, 950 Mason St; ⏲ 6-11:45pm Sun-Thu, to 12:45am Fri & Sat) Tonight's San Francisco weather: foggy, about 50 degrees, with a 100% chance of tropical rainstorms every 20 minutes on the lower level of the Fairmont Hotel. Rain only falls on the indoor pool, while you sip your Hurricane from a plastic coconut inside a grass hut.

Bigfoot Lodge (Map pp88-9; ☎ 415-440-2355; www.bigfootlodge.com; 1750 Polk St; ⏲ 3pm-2am) Cure cabin fever at this log-cabin bar with happy hours from 3pm to 7pm, when everyone's telling tall tales in the shadow of an 8ft Sasquatch and getting nicely toasted on Toasted Marshmallows – vanilla vodka, Bailey's and a flaming marshmallow.

Top of the Mark (Map pp88-9; ☎ 415-616-6916; www.topofthemark.com; 999 California St; cover $5-10; ⏲ 5pm-midnight Sun-Thu, 4pm-1am Fri & Sat) Sashay across the dance floor and feel on top of the world overlooking SF. Cocktails will set you back $16 plus cover, but watch the sunset and then try to complain.

THE MARINA

California Wine Merchant (Map pp94-5; ☎ 415-567-0646; www.californiawinemerchant.com; 2113 Chestnut St; ⏲ 10am-midnight Mon-Wed, to 1:30am Thu-Sat, 11am-11pm Sun) Pair local wines by the glass with mild flirting in this wine cave, and be surprised by the subtleties of Central Coast pinots and playboys improving their game.

MatrixFillmore (Map pp94-5; ☎ 415-563-4180; 3138 Fillmore St; ⏲ 6pm-2am) The one bar in town where the presumption is that you're straight and interested. Modern and sleek, if not especially subtle – and the same can be said of the crowd.

SOUTH OF MARKET (SOMA)

Eagle (Map pp88-9; ☎ 415-626-0880; cnr 12th & Harrison Sts) The quintessential gay leather bar, with a happening heated outdoor patio scene to warm all that exposed skin, and occasional live bands. The staff are consistently friendly and clientele tolerant of straight hipsters.

House of Shields (Map pp88-9; ☎ 415-392-7732; 39 New Montgomery St) Mind the decorative taxidermy on your way to snag a coveted mahogany booth to watch live bands with a stein and a shot, and stand your ground until closing.

City Beer Store & Tasting Room (Map pp88-9; ☎ 415-503-1033; 1168 Folsom St; noon-9pm Tue-Sat, to 6pm Sun) Exceptional local and Belgian microbrewed beer with killer cheese pairings, served in a spiffy brick bar that'll win over lounge-lizard friends – the floor's not sticky and it's not even stinky.

111 Minna (Map pp88-9; ☎ 415-431-1200; www.111minnagallery.com; 111 Minna St; noon-10pm Tue-Wed, noon-2am Thu-Fri, 5pm-2am Sat) Art and cocktails make other pairings possible at 111 Minna: graffiti artists mingle with webmasters, corporate events share the calendar with nonprofit fundraisers and fly DJs woo shy wallflowers.

THE MISSION

our pick **Zeitgeist** (Map pp96-7; ☎ 415-255-7505; 199 Valencia St; 9am-2am) The beer garden (minus the garden) is the place to be on a balmy Mission night, with generous pitchers and perfect pints of microbrews pulled by tough lady bartenders who out-sass biker regulars, and late-night munchies courtesy of the Tamale Lady.

Make-Out Room (Map pp96-7; ☎ 415-647-2888; 3225 22nd St) Between the generous pours and Pabst beer specials, the Make-Out has convinced otherwise sane people to leap onstage and read from their teen journals for Get Mortified nights and sing along to peculiar bands with catchy sounds, from punk fiddle to ukulele honky-tonk.

Elixir (Map pp96-7; ☎ 415-552-1633; www.elixirsf.com; 3200 16th St) Drinking is good for the environment at SF's first certified green bar, with your choice of organic, green and even biodynamic cocktails – get the Rancho Ancho No 2, with organic peach and lime juices, 4 Copas organic tequila and ancho chili.

Medjool (Map pp96-7; ☎ 415-550-9055; www.medjoolsf.com; 2522 Mission St; 5-10pm Sun-Thu, to 2am Fri & Sat) Well-muddled mojitos and tasty Middle Eastern mezze platters with rooftop panoramas of old Mission cinema marquees. Go early for sunsets and prime spots by heat lamps.

Latin American Club (Map pp96-7; ☎ 415-647-2732; 3286 22nd St; 6pm-2am Sun-Thu, 5pm-2am Fri & Sat) Too spiffy to be a dive, too cheap for high-maintenance dates, just right for killer margaritas and $6 cocktails with friends who still understand you when you slur.

Doc's Clock (Map pp96-7; ☎ 415-824-3627; www.docsclock.com; 2575 Mission St; 6pm-2am Mon-Sat, 8pm-2am Sun) Laid-back Mission crowds throng this corridor of a dive bar for $1 Pabst, shuffleboard grudge matches and neighborhood events like Barbie Mutilation Nights and Doggie Happy Hour.

Casanova Lounge (Map pp96-7; ☎ 415-863-9328; 527 Valencia St) Arrive early to score a couch under the nudie black velvet paintings and commandeer the indie music jukebox, until the DJs take over around 9pm or 10pm and it's too loud to chat up that film-school hottie.

THE CASTRO

Lime (Map pp96-7; ☎ 415-621-5256; 2247 Market St; 5pm-midnight Mon-Thu & Sun, 5-9pm Fri & Sat) Perch atop the outer-space fungi that passes for seating and slurp a key lime martini or two amid cute Castro boys and their strictly platonic girlfriends. At brunch, order the bottomless $6 mimosa at your own risk.

440 Castro (Map pp96-7; ☎ 415-621-8732; www.daddysbar.com; 440 Castro St) Just your friendly neighborhood bar, if your neighborhood

HOT TICKETS

Big events sell out fast in SF. Scan the free weeklies, the *San Francisco Bay Guardian* and the *SF Weekly*, and see what half-price and last-minute tickets you can find at **TIX Bay Area** (Map pp88-9; ☎ 415-433-7827; Union Sq at 251 Stockton St; 11am-6pm Tue-Thu, to 7pm Fri & Sat). Tickets are sold on the day of the performance for cash only. For tickets to theater shows and big-name concerts in advance, call **Ticketmaster** (☎ 415-421-8497) or **BASS** (☎ 415-478-2277).

consists mostly of bears (burly gay men) wearing nothing but boxer briefs and boots on Mondays and taking advantage of $2 or $2.50 beer specials most nights.

The Mint (Map pp96-7; ☎ 415-626-4726; www.themint.net; 1942 Market St; 🕑 4pm-2am) Show tunes are serious stuff at karaoke sessions starting at 9pm nightly, where it takes courage and a vodka gimlet to attempt Barbra Streisand. Prepare to be upstaged by a banker with a boa and a mean falsetto.

Orbit Room Cafe (Map pp96-7; ☎ 415-252-9525; 1900 Market St; 🕑 8am-midnight Sun, 7am-midnight Mon-Thu, 7am-2am Fri & Sat) Bartenders keep busy here inventing their next custom cocktail with house-infused spirits and fresh juices, so don't go expecting bar banter or speedy service, and mingle with standing-room crowds gushing over their drinks.

Moby Dick (Map pp96-7; ☎ 415-861-1199; www.mobydicksf.com; 4049 18th St; 🕑 2pm-2am Wed, noon-2am Sat & Sun) A gay dive bar with sharks circling the pool table, the occasional sailor at the bar, two-for-one frozen margaritas that'll shiver your timbers and an aquarium with fish flitting past something that's great and white but definitely not a whale.

Transfer (Map pp96-7; ☎ 415-861-7499; 198 Church St) Once seedier than the guy trying to sell late-night MUNI transfers out front, this divey, pan-sexual joint has been prettified in a smeared-lipstick Courtney Love way without alienating the lifers swilling tequila at the bar.

THE HAIGHT

Toronado (Map pp96-7; ☎ 415-863-2276; 547 Haight St; 🕑 11:30am-2am) Bow before the chalkboard altar listing 46 beers on tap and hundreds more bottled, including spectacular seasonal microbrews. Bring cash, come early and stay late, with a sausage from Rosamunde next door to accompany ale made by Trappist monks.

Aub Zam Zam (Map pp96-7; ☎ 415-861-2545; 1633 Haight St; 🕑 3pm-2am) Arabesque arches, jazz on the jukebox and enough paisley to make Prince feel right at home pay homage to the purist Persian charm of dearly departed cocktail fascist Bruno, who'd throw you out for ordering a vodka martini.

Noc Noc (Map pp96-7; ☎ 415-861-5811; 557 Haight St) Who's there? Dreadlocked graffiti artists, electronica DJs and *Mad Max*–inspired fashion designers, that's who. This place looks like a post-apocalyptic cartoon cave dwelling, and serves a sake cocktail that'll keep you buzzed until the next Burning Man.

Mad Dog in the Fog (Map pp96-7; ☎ 415-863-2276; 530 Haight St; 🕑 11:30am-2am Mon-Fri, 10am-2am Sat & Sun) Footie fans watch matches live on GMT, and know-it-alls arrive by 8:30pm Tuesdays and Thursdays to compete for free beer on Trivia Nights. There's no hard liquor or credit-card machine, but cash will get you beer, darts and occasionally live rockabilly.

THE RICHMOND

Rohan Lounge (Map p91; ☎ 415-221-5095; 3809 Geary Blvd; 🕑 6pm-midnight Mon-Thu, 6pm-2am Fri & Sat, 6-11pm Sun) Soju sophistication, with Korean spirits mixed with watermelon juice for Bond Girl–worthy *soju*-tinis and inspired bar bites from garlic edamame to the kimchi sampler.

Plough & Stars (Map p91; ☎ 415-751-1122; 116 Clement St; 🕑 4pm-2am Mon, 2pm-2am Tue-Thu, noon-2am Fri-Sun) The Emerald Isle by the Golden Gate. Jigs are to be expected after the first couple of rounds and rousing Irish fiddle tunes played most nights by top Celtic talent.

Beach Chalet Brewery (Map p91; ☎ 415-386-8439; www.beachchalet.com; 1000 Great Hwy; 🕑 9am-10pm Mon-Fri, 10am-11pm Sat, 10am-10pm Sun) Brews with views: sunsets over the Pacific, plus recently restored 1930s WPA frescoes downstairs showing a condensed history of San Francisco.

ENTERTAINMENT

You don't have to wait behind velvet ropes, wear the right designers or sweet-talk your way into VIP lounges to have a good time in SF – how very LA. SF's eclectic bars, dance clubs and cutting-edge concert spaces take a come-as-you-are attitude, and many San Franciscans don't even dress up for the opera, symphony, ballet and theatre (pity, really). But if you really want to see SF all gussied up, hit the drag scene.

Nightclubs

El Rio (off Map pp96-7; ☎ 415-282-3325; www.elriosf.com; 3158 Mission St; admission $3-8; 🕑 5pm-2am Mon-Thu, 1pm-2am Fri-Sun) Free-form funky grooves worked by regulars of every conceivable ethnicity and orientation. Arrive early for prime garden seating, 'Totally Fabulous Happy Hour' from 4pm to 9pm Tuesday to Friday and free oysters on the half shell on Fridays at 5:30pm.

Mighty (off Map pp88-9; ☎ 415-626-7001; www.mighty119.com; 119 Utah St; admission $10; 🕑 10pm-4am Fri-Sun) The weekly house parties here book high-caliber DJs, yet no one cops an attitude – it's just a Mighty fine time with three long bars, a vast dance floor and getting-to-know-you balcony.

Endup (Map pp88-9; ☎ 415-646-0999; www.theendup.com; 401 6th St; 10pm-6am Mon & Thu-Sat, 6am-2am Sun) Everyone ends up here sooner or later for Fag Fridays, definitive Sunday tea dances (since 1973!), reggae Saturdays and/or all-star lady DJs for marathon Minx Thursdays.

Mezzanine (Map pp88-9; ☎ 415-625-8880; www.mezzaninesf.com; 444 Jessie St) Brag about seeing biggish acts in a smallish place for cover ranging from nada to $15, with Mos Def, Dandy Warhols, Nas, the Slits and Method Man blowing the roof clean off the Mezzanine.

Cat Club (Map pp88-9; ☎ 415-703-8965; www.catclubsf.com; 1190 Folsom St; admission after 10pm $5; 9pm-3am Tue & Thu-Sat) You never really know your friends until you've seen them belt out a-ha's 'Take On Me' at legendary mixed 1984 Thursday nights, or perform 'Rapper's Delight' at old-school hip-hop Hot Pants lesbian Fridays on the second and fourth Fridays.

Bar on Castro (Map pp96-7; ☎ 415-626-7220; www.thebarsf.com; 456 Castro St; 4pm-2am Mon-Fri, 2pm-2am Sat & Sun) You haven't been to the Castro until you've passed the Bar. Relentless beats and shameless drink specials served by hottie bartenders help explain the three naked men fanning themselves out front on a recent Saturday night.

Annie's Social Club (Map pp88-9; ☎ 415-974-1585; www.anniessocialclub.com; 917 Folsom St; admission free or $5-8; 4pm-2am Mon-Fri, 8pm-2am Sat) Punk Rock and Schlock Karaoke nights require you to murder songs and throw in some cheeky pogo burlesque, and live punk shows do wonders for flagging street creds.

The Café (Map pp96-7; ☎ 415-861-3846; www.cafesf.com; 2369 Market St; 4pm-2am Mon-Fri, 3pm-2am Sat, 2pm-2am Sun) Anyone in hot pants is welcome on the dance floor, though Fridays favor fellas and every third Saturday shows lesbians the love. Cover can be up to $6, but '2 for 1' drinks from 5pm to 9pm compensate.

1015 Folsom (Map pp88-9; ☎ 415-431-1200; www.1015.com; 1015 Folsom St; admission from $10; 10pm-6am Thu-Sun) When other clubs close, this one thumps on with five dance floors, a diverse crowd, tight security (ie no drugs or weapons) and international DJ sets that bring on happy hoarseness by 3am.

Harry Denton's Starlight Room (Map pp88-9; ☎ 415-395-8595; www.harrydenton.com; 450 Powell St, 21st fl; 4:30pm-2am) The obligatory panoramic top-floor hotel bar with a disco floor, only this one's got drag-show Sunday brunches and the perfect $10 Cable Car: spiced rum with lemon juice and a cinnamon-sugar rim. The cover varies and is often free.

Live Music

our pick **The Fillmore** (off Map pp94-5; ☎ 415-346-6000; www.thefillmore.com; 1805 Geary Blvd; admission $20-40; box office 10am-4pm Sun, show nights 7:30-10pm) The legendary venue that launched the psychedelic era has the posters to prove it upstairs, and hosts arena acts in a 1250-seat venue where you can squeeze in next to the stage.

Warfield (Map pp88-9; ☎ 415-775-7722; www.livenation.com; 982 Market St; box office at the Fillmore 10am-4pm Sun, show nights 7:30-10pm) Originally a vaudeville theater but now an obligatory stop for comedians like Margaret Cho and Chelsea Handler, and indie rockers from Iggy Pop to Cat Power.

Yoshi's (off Map pp94-5; ☎ 415-655-5600; www.yoshis.com; 1330 Fillmore St; shows 8pm & 10pm, Sun 7pm & 9pm) The legendary East Bay jazz venue has opened a fabulous new restaurant/club in the heart of the historic African and Japanese American Fillmore jazz district, bringing the biggest names in jazz to an intimate venue with exciting seasonal Japanese cuisine.

Great American Music Hall (Map pp88-9; ☎ 415-885-0750; www.gamh.com; 859 O'Farrell St; admission $12-35; box office 10:30am-6pm Mon-Fri, to 9pm weekday show nights, 6-9pm weekend show nights) Previously a bordello and a dance hall, this ornate venue now hosts rock, country, jazz and world music artists. Arrive early to stake your claim to front-row balcony seats with a pint and a passable burger.

12 Galaxies (Map pp96-7; ☎ 415-970-9777; www.12galaxies.com; 2565 Mission St; admission $8-20; 4pm-2am Mon-Fri, 11am-2am Sat & Sun) List smart songwriters on the cusp of breakthrough to the mainstream, and there you have the lineup at 12 Galaxies – handy to dive bars and cheap Mission eateries too.

Bottom of the Hill (off Map pp96-7; ☎ 415-621-4455; www.bottomofthehill.com; 1233 17th St; admission $5-12; 8:30pm-2am Sat-Tue, 4pm-2am Wed-Fri) Top of the list for fun bills featuring California bands like LA's slick post-punk Urinals and the lo-fi surf stylings of locals The Traditional Fools in *Rolling Stone*'s favorite SF venue.

Slim's (Map pp88-9; ☎ 415-621-3330; www.slims-sf.com; 333 11th St; admission $13-35; box office

10:30am-6pm Mon-Fri) Rock legends like The Damned and pure entertainment like Dread Zeppelin and Gogol Bordello play shows for all ages, though shorties may get swallowed in the mosh pit. Come early for upstairs seating along the balcony with dinner.

Hotel Utah (Map pp88-9; www.thehotelutahsaloon.com; 500 4th St; ⌚ 11:30am-2am Mon-Fri, 6pm-2am Sat & Sun) Whoopi Goldberg and Robin Williams broke in the stage of this historic Victorian hotel back in the '70s, and the thrill of finding SF's top hidden talents draws crowds to singer-songwriter Open Mic Mondays and obscure bands with promising names: A Decent Animal, Fleeting Trance, Room for a Ghost.

Cafe du Nord (Map pp96-7; ☎ 415-861-5016; www.cafedunord.com; 2170 Market St; admission $7-15; ⌚ 7pm-2am) A 1930s downstairs speakeasy that serves 'em short and strong with live rockabilly, singer-songwriters and comedians, plus pulled-on-stage performances by the regular crowd of off-duty musicians and famous novelists.

Elbo Room (Map pp96-7; ☎ 415-552-7788; www.elbo.com; 647 Valencia St; admission $5-8; ⌚ 5pm-2am) Jazz, funk, soul and alterna-bands play on the upstairs stage for a groovy crossover clientele – the *New York Times* calls it 'a Benetton ad coming to life.'

Rickshaw Stop (Map pp88-9; ☎ 415-861-2011; www.rickshawstop.com; 155 Fell St; admission $7-12; ⌚ 6pm-2am) Noise-poppers, eccentric rockers and crafty DJs cross-pollinate hemispheres with something for everyone: bad-ass banghra nights, Latin explosion bands, 'homofabulous' Rebel Girl for the ladies on third Saturdays and bouncy Cockblock on second Saturdays.

Ritespot Café (Map pp96-7; ☎ 415-552-6066; www.ritespotcafe.net; 2099 Folsom St; ⌚ 6pm-2am) A dive with a difference: it's a supper club with white tablecloths and experimental bands in the corner, from Gypsy jazz to Toshio Hirano (aka the Japanese Hank Williams). Staff is casual and friendly, though stern with loud talkers during sets.

Bimbo's 365 Club (Map pp94-5; ☎ 415-474-0365; www.bimbos365club.com; 1025 Columbus Ave; tickets $15-40; ⌚ shows 7pm & 8pm) Anything goes behind these plush lounge velvet curtains, as it has since 1951. Recent bills featured manic Cambodian-Californian dance band Dengue Fever, the occasional singer-songwriter like Iron & Wine, and several full swing bands catering to North Beach's lindy hopping/rockabilly set.

Amnesia (Map pp96-7; ☎ 415-970-0012; www.amnesiathebar.com; 853 Valencia St; ⌚ 6pm-2am) A teensy bar featuring nightly local music acts that may be playing in public for the first time, so show hardworking bands some love and buy that shy rapper a drink.

Theater

San Francisco was brought back to its feet after the 1906 earthquake by its scrappy theater venues, and they've been keeping audiences on their feet ever since.

American Conservatory Theater (Map pp88-9; ACT; ☎ 415-749-2228; act-sf.org; 415 Geary St) San Francisco's most famous mainstream venue has put on original landmark productions of Tony Kushner's *Angels in America* and Robert Wilson's *Black Rider,* with a libretto by William S Burroughs and music by the Bay Area's own Tom Waits.

Magic Theatre (Map pp94-5; ☎ 415-441-8822; www.magictheatre.org; 3rd fl, Bldg D, Fort Mason Center; ⌚ shows 8pm) Probably the city's most adventurous large theater, staging provocative plays by Bill Pullman, Terrence McNally, Edna O'Brien, David Mamet and longtime playwright-in-residence Sam Shepard, plus staged works written by teenagers.

Beach Blanket Babylon (Map pp92-3; ☎ 415-421-4222; www.beachblanketbabylon.com; 678 Green St; admission $25-78; ⌚ 8pm Wed-Thu, 7pm & 10pm Fri & Sat, 2pm & 5pm Sun) San Francisco's longest-running comedy cabaret still packs them in with giant hats, killer drag and cutting satire. Spectators must be 21-plus, except at matinees.

Musicals and Broadway spectaculars play at a number of downtown theaters. Call ☎ 415-512-7770 for tickets for the **Orpheum Theatre** (Map pp88-9; ☎ 415-551-2000; 1192 Market St), recently restored to rococo splendor and showing world-class comedy acts and hit musicals; **Curran Theatre** (Map pp88-9; ☎ 415-551-2000; 445 Geary St) with Broadway-style opulence, though avoid the balcony seats with limited legroom; and **Golden Gate Theatre** (Map pp88-9; ☎ 415-551-2000; 1 Taylor St at Market St), touring Broadway shows in slightly shabby 1920s glamour.

San Francisco has many small theater spaces that host solo and experimental shows, including:

Cobb's Comedy Club (Map pp92-3; ☎ 415-928-4320; www.cobbscomedyclub.com; 915 Columbus Ave; admission $10-35 plus a 2-drink minimum; ⌚ 8pm & 11pm) Bumper-to-bumper shared tables make for an intimate (and vulnerable) audience for stand-up acts.

THE ULTIMATE SF FASHION STATEMENT

San Francisco toughs and salty dogs have been getting tattooed since before California was a state, and today you'll see piercings and tattoos on everyone from Mission baristas to downtown venture capitalists. If you want to take home a permanent souvenir of your time in SF, the following shops are well-respected locally for being personable, professional, sterile and creative:

- **Cold Steel America** (Map pp96-7; ☎ 415-933-7233; 1783 Haight St) Body art options range from namesake steel to wood, horn, bone and glass.
- **Black & Blue Tattoo** (Map pp96-7; ☎ 415-626-0770; www.blackandbluetattoo.com; 381 Guerrero St) Highly regarded for art without attitude; women-owned and operated. Reviewing artists' books and consulting before you commit is recommended.
- **Braindrops** (Map pp96-7; ☎ 415-621-4162; www.braindrops.net; 1324 Haight St; noon-8pm Mon-Sat, to 7pm Sun) New Yorkers and Berliners fly in for original designs by top tattoo artists – bring design ideas to your consult or trust them to make suggestions.

Exit Theatre (Map pp88-9; ☎ 415-673-3847; www.sffringe.org; 156 Eddy St; admission $15-20; box office 30min before shows) Hosts the SF Fringe Festival and avant-garde productions year-round.

Intersection for the Arts (Map pp96-7; ☎ 415-626-2787; www.theintersection.org; 446 Valencia; admission $5-20; 7pm or 8pm) Ambidextrous art space with famous playwrights-in-residence, a major jazz showcase and an excellent upstairs gallery since 1965.

Marsh (Map pp96-7; ☎ 415-641-0235; www.themarsh.org; 1062 Valencia St; tickets $8-35; 8pm Thu-Sun) A breeding ground for SF's comedy and dramatic talent, with one-acts and one-person shows.

Punch Line (Map pp88-9; ☎ 415-397-4337; www.punchlinecomedyclub.com; 444 Battery St; admission $8-20, plus 2-drink minimum; 9pm Sun-Thu, 9pm & 11pm Fri & Sat) Turns unknown comics into known names – Chris Rock, Ellen DeGeneres and David Cross, to name a few.

Theatre Rhinoceros (Map pp96-7; ☎ 415-861-5079; 2926 16th St) SF's premier queer theater venue, with original and touring productions.

CLASSICAL MUSIC & OPERA

Davies Symphony Hall (Map pp88-9; ☎ 415-864-6000; www.sfsymphony.org; 201 Van Ness Ave; box office 10am-6pm Mon-Fri, noon-6pm Sat) Conducted by Michael Tilson Thomas, the San Francisco Symphony performs from September to May here – don't miss Beethoven.

War Memorial Opera House (Map pp88-9; ☎ 415-864-3330; www.sfopera.com; 301 Van Ness Ave; box office 10am-6pm Mon-Fri) San Francisco Opera performs here from September to mid-December. Student tickets and standing-room tickets go on sale two hours before performances.

Herbst Theatre (Map pp88-9; ☎ 415-392-4400; www.performances.org; 401 Van Ness Ave; box office 1hr before performances) The UN Charter was signed here in 1945; now it hosts classical performances and the City Arts & Lectures series.

DANCE

San Francisco Ballet (☎ 415-861-5600 information, 415-865-2000 tickets; www.sfballet.org; tickets $7-100) This reknowned company performs at the War Memorial Opera House, Herbst Theater and Yerba Buena Center for the Arts (p107).

ODC Theater (Map pp96-7; ☎ 415-863-9834; www.odctheater.org; 3153 17th St) Modern dance nearly every weekend year-round featuring local and international artists.

Theater Artaud (Map pp96-7; ☎ 415-626-4370; www.artaud.org/theater; 450 Florida St; tickets $15-25) Frequently hosts performances by local choreographers and dance troupes.

Cinemas

Raucous, interactive crowds at vintage rep cinemas make movie-going an unforgettable SF experience.

our pick **Castro Theatre** (Map pp96-7; ☎ 415-621-6120; 429 Castro St; adult/child/senior $9.50/7/7) Showtunes on a Wurlitzer are the overture to independent cinema, silver-screen classics and unstoppable audience participation, plus the Gay and Lesbian Film Festival in June (see p116).

Sundance Kabuki Cinema (Map pp86-7; ☎ 415-929-4650; www.sundancecinemas.com/kabuki; 1881 Post St; admission $9.50-11) Trendsetting green multiplex with GMO-free popcorn, reserved seating in cushy seats made with recycled materials and the frankly brilliant Balcony Bar, where you can slurp seasonal cocktails during your movie. Charges $1.50 more per ticket than chains, because there are no ads. Hosts the revered

San Francisco International Film Festival each April (p116).

Roxie Cinema (Map pp96-7; ☎ 415-863-1087; www.roxie.com; 3117 16th St; evening/matinee $9/6) Independent gems, insightful documentaries and rare film noir you won't find elsewhere, in a landmark 1909 cinema recently restored and upgraded with Dolby sound.

Balboa Theater (Map p91; ☎ 415-221-8184; www.balboamovies.com; 3630 Balboa St; double-features adult/child/senior $9/6.50/6.50) Double-features perfect for foggy weather, including film fest contenders selected by the director of the Telluride Film Festival, in a renovated 1926 art-deco cinema.

Red Vic Movie House (Map pp96-7; ☎ 415-668-3994; www.redvicmoviehouse.com; 1727 Haight St; adult/senior/matinee $8.50/5/6.50) Collectively owned and operated cinema draws crowds with cult classics, surf documentaries, local and forgotten gems, couches and popcorn with optional brewer's yeast.

Sports

San Francisco 49ers (off Map pp86-7; ☎ 415-656-4900; www.49ers.com; Candlestick Park; tickets from $59; season Aug-Dec) One of the most successful teams in National Football League history, with no fewer than five Super Bowl championships. Home for the 49ers is the cold and windy Candlestick Park, off Hwy 101 in the southern part of the city. The park officially reverted to its original name in 2008, after naming rights were leased to 3 Com and Monster, and San Franciscans refused for 12 years to acknowledge the corporate name changes.

San Francisco Giants (Map pp88-9; ☎ 415-972-2000; http://sanfrancisco.giants.mlb.com; AT&T Park; tickets Mon-Thu/Fri & Sat/premium games from $10/17/25; season Apr-Oct) The city's National League baseball team draws crowds to AT&T Park and its solar-powered scoreboard. Locals annoyed by the park's merger-initiated corporate name changes (from Pac Bell to SBC to AT&T) refer to it as 'Giants' Stadium.' Outside the park, the Waterfront Promenade offers a free view of right field.

SHOPPING

San Francisco has big department stores and name-brand boutiques around Union Sq, including **Macy's** (Map pp88-9; ☎ 415-397-3333; www.macys.com; 170 O'Farrell Street), the sprawling new **Westfield Shopping Centre** (Map pp88-9; www.westfield.com/sanfrancisco; 865 Market St; 9:30am-9pm Mon-Sat, 10am-7pm Sun). But special, only-in-SF scores are found in the Haight, the Castro, the Mission and Hayes Valley (west of Civic Center).

Here's where to go for what on the major shopping thoroughfares:

Castro St Men's style, housewares and gifts for a good cause.
Clement St Foodie finds, books, Chinese herbal remedies and fun T-shirts.
Grant St Tea, paper lanterns and cheapo souvenirs.
Haight St Music, vintage, drag, shoes and tie-dye that just won't die.
Hayes Valley Indie designers and high-style housewares.
Union St Fine wines and flirty dresses.
Valencia St Local designers, pirate supplies, thrift and books.

Clothing & Accessories

our pick **Piedmont Boutique** (Map pp96-7; ☎ 415-864-8075; 1452 Haight St; 11am-7pm) Glam up or get out at this supplier of drag fabulousness: pleather hot pants, airplane earrings and a wall of feather boas.

MAC (Map pp88-9; ☎ 415-863-3011; 387 Grove St; 11am-7pm Mon-Sat, noon-6pm Sun) Impeccably structured looks for men from Belgian minimalist Dries Van Noten and Tsumori Chisato's Japanese luxe for the ladies; superb 40% to 75% off sales rack.

Velvet da Vinci (Map pp88-9; ☎ 415-441-0109; www.velvetdavinci.com; 2015 Polk St; noon-6pm Tue-Sat, to 4pm Sun) Ingenious jewelry by local and international artisans: Julia Turner's satellite-dish ring, Ben Neubauer's cage earrings, a drinking flask bracelet by William Clark.

Doe (Map pp96-7; ☎ 415-558-8588; www.doe-sf.com; 629a Haight St; noon-7pm Mon-Sat, to 6pm Sun) Local designers and handmade jewelry for women, men's limited-edition tees and hoodies, and cutie-pie kids' stuff.

Residents Apparel Gallery (Map pp88-9; ☎ 415-621-7718; www.ragsf.com; 541 Octavia St; noon-7pm Mon-Sat, to 5pm Sun) Local designers at design-school prices make eclectic SF chic easy at this certified green cooperative boutique.

Community Thrift (Map pp96-7; ☎ 415-861-4910; www.communitythrift.bravehost.com; 623 Valencia St; 10am-6:30pm) Vintage home furnishing scores and local retailer overstock, all sold to benefit local charities.

Jeremy's (Map pp88-9; ☎ 415-882-4929; www.jeremys.com; 2 South Park Ave; 11am-6pm Mon-Sat, to 5pm Sun) Window displays, photo shoot ensembles and department store customer returns translate to jaw-dropping bargains on major designers for men and women.

Sunhee Moon (Map pp96-7; ☎ 415-355-1800; www.sunheemoon.com; 3167 16th St; 🕒 noon-7pm Mon-Fri, to 6pm Sat & Sun) Local designer specializing in simple shapes and vibrant solids to flatter petites and curves alike.

Nancy Boy (Map pp88-9; ☎ 415-552-3802; www.nancyboy.com; 347 Hayes St; 🕒 11am-6pm Mon-Fri, to 7pm Sat & Sun) Wear these highly effective moisturizers, pomades and sun balms with pride, all locally made with plant oils and tested on boyfriends, never animals.

Dema (Map pp96-7; ☎ 415-206-0500; www.godemago.com; 1038 Valencia St; 🕒 11am-7pm Mon-Fri, noon-6pm Sat & Sun) Wear-everywhere shifts in vintage-inspired prints by local designer Dema, plus clever cardigans and Orla Kiely tees.

Upper Playground (Map pp96-7; ☎ 415-861-1960; www.upperplayground.com; 220 Fillmore St; 🕒 11am-7pm) Skate gear and the best SF nonsouvenirs: Grotesk Golden State hoodies, knit MUNI caps, 'I'm in a San Francisco State of Mind' tees.

Delilah Crown (Map pp92-3; ☎ 415-765-9060; www.delilahcrown.com; 524 Green St; 🕒 11am-6:30pm Tue-Sat, noon-5pm Sun) Casual flair with crafty details – pintucking, contrasting buttons, vintage patterns – for women and babies from SF designer Kristina De Pizzol.

Mingle (Map pp94-5; ☎ 415-674-8811; www.mingleshop.com; 1815 Union St; 🕒 11am-6:30pm Mon & Wed-Fri, noon-6pm Tue, 10am-7pm Sat, 11am-6pm Sun) Break up the H&M monotony with original designs by local designers: hot Heidi dirndl dresses, screen-printed tees, horn-button handbags.

Madame S & Mr S Leather (Map pp88-9; ☎ 415-863-9447, 415-863-7764; www.madame-s.com, www.mr-s-leather.com; 385 8th St; 🕒 11am-7pm) S&M superstore, with such musts as leashes, dungeon furniture and for that special someone, a chrome-plated codpiece.

Wasteland (Map pp96-7; ☎ 415-863-3150; www.thewasteland.com; 1660 Haight St; 🕒 11am-8pm) The catwalk of thrifting: psychedelic Pucci prints, deconstructed Yohji Yamamoto coats and a steady supply of go-go boots.

Margaret O'Leary (Map pp88-9; ☎ 415-391-1010; www.margaretoleary.com; 1 Claude Lane; 🕒 10am-5pm Tue-Sat) Local designer specializing in ultrasoft knitwear with a sleek urban edge – perfect for a town where sweaters are a must and frumpiness the ultimate fashion crime.

Sui Generis (Map pp96-7; ☎ 415-436-9661; 218 Church St; 🕒 noon-7pm Tue-Thu, to 8pm Fri & Sat, to 4pm Sun) Fedoras, windbreakers, Pendleton wool shirts and other select vintage for small–medium men.

Wine & Food

Ferry Plaza Farmers Market (Map pp88-9; ☎ 415-291-3276; www.cuesa.org; Ferry Bldg; 🕒 10am-2pm Tue, 8am-2pm Sat) While locals grouse that prices are higher here than at neighborhood farmers markets, this one offers local specialty foods that tantalize professional chefs and semiprofessional eaters alike. Indoors there are local gourmet shops selling wild-harvested mushrooms, sustainably farmed Marin caviar and an embarrassment of cheeses.

Ferry Plaza Wine Merchant (Map pp88-9; ☎ 415-391-9400; www.fpwm.com; 1 Ferry Plaza; 🕒 11am-8pm Mon-Wed, 10am-9pm Thu-Fri, 8am-9pm Saturday, 10am-7pm Sun) Part tasting room, part wine bar, totally tasty (hic). Staff are knowledgeable and the wine list is written in a colloquial way to make nonsnobs feel welcome.

Heart of the City Farmers Market (Map pp88-9; ☎ 415-558-9455; UN Plaza; 🕒 7am-5pm Sun & Wed year-round) A growing number of local farmers and producers sell sustainably sourced California produce here at bargain prices.

PlumpJack Wines (Map pp94-5; ☎ 415-346-9870; www.plumpjack.com; 3201 Fillmore St; 🕒 11am-8pm Mon-Fri, 10am-8pm Sat, 11am-6pm Sun) Large selection under $15 at the distinctive wine boutique owned by San Francisco Mayor Gavin Newsom.

Recchiuti Chocolates (Map pp88-9; ☎ 415-834-9494; www.recchiuticonfections.com; 1 Ferry Bldg; 🕒 10am-6pm Mon-Tue, to 7pm Wed-Fri, 8am-6pm Sat, 10am-5pm Sun) Scintillating SF-made chocolates, including fleur de sel caramels, gourmet s'more bites and edible chocolate paintings by local artist Rex Ray.

Gifts & Housewares

our pick **Under One Roof** (Map pp96-7; ☎ 415-503-2300; www.underoneroof.org; 518S Castro St; 🕒 10am-8pm Mon-Sat, 11am-7pm Sun) AIDS service organizations get 100% of the proceeds from goods donated by local designers and retailers, so show volunteer salespeople some love for raising $11 million to date.

Rare Device (Map pp96-7; ☎ 415-863-3969; www.raredevice.net; 1845 Market St; 🕒 noon-7pm Tue, Wed, Fri & Sat, to 9pm Thu, to 6pm Sun) Something unique, locally designed and well under $75 for everyone: webmaster-chic manbags, felted candy bowls, SF silver fog necklaces, retro letterpress prints of Painted Ladies.

Park Life (Map p91; ☎ 415-386-7275; www.parklifestore.com; 220 Clement St; 🕒 11am-8pm Mon-Thu, noon-8pm Fri & Sat) Design store, indie publisher and art gallery with gift options: smiling cupcake tees, Park Life's catalog of SF jazz portraitist Ian Johnson and librarian-chic laser-cut necklaces that command READ.

Polk-a-Dot (Map pp88-9; ☎ 415-346-0660; 1742 Polk St; ⏰ 11:30am-6:30pm Mon-Sat, noon-6pm Sun) Stationery, toys and delightful dead stock overflow doll-size chests of drawers: antique mah-jong tiles, wooden nuns, badges for diminutive sheriffs.

Human Rights Campaign Action Center & Store (Map pp96-7; ☎ 415-431-2200; www.hrc.org; 600 Castro St) Signature HRC boxer briefs, accessories and tees designed by Marc Jacobs, Heatherette and other fashion-forward-thinkers, with proceeds supporting civil rights initiatives.

Atys (Map pp94-5; ☎ 415-441-9220; www.atysdesign.com; 2149b Union St; ⏰ 11am-6:30pm Mon-Sat, noon-5pm Sun) Designer version 2.0 of essential household goods: elephant-shaped 'Hannibal' tape dispensers, streamlined Alessi espresso makers, locally designed 'Wooly Hoodwinks' stuffed animals made of reclaimed tweeds.

Studio (Map pp88-9; ☎ 415-931-3130; www.studiogallerysf.com; 1718a Polk St; ⏰ 11am-8pm Wed-Fri, to 6pm Sat-Sun) Winsome locally made arts and crafts at bargain prices, including Toru Sugita's SF cityscape etchings, Joanna Mendicino's white bird vases and silver-link necklaces in the shape of a serotonin molecule.

Cameras

Adolph Gasser (Map pp88-9; ☎ 415-495-3852; www.gassers.com; 181 2nd St; ⏰ 9am-6pm Mon-Fri, 10am-5pm Sat) A huge range of new and used photographic and video equipment; also processes film.

Music

Aquarius Records (Map pp96-7; ☎ 415-647-2272; www.aquariusrecords.org; 1055 Valencia St) Since 1970 this SF music scene institution has specialized in local bands, rare finds and genre-defying sounds: Japanese doom bands, Finnish psychedelia group Paavoharju, sections dedicated to 'trance space bliss innerspace drone,' and oodles of John Cale.

Amoeba Records (Map pp96-7; ☎ 415-831-1200; www.amoeba.com; 1855 Haight St; ⏰ 10:30pm-10pm Mon-Sat, 11am-9pm Sun) Bowling-alley-turned-superstore of new and used records in all genres, plus free in-store concerts and Music We Like 'zine for great new finds.

Outdoor Gear

SFO Snowboarding & FTC Skateboarding (Map pp96-7; ☎ 415-626-1141; www.sfosnow.com; 1630 Haight St; ⏰ 11am-7pm Mon-Sat, to 6pm Sun) State-of-the-art gear, snowboards and skateboards, some with designs by local artists.

Sports Basement (Map pp94-5; ☎ 415-437-0100; www.sportsbasement.com; 610 Mason St; ⏰ 9am-8pm Mon-Fri, 8am-7pm Sat & Sun) There's 70,000 sq ft of sports and camping equipment housed in the Presidio's former US Army PX; free coffee and hot cider while you shop.

For locally designed surf gear, check out **Mollusk** (off Map p91; ☎ 415-564-6300; www.mollusksurfshop.com; 4500 Irving St; ⏰ 9am-7pm) and **Aqua** (Map pp96-7; ☎ 415-876-2782; www.aquasurfshop.com; 1742 Haight St; ⏰ 3-7pm Wed-Fri, 10am-6pm Sat & Sun); see the boxed text, p111.

GETTING THERE & AWAY

Air

The Bay Area has three major airports: **San Francisco International Airport** (SFO; ☎ 650-821-8211), on the west side of the bay; Oakland International Airport (see p168), a few miles across the bay on the east side; and San José International Airport (p188), at the southern end of the bay. The majority of international flights use SFO. Travelers from other US cities may find cheaper flights into Oakland on discount airlines such as JetBlue and Southwest.

SFO is on the Peninsula, 14 miles south of downtown San Francisco, off Hwy 101. Improvements over the last decade include a new international terminal and a BART extension directly to the airport. All three SFO terminals have ATMs and information booths on the lower level, and **Travelers' Aid information booths** (⏰ 9am-9pm) on the upper level. The airport paging and information line is staffed 24 hours; call from any white courtesy phone.

Bus

All bus services arrive at and depart from the **Transbay Terminal** (Map pp88-9; 425 Mission St at 1st St), two blocks south of Market St. **AC Transit** (☎ 415-817-1717, 511; www.actransit.org) buses run to/from the East Bay; **Golden Gate Transit** (☎ 415-455-2000, 511; www.goldengatetransit.org) buses run north to Marin and Sonoma counties; and **SamTrans** (☎ 800-660-4287; www.samtrans.com) travels to Palo Alto and along the coast.

Greyhound (☎ 800-231-2222; www.greyhound.com; 425 Mission St) buses also leave from the Transbay Terminal, with multiple buses daily to Los Angeles ($45.50, eight to 12 hours) and other destinations.

Car & Motorcycle

All major car-rental operators are represented at the airports, and many have downtown offices.

Alamo (Map pp88-9; ☎ 415-693-0191, 800-327-9633; www.goalamo.com; 750 Bush St; 🕑 7am-7pm)

Avis (Map pp88-9; ☎ 415-885-5011, 800-331-1212; www.avis.com; 675 Post St; 🕑 6am-6pm)

Budget (Map pp88-9; ☎ 415-957-9998, 800-527-0700; www.budget.com; 821 Howard St; 🕑 7:30am-5:30pm Mon-Fri, 8am-2pm Sat-Sun)

Dollar (Map pp88-9; ☎ 866-434-2226, 800-800-4000; www.dollarcar.com; 364 O'Farrell St; 🕑 7am-7pm)

Hertz (Map pp88-9; ☎ 415-771-2200, 800-654-3131; www.hertz.com; 433 Mason St; 🕑 6am-6pm Mon-Thu, to 8pm Fri & Sat)

Thrifty (Map pp88-9; ☎ 415-788-8111, 800-367-2277; www.thrifty.com; 520 Mason St; 🕑 7am-7pm)

Ferry

The opening of the Bay Bridge (in 1936) and the Golden Gate Bridge (in 1937) spelled the near demise of the ferries, although in recent years they have enjoyed a modest revival for both commuters and tourists. For Alcatraz Cruises, see p85.

Blue & Gold Fleet Ferries (Map pp88-9; ☎ 415-705-5555, 415-705-8200; www.blueandgoldfleet.com) The Alameda–Oakland Ferry runs from the Ferry Building to Jack London Sq in Oakland ($6.25, 30 minutes). Ferries to Tiburon, Sausalito and Angel Island (see p152) run from Pier 41 at Fisherman's Wharf.

Golden Gate Ferries (☎ 415-923-2000; www.goldengateferry.org; 🕑 6am-10pm Mon-Fri, 10am-6pm Sat & Sun) Regular services run from the Ferry Building to Larkspur and Sausalito in Marin County (see p151). Transfers are available to MUNI bus services, and bicycles are permitted.

Vallejo Ferries (☎ 415-773-1188; one way adult/child $15/7.50) Blue & Gold also operates the Vallejo Ferry from the Ferry Building on weekdays and from Pier 39 at Fisherman's Wharf on weekends and holidays, for bay cruises and connections to the Six Flags Marine World theme park in Vallejo (p179).

Train

CalTrain (☎ 800-660-4287) links San Francisco to the South Bay, including Palo Alto (Stanford University) and San Jose. The CalTrain terminal (Map pp88–9) is at the corner of 4th and Townsend Sts. MUNI's N-Judah streetcar line runs to and from the CalTrain station.

The nearest **Amtrak** (☎ 800-872-7245) terminals are in Emeryville and Oakland (see p169), with bus service to San Francisco's Ferry Building.

GETTING AROUND

To/From the Airport

The direct 30-minute **Bay Area Rapid Transit** (BART; ☎ 415-989-2278) train service runs from the airport to downtown San Francisco ($5.15), connecting to Oakland via the AirBART shuttle (p726).

The express bus KX ($4, 30 minutes) and slower local bus 292 ($1.50, 50 minutes) run by **SamTrans** (☎ 800-660-4287) leave from the SFO BART station and drop you at San Francisco's Transbay Terminal (see opposite).

Door-to-door shuttle vans are cheaper than cabs if you're traveling alone. They pick up/drop off from any San Francisco location to/from SFO, but they usually take some time circulating to different hotels to pick up more passengers. Call for a reservation for pickups in SF; at SFO, vans leave frequently from the baggage claim level outside all terminals. One-way fares are $15 to $20.

American Airporter Shuttle (☎ 415-202-0733, 800-282-7758)

Quake City (☎ 415-255-4899)

Super Shuttle (☎ 415-558-8500; www.supershuttle.com)

Bicycle

San Francisco is bike-able, but traffic downtown can be dangerous; bicycling is best east of Van Ness Ave and across the bay. For bike shops and rentals, see p111. Bicycles are allowed on BART, but there are restrictions. During morning commute hours (7am to 9am), bikes are allowed in the Embarcadero Station only for trips to the East Bay. During evening commute hours (4:30pm to 6:45pm), bicyclists are not allowed on trains to the East Bay, and bicyclists traveling into San Francisco in commute hours must exit at the Embarcadero Station.

Car & Motorcycle

If at all possible, avoid driving in San Francisco: traffic is a given, parking meter readers are ruthless and street parking is harder to find than true love in a SoMa bar at 3am. Gas prices are rising steadily, and driving on these hills means shifting gears and applying brakes often – and contending with drivers who think they're Steve McQueen in *Bullitt*. But if you're planning a break in wine country or the redwoods, you might want your own wheels; see above for rental agencies. Before you set out to any bridge or other traffic choke-point, call ☎ 511 toll-free for a traffic update. **AAA** (Map pp88-9; ☎ 415-565-2012, emergency road service & towing 800-222-4357; www.aaa.com; 150 Van Ness Ave) can help members with roadside service.

Parking restrictions in San Francisco are strictly enforced. When parking in SF on hill streets (with a grade as slight as 3%), you must curb your wheels toward the street when facing uphill, toward the curb on a downhill. Failure to do so can result in fines. Parking in bus stops and blue wheelchair spots can leave you with fines of $250 or more. Blocking a rush-hour lane, a downtown loading zone (yellow) or a driveway can result in a costly tow. Beware also of street-cleaning days and signs in residential neighborhoods indicating a residential permit system (tickets $35). If you suspect your car has been towed, call **AutoReturn** (Map pp88-9; ☎ 415-558-7411; Rm 145, 850 Bryant St).

Some of the cheaper downtown parking garages are **Sutter-Stockton Garage** (Map pp88-9; ☎ 415-982-7275; cnr Sutter & Stockton Sts), **Ellis-O'Farrell Garage** (Map pp88-9; ☎ 415-986-4800; 123 O'Farrell St) and **Fifth & Mission Garage** (Map pp88-9; ☎ 415-982-8522; 833 Mission St), near Yerba Buena Gardens. The parking garage under Portsmouth Sq in Chinatown is reasonably priced for shorter stops; ditto for the **St Mary's Square Garage** (☎ 415-956-8106; California St), under the square, at Grant and Kearny Sts. Daily rates range between $18 and $28.

Public Transportation

BART

The **Bay Area Rapid Transit system** (BART; ☎ 415-989-2278; www.bart.gov; 🕑 4am-midnight Mon-Fri, 6am-midnight Sat, 8am-midnight Sun) is a subway system linking SFO, the Mission District, downtown, San Francisco and the East Bay. Downtown, the BART route runs beneath Market St, and it's a quick 10-minute ride to the Mission District; take any train heading south. BART is convenient, economical and generally quite safe, although caution is required around some BART stations at night.

One-way fares start at $1.25 within San Francisco, and range between $2 and $5 from downtown to various outlying areas. From San Francisco BART stations, half-price transfers ($1) are available for MUNI bus and streetcar services, and should be bought at white MUNI ticket machines before you exit the BART paid area.

MUNI

San Francisco's principal public-transportation system is the **San Francisco Municipal Railway** (MUNI; ☎ 415-673-6864; www.sfmuni.com; tickets adult/5-17yr/senior $1.50/50¢/50¢; 🕑 5am-late night weekdays, reduced schedules weekends), which operates nearly 100 bus lines (many of them electric trolley buses), Metro streetcars, historic streetcars and the famous cable cars. The detailed *Street & Transit Map* costs $3 and is available at newspaper stands around Union Sq. A timetable or electronic display is provided at some bus stops, but don't expect your bus to always be on time.

Standard MUNI fares are $1.50 for buses or streetcars and $5 for cable cars. Tickets are available on board, but you'll need exact change on buses and streetcars. Tickets are valid until the expiration time noted on your ticket, and you can then use them for two connecting trips within about 90 minutes or so. However, they are *not* transferable to cable cars. Hang onto your ticket even if you're not planning to use it again – if you're caught without one by the transit police, you're subject to a $75 fine.

A one-day ($11) or three-day ($18) MUNI Passport allows unlimited travel on all MUNI transportation, including cable cars; the seven-day ($24) Passport requires an additional $1 payment on cable cars. Passports can be purchased at the MUNI kiosk at the Powell St cable car stop on Market, from the half-price ticket kiosk on Union Sq and from a number of hotels. Monthly MUNI Fast Passes are good for buses, streetcars and cable cars. They cost $45 for adults, $10 for seniors and students, and can be purchased from shops with the MUNI Pass sign.

Taxi

Fares start at $3.30 at the flag drop and run about $2.25 per mile. Add at least 10% to the taxi fare as a tip (starting at $1, even for fares under $6).

These taxi companies have 24-hour dispatches:

Arrow Taxicab (☎ 415-648-3181)
De Soto Cab (☎ 415-970-1300)
Green Cab (☎ 415-626-4733; www.greencab.com) Hybrid, fuel-efficient vehicles; worker-owned collective with eight vehicles currently in circulation.
Luxor Cab (☎ 282-4141)

San Francisco Bay Area

Based on the number of people who will tell you they're from San Francisco, you could think that the City by the Bay was inhabited by several million. When pressed, many folks will explain that they actually live in the 'Bay Area,' which embraces the many cities and towns to the north, east and south of San Francisco's 7-sq-mile peninsula. But unlike most bedroom and commuter communities fanning out from a major city, the region surrounding San Francisco encompasses numerous destinations in their own right.

The Bay Area has a bonanza of natural vistas and close-by wildlife. You can cross the Golden Gate Bridge to Marin and visit wizened ancient redwoods body-blocking the sun, and herds of elegant elk prancing along the bluffs of Tomales Bay. Gray whales show some fluke off the cape of wind-scoured Point Reyes, and hawks surf the skies in the pristine hills of the Marin Headlands.

On the cutting edge of intellectual thought, the scholarly halls of Palo Alto and UC Berkeley draw academics and students from around the world, and the city of Berkeley sparked the locavore food movement and continues to be on the forefront of environmental and left-leaning political causes. Down south, the technology hotspot of Silicon Valley lures computer geeks and the entrepreneurs who love them.

Perhaps most importantly, when the fog creeps in and chills San Francisco, the rest of the Bay Area can be balmy enough for swimming or outdoor dining, something that drives many to escape the glittery big city on a frigid summer day.

HIGHLIGHTS

- **Closest encounter with marine mammals** Spying on the elephant seals at Año Nuevo State Reserve (p193)
- **Best outdoor buzz** Hiking or biking the perimeter of panoramic Angel Island (p152)
- **Best wildlife bonanza** Cavorting with elk and gray whales at the Point Reyes National Seashore (p160)
- **Tastiest food trail** Feasting your way through Berkeley's delectable Gourmet Ghetto (p175)
- **Best chill-out hideaway** Cooling off with a cannonball splash at blissful Bass Lake (p158)

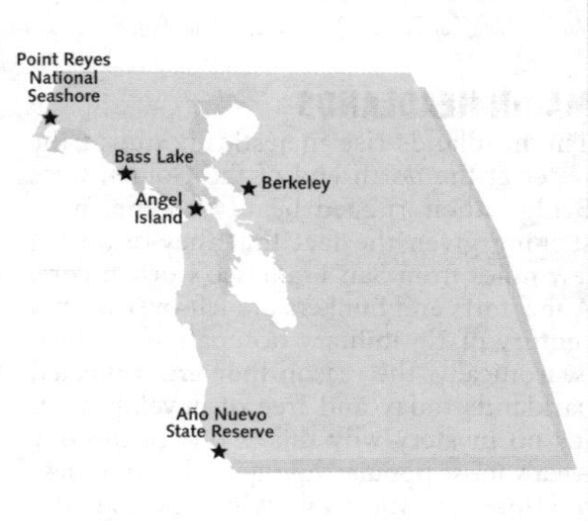

MARIN COUNTY

If there's a part of the Bay Area that consciously attempts to live up to the California dream, it's Marin County. Just across the Golden Gate Bridge from San Francisco, the region has a wealthy population which cultivates a seemingly laid-back lifestyle. Towns may look like idyllic rural hamlets, but the shops cater to cosmopolitan and expensive tastes. The 'common' folk here eat organic, vote Democrat and drive hybrids.

Geographically, Marin County is a near mirror image of San Francisco. It's a south-pointing peninsula that nearly touches the north-pointing tip of the city, and is surrounded by ocean and bay. But Marin is wilder, greener and more mountainous. Redwoods grow on the coast side of the hills, the surf crashes against cliffs, and hiking and biking trails crisscross the blessed scenery of Point Reyes, Muir Woods and Mt Tamalpais. Nature is what makes Marin County such an excellent day trip from San Francisco.

Busy Hwy 101 heads north from the Golden Gate Bridge ($6 toll when heading back into San Francisco), spearing through Marin's middle; quiet Hwy 1 winds its way along the sparsely populated coast. In San Rafael, Sir Francis Drake Blvd cuts across west Marin from Hwy 101 to the ocean.

Hwy 580 comes in from the East Bay over the Richmond–San Rafael bridge ($4 toll for westbound traffic) to meet Hwy 101 at Larkspur.

For tourist information for the entire county, contact the **Marin County Visitors Bureau** (☎ 415-925-2060, 866-925-2060; www.visitmarin.org; 1 Mitchell Blvd, San Rafael; ⌚ 9am-5pm Mon-Fri).

MARIN HEADLANDS

The headlands rise majestically out of the water at the north end of the Golden Gate Bridge, their rugged beauty all the more striking given the fact that they're only a few miles from San Francisco's urban core. A few forts and bunkers are left over from a century of US military occupation – which is, ironically, the reason they are protected parklands today and free of development. It's no mystery why this is one of the Bay Area's most popular hiking and biking destinations. As the trails wind through the scenic headlands, they afford stunning views of the sea, the Golden Gate Bridge and San Francisco, leading to isolated beaches and secluded spots for picnics.

Orientation & Information

After crossing the Golden Gate Bridge, exit immediately at Alexander Ave, then dip left under the highway and head out west for the expansive views and hiking trailheads. Conzelman Rd snakes up into the hills, where it eventually forks. Conzelman Rd continues west, becoming a steep, one-lane road as it descends to Point Bonita, from where it continues to Rodeo Beach and Fort Barry. McCullough Rd heads inland, joining Bunker Rd toward Rodeo Beach.

Information is available from the **Golden Gate National Recreation Area** (GGNRA; ☎ 415-561-4700; www.nps.gov/goga) and the **Marin Headlands Visitors Center** (☎ 415-331-1540; www.nps.gov/goga/marin-headlands.htm; ⌚ 9:30am-4:30pm), in an old church off Bunker Rd near Fort Barry.

Sights

About 2 miles along Conzelman Rd is **Hawk Hill**, where thousands of migrating birds of prey soar along the cliffs from late summer to early fall. At the end of Conzelman Rd is the **Point Bonita Lighthouse** (⌚ 12:30-3:30pm Sat-Mon), a breathtaking half-mile walk from the parking area (which has limited spaces). From the tip of Point Bonita, you can see the distant Golden Gate Bridge and beyond it the tips of the San Francisco skyline. It's an uncommon vantage point of the baycentric city, and harbor seals haul out nearby in season. To visit the promontory on one of the free twice-monthly full-moon tours, call ☎ 415-331-1540 to reserve a spot.

File past guard shacks with uniformed mannequins to witness the area's not-too-distant military history at the **Nike Missile Site**

FAST FACTS

Population of Berkeley 101,500

Average temperature low/high in Berkeley Jan 43/56°F, Jul 54/70°F

Downtown Berkeley to Sacramento 80 miles, 1½ hours

San Jose to San Francisco 45 miles, one hour

San Francisco to Point Reyes Lighthouse 55 miles, 2½ hours

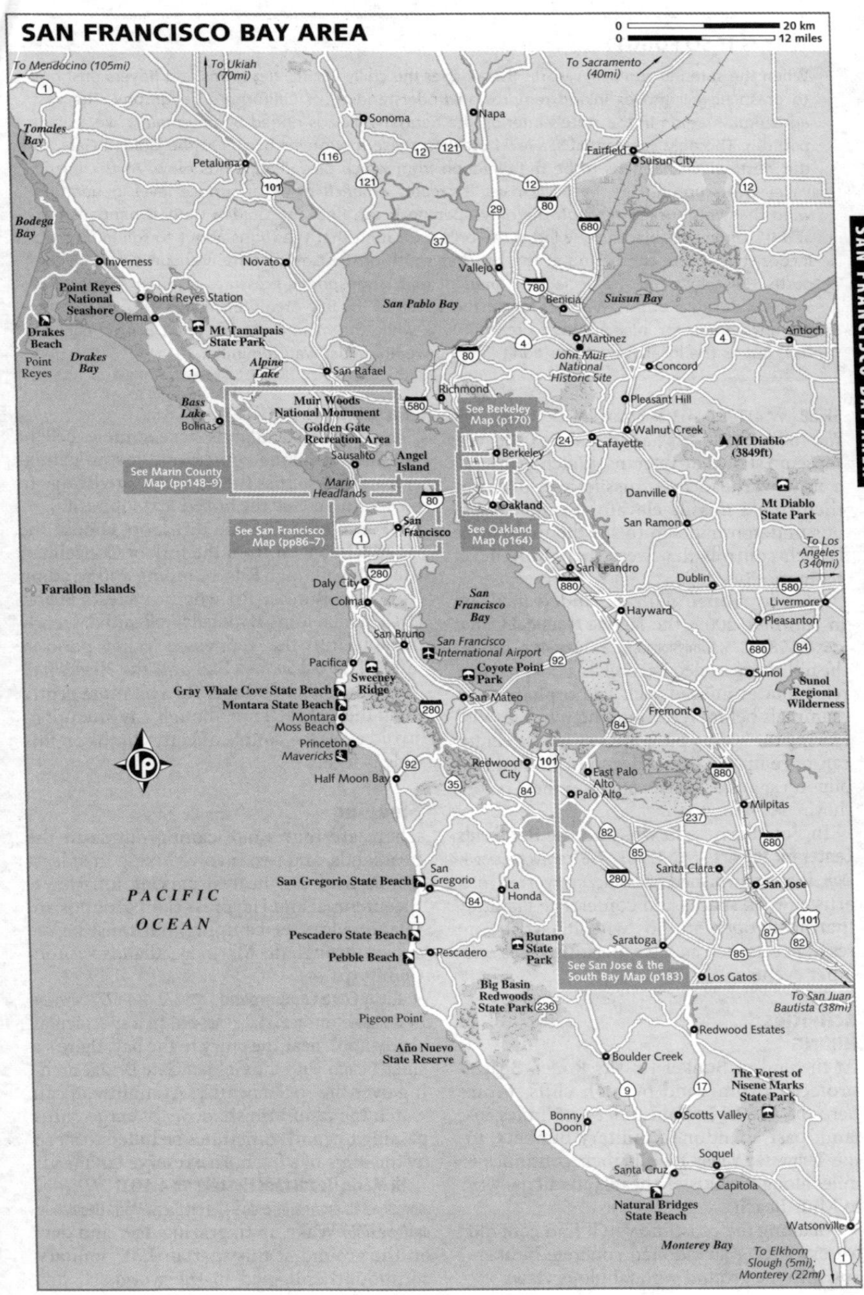
SAN FRANCISCO BAY AREA
20 km
12 miles
To Mendocino (105mi)
To Ukiah (70mi)
To Sacramento (40mi)
Tomales Bay
Sonoma
Napa
Petaluma
Fairfield
Suisun City
Bodega Bay
Inverness
Novato
Vallejo
Point Reyes National Seashore
Point Reyes Station
Olema
San Pablo Bay
Benicia
Suisun Bay
Drakes Beach
Mt Tamalpais State Park
Martinez
Antioch
Point Reyes
Drakes Bay
Alpine Lake
San Rafael
John Muir National Historic Site
Concord
Bass Lake
Bolinas
Muir Woods National Monument
Golden Gate Recreation Area
Richmond
See Berkeley Map (p170)
Pleasant Hill
Walnut Creek
Mt Diablo (3849ft)
Lafayette
Sausalito
Angel Island
Berkeley
See Marin County Map (pp148-9)
Marin Headlands
Oakland
Danville
Mt Diablo State Park
See San Francisco Map (pp86-7)
San Francisco
See Oakland Map (p164)
San Ramon
To Los Angeles (340mi)
San Leandro
Farallon Islands
Daly City
Dublin
Colma
San Francisco Bay
Livermore
Hayward
Pleasanton
San Bruno
San Francisco International Airport
Pacifica
Coyote Point Park
Sweeney Ridge
Sunol
Gray Whale Cove State Beach
San Mateo
Sunol Regional Wilderness
Montara State Beach
Fremont
Montara
Moss Beach
Princeton
Mavericks
Redwood City
East Palo Alto
Half Moon Bay
Palo Alto
Milpitas
Santa Clara
San Jose
San Gregorio State Beach
San Gregorio
La Honda
PACIFIC OCEAN
Pescadero State Beach
Butano State Park
Saratoga
Pebble Beach
Pescadero
See San Jose & the South Bay Map (p183)
Los Gatos
Big Basin Redwoods State Park
To San Juan Bautista (38mi)
Pigeon Point
Redwood Estates
Año Nuevo State Reserve
Boulder Creek
The Forest of Nisene Marks State Park
Bonny Doon
Scotts Valley
Soquel
Santa Cruz
Capitola
Natural Bridges State Beach
Watsonville
Monterey Bay
To Elkhorn Slough (5mi); Monterey (22mi)

WHY IS IT SO FOGGY?

When the summer sun's rays warm the air over the chilly Pacific, fog forms and hovers offshore; to grasp how it moves inland requires an understanding of California's geography. The vast agricultural region in the state's interior, the Central Valley, is ringed by mountains, like a giant bathtub. The only substantial sea-level break in these mountains occurs at the Golden Gate, to the west, which happens to be the direction from which prevailing winds blow. As the inland valley heats up and the warm air rises, it creates a deficit of air at surface level, generating wind that gets sucked through the only opening it can find: the Golden Gate. It happens fast and it's unpredictable. Gusty wind is the only indication that the fog is about to roll in. But it's inconsistent: there can be fog at the beaches south of the Golden Gate and sun a mile to the north. Hills block fog – especially at times of high atmospheric pressure, as often happens in summer. Because of this, weather forecasters speak of the Bay Area's 'microclimates.' In July it's not uncommon for inland areas to reach 100°F, while the mercury at the coast barely reaches 70°F. But as the locals say, if you don't like the weather, just wait a minute.

SF-88 (☎ 415-331-1453; admission free; 🕑 12:30-3:30pm Wed-Fri & 1st Sat of month), a fascinating Cold War museum staffed by veterans. Watch them cock a now-warhead-free missile into position, then ride a missile elevator to the cavernous underground silo to see the multikeyed launch controls that were thankfully never set in motion.

Due to reopen with expanded facilities in summer 2009, the **Marine Mammal Center** (☎ 415-289-7335; admission free; 🕑 10am-4pm), set on the hill above Rodeo Lagoon, is a hospital that rehabilitates injured, sick and orphaned sea mammals before returning them to the wild. During the spring pupping season the center can have up to several dozen orphaned seal pups on site and you can often see them before they're set free.

In Fort Barry, you will find the **Headlands Center for the Arts** (☎ 415-331-2787; www.headlands.org). It's a refurbished barracks converted into artists' work spaces and conference facilities that hosts open studios with its artists-in-residence as well as talks, performances and other events.

Activities

HIKING

At the end of Bunker Rd sits Rodeo Beach, protected from wind by high cliffs. From here the **Coastal Trail** meanders 3.5 miles inland, past abandoned military bunkers, to the **Tennessee Valley Trail**. It then continues 6 miles along the blustery headlands all the way to Muir Beach.

All along the coastline you'll find cool old battery sites – abandoned concrete bunkers dug into the ground with fabulous views.

MOUNTAIN-BIKING

The Marin Headlands have some excellent mountain-biking routes, and it's an exhilarating ride across the Golden Gate Bridge to reach them (see the boxed text, opposite).

For a good 12-mile dirt loop, choose the **Coastal Trail** west from the fork of Conzelman and McCullough Rds, bumping and winding down to Bunker Rd where it meets **Bobcat Trail**, which joins **Marincello Trail** and descends steeply into the Tennessee Valley parking area. The **Old Springs Trail** and the **Miwok Trail** take you back to Bunker Rd a bit more gently than the Bobcat Trail, though any attempt to avoid at least a couple of hefty climbs on this ride is futile.

Sleeping

There are four small campgrounds in the headlands, and two involve hiking in at least 1 mile from the nearest parking lot. Hawk, Bicentennial and Haypress campgrounds are inland, with free camping, but must be reserved through the Marin Headlands Visitors Center (p144).

Kirby Cove Campground (☎ 877-444-6777; www.recreation.gov; tent sites $25; 🕑 Apr-Oct) In a spectacular shady nook near the entry to the bay, there's a small beach with the Golden Gate Bridge arching over the rocks nearby. At night you can watch the phantom shadows of cargo ships passing by (and sometimes be lulled to sleep by the dirge of a fog horn); reserve far ahead.

HI Marin Headlands Hostel (☎ 415-331-2777; www.norcalhostels.org/marin; Bldg 941, Fort Barry, Marin Headlands; dm/r $22/66) Wake up to grazing deer and dew on the ground at this spartan 1907 military compound snuggled in the woods. It has comfortable beds and a well-stocked kitchen, and guests can gather round a fireplace in the common room, shoot pool or play ping-pong. Most importantly, the hostel is surrounded by hiking trails.

Getting There & Away

By car, take the Alexander Ave exit just after the Golden Gate Bridge and dip left under the freeway. Bicycles take roughly the same route, although when bike traffic moves on the west side of the bridge there's no need to pass under the freeway. Conzelman Rd, to the right, takes you up along the bluffs; you can also take Bunker Rd, which leads to the headlands through a one-way tunnel.

Golden Gate Transit (☎ 415-455-2000, 511; www.goldengatetransit.org) bus 2 leaves from the corner of Pine and Battery Sts in the Financial District to Sausalito and the Headlands ($3.75). On Sunday and holidays **MUNI** (☎ 415-673-6864, 511) bus 76 runs from the Caltrain depot in San Francisco to Fort Barry and Rodeo Beach.

SAUSALITO

pop 7228

Perfectly arranged on a secure little harbor on the bay, Sausalito is undeniably lovely. Named for the 'tiny willows' that once populated the banks of its creeks, it's a tiny settlement of pretty houses that tumble neatly down a green hillside into a well-heeled downtown. Much of the town affords the visitor uninterrupted views of San Francisco and Angel Island, and due to the ridgeline at its back, fog generally skips past it.

Sausalito began as a 19,000-acre land grant to an army captain in 1838. When it became the terminus of the train line down the Pacific coast, it entered a new stage as a busy lumber port with a racy waterfront. Dramatic changes came in WWII when Sausalito became the site of Marinship, a huge shipbuilding yard. After the war a new bohemian period began, with a resident artists' colony living in 'arks' (houseboats moored along the bay). You'll still see dozens of these floating abodes.

Sausalito today is a major tourist haven, jam-packed with T-shirt shops and costly boutiques. It's the first town you encounter after crossing the Golden Gate Bridge from San Francisco, so daytime crowds turn up in droves and make parking difficult. Ferrying over from San Francisco makes a more relaxing excursion.

Orientation & Information

Sausalito is actually on Richardson Bay, a smaller bay within San Francisco Bay. The commercial district is essentially one street, Bridgeway Blvd, on the waterfront. The ferry terminal and Humboldt Park mark the town center. The **Sausalito Visitors Center** (☎ 415-332-0505; 780 Bridgeway Blvd; 🕑 11:30am-4pm Tue-Sun) has local information and there's also an information kiosk at the ferry terminal.

Sights

Plaza de Viña Del Mar Park, near the ferry terminal, has a fountain flanked by 14ft-tall elephant statues from the 1915 Panama-Pacific Exposition in San Francisco. Opposite Johnson St, be sure to check out **Ark Row**, where several houseboats remain from Sausalito's bohemian days.

One of the coolest things in town, fascinating to both kids and adults, is the Army Corps of Engineers' **Bay Model Visitor Center** (☎ 415-332-3871; 2100 Bridgeway Blvd; admission free; 🕑 9am-4pm Tue-Fri, 10am-5pm Sat & Sun; ♿). Housed in one of

HIKING & BIKING THE BRIDGE

Walking or cycling across the Golden Gate Bridge to Sausalito is a fun way to avoid traffic, get some great ocean views and bask in that refreshing Marin County air. It's a fairly easy journey, mostly flat or downhill when heading north from San Francisco (biking back to the city involves one big climb out of Sausalito). You can also simply hop on a ferry back to SF (see p151).

The trip is about 4 miles from the south end of the bridge and takes less than an hour. Pedestrians have access to the bridge's east walkway between 5am and 9pm daily (until 6pm in winter). Cyclists generally use the west side, except on weekdays between 5am and 3:30pm, when they must share the east side with pedestrians (who have the right-of-way). After 9pm (6pm in winter), cyclists can still cross the bridge on the east side through a security gate.

For more information, contact the **San Francisco Bicycle Coalition** (☎ 415-431-2453; www.sfbike.org) or visit the bridge website (http://goldengatebridge.org/bikesbridge/bikes.php).

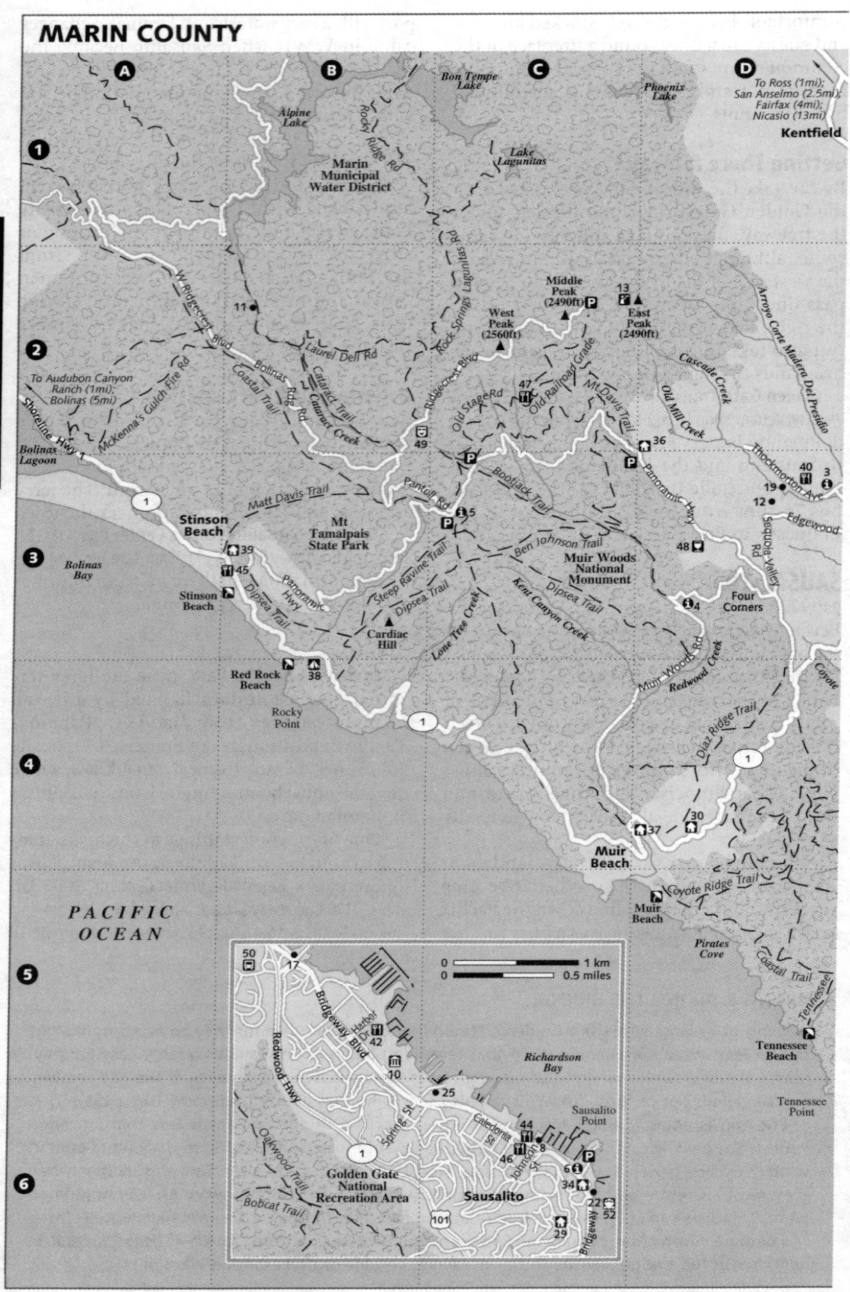
MARIN COUNTY
To Ross (1mi); San Anselmo (2.5mi); Fairfax (4mi); Nicasio (13mi)
Kentfield
Bon Tempe Lake
Phoenix Lake
Alpine Lake
Lake Lagunitas
Marin Municipal Water District
Rocky Ridge Rd
Rock Springs Lagunitas Rd
W Ridgecrest Blvd
Middle Peak (2490ft)
West Peak (2560ft)
East Peak (2490ft)
Laurel Dell Rd
Ridgecrest Blvd
Old Stage Rd
Old Railroad Grade
Mt Davis Trail
Cascade Creek
Old Mill Creek
Arroyo Corte Madera Del Presidio
Thockmorton Ave
Edgewood
Sequoia Valley Rd
To Audubon Canyon Ranch (1mi); Bolinas (5mi)
McKenna's Gulch Fire Rd
Bolinas Rdg Rd
Coastal Trail
Cataract Trail
Cataract Creek
Shoreline Hwy 1
Bolinas Lagoon
Matt Davis Trail
Pantoll Rd
Bootjack Trail
Panoramic Hwy
Stinson Beach
Mt Tamalpais State Park
Ben Johnson Trail
Muir Woods National Monument
Bolinas Bay
Steep Ravine Trail
Dipsea Trail
Cardiac Hill
Lone Tree Creek
Kent Canyon Creek
Four Corners
Muir Woods Rd
Redwood Creek
Coyote
Red Rock Beach
Rocky Point
Diaz Ridge Trail
Muir Beach
Coyote Ridge Trail
Pirates Cove
Coastal Trail
Tennessee
Tennessee Beach
Tennessee Point
PACIFIC OCEAN
0 1 km
0 0.5 miles
Bridgeway Blvd
Harbor Dr
Redwood Hwy
Richardson Bay
Spring St
Caledonia St
Sausalito Point
Johnson St
Oakwood Trail
Bobcat Trail
Golden Gate National Recreation Area
Sausalito
Bridgeway

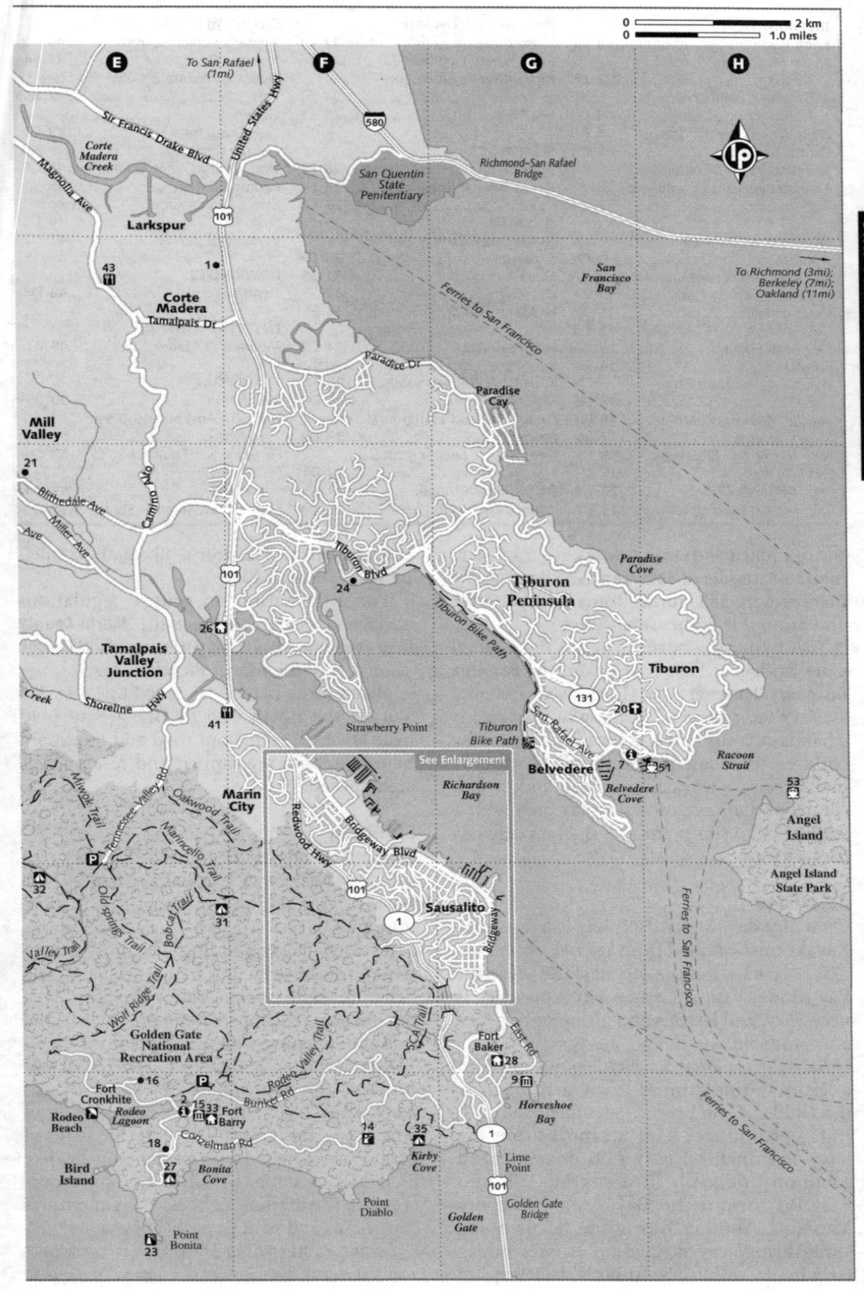

0 2 km
0 1.0 miles
E
F
G
H
To San Rafael (1mi)
580
Sir Francis Drake Blvd
United States Hwy
Corte Madera Creek
Magnolia Ave
San Quentin State Penitentiary
Richmond–San Rafael Bridge
Larkspur
101
43
1
Corte Madera
Tamalpais Dr
San Francisco Bay
To Richmond (3mi); Berkeley (7mi); Oakland (11mi)
Ferries to San Francisco
Paradise Dr
Paradise Cay
Mill Valley
21
Camino Alto
Blithedale Ave
Miller Ave
Ave
Tiburon Blvd
24
Paradise Cove
Tiburon Peninsula
Tiburon Bike Path
26
Tamalpais Valley Junction
Tiburon
131
20
Creek
Shoreline Hwy
41
Strawberry Point
Tiburon Bike Path
San Rafael Ave
See Enlargement
Richardson Bay
Belvedere
7
51
Racoon Strait
Belvedere Cove
53
Miwok Trail
Tennessee Valley Rd
Oakwood Trail
Marin City
Redwood Hwy
Bridgeway Blvd
Angel Island
Marincello Trail
Angel Island State Park
32
Old Springs Trail
Bobcat Trail
31
Sausalito
Bridgeway
Valley Trail
Wolf Ridge Trail
Ferries to San Francisco
SCA Trail
Rodeo Valley Trail
East Rd
Golden Gate National Recreation Area
Fort Baker
28
9
16
Fort Cronkhite
Bunker Rd
2
15
33
Fort Barry
Rodeo Beach
Rodeo Lagoon
14
35
Horseshoe Bay
Ferries to San Francisco
18
Conzelman Rd
Kirby Cove
Lime Point
Bird Island
27
Bonita Cove
Point Diablo
Golden Gate
Golden Gate Bridge
23
Point Bonita

INFORMATION
Book Passage....1 E2
Marin Headlands Visitors Center....2 E6
Mill Valley Chamber of Commerce....3 D3
Muir Woods Ranger Station....4 D3
Pantoll Station....5 C3
Sausalito Visitors Center....6 C6
Tiburon Peninsula Chamber of Commerce....7 G4

SIGHTS & ACTIVITIES
Ark Row....8 C6
Bay Area Discovery Museum....9 G6
Bay Model Visitor Center....10 B5
Cataract Falls....11 B2
Dipsea Steps....12 D3
East Peak Summit....13 C2
Hawk Hill....14 F6
Headlands Center for the Arts....15 E6
Marine Mammal Center....16 E6
Mike's Bikes....17 B5
Nike Missile Site SF-88....18 E6
Old Mill Park....19 D3
Old St Hilary's Church....20 G4
Outdoor Art Club....21 E3
Plaza de Viña Del Mar Park....22 C6
Point Bonita Lighthouse....23 E6
Richardson Bay Audubon Center....24 F3
Sea Trek....25 C6

SLEEPING
Acqua Hotel....26 E3
Bicentennial Campground....27 E6
Cavallo Point....28 G5
Gables Inn....29 C6
Green Gulch Farm & Zen Center....30 D4
Hawk Campground....31 E5
Haypress Campground....32 E5
HI Marin Headlands Hostel....33 E6
Hotel Sausalito....34 C6
Inn Above Tide....(see 52)
Kirby Cove Campground....35 F6
Mountain Home Inn....36 D2
Pantoll Station Campground....(see 5)
Pelican Inn....37 D4
Steep Ravine Environmental Campground....38 B4
Stinson Beach Motel....39 B3
Water's Edge Hotel....(see 51)

EATING
Avatar's Punjab Burritos....40 D3
Buckeye Roadhouse....41 F4
Depot Bookstore & Cafe....(see 3)
Fish....42 B5
Guaymas....(see 51)
Lark Creek Inn....43 E2
Murray Circle....(see 28)
North Point Coffee Company....44 C6
Parkside Cafe....45 B3
Sam's Anchor Cafe....(see 51)
Sushi Ran....46 C6
West Point Inn....47 C2

DRINKING
German Tourist Club....48 D3

ENTERTAINMENT
Mountain Theater....49 B2

TRANSPORT
Bus Station....50 B5
Ferries to Angel Island & San Francisco....51 H4
Ferries to San Francisco....52 C6
Ferries to Tiburon & San Francisco....53 H4
Muir Woods Summer Shuttle..(see 52)

the old Marinship warehouses, it's a 1.5-acre hydraulic model of San Francisco Bay and the delta region. Self-guided tours take you over and around it as the water flows.

Just under the north tower of the Golden Gate Bridge, at East Fort Baker, the **Bay Area Discovery Museum** (☎ 415-339-3900; adult/child $10/8; 9am-4pm Tue-Fri, 10am-5pm Sat & Sun;) is a hands-on museum specifically designed for children. Permanent (multilingual) exhibits include a wave workshop, a small underwater tunnel and a large outdoor play area with a shipwreck to romp around. A small café has healthy nibbles.

Activities

On a nice day, Richardson Bay is irresistible. Kayaks can be rented from **Sea Trek** (☎ 415-488-1000; Schoonmaker Marina; kayaks per hr $20), near the Bay Model Visitor Center. No experience is necessary, and lessons and group outings are also available.

Sausalito is great for **bicycling**, whether for a leisurely ride around town, a trip across the Golden Gate Bridge (see the boxed text, p147) or a longer-haul journey. From the ferry terminal, an easy option is to head south on Bridgeway Blvd, veering left onto East Rd toward the Bay Area Discovery Museum. Another nice route heads north along Bridgeway Blvd, then crosses under Hwy 101 to Mill Valley. At Blithedale Ave, you can veer east to Tiburon; a bike path parallels parts of Tiburon Blvd.

For information on routes, regulations and group rides, contact the **Marin County Bike Coalition** (☎ 415-456-3469; www.marinbike.org), publisher of the *Marin Bicycle Map*.

Mike's Bikes (☎ 415-332-3200; 1 Gate 6 Rd; 24hr $40), at the north end of Bridgeway Blvd near Hwy 101, rents out road and mountain bikes. Supplies are limited and reservations aren't accepted.

Sleeping

Gables Inn (☎ 415-289-1100, 800-966-1554; www.gablesinnsausalito.com; 62 Princess St; r incl breakfast $175-645; wi-fi) Tranquil and inviting, this inn has nine guest rooms in a historic 1869 home, and six in a newer building. The more expensive rooms have Jacuzzi baths, fireplaces and balconies with spectacular views, but even the smaller, cheaper rooms are stylish and tranquil. Evening wine is included.

Hotel Sausalito (☎ 415-332-0700, 888-442-0700; www.hotelsausalito.com; 16 El Portal; r $155-195, ste $265-285;) Steps away from the ferry in the middle of downtown, this grand 1915 hotel has loads of period charm paired with modern touches like iPod docking stations. Each guest room is decorated in Mediterranean hues, with sumptuous bathrooms and park or partial bay views.

Cavallo Point (☎ 415-339-4700; www.cavallopoint.com; 601 Murray Circle, Fort Baker; r from $275; wi-fi)

Spread out over 45 acres of the Bay Area's most scenic parkland, Cavallo Point is a brand new, buzz-worthy lodge that flaunts a green focus, a full service spa and easy access to outdoor activities. Choose from richly renovated rooms in the landmark Fort Baker officers' quarters or more contemporary solar-powered accommodations with exquisite bay views (including a turret of the Golden Gate Bridge).

Inn Above Tide (☎ 415-332-9535, 800-893-8433; www.innabovetide.com; 30 El Portal; r $305-585, ste $675-1025; wi-fi) Also at the ferry terminal, ensconce yourself in one of the 29 modern and spacious rooms – most with private decks and wood-burning fireplaces – that practically levitate out over the water. With envy-inducing bay views from your window, scan the horizon with the in-room binoculars.

Eating

Bridgeway Blvd is packed with moderately priced cafés, a few budget ethnic food options and some more expensive bay view restaurants.

Sushi Ran (☎ 415-332-3620; 107 Caledonia St; sushi $4-21) Many Bay Area residents claim this place is the best sushi spot around. A wine and sake bar next door eases the pain of the long wait for a table.

North Point Coffee Company (☎ 415-331-0777; 1250 Bridgeway Blvd; sandwiches $7-10; 6:30am-7:30pm Mon-Wed, to 9:30pm Thu, to 8:30pm Fri & Sat) For a tranquil respite from the tourist-saturated strip near the ferry terminal, walk a few blocks northwest of the dock and kick back here with a panini sandwich and a frothy espresso. The back brick patio fronts a peaceful and undeveloped stretch of bay shoreline.

Fish (☎ 415-331-3474; 350 Harbor Dr; mains $12-25; 11:30am-8:30pm;) Chow down on seafood sandwiches, oysters and Dungeness crab roll with organic local butter at redwood picnic tables facing Richardson Bay. A local leader in promoting fresh and sustainably caught fish, it has wonderful wild salmon in season, and refuses to serve the farmed stuff. Cash only.

Murray Circle (☎ 415-339-4750; 601 Murray Circle, Fort Baker; mains $16-22; breakfast, lunch & dinner) At the Cavallo Point lodge, dine on locally sourced meats, seafood and produce like grass-fed organic burgers or slow-roasted eggplant ravioli in a clubby dining room topped by a pressed-tin ceiling. Reservations recommended for lunch and dinner, though walk-ins can be seated on the panoramic-view balcony.

Getting There & Away

Driving to Sausalito from San Francisco, take the Alexander Ave exit (the first exit after the Golden Gate Bridge) and follow the signs into Sausalito. There are five municipal parking lots in town, and street parking is difficult to find.

Golden Gate Transit (☎ 415-455-2000; www.goldengatetransit.org) bus 10 runs daily to Sausalito from San Francisco ($3.75). Catch it from the Transbay Terminal.

The ferry is a fun and easy way to travel to Sausalito. **Golden Gate Ferries** (☎ 415-455-2000; one way $7.45) operate to and from the San Francisco Ferry Building. The ferries operate six to nine times daily and the trip takes 30 minutes. The **Blue & Gold Fleet** (☎ 415-705-8200; Pier 41, Fisherman's Wharf; one way $9.25) sails to Sausalito year-round and you can transport bicycles for free.

TIBURON

pop 8700

At the end of a small peninsula pointing out into the center of the bay, Tiburon is blessed with gorgeous views, much like Sausalito. The name comes from the Spanish Punta de Tiburon (Shark Point). Take the ferry from San Francisco, browse the shops on Main St, grab a bite to eat and you've seen Tiburon. The town is also the jumping-off point for nearby Angel Island (see p152).

Orientation & Information

The central part of town is comprised of Tiburon Blvd, with Juanita Lane and charming Main St arcing off. Main St, which is also known as Ark Row, is where the old houseboats have taken root on dry land and metamorphosed into classy shops and boutiques.

The **Tiburon Peninsula Chamber of Commerce** (☎ 415-435-5633; www.tiburonchamber.org; 96b Main St; 8am-4pm Mon-Fri) can provide information about the area.

Sights & Activities

There are great views from the lovely hillside surrounding **Old St Hilary's Church** (☎ 415-435-1853; 201 Esperanza; 1-4pm Wed-Sun Apr-Oct), a fine 19th-century example of Carpenter Gothic.

The **Angel Island-Tiburon Ferry** (☎ 415-435-2131; adult/child $20/10) runs sunset cruises on Friday and Saturday evenings from May to mid-October. Reservations are recommended.

Back toward Hwy 101 the **Richardson Bay Audubon Center** (☎ 415-388-2524; 376 Greenwood

DETOUR: ANGEL ISLAND

Angel Island (☎ 415-435-1915; www.parks.ca.gov/?page_id=468), in San Francisco Bay, has a mild climate with fresh bay breezes that make the island pleasant for hiking and biking. For a unique treat, picnic in a protected cove overlooking the close but immeasurably distant urban surroundings. The island's varied history – it was a hunting and fishing ground for the Miwok people, served as a military base, an immigration station, a WWII Japanese internment camp and a Nike missile site – has left it with some evocative old forts and bunkers to poke around in. There are 12 miles of roads and trails around the island, including a hike to the summit of 781ft **Mt Livermore** (no bikes) and a 5-mile perimeter trail.

Recently closed for major renovations but set to reopen in early 2009, the **Immigration Station**, which operated from 1910 to 1940, was the Ellis Island of the west coast. But this facility was primarily a screening and detention center for Chinese immigrants, who were at that time restricted from entering the US under the jingoistic Chinese Exclusion Act. Many detainees were held here for long periods before ultimately being returned home, and one of the most unusual sights here is the sad and longing Chinese poetry etched into the barrack walls.

In October 2008, a human-caused fire scorched half the island in a spectacular nighttime wildfire. Miraculously, no buildings were damaged, and rangers expect a healthy rejuvenation of the land. The campgrounds were temporarily closed as this book went to press, but were expected to reopen by spring 2009.

On weekends, **Sea Trek Ocean Kayaking** (☎ 415-488-1000, www.seatrekkayak.com; tours per person 2½hr/overnight $75/140) offers guided kayaking excursions around Angel Island. Tours include equipment and instructions, and May through October is the best time to paddle.

You can camp on the island, and when the last ferry sails off for the night, the island's your own – well, except for the very persistent raccoons. The dozen hike-, bike- or kayak-in **campsites** (☎ 800-444-7275; www.reserveamerica.com; tent sites $20) are usually reserved months in advance. Near the ferry dock, there's a café that specializes in barbecued oysters.

From San Francisco, take a **Blue & Gold Fleet** (☎ 415-705-8200) ferry from Pier 41 or the Ferry Building. From May to September there are three ferries a day on weekends and two on weekdays; during the rest of the year the schedule is reduced. Round-trip tickets cost $18 for adults and $11.50 for children.

From Tiburon, take the **Angel Island-Tiburon Ferry** (☎ 415-435-2131; www.angelislandferry.com), which costs $13.50 for the round-trip; add $1 for bicycles.

You can rent bicycles at Ayala Cove (per hour/day $10/35), and there are **tram tours** (☎ 415-897-0715; tours $13.50) around the island. Schedules vary seasonally; go to www.angelisland.com for more information.

Beach Rd; 🕑 9am-5pm Mon-Sat), off Tiburon Blvd, is home to a huge variety of waterbirds.

Sleeping & Eating

Water's Edge Hotel (☎ 415-789-5999, 877-789-5999; www.watersedgehotel.com; 25 Main St; r incl breakfast $169-399; wi-fi) This hotel, with its deck extending out over the bay, is exemplary for its tasteful modernity. Rooms have an elegant minimalism that combines comfort and style, and all afford an immediate view of the bay. The rooms with rustic high wood ceilings are quite romantic.

Guaymas (☎ 415-435-6300; 5 Main St; mains $14-25; lunch & dinner) Steps from the ferry, noisy Guaymas packs in a fun, boisterous crowd. Margaritas energize the place, and solid Mexican seafood dishes help keep people upright.

Sam's Anchor Cafe (☎ 415-435-4527; 27 Main St; mains $17-27; 11am-10pm Mon-Fri, 9:30am-10pm Sat & Sun) Even shambling little shacks like this one have unbeatable views. Sam's has been slinging seafood and burgers since 1920. On a warm afternoon, you can't beat a cocktail or a tasty plate of sautéed prawns on the deck.

Getting There & Away

Golden Gate Transit (☎ 415-455-2000; www.goldengatetransit.org) commute bus 8 runs direct between San Francisco and Tiburon ($3.75) during the week.

On Hwy 101, look for the off-ramp for Tiburon Blvd, E Blithedale Ave and Hwy 131;

driving east, it leads into town and intersects with Juanita Lane and Main St.

Blue & Gold Fleet (☎ 415-705-8200; Pier 41, Fisherman's Wharf; one way $11) sails daily from San Francisco to Tiburon; ferries dock right in front of the Guaymas restaurant on Main St. You can transport bicycles for free. From Tiburon, ferries also connect regularly to Angel Island.

MILL VALLEY

pop 13,400

Nestled under the redwoods at the base of Mt Tamalpais, tiny Mill Valley is one of the Bay Area's most picturesque hamlets. Mill Valley was originally a logging town, its name stemming from an 1830s sawmill that was the first in the Bay Area to provide lumber. Though the 1892 Mill Valley Lumber Company still greets motorists on Miller Ave, the town's a vastly different place today, packed with wildly expensive homes, fancy cars and pricey boutiques.

Mill Valley also served as the starting point for the scenic railway that carried visitors up Mt Tam (see p155). The tracks were removed in 1940, and today the Depot Bookstore & Cafe occupies the space of the former station.

Visitor information is available from the **Mill Valley Chamber of Commerce** (☎ 415-388-9700; www.millvalley.org; 85 Throckmorton Ave; 9am-noon Tue-Fri).

Sights & Activities

Said to have been founded by 35 Mill Valley ladies determined to preserve the local environment, the private **Outdoor Art Club** (☎ 415-388-9886; www.outdoorartclub.org; cnr W Blithedale & Throckmorton Aves) is housed in a landmark 1904 building designed by Bernard Maybeck.

Several blocks west of downtown along Throckmorton Ave is **Old Mill Park**, perfect for a picnic. Here you'll also find a replica of the town's namesake sawmill. Just past the bridge at Old Mill Creek, the **Dipsea Steps** mark the start of the Dipsea Trail.

Each October the **Mill Valley Film Festival** (www.mvff.com) presents an innovative, internationally regarded program of independent films.

Tennessee Valley Trail, in the Marin Headlands, offers beautiful views of the rugged coastline and is one of the most popular hikes in Marin (expect crowds on weekends). It has easy, level access to the beach and ocean, and is a short 3.8 miles, though it can get windy. From Hwy 101, take the Mill Valley–Stinson Beach–Hwy 1 exit and turn left onto Tennessee Valley Rd from the Shoreline Hwy; follow it to the parking lot and trailhead.

A more demanding option is the 7-mile **Dipsea Trail**, which climbs over the coastal range and down to Stinson Beach, cutting through a corner of Muir Woods. The trail starts at Old Mill Park with a climb up 676 steps in three separate flights, and includes a few more steep ups and downs before reaching the ocean.

Sleeping

Acqua Hotel (☎ 415-380-0400, 888-662-9555; www.marinhotels.com/acqua.html; 555 Redwood Hwy; r incl breakfast from $169; wi-fi) With views of the bay and Mt Tam, and a lobby with a soothing fireplace and fountain, the Acqua doesn't lack for pleasant indoor/outdoor eye candy. Contemporary rooms are sleekly designed with beautiful fabrics.

Mountain Home Inn (☎ 415-381-9000; www.mtnhomeinn.com; 810 Panoramic Hwy; r incl breakfast $195-345) Set amidst redwood, spruce and pine tress on a ridge of Mt Tam, this retreat is both modern and rustic. The larger (more expensive) rooms are rugged beauties, with unfinished timbers forming columns from floor to ceiling as though the forest is shooting up through the floor. Smaller rooms are cozy dens for two. A lack of televisions and the positioning of a good local trail map on the dresser make it clear that it's a place to breathe and unwind.

Eating & Drinking

Avatar's Punjab Burritos (15 Madrona St; mains $6-9; 11am-8pm Mon-Sat) For a quick bite, try a tasty burrito of lamb and curry or spicy veggies.

Depot Bookstore & Cafe (87 Throckmorton Ave; meals under $10; 7am-7pm daily) Smack in the town center, Depot serves cappuccinos, sandwiches and light meals. The bookstore sells lots of local publications, including trail guides.

Buckeye Roadhouse (☎ 415-331-2600; 15 Shoreline Hwy; mains $13-30; 11:30am-10pm Mon-Sat, 10:30am-10pm Sun) Originally opened as a roadside stop in 1932, the Buckeye is a Marin County gem, and its upscale American cuisine is in no danger of being compared to truck-stop fare. Stop off for chili-lime 'brick' chicken, baby back ribs or oysters Bingo before getting back on the highway.

DETOUR: GERMAN TOURIST CLUB

A private club that occasionally shares its sudsy love, the **German Tourist Club** (☎ 415-388-9987; www.touristclubsf.org; 🕑 1-6pm 1st, 3rd & 4th weekends of the month), or Nature Friends (Die Naturefreunde), has a gorgeous beer garden patio overlooking Muir Woods and Mt Tam that's a favored spot for parched Marin hikers. By car, turn onto Ridge Ave from Panoramic Hwy, park in the gravel driveway at the end of the road and start the 0.3-mile walk downhill. You can also hike in on the Sun Trail from Panoramic – a half-hour of mostly flat trail with views of the ocean and Muir Woods.

Getting There & Away

From San Francisco or Sausalito, take Hwy 101 north to the Mill Valley–Stinson Beach–Hwy 1 exit. Follow Hwy 1 (also called the Shoreline Hwy) to Almonte Blvd (which becomes Miller Ave), then follow Miller Ave into downtown Mill Valley.

From the north, take the E Blithedale Ave exit from Hwy 101, then head west into downtown Mill Valley.

Golden Gate Transit (☎ 415-455-2000; www.goldengatetranist.org) bus 4 runs directly from San Francisco to Mill Valley ($3.75) on weekdays.

LARKSPUR, SAN ANSELMO & CORTE MADERA

The inland towns of Larkspur, Kentfield, Corte Madera, Ross, San Anselmo and Fairfax evoke charmed small-town life, even though all are clustered around busy Hwy 101 and Sir Francis Drake Blvd. Some very fine restaurants here await hungry hikers.

In **Larkspur**, window-shop along Magnolia Ave or explore the redwoods in nearby Baltimore Canyon. On the east side of the freeway is the hulking mass of **San Quentin State Penitentiary**, California's oldest and most notorious prison, founded in 1852. Johnny Cash recorded an album here in 1969 after scoring a big hit with his live *Folsom Prison* album a few years earlier.

San Anselmo has a cute, small downtown area along San Anselmo Ave, including several antique shops. **Corte Madera** is home to one of the Bay Area's best bookstores, **Book Passage** (☎ 415-927-0960; 51 Tamal Vista Blvd), in the Marketplace shopping center. It has a strong travel section, plus frequent author appearances.

The **Lark Creek Inn** (☎ 415-924-7766; 234 Magnolia Ave, Larkspur; mains $22-35) is in a lovely spot and offers a fine-dining experience. It's housed in an 1888 Victorian house tucked away in a redwood canyon, and the farm-fresh American food (like the organic chicken roulade, pork loin chop, and heirloom squash and tomato tart) is gratifying.

After a lot of kitchen turnover, **Fork** (☎ 415-453-9898; 198 Sir Francis Drake Blvd, San Anselmo; prix fixe $42-59; 🕑 dinner Tue-Sat) has hit the jackpot with chef Nathan Lockwood, who's transformed this Marin foodie heaven into a scrumptious home for Italian-Mediterranean cuisine. The perfect pasta is freshly made daily, and while the focus is on the newer three- to five-course menu, you can still comb through the à la carte appetizers to eat small-plate style.

Golden Gate Transit (☎ 415-455-2000; www.goldengatetransit.org) runs a daily ferry service from the Ferry Building in San Francisco to Larkspur Landing on E Sir Francis Drake Blvd, directly east of Hwy 101. The trip takes 50 minutes and costs $7.45. You can take bicycles on the ferry.

SAN RAFAEL

pop 55,600

The oldest and largest town in Marin, San Rafael is slightly less upscale than most of its neighbors but doesn't lack atmosphere. It's a common stop for travelers on their way to Point Reyes. Just north of San Rafael, Lucas Valley Rd heads west to Point Reyes Station, passing George Lucas' Skywalker Ranch. Fourth St, San Rafael's main drag, is lined with cafés and shops. If you follow it west out of downtown San Rafael, it meets Sir Francis Drake Blvd and continues west to the coast.

Sights & Activities

The town began with **Mission San Rafael Arcángel** (☎ 415-454-8141; 1104 5th Ave), founded in 1817, which served as a sanitarium for Native Americans suffering from European diseases. The present building is a replica dating from 1949.

Designed by Frank Lloyd Wright, the **Marin County Civic Center** (☎ 415-472-3500) is a long, beautiful structure blending into the hills directly east of Hwy 101; exit on N San Pedro Rd, 2 miles north of San Rafael. Tours ($5) begin here Wednesday at 10:30am. The center hosts regular concerts and events, including a **farmers market** every Thursday and Sunday morning. In 1970, it was the scene of a high-profile shootout where black political activists freed prisoners on trial and four people were killed, including the judge.

Rafael Film Center (☎ 415-454-1222; 1118 4th St) is a restored downtown cinema offering innovative art-house programming in state-of-the-art surroundings.

China Camp State Park (☎ 415-456-0766), about 4 miles east of San Rafael, is a pleasant place to stop for a picnic or short hike. From Hwy 101, take the N San Pedro Rd exit and continue 3 miles east. A Chinese fishing village once stood here, and a small museum exhibits interesting artifacts from the settlement.

Sleeping & Eating

China Camp State Park (☎ 800-444-7275; www.reserveamerica.com; tent sites $25) The park has 30 walk-in campsites with pleasant shade.

Panama Hotel (☎ 415-457-3993; www.panamahotel.com; 4 Bayview St; r $135-150; wi-fi) The 10 artsy rooms at this B&B in a building dating from 1910 each have their own unique style and charming decor like crazy quilts and vibrant accent walls. The hotel restaurant has an inviting courtyard patio.

Gerstle Park Inn (☎ 415-721-7611, 800-726-7611; www.gerstleparkinn.com; 34 Grove St; r incl breakfast $189-255; wi-fi) Hone your croquet swing at this lovely 1880s home set beside a mini redwood grove and encircled by a lush mature garden. A gracious assemblage of suites and cottages filled with antiques, you'll lack for nothing here.

Sol Food Puerto Rican Cuisine (☎ 415-451-4765; Lincoln Ave & 3rd St; mains $7-11; lunch & dinner) Lazy ceiling fans, a profusion of tropical plants and the pulse of Latin rhythms create a soothing atmosphere for delicious dishes like a *jibaro* sandwich (thinly sliced steak served on green plantains) and other island-inspired entrées concocted with *plátanos*, organic veggies and free range meats.

Getting There & Away

Numerous **Golden Gate Transit** (☎ 415-923-2000; www.goldengatetransit.org) buses operate between San Francisco and the San Rafael Transit Center at 3rd and Hetherton Sts ($4.55, 1 hour).

MT TAMALPAIS STATE PARK

Standing guard over Marin County, majestic Mt Tamalpais (Mt Tam) has breathtaking 360-degree views of ocean, bay and hills rolling into the distance. The rich, natural beauty of 2571ft Mt Tam and its surrounding area is inspiring – especially considering that it lies within an hour's drive from one of the state's largest metropolitan areas.

Mt Tamalpais State Park was formed in 1930, partly from land donated by congressman and naturalist William Kent (who also donated the land that became Muir Woods National Monument in 1907). Its 6300 acres are home to deer, foxes, bobcats and many miles of hiking and biking trails.

Mt Tam was a sacred place to the coastal Miwok people for thousands of years before the arrival of European and American settlers. By the late 19th century, San Franciscans were escaping the bustle of the city with all-day outings on the mountain, and in 1896 the 'world's crookedest railroad' (281 turns) was completed from Mill Valley to the summit. Though the railroad was closed in 1930, Old Railroad Grade is today one of Mt Tam's most popular and scenic hiking and biking paths.

Orientation & Information

Panoramic Hwy climbs from Mill Valley through the park to Stinson Beach. **Pantoll Station** (☎ 415-388-2070; 801 Panoramic Hwy) is the park headquarters. Detailed park maps are sold here.

Sights

From Pantoll Station, it's 4.2 miles by car to **East Peak Summit**; take Pantoll Rd and then panoramic Ridgecrest Blvd to the top. Parking is $6 and a 10-minute hike leads to a fire lookout at the very top and awesome sea-to-bay views.

The park's natural-stone, 4000-seat **Mountain Theater** (☎ 415-383-1100) hosts the annual 'Mountain Play' series on six Sundays between mid-May and late June. Free shuttles are provided from Mill Valley. Free **astronomy programs** (☎ 415-455-5370) also take place here monthly around the new moon.

Activities

HIKING

The park map is a smart investment, as there are a dozen worthwhile hiking trails in the area. From Pantoll Station, the **Steep**

Ravine Trail follows a wooded creek on to the coast (about 2.1 miles each way). For a longer hike, veer right (northwest) after 1.5 miles onto the **Dipsea Trail**, which meanders through trees for 1 mile before ending at Stinson Beach. Grab some lunch, then walk north through town and follow signs for the **Matt Davis Trail**, which leads 2.7 miles back to Pantoll Station, making a good loop. The Matt Davis Trail continues on beyond Pantoll Station, wrapping gently around the mountain with superb views.

Another worthy option is **Cataract Trail**, which runs along Cataract Creek from the end of Pantoll Rd; it's approximately 3 miles to Alpine Lake. The last mile is a spectacular rooty staircase as the trail descends alongside **Cataract Falls**.

MOUNTAIN-BIKING

Bikers must stay on the fire roads (and off the single-track trails) and keep to speeds under 15mph. Rangers are prickly about these rules, and a ticket can result in a steep fine.

The most popular ride is the **Old Railroad Grade**. For a sweaty, 6-mile, 2280ft climb, start in Mill Valley at the end of W Blithedale Ave and bike up to East Peak. It takes about an hour to reach the West Point Inn (see right) from Mill Valley. For an easier start, begin partway up at the Mountain Home Inn (see p153) and follow the **Gravity Car Grade** to the Old Railroad Grade and the West Point Inn. From the Inn, it's an easy half-hour ride to the summit.

From just west of Pantoll Station, bikers can either take the **Deer Park fire road**, which runs close to the Dipsea Trail, through giant redwoods to the main entrance of Muir Woods, or the southeastern extension of the **Coastal Trail**, which has breathtaking views of the coast before joining Hwy 1 about 2 miles north of Muir Beach. Either option requires a return to Mill Valley via Frank Valley/Muir Woods Rd, which climbs steadily (800ft) to Panoramic Hwy and then becomes Sequoia Valley Rd as it drops toward Mill Valley. A left turn on Wildomar and two right turns at Mill Creek Park lead to the center of Mill Valley at the Depot Bookstore & Cafe.

For further information on bike routes and rules, contact the **Marin County Bike Coalition** (☎ 415-456-3469; www.marin bike.org).

Sleeping & Eating

Pantoll Station Campground (☎ 415-388-2070; tent sites $15) From the parking lot it's a 100yd walk or bike ride to the campground, with 16 first-come, first-served tent sites but no showers.

Steep Ravine Environmental Campground (☎ 800-444-7275; www.reserveamerica.com; campsites/cabins $15/60) Just off Hwy 1, about 1 mile south of Stinson Beach, this jewel has 6 beachfront campsites and several rustic five-person cabins overlooking the ocean. Both options are booked out months in advance and reservations can be made up to seven months ahead.

West Point Inn (☎ inn 415-388-9955, reservations 415-646-0702; www.westpointinn.com; per person r or cabin $50; 🕑 closed Mon) Load up your sleeping bag and hike in to this rustic 1904 hideaway built as a stopover for the Mill Valley and Mt Tamalpais Scenic Railway. It also hosts monthly pancake breakfasts ($10) during the summer as a hearty reward for all those switchbacks.

Getting There & Away

To reach Pantoll Station by car, take Hwy 1 to the Panoramic Hwy and look for the Pantoll signs. **West Marin Stagecoach** (☎ 415-526-3239; www.co.marin.ca.us/depts/PW/main/marintransit/stage.html) route 61 runs daily minibuses ($2) from Marin City (via Mill Valley) to both the Pantoll Station and Mountain Home Inn.

MUIR WOODS NATIONAL MONUMENT

Walking through an awesome stand of the world's tallest trees is an experience to be had only in Northern California and a small part of southern Oregon. The old-growth redwoods at **Muir Woods** (☎ 415-388-2595; www.nps.gov/muwo; admission $5; 🕑 8am-sunset), just 12 miles north of the Golden Gate Bridge, is the closest redwood stand to San Francisco. The trees were initially eyed by loggers, and Redwood Creek, as the area was known, seemed ideal for a dam. Those plans were halted when congressman and naturalist William Kent bought a section of Redwood Creek and, in 1907, donated 295 acres to the federal government. President Theodore Roosevelt made the site a national monument in 1908, the name honoring John Muir, naturalist and founder of environmental organization the Sierra Club.

Muir Woods can become quite crowded, especially on weekends. Try to come midweek, early in the morning or late in the afternoon, when tour buses are less of a problem.

Even at busy times, a short hike will get you out of the densest crowds and onto trails with huge trees and stunning vistas.

Hiking

The 1-mile **Main Trail Loop** is a gentle walk alongside Redwood Creek to the 1000-year-old trees at **Cathedral Grove**; it returns via **Bohemian Grove**, where the tallest tree in the park stands 254ft high. The **Dipsea Trail** is a good 2-mile hike up to the top of aptly named **Cardiac Hill**.

You can also walk down into Muir Woods by taking trails from the Panoramic Hwy, such as the **Bootjack Trail** from the Bootjack picnic area, or from Mt Tamalpais' Pantoll Station campground, along the **Ben Johnson Trail**.

Getting There & Away

Because parking can be such a headache during busy periods, consider taking the summer shuttle operated by **Golden Gate Transit** (www.goldengatetransit.org; round-trip adult/child $3/1; weekends & holidays late May-Aug). The 40-minute shuttle connects with four Sausalito ferries arriving from San Francisco.

To get there by car, drive north on Hwy 101, exit at Hwy 1 and continue north along Hwy 1/Shoreline Hwy to the Panoramic Hwy (a right-hand fork). Follow that for about 1 mile to Four Corners, where you turn left onto Muir Woods Rd (there are plenty of signs).

THE COAST

Muir Beach

pop 300

The turnoff to Muir Beach from Hwy 1 is marked by the longest row of mailboxes on the North Coast. Muir Beach is a quiet little town with a nice beach, but it has no direct bus service. Just north of Muir Beach there are superb views up and down the coast from the **Muir Beach Overlook**; during WWII, watch was kept from the surrounding concrete lookouts for invading Japanese ships.

Pelican Inn (☎ 415-383-6000; www.pelicaninn.com; 10 Pacific Way; r incl breakfast from $190) is the only commercial establishment in Muir Beach. The downstairs restaurant and pub is an Anglophile's dream and perfect for pre- or post-hike nourishment (mains $11 to $29).

Green Gulch Farm & Zen Center (☎ 415-383-3134; www.sfzc.com; 1601 Shoreline Hwy; s $85-115, d $145-175, d cottage $200) is a Buddhist retreat in the hills above Muir Beach. The center's accommodations are elegant, restful, modern and Japanese in style, and delicious buffet-style vegetarian meals are included. A hilltop retreat cottage is 25 minutes away by foot.

Stinson Beach

pop 750

Positively buzzing on warm weekends, Stinson Beach is 5 miles north of Muir Beach. The town flanks Hwy 1 for about three blocks and is densely packed with galleries, shops, eateries and B&Bs. The beach itself is often blanketed with fog, and when the sun's shining it's blanketed with surfers, families and gawkers. Nevertheless it's nice, with views of Point Reyes and San Francisco on clear days, and the beach is long enough for a vigorous stroll. From San Francisco it's nearly an hour's drive, though on weekends plan for toe-tapping traffic delays.

Three-mile-long **Stinson Beach** is a popular surf spot, but swimming is advised from late May to mid-September only; for updated weather and surf conditions call ☎ 415-868-1922. The beach is one block west of Hwy 1.

Around 1 mile south of Stinson Beach is **Red Rock Beach**. It's a clothing-optional beach that attracts smaller crowds, probably because it's accessed by a steep trail from Hwy 1.

About 3.5 miles north of town on Hwy 1, in the hills above the Bolinas Lagoon, the **Audubon Canyon Ranch** (☎ 415-868-9244; www.egret.org; donations requested; 10am-4pm Sat, Sun & holidays mid-Mar–mid-Jul) is a major nesting ground for great blue herons and great egrets.

Stinson Beach Motel (☎ 415-868-1712; www.stinsonbeachmotel.com; 3416 Hwy 1; r $90-225) is managed by a muscle man named Frodo. This 70-year-old motel is a collection of remodeled beach cottages surrounded by gardens. Nothing fancy, but it's only two blocks from the beach.

Parkside Cafe (☎ 415-868-1272; 43 Arenal Ave; mains $9-19; 7:30am-4pm & 5-9pm Mon-Fri, 8am-4pm & 5-9pm Sat & Sun) is famous for its hearty breakfasts and lunches, and noted far and wide for its excellent coastal cuisine. Reservations are recommended for dinner.

West Marin Stagecoach (☎ 415-526-3239; www.co.marin.ca.us/depts/PW/main/marintransit/stage.html) route 61 runs daily minibuses ($2) from Marin City; the 62 route runs three days a week from San Rafael.

Bolinas

pop 1250

For a town that is so famously unexcited about tourism, 4 offers some fairly tempting attractions for the visitor. Known as Jugville during the Gold Rush days, the sleepy beachside community is home to writers, musicians and fisherfolk, and it is deliberately hard to find. The highway department used to put up signs at the turnoff from Hwy 1, and locals kept taking them down, so the highway department finally gave up.

SIGHTS & ACTIVITIES

Bolinas Museum (☎ 415-868-0330; www.bolinasmuseum.org; 48 Wharf Rd; ⏲ 1-5pm Fri, noon-5pm Sat & Sun) has exhibits showcasing local artists as well as highlighting the region's history.

Surfing's popular in these parts, and from its shop behind the post office **2 Mile Surf Shop** (☎ 415-868-0264; 22 Brighton Ave) rents boards and wet suits and also gives lessons.

There are tide pools along some 2 miles of coastline at **Agate Beach**, around the end of Duxbury Point.

Formerly the Point Reyes Bird Observatory, **PRBO Conservation Science** (☎ 415-868-0655; ⏲ 9am-5pm), off Mesa Rd west of downtown, has bird-banding and netting demonstrations, monthly guided walks, a visitors center and nature trail. Banding demonstrations are held in the morning every Tuesday to Sunday from May to late November and on Wednesday, Saturday and Sunday the rest of the year.

Beyond the observatory is the Palomarin parking lot and access to various **walking trails** in the southern part of the Point Reyes National Seashore (see p160), including the easy (and popular) 3-mile trail to lovely **Bass Lake**. A sweet inland spot buffered by tall trees, this small lake is perfect for a pastoral swim on a toasty day. You can dive in wearing your birthday suit (or not), bring an inner tube to float about, or do a long lap all the way across.

If you continue on 1.5 miles northwest, you'll reach the unmaintained trail to **Alamere Falls**, a fantastic flume plunging 50ft off a cliff and down to the beach. But sketchy beach access makes it more enjoyable to walk another 1.5 miles to **Wildcat Beach** and then backtrack a mile on sand.

SLEEPING & EATING

Smiley's Schooner Saloon & Hotel (☎ 415-868-1311; www.coastalpost.com/smileys; 41 Wharf Rd; r $74-84; wi-fi) This is a crusty old place dating back to 1851, with simple but decent rooms. The bar has live bands on weekends and is frequented by plenty of salty dogs and grizzled deadheads.

Blue Heron Inn (☎ 415-868-1102; www.blueheron-bolinas.com; 11 Wharf Rd; r incl breakfast $158) This inn has two rooms, one queen and one king, tastefully decorated with antiques. The small restaurant does take-out food on Monday nights.

Bolinas People's Store (☎ 415-868-1433; 14 Wharf Rd; ⏲ 8:30am-6:30pm) An awesome little co-op grocery store hidden behind the community center that serves Fair Trade coffee and sells organic produce, fresh soup and excellent tamales. Eat at the tables in the shady courtyard, and have a rummage through the Free Box, a shed full of clothes and other waiting-to-be-reused items.

GETTING THERE & AWAY

Route 61 of the **West Marin Stagecoach** (☎ 415-526-3239; www.co.marin.ca.us/depts/PW/main/marintransit/stage.html) goes daily ($2) from the Marin City transit hub to downtown Bolinas; the 62 route runs three days a week from San Rafael. By car, follow Hwy 1 north from Stinson Beach and turn west (left) for Bolinas at the first road north of the lagoon.

Olema & Nicasio

About 10 miles north of Stinson Beach near the junction of Hwy 1 and Sir Francis Drake Blvd, **Olema** was the main settlement in West Marin in the 1860s. Back then, there was a stagecoach service to San Rafael and there were *six* saloons. In 1875, when the railroad was built through Point Reyes Station instead of Olema, the town's importance began to fade. In 1906 it gained distinction once again as the epicenter of the Great Quake.

The **Bolinas Ridge Trail**, a 12-mile series of ups and downs for hikers or bikers, starts about 1 mile west of Olema, on Sir Francis Drake Blvd. It has great views.

About a 15-minute drive inland from Olema, at the geographic center of Marin County, is **Nicasio**, a tiny town with a low-key rural flavor and a cool saloon and music venue. It's at the west end of Lucas Valley Rd, 10 miles from Hwy 101.

The six-room **Olema Inn** (☎ 415-663-9559; www.theolemainn.com; 10000 Sir Francis Drake Blvd; r incl breakfast $148-222) is a very stylish and peaceful country retreat. Rooms retain some of the building's antiquated charm, but are up to modern standards of comfort. The almost-entirely organic restaurant (mains $30 to $34) can set you up with Hog Island oysters, a small plate meal or something from the extensive list of smaller-scale California wineries. Lunch is served on weekends and dinner is served nightly except Tuesday.

Six miles east of Olema on Sir Francis Drake Blvd, **Samuel P Taylor State Park** (☎ 415-488-9897; www.reserveamerica.com; tent & RV sites $25) has beautiful, secluded campsites in redwood groves.

In the town center, **Rancho Nicasio** (☎ 415-662-2219; mains $16-32; lunch Mon-Thu, dinner daily, brunch Sat & Sun) is the local fun spot. It's a rustic saloon that regularly attracts local and national blues, rock and country performers.

Route 68 of the **West Marin Stagecoach** (☎ 415-526-3239; www.co.marin.ca.us/depts/PW/main/marintransit/stage.html) runs daily to Olema and Samuel P Taylor State Park from the San Rafael Transit Center ($2).

Point Reyes Station

pop 820

Though the railroad stopped coming through in 1933 and the town is small, Point Reyes Station is nevertheless the hub of West Marin. Dominated by dairies and ranches, the region was invaded by artists in the 1960s. Today it's an interesting blend of art galleries and tourist shops. The town has a rowdy saloon and the occasional smell of cattle on the afternoon breeze.

The weekly *Point Reyes Light* has local news and helpful listings of events, restaurants and lodgings.

Cute little cottages, cabins and B&Bs are plentiful in and around Point Reyes. The **West Marin Chamber of Commerce** (☎ 415-663-9232; www.pointreyes.org) has numerous listings.

A romantic refuge called the Sea Star Cottage is at the end of a small pier on Tomales Bay, while **Holly Tree Inn** (☎ 415-663-1554, 800-286-4655; www.hollytreeinn.com; Silverhills Rd; r $130-180, cottages $190-265), off Bear Valley Rd, has four rooms and three private cottages in a beautiful country setting.

Don't leave town without sampling something buttery from the **Bovine Bakery** (☎ 415-663-9420; 11315 Hwy 1; 6:30am-5pm Mon-Thu, 7am-5pm Sat & Sun), possibly the best bakery in Marin. A bear claw and an organic coffee are a good way to kick off your morning.

A local market in an old barn, **Tomales Bay Foods and Cowgirl Creamery** (☎ 415-663-9335; 80 4th St; tours $3; store 10am-6pm Wed-Sun, tours 11:30am Fri, $3) sells picnic items, including gourmet cheeses and organic produce. Reserve a spot in advance for the small-scale artisanal cheesemaker's Friday tour, where you can watch the curd-making and cutting, then sample a half dozen of the fresh and aged cheeses. All of the milk is local and organic, with vegetarian rennet in the cheese.

The lively community center, **Dance Palace** (☎ 415-663-1075; 503 B St), has weekend events, movies and live music. **Western Saloon** (☎ 415-663-1661; cnr Shoreline Hwy & 2nd St) is a rustic 1906 saloon with occasional live bands. Prince Charles stopped in here for an impromptu pint during a local visit in 2006.

Hwy 1 becomes Main St in town, running right through the center. Route 68 of the **West Marin Stagecoach** (☎ 415-526-3239; www.co.marin.ca.us/depts/PW/main/marintransit/stage.html) runs here daily from the San Rafael Transit Center ($2), and the 62 route goes south to Bolinas and Stinson Beach on Tuesday, Thursday and Saturday.

Inverness

pop 1400

This tiny town, the last outpost on your journey westward, is spread along the west side of Tomales Bay. It's got good places to eat and, among the surrounding hills and picturesque shoreline, multiple rental cottages and quaint B&Bs. Several great beaches are only a short drive north.

Blue Waters Kayaking (☎ 415-669-2600; www.bwkayak.com; 12938 Sir Francis Drake Blvd; kayak rental 2/4hr $30/45), at the Golden Hinde Inn, offers various Tomales Bay cruises, or you can rent a kayak and paddle around secluded beaches and rocky crevices on your own; no experience necessary.

Family friendly **Inverness Valley Inn** (☎ 415-669-7250, 800-416-0405; www.invernessvalleyinn.com; 13275 Sir Francis Drake Blvd; r $170-195; wi-fi) is hidden away in the woods, just a mile from town. It offers clean, modern kitchenette rooms in A-frame structures, and has tennis courts, horseshoe pitches and barbecue pits. It's past the town, on the way down the Pt Reyes Peninsula.

From Hwy 1, Sir Francis Drake Blvd leads straight into Inverness. Route 68 of the **West Marin Stagecoach** (☎ 415-526-3239; www.co.marin.ca.us/depts/PW/main/marintransit/stage.html) makes daily stops here from San Rafael ($2).

Point Reyes National Seashore

The windswept peninsula Point Reyes is a rough-hewn beauty that has always lured marine mammals and migratory birds as well as scores of shipwrecks. It was here in 1579 that Sir Francis Drake landed to repair his ship the *Golden Hind*. During his five-week stay he mounted a brass plaque near the shore claiming this land for England. Historians believe this occurred at **Drakes Beach** and there is a marker there today. In 1595 the first of scores of ships lost in these waters, the *San Augustine*, went down. She was a Spanish treasure ship out of Manila laden with luxury goods such as porcelain, and to this day bits of her cargo wash up on the shore. Despite modern navigation, the dangerous waters here continue to claim the odd boat.

Point Reyes National Seashore has 110 sq miles of pristine ocean beaches, and the peninsula offers excellent hiking and camping opportunities. Be sure to bring warm clothing, as even the sunniest days can quickly turn cold and foggy.

INFORMATION

The park headquarters, **Bear Valley Visitor Center** (☎ 415-464-5100; Bear Valley Rd; ⌚ 9am-5pm Mon-Fri, 8am-5pm Sat & Sun), is near Olema and has information and maps. You can also get information at the Point Reyes Lighthouse and the **Ken Patrick Center** (☎ 415-669-1250; ⌚ 10am-5pm Sat, Sun & holidays) at Drakes Beach (longer hours in summer).

SIGHTS & ACTIVITIES

For an awe-inspiring view, follow the **Earthquake Trail** from the park headquarters at Bear Valley. The trail reaches a 16ft gap between the two halves of a once-connected fence line, a lasting testimonial to the power of the 1906 earthquake that was centered in this area. Another trail leads from the visitors center a short way to **Kule Loklo**, a reproduction of a Miwok village.

Explore the landscape on horseback with a trail ride at **Five Brooks Stables** (☎ 415-663-1570; www.fivebrooks.com; trail rides from $40). Take a slow amble through a pasture or ascend over 1000ft to Inverness Ridge for views of the Olema Valley. If you can stay in the saddle for six hours, ride along the coastline to Wildcat Beach via Alamere Falls (see p158).

Limantour Rd, off Bear Valley Rd about 1 mile north of Bear Valley Visitor Center, leads to the Point Reyes Hostel (opposite) and **Limantour Beach**, where a trail runs along Limantour Spit with Estero de Limantour on one side and Drakes Bay on the other. The **Inverness Ridge Trail** heads from Limantour Rd up to 1282ft Mt Vision, from where there are spectacular views of the entire national seashore. You can drive almost to the top of Mt Vision from the other side.

About 2 miles past Inverness, Pierce Point Rd splits off to the right from Sir Francis Drake Blvd. From here you can get to two nice swimming beaches on the bay: Marshall Beach

SHAKE, RATTLE & ROLL

Curious to find a few places where the earth shook? Visit these notorious spots in and around the Bay Area:

- The **Earthquake Trail** (above) at Point Reyes National Seashore shows the effects of the big one in 1906.
- Forty-two people died when the Cypress Freeway collapsed in West Oakland, one of the most horrifying and enduring images of the 1989 Loma Prieta quake. The **Cypress Freeway Memorial Park** at 14th St and Mandela Parkway commemorates those who perished and those who helped rescue survivors.
- The Hayward Fault runs just beneath **Memorial Stadium** (p177) at UC Berkeley.
- Near Aptos in Santa Cruz County, a sign on the Aptos Creek Trail in the **Forest of Nisene Marks State Park** (☎ 831-763-7062; www.parks.ca.gov/default.asp?page_id=666) marks the actual epicenter of the Loma Prieta quake, and on the Big Slide Trail a number of fissures can be spotted.

GRAY WHALES

Gray whales may be seen at various points along the California coast, and the Point Reyes Lighthouse is a superb viewpoint for observing these huge creatures on their annual 6000-mile migration. During summer, the whales feed in the Arctic waters between Alaska and Siberia. Around October, they start to move south down the Pacific coast of Canada and the USA to sheltered lagoons in the Gulf of California, by the Mexican state of Baja California.

The whales, led by the pregnant cows, pass Point Reyes in December and January. They're followed by pods of females and courting males, usually in groups of three to five, and then by the younger whales. The whales spend about two months around Baja California, during which time the pregnant whales give birth to calves 15ft or 16ft long and weighing 2000lb to 2500lb. The newborn whales put on 200lb a day, and in February the reverse trip begins.

Gray whales live up to 50 years, grow to 50ft in length and weigh up to 45 tons. Spotting whales is a simple combination of patience and timing. Spouting, the exhalation of moist warm air, is usually the first sign that a whale is about. A series of spouts, about 15 seconds apart, may be followed by a sight of the creature's tail as the whale dives. If you're lucky, you may see whales spy-hopping (sticking their heads out of the water to look around) or even breaching (leaping clear out of the water). Bring binoculars as whales are typically a quarter- to a half-mile out to sea, though they're closer to shore on the southbound leg of the journey.

See p113 for information on whale-watching boats leaving from San Francisco.

requires a mile-long hike from the parking area, while Hearts Desire, in **Tomales Bay State Park**, is accessible by car.

Pierce Point Rd continues to the huge windswept sand dunes at **Abbotts Lagoon**, full of peeping killdeer and other shorebirds. At the end of the road is Pierce Point Ranch, the trailhead for the 3.5-mile Tomales Point Trail through the **Tule Elk Reserve**. The plentiful elk are an amazing sight, standing with their big horns against the backdrop of Tomales Point, with Bodega Bay to the north, Tomales Bay to the east and the Pacific Ocean to the west.

The **Point Reyes Lighthouse** (☎ 415-669-1534; 🕑 10am-4:30pm Thu-Mon) is at the very end of Sir Francis Drake Blvd. This spot, with its wild terrain and ferocious winds, feels like the end of the earth and offers the best **whale-watching** along the coast. The lighthouse sits below the headlands; to reach it requires descending over 300 stairs. Nearby **Chimney Rock** is a fine short hike, especially in spring when the wildflowers are blossoming. A nearby viewing area allows you to spy on the park's **elephant seal colony**.

On good weather weekends and holidays from late December through mid-April, the road to Chimney Rock and the lighthouse is closed to private vehicles. Instead you must take a shuttle ($5; children under 12 free) from Drakes Beach.

Keep back from the water's edge at the exposed North Beach and South Beach, as people have been dragged in and drowned by frequent rogue waves.

SLEEPING & EATING

Wake up to deer nibbling under a blanket of fog at one of Point Reyes' four hike-in **campgrounds** (☎ 415-663-8054; www.nps.gov/pore/planyourvisit/camping.htm; tent sites $15), each with pit toilets, water and tables. Reaching the campgrounds requires a 2- to 6-mile hike or bike ride.

Point Reyes Hostel (☎ 415-663-8811; www.norcalhostels.org/reyes; dm/r $20/58) Just off Limantour Rd, this rustic HI property has bunkhouses with warm and cozy front rooms, big view windows and outdoor areas with hill vistas. It's in a beautiful secluded valley 2 miles from the ocean and surrounded by lovely hiking trails.

Drakes Bay and nearby Tomales Bay are famous for excellent oysters. Stop by **Drakes Bay Family Farms** (☎ 415-669-1149; 17171 Sir Francis Drake Blvd, Inverness; 1 dozen oysters to go/on the half shell $10/18; 🕑 8am-4:30pm) to do some on-the-spot shucking and slurping, or pick some up to grill later.

GETTING THERE & AWAY

By car you can get to Point Reyes a few different ways. The curviest is along Hwy 1, through Stinson Beach and Olema. More direct is to exit Hwy 101 in San Rafael and follow Sir Francis Drake Blvd all the way to the tip of Point Reyes. For the latter route, take the Central San Rafael exit and head west on 4th St, which turns into Sir Francis Drake Blvd. By either route, it's about 1½ hours to Olema from San Francisco.

Just north of Olema, where Hwy 1 and Sir Francis Drake Blvd come together, is Bear Valley Rd; turn left to reach the Bear Valley Visitor Center. If you're heading to the further reaches of Point Reyes, follow Sir Francis Drake Blvd through Point Reyes Station and out onto the peninsula, about an hour's drive.

West Marin Stagecoach (☎ 415-526-3239; www.co.marin.ca.us/depts/PW/main/marintransit/stage.html) route 68 makes daily stops at the Bear Valley Visitor Center from San Rafael ($2).

EAST BAY

Berkeley and Oakland, collectively and affectionately called the 'five and dime,' after their 510 area code, are what most San Franciscans think of as the East Bay, though the area includes numerous other suburbs that swoop up from the bayside flats into exclusive enclaves in the hills. While many residents of the 'West Bay' would like to think they needn't ever cross the Bay Bridge or take a BART train under water, it is undeniable that the city would be incomplete if it didn't have its East Bay. Museums, celebrity restaurants, universities, woodsy parklands and better weather are just some ways the East Bay lures travelers from San Francisco.

OAKLAND

pop 398,000

Named for the grand oak trees that once lined its streets, Oakland is to San Francisco what Brooklyn is to Manhattan. To some degree a less expensive alternative to the nearby city of hills, it's often where bohemian refugees have fled to escape pricey San Francisco housing costs. An ethnically diverse city, it has a strong African American community and a long labor union history. Urban farmers raise chickens in their backyard or occupy abandoned lots to start community gardens, families find more room to stretch out, and self-satisfied residents thumb their noses at San Francisco's fog while basking in a sunny Mediterranean climate.

Orientation

The two main freeways through Oakland are I-880 and I-580, which parallel each other. Both split off from I-80 at the east end of the Bay Bridge and head south. Adding to the city's maze of freeways, the short Hwy 980 runs right through downtown. The Bay Bridge lets you off in West Oakland, a heavily industrial area with enormous portside cranes, residential pockets and housing projects. Downtown and Lake Merritt are southeast of there.

Broadway is the backbone of downtown Oakland, running from Jack London Sq at the waterfront all the way north to Piedmont and Rockridge. Telegraph Ave branches off Broadway at 15th St and heads north straight to Berkeley via the Temescal neighborhood (located between 40th St and 51st St). San Pablo Ave also heads north from downtown into Berkeley. Running east from Broadway is Grand Ave, leading to the Lake Merritt commercial district. Large regional parks rise into the hills along the city's eastern border.

Downtown BART stations are on Broadway at both 12th and 19th Sts; other stations are near Lake Merritt, Rockridge and Temescal (MacArthur station).

Emeryville is a separate bite-sized city, wedged between Oakland and south Berkeley on I-80.

Information

Oakland's daily newspaper is the *Oakland Tribune*. The free weekly *East Bay Express* has good Oakland and Berkeley listings.

Marcus Bookstore (☎ 510-652-2344; 3900 Martin Luther King Jr Way) Great for African American literature or history.

Oakland Convention & Visitors Bureau (☎ 510-839-9000; www.oaklandcvb.com; 463 11th St; 🕒 8:30am-5pm Mon-Fri) Between Broadway and Clay St.

Sights & Activities

DOWNTOWN

Oakland's downtown is full of historic buildings and a growing number of colorful local businesses. With such easy access from San Francisco via BART and the ferry, it's worth spending part of a day exploring here – and nearby Chinatown and Jack London Sq – on foot or by bicycle.

The pedestrianized **City Center**, between Broadway and Clay St, 12th and 14th Sts, forms the heart of downtown Oakland. The twin towers of the **Ronald Dellums Federal Building** are on Clay St, just behind it. Highlighting the skyline is the 1923 **Tribune Tower** (13th & Franklin Sts), an Oakland icon that's home to the *Oakland Tribune* newspaper. The beautiful, refurbished 1914 beaux arts **City Hall** (14th & Clay Sts) is another urban gem.

Old Oakland, along Washington St between 8th and 10th Sts, is lined with historic buildings dating from the 1860s to the 1880s. The buildings have been restored and some restaurants and hotels have opened up here. The area also hosts a lively **farmers market** every Friday morning. Also in the neighborhood, kid-produced artwork lines the walls of the **Museum of Children's Art** (☎ 510-465-8770; 538 9th St; admission free; 🕑 10am-5pm Tue-Fri, noon-5pm Sat & Sun), and drop-in art classes ($7 for kids) are a fun way to pass a rainy day.

East of Broadway and bustling with commerce, **Chinatown** centers on Franklin and Webster Sts, as it has since the 1870s. It's much smaller than the San Francisco version and not set up as a tourist trap.

Rotating exhibits on local black history are a highlight of the **African American Museum & Library at Oakland** (☎ 510-637-0200; www.oaklandlibrary.org/AAMLO; 659 14th St; admission free; 🕑 noon-5:30pm Tue-Sat), which is also a regional history archive.

From May through October, the City of Oakland runs a number of free 90-minute **walking tours** (☎ 510-238-3234; www.oaklandnet.com/walkingtours), with eight themes, including the waterfront and black history. Tours begin at 10am Wednesday and Saturday; reservations recommended.

JACK LONDON SQUARE

Currently a chaotic flurry of condo and retail construction that's poised to alter the waterfront, the area where writer and adventurer Jack London once raised hell now bears his name. It's now a tourist-oriented shopping mall dotted with chain restaurants, chain stores and gift shops. Still, the pretty waterfront location is worth a stroll, especially when the Sunday **farmers market** (🕑 10am-2pm) takes over. Catch a ferry from San Francisco and you'll land just paces away.

A replica of Jack London's **Yukon cabin** stands in an awkward spot near a parking lot at the eastern end of the square. It's partially built from the timbers of a cabin London lived in during the Yukon gold rush. Oddly, people throw coins inside as if it's a fountain. Another interesting stop, adjacent to the tiny cabin, is Heinold's First & Last Chance Saloon (see p167).

Franklin D Roosevelt's 'floating White House,' the 165ft **USS Potomac** (☎ 510-627-1215; www.usspotomac.org; admission $7; 🕑 10:30am-2:30pm Wed & Fri, noon-3:30pm Sun), is moored at Clay and Water Sts by the ferry dock, and is open for dock-side tours. Two-hour history **cruises** (☎ 866-468-3399; adult/child $40/20) are also held several times a month from May through early November.

LAKE MERRITT

An urban respite, Lake Merritt is a popular place to stroll or go running (a 3.5-mile track circles the lake). The two main commercial streets skirting Lake Merritt are **Lakeshore Ave** on the eastern edge of the lake and **Grand Ave**, running along the north shore.

Lakeside Park, at the northern end of the saltwater lake, includes **Children's Fairyland** (☎ 510-238-6876; admission $6; 🕑 10am-4pm Mon-Fri, to 5pm Sat & Sun summer, 10am-4pm Wed-Sun spring & fall, 10am-4pm Fri-Sun winter), which dates from 1950 and has charming fairy-tale-themed train, carousel and mini Ferris wheel rides. For a spin around the lake, the **Lake Merritt Boating Center** (☎ 510-238-2196; 🕑 Fri-Sun winter, daily spring-fall; ♿) rents canoes, rowboats, kayaks, pedal boats and sailboats for $8 to $15 per hour.

Near the southern end of the lake and one block from the Lake Merritt BART station is the **Oakland Museum of California** (☎ 510-238-2200; 1000 Oak St; adult/child/student $8/free/5, 2nd Sun each month free; 🕑 10am-5pm Wed-Sat, noon-5pm Sun, 10am-9pm 1st Fri each month), which has rotating exhibitions on artistic and scientific themes, and excellent permanent galleries dedicated to the state's diverse ecology and history as well as California art.

PIEDMONT AVE & ROCKRIDGE

North of downtown Oakland, Broadway becomes a lengthy strip of car dealerships called Broadway Auto Row. Just past that is Piedmont Ave, wall-to-wall antique stores, coffeehouses, fine restaurants and an art cinema. At the end of Piedmont Ave, **Mountain View Cemetery** (☎ 510-658-2588; 5000 Piedmont Ave) is perhaps the most serene and lovely artificial landscape in all the East Bay. Designed by Frederic Law Olmstead, the architect of New York City's Central Park, it's great for walking and the views are stupendous.

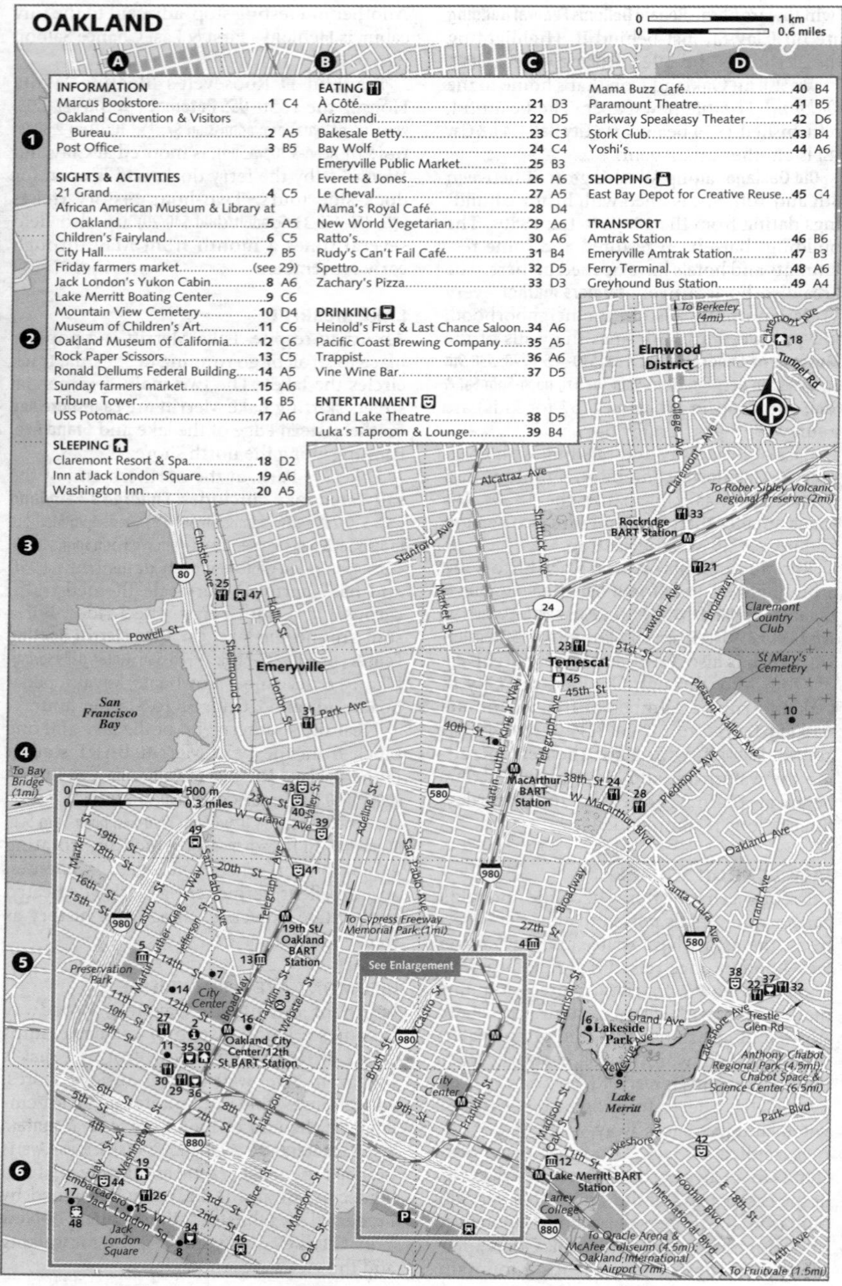
OAKLAND
0 1 km
0 0.6 miles
A
B
C
D
1
2
3
4
5
6
INFORMATION
Marcus Bookstore.....1 C4
Oakland Convention & Visitors Bureau.....2 A5
Post Office.....3 B5
SIGHTS & ACTIVITIES
21 Grand.....4 C5
African American Museum & Library at Oakland.....5 A5
Children's Fairyland.....6 C5
City Hall.....7 B5
Friday farmers market.....(see 29)
Jack London's Yukon Cabin.....8 A6
Lake Merritt Boating Center.....9 C6
Mountain View Cemetery.....10 D4
Museum of Children's Art.....11 C6
Oakland Museum of California.....12 C6
Rock Paper Scissors.....13 C5
Ronald Dellums Federal Building.....14 A5
Sunday farmers market.....15 A6
Tribune Tower.....16 B5
USS Potomac.....17 A6
SLEEPING
Claremont Resort & Spa.....18 D2
Inn at Jack London Square.....19 A6
Washington Inn.....20 A5
EATING
À Côté.....21 D3
Arizmendi.....22 D5
Bakesale Betty.....23 C3
Bay Wolf.....24 C4
Emeryville Public Market.....25 B3
Everett & Jones.....26 A6
Le Cheval.....27 A5
Mama's Royal Café.....28 D4
New World Vegetarian.....29 A6
Ratto's.....30 A6
Rudy's Can't Fail Café.....31 B4
Spettro.....32 D5
Zachary's Pizza.....33 D3
DRINKING
Heinold's First & Last Chance Saloon.....34 A6
Pacific Coast Brewing Company.....35 A5
Trappist.....36 A6
Vine Wine Bar.....37 D5
ENTERTAINMENT
Grand Lake Theatre.....38 D5
Luka's Taproom & Lounge.....39 B4
Mama Buzz Café.....40 B4
Paramount Theatre.....41 B5
Parkway Speakeasy Theater.....42 D6
Stork Club.....43 B4
Yoshi's.....44 A6
SHOPPING
East Bay Depot for Creative Reuse.....45 C4
TRANSPORT
Amtrak Station.....46 B6
Emeryville Amtrak Station.....47 B3
Ferry Terminal.....48 A6
Greyhound Bus Station.....49 A4
To Berkeley (4mi)
Elmwood District
Claremont Ave
Tunnel Rd
College Ave
Alcatraz Ave
To Rober Sibley Volcanic Regional Preserve (2mi)
Rockridge BART Station
Shattuck Ave
Stanford Ave
Christie Ave
Hollis St
Market St
Lawton Ave
Broadway
Claremont Country Club
Powell St
Shellmound St
Emeryville
Horton St
Park Ave
Temescal
51st St
45th St
40th St
St Mary's Cemetery
Pleasant Valley Ave
San Francisco Bay
To Bay Bridge (1mi)
Martin Luther King Jr Way
Telegraph Ave
MacArthur BART Station
38th St
W MacArthur Blvd
Piedmont Ave
Adeline St
San Pablo Ave
Oakland Ave
Santa Clara Ave
Grand Ave
To Cypress Freeway Memorial Park (1mi)
27th St
500 m
0.3 miles
23rd St
W Grand Ave
Valley St
19th St
18th St
16th St
15th St
20th St
Castro St
Jefferson St
19th St/ Oakland BART Station
Preservation Park
14th St
11th St
12th St
10th St
9th St
City Center
Franklin St
Webster St
Oakland City Center/12th St BART Station
6th St
5th St
4th St
8th St
7th St
Harrison St
Washington St
Clay St
3rd St
2nd St
Alice St
Madison St
Oak St
Embarcadero W
Jack London Sq
Jack London Square
See Enlargement
Brush St
Lakeside Park
Bellevue Ave
Lake Merritt
Lakeshore Ave
Trestle Glen Rd
Anthony Chabot Regional Park (4.5mi); Chabot Space & Science Center (6.5mi)
Park Blvd
Madison St
Oak St
11th St
Lake Merritt BART Station
Laney College
International Blvd
Foothill Blvd
E 18th St
14th Ave
To Oracle Arena & McAfee Coliseum (4.5mi); Oakland International Airport (7mi)
To Fruitvale (1.5mi)

One of Oakland's most popular shopping areas is **Rockridge**, a lively, upscale neighborhood. It is centered on College Ave, which runs from Broadway all the way to the UC Berkeley Campus. College Ave is lined with clothing boutiques, good bookstores, a vintage record shop, several pubs and cafés, and quite a few upscale restaurants – maybe the largest concentration in the Bay Area. You could easily spend a satisfying afternoon or evening browsing, eating and drinking here. Exiting BART at the Rockridge station puts you in the thick of things.

THE OAKLAND HILLS

East of downtown and the I-580, the streets become convoluted, winding through exclusive communities such as Montclair before reaching the ridgeline, where a series of parks edge the hills and cyclists lick their chops.

Stargazers will go gaga over the **Chabot Space & Science Center** (☎ 510-336-7300; www.chabotspace.org; 10000 Skyline Blvd, Oakland; adult/child $13/9; 10am-5pm Wed & Thu, to 10pm Fri & Sat, 11am-5pm Sun;), a science and technology center in the Oakland Hills with loads of exhibits on subjects such as space travel and eclipses, as well as cool **planetarium shows**. When the weather's good, check out the free Friday and Saturday evening viewings using a 20in refractor telescope.

The large parks of the Oakland Hills are ideal for day hiking. Information is available from the **East Bay Regional Parks District** (www.ebparks.org). The district manages 65 regional parks, preserves and recreation areas in the Alameda and Contra Costa counties, which contain some 1150 miles of trails.

Off Hwy 24, **Robert Sibley Volcanic Regional Preserve** is the northernmost of the Oakland Hills parks. It has great views of the Bay Area from its Round Top Peak (1761ft), an old volcano cone. From Sibley, Skyline Blvd runs south past **Redwood Regional Park** and adjacent **Joaquin Miller Park** to **Anthony Chabot Regional Park**. A hike or mountain-bike ride through the groves and along the hilltops of any of these sizable parks will make you forget you're in an urban area. At the southern end of Chabot Park is the enormous **Lake Chabot**, with an easy trail along its shore and canoes, kayaks and other boats for rent from the **Lake Chabot marina** (☎ 510-247-2526).

AC Transit bus 53 runs daily from the Fruitvale BART station to Joaquin Miller Park.

SPEAK SOFTLY & CARRY A BIG CANVAS

On the first Friday evening of the month, gallery-hop through downtown and Temescal as part of the **Oakland Art Murmur** (www.oaklandartmurmur.com; 6-10pm). Good bets include visual and performing arts at **21 Grand** (☎ 510-444-7263; 416 25th St) and crafty DIY art activities at **Rock Paper Scissors** (☎ 510-238-9171; 2278 Telegraph Ave).

FRUITVALE

Take the BART train to Fruitvale and indulge in a carnival of food and festivities. Formerly known as E 14th St and once a neglected part of town, Latino and Asian immigrants have turned a 3-mile stretch of **International Blvd** into a great place to stroll on a Sunday afternoon. You'll find an impressive fleet of excellent taco trucks parked along Fruitvale Ave or at the corner of High St and International Blvd. The Bay Area's best pho (Vietnamese noodle soup) joints are just blocks away.

Sleeping

Most Oakland sleeping options are cookie cutter chain hotels, though there are a few spiffy places downtown and in the hills.

Anthony Chabot Regional Park (☎ 510-639-4751; www.ebparks.org/parks/anthony_chabot; tent sites $18, RV sites with hookups $23-25) A few miles south of Oakland off I-580, the 5000-acre park has 75 campsites open year-round. Reservations ($8 service charge) can be arranged by calling ☎ 888-327-2757 or online at www.reserveamerica.com.

Inn at Jack London Square (☎ 510-452-4565; www.innatthesquare.com; 233 Broadway; r $119; wi-fi) Close by the waterfront and handy for the Amtrak train station, this older 100-room hotel is a bit worn around the edges but has nice amenities, including an in-house restaurant and a pleasant swimming pool. Rooms facing the pink-geranium-dotted courtyard are the most tranquil.

our pick **Washington Inn** (☎ 510-452-1776; www.thewashingtoninn.com; 495 10th St; r incl breakfast $129-149; wi-fi) Small and modern with a boutique feel, this historic downtown lodging offers updated comfort and character, with a lobby and guest rooms that project snazz and efficient sophistication. The carved lobby bar

WHAT THE...?

Burning Man (p374) only happens once a year, but ingenious arts and recycling are a way of life at the **East Bay Depot for Creative Reuse** (510-547-6470; www.creativereuse.org; 4695 Telegraph Ave; 11am-6pm), a favorite Bay Area spot to pick up material for the big shebang at Big Rock City. Scavenge a few hundred yards of fabulous upholstery fabric and bags of beads or forage through piles of found photos and fake flowers.

For those who can't wait until August, the annual **Maker Faire** (www.makerfaire.com) is a wacky two-day DIY expo and carnival held on the Peninsula in May. At this family-friendly science and art event showing off playful and irreverent inventions, you can gawk at power tool drag races, flame-belching robots, pulsating Tesla coils and all kinds of geeky cool contraptions.

is perfect for a predinner cocktail, and you're spoiled for choice with several fine restaurants within a few block radius.

Claremont Resort and Spa (510-843-3000, 800-551-7266; www.claremontresort.com; 41 Tunnel Rd; r $269-409; wi-fi) Oakland's classy crème de la crème, the Claremont is a glamorous white 1915 building with elegant restaurants, a fitness center, swimming pools, tennis courts and a full-service spa (room/spa packages are available). The bay view rooms are superb.

If you like B&Bs, the **Berkeley and Oakland Bed & Breakfast Network** (510-547-6380; www.bbonline.com/ca/berkeley-oakland) has listings of 15 private homes that rent rooms, suites and cottages; prices start from $90 per night and many have a two-night-minimum stay. Advance reservations are recommended, and most homes are nonsmoking.

Eating

DOWNTOWN & JACK LONDON SQUARE

Ratto's (510-832-6503; 821 Washington St; sandwiches from $5; 9am-5:30pm Mon-Fri, 10:30am-5pm Sat) If you want to eat outside on a sunny day, grab a sandwich from Ratto's, a vintage Oakland grocery (since 1897) with a deli counter that attracts a devoted lunch crowd.

Le Cheval (510-763-8495; 1007 Clay St; mains $8-13; 11am-9:30pm Mon-Sat, 5-9:30pm Sun) A large and airy downtown Vietnamese institution with well-worn parquet floors, a lightning-fast kitchen and acoustical tiles forming an oddly hypnotic checkerboard pattern on the ceiling. Feast on a five-course menu of beef ($28) or seafood ($21), or one of its many excellent vegetarian dishes.

New World Vegetarian (510-893-2061; 464 8th St; mains $9-13; lunch & dinner; V) Vegan cuisine covering an international spectrum, where diners can choose from Italian, Mexican and all sorts of Asian-inspired dishes. The tofu and veggie bird nest is supercrispy and especially fun for munching.

Everett & Jones (510-663-2350; 126 Broadway; lunch mains $7-9, dinner mains $12-21; 11am-10pm Mon-Thu, to midnight Fri, noon-midnight Sat, noon-10pm Sun) In Jack London Sq, follow your nose to this awesome barbecue restaurant. Order some ribs dripping in spicy sauce, with Southern comfort food sides like corn bread and greens, and wash it down with Sistah Ale.

LAKE MERRITT

Arizmendi (510-268-8849; 3265 Lakeshore Ave; pizza slices $3; 7am-7pm Tue-Sat, to 3pm Mon) Great for breakfast or lunch but beware – this bakery co-op is not for the weak-willed. The gourmet vegetarian pizza, yummy fresh breads and amazing scones ($2) are mouthwateringly addictive.

Spettro (510-451-7738; 3355 Lakeshore Ave; mains $13-16; dinner;) Spettro has a quirky decor and friendly attitude that keeps fans coming back for its homespun, culturally mixed cuisine. Pizzas, stir-fries and chili Colorado give an idea of the unusual mix offered.

PIEDMONT AVE & ROCKRIDGE

Some of the East Bay's finest restaurants are in these two hopping shopping areas along College and Piedmont Aves.

À Côté (510-655-6469; 5478 College Ave; dishes $7-16; dinner) This small plates eatery with individual and friendly communal tables is one of the best restaurants along College Ave. What the menu calls 'flatbread' is actually pizza for the gods. Mussels with Pernod is a signature dish.

Zachary's Pizza (510-655-6385; 5801 College Ave; pizzas from $12) Patrons have been drooling over Zachary's deep-dish Chicago-style stuffed pizzas for 25 years, though the thin-crust pizzas are pretty damn good too, if not better. Expect a long wait for a table.

Bay Wolf (☎ 510-655-6004; 3853 Piedmont Ave; lunch mains $10-20, dinner mains $15-25; lunch Mon-Fri, dinner daily) The menu changes each fortnight at this deservedly famous three-decade-old eatery, but the emphasis is always Mediterranean. It attracts a well-to-do crowd, but dining on the plant-shrouded, heated front porch is a charming, relaxed experience. Reservations are recommended.

TEMESCAL & EMERYVILLE

our pick **Bakesale Betty** (☎ 510-985-1213; 5098 Telegraph Ave; pastries from $2, sandwiches $6-8; 7am-7pm Mon-Sat, to 3pm Sun) An Aussie expat and Chez Panisse alum, Betty Barakat (in signature blue wig) has patrons licking their lips and lining up out the door for her heavenly scones, strawberry shortcake and scrumptious fried chicken sandwiches. Rolling pins dangle from the ceiling, and blissed-out locals sit down at ironing-board sidewalk tables to savor buttery baked goods and specialties like sticky date pudding.

Rudy's Can't Fail Café (☎ 510-594-1221; 4081 Hollis St, Emeryville; mains $6-10; 7am-1am;) A modern diner with tables crafted from board games and strange toys under glass, Rudy's has a goofy punk rock feel, possibly because an owner is the bassist from Green Day. Show up for huevos or tofu rancheros all day, or just chow down on a big burger.

Mama's Royal Café (☎ 510-547-7600; 4012 Broadway; mains $8-11; 7am-3pm Mon-Fri, 8am-3pm Sat & Sun) One of the best brunch spots in Oakland, it gets insanely busy on weekends as folks eat up omelets with gourmet ingredients like goat cheese, smoked salmon and portobello mushrooms (as well as a bunch of tofu options). Angle for one of the worn wooden booths in the middle room, where Sherry, a veteran 30-year employee, mounts a rotating display of vintage and hand-sewn aprons. Cash only.

To satisfy a group of finicky eaters, cross the Amtrak tracks to the indoor **Emeryville Public Market** (5959 Shellmound St, Emeryville; 7am-9pm Mon-Sat, to 8pm Sun) and choose from dozens of ethnic food stalls dishing out a huge range of international cuisines. Prices range from $6 to $8.

Drinking

Trappist (☎ 510-238-8900; 460 8th St; Wed-Sun) The specialty at this dignified brick and wood-paneled pub the size of a child's shoebox is Belgian ales. More than a dozen drafts rotate through the taps, with serving sizes varying based on alcohol content and special glasses for each brew.

Pacific Coast Brewing Company (☎ 510-836-2739; 906 Washington St) Right in the heart of Old Oakland, this place serves full meals alongside its own tasty brews. Try the Gray Whale Ale.

Heinold's First & Last Chance Saloon (☎ 510-839-6761; 48 Webster St) An 1883 bar constructed from wood scavenged from an old whaling ship, you really have to hold on to your beer here. Keeled to a severe slant during the 1906 earthquake, the building's 20% grade might make you feel self-conscious about stumbling before you even order. But its big claim to fame is that author Jack London was a regular patron.

Entertainment

LIVE MUSIC

Stork Club (☎ 510-444-6174; 2330 Telegraph Ave) The Stork is a funky dive catering to the East Bay's indie-rock scene with an eclectic lineup of punk, experimental, lo-fi, spoken word, country and other performers.

Mama Buzz Café (☎ 510-465-4073; 2318 Telegraph Ave; wi-fi) On the same block as the Stork Club, this DIY-feel alternative arts space has an eclectic roster of free nightly shows, as well as a low-key hipster café serving organic produce and Fair Trade java. Food service can be a tad frosty.

Yoshi's (☎ 510-238-9200; 510 Embarcadero W; shows $14-30) Yoshi's has a solid jazz calendar, with talent from around the world passing through on a near-nightly basis. Often, touring artists will stop in for a stand of two or three nights. It's also a Japanese restaurant, so you might enjoy a sushi plate before the show.

DJS

Luka's Taproom & Lounge (☎ 510-451-4677; 2221 Broadway) Go downtown to get down. DJs spin nightly, with a soulful mix of hip-hop, reggae, funk and house; there's generally a $10 cover on Fridays and Saturdays.

THEATERS & CINEMAS

Paramount Theatre (☎ 510-465-6400; www.paramounttheatre.com; 2025 Broadway) This massive 1931 art-deco masterpiece shows classic films a few times each month and is also home to the Oakland East Bay Symphony (☎ 510-444-0801) and Oakland Ballet (☎ 510-530-7516). It periodically books big-name concerts.

Tours ($5) are given at 10am on the first and third Saturdays of the month.

Grand Lake Theatre (☎ 510-452-3556; 3200 Grand Ave) In Lake Merritt, this 1926 beauty lures you in with its huge corner marquis (which sometimes displays left-leaning political messages) and keeps you coming with a fun balcony, free popcorn on weekdays and a Wurlitzer organ playing the pipes on weekends.

Parkway Speakeasy Theater (☎ 510-814-2400; 1834 Park Blvd; 🚼) Located two blocks east of Lakeshore Ave, this great, laid-back movie house shows quality second-run films in a comfy setting, and serves beer, wine, sandwiches and pizza. Family Night Sundays are for parents and kids.

SPORTS

Sports teams play at McAfee Coliseum or the Oracle Arena off I-880 (Coliseum/Oakland Airport BART station).

Golden State Warriors (☎ 510-986-2200) The Bay Area's NBA basketball team.

Oakland A's (☎ 510-638-4900) The Bay Area's American League baseball team.

Raiders (☎ 510-864-5000) Oakland's NFL team attracts a particularly rabid brand of fan.

Getting There & Away

AIR

Oakland International Airport (OAK; ☎ 510-563-3300; www.flyoakland.com) is directly across the bay from San Francisco International Airport, and it's usually less crowded and less expensive to fly here. Southwest Airlines has a large presence.

BART

Within the Bay Area, the most convenient way to get to Oakland and back is by **BART** (☎ 510-465-2278, 511; www.bart.gov). Trains run on a set schedule from 4am to midnight on weekdays, 6am to midnight on Saturday and 8am to midnight on Sunday. There are five different routes, operating at 15- or 20-minute intervals on average.

To downtown Oakland, catch a Richmond or Pittsburg/Bay Point train. Fares to the 12th or 19th St stations from downtown San Francisco are $2.90. From downtown to Lake Merritt ($2.90) or the Oakland Coliseum/Airport station ($3.55), catch a BART train that is heading for Fremont or Dublin/Pleasanton. Rockridge ($3.30) is on the Pittsburg/Bay Point line. Between Oakland and downtown Berkeley you can catch a Fremont–Richmond train ($1.50).

For AC Transit connections, take a transfer from the white AC Transit machines in the BART station to save 25¢ off the bus fare.

BUS

Regional company **AC Transit** (☎ 510-817-1717, 511; www.actransit.org) runs convenient buses from San Francisco's Transbay Terminal, at Mission and 1st Sts, to downtown Oakland and Berkeley, and between the two East Bay cities. Scores of buses go to Oakland from San Francisco during commute hours (fares $3.50), but only the 'O' line runs both ways all day and on weekends; you can catch the 'O' line at the corner of 5th and Washington Sts in downtown Oakland.

After BART trains stop, late-night transportation between San Francisco and Oakland is with the 800 line, which runs hourly from Market St and the Transbay Terminal in San Francisco to the corner of 14th St and Broadway.

Between Berkeley and downtown Oakland (fares $1.75), take the fast and frequent new 1R bus along Telegraph Ave between the two city centers. Alternatively, take bus 15 that runs via Martin Luther King Jr Way. Bus 51, which runs along Broadway in Oakland and then along College Ave in Berkeley, is less direct but has some handy stops, including Rockridge, the UC Berkeley campus and the Berkeley Marina.

Greyhound (☎ 510-832-4730; 2103 San Pablo Ave) operates direct buses from Oakland to Vallejo, San Francisco, San Jose, Santa Rosa and Sacramento (the San Francisco terminal has many more direct-service options). The station is pretty seedy.

CAR & MOTORCYCLE

From San Francisco by car, cross the Bay Bridge and enter Oakland via one of two ways: I-580, which leads to I-980 and drops you near the City Center; or I-880, which curves through West Oakland and lets you off near the south end of Broadway. I-880 then continues to the coliseum, the Oakland International Airport and, eventually, San Jose.

FERRY

With splendid bay views, ferries are the most enjoyable way of traveling between San

Francisco and Oakland, though also the slowest and most expensive. From San Francisco's Ferry Building, the **Alameda-Oakland ferry** (☎ 510-522-3300; www.eastbayferry.com) sails to Jack London Sq about 12 times a day on weekdays and six to nine times a day on weekends. The trip takes about 30 minutes, and the one-way fare is $6.25. Ferry tickets include a free transfer, which you can use on AC Transit buses from Jack London Sq.

TRAIN

Oakland is a regular stop for Amtrak trains operating up and down the coast. From Oakland's **Amtrak station** (☎ 800-872-7245; 245 2nd St) in Jack London Sq, you can catch AC Transit bus 72 to downtown Oakland, or take a ferry across the bay to San Francisco.

Amtrak passengers with reservations on to San Francisco need to disembark at the **Emeryville Amtrak station** (☎ 510-450-1081; 5885 Horton St), one stop away from Oakland. From there, an Amtrak bus shuttles you to San Francisco's Transbay Terminal.

Getting Around

A taxi from Oakland International Airport to downtown Oakland costs about $30, to downtown San Francisco about $50. **SuperShuttle** (☎ 800-258-3826; www.supershuttle.com) is one of many door-to-door shuttle services operating out of Oakland International Airport. One-way service to San Francisco destinations costs about $27 for the first person and $10 for the second. East Bay service destinations are also served. Reserve ahead.

A cheap, easy transportation option is BART. Air-BART buses run between the airport and the Coliseum/Oakland Airport BART station every 10 minutes until midnight. Tickets cost $3 with exact change or a BART ticket of that value.

AC Transit (☎ 510-817-1717, 511) has a comprehensive bus network within Oakland. Bus 13 will take you from 14th St downtown to Lake Merritt and Lakeshore Ave. From Broadway downtown, bus 12 goes to Grand Ave; bus 59 runs from Jack London Sq to the Piedmont district; and bus 51 heads to UC Berkeley by way of Rockridge. Fares are $1.75 and exact change is required.

Within Emeryville, the free **Emery Go Round** (www.emerygoround.com) shuttle runs a circuit that includes the Emeryville Amtrak station and MacArthur BART.

BERKELEY

pop 101,500

As the birthplace of the Free Speech and disability rights movements, and the home of the hallowed halls of the University of California, Berkeley is no bashful wallflower. A national hotspot of (mostly left-of-center) intellectual discourse and one of the most vocal activist populations in the country, this infamous college town has an interesting mix of graying progressives and idealistic undergrads. It's easy to stereotype 'Beserkeley' for some of its recycle-or-else PC crankiness, but the city is often on the forefront of environmental and political issues that eventually go mainstream.

The city is also home to a large South Asian community, as evidenced by an abundance of sari shops on University Ave and a large number of excellent Indian restaurants.

Orientation

Approximately 13 miles east of San Francisco, Berkeley is bordered by the bay to the west, the hills to the east and Oakland to the south. I-80 runs along the town's western edge, next to the marina; from here University Ave heads east to downtown and the campus.

Shattuck Ave crosses University Ave one block west of campus, forming the main crossroads of the downtown area. Immediately to the south is the downtown shopping strip and the Berkeley BART station. In North Berkeley, Shattuck becomes the Gourmet Ghetto.

San Pablo Ave is another major thoroughfare, crossing University Ave several blocks east of I-80. Heading north, San Pablo leads to Albany, El Cerrito, Richmond and other towns. To the south it takes you straight into downtown Oakland (about 5 miles).

Information

Alta Bates Summit Medical Center (Map p170; ☎ 510-204-4444; 2450 Ashby Ave) 24-hour emergency services.

Berkeley Convention & Visitors Bureau (Map p172; ☎ 510-549-7040, 800-847-4823; www.visitberkeley.com; 2015 Center St; 🕑 9am-5pm Mon-Fri) This helpful bureau has a free visitors guide and also sells the useful book *41 Walking Tours of Berkeley*.

Berkeley Historical Society (Map p172; ☎ 510-848-0181; 1931 Center St; tours $10) Offers excellent walking tours several times monthly, exploring eclectic themes.

UC Berkeley Visitor Services Center (Map p172; ☎ 510-642-5215; www.berkeley.edu/visitors; 101

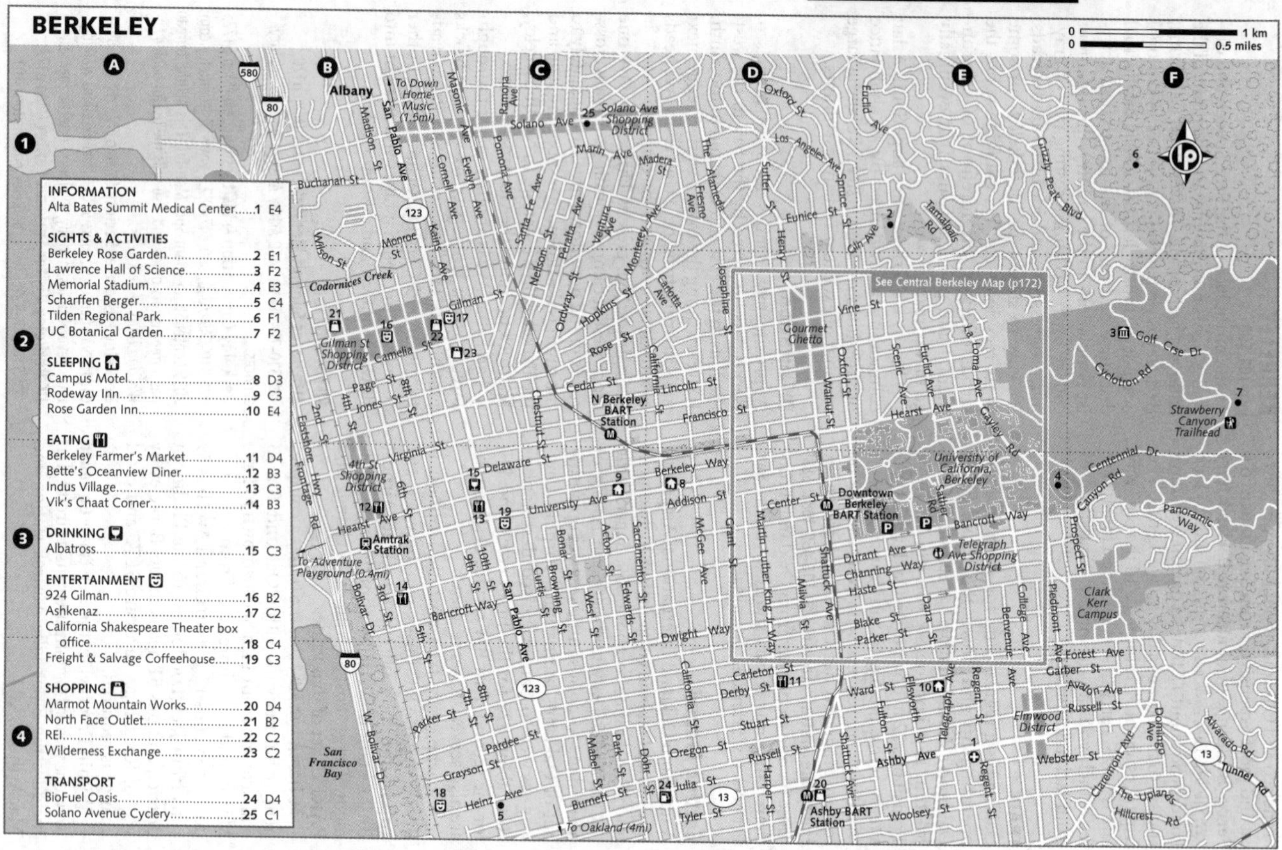
BERKELEY
0 1 km
0 0.5 miles
INFORMATION
Alta Bates Summit Medical Center....1 E4
SIGHTS & ACTIVITIES
Berkeley Rose Garden....2 E1
Lawrence Hall of Science....3 F2
Memorial Stadium....4 E3
Scharffen Berger....5 C4
Tilden Regional Park....6 F1
UC Botanical Garden....7 F2
SLEEPING
Campus Motel....8 D3
Rodeway Inn....9 C3
Rose Garden Inn....10 E4
EATING
Berkeley Farmer's Market....11 D4
Bette's Oceanview Diner....12 B3
Indus Village....13 C3
Vik's Chaat Corner....14 B3
DRINKING
Albatross....15 C3
ENTERTAINMENT
924 Gilman....16 B2
Ashkenaz....17 C2
California Shakespeare Theater box office....18 C4
Freight & Salvage Coffeehouse....19 C3
SHOPPING
Marmot Mountain Works....20 D4
North Face Outlet....21 B2
REI....22 C2
Wilderness Exchange....23 C2
TRANSPORT
BioFuel Oasis....24 D4
Solano Avenue Cyclery....25 C1
See Central Berkeley Map (p172)
University of California, Berkeley
Downtown Berkeley BART Station
N Berkeley BART Station
Ashby BART Station
Amtrak Station
Albany
San Francisco Bay
Strawberry Canyon Trailhead
Clark Kerr Campus
Gourmet Ghetto
Telegraph Ave Shopping District
Solano Ave Shopping District
Gilman St Shopping District
4th St Shopping District
Elmwood District
To Down Home Music (1.5mi)
To Adventure Playground (0.4mi)
To Oakland (4mi)

University Hall, 2200 University Ave) Campus maps and information are available. Free 90-minute campus tours are given at 10am Monday to Saturday and 1pm Sunday.

Sights & Activities

UNIVERSITY OF CALIFORNIA, BERKELEY

The Berkeley campus of the University of California (UCB, called 'Cal' by both students and locals) is the oldest university in the state. The decision to found the college was made in 1866, and the first students arrived in 1873. Today UCB has over 30,000 students, more than 1000 professors and more Nobel laureates than you could point a particle accelerator at.

From Telegraph Ave, enter the campus via Sproul Plaza and Sather Gate, a center for people-watching, soapbox oration and pseudotribal drumming. Or you can enter from Center St and Oxford Lane, near the downtown BART station.

The **Campanile** (Map p172; elevator rides $2; ⌚ 10am-4pm Mon-Fri, to 5pm Sat, to 1:30pm & 3-5pm Sun), which is officially called Sather Tower, was modeled on St Mark's Basilica in Venice. The 328ft spire offers fine views of the Bay Area, and at the top you can stare up into the carillon of 61 bells, ranging from the size of a cereal bowl to that of a Volkswagen. Recitals take place daily at 7:50am, noon and 6pm, with a longer piece performed at 2pm on Sunday.

UC Berkeley Art Museum (Map p172; ☎ 510-642-0808; 2626 Bancroft Way; adult/student $8/5, 1st Thu each month free; ⌚ 11am-5pm Wed-Sun) has 11 galleries showcasing a huge range of works, from ancient Chinese to cutting-edge contemporary. The complex also houses a bookstore, café and sculpture garden, and the much-loved Pacific Film Archive (see p176).

The **Museum of Paleontology** (Map p172; ☎ 510-642-1821; www.ucmp.berkeley.edu; admission free; ⌚ 8am-10pm Mon-Thu, to 5pm Fri, 10am-5pm Sat, 1-10pm Sun), in the ornate Valley Life Sciences Building, is a research facility. Though it's mostly closed to the public, you can see a number of fossil exhibits in the atrium, including a *Tyrannosaurus rex* skeleton.

Bancroft Library (Map p172; ☎ 510-642-3781; http://bancroft.berkeley.edu; ⌚ 9am-5pm Mon-Fri) houses, among other gems, the papers of Mark Twain, a copy of Shakespeare's First Folio and the records of the Donner Party (see the boxed text, p367). Its small public exhibits of historical Californiana include the surprisingly small gold nugget that sparked the 1849 Gold Rush. You must register to use the library and, to do so, you need to be 18 (or to have graduated from high school) and present two forms of identification (one with a photo). Stop by the registration desk on your way in.

South of the Campanile in Kroeber Hall, the **Phoebe Hearst Museum of Anthropology** (Map p172; ☎ 510-643-7649; admission free; ⌚ 10am-4:30pm Wed-Sat, noon-4pm Sun) includes exhibits from indigenous cultures around the world, including ancient Peruvian, Egyptian and African items. There's also a large collection highlighting native Californian cultures.

SOUTH OF CAMPUS

Telegraph Ave is undeniably the throbbing heart of studentville in Berkeley, the sidewalks crowded with undergrads, postdocs and youthful shoppers squeezing their way past throngs of vendors, buskers and homeless people. Numerous cafés and budget food options cater to students, and most of them are very good.

The frenetic energy buzzing from the university's Sather Gate on any given day is a mixture of youthful posthippies reminiscing about days before their time and young hipsters and punk rockers who sneer at tie-dyed nostalgia. Ponytailed panhandlers press you for change, and street stalls hawk everything from crystals to bumper stickers to self-published tracts.

Just east of Telegraph, between Haste St and Dwight Way, is **People's Park** (Map p172), a marker in local history as a political battleground between residents and the city and state government in the late 1960s. The park has since served mostly as a gathering spot for Berkeley's homeless. A publicly funded restoration spruced it up a bit, and occasional festivals do still happen here, but it's rather run-down.

On the park's southeast end stands Bernard Maybeck's impressive 1910 **First Church of Christ Scientist** (Map p172; ☎ 510-845-7199; 2619 Dwight Way; ⌚ services Sun), which uses concrete and wood in its blend of Arts and Crafts, Asian and Gothic influences. Maybeck was a professor of architecture at UC Berkeley and designed San Francisco's Palace of Fine Arts, plus many landmark homes in the Berkeley Hills. Free tours happen the first Sunday of every month at 12:15pm.

To the southeast of the park is the beautifully understated, redwood-infused 1910

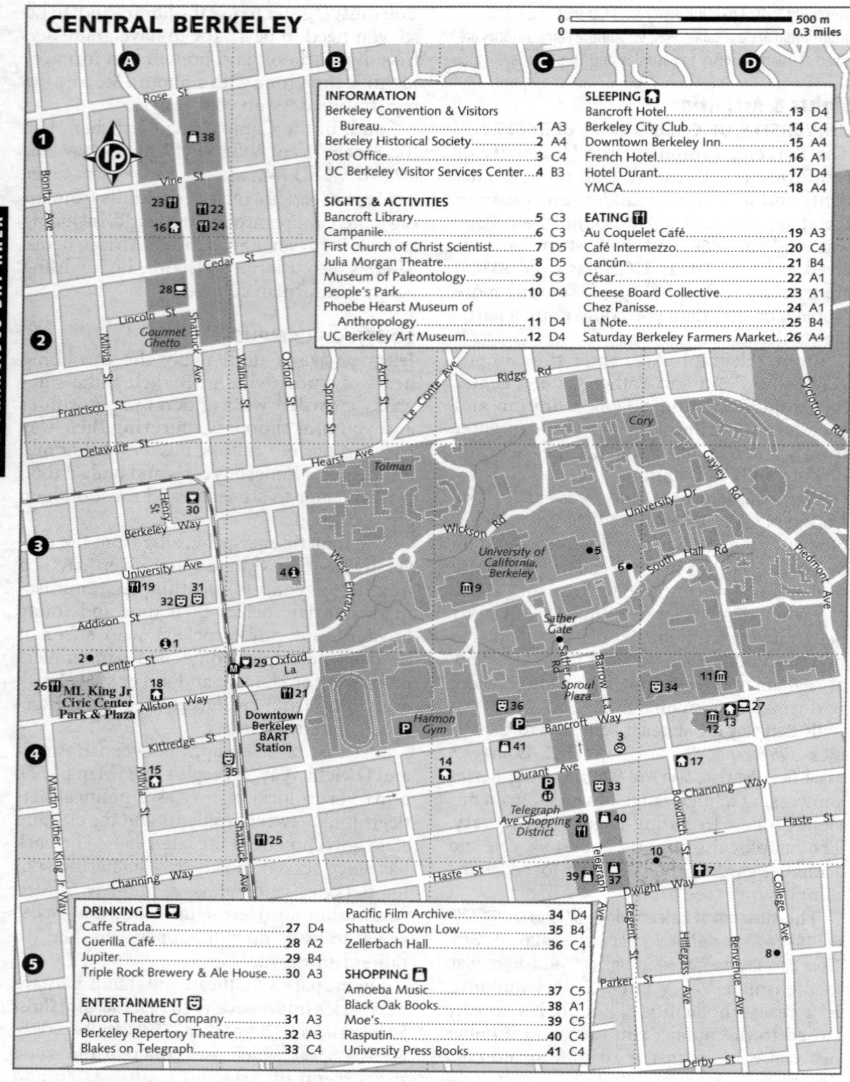

Julia Morgan Theatre (Map p172; ☎ 510-845-8542; 2640 College Ave), a performance space (formerly a church) created by Bay Area architect Julia Morgan, who designed numerous Bay Area buildings and, most famously, the Hearst Castle (see p472). South along College Ave is the **Elmwood District**, a charming nook of shops and restaurants that offers a calming alternative to the frenetic buzz around Telegraph Ave. Continue further south and you'll be in Rockridge.

DOWNTOWN

Berkeley's downtown, which is centered on Shattuck Ave between University Ave and Dwight Way, has far fewer traces of the city's tie-dyed reputation. The area has emerged as a bustling neighborhood with numerous shops and restaurants, restored public buildings and a burgeoning arts district. At the center of that district are the acclaimed thespian stomping grounds of the Berkeley Repertory Theatre (see p177) and the Aurora Theatre Company (see p177); a few good movie houses are nearby.

NORTH BERKELEY

Not too far north of campus is a neighborhood filled with lovely garden-front homes, parks and an incredible concentration of some of the best restaurants in California. The popular **Gourmet Ghetto** (Map p172) stretches along Shattuck Ave north of University Ave for several blocks, anchored by Chez Panisse. Northwest of here, **Solano Ave** (Map p170), which crosses from Berkeley into Albany, is lined with lots of funky shops and more good restaurants.

On Euclid Ave just south of Eunice St is the **Berkeley Rose Garden** (Map p170) and its eight terraces of Technicolor explosions. Here you'll find quiet benches and a plethora of almost perpetually blooming roses arranged by hue. Across the street is a picturesque park with a children's playground (including a very fun concrete slide about 100ft long).

THE BERKELEY HILLS

In the hills east of town is Berkeley's crown jewel, **Tilden Regional Park** (Map p170; ☎ 510-843-2137). The 2079-acre park has more than 30 miles of trails of varying difficulty, from paved paths to hilly scrambles, including part of the magnificent Bay Area Ridge Trail. Other attractions include a miniature steam train ($2), a children's farm, a wonderfully wild-looking botanical garden, an 18-hole **golf course** (☎ 510-848-7373) and environmental education center. **Lake Anza** is a favorite area for picnics, and from spring through late fall you can swim here for $3.50. AC Transit bus 67 runs to the park on weekends and holidays from the downtown BART station, but only stops at the entrances on weekdays.

The **Lawrence Hall of Science** (Map p170; ☎ 510-642-5132; Centennial Dr; adult/child $11/9; 🕔 10am-5pm daily; ♿), near Grizzly Peak Blvd, is named after Ernest Lawrence, who won the Nobel Prize for his invention of the cyclotron particle accelerator. He was a key member of the WWII Manhattan Project, and he's also the name behind the Lawrence Berkeley and Lawrence Livermore laboratories. The Hall of Science has a huge collection of interactive exhibits for kids and adults on subjects including earthquakes and nanotechnology, and outside there's a 60ft model of a DNA molecule. AC Transit bus 65 runs to the hall from the downtown BART station. You can also catch the university's Bear Transit shuttle (H line) from the Hearst Mining Circle.

Another great find in the hills is the **UC Botanical Garden** (Map p170; ☎ 510-643-2755; 200 Centennial Dr; adult/5-12yr $7/2, 1st Thu each month free; 🕔 9am-5pm), in Strawberry Canyon, below the Hall of Science. With 34 acres and more than 12,000 species of plants, the garden is one of the most varied collections in the USA. It can be reached via the Bear Transit shuttle H line.

The nearby fire trail is a woodsy walking loop around Strawberry Canyon that has great views of town and the off-limits Lawrence Berkeley National Laboratory. Enter at the trailhead at the parking lot on Centennial Dr just southwest of the Botanical Garden; you'll emerge near the Lawrence Hall of Science.

WEST BERKELEY

Fancy yourself a modern Willie Wonka? Don a hairnet and inspect the **Scharffen Berger** (Map p170; ☎ 510-981-4066; www.scharffenberger.com/factory.asp;

A LITTLE CHICKEN FEED WITH THAT FILL UP?

A women's worker-owned co-op, the **BioFuel Oasis** (Map p170; ☎ 510-665-5509; 1441 Ashby Ave; www.biofueloasis.com) is set to open a beautiful new station in fall 2008, pumping biodiesel fuel brewed from locally sourced waste vegetable oil. One of the largest retailers of biodiesel on the West Coast, their new home – which was renovated with salvaged building materials – will be both a sustainable fuel station and an urban farming depot. Landscaped by native and edible plants, with solar-powered pumps, folks will be able to drop off their used veggie oil, shop for books on urban beekeeping, pick up bulk organic chicken feed or just nose around for some 'bio-bling.'

Hours are expected to be Tuesday through Saturday, but check the website for updates.

TOP 5 KIDS' DESTINATIONS IN THE EAST BAY

At these family-friendly spots in Oakland and Berkeley, opportunities abound for unfettered art projects, outside-the-box educational programs and all sorts of cool outdoor exploration. As long as children are supervised by an adult, none of these choices have age restrictions.

- Carousel, steam train and horse-drawn train rides at **Tilden Regional Park** (p173)
- **Museum of Children's Art** (p163) For children 18 months and up.
- At Lake Merritt, **Children's Fairyland** (p163) and the paddleboats at the **Lake Merritt Boating Center** (p163)
- **Chabot Space & Science Center** (p165)
- **Adventure Playground** (right)

914 Heinz Av; admission free;) chocolate factory, where you can learn how cacao is transformed into the confections you love, and then nibble on product samples (the Gianduja, with dark chocolate and hazelnuts, is especially yummy). Tours are free but advance reservations are recommended and kids must be 10 or older.

San Pablo Ave was formerly US Rte 40, the main thoroughfare from the east before I-80 came along. The area north of University Ave is still lined with a few older motels, diners and atmospheric dive bars with neon signs. South of University Ave are pockets of trendiness, such as the short stretch of gift shops and cafés around Dwight Way.

Hidden within an industrial area near I-80 lies a three-block area known as the **4th St Shopping District** (Map p170), offering shaded sidewalks for upscale shopping or just strolling, and a few good restaurants too. It's often very hard to park in this area, especially on weekends.

At the west end of University Ave is the **Berkeley Marina** (Map p170), frequented by squawking seagulls, silent types fishing from the pier, unleashed dogs and, especially on windy weekends, lots of colorful kites. Construction of the marina began in 1936, though the pier has much older origins. It was originally built in the 1870s, then replaced by a 3-mile-long ferry pier in 1920 (its length was dictated by the extreme shallowness of the bay). Part of the original pier is now rebuilt, affording visitors sweeping bay views.

Also at the marina is one of the coolest play spaces in the country, the **Adventure Playground** (510-981-6720; 11am-4pm Sat & Sun;), a free outdoor park encouraging creativity and cooperation where supervised kids of any age can help build and paint their own structures. Dress the tykes in play clothes, because they *will* get dirty.

Sleeping

For B&B options, see the Berkeley & Oakland Bed & Breakfast Network (p166).

YMCA (Map p172; 510-848-6800; 2001 Allston Way; s $45-60, d $65-85; wi-fi) In the midst of remodeling its 100-year-old building when we stopped in, the downtown Y is still the best budget option in town. Rates for the dorm-like private rooms (all with shared bathroom) include use of the sauna, pool and fitness center, and kitchen facilities, and wheelchair accessible rooms are available as well. Corner rooms 310 and 410 boast enviable bay views.

Rodeway Inn (Map p170; 510-848-3840, 800-608-7329; www.berkeleyri.com; 1461 University Ave; r $110-120; wi-fi) This comfortable chain motel isn't anything exciting, but it's convenient to campus and has been newly renovated.

Campus Motel (Map p170; 510-841-3844; www.campusmotel.com; 1619 University Ave; r incl breakfast $110-130; wi-fi) Also a few blocks from campus, this small, well-kept 1950s establishment was recently renovated and updated. Modern rooms now have plasma TVs and kitchenettes.

our pick **Berkeley City Club** (Map p172; 510-848-7800; www.berkeleycityclub.com; 2315 Durant Ave; r/ste incl breakfast from $150/225; wi-fi) Designed by Julia Morgan, the architect of Hearst Castle, the 36 rooms in this 1929 historic landmark building were recently remodeled, and the entire premises (which is also a private club) feels like a glorious time warp to a more refined era. A full-time gardener tends the lush and serene Italianate courtyards, gardens and terraces, and the indoor pool is stunning. Elegant Old World rooms contain no TVs, and those with numbers ending in 4 and 8 have to-die-for views of the bay and the Golden Gate Bridge.

Rose Garden Inn (Map p170; 510-549-2145, 800-922-9005; www.rosegardeninn.com; 2740 Telegraph Ave; r incl breakfast $139-205; wi-fi) The decor flirting with flowery, this cute place is a few blocks away from the Telegraph Ave action and very peaceful. Two old houses are surrounded by pretty gardens.

Bancroft Hotel (Map p172; ☎ 510-549-1000, 800-549-1002; www.bancrofthotel.com; 2680 Bancroft Way; r incl breakfast $149; wi-fi) A gorgeous 1928 Arts and Crafts building that was originally a women's club, it's just across the street from campus and two blocks from Telegraph Ave. It has 22 comfortable, beautifully furnished rooms.

Also worth noting:

French Hotel (Map p172; ☎ 510-548-9930; 1538 Shattuck Ave; r from $95; wi-fi) Right in the Gourmet Ghetto, the modern brick building has 18 very straightforward rooms and a popular café downstairs.

Downtown Berkeley Inn (Map p172; ☎ 510-843-4043; www.downtownberkeleyinn.com; 2001 Bancroft Way; r $119-129;) A 27-room budget boutique-style hotel with good-sized rooms and correspondingly ample plasma TVs.

Hotel Durant (Map p172; ☎ 510-845-8981; www.hoteldurant.com; 2600 Durant Ave; r incl breakfast from $149; wi-fi) Located a block from campus, this classic 1928 hotel was renovating at time of research; plans include going more modern and green.

Eating

Jackpot! Telegraph Ave is packed with cafés, pizza counters and cheap restaurants, and Berkeley's Little India runs along the University Ave corridor. Many more restaurants can be found downtown along Shattuck Ave near the BART station. The section of Shattuck Ave north of University Ave is the 'Gourmet Ghetto,' home to lots of excellent eating establishments including California cuisine landmark Chez Panisse.

AROUND CAMPUS

Café Intermezzo (Map p172; ☎ 510-849-4592; 2442 Telegraph Ave; mains $6) Mammoth salads draw a constant crowd, and we're not talking about delicate little rabbit food plates. Bring a friend, or you might drown while trying to polish off a Veggie Delight heaped with beans, hard-boiled egg and avocado.

Cancún (Map p172; ☎ 510-549-0964; 2134 Allston Way; mains $5-10; lunch & dinner) Not to be confused with the popular SF *taquería* chain, Cancún fills you up with tasty burritos, tostadas and quesadillas, and challenges your adventuresome taste buds with a huge salsa bar. Options include strawberry, pineapple, chipotle, tomatillo, mango, pumpkin and the blisteringly hot *infierno*.

Au Coquelet Café (Map p172; ☎ 510-845-0433; 2000 University Ave; mains $6-9; 6am-1am Mon-Fri, 7am-1am Sat & Sun) Open till late, Au Coquelet is a popular stop for postmovie meals or late-night studying (no wi-fi here though). The front section serves coffee and café pastries while the skylit and spacious back room does a big range of omelets, pastas, sandwiches, burgers and salads.

NORTH BERKELEY

Cheese Board Collective (Map p172; ☎ 510-549-3183; 1504 & 1512 Shattuck Ave; pizza slice $2.55) Stop in to take stock of the over 300 cheeses available at this worker-owned business, and scoop up some fresh bread to make a picnic lunch. Or sit down for a slice of the fabulously crispy one-option-per-day veggie pizza just next door, where live music's often featured.

César (Map p172; ☎ 510-883-0222; 1515 Shattuck Ave; tapas $4-10; lunch & dinner) This airy tapas bar turns out simple and delicious small dishes that change with the season. It's jammed at mealtimes, but is a perfect spot for an impromptu *bocadillo* (filled roll), a slow-cooked paella ($18) or a glass of wine with friends.

Chez Panisse (Map p172; ☎ restaurant 510-548-5525, café 510-548-5049; 1517 Shattuck Ave; restaurant $55-85, café mains $18-28; restaurant dinner Mon-Sat, café lunch & dinner Mon-Sat) Foodies come to worship here at the Church of Alice Waters, the inventor of California cuisine. The restaurant is as good and popular as it ever was, and despite its fame the place has retained a welcoming atmosphere. It's in a lovely Arts and Crafts house and you can choose to pull all the stops with a prix-fixe meal downstairs, or go less expensive and a tad less formal in the café upstairs. Reserve weeks ahead.

DOWNTOWN & WEST BERKELEY

Vik's Chaat Corner (Map p170; 724 Allston Way; dishes $4-7; 11am-6pm Tue-Sun) This very popular *chaat* house in a large, stark warehouse space gets mobbed at lunchtime by regulars that include an equal number of hungry office workers and Indian families. Try a *cholle* (spicy garbanzo curry) or one of the many filling *dosas* (savory crepes) from the weekend menu.

Indus Village (Map p170; ☎ 510-549-5999; 1920 San Pablo Ave; mains $5-8; lunch & dinner) Pull up a handmade chair adorned like a rainbow-hued throne at this small Pakistani restaurant painted with murals of rural life. Try the *baingnan bharta* (creamed eggplant baked in a clay pot) or a halal meat dish and sip a cup or two of chai.

Bette's Oceanview Diner (Map p170; ☎ 510-644-3230; 1807 4th St; mains $5-10; 🕑 breakfast & lunch, to 4pm Sat & Sun) A buzzing breakfast spot, especially on the weekends, serving yummy baked soufflé pancakes and German-style potato pancakes with applesauce, plus eggs and sandwiches. Superfresh food and a nifty diner interior make it worth the wait.

La Note (Map p172; ☎ 510-843-1535; 2377 Shattuck Ave; mains $9-20; 🕑 breakfast & lunch daily, dinner Thu-Sat) A rustic country-French bistro downtown with excellent breakfasts. Come by to wake up to a big bowl of café au lait paired with oatmeal raspberry pancakes or lemon gingerbread pancakes with poached pears. Anticipate a wait on weekends.

On Saturdays from 10am to 3pm year-round, pick up some organic produce or tasty prepared food at the downtown **Berkeley Farmers Market** (Map p172)at Center St and MLK Way, and sit down to munch at MLK Park across from city hall.

Drinking

CAFÉS

our pick Guerilla Café (Map p172; ☎ 510-845-2233; 1620 Shattuck Ave) Exuding a retro 1970s flavor, this small and sparkling café has a creative political vibe, with polka-dot tiles on the counter handmade by one of the artist-owners and order numbers spotlighting guerillas and liberation revolutionaries. Organic and Fair Trade ingredients feature in the breakfasts and panini sandwiches, and locally roasted Blue Bottle coffee is served. Occasional film screenings pack the place, as do live music or DJ sessions on some weekend afternoons.

Caffe Strada (Map p172; 2300 College Ave; wi-fi) A popular, student-saturated hangout with an inviting shaded patio and strong espressos. Try the signature white chocolate mocha.

BARS

Albatross (Map p170; 1822 San Pablo Ave) A block north of University Ave, Berkeley's oldest pub is one of the most inviting and friendly in the entire Bay Area. Some serious darts are played here, and poker games and Trivial Pursuit will be going on around many of the worn-out tables.

Jupiter (Map p172; 2181 Shattuck Ave) This downtown pub has loads of regional microbrews, a beer garden, good pizza and live bands most nights. Sit upstairs for a bird's-eye view of bustling Shattuck Ave.

Triple Rock Brewery & Ale House (Map p172; 1920 Shattuck Ave) Opened in 1986, Triple Rock was one of the country's first brewpubs. The house beers and pub grub are quite good, and the antique wooden bar and rooftop sun deck are delightful.

Entertainment

LIVE MUSIC

Berkeley has plenty of intimate live music venues. Cover charges range from $5 to $20, and a number of venues are all-ages or 18 and over.

Blakes on Telegraph (Map p172; ☎ 510-848-0886; 2367 Telegraph Ave) Rancid, Green Day and other groups jammed here before they made it big. It's an 18-plus venue and superclose to campus, with live shows a few nights a week blasting out rock, rap, reggae, blues or jazz sounds.

924 Gilman (Map p170; ☎ 510-525-9926; 924 Gilman St; 🕑 Fri-Sun) This volunteer-run and booze-free all-ages space is a West Coast punk rock institution. Take AC Transit bus 9 from Berkeley BART.

Freight & Salvage Coffeehouse (Map p170; ☎ 510-548-1761; 1111 Addison St) Just off San Pablo Ave, this legendary club welcomes all ages and has great traditional folk and world music, but no alcohol. A new location twice the size is in the works downtown at 2020 Addison St, and scheduled to open in 2009.

Shattuck Down Low (Map p172; ☎ 510-548-1159; 2284 Shattuck Ave) A fun multiethnic crowd fills this basement space that often books big name bands. Locals love the Tuesday karaoke nights and the smokin' all-levels-welcome salsa on Wednesdays.

Ashkenaz (Map p170; ☎ 510-525-5054; 1317 San Pablo Ave; 🚸) Ashkenaz is a 'music and dance community center' attracting activists, hippies and fans of folk, swing and world music who love to dance (lessons offered).

CINEMAS

Pacific Film Archive (Map p172; ☎ 510-642-1124; 2575 Bancroft Way; adults/students/seniors $9.50/6.50/6.50) A world-renowned film center with an ever-changing schedule of international and classic films, cineastes should seek this place out. The spacious theater has seats that are comfy enough for hours-long movie marathons.

THEATER & DANCE

California Shakespeare Theater (Map p170; ☎ 510-548-9666; www.calshakes.org; box office 701 Heinz Ave) Headquartered in Berkeley, with a fantastic outdoor amphitheater further east in Orinda, 'Cal Shakes' is a warm-weather tradition of al fresco Shakespeare (and other classic) productions, with a season that lasts from about June through September.

Aurora Theatre Company (☎ 510-843-4822; www.auroratheatre.org; 2081 Addison St) An intimate downtown theater, it performs contemporary and thought-provoking plays staged with a subtle chamber-theater aesthetic.

Berkeley Repertory Theatre (Map p172; ☎ 510-647-2949; 2025 Addison St) Downtown is home to this highly respected company that has produced bold versions of classical and modern plays since 1968.

Zellerbach Hall (Map p172; ☎ 510-642-9988) On the south end of campus near Bancroft Way and Dana St, Zellerbach Hall features dance events, concerts and performances of all types by national and international artists. The on-site Cal Performances Ticket Office sells tickets without a handling fee.

SPORTS

Memorial Stadium (Map p170), which dates from 1923, is the university's 76,000-seat sporting venue, and the Hayward Fault runs just beneath it (see the boxed text, p160). On alternate years, it's the site of the famous football frenzy between the UC Berkeley and Stanford teams.

Call **Cal Athletic Ticket Office** (☎ 800-462-3277) for ticket information on all UC Berkeley sports events, and keep in mind that some sell out weeks in advance.

Shopping

Branching off the UC campus, Telegraph Ave caters mostly to students, hawking a steady dose of urban hippie gear, handmade sidewalk-vendor jewelry and head-shop paraphernalia. Audiophiles will swoon over the music stores. Other shopping corridors include College Ave in the Elmwood District, 4th St (north of University Ave) and Solano Ave.

BOOKS

Moe's (Map p172; ☎ 510-849-2087; 2476 Telegraph Ave) A longstanding local favorite, Moe's offers four floors of new, used and remaindered books for hours of browsing.

University Press Books (Map p172; ☎ 510-548-0585; 2430 Bancroft Way) This academic and scholarly stop across the street from campus stocks academic works by UC Berkeley professors and from other academic and museum publishers.

Black Oak Books (Map p172; ☎ 510-486-0698; 1491 Shattuck Ave) A fine store in North Berkeley with new and used selections and a full calendar of author appearances.

MUSIC

Amoeba Music (Map p172; ☎ 510-549-1125; 2455 Telegraph Ave) If you're a music junkie you might plan on spending a few hours at the original Berkeley branch of Amoeba Music, packed with massive quantities of new and used CDs, DVDs, tapes and records (yes, lots of vinyl).

Rasputin (Map p172; ☎ 800-350-8700; 2401 Telegraph Ave) Also on Telegraph Ave, Rasputin is another large store full of new and used releases.

Down Home Music (☎ 510-525-2129; 10341 San Pablo Ave, El Cerrito) North of Berkeley in El Cerrito, this world-class store for roots, blues, folk, Latin and world music is affiliated with the Arhoolie record label, which has been issuing landmark recordings since the early 1960s.

OUTDOOR GEAR

North Face Outlet (Map p170; ☎ 510-526-3530; cnr 5th & Gilman Sts) Discount store for the well-respected Bay Area–based brand of outdoor gear. It's a few blocks west of San Pablo Ave.

Marmot Mountain Works (Map p170; ☎ 510-849-0735; 3049 Adeline St) Marmot has climbing, ski and backpacking equipment.

Also try the large and busy **REI** (Map p170; ☎ 510-527-4140; 1338 San Pablo Ave) or **Wilderness Exchange** (Map p170; ☎ 510-525-1255; 1407 San Pablo Ave) for new and used gear.

Getting There & Away

BART

The easiest way to travel between San Francisco, Berkeley, Oakland and other East Bay points is on **BART** (☎ 510-465-2278, 511; www.bart.gov). Trains run approximately every 10 minutes from 4am to midnight on weekdays, with limited service from 6am on Saturday and from 8am on Sunday.

To get to Berkeley, catch a Richmond-bound train to one of three BART stations: Ashby (Adeline St and Ashby Ave), Downtown Berkeley (Shattuck Ave and Center St) or

North Berkeley (Sacramento and Delaware Sts). The fare ranges from $3.40 to $3.75 between Berkeley and San Francisco, and is $1.50 between Berkeley and downtown Oakland. After 8pm on weekdays, 7pm on Saturday and all day Sunday, there is no direct service operating from San Francisco to Berkeley; instead, catch a Pittsburg/Bay Point train and transfer at 12th St station in Oakland.

A BART-to-Bus transfer ticket, available from white AC Transit machines near the BART turnstiles, reduces the connecting bus fare to $1.50.

BUS

The regional company **AC Transit** (☎ 510-817-1717, 511; www.actransit.org) operates a number of buses from San Francisco's **Transbay Terminal** (Mission & 1st Sts) to the East Bay. The F line leaves from the Transbay Terminal to the corner of University and Shattuck Aves approximately every half-hour ($3.50, 30 minutes).

Between Berkeley and downtown Oakland ($1.75), take the fast and frequent new 1R bus along Telegraph Ave between the two city centers, or bus 15 that runs via Martin Luther King Jr Way. Bus 51 travels along Broadway in Oakland and then along College Ave in Berkeley, past the UCB campus and down to the Berkeley Marina.

CAR & MOTORCYCLE

With your own wheels you can approach Berkeley from San Francisco by taking the Bay Bridge and then following either I-80 (for University Ave, downtown Berkeley and the UCB campus) or Hwy 24 (for College Ave and the Berkeley Hills). Note that numerous barriers have been set up to prevent car traffic from traversing residential streets at high speeds, so zigzagging may be necessary in some neighborhoods.

TRAIN

Though **Amtrak** (☎ 800-872-7245) does stop in Berkeley, the shelter (University Ave and 3rd St) is not staffed and direct connections are few. More convenient is the nearby **Emeryville Amtrak station** (☎ 510-450-1081; 5885 Horton St), a few miles south of the Berkeley stop.

To reach Emeryville station from downtown Berkeley, take BART to the MacArthur station and from there take AC Transit bus 57 or the free Emery Go Round bus (BART Shopper or Powell route) to the train station.

Getting Around

Public transport, biking and walking are the best options for getting around central Berkeley. For instance, walking from the downtown Berkeley BART station to Telegraph Ave takes about 10 minutes. Cycling is a popular means of transportation, and safe and well-marked 'bicycle boulevards' with signed distance information to landmarks make crosstown journeys very easy. Just north of Berkeley, **Solano Avenue Cyclery** (Map p170; ☎ 510-524-1094; 1554 Solano Ave, Albany; ⌚ Mon-Sat) has 24-hour mountain- and road-bike rentals for $35 to $45.

AC Transit operates public buses in and around Berkeley, and UC Berkeley's **Bear Transit** (☎ 510-642-5149) runs a shuttle from the downtown BART station to various points on campus ($1). From its stop at the Hearst Mining Circle, the H Line runs along Centennial Dr to the higher parts of the campus ($1).

MT DIABLO STATE PARK

Collecting a light dusting of snowflakes on the coldest days of winter, at 3849ft Mt Diablo is more than 1000ft higher than Mt Tamalpais in Marin County. On a clear day (early on a winter morning is a good bet) the views from Diablo's summit are vast and sweeping. To the west you can see over the bay and out to the Farallon Islands; to the east you can see over the Central Valley to the Sierra Nevada.

The **state park** (☎ 925-837-2525; www.mdia.org; per vehicle $6; ⌚ 8am-sunset) has 50 miles of hiking trails, and can be reached from Walnut Creek or Danville. You can also drive to the top if you wish, where there's a **visitors center** (⌚ 10am-4pm Wed-Sun). The park office is at the junction of the two entry roads. Simple **campsites** (☎ 800-444-7275; www.reserveamerica.com; tent & RV sites $15-20) have no water during times of drought.

DANVILLE

pop 41,700

Set in the shadow of Mt Diablo, Danville is the archetype of the perfect upper-middle-class Californian suburb. Check out the surprisingly impressive automobile collection in the **Blackhawk Museum** (☎ 925-736-2277; 3700 Blackhawk Plaza Circle; adult/student $10/7; ⌚ 10am-5pm Wed-Sun). The museum includes six different galleries, two of which are devoted to cars –

about 90 of them all told, including many one-of-a-kind models.

Eugene O'Neill National Historic Site (☎ 925-838-0249; www.nps.gov/euon; admission free; tours 10am & 12:30pm Wed-Sun) is an interesting stop too. The famed playwright built Tao House with his 1936 Nobel Prize money and wrote *The Iceman Cometh* and *Long Day's Journey into Night* while living here between 1937 and 1944. You must book in advance, as all visitors are shuttled in from downtown Danville.

JOHN MUIR NATIONAL HISTORIC SITE

Less than 15 miles north of Walnut Creek, the **John Muir residence** (☎ 925-228-8860; www.nps.gov/jomu; 4202 Alhambra Ave, Martinez; adult/child $3/free; 10am-5pm Wed-Sun) sits in a pastoral patch of farmland in bustling, modern Martinez. Though he wrote of sauntering the High Sierra with a sack of tea and bread, it may be a shock for those familiar with the iconic Sierra Club founder's ascetic weather-beaten appearance that the house (built by his father-in-law) is a model of Victorian Italianate refinement, with a tower cupola, a daintily upholstered parlor and splashes of fussy white lace. His 'scribble den' has been left as it was during his life, with crumbled papers overflowing from wire wastebaskets and dried bread balls – his preferred snack – resting on the mantelpiece. Acres of his fruit orchard still stand, and visitors can enjoy seasonal samples. The grounds include the 1849 **Martinez Adobe**, part of the rancho on which the house was built. The park is just north of Hwy 4.

VALLEJO

pop 117,000

For one week in 1852 Vallejo was officially the California state capital – but the fickle legislature changed its mind. It tried Vallejo a second time in 1853, but after a month moved on again (to Benicia). That same year, Vallejo became the site of the first US naval installation on the West Coast (Mare Island Naval Shipyard, now closed). **Vallejo Naval & Historical Museum** (☎ 707-643-0077; 734 Marin St; admission $2; 10am-4:30pm Tue-Sat) tells the story.

The town's biggest tourist draw, though, is **Six Flags Discovery Kingdom** (☎ 707-644-4000; www.sixflags.com/discoverykingdom; adult/child under 4ft $45/30; 10am-8pm Fri-Sun spring & fall, to 10pm daily summer, variable weekend & holiday hours Dec), a modern wildlife and theme park offering mighty coasters and other rides alongside animal shows featuring sharks, killer whales and sea lions. Discounts are available on the park's website. Exit I-80 at Hwy 37 westbound, 5 miles north of downtown Vallejo. Parking is $15.

For people trying to keep costs low while visiting the Wine Country, Vallejo is a good budget lodging option. It's only 20 minutes from Napa and motel rooms off the freeway cost around $50 to 100 in the high season.

Blue & Gold Fleet (☎ 415-705-8200; one way adult/child $15/7.50) runs ferries from San Francisco's Pier 41 at Fisherman's Wharf and the Ferry Building to Vallejo.

DETOUR: LIVERMORE WINE COUNTRY

In-the-know wine-lovers venture an hour east of foggy San Francisco to tour the warm, rolling hills and fertile vine-staked valleys of the Livermore Valley, where more than 40 wineries invite you to taste their wares in one of the oldest wine-producing regions in the country. Weekends are the best time to sashay through these oak-dotted hills and farmlands of grazing cows, when tasting rooms fling open their doors and giddy visitors can sample tasting flights. See www.livermorewine.com for a winery area map.

THE PENINSULA

South of San Francisco, squeezed tightly between the bay and the coastal foothills, a vast swath of suburbia continues to San Jose and beyond. Dotted within this area are Palo Alto, Stanford University and Silicon Valley, the center of the Bay Area's immense tech industry. West of the foothills, Hwy 1 runs down the Pacific coast via Half Moon Bay and a string of beaches to Santa Cruz. Hwy 101 and I-280 both run to San Jose, where they connect with Hwy 17, the quickest route to Santa Cruz. Any of these routes can be combined into an interesting loop or extended to the Monterey Peninsula.

And don't bother looking for Silicon Valley on the map – you won't find it. Because silicon chips form the basis of modern microcomputers, and the Santa Clara Valley – stretching from Palo Alto down through Mountain View, Sunnyvale, Cupertino and Santa Clara to San Jose – is thought of as the birthplace of the microcomputer, it's been dubbed 'Silicon Valley.' The Santa Clara Valley is wide and flat, and its towns are essentially a string of shopping centers and industrial parks linked by a maze of freeways. It's hard to imagine that even after WWII this area was still a wide expanse of orchards and farms.

SAN FRANCISCO TO PALO ALTO

South of the San Francisco peninsula, I-280 is the dividing line between the densely populated South Bay area and the rugged and lightly populated Pacific coast. With sweeping views of hills and reservoirs, I-280 is a more scenic choice than crowded Hwy 101, which runs through miles of boring business parks. Unfortunately, these parallel north–south arteries are both clogged with traffic during commute times and often on weekends.

Less than 10 miles south of San Francisco is **Colma** (population 1200), a 2 sq mile town where the living are a small minority. Most of Colma has been covered by graveyards since San Francisco banned cemeteries within the city limits, and more than a million stiffs reside here. The dead outnumber the living by more than 1000 to 1.

A historic site where European explorers first set eyes on San Francisco Bay, **Sweeney Ridge** (www.nps.gov/goga/planyourvisit/upload/sb-sweeney-2008.pdf), straddles a prime spot between Pacifica and San Bruno, and offers hikers unparalleled ocean and bay views. From I-280, exit at Sneath Lane and follow it 2 miles west until it dead ends at the trailhead.

Right on the bay at the northern edge of San Mateo, 4 miles south of San Francisco International Airport, is **Coyote Point Park** (per vehicle $5). The main attraction is the **Coyote Point Museum** (☎ 650-342-7755; www.coyoteptmuseum.org; adult/child $7/3; 🕑 10am-5pm Tue-Sat, noon-5pm Sun), with innovative exhibits for kids and adults concentrating on ecological and environmental issues. Exit Hwy 101 at Coyote Point Dr.

PALO ALTO

pop 56,840

A leafy college town that's home to prestigious Stanford University and the headquarters of Hewlett-Packard, Palo Alto is considered the brain trust of Silicon Valley. It can be said that Silicon Valley started here just before WWII, when Stanford recruited several esteemed professors from MIT. An international mix of world-class academics and technology entrepreneurs gives the town an affluent and quasi-cosmopolitan air, its relaxed California affluence characterized by BMW convertibles and expensive sandals.

Orientation

Palo Alto is bordered by Hwy-101 on its northeast edge and I-280 to the southwest. In between it's bisected by El Camino Real, which also divides the town from the campus. University Ave is Palo Alto's main street and continues, with a name change to Palm Dr, straight into the heart of the Stanford campus. The extensive Stanford Shopping Center is on El Camino Real just north of campus.

Information

Chamber of Commerce (☎ 650-324-3121; www.paloaltochamber.com; 122 Hamilton Ave; 🕑 9am-5pm Mon-Fri)

Palo Alto Weekly (www.paloaltoonline.com) A community newspaper (and website) with entertainment listings.

Sights & Activities

STANFORD UNIVERSITY

Sprawled over 8200 leafy acres, **Stanford University** (www.stanford.edu) was founded by Leland Stanford, one of the Central Pacific Railroad's 'Big Four' founders and a former governor of California. When the Stanfords' only child died of typhoid during a European tour in 1884, they decided to build a university in his memory. Stanford University was opened in 1891, just two years before Leland Stanford's death, but the university grew to become a prestigious and wealthy institution. The campus was built on the site of the Stanfords' horse-breeding farm, and as a result, Stanford is still known as 'The Farm.'

The main booth for Stanford's **Visitor Information Services** (VIS; ☎ 650-723-2560; 🕑 8am-5pm Mon-Fri, 9am-5pm Sat & Sun) is in the lobby of Memorial Auditorium. Free one-hour walking tours of the campus depart from Memorial Auditorium daily at 11am and 3:15pm, except during the winter break (mid-December through early January) and some holidays. Parking can be a real pain. Meters are $1.50 per hour, and if carrying that much change sounds unwieldy, buy an all-day parking permit ($12) from VIS.

Auguste Rodin's *Burghers of Calais* bronze sculpture marks the entrance to the **Main Quad**, an open plaza where the original 12 campus buildings, a mix of Romanesque and Mission revival styles, were joined by the **Memorial Church** (also called MemChu) in 1903. The church is noted for its beautiful mosaic-tiled frontage, stained-glass windows and four organs with over 8000 pipes.

A campus landmark at the east of the Main Quad, the 285ft-high **Hoover Tower** (10am-4:30pm, closed during final exams, breaks btwn sessions & some holidays; adult/child $2/1) offers superb views. The tower houses the university library, offices and part of the right-wing Hoover Institution on War, Revolution & Peace (where Donald Rumsfeld caused a university-wide stir by accepting a position after he resigned as Secretary of Defense). At the entrance level there are exhibits on President Herbert Hoover, who was among the first class of students to attend Stanford in 1891.

The **Cantor Center for Visual Arts** (650-723-4177; 328 Lomita Dr; admission free; 11am-5pm Wed & Fri-Sun, to 8pm Thu) is a large museum originally dating from 1894. Its collection spans works from ancient civilizations to contemporary art, sculpture and photography, and rotating exhibits are eclectic in scope.

Immediately south is the open-air **Rodin Sculpture Garden**, which boasts the largest collection of bronze sculptures by Auguste Rodin outside of Paris, including reproductions of his towering *Gates of Hell*. More sculpture can be found around campus, including pieces by Andy Goldsworthy and Maya Lin. Pick up a free outdoor sculpture leaflet at the museum or at http://museum.stanford.edu/view/outdoor_sculpture.html.

The **Red Barn**, part of Leland Stanford's original farm, stands just west of campus. It's here that Eadweard Muybridge, under patronage of Leland Stanford, photographed moving horses in a study that led to the development of motion pictures. Hiking and biking trails lead from the barn into the foothills west of campus.

STANFORD LINEAR ACCELERATOR CENTER

Few drivers speeding along I-280 realize that things are speeding by beneath them at far higher velocities. The **Stanford Linear Accelerator Center** (SLAC; 650-926-2204; www.slac.stanford.edu; 2575 Sand Hill Rd), run by the university for the US Department of Energy, goes right under the freeway. Positrons (positively charged subatomic particles) hurtle down a straight 2-mile path in a 4in diameter linac (an accelerator beam tube), on their way to high-speed impacts at the other end of the tube. Experiments at SLAC have resulted in the discovery of the existence of further subatomic particles, including quarks, and have gained the facility four Nobel Prizes so far. At 2 miles long, SLAC's Klystron Gallery is one of the world's longest buildings. Because of major construction, SLAC was temporarily closed to visitors at time of research, but was expected to reopen soon. Check the website for updated visitor information. SLAC is about 2 miles west of campus, east of I-280.

NASA-AMES EXPLORATION CENTER

Space buffs will want to stop by the **NASA-Ames Exploration Center** (Map p183; 650-604-6274; www.nasa.gov/centers/ames; admission free; 10am-4pm Tue-Fri, noon-4pm Sat & Sun;), an aerospace research center that has contributed to discoveries in hyper-velocity flight. Inside is a mock-up of the international space station, a Mercury capsule, a moon rock, astronaut suits and the Immersive Theater with a circular screen that shows awesome footage from the ongoing Mars mission. From Hwy 101, turn off a few miles south of Palo Alto at the Moffett Blvd/NASA Pkwy exit, turn right at the stop sign in front of the main gate and then head for the big tent.

Sleeping

Hidden Villa (650-949-8648; www.hiddenvilla.org; 26870 Moody Rd; dm $21-24, cabin from $60; Sep-May) This HI hostel tucked away in a calm, pastoral setting in Los Altos Hills, 2 miles west of I-280, is the country's oldest hostel (it opened in 1937), and part of an organic farm and environmental educational center. The modern dormitory was completely rebuilt in 2001, but the private cabins are more rustic (and are heated) and also more romantic. The location is stellar, with many hiking trails, but there's no public transport nearby.

Cardinal Hotel (650-323-5101; www.cardinalhotel.com; 235 Hamilton Ave; r without bath $80-90, with bath $150-180; wi-fi) In the downtown area, this restored 1924 hotel oozes historic California character with its pristine Mission-style lobby (check out the original elevator and old wooden phone booths). Guest rooms cooled by ceiling fans are small but elegant and spotless.

our pick **Cowper Inn B&B** (650-327-4475; www.cowperinn.com; 705 Cowper St; r incl breakfast $175; wi-fi)

On a shady street two blocks from University Ave, this homey B&B has 13 antique-filled rooms in two gorgeous Arts and Crafts and Victorian houses. Two rooms with shared bathroom cost $105 to $125.

Creekside Inn (☎ 650-493-2411, 800-492-7335; www.creekside-inn.com; 3400 El Camino Real; r $229-279; wi-fi) Primarily serving business travelers, this lushly landscaped Arts and Crafts retreat has comfortable modern rooms – all with patio or balcony – and extensive amenities including a free limited car service, an on-site restaurant and a handy deli/store. Deluxe rooms overlook tranquil Matadero Creek, and all rates drop by $100 on Friday and Saturday.

Garden Court Hotel (☎ 650-322-9000, 800-824-9028; www.gardencourt.com; 520 Cowper St; r $299-379; wi-fi) Fresh fruit, good mattresses and free truffles at reception round out this modern and luxurious Mediterranean-style hotel in a prime spot downtown. Quieter interior rooms have balconies facing a pretty courtyard.

Eating

Café Brioche (☎ 650-326-8640; 445 California Ave; breakfast & lunch $8-12, dinner $14-25; 9am-3pm & 5:30-9pm) Though there's often a wait for weekend brunch at this French bistro, the grilled chicken and avocado omelet, huevos rancheros, oatmeal-rolled French toast and other yummy egg and tofu scrambles are definitely worth it. Sit inside under muraled walls or at one of the cute sidewalk tables.

Thaiphoon (☎ 650-323-7700; 543 Emerson St; mains $8-13; lunch Mon-Sat, dinner daily) Wicker chairs and a burbly Buddha fountain give this excellent Thai place a contemporary tropical feel. Popular dishes include yellow curry chicken and spicy veggies with tofu and Thai basil.

Tamarine (☎ 650-325-8500; 546 University Ave; dishes $10-25; 11:30am-2:30pm & 5:30-9:30pm) With a contemporary sea-green dining room illuminated by dramatic minichandeliers, this modern Vietnamese place is one of Palo Alto's most beautiful restaurants. The dishes have a slight seafood bias and are finely prepared in the style of California cuisine. Most mains are suitable for sharing, and this is one of the Bay Area's best destinations for exotic cocktails.

Osteria (☎ 650-328-5700; 247 Hamilton Ave; mains $16-26; lunch Mon-Fri, dinner Mon-Sat) Loyal fans crowd into this intimate little restaurant for excellent Northern Italian and fabulous homemade pasta. The service is very friendly, but you'll often have to wait for your table (even if you have reservations).

Also recommended:

Palo Alto Creamery (☎ 650-323-3131; 566 Emerson St; mains $7-17; 7am-10pm) A sparkling chrome and red booth beauty from 1923 that's famous for its frothy milkshakes ($6) and hefty hamburgers. Later hours on weekends.

Empire Grill & Tap Room (☎ 650-321-3030; 661 Emerson; mains $10-17) Eat pizza, sandwiches and sturdy meat-and-potato platters on the shaded upscale patio; 25 beers on tap.

St Michael's Alley (☎ 650-326-2530; 806 Emerson St; mains $16-25; lunch Tue-Fri, dinner Tue-Sat, brunch Sat & Sun) California cuisine in a romantic and quaint dining room; an extensive wine list with lots of Santa Clara County choices.

Drinking

Antonio's Nut House (321 S California Ave) The Nut House stands out in orderly, gentrified Palo Alto, as it's a down-to-earth, beer-and-peanuts sort of place. Those nuts are dispensed from a huge mechanical gorilla, so watch out.

Rose and Crown (547 Emerson St) Tucked away off to the side of a parking lot, this friendly ale house carries 21 fine beers on tap from a bar checkered with soccer team scarves. It's a friendly spot for a fine Belgian brew or a British pint of Old Speckled Hen, and the pub food (including homemade curry on Mondays) and Tuesday trivia night reel in the regulars.

Entertainment

Palo Alto Bowl (☎ 650-948-1031; 4329 El Camino Real) This is the real deal if you're hankering to knock a few back (meaning pins). Stop by on Friday and Saturday nights, when the sound system revs up, the disco lights and fog machine are turned on and you can go nuts until 1am.

Stanford Theatre (☎ 650-324-3700; 221 University Ave) This restored 1925 movie house screens some vintage Hollywood gems and international classics, accompanied by a 'mighty' Wurlitzer organ.

Getting There & Around

Palo Alto is about 35 miles south of San Francisco and 15 miles north of San Jose. The easiest way to get here from either end of the Peninsula is via **Caltrain** (☎ 800-660-4287, 650-817-1717), which stops in Menlo Park, Palo Alto and Stanford (for football games only), with faster 'Baby Bullet' commuter service at

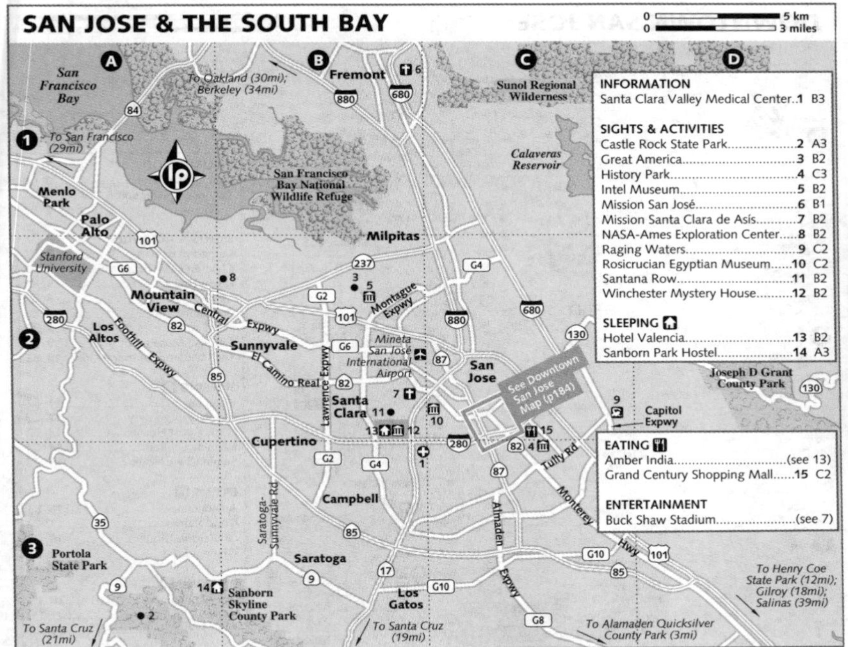

the Palo Alto station. Departures are every 30 or 60 minutes on weekdays and hourly on Saturdays and Sundays. San Francisco to Palo Alto takes about an hour (40 minutes on the baby bullet) and costs $5.75. Palo Alto to San Jose takes 20 to 30 minutes and costs $4. Palo Alto's Caltrain Station is beside Alma St, just north of University Ave.

Buses arrive at and depart from the Palo Alto Transit Center, adjacent to the Caltrain station. From Palo Alto, **SamTrans** (☎ 800-660-4287, 650-817-1717; www.samtrans.com) bus 390 runs to the Daly City BART station ($1.50), and bus KX goes to San Francisco's Transbay Terminal via San Francisco International Airport ($4). Both operate about every half-hour daily.

VTA (☎ 408-321-2300) serves Palo Alto and the Santa Clara Valley. Bus 22 runs from Palo Alto to San Jose ($1.75).

Marguerite (☎ 650-724-4309) is Stanford University's free public shuttle, providing service from Caltrain's Palo Alto and California Ave stations to the campus. Buses run about every 15 minutes until 8:30pm, and every 20 minutes between 8pm and 1:30am (until 2:30am Fridays and Saturdays).

There's free two-hour car parking all over town, or you can park all day for $2 at Caltrain stations, though it's difficult to find a spot on weekdays. See p180 for information about parking on campus.

SAN JOSE

pop 904,500

Though culturally diverse and historic, San Jose has always been in San Francisco's shadow, awash in Silicon Valley's suburbia. Founded in 1777 as El Pueblo de San José de Guadalupe, San Jose is California's oldest Spanish civilian settlement. Though it has recently prospered, its downtown is small and scarcely used for a city of its size. Industrial parks, high-tech computer firms and look-alike housing developments have sprawled across the city's landscape, taking over where farms, ranches and open spaces once spread between the bay and the surrounding hills.

The city seems to shrug its shoulders at comparisons to San Francisco, and has taken a refreshingly modest approach to establishing its own cultural niche within the greater Bay Area. San Jose's fun nightlife district is called

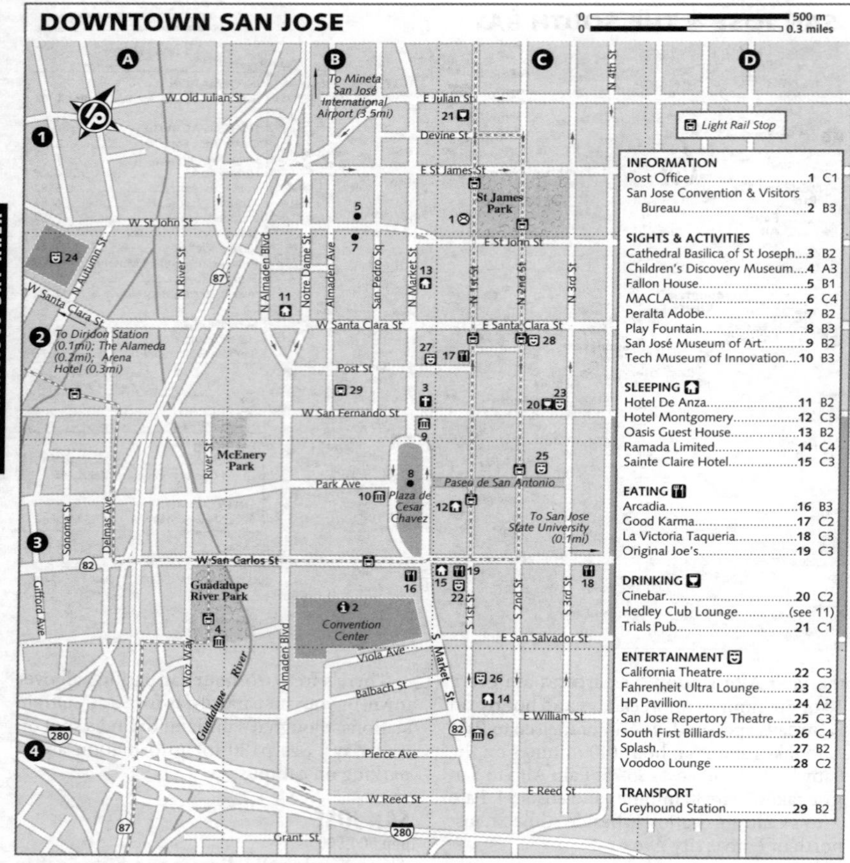

SoFA (South of First Area), which clearly plays on SF's SoMa and gets the upper hand in terms of wit.

Orientation

Downtown San Jose is at the junction of Hwy 87 and I-280. Hwy 101 and I-880 complete the box. Running roughly north–south the length of the city, from the old port town of Alviso on the San Francisco Bay all the way downtown, is 1st St; south of I-280, its name changes to Monterey Hwy.

San Jose State University is immediately east of downtown, and the SoFA district, with numerous nightclubs, restaurants and galleries, is on a stretch of S 1st St south of San Carlos St.

Mineta San José International Airport is at the intersection of Hwys 87 and 101, north of the city center, and planes fly just overhead downtown.

Information

To find out what's happening and where, check out the free weekly **Metro** (www.metroactive.com) newspaper, the biweekly **Wave** (www.thewavemag.com) or the Thursday 'Eye' section of the daily *San Jose Mercury News*.

San Jose Convention & Visitors Bureau (Map p184; ☎ 408-295-9600, 800-726-5673; www.sanjose.org; 150 W San Carlos St; 🕒 8am-5pm Mon-Fri) Inside the San Jose Convention Center.

Santa Clara Valley Medical Center (Map p183; ☎ 408-885-5000; 751 S Bascom Ave; 🕒 24hr)

Sights & Activities

PLAZA DE CESAR CHAVEZ

This leafy square in the center of downtown, which was part of the original plaza of El Pueblo de San José de Guadalupe, is the oldest public space in the city. It's named after Cesar Chavez – founder of the United Farm Workers, who lived part of his life in San Jose – and is surrounded by museums, theaters and hotels.

At the top of the plaza is the **Cathedral Basilica of St Joseph** (Map p184; 80 S Market St), the pueblo's first church. Originally constructed of adobe brick in 1803, it was replaced three times due to earthquakes and fire; the present building dates from 1877.

TECH MUSEUM OF INNOVATION

This excellent **technology museum** (Map p184; ☎ 408-294-8324; www.thetech.org; 201 S Market St; museum & 1 IMAX theater admission $8; 10am-5pm;), opposite Plaza de Cesar Chavez, examines subjects from robotics to space exploration to genetics. The museum also includes an IMAX dome theater, which has shows on the hour from 10am to 5pm daily.

SAN JOSE MUSEUM OF ART

With a strong permanent collection of 20th-century works and a variety of imaginative changing exhibits, the city's central **art museum** (Map p184; ☎ 408-271-6840; www.sjmusart.org; 110 S Market St; adult/child $8/5; 11am-5pm Tue-Sun) is one of the Bay Area's finest. The main building started life as the post office in 1892, was damaged by the 1906 earthquake and became an art gallery in 1933. A modern wing was added in 1991.

MACLA

A cutting-edge gallery highlighting themes by both established and emerging Latino artists, **MACLA** (Movimiento de Arte y Cultura Latino Americana; Map p184; ☎ 408-998-2783; www.maclaarte.org; 510 S 1st St; admission free; noon-7pm Wed & Thu, noon-5pm Fri & Sat) is one of the best community arts spaces in the Bay Area, with open-mic performances, hip-hop, punk and other live shows, and well-curated and thought-provoking visual arts exhibits.

SANTANA ROW

An upscale Main St–style mall that opened in 2002, Santana Row (Map p183) is a mixed-use space west of downtown with shopping, dining and entertainment along with a boutique hotel, lofts and apartments. Restaurants spill out onto sidewalk terraces, and public spaces have been designed to invite loitering and promenading. At its heart is a pedestrian-friendly thoroughfare with Mediterranean style and architecture. On warm evenings, the area swarms with an energetic crowd that's sorely lacking in the city's downtown core.

PERALTA ADOBE & FALLON HOUSE

These historic San Jose **houses** (Map p184; ☎ 408-918-1047; admission $6), sitting across the road from each other near San Pedro Sq, represent two very different early architectural styles. Both houses are open by advance appointment only, with a 10-person minimum.

The **Peralta Adobe**, the city's oldest building, is the last survivor from the original Spanish pueblo, and its two basic rooms have been furnished as they might have been during that time. Luis Maria Peralta came to the Bay Area at age 16 and died an American citizen and a millionaire, the owner of a large chunk of the East Bay.

Thomas Fallon married the daughter of an important Mexican landowner, built the fine Victorian **Fallon House** in 1854–55 and went on to become mayor of San Jose. There are 15 furnished rooms.

HISTORY PARK

Historic buildings from all over San Jose have been brought together in this open-air **history museum** (Map p183; ☎ 408-287-2290; www.historysanjose.org; cnr Senter Rd & Phelan Ave; admission free; noon-5pm Tue-Sun), southeast of the city center in Kelley Park. The centerpiece is a dramatic half-scale replica of the 237ft-high 1881 **Electric Light Tower**. The original tower was a pioneering attempt at street lighting, intended to illuminate the entire town center. It was a complete failure but, lights or not, was left standing as a central landmark until it toppled over in 1915 because of rust and wind. Other buildings include an 1888 **Chinese temple** and the **Pacific Hotel**, which has rotating exhibits inside. The **Trolley Restoration Barn** restores historic trolley cars to operate on San Jose's light-rail line. The trolleys are also run along the park's own short line.

Tours ($6) are offered on weekends between 12:30pm and 2pm, and many of the buildings are closed during the week.

WHAT THE...?

An odd structure purposefully commissioned to be that way by the heir to the Winchester rifle fortune, the **Winchester Mystery House** (Map p183; ☎ 408-247-2101; www.winchestermysteryhouse.com; 525 S Winchester Blvd; adult/child $23.95/17.95; 🕑 9:30am to 5pm, to 7pm summer) is a ridiculous Victorian mansion with 160 rooms of various sizes and little utility, with dead-end hallways and a staircase that runs up to a ceiling all jammed together like a toddler playing architect. Apparently, Sarah Winchester spent 38 years constructing this mammoth white elephant because the spirits of the people killed by Winchester rifles told her to. No expense was spared in the construction and the extreme results sprawl over 4 acres. Tours start every 30 minutes, and the standard hour-long guided mansion tour includes a self-guided romp through the gardens as well as entry to an exhibition of guns and rifles. It's west of central San Jose and just north of I-280, across the street from Santana Row.

ROSICRUCIAN EGYPTIAN MUSEUM

This unusual and educational **Egyptian Museum** (Map p183; ☎ 408-947-3636; www.egyptianmuseum.org; 1342 Naglee Ave; adult/child/student $9/5/7; 🕑 10am-5pm Mon-Wed & Fri, to 8pm Thu, 11am-6pm Sat & Sun) is one of San Jose's more interesting attractions, with an extensive collection that includes statues, household items and mummies. There's even a two-room, walk-through reproduction of an ancient subterranean tomb. The museum is the centerpiece of **Rosicrucian Park** (cnr Naglee & Park Aves), west of downtown San Jose.

HIKING & CYCLING

There are several parks in the hills around San Jose, each laced with a network of hiking and biking trails.

Almaden Quicksilver County Park (off Map p183; ☎ 408-268-3883) is south of town at the site of the old New Almaden mercury mine. Don't eat fish from the reservoirs, but do check out the trails, spring wildflower displays and a mining museum. From San Jose, head south via the Almaden Expressway.

West of San Jose lies **Castle Rock State Park** (Map p183; ☎ 408-867-2952; parking fee $6), where hiking trails are alternately lush and sun-drenched, providing beautiful ocean vistas. The park is on Hwy 35 in the Santa Cruz mountains (p451), just south of the intersection with Hwy 9.

San Jose for Children

Downtown, the technology-focused **Children's Discovery Museum** (Map p184; ☎ 408-298-5437; www.cdm.org; 180 Woz Way; admission $8; 🕑 10am-5pm Tue-Sat, noon-5pm Sun; 🚸) has hands-on science and space displays, plenty of toys and some pretty cool play-and-learn areas such as the kooky 'Alice's Wonderland.' The museum is on Woz Way, which is named after Steve Wozniak, the cofounder of Apple.

On hot days, kids can cavort among the 22 minigeysers that climb and fall at the **play fountain** (Map p184; Plaza de Cesar Chavez) on downtown's central square.

Kids can romp and whoop it up at two nearby theme parks. **Raging Waters** (☎ 408-238-9900; 2333 South White Rd; adult/child under 48in $30/22; 🕑 May-Sep; 🚸), a water park inside Lake Cunningham Regional Park, has fast water slides, a tidal pool and a nifty water fort.

If you can handle the shameful product placements, **Great America** (Map p183; ☎ 408-988-1776; www.pgathrills.com; adult/child under 48in $52/35; 4701 Great America Pkwy, Santa Clara; 🕑 Mar-Oct; 🚸) has roller coasters and other thrill rides. Note that online tickets cost much less than walk-up prices listed here; parking costs $10 but it's also accessible by public transit.

Sleeping

Conventions and trade shows keep the downtown hotels busy year-round, and midweek rates are usually higher than weekends. There's a string of older motels south of downtown on Monterey Hwy, though the motels along the Alameda are generally in better shape. More are found on N 1st St near the airport.

Henry Coe State Park (off Map p183; ☎ 408-779-2728, reservations 800-444-7275; www.coepark.org; sites $12) Southeast of San Jose near Morgan Hill, this huge state park has 20 drive-in campsites at the top of an open ridge overlooking the hills and canyons of the park's backcountry. There are no showers. To reserve, call at least two days in advance.

Sanborn Park Hostel (Map p183; ☎ 408-741-0166; www.sanbornparkhostel.org; 15808 Sanborn Rd, Saratoga; dm & r per person adult/child $14/7; 🕑 Fri & Sat) This remote hostel is in an amazingly beautiful 1908 log building among dense redwoods in 3600-acre Sanborn County Park, 12 miles southwest of San Jose. From Saratoga, drive west on Hwy 9 and look for signs to the park. If you don't have a car, the hostel will pick you up from downtown Saratoga; call before 9pm. Note that the hostel only opens on weekends unless there's a group of at least 10, when spaces may become available.

Oasis Guest House (Map p184; ☎ 661-709-9392; moroccos@live.com; 86 N Market St; s/d $75/120; wi-fi) Draped in colorful fabrics with tall common areas brightened with skylights, this new private hostel is run by the owners of a Moroccan restaurant downstairs. A tad lived-in, there are 10 private rooms (with sinks) and shared bathrooms, a kitchen for light cooking, and the friendly owners include a free meal at the restaurant.

Hotel Montgomery (Map p184; ☎ 408-282-8800, 866-823-0530; www.hotelmontgomerysj.com; 211 S 1st St; r weekend/midweek from $129/179; wi-fi) Built in 1911, the Montgomery combines the stately grandeur of a traditional downtown hotel with the cutting-edge exuberance of contemporary design concepts. A beautiful property, the rooms are sizable and comfortable. In addition to amenities such as bathrobes, there's a small fitness room and pair of bocce ball courts. Watch the lobby video showing how the hotel was moved 189ft in 2000.

our pick **Sainte Claire Hotel** (Map p184; ☎ 408-295-2000, 866-870-0726; www.thesainteclaire.com; 302 S Market St; r weekend/midweek from $139/209; wi-fi) Stretched leather ceilings top off the drop-dead beautiful lobby at this 1926 landmark hotel overlooking Plaza de Cesar Chavez. Guest rooms, while smallish, are modern and smartly designed, and bathrooms have hand-painted sky murals, dark wood vanities and restored tile floors.

Hotel De Anza (Map p184; ☎ 408-286-1000, 800-843-3700; www.hoteldeanza.com; 233 W Santa Clara St; r $149-249; wi-fi) This downtown hotel is a restored art-deco beauty, although contemporary stylings overwhelm the place's history. Guest rooms offer plush comforts (the ones facing south are a tad larger) and full concierge service is available.

Also recommended:

Ramada Limited (Map p184; ☎ 408-298-3500, 866-962-6700; www.ramadasanjose.com; 455 S 2nd St; r $85-109; wi-fi) Basic chain at the edge of the busy SoFA nightlife district, with a pleasant pool.

Arena Hotel (off Map p184; ☎ 408-294-6500; www.pacifichotels.com; 817 The Alameda; r incl breakfast $109-130; wi-fi) A few blocks from the HP Pavilion, this prefab-feel motel has good amenities and Jacuzzi tubs and kitchenettes in all rooms.

Hotel Valencia (Map p183; ☎ 408-551-0010, 866-842-0100; www.hotelvalencia.com; 355 Santana Row; r $209-329; wi-fi) This modern and quiet 212-room hotel evokes European luxury.

Eating

There are plenty of places to choose from along S 1st St and on San Pedro St by San Pedro Sq. Vietnamese restaurants are gathered along E Santa Clara St from 4th to 12th Sts. Santana Row also has several good restaurants.

La Victoria Taqueria (Map p184; ☎ 408-298-5335; 140 E San Carlos St; mains $2.50-4.50; 7am-2:30am Sun-Wed, to 3am Thu-Sat) Half a block from San Jose State University and open till the wee hours, patrons queue up inside this bright and clean old Victorian house for their fill of good burritos (breakfast burritos available until 11am) and tacos. Boosters swear by its mysterious spicy orange sauce.

Good Karma (Map p184; ☎ 408-294-2694; 37 S 1st; mains $5.50-7.50; 11am-9pm Mon-Sat, noon-7pm Sun; V) Centrally located with a laid-back DIY feel, the vegan Good Karma serves Asian and American comfort food in a small space adorned with work by local artists. At the deli-style counter, order ginger tofu with shiitake mushrooms or just a dreamy serving of dairy-free mashed potatoes.

Original Joe's (Map p184; ☎ 408-292-7030; 301 S 1st St; mains $13-30) Waiters in bow ties flit about this busy 1950s San Jose landmark, serving standard Italian dishes to locals and conventioneers. The newly remodeled dining room is a curious but tasteful hodgepodge of '50s brick, contemporary wood paneling and 5ft-tall Asian vases. Expect a wait.

Amber India (Map p183; ☎ 408-248-5400; No 1140, 377 Santana Row; dinner $13-33) The cooking at this upscale Indian restaurant is superb, offering a full complement of kebabs, curries and tandooris. Presentation is highly styled, with artsy china and groovy paintings on the walls. Whet your whistle with an exotic cocktail as you feast on the delectable butter chicken.

Arcadia (Map p184; ☎ 408-278-4555; 100 W San Carlos St; lunch $10-32, dinner $17-44) Chef Michael Mina, San Francisco's biggest celebrity chef, has opened this fine New American steakhouse restaurant in the Marriott Hotel. It's not the daring, cutting-edge style Mina is known for, but it's slick, expensive and, of course, very good.

Grand Century Shopping Mall (Map p183; 1001 Story Rd) For Vietnamese fare, the food court here offers an Americanized version of dining at food stalls in the markets of Saigon, with noodle soups, rice plates, baguette sandwiches, spring rolls and sweet bean puddings.

Drinking

Cinebar (Map p184; 69 E San Fernando; 6am-2am) A hip dive bar where patrons down bottled beer and all kinds of hard liquor, and closing time lasts a mere four hours. Black-and-white murals of film and music legends stare out from the walls, and there's pool table too.

Trials Pub (Map p184; 265 N 1st St) If you seek a well-poured pint in a supremely comfortable atmosphere, Trials Pub, north of San Pedro Sq, has many excellent ales on tap (try a Fat Lip), all served in a warm and friendly room with no TVs. There's good pub food too.

Hedley Club Lounge (Map p184; 233 W Santa Clara St) Also downtown, inside the elegant 1931 Hotel De Anza, Hedley Club is a good place for a quiet drink in swanky art-deco surroundings. Jazz combos play Friday and Saturday nights.

Entertainment

CLUBS

The biggest conglomeration of clubs is on S 1st St, aka SoFA, and around S 2nd at San Fernando. Raucous club-goers pack the streets on Friday and Saturday nights.

Voodoo Lounge (Map p184; ☎ 408-286-8636; 14 S 2nd St) Red brick walls and faux leopard-skin sofas adorn this midsized club hosting live music or DJs most nights. Survey the scene from the 2nd-floor balcony or lounge in a cozy corner behind the loft bar.

South First Billiards (Map p184; 420 S 1st St) It's a great place to shoot some stick, and a welcoming club to boot. Free rock shows on Friday and Saturday always draw a fun crowd.

Splash (Map p184; ☎ 408-993-0861; 65 Post St; Thu-Sun) Raise the roof at this supermixed club where straight couples bump and grind alongside unshirted boys in heated lip lock. This two-story dance spot gets down on a street that was once home to the city's red-light district.

Fahrenheit Ultra Lounge (Map p184; ☎ 408-998-9998; 99 E San Fernando St) Expect short party dresses, velvet ropes and clubbers enjoying bottle service and small-plates menu at this buzzing dance club. DJs play a mix and mash-ups of top 40, house and hip-hop, and flair bartenders play with fire as they pour drinks.

THEATERS

California Theatre (Map p184; 345 S 1st St) The absolutely stunning Spanish interior of this landmark entertainment venue is cathedral worthy. The theater is home to Opera San José, Symphony Silicon Valley and an ongoing classic film series, and is a venue for the city's annual film festival, **Cinequest** (☎ 408-295-3378; www.cinequest.org), held in late February or early March.

San Jose Repertory Theatre (Map p184; ☎ 408-367-7255; www.sjrep.com; 101 Paseo de San Antonio; tickets $30-59) Steaming ahead in its third decade, this company offers a full season of top-rated productions in a contemporary 525-seat venue downtown.

SPORTS

HP Pavilion (Map p184; ☎ 408-287-9200; cnr Santa Clara & N Autumn Sts; tickets $20-175) The fanatically popular San Jose Sharks, the city's NHL (National Hockey League) team, plays at the HP Pavilion, a massive glass-and-metal stadium. The NHL season runs from September to April.

Buck Shaw Stadium (Map p183; http://sjearthquakes.mlsnet.com; 500 El Camino Real, Santa Clara; tickets $20-60) Located at Santa Clara University, this is the new temporary home for the San Jose Earthquakes Major League Soccer team; games run from February through October.

Getting There & Away

Caltrain (www.caltrain.com), a double-decker commuter rail service that operates up and down the Peninsula, is your best bet between San Jose and San Francisco; see p182.

AIR

Two miles north of downtown, between Hwy 101 and I-880, is **Mineta San José International Airport** (SJC; Map p183; ☎ 408-277-4759; www.sjc.org). The airport has grown busier as the South Bay gets more crowded, with numerous domestic flights at two terminals (free wi-fi).

BART

To access the BART system in the East Bay, bus 180, operated by **VTA** (☎ 408-321-2300; www.vta.org), runs daily between the Fremont BART station and downtown ($3.50).

BUS

Greyhound buses to San Francisco ($7.25, 90 minutes) and Los Angeles ($45.50 to $62, seven to 10 hours) leave from the **Greyhound station** (Map p184; ☎ 408-295-4151; 70 Almaden Ave).

The VTA Hwy 17 Express bus plies a handy daily route between Diridon Station and Santa Cruz ($4, one hour).

CAR & MOTORCYCLE

San Jose is right at the bottom end of the San Francisco Bay, about 40 miles from Oakland (via I-880) or San Francisco (via Hwy 101 or I-280). Expect lots of traffic at all times of day on Hwy 101. Although I-280 is slightly longer, it's much prettier and usually less congested. Heading south, Hwy 17 leads over the hill to Santa Cruz.

On weekends until 6pm, parking is free in city-owned lots and garages downtown.

TRAIN

Between San Jose and San Francisco, **Caltrain** (☎ 800-660-4287) makes over three dozen trips daily (fewer on weekends); the 60-minute (on the Baby Bullet commuter trains) to 90-minute journey costs $7.50 each way and bicycles can be brought on designated cars. San Jose's terminal, **Diridon Station** (off Map p184; 65 Cahill St) is just south of the Alameda.

Diridon Station also serves as the terminal for **Amtrak** (☎ 408-287-7462), serving Seattle, Los Angeles and Sacramento, and Altamont Commuter Express (ACE; www.acerail.com), which runs to Great America, Livermore and Stockton.

VTA runs a free weekday shuttle (known as the Downtown Area Shuttle or DASH) from the station to downtown.

Getting Around

From the airport, VTA Airport Flyer shuttles run every 10 to 15 minutes to the Metro/Airport Light Rail station, where you can catch the San Jose light-rail to downtown San Jose. VTA buses run all over Silicon Valley. Fares for buses (except express lines) and light-rail trains are $1.75 for a single ride and $5 for a day pass.

SuperShuttle (☎ 408-558-9500) offers door-to-door bus service to most Silicon Valley destinations; fares start at $19.

The main San Jose light-rail line runs 20 miles north–south from the city center. Heading south gets you as far as Almaden and Santa Teresa. The northern route runs to the Civic Center, the airport and Baypointe, where it connects with another line that heads west past Great America to downtown Mountain View.

AROUND SAN JOSE

Mission Santa Clara de Asís

The eighth mission in California, **Mission Santa Clara de Asís** (Map p183; ☎ 408-554-4023; 6am-8pm daily) is located on the Santa Clara University campus, west of downtown San Jose. The mission started life in 1777, on the Guadalupe River. Floods forced the first move; the second site was only temporary; the third church burned; while the fourth church, a substantial adobe construction, was finished in 1784, but an earthquake in 1818 forced the move to the present site. That church, the fifth, was completed in 1822, but in 1926 it burned down, so the present church – an enlarged version of the 1822 church, completed in 1928 – is the sixth church on the fifth site.

Many of the roof tiles came from the earlier buildings, and the church is fronted by a wooden cross from the original mission of 1777. The only remains from the 1822 mission are a nearby adobe wall and an adobe building. The first college in California was opened at the mission in 1851. The college grew to become Santa Clara University, and the mission church is now the college chapel. Santa Clara University is within walking distance of the Santa Clara Caltrain station.

Mission San José

Founded in 1797, the **Mission San José** (Map p183; ☎ 510-657-1797; 43300 Mission Blvd, Fremont; museum & church 10am-5pm daily, mass 8am Mon-Fri) was the 14th California mission, and it's located in Fremont, not present-day San Jose. Its large Native American population and fertile agricultural lands made it one of the most successful, until a major earthquake struck in 1868, virtually leveling the mission's original 1809 church, which was then replaced by a wooden one. In 1979, the wooden church was sold and moved to San Mateo. The adobe church seen today is a reasonably faithful reconstruction of the 1809 structure. A statue of St Bonaventure, in a side altar, dates from around 1808. The adjacent living quarters, now housing a small mission museum, are original.

The mission is at the foot of Mission Peak Regional Preserve. From I-880 or I-680, take the Mission Blvd exit to Washington Blvd.

Intel Museum

At the company's headquarters, the **Intel Museum** (Map p183; ☎ 408-765-0503; www.intel.com/museum; 2200 Mission College Blvd, Santa Clara; admission free; 🕐 9am-6pm Mon-Fri, 10am-5pm Sat) has displays on the birth and growth of the computer industry with special emphasis, not surprisingly, on Intel's involvement. Call ahead if you want to schedule a guided tour.

SAN FRANCISCO TO HALF MOON BAY

One of the real surprises of the Bay Area is how fast the urban landscape disappears along the rugged and largely undeveloped coast. The 70-mile stretch of coastal Hwy 1 from San Francisco to Santa Cruz is one of the most beautiful motorways anywhere. For the most part a winding two-lane blacktop, it passes beach after beach, many of them little sandy coves hidden from the highway. Most beaches along Hwy 1 are buffeted by wild and unpredictable surf, making them more suitable for sunbathing (weather permitting) than swimming. The state beaches along the coast don't charge an access fee, but parking can cost a few dollars.

A cluster of isolated and supremely scenic HI hostels, at Point Montara (22 miles south of San Francisco) and Pigeon Point (36 miles), make this an interesting route for cyclists, though narrow Hwy 1 itself can be stressful, if not downright dangerous, for inexperienced cyclists.

Pacifica & Devil's Slide

Pacifica and Point San Pedro, 15 miles from downtown San Francisco, signal the end of the urban sprawl. South of Pacifica is Devil's Slide, an unstable cliff area through which Hwy 1 winds and curves. Drive carefully, especially at night and when it is raining, as rock and mud slides are frequent. Heavy winter storms often lead to the road's temporary closure. A tunnel will soon bypass this dramatic stretch of the highway.

In Pacifica, collecting a suntan or catching a wave are the main attractions at **Rockaway Beach** and the more popular **Pacifica State Beach** (also known as Linda Mar Beach), where the nearby **Nor-Cal Surf Shop** (☎ 650-738-9283; 5460 Coast Hwy) rents surfboards ($17 per day) and wet suits.

Gray Whale Cove to Mavericks

One of the coast's popular 'clothing-optional' beaches is **Gray Whale Cove State Beach** (☎ 650-726-8819), just south of Point San Pedro. There are steps down to the beach from a parking lot ($5). **Montara State Beach** is just a half-mile south. From the town of Montara, 22 miles from San Francisco, trails climb up from the Martini Creek parking lot into **McNee Ranch State Park**, which has hiking trails aplenty.

Point Montara Lighthouse HI Hostel (☎ 650-728-7177; www.norcalhostels.org/montara; cnr Hwy 1 & 16th St; dm $20-25, r $59-93) started life as a fog station in 1875. The hostel is adjacent to the current lighthouse, which dates from 1928. This very popular hostel has a living room, kitchen facilities and an international clientele. There are a few private rooms for couples or families. Reservations are a good idea anytime, but especially on weekends during summer. SamTrans bus 294 will let you off at the hostel if you ask nicely. Montara has a number of B&Bs too, including the **Goose & Turrets** (☎ 650-728-5451; http://goose.montara.com; 835 George St; r $145-190) and the **Farallone Inn** (☎ 650-728-8200, 800-818-7319; www.faralloneinn.com; 1410 Main St; r $85-195).

DETOUR: HIGHWAY 84

Inland, large stretches of the hills are protected in a patchwork of parks that, just like the coast, remain remarkably untouched despite the huge urban populations only a short drive to the north and east. Heading east toward Palo Alto, Hwy 84 winds its way through thick stands of redwood trees and several local parks with mountain-biking and hiking opportunities.

A mile in from San Gregorio State Beach on Hwy 1, kick off your shoes and stomp your feet to live bluegrass, Celtic and folk music on the weekends at the landmark **San Gregorio General Store** (☎ 650-726-0565), and check out the wooden bar singed by area branding irons.

Eight miles east is the tiny township of **La Honda**, former home to *One Flew Over the Cuckoo's Nest* author Ken Kesey, and the launching spot for his 1964 psychedelic bus trip immortalized in Tom Wolfe's *The Electric Kool-Aid Acid Test*. Housed in an old blacksmith's shop, **Apple Jack's Inn** (☎ 650-747-0331) is a rustic, down-home bar offering live music on weekends and lots of local color.

South of the lighthouse, **Fitzgerald Marine Reserve** (☎ 650-363-4020) at Moss Beach is an extensive area of natural tidal pools. Feel free to walk out and explore the pools at low tide, though be careful, as it's slippery. Also, it's illegal to remove any creatures, shells or even rocks – this is a marine reserve, after all. From Hwy 1 in Moss Beach, turn west onto California Ave and drive to the end. SamTrans bus 294 stops along Hwy 1.

Moss Beach Distillery (☎ 650-728-5595; cnr Beach Way & Ocean Blvd; lunch $17-30, dinner $30-50) is a 1927 landmark overlooking the ocean. In fair weather the deck here is the best place for miles around to have a leisurely cocktail or glass of vino.

South of here is a stretch of coast called Pillar Point. Fishing boats bring in their catch at the Pillar Point Harbor, some of which gets cooked up in seafront restaurants at Princeton such as **Barbara's Fishtrap** (281 Capistrano Rd), off Hwy 1, a true old-time fisherman's rest.

At the western end of Pillar Point is **Mavericks**, a serious surf break that attracts the world's top big-wave riders to battle its huge, steep and very dangerous waves. The annual Mavericks surf contest, called on a few days' notice when the swells get huge, is held between December and March.

HALF MOON BAY

pop 12,200

Developed as a beach resort back in the Victorian era, Half Moon Bay is the main coastal town between San Francisco (28 miles north) and Santa Cruz (40 miles south). Its long stretches of beach still attract rambling weekenders and hearty surfers. Half Moon Bay spreads out along Hwy 1 (called Cabrillo Hwy in town), but despite the development it's still relatively small. The main drag is a five-block stretch called Main St lined with shops, cafés, restaurants and a few upscale B&Bs. Visitor information is available from the **Half Moon Bay Coastside Chamber of Commerce** (☎ 650-726-8380; www.halfmoonbaychamber.org; 235 Main St; 9am-5pm Mon-Fri).

Pumpkins are a major deal around Half Moon Bay, and the pre-Halloween harvest is celebrated in the annual **Art & Pumpkin Festival** (☎ 650-726-9652). The mid-October event kicks off with the World Championship Pumpkin Weigh-Off, where the bulbous beasts can bust the scales at over 1000lb.

Around 1 mile north of the Hwy 92 junction, **Sea Horse Ranch** (☎ 650-726-9903) offers daily horseback rides along the beach. A two-hour ride is $75; early-bird specials start at 8am and cost just $45.

Sleeping & Eating

Half Moon Bay State Beach (☎ 800-444-7275; www.reserveamerica.com; tent & RV sites $25; wi-fi) Just west of town on Kelly Ave, this inexpensive overnight option has spartan campsites and pay showers.

San Benito House (☎ 650-726-3425; www.sanbenitohouse.com; 356 Main St; r incl breakfast $99-196; wi-fi) On the other end of the scale, this traditional Victorian inn is popular with honeymooners and has 12 neatly antiquated rooms.

Flying Fish Grill (☎ 650-712-1125; cnr Hwy 92 & Main St; mains $11-15) For superfresh seafood right in the center of town, the Flying Fish has excellent fresh cod or salmon tacos, which you can take out or eat in.

Pasta Moon (☎ 650-726-5125; 315 Main St; mains $14-25) If you're in the mood for romantic Italian, come here for yummy housemade pasta, organic produce, locally sourced ingredients and all-Italian wine list.

Getting There & Away

SamTrans (☎ 800-660-4287) bus 294 operates from the Hillsdale Caltrain station to Half Moon Bay, and up the coast to Moss Beach and Pacifica, daily until about 6pm ($1.50).

HALF MOON BAY TO SANTA CRUZ

With its long coastline, mild weather and abundant fresh water, this area has always been prime real estate. When Spanish missionaries set up shop along the California coast in the late 1700s, it had been Ohlone Indian territory for thousands of years. Pescadero was formally established in 1856, when it was mostly a farming and dairy settlement, although its location along the stagecoach route – now called Stage Rd – transformed it into a popular vacation destination. The Pigeon Point promontory was an active whaling station until 1900, when Prohibition-era bootleggers favored the isolated regional beaches for smuggling booze.

Pescadero

pop 2050

A foggy speck of coastside crossroads between the cities of San Francisco and Santa Cruz, 150-year-old Pescadero is a close-knit rural town of sugar-lending neighbors and community pancake breakfasts. But on weekends the tiny downtown strains its seams with long-distance cyclists panting for carbohydrates and day-trippers dive-bombing in from the ocean-front highway. They're all drawn to the winter vistas of emerald-green hills parched to burlap brown in summer, the wild Pacific beaches populated by seals and pelicans, and the food at a revered destination restaurant. With its cornucopia of tide-pool coves and parks of sky-blotting redwood canopy, city dwellers come here to slow down and smell the sea breeze wafting over fields of bushy artichokes.

SIGHTS & ACTIVITIES

A number of pretty sand beaches speckle the coast, though one of the most interesting places to stop is **Pebble Beach**, a tide pool jewel barely one mile south of Pescadero Creek Rd. As the name implies, the shore is awash in bite-sized eye candy of agate, jade and carnelians, and sandstone troughs are pockmarked by groovy honeycombed formations called tafoni. Bird-watchers enjoy **Pescadero Marsh Reserve**, across the highway from Pescadero State Beach, where numerous species feed year-round.

About 5 miles south of Pescadero, bobcats and full-throated coyotes reside discreetly in a dense redwood canyon at **Butano State Park** (☎ 650-879-2040; parking fee $6). The hiking is also excellent further down the coast at Big Basin Redwoods State Park (p452), with the easiest access from Santa Cruz.

Five miles south along the coast, the 115ft **Pigeon Point Light Station** (☎ 650-879-2120) is one of the tallest lighthouses on the West Coast. The 1872 landmark had to close access to the Fresnel lens when chunks of its cornice began to rain from the sky, but the beam still flashes brightly and the bluff is a prime though blustery spot to scan for breaching gray whales. The hostel here (below) is one of the best in the state.

SLEEPING & EATING

Green Oaks Creek Farm & Retreat (☎ 650-879-1009; www.greenoakscreek.com; 2060 Cabrillo Hwy; camping per person $5, yurt incl breakfast $150) A working organic farm living lightly on the land, where there's a communal kitchen built with straw bales, a composting toilet, an outdoor shower and a medicinal herb garden. Pitch a tent between the Santa Cruz Mountains and clusters of towering eucalyptus and redwood trees, or get pampered with a B&B farmstay in the yurt.

Pigeon Point Lighthouse Hostel (☎ 650-879-0633; www.norcalhostels.org/pigeon; dm/r $20/55) Not your workaday HI outpost, this highly coveted coastside hostel is all about location, location, location. Check-in early to snag a spot in

THE CULINARY COAST

Pescadero is renowned for Duarte's Tavern (see above), but loads of other scrumptious tidbits are very close by.

- **Phipps Country Store** (☎ 650-879-0787; 2700 Pescadero Creek Rd) Peek inside the shop, known universally as 'the bean store,' to marvel at whitewashed bins overflowing with dried heirloom varieties with names like Eye of the Goat, Painted Lady and Desert Pebble.
- **Arcangeli Grocery/Norm's Market** (☎ 650-879-0147; 287 Stage Rd; sandwiches $6) Create a picnic with made-to-order deli sandwiches, homemade artichoke salsa and a chilled bottle of California wine. And don't go breezing out the door without nabbing a crusty loaf of the famous artichoke garlic herb bread, fresh-baked almost hourly.
- **Harley Farms Cheese Shop** (☎ 650-879-0480; 250 North St) Follow the cool wooden cut-outs of the goat and the Wellington-shod girl with the faraway eyes. Another local food treasure with creamy artisanal goat cheeses festooned with fruit, nuts and a rainbow of edible flowers. Weekend farm tours by reservation.
- **Swanton Berry Farm** (☎ 650-469-8804; Coastways Ranch, 640 Cabrillo Hwy) To get a better appreciation of the rigors and rewards of farm life, smoosh up your shirtsleeves and harvest some fruit at this organic pick-your-own farm near Año Nuevo. It's a union outfit (operated by Cesar Chavez's United Farm Workers), with buckets of seasonal strawberries, kiwis and olallieberries ripe for the plucking.
- **Bonny Doon Tasting Room** (☎ 831-425-4518; 10 Pine Flat Rd, Bonny Doon; tasting $5) Stop by for a taste of the local grapes (and check out the crazy bottle labels!) at this popular winery 8 miles north of Santa Cruz, off Hwy 1.

ELEPHANT SEALS

Elephant seals follow a precise calendar: between September and November young seals and the yearlings, who left the beach earlier in the year, return and take up residence. In November and December, the adult males return and start the ritual struggles to assert superiority; only the largest, strongest and most aggressive 'alpha' males gather a harem. From December through February, the adult females arrive, pregnant from last year's beach activities, give birth to their pups and, about a month later, mate with the dominant males.

At birth an elephant seal pup weighs about 80lb, and while being fed by its mother it puts on about 7lb a day. A month's solid feeding will bring the pup's weight up to about 300lb, but around March the females depart, abandoning their offspring on the beach. For the next two to three months the young seals, now known as 'weaners,' lounge around in groups known as 'pods,' gradually learning to swim, first in the rivers and tidal pools, then in the sea. In April, the young seals depart, having lost 20% to 30% of their weight during this prolonged fast.

the outdoor hot tub, and contemplate roaring waves as the lighthouse beacon races through a starburst sky.

The Tower (☎ 650-879-0841, 888-217-0261; www.thetowerpescadero.com; 785 North St; d $135-160) At this quirky hybrid fire lookout/water tower, a two-level apartment crowns a three-story wooden aerie with panoramic views of endless fields and undulating hills. Ivy, the Bennett family pig, adores people and easily wins the heart of even the most skeptical guest.

our pick **Duarte's Tavern** (☎ 650-879-0464; 202 Stage Rd; mains $12-40) You'll rub shoulders with fancy-pants foodies, spandex-swathed cyclists and dusty cowboys in spurs at this casual and surprisingly unpretentious fourth-generation family restaurant. Duarte's (pronounced DOO-arts) is the culinary magnet of Pescadero, and for many the town and eatery are synonymous. Feast on crab cioppino and a half-and-half split of the cream of artichoke and green chili soups, and bring it on home with a wedge of olallieberry pie. Except for the unfortunate lull of Prohibition, the wood-paneled bar has been hosting the locals and their honored guests since 1894.

GETTING THERE & AWAY

By car, the town is 3 miles east from Hwy 1 on Pescadero Creek Rd, south of San Gregorio State Beach.

Año Nuevo State Reserve

More raucous than a full-moon beach rave, thousands of boisterous elephant seals party down year-round on the dunes of Año Nuevo point, their squeals and barks reaching fever pitch during the winter pupping season. The beach is 5 miles south of Pigeon Point and 27 miles north of Santa Cruz. Check out the park's live **SealCam** (www.parks.ca.gov /popup/main.asp).

Elephant seals were just as fearless two centuries ago as they are today, but unfortunately, club-toting seal trappers were not in the same seal-friendly category as camera-toting tourists. Between 1800 and 1850, the elephant seal was driven to the edge of extinction. Only a handful survived around the Guadalupe Islands off the Mexican state of Baja California. With the availability of substitutes for seal oil and the conservationist attitudes of more recent times, the elephant seal has made a comeback, reappearing on the Southern California coast from around 1920. In 1955 they returned to Año Nuevo Beach, and today the reserve is home to thousands in the peak season.

In the midwinter peak season, during the mating and birthing time from December 15 to the end of March (see the boxed text, above), you must plan well ahead because visitors are only permitted access through heavily booked guided tours. For the busiest period, mid-January to mid-February, it's recommended you book eight weeks ahead. Although the **park office** (☎ 650-879-2025; www.parks.ca.gov/?page_id=523) can advise on your chances of getting a place, bookings can only be made by calling ☎ 800-444-4445. Tours cost $5, plus $6 for parking. From the ranger station it's a 3- to 5-mile round-trip hike on sand, and the visit takes two to three hours. If you haven't booked, bad weather can sometimes lead to last-minute cancellations. The rest of the year, advance reservations aren't necessary, but visitor permits from the entrance station are required; arrive before 3pm. No dogs are permitted on-site. There's another, more convenient viewing site further south; see the boxed text, p472.

Wine Country

America's premier viticulture region has earned its reputation among the world's best, but the concept of 'Wine Country *style*' has been so thoroughly hyped in television cooking shows, glossy-magazine spreads and Hollywood movies that one basic concept has been lost: Wine Country is about farming, not lifestyle. It is from the land that all Wine Country lore springs – and what land it is. Rolling hills, dotted with century-old oaks, turn the color of lion's fur under the hot summer sun. Swaths of vineyards carpet the hillsides as far as the eye can see. Where they end, lush redwood forests follow serpentine rivers to the sea.

The temperate climate is perfect for grapes. Settlers began the tradition in the mid-19th century, but it wasn't until 1976 that the region won worldwide acclaim in Paris, when two Napa Valley wines outscored a venerable collection of French Bordeaux in a blind tasting. Today there are over 500 wineries in Napa and Sonoma Counties. But it's quality, not quantity, that sets the region apart.

With great wines come great food. Enter Wine Country style. Napa has become an outpost of San Francisco's top-end culinary scene and its attendant trends. Sonoma prides itself on agricultural diversity, with goat-cheese farms, pick-your-own orchards and roadside strawberry stands. This is the real Wine Country. Forget the style-seekers, the wine snobs, the Hummers and the hairdos. Get lost on the back roads, and fill the car with the season's sweetest fruits. As you picnic atop a sun-dappled hillside, the pastoral landscape unfurling below you, grab a hunk of dirt and know firsthand the thing of greatest meaning in Wine Country.

HIGHLIGHTS

- **Jaw-droppingest winery** Castello di Amoroso (p228)
- **Biggest bite of the Nor-Cal food scene** Oxbow Public Market (p229)
- **Weirdest physical sensation** Being buried in mud in Calistoga (p236)
- **Happiest place for kids to chase chickens** Frog's Leap (p227)
- **Easiest place to get lost** Russian River Valley (p207)
- **Safest road to fall off your bike drunk between wineries** West Dry Creek Rd (p210)
- **Coolest event for meeting locals** Occidental Farmers Market (p214)
- **Hardest place to keep goats from eating your lunch** Casa Nuestra (p228)
- **Worst spot to get caught in a snowstorm while hiking** Robert Louis Stevenson State Park (p239)

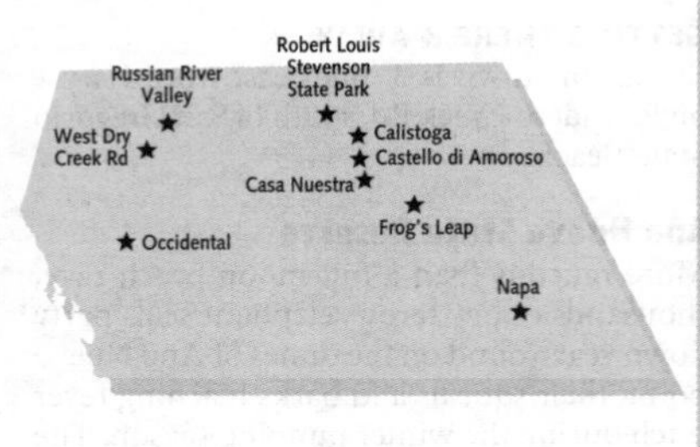

FAST FACTS

Population of city of Napa 74,966

Population of town of Sonoma 7350

Average temperature low/high in Napa Jan 37°/54°, Jul 53°/82°

San Francisco to downtown Sonoma 44 miles, 60 to 90 minutes

Downtown Sonoma to downtown Napa 15 miles, 25 minutes

Downtown Napa to Calistoga 26 miles, 45 to 90 minutes

WINE TASTING

To help you discover the real Wine Country, we've avoided the factories and listed family-owned boutique houses (which produce fewer than 20,000 cases annually) and mid-sized houses (20,000 to 60,000 cases annually). Why does it matter? Think of it. If you were to attend two dinner parties, one for 10 people, one for 1000, which would have the better food? Small wineries maintain tighter control over the grapes. Also, you won't easily find these wines elsewhere, except at high-end restaurants and shops in New York, LA and San Francisco.

Tastings are called 'flights' and include four to six different wines. Napa wineries charge $10 to $40 per flight. In Sonoma Valley, tastings cost $5 to $10, often refundable with purchase. In Sonoma County, tastings are sometimes free, or $5 to $10. You must be 21 to taste.

Do not drink and drive. The curvy roads are dangerous, and police monitor traffic, especially on Napa's Hwy 29.

To avoid burnout, visit no more than three wineries per day. Most open daily from 10am or 11am to 4:30pm or 5pm, but call ahead if you've got your heart set, or absolutely want a tour, especially in Napa, where law requires that some wineries accept visitors only by appointment. If you're buying, ask if the winery has a wine club, which is usually free to join and provides discounts.

Regarding picnics, zoning in Napa prohibits picnicking at most wineries. But in Sonoma, every place allows it. Just remember to buy a bottle of your host's wine.

GETTING THERE & AWAY

Napa and Sonoma counties each have an eponymous city and valley. So, the town of Sonoma is in Sonoma County, at the southern end of Sonoma Valley. The same goes for the city, county and valley of Napa.

From San Francisco, public transportation gets you to the valleys, but it's insufficient for vineyard-hopping. For public-transit information, dial ☎ 511 from Bay Area telephones, or get information online at http://tran sit.511.org.

Both valleys are 90 minutes' drive from San Francisco. Napa, the further inland of the two, has nearly 300 wineries and attracts the most visitors (expect heavy traffic on summer weekends). Sonoma County has 260 wineries, 70 in Sonoma Valley, which is less commercial and less congested than Napa. If you have time to visit only one valley, see Sonoma.

Bus

Golden Gate Transit (☎ 415-923-2000; www.goldengate.org) operates bus 70/80 from San Francisco to Petaluma ($8) and to Santa Rosa ($8.80); catch it at 1st and Mission Sts, across from the Transbay Terminal in San Francisco.

Greyhound (☎ 800-231-2222; www.greyhound.com) operates from San Francisco to Santa Rosa ($21 to 26) and Vallejo ($16 to 20); transfer for local buses.

Napa Valley Vine (☎ 800-696-6443, 707-251-2800; www.nctpa.net) operates bus 10 from the Vallejo Ferry Terminal and Vallejo Transit bus station, through Napa to Calistoga ($2.75); it also runs free trolleys in Napa (p197).

Sonoma Airporter (☎ 707-938-4246, 800-611-4246; www.sonomaairporter.com) operates door-to-door shuttle service ($50) between San Francisco Airport (SFO) and Sonoma Valley.

Car

From San Francisco, take Hwy 101 north, then Hwy 37 east to Hwy 121 north; continue to the junction of Hwys 12 and 121. For Sonoma Valley, take Hwy 12 north; for Napa Valley, take Hwy 12/121 east. Plan 70 minutes in light traffic, two hours during weekday commute times.

Hwy 12/121 splits south of Napa: Hwy 121 turns north and joins with Hwy 29 (aka St Helena Hwy); Hwy 12 merges with southbound Hwy 29. Hwy 29 backs up weekdays 4pm to 7pm, slowing return trips to San Francisco.

From the East Bay (or from downtown San Francisco), take I-80 east to Hwy 37 west (north of Vallejo), then northbound Hwy 29.

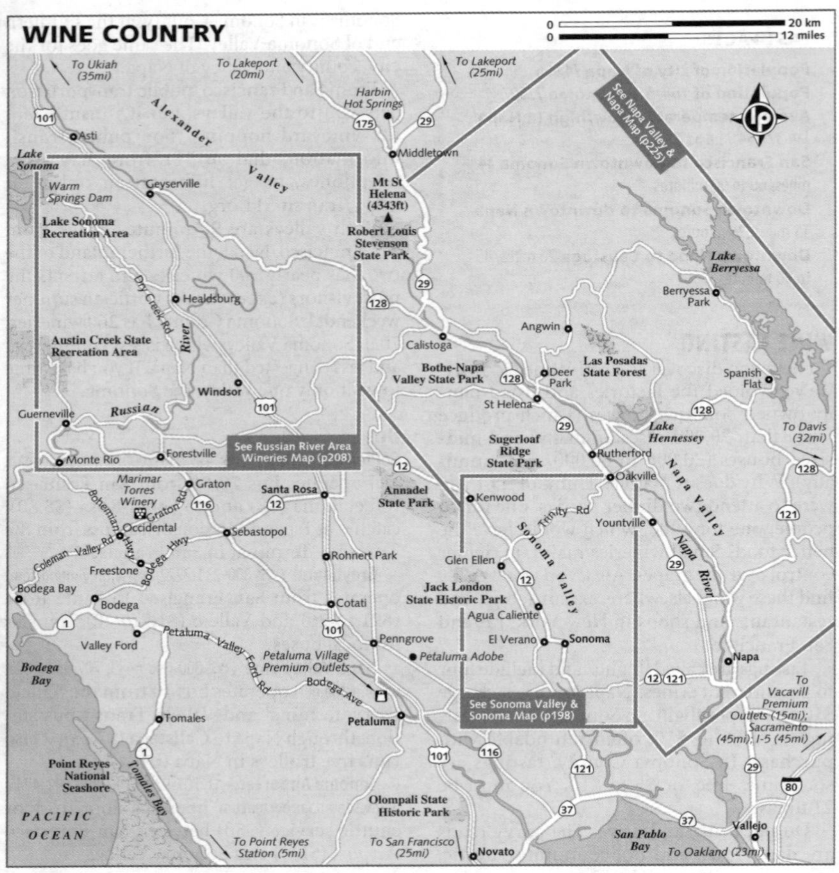

From Santa Rosa, take Hwy 12 east to access the northern end of Sonoma Valley. From Petaluma and Hwy 101, take Hwy 116 east.

Trains

Amtrak (☎ 800-872-7245; www.amtrak.com) trains travel to Martinez (south of Vallejo), with connecting buses to Napa (45 minutes), Santa Rosa (1¼ hours) and Healdsburg (1¾ hours).

BART trains (☎ 415 989-2278; www.bart.gov) run from San Francisco to El Cerrito (30 minutes). Transfer to **Vallejo Transit** (☎ 707-648-4666; www.vallejotransit.com) for Vallejo (30 minutes), then take Napa Valley Vine buses (p195) to Napa and Calistoga.

GETTING AROUND

You'll need a car to winery hop. If you can't or don't want to rent one, plan to visit tasting rooms in major hub towns, such as Napa or Sonoma.

Bicycle

Touring Wine Country by bicycle is unforgettable. Stick to the back roads. We most love pastoral West Dry Creek Rd, northwest of Healdsburg in Sonoma County. Through Sonoma Valley, take Arnold Dr instead of Hwy 12; through Napa Valley, take the Silverado Trail instead of Hwy 29.

Cycling between wineries isn't demanding – the valleys are mostly flat – but crossing between Napa and Sonoma Valleys is intense, particularly via steep Oakville Grade and Trinity Rd (between Oakville and Glen Ellen).

Bicycles, in boxes, can be checked on Greyhound buses for $20 to $30; bike boxes cost $10. You can transport bicycles on Golden Gate Transit buses, which usually have free racks available (first-come, first-served). For rentals, see Tours below.

Car

Shortcuts between Napa and Sonoma Valleys: from Oakville, take Oakville Grade to Trinity Rd; from St Helena, take Spring Mountain Rd into Calistoga Rd; from Calistoga, take Petrified Forest Rd to Calistoga Rd.

Public Transportation

Downtown Napa Trolley (☎ 800-696-6443, 707-251-2800; www.nctpa.net) is free and makes a downtown loop, every 20 minutes, 11am to 6pm Monday through Wednesday, until 8pm Thursday and Sunday, and to 10pm Friday and Saturday.

Sonoma County Transit (☎ 707-576-7433, 800-345-7433; www.sctransit.com) operates buses from Santa Rosa to Petaluma (70 minutes), Sonoma (1¼ hours) and western Sonoma County, including the Russian River Valley towns (30 minutes).

Train

A cushy, if touristy, way to see Wine Country, the **Napa Valley Wine Train** (☎ 707-253-2111, 800-427-4124; www.winetrain.com; adult/child under 12 $50/25, incl lunch adult/child $40/23, incl dinner adult/child $48/23) offers three-hour daily trips in vintage Pullman dining cars, from Napa to St Helena and back. Trains depart from McKinstry St near 1st St.

TOURS

For balloons and airplane rides, see the boxed text, p232.

Bicycle

Guided tours start around $90 per day including bikes, tastings and lunch. Daily rentals cost $25 to $40; make reservations.

Backroads (☎ 800-462-2848; www.backroads.com) All-inclusive guided biking and walking.

Calistoga Bike Shop (☎ 707-942-9687, 866-942-2453; www.calistogabikeshop.com; 1318 Lincoln Ave, Calistoga) Wine-tour rental package ($79) includes wine-carrying baskets; if you buy multiple bottles they'll pick them up for you.

Getaway Adventures (☎ 707-568-3040, 800-499-2453; www.getawayadventures.com) Great guided tours, some combined with kayaking. Locations in Petaluma, Calistoga and Healdsburg. Single- and multi-day trips.

Good Time Touring (☎ 707-938-0453, 888-525-0453; www.goodtimetouring.com) Tours Sonoma Valley, Dry Creek and West County Sonoma.

Napa Valley Adventure Tours (☎ 707-259-1833, 877-548-6877; www.napavalleyadventuretours.com; Oxbow Public Market, 610 1st St, Napa) Guides bike tours between wineries, as well as off-road trips, hiking and kayaking. Daily rentals, too.

Napa Valley Bike Tours (☎ 707-944-2953, 800-707-2453; www.napavalleybiketours.com; 6488 Washington St, Yountville) Daily rentals; easy and moderately difficult tours.

Sonoma Valley Cyclery (Map p198; ☎ 707-935-3377; 20093 Broadway, Sonoma) Daily rentals; Sonoma Valley guides.

Jeeps

Wine Country Jeep Tours (☎ 707-546-1822, 800-539-5337; www.jeeptours.com; 3hr tour $75) Tour Wine Country's back roads and boutique wineries by Jeep, year-round at 10am and 1pm. Also operates tours of Sonoma Coast.

Limousine

Antique Tours Limousine (☎ 707-226-9227; www.antiquetours.net) Fancy a drive in a 1947 Packard convertible limousine? Antique Tours charges $130 per hour (minimum five hours). Ask for Thad.

Beau Wine Tours (☎ 707-938-8001, 800-387-2328; www.beauwinetours.com) Winery tours in sedans and stretch limos; charges $70 to $100 per hour (three-hour minimum weekdays, six hours weekends).

Flying Horse Carriage Company (☎ 707-849-8989; www.flyinghorse.org; 4hr tours per person $145) Clip-pety-clop through the Alexander Valley in a horse-drawn carriage. Includes a picnic.

Magnum Tours (☎ 707-753-0088; www.magnumwinetours.com) Sedans and specialty limousines from $65 to $100 per hour (four-hour minimum, five hours on Saturdays). Exceptional service.

SONOMA VALLEY

We have a soft spot for Sonoma's folksy ways. Unlike in fancy-pants Napa, nobody cares if you drive a clunker and vote Green. Locals call it 'Slow-noma.' Anchoring the bucolic 17-mile-long Sonoma Valley, the town of Sonoma makes a great jumping-off point for exploring Wine Country – it's only an hour from San Francisco – and has a marvelous sense of place, with storied 19th-century historical

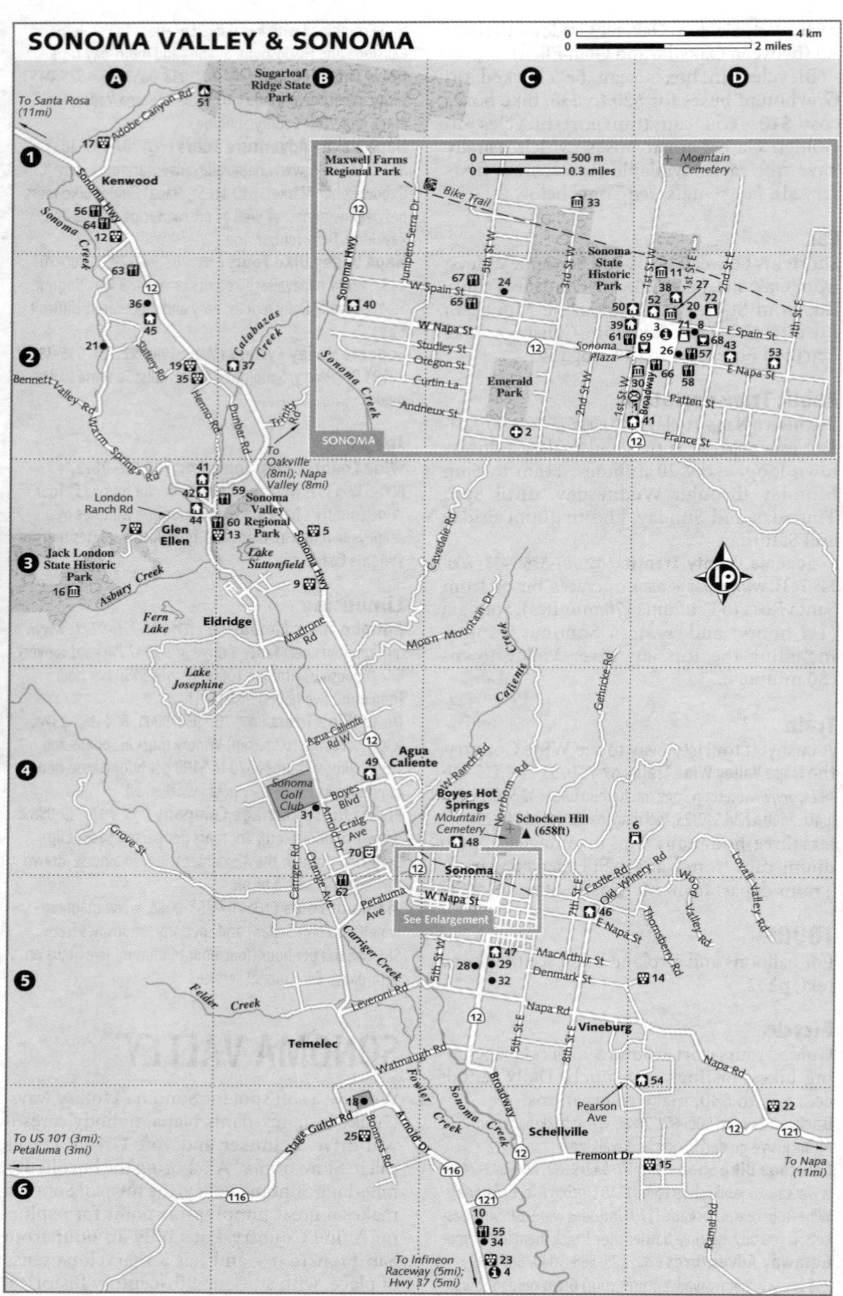
SONOMA VALLEY & SONOMA
0 4 km
0 2 miles
Sugarloaf Ridge State Park
To Santa Rosa (11mi)
Adobe Canyon Rd
Kenwood
Sonoma Hwy
Sonoma Creek
Calabazas Creek
Bennett Valley Rd
Warm Springs Rd
Stuart Rd
Henno Rd
Dunbar Rd
Trinity Rd
To Oakville (8mi); Napa Valley (8mi)
London Ranch Rd
Glen Ellen
Sonoma Valley Regional Park
Jack London State Historic Park
Lake Suttonfield
Asbury Creek
Fern Lake
Eldridge
Madrone Rd
Moon Mountain Dr
Lake Josephine
Cavedale Rd
Caliente Creek
Gehricke Rd
Agua Caliente Rd W
Agua Caliente
W Ranch Rd
Norrbom Rd
Boyes Hot Springs
Mountain Cemetery
Schocken Hill (658ft)
Sonoma Golf Club
Boyes Blvd
Arnold Dr
Craig Ave
Grove St
Carriger Rd
Orange Ave
Petaluma Ave
W Napa St
See Enlargement
Sonoma
7th St E
Castle Rd
Old Winery Rd
Wood Valley Rd
Lovall Valley Rd
E Napa St
Thornsberry Rd
MacArthur St
Denmark St
5th St W
Carriger Creek
Leveroni Rd
Felder Creek
Napa Rd
Vineburg
Temelec
5th St E
8th St E
Watmaugh Rd
Fowler Creek
Sonoma Creek
Broadway
Pearson Ave
Napa Rd
Stage Gulch Rd
Bonness Rd
Arnold Dr
Schellville
Fremont Dr
To Napa (11mi)
To US 101 (3mi); Petaluma (3mi)
Ramal Rd
To Infineon Raceway (5mi); Hwy 37 (5mi)
Maxwell Farms Regional Park
0 500 m
0 0.3 miles
Mountain Cemetery
Bike Trail
Juniper Serra Dr
5th St W
3rd St W
Sonoma State Historic Park
1st St W
1st St E
2nd St E
4th St E
W Spain St
W Napa St
Studley St
Oregon St
Curtin La
Andrieux St
Emerald Park
2nd St W
Sonoma Plaza
E Spain St
E Napa St
Patten St
Broadway
France St
SONOMA

INFORMATION
Chanticleer Books & Prints......(see 57)
Readers' Books......................(see 57)
Sonoma Post Office..................**1** D2
Sonoma Valley Hospital..............**2** C2
Sonoma Valley Visitors Bureau...**3** D2
Sonoma Valley Visitors Bureau (Southern Branch)..................**4** C6
Sunflower Café......................(see 39)

SIGHTS & ACTIVITIES
Arrowood................................**5** B3
Bartholomew Park.....................**6** D4
Bear Flag Monument................(see 3)
Benziger....................................**7** A3
Blue Wing Inn..........................**8** D2
BR Cohn....................................**9** B3
City Hall..................................(see 3)
Cornerstone Gardens...............**10** C6
Depot Park Museum.................**11** D2
Family Wineries.......................**12** A1
Figone's Olive Oil....................**13** B3
Gundlach-Bundschu..................**14** D5
Homewood..............................**15** D6
Jack London Museum...............**16** A3
Kaz..**17** A1
Landmark...............................(see 17)
Los Arroyos Golf Course..........**18** B6
Loxton.....................................**19** A2
Mission San Francisco Solano de Sonoma..............................**20** D2
Morton's Warm Springs Resort..**21** A2
Nicholson Ranch.......................**22** D6
Olive Press...............................**23** C6
Ramekins Sonoma Valley Culinary School.....................................**24** C2
Robledo....................................**25** B6
Sebastiani Theater....................**26** D2
Sonoma Barracks......................**27** D2
Sonoma Valley Cyclery.............**28** C5
Sonoma Valley High School.......**29** C5
Sonoma Valley Museum of Art..**30** D2
Spa at Sonoma Mission Inn.......**31** B4
Toscano Hotel........................(see 27)
Traintown..................................**32** C5
Vallejo Home............................**33** C1
Vintage Aircraft Company.........**34** C6
Wellington................................**35** A2
Wildwood Farm Nursery Sculpture Garden..................................**36** A2
Wine Country Chocolates Tasting Bar...(see 23)

SLEEPING
Beltane Ranch...........................**37** B2
Bungalows 313..........................**38** D2
El Dorado Hotel........................**39** C2
El Pueblo Inn............................**40** B2
Gaige House.............................**41** A3
Glen Ellen Cottages..................**42** A3
Hidden Oak Inn........................**43** D2
Jack London Lodge...................**44** A3
Kenwood Inn & Spa..................**45** A2
Les Petites Maisons..................**46** C5
MacArthur Place.......................**47** C5
Sonoma Chalet..........................**48** C4
Sonoma Creek Inn.....................**49** B4
Sonoma Hotel............................**50** C2
Sugarloaf Ridge State Park........**51** A1
Swiss Hotel...............................**52** D2
Victorian Garden Inn................**53** D2
Windhaven Cottage...................**54** D5

EATING
Angelo's Wine Country Deli.....**55** C6
Cafe Citti..................................**56** A1
Café La Haye............................**57** D2
Cheesemaker's Daughter........(see 58)
Della Santina's..........................**58** D2
Farmers Market.......................(see 11)
fig café....................................(see 42)
Garden Court Cafe....................**59** B3
girl & the fig...........................(see 50)
Glen Ellen Inn..........................(see 42)
Glen Ellen Village Market..........**60** B3
Harvest Moon Café....................**61** C2
Juanita Juanita..........................**62** B5
Kenwood Restaurant & Bar.......**63** A2
Mayo Winery Reserve Room.....**64** A1
Pearl's Homestyle Cooking.......**65** C2
Shiso..**66** D2
Sonoma Market........................**67** C2
Taste of the Himalayas...........(see 68)
Yeti...(see 13)

DRINKING
Murphy's Irish Pub...................**68** D2
Steiner's...................................**69** D2
Swiss Hotel.............................(see 52)

ENTERTAINMENT
Little Switzerland......................**70** B4

SHOPPING
Artifax.....................................**71** D2
Earthworks..............................(see 39)
La Haye Art Center..................(see 57)
Sign of the Bear......................(see 69)
Vella Cheese Co........................**72** D2
Wine Exchange of Sonoma.....(see 71)

sights surrounding the state's largest town square. Halfway up-valley, tiny Glen Ellen is right out of a Norman Rockwell painting, in stark contrast to the valley's northernmost town, Santa Rosa, the workaday urban center best known for its traffic. If you've more than a day, explore Sonoma's quiet, rustic side along the Russian River Valley (p207) and work your way to the sea.

Sonoma Hwy/Hwy 12 is lined with wineries and runs from Sonoma to Santa Rosa, then to western Sonoma County; Arnold Dr has less traffic (but few wineries) and runs parallel, up the valley's western side to Glen Ellen.

SONOMA VALLEY WINERIES

Rolling grass-covered hills rise from 17-by-7-mile-long Sonoma Valley. Its 72 wineries get less attention than Napa's, but many are equally good. If you love zinfandel and syrah, you're in for a treat.

Picnicking is allowed at Sonoma wineries. Get maps and discount coupons in the town of Sonoma (p202) or, if you're approaching from the south, the **Sonoma Valley Visitors Bureau** (☎ 707-935-4747; www.sonomavalley.com; Cornerstone Gardens, 23570 Hwy 121; 9am-4pm), off Hwy 121 on the grounds of Cornerstone Gardens (p203).

The following are in south–north order. Plan at least five hours to visit the valley from

LIMOUSINE PROS & CONS

Hiring a limousine lets you drink with no fear of drink-driving. But bear in mind that most wineries don't allow limousines because those who hire them tend to get messy. Also, limo drivers hit wineries with which they have arrangements, and we don't always agree they're the best. To get under the skin of Wine Country and see the small-production wineries and out-of-the-way places that make the region special, select a designated driver, or simply avoid getting wasted, and you'll have more options.

NAPA OR SONOMA?

Napa and Sonoma valleys run parallel, a few miles apart, separated by the narrow, imposing Mayacamas Mountains. The two couldn't be more different. It's easy to mock aggressively sophisticated Napa, its monuments to ego, trophy homes and trophy wives, $1000-a-night inns, $30+ tastings and wine-snob visitors, but Napa makes some of the world's best wines. Constrained by its geography, it stretches along a single valley, so it's easy to visit. Drawbacks are high prices and heavy traffic, but there are 200 nearly side-by-side wineries. And the valley is gorgeous.

Sonoma County is much more down-to-earth and politically left leaning. You'll see lots more rusted-out pick-ups. Though becoming gentrified, Sonoma lacks Napa's chic factor, and locals like it that way. The wines are more approachable, but the county's 260 wineries are spread out (see A Wine Country Primer, p211). If you're here on a weekend, head to Sonoma (County or Valley), which gets less traffic, but on a weekday, see Napa, too. Ideally schedule two to four days: one for each valley, and one or two additional for western Sonoma County.

Spring and fall are the best times to visit. Summers are hot, dusty and crowded. Fall brings fine weather, harvest time and the 'crush,' the pressing of the grapes, but lodging prices skyrocket. If you're on a budget, the suburban town of Vallejo is about 20 minutes from downtown Napa and has motels off the freeway for about $50 to $100 during high season.

bottom to top. For other Sonoma County wineries, see the Russian River Valley section

Nicholson Ranch

Unfiltered pinot noir and chardonnay are the standouts at **Nicholson Ranch** (☎ 707-938-8822; www.nicholsonranch.com; 4200 Napa Rd; tastings $10; 🕑 10am-6pm), known for its high-end fruit and artisinal craftsmanship. The well-structured, earthy pinot isn't overly berried, more Burgundian than Californian; the chardonnay is light and creamy, never buttery or cloying. The lesser-known pinot-noir rosé makes a terrific back-porch wine. Lovely picnic grounds abut a lily pond and the Mayacamas Mountains. Bottles cost $20 to $50.

Homewood

'Da redder, da better' at **Homewood** (☎ 707-996-6353; www.homewoodwinery.com; 23120 Burndale Rd at Hwy 121/12; tastings free), a tiny Carneros District winery that makes fruit-forward, vineyard-designate wines. The tasting room is a garage, where you'll get a warm welcome from Oliver, the resident golden Labrador. Ask about the 'vertical tastings,' in which you sample the same wines from the same vineyards, but different years. Dogs welcome. Bottles cost $16 to $32.

Robledo

Sonoma Valley's feel-good winery, **Robledo** (☎ 707-939-6903; www.robledofamilywinery.com; 21901 Bonness Rd; tastings $5-10; 🕑 by appointment only) was founded by a former grape-picker from Mexico who worked his way up to vineyard manager, then land owner, now vintner. His kids run the place. The wine is excellent, including a crisp, no-oak sauvignon blanc; jammy syrah; bold, spicy, lingering cabernet; and bright-fruit pinot. The windowless tasting room has hand-carved Mexican furniture, but ugly fluorescents. The winery is off Hwy 116. Bottles cost $15 to $40.

Gundlach-Bundschu

One of Sonoma Valley's oldest and prettiest, **Gundlach-Bundschu** (☎ 707-938-5277; www.gunbun.com; 2000 Denmark St; tastings $5-10) was founded in 1858 by Bavarian immigrant Jacob Gundlach. Rieslings and gewürztraminers are the signatures, but 'Gun-Bun' was the first in America to produce 100% merlot. Tours of the 2000-barrel cave ($20) are available Friday to Sunday. Up a winding road, it's a good bike-to winery, with picnicking, hiking and a small lake. Bottles cost $22 to $40.

Benziger

If you're new to wine, make **Benziger** (☎ 707-935-3000, 888-490-2739; www.benziger.com; 1883 London Ranch Rd, Glen Ellen; tastings $5-10; 👶) your first stop for Sonoma's best crash course in winemaking. The worthwhile, nonreservable tour ($10) includes an open-air tram ride through biodynamic vineyards, and a four-wine tasting. Little ones love the peacocks. The large-production wine's OK (head for the reserves); the tour's the thing. Bottles cost $15 to $80.

Loxton

Say g'day to Chris, the Aussie winemaker, at **Loxton** (☎ 707-935-7221; www.loxtonwines.com; 11466 Dunbar Rd, Glen Ellen; tastings free), a no-frills winery with million-dollar views. The 'tasting room' is actually a small warehouse, where you can taste wonderful syrah. There's terrific port; non-oaky, fruit-forward chardonnay; and good zinfandel. Bottles cost $15 to $25.

Landmark

Though it looks like a suburban house, **Landmark** (☎ 707-833-0053; www.landmarkwine.com; 101 Adobe Canyon Rd, Kenwood; tastings $5;) surrounds a lovely mission-style fountain courtyard abutting a big lawn dotted with oaks, perfect for picnicking. Classic Burgundy-style chardonnay is the draw, and it's damn good – famed Helen Turley is the original consulting winemaker. Also noteworthy, an elegant Sonoma Coast pinot noir. Call about horsedrawn-wagon rides; there's boccie and Popsicles for kids. Bottle cost $27 to $65.

Wellington

Known for port (including a white) and meaty reds, **Wellington** (☎ 707-939-0708; www.wellingtonvineyards.com; 11600 Dunbar Rd, Glen Ellen; tastings $5) makes great zinfandel, one from vines planted in 1892 – wow, what color! The noir de noir is a cult favorite. Alas, servers have vineyard views, while you face the warehouse. Bottles cost $15 to $30.

Kaz

Sonoma's cult favorite, supercool **Kaz** (☎ 707-833-2536; www.kazwinery.com; 233 Adobe Canyon Rd, Kenwood; tastings $2;) is about blends: whatever's in the vineyard goes into the wine – and they're blended at crush, not during fermentation. Expect lesser-known varietals like alicante bouchet and lenoir, and a worthwhile cabernet-merlot blend. Kids can sample grape juice and mold Play-Doh. Dogs welcome. Bottles cost $10 to $40.

Also consider:

Arrowood (☎ 707-935-2600; www.arrowoodvineyards.com; 14347 Sonoma Hwy; tastings $5-10) Excellent cabernet and chardonnay; stunning views.

BR Cohn (☎ 707-938-4064; www.brcohn.com; 15000 Sonoma Hwy; tastings $5-10) Good cabernet, great olive oil, fun summer concerts.

Family Wineries (☎ 707-433-0100; www.familywines.com; 9380 Sonoma Hwy at Laurel Ave; tastings $5-10) Several wineries under one roof, good for half-day-trippers. Standouts: David Noyes pinot noir and Tandem chardonnay.

SONOMA & AROUND

pop 9900

Fancy boutiques may lately be replacing hardware stores, but Sonoma still retains an old-fashioned charm, thanks to the plaza – California's largest town square – and its surrounding frozen-in-time historic buildings. You can drink openly on the plaza (a rarity in California parks), and while swilling wine here during our last visit, we spotted a rooster ambling across the road. Ah, Sonoma…

Sonoma has a rich history. In 1846 it was the site of a second American revolution, this time against Mexico, when General Mariano Guadalupe Vallejo deported all foreigners from California, prompting outraged American frontiersmen to occupy the Sonoma presidio and declare independence (see p39). They dubbed California the Bear Flag Republic after the battle flag they'd fashioned.

The republic was short-lived. The Mexican-American War broke out a month later, and California was annexed by the US. The revolt gave California its flag, which remains emblazoned with the words 'California Republic' beneath a muscular brown bear. Vallejo was initially imprisoned, but ultimately returned to Sonoma and played a major role in the region's development.

Orientation & Information

Sonoma Hwy (Hwy 12) runs through town. Sonoma Plaza, laid out by General Vallejo in 1834, is the heart of downtown, lined with hotels, restaurants and shops. Pick up a walking-tour brochure from the visitors bureau.

TOP KID-FRIENDLY WINERIES

- **Kaz** (left) Play-Doh and grape juice
- **Benziger** (opposite) Open-air tram ride and peacocks
- **Landmark** (left) Horsedrawn-wagon rides and Popsicles
- **Sterling** (p228) Gondola rides and crayons
- **Frog's Leap**(p227) Cats, chickens and croquet

Immediately north along Hwy 12, expect a suburban landscape.

BOOKSTORES

Chanticleer Books & Prints (☎ 707-996-7613; 127 E Napa St; ⏲ Wed-Sun) Antiquarian, first editions and California history.

Readers' Books (☎ 707-939-1779; 130 E Napa St) Independent bookseller.

EMERGENCY & MEDICAL SERVICES

Police, fire, ambulance (☎ 911) Emergencies.

Sonoma Valley Hospital (☎ 707-935-5000; 347 Andrieux St; ⏲ 24hr)

INTERNET ACCESS

Sunflower Caffe (☎ 707-996-6645; www.sonomasunflower.com; 421 1st St W)

MEDIA

KRSH 95.5 and 95.9 FM Eclectic music, locally programmed.

KSVY 91.3 FM Community radio; world music to local politics.

POST

Sonoma post office (☎ 800-275-8777; www.usps.com; 617 Broadway; ⏲ Mon-Fri)

TOURIST INFORMATION

Sonoma Valley Visitors Bureau (☎ 707-996-1090; www.sonomavalley.com; 453 1st St E; ⏲ 9am-6pm Jul-Sep, to 5pm Oct-Jun) Arranges accommodations; has a good walking-tour pamphlet and information on events. There's another location at Cornerstone Gardens (opposite).

WINE COUNTRY

Sights

SONOMA PLAZA & AROUND

Smack in the plaza's center, the Mission-revival-style **City Hall** (1906–08) has identical facades on four sides, reportedly because plaza businesses all demanded City Hall face their direction. At the plaza's northeast corner, the **Bear Flag Monument** marks Sonoma's moment of revolutionary glory.

Other noteworthy buildings include the **Sebastiani Theatre** (476 1st St E), a 1934 Mission-revival cinema that screens art house and revival films, and sometimes stages live theater and musical productions. Check its site for current listings. Just off the plaza, **Blue Wing Inn** (139 E Spain St) was built by Vallejo around 1840 to house visiting soldiers and travelers. It later served as a hotel, saloon and stagecoach depot.

On the plaza's north side, next to the Sonoma Barracks, **Toscano Hotel** (20 E Spain St) opened as a store and library in the 1850s, then became a hotel in 1886. Peek into the lobby from 10am to 5pm; except for the traffic outside, you'd swear you'd stepped back in time. Free tours 1pm through 4pm, weekends and Mondays.

Vallejo's first Sonoma home, **La Casa Grande**, was built around 1835 along this side of the plaza, but burned in 1867. The only remains are the servants' quarters, where the general's Native American servants lived.

SONOMA STATE HISTORIC PARK

The mission, Sonoma Barracks and Vallejo Home are part of **Sonoma State Historic Park** (☎ 707-938-1519; www.parks.ca.gov; adult/child under 17 $2/free; ⏲ 10am-5pm).

The **Mission San Francisco Solano de Sonoma** (E Spain St), at the plaza's northeast corner, was built in 1823, in part to forestall the Russian coastal colony at Fort Ross from moving inland. The mission was the 21st and final California mission and the only one built during the Mexican period (the rest were founded by the Spanish; p37). It marks the northernmost point on El Camino Real. Five of the mission's original rooms remain. The not-to-be-missed chapel dates from 1841.

The adobe **Sonoma Barracks** (E Spain St) were built by Vallejo between 1836 and 1840 to house Mexican troops. The barracks later became American military quarters. Now a museum, the barracks houses displays on life during the Mexican and American periods.

A half-mile northwest, the **Vallejo Home**, otherwise known as Lachryma Montis (Latin for 'Tears of the Mountain'), was built in 1851–52 for General Vallejo. It's named for the spring on the property; the Vallejo family later made a handy income piping water to town. The property remained in the family until 1933, when the state of California purchased it, retaining much of its original furnishings. A bike path leads to the house from downtown.

Admission here includes entry to the **Petaluma Adobe** (Map p196; ☎ 707-762-4871; 3325 Adobe Road, Petaluma; adults $2, under 16 free; ⏲ 10am-5pm), a historic ranch 15 miles away in suburban Petaluma.

DEPOT PARK MUSEUM

Two blocks north of the plaza is the **Depot Park Museum** (☎ 707-938-1762; www.vom.com/depot;

270 1st St W; admission free; 1-4:30pm Wed-Sun). It has art and exhibits from pioneer days, with an emphasis on the Bear Flag Republic. Check out the century-old hand-painted theater curtain.

TRAINTOWN

Little kids love **Traintown** (707-938-3912; www.traintown.com; 20264 Broadway; 10am-5pm daily in summer, Fri-Sun only mid-Sep–late May), one mile south of the plaza. A miniature steam engine makes 20-minute loops ($4.25), and there are vintage amusement-park rides, including a carousel and a Ferris wheel; each ride costs $2.

BARTHOLOMEW PARK

The top in-town outdoors destination is **Bartholomew Park** (707-935-9511; www.bartholomewparkwinery.com; 1000 Vineyard Lane), off Castle Rd, where you can hike and picnic beneath giant oaks. There's an OK winery, too, but its real draw is the free Sonoma Valley museum. The Palladian Villa at the park's entrance is a turn-of-the-20th-century replica of Count Haraszthy's original residence, open 10am to 4pm on Wednesdays and weekends. For information, call the **Bartholomew Park Foundation** (707-938-2244).

CORNERSTONE GARDENS

There's nothing traditional about **Cornerstone Gardens** (707-933-9474, 707-933-3010; www.cornerstonegardens.com; 23570 Hwy 121; admission free; 10am-5pm), which showcases the work of 25 renowned avant-garde landscape designers. We especially love Pamela Burton's 'Earth Walk,' which descends into the ground; and McCrory and Raiche's 'Rise,' which exaggerates space. Afterward, explore top-notch garden shops, and refuel at the on-site café.

SONOMA VALLEY MUSEUM OF ART

While this 8000-sq-ft **museum** (707-939-7862; www.svma.org; 551 Broadway; adult/family $5/8, free Sun; 11am-5pm Thu-Sun) presents compelling work by local and national artists, the standout is October's Día de los Muertos exhibition. Call about live-music series.

WILDWOOD FARM NURSERY SCULPTURE GARDEN

Tripped-out abstract sculptures, large and small, fill flowering gardens at **Wildwood** (707-833-1161, 888-833-4181; www.wildwoodmaples.com; 10300 Sonoma Hwy, Kenwood; 9am-4pm Wed-Sun, to 2pm Tue), a nursery for exotic plants and Japanese maples.

FARMERS MARKET

The **farmers market** meets Fridays 9am to noon at Depot Park and, April to October, Tuesdays 5:30pm to 8pm on the plaza.

Activities

Many local inns provide bicycles, or you can rent one from **Sonoma Valley Cyclery** (707-935-3377; www.sonomacyclery.com; 20091 Broadway; 10am-6pm Mon-Sat, to 4pm Sun) for $6 per hour, $25 per day.

Hit the trail with **Triple Creek Horse Outfit** (707-887-8700; www.triplecreekhorseoutfit.com), April through October. One- and two-hour rides through Jack London State Historic Park or Sugarloaf Ridge State Park cost $60/90. Reservations required.

Doctor your swing at the public, nine-hole **Los Arroyos Golf Course** (707-938-8835; 5000 Stage Gulch Rd), $20 on weekends. Play tennis at **Sonoma Valley High School** (707-933-4010; 20000 Broadway) weekends and after 5pm weekdays.

Few Wine Country spas compare with glitzy **Spa at Sonoma Mission Inn** (707-938-9000, 877-289-7354; www.fairmont.com/sonoma; 100 Boyes Blvd). Book two treatments and get free access to the Romanesque bathhouse.

Dudes who dig cars love **Infineon Raceway** (800-870-7223; www.infineonraceway.com), at the intersection of Hwys 37 and 121 . There are events year-round, from the NASCAR Cup to the Superbike Showdown. At resident **Jim Russell Racing School** (800-733-0345; www.jimrussellusa.com) you can learn racing techniques using your own vehicle.

Festivals & Events

For up-to-date event listings, see www.sonomacounty.com.

Sonoma Valley Olive Festival (www.sonomavalley.com/olivefestival) December through February

Sonoma Valley Film Festival (www.sonomafilmfest.org) April

Sonoma Lavender Festival (www.sonomalavender.com) Mid-June

Sonoma Valley Harvest Wine Auction (www.sonomavalleywine.com/harvest_main.asp) Labor Day weekend

Courses

Ramekins Sonoma Valley Culinary School (707-933-0450; www.ramekins.com; 450 W Spain St) offers demonstrations and hands-on classes for home chefs. Ask about winemaker dinners.

Sleeping

Off-season rates plummet. Reserve ahead. Several noteworthy historic hotels line the plaza. Ask about parking.

Also consider Glen Ellen (p206) and, if counting pennies, Santa Rosa (p219).

Sugarloaf Ridge State Park (☎ 707-833-5712, reservations 800-444-7275; www.reserveamerica.com; 2605 Adobe Canyon Rd; sites $20-25) Sonoma's nearest campground is this 50-site park, with drive-in sites and great hiking, north of Kenwood.

Sonoma Chalet (☎ 707-938-3129; www.sonomachalet.com; 18935 5th St W; r without bath $125, r with bath $140-180, cottages $190-225;) An old farmstead surrounded by rolling hills, Sonoma Chalet has rooms in a Swiss-chalet-style house adorned with little balconies and country-American bric-a-brac. We especially love the free-standing cottages; Laura's has a wood-burning fireplace. Breakfast is served on a deck overlooking a nature preserve. No air-con in rooms with shared bath.

Sonoma Creek Inn (☎ 707-939-9463, 888-712-1289; www.sonomacreekinn.com; 239 Boyes Blvd; r $129-189; wi-fi) This cute-as-a-button motel has cheery, retro-Americana rooms, with primary colors and country quilts. It's not downtown; valley wineries are a short drive.

Swiss Hotel (☎ 707-938-2884; www.swisshotelsonoma.com; 18 W Spain St; r Mon-Fri $150-170, Sat & Sun $200-240;) It opened in 1905, so you'll forgive the wavy floors. Think knotty pine and wicker. In the morning sip coffee on the shared plaza-view balcony. Downstairs there's a raucous bar and restaurant.

El Pueblo Inn (☎ 707-996-3651, 800-900-8844; www.elpuebloinn.com; 896 W Napa St; r $154-299; wi-fi) One mile west of downtown, family-owned El Pueblo has surprisingly cush rooms with great beds. The big lawns and the heated pool are perfect for kids; moms like the small spa.

Windhaven Cottage (☎ 707-938-2175; www.windhavencottage.com; 21700 Pearson Ave; cottage $155-165; wi-fi) Great-bargain Windhaven has two units: a hideaway cottage with vaulted wooden ceilings and a fireplace; and a handsome 800-sq-ft studio. We prefer the romantic cottage. Both have hot tubs. Tennis, bicycles and barbecues sweeten the deal.

Les Petites Maisons (☎ 707-933-0340, 800-291-8962; www.thegirlandthefig.com/lespetitesmaisons; 1190 E Napa St; cottages $165-250; wi-fi) A mile east of the plaza, each of the four colorful, inviting cottages has a bedroom, a living room, a kitchen and a barbecue, with comfy furniture, stereos, DVDs and bicycles.

El Dorado Hotel (☎ 707-996-3030, 800-289-3031; www.hoteleldorado.com; 405 1st St W; r Mon-Fri/Sat & Sun $175/195;) Swanky touches like high-end linens and flat-panel TVs make up for the rooms' compact size, as do private balconies overlooking the plaza or the rear courtyard (we prefer the plaza view, despite the noise). Wi-fi in lobby.

Sonoma Hotel (☎ 707-996-2996; www.sonomahotel.com; 110 W Spain St; r $175-200;) This spiffy vintage-1880s hotel is decked with Spanish-colonial and American-country-crafts furnishings. There's no elevator. Wi-fi in lobby.

MacArthur Place (☎ 707-938-2929, 800-722-1866; www.macarthurplace.com; 29 E MacArthur St; r from $350, ste from $450; wi-fi) Built on the grounds of a former estate, with gorgeous 150-year-old plantings, splurge-worthy MacArthur is Sonoma's top inn, with sumptuous rooms in a historic house and outlying cottages. Spa suites have double-size bathtubs and private gardens with outdoor hot tubs – perfect for a kiss-and-make-up weekend.

Also consider:

Bungalows 313 (☎ 707-996-8091; www.bungalows313.com; 313 1st St E; d $229-319, q $379-469; wi-fi) Century-old brick farmhouse and bungalows with kitchens. Gorgeous gardens. Best for couples.

Hidden Oak Inn (☎ 707-996-9863, 877-996-9863; www.hiddenoakinn.com; 214 E Napa St; r incl breakfast $175-195; wi-fi) B&B circa 1914.

Victorian Garden Inn (☎ 707-996-5339; www.victoriangardeninn.com; 316 E Napa St; r incl breakfast $189-329, cottage $369; wi-fi) Farmhouse B&B with homey rooms, built in 1870.

Eating

Also see Glen Ellen, p207.

Pearl's Homestyle Cooking (☎ 707-996-1783; 561 5th St W; mains $7-10; 7am-2:30pm;) In a strip mall across from Safeway's west-facing wall, Pearl's dishes up giant American breakfasts. Look for the kitty-cat out front.

Juanita Juanita (☎ 707-935-3981; 19114 Arnold Dr; mains $7-15 11am-8pm;) Dig the crazy mural outside this drive-in Mexican, which makes winning tostadas, garlic-garlic burritos and fiery *chile verde* (green chili stew with pork or chicken). Dog-friendly patio. Beer and wine.

Come-to-Jesus Taco Truck (Hwy 12; meals under $10) For late-night Mexican, find the truck among the mobile *taquerías* (Mexican fast-food restaurants) on Hwy 12's east side, between Boyes Blvd and Agua Caliente. Look to the Lord for the best tacos; he's painted on the back of the truck.

Angelo's Wine Country Deli (707-938-3688; 23400 Arnold Dr; sandwiches $6; 9am-5pm Tue-Sun) Look for the cow on the roof of this roadside deli, a fave for fat sandwiches and homemade jerky. In spring, look for the little lambs grazing outside.

Taste of the Himalayas (707-996-1161; 464 1st St E; mains $9-17; Tue-Sun) Down an alley next to the Sebastiani Theatre, sample spicy curries and tandoori meats. Between 11am and 3:30pm there's a garbanzo-bean-heavy, all-you-can-eat buffet ($10).

girl & the fig (707-938-3634; www.thegirlandthefig.com; 110 W Spain St; lunch mains $10-15, dinner mains $17-26) For a festive evening, book a garden table at this soulful French-provincial bistro, known for its hearty cooking and party atmosphere. We love the small plates ($10 to $14), especially the steamed mussels with matchstick fries, and duck confit with lentils. The weekday three-course prix-fixe menu costs $32; add $8 for wine. Stellar cheeses. Reservations essential.

Della Santina's (707-935-0576; www.dellasantinas.com; 135 E Napa St; mains $11-17) The waiters have been at Della Santina's forever, and its 'specials' never change (*penne con funghili* and veal parmigiana), but the food is consistent ($12 plates of pasta pesto, $15 rotisserie chickens) and the brick courtyard is charming, especially on warm evenings. Try the *delizia* for dessert.

Shiso (707-933-9331; www.shisorestaurant.com; 522 Broadway; mains $11-22; lunch Wed-Sat, dinner Tue-Sun) Booths line the walls at this Cal-Japanese, with good sushi, kobe-beef tataki and great pork lettuce cups. Set lunch menus cost $9 to $12.

Café La Haye (707-935-5994; www.cafelahaye.com; 140 E Napa St; mains $15-25; dinner Tue-Sat) Despite a recent change in ownership, La Haye remains one of Sonoma's top tables for earthy New American cooking, made with produce sourced from within 60 miles. The tiny room is cheek-by-jowl and service borders on perfunctory, but the clean simplicity and flavor-packed cooking make it foodies' first choice. Reservations essential.

Harvest Moon Cafe (707-933-8160; www.harvestmooncafesonoma.com; 487 1st St W; mains $18-25; dinner) Inside an 1836 adobe, this casual bistro uses local ingredients in its changing menu, with dishes like duck risotto with Bellwether Farms ricotta. Lovely back patio.

For Sonoma's best groceries and sandwiches, visit **Sonoma Market** (707-996-3411; 500 W Napa St; sandwiches $7). Skip the Cheese Shop on the plaza; **Cheesemaker's Daughter** (707-996-4060; 127 E Napa St; Tue-Sun) has better European and local cheeses.

Drinking

Steiner's (707-996-3812; 456 1st St W) Open since 1927, Steiner's is Sonoma's oldest bar, and crowded on Sunday afternoons with cyclists and motorcyclists. Dig the taxidermy mountain lions.

Swiss Hotel (707-938-2884; 18 W Spain St) Locals and tourists crowd side-by-side at the 1909 Swiss Hotel for afternoon cocktails. There's OK food, but the bar's the thing.

Murphy's Irish Pub (707-935-0660; www.sonomapub.com; 464 1st St E) Don't ask for Bud – only *real* brews here. Good hand-cut fries and shepherd's pie too. Live music Thursday, through Sunday evenings.

Entertainment

Free jazz concerts happen on the plaza every second Tuesday, June to September, 6pm to 8pm; arrive early and bring a picnic. The Sonoma Valley Museum of Art (p203) hosts live-music events.

Little Switzerland (707-938-9990; www.lilswiss.com; 401 Grove St; Fri-Sun;) Long before Sonoma became 'Wine Country,' locals drank at this old-fashioned beer garden. Live bands play Latin music Friday evenings, jazz, swing or zydeco on Saturdays and – the great tradition – polka on Sunday afternoons, when you can bring the family. It sometimes serves barbecue; call ahead.

Shopping

La Haye Art Center (707-996-9665; 148 E Napa St; Fri-Mon) See the work of five local artists – a bronze sculptor, a potter and three painters – inside a former foundry.

Vella Cheese Co (707-928-3232; 315 2nd St E) Known for its dry-jack cheeses (made here since the 1930s), Vella also makes good Mezzo Secco with cocoa-powder-dusted rind. Staff will vacuum-pack for shipping.

Sign of the Bear (☎ 707-996-3722; 435 1st St W) Kitchen-gadget freaks: make a beeline to this indie cookware store.

Wine Exchange of Sonoma (☎ 800-938-1794; Suite C, 452 1st St E; 10am-6pm) If you can't make it to the wineries, sample local vintages for $1 to $2 per ounce at this wine shop, which also carries international beers.

Earthworks (☎ 707-935-0290; 403 1st St W) Cool consignment jewelry and art glass.

Artifax (☎ 707-996-9494; 450c 1st St E) Unusual Asian artifacts, rare beads and spiritual objects.

GLEN ELLEN

pop 990

Sleepy Glen Ellen is a snapshot of old Sonoma, with white picket fences, tiny cottages and ramshackle 19th-century brick buildings beside a poplar-lined creek. When downtown Sonoma is jammed, you can wander quiet Glen Ellen and feel far from civilization. It's ideal for a leg-stretching stopover between wineries or a romantic overnight – the nighttime sky blazes with stars.

Arnold Dr is the main drag and the valley's back-way route. Kenwood is just north, along Hwy 12, but has no town center like Glen Ellen's. For services, drive 8 miles to Sonoma.

Glen Ellen's biggest draws are Jack London State Historic Park (opposite) and Benziger winery (p200); several interesting shops line Arnold Dr.

Two great family-friendly alternatives to wine tasting: **Figone's Olive Oil** (☎ 707-938-3164; www.figoneoliveoil.com; 14301 Arnold Dr) presses its own extra-virgin olive oil; come in November or December to watch. You can sample year-round. Our favorite is infused with Meyer lemon – great for salads. Next door, compare chocolates of varying percentages of cacao at **Wine Country Chocolates Tasting Bar** (☎ 707-996-1010; www.winecountry chocolates.com).

There's fantastic hiking (when it's not blazingly hot) at **Sugarloaf Ridge State Park** (☎ 707-833-5712; www.parks.ca.gov; 2605 Adobe Canyon Rd, Kenwood; per car $6). On clear days, Bald Mountain has drop-dead views to the sea, while Bushy Peak Trail peers into Napa Valley. Both are moderately strenuous; plan four hours round-trip.

On hot days, families cool off in mineral-spring-fed swimming pools at **Morton's Warm Springs Resort** (☎ 707-833-5511, 800-551-2177; www.mortonswarmsprings.com; 1651 Warm Springs Rd; adult/child 3-12 $8/7; 10am-6pm Tue-Sun Jun-Aug, Sat, Sun & holidays only May & Sep, closed Oct-Apr), in Kenwood. Take Sonoma Hwy to Warm Springs Rd, and turn west.

Sleeping

Jack London Lodge (☎ 707-938-8510; http://jacklondonlodge.com; 13740 Arnold Dr; r Mon-Fri/Sat & Sun $120/180; wi-fi) An old-fashioned wood-sided motel, this is a weekday bargain. The well-kept rooms are decorated with some antiques; outside there's a Jacuzzi. The saloon is good for billiards.

Glen Ellen Cottages (☎ 707-996-1174; www.glenelleninn.com; 13670 Arnold Dr; cottage Mon-Fri/Sat & Sun $149/239;) Hidden behind the Glen Ellen Inn, these five creek-side cottages are designed for romance. Features include oversized jetted tubs, steam showers and gas fireplaces. In-room fruit and cookies greet your arrival.

our pick **Beltane Ranch** (☎ 707-996-6501; www.beltaneranch.com; 11775 Sonoma Hwy; r incl breakfast $150-220; wi-fi) Surrounded by horse pastures, Beltane is a throwback to 19th-century Sonoma. The cheerful, lemon-yellow 1890s ranch house occupies 100 acres and has double porches lined with swinging chairs and white wicker. Though this is technically a B&B, each unfussy, country-Americana-style room has a private entrance – nobody will make you pet the cat after dinner. Have breakfast in bed. No phones or TVs mean zero distraction from pastoral bliss.

Gaige House (☎ 707-935-0237, 800-935-0237; www.gaige.com; 13540 Arnold Dr; r incl breakfast $295-395, ste $550-695;) For a hideout with your lover, it's hard to beat Gaige House. The 1890 house contains five of the 22 rooms, which are decked out in Asian style with European-antique accents. But the best are the Japanese-style spa suites with all the latest bells and whistles, including freestanding tubs made from hollowed-out granite boulders. Breakfast is lavish.

Kenwood Inn & Spa (☎ 707-833-1293, 800-353-6966; www.kenwoodinn.com; 10400 Sonoma Hwy, Kenwood; r incl breakfast $375-525, ste $550-700;) Lush gardens surround ivy-covered bungalows at this gorgeous inn, which feels like a Mediterranean château. A recent ownership change resulted in a downgrading of amenities, but the facilities remain some of the best-looking in the Wine Country. There are two hot tubs (one with a waterfall) and an on-site spa. Book an upstairs balcony room.

Eating

Cafe Citti (☎ 707-833-2690; 9049 Sonoma Hwy; mains $8-15) Locals flock to this mom-and-pop Italian-American deli-trattoria, where you order at the counter then snag yourself a seat on the deck. Go for the roasted chicken, homemade gnocchi and ravioli. At lunch there are housebaked focaccia-bread sandwiches and pizzas with marinara just like Mama made.

fig café (☎ 707-938-2130; www.thefigcafe.com; mains $12-20; 13690 Arnold Dr; brunch Sat & Sun, dinner Fri-Mon) It's worth a trip to Glen Ellen for the fig's earthy California-Provençal comfort food, like flash-fried calamari with spicy lemon aioli, chopped salad, *moules-frites* (mussels and French fries), lamb stew and pot roast. All wines cost $7 by the glass; bottles are under $38.

Mayo Winery Reserve Room (☎ 707-833-5544; www.mayofamilywinery.com; 9200 Sonoma Hwy, Kenwood; 7-course menus $25; 11am-5pm, by reservation only) Wish you could sample a seven-course menu paired with wine, but lack the cash? Here's your chance – for $25. Portions are tiny, but the food is great – wild boar, duck pâté, prawns and other rich foods that pair with big zins and fat cabs.

Also recommended:

Garden Court Cafe (☎ 707-935-1565; 13647 Arnold Dr; mains $9-12; 7:30am-2:30pm Wed-Mon) Basic breakfasts, sandwiches and salads.

Glen Ellen Inn (☎ 707-996-6409; www.glenelleninn.com; 13670 Arnold Dr; lunch mains $10-13, dinner mains $19-22; lunch Fri-Tue, dinner nightly) Oysters, martinis and grilled steaks. Lovely garden, full bar.

Kenwood Restaurant & Bar (☎ 707-833-6326; www.kenwoodrestaurant.com; 9900 Sonoma Hwy, Kenwood; mains $14-26; 11:30am-9pm Wed-Sun) Skirt-and-sweater favorite for French-California vineyard-view lunches.

Yeti (☎ 707-996-9930; 14301 Arnold Dr; mains $10-22; 8:30am-9:30pm) Indian on a creek-side patio. Great naan.

Buy groceries and picnics at **Glen Ellen Village Market** (☎ 707-996-6728; 13751 Arnold Dr; 6am-9pm).

JACK LONDON STATE HISTORIC PARK

Napa has Robert Louis Stevenson, but Sonoma's got Jack London. This 1400-acre **park** (☎ 707-938-5216; www.parks.ca.gov; off Hwy 12, Glen Ellen; parking $6; 10am-5pm) traces the last years of the author's life.

Changing occupations from Oakland fisherman to Alaska gold prospector to Pacific yachtsman – and novelist on the side – London (1876–1916) ultimately took up farming. He bought Beauty Ranch in 1905 and moved there in 1910. With his second wife, Charmian, he lived and wrote in a small cottage while his mansion, Wolf House, was under construction. On the eve of its completion in 1913, it burned down. This disaster devastated London, and although he toyed with rebuilding, he died before construction got underway. The widow Charmian built the House of Happy Walls, which has been preserved as a **museum**. It's a half-mile walk from there to the remains of Wolf House, passing London's **grave** along the way. Other paths wind around the farm to the **cottage** where he lived and worked. Miles of trails (some of which are open to mountain bikes) weave through oak-dotted woodlands, between 600ft and 2300ft elevation. Watch out for poison oak (shiny red or green leaves that release a poisonous oil, causing a rash and itching; wash with Tecnu-brand soap if exposed).

RUSSIAN RIVER AREA

Lesser-known west Sonoma County was formerly famous for its apple farms and vacation cottages. Lately vineyards are replacing the orchards, and the Russian River has now taken its place among California's important wine appellations for superb pinot noir.

'The River,' as locals call it, has long been a summertime weekend destination for Northern Californians, who come to canoe, wander country lanes, taste wine, hike redwood forests and live at a lazy pace. In winter the river floods, and nobody's here.

The Russian River begins in the mountains north of Ukiah, in Mendocino County, but the most famous sections lie southwest of Healdsburg, where it cuts a serpentine course toward the sea. Just north of Santa Rosa, River Rd, the lower valley's main artery, connects Hwy 101 with coastal Hwy 1 at Jenner. Hwy 116 heads northwest from Cotati through Sebastopol and on to Guerneville. Westside Rd connects Guerneville and Healdsburg. West County's winding roads get confusing; carry a map.

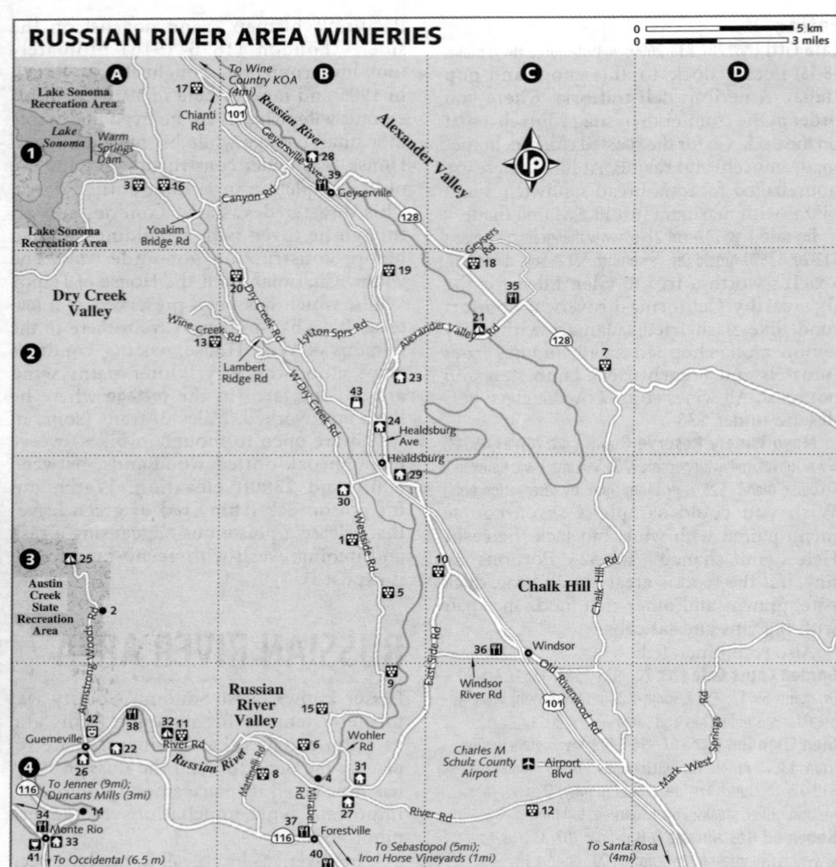

RUSSIAN RIVER AREA WINERIES

Outside Sonoma Valley, Sonoma County's wine-growing regions encompass several diverse areas, each famous for different reasons (see A Wine Country Primer, p211). Pick up the free, useful *Russian River Wine Road* map (www.wineroad.com) in tourist-brochure racks.

Russian River Valley

Nighttime coastal fog drifts up the Russian River Valley, then clears around midday. Pinot noir does beautifully here, as does chardonnay, which also grows in hotter regions but prefers the longer 'hang time' of cooler climes. The highest concentration of wineries is along Westside Rd, between Guerneville and Healdsburg. Some are photogenic and historic but corporately owned, such as **Hop Kiln Winery** (☎ 707-433-6491; www.hopkilnwinery.com; 6050 Westside Rd). Several are downright unfriendly; trust your instincts. Skip Rocchioli. The following are laid out west–east, from south of Guerneville toward Healdsburg.

HARTFORD FAMILY WINERY

Surprisingly upscale **Hartford Family** (☎ 707-887-1756; www.hartfordwines.com; 8075 Martinelli Rd, Forestville; tastings free) sits in a pastoral valley surrounded by redwood-forested hills on one of the area's prettiest back roads. It specializes in single-vineyard pinot (eight kinds), chardonnay and zinfandel, some from old-vine

SIGHTS & ACTIVITIES
Armida Winery.....1 B3
Armstrong Woods State Reserve..2 A3
Bella Vineyards.....3 A1
Burke's Canoe Trips.....4 B4
De la Montanya.....5 B3
Gary Farell.....6 B4
Hanna.....7 C2
Hartford Family Winery.....8 B4
Hawkes.....(see 35)
Hop Kiln Winery.....9 B4
J Winery.....10 C3
Korbel.....11 A4
Locals Tasting Room.....(see 39)
Martinelli.....12 C4
Michel-Schlumberger.....13 A2
Northwood Golf Course.....14 A4
Porter Creek.....15 B4
Preston Vineyards.....16 A1
Silver Oak.....17 A1
Stryker Sonoma.....18 C2
Trentadue.....19 B2
Unti Vineyards.....20 B2

SLEEPING
Alexander Valley RV Park.....21 C2
Applewood Inn.....22 A4
Belle de Jour Inn.....23 B2
Best Value Inn.....(see 29)
Best Western Dry Creek Inn.....24 B2
Bullfrog Pond.....25 A3
Creekside Inn & Resort.....26 A4
Farmhouse Inn.....27 B4
Geyserville Inn.....28 B1
Highland Dell.....(see 33)
L&M Motel.....29 B3
Madrona Manor.....30 B3
Raford House.....31 B4
Rio Villa Beach Resort.....(see 34)
Schoolhouse Canyon Campground.....32 A4
Village Inn & Lodge.....33 A4

EATING
Applewood Inn Restaurant.....(see 22)
Cafe Les Jumelles.....34 A4
Diavola.....(see 39)
Farmhouse Inn.....(see 27)
Highland Dell.....(see 33)
Jimtown Store.....35 C2
Madrona Manor.....(see 30)
Mirepoix.....36 C3
Mosaic.....37 B4
Nit's Thai Creations.....38 A4
Santi.....39 B1
Sophie's Cellars.....(see 34)
Stella's Café.....40 B4

DRINKING
Pink Elephant.....41 A4
Stumptown Brewery.....(see 38)

ENTERTAINMENT
Coffee Bazaar.....42 A4

SHOPPING
Gardener.....43 B2

fruit. The gardens have umbrella tables for picnicking. Bottles cost $23 to $65.

IRON HORSE

Atop a hill with drop-dead views over the county, **Iron Horse Vineyards** (☎ 707-887-1507; www.ironhorsevineyards.com; 9786 Ross Station Rd, Sebastopol; tastings $10; 10am-3:30pm) is known for sparkling wines and pinot noir, which the White House often pours. The outdoor tasting room is refreshingly unfussy: when you're done with your wine, pour it in the grass. Located off Hwy 116. Bottles cost $18 to $50.

MARIMAR TORRES

Marimar Torres (Map p196; ☎ 707-823-4365; www.marimarestate.com; 11400 Graton Rd, Sebastopol; tastings $10) specializes in pinot – seven different varieties – and chardonnay, all organically grown. The Spanish-style hilltop tasting room has a knockout vineyard-view terrace, lovely for picnics. Call ahead for tapas and wine pairings ($25). Bottles cost $29 to $52.

PORTER CREEK

Porter Creek (☎ 707-433-6321; www.portercreekvineyards.com; 8735 Westside Rd; tastings free) is classic old-school Northern California. Inside a vintage-1920s garage, the tasting bar is a former bowling-alley lane plunked atop two barrels. The grapes are organically grown, and equipment runs on biodiesel. High-acid, food-friendly pinot noir and chardonnay are the specialties, but there's a silky zinfandel and other Burgundy- and Rhône-style wines, too. Check out the aviary and the yurt. Bottles cost $24 to $65.

DE LA MONTANYA

On weekends you can meet the practical-joker winemaker at this tiny **winery** (☎ 707-433-3711; www.dlmwine.com; 2651 Westside Rd at Foreman Lane; tastings free; Mon-Thu by appointment only, Fri-Sun 11am-5pm), known for 17 small-batch varieties made with estate-grown fruit. Viognier is the signature white, Portivo the red. The 'summer white' blend and the gewürztraminer are great back-porch wines, infinitely drinkable. Bottles cost $20 to $58.

ARMIDA WINERY

Taste inside a geodesic dome at **Armida** (☎ 707-433-2222; www.armida.com; 2201 Westside Rd; tastings free, reserves $10). Head directly to the zinfandel – 'Poizin: the Wine to Die For' is tops. Before you keel over, enjoy a game of boccie, then picnic on the deck beneath moss-covered oaks while taking in the views. Bottles cost $12 to $30.

J WINERY

Swanky **J** (☎ 707-431-3646; www.jwine.com; 11447 Old Redwood Hwy; tastings $10) makes crisp sparkling wines – one of Wine Country's best – a terrific pinot noir and a lesser-known pinot gris. The tasting bar is straightforward, but we recommend the food pairings, served on the 'J Terrace' ($35; no reservations) and in education-intensive 'Bubble Room' sessions ($55; reservations required). Bottles range from $28 to $40.

Also consider:

Gary Farrell (☎ 707-473-2900; www.garyfarrellwines.com; 10701 Westside Rd; tastings $5) Elegant chardonnay and pinot by a big-name winemaker; tasting room in second-growth redwoods.

Korbel (☎ 707-824-7316, 707-824-7000; www.korbel.com; 13250 River Rd; tastings free) *Gorgeous* rose gardens (April to October), but the champagne's just OK. On-site deli and picnicking.

Martinelli (☎ 707-525-0570; www.martinelliwinery.com; 3360 River Rd, Windsor; tastings free) Celeb consulting winemaker Helen Turley; standout pinot noir and good syrah, sauvignon blanc and chardonnay.

Dry Creek Valley

Hemmed in by 2000ft-high mountains, Dry Creek Valley is relatively warm, ideal for sauvignon blanc, zinfandel and (in spots) cabernet sauvignon. It's west of Hwy 101, between Healdsburg and Lake Sonoma. Dry Creek Rd is the main thoroughfare. Parallel-running West Dry Creek Rd is an undulating country lane with no center stripe – one of Sonoma's great back roads, ideal for biking. The following are in north–south order.

BELLA VINEYARDS

Atop the valley's north end, always-fun **Bella** (☎ 707-473-9171, 866-572-3552; www.bellawinery.com; 9711 W Dry Creek Rd; tastings $5) has caves built into the hillside. The estate-grown grapes include 110-year-old vines from the Alexander Valley. The focus is on big reds – zin and syrah – but there's terrific rosé, an ideal barbecue wine, and late-harvest zin that goes fabulously with brownies. The wonderful vibe and dynamic staff make Bella special. Bottles cost $15 to $35.

PRESTON VINEYARDS

Preston Vineyards (☎ 707-433-3327, 800-305-9707; www.prestonvineyards.com; 9282 W Dry Creek Rd; tastings $5, refundable with purchase) is a 19th-century organic farm. A weathered picket fence frames the farmhouse's tasting room, where candy-colored walls and tongue-in-groove ceilings set a country mood. The signature is citrusy sauvignon blanc, but try the Rhône varietals and small-lot wines: mourvèdre, viognier, cinsault and cult-favorite barbera. Lou Preston is known for his bread: picnic in the shade of the walnut tree, then play boccie. Bottles cost $16 to $28.

UNTI VINEYARDS

Inside a fluorescent-lit windowless garage, **Unti** (☎ 707-433-5590; www.untivineyards.com; 4202 Dry Creek Rd; 🕑 Sat & Sun, by appointment Mon-Fri) makes all estate-grown reds, including a Châteauneuf-du-Pape-style granache, a slutty syrah – powerful and compelling – and a 100% sangiovese, favored by oenophiles. If you love wine, don't miss Unti. Bottles cost $16 to $30.

MICHEL-SCHLUMBERGER

Well off the beaten path, this **winery** (☎ 800-447-3060; www.michelschlumberger.com; 4155 Wine Creek Rd; tours $15-30, tastings $5; 🕑 by appointment) is a leader in organic farming and makes superb Bordeaux-style wines – cabernet sauvignon, chardonnay and syrah – all in French oak, a rarity in California. We love the 'green tour' ($30), an hour-long walk through the 100-acre estate, focusing on local ecology and sustainable wine-making, and culminating with a hilltop tasting. Bottles cost $21 to $55.

Alexander Valley

Bucolic Alexander Valley flanks the Mayacamas Mountains immediately west of Napa, with postcard-perfect vistas and wide-open vineyards. Summers are hot, perfect for cabernet sauvignon, merlot and warm-weather chardonnay, but there's also fine sauvignon blanc and zinfandel. For events info, including First Weekend happenings, visit www.alexandervalley.org. The following are in north–south order.

STRYKER SONOMA

Wow! What a view from the hilltop concrete-and-glass tasting room at **Stryker Sonoma** (☎ 707-433-1944; www.strykersonoma.com; 5110 Hwy 128; tastings free). Plan to picnic. The standouts are fruit-forward zinfandel and sangiovese, which you can't buy anywhere else. Bottles cost $20 to $48.

HAWKES

The tasting room at **Hawkes** (☎ 707-433-4295; www.hawkeswine.com; 6734 Hwy 128; tastings $5) opened in 2007, but it's been growing top-end cabernet grapes for decades. The single-vineyard cab is damn good, as is the blend; there's also a clean-and-crisp, nonmalolactic chardonnay. Peruse the cool teapot collection between sips. Bottles cost $20 to $60.

HANNA

Abutting oak-studded hills, **Hanna** (☎ 707-431-4310, 800-854-3987; http://hannawinery.com; 9280 Hwy 128;

A WINE COUNTRY PRIMER

When people talk about Sonoma, they're referring to the *whole* county, which unlike Napa is huge. It extends all the way from the coast, up the Russian River Valley, into Sonoma Valley and eastward to Napa Valley; in the south it stretches from San Pablo Bay (an extension of San Francisco Bay) to Healdsburg in the north. It's essential to break Sonoma down by district.

West County refers to everything west of Hwy 101 and includes the **Russian River Valley** and the coast. **Sonoma Valley** stretches north–south along Hwy 12. In northern Sonoma County, **Alexander Valley** lies east of Healdsburg, and **Dry Creek Valley** lies north of Healdsburg. In the south, **Carneros** straddles the Sonoma–Napa border, north of San Pablo Bay. Each region has its own particular wines; what grows where depends upon the weather.

Inland valleys get hot; coastal regions stay cool. In West County and Carneros, nighttime fog blankets the vineyards. Burgundy-style wines do best, particularly pinot noir and chardonnay. Further inland, Alexander, Sonoma and much of Dry Creek Valleys (as well as Napa Valley) are fog-protected. Here, Bordeaux-style wines thrive, especially cabernet sauvignon, sauvignon blanc, merlot and other heat-loving varieties. For California's famous cabernets, head to Napa. Zinfandel and Rhône-style varieties, such as syrah and viognier, grow in both regions, warm and cool. In cooler climes, resultant wines are lighter, more elegant; in warmer areas they are heavier and more rustic.

As you drive around, notice the bases of the grapevines. The fatter they are, the older they are. 'Old vine' grapes yield a richness, a depth of color and a complexity of flavor not found in grapes from younger vines.

A few basics: wineries and vineyards are not the same. Grapes grow in a vineyard, then get fermented at a winery. Wineries that grow their own grapes are called estates, as in 'estate-grown' or 'estate-bottled,' but estates, too, often ferment grapes from other vineyards. When vintners speak of 'single-vineyard' or 'vineyard-designate' wines, they mean that the grapes all originated from the same vineyard, which allows for tighter quality control. 'Single varietal' means all the grapes are the same variety (such as 100% merlot), but may come from different vineyards. Reserve wines are the vintner's special wines; only a few are made, and they're usually available only at the winery.

But it all comes down to personal taste. If you don't like cabernet, who cares how well it grows in Napa? And if you're a neophyte, uncertain of what to try, don't be afraid to ask questions. Vintners love to share their knowledge with interested visitors. If you don't know how to taste wine or what to look for, ask the person behind the tasting-room counter to help you discover what you like. Just remember to spit out the wine once you've tasted it; the slightest buzz will diminish your capacity to distinguish one from another.

The hands-down best place for a crash course is Copia (p229), in Napa. For a handy-dandy reference on the road, pick up a copy of Jancis Robinson's *Concise Wine Companion* (2001, Oxford University Press) to carry in the car.

tastings $5; 10am-4pm) resembles a Tuscan-style train depot. At the bar, look out for estate-grown merlot and cabernet, as well as big-fruit zins and syrah. There's an appointment-only sit-down tasting of reserve wine, cheese and charcuterie available for $25. There are stellar views and good picnicking. Bottles cost $18 to $52.

Also consider:

Silver Oak (800-273-8809; www.silveroak.com; 24625 Chianti Rd; tastings $10; Mon-Sat) Sister to the legendary Napa winery; the Alexander Valley cabernet is similarly luxurious, but more fruit-forward.

Trentadue (707-433-3104, 888-332-3032; www.trentadue.com; 19170 Geyserville Ave; port tastings $5) Specializes in ports (ruby, not tawny); chocolate port makes a great gift.

SEBASTOPOL

pop 7550

Grapes have replaced apples as the new cash crop, but Sebastopol's farm-town identity remains rooted in the apple – evidence the much-heralded summertime Gravenstein Apple Fair. Town center feels suburban because of traffic, but a hippie tinge gives it color.

WINE COUNTRY

Orientation & Information

Hwys 116 and 12 form Sebastopol's major intersection. Hwy 116 becomes Main St through town; southbound traffic uses Main St, northbound traffic Petaluma Ave. At Main St's northern end, the road turns 90 degrees and becomes Healdsburg Ave, continues northward, then becomes Gravenstein Hwy N toward Forestville and Guerneville. At town's south end, Main St becomes Gravenstein Hwy S and heads toward Hwy 101 and Sonoma.

Sebastopol Area Chamber of Commerce & Visitors Center (☎ 707-823-3032, 877-828-4748; www.sebastopol.org; 265 S Main St; 10am-4pm Mon-Fri) has maps, information and exhibits.

Festivals & Events

Apple Blossom Festival (www.sebastopol.org) April
Gravenstein Apple Fair (www.farmtrails.org/applefair.html) August
Celtic Festival (http://cumuluspresents.com/celtic) Late September

Sights & Activities

East of the plaza, **Sebastopol Center for the Arts** (☎ 707-829-4797; www.sebarts.org; 6780 Depot St; admission free; 10am-5pm Mon-Fri, 1-4pm Sat & Sun) hosts exhibitions by California artists and free art walks the first Thursday of each month.

The **farmers market** (cnr Petaluma & McKinley Aves; 10am-1:30pm Sun Apr–mid-Dec) meets at the downtown plaza. Surrounding Sebastopol, look for family-friendly farms, gardens, animal sanctuaries and pick-your-own orchards. For a countywide list, pick up the free **Sonoma County Farm Trails Guide** (www.farmtrails.org), in which you'll find listings like the **Hallberg Butterfly Gardens** (☎ 707-823-3420; www.hallbergbutterflygardens.org; 8687 Oak Grove Rd; suggested donation $5; by appointment Wed-Sun Apr-Oct); and **Kozlowski Farms** (☎ 707-887-1587; 800-473-2767; www.kozlowskifarms.com; 5566 Gravenstein Hwy N; 9am-5pm Mon-Fri), which makes lip-smacking jams and apple pie.

Sleeping

Sebastopol is good for get-up-and-go travelers exploring Russian River Valley and the coast.

Raccoon Cottage (☎ 707-545-5466; www.raccooncottage.com; 2685 Elizabeth Ct; cottage incl breakfast $115-130) Stay in a small cottage, off Vine Hill Rd, amid oaks, fruit trees and gardens.

Sebastopol Inn (☎ 707-829-2500, 800-653-1082; www.sebastopolinn.com; 6751 Sebastopol Ave; r $119-169; wi-fi) We like this independent, *non*-cookie-cutter motel for its quiet, off-street location, reasonable rates and good-looking rooms with solid-pine furniture. Outside are grassy areas and a hot tub.

Holiday Inn Express (☎ 707-829-6677, 800-465-4329; www.winecountryhi.com; 1101 Gravenstein Hwy S; r $129-199; wi-fi) This modern hotel feels generic, but has in-room refrigerators, coffee makers and a hot tub.

Vine Hill Inn (☎ 707-823-8832; www.vine-hill-inn.com; 3949 Vine Hill Rd; r incl breakfast $170; wi-fi) Mature landscaping surrounds this four-room 1897 Victorian farmhouse, with gorgeous vineyard views, just north of town off Hwy 116. Breakfast is made with eggs from the barn's chickens. Two rooms have Jacuzzis.

Eating

Viva Mexicana (☎ 707-823-5555, 707-829-5555; 841 Gravenstein Hwy S; mains $5-8; 8am-8pm; V) This tiny roadside *taquería* has outdoor tables, and veggie-heavy burritos with homemade salsa.

Mom's Apple Pie (☎ 707-823-8330; 4550 Gravenstein Hwy N; whole pies $6-14; 10am-6pm) Pie's the thing here. Apple is predictably good, but blueberry is our fave, best with vanilla ice cream. Yum, that flaky crust!

East-West Cafe (☎ 707-829-2822; 128 N Main St; meals $7-11; 8am-9pm; V) At this unfussy café there's everything from grass-fed burgers to macrobiotic wraps, stir-fries to *huevos rancheos* (corn tortilla with fried egg and chili-tomato sauce). Try the blue-corn pancakes.

Slice of Life (☎ 707-829-6627; www.thesliceoflife.com; 6970 McKinley St; mains under $10; 11am-9pm Tue-Sun; V) This terrific vegan-vegetarian kitchen doubles as a pizzeria. Breakfast all day. Great smoothies and date shakes.

K&L Bistro (☎ 707-823-6614; www.klbistro.com; 119 S Main St; lunch $9-18, dinner $16-28; lunch & dinner Tue-Sat) Sebastopol's top table is celebrated for down-to-earth provincial Cal-French cooking and a convivial – if loud – bistro atmosphere, with classic dishes like mussels and French fries, and grilled steaks with red-wine reduction. Tables are tight, but the crowd is friendly. Make reservations.

Hopmonk Tavern (☎ 707-829-9300; www.hopmonk.com; 230 Petaluma Ave; mains $10-20) Inside a converted 1903 railroad station, Hopmonk's competent cooking is designed to pair with beer – 76 varieties – served in type-specific

TASTING ROOM ETIQUETTE

If you've never gone wine tasting, here are some basics to help you avoid awkward moments and dirty looks.

- Don't smoke. Not in the gardens either. Wait until you're off the property.
- Wear no perfume and avoid scented soaps. Nothing annoys winemakers so much as a cloud of cologne. Wine tasting requires there be no olfactory distractions.
- Avoid getting shit-faced. If you're serious about tasting or worried about drinking too much, use the spit buckets. Besides, a buzz gets in the way of properly assessing a wine. It's OK to get giggly, of course.
- Embrace sensuality. Linger over the wine's aroma and color before you sip. There's no need to rush. This *is* Wine Country, after all.
- Don't chew gum. 'Nuf said.
- Check your criticism. You might be standing in front of the winemaker.
- Be open to unfamiliar wines. You may think you only like, say, merlot, but allow your host to show you other wines, too. In Anderson Valley (p270), for example, there are fantastic Alsatian-style wines like gewürztraminer, which most wrongly assume to be sweet. Let yourself be surprised.
- Don't be afraid to ask questions. There's nothing wrong with not knowing what you're doing. Starry-eyed enthusiasm is charming, and most winemakers love helping visitors understand what they're tasting. But if you don't get assistance, or if you find the place snooty, leave. There are hundreds of others who'd love to help you.
- If you picnic at a winery, buy a bottle of your host's wine.
- Take wine tasting lightly. Don't be intimidated by snobs who insist it takes years to appreciate the art of oenology. Maybe it does, but you've got to start somewhere. Now's your chance.

glassware. Great burgers, fried calamari, charcuterie platters and organic salads.

Saint Rose (☎ 707-829-5898; http://cafesaintrose.blogspot.com; 9890 Bodega Hwy; mains $18-22; 🕑 Wed-Sun dinner, Sat & Sun brunch) This kick-back-casual, funky little roadhouse surprises with high-concept, seasonal-regional cooking geared for foodies, not the steak-and-potatoes set. The daily-changing menu is short, but lists few familiar dishes – instead of steak and chicken, expect braised pork shanks and hibachi-grilled poussin. Though dishes sometimes miss, the quirky culinary viewpoint gives insight into the experimental side of Northern California's food scene. The sun-dappled back patio feels like a secret garden. Make reservations.

Independent **Fiesta Market** (☎ 707-823-9735; 550 Gravenstein Hwy N) carries the best groceries and picnics.

Goodbye Ben & Jerry, hello **Screamin' Mimi** (☎ 707-823-5902; 6902 Sebastopol Ave; 🕑 11am-10pm) for rich homemade ice cream. There's also **Sebastopol Cookie Co** (☎ 707-824-4040; 168 N Main St).

Drinking & Entertainment

Hopmonk Tavern (☎ 707-829-9300; www.hopmonk.com; 230 Petaluma Ave) An always-fun beer garden with 76 American and European craft brews – several housemade. Top-notch pub grub. Live music most nights; Tuesday is open mic.

Ace-in-the-Hole Pub (☎ 707-829-1223; cnr Hwy 116 & Graton Rd; 🕑 11:30am-9pm Sun-Thu, to 10pm Fri & Sat) America's first cider pub hosts live music daily. Great barbecued oysters and hand-cut fries.

Jasper O'Farrell's (☎ 707-823-1389; 6957 Sebastopol Ave) There's live music Friday and Saturday at this Irish-style bar with billiards.

Hardcore Espresso (☎ 707-823-7588; 1798 Gravenstein Hwy S; 🕑 6am-7pm) Meet local hippies and art freaks over coffee and smoothies at this classic Nor-Cal off-the-grid, indoor-outdoor coffeehouse that's essentially a corrugated-metal-roofed shack surrounded by umbrella tables. The organic coffee is the town's best.

Coffee Catz (☎ 707-829-6600; 6761 Sebastopol Ave; 🕑 7am-10pm Fri & Sat, to 6pm Sun-Thu) This roastery and café, east of downtown in a historic rail

DETOUR: GRATON

A portrait of West County's offbeat arts and food scenes, teeny-tiny Graton (population 1815) wasn't on tourists' radar until Martha Stewart profiled an antiques shop here in 2008. She overlooked the rest of town, but we love the entire one-block-long place. Go 4 miles north of Sebastopol on Hwy 116, then a half-mile west via Graton Rd.

Far West Trading Co (☎ 707-823-4880; www.farwesttradingcompany.com; 9060 Graton Rd; Tue-Sun) carries top-end Asian home furnishings and has an inviting tea bar with imported loose-leaf teas you can sample in the garden. Contemporary California artists show at **Graton Gallery** (☎ 707-829-8912; 9050 Graton Rd). Martha loves browsing bric-a-brac at **Mr Ryder & Co Art & Antiques** (☎ 707-824-8221; 9040 Graton Rd). So do we.

Part general store, part café, **Willow Wood Market** (☎ 707-823-0233; 9020 Graton Rd; mains $8-17; 8am-9pm Mon-Sat, 9am-3pm Sun) serves knockout California comfort food, like smoked-trout salad, polenta with goat cheese, and roasted chicken; sit in the garden. Surprisingly cosmopolitan **Underwood Bar & Bistro** (☎ 707-823-7023; 9113 Graton Rd; tapas $8-15, mains $21-26; lunch Tue-Sat, dinner Tue-Sun) draws accolades for Mediterranean-style small plates; bon vivants fill the hoppin' bar.

barn (Gravenstein Station), hosts acoustic music Thursday to Sunday; open mic is Wednesday.

Main Street Theatre (☎ 707-823-0177; www.the-rep.com; 104 N Main St) Presents repertory and new drama.

Shopping

Antique shops line Gravenstein Hwy S toward Hwy 101.

Antique Society (☎ 707-829-1733; 2661 Gravenstein Hwy S) This 20,000sq-ft space features 125 vendors.

Midgley's Country Flea Market (☎ 707-823-7874; 2200 Gravenstein Hwy S; 6:30am-4:30pm Sat & Sun) The region's largest flea market.

Downtown there's **Copperfield's Books** (☎ 707-823-2618; www.copperfields.net; 138 N Main St), which hosts literary events; and legendary **Incredible Records** (☎ 707-824-8099; 112 N Main St).

OCCIDENTAL

pop 1270

Our favorite West County town is a haven of artists, back-to-the-landers and counterculturalists. Historic 19th-century buildings line a single main drag, easy to explore in an hour. Check out the **Bohemian Connection** (www.bohemianconnection.com) for information.

Meet the whole community at the detour-worthy **farmers market** (☎ 707-793-2159; www.occidentalfarmersmarket.com, 4pm-dusk Fridays, Jun-Oct), with musicians, craftspeople and – the star attraction – **Gerard's Paella** (www.gerardspaella.com) of TV-cooking-show fame. Our favorite scenic drive, **Coleman Valley Rd**, heads west through redwoods and pastoral valleys, then atop 1400ft rolling hills before reaching Bodega Bay (p250).

At Christmastime, Bay Area families flock to Occidental to buy trees. The town decorates to the nines, and there's weekend cookie-decorating and caroling at the Union Hotel's Bocce Ballroom. (Locals whisper that many Christmas-tree farms are tax write-offs.)

our pick **Renga Arts** (☎ 707-874-9407; www.rengaarts.com; 3605 Bohemian Hwy; Fri-Mon) All the cool stuff here is made from reclaimed materials, including handbags, jewelry, birdhouses and benches.

Aubergine (☎ 707-874-9034; 3690 Bohmenian Hwy; Thu-Mon) carries slim-fitting second-hand European clothes. **Verdigris** (☎ 707-874-9018; www.1lightartlamps.com; 72 Main St; Thu-Mon) crafts gorgeous art lamps.

Three miles south in Freestone, a Zen-like tranquility prevails at **Osmosis Enzyme Bath & Massage** (☎ 707-823-8231; www.osmosis.com; 209 Bohemian Hwy; 9am-9pm), which indulges patrons with dry-enzyme baths of aromatic cedar fibers (bath-and-blanket wrap $85), lovely gardens for tea and meditation, plus outdoor massages. Make reservations.

Rooms at the **Occidental Hotel** (☎ 707-874-3623, 877-867-6084; www.occidentalhotel.com; 3610 Bohemian Hwy; r $100-125, 2-bedroom ste with kitchen Mon-Fri/Sat & Sun $160/190) haven't been redecorated in years, but they're clean. We prefer the simple country B&B rooms at Freestone's **Green Apple Inn** (☎ 707-874-2526; 520 Bohemian Hwy, Freestone; r incl breakfast $99-109) or Valley Ford Hotel (opposite).

A beautifully restored 1876 Victorian, the **Inn at Occidental** (☎ 707-874-1047, 800-522-6324; www.innatoccidental.com; 3657 Church St; r incl breakfast

WINE COUNTRY

$229-339; ☒ ☒ ☐) – one of Sonoma's finest – is full of collectible antiques. Rooms have gas fireplaces, feather beds and rich color schemes.

Foodies: consider nearby Graton (see the boxed text, opposite). **Bohemian Market** (☎ 707-874-3312; 3633 Main St) has the best groceries. In Freestone, **Wild Flour Bakery** (☎ 707-874-3928; 140 Bohemian Hwy; ⏲ 8am-6pm Fri-Mon) makes artisinal brick-oven breads, scones and coffee.

Come for big plates of comfort food at **Howard Caffe & Espresso Bar** (☎ 707-874-2838; 75 Main St; meals under $10; ⏲ breakfast & lunch; ♿); there's also a juice bar, terrific breakfast and wi-fi.

Worth a special trip, **Bistro des Copains** (☎ 707-874-2436; 3728 Bohemian Hwy; mains $21-24; ⏲ dinner) draws bon vivants for its Cal-French country cooking, like steak-*frites* and roast duck. Great wines; free corkage Tuesday nights for Sonoma vintages.

Negri's (☎ 707-823-5301; 3700 Bohemian Hwy; meals $10-20; ♿) and the **Union Hotel** (☎ 707-874-3555; 3703 Bohemian Hwy; meals $10-20; ♿) serve six-course family-style dinners. The Union is slightly better (neither is great) and has a hard-to-beat lunch special – a whole pizza, salad and a soda for $12 – in its 1869 saloon; at dinner, sit in the Bocce Ballroom. There's live music weekends.

GUERNEVILLE & AROUND

Pop 5570

The Russian River's biggest vacation-resort town, Guerneville gets packed summer weekends with party-hardy gay boys, sun-worshipping lesbians and long-haired beer-drinking Harley riders, earning it the nickname 'Groinville.' The gay scene has died back since the unfortunate closure of Fife's, the world's first gay resort, but fun-seeking crowds still come to canoe, hike redwoods and hammer cocktails poolside.

Downriver, some areas are sketchy (due to drugs). The local chamber of commerce has chased most of the tweakers from Main St in Guerneville, but some off-the-beaten path areas remain sketchy. If some woodsy locales feel creepy – especially campgrounds – they probably are.

Four miles downriver, tiny Monte Rio has a sign over Hwy 166 declaring it 'Vacation Wonderland' – an overstatement, but the dog-friendly beach is a hit with families. Further west, idyllic Duncans Mills is home to a few dozen souls, but has charming historic buildings. Upriver, east of Guerneville, Forestville feels more like mellow Wine Country.

Orientation & Information

Get information and lodging referrals:

Russian River Chamber of Commerce & Visitor Center (☎ 707-869-9000, 877-644-9001; www.russianriver.com; 16209 1st St, Guerneville; ⏲ 10am-5pm Mon-Sat, to 4pm Sun)

Russian River Visitor Information Center (☎ 707-869-4096; ⏲ 10am-3:45pm) At Korbel Cellars.

Sights & Activities

A magnificent redwood forest 2 miles north of Guerneville, the 805-acre **Armstrong Redwoods State Reserve** (☎ 707-869-2015; www.parks.ca.gov; 17000 Armstrong Woods Rd; day use per vehicle $6) was set aside by a 19th-century lumber magnate. Walk or cycle in for free; pay only to drive in. Short interpretive trails lead into magical forests, with miles of backcountry trails and campgrounds. **Armstrong Woods Pack Station** (☎ 707-887-2939; www.redwoodhorses.com) leads year-round

DETOUR: VALLEY FORD

Valley Ford (population 60) is a tableau of rural California, with rolling hills dotted with grazing cows and manure lingering on the breeze – the forced sophistication of other Wine Country locales couldn't feel further away. It's ideal for a one-nighter or a lazy meal while exploring backroads.

Girly-girls like the linens, candles and garden trinkets at **Gabby Girl Boutique** (☎ 707-876-1933; 14430 Hwy 1; ⏲ Fri-Mon). **West County Design** (☎ 707-875-9140; 14390 Hwy 1) houses a stonemason's and custom-furniture-builder's shops, giving a glimpse of contemporary California home-furnishings styles.

We love the flavor-rich cooking at **Rocker Oysterfeller's** (☎ 707-876-1983; www.rockeroysterfellers.com; 14415 Hwy 1; mains $19-28; ⏲ dinner Wed-Sun, brunch Sun), with its barbecued oysters, local crab cakes, steaks and fried chicken. Great wine list, too. Stay the night at the adjoining **Valley Ford Hotel** (☎ 707-876-1983; www.vfordhotel.com; rooms Mon-Fri/Sat & Sun $129/199), a 19th-century hotel with good beds, soft linens and great rates.

2½-hour trail rides ($70), full-day rides and overnight treks. Reservations required.

Look for sandy beaches and swimming holes along the river. There's year-round fishing. Outfitters operate mid-May to early October, after which winter rains dangerously swell the river.

You can't beat **Burke's Canoe Trips** (☎ 707-887-1222; www.burkescanoetrips.com; 8600 River Rd, cnr Mirabel Rd, Forestville; Memorial Day-Sep;) for a day on the river. Self-guided canoe trips cost $59 per canoe and include shuttles back to your car. Camping in its riverside redwood grove costs $10 per person. Make reservations.

Johnson's Beach (☎ 707-869-2022; end of Church St, Guerneville) rents inner tubes, canoes, paddle-boats and watercraft.

King's Sport & Tackle (☎ 707-869-2156; www.guernevillesport.com; 16258 Main St, Guerneville) is *the* local source for fishing and river-condition information. It rents kayaks ($30 to $55) and canoes ($55).

The 1920s-vintage Alistair MacKenzie–designed **Northwood Golf Course** (☎ 707-865-1116; www.northwoodgolf.com; 19400 Hwy 116, Monte Rio) is a par-36, nine-hole course.

Pee Wee Golf & Arcade (☎ 707-869-9321; 16155 Drake Rd at Hwy 116; games $7; 11am-10pm Memorial Day-Labor Day, Sat & Sun Easter-Memorial Day), just south of the Hwy 116 bridge, is a kitschy, but tired, retro-1950s miniature-golf course. It rents bicycles ($30).

A **farmers market** meets downtown Wednesdays, June through September, 4pm to 7pm. Saturdays in summer, there's one at Monte Rio Beach, 11am to 2pm.

Festivals & Events

Women's Weekends (www.russianriverwomensweekends.com) Lesbians and liberal-minded grrrls in spring and fall.

Stumptown Days Parade, Rodeo & BBQ June

Russian River Blues Festival June

Lazy Bear Weekend Read: heavy, hairy gay men; mid-July.

Jazz on the River September

Russian River Food & Wine Fest September

Sleeping

Russian River has few budget sleeps; prices drop midweek. Weekends and holidays, book ahead. Many places don't have TVs. Because the river sometimes floods, some lodgings have cold linoleum or tile floors, so pack slippers.

GUERNVILLE

Bullfrog Pond (tent sites $15) Reached via a steep road out of Armstrong Redwoods, Bullfrog Pond has forested campsites with cold water, and primitive hike-in and equestrian backcountry campsites. All are first-come, first-served, year-round.

Johnson's Beach Resort (☎ 707-869-2022; www.johnsonsbeach.com; 16241 1st St; tent sites from $16, RV sites from $25-35, rustic cabins $50, per week $300) On the river in Guerneville, Johnson's has little to boast (think weeds and trailers) other than its central location. No dogs, no credit cards.

Highlands Resort (☎ 707-869-0333; www.highlandsresort.com; 14000 Woodland Dr; tent sites $25, r with/without bathroom $90/70, cottages $130-190;) Guerneville's mellowest all-gay resort sits on a wooded hillside, walkable to town, and has simply furnished rooms and little cottages with porches. The large pool and hot tub are clothing-optional (weekday/weekend day use $5/10). There's camping, too. Prices are lower on weekdays.

Schoolhouse Canyon Campground (☎ 707-869-2311; 12600 River Rd; tent sites $35) Two miles east of downtown Guerneville, Schoolhouse's tent sites are beneath tall trees, some bordering on the river. The baths could be cleaner, but the showers are hot (bring quarters) and the location quiet. Dogs allowed.

Riverlane Resort (☎ 707-869-2323, 800-201-2324; www.riverlaneresort.com; 16320 1st St; cabins $80-125;) Right downtown, Riverlane has cabins with kitchens, dated furniture and futons. Best for no-frills travelers or campers wanting an upgrade. Friendly service, heated pool, private beach and hot tub.

Russian River Resort (Triple-R; ☎ 707-869-0691, 800-417-3767; http://russianriverresort.com; cnr 4th & Mill St; r Mon-Fri $85-175, Sat & Sun $100-200; wi-fi) The most raucous gay resort. Triple-R's pool – free to nonguests – gets packed with suntan-oiled, cocktail-swilling gay boys. The motel-style rooms are clean, and you can bang the headboard without fear of disturbing anyone.

Creekside Inn & Resort (☎ 707-869-3623, 800-776-6586; www.creeksideinn.com; 16180 Neeley Rd; B&B r $98-175, cottages $130-165; wi-fi) Across the river from downtown, quiet and secluded-feeling Creekside has well-tended cottages with kitchens (some with fireplaces), and homey B&B rooms in the main house. Creekside is enviro-conscious: new 'green cottages' were built with solar panels. There's a hot tub and a pool beneath redwoods. Some air-con.

WINE COUNTRY

Applewood Inn (☎ 707-869-9093, 800-555-8509; www.applewoodinn.com; 13555 Hwy 116; r $195-345; wi-fi) A former estate on a wooded hilltop, the Applewood has marvelous Arts and Crafts–era detail, with dark wood and heavy furniture. Rooms sport Jacuzzis, couples' showers and top-end linens; some have fireplaces and air-con. Great hideaway.

Fern Grove Cottages (☎ 707-869-8105; www.ferngrove.com; 16650 River Rd; cabins incl breakfast $149-189, cabins with kitchen $199-239; wi-fi) Guerneville's cheeriest resort, Fern Grove has vintage-1920s pine-paneled cabins downtown, beneath redwoods. Some have Jacuzzis and fireplaces. Quality is in the details: the pool uses salt, not chlorine; the lovely English innkeeper provides concierge service; and breakfast includes homemade scones.

FORESTVILLE

Raford House (☎ 707-887-9573, 800-887-9503; www.rafordhouse.com; 10630 Wohler Rd; r $150-250; wi-fi) We love this B&B's secluded hilltop location, surrounded by tall palms and rambling vineyards. The 1880 Victorian's rooms are big and airy, done with lace and antiques; some have fireplaces. And wow, those sunset views!

Farmhouse Inn (☎ 707-887-3300, 800-464-6642; www.farmhouseinn.com; 7871 River Rd; cottages $285-465; wi-fi) Think love nest. The area's top resort has eight soothing rooms done with cush amenities like rainfall showers, saunas and wood-burning fireplaces. Its small on-site spa and the top-notch restaurant (p218) mean you may never leave the grounds. Check in early to maximize time.

MONTE RIO

Highland Dell (☎ 707-865-2300; http://highlanddell.com; 21050 River Blvd; r $109-214; wi-fi) Built in 1906 and redone in 2007 in the style of a grand lodge, the inn fronts right on the river. Above a giant dining room are several bright, fresh-looking rooms with comfy beds.

Village Inn & Lodge (☎ 707-865-2304; www.villageinn-ca.com; 20822 River Blvd; r $125-215; wi-fi) This charming, old-fashioned, 11-room resort inn sits beneath towering trees, right beside the river, and is run by a retired concierge who provides wonderful service. Some rooms have river views; all have fridges and microwaves.

Tea House Inn (☎ 707-865-2763; www.teahouseinn.com; 22746 Sylvan Way; teahouse incl breakfast $165) It looks like a suburban house outside, but inside the austere Japanese-teahouse decor is lovely, with shoji screens, kimonos and an altar with a ceiling-high madrone trunk. Soak beneath stars in the garden's hot tub.

Rio Villa Beach Resort (☎ 707-865-1143, 877-746-8455; www.riovilla.com; 20292 Hwy 116; r with kitchen $169-199, r without kitchen $139; wi-fi) Landscaping is lush at this small riverside resort with excellent sun exposure (you see redwoods, but you're not under them). Rooms are well kept but simple; the emphasis is on the outdoors, evident by the large riverside terrace, outdoor fireplace and barbecues.

Far Reaches (☎ 415-864-4554; www.russianrivercottage.com; Monte Rio; cottage $215; wi-fi) A peaceful respite on a wooded hillside, this hidden cottage features a meditation garden, lush plantings, a wraparound deck, Balinese furnishings, a kitchen, a stereo and an outdoor shower. Sleeps two to six. Book well ahead.

DUNCAN MILLS

Casini Ranch (☎ 707-865-2255, 800-451-8400; www.casiniranch.com; 22855 Moscow Rd, Duncan Mills; tent sites $26, RV sites partial/full hookups $31/34;) In quiet Duncans Mills, beautifully set on riverside ranchlands, Casini is popular with families. Amenities include hot showers and watercraft.

Eating

GUERNEVILLE

Coffee Bazaar (☎ 707-869-9706; 14045 Armstrong Woods Rd; dishes $3-6; 6am-8pm) This happenin' hangout has salads, sandwiches and pastries. It's attached to a bookstore.

Stumptown Brewery (☎ 707-869-0705; 15045 River Rd; meals $6-14; 2pm-9pm Mon, Thu & Fri, noon-9pm Sat & Sun) Mostly a bar, Stumptown has fish-and-chips, house-smoked meats and ribs.

Nit's Thai Creations (☎ 707-869-3576; mains $7-10; 15025 Old River Rd; Tue & Wed lunch, Thu-Sun lunch & dinner) Flavors sparkle at this Thai-owned restaurant, but spiciness is tailored to American palates; ask them to amp it up. The food is prettier than the room – except outside overlooking the river.

Main Street Station (☎ 707-869-0501; 16280 Main St; meals $8-15; breakfast, lunch & dinner;) This family-friendly pizzeria has evening jazz. Expect iceberg-lettuce salads. Breakfast, too.

Applewood Inn Restaurant (☎ 707-869-9093, 800-555-8509; www.applewoodinn.com; 13555 Hwy 116; mains $20-28; dinner) Cozy by the fire in the treetop-level dining room at Guerneville's best resort. The bold Euro-Cal cooking maximizes seasonal produce, with dishes like rack of lamb with minted *chimichuri* (garlic-parsley vinaigrette) and a roast chicken with bacon, corn, cabbage, lentils and mâche. Make reservations.

There's a taco truck at 16451 Main St.

FORESTVILLE

Stella's Cafe (☎ 707-887-2300; www.stellascafe.net; 5700 Gravenstein Hwy N; lunch mains $10-15, dinner mains $16-22; Wed-Sun) At Russian River Vineyards, chef-owned Stella's serves an eclectic menu with lunchtime salmon sandwiches, and halibut, paella and pork ribs at dinner.

Mosaic (☎ 707-887-7503; www.mosaiceats.com; 6675 Front St; lunch $8-10, dinner $21-30) The brick-red interior of this chef-owned roadhouse is inviting, but the outdoor garden inspires romance with its Japanese maples and towering redwood. Look for earthy, seasonal combos like duck breast with cherries, and pork tenderloin with stone-fruit compote. At lunch expect pizzas and salads.

Farmhouse Inn (☎ 707-887-3300; www.farmhouseinn.com; 7871 River Rd; mains $30-40; dinner Thu-Sun) One of Wine Country's best, the Farmhouse changes its seasonal Euro-Cal menu daily, using locally raised, organic ingredients like Sonoma lamb, wild salmon and rabbit. Details are impeccable, from aperitifs in the garden to the tableside cheese service. Make reservations.

MONTE RIO

Cafe Les Jumelles (☎ 707-865-9184; 20391 Hwy 116; mains $8-13; 7am-10pm, closed for dinner Mon;) Knotty-pine walls lend a woodsy feel to this standard American diner.

Highland Dell (☎ 707-865-2300; http://highlanddell.com; 21050 River Blvd; lunch mains $9-15, dinner mains $13-30; 2pm-9pm Mon-Sat, 10am-8pm Sun) A dramatic three-story-high chalet-style dining room with a river-view deck, Highland Dell makes good German – steaks, schnitzel, sauerbraten and sausage. Full bar.

Village Inn (☎ 707-865-2304; www.villageinn-ca.com; 20822 River Blvd; mains $15-24; dinner Wed-Sun) The straightforward steaks-and-seafood menu is basic American and doesn't distract from the wonderful river views. Great local wine list, full bar.

Sophie's Cellars (☎ 707-865-1122; www.sophiescellars.com; 20293 Hwy 116; 11am-7pm Thu-Tue) This stellar wine shop has an excellent cheese selection.

DUNCANS MILLS

Wine Tasting of Sonoma County (☎ 707-865-0565; 25179 Hwy 116; wine tastings $5; noon-6pm Wed-Mon) Sample local vino and cheeses alfresco at this little wine bar and shop.

Cape Fear Cafe (☎ 707-865-9246; 25191 Hwy 116; breakfast & lunch mains $8-15, dinner mains $16-25). This window-lined roadhouse has pastel walls and butcher-paper tablecloths, and serves big salads, house-smoked salmon, prime rib and shrimp grits. One of the best midrange spots along the river. Make reservations. There's breakfast, too.

Drinking & Entertainment

Stumptown Brewery (☎ 707-869-0705; 15045 River Rd, Guerneville) Guerneville's best straight bar is gay-friendly and has a foot-stompin' jukebox, a pool table, a riverside beer garden (great for smokers) and nine tap beers (three made on-site).

Rainbow Cattle Company (☎ 707-869-0206; 16220 Main St, Guerneville) The stalwart gay watering hole.

Russian River Resort (Triple-R; ☎ 707-869-0691; Fourth & Mill St, Guerneville) Where gay boys get hammered poolside. Bring a bathing suit.

Pink Elephant (☎ 707-865-0500; 9895 Main St, Monte Rio) West County's best neon flickers above this classic dive with weekend bands.

Kaya Organic Espresso (☎ 707-869-2230; 16626 Main St, Guerneville; 7am-2pm) Hippie kids strum guitars at this all-organic coffee shack.

Rio Theater (☎ 707-865-0913; cnr Bohemian Hwy & Hwy 116, Monte Rio) Inside an old riverside Quonset hut, the Rio shows first-run movies and has great hot dogs.

Main Street Station (☎ 707-869-0501; www.mainststation.com; 16280 Main, Guerneville; cover $3-6) Live jazz, blues and cabaret nightly in summer, weekends winter.

SANTA ROSA

pop 154,210

Wine Country's biggest city is known for traffic and suburban sprawl. It lacks small-town charm, but has reasonably priced accommodations and easy access to Sonoma County and Valley.

Santa Rosa claims two famous native sons – a world-renowned cartoonist and a celebrated horticulturalist – and you'll find enough museums, gardens and shopping for an afternoon. Otherwise, there ain't much to do, unless you're here in July during the

Sonoma County Fair (☎ 707-545-4200; www.sonomacountyfair.com), at the fairgrounds on Bennett Valley Rd.

Orientation & Information

The main shopping stretch is 4th St, which abruptly ends at Hwy 101 but reemerges on the other side at historic Railroad Sq. Downtown parking lots are free for the first 1½ hours. East of town, 4th St turns into Hwy 12 to Sonoma Valley.

Aroma Roasters (☎ 707-576-7765; 95 5th St, Railroad Sq; per 15min $1.50; 6am-11pm Mon-Thu, 7am-midnight Fri & Sat, 7am-10pm Sun) Internet access. Free wi-fi, but no electrical outlets.

California Welcome Center & Santa Rosa Visitors Bureau (☎ 707-577-8674, 800-404-7673; www.visitsantarosa.com; 9 4th St; 9am-5pm Mon-Sat, 10am-5pm Sun) At Railroad Sq, west of Hwy 101; take the downtown Santa Rosa exit off Hwy 12 or Hwy 101.

Santa Rosa Memorial Hospital (☎ 707-935-5000; 347 Andrieux St)

Sights & Activities

LUTHER BURBANK HOME & GARDENS

Pioneering horticulturist Luther Burbank (1849–1926) developed many hybrid plant species at his 19th-century Greek-revival home, at Santa Rosa and Sonoma Aves. The extensive **gardens** (☎ 707-524-5445; www.lutherburbank.org; admission free; 8am-dusk) are lovely. The house and adjacent **Carriage Museum** (guided tour adult/child/senior $5/free/4, self-guided cell-phone audio tour adult/senior $5/4; 10am-3:30pm Tue-Sun Apr-Oct) have displays on Burbank's life and work.

Across the street from Burbank's home, Julliard Park has a **playground**.

CHARLES M SCHULZ MUSEUM

Charles Schulz, creator of *Peanuts* cartoons, was a long-term Santa Rosa resident. Born in 1922, he published his first drawing in 1937, introduced the world to Snoopy and Charlie Brown in 1950, and produced Peanuts cartoons until just before his death in 2000.

At the **museum** (☎ 707-579-4452; www.schulzmuseum.org; 2301 Hardies Lane; adult/child & senior $8/5; 11am-5pm Mon-Fri, 10am-5pm Sat & Sun, closed Tue Sep-May) a glass wall overlooks a courtyard with a Snoopy labyrinth. Exhibits include Peanuts-related art and Schulz's actual studio. Skip Snoopy's Gallery gift shop; the museum has the good stuff.

REDWOOD EMPIRE ICE ARENA

This **skating rink** (☎ 707-546-7147; www.snoopyshomeice.com; adult/child incl skates $12/10;) was formerly owned and deeply loved by Schulz. It's open most afternoons (call for schedules). Bring a sweater.

FARMERS MARKET

Sonoma County's largest **farmers market** meets Wednesday, 5pm to 8:30pm, mid-May through August, at 4th and B Sts.

Sleeping

Motels line Cleveland Ave, fronting Hwy 101's western side, between the Steele Lane and Bicentennial Lane exits. Skip Motel 6 – we've heard reports of nearby gang activity.

Hillside Inn (☎ 707-546-9353; www.hillside-inn.com; 2901 4th St; s/d/q $70/82/90; wi-fi) Santa Rosa's best-kept motel is closest to Sonoma Valley; add $4 for kitchens. Some furnishings are dated, but everything is scrupulously maintained, with nary a cock-eyed lampshade.

Sandman Hotel (☎ 707-544-8570; www.sonoma.com/lodging; 3421 Cleveland Ave; s/d $84/94; wi-fi) Cleveland Ave's reliable budget choice.

Best Western Garden Inn (☎ 707-546-4031, 888-256-8004; www.thegardeninn.com; 1500 Santa Rosa Ave; r $109-129; wi-fi) Book a room in back for quiet, up front for privacy, at this well-kept cookie-cutter motel, south of downtown. The street gets seedy by night (think hookers), but the hotel is secure, clean and comfortable.

Hotel La Rose (☎ 707-579-3200; www.hotellarose.com; 308 Wilson St; r Mon-Fri $129-179, Sat & Sun $209-279; wi-fi) At Railroad Sq, this charming 1907 hotel has rooms with marble baths, sitting areas with thick carpeting and wing chairs, and supercomfy mattresses with feather beds. Great for a moderate splurge. There's a rooftop hot tub.

Flamingo Resort Hotel (☎ 707-545-8530, 800-848-8300; www.flamingoresort.com; 2777 4th St; r $139-219;) This Mid-Century Modern hotel sprawls over 11 acres and doubles as a conference center. Rooms are motel-generic, but what a gigantic pool! – and it's kept at 82° year-round. On-site health-club and gym. Prices skyrocket summer weekends.

Vintners Inn (☎ 707-575-7350, 800-421-2584; www.vintnersinn.com; 4350 Barnes Rd; r $200-350;) Built in the 1980s, Vintners Inn sits on the rural outskirts of town (near River Rd) and appeals to the gated-community crowd. Rooms' amenities are business-class generic,

OUTLET SHOPPING

Max out your credit cards on last season's close-outs.

Napa Premium Outlets (Map p225; ☎ 707-226-9876; www.premiumoutlets.com; 629 Factory Stores Dr, Napa) 50 stores

Petaluma Village Premium Outlets (Map p196; ☎ 707-778-9300; www.premiumoutlets.com; 2200 Petaluma Blvd North, Petaluma) 60 stores, Sonoma County

St Helena Marketplace (Map p225; ☎ 707-963-7282; www.sthelenapremieroutlets.com; 3111 N St Helena Hwy, St Helena) Eight stores

Vacaville Premium Outlets (Map p196; ☎ 707-447-5755; www.premiumoutlets.com/vacaville; 321 Nut Tree Rd, Vacaville) 120 stores, northeast of the Wine Country on I-80

but have private garden-view patios, king beds and high-thread-count sheets. Check for last-minute specials.

There are 30 campsites 4 miles from downtown at **Spring Lake Regional Park** (☎ 707-539-8092, reservations 707-565-2267; www.sonoma-county.org/parks; 5585 Newanga Ave; sites $20); make reservations ($7 fee) 10am to 3pm weekdays. The park is open year-round: the campground operates daily May to September, weekends October to April. Take 4th St eastbound, turn right on Farmer's Lane, pass the first Hoen St and turn left on the *second* Hoen St, continue straight, then left on Newanga Ave.

WINE COUNTRY

Eating

Taqueria Las Palmas (☎ 707-546-3091; 415 Santa Rosa Ave; dishes $4-7; 9am-9pm; V) For Mexican, this is the real deal, with standout *carnitas* (barbecued pork), homemade salsas and veggie burritos.

Pho Vietnam (☎ 707-571-7687; No 8, 711 Stony Point Rd; dishes $6-8; 10am-8:30pm Mon-Sat, to 7:30pm Sun) Fantastic noodle bowls and rice plates at a hole-in-the-wall shopping-center restaurant, just off Hwy 12, west of downtown.

Rosso Pizzeria & Wine Bar (☎ 707-544-3221; 53 Montgomery St, Creekside Shopping Centre; pizzas $12-15; 11:30am-10pm) Crispy brick-oven pizzas, inventive salads and a standout wine list make Rosso worth seeking out.

Zazu (☎ 707-523-4814; www.zazurestaurant.com; 3535 Guerneville Rd; mains $19-26; dinner Wed-Sun) In a raucous roadhouse 10 minutes west of downtown, chef-owner John Stewart's Cal-Ital cooking packs a wallop, with invigorating flavors and sure-handed dynamic style. Every dish sings, from the hand-thrown pizzas to slow-roasted balsamic pork shoulder. His competition isn't Sonoma chefs, but Tuscan grandmothers. Wednesday, Thursday and Sunday are pizza-and-pinot nights, with wine flights paired for pizza.

Also consider:

Mac's Delicatessen (☎ 707-545-3785; 630 4th St; dishes under $10; breakfast & lunch Mon-Sat) Bagels and lox, fat sandwiches and chicken-noodle soup.

Traverso's Gourmet Foods (☎ 707-542-2530; www.traversos.com; 106 B St; 9:30am-5:30pm Mon-Sat) Old-fashioned Italian deli and wine shop.

Willi's Wine Bar (☎ 707-528-3096; www.williswinebar.net; dishes $9-15; 11:30am-9:30pm Tue-Sat, 5pm-9pm Sun & Mon) Great small plates and wine flights.

Drinking

Last Day Saloon (☎ 707-545-2343; www.lastdaysaloon.com; 120 5th St) Live bands most nights; cover ranges $5 to $15, but sometimes free. Karaoke Mondays.

Aroma Roasters (☎ 707-576-7765; 95 5th St, Railroad Sq; 6am-11pm Mon-Thu, to midnight Fri & Sat; 7am-10pm Sun) Town's hippest café; serves no booze.

Russian River Brewing Co (☎ 707-545-2337; 729 4th St) Drink locally crafted brews in an industrial space or on the sidewalk with the dudes.

Third Street Aleworks (☎ 707-523-3060; 610 3rd St) This giant brew pub gets packed weekends and game days. Great garlic fries. Big smokers patio and half-a-dozen pool tables.

HEALDSBURG

pop 10,960

Once a sleepy ag town best known for its Future Farmers of America parade, Healdsburg has emerged as northern Sonoma County's hot new destination. Foodie-scenester restaurants and cafés, wine-tasting rooms and chic boutiques line Healdsburg Plaza, the town's sun-dappled central square (bordered by Healdsburg Ave and Center, Matheson and Plaza Sts). Traffic grinds to a halt summer weekends, when second-home-owners and tourists jam downtown. Old-timers aren't happy with the change, but Healdsburg remains rooted in its agrarian traditions and retains its historic look and color. Healdsburg is a must-visit, if only to stroll the pretty tree-lined streets, sample locavore cooking and soak up the Nor-Cal-now flavor.

Information

Copperfield's Books (☎ 707-433-9270; 104 Matheson St) Sells guidebooks and maps.

Healdsburg Chamber of Commerce & Visitors Bureau (☎ 707-433-6935, 800-648-9922; www.healdsburg.org; 217 Healdsburg Ave; 9am-5pm Mon-Fri, to 3pm Sat, 10am-2pm Sun) A block south of the plaza. Has winery maps and information on hot-air ballooning, golf, tennis, spas and nearby farms (get the *Farm Trails* brochure); 24-hour walk-up booth.

Healdsburg Public Library (☎ 707-433-3772; www.sonoma.lib.ca.us; cnr Piper & Center Sts; 10am-6pm Mon & Wed, to 9pm Tue & Thu-Sun) Free internet access.

Levin & Company (☎ 707-433-1118; 306 Center St) Fiction and CDs; co-op art gallery.

Sights

East of the plaza, **Healdsburg Museum** (☎ 707-431-3325; www.healdsburgmuseum.org; 221 Matheson St; donation requested; 11am-4pm Thu-Sun) is worth a visit for a glimpse of Healdsburg's past. Exhibits include Native American basketry and compelling installations on northern Sonoma County history. Pick up a historic-homes walking-tour pamphlet.

The **Sonoma County Wine Library**, inside Healdsburg's public library, is one of the top oenology references in California. Community-driven **Plaza Arts Center** (☎ 707-431-1970; www.plazaartscenter.org; 130 Plaza St; 11am-5pm) spotlights California artists.

Part gallery, part tasting room, **Artiste** (☎ 707-433-1920; www.artiste.com; 439 Healdsburg Ave; $5 tastings; 11am-5:30pm) blends wines inspired by paintings by contemporary California artists; there's also DIY painting (call ahead).

Summertime **farmers markets** (☎ 707-431-1956; www.healdsburgfarmersmarket.org) are held on **Healdsburg Plaza** (4pm-6:30pm Tue Jun-Oct) and the **municipal parking lot** (cnr Vine & North Sts; 9am-noon Sat May-Nov).

Eight miles north, tiny photo-op-ready, one-block-long Geyserville is home to **Locals Tasting Room** (☎ 707-857-4900; www.tastelocalwines.com; Geyserville Ave & Hwy 128), which represents seven small-production indie wineries.

Free summer concerts are held Tuesday afternoons on the plaza.

Activities

River's Edge Kayak & Canoe Trips (☎ 707-433-7247; www.riversedgekayakandcanoe.com; 20 Healdsburg Ave) rents canoes ($35/$60 per half/full day) and kayaks ($55/$85) April to September, including transportation. Call about guided trips.

Getaway Adventures (☎ 707-763-3040, 800-499-2453; www.getawayadventures.com) guides spectacular morning vineyard cycling in Alexander Valley, followed by lunch and optional canoeing on Russian River ($150 to $175).

Healdsburg Spoke Folk Cyclery (☎ 707-433-7171; www.spokefolk.com; 201 Center St) rents touring, racing and tandem bicycles.

Relish Culinary School (☎ 707-431-9999, 877-759-1004; www.relishculinary.com) teaches courses for home chefs, and operates out of local kitchens.

Murphy Goode winery (☎ 707-431-7644; www.murphygoodewinery.com; 209 Matheson St) offers free tastings if you bring the online coupon. Good *fumé blanc* (aka sauvignon blanc) and oaky chardonnay.

Festivals & Events

Russian River Wine Road Barrel Tasting (www.wineroad.com) March

Future Farmers Parade (www.healdsburgfair.org) May

Healdsburg Jazz Festival (www.healdsburgjazzfestival.org) Late May to early June

Healdsburg Harvest Century Bicycle Tour (www.healdsburg.org) Mid-July

Wine & Food Affair (www.wineroad.com/events) November

Sleeping

Healdsburg is expensive; rates plummet in fall, winter and spring.

Most Healdsburg B&Bs are within walking distance of the plaza, and there are two noteworthy B&Bs in the surrounding countryside. Two older motels lie south of the plaza, two to the north at Hwy 101's Dry Creek exit. For campsites, also see Lake Sonoma, p267.

Alexander Valley RV Park (☎ 707-431-1453, 800-640-1386; 2411 Alexander Valley Rd; tent/RV sites $35/45; Mar-Nov) Four miles northeast of Healdsburg, this campground has mixed-use sites with hookups. Some are shadeless.

Cloverdale Wine Country KOA (☎ 707-894-3337, 800-368-4558; www.winecountrykoa.com; 1166 Asti Ridge Rd, Cloverdale; tent/RV sites from $35/55, 1-/2-bedroom cabins $72/82; wi-fi) Six miles from the Central Cloverdale exit off Hwy 101, KOA's amenities include hot showers, a swimming pool and a hot tub, nature trails, a laundry, paddleboats and bicycles.

Best Western Dry Creek Inn (707-433-0300, 800-222-5784; www.drycreekinn.com; 198 Dry Creek Rd; r $139-239; wi-fi) Town's top motel has good service and an outdoor hot tub. New rooms have jetted tubs and gas fireplaces. Check for weekday discounts.

Geyserville Inn (707-857-4343, 877-857-4343; www.geyservilleinn.com; 21714 Geyserville Ave, Geyserville; r $149-229; wi-fi) Eight miles north of Healdsburg, this immaculately kept top-end motel is surrounded by vineyards. It has unexpectedly smart furnishings, such as overstuffed side chairs and fluffy feather pillows. Be sure to request a remodeled room. Hot tub. Great value.

Belle de Jour Inn (707-431-9777; www.belledejourinn.com; 16276 Healdsburg Ave; r $225-295, ste $355;) Belle de Jour's bright and airy rooms have American-country furnishings, with extra touches like sun-dried sheets, hammocks and CD players. The manicured gardens are perfect for a lovers' tryst.

Madrona Manor (707-433-4231, 800-258-4003; www.madronamanor.com; 1001 Westside Rd; r & ste $260-460; wi-fi) The first choice for lovers of country inns and stately manor homes, the regal 1881 Madrona Manor exudes Victorian elegance. Surrounded by 8 acres of woods and gardens, the hilltop mansion is decked out with many original furnishings. There are also rooms in a carriage house, a cottage and a former schoolhouse. A mile west of Hwy 101, it's convenient to Westside Rd's wineries.

Hotel Healdsburg (707-431-2800, 800-889-7188; www.hotelhealdsburg.com; 25 Matheson St; r incl breakfast $260-490; wi-fi) Smack on the plaza, the chic HH has a coolly minimalist style and all the requisite top-end bells and whistles. Wear Armani and blend right in. The ultracushy rooms in muted earth tones have deliciously comfy beds and bathrooms with extra-deep tubs. Downstairs there's a full-service spa.

Healdsburg Inn on the Plaza (707-433-6991, 800-431-8663; www.healdsburginn.com; 110 Matheson St; Sat & Sun $300-375; wi-fi) This spiffy B&B has fresh-looking rooms with fine linens and gas fireplaces; some have jetted tubs for two. The location on the plaza explains the price.

Also consider:

Best Value Inn (707-433-5548; www.bestvalueinn.com; 74 Healdsburg Ave; r $119-159;) Cookie-cutter motel; request a new room.

Camellia Inn (707-433-8182, 800-727-8182; www.camelliainn.com; 211 North St; r $119-239; wi-fi) Italianate 1869 house; one room accommodates families.

George Alexander House (707-433-1358, 800-310-1358; www.georgealexanderhouse.com; 423 Matheson St; r $180-350; wi-fi) Queen Anne from 1905 with Victorian and Asian antiques; also a sauna.

Haydon Street Inn (707-433-5228, 800-528-3703; www.haydon.com; 321 Haydon St; r $190-295, cottage $395; wi-fi) Two-story Queen Anne with big front porch and a cottage out back.

Honor Mansion (707-433-4277, 800-554-4667; www.honormansion.com; 891 Grove St; r $230-400, ste $325-600; wi-fi) Victorian mansion circa 1883; spectacular grounds.

L&M Motel (707-433-6528; www.landmmotel.com; 70 Healdsburg Ave; r $100-130; wi-fi) Simple, clean motel rooms; big lawns and barbecue grills great for families. Dry sauna and Jacuzzi.

Piper Street Inn (707-433-8721, 877-703-0370; www.piperstreetinn.com; 402 Piper St; r $175-195; wi-fi) Two rooms: a homey bedroom, a garden cottage.

Eating

Healdsburg is the gastronomic capital of Sonoma County – the hardest decision may be where to eat. Reservations essential.

BUDGET

Flaky Cream Coffee Shop (707-433-3895; Healdsburg Shopping Center, 441 Center St; dishes $3-7; breakfast & lunch) The bacon-and-egg breakfasts are OK, but we most love this greasy spoon's doughnuts. Yum.

Jimtown Store (707-433-1212; www.jimtown.com; 6706 Hwy 128; sandwiches under $10) If you're heading to Alexander Valley, don't miss Jimtown – one of our favorite stopovers – famous for its picnic supplies and sandwiches made using housemade flavor-packed spreads (eg artichoke, olive and caper; fig and olive).

Oakville Grocery (707-433-3200; www.oakvillegrocery.com; 124 Matheson St; sandwiches around $10; 8am-6pm) Oakville carries top-of-the-line smoked fish, gourmet sandwiches, salads, caviar and picnics. It's crowded and overpriced, but the plaza-view terrace is a great spot for vino and people-watching.

MIDRANGE

Bovolo (707-431-2962; www.bovolorestaurant.com; 106 Matheson St; mains $10-15; 9am-6pm Thu-Tue, to

WINE COUNTRY

9pm Sat & Sun) Bovolo serves 'slow food fast,' including knockout housemade antipasti and salumi (cured pork) platters, hot savory sandwiches, hand-thrown pizzas and hand-turned gelato. Order at the counter and sit outside or in. Great local wine selection. Breakfasts are tops, with apple fritters, walnut pancakes and housemade bacon.

Santi (☎ 707-857-1790; www.tavernasanti.com; 21047 Geyserville Ave, Geyserville; lunch mains $9-14, dinner mains $15-25; 🕑 lunch Wed-Sat, dinner nightly) Never-fussy, always-popular Santi cooks *bellissima* rustic northern-Italian cooking, like spaghetti calabrese and osso bucco, worth the 10-minute drive north. On balmy evenings, hold hands by candlelight on the big wooden deck.

Zin (☎ 707-473-0946; www.zinrestaurant.com; 344 Center St; lunch mains $8-14, dinner mains $16-25; 🕑 lunch Mon-Fri, dinner nightly; 🚼) Ever-reliable Zin makes hearty Cal-American comfort food (some with produce from its own gardens) designed to pair with zinfandel and other local varietals. Think pot roast and apple pie. Fun wine bar, good service.

Diavola (☎ 707-814-0111; www.diavolapizzera.com; 21021 Geyserville Ave, Geyserville; pizzas $12-15; 🕑 11:30am-9pm Wed-Mon; 🚼) An ideal stopover while wine tasting in the Alexander Valley, Diavola makes homemade salumi and thin-crust pizzas in a 19th-century brick-walled building. Fun, and loud enough to drown out the kids. Beer and wine.

Mirepoix (☎ 707-838-0162; www.restaurantmirepoix.com; 275 Windsor River Rd, Windsor; mains $14-23; 🕑 11:30am-9pm Tue-Sat) Worth the 6-mile drive to Windsor, this tiny chef-owned bistro in a converted house scores high marks for its provincial-French cooking, like *croques madames*, steak *au poivre* and sweetbreads. Many wines in the $20 to $30 range.

Barndiva (☎ 707-431-0100; www.barndiva.com; 231 Center St; lunch mains $14-18, dinner mains $16-25; 🕑 noon-11pm Wed-Sun) Barndiva's cavernous dining room and giant bar have an austerely sexy lounge vibe. The nontraditional menu is 'flavor profiled,' with food to fit your mood: from light to spicy to comfort cooking. Despite the aggressive style, there's substance behind the New American cooking, all made with sustainably farmed ingredients. On Sunday there's brunch in the garden.

Scopa (☎ 707-433-5282; www.scopahealdsburg.com; 109A Plaza St; mains $15-20; 🕑 dinner Tue-Sun) A newcomer in 2008 from a former chef of Santi, Scopa makes rustic Italian dishes like tomato-braised chicken with sautéed greens and toasted polenta. The exposed wooden tables are cheek-by-jowl, but the lively crowd and good wine prices (many under $40) create a convivial atmosphere.

TOP END

Madrona Manor (☎ 707-433-4231, 800-258-4003; www.madronamanor.com; 1001 Westside Rd; prix fixe $60-79; 🕑 dinner) You'd be hard-pressed to find a lovelier place to pop the question than on the mansion's garden-view veranda, while supping on sophisticated Euro-Cal cooking.

our pick **Cyrus** (☎ 707-433-3311; www.cyrusrestaurant.com; 29 North St; prix fixe $78-102; 🕑 dinner Wed-Mon) Napa's venerable French Laundry (p233) has stiff competition in swanky Cyrus, an ultra-chic dining room in the great tradition of the French country auberge. The emphasis is on luxury foods – foie gras, caviar, lobster – expertly prepared with a French sensibility and flavored with global spices, as in the signature Thai-marinated lobster. The staff moves as if in a ballet, ever intuitive of your pace and tastes. From the caviar cart to the cheese course, Cyrus is one meal to remember. If you're a serious foodie, don't miss it.

Also consider the following:

Bistro Ralph (☎ 707-433-1380; 109 Plaza St; lunch mains $10-18, dinner mains $18-30; 🕑 Mon-Sat) Long-standing French bistro fave. Great martinis.

Ravenette Cafe (☎ 707-431-1770; 117 North St; meals $18; 🕑 dinner Thu-Sat, brunch Sun) Euro-Cal comfort foods, great prices. Six tables, no reservations.

Willi's Seafood & Raw Bar (☎ 707-433-9191; www.willisseafood.net; 403 Healdsburg Ave; small plates $9-13; 🕑 11:30am-9:30pm) Oysters and small plates. Thirty wines by the glass. NB: prices add up.

SELF-CATERING

Anstead's Marketplace & Deli (☎ 707-431-0530; 428 Center St) An indie alternative for groceries, organic produce, picnics and sandwiches. It's more reasonable than the Oakville Grocery (but not as fancy).

Healdsburg's finest bakery, **Downtown Bakery & Creamery** (☎ 707-431-2719; www.downtownbakery.net; 308a Center St; 🕑 7am-5:30pm), creates scrumptious pastries. **Costeaux French Bakery & Cafe** (☎ 707-433-1913; www.costeaux.com; 417 Healdsburg Ave; 🕑 7am-4pm Mon-Sat, to 1pm Sun) makes fresh bread and good boxed lunches, and the **Cheese Shop** (☎ 707-433-4998; www.doraliceimports.com; 423 Center St; 🕑 Mon-Sat) has a top-notch selection of imported and local cheeses.

Drinking & Entertainment

Flying Goat Coffee (☎ 707-433-9081; www.flyinggoatcoffee.com; 324 Center St; 🕑 7am-6pm) See ya later, Starbucks. Flying Goat is what coffee should be – fair-trade and locally roasted. This is where to meet locals.

Bear Republic Brewing Company (☎ 707-433-2337; 345 Healdsburg Ave; 🕑 11:30am-late) Bear Republic features handcrafted award-winning ales, a (so-so) pub-style menu and live music weekends.

Barndiva (☎ 707-431-0100; www.barndiva.com; 231 Center St; 🕑 Wed-Sun) For swanky cocktails – think blood-orange margaritas – you can't beat Barndiva. NB: drinks cost over $10.

Raven Theater & Film Center (☎ 707-433-5448; www.raventheater.com; 115 N Main St) The Raven hosts concerts, events and first-run art-house screenings.

Shopping

Fideaux (☎ 707-433-9935; 43 North St) For dog- and cat-fetishist items, here's a storeful of them.

Jimtown Store (☎ 707-433-1212; www.jimtown.com; 6706 Hwy 128) Behind the deli and café, browse carefully chosen antique bric-a-brac, candles and Mexican oilcloths at this roadside store in Alexander Valley.

Gardener (☎ 707-431-1063; www.thegardener.com; 516 Dry Creek Rd) If you love garden stores, don't miss this beauty, with fab furniture and imported terra-cotta.

NAPA VALLEY

The birthplace of modern-day Wine Country is famous for regal cabernets, sauvignons, château-like wineries and a fabulous culinary scene. But Napa is a victim of its own success, with traffic jams, a monoculture of cabernet grapes and impossible land prices. Here's how it happened.

In 1968, Napa was declared the 'Napa Valley Agricultural Preserve,' effectively blocking future valley development for nonagricultural purposes. The law stipulates no subdivision of valley-floor land under 40 acres. This succeeded in preserving the valley's natural beauty, but sent land values through the roof. Only the very rich could afford to build. Hence so many architecturally jaw-dropping wineries: people construct monuments to ego. Major corporations are the other big players, and as they did in California's Central Valley, they're eating up the land.

Still, Napa remains visually gorgeous, and if you have the time, you should come. Be prepared to open your wallet – wide.

Orientation

Napa Valley is 30-miles long and 5-miles wide at its widest point (the city of Napa), 1 mile at its narrowest (Calistoga). Two roads run north–south: Hwy 29 (St Helena Hwy) and the more scenic Silverado Trail, a mile east. Drive up one, down the other.

An American Automobile Association study determined that Napa Valley is the 8th most congested rural vacation destination in America. Summer and fall weekend traffic is unbearable, especially on Hwy 29 between Napa and St Helena. Plan accordingly.

Cross-valley roads that link Silverado Trail with Hwy 29 – including Yountville, Oakville and Rutherford crossroads – are bucolic and get less traffic. For scenery, the Oakville Grade and rural Trinity Rd (which leads southwest to Hwy 12 in Sonoma Valley) are narrow, curvy and beautiful – but treacherous in rainstorms. Mt Veeder Rd leads through pristine countryside west of Yountville.

Note: cops watch like hawks for traffic violators (especially if you're brown, so say locals). *Don't drink and drive.*

The city of Napa anchors the valley, but the real work happens up-valley. Napa isn't as pretty as other towns, but has some noteworthy sights, among them Copia (p229) and Oxbow Public Market (p229). Scenic towns include St Helena, Yountville and Calistoga – the latter more famous for water than wine.

NAPA VALLEY WINERIES

Cab is king in Napa. No varietal captures imaginations like the fruit of the cabernet-sauvignon vine – Bordeaux is the French equivalent – and no wine fetches a higher price. Napa farmers can't afford *not* to grow cabernet. Other heat-loving varieties, such as sangiovese and merlot, also thrive here.

Napa's wines merit their reputation among the world's finest. If you love deep-red wines with complex noses and luxurious finishes, you're gonna freak out in Napa. (Though in Napa, you don't 'freak out' per se, you *delight* or *luxuriate*, but you definitely don't freak. Dude, where do you think you are, Sonoma?)

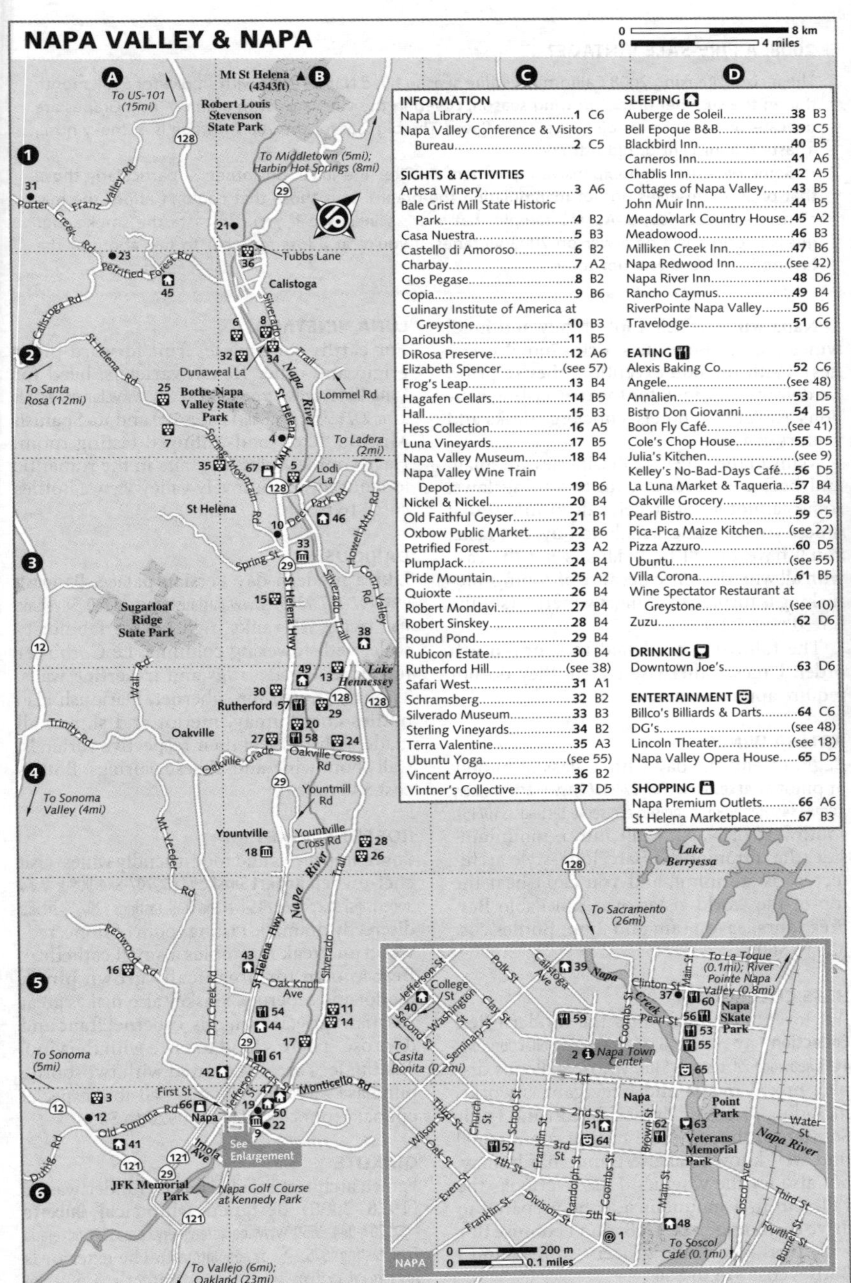
NAPA VALLEY & NAPA
0 8 km
0 4 miles
A
B
C
D
1
2
3
4
5
6
INFORMATION
Napa Library....1 C6
Napa Valley Conference & Visitors Bureau....2 C5
SIGHTS & ACTIVITIES
Artesa Winery....3 A6
Bale Grist Mill State Historic Park....4 B2
Casa Nuestra....5 B3
Castello di Amoroso....6 B2
Charbay....7 A2
Clos Pegase....8 B2
Copia....9 B6
Culinary Institute of America at Greystone....10 B3
Darioush....11 B5
DiRosa Preserve....12 A6
Elizabeth Spencer....(see 57)
Frog's Leap....13 B4
Hagafen Cellars....14 B5
Hall....15 B3
Hess Collection....16 A5
Luna Vineyards....17 B5
Napa Valley Museum....18 B4
Napa Valley Wine Train Depot....19 B6
Nickel & Nickel....20 B4
Old Faithful Geyser....21 B1
Oxbow Public Market....22 B6
Petrified Forest....23 A2
PlumpJack....24 B4
Pride Mountain....25 A2
Quioxte....26 B4
Robert Mondavi....27 B4
Robert Sinskey....28 B4
Round Pond....29 B4
Rubicon Estate....30 B4
Rutherford Hill....(see 38)
Safari West....31 A1
Schramsberg....32 B2
Silverado Museum....33 B3
Sterling Vineyards....34 B2
Terra Valentine....35 A3
Ubuntu Yoga....(see 55)
Vincent Arroyo....36 B2
Vintner's Collective....37 D5
SLEEPING
Auberge de Soleil....38 B3
Bell Epoque B&B....39 C5
Blackbird Inn....40 B5
Carneros Inn....41 A6
Chablis Inn....42 A5
Cottages of Napa Valley....43 B5
John Muir Inn....44 B5
Meadowlark Country House....45 A2
Meadowood....46 B3
Milliken Creek Inn....47 B6
Napa Redwood Inn....(see 42)
Napa River Inn....48 D6
Rancho Caymus....49 B4
RiverPointe Napa Valley....50 B6
Travelodge....51 C6
EATING
Alexis Baking Co....52 C6
Angele....(see 48)
Annalien....53 D5
Bistro Don Giovanni....54 B5
Boon Fly Café....(see 41)
Cole's Chop House....55 D5
Julia's Kitchen....(see 9)
Kelley's No-Bad-Days Café....56 D5
La Luna Market & Taqueria....57 B4
Oakville Grocery....58 B4
Pearl Bistro....59 C5
Pica-Pica Maize Kitchen....(see 22)
Pizza Azzuro....60 D5
Ubuntu....(see 55)
Villa Corona....61 B5
Wine Spectator Restaurant at Greystone....(see 10)
Zuzu....62 D6
DRINKING
Downtown Joe's....63 D6
ENTERTAINMENT
Billco's Billiards & Darts....64 C6
DG's....(see 48)
Lincoln Theater....(see 18)
Napa Valley Opera House....65 D5
SHOPPING
Napa Premium Outlets....66 A6
St Helena Marketplace....67 B3
Mt St Helena (4343ft)
Robert Louis Stevenson State Park
To US-101 (15mi)
To Middletown (5mi); Harbin Hot Springs (8mi)
Porter
Franz Valley Rd
Creek Rd
Petrified Forest Rd
Calistoga Rd
Tubbs Lane
Calistoga
Silverado Trail
St Helena Rd
Dunaweal La
To Santa Rosa (12mi)
Bothe-Napa Valley State Park
Napa River
St Helena Hwy
Lommel Rd
To Ladera (2mi)
Spring Mountain Rd
Lodi La
Deer Park Rd
Howell Mtn Rd
St Helena
Spring St
Conn Valley Rd
Sugarloaf Ridge State Park
Wall Rd
Lake Hennessey
Rutherford
Trinity Rd
Oakville
Oakville Grade
Oakville Cross Rd
To Sonoma Valley (4mi)
Yountmill Rd
Yountville
Yountville Cross Rd
Mt Veeder Rd
Lake Berryessa
To Sacramento (26mi)
Redwood Rd
Dry Creek Rd
Oak Knoll Ave
To Sonoma (5mi)
Trancas St
Monticello Rd
First St
Jefferson St
Old Sonoma Rd
Napa
Imola Ave
See Enlargement
Duhig Rd
JFK Memorial Park
Napa Golf Course at Kennedy Park
To Vallejo (6mi); Oakland (23mi)
Jefferson St
College St
Second St
Washington St
Polk St
Calistoga Ave
Clay St
Seminary St
Napa Creek
Clinton St
Main St
Coombs St
Pearl St
To La Toque (0.1mi); River Pointe Napa Valley (0.8mi)
Napa Skate Park
To Casita Bonita (0.2mi)
Napa Town Center
1st
Third St
Church St
School St
2nd St
Point Park
Water St
Napa River
Wilson St
Oak St
Franklin St
3rd St
Randolph St
Brown St
Veterans Memorial Park
4th St
Even St
Division St
5th St
Soscol Ave
Third St
Fourth St
Burnell St
To Soscol Café (0.1mi)
0 200 m
0 0.1 miles
NAPA

WINE COUNTRY

2008: A FIRE-SALE VINTAGE?

The record-breaking 2008 California wildfire season filled Napa's skies with smoke for a full month during the summer grape-growing season, covering the vineyards with a film of ash. Grapes are delicate: any change in soil affects their flavor. The big fear for the 2008 vintage is a smoky nose, a taste reminiscent of old ashtray.

Some wineries used expensive equipment to filter the juice, but others – particularly those that pride themselves on not manipulating the grapes, plus those that couldn't afford the machinery – chose not to. As you sample that year's wines, see if you can taste the smoke. Our guess is prices will be lower on 2008 vintages. If you're at a loss for what to talk about at the tasting bar, this is one hot topic.

Napa wineries sell a lot of 'buy and hold' wines (versus Sonoma's 'drink now' varieties). With the odd exception, they're pricy. To defray costs, look for the free-tasting coupons available at hotels, concierge desks and visitors centers.

Many of the valley's 230 wineries are small, and because of strict county-zoning laws, some cannot legally receive drop-in visitors; unless you've come strictly to buy, not taste, you'll have to call first. This is *not* the case with all wineries. Also because of zoning, picnicking is forbidden at most wineries (see the boxed text, p228).

The following are listed in south–north order. Unless otherwise stated, they do not require appointments.

WINE COUNTRY

ARTESA WINERY

Begin or end the day with a glass of bubbly or pinot at **Artesa** (☎ 707-224-1668; www.artesawinery.com; 1345 Henry Rd; nonreserve/reserve tastings $10/15), southwest of Napa. Built into a mountainside, the ultramodern Barcelona-style architecture is stunning, and you can't beat the top-of-the-world vistas over San Pablo Bay. Free tours leave 11am and 2pm. Bottles cost $20 to $60.

HESS COLLECTION

Art lovers shouldn't miss the modern **Hess Collection** (☎ 707-255-8584; www.hesscollection.com; 4411 Redwood Rd; tastings $10), whose galleries display mixed-media and large-canvas works, including pieces by Francis Bacon and Louis Soutter. In the cave-like tasting room you'll find well-known cabernet and chardonnay, but also try the viognier. Hess overlooks the valley from a mountainside; be prepared to drive a winding road. (NB: don't confuse this with Hess Select, the grocery-store brand.) Bottles cost $15 to $60.

LUNA VINEYARDS

For earthy sangiovese, fruit-forward pinot grigio and other Italian varietals, head for **Luna Vineyards** (☎ 707-255-2474; www.lunavineyards.com; 2921 Silverado Trail; tastings $15) and its Spanish Mission–like wood-ceilinged tasting room. Have your last glass upstairs in the romantic lookout tower for lovely valley views. Bottles cost $16 to $40.

DARIOUSH

Like a modern-day Persian palace, **Darioush** (☎ 707-257-2345; www.darioush.com; 4240 Silverado Trail; tastings $25) ranks high on the fabulosity scale, with towering columns, Le Corbusier furniture, Persian rugs and travertine walls. Though known for cabernet, Darioush also bottles chardonnay, merlot and shiraz, all made with 100% of their respective varietals. Call about wine-and-cheese pairings. Bottles cost $40 to $80.

ROBERT SINSKEY

For hilltop views and food-friendly wines, visit chef-owned **Robert Sinskey** (☎ 707-944-9090; www.robertsinskey.com; 6320 Silverado Trail; tastings $20), whose discreetly dramatic tasting room of stone, redwood and teak resembles a small cathedral. Best known for organically grown pinot, merlot and cabernet, Sinskey also makes great Alsatian varietals, vin gris, cabernet franc and dry rosé. There's food to taste with the vino. Tasting fees are discounted with two-bottle purchase – a rarity in Napa. Call about special culinary tours. Bottles cost $20 to $85.

QUIXOTE

Famed architect Friedensreich Hundertwasser (1928–2000) designed whimsical **Quixote** (☎ 707-944-2659; www.quixotewinery.com; 6126 Silverado Trail; tastings $25; by appointment). The exterior is a riot of color, with the architect's signature gold-leaf onion dome crowning the building. No two windows are alike, no lines straight, no surfaces perfectly level. Tour it, by appointment only, on weekdays. Weekends, you can only glimpse it while sampling 100% organic fine petite sirah and cabernet. Bottles cost $40 to $60.

ROBERT MONDAVI

This huge, corporately owned **winery** (☎ 888-766-6328; www.robertmondavi.com; 7801 Hwy 29, Oakville; tour $25) draws oppressive crowds, but if you know nothing about wine and plan *not* to visit Copia (p229), learn about wine-making here on a guided tour. Otherwise, skip it unless you're here for one of the wonderful summer **concerts**, ranging from classical and jazz to R&B and Latin; call for schedules. Bottles cost $18 to $50; annual case production is 300,000.

PLUMPJACK

Founded by San Francisco's Mayor, Gavin Newsom, **PlumpJack** (☎ 707-945-1220; www.plumpjackwinery.com; 621 Oakville Cross Rd, Oakville; tastings $10) is one of Napa's less pretentious boutique wineries, whose whimsical, fashion-forward design sets a fun mood. The smoky, caramely, estate-grown cabernet is the standout, but there's also big fat syrah. PlumpJack also operates top-flight restaurants in San Francisco and Lake Tahoe's Squaw Valley. Bottles cost $26 to $74.

NICKEL & NICKEL

An offshoot of famous Far Niente, **Nickel & Nickel** (☎ 707-967-9600; www.nickelandnickel.com; 8164 St Helena Hwy, Oakville; tour $40; by appointment) occupies a 19th-century farmstead, including a weathered red barn dating to 1775 and an 1884 farmhouse, where you taste elegant single-vineyard, single-varietal wines, all from the same plot of earth (called a '*terroir* tasting'). The tour and six-wine flight are expensive, but these are great wines. Reservations essential. Bottles cost $45 to $140.

RUBICON ESTATE

The former Inglenook **estate** (☎ 707-968-1100; www.rubiconestate.com; 1991 St Helena Hwy, Rutherford; mandatory tour $25; by appointment) is owned by filmmaker Francis Ford Coppola. The tour ($25) focuses on the striking 1887 château, its parklike grounds, and a small film- and wine-making museum. The Rubicon label is solid, but you can find better; it's the setting that's great. Bottles cost $28 to $125.

FROG'S LEAP

our pick **Frog's Leap** (☎ 707-963-4704, 800-959-4704; www.frogsleap.com; 8815 Conn Creek Rd; tours & tastings free, by appointment;) If you see only one Napa winery, make it to Frog's Leap. Meandering paths wind through magical gardens and fruit-bearing orchards – pick peaches in July – surrounding an 1884 barn and farmstead with cats and chickens. But more than anything, it's the vibe that's wonderful: casual and down-to-earth, with a major emphasis on *fun*. Sauvignon blanc is its best-known wine, but the merlot merits attention. There's also a dry, restrained cabernet – a style atypical in Napa. All are organically grown. NB: you *must* make an appointment (which includes a *free* tour and tasting). Bottles cost $18 to $40.

HALL

One of Napa's up-and-coming wineries, **Hall** (☎ 707-967-2620; www.hallwines.com; 401 St Helena Hwy, St Helena; tastings $15) specializes in cabernet franc, sauvignon blanc, merlot and cabernet sauvignon. There's a cool abstract-sculpture garden and a lovely picnic area shaded by mulberry trees (with wines by the glass). In 2008 construction began on a long-awaited Frank Gehry–designed visitors center, due to open in 2010. Tours ($30) include barrel tastings and a glimpse of the new all-green-constructed winery building. Bottles cost $28 to $75.

CHARBAY

Most know **Charbay** (☎ 707-963-9327; www.charbay.com; 4001 Spring Mountain Rd, St Helena; tastings $20; by appointment) for its top-shelf flavored vodkas and spirits, made by a master 12th-generation Serbian distiller. Alas, by law you can't sample the spirits, but you can taste excitingly crisp aperitif wines, including a brandy-infused chardonnay, a lip-smacking sangria-like rosé and excellent ports. Charbay is old Napa: the winery is a farm and a garage with plastic chairs and tables, a giant alembic still in the driveway and a yappy dog to greet you. Bottles cost $25 to $75

PRIDE MOUNTAIN

High atop Spring Mountain, cult-favorite **Pride** (☎ 707-963-4949; www.pridewines.com; 4026 Spring

Mountain Rd, St Helena; tastings $5; by appointment) straddles the Napa-Sonoma border and bottles vintages under both appellations. The well-structured cabernet sauvignon and the big merlot are the best-known wines, but there's also an elegant viognier (perfect with oysters) and a standout cab franc, heavy with blueberry and violet, available only at the winery. Picnicking here is spectacular (choose Viewpoint for drop-dead vistas, or Ghost Winery for shade and the historic ruins of a 19th-century winery), but you must first have a tasting appointment. Bottles cost $42 to $66.

CASA NUESTRA

our pick **Casa Nuestra** (☎ 707-963-5783; www.casanuestra.com; 3451 Silverado Trail, St Helena; tastings $5, refundable with purchase; call ahead for opening hours;) A peace flag and a picture of Elvis greet your arrival in the tasting barn at this old-school, '70s-vintage, mom-and-pop outfit, which produces unusual blends and interesting varietals (including good chenin blanc) and 100% cabernet franc. Vineyards are all-organic and the sun provides the power. Best of all, you can picnic free (call ahead and buy a bottle) beneath weeping willows, beside two happy goats. Bottles cost $20 to $45.

LADERA

High on the flanks of Howell Mountain, **Ladera** (☎ 707-965-2445, 866-523-3728; www.laderavineyards.com; 150 White Cottage Rd S, Angwin; tastings $15, tour & tasting $25; by appointment) makes wonderful, little-known, estate-grown cabernet sauvignon. Make an appointment to visit this well-off-the-beaten-path 19th-century stone-walled winery. There's only one tour at a time: yours. Tasting fees refunded with purchase. Bottles cost $25 to $65.

> **A LOVELY SPOT FOR A PICNIC**
>
> Unlike Sonoma, there aren't many places to picnic legally in Napa. Here's a short list of spots, but call ahead and remember to buy a bottle (or glass, if available) of your host's wine. Bon appétit!
>
> - **Casa Nuestra** (above)
> - **Hall** (p227)
> - **Napa Valley Museum** (p232)
> - **Pride Mountain Vineyards** (p227)
> - **Rutherford Hill** (Map p225; ☎ 707-963-1871; www.rutherfordhill.com; 200 Rutherford Hill Rd; bottles $15-150)
> - **Vincent Arroyo** (opposite)

SCHRAMSBERG

Up a wooded lane off Hwy 29, **Schramsberg** (☎ 707-942-4558; www.schramsberg.com; 1400 Schramsberg Rd; tastings $35; by appointment) makes some of California's best brut sparkling wines, and in 1972 was the first domestic wine served at the White House. Blanc de blancs is the signature. The appointment-only tasting and tour (book well ahead) is expensive, but you'll sample all the *tête de cuvées*, not just the low-end wines. Tours include a walk through the caves; bring a sweater. Located off Peterson Dr. Bottles cost $20 to $100.

CASTELLO DI AMOROSO

our pick **Castello** (☎ 707-967-6272; www.castellodiamorosa.com; 4045 N St Helena Hwy, Calistoga; tastings/tours $10/30;) For over-the-top grandeur, this place wins hands-down. It took 14 years to build this perfectly replicated 12th-century Italian castle, complete with moat, hand-cut stone walls, ceiling frescoes by Italian artisans, Roman-style cross-vault brick catacombs and a torture chamber with period equipment. So picture-ready is the castle that on our last visit Disney was filming. You can taste without an appointment, but you'd be crazy to miss the tour. Oh, the wine? Some very respectable Italian varietals, including a velvety Tuscan blend, and a merlot blend that goes great with pizza. Bottle cost $25 to $40.

STERLING

The reason to visit **Sterling Vineyards** (☎ 707-942-3300, 800-726-6136; www.sterlingvineyards.com; 1111 Dunaweal Lane, Calistoga; adult/child under 3yr/child 3-21yr $20/free/10;) is to ride a gondola to its hilltop winery for superb valley views. Modeled after a Greek villa, the winery is architecturally interesting, but the wine is just OK. Come for the gondola. The website has discount coupons. Bottles cost $15 to $45.

CLOS PEGASE

Clos Pegase (☎ 707-942-4981; www.clospegase.com; 1060 Dunaweal Lane; tastings $10) has a $65 million modern-art collection with works by Jean

WINE COUNTRY

Dubuffet and Henry Moore – though there may be a rack of sweatshirts obscuring the Francis Bacon in the gift shop. On the tasting bar, look for food-friendly chardonnay, pinot noir, merlot and cabernet sauvignon. Free tours at 11:30am and 2pm. Bottles cost $18 to $38.

VINCENT ARROYO

The tasting room at **Vincent Arroyo** (☎ 707-942-6995; www.vincentarroyo.com; 2361 Greenwood Ave, Calistoga; tastings free; 🕑 by appointment) is a garage, where you may even meet Mr Arroyo, known for his all-estate-grown petite sirah and cabernet sauvignon. These wines are distributed nowhere else and are so consistently good that 75% of production is sold before it's bottled. Tastings are free, but appointments are required. Bottles cost $22 to $45.

Also consider:

Elizabeth Spencer (☎ 707-963-6067; www.elizabethspencerwines.com; 1165 Rutherford Rd, Rutherford; tastings $15-25) Taste inside an 1872 railroad depot or an outdoor garden. Small-lot wines include monster-sized pinot noir, and a well-priced grapefruit-y sauvignon blanc. Bottles $20 to $85.

Hagafen Cellars (☎ 888-424-2336; www.hagafen.com; 4160 Silverado Trail; tastings $5-10) All-kosher wines. Tasty late-harvest dessert chardonnay. Print free tasting coupons online. Bottles $16 to $50.

Round Pond (☎ 888-302-2575; www.roundpond.com; 875 Rutherford Rd, Rutherford; tastings $25; 🕑 by appointment) Fantastic food pairings on a vineyard-view stone patio. We especially love the tastings of olive oil and red-wine vinegar, and guided tours ($30) of the olive mill. Bottles $26 to $60.

Terra Valentine (☎ 707-967-8340; www.terravalentine.com; 3787 Spring Mountain Rd, St Helena; tastings $30; 🕑 by appointment) Sweeping vistas from a churchlike hillside winery. Sit-down tastings, paired with chocolate and cheese, in a lovely library. Big, balanced cabernets. Bottles $30 to $40.

NAPA

pop 75,000

The valley's workaday hub was once a nothing-special city of storefronts, Victorian cottages and riverfront warehouses, but booming real-estate values caused an influx of new money that transformed Napa into a happening city of arts and food. Napa is home to Copia and Oxbow Public Market – reason enough to visit – and the terminus of the Napa Valley Wine Train (p197).

Orientation & Information

Napa lies between Silverado Trail and St Helena Hwy/Hwy 29. For downtown, exit Hwy 29 at 1st St and drive east. Napa's main drag, 1st St, is lined with shops and restaurants.

Napa Library (☎ 707-253-4241; www.co.napa.ca.us; 580 Coombs St; 🕑 10am-9pm Mon-Thu, to 5:30pm Fri, to 5pm Sat, 2-9pm Sun) Email connections.

Napa Valley Conference & Visitors Bureau (☎ 707-226-7459; www.napavalley.org; 1310 Napa Town Center; 🕑 9am-5pm) The biggest information center is in a mall between 1st and Pearl Sts, two blocks west of Main St. Pick up the free *Inside Napa Valley,* with its almost-comprehensive winery guide. Staff will make same-day reservations, but not advance.

Sights & Activities

Named for the Roman god of abundance, **Copia: The American Center for Wine, Food & the Arts** (☎ 707-259-1600; www.copia.org; 500 1st St; admission free; 🕑 10am-6pm; 🚸) is a $50-million cultural center, bringing together all things Wine Country. Interactive exhibits include wine-tasting stations, preparing you to visit wineries unafraid. Fascinating installations tackle the question, 'What is American food?' Look for free food samplings and cooking demonstrations. The extensive gardens include one for children (with roosters and a beanstalk tipi) and a 'wine garden' planted with flora used to describe wine, from lemons to tobacco. The café serves great salads and sandwiches (under $10); Julia's Kitchen (see p231) provides white-tablecloth service. Check the website for outdoor concerts, forums, barbecues and films. Budget three to four hours.

Next door, **Oxbow Public Market** (☎ 707-226-6529; www.oxbowpublicmarket.com; 610 1st St; admission free; 🕑 9am-7pm Mon-Sat, to 8pm Tue, 10am-5pm Sun; 🚸) opened in 2008, showcasing all things culinary – from produce stalls to kitchen stores to fantastic edibles. We particularly like Pica-Pica (see p231); Whole Spice (☎ 707-256-0700; www.wholespice.com) for hard-to-find herbs and spices; and Fatted Calf (☎ 707-256-3684; www.fattedcalf.com) for delectable charcuterie. Kids love the burgers at Taylor's Auto Refresher (see p234).

At supercool **Vintners' Collective** (☎ 707-255-7150; www.vintnerscollective.com; 1245 Main St; tastings $15-25; 🕑 11am-6pm Wed-Mon), sample tiny-scale-production high-end wines from 18 wineries too small to have their own tasting rooms. If you can't make it up-valley, VC is the perfect alternative. Want the skinny on Napa? Talk to Doug – he knows all the gossip.

WINE COUNTRY

In Carneros, see one of Northern California's best modern-art collections at 217-acre **DiRosa Preserve** (☎ 707-226-5991; www.dirosapreserve.org; 5200 Carneros Hwy; admission $3; 9:30am-3pm Tue-Fri, tours by appointment Tue-Sat), where there's an outdoor sculpture garden, a 35-acre lake and indoor galleries.

Perfect your asanas at **Ubuntu Yoga** (☎ 707-251-5656; www.ubuntunapa.com; 1140 Main St); drop-in classes cost $18.

Sleeping

Summer demand exceeds supply. Weekend rates skyrocket. Also try Calistoga (p237).

Chablis Inn (☎ 707-257-1944; 800-443-3490; www.chablisinn.com; 3360 Solano Ave; r Mon-Fri $99-119, Sat & Sun $159-179; wi-fi) This well-kept two-story motel is good value. Hot tub.

RiverPointe Napa Valley (☎ 707-252-4200, 877-258-2282; www.riverpointenapa.com; 500 Lincoln Ave; studios $115, 1-bedroom r $187-250;) Lush landscaping cleverly disguises an 11-acre high-end trailer park. Take heart: all 100 units are spotless – if boxy – and once you get over the mobile-home thing, they're actually comfortable. All have kitchenettes. Wi-fi in lobby.

John Muir Inn (☎ 707-257-7220, 800-522-8999; www.johnmuirnapa.com; 1998 Trower Ave; r incl breakfast Mon-Fri $150-210, Sat & Sun $170-240; wi-fi) The best of the generic hotels lining Hwy 29, John Muir's spotless rooms have marble baths and comfy mattresses. Breakfast is next door at Marie Callender's coffee shop.

Napa River Inn (☎ 707-251-8500, 877-251-8500; www.napariverinn.com; 500 Main St; r Mon-Fri $169-289, Sat & Sun $199-289; wi-fi) On the river in the historic 1884 Hatt Building, the inn has upper-midrange rooms with extras like triple-sheeted beds, quality fabrics and bathrobes; for $25, get a doggie bed, cookies and chardonnay biscuits.

Casita Bonita (☎ 707-259-1980, 707-738-5587; www.lacasitabonita.comq $225-300; wi-fi) What a bargain! This smartly decorated two-bedroom cottage has a full kitchen, a dining room, a living room and a veggie garden shaded with lemon and plum trees – kids love the chickens. It's perfect for two couples or a family, and includes a free tasting at Vintner's Collective (p229).

Cottages of Napa Valley (☎ 707-252-7810; www.napacottages.com; 1012 Darns Lane; d $375-455, q $450-600; wi-fi) Originally constructed in the 1940s and rebuilt with top-end amenities in 2005, these eight cottages are ideal for a romantic hideaway, with extra-long soaking tubs, gas fireplaces, and outdoor fire pits beneath towering pines. Cottages 4 and 8 have private porches and swinging chairs. The only drawback is traffic noise, but interiors are silent.

Milliken Creek Inn (☎ 707-255-1197, 888-622-5775; www.millikencreekinn.com; 1815 Silverado Trail; r incl breakfast $375-775; wi-fi) Understatedly elegant Milliken Creek combines small-inn charm, fine-hotel service and B&B intimacy. The impeccably styled, English Colonial rooms have top-flight amenities – flat-panel TVs, fireplaces, ultrahigh-thread-count linens – but the beauty is in details like evening candles in your room and breakfast in bed. Book a river-view room.

our pick **Carneros Inn** (☎ 707-299-4900; www.thecarnerosinn.com; 4048 Sonoma Hwy; r Mon-Fri $505-595, Sat & Sun $630-705; wi-fi) The pinnacle of chic for the under-50s, Carneros Inn's snappy design aesthetic and retro small-town-agricultural theme shatters the predictable Wine Country mold. The semidetached, corrugated-metal units look like itinerant housing, but inside are cherry-wood floors, ultrasuede headboards, bright white duvets, leather club chairs, wood-burning fireplaces, heated-tile bathroom floors, giant soaking tubs and indoor-outdoor showers. Splurge on a vineyard-view room.

Also recommended:

Belle Epoque B&B (☎ 707-257-2161, 800-238-8070; www.labelleepoque.com; 1386 Calistoga Ave; r incl breakfast $299-379; wi-fi) Formal-fancy 1893 Victorian.

Blackbird Inn (☎ 707-226-2450, 888-567-9811; www.blackbirdinnnapa.com; 1775 1st St; r incl breakfast $175-250; wi-fi) Gorgeous, eight-room Arts and Crafts–style house.

Napa Redwood Inn (☎ 707-257-6111, 877-872-6272; www.napavalleyredwoodinn.com; 3380 Solano Ave; r Mon-Fri $90-110, Sat & Sun $140-150; wi-fi) Generic freeway-side motel.

Travelodge (☎ 707-226-1871; www.travelodge.com; 853 Coombs St at 2nd St; r Mon-Fri/Sat & Sun $110/150;) Thin-walled budget option; 3rd-floor rooms quietest.

Eating

July to mid-August, look for the peach stand at Deer Park Rd and Silverado Trail (across Deer Park Rd from Stewart's farmstand) for juicy-delicious heirloom varieties.

Soscol Café (☎ 707-252-0651; 632 Soscol Av; dishes $5-8; 6am-2pm Mon-Sat, 7am-1pm Sun) The ultimate greasy-spoon diner, Soscol makes massive huevos rancheros, and chicken-fried steak and eggs. Not a high heel in sight.

Pica-Pica Maize Kitchen (☎ 707-515-0633; picapicakitchen.com; Oxbow Market, 610 1st St; dishes $6-9; ⏲ 9am-8pm Mon-Sat, 10am-6pm Sun; V) Venezuelan-style (wheat- and gluten-free) corn-flour tortillas are topped with grilled veggies, meat and savory sauces. Order at the counter.

Alexis Baking Co (☎ 707-258-1827; www.alexisbakingcompany.com; 1517 3rd St; dishes $6-10; ⏲ breakfast & lunch; 👶 V) Our fave spot for scrambles, granola, focaccia-bread sandwiches, big cups of joe and boxed lunches to go.

Boon Fly Cafe (☎ 707-299-4870; www.theboonflycafe.com; 4048 Sonoma Hwy; mains $10-20; ⏲ 7am-9pm) For New American comfort food done well, make a beeline to Boon Fly – but avoid peak meal times. At breakfast, try homemade doughnuts or brioche French toast; at lunch and dinner, grilled Reubens, roasted chicken, and spinach salads. Save room for warm chocolate-chip cookies.

Pizza Azzuro (☎ 707-255-5552; www.azzuropizzeria.com; 1260 Main St; mains $11-15; 👶 V) The new location of this Napa classic is deafeningly loud, but the tender-crusted pizzas and salad-topped 'manciata' bread make it worth bearing. Good Caesar salad and pastas.

Pearl Bistro (☎ 707-224-9161; www.therestaurantpearl.com; 1339 Pearl St; mains $14-19; ⏲ Tue-Sat) Meet locals at this dog-friendly bistro with red-painted concrete floors, pinewood tables and open-rafter ceilings. The winning down-to-earth cooking includes double-cut pork chops, chicken verde with polenta, steak tacos and the specialty, oysters.

Annalien (☎ 707-224-8319; www.restaurantannalien.com; 1142 Main St; mains $14-22; ⏲ Tue-Sat) The Saigon-style street food is pricier than Vietnam's, but nowhere else in Napa will you find *banh xeo* (crepes with chicken and shrimp). Great five-spice quail.

Bistro Don Giovanni (☎ 707-224-3300; www.bistrodongiovanni.com; 4110 Howard Lane at Hwy 29; mains $15-25) This long-running-favorite, trattoria-style roadhouse cooks up modern-Italian pastas, crispy pizzas and wood-roasted meats. Reservations essential. Weekends get packed – and loud. For vineyard-view seats, request tables 50 to 59 or 70 to 79.

Ubuntu(☎ 707-251-5656; www.ubuntunapa.com; 1140 Main St; mains $15-25; ⏲ dinner; V) Chef Jeremy Fox elevates vegetarian cooking to high art, and is the second-ever guest chef to present an all-veg menu at the prestigious James Beard House. Incorporating ultrafresh ingredients from the restaurant's biodynamic gardens, he ekes out subtle variations in flavor, then elongates them with nut oils and other natural fats. For the maximum experience, order the tasting menu with wines. At $125 it's no bargain, but at last vegetarians have a splurge-worthy option on par with Napa's top tables.

La Toque (☎ 707-257-5157; www.latoque.com; 1314 McKinstry St; 2-/3-/4-course menu $49/68/88; ⏲ dinner) Napa's unsung hero of Gallic cooking, chef Ken Frank, exquisitely crafts haute-contemporary French cuisine, and is a master with foie gras and truffles. The artistry is mirrored in the wine director's accompanying selections. Service is refreshingly unpretentious. La Toque isn't for everyone, but if you're a foodie this might be your trip's best meal. Men: wear a jacket. Reservations essential.

Also recommended:

Angele (☎ 707-252-8115; www.angelerestaurant.com; 540 Main St; lunch mains $10-24, dinner mains $18-28) Perfect provincial French on a river-view patio. Beautiful *cassoulet*; great burgers.

Cole's Chop House (☎ 707-224-6328; www.coleschophouse.com; 1122 Main St; mains $20-50; ⏲ dinner) Napa's best steaks.

Julia's Kitchen (☎ 707-265-5700; www.juliaskitchen.org; Copia, 500 First St; mains $19-35, 4-course tasting $60; ⏲ lunch Wed-Mon, dinner Wed-Sun) Swank Cal-French; Thursday evening's three-course prix fixe costs $35 – a bargain.

Kelley's No-Bad-Days Cafe (☎ 707-258-9666; 958 Pearl St; mains $12-20; ⏲ Wed-Sat; 👶) Mish-mash American, with Mexican-Thai spicing. Live music and no corkage Thursdays.

Villa Corona (☎ 707-447-7683; www.villacoronamex.com; 3614 Bel Air Plaza; dishes $5-9; ⏲ 9am-9pm Mon-Sat, to 8pm Sun; 👶) Hole-in-the-wall Mexican with burritos and chimichangas. Behind Lamplighter Lounge on Trancas, just east of Hwy 29.

Zuzu (☎ 707-224-8555; www.zuzunapa.com; 829 Main St; small plates $6-14; ⏲ lunch Mon-Fri, dinner nightly) Small plates, big waits.

Drinking

Downtown Joe's (☎ 707-258-2337; 902 Main St at 2nd St; wi-fi) Live music plays Thursday to Sunday, and TV sports show nightly at this often-packed microbrewery-restaurant.

Entertainment

Silo's Jazz Club (☎ 707-251-5833; www.silosjazzclub.com; Napa River Inn, 530 Main St; cover $10-20;

FLYING & BALLOONING

Wine Country is stunning from the air – a multihued tapestry of undulating hills, deep valleys and rambling vineyards. Make reservations.

The **Vintage Aircraft Company** (Map p198; ☎ 707-938-2444; www.vintageaircraft.com; 23982 Arnold Dr) flies over Sonoma in a vintage biplane with an awesome pilot who'll do loop-de-loops on request (add $50). Twenty-minute tours cost $175/265 for one/two adults.

Napa Valley's signature hot-air balloon flights leave early, around 6am or 7am, when the air is coolest; they usually include a champagne breakfast on landing. Adults pay about $200 to $250, and kids $130 to $150. Call **Balloons above the Valley** (☎ 707-253-2222, 800-464-6824; www.balloonrides.com) or **Napa Valley Balloons** (☎ 707-944-0228, 800-253-2224; www.napavalleyballoons.com), both in Yountville.

Tue-Thu 4pm-10pm, Fri-Sat to midnight) A cabaret-style wine and beer bar, Silo's hosts local jazz luminaries Wednesday through Saturday from 7pm to 10pm, including the Bay Area's preeminent cabaret duo, Wesla and Mike Whitfield, who perform classics from the Great American Songbook most Friday and Saturday nights. Call for the current lineup. Table reservations recommended on weekends.

Napa Valley Opera House (☎ 707-226-7372; www.nvoh.org; 1030 Main St) This restored vintage-1880s opera house stages straight plays, comedy and live musicians like Ravi Shankar.

Billco's Billiards & Darts (☎ 707-226-7506; 810 Randolph St; noon-1am) The mostly men-in-khakis crowd swills beer, shoots pool and throws darts.

YOUNTVILLE

pop 2900

Say *yawnt*-ville. This once quiet town, 9 miles north of Napa, gets overrun with tourists most afternoons, but outstanding restaurants justify fighting traffic. If you're not into food, consider skipping it. Most businesses are on Washington St, including a bank. There are some good inns here – one of which is great – but St Helena and Calistoga generally make better bases.

Yountville's modernist 40,000-sq-ft **Napa Valley Museum** (☎ 707-944-0500; www.napavalleymuseum.org; 55 Presidents Circle; adult/child $4.50/2.50; 10am-5pm Wed-Mon), off California Dr, chronicles cultural history and showcases local paintings. Good picnicking outside.

The only worthwhile shop at V Marketplace is TV-chef Michael Chiarello's **Napa Style** (☎ 707-945-1229; 6525 Washington St), but it's overpriced.

Sleeping

Maison Fleurie (☎ 707-944-2056, 800-788-0369; www.maisonfleurienapa.com; 6529 Yount St; r incl breakfast $130-285; wi-fi) The rooms at this country inn are located inside an ivy-covered, turn-of-the-20th-century home and carriage house, which are decorated in French-provincial style. There's a big breakfast, as well as afternoon wine and hors d'oeuvres. Outdoor hot tub.

Napa Valley Railway Inn (☎ 707-944-2000; www.napavalleyrailwayinn.com; 6523 Washington St; r $140-210;) Sleep in a converted railroad car, part of two short trains parked at a central platform. They've little privacy, but are moderately priced. Kids love 'em.

Petit Logis (☎ 707-944-2332, 877-944-2332; www.petitlogis.com; 6527 Yount St; r Mon-Fri $195-245, Sat & Sun $235-275; wi-fi) This cedar-sided inn has five individually decorated rooms. Think white wicker furniture and dusty-rose fabric. Add $20 for breakfast for two.

Napa Valley Lodge (☎ 707-944-2468; www.napavalleylodge.com; 2230 Madison St at Washington St; r $299-450; wi-fi) It looks like a condo complex, but rooms are spacious and modern (some with fireplaces); beds have comfortable pillow-top mattresses. Hot tub, sauna and exercise room.

Poetry Inn (☎ 707-944-0646; www.poetryinn.com; 6380 Silverado Trail; r incl breakfast $640-1400; wi-fi) There's no better view of the Napa Valley than from this understatedly chic, three-room inn, located high on the valley wall east of Yountville. The rooms are decorated in Arts and Crafts–inspired style, and feature private balconies, wood-burning fireplaces, 1000-thread-count sheets and enormous baths with indoor-outdoor showers. Bring a ring.

Eating

French is the dominant paradigm. Make reservations.

Bouchon Bakery (☎ 707-944-2253; 6528 Washington St; dishes $3-9; 7am-7pm) Bouchon makes perfect French pastries and strong coffee. Order at the counter and sit outside, or pack a bag to go.

Bistro Jeanty (☎ 707-944-0103; www.bistrojeanty.com; 6510 Washington St; mains $16-29) A bistro is classically defined as serving comfort food to weary travelers, and that's exactly what French-born chef-owner Philippe Jeanty does, with great cassoulet, coq au vin, steak-*frites*, braised pork with lentils, and scrumptious tomato soup.

Bouchon (☎ 707-944-8037; www.bouchonbistro.com; 6534 Washington St; mains $17-36) At celeb chef Thomas Keller's French brasserie, everything from food to decor is so authentic, from zinc bar to white-aproned waiters, you'd swear you were in Paris – even the Bermuda-shorts-clad Americans look out of place. On the menu: giant platters of oysters, onion soup, roasted chicken, leg of lamb, trout with almonds, runny cheeses and profiteroles for dessert, all impeccably prepared.

Mustards Grill (☎ 707-944-2424; www.mustardsgrill.com; 7399 St Helena Hwy; mains $18-24;) The valley's long-standing, archetypal roadhouse serves up wood-fired California comfort food – roasted meats, lamb shanks, pork chops, hearty salads and sandwiches. Great crowd-pleaser.

Ad Hoc (☎ 707-944-2487; http://adhocrestaurant.com; 6476 Washington St; prix-fixe meals $48; dinner) Another winning formula by Yountville's culinary oligarch, Thomas Keller. Ad Hoc serves the master's favorite American home cooking in a four-course prix-fixe menu. One drawback: the daily-changing menu is set, with no choices.

French Laundry (☎ 707-944-2380; www.frenchlaundry.com; 6640 Washington St; prix fixe incl service charge $240; dinner nightly, lunch Fri-Sun) The pinnacle of California dining, Thomas Keller's French Laundry is epic, a high-wattage culinary experience on par with the world's best. Book two months ahead at 10am sharp. Avoid booking before 7pm; first-service seating moves faster than the second – sometimes too fast.

Drinking & Entertainment

Pancha's (☎ 707-944-2125; 6764 Washington St) Swill tequila at this dive. Vineyard workers come early, restaurant waiters late.

Lincoln Theater (☎ 707-944-1300, 866-944-9199; www.lincolntheater.org; 100 California Dr) Various artists play this 1200-seat theater, including the Napa Valley Symphony.

OAKVILLE & RUTHERFORD

But for its famous grocery, you'd drive through Oakville (pop 500) and never know you'd missed it. This is the middle of the grapes – vineyards sprawl in every direction. Rutherford (pop 525) is more conspicuous, but really, it's the wineries that put these towns on the map.

Sleeping

There is no budget lodging.

Rancho Caymus (☎ 707-963-1777, 800-845-1777; www.ranchocaymus.com; 1140 Rutherford Rd, Rutherford; r $250-400; wi-fi) Reminiscent of California's missions, this hacienda-style inn scores high marks for its tiled fountain courtyard, and rooms' kiva-style fireplaces, oak-beamed ceilings and wood floors. Winter rates drop nearly $100.

Auberge du Soleil (☎ 707-963-1211, 800-348-5406; www.aubergedusoleil.com; 180 Rutherford Hill Rd; r $600-1025, ste $1200-2200; wi-fi) The top splurge for a no-holds-barred romantic weekend, Auberge's hillside cottages are second to none, with a terra-cotta Mediterranean-inspired decor, wood-burning fireplaces, sound systems, stocked fridges, vineyard-view patios, sumptuous beds and top-flight amenities by Dr Hauschka. Less-expensive rooms feel comparatively cramped; book a suite. Excellent guests-only spa.

Eating

Oakville Grocery & Cafe (☎ 707-944-8802; www.oakvillegrocery.com; 7856 Hwy 29, Oakville; 8am-5:30pm) The definitive Wine Country deli sells stinky cheeses, charcuterie meats, fresh-baked bread, olives, wine and lunch boxes ($18) you can order ahead. There are three tables outside, but ask where to picnic nearby.

La Luna Market & Taqueria (☎ 707-963-3211, 707-967-3497; 1153 Rutherford Rd, Rutherford; dishes $4-6; 8am-7:30pm) Wondering where the Mexican day-laborers eat? Look no further for honest burritos with homemade hot sauce.

Rutherford Grill (☎ 707-963-1792; www.hillstone.com; 1180 Rutherford Rd, Rutherford; mains $15-30) Yes, it's a chain (Houston's), but to rub shoulders with winemakers, snag a stool for lunch at the bar. The food is consistent – ribs, rotisserie chicken, outstanding grilled artichokes – and there's no corkage fee, so you can chug-a-lug that bottle you just bought down the road.

Auberge du Soleil (☎ 707-963-1211; www.aubergedusoleil.com; 180 Rutherford Hill Rd, Rutherford; mains breakfast $16-18, lunch $20-34, 4-/6-course prix-fixe dinner $90/125) Auberge's Euro-Cal cooking is expertly prepared with an easy, elegant style. It's one of the valley's best for a swanky breakfast, lazy lunch or a will-you-wear-my-ring dinner. Valley views are mesmerizing from the terrace – *don't* sit inside. Make reservations; arrive before sunset. For the full experience, order the tasting menu paired with wines.

ST HELENA

pop 5900

You'll know you're arriving when traffic halts. St Helena (say ha-*lee*-na) is the Rodeo Dr of Napa, with fancy boutiques lining Main St (Hwy 29). The historic downtown is good for a stroll, with great window-shopping, but parking is next-to-impossible summer weekends. Carry your platinum card.

The **chamber of commerce** (☎ 707-963-4456, 800-799-6456; www.sthelena.com; Suite A, 1010 Main St; ⏰ 10am-5pm Mon-Fri, 11am-3pm Sat) has information and lodging assistance.

WINE COUNTRY

Sights & Activities

Silverado Museum (☎ 707-963-3757; www.silveradomuseum.org; 1490 Library Lane; admission free; ⏰ noon-4pm Tue-Sun) contains a fascinating collection of Robert Louis Stevenson memorabilia. In 1880 the author – then sick, penniless and unknown – stayed in an abandoned bunkhouse at the old Silverado Mine with his wife, Fanny Osbourne. His novel *The Silverado Squatters* is based on his time there. To reach Library Lane, turn east off Hwy 29 at the Adams St traffic light and cross the railroad tracks.

The **Culinary Institute of America at Greystone** (☎ 707-967-2320; www.ciachef.edu/california; 2555 Main St; cooking demonstration $12.50; ⏰ 10am-5pm), a continuing-education campus for food and wine professionals, occupies the Christian Brothers' 1889 château and offers public cooking demonstrations, Friday through Monday.

A **farmers market** (www.sthelenafarmersmkt.org; ⏰ 7:30am-noon Fri May-Oct) meets at Crane Park, half a mile south of downtown.

Sleeping

Hotel St Helena (☎ 707-963-4388; www.hotelsthelena.net; 1309 Main St; r with bath $125-225, without bath $95-155; ❄) Decorated with period furnishings, this 1881 hotel sits right downtown. Rooms are tiny but a bargain, especially those with shared bathrooms.

El Bonita Motel (☎ 707-963-3216, 800-541-3284; www.elbonita.com; 195 Main St; r $140-249; ❄ 💻 🏊) Book in advance to secure a room at this sought-after motel, with up-to-date rooms (quietest are in back), attractive grounds, a hot tub and a sauna.

Meadowood (☎ 707-963-3646, 800-458-8080; www.meadowood.com; 900 Meadowood Lane; r from $650; ❄ 👶 🏊 wi-fi) Hidden in a wooded dell with towering pines and miles of hiking, Napa's grandest resort has cottages and rooms in satellite buildings surrounding a croquet lawn. We most like the hillside fireplace cottages; lawn-view rooms lack privacy but are good for families, with room to play outside. The vibe is country club, with white-clapboard buildings reminiscent of New England. Wear linen and play *Great Gatsby*. Kids love the mammoth pool.

Also consider the following:

Eagle & Rose Inn (☎ 707-963-1532; www.eagleandroseinn.com; 1431 Railroad Ave; motel r $169, hotel r with kitchenette $169-189; ❄ wi-fi) Twelve-room in-town hotel (with kitchenettes), and five-room motel, 1 mile north.

Harvest Inn (☎ 707-963-9463, 800-950-8466; www.harvestinn.com; 1 Main St; r incl breakfast $269-469; ❄ 🏊 wi-fi) Former estate with satellite buildings. The new one is generic; we prefer the vineyard-view king rooms, with their private hot tubs. Sprawling gardens.

Eating

Taylor's Auto Refresher (☎ 707-963-3486; www.taylorsrefresher.com; 933 Main St; dishes $6-14; ⏰ 10:30am-9pm; 👶) Wiggle your toes in the grass while you munch on all-natural burgers, Cobb salads and fried calamari at this classic roadside drive-in. Expect big waits weekends.

Model Bakery (☎ 707-963-9731; 1357 Main St; dishes $5-10; ⏰ Tue-Sun) Great scones, muffins, salads, gelato, pizzas, sandwiches and strong coffee.

Armadillo's (☎ 707-963-8082; 1304 Main St; mains $7-12) Sunny Mexican with reasonable prices.

Cook St Helena (☎ 707-963-7088; 1310 Main St; lunch mains $9-18, dinner mains $15-23; ⏰ Tue-Sat) Locals crowd the counter at this tiny storefront bistro, which makes BLTs, burgers and pasta at lunch, and melt-off-the-bone ribs and Italian-derivative mains at dinner. They're not on the menu, but request the butter-braised brussels sprouts – fantastic.

Market (☎ 707-963-3799; www.marketsthelena.com; 1347 Main St; mains $10-23; ⏰ 11:30am-10pm) We love the big portions of simple, fresh American cooking at Market. Maximizing the season's best produce, the chef creates enormous, inventive salads and soul-satisfying mains like buttermilk fried chicken. The stone-walled dining room dates to the 19th century, as does the ornate backbar, where cocktails are muddled to order. Nothing is over $23, and the wine markup never exceeds $14.

Cindy's Backstreet Kitchen (☎ 707-963-1200; www.cindysbackstreetkitchen.com; 1327 Railroad Ave; mains $15-21) The inviting retro-homey decor complements the menu's Cal-American comfort food, like avocado-and-papaya salad, wood-fired duck, steak with French fries, and the simple grilled burger. The bar makes a mean mojito.

Terra (☎ 707-963-8931; www.terrarestaurant.com; 1345 Railroad Ave; mains $20-30; ⏰ dinner Wed-Mon) Inside an 1884 stone building, Terra wows diners with its seamlessly blended Japanese, French and Italian culinary styles. The signature is a stellar broiled sake-marinated black cod and shrimp dumplings in shiso broth. This is one of Wine Country's best; it's pricy, but you won't soon forget what you ate.

Martini House (☎ 707-963-2233; www.martinihouse.com; 1245 Spring St; lunch mains $14-26, dinner mains $33-40; ⏰ lunch Fri-Sun, dinner nightly) One of Wine Country's most handsome dining rooms, Martini House occupies a 1923 California Arts and Crafts–style house, with food as fine as the room is gorgeous. Celeb chef-owner Todd Humphries is a master with mushrooms; consider ordering his signature tasting menu ($60). Book a table in the grand main dining room or the romantic, sun-dappled garden. Drinkers: see the supercool downstairs bar.

Wine Spectator Greystone Restaurant (☎ 707-967-1010; www.ciachef.edu; 2555 Main St; mains $27-36) Inside the renowned Culinary Institute of America, head directly to the gorgeous patio bar for cocktails or garden-view lunch, or sit inside and watch the chefs in the open kitchen. The menu is pure California, with a broad selection of local wines and microbrews.

Sunshine Foods (☎ 707-963-7070; 1115 Main St) Carries the town's best groceries.

Before the advent of fancy-food stores, there was **Napa Valley Olive Oil Mfg Co** (☎ 707-963-4173; 835 Charter Oak St; ⏰ 8am-5:30pm), an old-fashioned Italian market with succulent prosciutto and salami, meaty olives, fresh bread, nutty cheeses and of course olive oil. Yellowed business cards from 50 years ago adorn the walls, and the owner knows everyone in town. He'll lend you a knife and a board to make a picnic at the rickety wooden tables outside in the grass.

OLIVE-OIL TASTING

When you weary of wine tasting, pop in to one of the following olive-oil mills and dip some crusty bread. The harvest and pressing happen in November.

- **BR Cohn** (p201) Free tastings.
- **Round Pond** (p229) Ninety-minute mill tour and tasting $25.
- **Figone's Olive Oil** (p206) Free tastings.
- **Olive Press** (Map p198; ☎ 707-939-8900; www.theolivepress.com; 24724 Arnold Dr, Sonoma) Free tastings.

Shopping

Main St is lined with high-end boutiques (think $100 socks), but some mom-and-pop shops remain. Also see Outlet Shopping, p220.

Diva Perfumes (☎ 707-963-4057; 1309 Main St) If you can't get to Paris, get hard-to-find perfumes here.

Campus Store (☎ 707-967-2309; 2555 Main St) Inside the Culinary Institute, the campus store carries a huge selection of cookbooks and gadgets.

Woodhouse Chocolates (☎ 800-966-3468; 1367 Main St) Woodhouse looks more like Tiffany & Co than a candy shop, and the chocolates are priced accordingly: $75 per pound. Welcome to St Helena.

Footcandy (☎ 877-517-4606; 1239 Main St) Strappy sandals are displayed as if in a museum – or a set from *Sex in the City*.

Martin Showroom (☎ 707-967-8787; 1350 Main St) One-of-a-kind home furnishings.

Main Street Books (☎ 707-963-1338; 1315 Main St; ⏰ Mon-Sat) Sells good used books.

CALISTOGA

pop 5200

The least gentrified town in Napa Valley feels refreshingly simple, with an old-fashioned main street lined with shops, not boutiques, and a diverse mix of characters wandering the sidewalks. Bad hair? No problem.

Fancy-pants St Helena couldn't feel further away. Most tourists don't make it this far north. You should.

Famed 19th-century author Robert Louis Stevenson said of Calistoga, 'the whole neighborhood of Mt St Helena is full of sulfur and boiling springs…Calistoga itself seems to repose on a mere film above a boiling, subterranean lake.' Indeed, it does. Calistoga is synonymous with the mineral water bearing its name, bottled here since 1924. Its springs and geysers have earned it the nickname the 'hot springs of the West.' Plan to visit one of the town's spas, where you can indulge in the local specialty: a hot-mud bath, made of the volcanic ash from nearby volcanic Mt St Helena.

The town's odd name comes from Sam Brannan, who founded Calistoga in 1859, believing it would develop like the New York spa town of Saratoga. Apparently Sam liked his drink and at the founding ceremony tripped on his tongue, proclaiming it the 'Cali-stoga' of 'Sara-fornia.' The name stuck.

Orientation & Information

Calistoga's shops and restaurants line Lincoln Ave.

Hwys 128 and 29 run together from Rutherford through St Helena; in Calistoga, they split. Hwy 29 turns east and becomes Lincoln Ave, continuing across Silverado Trail, toward Clear Lake. Hwy 128 continues north as Foothill Blvd (not St Helena Hwy).

Chamber of Commerce & Visitors Center (☎ 707-942-6333, 866-306-5588; www.calistogachamber.com; 1458 Lincoln Ave; 🕒 10am-5pm)

Coperfield's Bookshop (☎ 707-942-1616; 1330 Lincoln Ave)

Sights & Activities

The picturesque **City Hall**, on Washington St, was built in 1902 as the Bedlam Opera House. Today it houses offices.

Across the street, and created by an ex-Disney animator (whose Oscar is on display), **Sharpsteen Museum** (☎ 707-942-5911; www.sharpsteen-museum.org; 1311 Washington St; admission free; 🕒 11am-4pm; 👶) has a fabulous diorama of the town in the 1860s, a big Victorian dollhouse, a full-size horse-drawn carriage, cool taxidermy and a restored cottage from Brannan's original resort. (The only Brannan cottage still at its original site is at 106 Wapoo Ave, near the Brannan Cottage Inn.)

Calistoga is famous for **hot-spring spas** and **mud-bath emporiums**, where you're buried in hot mud and emerge feeling supple, detoxified and enlivened. (The mud is made with volcanic ash and peat; the higher the ash content, the better the bath.)

Packages take 60 to 90 minutes and cost $75 to $85. You start semisubmerged in hot mud, then soak in hot mineral water. A steam bath and blanket-wrap follow. The treatment can be extended with a massage, increasing the cost to $120 or more.

Baths can be taken solo or, at some spas, as couples. Variations include thin, painted-on clay-mud wraps (called 'fango' baths, good for those uncomfortable sitting in mud), herbal wraps, seaweed baths and various massage treatments. Discount coupons are sometimes available from the visitors center. Book ahead, especially on summer weekends. Reservations essential at all spas.

The following spas in downtown Calistoga offer one-day packages. Some also offer discounted spa-lodging packages.

Calistoga Spa Hot Springs (☎ 707-942-6269, 866-822-5772; www.calistogaspa.com; 1006 Washington St; 🕒 appointments 8:30am-4:30pm Tue-Thu, to 9pm Fri-Mon; 👶) Traditional mud baths and massage at a motel complex with two huge swimming pools where kids can play while you soak (pool passes $25).

Dr Wilkinson's Hot Springs (☎ 707-942-4102; www.drwilkinson.com; 1507 Lincoln Ave; 🕒 appointments 8:30am-4pm Mon-Fri, to 5pm Sat-Sun) Fifty years running; 'the doc' uses more peat in its mud, making it less heavy.

Golden Haven Hot Springs (☎ 707-942-6793; www.goldenhaven.com; 1713 Lake St; 🕒 8am-8pm) Old-school and unfussy; offers couples' mud baths and couples' massage.

ourpick Indian Springs (☎ 707-942-4913; www.indianspringscalistoga.com; 1712 Lincoln Ave; 🕒 8am-9pm) The longest continually operating spa and original Calistoga resort has concrete mud tubs and mines its own ash. Treatments include use of the huge, hot-spring-fed pool. Great cucumber body lotion.

Lavender Hill Spa (☎ 707-942-4495; www.lavenderhillspa.com; 1015 Foothill Blvd; 🕒 9am-9pm) Small, cute, two-room spa; good for couples' massages.

Mount View Spa (☎ 707-942-6877, 800-816-6877; www.mountviewhotel.com; 1457 Lincoln Ave; 🕒 9am-9pm) Traditional, full-service, 12-room spa good for those who prefer painted-on mud to submersion.

Spa Solage (☎ 707-226-0825; www.solagecalistoga.com; 755 Silverado Trail; 🕒 8am-8pm) Chichi, austere, top-end spa, with couples' rooms and a fango-mud bar for

DIY paint-on treatments. Also has zero-gravity chairs for blanket wraps, and a clothing-optional pool.

Hardcore mountain bikers can tackle **Oat Hill Mine Trail**, one of Northern California's most technically challenging trails, just outside town. Find information and rentals at **Calistoga Bike Shop** (☎ 707-942-9687, 866-942-2453; www.calistogabikeshop.com; 1318 Lincoln Ave), which rents full-suspension mountain bikes (per day $70), tandem bikes (per hour/day $20/65) and wine-touring packages with custom wine carriers (per day $35) – the staff will even pick up your vino for you.

Sleeping

Also see Safari West (p240).

Napa County Fairgrounds & RV Park (☎ 707-942-5111, 707-942-5221; www.napacountyfairgrounds.com; 1435 Oak St; tent sites $20, RV sites $30-33) A dusty RV park northwest of downtown.

Bothe-Napa Valley State Park (☎ 707-942-4575, reservations 800-444-7275; www.reserveamerica.com; tent & RV sites $20-25;) Three miles south, Bothe has shady camping near redwoods and gorgeous hiking.

Calistoga Inn & Brewery (☎ 707-942-4101; www.calistogainn.com; 1250 Lincoln Ave; r Mon-Fri/Sat & Sun $89/$139; wi-fi) Perfect for bargain-hunters, this historic hotel has 18 clean, basic rooms with shared bath. No TVs. Great bar downstairs.

Golden Haven Hot Springs (☎ 707-942-6793; www.goldenhaven.com; 1713 Lake St; r $99-135, r with kitchenette $135-169; wi-fi) This plain-Jane motel, better priced than those on Lincoln Ave, has spa-lodging packages.

Dr Wilkinson's Motel & Hideaway Cottages (☎ 707-942-4102; www.drwilkinson.com; 1507 Lincoln Ave; r $139-199, housekeeping cottages from $149; wi-fi) This good-value vintage-1950s motel has well-kept rooms facing a courtyard. There's no hot tub, but there are three pools (one indoors) – and, of course, mud baths. Doc Wilkinson's rents housekeeping units at its sister property, Hideaway Cottages.

Calistoga Spa Hot Springs (☎ 707-942-6269, 866-822-5772; www.calistogaspa.com; 1006 Washington St; r $142-162;) Great for families, who jam the place weekends, this motel-resort has generic rooms with kitchenettes and fantastic pools – two full-size, a kiddie-pool with a miniwaterfall and a huge adults-only Jacuzzi. Outside are barbecues and a snack bar. Wi-fi in lobby.

Brannan Cottage Inn (☎ 707-942-4200; www.brannancottageinn.com; 109 Wapoo Ave; r incl breakfast $175-200, ste $210-235; wi-fi) Sam Brannan built this 1860 cottage, listed on the National Register of Historic Places. Long on charm and friendly service, it's decorated with floral-print fabrics and simple country furnishings. Suites sleep four. Guests use the pool at nearby Golden Haven motel.

Mount View Hotel & Spa (☎ 707-942-6877, 800-816-6877; www.mountviewhotel.com; 1457 Lincoln Ave; r $179-329; wi-fi) Rooms in this historic hotel are done with Victorian antiques, supercomfy beds with down comforters, and gleaming white-tile baths, but it's unadventurous for young travelers.

Hotel d'Amici (☎ 707-942-1007; www.hoteldamici.com; 1436 Lincoln Ave; r $185-230;) All four rooms at this 2nd-floor hotel have crisp linens and lots of sunlight. In the morning there's continental breakfast. NB: there's no on-site staff and no elevator.

Chanric (☎ 707-942-4535; www.thechanric.com; 1805 Foothill Blvd; r incl breakfast $209-349; wi-fi) A converted Victorian close to the road, this B&B has small-ish rooms with modern furnishings, pricy for their size, but the owner makes a lavish three-course breakfast. Gay-friendly.

Meadowlark Country House (☎ 707-942-5651, 800-942-5651; www.meadowlarkinn.com; 601 Petrified Forest Rd; r incl breakfast $210-265, ste $284; wi-fi) On 20 acres west of town, Meadowlark has luxury rooms decorated in contemporary style, most with decks and Jacuzzis. Outside there's a hot tub, a sauna and a clothing-optional pool. The truth-telling innkeeper lives in another house, offers helpful advice, then vanishes when you want privacy. There's a superfabulous cottage for $425. Gay-friendly.

Indian Springs Resort (☎ 707-942-4913; www.indianspringscalistoga.com; 1712 Lincoln Ave; motel r $225-290, studio $250-315, 1-bedroom bungalow $280-335, 2-bedroom bungalow $350-410; wi-fi) The definitive Calistoga resort, Indian Springs has bungalows facing a central lawn with palm trees, shuffleboard, boccie, hammocks and Weber grills – not unlike an old-school Florida resort. Some bungalows sleep six. There are also top-end motel-style rooms. All have great beds.

Chateau De Vie (☎ 707-942-6446, 877-558-2513; www.cdvnapavalley.com; 3250 Hwy 128; r incl breakfast $229-429; wi-fi) Surrounded by vineyards, with gorgeous views of Mt St Helena, CDV has five modern B&B rooms with top-end amenities. The house is austerely decorated, with zero froufrou. There's wine every afternoon on the sun-dappled patio, a hot tub and a big pool. Gay-friendly.

Aurora Park Cottages (☎ 707-942-6733, 877-942-7700; www.aurorapark.com; 1807 Foothill Blvd; cottages incl breakfast $245-275; wi-fi) Six sunny-yellow cottages stand in a row beside flowering gardens. They're immaculate, with polished-wood floors, featherbeds and sundecks. The innkeeper couldn't be nicer. They're close to the road, but quiet at night.

Solage (☎ 707-226-0800, 866-942-7442; www.solagecalistoga.com; 755 Silverado Trail; r $425-625; wi-fi) The latest addition to Calistoga's spa-hotels ups the style factor, with swank semidetached cottages and a glam palm-tree-lined pool. Rooms are austere, with vaulted ceilings, putty-colored walls, zillion-thread-count linens, limestone vanities and pebble-floor showers. The landscaping hasn't grown in, so there's not much patio privacy, but rooms are top-notch.

Also consider these options:

Chelsea Garden Inn (☎ 707-942-0948; www.chelseagardeninn.com; 1443 2nd St; r incl breakfast $195-275; wi-fi) On a quiet street, five floral-print B&B rooms with private entrances and pretty gardens.

Cottage Grove Inn (☎ 707-942-8400, 800-799-2284; www.cottagegrove.com; 1711 Lincoln Ave; cottages $250-395; wi-fi) Romantic cottages for over-40s, with wood-burning fireplaces, two-person tubs and front porches with rocking chairs.

Garnett Creek Inn (☎ 707-942-9797; www.garnettcreekinn.com; r 1139 Lincoln Ave; r $175-270; wi-fi) Small, frilly rooms (think Laura Ashley), but there's a big veranda and in-room breakfast.

Wine Way Inn (☎ 707-942-0680, 800-572-0679; www.winewayinn.com; 1019 Foothill Blvd; r $150-200; wi-fi) Small B&B in 1910 house, owned by a lovely English couple.

Eating

Buster's Southern BBQ (☎ 707-942-5605; www.busterssouthernbbq.com; 1207 Foothill Blvd; dishes $8-10; 9am-8pm Mon-Sat, 10:30am-6pm Sun;) The sheriff eats lunch at this indoor-outdoor barbecue joint, which serves smoky ribs, chicken, tri-tip steak and burgers. Beer and wine.

Hydro Grill (☎ 707-942-9777; 1403 Lincoln Ave; mains $8-19; 8:30am-10pm;) When it's good it's great, but Hydro occasionally misses. Still, we'll return for the (sometimes) awesome grilled artichoke with lime aioli, cornmeal-crusted *chile rellenos*, and grilled-salmon salad. Kids like the burgers and mac and cheese.

Wappo Bar & Bistro (☎ 707-942-4712; www.wappobar.com; 1226b Washington St; lunch $10-15, dinner $17-27) On a warm night, Wappo's flower-filled outdoor patio ranks as the most romantic spot in town. While the 'global cuisine'– a mishmash of Indian, Italian, Thai, French and Spanish – shows creativity, it lacks culinary discipline. Service can be slow, but what a lovely spot to linger. Beer and wine.

All Seasons Bistro (☎ 707-942-9111; www.allseasonsnapavalley.net; 1400 Lincoln Ave; lunch mains $10-15, dinner mains $18-24; lunch Fri-Mon, dinner nightly) The dining room looks like a white-table-cloth soda fountain, but All Seasons makes some of the best food in town, from simple steak-*frites* to composed dishes like corn-meal-crusted scallops with summer succotash, all using sustainably grown ingredients. Great wine list.

Solbar (☎ 707-226-0850; www.solagecalistoga.com; 755 Silverado Trail; lunch $10-20, dinner $18-28) At last Calistoga has a dining room on par with down-valley restaurants. The look is spare, with concrete floors, exposed-wood tables and soaring ceilings. Flavors are clean and bright, maximizing the use of seasonal produce. Each dish is elegantly composed on the plate, with a strong interplay of sweet, salt and acid, as in the wine-braised short-ribs with pungent gremolata and creamy risotto. The chef is a master with fish. Book outside on a warm night.

Calistoga Inn & Brewery (☎ 707-942-4101; www.calistogainn.com; 1250 Lincoln Ave; dishes $12-26) Locals crowd the outdoor beer garden here on Sundays. Midweek we prefer the country dining room and its big oakwood tables, a homey spot for pot roast and other simple American dishes. There's live music on summer weekends.

Also consider:

Checkers (☎ 707-942-9300; 1414 Lincoln Ave; pizzas $8-14, mains $11-16;) Salads, pizza and beer. Good, not great.

Puerto Vallarta (☎ 707-942-6563; 1473 Lincoln Ave; dishes $8-10;) Good burritos.

Drinking

English Garden Tea Room (☎ 707-942-4262; 1107 Cedar St; 10am-7pm) Take your mum to high tea at this tiny tea room with rose-patterned china and silver service.

WINE COUNTRY

WHAT THE...?

When you weary of wine snobs and the parvenu, travel back in time, before the advent of 'Wine Country,' at these left-over pockets of roadside Americana kitsch.

- **Old Faithful Geyser** (right)
- **Pee Wee Golf** (p216)
- **Petrified Forest** (right)
- **Traintown** (p203)

Hydro Grill (☎ 707-942-9777; 1403 Lincoln Ave) Live music plays weekend evenings at this hoppin' corner bar-restaurant.

Solbar (☎ 707-226-0850; 755 Silverado Trail) Sip cocktails and wine on cane sofas beside outdoor fireplaces and a palm-lined pool. Wear white.

Brannan's Grill (☎ 707-942-2233; www.brannansgrill.com; 1374 Lincoln Ave) Calistoga's most handsome restaurant is primarily a steak house, but the mahogany bar is great for martinis, especially on weekends, when jazz combos play.

Susie's Bar (☎ 707-942-6710; 1365 Lincoln Ave) Turn your baseball cap sideways, do shots and shoot pool while the juke box blares classic rock and country and western.

Shopping

Candy Cellar (☎ 707-942-6990; 1367 Lincoln Ave; 10am-9pm) Get a teeth-grinding sugar rush on homemade fudge.

Wine Garage (☎ 707-942-5332; www.winegarage.net; 1020 Foothill Blvd) Every bottle costs under $25 at this cool wine store, formerly a service station.

Calistoga Pottery (☎ 707-942-0216; www.calistogapottery.com; 1001 Foothill Blvd) Winemakers aren't the only artisans in Napa. Watch a potter throw vases, bowls and plates, all for sale.

Ca'toga Galleria d'Arte (☎ 707-942-3900; www.catoga.com; 1206 Cedar St) This gallery specializes in trompe l'oeil painting; on weekends you can tour the artist's over-the-top villa (call ahead).

AROUND CALISTOGA

Bale Grist Mill & Bothe-Napa Valley State Parks

There's good picnicking at **Bale Grist Mill State Historic Park** (☎ 707-963-2236; adult/child under 16 $2/free;), which features a 36ft water-powered mill wheel dating from 1846 – the largest still operating in North America. Watch it grind corn and wheat into flour Saturdays and Sundays; call for times. In early October, look for the living-history festival, **Old Mill Days**.

A mile-long trail leads to adjacent **Bothe-Napa Valley State Park** (☎ 707-942-4575; per car $6; 8am-sunset;), where there's a **swimming pool** (adult/child $3/1; summer only) and lovely hiking through redwood groves and horseback-riding. **Triple Creek Horse Outfit** (☎ 707-996-8566; www.triplecreekhorseoutfit.com) guides 60- and 90-minute rides, April through October, for $60/$70; reservations required.

Admission to one park includes the other. If you're not traveling solo, go to Bothe first, and pay only $6 instead of the per-head charge at Bale Grist Mill.

The mill and both parks are on Hwy 29/128, midway between St Helena and Calistoga.

Old Faithful Geyser

Calistoga's miniversion of Yellowstone's Old Faithful shoots boiling water 60ft to 100ft into the air, every 45 minutes. The vibe is pure roadside Americana, with folksy hand-painted interpretive exhibits, picnicking and a little petting zoo.

The **geyser** (☎ 707-942-6463; www.oldfaithfulgeyser.com; 1299 Tubbs Lane; adult/child under 6yr/child 6-12yr/senior $8/free/3/7; 9am-6pm summer, to 5pm winter;) is 2 miles north of town, off Silverado Trail. Look for discount coupons around town.

Petrified Forest

Three million years ago, a volcanic eruption at nearby Mt St Helens blew down a stand of redwoods between Calistoga and Santa Rosa. The trees fell in the same direction, away from the blast, and were covered in ash and mud. Over the millennia, the mighty giants' trunks turned to stone; gradually the overlay eroded, exposing them. The first stumps were discovered in 1870. A monument marks Robert Louis Stevenson's 1880 visit. He describes it in *The Silverado Squatters*.

The **petrified forest** (☎ 707-942-6667; www.petrifiedforest.org; 4100 Petrified Forest Rd; adult/child/senior $6/3/5; 9am-7pm summer, to 5pm winter) is 5 miles northwest of town off Hwy 128. Check online for 15%-off coupons.

Robert Louis Stevenson State Park

The long-extinct volcanic cone of Mt St Helena marks the valley's end, 8 miles north of Calistoga. The undeveloped **state park**

(☎ 707-942-4575; www.parks.ca.gov; admission free) on Hwy 29 often gets snow in winter.

It's a strenuous 5-mile climb to the peak's 4343ft summit, but what a view – 200 miles on a clear winter's day. Check conditions before setting out. Also consider 2.2-mile one-way Table Rock Trail (go south from the summit parking area) for drop-dead valley views. Temperatures are best in wildflower season, February to May; fall is prettiest, when the vineyards change colors.

The park includes the site of the Silverado Mine where Stevenson and his wife honeymooned in 1880.

Safari West

Giraffes in Wine Country? Whadya know! **Safari West** (☎ 707-579-2551, 800-616-2695; www.safariwest.com; 3115 Porter Creek Rd; adult/child $65/30;) covers 400 acres and protects zebras, cheetahs and other exotic animals, which mostly roam free. See them on a guided three-hour safari in open-sided jeeps; reservations required. You'll also walk thorough an aviary and a lemur condo. The reservations-only café serves lunch and dinner. If you're feeling adventurous, stay overnight in nifty canvas-sided **tent cabins** (cabins incl breakfast $230-255), right in the preserve.

California Flavor

Fresh seasonal produce is a California specialty

JERRY ALEXANDER

Harvest time in Half Moon Bay (p191)

THOMAS W

Could it be mere coincidence that on a map California looks like one big, drooling tongue? The Golden State has seen booms and busts, sunsets and Hollywood starlets come and go, but its shining glory remains the same: California flavor. As you travel from surfer-worthy fish tacos to Olympian gourmet feats on seasonal tasting menus, you'll frequently have cause to compliment the chef. When you do, you'll find that California cooks are generous about sharing credit for a memorable dish with the stellar ingredients brought to them by local producers – many cheesemakers, wineries, farms, ranches and fisheries are credited by name on California menus. Chefs elsewhere often gripe about catering to vegetarians, but California produce is so fresh and flavorful that it's often a menu scene-stealer and doesn't need to be hidden under slabs of meat or heavy sauces.

So how do you wash down a bite of bliss? Discover your new favorite drink in California, from seasonal microbrews at solar-powered Anderson Valley Brewery Co (p270) to audacious cabernets at the latest Frank Gehry–designed Napa Valley project at Hall winery (p227) – and to detox afterwards, perhaps a bracing shot of wheatgrass juice from a SoCal juice bar. Raise a toast to the Californians who made it all possible: Native Americans for their stewardship of these rich coastal lands; farmers, laborers and chefs, who bring seasonal flavors to the table; and the ordinary Californians whose extraordinary palates make any California road trip a nonstop taste adventure.

WETTEST OF THE WEST

Legend has it that the martini was invented in San Francisco when a local lush needed a drink to tide him over on a trip across the Bay to Martinez. A likely story...but hey, we'll drink to that. The 1990s dot-com boom revived retro martini bars, and recently San Francisco distilleries Junipero and 209 Gin have kicked off a full-scale gin comeback. Across the Bay, Hangar vodka and Berkeley-produced Takara sake provide the local raw materials for ever-popular cosmos and sake-tinis. Irish coffee (coffee, cream, sugar and Irish whiskey) is another beloved tradition for foggy North Beach nights, while margaritas (tequila, lime, Cointreau, ice and salt) inspire pub crawls in the balmy Mission.

SAN FRANCISCO BAY AREA

Although San Francisco ballooned from a sleepy cove of 800 in 1849 to a Gold Rush boomtown of 25,000 by 1850, there was only one woman per 100 men – but there were 500 saloons and hundreds of eateries, ranging from ubiquitous Chinese noodle shops to struck-it-rich French fine dining. The first Italian restaurant in America opened in San Francisco's North Beach in 1886, serving the ever-popular cioppino (Dungeness crab stew). Steam-brewing methods pioneered in San Francisco produced signature amber ales that are still on tap across the city.

Even 160 years after that boom went bust, there's still one restaurant for every 28 San Franciscans – that's 10 times more than any other North American city. All that competition keeps chefs innovating and prices lower than you'd find for equivalent dining experiences elsewhere. Chinese, Mexican,

top five TRENDY SF RESTAURANT INGREDIENTS

Meyer lemon
A sweet local citrus, used with or without its thick rind

Toybox carrots
Tiny, flavorful carrots in unexpected hues of purple, yellow and white

Huitlacoche
Corn fungus, a traditional Mexican delicacy

Fennel
Anise-flavored vegetable used for its herbal fronds and crunchy bulb

Gem lettuce
Small lettuce with flavor midway between butter lettuce and mesclun greens

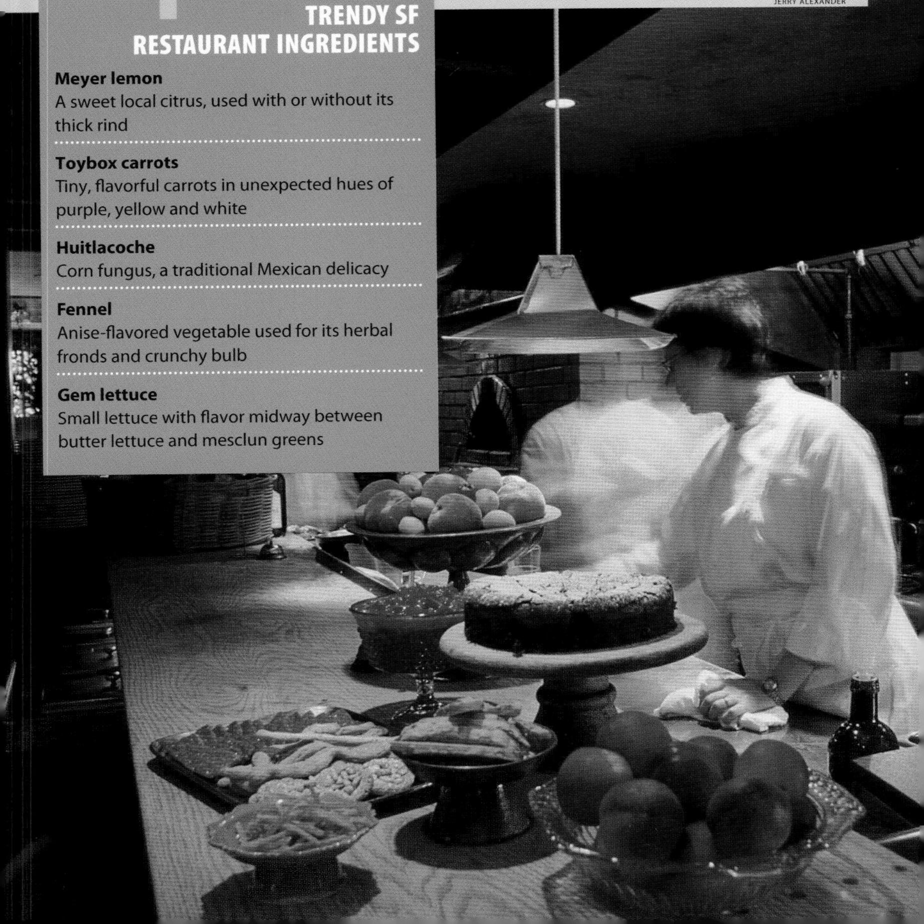

Iconic Berkeley restaurant Chez Panisse (p175)
JERRY ALEXANDER

French and Italian restaurants remain perennial local favorites, along with more recent San Francisco crazes for sushi, tandoori and pho (Vietnamese noodles). San Francisco has more award-winning chefs per capita than any other US city (sorry, New York), but the most iconic local culinary figure is Alice Waters, who in 1971 began converting steakhouse-trained taste buds to local, sustainable fine dining at Berkeley's Chez Panisse (p175). Today the number one SF tourist attraction is no longer the Golden Gate Bridge, but the local, sustainable, seasonal bounty at Bay Area farmers markets.

NORTH COAST & THE SIERRAS

Nature has been kind to this landscape, which manages to be both rugged and lush, yielding bonanzas of mountain honey, wild blackberries, chanterelle mushrooms and other wild-crafted delicacies. Stop by roadside inn restaurants and saloons, and you'll see how Northern California cuisine has catered to equally rugged appetites and downright lushes since the gold-mining days. Lacking the patience for agriculture or families for consolation, miners cultivated a taste for fast food, faster women and strong drink. Takeout, breweries and bordellos flourished; public health did not. But there were also competing culinary forces at work in seasonal, local, wild-crafted Ohlone

Sustainably farmed oysters
Slurp them out of the shell at Hog Island (p123)

Olallieberries
Juicy relatives of the blackberry burst onto the roadside scene from August through October

Wild mushrooms
Appearing on NorCal restaurant menus in November and December

Sustainably farmed abalone
The prized dish of Native Americans, now readily accessible from 15 California coastal farms

Venison
Overpopulation has made deer-herd thinning a necessity, so enjoy venison sausages and dry-rubbed steaks in fall during the hunting season

North Coast delights: ocean-fresh oysters
JERRY ALEXANDER

Farmers markets across the state showcase fresh regional produce

HANAN ISACHAR

and Miwok cuisine. In addition to fishing, hunting game, gathering wild mushrooms and berries, and making bread from acorn flour, these indigenous Californians also tended orchards and cultivated foods.

In the 1970s, San Francisco hippies burned out on the hectic Haight headed back to the land of the North Coast, combining Gold Rush hedonism with the seasonal tendencies of Native American cuisine. Bakeries and breweries flourished as '70s homesteaders introduced healthy wheat germ and hearty microbrews into the NorCal diet. Early adopters of pesticide-free farming, hippie homesteaders created an organic cuisine that was health-minded yet attuned to the immediate needs of the munchies – marijuana remains a major North Coast crop.

THE RICHEST DISH IN CALIFORNIA

One notable holdover from Gold Rush cuisine is Placerville's 'hangtown fry,' a scramble of eggs, bacon and oysters. It may sound like a greasy-spoon special, but this dish was strictly for miners who struck it rich. Oysters were brought 100 miles from San Francisco to Placerville packed in ice, and the bacon arrived packed in salt from the East Coast, but the most expensive ingredients were the eggs, which in 1849 California cost $10 a dozen – the equivalent of $272 today.

WINE COUNTRY

California might still be a Mexican province guzzling Australian wines except for one drunken night in Sonoma in 1846. Under the influence of local wine, a group of frontier rabble-rousers decided to seize the state government from Mexican authorities (p39). To everyone's surprise they succeeded, and California history and Sonoma's reputation for drink were made. One hundred and thirty years later, neighboring Napa Valley kicked off another revolution at the 1976 Paris Tasting, aka the 'World Cup of Wine,' when a Stag's Leap cabernet sauvignon and a Chateau Montelena chardonnay beat home-terroir French favorites.

With the international reputation of California wines came woozy Wine Country visitors in need of food, and local cheesemakers and restaurateurs were quick to oblige. By the 1930s Sonoma was supplying excellent jack cheese to accompany local wine – but local chefs had more unusual pairings in mind. Chef Thomas Keller transformed Yountville's 1900-saloon-turned-

top five TASTIEST WINE-TASTING ROOMS

Mayo Winery Reserve Room (p207)
Savor a seven-course tasting menu with your cab and zin tasting for about a 10th the price of French Laundry

J (p209)
Creative starters and delightful twin bites of sushi to accompany your sparkling-wine sampler

Homewood (p200)
Unconventional blends like the Flying Wizzbanger taste even more outrageous with a chocolate pairing

Marimar Torres (p209)
California goes Catalan with pairings of organic wines and the winegrower's own family-recipe tapas

Copia (p229)
Going back to school sounds delicious at Napa's cultural center, with free cooking demos and wine tastings

World-class wines in the Napa Valley (p224)
JERRY ALEXANDER

California is reknowned for its innovative and sophisticated cuisine BRENT WINEBRENNER

restaurant French Laundry (p233) into an international foodie landmark in 1994, showcasing local produce and casual elegance in multicourse feasts. Other chefs eager to make their names and fortunes among free-spending wine-tasters flocked to the area, and those who offer the best ratio of price to quality are featured in the Wine Country chapter (p194). But for all the airs Wine Country has put on over the years, you can still find respectable cheap Mexican food at Sonoma's Come-to-Jesus Taco Truck (p205).

METRO LOS ANGELES

Most of California's produce is grown in the hot, irrigated Central Valley, south of the Bay Area, but road-tripping foodies tend to bolt through this sunny stretch of fast-food speed traps to reach Los Angeles in time for dinner. Authenticity-trippers know exactly where to go: directly to Koreatown for tender *kalbi* (marinated barbecued beef short ribs) and strong *soju* (barley spirits), East LA for tacos *al pastor* (with marinated fried pork) and margaritas on the rocks, and Little Tokyo for sashimi faceted like diamonds and palate-purifying *junmai* sake.

But what would Los Angeles be without celebrity? Wolfgang Puck launched the celebrity-chef trend when he opened the

TASTY SEAFOOD... BUT IS IT SUSTAINABLE?

To judge your seafood options in California restaurants, download a portable list of best choices and options to avoid (either to your phone or as a wallet-sized printout) from the Seafood Watch Program of the Monterey Bay Aquarium (p455) at www.mbayaq.org/cr/SeafoodWatch.asp.

star-spangled Spago (p557) on the Sunset Strip in 1982, followed by Nobu Matsuhisa of Nobu (with partner Robert De Niro; p557) and most recently by reality-restaurateur Gordon Ramsay, of *Hell's Kitchen* fame, at the London West Hollywood. Being seen at a trendy restaurant may be enough in New York, but in LA it's better to be glimpsed slipping past a VIP lounge rope or dashing through dining rooms to a private chef's table. The drinking and dining experience may seem anticlimactic, especially if you don't recognize any of your fellow VIPs. But this being LA, you can always rescue a night out at mom-and-pop drive-throughs and Hollywood late-night diners that haven't changed since Technicolor was introduced... and hey, isn't that Lindsay Lohan?

top five STAR-STUDDED SOCAL SOCIALS

National Date Festival
Score a famous date at Indio's February festival to its prime local product (p659)

Santa Barbara Vintner's Fest
(www.sbcountywines.com) California's other wine country, as featured in the movie *Sideways* and this April celebration

Taste of the Nation
(www.tasteofthenation.com) June heats up in Culver City with this fundraiser to end child hunger, with chefs including *Top Chef* star Tom Colicchio

American Wine & Food Festival
(www.awff.org) September's glam foodie fundraiser is held (where else?) on the backlot at Universal Studios (p539)

Wine and dine LA
(www.dinela.com) In September, 40 rising star chefs show off and celebrate California wines with creative pairing menus

Historic Bob's Big Boy (p559) in Burbank, LA.
DAVID PEEVERS

North Coast

On northern California's coast, craggy sienna cliffs tower over windswept beaches and rocky coves. The ocean crashes cold and dramatic against the shores. Land of spotted owls, Mary Jane, timber wars, tie-dye and flannel shirts, this is the antithesis of Southern California in almost every way. Expect laid-back, idiosyncratic villages, and hope for the fog to lift so you can be sun-warmed as you roam isolated sand-spits or coastal redwoods.

Considering their proximity to the hubbub of the Bay Area, Sonoma and Mendocino counties remain unspoiled, even as swank B&Bs cater to city folks. The austere coastal bluffs here are some of the most spectacular in the country, and each of the small towns along the way has a distinct feel and local scene.

When you reach the Redwood Empire, where Hwy 1 ends its long trek from Southern California and cuts inland to join Hwy 101, the land along the Pacific – called the Lost Coast – has no highway and is truly one of the state's best-preserved natural gifts. Continue working your way north through Humboldt County and you'll journey beneath towering redwoods, the tallest trees in the world, and reach the small but vibrant harborside cities of Eureka and Arcata.

Coastal lagoons and marshes yield once again to giant, ancient trees and roaming elk, and you're back in the woods, twisting and turning your way toward low-key Del Norte County and its pristine, little-visited redwood forests. This marks the beginning of the Pacific Northwest and the northernmost end of California, a world away from the megalithic economies of the south.

HIGHLIGHTS

- **Most humbling hike** Be magnificently outnumbered by the elk and the owls on the Lost Coast Trail (p282)
- **Coolest art lesson** Find out about the hottest art up and down the coast at the hopping Mendocino Art Center (p260)
- **Most sustainable holiday** Volunteer at the Solar Living Center (p268) in Hopland
- **Funkiest seaside village** Chew the fat with interesting locals at Arena Cove in Point Arena (p256)
- **Most peaceful communion with nature** Listen to the quiet on the fern-laden forest floor of primeval Rockefeller Forest (p278) or Redwood National and State Parks (p292)

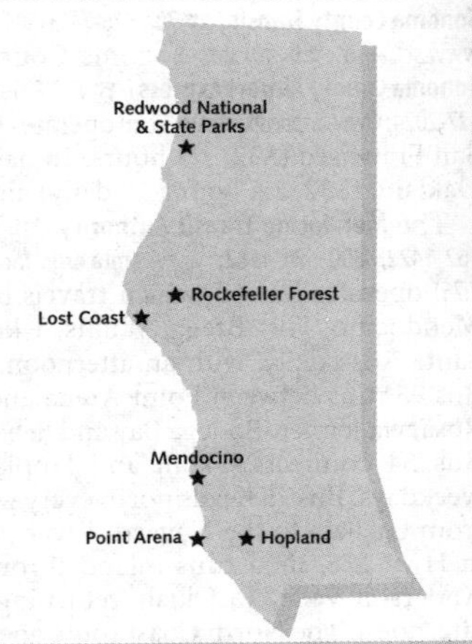

FAST FACTS

Population of Mendocino 1000

Average temperature low/high in Mendocino Jan 47/60°F, Jul 50/71°F

Mendocino to San Francisco 155 miles, 3¼ hours

Mendocino to Los Angeles 530 miles, nine hours

Mendocino to Eureka 145 miles, three hours

Mendocino to Crescent City 230 miles, 4½ hours

GETTING AROUND

Hwy 101 is the faster, inland route. Hwy 1 hugs the coast, then cuts inland and ends at Leggett, where it joins Hwy 101.

Amtrak (☎ 800-872-7245; www.amtrakcalifornia.com) operates the *Coast Starlight* between Los Angeles and Seattle (see p738), with connecting buses to several North Coast towns including Leggett ($56, five hours, two daily) and Garberville ($61, five hours, 2½ daily.

Greyhound (☎ 800-231-2222; www.greyhound.com) runs buses from San Francisco to Santa Rosa ($19, 1¾ hours, one daily), Ukiah, ($32.50, three hours, one daily) Willits ($32.50, 3½ hours, one daily), Rio Dell (near Fortuna, $42, six hours, one daily), Eureka ($42, 6¾ hours, one daily) and Arcata ($42, seven hours, one daily). In Santa Rosa, **Golden Gate Transit** (☎ 707-541-2000, 415-923-2000; www.goldengatetransit.org) bus 80 serves San Rafael ($5.55, 1½ hours) and San Francisco ($8.80, 1¼ hours, 19 times daily), **Sonoma County Transit** (☎ 707-576-7433, 800-345-7433; www.sctransit.com) serves Sonoma County, and **Sonoma County Airport Express** (☎ 707-837-8700, 800-327-2024; www.airportexpressinc.com) operates buses to San Francisco ($32, 2¼ hours, 15 daily) and Oakland ($32, 2¼ hours, 10 daily) airports.

The **Mendocino Transit Authority** (MTA; ☎ 707-462-1422, 800-696-4682; www.4mta.org; fares $3.25-7.75) operates bus 65, which travels between Mendocino, Fort Bragg, Willits, Ukiah and Santa Rosa daily, with an afternoon return. Bus 95 runs between Point Arena and Santa Rosa, via Jenner, Bodega Bay and Sebastopol. Bus 54 connects Ukiah and Hopland on weekdays. Bus 75 heads north every weekday from Gualala to the Navarro River junction at Hwy 128, then runs inland through the Anderson Valley to Ukiah, returning in the afternoon. The North Coast route goes north from Navarro River junction to Albion, Little River, Mendocino and Fort Bragg, Monday to Friday.

North of Mendocino County, the **Redwood Transit System** (☎ 707-443-0826; www.hta.org) operates buses ($2.50) Monday through Saturday between Scotia and Trinidad (2½ hours), stopping en route at Eureka (1¼ hours) and Arcata (1½ hours). **Redwood Coast Transit** (☎ 707-464-9314; www.redwoodcoasttransit.org) runs buses Monday to Saturday between Crescent City, Klamath ($1, one hour, two daily) and Arcata ($20, two hours, two daily), with numerous stops along the way.

COASTAL HIGHWAY 1

Down south it's called the 'PCH,' or Pacific Coast Hwy, but North Coast locals simply call it 'Hwy 1.' However you label it, say hello to the fabulous coast road, which cuts a serpentine course on isolated cliffs high above the crashing surf. Stop along the way to comb fog-shrouded beaches, gaze at churning white-caps and listen for the braying of sea lions on the wind. From December to April, keep your eyes peeled for migrating gray whales; you should be able to spot them from almost any headland.

Coastal accommodations (including campgrounds) fill up from Memorial Day to Labor Day and on fall weekends, and often require two-night stays, so reserve ahead. Try to visit during spring or fall, especially September and October when the fog lifts, the ocean sparkles and most other visitors have gone home.

BODEGA BAY

pop 1450

Perched on gorgeous windswept coastal bluffs, the village of Bodega Bay attracts visitors for its nearby beaches, tide pools, whale-watching, fishing, surfing and seafood. Decidedly laid-back, here surfers mingle with visiting city slickers, all soaking up the beauty of this peaceful hamlet.

Originally inhabited by the Pomo people, the bay takes its name from Juan Francisco de la Bodega y Quadra, captain of the Spanish sloop *Sonora*, which entered the bay in 1775. The area was then settled by Russians in the early 19th century, and farms were established to grow wheat for the Russian fur-trapping empire, which stretched from Alaska all the

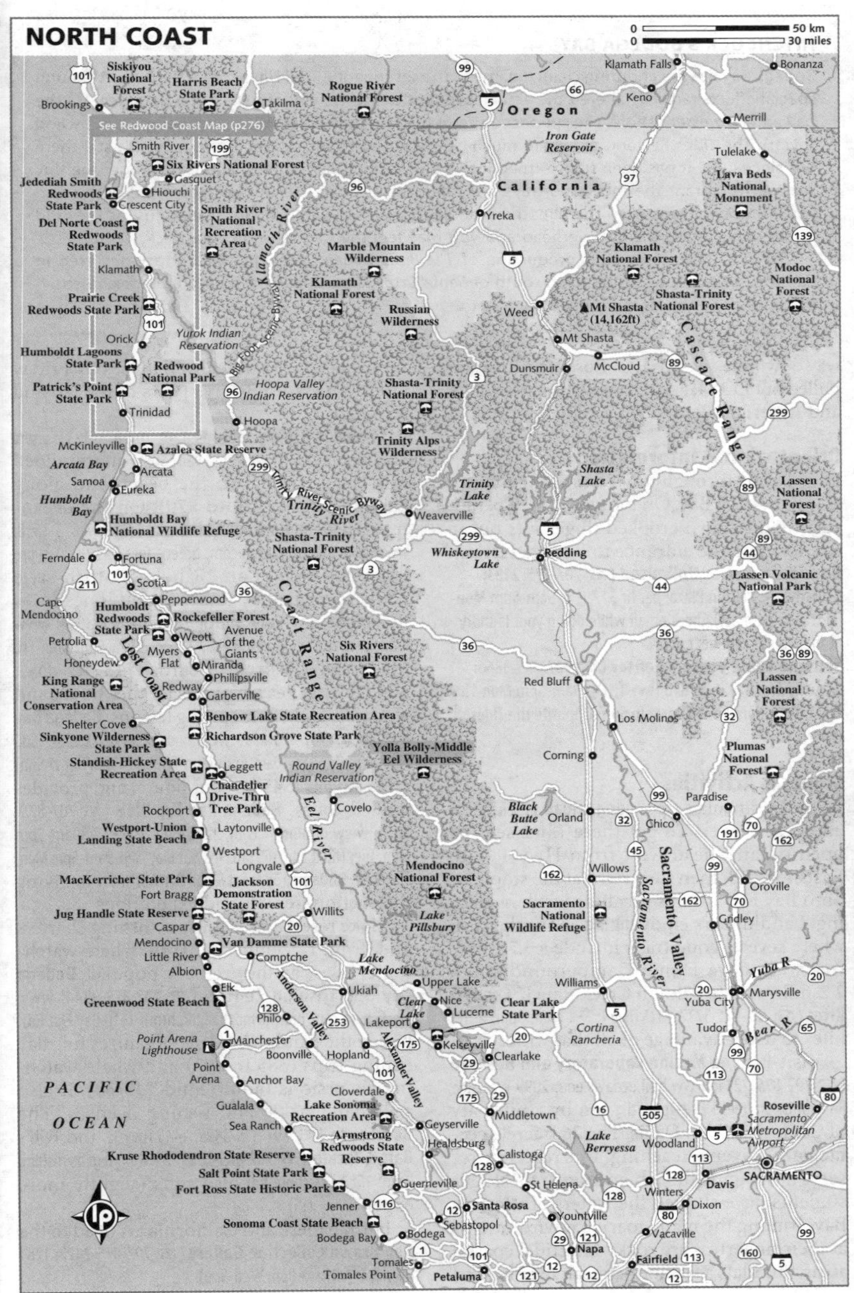
NORTH COAST
0 50 km
0 30 miles
See Redwood Coast Map (p276)
Oregon
California
PACIFIC
OCEAN
Siskiyou National Forest
Harris Beach State Park
Rogue River National Forest
Brookings
Takilma
Klamath Falls
Bonanza
Keno
Merrill
Iron Gate Reservoir
Tulelake
Lava Beds National Monument
Smith River
Six Rivers National Forest
Gasquet
Hiouchi
Jedediah Smith Redwoods State Park
Crescent City
Del Norte Coast Redwoods State Park
Smith River National Recreation Area
Klamath River
Yreka
Marble Mountain Wilderness
Klamath National Forest
Modoc National Forest
Shasta-Trinity National Forest
Klamath
Prairie Creek Redwoods State Park
Big Foot Scenic Byway
Russian Wilderness
Weed
Mt Shasta (14,162ft)
Mt Shasta
Orick
Yurok Indian Reservation
Humboldt Lagoons State Park
Redwood National Park
Patrick's Point State Park
Trinidad
Hoopa Valley Indian Reservation
Hoopa
Dunsmuir
McCloud
Cascade Range
Trinity Alps Wilderness
McKinleyville
Azalea State Reserve
Arcata Bay
Arcata
Samoa
Eureka
Humboldt Bay
Trinity River Scenic Byway
Trinity River
Trinity Lake
Shasta Lake
Lassen National Forest
Weaverville
Humboldt Bay National Wildlife Refuge
Whiskeytown Lake
Redding
Ferndale
Fortuna
Scotia
Lassen Volcanic National Park
Cape Mendocino
Pepperwood
Humboldt Redwoods State Park
Rockefeller Forest
Coast Range
Petrolia
Weott
Avenue of the Giants
Myers Flat
Honeydew
Miranda
Lost Coast
Phillipsville
Six Rivers National Forest
King Range National Conservation Area
Redway
Garberville
Red Bluff
Shelter Cove
Benbow Lake State Recreation Area
Los Molinos
Sinkyone Wilderness State Park
Richardson Grove State Park
Standish-Hickey State Recreation Area
Leggett
Yolla Bolly-Middle Eel Wilderness
Round Valley Indian Reservation
Corning
Plumas National Forest
Chandelier Drive-Thru Tree Park
Rockport
Covelo
Paradise
Westport-Union Landing State Beach
Laytonville
Eel River
Black Butte Lake
Orland
Chico
Westport
Longvale
Willows
Sacramento Valley
Sacramento River
MacKerricher State Park
Jackson Demonstration State Forest
Mendocino National Forest
Oroville
Fort Bragg
Jug Handle State Reserve
Willits
Lake Pillsbury
Sacramento National Wildlife Refuge
Gridley
Caspar
Mendocino
Van Damme State Park
Little River
Comptche
Albion
Lake Mendocino
Yuba R
Elk
Anderson Valley
Ukiah
Upper Lake
Williams
Marysville
Greenwood State Beach
Clear Lake
Nice
Lucerne
Clear Lake State Park
Yuba City
Philo
Lakeport
Cortina Rancheria
Tudor
Point Arena Lighthouse
Manchester
Alexander Valley
Kelseyville
Bear R
Boonville
Hopland
Clearlake
Point Arena
Anchor Bay
Cloverdale
Gualala
Lake Sonoma Recreation Area
Middletown
Roseville
Sea Ranch
Geyserville
Lake Berryessa
Sacramento Metropolitan Airport
Armstrong Redwoods State Reserve
Healdsburg
Woodland
Kruse Rhododendron State Reserve
Calistoga
SACRAMENTO
Salt Point State Park
Guerneville
Davis
Fort Ross State Historic Park
St Helena
Winters
Jenner
Santa Rosa
Dixon
Sebastopol
Yountville
Sonoma Coast State Beach
Bodega
Bodega Bay
Vacaville
Napa
Fairfield
Tomales
Tomales Point
Petaluma

HITCHCOCK'S BODEGA BAY

Bodega Bay has the enduring claim to fame as the setting for Alfred Hitchcock's *The Birds*. Although special effects radically altered the actual layout of the town, you can still get a good feel for the bay and its western shore, the supposed site of the farm owned by Mitch Brenner (played by Rod Taylor). The Tides Restaurant, where much avian-caused havoc occurs in the movie, is still there but since 1962 it has been transformed into a vast restaurant complex, and is no longer the tiny seaside restaurant the movie portrays. Venture 5 miles inland to the tiny town of Bodega and you'll find two icons from the film: the schoolhouse and the church. Both stand just as they did in the movie – see a crow overhead and you may feel the hair raise on your neck.

Coincidentally, right after production of *The Birds* began, a real-life bird attack occurred in Capitola, the sleepy seaside town south of Santa Cruz. Thousands of seagulls ran amok, destroying property and attacking people.

way down the coast to Fort Ross. The Russians pulled out in 1842, abandoning fort and farms, and American settlers moved in.

Orientation & Information

Hwy 1 runs through town and along the east side of Bodega Bay. On the west side, a peninsula resembling a crooked finger juts out to sea, forming the entrance to Bodega Harbor.

Business Services Unlimited (☎ 707-875-2183; 1400 Hwy 1, Pelican Plaza; per hr $12; ⏰ 9am-5pm Mon-Fri, 10am-2pm Sat) Check email while doing your laundry at the launderette next door.

Sonoma Coast Visitors Center (☎ 707-875-3866; www.bodegabay.com; 850 Hwy 1; ⏰ 9am-5pm Mon-Thu & Sat, 9am-6pm Fri, 10am-5pm Sun) Opposite the Tides Wharf.

Sights & Activities

At the peninsula's tip, **Bodega Head** rises 265ft above sea level. To get there (and see the open ocean), head west from Hwy 1 onto Eastshore Rd, then turn right at the stop sign onto Bay Flat Rd. It's great for whale-watching. Landlubbers enjoy **hiking** above the surf, where several good trails include a 3.75-mile trek to Bodega Dunes Campground and a 2.2-mile walk to Salmon Creek Ranch. **Candy & Kites** (☎ 707-875-3777; 1415 Hwy 1; ⏰ 10am-5pm) sells kites to take advantage of all that wind.

Visit **Bodega Marine Laboratory and Reserve** (☎ 707-875-2211; www.bml.ucdavis.edu; 2099 Westside Rd; admission free; ⏰ 2-4pm Fri), run by University of California (UC) Davis. The 263-acre, spectacularly diverse teaching and research reserve surrounds the lab and since the 1920s students have studied the waters off Bodega Bay. Among the many marine environments at their fingertips are rocky intertidal coastal areas, mudflats and sandflats, salt marsh, sand dunes and freshwater wetlands. On Friday afternoons docents give tours of the lab and its aquaria.

Chanslor Riding Stables (☎ 707-875-3333; www.chanslor.com; 2660 Hwy 1; ⏰ 9am-5pm) offers guided horseback riding on the beach and along Salmon Creek ($30 to $70). On the oceanfront, **Bodega Harbour Golf Links** (☎ 707-875-3538; www.bodegaharbourgolf.com; greens fees $45-90; ⏰ pro shop 6:30am-5pm) is an 18-hole Scottish-style course designed by Robert Trent Jones Jr.

Bodega Bay Surf Shack (☎ 707-875-3944; www.bodegabaysurf.com; 1400 Hwy 1; ⏰ 10am-6pm Mon-Fri, 9am-7pm Sat & Sun) rents boards ($13 per day), windsurfing gear, bicycles ($5 per hour) and wet suits, and offers surfing lessons. **Bodega Bay Kayak** (☎ 707-875-8899; www.bodegabaykayak.com; 1580 Eastshore Rd; ⏰ 10am-6pm Mon-Fri, 9am-7pm Sat & Sun) rents kayaks ($45 for four hours) and provides guided tours. **Bodega Bay Pro Dive** (☎ 707-875-3054; www.bbprodive.com; 1275 Hwy 1; ⏰ 7:30am-5pm Mon, Tue, Thu & Sun, to 7pm Fri & Sat May-Sep, 9am-5pm Mon, Thu & Fri, 7:30am to 5pm Sat & Sun Oct-Apr) offers diving instruction, rentals and expeditions.

Make reservations for sportfishing charters and, from December to April, whale-watching cruises, as they're very popular. **Bodega Bay Sportfishing Center** (☎ 707-875-3344; www.usafishing.com/bodegasportfishing.html; 1410 Bay Flat Rd), beside the Sandpiper Cafe, organizes full-day fishing trips ($85 to $95) and whale-watching excursions (adult/child $35/30); it also sells bait, tackle and fishing licenses. The **Boathouse** (☎ 707-875-3495; 1445 Hwy 1) and **Will's Bait & Tackle** (☎ 707-875-2323; www.bodegabayfishing.com; 1580 Eastshore Rd) also runs (slightly more expensive) trips.

For Japanese and California art head to the **Ren Brown Collection Gallery** (☎ 707-875-2922; 1781 Hwy 1; ⏰ 10am-5pm Wed-Sun).

Pick up the excellent *Farm Trails* (www.farmtrails.org) guide at the Sonoma Coast Visitors Center to tour local ranches, orchards, farms and apiaries.

Festivals & Events

The **Bodega Bay Fishermen's Festival** (☎ 707-875-3866; www.bbfishfest.com) in April is the big annual event and includes the blessing of the fleet, a flamboyant parade of vessels, an arts-and-crafts fair, kite-flying and feasting. The **Bodega Bay Grange Crab Cioppino Feed** (☎ 707-875-3695) and the Tide Restaurant's **Dungeness Crab Feed** (☎ 707-875-3652) occur in January.

Sleeping

Branscomb's Bodega Bay Inn (☎ 707-875-3388, 888-875-8733; www.bodegabayinn.com; 1588 Eastshore Rd; r incl breakfast $70-220; wi-fi) Local art fills this converted house, packed with eclectic, folksy furnishings. The big garden courtyard is a blooming treat.

Bodega Harbor Inn (☎ 707-875-3594; www.bodegaharborinn.com; 1345 Bodega Ave; r $80-155) Half a block past Hwy 1, this modest blue-and-white shingled hotel is furnished with both real and faux antiques and has a cheery feel. One room has wheelchair access.

Bodega Bay Lodge & Spa (☎ 707-875-3525, 888-875-2250; www.bodegabaylodge.com; 103 Hwy 1; r $235-360; 💻 🏊) Bodega's best, this small oceanfront resort has indulgent treats, such as evening wine tastings, ocean-view swimming pool, whirlpool spa and fitness club. Luxurious rooms overlook marshland and dunes to the sea beyond, some have fireplaces. The fancy Duck Club restaurant is located here.

Campgrounds fill up early in the day. **Sonoma County Regional Park** (☎ information 707-875-3540, reservations 707-565-2267; www.sonoma-county.org/parks; sites $20) operates **Doran Park** (201 Doran Beach Rd), which is best for tents, and **Westside Regional Park** (2400 Westshore Rd), best for RVs. Both have windy exposures, beaches, hot showers and boat ramps.

Eating & Drinking

Dog House (☎ 707-875-2441; 573 Hwy 1; dishes $5-9; 🕑 11am-6pm) Load up on Vienna beef dogs, hand-cut fries and *real* shakes made with hand-scooped ice cream. There's even a view.

Spud Point Crab Company (☎ 707-875-9472; 1860 Westshore Rd; dishes $7-10; 🕑 9am-5pm Thu-Tue) In the classic tradition of dockside crab shacks, you can get sandwiches and salty-sweet crab cocktails served at picnic tables overlooking the marina.

Sandpiper Dockside Cafe & Restaurant (☎ 707-875-2278; 1410 Bay Flat Rd; mains $12-20; 🕑 8am-8pm) Popular with the locals, Sandpiper serves breakfast, straightforward seafood with a water-level view of the bay and *great* chowder. To get there, turn seaward from Hwy 1 onto Eastshore Rd and go straight at the stop sign to the marina.

Terrapin Creek Cafe & Restaurant (☎ 707-875-2700; 1580 Eastshore Dr; mains $18-20; 🕑 lunch Thu-Sun, dinner Wed-Sun; V) This colorful little café, formerly the renowned Seaweed Cafe, is still dedicated to preserving slow food using farm-fresh greens, seafood and poultry, most from within 30 miles of the restaurant. Try everything from braised organic tofu to chicken and dumplings with a twist.

Duck Club (☎ 707-875-3525; 103 Hwy 1; breakfast $9-13, dinner mains $18-35; 🕑 breakfast & dinner) The town's fanciest restaurant, in the Bodega Bay Lodge, serves a loosely Cal-French menu. It's the kind of place you could take your in-laws – delicious and predictable.

Gourmet Au Bay (☎ 707-875-9875; 913 Hwy 1; 🕑 11am-6pm Thu-Tue) Sit on the back deck of this wine bar and sniff salt air with your zinfandel.

For dockside seafood, **Tides Wharf & Restaurant** (☎ 707-875-3652; 835 Hwy 1; mains breakfast $6-12, lunch $12-22, dinner $16-25) and **Lucas Wharf Restaurant & Bar** (☎ 707-875-3522; 595 Hwy 1; mains $15-25; 🕑 lunch & dinner) both have views, clam chowder, fried fish and coleslaw.

SONOMA COAST STATE BEACH

Stretching 17 miles north from Bodega Head to Vista Trail, glorious **Sonoma Coast State Beach** (☎ 707-875-3483) is actually a series of beaches separated by sere, beautiful rocky headlands. Some beaches are tiny, hidden in little coves, while others stretch far and wide. Most of the beaches are connected by vista-studded coastal **hiking trails** that wind along the bluffs.

Heading north along the coast, some of the more exquisite beaches – but how do you judge?! – include **Bodega Dunes**; 2-mile **Salmon Creek Beach**; sandy **Portuguese** and **Schoolhouse Beaches**; **Duncan's Landing**, where small boats unload; **Shell Beach**, for tide-pooling and beachcombing; and impressive **Goat Rock**, with its harbor-seal colony at the mouth of the Russian River.

The surf is often too treacherous to wade. Keep an eye on children.

A mile north of Bodega Bay, pretty **Bodega Dunes Campground** (☎ 800-444-7275; www.reserveamerica.com; tent & RV sites $25) has high dunes and hot showers. Another 5 miles north, year-round **Wright's Beach Campground** (☎ 800-444-7275; www.reserveamerica.com; tent & RV sites $25-35) has popular beachside sites but they lack privacy.

On Willow Creek Rd, inland from Hwy 1 on the southern side of the Russian River Bridge, are two beautiful first-come, first-served environmental campgrounds, Willow Creek and Pomo Canyon (tent sites $20), under a cathedral-like grove of second-growth redwoods. To reach the sites, walk the **Pomo Canyon trail** and emerge into wildflower-studded meadows with exquisite views of the Russian River and vistas south as far as Pt Reyes on a clear day. Willow Creek has no water; Pomo Canyon has cold-water faucets. Both are usually open April to November.

JENNER

pop 254

Perched on the hills looking out to the Pacific and above the mouth of the Russian River, tiny, quiet Jenner offers convenient access to the coast and the Russian River wine region (see p208). A **harbor-seal colony** sits at the river's mouth; pups are born from March to August. Heading north on Hwy 1 you will begin driving on one of the most beautiful, windy stretches of California highway. You'll also probably lose cell-phone service – a blessing?

Jenner Inn & Cottages (☎ 707-865-2377, 800-732-2377; www.jennerinn.com; 10400 Hwy 1; r creekside $108-178, ocean-view $168-278, cottages $188-278; 💻) offers quaint riverside cottages and ocean-view guestrooms. Rates include breakfast and afternoon tea. Some are pet-friendly.

our pick River's End (☎ 707-865-2484; www.rivers-end.com; 11048 Hwy 1; mains lunch $13-26, dinner $25-39; 🕒 lunch & dinner Thu-Mon; Ⓥ) Unwind in style at the picture-perfect restaurant, perched on a cliff overlooking the river's mouth and the grand sweep of the Pacific Ocean. It serves world-class meals at world-class prices, but you could also consider simply sharing a delectable appetizer or dessert with an award-winning glass of wine, and watching the sun set in the silence. Its ocean-view cottages and comfortable rooms have no TVs or phones (rooms and cottages $130 to $175).

FORT ROSS STATE HISTORIC PARK

In March 1812, a group of 25 Russians and 80 Alaskans (including members of the Kodiak and Aleutian tribes) built a wooden fort here, near a Kashaya Pomo village. The southernmost outpost of the 19th-century Russian fur trade on America's Pacific coast, Fort Ross was established as a base for sea-otter hunting operations and trade with Alta California, and for growing crops for Russian settlements in Alaska. The Russians dedicated the fort in August 1812 and occupied it until 1842, when it was abandoned because the sea otter population had been decimated and agricultural production had never taken off.

Today, 11 miles north of Jenner, on a beautiful point, **Fort Ross State Historic Park** (☎ 707-847-3286; 19005 Hwy 1; per car $6; 🕒 10am-4:30pm) presents an accurate reconstruction of the fort. The original buildings were sold, dismantled and carried off to Sutter's Fort (p422) during the Gold Rush. The **visitors center** (☎ 707-847-3437) has historical displays and an excellent bookshop on Californian and Russian history and nature. Ask about hikes to the Russian cemetery.

On **Fort Ross Heritage Day**, the last Saturday in July, costumed volunteers bring the fort's history to life; check the website or call for other special events.

Reef Campground (☎ 707-847-3286; day use $6, tent & RV sites $15; 🕒 Apr-Oct), 2 miles south of the park, has first-come, first-served campsites (cold water, no showers) in a sheltered seaside gully beneath redwoods.

Timber Cove Inn (☎ 707-847-3231, 800-987-8319; www.timbercoveinn.com; 21780 N Hwy 1; r midweek/weekend from $78/110, r with ocean-view from $178/222), a dramatic and quirky '60s-modern seaside inn, was once a top-of-the-line luxury lodge but today is rather plain. The architectural shell is still stunning and the views gorgeous. You'll either love it or hate it.

Stillwater Cove Regional Park (☎ information 707-847-3245, reservations 707-565-2267; www.sonoma-county.org/parks; 22455 N Hwy 1; tent & RV sites $20), 2 miles north of Timber Cove, has hot showers and hiking under Monterey pines. Sites 1, 2, 4, 6, 9 and 10 have ocean views.

SALT POINT STATE PARK

Sandstone cliffs drop precipitously down to the sea at the 6000-acre **Salt Point State Park** (☎ 707-847-3221, 800-444-7275; day use $6). Hiking trails head inland to crisscross grasslands and wooded hills, connecting pygmy forests and coastal coves rich with tidepools. The park is bisected by the San Andreas fault – the rock on the east side of the park is vastly different from that on the west. The notable geology includes *tafonis* (honeycombed-sandstone formations) near Gerstle Cove.

For views of the pristine coastline, walk to the platform overlooking **Sentinel Rock**; it's just a short stroll from the Fisk Mill Cove parking lot, at the park's north end. Just south, **Stump Beach** has picnic areas with fire pits. Further south, look for seals lazing at **Gerstle Cove Marine Reserve**, one of California's first underwater parks; tread lightly around tidepools, and don't lift the rocks: even a glimpse of sunlight can kill some critters.

If you're here in spring, a visit to **Kruse Rhododendron State Reserve** (☎ 707-847-3221) is a must. Growing abundantly in the forest's filtered light, the rhododendrons reach heights of over 30ft, with magnificent displays of pink blossoms; turn east from Hwy 1 onto Kruse Ranch Rd, then follow the signs.

Two campgrounds, **Woodside** and **Gerstle Cove** (☎ 800-444-7275; www.reserveamerica.com; day use $6, tent & RV sites $25), both signposted off Hwy 1, have cold water. Woodside is protected by Monterey pines; Gerstle Cove's trees burned a decade ago, so it's more exposed. Walk-in **environmental campsites** (sites $15) are half a mile from the parking area, on Woodside campground's east side.

The **Salt Point Lodge** (☎ 707-847-3234, 800-956-3437; www.saltpointlodgebarandgrill.com; 23255 Hwy 1; r $120-130) has basic motel rooms, some with views, and a restaurant.

SEA RANCH

The upmarket subdivision of Sea Ranch sprawls understatedly along the coast for 10 miles. Strict zoning laws require that houses are constructed of weathered wood only, so despite its size, the scale and feel is windswept-coast. Except for a lodge and small store, it's almost entirely residential. There's no commercial area, so for gasoline go to Gualala.

After years of litigation, public throughways onto private beaches have been legally mandated. Hiking trails lead from roadside parking lots to the sea and along the bluffs (don't trespass on adjacent lands, though). **Stengel Beach** (Hwy 1 mileage marker 53.96) has a beach-access staircase, **Walk-On Beach** (mileage marker 56.53) provides wheelchair access and **Shell Beach** (mileage marker 55.24) also has beach-access stairs; parking costs $4 and no RVs or trailers are allowed. For hiking details, including maps, contact the **Sea Ranch Association** (☎ 707-785-2444; www.tsr a.org).

Sea Ranch Lodge (☎ 707-785-2371, 800-732-7262; www.searanchlodge.com; 60 Sea Walk Dr; r incl breakfast $180-400; wi-fi), a marvel of '60s-modern California architecture, has spacious, luxurious rooms, many with dramatic views to the ocean; some have hot tubs and fireplaces. At the time of writing, the entire lodge was slated for teardown and rebuild in an even more decadent vein. The fine contemporary **restaurant** (mains lunch $12-16, dinner $22-26; 🕑 8am-9pm; Ⓥ) serves everything from duck breast to local fish tacos. North of the lodge you'll see Sea Ranch's iconic nondenominational chapel; it's on the inland side of Hwy 1, mileage marker 55.66.

Depending on the season, it can be surprisingly affordable to rent a house in Sea Ranch; contact **Rams Head Realty** (☎ 707-785-2427, 800-785-3455; www.ramshead-realty.com), **Sea Ranch Rentals** (☎ 707-884-4235; www.searanchrentals.com), **Sea Ranch Vacation Rentals** (☎ 800-643-8899; www.searanch getaway.com) or **Sea Ranch Escape** (☎ 888-732-7262; www.searanch escape.com).

For crusty artisanal breads and delicious pastries, visit **Two Fish Baking Co** (☎ 707-785-2443; 355090 Verdant View Dr; 🕑 7am-2pm Wed-Sun), off Annapolis Rd.

GUALALA

pop 2030

Founded as a lumber-mill town during the 1860s, bustling, tiny Gualala is the region's commercial center. **Redwood Coast Chamber of Commerce** (☎ 707-884-1080, 800-778-5252; www.red woodcoastchamber.com) has local business information. The **Dolphin Arts Gallery** (☎ 707-884-3896; 39225 Hwy 1; 🕑 10am-5pm), behind the Gualala Hotel, has maps and limited information.

Inland along Old State Rd, at the south end of town, **Gualala Arts Center** (☎ 707-884-1138; www .gualalaarts.org; 🕑 9am-4pm Mon-Fri, noon-4pm Sat & Sun), beautifully built entirely by volunteers, hosts changing exhibitions, organizes the Art in the Redwoods Festival in late August and has loads of info on art in Mendocino County.

The 195-acre **Gualala Point Regional Park** (☎ 707-785-2377, reservations 707-565-2267; www .sonoma-county.org/parks; 42401 Hwy 1; day use $5, tent & RV sites $20), a mile south of town, has good camping facilities under the redwoods and wooded hiking trails up the sandy banks of the Gualala River.

In summer a sand spit forms at the mouth of the river, cutting it off from the ocean and turning it into a warm-water lake. **Adventure Rents** (☎ 707-884-4386, 888-881-4386; www.adventurerents.com) rents canoes and kayaks and provides instruction.

Inland along Old State Rd you can camp and hike at **Gualala River Redwood Park** (☎ 707-884-3533; www.gualalapark.com; day use $6, tent & RV sites $22-42; Memorial Day-Labor Day).

Ocean-view inns line the main drag. The first choice is the straightforward **Surf Motel** (☎ 707-884-3571, 888-451-7873; 39170 S Hwy 1; r $95-120, r with ocean views $135-179), which has cute touches like denim bedspreads.

There's no place like **St Orres Inn** (☎ 707-884-3303; www.saintorres.com; 36601 Hwy 1; B&B $95-135, cottages from $140), famous for its unusual Russian-inspired architecture: dramatic rough-hewn timbers and copper domes. On the property's 90 acres, hand-built cottages range from rustic to luxurious. The inn's fine **restaurant** (☎ 707-884-3335; mains $40; open dinner) serves inspired California cuisine in one of the coast's most romantic rooms.

Hit **Laura's Bakery & Taqueria** (☎ 707-884-3175; 38411 Robinson Reef Rd at Hwy 1; mains $7-12; 7am-7pm Mon-Sat; V) for a spicy fix of Mexican food, at the north end of town. Slow-smoked meats and Texas-style, wood-pit barbecue are the specialties at **Bones Roadhouse** (☎ 707-884-1188; 38920 S Hwy 1; mains $9-18; lunch & dinner), where tin mobiles hang from the ceiling and rustic Americana make the place a living sculpture.

Everybody loves **Pangaea** (☎ 707-884-9669; 39165 S Hwy 1; mains $27-35; dinner Wed-Sun; V), where the eclectic, soulful menu features dishes like pork confit with polenta, and halibut with corn succotash. Make reservations.

Get freshies at the **farmers market** (Gualala Community Center; 10am-12:30pm Sat Jun-Oct).

NORTH COAST

ANCHOR BAY

pop 500

Quiet Anchor Bay has several inns south of town, a tiny shopping center and, heading north, a string of secluded, hard-to-find beaches. It makes an excellent jumping-off point for exploring the area.

Seven miles north of town, pull off at mileage marker 11.41 for **Schooner Gulch** (☎ 707-937-5804). A trail into the forest leads down cliffs to a sandy beach with tidepools. Bear right at the fork in the trail to reach iconic **Bowling Ball Beach**, the next beach north, where at low tide rows of big, round rocks resemble bowling balls. Consult tide tables for Arena Cove. The forecast low tide must be lower than +1.5ft on the tide chart; otherwise the rocks remain covered with water.

Mar Vista Cottages (☎ 707-884-3522, 877-855-3522; www.marvistamendocino.com; 35101 S Hwy 1; 1-bedroom cottages $155-245, 2-bedroom cottages $255-295;) is an experience. The rambling 9-acre grounds hold barbecues, a redwood soaking tub, goats and an organic vegetable garden (human grazing encouraged). Simple, spotless, retro-cozy 1930s vacation cottages have old-fashioned kitchens and sumptuously comfy beds. There's a great beach across the road. Dogs welcome.

Overlook the synthetic flowers and acrylic decor at **Whale Watch Inn** (☎ 707-884-3667; www.whalewhatchinn.com; 35100 S Hwy 1; r incl breakfast $180-300;) and you'll see perhaps the best views of any hotel along the coast, and it's got a private beach. The octagonal common lounge with fireplace is the perfect place to unwind.

Perched on an inland hillside beneath towering trees, surrounded by lovely gardens, **North Coast Country Inn** (☎ 707-884-4537, 800-959-4537; www.northcoastcountryinn.com; 34591 S Hwy 1; r incl breakfast $195-225;) has a gregarious owner, a hot tub, and six spacious country-style rooms with fireplaces, board games and private entrances.

Stock up on veggies and organics at **Anchor Bay Store** (☎ 707-884-4245; Hwy 1; 8am-7pm). There are two so-so eateries next door.

POINT ARENA

pop 400

This laid-back little town combines creature comforts with relaxed, eclectic California living. It's a great place to chill for a few days and soak up the local rhythms. Sit by the docks a mile west of town at Arena Cove and watch surfers mingle with fishermen and hippies.

The **public library** (☎ 707-882-3114; 225 Main St; noon-6pm Mon-Fri, to 3pm Sat) has free internet access.

Two miles north of town, 1908 **Point Arena Lighthouse** (☎ 707-882-2777; www.pointarenalighthouse.com; adult/child $5/1; 10am to 3.30pm) stands 10 stories high and is the only lighthouse in California you can ascend. Check in at the museum, then climb the 145 steps to the top and see the Fresnel lens

THAR SHE BLOWS!

Every year, from December to February, the California Gray Whale (*Eschrictius robustus*) makes its steady journey down the coast from its summer feeding ground in the Arctic to breeding grounds in Baja California. From mid-March to April, they return north, taking the 12,000-mile round-trip at a steady 4mph to 5mph, sometimes for up to 20 hours per day. Once near extinction with only 1000 at the turn of the 19th century, they were protected in 1937 by international agreement, and now number as many as 20,000. Their Atlantic and Korean brethren have not been so lucky.

Watch for spouts, sounding and breaching whales and pods. Anywhere coastal will do, but following are some of the north coast's hottest watching spots:

- Bodega Head (p250)
- Mendocino Headlands State Park (p260)
- Jug Handle State Reserve (p263)
- MacKerricher State Park (p266)
- Shelter Cove & The Lost Coast (p280)
- Trinidad Head Trail (p291)
- Klamath River Overlook (p295)

and the jaw-dropping view. At the time of writing the lighthouse was going through $1.5-million renovations.

For fabulous bird-watching, hiking on terraced rock past sea caves and access to hidden coves, head 1 mile down Lighthouse Rd from Hwy 1 and look for the Bureau of Land Management (BLM) signs on the left indicating the 1132-acre **Stornetta Public Lands** (☎ 707-468-4000).

Visit the **B Bryan Preserve** (☎ 707-882-2297; www.bbryanpreserve.com; cottage $165) for a glimpse of zebra and antelope. Reserve ahead for the 1½ hour tour (adult/child $20/10).

The **Sea Shell Inn** (☎ 707-882-2000; 135 Main St; s & d $55-70, tr $90; wi-fi) is one of the cheapest motels within a hundred miles.

A cluster of small, modern rooms overlook Arena Cove at friendly **Wharf Master's Inn** (☎ 707-882-3171, 800-932-4031; www.wharfmasters.com; 785 Port Rd; r $85-195;). Next door, soak up old-world oceanside charm at the **Coast Guard House Inn** (☎ 707-882-2442; www.coastguardhouse.com; 695 Arena Cove; r $155-225), a 1901 Cape Cod–style house and cottage, with water-view rooms.

The plain three-bedroom former **Coast Guard homes** (☎ 707-882-2777; houses $125-210), at the lighthouse, make for a quiet, wind-swept getaway.

Lighthouse Pointe (☎ 707-882-2440; 22900 Shoreline Hwy; tent/RV sites $30/45), at the turnoff from Hwy 1, has hot showers, a convenience store, laundry and hot tub.

Carlini's Cafe (☎ 707-882-2942; 206 Main St; dishes $5-8; breakfast & lunch Thu-Tue), a warm, friendly diner, serves delicious breakfasts. Kenny at **Pizzas N Cream** (☎ 707-882-1900; 790 Port Rd; pizzas $10-18; lunch & dinner; V), in Arena Cove, whips up exquisite pizzas and fresh salads – ice cream, too!

our pick **Franny's Cup and Saucer** (☎ 707-882-2500; 213 Main St; pastries $1-5; 8am-4pm Wed-Sat; V) is like entering a real-word version of the patisserie in the movie *Chocolat*. Franny and her mother, Barbara, handcraft exquisite concoctions in a cheery small storefront trimmed with artsy knickknacks. Try the key-lime torte topped with fresh blackberries.

Pick up sandwiches, coffee and organic groceries at the **Record** (☎ 707-882-3663; 265 Main St; 7am-7pm Mon-Sat, 8am-6pm Sun).

Arena Cinema (☎ 707-882-3456; 214 Main St) shows mainstream, foreign and art films in a beautifully restored movie house. Sue, the ticket seller, has been in that booth for 40 years. Got a question about Point Arena? Ask Sue.

MANCHESTER

Follow Hwy 1 7 miles north of Point Arena, through gorgeous rolling fields dropping down from the hills to the blue ocean, and a turnoff leads to **Manchester State Beach**, a long, wild stretch of sand. The area around here is remote and beautiful (only one grocery store), but it's a quick drive to Point Arena for more elaborate provisions.

Ross Ranch (☎ 707-877-1834; www.elkcoast.com/rossranch) at Irish Beach, another 5 miles to the north, arranges two-hour horseback beach ($60) and mountain ($50) rides; reservations recommended.

our pick **Victorian Gardens** (☎ 707-882-3606; www.innatvictoriangardens.com; 14409 S Hwy 1; r $240-310) Have a decadently bucolic rest at this lovingly restored 1904 farmhouse on 92 exquisitely situated acres just north of Manchester. Every detail from the deluxe bathrooms to the soothing views has been seen to. For larger groups, the owners can prepare five-course authentic Italian dinners with carefully paired wines.

Rent a beach house at **Irish Beach Vacation Rentals** (☎ 707-882-2467; www.irishb each.com).

Mendocino Coast KOA (☎ 707-882-2375, 800-562-4188; www.manchesterbeachkoa.com; tent/RV sites from $35/50, cabins $68-78; wi-fi) has densely packed campsites beneath enormous Monterey pines plus a cooking pavilion, hot showers, hot tub and bicycles.

A quarter-mile west, the sunny, exposed campground at **Manchester State Park** (☎ 707-882-2463; tent & RV sites $15) has cold water and quiet right by the ocean. Ten nonreservable **environmental campsites** (tent sites $15) hide in the dunes a 1.5-mile walk from the parking area; these have untreated creek water.

ELK

pop 250

Teeny Elk perches on the brink of cliffs overlooking some of the most dramatic coastline in California – mesmerizing rock formations jut out of the Pacific. Elk's **visitors center** (5980 Hwy 1; 11am-1pm Sat & Sun mid-Mar–Oct) has exhibits on the town's logging past. At the southern end of town, **Greenwood State Beach** (☎ 707-877-3458) sits where Greenwood Creek meets the sea. **Force 10** (☎ 707-877-3505; www.force10tours.com) guides ocean-kayaking tours ($115).

Tucked into a tiny clapboard house looking across the road to the ocean, the **Elk Studio Gallery & Artist's Collective** (☎ 707-877-1128; www.artists-collective.net; 6031 S Hwy 1; 10am-5pm) is festooned with everything from carvings and pottery to photography and jewelry. Peek upstairs into the working print and photo studio.

Several upmarket B&Bs take advantage of the views. **Griffin House** (☎ 707-877-3422; www.griffinn.com; 5910 S Hwy 1; cottages $130-160, ocean-view cottages $198-288;) is an unpretentious cluster of simple, powder blue bluffside cottages with wood-burning stoves.

Tucked on a hill beneath pines and eucalyptus, **Elk Cove Inn** (☎ 707-877-3321, 800-275-2967; www.elkcoveinn.com; 6300 S Hwy 1; r $135-195, r with ocean views $295-395) has fine linens and a spa.

A new-age feel pervades the Buddha-dotted grounds and ocean-view cottages at **Greenwood Pier Inn** (☎ 707-877-9997; www.greenwoodpierinn.com; 5928 S Hwy 1; d $175-325). Its café is open for lunch and dinner.

Harbor House Inn (☎ 707-877-3203, 800-720-7474; www.theharborhouseinn.com; 5600 S Hwy 1; r & cottages incl breakfast $315-490), in a 1915 Arts and Crafts–style mansion built by the town's lumber baron, has gorgeous cliff-top gardens and a private beach. Rates include a superb four-course dinner for two.

Everyone swears by excellent **Queenie's Roadhouse Cafe** (☎ 707-877-3285; 6061 S Hwy 1; dishes $6-10; 8am-3pm Thu-Mon; V) for a creative range of breakfast (try the wild rice waffles) and lunch treats. Sweet, little **Bridget Dolan's** (☎ 707-877-1820; 5910 S Hwy 1; dishes $10-15; dinner) serves straight-forward cookin' like pot pies, and bangers and mash.

VAN DAMME STATE PARK

Three miles south of Mendocino, this **park** (Map p264; ☎ 707-937-5804, 707-937-5397; www.parks.ca.gov; day use $6) is known for its **pygmy forest**, where the acidic soil and an impenetrable layer of hardpan just below the surface create a bonsai forest with decades-old trees growing only several feet high. A wheelchair-accessible boardwalk provides access to the forest. To get there, turn east off Hwy 1 onto Little River Airport Rd, a half-mile south of Van Damme State Park, and drive for 3 miles. Alternatively, hike or bike up from the campground on the 3.5-mile **Fern Canyon Scenic Trail**, which crosses back and forth over Little River.

The **visitors center** (☎ 707-937-4016; 10am-4pm summer, 10am-4pm Sat & Sun fall-spring) has nature exhibits, videos and programs; a half-hour marsh loop trail starts nearby.

For sea-cave kayaking tours ($50), contact **Lost Coast Kayaking** (☎ 707-937-2434; www.lostcoastkayaking.com).

Two pretty **campgrounds** (☎ 800-444-7275; www.reserveamerica.com; tent & RV sites $20-25) have hot showers: one is just off Hwy 1, the other is in a highland meadow. Ten **environmental campsites** (tent sites $15) lie just under a 2-mile hike up Fern Canyon; there's untreated creek water.

MENDOCINO

pop 1000

Picture-perfect Mendocino sits perched on a rocky headland jutting out to sea. Small cottages surrounded by blossoming gardens line narrow, sandy streets. Stand almost anywhere in town and you can see the crashing waves of the Pacific. The whole of Mendocino is listed on the National Register of Historic Places. With New England–style water towers and Victorian architecture, the town has served as the backdrop for over 50 films, including *East of Eden* (1954) and *The Majestic* (2001). It's the perfect place to bring your sweetie for a romantic getaway.

Built by transplanted New Englanders in the 1850s, Mendocino thrived late into the 19th century, with ships transporting redwood timber from here to San Francisco. The mills shut down in the 1930s, and the town fell into disrepair until it was rediscovered in the 1950s by artists and bohemians. Today the culturally savvy, politically aware, well-traveled citizens welcome visitors, but eschew corporate interlopers – don't look for a Big Mac or try to use your cell phone. To avoid crowds, come midweek or in the low season, when the vibe is mellower – and prices more reasonable.

Information

Ford House Visitors Center & Museum (Map p259; ☎ 707-937-5397; www.gomendo.com; 735 Main St; suggested donation $2; 🕑 11am-4pm) Maps, books,

STAR OF THE SILVER SCREEN

Over 50 films for TV and the silver screen have been shot around tiny Mendocino village, starting with *The Promise,* a 1916 silent film about a train wreck. Some of the best-known movies made here include *East of Eden* (1954) and *Rebel Without a Cause* (1955), both starring James Dean; *The Island of the Blue Dolphins* (1964), filmed on the southern Mendocino coast; and the *Murder, She Wrote* TV series (1984–96), starring Angela Lansbury. Most recently, *The Majestic* (2001) with Jim Carrey included scenes shot at Point Cabrillo Lighthouse and Fort Bragg's Skunk Train depot. Pick up the *Films Made in Mendocino County* brochure to find more film sites – a great chance for photo ops posing as your favorite starlet.

information and exhibits including a scale model of 1890 Mendocino.

Gallery Books (Map p259; ☎ 707-937-2665; 319 Kasten St)

Mendocino Coast Clinics (Map p264; ☎ 707-964-1251; 205 South St; 🕑 9am-5pm Mon-Fri, to 8pm Wed, 9am-1pm Sat) Nonemergencies.

Moody's Coffee Bar (Map p259; ☎ 707-933-4843; Lansing St; per min 10¢; 🕑 6am-8pm) Internet and the *New York Times.*

Moore Used Books (Map p259; ☎ 707-937-1537; 990 Main St)

Sights

Mendocino is lined with all kinds of interesting galleries, which hold **openings** on the second Saturday of each month from 5pm to 8pm. The mothership, **Mendocino Art Center** (Map p259; ☎ 707-937-5818, 800-653-3328; www.mendocinoartcenter.org; 45200 Little Lake St; 🕑 10am-5pm Apr-Oct, 10am-4pm Wed-Sat Nov-Mar), hosts exhibitions, arts-and-crafts fairs, theater and a nationally recognized program of over 200 art classes. It has dorm rooms for enrollees.

The 1861 **Kelley House Museum** (Map p259; ☎ 707-937-5791; www.kelleyhousemuseum.org; 45007 Albion St; admission $2; 🕑 11am-3pm Thu-Tue Jun-Sep, Fri-Mon Oct-May) has a research library and changing exhibits on early California and Mendocino. In summer the museum hosts **walking tours** (tours $10; 🕑 Fri-Mon).

At the 1852 **Kwan Tai Temple** (Map p259; 45160 Albion St), peer in the window to see the old Chinese altar.

The restored 1909 **Point Cabrillo Lighthouse** (Map p264; ☎ 707-937-6122; www.pointcabrillo.org; Point Cabrillo Dr; admission free; 🕑 11am-4pm Mar-Oct, Fri-Mon Nov-Dec, Sat & Sun Jan-Feb) stands on a 300-acre wildlife preserve north of town, between Russian Gulch and Caspar Beach. On weekends you can visit the old lightkeeper's home, too. Guided walks leave at 11am on Sundays from June to September.

Activities

Spectacular **Mendocino Headlands State Park** (Map p259; ☎ 707-837-5804) surrounds the village, with trails crisscrossing the bluffs and rocky coves. Ask at the visitors center about guided weekend walks, including spring wildflower walks and whale-watching.

Catch A Canoe & Bicycles, Too! (Map p259; ☎ 707-937-0273, 800-331-8884; www.stanfordinn.com; Comptche-Ukiah Rd & Hwy 1; 🕑 9am-5pm) rents bikes, kayaks and canoes for trips up the 8-mile Big River tidal estuary, the longest undeveloped estuary in Northern California. No highways or buildings, only beaches, forests, marshes, streams, abundant wildlife and historic logging sites, including century-old train trestles and log dams.

Tiny Albion (Map p264), hugging the north side of the Albion River mouth, 5 miles south of Mendocino, has a navigable river and ocean bay for **kayaking**.

Sweetwater Garden Spa (Map p259; ☎ 707-937-4140, 800-300-4140; 955 Ukiah St; 1hr private tub-and-sauna $23, public tub $10, public tub on Wed $8.50; 🕑 noon-10pm Sun-Fri, to 11pm Sat) offers massage, bodywork, hot tubs and sauna; ask for an outdoor tub.

Festivals & Events

For the complete list of festivals, check with the visitors center or www.gome ndo.com.

Taste Mendocino (www.mendocino.com/taste-mendocino.html) Combines the Crab & Wine Days Festival in January, the Wine & Mushroom Festival in November and a series of food, wine and whale events running from November to March.

Mendocino Whale Festival (www.mendowhale.com) Early March, with wine and chowder tastings, whale-watching and music.

Mendocino Music Festival (www.mendocinomusic.com) Mid-July, with orchestral and chamber music on the headlands, children's matinees and open rehearsals.

Mendocino Coast Christmas Festival (☎ 707-964-1228) Candlelight inn tours and music.

Sleeping

Standards are high and so are prices; 2-day minimums on weekends. Fort Bragg, 10 miles north, has cheaper lodgings (see p265).

BUDGET

Russian Gulch State Park (Map p264; ☎ reservations 800-444-7275; www.reserveamerica.com; tent & RV sites $20-25) In a wooded canyon 2 miles north of town, Russian Gulch has secluded drive-in sites and hot showers, a sandy beach, a small waterfall and Devil's Punch Bowl, a collapsed sea arch.

Mendocino Campground (Map p259; ☎ 707-937-3130; www.mendocino-campground.com; Comptche-Ukiah Rd; tent sites $25-35; Apr-Oct) High above Hwy 1, this woodsy option has 60 sites (some with views), hot showers and forested trails. Dogs welcome.

Caspar Beach RV Park (Map p264; ☎ 707-964-3306; www.casparbeachrvpark.com; 14441 Cabrillo Dr; tent sites $25/RV sites $30-35) In a sheltered gully beside Caspar Beach, 3.5 miles north of Mendocino.

Blue Heron Inn (Map p259; ☎ 707-937-4323; www.theblueheron.com; 390 Kasten St; r $95-115) Spartan rooms above a restaurant have crisp linens; some shared bathrooms.

About 5 miles south of town, Albion has bare, exposed riverside camping: **Schooner's Landing Campground** (Map p264; ☎ 707-937-5707; tent & RV sites $35-45) and **Albion River Campground** (Map p264; ☎ 707-937-0606; www.albionrivercampground.com; 34500 Hwy 1; tent sites $25, RV with/without hookup $30/35).

MIDRANGE

All B&B rates include breakfast; only a few places have TVs. For a range of cottages and B&Bs, contact **Mendocino Coast Reservations** (Map p259; ☎ 707-937-5033, 800-262-7801; www.mendocinovacations.com; 45084 Little Lake St; 9am-5pm).

Sweetwater Spa & Inn (Map p259; ☎ 707-937-4076, 800-300-4140; www.sweetwaterspa.com; 44840 Main St; r & cottages $70-295) owns a variety of accommodations, both in and near town. Some are run-down, so check closely.

Mendocino Hotel (Map p259; ☎ 707-937-0511, 800-548-0513; www.mendocinohotel.com; 45080 Main St; r with bath $135-295, without bath $95-125, ste $325-395; wi-fi) Built in 1878 as the town's first hotel, it's like a piece of the Old West. Modern garden suites sit behind the main building. Some wheelchair accessible.

Headlands Inn (Map p259; ☎ 707-937-4431; www.headlandsinn.com; cnr Albion & Howard Sts; r $129-229) Homey saltbox with featherbeds and fireplaces. Quiet dormer rooms have sea views and staff will bring you the gourmet breakfast in bed.

Sea Gull Inn (Map p259; ☎ 707-937-5204, 888-937-5204; www.seagullbb.com; 44960 Albion St; r $130-165, barn $185; wi-fi) Cozy, with pristine white bedspreads and organic breakfasts, right in the thick of the action.

Blackberry Inn (Map p259; ☎ 707-937-5281, 800-950-7806; www.mendocinomotel.com; 44951 Larkin Rd; r $145-205; wi-fi) Above town on a hill, the Blackberry looks like a row of Old West storefronts. Many of the Americana-style rooms have distant ocean views and fireplaces.

Alegria (Map p259; ☎ 707-937-5150, 800-780-7905; www.oceanfrontmagic.com; 44781 Main St; r $159-189, r with ocean view $239, cottages $179-269) Perfect for a romantic hideaway, rooms have ocean-view decks and wood-burning fireplaces; outside a gorgeous path leads to a private beach. Ever-so-friendly innkeepers rent simpler rooms in a 1900s Arts and Crafts place across the street.

MacCallum House Inn (Map p259; ☎ 707-937-0289, 800-609-0492; www.maccallumhouse.com; 45020 Albion St; r & cottages $165-425, ste $265-425;) Stay in an 1882 refurbished barn, a cottage or 20th-century luxury home; all have cushy extras like robes, DVD players, stereos and plush linens. Pets welcome. Also has a hoppin' bar and terrific restaurant.

Lighthouse Inn at Point Cabrillo (Map p264; ☎ 707-937-6124; 866-937-6124; http://mendocinolighthouse.pointcabrillo.org; Point Cabrillo Dr; r $177-272) On 300 acres, in the shadow of Point Cabrillo Lighthouse, the light keeper's house and several cottages have been turned into B&B rooms. Rates include a private night tour of the lighthouse and a five-course breakfast.

Joshua Grindle Inn (Map p259; ☎ 707-937-4143, 800-474-6353; www.joshgrin.com; 44800 Little Lake Rd; r $179-259) Mendocino's oldest B&B has bright, airy, uncluttered rooms in an 1869 house, a weathered saltbox cottage and water tower. Enjoy goodies like fluffy muffins, warm hospitality and gorgeous gardens.

Whitegate Inn (Map p259; ☎ 707-937-4892; www.whitegateinn.com; 499 Howard St; r $180-290; wi-fi) It's like staying in your old auntie's house: picket fence, bric-a-brac, chandeliers, overstuffed chairs and a gazebo out back in the lush garden. Plus fresh-baked afternoon treats.

Packard House (Map p259; ☎ 707-937-2677, 888-453-2677; www.packardhouse.com; 45170 Little Lake St; r $190-275) Decked out in contemporary style, this place is Mendocino's chic B&B choice – sleek and elegant, with beautiful fabrics, colorful minimalist paintings and limestone bathrooms.

Stanford Inn by the Sea (Map p259; ☎ 707-937-5615, 800-331-8884; www.stanfordinn.com; cnr Hwy 1 & Comptche-Ukiah Rd; r $195-305; wi-fi) This masterpiece of a lodge standing on 10 lush acres has wood-burning fireplaces, original art, stereos and top-quality mattresses in every room. Solarium-enclosed pool and hot tub open 24 hours. Pets welcome.

Also recommended:

John Dougherty House (Map p259; ☎ 707-937-5266; 800-486-2104; www.jdhouse.com; 571 Ukiah St; r $130-275) Stylish and sleeker than most.

Glendeven (Map p264; ☎ 707-937-0083, 800-822-4536; www.glendeven.com; 8205 N Hwy 1; r $135-320; wi-fi) Elegant estate 2 miles south of town.

Fensalden (Map p264; ☎ 707-937-4042, 800-959-3850; www.fensalden.com; 33810 Navarro Ridge Rd, Albion; r $150-200, bungalow $253) An 1880s stagecoach stop, 8 miles south of town. Supercool bungalow sleeps four.

Agate Cove Inn (Map p259; ☎ 707-937-0551, 800-527-3111; www.agatecove.com; 11201 Lansing St; r $210-259; wi-fi) On a spectacular bluff.

Eating

Mendocino's excellent restaurants fill up – make reservations.

Tote Fete (Map p259; ☎ 707-937-3383; 1045 Lansing St; dishes $4-8; 7:30am-7pm Mon-Sat, to 6pm Sun) Dishes out great salads and sandwiches – try the pesto, asiago and artichoke.

Mendocino Market (Map p259; ☎ 707-937-3474; 45051 Ukiah St; sandwiches $6-9; 9am-5pm Mon-Fri, 11am-4pm Sat & Sun; wi-fi) Pick up deli sandwiches and picnics here.

Mendo Burgers (Map p259; ☎ 707-937-1111; 10483 Lansing St; meals $6-9; 11am-4:30pm Thu-Tue; V) Behind Mendocino Bakery; makes great burgers, hand-cut fries, and veggie burgers, too.

Lu's Kitchen (Map p259; ☎ 707-937-4939; 45013 Ukiah St; dishes $8-10; 11:30am-5:30pm; V) Rustles up fab organic-veggie burritos in a tiny shack; outdoor-only tables.

Ravens (Map p259; ☎ 707-937-5615; www.stanfordinn.com; Stanford Inn, Comptche-Ukiah Rd; breakfast $11-15, mains $22-35; breakfast & dinner; V) Haute-contemporary cuisine meets vegetarianism at Ravens, where the produce comes from the inn's own organic gardens. Omnivores may foreswear meat after dining here, as there's everything from sea-palm strudel to pizza. Good view, too.

Mendocino Cafe (Map p259; ☎ 707-937-6141; 10451 Lansing St; lunch mains $12-15, dinner mains $12-24; lunch & dinner; V) One of Mendocino's few mid-priced dinner spots also serves lovely alfresco lunches on its ocean-view deck surrounded by roses. Try the fish tacos or Thai burrito. At dinner there's grilled steak and seafood.

Moosse Cafe (Map p259; ☎ 707-937-4323; 390 Kasten St; mains lunch $12-16, dinner $22-28; V) The blond woodwork and starched linen napkins set a relaxed yet elegant tone for top-notch Cal-French cooking. Try the cioppino in saffron-fennel-tomato broth at dinner; lunch is more casual.

MacCallum House Restaurant (Map p259; ☎ 707-937-0289; 45020 Albion St; café dishes $12-16, mains $25-37; breakfast & dinner; V) Sit on the veranda or fireside for a romantic dinner of all-organic duck, fish or risotto primavera. The bar menu is one of Mendocino's few bargains. Great breakfasts.

Ledford House (Map p264; ☎ 707-937-0282; 3000 N Hwy 1, Albion; bistro meals $15-18, mains $22-30; dinner Wed-Sun; V) Watch the water pound the rocks and the sun set out of the Mendocino hubbub (8 miles south) at this organic Cal-Med bistro. Try the cassoulet or the gnocchi. This local hangout gets hoppin' with live jazz most nights.

our pick **Cafe Beaujolais** (Map p259; ☎ 707-937-5614; 961 Ukiah St; mains $27-40; lunch Wed-Sun, dinner daily; V) In a laid-back yet elegant house built in 1896, Mendocino's iconic California-cuisine restaurant serves innovative, refined and inspired cooking, using organic meats and produce. How about pan-roasted California sturgeon with housemade tagliatelle? Or key-lime cheesecake?

Corners of the Mouth (Map p259; ☎ 707-937-5345; 45016 Ukiah St; 8am-8pm) carries natural foods. **Mendosa's** (Map p259; ☎ 707-937-5879; 10501 Lansing St; 8am-9pm) sells basics and good meat. Get fresh, local produce at the **farmers market** (Howard & Main St; noon-2pm Fri May-Oct).

Drinking

Have cocktails at the Mendocino Hotel (p261) or the Grey Whale Bar at the MacCallum House Inn (p261).

Patterson's Pub (Map p259; ☎ 707-937-4782; 10485 Lansing St) This boisterous, inviting Irish-style has an appealing menu of beans and rice, seafood and salads ($7 to $13) before 9:30pm.

Do shots with rowdy locals at **Dick's Place** (Map p259; ☎ 707-937-5643; 45080 Main St).

Entertainment

Mendocino Theatre Company (Map p259; ☎ 707-937-4477; www.1mtc.org; 45200 Little Lake St) Performs contemporary plays.

Shopping

Highlight (Map p259; ☎ 707-937-3132; 45052 Main St) Stands out for its exquisite wood artists. Tables, chairs and chests are functional sculpture at its best.

Color & Light Glass (Map p259; ☎ 707-937-1003; 10525 Ford St; Fri-Tue) Inside an artist's studio, see original fused and stained-glass works.

Out of This World (Map p259; ☎ 707-937-3335; 451000 Main St) Birders, astronomy buffs and science geeks: head directly to this telescope, binocular and science-toy shop.

Articles (Map p259; ☎ 707-937-3891; 611 Albion St; Thu-Tue) Check out cool crafts inside an old water tower you can ascend.

Lark in the Morning (Map p259; ☎ 707-937-5275; 45011 Ukiah St; Mon-Sat) Carries all manner of musical instruments.

Mendocino Jams & Preserves (Map p259; ☎ 707-937-1037; 440 Main St) Offers tastes of its goodies. Try the ketchup.

Mendocino Wine Co (Map p259; ☎ 800-860-3347; 45070 Main St) Sample zinfandel, syrah and cabernet ($5).

Reflections (Map p259; ☎ 707-937-0173; 45050 Main St; Thu-Mon) Specializes in handmade kaleidoscopes.

JUG HANDLE STATE RESERVE

Between Mendocino and Fort Bragg, Jug Handle (Map p264) preserves an **ecological staircase** that you can view on a 5-mile (round-trip) self-guided nature trail. Five wave-cut terraces ascend in steps from the seashore, each 100ft and 100,000 years removed from the previous one, and each with its own distinct geology and vegetation. One of the terraces has a pygmy forest, similar to the better-known example at Van Damme State Park (p258). Pick up a printed guide detailing the area's geology, flora and fauna from the parking lot. The reserve is also a good spot to stroll the headlands, whale-watch or lounge on the beach. It's easy to miss the entrance; watch for the turnoff, just north of Caspar.

Opposite the reserve, **Annie's Jughandle Beach B&B** (Map p264; ☎ 707-964-1415, 800-964-9957; Hwy 1, mileage marker 55; r incl breakfast $140-240) is an 1880s farmhouse with cheery rooms, some with Jacuzzis and gas fireplaces.

Jug Handle Creek Farm and Nature Center (Map p264; ☎ 707-964-4630; http://jughandle.creek.org; tent sites $12, r & cabins adult $35-40, child $15, student $28-33) is a nonprofit 39-acre farm with rustic cabins and hostel rooms in a 19th-century farmhouse. Call ahead about work-stay discounts. Drive 5 miles north of Mendocino to Caspar; the farm is on the east side of Hwy 1. Take the second driveway after Fern Creek Rd.

FORT BRAGG

pop 13,840

Although it's less charming than Mendocino, Fort Bragg makes an excellent base for exploring the coast, and serves as a jumping-off point for whale-watching and deep-sea fishing excursions. With the tearing down of the oceanfront lumber mill, the opening up of 10 miles of headlands and an influx of artists, the city is going through a bit of a renaissance. Overlook the strip malls and stick to downtown.

The fort established here in 1857 was named for Colonel Braxton Bragg, a veteran of the Mexican War. Ostensibly used to 'supervise' the local Pomo, it was abandoned a decade later. A lumber company was established in 1885, and the California Western Railroad (later nicknamed the 'Skunk Train') was built to haul giant redwoods from forest to coast.

Orientation & Information

Twisting Hwy 20 provides the main access to Fort Bragg from the east, and most facilities are near Main St, a 2-mile stretch of Hwy 1. Franklin St runs parallel, one block east. Fort Bragg's wharf lies at Noyo Harbor – the mouth of the Noyo River – south of downtown.

Cheshire Books (☎ 707-964-5916; 345 N Franklin St) Independent since 1972.

Fort Bragg-Mendocino Coast Chamber of Commerce (☎ 707-961-6300, 800-726-2780; www.fortbragg.com, www.mendocinocoast.com; 332 N Main St; per 15min $1; 9am-5pm Mon-Fri, to 3pm Sat) Internet access.

Mendocino Coast District Hospital (Map p264; ☎ 707-961-1234; 700 River Dr; 24hr) Emergency room.

Sights & Activities

Fort Bragg's pride and joy, the vintage **Skunk Train** (☎ 707-964-6371, 866-866-1690; www.skunktrain.com; adult/3-11yr $47/22) got its nickname in 1925 for its stinky gas-powered steam engines but today the historic steam and diesel locomotives are odorless. Passing through

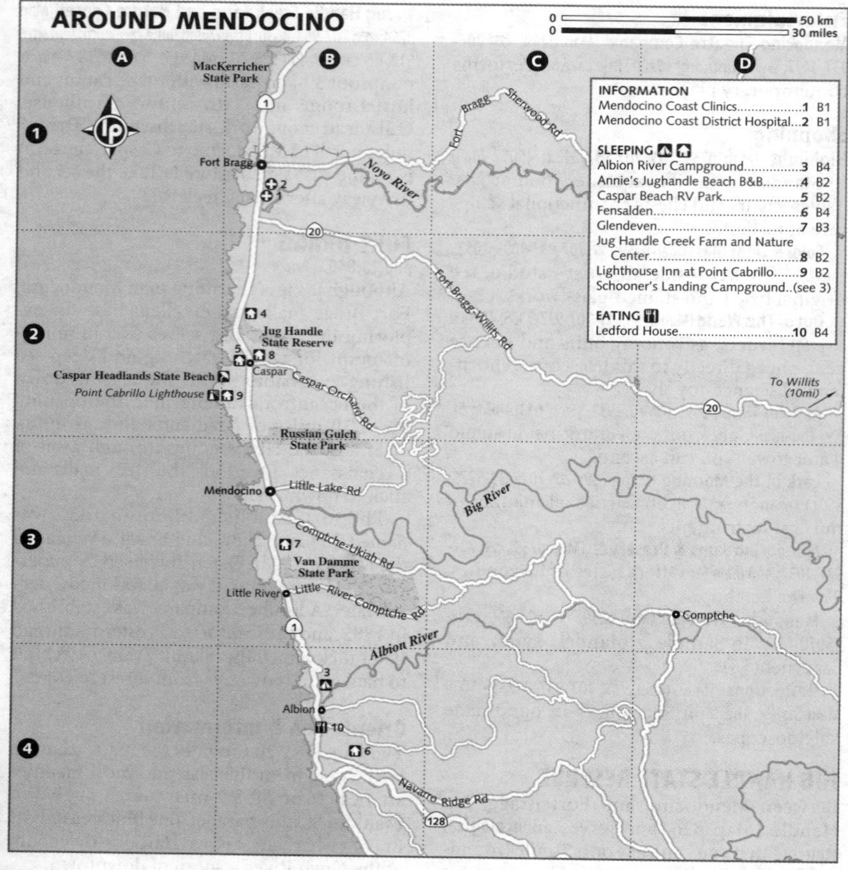

redwood-forested mountains, along rivers, over bridges and through deep mountain tunnels, the trains run from both Fort Bragg and Willits (p274) to the midway point of Northspur, where they turn around (if you want to go to Willits, plan to spend the night). The depot is downtown at the foot of Laurel St, one block west of Main St.

The **Guest House Museum** (☎ 707-964-4251; 343 N Main St; admission $2; 1-3pm Mon, 11am-2pm Tue-Fri, 10am-4pm Sat & Sun summer, 11am-3pm Thu-Sun winter), a majestic Victorian structure built in 1892, displays historical photos and relics of Fort Bragg's history.

Literally and figuratively on the other side of the street, the **Triangle Tattoo & Museum** (☎ 707-964-8814; www.triangletattoo.com; 356B N Main St; admission free; noon-7pm) shows multicultural international tattoo art. Next door, **Northcoast Artists Gallery** (☎ 707-964-8266; 362 N Main St; 10am-6pm), an excellent local arts cooperative, has the useful *Fort Bragg Gallery & Exhibition Guide,* which directs you to other galleries around town. Openings are the first Fridays of the month. Antique and book stores line Franklin St, one block east.

Glass Beach is named for the sea-polished glass lying on the sands. Take the headlands trail from Elm St, off Main St, but don't walk barefoot. Nearby **North Coast Brewing Co** (☎ 707-964-2739; 455 N Main St) offers brewery tours Monday to Saturday; call ahead. The walk along the **Pudding Creek Trestle**, north of downtown, is fun for the whole family.

Small boats at Noyo Harbor offer coastal and whale-watching cruises and deep-sea fishing trips. Try **Noyo Fishing Center** (☎ 707-964-3000; www.fortbraggfishing.com; 32440 N Harbor Dr).

A Northern California hidden gem, **Mendocino Coast Botanical Gardens** (☎ 707-964-4352; www.gardenbythesea.org; 18220 N Hwy 1; adult/child/teen/senior $10/2/4/7.50; 9am-5pm Mar-Oct, to 4pm Nov-Feb) displays native flora, rhododendrons and heritage roses along serpentine paths on 47 seafront acres south of town. Primary trails are wheelchair-accessible.

Festivals & Events

Fort Bragg Whale Festival (www.mendowhale.com) Held on the 3rd weekend in March, with microbrew tastings, crafts fairs and whale-watching trips.

Rhododendron Show (☎ 707-964-4435) Takes place in late April or early May.

World's Largest Salmon BBQ (www.salmonrestoration.org) Held at Noyo Harbor on the Saturday nearest 4th of July.

Paul Bunyan Days (www.paulbunyandays.com) Held on Labor Day weekend in September, celebrate California's logging history with a logging show, square dancing, parade and fair.

Sleeping

Fort Bragg's lodging is cheaper than Mendocino's, but most of the motels along noisy Hwy 1 don't have air-conditioning so you'll hear traffic through your open windows. Most B&Bs do not have TVs and they all include breakfast. The usual chains abound.

Colombi Motel (☎ 707-964-5773; www.colombimotel.com; 647 Oak St; 1- & 2-bedroom units $45-125) All units have two rooms – a bedroom and kitchen or two bedrooms – at this sparkling-clean motel, the best bargain on the Mendocino Coast. Check in at the Colombi Market on the corner of Oak and Harold Sts. A launderette's adjacent.

Beachcomber Motel (☎ 707-964-2402, 800-400-7873; www.thebeachcombermotel.com; 1111 N Main St; r $79-130, r with kitchen $79-159, with ocean view $109-139) On the inland side of Hwy 1 with cozy furniture; book upstairs for privacy.

Grey Whale Inn (☎ 707-964-0640, 800-382-7244; www.greywhaleinn.com; 615 N Main St; r $100-195; wi-fi) Built in 1915, this oceanside shingled behemoth has huge rooms and a relaxed feel. Penthouse suites have sweeping views.

Lodge at Noyo River (☎ 707-964-8045, 800-628-1126; www.noyolodge.com; 500 Casa del Norte Dr; r $110-300) Spacious rooms and modern suites with over-sized tubs fill a 19th-century lumber-baron's house, overlooking Noyo Harbor.

Shoreline Cottages (☎ 707-964-2977; www.shoreline-cottage.com; 18725 N Hwy 1; r $115-125; wi-fi) Low-key and pet-friendly four-person rooms and cottages with kitchens surround a central tree-filled lawn.

Rendezvous Inn (☎ 707-964-8142, 800-491-8142; www.rendezvousinn.com; 647 N Main St; r $120; wi-fi) Rooms are spartan, but Fort Bragg's best chef cooks breakfast.

Weller House Inn (☎ 707-964-4415, 877-893-5537; www.wellerhouse.com; 524 Stewart St; r $130-195; wi-fi) Rooms in this beautifully restored 1886 mansion have down comforters, good mattresses and fine linens. The water tower is the tallest structure in town – and it has a hot tub at the top! Breakfast in the massive redwood ballroom.

Also consider:

Beach House Inn (☎ 707-961-1700, 888-559-9992; www.beachinn.com; 100 Pudding Creek Rd; r $90-150) North of town, perched on a hill over the creek.

Anchor Lodge (☎ 707-964-4283; www.silversatthewharf.com; 32260 N Harbor Dr; r $65, r with ocean view $95, with kitchen $100) At Noyo Harbor, basic rooms under the Wharf Restaurant have water views.

Eating

Headlands Coffeehouse (☎ 707-964-1987; 120 E Laurel St; dishes $4-8; breakfast, lunch & dinner; wi-fi) The town's best café has Belgian waffles, homemade soups, veggie-friendly salads, panini and lasagna.

La Playa (☎ 707-964-4074; 542 N Main St; mains $6-12; 10am-9pm Mon-Sat) Down-home, no-frills Mexican cookin' right by the train tracks – try the *carne asada* (seasoned, roasted beef)

Eggheads (☎ 707-964-5005; 326 N Main St; meals $8-13; breakfast & lunch Thu-Tue) Enjoy the *Wizard of Oz* theme as you tuck into one of 50 varieties of omelet, crepe or burrito, some with local Dungeness crab.

Chapter & Moon (☎ 707-962-1643; 32150 N Harbor Dr; mains $8-18; 8am-8pm) Overlooking Noyo Harbor, this small café serves blue-plate American cooking: chicken and dumplings, meatloaf with mashers, and fish with yam chips. Save room for fruit cobbler.

Cafe 1 (☎ 707-964-3309; 735 N Main St; mains $9-12; breakfast & lunch; V) Locals come for great organic breakfasts, like the hippie scramble (seasonal veggies with braised tofu).

Piaci Pub & Pizzeria (☎ 707-961-1133; 120 W Redwood Ave; pizza $9-12; lunch Mon-Fri, dinner daily) This is the place for thin-crust pizzas, focaccia sandwiches, local wines and great microbrews.

Mendo Bistro (☎ 707-964-4974; 301 N Main St; dishes $11-20; dinner) Upstairs in the Company Store building, lively Mendo Bistro serves good crab cakes, steaks, roasted chicken and housemade pasta. Request a window table.

Nit's Cafe (☎ 707-964-7187; 322 N Main; mains lunch $13-17, dinner $22; lunch Tue-Fri, dinner Tue-Sat; V) This tiny storefront café gets packed. The Thai-born chef-owner wows with imaginative, wonderfully spiced French-Thai cooking. Reserve ahead.

The Restaurant (☎ 707-964-9800; 418 N Main St; mains $24; dinner Thu-Mon) Locals flock to this relaxed downtown dining room for consistently excellent tasties like blackened Pacific rockfish.

Rendezvous Inn (☎ 707-964-8142; 647 N Main St; mains $22-35; dinner Wed-Sun; V) Rustic charm meets big-city cooking: expertly prepared, down-to-earth, French-provincial cooking in a redwood-paneled, Arts and Crafts–style house. If you're a foodie, don't miss it. Make reservations.

Skip the overpriced Wharf Restaurant (aka Silver's), and head next door to unpretentious **Cap'n Flint's** (☎ 707-964-9447; 32250 N Harbor Dr; mains $11; 11am-9pm) to eat the same fried fish for less. **Sharon's by the Sea** (☎ 707-962-0680; 32096 N Harbor Dr; mains lunch $6-17, dinner $11-24) is one of the best options for seafood.

For the best groceries, visit **Harvest Market** (☎ 707-964-7000; cnr Hwys 1 & 20; 5am-11pm). A **farmers market** (☎ 707-937-4330; cnr Laurel & Franklin Sts; 3:30-6pm Wed May-Oct) meets downtown, near **Cowlick's Ice Cream** (☎ 962-9271; 250b Main St).

Drinking & Entertainment

Locals cherish their indie cafés. When Starbucks arrived in 2005, the townspeople started wearing T-shirts emblazoned with a Starbucks-like logo reading 'Corporate Coffee Sucks!'

Headlands Coffeehouse (☎ 707-964-1987; www.headlandscoffeehouse.com; 120 E Laurel St; wi-fi) This not-to-be-missed, earthy café features live music every evening – jazz, folk and classical – and jazz jams on Sunday afternoons.

Caspar Inn (☎ 707-964-5565; 14957 Caspar Rd; live entertainment cover Tue-Sat, $3-25) Five miles south of Fort Bragg, off Hwy 1, this jumpin' roadhouse rocks out the reggae, hip-hop, rockabilly, R&B and world beat. It's worth the drive.

Sample some of the microbrews at **North Coast Brewing Company** (☎ 707-964-3400; 444 N Main St) or do shots at **Old Coast Hotel** (☎ 707-961-4488; 101 N Franklin St).

Opera Fresca (☎ 707-937-3646, 888-826-7372; www.operafresca.com) performs full operas year-round. **Gloriana Opera Company** (☎ 707-964-7469; www.gloriana.org; 721 N Franklin St) stages musical theater and operettas. **Footlighters Little Theater** (☎ 707-964-3806; 248 E Laurel St) presents 1890s-style musicals, comedy and melodrama.

Getting There & Around

Mendocino Transit Authority (MTA; ☎ 707-462-1422, 800-696-4682; www.4mta.org) runs local route 5 'BraggAbout' buses between Noyo Harbor and Elm St, north of downtown ($1). Service runs throughout the day.

Fort Bragg Cyclery (☎ 707-964-3509; www.fortbraggcyclery.com; 221a N Main St) rents bicycles.

MACKERRICHER STATE PARK

Three miles north of Fort Bragg, the **MacKerricher State Park** (Map p264; ☎ 707-964-9112; www.parks.ca.gov) preserves 9 miles of pristine rocky headlands, sandy beaches, dunes and tidepools.

The **visitors center** (10am-6pm Sat & Sun summer, 11am-3pm Sat & Sun rest of year) sits next to the whale skeleton at the park entrance. Hike the **Coastal Trail** along dark-sand beaches and see rare and endangered plant species (tread lightly). **Lake Cleone** is a 30-acre freshwater lake stocked with trout and visited by over 90 species of birds. At nearby **Laguna Point** an interpretive disabled-accessible boardwalk overlooks harbor seals and, from December to April, migrating whales. **Ricochet Ridge Ranch** (☎ 707-964-7669; www.horse-vacation.com; 24201 N Hwy 1) offers horseback-riding trips through redwoods or along the beach ($45 for 90 minutes).

Popular **campgrounds** (☎ 800-444-2725; www.reserveamerica.com; tent & RV sites $20-25), nestled in pine forest, have hot showers and water; the first-choice reservable tent sites are numbers 21 to 59. Ten superb, secluded walk-in tent sites (numbers 1 to 10; sites $25) are first-come, first-served.

WESTPORT

pop 400

The last hamlet before the Lost Coast (p280), sleepy Westport feels like a frontier settlement. A turn-of-the-20th-century shipping port, it once had the longest logging chute in California. Today there's little here except for romantic beaches and abundant peace.

Bring a picnic to **Pacific Star Winery** (☎ 707-964-1155; 33000 N Hwy 1; tastings free; 🕑 11am-5pm) and sample Italian-style wines from atop stunning ocean-view bluffs.

Head 1.5 miles north of town for the ruggedly beautiful **Westport-Union Landing State Beach** (☎ 707-937-5804; tent sites $14), which extends for 3 miles on coastal bluffs. A rough hiking trail leaves the primitive campground (with water) and passes by tidepools and streams, accessible at low tide. A mile south, **Westport Beach RV & Camping** (☎ 707-964-2964; www.westportbeachrv.com; 37700 N Hwy 1; tent sites $25, RV sites with hookups $35-40, without $25) has showers and beachside tent camping.

Simple accommodations in town include the blue and red, plastic-flower-festooned **Westport Inn** (☎ 707-964-5135; 37040 N Hwy 1; r incl breakfast from $65).

Further north lie two wonderful rural retreats. The secluded **DeHaven Valley Inn** (☎ 707-961-1660, 877-334-2836; www.dehavenvalleyinn.com; 39247 N Hwy 1; r $115-150, cottages $155-165) is an 1875 house on 20 acres. There are comfy rooms – one of whch has a fireplace – and gorgeous mountain views.

our pick **Howard Creek Ranch** (☎ 707-964-6725; www.howardcreekranch.com; 40501 N Hwy 1; r $90-165, ste $125-200, cabins $75-200; wi-fi) On 60 stunning acres of forest and farmland abutting the wilderness, Howard Creek Ranch has accommodations in the 1880s farmhouse or the carriage barn, whose way-cool redwood rooms have been expertly handcrafted by the owner. Rates include full breakfast. Bring hiking boots, not high heels.

Want to rent a house? Consider the pet-friendly, two-bedroom, 1832 **Westport House** (☎ 707-937-4007; www.vrbo.com/61409; per night $250), overlooking pounding surf, or the four-bedroom **Seagate Vacation Rental** (☎ 530-873-6793; www.vrbo.com/30340; 36875 N Hwy 1; per night $275).

ALONG HIGHWAY 101

North of Santa Rosa, Hwy 101 heads through a series of fertile valleys along the Russian River, intersecting with Hwy 1 in Leggett. Although Hwy 101 may not look as enticing as the coastal route, it's faster and less winding, leaving you time along the way to detour into Sonoma and Mendocino counties' wine regions, explore pastoral Anderson Valley, splash about Clear Lake or soak at hot-springs resorts outside Ukiah – time well spent indeed!

LAKE SONOMA

Formed by Warm Springs Dam in 1983, Lake Sonoma has two major arms, 4 miles and 8 miles long, and many smaller coves. The 319ft-high, 3000ft-long dam is at the lake's east end. To get there from Hwy 101, take the Dry Creek Rd exit north of Healdsburg and head northwest for 11 miles through gorgeous vineyards (see p208).

The **visitors center** (☎ 707-433-9483; www.parks.sonoma.net/laktrls.html; 🕑 8am-4pm Mon-Fri) has historical exhibits on local Pomo tribe culture, maps, and information on fishing, boating, camping and hiking over 40 miles of trails. Behind the center is a fish hatchery. Two miles further along, the **marina** (☎ 707-433-2200) rents everything from canoes to houseboats.

Liberty Glen Campground has 113 unreserved sites, hot showers and panoramic vistas. Primitive boat-in and hike-in campsites dot the lakeside; contact the park for reservations and camp permits.

HOPLAND

pop 820 / elev 486ft

Cute Hopland is the gateway to Mendocino County's wine country. Hops were first grown here in 1866, but Prohibition brought the industry temporarily to a halt. In 1983, the Mendocino Brewing Company opened up the first brewpub licensed in California since Prohibition and put Hopland back on the map. Now wine tasting is the primary draw.

Sights & Activities

Don't miss **Fetzer Vineyards Organic Gardens** (☎ 800-846-8637; www.fetzer.com; 13601 Eastside Rd; 🕑 9am-5pm), overseen by Kate Frey, gold-medal winner at England's 2005 Chelsea Flower Show.

Graziano Family of Wines (☎ 707-744-8466; www.grazianofamilyofwines.com; 13251 S Hwy 101; 🕑 10am-5pm) specializes in 'Cal-Ital' wines – nebbiolo, dolcetto, barbera and sangiovese – at some great prices. **McDowell Valley Vineyards** (☎ 707-744-8911; www.mcdowellsyrah.com; 13380 S Hwy 101; 🕑 11am-5pm Mon-Fri, from 10am Sat & Sun) is famous for Rhône varietals and makes luscious, jammy reds and a lovely rosé. Two miles north, the fun-to-visit **Jepson Vineyards**

SUSTAINABLE HOPLAND

Located in a spectacular 12-acre renewable energy and sustainable living demonstration site, **Solar Living Institute** (☎ 707-744-2017; www.solarliving.org; 13771 S Hwy 101; suggested donation $1-5; 10am-6pm;) educates by example. Take a tour or attend a hands-on workshop on renewable energy, green building or organic gardening. Or volunteer there! Kids' areas include a solar-powered miniature **carousel** (rides $1; noon-4pm). Students and volunteers can camp on-site; register a week in advance. The annual **SolFest** in August adds great food and family fun.

(☎ 800-516-7342; www.jepsonwine.com; 10400 S Hwy 101) makes chardonnay and brandy in its giant alembic still; tours by appointment.

Drop in to **SIP! Mendocino** (☎ 707-744-8375; 13420 S Hwy 101; 11am-6pm), where fun, friendly proprietors guide you through a tour of 18 wines with delectable appetizer pairings and a blossom-filled courtyard.

Visit **Brutocao Schoolhouse Plaza** (☎ 707-744-2000; 13500 S Hwy 101; 11am-8pm) to play boccie. **Hopland Women's Festival** takes place on Memorial Day.

Sleeping & Eating

Fetzer Valley Oaks Inn (☎ 707-744-7413, 800-846-8637; www.fetzer.com; 13601 Eastside Rd; r $169, ste $195-270, cottage $220;) Once a 19th-century carriage house, this inn on the Fetzer Vineyards' grounds has ever-so-charming rooms with redwood paneling, supercomfy beds and superb vineyard views from private terraces.

Hopland Inn (☎ 707-744-1890, 800-266-1891; www.hoplandinn.com; 13401 S Hwy 101; r $180;) This Victorian beauty was established in 1890 and still has excellent, comfy rooms with period furnishings.

Munchies (☎ 707-744-1600; 13275 S Hwy 101; sandwiches $6; breakfast & lunch; V) Excellent juice, gelato, pastries, espresso and picnic baskets. Bicycles for rent.

Bluebird Cafe (☎ 707-744-1633; 13340 S Hwy 101; breakfast & lunch $5-12, dinner $12-17; breakfast & lunch daily, dinner Fri-Sun; V) This classic American diner serves heavy breakfasts, giant burgers and homemade pie.

Drinking

Mendocino Brewing Company (☎ 707-744-744-1015; 13351 S Hwy 101; 1-8pm Mon, Wed, Thu, from noon Fri-Sun) One of Northern California's best-known brewpubs is moribund: the beer is made in Ukiah now and the bar shuts at eight friggin' o'clock. Still, if you love beer, get some take-out food from the Bluebird or Munchies, bring it to the garden, order a pint and listen to the crickets.

CLEAR LAKE

pop 14,728 / elev 1326ft

With over 100 miles of shoreline, Clear Lake is the largest naturally occurring freshwater lake in California (Tahoe is bigger, but crosses the Nevada state line). In summer the warm water thrives with algae, giving it a murky green appearance and creating a fabulous habitat for fish – especially bass – and tens of thousands of birds. Mt Konocti, a 4200ft-tall dormant volcano, lords over the scene. Alas, the human settlements don't always live up to the grandeur and thousands of acres near the lake burned in the wildfires of 2008.

Orientation & Information

Locals refer to 'upper lake' (the northwest portion) and 'lower lake' (the southeast portion). Lakeport (population 5240) sits on the northwest shore, a 45-minute drive east of Hopland along Hwy 175 (off Hwy 101); Kelseyville (population 3000) is 7 miles south. Clearlake, off the southeastern shore, is the biggest (and ugliest) town.

Hwy 20 links the north-shore hamlets of Nice (the northernmost town) and Lucerne, 4 miles southeast. Middletown, a cute village, lies 20 miles south of Clearlake at the junction of Hwys 175 and 129, 40 minutes north of Calistoga.

Lake County Visitor Information Center (☎ 707-263-9544, 800-525-3743; www.lakecounty.com; 6110 E Hwy 120, Lucerne; 9am-6pm Mon-Thu & Sat, to 7pm Fri, 10am-5pm Sun) has complete information.

Sights & Activities

In Lakeport, the 1871 **Old County Courthouse** (255 N Main St) holds **Lake County Museum** (☎ 707-263-4555; 10am-4pm Wed-Sat, from noon Sun), with Pomo artifacts and historical exhibits.

Six miles from Lakeport, **Clear Lake State Park** (☎ 707-279-4293; 5300 Soda Bay Rd, Kelseyville; per car $6), on the lake's west shore, is idyllic and gorgeous, with hiking trails, fishing, boating and camping. The **bird-watching** is extraordinary. The **visitors center** has geological and historical exhibits. **Taylor Planetarium & Observatory** (☎ after 3pm 707-279-8372; 5727 Oak Hills Lane, Kelseyville; donation $3) offers occasional stargazing programs.

In Lower Lake the conservation group **Redbud Audubon Society** (☎ 707-994-1545; www.redbudaudubon.org) leads birding walks. Check out the restored 19th-century classroom at **Lower Lake Historical Schoolhouse Museum** (☎ 707-995-3565; 16435 Morgan Valley Rd; 🕑 11am-4pm Wed-Sat).

Docked in Lucerne on the north shore, **Clear Lake Queen** (☎ 707-994-5432; www.paddlewheel.com; 2/3hr cruise $17/20), an elegant, three-story paddlewheel steamboat, offers sightseeing cruises, with decent dining, a bar and live music. Reservations essential.

Many outfits rent boats, including **On the Waterfront** (☎ 707-263-6789; 60 3rd St, Lakeport) and Konocti Harbor Resort & Spa in Kelseyville.

From north to south, the following four wineries are the best; some offer tours by appointment.

Ceago Vinegarden (☎ 707-274-1462; 5115 E Hwy 20, Nice; 🕑 10am-6pm) Ceago (cee-*ay*-go) occupies a spectacular spot on the north shore, and pours biodynamic, fruit-forward wines.

Wildhurst Vineyards (☎ 707-279-4302; 3855 Main St, Kelseyville; 🕑 10am-5pm) The best wine on the lake, but lacks atmosphere. Try the sauvignon blanc.

Ployez Winery (☎ 707-994-2106; 1171 S Hwy 29, Lower Lake; 🕑 11am-5pm) Above-average *méthode champenoise* sparkling wines; surrounded by farmland.

Guenoc & Langtry Estate Vineyards (☎ 707-987-9127; 21000 Butts Canyon Rd, Middletown; 🕑 11am-5pm) The most beautiful vineyard. Try the port.

Sleeping & Eating

Make reservations on weekends and during summer.

LAKEPORT & KELSEYVILLE

Konocti Harbor Resort & Spa (☎ 707-279-4281, 800-660-5253; www.konoctiharbor.com; 8727 Soda Bay Rd, Konocti Bay; r $89-199, apt & beach cottages $199-349, ste $259-399; wi-fi) On Konocti Bay, 4 miles from Kelseyville, this gargantuan resort, famous for huge concerts, includes four pools, a fitness center, tennis, golf, marina and spa. Rates spike on concert nights.

Arbor House Inn (☎ 707-263-6444; www.arborhousebnb.com; 150 Clearlake Ave, Lakeport; r $120-160, ste $175; wi-fi) Decorated with dried flowers, this straightforward B&B feels like someone's house. Rooms are dark, but the innkeeper is friendly; there's a garden hot tub.

our pick **Lakeport English Inn** (☎ 707-263-4317; www.lakeportenglishinn.com; 675 N Main St, Lakeport; r $159-210, cottages $210;) The finest B&B at Clear Lake is an 1875 Carpenter Gothic with 10 impeccably furnished rooms, styled with a nod to the English countryside. Weekends take high tea (public welcome by reservation) – with real Devonshire cream.

Waterfront motels with boat slips include cottage-style **Mallard House** (☎ 707-262-1601; www.mallardhouse.com; 970 N Main St, Lakeport; r with kitchen $69-149, without $49-99; wi-fi) and well-kept **Skylark Shores Motel** (☎ 707-263-6151, 800-675-6151; www.skylarkshores.com; 1120 N Main St, Lakeport; r with kitchen 100-150, without $100; wi-fi).

Clear Lake State Park has four **campgrounds** (☎ 800-444-7275; www.reserveamerica.com; sites $15-30) with showers.

our pick **Sawshop Bistro** (☎ 707-278-0129; 3825 Main St, Kelseyville; small plates $10-12, mains $18-30; 🕑 dinner Tue-Sat) The best restaurant in Lake County serves a California-cuisine menu of wild salmon and rack of lamb, as well as a small-plates menu of sushi, lobster tacos, Kobe-beef burgers and flatbread pizzas. Laid-back atmosphere, too.

Park Place (☎ 707-263-0444; 50 3rd St, Lakeport; dinner mains $12-30; 🕑 lunch & dinner) Everything is made in-house at this cheerful café with outdoor dining. Consistently good cooking includes lunchtime soups and pastas, steak, duck and seafood at dinner.

The Mexican food at **TNT on the Lake** (☎ 707-263-4868; 1 1st St Lakeport; mains $8-12; 🕑 lunch & dinner) is nothing special, but the views are. For meatloaf and BLTs, visit **Ashley's** (☎ 707-263-1399; 155 N Main St, Lakeport; mains $8-17; 🕑 lunch & dinner).

Kelseyville hosts a **farmers market** (☎ 707-928-4685; Hwy 29 & Thomas Rd; 🕑 8:30am-noon first Sat May-Oct).

NORTH SHORE

Sea Breeze Resort (☎ 707-998-3327; www.seabreezeresort.net; 9595 Harbor Dr, Glenhaven; cottages with kitchen $130-150, without $100; 🕑 Apr-Oct;) Just south of Lucerne on a small peninsula, gardens surround seven spotless lakeside cottages. All have barbecues.

Gingerbread Cottage (☎ 707-274-0200, 888-880-5253; www.gingerbreadcottages.com; 4057 E Hwy 20, Nice; cottages $125-195;) Cottages on a hill face the lake, with good mattresses and extras like in-room sherry and bathrobes. Rent kayaks at the dock.

Featherbed Railroad Co (☎ 707-274-8378, 800-966-6322; www.featherbedrailroad.com; 2870 Lakeshore Blvd, Nice; cabooses incl breakfast $140-190;) A treat for train buffs and kids, Featherbed has 10 comfy, real cabooses on a grassy lawn. Some of the cabooses straddle the border between kitschy and tacky (the 'Easy Rider' has a mirrored ceiling), but they're great fun if you keep a sense of humor. There's a tiny beach across the road.

Tallman Hotel (☎ 707-275-2244, 866-708-5253; www.tallmanhotel.com; 9550 Main St, Upper Lake; d $150-190;) This swank little place in an award-winning restored 1890s building has an open, airy feeling. Garden rooms come with Japanese soaking tubs, all heated and cooled by an energy-efficient geothermal-solar system.

Get simple breakfasts, sandwiches, soups, salads and pastas at **Scotty's Garden Cafe** (☎ 707-274-0134; 6034 E Hwy 20, Lucerne; mains $4-10; 7am-7pm Sun & Mon, to 9pm Tue-Sat).

MIDDLETOWN

Harbin Hot Springs (☎ 707-987-2377, 800-622-2477; www.harbin.org; Harbin Hot Springs Rd; camping midweek/weekend $25/35, dm $35/50, s midweek $60-75, weekend $95-120, d midweek $90-190, weekend $140-260) Harbin is classic Northern California. Originally a 19th-century health spa and resort, it now has a retreat-center vibe and people come to unwind in silent, clothing-optional hot- and cold-spring pools. This is the birthplace of Watsu (floating massage) and there are wonderful body therapies as well as yoga, holistic-health workshops and 1160 acres of hiking. Accommodations are in Victorian buildings (which could use sprucing up) and share a common vegetarian-only kitchen. Food is available at the market, café and restaurant. Day-trippers are welcome; day rates are $20/25 (weekday/weekend) and require one member of your group to purchase a membership (one month $10).

The springs are 3 miles off Hwy 175. From Middletown, take Barnes St, which becomes Big Canyon Rd, and head left at the fork.

Drinking

Wet your whistle at **Mount St Helena Brewing Co** (☎ 707-987-3361; 21167 Calistoga Rd, Middletown) or **Carlos & Vinny's** (☎ 707-263-6493; 370 S Main St, Lakeport); live music on Friday and Saturday.

Entertainment

Konocti Harbor Resort & Spa (☎ 707-279-4281; 800-225-2277; www.konoctiharbor.com; 8727 Soda Bay Rd) Presents headliners like Lyle Lovett in an outdoor amphitheater and indoor concert hall.

Library Park, in Lakeport, has free lakeside Friday-evening **summer concerts**, from blues to rockabilly. Harbin Hot Springs (left) presents a surprising line-up of world music and dances.

Getting Around

Lake Transit (☎ 707-263-3334, 707-994-3334; www.laketransit.org) operates weekday routes between Middletown and Calistoga ($3, 35 minutes, three daily); on Thursday they connect through to Santa Rosa. Buses serve Ukiah ($3, two hours, four daily), from Clearlake via Lakeport ($1, 1¼ hours, seven daily).

ANDERSON VALLEY

Rolling hills surround pastoral Anderson Valley, famous for apple orchards, vineyards, pastures and quiet. Visitors come primarily to winery-hop, but there's good hiking and bicycling in the hills, and the chance to escape hectic civilization.

Orientation & Information

Boonville (population 1370) and Philo (population 1000) are the valley's principal towns. From Ukiah, winding Hwy 253 heads 20 miles south to Boonville. Equally scenic Hwy 128 twists and turns 60 miles between Cloverdale on Hwy 101, south of Hopland, and Albion on coastal Hwy 1. This is the route to Mendocino from San Francisco.

Anderson Valley Chamber of Commerce (☎ 707-895-2379; www.andersonvalleychamber.com) For tourist information.

KZYX FM Tune to 88.3, 90.7 or 91.5 for community radio.

Sights & Activities

The **Anderson Valley Historical Society Museum** (☎ 707-895-3207; www.andersonvalleymuseum.org; 12340 Hwy 128; 1-4pm Fri-Sun Feb-Nov), in a recently renovated little red schoolhouse west of Boonville, displays historical artifacts.

Anderson Valley Brewing Co (☎ 707-895-2337; www.avbc.com; 17700 Hwy 253; tours $5; 11am-6pm), east of the Hwy 128 crossroads, crafts award-winning beers in a Bavarian-style brewhouse. Tours leave at 1:30pm and 4pm daily; call ahead.

The valley's cool nights yield high-acid, fruit-forward, food-friendly wines. Pinot noir,

NORTH COAST

BOONTLING

Boonville is famous for its unique language, 'Boontling,' which evolved about the turn of the 20th century when Boonville was very remote. Locals developed the language to *shark* (stump) outsiders and amuse themselves. You may hear *codgie kimmies* (old men) asking for a horn of *zeese* (a cup of coffee) or some *bahl gorms* (good food). If you are really lucky, you'll spot the tow truck called Boont Region De-arkin' Moshe (literally 'Anderson Valley Un-wrecking Machine').

chardonnay and dry gewürztraminer flourish. Most **wineries** (www.avwines.com) sit outside Philo. Many are family-owned and offer tastings, some give tours:

Esterlina (☎ 707-895-2920; www.esterlinavineyards.com) For big reds, pack a picnic and head high up the rolling hills; call ahead.

Handley (☎ 707-895-3876, 800-733-3151; www.handleycellars.com; 3151 Hwy 128; 10am-6pm) The tasting room has cool tribal art and top wines include its pinot gris, Gewürztraminer and chardonnay.

Husch (☎ 800-554-8724; 4400 Hwy 128; 10am-5pm) Husch serves exquisite tastings inside a rose-covered cottage.

Lazy Creek (☎ 707-895-3623; 4741 Hwy 128) Surrounded by lovely gardens, romantic and tiny Lazy Creek is up a half-mile dirt road; it's open when the gate is (call ahead).

Navarro (☎ 707-895-3686; 5601 Hwy 128; 10am-6pm) The best option, and picnicking is encouraged.

For the best fruit, skip the obvious roadside stands and instead head to gorgeous **Apple Farm** (☎ 707-895-2333; www.philoapplefarm.com; 18501 Greenwood Rd, Philo; daylight hr) for organic preserves, chutneys, heirloom apples and pears. It also rents spiffy orchard cottages ($175 to $250), and hosts **cooking classes** with some of the Wine Country's best chefs.

Festivals & Events

Annual celebrations include the **Boonville Beer Festival** (www.avbc.com/news/boontbeerfest.html), **California Wool & Fiber Festival** (www.fiberfestival.com) and **Pinot Noir Festival** (www.avwines.com/pnf.htm), all in May, followed by the **Wild Iris Folk Festival** (☎ 707-895-3589) in June. Mid-September brings the **Mendocino County Fair** (www.mendocou ntyfair.com).

Sleeping

Accommodations fill on weekends.

Wellspring Retreat Center (☎ 707-895-3893; www.wellspringrenewal.org; Ray's Rd, Philo; tent sites $10, cabins from $40) For spiritual retreat, try these rustic cottages with shared bathrooms; bring bedding and towels. Reservations essential.

Hendy Woods State Park (☎ 707-937-5804, reservations 800-444-7275; www.reserveamerica.com; tent & RV sites $25, cabins $50) Bordered by the Navarro River on Hwy 128, west of Philo, the park has hiking, picnicking and a forested campground with hot showers.

Anderson Valley Inn (☎ 707-895-3325; www.avinn.com; 8480 Hwy 128, Philo; r $85-120, 2-bedroom ste with kitchen $140-180) This small motel has fresh-looking, good-value rooms.

Philo Pottery Inn (☎ 707-895-3069; www.philopotteryinn.com; 8550 Hwy 128, Philo; r $90-165) Made from unfinished redwood, this cozy 1888 B&B has comfy rooms and flower gardens. The house is the oldest structure in the entire valley and has a wonderful historic vibe.

Boonville Hotel (☎ 707-895-2210; www.boonvillehotel.com; 14040 Hwy 128; r $125-200, ste $225) Decked out in a contemporary American-country style with sea-grass flooring, pastel colors and fine linens that would make Martha Stewart proud, this historic hotel's rooms are safe for urbanites who refuse to abandon style just because they've gone to the country.

Other Place (☎ 707-895-3979; www.sheepdung.com; cottages $140-200;) Outside of town, 500 acres of ranch land surrounds private hilltop cottages. Dogs welcome.

Eating & Drinking

Boonville General Store (☎ 707-895-9477; 17810 Farrer Lane; dishes $5-8; 9am-3pm Thu-Mon) Opposite the Boonville Hotel. Stock up for picnics: sandwiches on homemade bread, thin-crust pizzas and organic cheeses.

Libby's (☎ 707-895-2646; 8651 Hwy 128, Philo; mains $6-12; lunch & dinner Tue-Sun) Miss Libby makes good Mexican.

Lauren's (☎ 707-895-3869; 14211 Hwy 128, Boonville; mains $8-14; dinner Tue-Sat; V) Locals pack Lauren's for eclectic homemade cookin'. Musicians sometimes jam.

our pick **Boonville Hotel** (☎ 707-895-2210; 14040 Hwy 128; mains $15-30; dinner Thu-Mon) Food-savvy travelers love the constantly changing New American menu featuring simple dishes done well, like roasted chicken and strawberry shortcake.

A **farmers market** (9:45am-noon Sat May-Oct) is held at the Boonville Hotel. **Boont Berry Farm** (707-895-3576; 13981 Hwy 128) has a small deli.

UKIAH

pop 15,500 / elev 639 ft

Ringed by 4000ft-high peaks, in the fertile Yokayo Valley, Ukiah means 'deep valley' in the Pomo language. During fall, orchards and vineyards explode with fruit. Although it's Mendocino's county seat, it's a simple place with affordable lodgings and great hiking nearby, making Ukiah a good base for hopping between outlying wineries, hot springs and nature reserves.

Orientation & Information

Running north–south, west of Hwy 101, State St is Ukiah's main drag. School St, near Perkins St, is good for strolling.

Bureau of Land Management (707-468-4000; 2550 N State St) Maps and information on backcountry camping, hiking and biking in wilderness areas.

Greater Ukiah Chamber of Commerce (707-462-4705; www.gomendo.com; 200 S School St; 9am-5pm Mon-Fri) One block west of State St; information on Ukiah, Hopland and Anderson Valley.

Sights

Don't miss **Grace Hudson Museum-Sun House** (707-467-2836; www.gracehudsonmuseum.org; 431 S Main St; donation $2; 10am-4:30pm Wed-Sat, from noon Sun), one block east of State St. The collection's mainstays are paintings by Grace Hudson (1865–1937), whose sensitive depictions of Pomo people complement the ethnological work and Native American baskets collected by her husband, John Hudson.

North of downtown, check out the **Redwood Tree Service Station** (859 N State St), a former gas station carved out of a redwood tree.

Festivals & Events

Special events include the **Redwood Empire Fair** (www.redwoodempirefair.com), on the second weekend of August, and the **Ukiah Country PumpkinFest** (707-463-6231) in late October, with an arts-and-crafts fair, children's carnival and fiddle contest.

Sleeping

Chains abound; resorts and campgrounds cluster around Ukiah (see opposite).

Sunrise Inn (707-462-6601; www.sunriseinn.net; 650 S State St; r $48-68;) Request one of the remodeled rooms at Ukiah's best budget motel.

our pick Robinson Creek Inn (707-468-9039; www.robinsoncreek.com; 1901 Boonville Rd; s $100, d $120-140;) Gorgeous gardens lead from the 1878 farmhouse at this inn to a swimming hole behind this country-casual, peaceful B&B-cum-flower farm. Breakfast includes eggs from the inn's own chickens.

Also consider:

Discovery Inn Motel (707-462-8873; www.5motels.com; 1340 N State St; r $74-95; wi-fi) Clean, but dated with a 75ft pool and four Jacuzzis.

Holiday Inn Express (707-462-5745, 800-465-4329; www.hiexpress.com/ukiahca; 1720 N State St; r $81-121; wi-fi) Expanded continental breakfast and laundry machines.

Sanford House B&B (707-462-1653; www.sanfordhouse.com; 306 S Pine St; s/d $95/175;)

Eating

Schat's Courthouse Bakery & Cafe (707-462-1670; 113 W Perkins St; mains lunch $3-7, dinner $8-14; breakfast, lunch & dinner Mon-Sat) Founded by Dutch bakers, Schat's makes a dazzling array of chewy, dense breads, sandwiches, wraps, big salads, dee-lish hot mains and homemade pastries.

Ruen Tong (707-462-0238; 801 N State St; mains $7-12; lunch & dinner; V) This little Thai spot is decked out with glittering decorations; try the pumpkin curry, spicy eggplant or barbecued salmon.

Oco Time (707-462-2422; 111 W Church St; mains lunch $7-10, dinner $8-16; lunch Tue-Fri, dinner Mon-Sat; V) Shoulder your way through the locals to get Ukiah's best sushi, noodle bowls and *oco* (grilled cabbage, egg and noodles). Yum.

Himalayan Cafe (707-467-9900; 1639 S State St; lunch buffet $8, dinner $8-14; V) South of downtown, tuck into delicately spiced Nepalese cooking – tandoori breads and curries.

our pick Patrona (707-462-9181; 130 W Standley St; mains lunch $10-15, dinner $15-28; lunch Mon-Fri, dinner Tue-Sat; V) Foodies flock to excellent Patrona for earthy, flavor-packed, seasonal-regional organic cooking. The unfussy menu includes dishes like roasted chicken, brined-and-roasted pork chops, housemade pasta and local wines. Make reservations and ask about the prix fixe.

Ukiah farmers market (cnr School & Clay Sts; 8:30am-noon Sat May-Oct, 3-6pm Tue Jun-Oct) has farm-fresh produce, crafts and entertainment. **Moore's Flour Mill & Bakery** (707-462-

6550; 1550 S State St; 🕑 7:30am-6pm Mon-Sat) grinds flour for its soft-style bread used on its deli sandwiches; great cookies, too.

Drinking & Entertainment

Dive bars and scruffy cocktail lounges line State St. Ask at the chamber of commerce about cultural events, including Sunday summer concerts at Todd Grove Park and local square dances.

Coffee Critic (☎ 707-462-6333; 476 N State St) Drop in for espresso, ice cream and occasional live music.

Ukiah Brewing Co (☎ 707-468-5898; 102 S State St) This local brewpub makes organic beer and draws weekend crowds for live music.

Mendocino College (☎ 707-468-3000; 1000 Hensley Creek Rd) Students present theater, dance and music.

Shopping

Ukiah's best shopping is along School St, near the courthouse. Step inside **Nomad's World** (☎ 707-462-4060; 111 S School St; 🕑 Mon-Sat) for cool jewelry and home furnishings. Browse a mishmash of antiques at **Ukiah Antique Mall** (☎ 707-462-5559; 116 N School St; 🕑 Mon-Sat).

Take turns trying on superfun vintage drag at **Ruby Slippers** (☎ 707-462-7829; 110 N School St; 🕑 Mon-Sat). The best bookstore in town is **Mendocino Book Co** (☎ 707-468-5940; 102 S School St; 🕑 Mon-Sat).

AROUND UKIAH

Ukiah Wineries

Pick up a wineries map from the Ukiah Chamber of Commerce. Fruit-forward reds from **Fife** (☎ 707-485-0323; www.fifevineyards.com; 3621 Ricetti Lane, Redwood Valley; 🕑 10am-5pm) include a peppery zinfandel and petite sirah, both affordable and food-friendly. And oh, the hilltop views! Bring a picnic.

Germain-Robin (☎ 707-462-0314; Unit 35, 3001 S State St; 🕑 by appointment) makes some of the world's best brandy, which is handcrafted by a fifth-generation brandy-maker from the Cognac region of France. It's just a freeway-side warehouse, but if you're into cognac, you gotta come.

Lolonis (☎ 925-938-8066; 1905 Rd D, Redwood Valley; 🕑 by appointment Apr-Sep) is known for big reds – cabernet, merlot and petite sirah – and for its signature Ladybug Red, some made with estate-grown old-vine grapes.

Vichy Hot Springs Resort

Opened in 1854, Vichy is the oldest continuously operating mineral-springs spa in California. The water's composition perfectly matches that of its famous namesake in Vichy, France. A century ago, Mark Twain, Jack London and Robert Louis Stevenson traveled here for the water's restorative properties, which ameliorate everything from arthritis to poison oak.

Today, the beautifully maintained historic **resort** (☎ 707-462-9515; www.vichysprings.com; 2605 Vichy Springs Rd; RV sites $35, lodge s/d $130/185, creekside s/d $185/235, cottages $270-375; ⛶ 🖳 wi-fi) has the only warm-water, naturally carbonated mineral baths in North America. Unlike others, Vichy requires swimsuits (rentals $2). Day use costs $27 for two hours, $45 for a full day.

Facilities include a swimming pool, outdoor mineral hot tub, 10 indoor and outdoor tubs with natural 100°F waters, and a grotto for sipping the effervescent waters. Massages and facials are available. Entry includes use of the 700-acre grounds, abutting Bureau of Land Management (BLM) lands; hiking trails lead to a 40ft waterfall, an old cinnabar mine and 1100ft peaks – great for sunset views.

The resort's suite and two cottages, built in 1854, are Mendocino County's three oldest structures. The cozy rooms have wooden floors, top-quality beds, breakfast and spa privileges, and no TVs. RV parking doesn't include breakfast or spa entry; there's no tent camping.

From Hwy 101, exit at Vichy Springs Rd and follow the state-landmark signs east for 3 miles. Ukiah is five minutes, but a world, away.

Orr Hot Springs

A clothing-optional resort that's beloved by locals, back-to-the-land hipsters, backpackers and liberal-minded tourists, **Orr Hot Springs** (☎ 707-462-6277; hotwater@pacific.net; sites $45-50, d $140-160, cottages $195-230; 🕑 10am-10pm; 🖳) has a communal redwood hot tub, private porcelain tubs, outdoor tile-and-rock heated pools, sauna, spring-fed rock-bottomed swimming pool, steam, massage and magical gardens. Day use costs $25, $20 on Mondays.

Accommodation includes use of the spa and communal kitchen; some cottages have kitchens. Reservations are essential.

To get there from Hwy 101, take N State St exit, go north a quarter of a mile to Orr

Springs Rd, then 9 miles west. The steep, winding mountain road takes 30 minutes to drive.

Montgomery Woods State Reserve

Two miles west of Orr, this 1140-acre **reserve** (☎ 707-937-5804) protects five old-growth redwood groves. A 2-mile loop trail crosses the creek, winding through the serene groves, starting near the picnic tables and toilets. Day use only; no camping.

Lake Mendocino

Amid rolling hills, 5 miles northeast of Ukiah, this tranquil 1822-acre artificial lake fills a valley, once the ancestral home of the Pomo people. On the lake's north side, **Pomo Visitors Center** (☎ 707-467-4200; Marina Dr; 9am-5pm Wed-Sun Apr-Sep, 1-5pm Sat & Sun Oct-Nov 15) is modeled after a Pomo roundhouse, with exhibits on tribal culture and the dam.

Coyote Dam, 3500ft long and 160ft high, marks the lake's southwest corner; the lake's eastern part is a 689-acre protected wildlife habitat. The **Army Corps of Engineers** (☎ 707-462-7581; www.spn.usace.army.mil/mendocino; 1160 Lake Mendocino Dr; 8am-4pm Mon-Fri) built the dam, manages the lake and provides recreation information. Its office is inconveniently located on the Lower Lake.

There are 300 **campsites** (☎ 877-444-6777; www.reserveusa.com; tent & RV sites $16-25), most with hot showers and primitive boat-in sites ($8).

City of Ten Thousand Buddhas

Three miles east of Ukiah, via Talmage Rd, the **City of Ten Thousand Buddhas** (☎ 707-462-0939; www.advite.com/sf; 2001 Talmage Rd; 8am-6pm) used to be a state mental hospital. Since 1976 it has been a lush, quiet 488-acre Chinese-Buddhist community. Don't miss the temple hall, which really does have 10,000 Buddhas! Be discreet. Stay for lunch in the vegetarian Chinese **restaurant** (4951 Bodhi Way; mains $10; lunch; V).

WILLITS

pop 5100 / elev 1800ft

Willits has a NorCal boho vibe. Ranching, timber and manufacturing may be its mainstays but tie-dye is de rigueur. For visitors, Willits' greatest claim to fame is as the eastern terminus of the Skunk Train. Fort Bragg is 35 miles away on the coast; allow an hour to navigate twisty Hwy 20.

You can check your email (free of charge) over an ice cream at **Sugar Magnolia** (☎ 707-459-0396; 212 S Main St; 11am-10pm Mon-Sat, noon-8pm Sun). **Willits Chamber of Commerce** (☎ 707-459-7910; www.willits.org; 239 S Main St; 10am-4pm Mon-Fri) has oodles of information.

Sights & Activities

The depot for the **Skunk Train** (☎ 707-459-5248, 866-457-5865; www.skunktrain.com) is on E Commercial St, three blocks east of Hwy 101. Trains run between Willits and Fort Bragg (for details, see p263).

The not-to-be-missed **Mendocino County Museum** (☎ 707-459-2736; 400 E Commercial St; by donation individual/family $2/5; 10am-4:30pm Wed-Sun) has an entire 1920s soda fountain and barber shop inside. You could spend an hour perusing Pomo and Yuki basketry and artifacts, or reading about local scandals and countercultural movements. Outside, the **Roots of Motive Power** (www.rootsofmotivepower.com) exhibit occasionally demonstrates steam logging and machinery.

Willits' most famous resident was the horse Seabiscuit, which grew up on **Ridgewood Ranch** (☎ 707-459-5992, reservations 707-459-7910; www.seabiscuitheritage.com; 16200 N Hwy 101; tours $15-25). Ninety-minute tours operate on Monday, Wednesday and Friday (June to September); on Saturday once a month there's a three-hour tour by reservation.

Set among giant redwood trees, **Brooktrails Golf Course** (☎ 707-459-6761; 24860 Birch St; greens fees 9/18 holes $12/18), off Sherwood Rd, 2 miles north of downtown, is one of Northern California's most picturesque nine-hole public courses.

Jackson Demonstration State Forest, 15 miles west of Willits on Hwy 20, offers day-use recreational activities, including educational hiking trails and mountain-biking.

Ten miles north of Willits, **Hwy 162/Covelo Rd** makes for a superb drive following the route of the Northwestern Pacific Railroad along the Eel River and through the Mendocino National Forest. The hour's journey through exquisite river canyons and rolling hills brings you to Covelo, known for its unusual round valley.

Festivals & Events

Willits Frontier Days & Rodeo (www.willitsfrontierdays.com) The first week in July, and dating from 1926, Willits' is 'the oldest continuous rodeo in California.'

Celtic Renaissance Faire (www.rustyswordproductions.com/willits_ren_faire.htm) Held in August, featuring Highland Scottish games, food, music, jugglers, arts and crafts.

Sleeping

Jackson Demonstration State Forest (☎ 707-964-5674; sites free) Campsites have barbecue pits and pit toilets, but no water. Get a permit from the on-site host.

Creekside Cabins & RV Resort (☎ 707-459-2521; www.creeksidecabinsandrvresort.com; 29801 N Hwy 101; tent sites $22, RV sites $35-45, cabins $175) Seven miles north of Willits; camp or stay in a six-person cabin.

Willits KOA Resort (☎ 707-459-6179, 800-562-8542; Hwy 20; tent/RV sites $28/40, cabins $72;) Two miles west of downtown, KOA has hiking and family-oriented activities.

Amendolia's Willits Creek Cabin (☎ 707-456-0201; willitscreekcabin@sbcglobal.net; 190 Bittenbender Lane; s/d $95/110) A 1930s mill-worker's cottage walkable to downtown, this vacation rental has a loft, gas fireplace and barbecue, and sleeps six.

Beside Still Waters Farm (☎ 707-984-6130, 877-230-2171; 30901 Sherwood Rd; cottages 1-bedroom $249-269, 2-bedroom $289) For a romantic splurge, stay in a luxurious B&B cottage with attentive proprietors on 21 acres.

Some of the in-town motels are dumps, so choose carefully. Ask about Skunk Train packages. Upmarket motels include the top-choice **Baechtel Creek Inn & Spa** (☎ 707-459-9063, 800-459-9911; www.baechtelcreekinn.com; 101 Gregory Lane; d incl breakfast $100-130;) and second-choice **Super 8 Motel** (☎ 707-459-3388, 800-800-8000; www.super8.com; 1119 S Main St; d from $79;). A cheaper option is **Best Value Inn Holiday Lodge** (☎ 707-459-5361, 800-835-3972; www.bestvalueinn.com; 1540 S Main St; d from $63;).

Eating

Phoenix Bread Co (☎ 707-456-9970; www.phoenixbreadcompany.com; 861 S Main St; dishes $6-10; 8am-8pm Wed-Mon) Next door to Safeway; concocts fantastic cheese-and-meat-stuffed country-style bread and finger-lickin' barbecue.

Anna's Asian House (☎ 707-459-6086; 47 Mendocino Ave; mains $6-12; lunch & dinner) For Szechuan cooking, made with no MSG and little oil.

our pick Purple Thistle (☎ 707-459-4750; 50 S Main St; mains $13-25; dinner) Willits' best; cooks up Cajun- and Japanese-inspired 'Mendonesian' cuisine, using fresh organic ingredients. Make reservations.

For quick eats, tiny **Ardella's Kitchen** (☎ 707-459-6577; 35 E Commercial St; meals $5-8; 6am-noon Tue-Sat) is tops for breakfast – and *the* place for gossip. For soup and sandwiches, visit **Loose Caboose** (☎ 707-459-1434; 10 Woods St; dishes $6-10; breakfast & lunch). **Gribaldo's Cafe** (☎ 707-459-2256; 1551 S Main St; dishes $6-12; breakfast, lunch & dinner) has cheap breakfasts and weekday breakfast-and-lunch buffets. For healthful Mexican, try **Burrito Exquisito** (☎ 707-459-5421; 42 S Hain St; dishes $7; lunch & dinner).

A **farmers market** (Willits City Park; 3-6pm Thu May-Oct) meets one block off Hwy 101. Pick up natural foods at the **Mariposa Market** (☎ 707-459-9630; 600 S Main St).

Drinking & Entertainment

Shanachie Pub (☎ 707-459-9194; 50B S Main St; Mon-Sat) and **Sugar Magnolia** (☎ 707-456-0396; 212 S Main) have live entertainment.

Willits Community Theatre (☎ 707-459-0895; www.allaboutwct.org; 212 S Main St) stages award-winning plays, poetry readings and comedy.

THE REDWOOD COAST

This sparsely touristed section of the state from Leggett to Crescent City provides world-class opportunities for hikes and wilderness experiences with nary a soul to pester you. So much of the coastal drive passes through deeply forested areas that you can lose perspective and forget that you're by the ocean. Though it's magical beneath the canopy of trees, stop at pullouts for views of the rocky coast and the wildflower-studded prairie lands. This is a more working-class region than its southern neighbors, so expect less gourmet and more down-home.

Information

Redwood Coast Heritage Trails (www.redwoods.info) gives a nuanced slant on the region with itineraries based around lighthouses, Native American culture, the timber and rail industries, and maritime life.

LEGGETT

pop 200

Leggett marks the redwood country's beginning and Hwy 1's end. There ain't much but an expensive gas station, pizza joint and two markets.

Visit 1000-acre **Standish-Hickey State Recreation Area** (☎ 707-925-6482; 69350 Hwy 101; day use $6), 1.5 miles to the north, for picnicking, swimming and fishing in the Eel River and

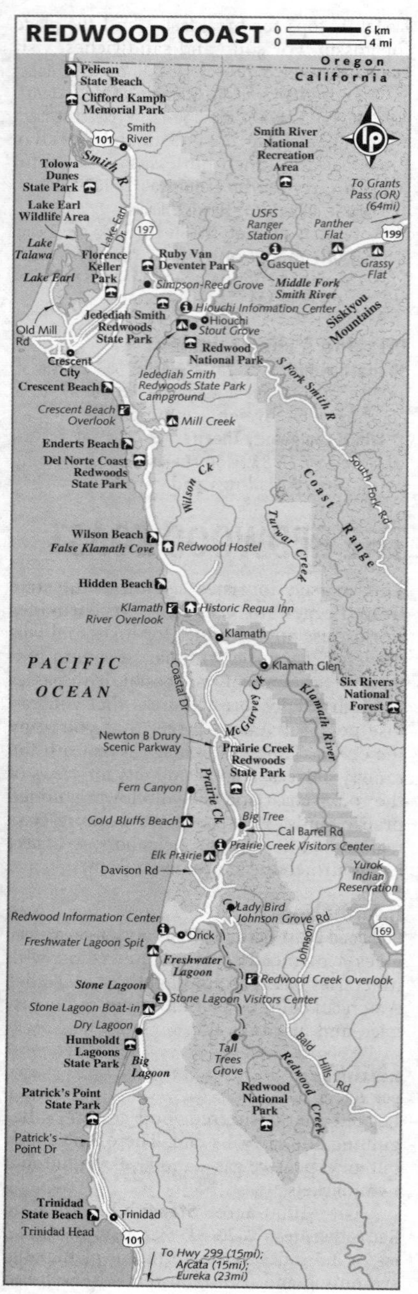

hiking trails among virgin and second-growth redwoods. Year-round **campgrounds** (☎ 800-444-7275; www.reserveamerica.com; tent & RV sites $15-20) with hot showers book up in summer. Avoid highway-side sites.

Chandelier Drive-Thru Tree Park (☎ 707-925-6363; www.drivethrutree.com; Drive-Thru Tree Rd; per car $3; 8am-dusk) has 200 private acres of virgin redwoods with picnicking and nature walks. And yes, there's a redwood with a square hole carved out, which cars can drive through. Only in America.

Across from the Confusion Hill tourist trap, **Redwoods River Resort** (☎ 707-925-6249; www.redwoodriverresort.com; 75000 Hwy 101; tent sites $22-28, RV sites $32-40, lodge r $95-145, cabins with kitchens $120-145;) has a range of lodgings, good for families.

For basic supplies, visit **Price's Peg House** (☎ 707-925-6444; 69501 Hwy 101; 8am-9pm).

RICHARDSON GROVE STATE PARK

Fifteen miles to the north, and bisected by the Eel River, serene **Richardson Grove** (☎ 707-247-3318; Hwy 101; per car $6) occupies 1400 acres of virgin forest. Many trees are over 1000 years old and 300ft tall, but there aren't many hiking trails. In winter, there's good fishing for silver and king salmon.

The **visitors center** (☎ 707-247-3318; 9am-2pm) sells books inside a 1930s lodge, which often has a fire going during cool weather. The park is primarily a **campground** (☎ reservations 800-444-7275; www.reserveamerica.com; tent & RV sites $15-20) with three separate areas with hot showers; some remain open year-round. Summer-only Oak Flat on the east side of the river is shady and has a sandy beach.

BENBOW LAKE

On the Eel River, 2 miles south of Garberville, the 1200-acre **Benbow Lake State Recreation Area** (☎ in summer 707-923-3238, in winter 707-923-3318; day use $6) holds a dam that forms 26-acre Benbow Lake. Events include **summer jazz** in June at the Benbow Inn and the **Summer Arts and Music Festival** (www.mateel.org), where music, food, arts and crafts line the lake for a weekend in May.

our pick **Benbow Inn** (☎ 707-923-2124, 800-355-3301; www.benbowinn.com; 445 Lake Benbow Dr; r $90-305, cottage $395-595; wi-fi) A monument to 1920s rustic elegance, the Redwood Empire's first luxury resort is a national historic landmark. Hollywood's elite once frolicked in the Tudor-style resort's lobby, where you can play chess by the crackling fire, and enjoy a complimentary afternoon tea and evening hors d'oeuvres. Rooms have top-quality beds and antique furniture. The window-lined dining room (breakfast and lunch $10 to $15, dinner mains $22 to $32) serves excellent meals.

Your only other options are the neighboring **RV Resort & Golf Course** (☎ 707-923-2777; www.benbowrv.com), or, across Hwy 101, the year-round riverside **campground** (☎ reservations 800-444-7275; www.reserveamerica.com; sites $23-28) – subject to bridge closures due to flooding – with one shower and highway noise.

DRIVE-THROUGH REDWOODS

What better way to bond with a redwood than driving through its belly? Three carved-out (but alive!) redwoods await along Hwy 101.

Chandelier Drive-Thru Tree Fold in your mirrors and inch forward, then cool off in the uberkitschy gift shop in Leggett.

Shrine Drive-Thru Tree Look up to the sky as you roll through, on the Ave of the Giants in Myers Flat. The least impressive of the three.

Tour Thru Tree Squeeze through then check out the emu off exit 769 in Klamath.

GARBERVILLE

pop 1800

Garberville looks like Main Street USA – until you notice the range of folks cruising the sidewalks. If you've ever wondered where all of the San Francisco hippies went, look no further. The hippies rub shoulders (but not much more) with old-guard fisher-logger types. Appearances can be deceiving. Leather-clad Harley riders might sidle up to the counter at a local eatery and order the tofu ranchero with a whole-wheat bagel. Redway lies 2 miles west.

Information

Garberville-Redway Area Chamber of Commerce (☎ 707-923-2613, 800-923-2613; www.garberville.org; 784 Redwood Dr; ⌚ 10am-4pm summer, Mon-Fri rest of year) Inside the Redwood Dr Center.

KMUD FM91 (www.kmud.org) Find out what's really happening by tuning in to community radio.

Treats (☎ 707-923-3554; 764 Redwood Dr; per min 15¢; ⌚ 8:30am-7pm) Internet and wi-fi.

Trees Foundation Office & Community Resource Center (☎ 707-923-4377; www.treesfoundation.org; 439 Melville Rd; ⌚ 10am-4pm Mon-Thu) Completely in-the-know on conservationist issues.

Festivals & Events

Renowned **Reggae on the River/Reggae Rising** (☎ 707-923-4583; www.reggaeontheriver.com, www.reggaerising.com) in early August draws huge crowds for reggae, world music, arts and craft fairs, camping and swimming in the river. Three-day passes ($175) go on sale March 1 and sell out; no single tickets.

Other annual events:

Avenue of the Giants Marathon (www.theave.org) Race in May.

Harley-Davidson Redwood Run (www.redwoodrun.com) Held in June.

Garberville Rodeo June rodeo.

Hemp Fest (☎ 707-923-3368) Celebrate all things hemp in November.

Winter Arts Faire (www.mateel.org/winterarts.php) A mid-December fair.

Sleeping

South of town, Benbow Inn (opposite) blows away the competition.

Best Western Humboldt House Inn (☎ 707-923-2771, 800-528-1234; 701 Redwood Dr; r incl breakfast $120-140; wi-fi) The best place in town, it has good beds, furnishings and refrigerators.

Also recommended:

Humboldt Redwoods Inn (☎ 707-923-2451; www.humboldtredwoodsinn.com; 987 Redwood Dr; r $60-100;)

Garberville Motel (☎ 707-923-2422; fax 707-923-2599; 948 Redwood Dr; r $70-85;)

Sherwood Forest (☎ 707-923-2721; www.sherwoodforestmotel.com; 814 Redwood Dr; r $70-85;) Of these three options, try this place first.

Eating

Amillia's (☎ 707-923-4340; 443 Melville Rd; mains $7-10; ⌚ 8am-6pm Mon-Fri; Ⓥ) Friendly gourmet-to-go comes from a changing menu of great sandwiches, salads and baked goods.

Woodrose Cafe (☎ 707-923-3191; 911 Redwood Dr; meals $7-12; ⌚ breakfast & lunch; Ⓥ) Garberville's best-loved restaurant; delicious breakfasts and tasty organic salads and sandwiches.

Calico's Deli & Pasta (☎ 707-923-2253; 808 Redwood Dr; dishes $7-13; ⌚ lunch & dinner) Housemade pasta and sandwiches.

Mateel Cafe (☎ 707-923-2030; 3342-3344 Redwood Dr, Redway; mains lunch $11-13, dinner $20-24; ⌚ lunch & dinner Mon-Fri; Ⓥ) Across from the Mateel Community Center in Redway; serves up

MEDICAL MARIJUANA: CULTIVATING CONFLICT

In 1996 California voters approved Proposition 215, which legalized the medicinal use of marijuana. With a doctor's note, patients could now legally grow pot or buy it at 'cannabis clubs' without fear of legal reprisal.

The North Coast has the ideal pot-growing climate. In Mendocino County, you might even spot Mary Jane growing in people's *front* yards. The law allows people to plant a 10ft-by-10ft plot. You can fit 20 plants in a plot that size. Each can yield $4000 on the black market, so one plot alone can bring in $80,000. Interestingly enough, the number of pot permits in Mendocino County coincides with the number of concealed-weapons permits: about 1300.

Legal conflicts abound. California's law directly contradicts federal drug laws, and in the USA federal law trumps state law – theoretically. In June 2005 the US Supreme Court ruled that federal agents could indeed enforce federal law and pursue medical-marijuana users. However, the justices did *not* specifically overturn Prop 215.

Local conflicts have also arisen. In the 1980s, while Nancy Reagan told America's kids to 'just say no,' Ronnie sprayed California's marijuana fields with the toxic herbicide paraquat. Young botanists retaliated by just saying no, thank you, and quietly began formulating new strains of genetically modified pot that grew well indoors – and they were *far* more potent than outdoor pot had ever been. Fast-forward to Mendocino, March 2004, when voters approved a new law banning the propagation of genetically modified organisms (GMOs) anywhere in the county. If this law is enforced, then technically Mendo's pot crops are illegal – under local law – in a county that overwhelmingly supported Prop 215. Go figure.

steaks and chops, stone-baked pizzas and organic salads.

our pick **Cecil's** (☎ 707-923-7007; 773 Redwood Dr; mains $18-27; dinner Thu-Mon) Specializes in tony Cajun cooking – crawfish *étouffée*, pecan catfish and pork chops with sweet-potato mashers. Occasional live music keeps this top spot busy.

Chautauqua Natural Foods (☎ 707-923-2452; 436 Church St; Mon-Sat) sells groceries. The **farmers market** (11am-3pm Fri May-Oct) sets up in the town square.

Drinking & Entertainment

Sip cocktails in elegant 1920s Tudor-style Benbow Inn (p276).

Flavors (☎ 707-923-717; 767 Redwood Dr) The town's popular coffee shop, with a range of pastries, soups and salads.

Garberville Theatre (☎ 707-923-3580; 766 Redwood Dr) Shows first-run movies.

Mateel Community Center (☎ 707-923-3368; www.mateel.org; 59 Rusk Lane, Redway) Hosts a diverse array of dances and events.

HUMBOLDT REDWOODS STATE PARK & AVENUE OF THE GIANTS

Don't miss this magical drive through California's largest redwood park, **Humboldt Redwoods State Park** (☎ 707-946-2409), which covers 53,000 acres – 17,000 of which are old-growth – and contains some of the world's most magnificent trees (see boxed text, p293). Exit Hwy 101 when you see the 'Avenue of the Giants' sign, take this smaller alternative to the interstate; it's an incredible, 32-mile, two-lane stretch. You'll find free driving guides at roadside signboards at both the avenue's southern entrance, 6 miles north of Garberville, near Phillipsville, and at the northern entrance, south of Scotia, at Pepperwood; there are access points off Hwy 101.

South of Weott, a volunteer-staffed **visitors center** (☎ 707-946-2263; 9am-5pm summer, 10am-4pm winter) shows videos and sells maps and books. Don't bypass its small, excellent **museum** housing the historic 1917 'Travel Log.'

Three miles north, the **California Federation of Women's Clubs Grove** is home to an interesting four-sided hearth designed by renowned San Franciscan architect Julia Morgan in 1931 to commemorate 'the untouched nature of the forest.'

Primeval **Rockefeller Forest**, 4.5 miles west of the avenue via Mattole Rd, appears as it did a century ago. You quickly walk out of site of cars and feel like you have fallen into the time of dinosaurs. It's the world's largest contiguous old-growth redwood forest, and contains about 20% of all such remaining trees. Check out the subtly variegated rings (count one for each year) on the cross sections of some of the downed giants that are left to mulch back into the earth over the next few hundred years.

In **Founders Grove**, north of the visitors center, the **Dyerville Giant** was knocked over in 1991 by another falling tree. A walk along its gargantuan 370ft length, with its wide trunk towering above, helps you appreciate how huge these ancient trees are.

The park has over 100 miles of trails for hiking, mountain-biking and horseback riding. Easy walks include short nature trails in Founders Grove and Rockefeller Forest and **Drury-Chaney Loop Trail** (with berry picking in summer). Challenging treks include popular **Grasshopper Peak Trail**, south of the visitors center, which climbs to the 3379ft fire lookout.

For a break from hiking, taste wine at **Riverbend Cellars** (☎ 707-943-9907; 12990 Ave of the Giants, Myers Flat; 11am-5pm) or tuck into a gourmet meal at the **Grove** (☎ 707-943-9930; 13065 Ave of the Giants, Myers Flat; lunch & dinner Thu-Mon).

The park runs three **campgrounds** (☎ reservations 800-444-7275; www.reserveamerica.com; tent & RV sites $15-20), with hot showers, two environmental camps, five trail camps, a hike/bike camp and an equestrian camp. Of the developed spots, Burlington Campground is open year-round beside the visitors center and near a number of trailheads. Hidden Springs Campground, 5 miles south, and Albee Creek Campground, on Mattole Rd past Rockefeller Forest, are open mid-May to early fall.

If the park's campsites are full, **Giant Redwoods RV & Campground** (☎ 707-943-3198; www.giantredwoodsrvcamp.com; 455 Boy Scout Camp Rd, Myers Flat; tent/RV sites $25/37) has showers, riverside sites and beaches.

Several towns along the avenue have simple lodgings of varying calibers and levels of hospitality. The best is the family-friendly **Miranda Gardens Resort** (☎ 707-943-3011; www.mirandagardens.com; 6766 Ave of the Giants, Miranda; cottages with kitchen $165-275, without $115-175;). The cozy, slightly rustic cottages have redwood paneling, and some have fireplaces. Across the street, **Avenue Cafe** (☎ 707-943-9945; 6743 Ave of the Giants, Miranda; mains $8-11; breakfast & lunch daily, dinner Mon-Sat) serves up basic diner food.

Vacation House in the Redwoods (☎ 707-722-4330; www.redwoodvisitor.org; 31117 Ave of the Giants, Pepperwood; cottage $145) is a lovely two-bedroom cottage surrounded by a sunny flower farm that sleeps up to five. A hammock, deck and hot tub sweeten the deal.

For great burgers, **Chimney Tree** (☎ 707-923-2265; 1111 Ave of the Giants, Phillipsville; burgers $6-10; 10am-7pm May-Sep; V) raises its own grass-fed beef. Alas, the fries are frozen, but those burgers…mmm-mmm!

Harley riders pack **Riverwood Inn** (☎ 707-943-3333; www.riverwoodinn.info; 2828 Ave of the Giants, Phillipsville; lunch Sat & Sun, dinner Wed-Mon), a haunted roadhouse that hosts blues, folk and rock bands, mixes up strong drinks – 32 tequilas! – and serves OK Mexican cooking. It also rents rooms ($55 to $80).

SCOTIA

pop 1000

Who do the environmental activists do battle with? Stop in at Scotia to see the Pacific Lumber Company (Palco), the world's largest redwood lumber mill and its company town. A bit spooky, hearing forklifts, smelling smokestacks and seeing all the felled redwoods in piles, but this is how the state got its redwood hot tubs. Times are changing, though. The mill sawed its last big tree in 1997 and no longer has a blade big enough to cut giant redwoods.

The **Scotia Museum & Visitors Center** (☎ 707-764-2222; www.palco.com; cnr Main & Bridge Sts; 8am-4:30pm Mon-Fri summer;), at the town's south end, offers free self-guided mill tours (Monday to Friday). In summer, go to the museum; otherwise head to the guardhouse at the mill's entrance and you'll be able to see the $25 million saw mill, which uses lasers, computers and robotics to maximize the amount of lumber generated from each log.

As you drive along Hwy 101 and see what appears to be a never-ending redwood forest, understand that this 'forest' sometimes consists of trees only a few rows deep, a carefully crafted illusion for tourists. Most of the old-growth trees have been cut. Once you've grasped Palco's party line about 'forestry stewardship,' log on to the website www.headwaterspreserve.org to learn about clear-cutting and the politics of the timber wars. Also tune in to community-radio station KMUD FM 90.3 and 91.1.

Tidy, deserted **Scotia Inn** (☎ 707-764-5683, 888-764-2248; www.scotiainn.com; 100 Main St; r $85-140), with its grand old-timey lobby, is adorned with floral wallpaper, lace curtains and nary a soul.

Hoby's Market (☎ 707-764-5331; 105 Main St) sells sandwiches and groceries. Rio Dell, across the river, has nothing-special motels and **Old**

Café 101 (☎ 707-764-3090; 70 Wildwood Ave; mains $6-8; 7am-8pm) with wi-fi.

LOST COAST

California's gorgeous Lost Coast extends from just north of Rockport where Hwy 1 cuts inland to the town of Ferndale in the north. One of the state's most untouched coastal areas, the region became 'lost' when the highway system bypassed it early in the 20th century.

The central and southern stretches fall respectively within the King Range National Conservation Area and the Sinkyone Wilderness State Park. Steep, rugged King Range rises over 4000ft, less than 3 miles from the coast, with near-vertical cliffs plunging to the sea. High rainfall causes frequent landslides; the area north of the King Range is more accessible, but the scenery less dramatic.

Although there are several one-horse rural settlements (Petrolia and Honeydew, for example), the only sizable community is Shelter Cove, an isolated unincorporated town on the coast.

You can explore the Lost Coast from many different points, most requiring backtracking by car or planning for a pick-up and shuttle back to your vehicle. The BLM website lists approved shuttle services and posts road and trail conditions and closures. Or, take a guided hike with a group like **Sanctuary Forest** (www.sanctuaryforest.org).

TEDDY ROOSEVELT'S ELK

Roosevelt elk are the largest of their kind, with males weighing up to 1000lb and carrying massive antlers. They are named in honor of US President Teddy Roosevelt, who established the national wildlife refuge system in the early 1900s, and made Washington's Olympic National Park a protected habitat for the endangered elk. By 1925 there were only 25 left; today, the population stands at over 1000. The elks' biggest threats are now from poachers and reckless drivers.

You'll see them on the Lost Coast and around Orick along Davison Rd, west of Hwy 101; in Elk Prairie, on the Newton B Drury Scenic Parkway; and at Gold Bluffs Beach, near Fern Canyon. Try to visit in the early morning and late evening, when the herds feed.

Check for ticks; Lyme disease is common. Don't jump fences or trespass, especially in October at harvest time; this is pot-growing country. In fall the weather is clear, if cool. Wildflowers bloom from April through May, and gray whales migrate from December through April. The warmest, driest months are June to August, but days are foggy. The weather can quickly change.

Shelter Cove

An unincorporated town 25 long miles west of Garberville, Shelter Cove is a patchwork of government-owned land and private property. In the late 19th and early 20th centuries it used to be the departure point for shipping the bark of the locally occurring tan oak. As the name suggests, the bark was used as a natural tanning agent before chemical agents were developed in the 1920s.

Fifty years ago, Southern California fast-talkers subdivided the land, built an airstrip and convinced investors to buy seaside plots. But they didn't tell buyers that a steep, winding, one-lane dirt road provided the only access. Today, there's still only one route in, but it is now paved; nevertheless, take care when it's foggy.

An encampment of restaurants and inns makes this a great spot for a break or a convenient base from which to explore.

The tidy, modern rooms at **Oceanfront Inn & Lighthouse** (☎ 707-986-7002; www.oceanfrontinnca.com; 10 Seal Court; r $125-145, ste with kitchen $175) have microwaves, refrigerators, and balconies overlooking the sea.

Charming **Tides Inn** (☎ 707-986-7900; www.sheltercovetidesinn.com; 59 Surf Pt; r $130-145, ste with kitchen $185) sits right above the crashing waves.

The best place to stay hands down is the sparkling, recently renovated, oceanfront **Shelter Cove Bed & Breakfast** (☎ 707-986-7161; www.sheltercovebandb.com; 148 Dolphin Dr; r $175-195), managed by supercool, design-savvy owners. Think love nest, and leave the kids at home.

Other recommendations:

Shelter Cove Beachcomber Inn (☎ 707-986-7551, 800-718-4789; 412 Machi Rd; r $65-105) Slightly inland and slightly worn; some apartments.

Marina Motel (☎ 707-986-7595; www.mariosofsheltercove.com; 533 Machi Rd; r $100) Basic.

Cliff House at Shelter Cove (☎ 707-986-7344; www.cliffhousesheltercove.com; 141 Wave Dr; ste with kitchen $169) Oceanfront.

Northern California Properties (☎ 707-986-7346; 101 Lower Pacific Dr) Rents vacation properties.

Shelter Cove RV Park, Campground & Deli (☎ 707-986-7474; 492 Machi Rd) has great fresh fish-and-chips, plus hot showers and outdoor tables. Sites are $25 to $35.

Have a sweet escape at **Cape Mendocino Tea** (☎ 707-986-1138; 1176 Lower Pacific Dr; dishes $5-15; 11am-4pm Sat-Mon), an old-school British-style teahouse with finger sandwiches.

First-choice **Cove Restaurant** (☎ 707-986-1197; 10 Seal Court; dishes $6-19; lunch & dinner Thu-Sun; V) has everything from veggie stir-fries to New York steaks.

Costa Cucina (☎ 707-986-7672; 205 Wave Dr; mains $7-12, pizza $15-25; breakfast, lunch & dinner Thu-Sun) serves a range of pizzas.

Get groceries and gasoline at **Shelter Cove General Store** (☎ 707-986-7733; 7272 Shelter Cove Rd), 2 miles beyond town.

Sinkyone Wilderness State Park

Named for the Sinkyone people who once lived here, this 7367-acre wilderness extends south of Shelter Cove along pristine coastline. The **Lost Coast Trail** continues along here for another 22 miles, from Whale Gulch south to Usal Beach Campground, taking at least three days. Many roads in the park are *not* maintained fall through spring and quickly become impassable. To get through you'll need a 4WD and a chainsaw. Seriously.

Near the park's northern end, **Needle Rock** (☎ 707-986-7711) serves as a remote visitors center and source of potable water, with gorgeous views up and down the coast. Friendly volunteer rangers sell maps and provide information, especially about road conditions. If you feel like getting out of the elements on your camping experience, rent its Barn Camp ($20), which gives you oceanfront shelter on a platform in a quaint weathered wooden barn.

To get here, drive west from Garberville and Redway, on Briceland-Thorn Rd, 21 miles through Whitethorn to Four Corners. Turn left (south) and continue for 3.5 miles down a very rugged road to the visitor center; it takes 1½ hours.

A great day hike goes north from Needle Rock to **Whale Gulch** (4.5 miles round-trip), where a small lagoon is studded with piles of driftwood.

Bear Harbor Campground lies south of Needle Rock and was used by smugglers during Prohibition – hard to get caught here! Now, you are more likely to be surrounded by the majestic Roosevelt elk that pass through in quiet, munching herds. Don't feed them.

There's also access to Usal Beach Campground at the south end of the park from Hwy 1: north of Westport, unpaved County Rd 431 begins from Hwy 1's milepost 90.88 and travels 6 miles up the coast to the campground.

North of the King Range

You can reach the Lost Coast's northern section year-round via paved, narrow Mattole Rd. Plan three hours to navigate the winding 68 miles through rolling grassland from Ferndale to the coast at Cape Mendocino, then inland to Humboldt Redwoods State Park and Hwy 101. The drive is enjoyable, but the Lost Coast's wild, spectacular scenery lies further south in the more remote regions.

You'll pass two tiny settlements. **Petrolia** is the site of California's first oil well, capped-off on private property. Pick blueberries at **Lost Coast Blueberries** (☎ 707-629-3563; 41774 Mattole Rd), but call ahead. There's also a post office and **store** (☎ 707-629-3455; 9am-5pm) with bear-canister rentals (cash only), gasoline, propane and kerosene. At **Honeydew** there's a semireliable gas station at the **post office** (☎ 707-629-3310; 9am-5pm).

Camp creekside with flush toilets and cold showers at **AW Way County Park** (☎ 707-445-7651; Mattole Rd; per vehicle $15), 6 miles southeast of Petrolia, on the road toward Honeydew.

King Range National Conservation Area

Stretching over 35 miles of virgin coastline, with ridge after ridge of mountainous terrain plunging down to the surf, the 60,000-acre wilderness tops out at namesake **King's Peak**. From the trailhead to the summit (round-trip 4 miles) climb to a height of 4087ft and reap the benefits of your labor with vistas in all directions. To the west, of course, you have the Pacific and Big Flat River Creek. To the east see as far as the Yolla Bolly Wilderness on a clear day.

Nine miles east of Shelter Cove in Whitethorn, the **BLM** (☎ 707-986-5400, 707-825-2300; 768 Shelter Cove Rd; 8am-4:30pm Memorial Day-Labor Day, 8am-4:30 Mon-Fri Sep-May) has maps and directions for trails and campsites; they're posted outside after hours. Information is also available from the BLM in Arcata (see p288).

The best way to see the Lost Coast is to hike. **Lost Coast Trail** follows 24 miles of coastline from Mattole Campground in the north, near Petrolia, to Black Sands Beach at Shelter Cove in the south. The prevailing northerly winds make it best to hike from north to south; plan three or four days. For information on backpacker shuttles, call the BLM or contact **Lost Coast Trail Transport Services** (☎ 707-986-9909; www.lostcoasttrail.com).

Highlights include an abandoned lighthouse at Punta Gorda, remnants of early shipwrecks, tidepools and abundant wildlife, including sea lions, seals and more than 300 bird species. The trail is mostly level, passing beaches and over rocky outcrops. Consult tide tables, as some outcroppings are passable only at low tide.

A good day hike starts at the Mattole Campground trailhead and travels 3 miles south along the coast to the **Punta Gorda lighthouse** (return against the wind). Mattole Campground is at the ocean end of Lighthouse Rd, 4 miles from Mattole Rd, southeast of Petrolia.

Or, go to the back of Wailaki Campground to reach the head of the **Chemise Mountain Trail.** This quick ascent of approximately 0.7 miles winds steadily through redwoods, madrones and tan oaks, and brings you to an overlook where ridge after ridge of the King Range stretches off into the distance, undisturbed by humankind.

Both Wailaki and Nadelos have developed **campgrounds** (tent & RV sites $8). There are another four campgrounds scattered around the range, plus multiple primitive walk-in sites. For camping outside developed campgrounds, you'll need a bear canister and free fire permit, both available from BLM offices.

Some claim that nearby Cape Mendocino is the westernmost point in the contiguous US. It's not. That honor belongs to Cape Alava, Washington.

FERNDALE

pop 1400

Twenty miles south of Eureka and nestled in rich agricultural plains, Ferndale has so well preserved its Victorian architecture that the entire town is listed as a state and federal historic landmark. Stroll along Main St and visit galleries, quaint emporia and soda fountains.

THE SOUNDS OF SILENCE

In the forests, soak up sweet solitude, but on the road, spin your dial for the eclectic reality of far northern life.

- **KMUD 91.1FM** Local institution 'redwood community radio' is also 88.3FM in Eureka
- **KHSU 90.5FM** Humboldt State's 'diverse public radio'
- **KSLG 94.1FM** Hot new alt-rock based in Ferndale
- **KLVG 103.7FM** 'Positive and encouraging' Christian radio
- **100.9FM** Get on your country twang
- **1610AM** Tune in for information on elk sightings

Although Ferndale relies on tourism, the town has refreshingly avoided becoming a tourist trap. It's a lovely place to spend the night.

Information

Ferndale Chamber of Commerce (☎ 707-786-4477; www.victorianferndale.org/chamber) A visitors guide is available around town.

Ferndale Library (☎ 707-786-9559; 807 Main St; 🕑 noon-5pm & 7-9pm Tue-Thu, noon-4pm Fri, noon-5pm Sat) Free internet access, one-hour limit.

Sights & Activities

As Ferndale's settlers became wealthy from dairy farming, some built ornate mansions called 'butterfat palaces.' **Shaw House** (703 Main St) was the first permanent structure in Ferndale. The town's founder, Seth Shaw, built the gabled Carpenter Gothic from 1854 to 1866. It was called 'Fern Dale' for the 6ft-tall ferns that grew there – hence the town's name. The **Gingerbread Mansion** (400 Berding St), an 1898 Queen Anne-Eastlake, is the town's most photographed building. The 1866, 32-room **Fern Cottage** (☎ 707-786-4835; www.ferncottage.org; Centerville Rd; adult/student $5/2.50; 🕑 10am-4pm Wed-Sun summer), west of town, was originally a Carpenter Gothic that grew as the family did. Only one family ever lived here, so nothing got thrown away, and it's all been preserved. Call ahead for winter hours.

The **Ferndale Museum** (☎ 707-786-4466; www.ferndale-museum.org; cnr Shaw & 3rd Sts; admission by donation; 11am-4pm Wed-Sat, 1-4pm Sun) is jam-packed with artifacts.

The **Kinetic Sculpture Museum** (580 Main St; admission free; 10am-5pm Mon-Sat, noon-4pm Sun;) houses fanciful, astounding kinetic sculptures used in the town's annual Kinetic Sculpture Race.

Half a mile from downtown via Bluff St, enjoy short tramps through fields of wildflowers, beside ponds, redwood groves and eucalyptus trees at 110-acre **Russ Park**. The **cemetery**, also on Bluff St, is way cool with graves dating to the 1800s and great views to the ocean. Five miles down Centerville Rd, **Centerville Beach** is one of the few off-leash dog beaches in Humboldt County.

Festivals & Events

This wee town has a packed social calendar.

Kinetic Sculpture Race (http://kineticgrandchampionship.com) Famous moving-sculpture race held in May.

Tour of the Unknown Coast (www.tucycle.org) Bicycle race in May.

Scandinavian Mid-Summer Festival Folk dancing and feasting in June.

Humboldt County Fair (www.humboldtcountyfair.org) Held in mid-August.

Victorian Village Oktoberfest & Harvest Day Let out your inner German.

Christmas celebrations The halls are decked and the lights are on.

Sleeping

Humboldt County Fairgrounds (707-786-9511; www.humboldtcountyfair.org; 1250 5th St; tent/RV sites $10/25) Turn west onto Van Ness St and go a few blocks for lawn camping with showers.

Francis Creek Inn (707-786-9611; www.franciscreekinn.com; 577 Main St; r from $85; wi-fi) White picket balconies front tidy, spartan rooms furnished with simple faux antiques.

Redwoods Suites (707-786-5000; www.redwoodsuites.com; 332 Ocean St; r from $85) This simple motel has a big lawn and miniature Victorian playhouse for kids.

Hotel Ivanhoe (707-786-9000; www.ivanhoe-hotel.com; 315 Main St; r $95-145) Ferndale's oldest hostelry opened in 1875. It has four antique-laden rooms and an Old West–style 2nd-floor gallery, perfect for morning coffee.

our pick **Victorian Inn** (707-786-4949, 888-589-1808; www.a-victorian-inn.com; 400 Ocean Ave; r $105-245; wi-fi) The bright, sunny rooms inside this venerable 1890 two-story, former bank building are comfortably furnished with thick carpeting, good linens and antiques.

Shaw House (707-786-9958, 800-557-7429; www.shawhouse.com; 703 Main St; r $135-185, ste $250-275) California's oldest B&B is also Ferndale's first grand home, set back on extensive grounds. Original details remain, including painted wooden ceilings. If you like B&Bs, this one's a charmer.

Gingerbread Mansion Inn (707-786-4000, 800-952-4136; www.gingerbread-mansion.com; 400 Berding St; r $135-205, ste $155-305; wi-fi) Ferndale's iconic B&B drips with gingerbread trim. The 11 exquisitely detailed rooms are decked out with high-end 1890s Victorian furnishings. Rates include high-tea service, evening wine and three-course breakfast. No kids under 12.

Collingwood Inn B&B (707-786-9219, 800-469-1632; www.collingwoodinn.com; 831 Main St, r $165-200, ste $210-225; wi-fi) This 1885 Hart House, surrounded by bodacious rose gardens, has four rooms with extras like feather beds, bathrobes and coffee delivered to your door. It's gay friendly, too.

Eating

Buttercream (707-786-4880; 385 Main St; dishes $5-7; lunch Tue-Sun) This country-style tea salon in the back of an antiques store serves a daily-changing menu of soup, salad and one main. Good muffins and French-press coffee, too.

Poppa Joe's (707-786-4180; 409 Main St; dishes $5-7; lunch & dinner Mon-Fri, 6am-noon Sat & Sun) You can't beat the atmosphere at this wacky diner, where trophy heads hang from the wall and old men play poker all day. The American-style breakfasts are good, too – especially the pancakes.

our pick **Curley's Grill** (707-786-9696; 400 Ocean Ave; mains $10-25; lunch & dinner) Sidle up to the Old West–style oak bar for a stellar cocktail or dig in to everything from steak sandwiches and meatloaf to the portabello mushroom tower and Niçoise salad, served on brightly colored Fiestaware.

Hotel Ivanhoe (707-786-9000; 315 Main St; mains $14-20; dinner Wed-Sun) For Italian-American food and prime rib, the Ivanhoe has a quiet dining room and occasional live music.

Pick up freshies at the **farmers market** (Victorian Inn, 400 Ocean Ave; 10:30am-2pm Sat May-Oct).

Entertainment

Ferndale Repertory Theatre (707-786-5483; www.ferndale-rep.org; 447 Main St) This top-shelf company produces excellent contemporary theatre in the historic Hart Theatre Building.

Shopping

Blacksmith Shop & Gallery (☎ 707-786-4216; www.ferndaleblacksmith.com; 455 & 491 Main St) From wrought-iron art to hand-forged furniture, this is the largest collection of contemporary blacksmithing in America.

Golden Gait Mercantile (☎ 707-786-4891; 421 Main St) Spend hours browsing the shelves of yesteryear's goods.

Hobart Gallery (☎ 707-786-9259; 393 Main St) Check out the mixed-media art here.

Silva's (☎ 707-786-4425; Victorian Inn, 400 Ocean Ave) Gorgeous jewelry.

HUMBOLDT BAY NATIONAL WILDLIFE REFUGE

This pristine **wildlife refuge** (☎ 707-733-5406; sunrise-sunset) protects wetland habitats for more than 200 species of birds migrating annually along the Pacific Flyway (see boxed text, p324). In one single day in 2004, there were a whopping 26,000 Aleutian cackling geese counted outside the visitors center!

The peak season for waterbirds and raptors runs September to March, for black brant geese and migratory shorebirds mid-March to late April. Gulls, terns, cormorants, pelicans, egrets and herons come year-round. Look for harbor seals offshore; bring binoculars. If it's open, drive out South Jetty Rd to the mouth of Humboldt Bay for a stunning perspective.

Pick up a map from the **visitors center** (1020 Ranch Rd; 8am-5pm). Exit Hwy 101 at Hookton Rd, 11 miles south of Eureka, turn north along the frontage road, on the freeway's west side. In April, look for the **Godwit Days** festival.

EUREKA

pop 26,200

Thriving Eureka hugs the shores of Humboldt Bay, the state's largest bay north of San Francisco. As you drive into the town along Hwy 101, Eureka's suburban strip is unimpressive. But venture into Old Town, a couple of blocks away, and discover colorful Victorians, impressive museums and a refurbished waterfront. Artists gravitate here: photographs, paintings and sculpture adorn restaurants, bars and public spaces.

Orientation & Information

The streets lie on a grid; numbered streets cross lettered streets. For the best window-shopping, head to the 300, 400 and 500 blocks of 2nd St, between D and G Sts.

Eureka Chamber of Commerce (☎ 707-442-3738, 800-356-6381; 2112 Broadway; 8:30am-5pm Mon-Fri) The main visitor information center is on Hwy 101.

Eureka-Humboldt County Convention and Visitors Bureau (☎ 707-443-5097, 800-346-3482; 1034 2nd St; 9am-5pm Mon-Fri) Maps and brochures.

Going Places (☎ 707-443-4145; 328 2nd St) Travel-oriented bookstore.

Has Beans (☎ 707-442-1535; 738 2nd St; per hr $8) On the cnr of I St; internet access and homemade pastries.

Pride Enterprises Tours (☎ 707-445-2117, 800-400-1849) Local historian leads outstanding tours. Licensed to guide in the national parks.

Six Rivers National Forest Headquarters (☎ 707-442-1721; 1330 Bayshore Way; 8am-4:30pm Mon-Fri) Maps and information.

Sights

Of Eureka's fine Victorian buildings the most famous is the ornate **Carson Mansion** (134 M St), the 1880s home of lumber baron William Carson. It took 100 men a full year to build. Today it's a private men's club. The pink house opposite, at 202 M St, is an 1884 Queen Anne Victorian designed by the same architects and built as a wedding gift for Carson's son.

The free *Eureka Visitors Map,* available at tourist offices, details walking tours and scenic drives, focusing on architecture and history. **Old Town**, along 2nd and 3rd Sts from C St to M St, was once Eureka's down-and-out area, but has been refurbished into a buzzing pedestrian district of galleries, shops, cafés and restaurants. The F Street Plaza and Boardwalk run along the waterfront at the foot of F St. Gallery **openings** fall on the first Saturday of every month.

One of only seven of its kind in America, the incredible **Blue Ox Millworks & Historic Park** (☎ 707-444-3437, 800-248-4259; www.blueoxmill.com; 1 X St; adult/child $7.50/3.50; 9am-5pm Mon-Fri, to 4pm Sat;) uses antique tools and mills to produce authentic gingerbread trim for Victorian buildings; one-hour self-guided tours take you through the mill and historical buildings, including a blacksmith shop and 19th-century skid camp. Kids love the oxen.

A relic of Eureka's recent past, the **Romano Gabriel Wooden Sculpture Garden** (315 2nd St) is enclosed by glass, between D and E Sts. For 30 years the brightly painted folk art in Gabriel's front yard delighted locals. After he died in 1977, the city moved the collection here.

The **Clarke Memorial Museum** (☎ 707-443-1947; 240 E St; admission by donation; ⌚ 11am-4pm Tue-Sat), in the former 1912 Bank of Eureka building, holds Native American artifacts and thousands of pieces on Humboldt County history.

Also in Old Town, there's **Humboldt Bay Maritime Museum** (☎ 707-444-9440; www.humboldtbaymaritimemuseum.com; 423 1st St; admission free; ⌚ 11am-4pm Wed-Sun) and **Discovery Museum** (☎ 707-443-9694; 517 3rd St; admission $4; ⌚ 10am-4pm Tue-Sat, from noon Sun;), a hands-on kids' museum.

Across Hwy 101, the excellent **Morris Graves Museum of Art** (☎ 707-442-0278; www.humboldtarts.org; 636 F St; admission by donation; ⌚ noon-5pm Wed-Sun) shows rotating exhibitions of California artists inside 1904 Carnegie library, the state's first public library. It hosts weekend jazz, dance and spoken-word performances (September to May).

Fort Humboldt State Historic Park (☎ 707-445-6567; 3431 Fort Ave; admission free; ⌚ 8am-5pm) lies off Broadway, south of downtown. The fort was established in 1853 on a bluff overlooking Humboldt Bay. Outdoor exhibits show how giant redwoods were felled.

Sequoia Park (☎ 707-442-6552; 3414 W St; zoo adult/child $4/2; ⌚ 10am-7pm May-Sep, to 5pm Oct-Apr), a 77-acre old-growth redwood grove, has biking and hiking trails, children's playground and picnic areas, and a small zoo.

Activities

Board the 1910 *Madaket*, America's oldest continuously operating passenger vessel, for a **harbor cruise** (☎ 707-445-1910; www.humboldtbaymaritimemuseum.com; adult/child $18/10, shorter cruise $10), and learn the history of Humboldt Bay. The *Madaket*, located at the foot of C St, originally ferried mill workers and passengers until the Samoa Bridge was built in 1972.

Hum-Boats Sail, Canoe & Kayak Center (☎ 707-443-5157; www.humboats.com; Startare Dr; ⌚ 9am-5pm Mon-Fri, 9am-6pm Sat & Sun Apr-Oct, 9am-2:30pm Nov-Mar), at Woodley Island Marina, rents kayaks and sailboats, and has lessons, tours, charters, sunset sails and full-moon paddles.

Northern Mountain Supply (☎ 707-445-1711; 125 W 5th St; ⌚ 10am-6pm Mon-Sat, noon-5pm Sat) sells canoes and kayaks, as well as renting camping and backpacking gear. **Pro Sport Center** (☎ 707-443-6328; 508 Myrtle Ave; ⌚ 10am-6pm Mon-Fri, 9am-6pm Sat, 10am-5pm Sun) has a full-service bike shop (no rentals) and sells camping gear; it also rents and sells kayaks and scuba, diving and skiing gear.

Festivals & Events

Summer concerts rock out the F Street Pier. Festivals include:

Redwood Coast Dixieland Jazz Festival (www.redwoodcoastmusicfestivals.org) In March.

Rhododendron Festival (☎ 707-498-8742) April flower festival.

Blues by the Bay (www.redwoodcoastmusicfestivals.org) Waterfront concerts in September.

Kinetic Sculpture Race (http://kineticgrandchampionship.com) The kooky-lovely race passes through Eureka on Memorial Day weekend in September, when folks on self-propelled contraptions travel 38 miles from Arcata to Ferndale.

Sleeping

Room rates run high midsummer; you can sometimes find cheaper in Arcata. Motels line Hwy 101. Most cost $60 to $100 and have no air-conditioning; choose places set back from the road. The cheapest are south of downtown on the suburban strip. For camping you could also try Samoa Peninsula (p287)

Eureka KOA (☎ 707-822-4243, 800-562-3136; www.koakampgrounds.com; 4050 N Hwy 101; tent sites $28, RV sites with hookups $32-35, without hookups $25, cabins $60; wi-fi) About halfway to Arcata, with all the standard KOA offerings.

Eagle House Inn (☎ 707-444-3344; www.eaglehouseinn.com; 139 2nd St; r $105-205;) This hulking Victorian hotel in Old Town has 24 rooms above a turn-of-the-century ballroom perfect for hide-and-seek. Rooms have opulent but not overly precious period furniture: carved headboards, floral-print carpeting and antique armoires.

Abigail's Elegant Victorian Mansion (☎ 707-444-3144; www.eureka-california.com; 1406 C St; r $145-215) Inside this National Historic Landmark that's practically a Victorian living-history museum, the sweet-as-could-be innkeepers lavish guests with warm hospitality.

our pick **Daly Inn** (☎ 707-445-3638, 800-321-9656; www.dalyinn.com; 1125 H St; r with bathroom $170-185, without bathroom $130) This impeccably maintained 1905 Colonial Revival mansion has individually decorated rooms with turn-of-the-20th-century European and American antiques. Guest parlors are trimmed with rare woods; outside are century-old flowering trees.

Hotel Carter (☎ 707-444-8067, 800-404-1390; www.carterhouse.com; 301 L St; r $190-233, ste $304-380, all incl breakfast; 🅟) Hotel Carter bears the standard for North Coast luxury. Recently constructed in period style, it's a Victorian look-alike. Rooms have top-quality linens and modern amenities; suites have in-room whirlpools and marble fireplaces. Rates include made-to-order breakfast, plus evening wine and hors d'oeuvres.

Carter House Victorians (☎ 707-444-8067, 800-404-1390; www.carterhouse.com; r $190-275, ste $350-450, cottages $595) Stay in one of three sumptuously decorated houses: a single-level 1900 house, a honeymoon-hideaway cottage or a replica of an 1880s San Francisco mansion, which the owner built himself, entirely by hand. Unlike elsewhere, you won't see the innkeeper unless you want to. Guests have an in-room breakfast or eat at the understatedly elegant restaurant.

Also consider:

Bayview Motel (☎ 707-442-1673, 866-725-6813; www.bayviewmotel.com; 2844 Fairfield St; r $85; wi-fi) Spotless rooms, some with patios overlooking Humboldt Bay.

Best Western Humboldt Bay Inn (☎ 707-443-2234, 800-521-6996; www.humboldtbayinn.com; 232 W 5th St; r $105-159; 🅟) Firm mattresses and thick carpeting. Request a quiet room.

Old Town B&B Inn (☎ 707-443-5235, 888-508-5235; www.oldtownbnb.com; 1521 3rd St; r $130-150) Built in1871; cozy rooms at Old Town's edge.

Ship's Inn (☎ 707-443-7583, 877-443-7583; www.shipsinn.net; 821 D St; r $130-175, cottages $160) Warmly modern furnishings.

Upstairs at the Waterfront (☎ 707-444-1301, 888-817-5840; www.upstairsatthewaterfront.com; 102 F St; r/ste $175/225) Victorian apartment above Café Waterfront.

Eating

Kyoto (☎ 707-443-7777; 320 F St; sushi $4-6, mains $15-25; ⏲ dinner Wed-Sat) Make reservations for the best sushi in Humboldt County, as the place is tiny, serves delicious, beautiful food and is guaranteed to be packed.

Ramone's (☎ 707-445-2923; 209 E St; dishes $6-10; ⏲ 7am-6pm Mon-Sat, 8am-4pm Sun) For grab-and-go sandwiches, good soups and wraps.

La Chapala (☎ 707-443-9514; 201 2nd St; dishes $6-14; ⏲ lunch & dinner) For Mexican, family-owned La Chapala makes strong margaritas and homemade flan.

Waterfront Café Oyster Bar & Grill (☎ 707-443-9190; 102 F St; mains lunch $8-13, dinner $13-25; ⏲ breakfast, lunch & dinner) Eureka's best lunch spot. Chowder! Also feast on steamed clams, fish and chips, and oysters.

our pick **Hurricane Kate's** (☎ 707-444-1405; 511 2nd St; mains lunch $9-14, dinner $16-25; ⏲ lunch & dinner; Ⓥ) Loud and bustling Kate's pumps out eclectic, tapas-style dishes, roast meats and wood-fired pizzas. The party atmosphere pervades the warm dining room and the full bar.

Café Marina & Woodley's Bar (☎ 707-443-2233; 601 Startare Dr; mains $10-16; ⏲ lunch & dinner) Across the water in Woodley Island Marina, this harborside bar and grill makes great Bloody Marys and straightforward American food, served on a deck overlooking the small-craft harbor. Perfect on a sunny day.

Restaurant 301 (☎ 707-444-8062; 301 L St; breakfast mains $11, dinner mains $18-29; ⏲ breakfast & dinner; Ⓥ) Eureka's most refined dining room offers a contemporary California menu using produce from its organic gardens. Fabulous wine list.

Cin Cin (☎ 707-444-3708; 421 E St; mains $12-28; ⏲ dinner Wed-Sun; Ⓥ) Get dressed up for this top-notch Italian joint. Delectable concoctions include *bistecca con porcini* (grilled fillet mignon topped with porcini, olive and truffle oil butter and asparagus; $28). Or sip one of the delicious wines at the copper bar, surrounded by local art.

O.H.'s Townhouse (☎ 707-443-4652; 206 W 6th St; mains $16-29; ⏲ dinner Tue-Sun) Carnivores: if you're hungry for steak, pick your own meat from the display case at this 1970s throwback with wood-veneer-paneled walls. The veggies suck; the steak's great.

Avalon (☎ 707-445-0500; 3rd & G Sts; mains $21-30; ⏲ dinner Tue-Sat; Ⓥ) Sophisticated Avalon's diverse California menu features everything from foie gras to fried calamari. Leave room for chocolate soufflé.

Pick up groceries at **Eureka Natural Foods** (☎ 707-442-6325; 1626 Broadway) or **Eureka Co-op** (☎ 443-6027; cnr 5th & L Sts). There are also two **farmers markets** (☎ 707-441-9999); Old Town Gazebo (cnr 2nd & F Sts; ⏲ 10am-1pm Tue Jun-Oct); Henderson Center (⏲ 10am-1pm Thu Jun-Oct).

Drinking

Shanty (☎ 707-444-2053; 213 2nd St; ⏲ noon-2am) The coolest spot in town is grungy and fun. Play pool, Donkey Kong, Ms Pac Man or Ping Pong, or kick it on the back patio with local 20- and 30-something hipsters. Shanty is gay friendly, but not gay per se.

Pearl (☎ 707-444-2017; 507 2nd St) Eureka's swankiest, most fashion-forward bar caters to the over-30 set, with live jazz weekends.

Lost Coast Brewery (☎ 707-445-4480; 617 4th St) Try the Downtown Brown Ale or tuck into tasty fried pub grub.

Casa Blanca (☎ 707-443-6190; 1436 2nd St; 4-9pm) Drink margaritas with a bay view; arrive before sunset.

321 Coffee (☎ 707-444-9371; 321 3rd St; 8am-9pm) Students sip French-press coffee and play chess at this living-room-like coffeehouse. Good soup.

Entertainment

Morris Graves Museum of Art (☎ 707-442-0278; www.humboldtarts.org; 636 F St; admission by donation; noon-5pm Wed-Sun) Hosts performing-arts events between September and May, usually on Saturday evenings and Sunday afternoons.

Arkley Center for the Performing Arts (☎ 707-442-1956; www.arkleycenter.com; 412 G St) Home to the Eureka Symphony and North Coast Dance, and stages musicals and plays.

Broadway Cinema (☎ 707-444-3456; Broadway) Has first-run movies. Near 14th St.

Club Triangle at Indigo Nightclub (☎ 444-2582; 535 5th St) On Sunday nights this place becomes the North Coast's big gay dance club. For gay events, log onto www.queerhu mboldt.com.

Getting There & Around

Horizon Air (☎ 800-547-9308; www.alaskaair.com), **United Express** (☎ 800-241-6522; www.united.com) and **Delta** (☎ 800-221-1212; www.delta.com) serve **Arcata-Eureka Airport** (ACV; ☎ 707-839-5401; 3561 Boeing Ave, McKinleyville), 20 miles north. The Greyhound station is in Arcata (see p290).

Eureka Transit Service (☎ 707-443-0826; www.eurekatransit.org) operates local buses ($1.30), Monday to Saturday.

SAMOA PENINSULA

A windswept beauty, 7 miles long and half a mile wide, Samoa Peninsula, the north spit of Humboldt Bay, is named for its resemblance to Pago Pago Harbor, Samoa. The shoreline road (Hwy 255) is a backdoor route between Eureka and Arcata. Reach the beach by walking west through the dunes.

Locals throng to **Samoa Dunes Recreation Area** (☎ 707-825-2300; sunrise-sunset), at the south end of the peninsula, for picnicking and fishing. For wildlife, head to **Mad River Slough & Dunes**; from Arcata, take Samoa Blvd west 3 miles, then turn right at Young St, the Manila turnoff. Continue to the community center parking lot, from where a trail passes mudflats, salt marsh and tidal channels. There are over 200 species of birds: migrating waterfowl in spring and fall, songbirds in spring and summer, shorebirds in fall and winter, and abundant waders year-round.

The 475-acre **Lanphere Dunes Preserve** protects one of the finest examples of dune succession on the entire Pacific coast. These undisturbed dunes reach heights exceeding 80ft. Because of the environment's fragility, access is by guided tour only. **Friends of the Dunes** (☎ 707-444-1397; www.friendsofthedunes.org) leads 2½-hour rain-or-shine walks through Lanphere, Manila and Ma-le'l Dunes. Bring a jacket and soft-soled shoes. Call or check the website for schedules and volunteer restoration workdays.

Walking trails cross **Ma-Le'l Dunes** (☎ 707-825-2300), immediately south of Lanphere Dunes. Access is from Young Lane, at the northern end of the peninsula, off Hwy 255. A couple of miles south of Lanphere Dunes, the 100-acre **Manila Dunes Recreation Area** (☎ 707-445-3309) is open to the public, with access from Peninsula Dr.

Camp at **Samoa Boat Ramp County Park** (☎ 707-445-7651; sites $15), on the peninsula's bay side, 4 miles south of Samoa Bridge. There's limited tent camping (it's mostly RVs) and few facilities, just some picnic tables, toilet and parking lot – but it has lovely views.

The West's last surviving lumber-camp cookhouse, the **Samoa Cookhouse** (☎ 707-442-1659; www.humboldtdining.com/cookhouse; off Samoa Blvd; breakfast/lunch/dinner $9/10/14) serves all-you-can-eat family meals, at long tables with checkered tablecloths. Kids eat half-price. Stop by the little museum. The cookhouse is five minutes northwest of Eureka, across the Samoa Bridge; follow the signs. From Arcata, take Samoa Blvd (Hwy 255).

ARCATA

pop 16,500

On a hill overlooking Humboldt Bay, patchouli-dipped Arcata appears to be a quaint, bustling burg built around a pretty central square. It's also a bastion of alternative lifestyles and liberal politics: in April 2003, the City Council not only voted to condemn the USA Patriot Act, but outlawed voluntary compliance with it.

Liberal or conservative, you'll appreciate the town's forward-thinking ecological practices. While the rest of the US is only just starting to consider the idea of sustainability, Arcata has been living it for years: garbage trucks run on biodiesel, recycling gets picked up by tandem bicycle, wastewater gets filtered clean in marshlands and almost every street has a bike lane.

Founded in 1850 by the Union Timber Company and originally called Union Town, Arcata was a base for nearby lumber camps. In the late 1850s when Bret Harte worked here as a journalist, the town became the setting for some of his Gold Rush–era stories. Today Humboldt State University (HSU) has redefined Arcata as a college town.

Orientation

Roads run on a grid, with numbered streets traveling east–west and lettered streets going north–south. G and H Sts run north and south (respectively) to HSU and Hwy 101. The plaza is bordered by G and H and 8th and 9th Sts.

Information

Check www.humboldtpride.org for GBLT events.

Bureau of Land Management (BLM; ☎ 707-825-2300; 1695 Heindon Rd) Information on the Lost Coast.

California Welcome Center (☎ 707-822-3619; www.arcatachamber.com; 1635 Heindon Rd; 9am-5pm) Two miles north of town, off Giuntoli Lane, Hwy 101's west side. Local and statewide information.

Humboldt Internet (☎ 707-825-4638; 750 16th St; per hr $3; 10am-5pm Mon-Fri) PC internet access.

Northtown Books (☎ 707-822-2384; 957 H St) New books, periodicals, maps and guides.

Tin Can Mailman (☎ 707-822-1307; 1000 H St) Used volumes on two floors.

NORTH COAST

Sights

Hippies, nerds, skaters, hikers, beggars, rednecks and squares troop through **Arcata Plaza**. Surrounding notable buildings include two National Historic Landmarks: the 1857 **Jacoby's Storehouse** (cnr H & 8th Sts) and the 1915 **Hotel Arcata** (cnr G & 9th Sts). Others are the vintage 1914 **Minor Theatre** (1013 10th St) and the 1854 **Phillips House Museum** (☎ 707-822-4722; www.arcatahistory.org; cnr 7th & Union Sts; admission by donation; noon-4pm Sun & by appointment), which has historical exhibits and runs tours.

On the northeastern side of town, **Humboldt State University** (HSU; ☎ 707-826-3011; www.humboldt.edu) is Arcata's current *raison d'être*. The **HSU Natural History Museum** (☎ 707-826-4479; www.humboldt.edu/~natmus; 1315 G St; adult/child $3/2; 10am-5pm Tue-Sat;) has kid-friendly interactive exhibits of fossils, live animals, a beehive, and cool tsunami and seismic displays.

On the shores of Humboldt Bay, **Arcata Marsh & Wildlife Sanctuary** has 5 miles of walking trails and outstanding birding. The **Redwood Region Audubon Society** (☎ 707-826-7031; www.rras.org; donation welcome) offers guided walks Saturdays at 8:30am, rain or shine, from the parking lot at I Street's south end. Friends of Arcata Marsh guide tours Saturdays at 2pm from the **Arcata Marsh Interpretive Center** (☎ 707-826-2359; 569 South G St; tours free; 9am-5pm).

At the east end of 11th and 14th Sts, **Redwood Park** has beautiful redwoods and picnic areas. Adjoining the park, **Arcata Community Forest**, a 575-acre old-growth forest, is crisscrossed by 10 miles of trails and roads good for hikers and mountain-bikers.

Northeast of Arcata, **Azalea State Reserve** (☎ 707-488-2041; Hwy 200) explodes with color from late April to late May; otherwise skip it.

Activities

If you're at all bohemian, visit **Finnish Country Sauna & Tubs** (☎ 707-822-2228; cnr 5th & J Sts; noon-10pm Sun-Thu, to 12:30am Fri & Sat), where you can sip chai fireside or in meditative outdoor gardens, then rent a private open-air redwood hot tub ($8 per half-hour) or sweat in a sauna. Reserve ahead, especially on weekends.

HSU Center Activities (☎ 707-826-3357), on the 2nd floor of the University Center, beside the campus clock tower, sponsors myriad workshops, outings and sporting-gear rentals; nonstudents welcome.

Community Yoga Center (☎ 707-440-2111; www.innerfreedomyoga.com; 890 G St; classes $10) offers drop-in classes. **Arcata Community Pool** (☎ 707-822-6801; 1150 16th St; adult/child $6.50/4.50) has a coed hot tub, sauna and exercise room.

Adventure's Edge (☎ 707-822-4673; www.adventuresedge.com; 650 10th St; 9am-6pm Mon-Sat, 11am-5pm Sun) rents, sells and services outdoor equipment. **Outdoor Store** (☎ 707-822-0321; 876 G St; 10am-6pm Mon-Sat, noon-5pm Sun) sells outdoor gear, and rents snowboards and kayaks.

Festivals & Events

Arcata's most famous event, the **Kinetic Sculpture Race** (http://kineticgrandchampionship.com), is held Memorial Day weekend: people on amazing self-propelled contraptions travel 38 miles from Arcata to Ferndale. The **Arcata Bay Oyster Festival** (www.oysterfestival.net) happens in June. September brings the **North Country Fair** (www.sameold peopl.org).

Sleeping

Arcata has affordable but limited lodgings. A brand-spanking-new bayside ecohostel is in the works; log on to www.eco-hostel.org for the latest. The nearest camping is Eureka KOA (p285).

Fairwinds Motel (☎ 707-822-4824; www.fairwindsmotelarcata.com; 1674 G St; s $70-75, d $75-90; wi-fi) OK rooms in this standard-issue motel, but noise from Hwy 101, right behind, is loud.

Hotel Arcata (☎ 707-826-0217, 800-344-1221; www.hotelarcata.com; 708 9th St; r $84-105, ste $105-155; wi-fi) Anchoring the plaza, the renovated 1915 brick landmark has friendly staff, high ceilings and comfortable, old-world rooms. Quietest face the back.

Lady Anne Inn (☎ 707-822-2797; www.humboldt1.com/ladyanne; 902 14th St; r $110-140) Roses line the walkway to this 1888 mansion full of Victorian bric-a-brac. The frilly rooms are pretty, but there's no breakfast.

Arcata Stay (☎ 707-822-0935, 877-822-0935; www.arcatastay.com; apt from $165) Live like a local in a beautifully furnished apartment or cozy cottage hideaway; all are walkable to the plaza and have kitchens and lots of privacy. Two-night minimum.

Other motels lie 2 miles north off Hwy 101's Giuntoli Lane exit. We recommend:

Motel 6 (☎ 707-822-7061, 800-466-8356; www.motel6.com; 4755 Valley West Blvd; s $50-56, d $56-62; ❄ 🏊)

North Coast Inn (☎ 707-822-4861, 800-406-0046; www.northcoastinn.com; 4975 Valley West Blvd; r $80-85; ❄ 🏊) Satisfactory option.

Best Western Arcata Inn (☎ 707-826-0313, 800-528-1234; www.bestwestern.com; 4827 Valley West Blvd; r $99; ❄ 🏊) First-choice motel.

Eating

Great food abounds in restaurants throughout Arcata, almost all casual.

Tomo Japanese Restaurant (☎ 707-822-1414; 708 9th St; sushi $3.25-7, dinner mains $15-18; 🕒 lunch Mon-Sat, dinner nightly; Ⓥ) In the Hotel Arcata, Tomo packs 'em in for the town's best sushi and tasty sakes.

Renata's Crèperie (☎ 707-825-8783; 1030 G St; dishes $5-8; 🕒 8am-3pm & 5-9pm Fri & Sat, 8am-3pm Wed, Thu & Sun; Ⓥ) We love Renata. She formerly served crepes out of a truck, but finally has permanent digs, and it's the new hot spot, with organic sweet and savory crepes, salads and coffee.

Japhy's Soup & Noodles (☎ 707-826-2594; 1563 G St; dishes $5-8; 🕒 11:30am-8pm Mon-Fri) Fill up on big salads, tasty coconut curry, cold noodle salads and great homemade soups, without breaking the bank!

Wildflower Cafe & Bakery (☎ 707-822-0360; 1604 G St; breakfast & lunch $5-8, dinner mains $15-16; 🕒 8am-8pm Sun-Wed; Ⓥ) Tops for vegetarians, this tiny storefront serves fab frittatas, pancakes and curries, and big crunchy salads.

Daybreak Cafe (☎ 707-826-7543; 768 18th St; mains $5-9; 🕒 7am-4pm; Ⓥ) The veggie-heavy breakfasts are tasty, with omelets and burritos, but the blueberry cornmeal pancakes take the prize.

Folie Douce (☎ 707-822-1042; 1551 G St; mains brunch $8-14, dinner $27-36; 🕒 Tue-Sat dinner, Sun brunch; Ⓥ) Just a slip of a place, but with an enormous reputation. The short but inventive menu features seasonally inspired bistro cooking, from Asian to Mediterranean, with an emphasis on local organics. Wood-fired pizzas ($14 to $19) are renowned. Sunday brunch, too. Reservations essential.

Arcata has good cheap eats:

Los Bagels (☎ 707-822-3150; 1061 I St; dishes $2.50-6; 🕒 Wed-Mon) Draws folks from all around.

Stars Hamburgers (☎ 707-826-1379; 1535 G St; burgers $3-5; 🕒 lunch & dinner) Uses grass-fed beef.

Rico's Tacos (☎ 707-826-2572; 686 F St; mains $5-7; 🕒 9am-9pm) Next to Safeway; town's best *taqueria* (Mexican fast-food restaurant).

Philly Cheese Steak Shoppe (☎ 707-825-7400; cnr 18th & G Sts; sandwiches $4-8; 🕒 11am-9pm) Ever-popular with hungry, cash-strapped students.

Redwood Yogurt (☎ 707-826-7677; 1573 G St; yogurt $2-4; 🕒 noon-8pm Mon-Sat) Makes its own frozen yogurt.

Bon Boniere (☎ 707-822-6388; 791 8th St; sundaes $6-8; 🕒 11am-10pm) Inside Jacoby's Storehouse; get ice-cream sundaes here.

Arcata Pizza & Deli (☎ 707-822-4650; 1057 H St; pizzas $16-20; 🕒 11am-1am Sun-Thu, to 3am Fri & Sat) Fill up after bar-hopping.

Don's Donuts (☎ 707-822-6465; 933 H St; donuts 80¢-$1.35, sandwiches from $6; 🕒 24hr) Get a Southeast-Asian sandwich.

Fantastic **farmers markets** (☎ 707-441-9999; Arcata Plaza (🕒 9am-2pm Sat Apr-Nov); Wildberries (🕒 3:30-6:30pm Tue Jun-Oct) set up on Arcata Plaza and outside **Wildberries Marketplace** (☎ 707-822-0095;

747 13th St; 7am-11pm), which has natural foods. Gigantic **Arcata Co-op** (707-822-5947; cnr 8th & I Sts; 6am-10pm) carries natural foods and is a community staple; check the kiosk out front.

Drinking

Dive bars and cocktail lounges line the plaza's northern side. Arcata is awash in coffeehouses.

Muddy Waters Coffee Co (707-826-2233; 1603 G St) A happenin' indie joint, with live music, beer and wine, too.

Cafe Mokka (707-822-2228; Finnish Country Sauna & Tubs, cnr 5th & J Sts) Has hearthside mellow acoustic music (usually European folk) on weekends; other nights, you can read international newspapers and join multilingual conversations.

Humboldt Brews (707-826-2739; 856 10th St) Has 13 brews on tap, fab fish tacos and bitchin' buffalo wings (pub grub $5 to $10). Live music Thursday to Saturday nights.

Plaza Grill (707-826-0860; 791 8th St) Upstairs in Jacoby's Storehouse; the handsomest bar in town.

Entertainment

Center Arts (707-826-4411, tickets 707-826-3928; www.humboldt.edu/~carts) You'd be amazed who shows up at this HSU division, from Diana Krall and Dave Brubeck to Lou Reed and Ani Difranco.

Jambalaya (707-822-4766; 915 H St) Hosts live music after 10pm Fridays and Saturdays.

Minor Theatre (707-822-3456; 1013 H St) Shows first-run and classic films.

Getting There & Around

See p287 for airport information. Book ahead with **Door-to-Door Airporter** (707-839-4186, 888-338-5497; www.doortodoorairporter.com) to go from the Arcata-Eureka Airport to Trinidad ($19), Arcata ($19), Eureka ($23) and Scotia ($65).

Redwood Transit System (707-443-0826; www.hta.org) has services to Trinidad ($2.50, one hour, five daily) and to Eureka ($2.50, 15 minutes, 25 daily). **Greyhound** (707-825-8934, 800-231-2222; www.greyhound.com; Mon-Sat) has services to San Francisco ($42, seven hours, one daily) and Ukiah ($41.50, 4¼ hours, one daily).

Arcata city buses (707-822-3775; Mon-Sat) stop at the **Arcata Transit Center** (707-825-8934; 925 E St at 9th St). For shared rides, read the bulletin board at the Arcata Co-op (above).

Revolution Bicycle (707-822-2562; 1360 G St) and **Life Cycle Bike Shop** (707-822-7755; 1593 G St; Mon-Sat) rent, service and sell bicycles.

Only in Arcata: borrow a bike from **Library Bike** (707-822-1122; www.arcata.com/greenbikes; 865 8th St) for a $20 deposit, which gets refunded when you return the bike – up to six months later! They're beaters, but they ride.

TRINIDAD

pop 400

Cheery Trinidad perches prettily on the side of the ocean, combining upscale homes with a mellow surfer vibe. Somehow it feels a bit off the beaten path even though tourism augments fishing to keep the economy going.

Trinidad gained its name when Spanish sea captains arrived on Trinity Sunday in 1775 and named the area La Santisima Trinidad (the Holy Trinity). It didn't boom, though, until the 1850s, when it became an important port for miners. Schooners from San Francisco brought supplies for inland gold fields, and carried back lumber from the North Coast.

Orientation & Information

Trinidad is small: approach via Hwy 101 or from the north via Patrick's Point Dr (which becomes Scenic Dr further south). To reach town, take Main St.

Beachcomber Café (707-677-0106; 363 Trinity St; per hr $5; 7am-4pm Mon-Thu, to 9pm Fri, 9am-4pm Sat & Sun) Internet access.

Information kiosk (cnr Patrick's Point Dr & Main St) Just west of the freeway. The pamphlet *Discover Trinidad* has an excellent map.

Trinidad Chamber of Commerce (707-667-1610; www.trinidadcalif.com) Information on the web, but no visitors center.

Sights & Activities

Trinidad Memorial Lighthouse (cnr Trinity & Edwards Sts), a replica of an 1871 lighthouse, sits on a gorgeous bluff overlooking the bay and **Trinidad Head**. The annual **Trinidad Fish Festival** is celebrated in June; it's one of the few times the lighthouse opens to visitors.

Half a block inland, **Trinidad Museum** (707-677-3883; 529b Trinity St; noon-3pm Fri-Sun May-Sep) holds exhibits on the area's history.

HSU Telonicher Marine Laboratory (707-826-3671; www.humboldt.edu/~marinelb; Ewing St; admission free; 9am-4:30pm Mon-Fri, noon-4pm Sat Sep–mid-May;), near Edwards St, has a touch tank, several aquariums (look for the giant Pacific octo-

NORTH COAST

pus), an enormous whale jaw and a cool three-dimensional map of the ocean floor.

The free town map at the information kiosk shows several fantastic hiking trails, most notably the **Trinidad Head Trail** with superb coastal views; excellent for whale-watching (December to April). Stroll along an exceptionally beautiful cove at **Trinidad State Beach**; take Main St and bear right at Stagecoach, then take the second turn left (the first is a picnic area) into the small lot.

Scenic Dr twists south along coastal bluffs, passing tiny coves with views back toward the bay. It peters out before reaching the broad expanses of **Luffenholtz Beach** (accessible via the staircase) and serene white-sand **Moonstone Beach**. Exit Hwy 101 at 6th Ave/Westhaven to get there. Further south Moonstone becomes **Clam Beach County Park**.

Trinidad is famous for its fishing. Arrange a trip through **Salty's Surf 'n' Tackle Tours** (☎ 707-677-0300; 332 Main St) or **Trinidad Bay Charters** (☎ 707-839-4743, 800-839-4744; www.trinidadbaycharters.net). The harbor is at the bottom of Edwards St, at the foot of Trinidad Head. A five-hour trip costs about $85.

Surfing is good year-round, but potentially dangerous: unless you know how to judge conditions and get yourself out of trouble – there are no lifeguards here – surf in better-protected Crescent City.

North Coast Adventures (☎ 707-677-3124; www.northcoastadventures.com;lesson per 2hr/day $50/90) gives sea- and river-kayaking lessons and guided ecotrips around the North Coast.

Sleeping

Many of the inns line Patrick's Point Dr, north of town.

Clam Beach (☎ 707-445-7491; tent sites per vehicle $10), south of town off Hwy 101, has excellent camping. Pitch your tent in the dunes (look for natural windbreaks). Facilities include pit toilets, cold water, picnic tables and fire rings.

View Crest Lodge (☎ 707-677-3393; www.viewcrestlodge.com; 3415 Patrick's Point Dr; tent/RV sites $16/26, 1-bedroom cottages $95-170) On a hill above the ocean on the inland side, some of the well-maintained, modern cottages have views and Jacuzzis; most have kitchens. Also a good campground.

Emerald Forest (☎ 707-677-3554; www.rvintheredwoods.com; 753 Patrick's Point Dr; tent sites $29, RV with hookup $30-41, without hookup $29; wi-fi) has shady campsites and friendly proprietors.

Trinidad Inn (☎ 707-677-3349; www.trinidadinn.com; 1170 Patrick's Point Dr; r $75-115) Sparklingly clean and attractively decorated rooms (many with kitchens) fill this upmarket, gray-shingled motel under tall trees.

Bishop Pine Lodge (☎ 707-677-3314; www.bishoppinelodge.com; 1481 Patrick's Point Dr; cottages with/without kitchen from $100/150) It feels like summer camp: rent free-standing redwood cottages in a grassy meadow. Expect woodsy charm and unintentionally retro-funky furniture.

our pick Trinidad Bay B&B (☎ 707-677-0840; www.trinidadbaybnb.com; 560 Edwards St; r incl breakfast from $200) Opposite the lighthouse, this gorgeous light-filled Cape Cod–style house overlooks the harbor and Trinidad Head. Breakfast is delivered to your uniquely styled room; afternoon cookies.

Lost Whale Inn (☎ 707-677-3425; www.lostwhaleinn.com; 3452 Patrick's Point Dr; r $200-285, ste $375, all incl breakfast;) Perched atop a grassy cliff, high above crashing waves and braying sea lions, this spacious, modern, light-filled B&B has jaw-dropping views out to the sea. The lovely gardens have a 24-hour hot tub.

Turtle Rocks Oceanfront Inn (☎ 707-677-3707; www.turtlerocksinn.com; 3392 Patrick's Point Dr; r incl breakfast $285-300) Next door to the Lost Whale, Turtle Rocks has stark, modern rooms with glass-paneled decks and ocean views.

Turtle Rocks Oceanfront Inn (☎ 707-677-3707; www.turtlerocksinn.com; 3392 Patrick's Point Dr; r incl breakfast $285-300) Next door to the Lost Whale, and equally as stunning, Turtle Rocks has modern rooms with glass-paneled decks and ocean views. Both places are right outside Patrick Point State Park.

Trinidad Retreats (☎ 707-677-1606; www.trinidadretreats.com) and **Redwood Coast Vacation Rentals** (☎ 707-496-8746; www.enjoytrinidad.com) handle local property rentals.

Eating & Drinking

Catch Café (☎ 707-677-0390; 355 Main St; mains $5-10; 11am-7pm Tue-Sat, to 5pm Sun; V) For mostly organic, good food fast: grab pizzettas, burgers, brown rice and veggies, homemade soups and vegan falafel. In the strip mall but relaxed with sunny outdoor tables.

Seascape Restaurant (☎ 707-677-3762; Trinidad Harbor; breakfast & lunch $8-10, dinner $11-22; breakfast, lunch & dinner) Sit in a vinyl booth and watch the fishermen from this harborside diner, which serves good breakfasts and standard-American seafood dishes.

NORTH COAST

our pick **Larrupin' Cafe** (☎ 707-677-0230; 1658 Patrick's Point Dr; mains $20-30; ⌚ dinner Thu-Tue) Everybody loves Larrupin, where Moroccan rugs, chocolate brown walls, gravity-defying floral arrangements and deep-burgundy Oriental carpets create a moody atmosphere perfect for a lovers' tryst. On the menu, expect consistently good mesquite-grilled seafood and meats. In summer book a table on the garden patio. No credit cards.

Moonstone Grill (☎ 707-677-1616; Moonstone Beach; mains $23-32; ⌚ dinner Wed-Sun) Enjoy drop-dead sunset views over a picture-perfect beach while supping on the likes of oysters on the half-shell, Pacific wild king salmon or spice-rubbed rib eye.

Katy's Smokehouse & Fishmarket (☎ 707-677-0151; 740 Edwards St; ⌚ 9am-6pm) Makes its own chemical-free smoked and canned fish, using line-caught sushi-grade seafood.

Beachcomber Café (☎ 707-677-0106; 363 Trinity St). Head here for the best homemade cookies and to meet locals. Friday rocks live music.

To put on a bit of the ritz, have a cocktail at Moonstone Grill.

PATRICK'S POINT STATE PARK

Coastal bluffs jut out to sea at 640-acre **Patrick's Point** (☎ 707-677-3570; 4150 Patrick's Point Dr; day use $6;), where sandy beaches abut rocky headlands. Five miles north of Trinidad, with supereasy access to dramatic coastal bluffs, it's a best-bet for families. Stroll scenic overlooks, climb giant rock formations, watch whales breach, gaze into tidepools, or listen to barking sea lions and singing birds from this manicured park.

Sumêg is an authentic reproduction of a Yurok village, with hand-hewn redwood buildings where Native Americans gather for traditional ceremonies. In the native plant garden you'll find species for making traditional baskets and medicines.

On **Agate Beach** look for stray bits of jade and sea-polished agate. Follow the signs to tidepools, but tread lightly and obey regulations. The 2-mile **Rim Trail**, a former Yurok trail around the bluffs, circles the point with access to huge rocky outcroppings. Don't miss **Wedding Rock**, one of the park's most romantic spots. Other trails lead around unusual formations like **Ceremonial Rock** and **Lookout Rock**.

The park's three well-tended **campgrounds** (☎ reservations 800-444-7275; www.reserveamerica.com; sites $20) have coin-operated hot showers. Penn Creek and Abalone campgrounds are more sheltered than Agate Beach.

HUMBOLDT LAGOONS STATE PARK

Stretching out for miles along the coast, **Humboldt Lagoons** (☎ 707-488-2041) has long, sandy beaches and a string of coastal lagoons. **Big Lagoon** and the even prettier **Stone Lagoon** are both excellent for kayaking and bird-watching. Sunsets are spectacular, with no manmade structures in sight. Picnic at Stone Lagoon's north end. The Stone Lagoon Visitors Center, on Hwy 101, has closed due to staffing shortages, but there's a toilet and a bulletin board displaying information.

A mile north, **Freshwater Lagoon** is also great for birding. South of Stone Lagoon, tiny **Dry Lagoon** (a freshwater marsh) has a fantastic day hike. Park at Dry Lagoon's picnic area and hike north on the unmarked trail to Stone Lagoon; the trail skirts the southwestern shore and ends up at the ocean, passing through woods and marshland rich with wildlife. It's about 2.5 miles one way, and mostly flat – and nobody takes it because it's unmarked.

All campsites are first-come, first-served. The park runs two **environmental campgrounds** (sites $12; ⌚ Apr-Oct); bring water. Stone Lagoon has six boat-in environmental campsites; Dry Lagoon has six walk-in campsites. Check in at Patrick's Point State Park, at least 30 minutes before sunset.

Humboldt County Parks (☎ 707-445-7651; tent sites $14) operates a lovely cypress-grove picnic area and campground beside Big Lagoon, a mile off Hwy 101, with flush toilets and cold water, but no showers.

Redwood Trails RV & Campground (☎ 707-488-2061; rv4fun.com/redwood.html; Hwy 101; tent/RV sites $17/30), opposite the turnoff to Dry Lagoon, has a general store, horseback rides and, if you're lucky, elk lazing in the meadow outside.

REDWOOD NATIONAL PARK

A patchwork of public lands jointly administered by the state and federal governments, **Redwood National and State Parks** are actually a string of parks, starting in the south at Redwood National Park and continuing north through Prairie Creek Redwoods (p294), Del Norte Coast Redwoods (p295) and ending with Jedediah Smith Redwoods (p298). Prairie Creek and Jedediah Smith Parks were originally land slated for clear-cutting, but in the '60s activists successfully

COAST REDWOODS: THE TALLEST TREES ON EARTH

Though they covered much of the northern hemisphere millions of years ago, redwood trees now grow only in China and two areas of California (and a small grove in Oregon). Coast redwoods *(Sequoia sempervirens)* are found in a narrow, 450-mile-long strip along California's Pacific coast between Big Sur and southern Oregon. They can live for 2200 years, grow to 378ft tall (the tallest tree ever recorded) and achieve a diameter of 22ft at the base, with bark up to 12in thick.

In summer 2006, researchers found three new record-breaking trees in Redwood National Park. The tallest, Hyperion, measures a whopping 378ft – that's nearly 40 stories tall! Coming in a close second and third are Helios at 376ft and Icarus at 371ft. These just-discovered trees displace the old record-holder, the 370ft-high Stratosphere Giant in Rockefeller Forest (p278). But the trees bear no signs, so you won't be able to find them – too many boot-clad visitors would compact the delicate root systems, so the park's not telling where they are.

The tallest trees reach their maximum height some time between 300 and 700 years of age. Because they're narrow at their bases, they generally aren't the ones you notice as you walk through the forest. The dramatic, fat-trunked giants, which make such a visually stunning impact from the ground, are ancient, as much as 2000 years old. But they're not as tall as the younger ones because their tops have been blown off in intense storms over the centuries.

The structure of coast redwoods has been compared to a nail standing on its head. Unlike most trees, coast redwoods have no deep taproot and their root system is shallow in relation to their height – only 10ft to 13ft deep and spreading out 60ft to 80ft around the tree. The trees sometimes fall due to wind, but they are very flexible and usually sway in the wind as if they're dancing.

What gives these majestic giants their namesake color? It's the redwoods' high tannin content. It also makes their wood and bark resistant to insects and disease. The thick, spongy bark also has a high moisture content, enabling the ancient trees to survive many naturally occurring forest fires.

Coast redwoods are the only conifers in the world that can reproduce not only by seed cones, which grow to about the size of an olive at the ends of branches, but also by sprouting from their parents' roots and stumps, using the established root systems. Often you'll see a circle of redwoods standing in a forest, sometimes around a wide crater; this 'fairy ring' is made up of offspring that sprouted from one parent tree, which may have deteriorated into humus long ago. Burls, the large bumpy tissue growths on trunks and fallen logs, are a third method of reproduction.

Today only 4% of the North Coast's original two million acres of ancient redwood forests remain standing. Almost half of these old-growth forests are protected in Redwood National and State Parks.

protected them and today all these parks are an International Biosphere Reserve and World Heritage Site. At one time the national park was to absorb at least two of the state parks, but that did not happen, and so the cooperative structure remains.

Little-visited compared to their southern brethren, the world's tallest living trees have been standing here for time immemorial, predating the Roman Empire by over 500 years. Prepare to be impressed.

The small town of **Orick** (population 650), at the southern tip of the park, in a lush valley, is barely more than a few storefronts and a vast conglomeration of woodcarving.

Orientation & Information

Unlike most national parks, there are no fees and no highway entrance stations at Redwood National Park, so it's imperative to pick up the free map at the park headquarters (p296) in Crescent City or at the **Redwood Information Center** (Kuchel Visitors Center; ☎ 707-464-6101, ext 5265; www.nps.gov/redw; Hwy 101; 9am-5pm Mar-Oct, to 4pm Nov-Feb) in Orick. Rangers here issue permits to visit Tall Trees Grove. For in-depth redwood ecology, buy the excellent official park handbook.

Reserve park campgrounds in advance, lest you be relegated to the less-attractive nearby private RV parks.

Sights & Activities

Just north of the visitors center, turn east onto Bald Hills Rd and travel 2 miles to **Lady Bird Johnson Grove**, one of the park's most spectacular groves, accessible via a gentle 1-mile loop trail. Continue for another 5 miles up Bald Hills to **Redwood Creek Overlook**. On the top of the ridgeline at 2100ft get views over the forest and the entire watershed – provided it's not foggy. Just past the overlook lies the gated turnoff for **Tall Trees Grove**, location of several of the world's tallest trees. Rangers issue only 50 vehicle permits per day, but they rarely run out. Pick one up, along with the gate-lock combination, from the visitors centers. Allow four hours for the round-trip, which includes a 6-mile drive down a rough dirt road (speed limit 15mph) and a steep 1.3-mile one-way hike, which descends 800ft to the grove.

Several longer trails include the awe-inspiring **Redwood Creek Trail**, which also reaches Tall Trees Grove. You'll need a free backcountry permit to hike and camp, accessible only from Memorial Day to Labor Day, when summer footbridges are up. Otherwise, there's no way across the creek.

You can also come on horseback; phone **Redwood Trails** (☎ 707-488-2061). There's primitive camping in the park; inquire at visitors centers.

PRAIRIE CREEK REDWOODS STATE PARK

Famous for virgin redwood forests and unspoiled coastline, this 14,000-acre section of Redwood National and State Parks has 70 miles of hiking trails and spectacular scenic drives. Pick up maps and information and sit by the river-rock fireplace at **Prairie Creek Visitors Center** (☎ 707-464-6101, ext 5300; 9am-5pm Mar-Oct, 10am-4pm Nov-Feb;). Kids will love the taxidermy dioramas with their push-button, light-up displays. Outside, elk roam grassy flats.

Sights & Activities

The 8-mile **Newton B Drury Scenic Parkway** runs parallel to Hwy 101, passing through untouched ancient redwood forests. It's worth the short detour off the freeway to view the magnificence of these trees. Numerous trails branch off from roadside pullouts. Intersecting scenic drives include the 3-mile-long **Cal Barrel Rd**, which joins the parkway just north of the visitors center.

There are 28 mountain-biking and hiking trails through the park, from simple to strenuous. If you're tight on time or have mobility impairments, stop at **Big Tree**, an easy 100yd walk from the car park. Several other short nature trails start near the visitors center, including the Revelation Trail and Elk Prairie Trail. Stroll the recently reforested logging road on the **Ah-Pah Interpretive Trail** at the park's north end. The truly spectacular 11.5-mile **Coastal Trail** goes through primordial redwoods, and the 3.5-mile **South Fork–Rhododendron–Brown Creek Loop** is particularly beautiful in spring when rhododendrons and wildflowers bloom. Approach from the Brown Creek to South Fork direction – unless you like tramping uphill.

The **Coastal Drive** follows Davison Rd to Gold Bluffs. Go west 3 miles north of Orick and double back north along a sometimes-rough gravel road for 3.5 miles over the coastal hills to the **fee station** (per vehicle $6), then head up the coast to exquisite **Gold Bluffs Beach**, excellent for picnicking or camping. One mile ahead, take an easy half-mile trail to prehistoric-looking **Fern Canyon**, whose 60ft fern-covered sheer-rock walls can be seen in Steven Spielberg's *Jurassic Park 2: The Lost World*.

Eating

There are no motels or cabins.

Gold Bluffs Beach (no reservations; tent sites $15) This campground sits between 100ft cliffs and wide-open ocean, but there are some windbreaks and solar-heated showers. Look for sites up the cliff under the trees.

Elk Prairie Campground (☎ reservations 800-444-7275; www.reserveamerica.com; tent & RV sites $15-20) Elk roam this popular campground, where you can sleep under redwoods or at the prairie's edge. There are hot showers and some hike-in sites and a shallow creek to splash in. Sites 1–7 and 69–76 are on grassy prairies and get full sun; sites 8–68 are wooded. To camp in a mixed redwood forest, book sites 20–27.

The park also has three backcountry **campsites** (per person $3), as well as one **environmental campsite** (per person $12).

KLAMATH

pop 1420

Tiny Klamath's most noticeable landmark is the Klamath River Bridge where golden California bears stand sentry at the southern end of town. There's not much here except

NORTH COAST

WHAT THE...?

It's hard to miss the giant statues of Paul Bunyan and Babe the Blue Ox towering over the parking lot at **Trees of Mystery** (☎ 707-482-2251; www.treesofmystery.net; 15500 Hwy 101; adult/child/senior $13.50/6.50/10; 🕑 8am-7pm Jun-Aug, 9am-4pm Sep-May; ♿), a shameless tourist trap with a gondola running through the redwood canopy. The **End of the Trail Museum** located behind the Trees of Mystery gift shop has an outstanding collection of Native American arts and artifacts, and it's *free*.

water and trees, making it an excellent base for outdoor adventurers.

For information or to learn about August's Salmon Festival, contact the **Klamath Chamber of Commerce** (☎ 800-200-2335; www.klamathcc.org). For hiking maps, stop by the Redwood National and State Parks Headquarters in Crescent City (p296) or the Redwood Information Center in Orick (p293).

Sights & Activities

The mouth of the **Klamath River** is a dramatic sight. Marine, riparian, forest and meadow ecological zones all converge: the birding is exceptional! For the best views, head north of town to Requa Rd and the **Klamath River Overlook** and picnic on high bluffs above driftwood-strewn beaches. On a clear day, this is one of the most spectacular viewpoints on the North Coast, and one of the best whale-watching spots in California. For a good hike, head north along the Coastal Trail. You'll have the sand to yourself at **Hidden Beach**; access the trail at the northern end of Motel Trees.

Just south of the river, on Hwy 101, follow signs for the scenic **Coastal Drive**, a narrow, winding country road (unsuitable for RVs and trailers) atop extremely high cliffs over the ocean. Come when it's not foggy, and mind your driving. Though technically in Redwood National Park, it's much closer to Klamath.

Book jet-boat excursions and fishing trips at **Klamath Jet Boat Tours** (☎ 707-482-5822; www.jetboat tours.com).

Sleeping & Eating

Woodsy Klamath is cheaper than Crescent City, but there aren't as many places to eat or buy groceries, and there's nothing to do at night but play cards.

Motel Trees (☎ 707-482-3152, 800-848-2982; www.treesofmystery.com; 15495 Hwy 101 S; s/d/q $55/76/98) Opposite Trees of Mystery; standard-issue rooms alternate with theme rooms.

Ravenwood Motel (☎ 707-482-5911, 866-520-9875; www.ravenwoodmotel.com; 131 Klamath Blvd; r/ste with kitchen $65/115) The spotlessly clean rooms are better than anything in Crescent City and individually decorated with furnishings and flair you'd expect in a city hotel, not a small-town motel.

Woodland Villa Cabins (☎ 707-482-2081, 888-866-2466; www.klamathusa.com; 15870 Hwy 101; cottages with kitchen $135-145, without kitchen $80-90; wi-fi) Rent modest, cozy, lovingly tended cottages. There's a picnic area and small market on-site.

our pick **Historic Requa Inn** (☎ 707-482-1425, 866-800-8777; www.requainn.com; 451 Requa Rd; r incl breakfast $90-140; wi-fi) North of town, this quaint 1914 inn sits atop the riverbank at the edge of the national park; many of the charming country-style rooms have mesmerizing views, as does the dining room, where guests have breakfast and dinner (Tuesday to Saturday). After a day hiking, play Scrabble by a roaring fire or take a hot tub.

If park campgrounds are full, pitch a tent at **Kamp Klamath** (☎ 707-482-0227, 866-552-6284; www.kampklamath.com; 1661 W Klamath Beach Rd; tent/RV sites $20/22), a 33-acre campground on the river's south shore.

Klamath River Cafe (☎ 707-482-1000; 164 Klamath Blvd; mains $5-8; 🕑 breakfast & lunch daily, dinner Mon-Thu) rustles up reliable specials and homemade desserts. **Forest Cafe** (☎ 707-482-5585; 15499 Hwy 101; mains $10-21; 🕑 breakfast, lunch & dinner Thu-Mon; wi-fi), across from Trees of Mystery, serves plain old American cooking under a ceiling covered with plastic flowers. **Steelhead Lodge** (☎ 707-482-8145; 330 Terwer Riffle Rd; mains $16-25; 🕑 dinner daily Jun-Oct, Fri-Sun Nov-May), 3 miles upriver in Klamath Glen, grills big, juicy steaks and serves strong drinks. It also rents clean, basic motel rooms with kitchens (rooms from $75).

DEL NORTE COAST REDWOODS STATE PARK

Marked by steep canyons and dense woods, half the 6400 acres of this **park** (vehicle day-use fee $6) are virgin redwood forest, crisscrossed by 15 miles of hiking trails. Even the most cynical of redwood-watchers can't help but be moved.

Pick up maps and inquire about guided walks at the Redwood National and State Parks Headquarters in Crescent City (right) or the Redwood Information Center in Orick (p293).

Hwy 1 winds in from the coast at rugged, dramatic **Wilson Beach**, and traverses the dense forest, with groves stretching off as far as you can see.

Picnic on the sand at **False Klamath Cove**. Heading north, tall trees cling precipitously to canyon walls that drop to the rocky, timber-strewn coastline, and it's almost impossible to get to the water, except via gorgeous but steep Damnation Trail or Footsteps Rock Trail. Hwy 1 winds in from the coast at rugged, dramatic **Wilson Beach**, and traverses the dense forest, with groves stretching off as far as you can see.

Hike via the Coastal Trail (or the Crescent Beach Trail from the north) to **Enderts Beach** for magnificent tidepools at low tide (tread lightly and obey posted regulations).

Crescent Beach Overlook and picnic area has superb wintertime whale-watching. At the park's north end, watch the surf pound at **Crescent Beach**, just south of Crescent City via Enderts Beach Rd.

our pick **HI Redwood Hostel** (☎ 707-482-8265, 800-909-4776; www.norcalhostels.org; 14480 Hwy 101; dm/d $21/52; reception 8am-10am & 5-10pm Mar-Nov) is a rambling 1908 farmhouse on a bluff overlooking False Klamath Cove. The window-lined kitchen is glorious at breakfast, when the sun lights up the churning surf outside. It's quite special, so reserve well in advance.

Mill Creek Campground (☎ 800-444-7275; www.reserveamerica.com; tent sites $20) has hot showers and 145 sites in a redwood grove, 2 miles east of Hwy 101, 7 miles south of Crescent City. Sites 1–74 are woodsier; sites 75–145 sunnier. Hike-in sites are prettiest.

NORTH COAST

CRESCENT CITY

pop 8800

On a crescent-shaped bay, Crescent City is California's last big town north of Arcata. Though founded in 1853 as a seaport for inland gold mines, it retains few old buildings: half the town was destroyed by a tsunami in 1964 (see opposite). Completely rebuilt, it lacks charm, and is best only as a resupply point near the national and state parks. The local economy depends heavily on fishing, logging and the Pelican Bay maximum-security prison, just north of town.

Orientation & Information

Hwy 101 splits into two parallel one-way streets, with the southbound traffic on L St, northbound on M St. To see the major sights, turn west on Front St toward the lighthouse. Downtown is centered along 3rd St.

Crescent City-Del Norte Chamber of Commerce (☎ 707-464-3174, 800-343-8300; www.northerncalifornia.net; 1001 Front St; 9am-5pm daily summer, Mon-Fri rest of year) Local information.

Redwood National & State Parks Headquarters (☎ 707-464-6101; 1111 2nd St; 9am-5pm Oct-May, to 6pm Jun-Sep) On the corner of K St; rangers and information about all four parks under its jurisdiction.

Sights & Activities

The 1856 **Battery Point Lighthouse** (☎ 707-464-3089; www.delnortehistory.org/lighthouse), at the south end of A St, still operates on a tiny, rocky island that you can easily reach at low tide. From April to September, tour the **museum** (adult/child $3/1; 10am-4pm Mon-Sat May-Sep); hours vary with tides and weather.

North Coast Marine Mammal Center (☎ 707-465-6265; www.nothcoastmarinemammal.org; 424 Howe Dr; by donation; 10am-5pm), just east of Battery Point, is where injured seals, sea lions and dolphins recuperate after being rescued.

Beachfront Park (Howe Dr), between B and H Sts, has a great harborside beach for little ones, with no big waves. Further east on Howe Dr, near J St, you'll come to **Kidtown**, with slides and swings and a make-believe castle. For a scenic drive, head north on Pebble Beach Dr, which ends at **Point St George**, and walk through grassy dunes.

Rent a board from **Rhyn Noll Surf & Skate** (☎ 707-465-4400; 275 L St; boards/body boards/wetsuits per day $15/7.50/10) to surf at **Crescent Beach**. **Bikes & Trikes** (☎ 707-954-5078; 400 Front St; bikes per day $10) rents (and delivers) bikes. Go whale-watching or deep-sea fishing aboard the **Tally Ho II** (☎ 707-464-1236; 3hr whale-watching $45, half-day fishing $100). There's weekend glow-in-the-dark bowling at **Tsunami Lanes** (☎ 707-464-4323; 760 L St; per game $2-3, shoe rental $2).

Del Norte County Fair takes place in August.

Sleeping

Most people stop here for one night while traveling; motels are overpriced.

CRESCENT CITY'S GREAT TSUNAMI

On March 28, 1964, most of downtown Crescent City was destroyed by a great tsunami (tidal wave). At 3:36am, a giant earthquake occurred on the north shore of Prince William Sound in Alaska. Measuring 9.2 on the Richter scale, the quake was the most severe ever recorded in North America. The first of the ensuing giant ocean swells reached Crescent City only a few hours later.

Officials warned the sheriff's office, and at 7:08am evacuation of the waterfront began. The waves arrived an hour later. The first two were small, only about 13ft above the tide line, and many rejoiced, thinking the worst had passed. Then the water receded until the bay was emptied, leaving boats that had been anchored offshore sitting in the mud. Frigid water surged in, rising all the way up to 5th St, knocking buildings off their foundations, carrying away cars, trucks and anything else in its path. By the time the fourth and final wave receded, 29 blocks of town were destroyed, with more than 300 buildings displaced. Five gasoline storage tanks exploded. Eleven people died, three of whom were never found.

Many old-timers are still remembered for their heroic acts during and after the waves, helping to save their neighbors and later rebuild the town. The little shopping center that replaced many of the destroyed buildings bears an appropriate name – Tsunami Landing, and you'll see signs warning 'Tsunami Zone' throughout the region.

Curly Redwood Lodge (☎ 707-464-2137; www.curlyredwoodlodge.com; 701 Hwy 101 S; r $64-69) Aficionados of '50s-modern love this motel, the rooms of which are paneled with the lumber of just a single giant curly redwood, but the place needs upgrades.

Castle Island Getaway (☎ 707-465-5102; www.castleislandgetaway.com; 1830 Murphy Ave; r $100-150; 💻) Two blocks from the ocean, this B&B has three rooms (reservations required) in a home owned by a charming innkeeper; the upstairs suite has the most space.

Cottage by the Sea (☎ 707-464-9068, 877-642-2254; www.waterfrontvacationrental.com; 205 South A St; cottage with kitchen $150) Near the lighthouse, this sparkling-clean cottage is decorated with piles of pillows. It's by the sea but has no view.

Also consider:

Crescent Beach Motel (☎ 707-464-5436; www.crescentbeachmotel.com; 1455 Hwy 101 S; r $70-100) South of town, a basic motel with some stunning ocean views.

Anchor Beach Inn (☎ 707-464-2600; www.anchorbeachinn.com; 880 Hwy 101 S; r $85-105; ❄ 💻) Microwave, DSL, soundproof walls and personality-free.

Hampton Inn (☎ 707-465-5400; www.hamptoninn.com; 100 A St; r $169-209; ❄ 💻 🏊) Corporate-style but with ocean-view rooms.

The county operates two reservable **campgrounds** (☎ 707-464-7230; sites $10) just outside town. **Florence Keller Park** (3400 Cunningham Lane) has 50 sites in a beautiful redwood grove (take Hwy 101 north to Elk Valley Cross Rd and follow the signs). **Ruby Van Deventer Park** (4705 N Bank Rd) has 18 sites along the Smith River, off Hwy 197.

Eating & Drinking

Tomasini's (☎ 707-464-2909; 960 3rd St; dishes $4-8; 🕒 breakfast & lunch; Ⓥ) Stop in for salads, sandwiches or jazz on weekend nights.

Good Harvest Cafe (☎ 707-465-6028; 700 Northcrest Dr; dishes $4-8; 🕒 breakfast & lunch; Ⓥ) On the corner of Hwy 101; the city's best breakfast and lunch, with homemade soups, smoothies, sandwiches and great salads.

Thai House (☎ 707-464-2427; 105 N St; dishes $8-11; 🕒 lunch & dinner; Ⓥ) Behind Safeway; get surprisingly good Thai and Vietnamese cooking, with a few Chinese dishes as well.

Beachcomber Restaurant (☎ 707-464-2205; 1400 Hwy 101 S; meals $13-19; 🕒 dinner, closed Wed) For fish dinners, the Beachcomber has full ocean views, vinyl booths, and straightforward preparations of seafood and meat.

Stock up on organics at **Harvest Natural Foods** (☎ 707-464-1926; 265 L St; 🕒 10am-6pm Mon-Sat, from 9am Sun). Get strong coffee at **Java Hut** (☎ 707-465-4439; 437 Hwy 101 N; 🕒 5am-10pm).

Entertainment

The town's tiny music scene plays at **Pizza King** (☎ 707-464-4890; 1348 Front St).

Getting There & Around

United Express (☎ 800-241-6522) flies into tiny **Crescent City Airport** (CEC; ☎ 707-464-5750), north of town. Rent a vehicle, by reservation only, at **Hertz** (☎ 707-464-5750, 800-654-3131). **Redwood Coast**

DETOUR: SMITH RIVER NATIONAL RECREATION AREA

West of Jedediah Smith Redwoods, the Smith River, the state's last remaining undammed waterway, runs right beside Hwy 199. Originating high in the Siskiyou Mountains, its serpentine course cuts through deep canyons beneath thick forests. Chinook salmon and steelhead trout annually migrate up its clear waters. Camp, hike, raft and kayak; check regulations if you want to fish. Stop by the **Six Rivers National Forest Headquarters** (☎ 707-457-3131; www.fs.fed.us/r5/sixrivers; 10600 Hwy 199, Gasquet; 🕒 8am-4:30pm daily summer, Mon-Fri fall-spring) to get your bearings. Pick up pamphlets for the **Darlingtonia Trail** and **Myrtle Creek Botanical Area**, both easy jaunts into the woods where you can see rare plants and learn about the area's geology.

Patrick Creek Lodge (☎ 707-457-3323; www.patrickcreeklodge.net; r $100-140), a 1926 log-cabin-style roadhouse, has simple accommodations and serves three good meals a day (lunch $7 to $12, dinner $17 to $25).

Transit (☎ 707-464-9314; www.redwoodcoasttransit.org) serves Crescent City with local buses ($1), and runs buses Monday to Saturday to Klamath ($1, one hour, two daily) and Arcata ($20, two hours, two daily) with stops in between.

TOLOWA DUNES STATE PARK & LAKE EARL WILDLIFE AREA

Two miles north of Crescent City, this **state park and wildlife area** (☎ 707-464-6101, ext 5112; 🕒 sunrise-sunset) encompasses 10,000 acres of wetlands, dunes, meadows and two lakes, **Lake Earl** and **Lake Tolowa**. This major stopover on the Pacific Flyway route brings over 250 species of birds (see boxed text, p324). Listen for the whistling, warbling chorus. On land, look for coyotes and deer; at sea, spot whales, seals and sea lions. Angle for trout, or hike or ride 20 miles of trails.

In summer ask about guided walks. The best wetlands trails lie at the northern portion of the park, where a delicate balance exists between freshwater and marine habitats. Pick up information from the Crescent City visitors centers. All is green and lush in spring and early summer; in winter it's wet; and in summer and fall it's dry.

The park and wildlife area is a patchwork of lands administered by California State Parks and the Department of Fish and Game (DFG). The DFG focuses on single-species management, hunting and fishing; the State Parks' focus is on ecodiversity and recreation. You might be hiking a vast expanse of pristine dunes, then suddenly hear a shotgun or a whining 4WD. Strict regulations limit where and when you can hunt and drive; trails are clearly marked.

There are two primitive, nonreservable **campgrounds** (tent sites $10): a walk-in environmental campground (no water) and an equestrian campsite (nonpotable well water). Register at the Jedediah Smith or Del Norte Coast Redwoods State Park campgrounds. Bring firewood and mosquito repellent in spring and early summer.

JEDEDIAH SMITH REDWOODS STATE PARK

California's northernmost redwood park, **Jedediah Smith** (day use $6) sits 10 miles northeast of Crescent City (via Hwy 101 east to Hwy 197). The redwood stands are so dense that few trails penetrate the park, but the outstanding 11-mile **Howland Hill scenic drive** cuts through otherwise inaccessible areas (take Hwy 199 to South Fork Rd; turn right after crossing two bridges). It's a rough road, impassable for RVs, but if you can't hike, it's the best way to see the forest.

Along Hwy 199, signs announce the names of the groves. Pull over – there's rarely a trail, but overlooks give glimpses of the forest's lush diversity.

Stop for a stroll under enormous trees in **Simpson-Reed Grove**. If it's foggy at the coast it may be sunny here. There's a **swimming hole** and picnic area near the park entrance. An easy half-mile trail, departing from the far side of the campground, crosses the **Smith River** via a summer-only footbridge, leading to **Stout Grove**, the park's most famous grove. The **visitors center** (☎ 707-464-6101, ext 5113; 🕒 10am-4pm daily summer, Sat & Sun fall & spring) sells hiking maps and nature guides. If you wade in the river, be careful in spring when currents are swift and the water cold.

The popular **campground** (☎ reservations 800-444-7275; www.reserveamerica.com; tent & RV sites $20) has gorgeous sites tucked through the redwoods beside the Smith River. Offers hot showers.

Just east, **Hiouchi Information Center** (☎ 707-458-3294; 🕑 9am-5pm mid-Jun–mid-Sep) stocks maps and books. Families may borrow free activity backpacks with projects for kids. When the visitors centers are closed, go to the Redwood National and State Parks Headquarters in Crescent City (p296).

A mile east of the park in Hiouchi, rent inner tubes, inflatable kayaks and mountain bikes at **Lunker Fish Trips** (☎ 707-458-4704, 800-248-4704; 2590 Hwy 199), one of the North Coast's finest steelhead-fishing guides (fishing is best September to April).

Hiouchi Hamlet RV Resort (☎ 707-458-3321, 800-722-9468; www.hiouchirv.com; tent sites $22-25, RV sites $33-36) also has a small market where you can pick up supplies and fishing licenses. Over the street, **Hiouchi Motel** (☎ 707-458-3041, 888-881-0819; www.hiouchimotel.com; 2097 Hwy 199; s $50, d $65-70; 💻) has straightforward motel rooms.

Continue along Hwy 199 to **Gasquet** for stellar views of the region.

PELICAN BEACH STATE PARK

Never-crowded **Pelican State Beach** (☎ 707-464-6101, ext 5151) occupies five coastal acres on the Oregon border. There are no facilities, but it's great for kite flying; pick one up at the shop just over the border in Oregon.

The best reason to visit is to stay at secluded, charming **Casa Rubio** (☎ 707-487-4313; www.casarubio.com; 17285 Crissey Rd; r $88-158; 💻), where three of the four ocean-view rooms have kitchens. Next door, **Nautical** (☎ 707-487-5006; 16850 Hwy 101 N; mains $19-29; 🕑 dinner) has spectacular sunset views and stylized Cal-French cooking.

Sea Escape (☎ 707-487-7333; www.seaescape.us; 15370 Hwy 101 N; r $95-135; wi-fi) has clean motel-style suites, some with ocean views and kitchens. **White Rock Resort** (☎ 707-487-1021, 888-487-4659; www.whiterockresort.com; 16800 Hwy 101 N; r $200-250) has four-person 'cottages' (converted mobile homes).

Pitch a tent by the ocean (no windbreaks) at **Clifford Kamph Memorial Park** (☎ 707-464-7230; 15100 Hwy 101; tent sites $5); no RVs.

Northern Mountains

When visitors envision Northern California – even when Californians picture Northern California – their mental images are of cable cars, foggy wharfs, redwoods, grapevines, wild coasts and a tall orange bridge…all beautiful and true. But there is another, wilder Northern California, remote and mountainous, pristine and thinly populated.

Vast expanses of untamed wilderness cover the Northern Mountains region. The terrain courses with rivers and streams. Unspoiled cobalt lakes grace alpine peaks. An enormous variety of species, some found nowhere else in the world, inhabit its isolated reaches. Intimate towns beckon with charm and lore. You'll encounter all the natural splendor of Yosemite and all the '49er romance of the Gold Country, but without the crowds. Even at the peak of summer, the region's biggest draws, Mt Shasta and Lassen Volcanic National Park, remain accessible and calm.

What has safeguarded the beauty and vibrancy of the Northern Mountains thus far is this: of the approximately 24,000 sq miles that comprise the region, roughly 65% is protected national forest. Still, where growth is possible it is flourishing, and recently public land has been exposed to private development. Ex-urbanites are drawn here in the hope of mining this era's gold – space and tranquillity. For now, however, the Northern Mountains remain California's most untouched and wild frontier.

HIGHLIGHTS

- **Sweetest mountain village** Explore the wilds of nearby mountains from the shelter of bucolic Weaverville (p325)
- **Most dramatic volcanic adventure** Camp, hike and boat on the desolate crags of Lassen Volcanic National Park (p306)
- **Easiest blast to the past** Re-create history on McCloud's narrow-gauge Shasta Sunset Dinner Train (p322)
- **Mellowest afternoon outing** Grab an inner tube and float down the Feather River in Quincy (p311)
- **Cushiest alpine hideaway** Stay in an isolated fire lookout near the slopes of Mt Shasta (p316)

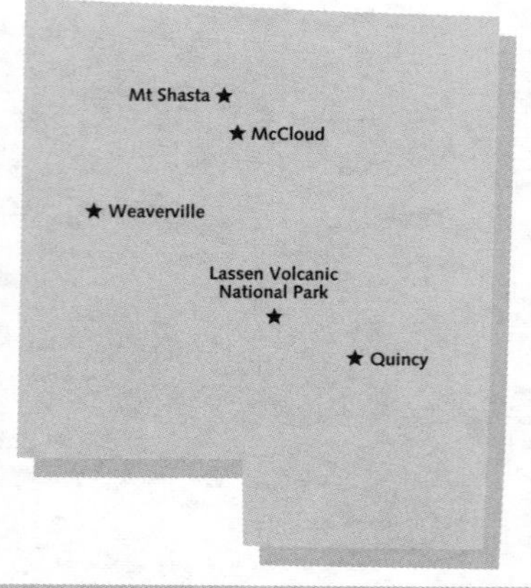

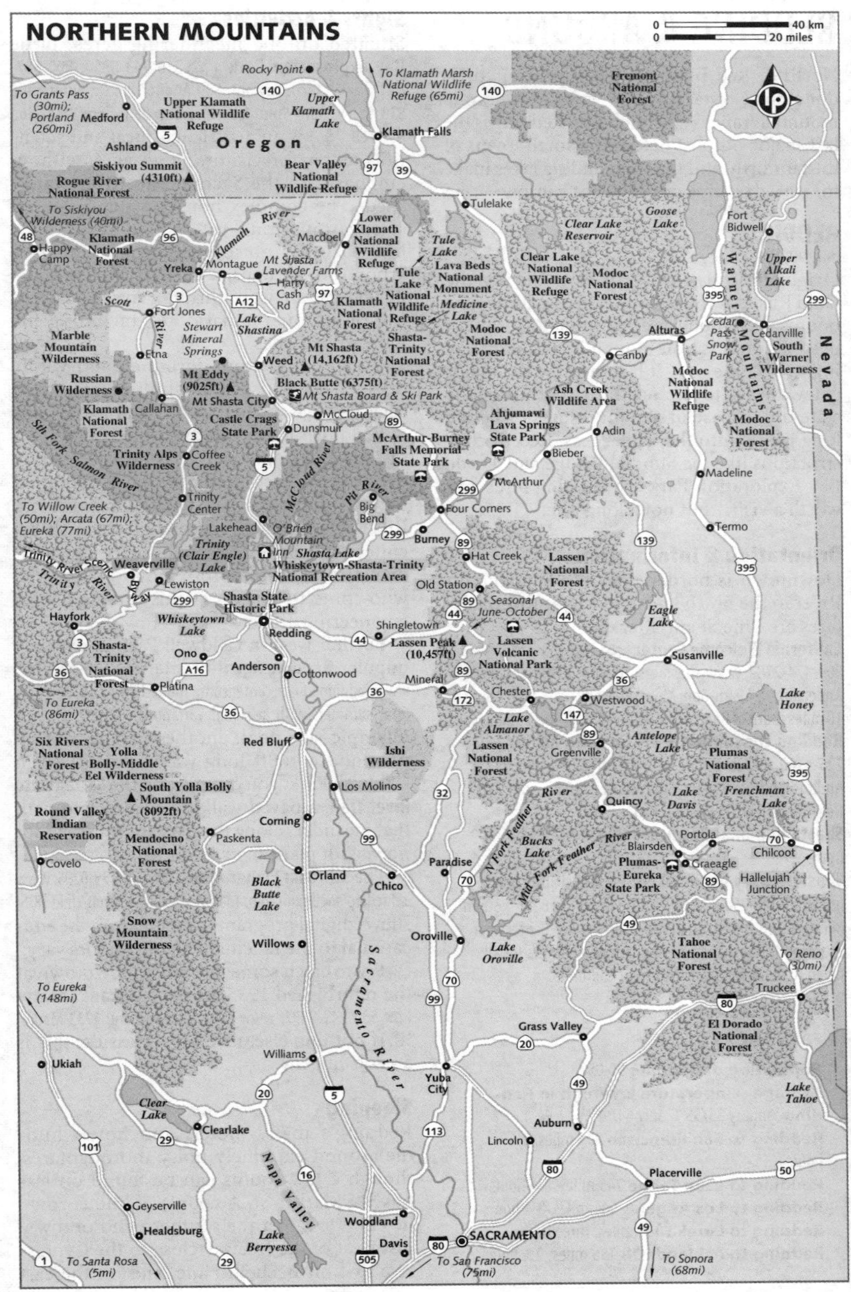
NORTHERN MOUNTAINS
0 40 km
0 20 miles
Oregon
Nevada
Rocky Point
To Klamath Marsh National Wildlife Refuge (65mi)
Fremont National Forest
To Grants Pass (30mi); Portland (260mi)
Medford
Upper Klamath National Wildlife Refuge
Upper Klamath Lake
Klamath Falls
Ashland
Siskiyou Summit (4310ft)
Bear Valley National Wildlife Refuge
Rogue River National Forest
To Siskiyou Wilderness (40mi)
Klamath River
Tulelake
Goose Lake
Fort Bidwell
Clear Lake Reservoir
Happy Camp
Klamath National Forest
Macdoel
Lower Klamath National Wildlife Refuge
Tule Lake
Upper Alkali Lake
Yreka
Montague
Mt Shasta Lavender Farms
Harry Cash Rd
Lava Beds National Monument
Clear Lake National Wildlife Refuge
Modoc National Forest
Warner Mountains
Scott River
Fort Jones
Lake Shastina
Klamath National Forest
Tule Lake National Wildlife Refuge
Medicine Lake
Alturas
Cedar Pass Snow Park
Cedarvillle
Marble Mountain Wilderness
Stewart Mineral Springs
Etna
Mt Shasta (14,162ft)
Shasta-Trinity National Forest
Modoc National Forest
South Warner Wilderness
Weed
Canby
Russian Wilderness
Mt Eddy (9025ft)
Black Butte (6375ft)
Mt Shasta Board & Ski Park
Ash Creek Wildlife Area
Modoc National Wildlife Refuge
Mt Shasta City
Klamath National Forest
Callahan
McCloud
Castle Crags State Park
Dunsmuir
Ahjumawi Lava Springs State Park
Adin
Modoc National Forest
5th Fork Salmon River
Coffee Creek
Trinity Alps Wilderness
McArthur-Burney Falls Memorial State Park
McCloud River
Bieber
McArthur
Madeline
Trinity Center
Pit River
Big Bend
Four Corners
To Willow Creek (50mi); Arcata (67mi); Eureka (77mi)
Lakehead
O'Brien Mountain Inn
Burney
Termo
Trinity (Clair Engle) Lake
Shasta Lake
Hat Creek
Lassen National Forest
Trinity River Scenic Byway
Weaverville
Whiskeytown-Shasta-Trinity National Recreation Area
Trinity River
Lewiston
Old Station
Shasta State Historic Park
Seasonal June-October
Hayfork
Whiskeytown Lake
Redding
Shingletown
Eagle Lake
Lassen Peak (10,457ft)
Lassen Volcanic National Park
Shasta-Trinity National Forest
Ono
Anderson
Susanville
Cottonwood
Mineral
Platina
Chester
Westwood
Lake Honey
To Eureka (86mi)
Lake Almanor
Antelope Lake
Six Rivers National Forest
Yolla Bolly-Middle Eel Wilderness
Red Bluff
Ishi Wilderness
Lassen National Forest
Greenville
Plumas National Forest
South Yolla Bolly Mountain (8092ft)
Los Molinos
River
Quincy
Lake Davis
Frenchman Lake
Round Valley Indian Reservation
Corning
N Fork Feather
Mendocino National Forest
Paskenta
Bucks Lake
Mid Fork Feather River
Portola
Blairsden
Chilcoot
Covelo
Paradise
Plumas-Eureka State Park
Graeagle
Orland
Chico
Hallelujah Junction
Black Butte Lake
Snow Mountain Wilderness
Willows
Oroville
Lake Oroville
Tahoe National Forest
To Reno (30mi)
Sacramento River
To Eureka (148mi)
Truckee
El Dorado National Forest
Grass Valley
Williams
Ukiah
Yuba City
Lake Tahoe
Clear Lake
Clearlake
Auburn
Lincoln
Napa Valley
Placerville
Geyserville
Woodland
Healdsburg
Lake Berryessa
Davis
SACRAMENTO
To Santa Rosa (5mi)
To San Francisco (75mi)
To Sonora (68mi)

REDDING & AROUND

North of Red Bluff the dusty central corridor along I-5 starts to give way to panoramic mountain ranges on either side. Redding is the last major outpost before the small towns of the far north, and the surrounding lakes make for easy day trips or overnight camps.

REDDING

pop 90,050 / elev 557ft

Originally called Poverty Flats during the Gold Rush for its lack of wealth, Redding now booms with modern development. A tourist destination it is not, though it is eagerly trying to become one. It is, however, the major gateway city to the northeast corner of the state and so a useful spot for restocking before long jaunts into the wilderness. Recent constructions like the Sundial Bridge and Turtle Bay Exploration Park are enticing lures and worth a visit…but not a long one.

Orientation & Information

Downtown is bordered by the Sacramento River to the north and east. Major thoroughfares are Pine St and Market St.

California Welcome Center (☎ 530-365-1180, 800-474-2782; www.shastacascade.org; 1699 Hwy 273, Anderson; 9am-6pm Mon-Sat, from 10am Sun) About 10 miles south of Redding, in Anderson's Prime Outlets Mall.

Redding Convention & Visitors Bureau (☎ 530-225-4100, 800-874-7562; www.visitredding.com; 777 Auditorium Dr; 9am-6pm Mon-Fri, 10am-5pm Sat) Near Turtle Bay Exploration Park.

Shasta Regional Hospital (☎ 530-244-5400; 1100 Butte St)

Shasta-Trinity National Forest Headquarters (☎ 530-226-2500; 3644 Avtech Pkwy; 8am-4:30pm Mon-Fri) South of town in the USDA Service Center near the airport. Has maps and free camping permits for all seven national forests in Northern California.

> **FAST FACTS**
>
> **Population of Redding** 90,050
>
> **Average temperature low/high in Redding** January 35/55°F, July 64/98°F
>
> **Redding to San Francisco** 215 miles, 3½ hours
>
> **Redding to Lake Tahoe** 245 miles, 4¼ hours
>
> **Redding to Los Angeles** 545 miles, 8¼ hours
>
> **Redding to Eureka** 150 miles, three hours
>
> **Redding to Ashland, OR** 135 miles, 2¼ hours

Sights & Activities

Situated on 300 meandering acres, **Turtle Bay Exploration Park** (☎ 530-243-8850, 800-887-8532; www.turtlebay.org; 800 Auditorium Dr; adult/child $13/9; 9am-5pm daily Mar-Oct, 9am-5pm Wed-Mon Nov-Feb;) is an artistic, cultural and scientific center for visitors of all ages, with an emphasis on the Sacramento River watershed. The complex houses art and natural science museums, interactive exhibits for kids focusing on forest ecology, extensive arboretum gardens, a butterfly house and a 22,000-gallon, walk-through river aquarium full of regional aquatic life, including the namesake turtles.

Resembling a run-aground (and wildly off-course) cruise ship, shimmering-white **Sundial Bridge** spans the river and is now one of Redding's marquee attractions. Completed in 2004, this impressive glass-deck pedestrian overpass connects the Turtle Bay Exploration Park to the north bank of the Sacramento River. Designed by renowned Spanish architect Santiago Calatrava, the bridge/sundial attracts visitors from around the world, who come to marvel at this unique feat of engineering artistry.

Further west in Caldwell Park, the hugely popular **Redding Aquatic Center** (☎ 530-245-7247; www.reddingaquaticcenter.com; adult/child $3.50/3; 1-5pm summer, with seasonal variations) contains an Olympic-size pool, another vast recreation pool and a 160ft-long water slide. Also in Caldwell Park, you can pick up the **Sacramento River Trail**, a paved walking and cycling path that meanders along the river for miles (13 for now, with plans to extend to 20).

The **Schreder Planetarium** (☎ 530-225-0295; www.schrederplanetarium.com; 1644 Magnolia Ave; adult/child $8/5) shows digital programs ranging from the educational to the fanciful. Opening hours vary.

Try to catch some live music downtown at the refurbished 1935 art-deco **Cascade Theatre** (☎ 530-243-8877; www.cascadetheatre.org; 1733 Market St). If nothing else, take a peek inside; this is a neon-lit gem.

Sleeping

Redding's many motels and hotels huddle around extremely noisy thoroughfares, though a few rooms can be found on less busy N Market St. A couple of 'motel rows' lie close to I-5 at the southern end of town: just west of the freeway close to the Cypress Ave exit on Bechelli Lane, and on the east

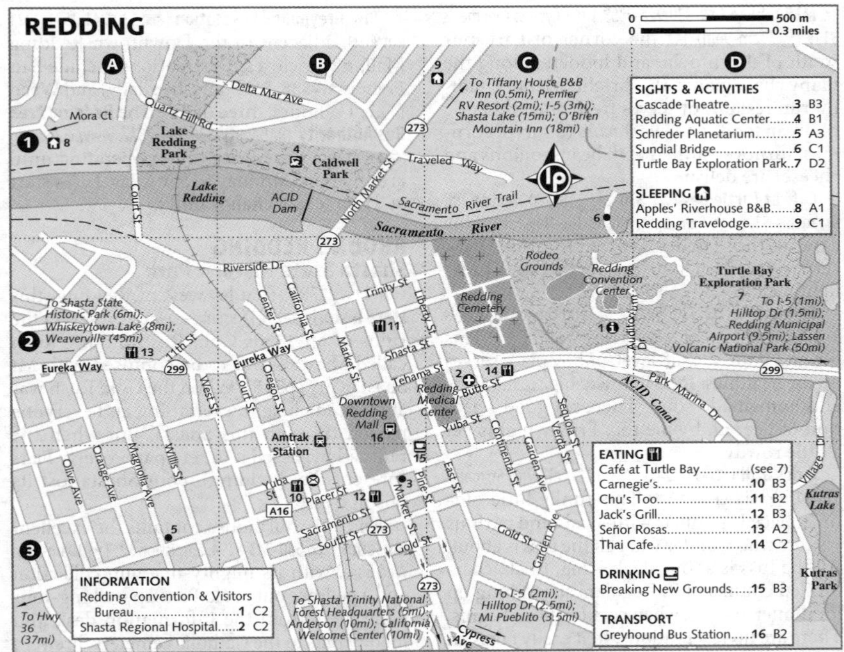

side of the freeway on Hilltop Dr. B&Bs offer a quiet alternative.

Apples' Riverhouse B&B (☎ 530-243-8440; www.applesriverhouse.com; 201 Mora Ct; r $95-110) Just steps from the Sacramento River Trail, this modern, suburban, ranch-style home has three comfortable upstairs rooms, two with decks. In the evening the sociable hosts invite you for cheese and wine. Bikes are yours to borrow.

Redding Travelodge (☎ 530-243-5291, 800-243-1106; www.reddingtravelodge.com; 540 N Market St; d $97; wi-fi) The best of the four motels on N Market St, the rooms here are particularly tidy and the staff friendly. A full breakfast at the adjoining restaurant is included.

Tiffany House B&B Inn (☎ 530-244-3225; www.tiffanyhousebb.com; 1510 Barbara Rd; r $110-120, cottage $150;) In a quiet cul-de-sac a mile north of the river, this Victorian cottage has an expansive garden with sweeping views. Cozy rooms are packed with antiques, rosebuds and ruffles. Affable hosts make a big yummy to-do over breakfast.

For another B&B option in the area, try O'Brien Mountain Inn (p306), located just 15 minutes north, off I-5 near Shasta Lake.

RV parks clump around the outskirts of town and include **Premier RV Resort** (☎ 530-246-0101; www.premierrvresorts.com; 280 N Boulder Dr; tent sites $37, RV sites $33-47) to the north. For good tent-camping options visit Whiskeytown Lake (p304) or Shasta Lake (p306).

Eating & Drinking

Thai Cafe (☎ 530-243-5523; 820 Butte St; mains $10-15; Mon-Sat) To mix it up after days of campstove cooking on the trail, hit this excellent Thai place with an extensive menu. The seafood mains (so far from the sea) are surprisingly fresh.

Chu's Too (☎ 530-244-2987; 1135 Pine St; mains $10-25; lunch & dinner Mon-Fri, dinner Sat) Though billed as Chinese, more than half the menu is Japanese. Along with all the sweet-and-sour standards there's an impressive fresh-caught array of sushi offerings.

Señor Rosas (☎ 530-241-8226; 2056 Eureka Way; meals $11; lunch Mon-Sat, dinner Fri; V) Run by a couple of gringos, this taco place is genuinely *delicioso*. Ingredients are fresh and organic, and there are more than a couple of veggie choices on the menu.

Mi Pueblito (☎ 530-224-9888; 916 E Cypress Ave; meals $11; 11am-9pm) At the corner of Larkspur south of downtown, and hidden among the many chain giants, this bright, friendly, family-run restaurant serves fresh and authentic Mexican food. The *huarraches* (a sort of cornmeal turnover stuffed with beans, onions and cheese) are delish.

Café at Turtle Bay (☎ 530-242-3181; 800 Auditorium Dr; meals $12; 8am-5pm, closed Tue Nov-Feb) This café at the Turtle Bay Exploration Park serves excellent gourmet coffee and great light meals.

Carnegie's (☎ 530-246-2926; 1600 Oregon St; meals $12; 10am-3pm Mon & Tue, to 11pm Wed-Fri; V) This hip and homey, split-level, pubby place serves up the healthiest food in town: big fresh salads and homemade soup. There's a good selection of beer and wine too. Friday nights get a little rowdy.

Jack's Grill (☎ 530-241-9705; 1743 California St; mains $15-31; dinner Mon-Sat) This funky little old-time place is popular with locals and curious visitors who wonder what all the fuss is about. All the fuss is about steak – big, thick, charbroiled chunks of it. Regulars start lining up for dinner at 4pm, when cocktail hour begins. There are no reservations, so it easily takes an hour to get a seat.

Breaking New Grounds (☎ 530-246-4563; 1320 Yuba St; 6am-7pm Mon-Thu, 6am-10pm Fri, 7am-4pm Sat; wi-fi) With a sort of relaxed living-room feel, this wi-fi café attracts a cross-section of local folks. Live acoustic music is featured on Friday nights.

Getting There & Around

Redding Municipal Airport (RDD; ☎ 530-224-4320; www.ci.redding.ca.us; 6751 Woodrum Circle) is 9.5 miles southeast of the city, just off of Airport Rd. Horizon Airlines flies daily to Los Angeles, Eureka/Arcata and Portland. United Express flies to San Francisco. Free wi-fi available.

The **Amtrak station** (☎ 800-872-7245; www.amtrak.com; 1620 Yuba St), one block west of the Downtown Redding Mall, is not staffed. For the *Coast Starlight* service, make advance reservations by phone or via the website, then pay the conductor when you board the train. Alternatively, visit a travel agency – in Redding try **Amtrak Travel Agency** (☎ 530-241-8701; 6392 Westside Rd). Amtrak travels to Oakland ($58, six hours), Sacramento ($35, four hours) and Dunsmuir ($21, 1¾ hours) once daily.

The **Greyhound bus station** (☎ 530-241-2531; 1321 Butte St), adjacent to the Downtown Redding Mall, never closes. Destinations include San Francisco ($38, 8½ hours, five daily) and Weed ($21, 1½ hours, three daily). The **Redding Area Bus Authority** (RABA; ☎ 530-241-2877; www.ci.redding.ca.us) has a dozen city routes operating until around 6pm Monday to Saturday. Fares start at $1.50 (exact change only).

AROUND REDDING

Shasta State Historic Park

On Hwy 299, 6 miles west of Redding, this **state historic park** (sunrise-sunset) preserves the ruins of an 1850s Gold Rush mining town called Shasta – not to be confused with Mt Shasta City (p315). When the Gold Rush was at its heady height, everything and everyone passed through this Shasta. But when the railroad bypassed it to set up in Poverty Flats (present-day Redding), poor Shasta lost its raison d'être.

An 1861 courthouse contains the excellent **museum** (☎ 530-243-8194; admission $2; 10am-5pm Wed-Sun), with its mighty-fine gun collection and a gallows out back. Pick up walking-tour pamphlets from the information desk and follow trails to the Catholic cemetery, brewery ruins and many other historic sites.

Whiskeytown Lake

Two miles further west on Hwy 299, sparkling **Whiskeytown Lake** (☎ 530-242-3400; www.nps.gov/whis; day use per vehicle $5) takes its name from an old mining camp. When the lake was created in the 1960s by the construction of a 263ft dam, designed for power generation and Central Valley irrigation, the few remaining buildings of old Whiskeytown were moved and the camp was submerged. Today, folks descend upon the lake's serene 36 miles of forested shoreline to camp, swim, sail, mountain-bike and pan for gold.

The **visitors center** (☎ 530-246-1225; 9am-6pm summer, 10am-4pm winter), on the northeast point of the lake just off Hwy 299, provides free maps and information on Whiskeytown and Whiskeytown-Shasta-Trinity National Recreation Area. Look for the schedules of ranger-led interpretive programs and guided walks. From the visitors center hike to roaring **Whiskeytown Falls** (3.4 miles round-trip) on a former logging road.

On the southern shore of the lake, **Brandy Creek** is ideal for swimming. Just off Hwy

THE FOREST THROUGH THE TREES

What characterizes, unites and defines the Northern Mountains region is, of course, mountains – great, densely green, richly forested mountains. The Northern Mountains cover an area roughly the size of West Virginia, and approximately 65% of that total landmass is thickly treed national forest. The most wild and delicate wilderness regions in California are found here, and the region is home to some of the world's richest biodiversity. The Klamath-Siskiyou ecoregion, for example, protects one of the four most diverse temperate coniferous forests on the globe.

Over the years, the wooded Northern Mountains territory – at least the part that's accessible to humans – has been the source of contentious struggles between loggers and environmentalists; however, until recently the area's most remote habitats have continued to thrive in pristine seclusion. Within the inner, roadless reaches of the area's five national forests, old-growth groves survive untouched, rivers and streams run clear, and wildlife remains mostly out of hunters' range.

In 2005 the US Forest Service celebrated its centennial anniversary. A little over 100 years ago President Theodore Roosevelt initiated the agency with the visionary objective of preserving and protecting, for perpetuity, the nation's richest treasure – its wild lakes, rivers and forests and the myriad creatures that inhabit them. 'Leave it as it is,' he said of the land. 'The ages have been at work on it and man can only mar it.'

Subsequent leaders have championed and furthered Roosevelt's cause. During his last term, President Clinton introduced the Roadless Area Conservation Rule, the most ecology-centric statute instated since the inception of the forest service a century ago. This rule was to permanently protect 58.5 million roadless acres of national forests from potential future road building, logging, drilling and mining.

In late 2003, however, President Bush revoked the Roadless Rule and established instead the controversial wildfire-prevention Healthy Forest Initiative, which promotes road development, logging, mining and drilling on 190 million acres of public lands across the country. Under this initiative, 5.6 million acres of Northern California's national forest lands – including the unique and fragile Klamath-Siskiyou habitat – could be opened to road building and the subsequent logging those roads allow.

Many concerned citizens and environmentalists nationwide feel the Healthy Forest Initiative promotes the wealth of the timber industry and not the health of the forests. Currently, activists are working to counteract this legislation and its potential effects. Their goal is to defend the wisdom of the national forests' original steward, Teddy Roosevelt, who recognized that 'To waste, to destroy our natural resources, to skin and exhaust the land…will result in undermining in the days of our children the very prosperity which we ought by right to hand down to them…'

299, on the northern edge of the lake, **Oak Bottom Marina** (☎ 530-359-2269) rents boats. On the western side of the lake, the **Tower House Historic District** contains the El Dorado mine ruins and the pioneer Camden House, open for summer tours.

Oak Bottom Campground (☎ 800-365-2267; tent/RV sites $12/25) is a privately run place with RV and tent camping. Most attractive are the walk-in sites right on the shore. **Primitive campsites** (summer/winter $10/5) surround the lake.

SHASTA LAKE

About 15 minutes north of Redding, the largest reservoir in California, **Shasta Lake** (www.shastalake.com), is home to the state's biggest population of nesting bald eagles. Surrounded on its several arms by hiking trails and campgrounds, the lake gets packed in summer.

The **ranger station** (☎ 530-275-1589; 14250 Holiday Rd; 8am-5pm Mon-Sat, 8am-4:30pm Sun summer, 8am-4:30pm Mon-Fri rest of year) offers free maps and information about fishing, boating and hiking. To get here, take the Mountaingate Wonderland Blvd exit off I-5, about 9 miles north of Redding, and turn right.

Sights & Activities

The colossal **Shasta Dam**, a 15-million-ton dam second only in size to Hoover Dam in Nevada, lies at the south end of the lake on Shasta Dam Blvd (Hwy 151). Built from 1938 to 1945, its 487ft spillway is as high as a 60-story building – three times higher than Niagara Falls. Woody Guthrie wrote 'This Land Is Your

Land' while he was here working on the dam. The **Shasta Dam Visitors Center** (☎ 530-275-4463; 8:30am-4:30pm) offers fascinating free guided tours of the structure's rumbling interior.

High in the limestone megaliths at the north end of the lake hide the prehistoric **Lake Shasta Caverns** (☎ 530-238-2341, 800-795-2283; www.lakeshastacaverns.com; adult/child $20/12; 9am-4pm Memorial Day to Labor Day, to 3pm Apr, May & Sep, restricted hours Oct-Mar). Tours of the crystalline caves operate daily and include a boat ride across Lake Shasta. Bring a sweater, as the temperature inside is 58°F year-round. To get there, take the Shasta Caverns Rd exit from I-5, about 15 miles north of Redding, and follow the signs for 1.5 miles.

Sleeping & Eating

All of the RV parks and resorts listed here have on-site restaurants.

US Forest Service (USFS) campgrounds (☎ 877-444-6777; www.reserveusa.com; tent sites $6-26) About half of the USFS campgrounds around the lake are open year-round. Free boat-in sites are first-come, first-served. Camping outside organized campgrounds requires a campfire permit from May to October, available free from any USF office.

Antlers RV Park & Campground (☎ 530-238-2322, 800-238-3924; www.shastalakevacations.com; 20679 Antlers Rd; tent & RV sites $17-35, cabins from $95;) East of I-5 in Lakehead, at the north end of the lake, this family-oriented campground has cabins, a country store and a marina renting watercraft and houseboats.

Lakeshore Inn & RV (☎ 530-238-2003, 888-238-2003; www.shastacamping.com; 20483 Lakeshore Dr; RV sites $20-33, cabins from $95; wi-fi) On the western side of I-5, this lakeside vacation park has a restaurant and tavern, horseshoes and basic cabins.

Holiday Harbor Resort (☎ 530-238-2383, 800-776-2628; www.lakeshasta.com; Holiday Harbor Rd; tent & RV sites $36; wi-fi) Primarily an RV campground (some tent camping), it also rents houseboats, and the busy marina offers parasailing and fishing-boat rentals. A little café (open 8am to 3pm) sits lakefront. It's off Shasta Caverns Rd, next to the lake.

our pick **O'Brien Mountain Inn** (☎ 530-238-8026, 888-799-8026; www.obrienmtn.com; Shasta Caverns Rd, O'Brien; r $140-175, ste $250-300, tree house $300; wi-fi) As a tribute to their love of music (both were involved in the LA music biz in prior lives), owners Greg and Teresa Ramsey have tastefully decked out each room with a musical theme: jazz, world beat, classical. The phenomenal and very romantic tree house has cherry-wood floors, skylights, a hot tub, a kitchen and fireplaces. Breakfast is an orchestrated symphony. From I-5, take exit 695 O'Brien/Shasta Caverns Rd.

Houseboats (www.shastalake.com) are a wildly popular lodging option. Most of them sleep six to 10 people and require a two-night minimum stay. If you want to rent one, make reservations as far in advance as possible, especially in the summer months. Boats usually sleep 10 to 16 adults and cost around $1400 to $8400 per week.

MT LASSEN & AROUND

The dramatic crags, volcanic formations and alpine lakes of Lassen Volcanic National Park remain surprisingly under-touristed and pristine when you consider that they are only a few hours from the Bay Area. Snowed in through most of winter, the park blossoms in late spring. While it is only 50 miles from Redding and thus close enough to be enjoyed on a day trip, to really do it justice you'll want to invest a few days exploring the area.

From Lassen Volcanic National Park you can take one of two very picturesque routes: Hwy 36, which heads east past Chester, Lake Almanor and historic Susanville; or Hwy 89, which leads southeast to the cozy mountain town of Quincy.

LASSEN VOLCANIC NATIONAL PARK

The dry, smoldering, treeless terrain within this 106,000-acre national park stands in stunning contrast to the cool, green conifer forest that surrounds it. Entering the park (especially from the southwest entrance) is to suddenly step into another world – or onto another planet. The lavascape here offers a fascinating glimpse into the earth's fiery core. In a fuming display, the terrain is marked by roiling hot springs, steamy mud pots, noxious sulfur vents, fumaroles, lava flows, cinder cones, craters and crater lakes.

In earlier times, the region was a summer encampment and meeting point for Native American tribes – namely the Atsugewi, Yana, Yahi and Maidu. They hunted deer and gathered plants for basket-making

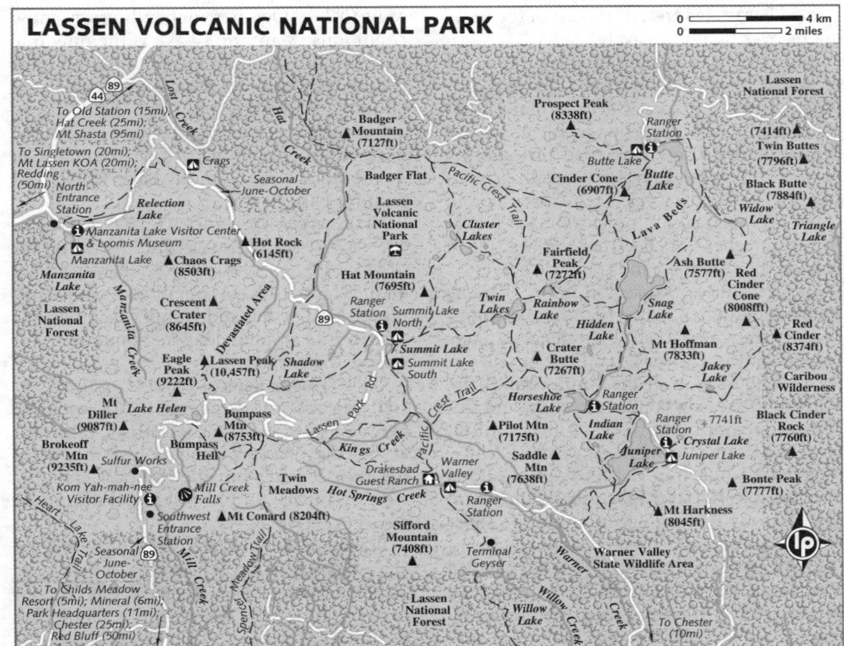

here. Some indigenous people still live near and work closely with the park to help educate visitors on their ancient history and contemporary culture.

If you're coming to Lassen National Park from the north on Hwy 89, you won't see many gas/food/lodgings signs after Mt Shasta City. Old Station makes a decent stop before entering the park. **Hat Creek Resort & RV Park** (☎ 800-568-0109; www.hatcreekrvresort.com; 12533 Hwy 44/89; tent & RV sites without/with hookups $22/38, r $90-180; wi-fi) sits along a fast-moving, trout-stocked creek. Some simple motel rooms and cabins have full kitchens. Stock up at the convenience store and deli, then eat on a picnic table by the river.

Information

Whether you enter at the north or southwest entrance, you'll be given a free map with general information.

Kom Yah-mah-nee Visitor Facility (☎ 530-595-4480; 9am-6pm Jun-Sep, hours vary Oct-May) About half a mile north of the park's southwest entrance, this handsome new center is certified by the US Green Building Council. It holds educational exhibits, a bookstore, an auditorium, a gift shop and a restaurant. Visitor information and maps available.

Manzanita Lake Visitors Center & Loomis Museum (☎ 530-595-4444, ext 5180; 9am-5pm Jun-Sep) Just past the entrance-fee station at the park's northern boundary. You can see exhibits and an orientation video inside the museum. During summer, rangers and volunteers lead programs dealing with geology, wildlife, astronomy and local culture. Visitor information and maps available.

Park Headquarters (☎ 530-595-4444; www.nps.gov/lavo; 38050 Hwy 36; 8am-4:30pm daily Jun-Sep, 8am-4:30pm Mon-Fri Oct-May) About a mile west of the tiny town of Mineral, it's the nearest stop for refueling and supplies.

Sights & Activities

Lassen Peak, the world's largest plug-dome volcano, rises 2000ft over the surrounding landscape to 10,457ft above sea level. Classified as an active volcano, its most recent eruption took place in 1915 when it blew a giant cloud of smoke, steam and ash 7 miles into the atmosphere. The national park was created the following year to protect the newly formed landscape. Some areas destroyed by the blast, including the aptly named **Devastated Area**, northeast of the peak, are recovering impressively.

Hwy 89, the road through the park, wraps around Lassen Peak on three sides and provides access to dramatic geothermal formations, pure lakes, gorgeous picnic areas and remote hiking trails. The road through the park is only open in summer, usually around June to October – it has been closed due to snow (as much as 40ft of it) well into July at times. Call ahead or check the NPS website to see whether the road and trails are open.

In total, the park has 150 miles of **hiking trails**, including a 17-mile section of the popular Pacific Crest Trail. Experienced hikers can attack the Lassen Peak Trail; it takes at least 4½ hours to make the 5-mile round-trip. Early in the season you'll need snow and ice-climbing equipment to reach the summit. Near the Kom Yah-mah-nee Visitor Facility, a gentler 2.3-mile trail leads through meadows and forest to **Mill Creek Falls**. Further north on Hwy 89, you'll recognize the roadside **Sulfur Works** by its bubbling mud pots, hissing steam vent, fountains and fumaroles. At **Bumpass Hell** a moderate 1.5-mile trail and boardwalk lead to an active geothermal area, with bizarrely colored pools and billowing clouds of steam.

The road and trails wind through cinder cones, lava and lush alpine glades, with views of Juniper Lake, Snag Lake and the plains beyond. Most of the lakes at higher elevations remain partially and beautifully frozen in summer, but leave time to fish, swim or boat on the lower **Manzanita Lake**, an emerald gem near the northern entrance.

Sleeping & Eating

The park has eight developed **campgrounds** (tent & RV sites $10-18), and there are many more in the surrounding Lassen National Forest. Campgrounds in the park are open from late May to late October, depending on snow conditions. Manzanita Lake is the only one with hot showers, but the two Summit Lake campgrounds, in the middle of the park, are also popular. **Reservations** (☎ 877-444-6777; www.recreation.gov) are permitted at Butte Lake in the northeast corner of the park, Manzanita Lake in the northwest, Summit Lake North and Summit Lake South.

Mt Lassen KOA (☎ 530-474-3133, 800-562-3403; www.koa.com; 7749 KOA Rd; tent sites $28, RV sites from $40, cabins $57-140; mid-Mar–Nov; wi-fi) Enjoy all the standard KOA amenities: a children's playground, a deli and laundry facilities. It's off Hwy 44 in Shingletown, about 20 miles west of the park.

Childs Meadow Resort (☎ 530-595-3383, 888-595-3383; www.childsmeadowresort.com; 41500 E Hwy 36, Mill Creek; d $60-70, cabins $75-150;) Rustic cabins sit at the edge of a spectacularly lush mountain meadow 9 miles outside the park's southwest entrance. An old-fashioned mountain resort experience.

Drakesbad Guest Ranch (☎ 530-529-1512, ext 120; www.drakesbad.com; Warner Valley Rd; r per person $155-185; Jun-early Oct; V) Seventeen miles northwest of Chester, this fabulously secluded place lies inside the park's southern boundary. Guests, many of whom are faithful repeat visitors, use the hot-springs-fed swimming pool or go horseback riding. Except in the main lodge, there's no electricity here (think kerosene lamps and campfires). Rates include country-style meals (vegetarian options available) and campfire barbecues every Wednesday. Ask about weekly discounts.

Getting There & Away

The park has two entrances. The northern entrance, at Manzanita Lake, is 50 miles east of Redding via Hwy 44. The southwest entrance is on Hwy 89 about 5 miles north of the junction with Hwy 36. From this junction it is 5 miles west on Hwy 36 to Mineral and 44 miles west to Red Bluff. Heading east on Hwy 36 Chester is 25 miles away and Susanville about 60 miles. Quincy is 65 miles southeast from the junction on Hwy 89.

Mt Lassen Transit (☎ 530-529-2722) buses between Red Bluff and Susanville run via Mineral, which is the stop closest to the park. There's no public transportation within the park or on the 5 miles between Hwy 36 and the park entrance.

DETOUR: WILD HORSE SANCTUARY

Since 1978, the **Wild Horse Sanctuary** (☎ 530-335-2241; www.wildhorsesanctuary.com; Shingletown; admission free; 9am-6pm Wed & Sat) has been sheltering horses and burros that would otherwise have been destroyed. To see them on the open plains, take a two- to three-day weekend pack trip in spring or summer. Shingletown lies 20 miles to the west of Lassen Volcanic National Park.

LASSEN NATIONAL FOREST

The vast, unspoiled **national forest** (www.fs.fed.us/r5/lassen) surrounding Lassen Volcanic National Park covers 1.2 million acres (1875 sq miles) of wilderness in an area called 'The Crossroads,' where the granite Sierra, volcanic Cascades, Modoc Plateau and Central Valley meet.

The forest contains 460 miles of **hiking trails**, including 120 miles of the Pacific Crest Trail, the 12-mile Spencer Meadows National Recreation Trail and the 3.5-mile Heart Lake National Recreation Trail. Special points of interest include a 600yd walk through the **Subway Cave** lava tube; the 1.5-mile volcanic **Spattercone Crest Trail**; **Willow Lake** and **Crater Lake**; 7684ft **Antelope Peak**; and the 900ft-high, 14-mile-long **Hat Creek Rim** escarpment.

The forest also contains three wilderness areas. The **Caribou Wilderness** and **Thousand Lakes Wilderness** are best visited from mid-June to mid-October. The **Ishi Wilderness**, at a much lower elevation in the Central Valley foothills east of Red Bluff, is more comfortable in spring and fall, as summer temperatures often climb to over 100°F.

The Lassen National Forest Supervisor's Office (p310) is in Susanville. Other ranger offices include **Eagle Lake Ranger District** (☎ 530-257-4188; 477-050 Eagle Lake Rd, Susanville), **Hat Creek Ranger District** (☎ 530-336-5521; 43225 E Hwy 299, Fall River Mills) and **Almanor Ranger District** (☎ 530-258-2141; 900 E Hwy 36, Chester), about a mile west of Chester.

LAKE ALMANOR AREA

Calm, turquoise Lake Almanor lies south of Lassen Volcanic National Park via Hwys 89 and 36. This man-made lake surrounded by lush meadows and tall pines was once little-visited, but is now a burgeoning mini Lake Tahoe. Properties are being snapped up, exclusive country clubs are mushrooming, and by the time you read this, a 3000-acre ski area, Dyer Mountain Resort, will be the area's new winter polestar.

The main town near the lake, Chester (population 2500, elevation 4528ft), seems like your average tiny burg – you could whiz right by and dismiss it as a few blocks of nondescript roadside storefronts. Don't – it's not. This robust little community has a fledgling art scene, decent restaurants and some comfy places to stay.

DETOUR: WESTWOOD & THE BIZZ JOHNSON TRAIL

A few miles east of Chester is Westwood, a tiny speck of a town that marks the beginning of the **Bizz Johnson Trail**, an extremely picturesque route that runs the remote 25.5 miles from Westwood to Susanville. Once part of the old Southern Pacific right-of-way, the wooden bridges and serenely crossing-free trail are traversable by foot, mountain bike, horseback or cross-country skis (no motorized vehicles allowed!). Do the trail in the Westwood–Susanville direction, as it's mostly downhill that way. Get trail guides at the chamber of commerce in Chester (below) or at the Susanville Railroad Depot (p310).

Information

Rent boats and water-sports equipment at any of the many places around the lake.

B&B Booksellers (☎ 530-258-2150; 140 Main St) A bookstore and gallery with free wi-fi access.

Bodfish Bicycles & Quiet Mountain Sports (☎ 530-258-2338; 152 Main St) Rents bicycles, cross-country skis and snowshoes, and sells canoes and kayaks. It's a great source of mountain-biking and bicycle-touring advice.

Chester & Lake Almanor Chamber of Commerce (☎ 530-258-2426, 800-350-4838; www.chester-lakealmanor.com; 529 Main St; ⌚ 9am-4pm Mon-Fri) Get information about lodging and recreation around the lake, in Lassen National Forest and in Lassen Volcanic National Park.

Lassen National Forest Almanor Ranger Station (☎ 530-258-2141; 900 E Hwy 36; ⌚ 8am-4:30pm Mon-Fri) About a mile west of town, with similar information to the chamber of commerce.

Sleeping & Eating

CHESTER

Cinnamon Teal Inn (☎ 530-258-3993; www.cinnamontealinn.net; 227 Feather River Dr; r with shared bath $70-80, r with private bath $120, cottage $130) This shady B&B a half-block back from Main St has river access from the verdant gardens. Fluffy feather beds dominate each quaint room, and the cottage has a fully equipped kitchen.

Timber House Lodge (☎ 530-258-2729; 501 Main St; r from $80) Small but decent rooms make this one of the area's best budget options. The adjoining family-style restaurant/bar (open for dinner Thursday to Saturday) is known for its steak, prime ribs and seafood.

our pick Bidwell House B&B (☎ 530-258-3338; www.bidwellhouse.com; 1 Main St; r with shared bath $85, r with private bath $115-165, cottage $175; wi-fi) Set back from the street, this historic summer home of pioneers John and Annie Bidwell is packed with antiques. The classic accommodations come with all the modern amenities (including a spa in some rooms) – no roughing it here. Enjoy goodies like a three-course breakfast, home-baked cookies and afternoon sherry.

St Bernard Lodge (☎ 530-258-3382; www.stbernardlodge.com; 44801 E Hwy 36, Mill Creek; d with shared bath $90-150) Located 10 miles west of Chester at Mill Creek, this old-world charmer has seven B&B rooms with views to the mountains and forest. Think knotty-pine paneling and quilted bedspreads. The tavern also serves lunch and dinner.

Knotbumper Restaurant (☎ 530-258-2301; 274 Main St; meals $8-10; ⏰ 11am-8pm Mon-Sat) This place has a generous deli menu, including tamale pies, shrimp salad sandwiches and other eclectic selections. On summer days, eat on the lively front porch.

Mt Fusion (☎ 530-258-3310; 605 Main St; mains $10-15; ⏰ lunch & dinner) This bright, forest-green restaurant at the western end of town serves up sizzling Mexican food.

AROUND THE LAKE

Book ahead for lakefront lodgings in summer. There are restaurants at the resorts.

Federal campgrounds (☎ reservations 877-444-6777; www.reserveusa.com; tent sites $12-20) These campgrounds lie within the surrounding Lassen and Plumas National Forests on the lake's southwest shore. Sites tend to be more tranquil than the RV-centric private campgrounds.

Knotty Pine Resort & Marina (☎ 530-596-3348; www.knottypine.net; 430 Peninsula Dr; weekly RV sites $175, r $195, 2-bedroom cabins with kitchen $155; 🐕) This full-service lakeside alternative, seven miles east of Chester, has simple cabins and rents boats, kayaks and canoes.

North Shore Campground (☎ 530-258-3376; www.northshorecampground.com; tent sites $33, RV sites $36-48, cabins $140-225; wi-fi) Two miles east of Chester on Hwy 36, these expansive, forested grounds stretch for a mile along the water. Ranch-style cabins have full kitchens.

Little Norway Resort (☎ 530-596-3225; 432 Peninsula Dr; cabins from $120) At Big Cove, eight miles east of Chester, off Hwy A13, Little Norway Resort has rustic cabins ranging from one- to four-bedroom, with fully equipped kitchens. It also rents boats, kayaks and canoes.

SUSANVILLE

pop 18,100 / elev 4258ft

This high desert plateau town is the Lassen County seat and site of two prisons. Not a tourist destination in itself, it does provide lots of basic services for the many travelers passing through – it lies 35 miles east of Lake Almanor and 85 miles northwest of Reno. Home to exceptionally friendly folk, it also holds its share of Wild West history. Tourist information can be found at the **Lassen County Chamber of Commerce** (☎ 530-257-4323; www.lassencountychamber.org; 84 N Lassen St; ⏰ 10am-4pm Mon-Fri), while the **Lassen National Forest Supervisor's Office** (☎ 530-257-2151; 2550 Riverside Dr; ⏰ 8am-4:30pm Mon-Fri) has maps and recreation information.

The restored **Susanville Railroad Depot**, south of Main St off Weatherlow St, sits beside the terminus of the Bizz Johnson Trail (see the boxed text, p309). The **visitors center** (☎ 530-257-3252; 601 Richmond Rd; ⏰ 10am-4pm May-Oct) rents bicycles and has brochures on mountain-biking trails in the area.

The town's oldest building, **Roop's Fort** (1853), is named after Susanville's founder, Isaac Roop. The fort was a trading post on the Nobles Trail, a California emigrant route. The town itself was named after Roop's daughter, Susan. Beside the fort is the tame **Lassen Historical Museum** (☎ 530-257-3292; 75 N Weatherlow St; admission by donation; ⏰ 10am-4pm Mon-Fri May-Oct).

The **Lassen County Fair** (☎ 530-251-8900; www.lassencountyfair.org) swings into gear in July.

Motels along Main St, none of them exceptional, average $50 to $75 per night. Try the **Roseberry House B&B** (☎ 530-257-5675; www.roseberryhouse.com; 609 North St; r/ste $110/135; 🚭) for more character. This sweet 1902 Victorian house is two blocks north of Main St. Striking dark-wood antique headboards and armoires combine with rosebuds and frill. Scrummy breakfasts are a treat.

Step through the door and back in time at the **Grand Café** (☎ 530-257-4713; 730 Main St; mains $9; ⏰ breakfast & lunch Mon-Sat). Established in 1909, this art-deco café is a time capsule with original wooden booths, green-and-black floor tiles, table lamps and a jukebox. The menu hasn't changed much over time either, featuring pancakes, soup, homemade bread and malts. The **Pioneer Café** (☎ 530-257-2311; 724 Main St) is older still: one saloon or another has been operating on this site since 1862. Today it's a combination bar, billiards room and inexpensive eatery.

Mt Lassen Transit (☎ 530-529-2722) buses leave Red Bluff at 8:30am Mon-Sat ($25, 4½ hours) and return from Susanville at 2pm. **Susanville City Buses** (☎ 530-252-7433) make a circuit around town (fare $1).

EAGLE LAKE

From late spring until fall this lovely lake, about 15 miles northwest of Susanville, attracts visitors who come to cool off, swim, fish, boat and camp. On the south shore of this, California's second-largest natural lake, you'll find a pristine 5-mile **recreational trail** and several busy **campgrounds** (☎ reservations 877-444-6777; www.recreation.gov; tent sites $18, RV sites $29-33) administered by Lassen National Forest and the **Bureau of Land Management** (BLM; ☎ 530-257-5381). Campgrounds for tent camping include Merrill, Aspen, Christie and Eagle. Merrill and Eagle also have RV sites. Nearby **Eagle Lake Marina** (☎ 530-825-3454; www.eaglelakerecreationarea.com) offers hot showers, laundry and boat rentals.

Eagle Lake RV Park (☎ 530-825-3133; www.eaglelakeandrv.com; 687-125 Palmetto Way; tent/RV sites $25/37, cabins $90-150; wi-fi), on the western shore, and **Mariners Resort** (☎ 530-825-3333; Stones Landing; RV sites $34-37, cabins $95-180), on the quieter north shore, both rent boats.

QUINCY

pop 5000 / elev 3432ft

Idyllic Quincy is nestled in a high valley in the northern Sierra, southeast of both Lassen Volcanic National Park and Lake Almanor via Hwy 89. Students from small, local Feather River College give this laid-back mountain town just enough of an edge to keep the atmosphere lively. Nearby Feather River, Plumas National Forest, Tahoe National Forest and their oodles of open space make Quincy an excellent base from which to explore.

Orientation & Information

Once in town, Hwy 70/89 splits into two one-way streets, with traffic on Main St heading east, and traffic on Lawrence St heading west. Jackson St runs parallel to Main St, one block south, and is another main artery. Just about everything you need is on, near or between these three streets, making up Quincy's low-key commercial district.

Mt Hough Ranger District Office (☎ 530-283-0555; 39696 Hwy 70; 🕑 8am-4:30pm Mon-Fri) Five miles west of town. Has maps and outdoors information.

Plumas County Visitors Bureau (☎ 530-283-6345, 800-326-2247; www.plumascounty.org; 550 Crescent St; 🕑 8am-5pm Mon-Sat) Half a mile west of town.

Plumas National Forest Headquarters (☎ 530-283-2050; 159 Lawrence St; 🕑 8am-4:30pm Mon-Fri) For maps and outdoors information.

Sights & Activities

Pop into the 1921 **Plumas County Courthouse**, at the west end of Main St, to see enormous interior marble posts and staircases, and a 1-ton bronze-and-glass chandelier in the lobby.

In the block behind the courthouse, the **Plumas County Museum** (☎ 530-283-6320; 500 Jackson St, at Coburn St; adult/child $1/50¢; 🕑 8am-5pm Mon-Sat, also 10am-4pm Sun May-Sep) has flowering gardens, as well as hundreds of historical photos and relics from the county's pioneer and Maidu days, its early mining and timber industries, and construction of the Western Pacific Railroad. Peruse local art at the **Plumas Art Gallery** (☎ 530-283-3402; 372 Main St; admission free; 🕑 11am-5:30pm Wed-Fri).

Pick up free walking and driving tour pamphlets from the visitors bureau to guide you through gorgeous surrounding **American Valley**. The Feather River Scenic Byway (Hwy 70) leads into the Sierra. In summer, the icy waters of county namesake **Feather River** (*plumas* is Spanish for feathers) are excellent for swimming, kayaking, fishing and floating in old inner tubes. The area is also a wonderland of winter activities, especially at Bucks Lake (p313). Rent cross-country ski gear and snowshoes at **Sierra Mountain Sports** (☎ 530-283-2323; 501 W Main St), across from the courthouse.

Festivals & Events

On the first weekend in July, quiet Quincy is host to the blow-out **High Sierra Music Festival** (www.highsierramusic.com). The four-day extravaganza brings a five-stage smorgasbord of art and music (rock, blues, folk, jazz). And contrary to local billing (some call it the Hippie Fest), the audience is not all that crunchy and not everyone is stoned. Festival-goers come from different walks of life, even different parts of the globe. If you plan to attend, reserve a room or campsite a couple of months in advance.

NORTHERN BITES

Northern California was propelled into culinary stardom by the Bay Area and Wine Country's fine restaurants, not by the mountain region's greasy spoons. Still, the area doesn't suffer from foodie famine. Don't expect concentrations of fine bistros here, but enjoy the sprinkling (like a fine dusting of cocoa powder over tiramisu) of exceptional restaurants you do find.

Try the area's top four recommended spots:

- **Café Le Coq** (right), Quincy
- **Café Maddalena** (p320), Dunsmuir
- **Trinity Café** (p318), Mt Shasta City
- **La Grange Café** (p326), Weaverville

Sleeping

Feather River Canyon Campgrounds (☎ reservations 877-444-6777; www.recreation.gov; tent & RV sites $15-20) Area campgrounds are administered through the Mt Hough Ranger District Office. They clump along the north fork of the Feather River west of Quincy – five are no-fee, but also have no piped water.

Pine Hill Motel (☎ 530-283-1670, 866-342-2891; www.pinehillmotel.com; 42075 Hwy 70; s/d/cabin from $69/75/150;) A mile west of downtown Quincy, a cooling emerald lawn surrounds this homey place. Each cozy unit is equipped with a microwave, coffeemaker and refrigerator. Some cabins have full kitchens.

Ada's Place (☎ 530-283-1954; www.adasplace.com; 562 Jackson St; cottages $100-145; wi-fi) Not a B&B, just a B. You're responsible for your own breakfast here – no problem, as each of the three cottage units has a full kitchen. It's very cozy, quiet and private, with a DSL internet connection.

our pick **Feather Bed B&B** (☎ 530-283-0102, 800-696-8624; www.featherbed-inn.com; 542 Jackson St, at Court St; s $120-130, d $131-152, cottages $179-190) Just behind the courthouse, this frilly pink 1893 Queen Anne home is choc full of antiques and cuteness – a teddy bear adorns every quilted bed. Gracious hosts make afternoon tea with cookies and guests can borrow bikes. The cottage is accessible for travelers with disabilities.

Quincy Courtyard Suites (☎ 530-283-1401; www.quincycourtyardsuites.com; 436 Main St; apt $129-159; wi-fi) Book a vacation rental in the beautifully renovated 1908 Clinch building in the heart of downtown. The warmly decorated apartments have spacious, modern kitchens and gas fireplaces.

Greenhorn Guest Ranch (☎ 800-334-6939; www.greenhornranch.com; 2116 Greenhorn Ranch Rd; adult/child/junior $250/117/183; May-Oct;) Not a 'dude' ranch but rather a 'guest' ranch: instead of slopping out stalls you'll be joining in mountain trail rides, riding lessons, even rodeo practice. Or you can just fish, hike, square dance and attend evening bonfires, cookouts and frog races. Meals included; weekly discounts available.

Eating & Drinking

Pangaea Café & Pub (☎ 530-283-0426; 461 W Main St; mains $8-12; lunch & dinner Mon-Fri; V wi-fi) Like a stranger you feel you've met before, this earthy spot feels warmly familiar. The specialty is panini, with a zillion flavorful, mostly veggie, combos. Microbrew choices are just as tempting. The cozy little nook in the back has a computer (internet $3 per hour). Live music most weekends.

Morning Thunder Café (☎ 530-283-1310; 557 Lawrence St; meals $9-15; breakfast & lunch; V) Homey. Hip. The best place in town for breakfast. The menu is mainly, though not exclusively, vegetarian. Try the vegetaters: roasted veg and potatoes smothered in cheese.

Moon's (☎ 530-283-0765; 497 Lawrence St; mains $11-24; dinner Tue-Sun) Follow the aroma of garlic to this welcoming little chalet with a charming ambience. Dig into choice steaks and Italian-American classics, including excellent pizza and rich lasagna.

Sweet Lorraine's (☎ 530-283-5300; 384 Main St; meals $12-21; lunch Mon-Fri, dinner Mon-Sat) On a warm day – or, better yet, evening – the patio here is especially sweet. The menu features light California cuisine (fish, poultry, soups and salads), but it's also known for its award-winning St Louis Ribs.

Ten-Two Dinner House (☎ 530-283-2817; 8270 Bucks Lake Rd; mains $14-17; dinner Thu-Mon) Eight miles from Quincy in Meadow Valley, on the road to Bucks Lake, the Ten-Two serves superb food with all-natural ingredients. The menu changes with the seasons. In summer sit outside by the creek. Reservations recommended.

our pick **Café Le Coq** (☎ 530-283-0114; 189 Main St; prix fixe menu lunch/dinner $17/32; lunch Mon-Fri, dinner Tue-Sat) The French owner and chef makes this little house surrounded by an enchanted garden feel like home. Delicious gourmet French meals are served inside or out.

Drunk Brush (☎ 530-283-9380; 438 Main St) This wine bar pours 25 wines by the glass, with another dozen by the bottle and a selection of beers. Sample delicious appetizer pairings in a welcoming, art-bedecked atmosphere.

Stock up on fresh organic produce at the lively **farmers market** (cnr Church & Main Sts, 5-8pm Thu mid-Jul–mid-Sep) and help support local sustainable agriculture.

BUCKS LAKE

elev 5000ft

Locals flock to this clear mountain lake surrounded by pine forests for fishing and boating. It's about 17 miles southwest of Quincy, via Bucks Lake Rd (Hwy 119), and is lined with beautiful **hiking trails**, including the Pacific Crest Trail, which passes through the adjoining 21,000-acre Bucks Lake Wilderness in the northwestern part of Plumas National Forest. **Bucks Lake Stables** (☎ 530-283-1147; 1540 Chandler Rd), on the north side of town, offers trail rides ($30 to $70) and overnight pack trips. In winter, the last 3 miles of Bucks Lake Rd are closed by snow, making it ideal for cross-country skiers.

Bucks Lake Lodge (☎ 530-283-2262; www.buckslakelodge.com; 16525 Bucks Lake Rd; d & cabins $109-119) rents boats and fishing tackle in summer and cross-country skis in winter. The restaurant is popular with locals. **Haskins Valley Inn** (☎ 530-283-9667; www.haskinsvalleyinn.com; 1305 Haskins Circle; r from $130; wi-fi) is actually a lakefront B&B with cozily overstuffed furnishings, Jacuzzis, fireplaces and a deck.

Five first-come, first-served **campgrounds** (tent & RV sites $16-20) are open from June to September. Get a map at the Plumas National Forest Headquarters or the ranger station, both in Quincy (p311).

MT SHASTA & AROUND

One hypnotic glimpse of Mt Shasta and you'll find it hard to stay away. Hike, mountain-bike, white-water raft, ski or snowshoe: take your pick as you explore the peak and surrounding Shasta-Trinity National Forest. At Mt Shasta's base sit three must-see towns: Dunsmuir, Mt Shasta City and McCloud. Each community has a distinct personality but all share a wild-mountain sensibility (plus first-rate restaurants and places to stay). In the same dramatic vicinity rise the snaggle-toothed peaks of Castle Crags, just 6 miles west of Dunsmuir.

Northeast of Mt Shasta, a long drive and a world away, is remote, eerily beautiful Lava Beds National Monument, a blistered badland of petrified fire. The contrasting cool wetlands of Klamath Basin National Wildlife Refuges are just west of Lava Beds.

Further east, high desert plateaus give way to the mountains of the northern Sierra. Folks in this remote area are genuinely happy to greet a traveler, even if they're a bit uncertain why you've come.

MT SHASTA

'When I first caught sight of it I was 50 miles away and afoot, alone and weary. Yet all my blood turned to wine, and I have not been weary since,' wrote naturalist John Muir in 1874. Mt Shasta's beauty is intoxicating, and the closer you get to her the headier you begin to feel. Dominating the landscape, the mountain is visible for more than 100 miles from many parts of northern California and southern Oregon. Though not California's highest peak (at 14,162ft it ranks fifth), Mt Shasta is especially magnificent because it rises alone on the horizon, unrivaled by other mountains.

Mt Shasta is part of the vast volcanic Cascade chain that includes Lassen Peak to the south and Mt St Helens and Mt Rainier to the north in Washington state. The presence of thermal hot springs indicates that Mt Shasta is dormant, not extinct. Smoke was seen puffing out of the crater on the summit in the 1850s, though the last eruption is believed to have been about 200 years ago. The mountain has two cones: the main cone has a crater about 200yd across; the younger, shorter cone on the western flank, called Shastina, has a crater about half a mile wide.

The mountain and surrounding **Shasta-Trinity National Forest** (www.fs.fed.us/r5/shastatrinity) are crisscrossed by trails and dotted with alpine lakes. It's easy to spend days or weeks camping, hiking, river rafting, skiing, mountain-biking and boating.

When European fur trappers arrived in the area in the 1820s, they encountered several Native American tribes, including the Shasta, Karuk, Klamath, Modoc, Wintu and Pit River. By 1851 hordes of Gold Rush miners had arrived, completely disrupting the tribes' traditional life. Later the newly completed railroad began to swiftly import workers and export timber for the booming lumber industry. And since Mt Shasta City (called Sisson at the time) was the only non-dry town around, it became *the* bawdy, good-time hangout for lumberjacks.

The lumberjacks have now been replaced by new-agers. Today Mt Shasta is a mecca for mystics: seekers are attracted to the peak's reported cosmic properties. In 1987 about 5000 believers from around the world convened here for the Harmonic Convergence, a communal meditation for peace. Reverence for the mountain is nothing new; for centuries Native Americans have honored the mountain as sacred, considering it to be no less than the Great Spirit's wigwam.

Information

Peak tourist season is from Memorial Day through Labor Day and also weekends during ski season (late November to mid-April). The ranger station and visitors bureau are in Mt Shasta City (opposite).

Sights & Activities

For activity operators and outfitters, see opposite.

VISITING THE MOUNTAIN

You can drive almost the whole way up the mountain via the Everitt Memorial Hwy (Hwy A10) and see exquisite views at any time of year. Simply head east on Lake St from downtown Mt Shasta City, then turn left onto Washington Dr and keep going. **Bunny Flat** (6860ft), which has a trailhead for Horse Camp and the Avalanche Gulch summit route, is a busy place with parking spaces, information signboards and a toilet. The section of highway beyond Bunny Flat is only open from about mid-June to October, depending on snows. This road leads to **Lower Panther Meadow**, where trails connect the campground to a Wintu sacred spring, in the upper meadows near the **Old Ski Bowl** (7800ft) parking area. Shortly thereafter is the highlight of the drive, **Everitt Vista Point** (7900ft), where a short interpretive walk from the parking lot leads to a stone-walled outcropping affording exceptional views of Lassen Peak to the south, the Mt Eddy and Marble Mountains to the west and the whole Strawberry Valley below.

Climbing the summit is best done between May and September, preferably in spring and early summer, when there's still enough soft snow on the southern flank to make footholds easier on the nontechnical route. Though the round-trip could conceivably be done in one day with 12 or more hours of solid hiking, it's best to allow at least two days and spend a night on the mountain. How long it actually takes to climb up and back depends on the route selected, the physical condition of the climbers and weather conditions (for weather information call ☎ 530-926-9613).

Although the hike to the summit from Bunny Flat is only about 7 miles, it is a vertical climb of more than 7000ft, so acclimatizing to the elevation is important. You'll need crampons, an ice ax and a helmet, all of which can be rented locally. Rock slides and unpredictable weather can be hazardous, so novices should contact the Mt Shasta Ranger Station for a list of available guides.

There's a charge to climb beyond 10,000ft: a three-day summit pass costs $20; an annual pass is $30. Contact the ranger station for details. You must obtain a free wilderness permit any time you go into the wilderness, whether on the mountain or in the surrounding area.

MT SHASTA BOARD & SKI PARK

On the south slope of Mt Shasta, off Hwy 89 heading toward McCloud, this winter skiing and snowboarding **sports park** (☎ snow reports 530-926-8686; www.skipark.com; lift tickets adult/child Mon-Thu $25/15, Fri-Sun $39/20; 9am-9pm Wed-Sat, 9am-4pm Sun-Tue winter, 10am-4pm Wed, Thu & Sun, 10am-9pm Fri & Sat late Jun-early Sep) opens depending on snowfall. The park has a 1390ft vertical drop, over two dozen alpine runs and 18 miles of cross-country trails. Rentals, instruction and weekly specials are available. It's Northern California's largest night-skiing operation.

In summer, the park offers scenic chairlift rides, paragliding flights, a 24ft climbing tower and Frisbee golf. Mountain-bikers take the chairlift up and come whooshing back down.

THE LAKES

There are a number of pristine mountain lakes near Mt Shasta. Some of them are accessible only by dirt roads or hiking trails and are great for getting away from it all.

The closest lake to Mt Shasta City is **Lake Siskiyou** (also the largest), 2.5 miles southwest on Old Stage Rd, where you can peer into **Box Canyon Dam**, a 200ft-deep chasm. Another 7 miles up in the mountains, southwest of

Lake Siskiyou on Castle Lake Rd, lies **Castle Lake**, an unspoiled gem surrounded by granite formations and pine forest. Swimming, fishing, picnicking and free camping are popular in summer; in winter, folks ice-skate on the lake. **Lake Shastina**, about 15 miles northwest of town off Hwy 97, is another beauty, favored by short-board windsurfers.

MT SHASTA CITY

pop 3630 / elev 3554ft

No town, no matter how lovely – and Mt Shasta City is lovely – could compete with the surrounding natural beauty here. Understandably, most visitors don't make a pilgrimage here to visit the fish hatchery; they come to meet the mountain. Still, downtown itself is charming: you can spend hours poking around bookstores, galleries and boutiques.

Orientation & Information

Orienting yourself is easy, with Mt Shasta looming over the east side of town. The downtown area is a few blocks east of I-5. Take the Central Mt Shasta exit, then drive east on Lake St past the visitors bureau, up to the town's main intersection at Mt Shasta Blvd, the principal drag.

Has Beans Coffeehouse (☎ 530-926-3602; 1011 S Mt Shasta Blvd; per hr $3; 🕒 5:30am-7pm; wi-fi) Check email here. Wi-fi free.

Mt Shasta Ranger Station (☎ 530-926-4511; 204 W Alma St; 🕒 8am-4:30pm) One block west of Mt Shasta Blvd. Issues wilderness and mountain-climbing permits, good advice, weather reports and all you need for exploring the area. Also sells topographic maps.

Mt Shasta Visitors Bureau (☎ 530-926-4865, 800-926-4865; www.mtshastachamber.com; 300 Pine St; 🕒 9am-5:30pm Mon-Sat, to 4:30pm Sun summer, 10am-4pm daily winter) Detailed information on recreation and lodging across Siskiyou County.

Sights & Activities

Sisson Museum (☎ 530-926-5508; 1 Old Stage Rd; admission free; 🕒 10am-4pm Mon-Sat, 1-4pm Sun Jun-Sep, 1-4pm Fri-Sun Oct-Dec, 1-4pm daily Apr & May), a half-mile west of the freeway, is full of curious mountaineering artifacts and old pictures. The changing exhibitions highlight history – geological and human – but also occasionally showcase local artists. Next door, the **Mt Shasta Fish Hatchery** (☎ 530-926-2215; 🕒 7am-sunset), the oldest operating hatchery in the west, maintains outdoor ponds full of thousands of rainbow trout that will eventually be released into lakes and rivers.

At **Mt Shasta City Park** (Nixon Rd), off Mt Shasta Blvd about a mile north of downtown, the headwaters of the Sacramento River gurgle up from the ground in a large, cool spring. The park also has walking trails, picnic spots, sports fields and courts, and a children's playground. East of downtown, the immense outdoor skating rink at **Shastice Park** (☎ 530-926-2494; adult/child 12yr and under/13-18yr $10/5/8, skate rentals $2; cnr Rockfellow & Adams Drs; 🕒 10am-noon Mon, 10am-noon & 3-5pm Tue, 3-4:30pm Thu, 3-9pm Fri, 1:30-9pm Sat, 1:30-5pm Sun) is open to ice skaters in winter and in-line skaters in summer.

Mt Shasta Resort (☎ 530-926-3052; www.mountshastaresort.com; 1000 Siskiyou Lake Blvd; greens fees $40-55) has a rolling, tree-lined, 18-hole golf course with expansive views. Fees are discounted for twilight play.

To head out hiking on your own, first stop by the ranger station or the visitors bureau for excellent free trail guides, including several access points along the **Pacific Crest Trail**. Gorgeous **Black Butte**, a striking, treeless, black volcanic cone, rises almost 3000ft. The 2.5-mile trail to the top takes at least 2½ hours for the round-trip. It's steep and rocky in many places, and there is neither shade nor water, so don't hike on a hot summer day. Wear good hiking shoes and bring plenty of water. Or try the 9-mile **Sisson-Callahan National Recreation Trail**, a historic route established in the mid-1800s by prospectors, trappers and cattle ranchers to connect the mining town of Callahan with the town of Sisson, now called Mt Shasta City.

OPERATORS & OUTFITTERS

Shasta Mountain Guides (☎ 530-926-3117; www.shastaguides.com) offers two-day guided climbs of Mt Shasta, all gear and meals included, for around $500. **Mt Shasta Mountaineering School** (☎ 530-926-6003, 800-797-6867; www.swsmtns.com; 210a E Lake St) conducts clinics and courses for serious climbers, or those looking to get serious.

For a uniquely Mt Shasta outdoor experience, try **Shasta Vortex Adventures** (☎ 530-926-4326; www.shastavortex.com; 400 Chestnut St). Its trips accent the spiritual quest as much as the physical journey.

Fifth Season Sports (☎ 530-926-3606; 300 N Mt Shasta Blvd, at Lake St) rents camping, mountain-climbing and backpacking gear, plus mountain bikes, skis, snowshoes and snowboards. Ski and snowboard rentals are also available

DETOUR: WEED & STEWART MINERAL SPRINGS

Just outside of Weed, **Stewart Mineral Springs** (☎ 530-938-2222; www.stewartmineralsprings.com; 4617 Stewart Springs Rd; mineral baths $25, sauna $17; 10am-6pm Sun-Wed, to 7pm Thu-Sat) is a popular alternative (read clothing-optional) hangout on the banks of a clear mountain stream. Locals come for the day and visitors from afar come for weeks. Henry Stewart founded these springs in 1875 after Native Americans revived him from a near-death experience. He attributed his recovery to the healthful properties of the mineral waters, said to draw toxins out of the body.

Today you can soak in a private claw-foot tub or steam in the dry-wood sauna. Other perks include massage, body wraps, meditation, a Native American sweat lodge and a riverside sunbathing deck. Dining and **accommodations** (tent & RV sites $20, tipis $30, r $65-85) are available. To reach the springs, go 10 miles north of Mt Shasta City on I-5, past Weed to the Edgewood exit, then turn left at Stewart Springs Rd and follow the signs.

While in the area, tickle your other senses at the **Mt Shasta Lavender Farms** (☎ 530-926-2651; www.mtshastalavenderfarms.com), 16 miles northwest of Weed, off Hwy A12, on Harry Cash Rd. You can harvest your own sweet flowers in the June and July blooming season. Or drink up the tasty porter at the **Weed Mt Shasta Brewing Company** (☎ 530-938-2394; 360 College Ave, Weed).

at **Sportsmen's Den Snowboard & Ski Shop** (☎ 530-926-2295; 402 N Mt Shasta Blvd) and **House of Ski & Board** (☎ 530-926-2359; 316 Chestnut St), which also rents bicycles. Ski and snowboard packages run about $25 a day. Bike rentals cost $30 for a full day.

Excellent **River Dancers Rafting & Kayaking** (☎ 530-926-3517, 800-926-5002; www.riverdancers.com; 302 Terry Lynn Ave) is run by active environmentalists who guide one- to five-day white-water rafting excursions down the area's rivers: the Klamath, Sacramento, Salmon, Trinity and Scott. **Osprey Outdoors Kayak School** (☎ 530-926-6310; www.ospreykayak.com; 2925 Cantara Loop Rd) has a reputation for quality classes. Expect to pay around $80 to $100 per adult per day for either River Dancers or Osprey.

Live a dream by seeing the area from a hot-air balloon with **Shasta Valley Balloons** (☎ 530-926-3612; 316 Pony Trail; rides $200).

Sleeping

Make reservations well in advance, especially on weekends and holidays, and during ski season.

CAMPING

The visitors bureau has details on over two dozen campgrounds around Mt Shasta. Check with the Mt Shasta and McCloud ranger stations about USFS campgrounds in the area. As long as you set up camp at least 200ft from the water and get a free campfire permit from a ranger station, you can camp beside many mountain lakes. Castle Lake (6450ft) and Gumboot Lake (6000ft) have free tent camping (purify your own drinking water) and are closed in winter. Lovely Toad Lake (7060ft), 18 miles from Mt Shasta City, isn't a designated camping area, but you may camp there if you follow the regulations. To get there, go down the 11-mile gravel road (4WD advised) and walk the last quarter-mile.

our pick **Historic Lookout & Cabin Rentals** (☎ 530-994-2184; www.fs.fed.us/r5/shastatrinity; up to 4 people per night $35) What better way to rough it in style than to bunk down in a restored fire lookout on the slopes of Little Mt Hoffman or Girard Ridge? Built from the 1920s to '40s, they come with cots, tables and chairs, have panoramic views and can accommodate four people.

Panther Meadows (tent sites free) Ten walk-in tent sites (no drinking water) sit at the timberline. They're 7 miles further up the mountain (at 7400ft), and are accessible from Everitt Memorial Hwy. No reservations here; arrive early to secure a site.

Horse Camp (per person without/with tent $3/5) This 1923 alpine lodge run by the Sierra Club is a 2-mile hike uphill from Bunny Flat, at 8000ft. Caretakers staff the hut from May to September only.

McBride Springs (tent sites $10) Easily accessible from Everitt Memorial Hwy, this campground has running water and pit toilets, but no showers. It's near mile-marker 4, at an elevation of 5000ft. Arrive early in the morning to secure a spot (no reservations).

Lake Siskiyou Camp-Resort (☎ 530-926-2618; www.lakesis.com; 4239 WA Barr Rd; tent/RV sites from $20/29, cabins $100-145) Tucked away on the shore of Lake Siskiyou, it has a swimming beach, as well as kayak, canoe, fishing boat and paddle boat rentals.

MOTELS

Many motels offer discount ski packages in winter and lower midweek rates year-round.

Finlandia Motel (☎ 530-926-5596; www.finlandiamotel.com; 1612 S Mt Shasta Blvd; r $60-120, with kitchen $89-150) An excellent deal, the standard rooms are…standard – clean and simple. The suites get a little chalet flair from vaulted pine-wood ceilings and mountain views. There's an outdoor hot tub and the Finnish sauna is available by appointment.

Strawberry Valley Inn (☎ 530-926-2052; http://strawberryvalleysuites.com;1142 S Mt Shasta Blvd; d from $90; 💻) The serenely understated rooms surround a garden courtyard. Enjoy all the intimate feel of a B&B without the have-to-chat-with-the-newlyweds-in-the-hall social pressure. A full vegetarian breakfast is included. In the evenings there's complimentary wine.

Strawberry Valley Court (☎ 530-926-2052; 305 Old McCloud Rd; cabins from $90) The Inn's equally cute sister property has a white picket fence and shady brick cabins with private garages.

Several modest motels stretch along S Mt Shasta Blvd. All have hot tubs and rooms cost between $60 and $140 in peak season:

Swiss Holiday Lodge (☎ 530-926-3446; www.snowcrest.net/swissholidaylge; 2400 S Mt Shasta Blvd; ❄ 🏊) Quiet.

Evergreen Lodge (☎ 530-926-2143; www.snowcrest.net/evergreenlodge; 1312 S Mt Shasta Blvd; ❄ 🏊) Friendly.

Mountain Air Lodge & Ski House (☎ 530-926-3411; 1121 S Mt Shasta Blvd) Old-fashioned, with a recreation room and complimentary breakfast.

B&BS

Mt Shasta Ranch B&B (☎ 530-926-3870; www.stayinshasta.com; 1008 WA Barr Rd, at Ream Ave; d with shared bath & kitchen from $70, d with private bath & kitchen $120, cottages $115-160; 👶) The rambling, country-style main house and everything in it is supersized – the rooms, the baths, the stone fireplace, the views. Soak in the hot-spring spa. Breakfast (also big) is included with rooms, but not cottages.

Dream Inn (☎ 530-926-1536, 877-375-4744; www.dreaminnmtshastacity.com; 326 Chestnut St; r with shared bath $80-110, ste $120-160; 💻) Made up of two houses in the center of town: one is a meticulously kept Victorian cottage stuffed with fussy knickknacks; the other a Spanish-style two-story with chunky raw-wood furniture and no clutter. A rose garden with koi pond joins the two properties. A hefty breakfast is included.

Alpenrose Cottage Guest House (☎ 530-926-6724; www.snowcrest.net/alpenrose; 204 E Hinckley St; s/d $70/90, cottage $175) You'll find this homey spot a few long blocks north of downtown. A hostel in its former life, this roomy two-bedroom house retains a communal feel. There's a mountain-view deck, wood-burning stoves, enchanting gardens and a shared kitchen.

ShasTao (☎ 530-926-4154; www.shastao.com; 3609 N Old Stage Rd; d $100-160; 💻 wi-fi) A pair of very mellow, affable philosophy professors runs this wooded, peaceful retreat. You won't find your granny's wallpaper here…or her library: they've got bookshelves stacked with titles from aestheticism to Zen. They also loan bikes and snowshoes. Vegetarian/vegan breakfast included.

our pick Shasta MountInn (☎ 530-926-1810; www.shastamountinn.com; 203 Birch St; r without/with fireplace $125/175; 💻) Only antique on the outside – inside, this Victorian farmhouse is all relaxed minimalism. Each airy room has a designer mattress and exquisite views of the luminous mountain. Enjoy the expansive garden, wrap-around deck and outdoor sauna.

RESORTS

Mt Shasta Resort (☎ 530-926-3030; www.mountshastaresort.com; 1000 Siskiyou Lake Blvd; r from $90, 1-/2-bedroom chalets from $154/193) Divinely situated, this upscale golf resort and spa has Arts and Crafts–style chalets nestled in the woods around the shores of Lake Siskiyou. Each has a kitchen and gas fireplace. Basic lodge rooms are near the golf course. The restaurant has excellent views and serves California cuisine.

Eating

Trendy restaurants and cafés here come and go with the snowmelt. Most of the following are tried and true, favored by locals and visitors alike.

Poncho & Lefkowitz (☎ 530-926-1102; 401 S Mt Shasta Blvd; meals $4-10; Ⓥ) A classy, wood-sided food cart – sort of a café on wheels. From juicy Polish sausage to veggie burritos, this combo Mexican-food/gourmet-hot-dog stand serves scrumptious treats.

Berryvale Grocery & Deli (☎ 530-926-3536; 305 S Mt Shasta Blvd; mains $9; 🕑 breakfast & lunch daily, dinner Mon-Fri; Ⓥ) Sells health-conscious groceries and organic produce. The excellent deli café serves good coffee and an array of tasty – and mostly veggie – salads, sandwiches and burritos.

Lily's (☎ 530-926-3372; 1013 S Mt Shasta Blvd; breakfast & lunch mains $9-15, dinner mains $15-22; ⏰ breakfast, lunch & dinner Mon-Fri, brunch & dinner Sat & Sun) Enjoy quality California cuisine in a cute, white, clapboard house. Outdoor tables overhung by flowering trellises are almost always full, especially for breakfast.

our pick **Trinity Café** (☎ 530-926-6200; 622 N Mt Shasta Blvd; mains $17-27; ⏰ dinner Tue-Sat) Trinity has long rivaled any big-city 'haute' spot. The owners, who hail from Napa, infuse the bistro with a Wine Country feel, not to mention an extensive, excellent wine selection. The organic menu ranges from delectable, perfectly cooked steaks to creamy-on-the-inside, crispy-on-the-outside polenta. The warm, mellow mood makes for an overall delicious experience.

Michael's Restaurant (☎ 530-926-5288; 313 N Mt Shasta Blvd; mains $27; ⏰ lunch & dinner Tue-Fri, dinner Sat) The few Italian places in town are all overpriced. Michael's is no exception, but the food here is comparably exceptional and the views of Mt Shasta gorgeous. The pasta is fresh – a rarity in these parts – and the desserts homemade.

KenZen (☎ 530-926-2345; 315 N Mt Shasta Blvd; meals $28; ⏰ dinner Tue-Sun) Don't be put off by the drab exterior of this first-rate sushi bar; inside it's all sleek mahogany and calm. The owner flies in just-caught, grade-A fish daily. The quality is excellent, though the import cost is reflected in the prices.

There are a couple of kitschy, breakfast-served-all-day options:

The Skillet (☎ 530-926-4047; 610 S Mt Shasta Blvd; mains $8; ⏰ breakfast, lunch & dinner) Mexican-leaning and serving good huevos rancheros; known for its huge portions.

Black Bear Diner (☎ 530-926-1411; 401 W Lake St; mains $8; ⏰ breakfast, lunch & dinner) Part of a cute bear-themed chain; nice view.

The **farmers market** (⏰ 3:30-6pm Mon) sets up on Mt Shasta Blvd during summer.

Drinking & Entertainment

Has Beans Coffeehouse (☎ 530-926-3602; 1011 S Mt Shasta Blvd; ⏰ 5:30am-7pm; 💻 wi-fi) This snug little hangout serves organic, locally roasted coffee. One computer is tucked away in the back corner (internet $3 per hour). There's live acoustic music some evenings.

Stage Door Coffeehouse & Cabaret (☎ 530-926-1050; www.stagedoorcabaret.com; 414 N Mt Shasta Blvd; ⏰ 7am-10pm Mon-Sat, to 7pm Sun; V wi-fi) Popular café-bar and theater. The menu features espresso, microbrews, wine and lots of veggie dishes. On Wednesday nights there are indie films; on weekends live music – anything from Celtic punk to bluegrass.

Mt Shasta Cinemas (☎ 530-926-1116; Mt Shasta Shopping Center, 118 Morgan Way) Shows first-run films.

Shopping

Visions Gallery (☎ 530-926-1189; 201 N Mt Shasta Blvd) In the Black Bear Building, it has skylit exhibition spaces and quality crafts.

Both **Village Books** (☎ 530-926-1678; 320 N Mt Shasta Blvd) and **Golden Bough Books** (☎ 530-926-3228; 219 N Mt Shasta Blvd) carry fascinating volumes about Mt Shasta, on topics from geology and hiking to folklore and mysticism, as does the Sisson Museum shop (p315).

Getting There & Around

Greyhound (☎ 800-231-2222; www.greyhound.com) buses heading north and south on I-5 stop opposite the Vet's Club (406 N Mt Shasta Blvd) and at the **depot** (☎ 530-938-4454; 628 S Weed Blvd) in Weed, 8 miles north on I-5. Services include Redding ($21, one hour and 20 minutes, three daily), Sacramento ($51, 5½ hours, three daily) and San Francisco ($61, 10½ hours, two or three times daily).

The **STAGE bus** (☎ 530-842-8295, 800-247-8243; www.co.siskiyou.ca.us) includes Mt Shasta City in its local I-5 corridor route (fares $1.05 to $8 depending on distance), which also serves McCloud, Dunsmuir, Weed and Yreka several times daily on weekdays only. Other buses connect at Yreka (see p328).

The **California Highway Patrol** (CHP; ☎ 530-842-4438) recorded report gives weather and road conditions for Siskiyou County.

DUNSMUIR

pop 1870 / elev 2289ft

Built by Central Pacific Railroad, Dunsmuir was originally named Pusher, for the auxiliary 'pusher' engines that muscled the heavy steam engines up the steep mountain grade. In 1886 Canadian coal baron Alexander Dunsmuir came to Pusher and was so enchanted that he promised the people a fountain if they would name the town after him. The fountain stands in the park today. Stop there to quench your thirst: it could easily be – as locals claim – 'the best water on earth.'

A more apt name for the town might have been Phoenix. Rising from the ashes (sometimes literally), this town has survived and triumphed over mythic-sized woes. Over the past century Dunsmuir has been subjected to avalanche, fire and flood, and in 1991 a toxic railroad spill damaged the river's aquatic life and people's morale. Long since cleaned up, the river has been restored to pristine levels and the community now prospers like never before.

Today artists, naturalists, urban refugees and native Dunsmuirians make up a thriving community. In its bawdy Gold Rush heyday five saloons and three brothels crowded downtown. Today shops, cafés, restaurants and galleries dot Dunsmuir and Sacramento Aves.

The **Dunsmuir Chamber of Commerce** (☎ 530-235-2177, 800-386-7684; www.dunsmuir.com; Suite 100, 5915 Dunsmuir Ave; 🕑 10am-3:30pm Tue-Sat) has free maps, walking-guide pamphlets and excellent information on outdoor activities.

Sights & Activities

On Dunsmuir Ave at downtown's north end stands what was once the town's pride: the **California Theater** (☎ 530-235-9934). In a grassroots community effort, this long-defunct, once-glamorous venue is being carefully restored to its original glory. First opened in 1926, the theater hosted stars like Clark Gable, Carole Lombard and the Marx Brothers. Today the lineup includes films, musical performances, theater groups and comedians.

Check out Jayne Bruck-Fryer's **Ruddle Cottage** (☎ 530-235-2022; 5815 Sacramento Ave; 🕑 10am-4pm May-Oct, 11am-4pm Nov-Apr) gallery. The artist makes each and every ingenious creation – from sculptures to jewelry – from recycled materials. The pretty fish hanging in the window? Dryer lint!

As you follow winding Dunsmuir Ave north over the freeway, look for **Dunsmuir City Park & Botanical Gardens** (☎ 530-235-4740; admission free; 🕑 dawn to dusk) with its local native plant gardens and a **vintage steam engine** in front. A forest path from the riverside gardens leads to a small waterfall, but **Mossbrae Falls** is the larger and more spectacular of Dunsmuir's waterfalls. To get there from Dunsmuir Ave, turn west onto Scarlett Way, passing under an archway marked 'Shasta Retreat.' Park by the railroad tracks (there's no sign), then walk north along the right-hand side of the tracks for a half-hour until you reach a railroad bridge built in 1901. Backtracking slightly from the bridge, you'll find a little path going down through the trees to the river and the falls. Be *extremely careful* of trains as you walk by the tracks – the river's sound can make it impossible to hear them coming.

The chamber of commerce stocks maps of **biking trails** and **swimming holes** on the Upper Sacramento River.

Sleeping

Cave Springs Resort (☎ 530-235-2721; www.cavesprings.com; 4727 Dunsmuir Ave; RV sites $22, cabins $45-63, r $54-69; 🐾 📡) Location, location, location. These very rustic cabins are nestled on a piney crag above the Sacramento River. Though mostly frequented by anglers, this place has romantic appeal: at night there's nothing but the sound of rushing water and the haunting whistle of trains. The motel rooms have more amenities but less character.

Railroad Park Resort (☎ 530-235-4440, 800-974-7245; www.rrpark.com; 100 Railroad Park Rd; tent/RV sites $22/30, caboose & boxcar ste $115-120; 📡) About a mile south of town off I-5, spend the night inside vintage railroad cars. The deluxe boxcars are furnished with antiques and claw-foot tubs; the cabooses are simpler. Enjoy tremendous views of Castle Crags, a peaceful creekside setting and tall pines shading the adjoining campground.

Cedar Lodge (☎ 530-235-4331; www.cedarlodge-dunsmuir.com; 4201 Dunsmuir Ave; r $69-79; 📡) At the far north end of town, this large, welcoming, woodsy property contains basic motel rooms, some with kitchens; all have microwave ovens and small refrigerators.

Dunsmuir Lodge (☎ 530-235-2884, 877-235-2884; www.dunsmuirlodge.net; 6604 Dunsmuir Ave; r $69-139; wi-fi) Toward the south entrance of town, the simple but tastefully renovated rooms have hardwood floors, big chunky blond-wood bed frames and tiled baths. A grassy communal picnic area overlooks the canyon slope.

Eating & Drinking

Cornerstone Bakery & Café (☎ 530-235-4677; 5759 Dunsmuir Ave; mains $8-9; 🕑 breakfast & lunch Wed-Mon, dinner Fri-Sun; Ⓥ) Smack in the middle of town, it serves smooth, strong coffee, espresso and chai. All the baked goods – including thick, gooey cinnamon rolls – are warm from the oven. Creative omelets include cactus. The wine list is extensive, as is the dessert selection.

Brown Trout Café & Gallery (☎ 530-235-0754; 5841 Sacramento Ave; mains $10; ⏰ breakfast & lunch; wi-fi) This casual, high-ceilinged, brick-walled hangout has a light, satisfying menu. Try the excellent Mexican mocha. Lunch highlights include specialty sandwiches (veggie with pesto or Jamaican jerk chicken) and salads (pear and blue cheese…yum). There's also a short wine and microbrew list.

our pick **Sengthongs Restaurant & Blue Sky Room** (☎ 530-235-4770; www.sengthongs.com; 5843 Dunsmuir Ave; mains $11-20; ⏰ lunch Mon-Fri summer, dinner Mon, Tue & Thu-Sat year-round) This funky joint serves up sizzling Thai, Lao and Vietnamese food and books first-rate jazz, reggae, salsa or blues most nights. Many dishes are simply heaping bowls of noodle-iciousness.

Railroad Park Dinner House (☎ 530-235-4440; Railroad Park Resort, 100 Railroad Park Rd; mains $15-25; ⏰ dinner Fri & Sat Apr-Nov) Set inside a vintage railroad car, this popular restaurant-bar offers trainloads of dining-car ambience and California cuisine.

our pick **Café Maddalena** (☎ 530-235-2725; 5801 Sacramento Ave; mains $20-25; ⏰ dinner Thu-Sun) This café put Dunsmuir on the foodie map. Though original owner Maddalena Sera no longer runs the café (rumor has it she is now Francis Ford Coppola's personal chef), Bret LaMott (of Trinity Café fame; p318) maintains the restaurant's stellar reputation. The menu, which changes weekly, features southern European and North African specialties, and the wine bar is stocked with rare Mediterranean labels.

Getting There & Away

Dunsmuir's **Amtrak station** (☎ 800-872-7245; www.amtrak.com; 5750 Sacramento Ave) is the only train stop in Siskiyou County and is not staffed. Buy tickets for the north–south *Coast Starlight* on board the train, but only after making reservations by phone or via the website. The *Coast Starlight* runs once daily to Redding ($21, 1¾ hours), Sacramento ($46, 5¾ hours) and Oakland ($59, eight hours).

The **STAGE bus** (☎ 530-842-8295, 800-247-8243) includes Dunsmuir in its local I-5 corridor route, which also serves Mt Shasta City ($1.75, 20 minutes), Weed ($3.15, 30 minutes) and Yreka ($4.85, 1¼ hours) several times daily on weekdays only. The bus runs on Dunsmuir Ave.

CASTLE CRAGS STATE PARK

The stars of this glorious state park alongside Castle Crags Wilderness Area are its soaring spires of ancient granite formed some 225 million years ago, with elevations ranging from 2000ft along the Sacramento River to more than 6500ft at the peaks. The crags are similar to the granite formations of the eastern Sierra, and Castle Dome here resembles Yosemite's famous Half Dome.

Rangers at the **park entrance station** (☎ 530-235-2684; day use per vehicle $6) have information and maps covering nearly 28 miles of **hiking trails**. There's also **fishing** in the Sacramento River at the picnic area on the opposite side of I-5.

If you drive past the campground you'll reach **Vista Point**, near the start of the strenuous 2.7-mile **Crags Trail**, which rises through the forest past the Indian Springs spur trail, then clambers up to the base of **Castle Dome**. You're rewarded with unsurpassed views of Mt Shasta, especially if you scramble the last hundred yards or so up into the rocky saddle gap. The park also has gentle **nature trails** and 8 miles of the **Pacific Crest Trail**, which passes through the park at the base of the crags.

The **campground** (☎ reservations 800-444-7275; www.reserveamerica.com; tent & RV sites $15-20) has running water, hot showers, and three spots that can accommodate RVs but have no hookups. Sites are shady, but suffer from traffic noise. You can camp anywhere in the Shasta-Trinity National Forest surrounding the park if you get a free campfire permit, issued at park offices.

MCCLOUD

pop 1600 / elev 3254ft

This small, historic mill town sits at the foot of the south slope of Mt Shasta. Quiet streets retain their simple charm. It's the closest settlement to Mt Shasta Board & Ski Park (p314), and is surrounded by abundant natural beauty.

Information

McCloud Chamber of Commerce (☎ 530-964-3113; www.mccloudchamber.com; 205 Quincy St; ⏰ 10am-4pm Mon-Fri)

McCloud Ranger District Office (☎ 530-964-2184; Hwy 89; ⏰ 8am-4:30pm Mon-Sat summer, 8am-4:30pm Mon-Fri rest of year) A quarter-mile east of town. Detailed information on camping, hiking and recreation.

Sights & Activities

The **Shasta Sunset Dinner Train** (☎ 530-964-2142, 800-733-2141; www.shastasunset.com; 328 Main St; adult/child $12/8; ⏲ 4pm Thu-Sat summer) offers one-hour, superscenic, open-air train rides through Mt Shasta's forested southern slopes, in addition to its dinner service (see p322). A tiny **historical museum** (admission free; ⏲ 11am-3pm Mon-Sat, 1-3pm Sun) sits opposite the depot.

The **McCloud River Loop**, a gorgeous, 6-mile, partially paved road along the Upper McCloud River, begins at Fowlers Camp, 5.5 miles east of town on Hwy 89, and re-emerges about 11 miles east of McCloud. Along the loop, turn off at **Three Falls** for a pretty trail that passes…yep, three lovely falls, and a riparian habitat for bird-watching in the Bigelow Meadow. The loop can easily be done by car, by bicycle or on foot, and has five first-come, first-served campgrounds.

Other good hiking trails include the **Squaw Valley Creek Trail** (not to be confused with the ski area near Lake Tahoe), an easy 5-mile loop trail south of town, with options for swimming, fishing and picnicking. Also south of town, **Ah-Di-Na** is the remains of a Native American settlement and historic homestead once owned by the William Randolph Hearst family. Sections of the **Pacific Crest Trail** are accessible from Ah-Di-Na Campground, off Squaw Valley Rd, and also up near Bartle Gap, offering head-spinning views.

Fishing and swimming are popular on remote **Lake McCloud** reservoir, 9 miles south of town on Squaw Valley Rd, which is signposted as Southern Ave in town. You can also go fishing on the Upper McCloud River (stocked with trout) and at the Squaw Valley Creek. **Friday's RV Retreat** (☎ 530-964-2878; Squaw Valley Rd; 2½-hour lesson $90), 6 miles south of McCloud near Squaw Valley Creek, has a fly-fishing school (all gear is provided).

Sleeping

Lodging in McCloud is taken seriously – all are excellent and reservations are recommended.

Go to the McCloud Ranger District Office for information on the half-dozen campgrounds nearby. Fowlers Camp is the most popular. The campgrounds have a range of facilities, from primitive (no running water and no fee) to developed (hot showers and fees of up to $20 per site). Ask about nearby fire-lookout cabins for rent – they give amazing, remote views of the area.

McCloud Dance Country RV Park (☎ 530-964-2252; www.mccloudrvpark.com; 480 Hwy 89, at Southern Ave; tent sites $14-24, RV sites $21-37, cabins $85-120; wi-fi) Chock-full of RVs, with sites under the trees. Cabins are basic but clean.

McCloud Century House Inn (☎ 530-964-2206; www.mccloudcenturyhouse.com; 433 Lawndale Ct; ste $50-135; 👪) This cozy getaway at the west end of town offers knickknack-filled suites with full kitchens.

Stoney Brook Inn (☎ 530-964-2300, 800-369-6118; www.stoneybrookinn.com; 309 W Colombero Dr; s/d with shared bathroom $53/79, with private bathroom $65/94, ste with kitchen $99-156) Smack in the middle of town, under a stand of pines, this alternative B&B also sponsors group retreats. Creature comforts include an outdoor hot tub, a sauna, a Native American sweat lodge and massage by appointment. Downstairs rooms are nicest. Vegetarian breakfast available.

McCloud River Lodge (☎ 530-964-2700; www.mccloudlodge.com; 140 Squaw Valley Rd; d $70-105) Tidy, new log cabins surround a lush central grassy area. Simple rooms have homey, plush, quilted beds. Accessible rooms for travelers with disabilities are available.

McCloud River Inn (☎ 530-964-2130, 800-261-7831; www.mccloudriverinn.com; 325 Lawndale Ct; r $96-175; ⊠) Rooms in this rambling, quaint Victorian are fabulously big – the bathrooms alone could sleep two. The relaxed and familial atmosphere guarantees that it books up quickly.

our pick **McCloud Hotel** (☎ 530-964-2822, 800-964-2823; www.mccloudhotel.com; 408 Main St; r $100-235; ⊠) This regal, block-long, butter-yellow, grand hotel opposite the depot first opened in 1916. The elegant historic landmark has been lovingly restored to a luxurious standard, and the included breakfast is taken very seriously. One room is accessible for travelers with disabilities.

Eating

McCloud's eating options are few. For more variety, make the 10-mile trip over to Mt Shasta City.

River Grill & Bar (☎ 530-964-2700; 140 Squaw Valley Rd; mains $6-17; ⏲ lunch Sat & Sun, dinner Wed-Mon) At the McCloud River Lodge, tuck into greasy-spoon diner basics here.

White Mountain Fountain Café (☎ 530-964-2005; 241 Main St; mains lunch $8, dinner $20-25; ⏲ breakfast & lunch daily, dinner Fri & Sat) Located in the Old

Mercantile Building, this old-fashioned little soda fountain serves burgers and shakes. Inventive three-course dinners on weekends include dishes like herbed balsamic New York steak with wild mushroom risotto.

Shasta Sunset Dinner Train (☎ 800-733-2141; www.shastasunset.com; 328 Main St; 3hr ride with multicourse dinner $98; 🕑 5:30pm Thu-Sat summer) Dine in elegance on this superscenic ride along Mt Shasta's southern slopes. These 1916-vintage restored dining cars chug along one of several archaic routes going west and east from McCloud. Trips are scaled back outside of summer.

Entertainment

McCloud Dance Country (☎ 530-964-2578; cnr Broadway & Pine Sts; per couple $20; 🕑 7pm Fri & Sat) Dust it up on the 5000-sq-ft maple dance floor in the 1906 Broadway Ballroom. Square dances, round dances, ballroom dancing – they do it all. Multiday packages run $35 to $255 per couple. Call ahead to see what's on and whether you need a reservation for the event.

MCARTHUR-BURNEY FALLS MEMORIAL STATE PARK

Beautiful **McArthur-Burney Falls Memorial State Park** (☎ 530-335-2777; www.parks.ca.gov; day use per vehicle $6) lies southeast of McCloud near the crossroads of Hwy 89 and Hwy 299 from Redding. The 129ft falls cascade with the same volume of water (100 million gallons per day) and at the same temperature (42°F) year-round. Clear, lava-filtered water surges over the top and also from springs in the waterfall's face.

A lookout point beside the parking lot also has trails going up and down the creek from the falls. The nature trail heading downstream leads to Lake Britton; other hiking trails include a portion of the Pacific Crest Trail. The scenes in the film *Stand By Me* (1986) where the boys dodge the train were shot on the Lake Britton Bridge trestle in the park.

The park's **campgrounds** (☎ 530-335-2777, summer reservations 800-444-7275; www.reserveamerica.com; day use $6, tent & RV sites $20) have hot showers and are open year-round.

About 10 miles northeast of McArthur-Burney Falls, the 6000-acre **Ahjumawi Lava Springs State Park** is known for its abundant springs, aquamarine bays and islets, and jagged flows of black basalt lava. It can only be reached by boats that are launched from Rat Farm, 3 miles north of the town of McArthur along a graded dirt road. Arrangements for primitive camping can be made by calling McArthur-Burney Falls Memorial State Park.

> **DETOUR: HAT CREEK RADIO OBSERVATORY**
>
> The **Hat Creek Radio Observatory** (☎ 530-335-2364; www.hcro.org; Bidwell Rd, Hat Creek; 🕑 9am-3pm Mon-Fri), 10 miles south of the crossroads of Hwy 89 from McCloud and Hwy 299 from Redding, uses radio telescopes designed to capture radio waves coming from outer space to research radio astronomy. Founded in 1950 and operated by UC Berkeley, the facility offers free tours – maybe they can make a collect call for you.

LAVA BEDS NATIONAL MONUMENT

Off Hwy 139, immediately south of Tule Lake National Wildlife Refuge, **Lava Beds National Monument** (☎ 530-667-8100; www.nps.gov/labe; 7-day entry per vehicle/hiker/biker $10/5/5) is a truly remarkable 72-sq-mile landscape of volcanic features – lava flows, craters, cinder cones, spatter cones, shield volcanoes and amazing lava tubes.

Lava tubes are formed when hot, spreading lava cools and hardens on the surfaces exposed to the cold air. The lava inside is thus insulated and stays molten, flowing away to leave an empty tube of solidified lava. Nearly 400 such tubular caves have been found in the monument, and many more are expected to be discovered. About two dozen or so are currently open for exploration by visitors.

On the south side of the park, the **visitors center** (☎ 530-667-2282, ext 230; 🕑 8am-6pm summer, 8:30am-5pm rest of year) has free maps, activity books for kids, and information about the monument and its volcanic features and history. Rangers loan flashlights, rent helmets and kneepads for cave exploration, and lead summer interpretive programs, including campfire talks and guided cave walks. To explore the caves, it's essential you use a high-powered flashlight, wear good shoes and long sleeves (lava is sharp), and not go exploring alone.

Near the visitors center, a short, one-way loop drive provides access to many lava-tube caves, with names like Labyrinth, Hercules Leg, Golden Dome and Blue Grotto. **Mushpot Cave**, the one nearest the visitors center, has lighting and informational signs.

The tall black cone of **Schonchin Butte** (5253ft) has a magnificent outlook accessed via a steep 1-mile hiking trail. Once you reach the top, you can visit the fire-lookout staff between June and September. **Mammoth Crater** is the source of most of the area's lava flows.

The weathered Modoc **petroglyphs** at the base of a high cliff at the far northeastern end of the monument, called Petroglyph Point, are thousands of years old. At the visitors center, be sure to take the leaflet explaining the origin of the petroglyphs and their probable meaning. Look for the hundreds of nests in holes high up in the cliff face, which provide shelter for birds that sojourn at the wildlife refuges nearby.

Also at the north end of the monument, be sure to go to the labyrinthine landscape of **Captain Jack's Stronghold**. A brochure will guide you through the breathtaking Stronghold trail.

Indian Well Campground (tent & RV sites $10), near the visitors center at the south end of the park, has water and flush toilets, but no showers. A couple of motels are on Hwy 139 in the nearby town of Tulelake (see p324).

KLAMATH BASIN NATIONAL WILDLIFE REFUGES

Of the six stunning national wildlife refuges in this group, Tule Lake and Clear Lake refuges are wholly within California, Lower Klamath refuge straddles the California-Oregon border, and the Upper Klamath, Klamath Marsh and Bear Valley refuges are across the border in Oregon. Bear Valley and Clear Lake (not to be confused with the Clear Lake just east of Ukiah) are closed to the public to protect their delicate habitats, but the rest are open during daylight hours.

These refuges provide habitats for a stunning array of birds migrating along the Pacific Flyway (see the boxed text, p324). Some stop over only briefly; others stay longer to mate, make nests and raise their young. The refuges are always packed with birds, but during the spring and fall migrations populations can rise into the hundreds of thousands.

The **Klamath Basin National Wildlife Refuges Visitors Center** (☎ 530-667-2231; http://klamathbasinrefuges.fws.gov; 4009 Hill Rd, Tulelake; ⌚ 8am-4:30pm Mon-Fri, 10am-4pm Sat & Sun) sits on the west side of the Tule Lake refuge, about 5 miles west of Hwy 139, near the town of Tulelake. Follow the signs from Hwy 139 or from Lava Beds National Monument. The center has a bookstore and interesting video program, as well as maps, information on recent bird sightings and updates on road conditions. It rents photo blinds. Be sure to pick up the excellent, free *Klamath Basin Birding Trail* brochure for detailed lookouts, maps, color photos and a species checklist.

The spring migration peaks during March, and in some years more than a million birds fill the skies. In April and May the songbirds, waterfowl and shorebirds arrive, some to stay and nest, others to build up their energy before they continue north. In summer, ducks, Canada geese and many other waterbirds are raised here. The fall migration begins in early September and by late October peak numbers of birds have departed. In cold weather, the area hosts the largest wintering concentration of bald eagles in the lower 48 states, with 1000 in residence at times from December to February. The Tule Lake and Lower Klamath refuges are the best places to see eagles and other raptors.

The Lower Klamath and Tule Lake refuges attract the largest numbers of birds year-round, and **auto trails** (drivable routes) have been set up; a free pamphlet from the visitors center shows the routes. Self-guided **canoe trails** have been established in three of the refuges. Those in the Tule Lake and Klamath Marsh refuges are usually open from July 1 to September 30; no canoe rentals are available. Canoe trails in the Upper Klamath refuge are open year-round; canoes can be rented at **Rocky Point Resort** (☎ 541-356-2287; 28121 Rocky Point Rd, Klamath Falls, OR; canoes, kayak & peddle boat rental

> **LOCAL VIEW ON LAVA BEDS**
>
> When asked which is her favorite cave or lava tube, NPS ranger Kristin 'Kale' Bowling responds 'whichever I'm in at the time.' Bowling is effusive in her descriptions of all of the varieties of caves: freezing, with skylights, with ferns, with glow-in-the-dark mineral deposits...the list goes on and on. And she's equally enthusiastic when describing the 14 species of bats found in the park. She's careful, though, to caution new cavers to check in with the visitors center before exploring: she wants no damage to the caver or to the fragile geological and biological resources in the park.

THE AVIAN SUPERHIGHWAY

California is on the Pacific Flyway, a migratory route for hundreds of species of birds heading south in winter and north in summer. There are birds to see year-round, but the best viewing opportunities are during the spring and fall migrations. Flyway regulars include everything from tiny finches, hummingbirds, swallows and woodpeckers to eagles, hawks, swans, geese, ducks, cranes and herons. Much of the flyway route corresponds with I-5 (or fly-5 in the birds' case), so a drive up the interstate in spring or fall is a show: great Vs of geese undulate in the sky and noble hawks stare from roadside perches.

In Northern California, established wildlife refuges safeguard wetlands used by migrating water fowl. The Klamath Basin National Wildlife Refuges offer extraordinary year-round bird-watching.

per hr/half-day/day $15/30/40), on the west side of Upper Klamath Lake in Oregon.

Camp at nearby Lava Beds National Monument (p323). A couple of RV parks and budget motels cluster on Hwy 139 near the tiny town of **Tulelake** (4035ft), including the friendly **Ellis Motel** (☎ 530-667-5242; 2238 Hwy 139; d without/with kitchen $75/95). Comfortable **Fe's B&B** (☎ 877-478-0184; www.fesbandb.com; 660 Main St; s/d with shared bath $60/70) has four simple rooms, with a big breakfast included.

MODOC NATIONAL FOREST

This **national forest** (www.fs.fed.us/.r5/modoc) covers almost two million spectacular, remote acres of California's northeastern corner. Fourteen miles south of Lava Beds National Monument, on the western edge of the forest, **Medicine Lake** is a stunning crater lake in a caldera (collapsed volcano) surrounded by pine forest, volcanic formations and campgrounds. The enormous volcano that formed the lake is the largest in area in California. When it erupted, it ejected pumice followed by flows of obsidian, as can be seen at **Little Glass Mountain**, east of the lake.

Pick up the excellent *Medicine Lake Highlands: Self-Guided Roadside Geology Tour* pamphlet from the McCloud Ranger District Office (p320) to find and learn about the glass flows, pumice deposits, lava tubes and cinder cones throughout the area. Roads are closed by snow from around mid-November to mid-June, but the area is still popular for winter sports, and accessible by cross-country skiing and snowshoeing.

The **Warner Mountains**, a spur of the Cascade Range on the east side of the forest, have extremely changeable weather: there've been snowstorms here in every season of the year, so always be prepared. The range divides into the North Warners and South Warners at **Cedar Pass** (elevation 6305ft), east of Alturas.

Remote **Cedar Pass Snow Park** (☎ 530-233-3323; http://cedarpasssnowpark.com; all day T-bar adult/child under 6yr/6-18yr $15/5/12, all-day rope tow $5; 10am-4pm Sat, Sun & holidays during ski season) offers downhill and cross-country skiing. The majestic **South Warner Wilderness** contains 77 miles of hiking and riding trails; the best time to use them is from July to mid-October.

Maps, campfire permits and information are all available at the **Modoc National Forest Supervisor's Headquarters** (☎ 530-233-5811; 800 W 12th St; 8am-5pm Mon-Fri) in Alturas, a small town that provides basic services, motels and family-style restaurants. It's also home to the **Modoc County Historical Museum** (☎ 530-233-6328; 600 South Main St; admission adult/child 16yr and under $2/free; 10am-4pm Tue-Sat May-Oct), with exhibits on Native American life in the area.

WEST OF I-5

West of I-5 you'll find some of the mountain area's most rugged towns and seductive wilderness.

The Trinity River Scenic Byway (Hwy 299) winds spectacularly along the Trinity River and beneath towering cliffs as it makes its way from the plains of Redding to the coastal redwood forests around Arcata. It provides a chance to cut through some of the Northern Mountains' most pristine wilderness and passes through the vibrant Gold Rush town of Weaverville.

Heavenly Hwy 3 (a highly recommended – although slower and windier – alternative route to I-5) heads north from Weaverville. This mountain byway transports you through the Trinity Alps – a stunning range of azure-laked peaks – past the shores of Lewiston and Trinity Lakes, over the Scott Mountains, and finally into emerald, mountain-rimmed Scott Valley. Rough and ready Yreka awaits you at the end of the line.

WEAVERVILLE

pop 3500 / elev 2011ft

In 1941 a reporter interviewed James Hilton, the British author of *Lost Horizon*. 'In all your wanderings,' the journalist asked the writer, 'what's the closest you've found to a real-life Shangri-La?' Sighing wistfully (one imagines), Hilton responded, 'A little town in northern California…a little town called Weaverville.'

Cute, flower-festooned Weaverville is the seat of Trinity County, a mountain and forest area that's 75% federally owned. With its almost 3300 sq miles, the county is roughly the size of Delaware and Rhode Island together, yet has a total population of only 13,000, and not one traffic light or parking meter.

Weaverville is a small gem of a town on the National Register of Historic Places and has a laid-back feel. You can easily spend a day here just strolling around the quaint storefronts and visiting art galleries, museums and historic structures.

Information

Trinity County Chamber of Commerce (☎ 530-623-6101, 800-487-4648; www.trinitycounty.com; 215 Main St; ⏰ 10am- 4pm) Knowledgeable staff with lots of useful information.

Weaverville Ranger Station (☎ 530-623-2121; 210 N Main St; ⏰ 8am-4:30pm Mon-Fri) Maps, information and permits for all lakes, national forests and wilderness areas in and near Trinity County.

Sights & Activities

Joss House State Historic Park (☎ 530-623-5284; cnr Hwy 299 & Oregon St; admission $2; ⏰ 10am-5pm Sat winter, 10am-5pm Wed-Sun rest of year), in the center of town, holds the oldest continuously used Chinese temple in California – it dates back to the 1870s. The rich blue and gold Taoist shrine contains an ornate altar, more than 3000 years old, which was brought here from China. Tours depart from 10am until 4pm, on the hour.

Next door, the **JJ Jackson Memorial Museum & Trinity County Historical Park** (☎ 530-623-5211; www.trinitymuseum.org; 508 Main St; donation requested; ⏰ 10am-5pm daily May-Oct, noon-4pm daily Apr & Nov-Dec 24, noon-4pm Tue & Sat Dec 26-Mar) has gold-mining and cultural exhibits, plus vintage machinery, amazing memorabilia, an old miner's cabin and a blacksmith's shop.

Stroll galleries like the **Highland Art Center** (☎ 530-623-5111; 691 Main St; ⏰ 10am-5pm Mon-Sat, 11am-4pm Sun), showcasing local artists.

Coffee Creek Ranch (☎ 530-266-3343, 800-624-4480; www.coffeecreekranch.com) in Trinity Center leads fishing and fully outfitted pack trips ($150 to $350) into the Trinity Alps Wilderness.

Festivals & Events

The **Ruth Rodeo** gets hopping in August, while the **Quilt Show** bedecks Main St in October. Contact the chamber of commerce for more information.

Sleeping

The ranger station has information on many USFS campgrounds in the area, especially around Trinity Lake. Commercial RV parks, some with tent sites, dot Hwy 299.

Red Hill Motel & Cabins (☎ 530-623-4331; 116 Red Hill Rd; d $42, cabins without/with kitchen $48/59) This very quiet and simple motel is tucked under ponderosa pines at the west end of town, just off Main St, next to the library.

Whitmore Inn (☎ 530-623-2509; www.whitmoreinn.com; 761 Main St; r $100-165; wi-fi) Settle into plush, cozy rooms in this downtown Victorian with wraparound deck and abundant gardens. One room is accessible for travelers with disabilities.

our pick **Weaverville Hotel** (☎ 800-750-8957; www.weavervillehotel.com; 203 Main St; r $100-260;) Play like you're in the Old West at this upscale hotel and historic landmark, refurbished in grand Victorian style. It's luxurious but not stuffy, and the very gracious owners take great care in looking after you. Guests may use the local gym, and breakfast at a neighboring café is on the house.

Carrville Inn B&B (p326) is well out of town but worth the effort to get to.

Eating

Trinideli (☎ 530-623-5856; 201 Trinity Lakes Blvd, at Center St; sandwiches $5-7; ⏰ 6:30am-5:30pm) Cheerful staff prepare decadent sandwiches, stuffed with all kinds of fresh goodness, with good vibes all around.

Noelle's Garden Café (☎ 530-623-2058; 252 Main St; mains $9; ⏰ breakfast & lunch; V) *The* best place for breakfast. Sit inside the cheery white clapboard house, or out on the adjoining vine-trellised deck when the weather is fair. Lunch on soups, sandwiches and salads – with lots of veggie options.

La Casita (☎ 530-623-5797; 254 Main St; mains $9; ⏰ lunch & dinner) Tucked right next door to

Noelle's, low-ceilinged little La Casita serves delicious, authentic Mexican classics.

our pick **La Grange Café** (☎ 530-623-5325; 315 N Main St; mains $15-30; lunch & dinner daily, breakfast Sun) Spacious yet intimate, this celebrated multi-star restaurant serves exceptional light, fresh and satisfying fare: fish, pasta and bodacious salads. The exceedingly friendly atmosphere in the restored brick pub and dining room keep it packed.

The lively organic **farmers market** (4:30-7:30pm Wed May-Oct) lines Main St in the warmer months. Stock up on natural foods at **Mountain Marketplace** (☎ 530-623-2656; 222 S Main St; 9am-6pm Mon-Fri, 10am-5pm Sat; V) or hit its juice bar and vegetarian deli.

Drinking & Entertainment

Red House (☎ 530-623-1635; 218 S Miner St; 7am-6pm Mon-Sat, 8:30am-3pm Sun) Airy, bambooey, light – definitely well feng-shuied. This inviting spot serves coffees, a wide selection of teas and light snacks. If you're in a hurry (rare in Weaverville) there's a drive-through window.

Mamma Llama (☎ 530-623-6363; 208 N Main St; 6am-6pm Mon-Fri, 7am-6pm Sat, 7am-3pm Sun; wi-fi) Excellent, roomy and relaxed chill spot under the white arcade. Get espresso, browse through the selection of books and CDs, or make yourself at home on the couch. Occasional live music.

Trinity Theatre (☎ 530-378-3411; 310 Main St) Plays first-run movies.

Getting There & Away

A local **Trinity Transit** (☎ 530-623-5438; fares 50¢) bus makes a Weaverville–Lewiston loop via Hwy 299 and Hwy 3 from Monday to Friday. Another one runs between Weaverville and Hayfork, a small town about 30 miles to the southwest on Hwy 3.

THE LAKES

Lewiston Lake

Pleasant **Lewiston** (population 1300) sits 26 miles west of Redding, around 5 miles off Hwy 299 on Trinity Dam Blvd. It's right beside the Trinity River, where there's good fishing below the dam. About 1.5 miles north, tiny Lewiston Lake is a serene alternative to the other area lakes because of its 10mph boat speed limit. The water is kept at a constant level, providing a nurturing habitat for fish and waterfowl. Migrating bird species sojourn here – early in the evening you may see ospreys and bald eagles diving for fish. The **Trinity River Fish Hatchery** (sunrise-sunset) traps juvenile salmon and steelhead and holds them until they are ready to be released into the river. The only marina on the lake, **Pine Cove Marina** (☎ 530-778-3838; 9435 Trinity Dam Blvd), has free information about the lake and its wildlife, boat and canoe rentals, potluck dinners and guided off-road tours.

Several commercial campgrounds dot the rim of the lake. For information on USFS campgrounds, contact the ranger station in Weaverville (p325). Near town there are a few quiet places, like **Old Lewiston Bridge RV Resort** (☎ 530-778-3894, 800-922-1924; 8460 Rush Creek Rd, at Turnpike Rd; tent/RV sites $14/26), with campsites beside the river bridge.

Tidy, simple **Lewiston Valley Motel** (☎ 530-778-3942; 4789 Trinity Dam Blvd; RV sites $20, s/d $50/60;) has an RV park and sits next to a gas station and convenience store. **Lakeview Terrace Resort** (☎ 530-778-3803; www.lakeviewterraceresort.com; RV sites $26, trailers $72, cabins $72-132;), 5 miles north of Lewiston, rents boats. In town, beside the river, the homey **Old Lewiston Inn B&B** (☎ 530-778-3385, 800-286-4441; www.theoldlewistoninn.com; Deadwood Rd; r $110-125;) is in an 1875 house and serves country-style breakfasts. Enjoy the hot tub, or ask about all-inclusive fly-fishing packages.

In the center of town, the 1862 **Lewiston Hotel** (☎ 530-778-6800; 125 Deadwood Rd; mains $9-26; dinner Wed-Sat) is no longer a functioning hotel. It's now a hangout with character, serving excellent drinks and dinners. If you're lucky, there may be live music and dancing. **Mountain Valley Grill** (☎ 530-778-3177; 4811 Trinity Dam Blvd; mains $9; lunch & dinner) serves up basics, from pancakes to pasta.

Trinity (Clair Engle) Lake

Placid Trinity Lake, California's third-largest reservoir, sits beneath dramatic snow-capped alps north of Lewiston Lake and attracts multitudes, who come for swimming, fishing and other water sports. Most of the campgrounds, RV parks, motels, boat rentals and restaurants line the west side of the lake.

Cozy **Pinewood Cove Resort** (☎ 530-286-2201, 800-988-5253; www.pinewoodcove.com; 45110 Hwy 3; tent sites $20-28, RV sites $28-40, A-frame cabins $88-126, loft cabins $103-147; campground Apr-Oct;), on the waterfront, is a popular place to stay, but doesn't provide bed linens.

our pick **Carrville Inn B&B** (☎ 530-266-3511; www.carrvilleinn.com; Carrville Loop Rd; r with shared bath $160, with private bath $180-195;) This B&B north of the lake provides elegant accommodations in a huge Victorian home with a broad porch and expansive, blossoming grounds. The charming barnyard is populated with the usual residents plus exotic extras: an emu, a llama and a potbellied pig. To get here take Hwy 3 to 6 miles past Trinity Center, then turn left on Carrville Loop Rd.

Trinity Alps Marina (530-286-2282, 800-824-0083; www.trinityalpsmarina.com; houseboats per week $1200-4300) rents fishing boats and houseboats. **NOLA's** (mains lunch $7-9, dinner $13-19; lunch & dinner May-Sep), the restaurant there, serves up tasty grilled trout, steaks and sandwiches.

The east side of the lake is quieter, with more secluded campgrounds, some accessible only by boat. The Weaverville Ranger Station (p325) has information on USFS campgrounds.

DETOUR: ALPEN CELLARS

Jaunt over to little-known, utterly picturesque **Alpen Cellars** (530-266-9513; www.alpencellars.com; 10am-4pm summer, by appointment Oct-May). Specializing in riesling, gewürztraminer, chardonnay and pinot noir, the vineyard is open for tours, tasting and picnicking on idyllic riverside grounds. To get there from Weaverville take Hwy 3 for about 35 miles to the north end of Trinity Lake (5 miles past Trinity Center), then turn right on East Side Rd; 8 miles further head left on East Fork Rd and continue for 2 miles.

KLAMATH & SISKIYOU MOUNTAINS

A dense conglomeration of rugged coastal mountains gives this region the nickname 'the Klamath Knot.' Wet coastal temperate rain forests give way to moist inland forests, creating an immense diversity of habitats for many species, some found nowhere else in the world. Around 3500 native plants live here. Local fauna includes the northern spotted owl, the bald eagle, the tailed frog, several species of Pacific salmon, and carnivores like the wolverine and the mountain lion. One theory for the extraordinary biodiversity of this area is that it escaped extensive glaciation during recent ice ages. This may have given species refuge and longer stretches of relatively favorable conditions during which to adapt.

The region also includes the largest concentration of wild and scenic rivers in the US: the Salmon, the Smith, the Trinity, the Eel and the Klamath, to name a few. The fall color change is magnificent.

Five main wilderness areas dot the Klamath Knot. The **Marble Mountain Wilderness** in the north is marked by high rugged mountains, valleys and lakes, all sprinkled with colorful geological formations of marble and granite, and a huge array of flora. The **Russian Wilderness** is 8000 acres of high peaks and isolated, beautiful mountain lakes. The **Trinity Alps Wilderness**, west of Hwy 3, is ripe for rafting, fishing, mountain-biking and hiking, and has more than 600 miles of trails. The **Yolla Bolly-Middle Eel Wilderness** in the south is little-visited, despite its proximity to the Bay Area, and so affords spectacular, secluded backcountry experiences. The **Siskiyou Wilderness**, closest to the coast, rises to heights of 7300ft, from which you can see the ocean. An extensive trail system crisscrosses the wilderness, but it is difficult to make loops.

The Trinity River Scenic Byway (Hwy 299) follows the rushing **Trinity River** to the Pacific coast and is dotted with lodges, RV parks and blink-and-you'll-miss-'em burgs. There's **river rafting** at Willow Creek, 55 miles west of Weaverville. **Big Foot Rafting Company** (530-629-2263, 800-722-2223; www.bigfootrafting.com) leads guided trips (from $79) and also rents rafts and kayaks (from $32 per day).

SCOTT VALLEY

North of Trinity Lake, Hwy 3 climbs along the gorgeous eastern flank of the Trinity Alps Wilderness to Scott Mountain Summit (5401ft) and then drops gracefully down into verdant Scott Valley, a bucolic agricultural area nestled between towering mountains. Here you can hike, bike or horse pack to a mountain lake. For a bit of history, pick up the *Trinity Heritage Scenic Byway* brochure from the Weaverville Ranger Station (p325) before taking this world-class drive.

Etna, toward the north end of the valley, is known for its **Bluegrass Festival** at the end of July, and tiny **Etna Brewing Company** (530-467-5277; 131 Callahan St; brewery tours free; pub 11am-6pm Wed-Sun, tours by appointment), with delicious beers and pub grub. If you're sticking around, try the **Motel Etna** (530-467-5338; 317 Collier Way; s/d $40/45). **Scott Valley Drug** (530-467-5335; 511 Main St; Mon-Sat) serves up old-fashioned ice-cream sodas.

Beyond Etna, **Fort Jones** is just 18 miles from Yreka. The **visitors center** (☎ 530-468-5442; 11943 Main St; 🕑 10am-5pm Tue-Sat, noon-4pm Sun) sits at the back of the Guild Shop mercantile. Down the street, a small **museum** (☎ 530-468-5568; 11913 Main St; donation requested; 🕑 Mon-Sat summer) houses Native American artifacts.

YREKA

pop 7400 / elev 2625ft

Inland California's northernmost town, Yreka (wy-*ree*-kah) was once a booming Gold Rush town. Most travelers only pass through en route to Oregon. Yreka – especially the quaint historic downtown – makes a good spot to stretch, eat and refuel before heading out into the hinterlands of the Scott Valley or the northeastern California wilderness.

Information

Klamath National Forest Supervisor's Office (☎ 530-842-6131; 1312 Fairlane Rd, at Oberlin Rd; 🕑 8am-4:30pm Mon-Fri) At the south edge of town, with the lowdown on recreation and camping.

Yreka Chamber of Commerce (☎ 530-842-1649, 800-669-7352; www.yrekachamber.com; 117 W Miner St; 🕑 9am-5pm summer, hours vary winter)

Sights & Activities

The **Siskiyou County Courthouse** (311 4th St) downtown was built in 1857 and has a collection of gold nuggets, flakes and dust in the foyer. Many blocks further to the south, the exceptionally well-curated **Siskiyou County Museum** (☎ 530-842-3836; 910 S Main St; admission $1; 🕑 9am-5pm Tue-Sat) brings together pioneer and Native American history. An outdoor section contains historic buildings brought from around the county. Behind the museum, the **Yreka Creek Greenway** has walking paths winding through the trees. The **Blue Goose Steam Excursion Train** (☎ 530-842-4146; www.yrekawesternrr.com; adult/child 2-12yr $20/12) hisses and chugs along a 100-year-old track.

About 25 miles north of Yreka on I-5, just across the Oregon border, Siskiyou Summit (elevation 4310ft) often closes in winter – even when the weather is just fine on either side. Call ☎ 530-842-4438 to check.

Sleeping

Motels, motels, motels. The **Best Western Miner's Inn** (☎ 530-842-4355; 122 E Miner St; d from $70; 🏊), at the Central Yreka exit, offers a bit more luxury than the rest. Folks at **Klamath Motor Lodge** (☎ 530-842-2751; www.klamathmotorlodge.net; 1111 S Main St; d from $70; 🏊) are especially friendly.

Klamath National Forest runs several campgrounds; the supervisor's office has information. RV parks cluster on the edge of town.

> **WHAT THE…?**
>
> Pop over to the **Willow Creek China Flat Museum** (☎ 530-629-2653; Hwy 299, Willow Creek; admission free, donations accepted; 🕑 10am-4pm Wed-Sun May-Sep, 11am-4pm Fri & Sat, noon-4pm Sun Oct-Apr) to take in its persuasive Bigfoot collection. Foot prints, hand prints, hair…it has all kinds of goodies to substantiate the ole boy's existence. In fact, namesake Bigfoot Scenic Byway (Hwy 96) starts here and heads north, winding through breathtaking mountain and river country.

Eating & Drinking

Join locals at fun **Klander's Deli** (☎ 530-842-3806; 211 S Oregon St; sandwiches $6; 🕑 breakfast & lunch Mon-Fri) for the long list of yummy sandwiches. **Grandma's House** (☎ 530-842-5300; 123 E Center St; breakfast & lunch mains $5-7, dinner mains $8-15; 🕑 breakfast, lunch & dinner) gets packed for its fresh, homestyle cooking. Look for the cutesy gingerbread house east of downtown between Main St and I-5. Hit **Angelini's Italian Restaurant** (☎ 530-842-5000; 322 W Miner St; mains lunch/dinner $15/25; 🕑 lunch & dinner) for wood-fired pizza.

Friendly natural-foods store and bakery **Nature's Kitchen** (☎ 530-842-1136; 412 S Main St; dishes $7; 🕑 breakfast & lunch Mon-Sat; V) serves healthy and tasty vegetarian dishes, fresh juices and good espresso. **Village Grind** (☎ 530-842-4607; 400 W Miner St; dishes $7; 🕑 7:30am-7pm Mon-Fri, 8am-7pm Sat, 8:30am-5pm Sun; wi-fi), an espresso bar and café, adds a little urbane dash with its attractive wooden floors and local art on the walls. It has nice light meals – omelets, salads, pizzas.

Getting There & Away

STAGE (☎ 530-842-8295, 800-247-8243; fares from $1.75) buses run throughout the region from a few different stops in Yreka. There are several daily services on weekdays along the I-5 corridor to Weed, Mt Shasta, McCloud and Dunsmuir. Other buses depart daily for Fort Jones (25 minutes), Greenview (35 minutes) and Etna in the Scott Valley (45 minutes), and, on Monday and Friday only, out to Klamath River (40 minutes) and Happy Camp (two hours).

Gold Country

Gold Country is where California was born. These hills were technically still Mexico when James Marshall caught a glimpse of a curiously shiny rock at John Sutter's Mill, starting the uproar that became California. The stampede of 300,000 '49ers who rushed these hills jump-started the new state's economy. They only got a fraction of the gold before the catastrophic environmental impacts caused a halt to the mining. The scars have healed beautifully though, leaving hills covered in pine, oak and a string of historic towns – some restored to lacy Victorian elegance, others wilting in the high heat. And, without discounting the subtle thrill of tales of bloodlust and banditry outlined on historical markers, the region's more tactile pleasures include an icy plunge into the swimming holes of California's powerful rivers, and tasting some of the state's most exciting wines.

Many small Gold Country cities compete in the region's beauty pageant but all have similar draws: antique shops, ice-cream parlors and small museums piled with Gold Rush artifacts. Accommodations options abound, from sleeping under the stars to the frills of countless B&Bs. Even if you are only passing through, working a bit of Hwy 49 into your itinerary has rich rewards.

HIGHLIGHTS

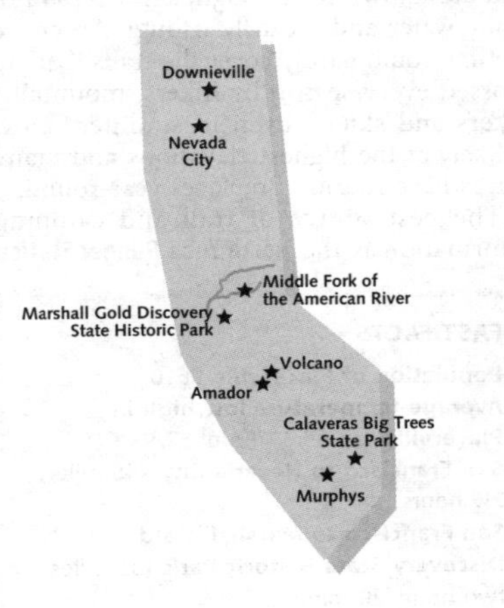

- **Best white-water rush** Rushing past canyons on frothing Class III rapids of the Middle Fork of the American River (p337)
- **Most haunting history lesson** Wandering to the river's edge near the famous find at Marshall Gold Discovery State Historic Park (p338)
- **Richest digging for your ears** Pulling vinyl from Nevada City's matchless record shop (p334)
- **Most down-to-earth wine tour** Sipping some of California's best wines, without a whiff of pretension, at Amador vineyards (p341)
- **Strangest sip** Mustering the courage to order a Moose Milk at the St George Hotel (p343) in Volcano
- **Best place to feel little** Craning upward at the big lumber in Calaveras Big Trees State Park (p345)
- **Best place to stare down a bandit** Pondering the portrait of the Gold Rush bandit Joaquin Murrieta at the Murphys Old Timers Museum (p346)
- **Most exhilarating lesson about gravity** Bombing down the best mountain-bike trails in the West in Downieville (p332)

NEVADA COUNTY & NORTHERN GOLD COUNTRY

From the time Rushers tore up the hills of Nevada County looking for loot, this part of Gold Country has always offered some of the state's greatest rewards. Back in the day, it spewed forth more gold than any other part of the mother lode, and the profit built one of the most picturesque remaining boomtowns in Nevada City. Get out of town and you'll find some of the loveliest wilderness in the state, as well as a clutch of historic parks and rusting relics of the long-gone miners. This is also a magnet for woodsy adrenaline junkies looking to bomb down single-track mountain-bike lanes or plunge into icy swimming holes that are remote enough to go suit-free.

NORTH YUBA RIVER

The northernmost segment of Hwy 49 follows the North Yuba River through some stunning, remote parts of the Sierra Nevada, which feel isolated from the rest of the state, and are known for a tough, short season of white water and great fly-fishing. An entire lifetime could hardly cover the trails that are crossed every season by hikers, mountain-bikers and skiers. Even in summer, snow is likely at the highest elevations and many places have roaring fireplaces year-round.

The best source of trail and camping information is the **North Yuba Ranger Station** (☎ 530-288-3231; 15924 Hwy 49; ⌚ 8am-4:30pm Mon-Fri) in Camptonville.

FAST FACTS

Population of Placerville 9610

Average temperature low/high in Placerville Jan 33/57°F, Jul 57/93°F

San Francisco to Nevada City 148 miles, 2½ hours

San Francisco to Marshall Gold Discovery State Historic Park 132 miles, two hours 20 minutes

Sacramento to Plymouth 38 miles, 45 minutes

Yosemite National Park to Columbia State Historic Park 62 miles, 1½ hours

Los Angeles to Murphys 355 miles, six hours

Sierra City

pop 300 / elev 4187ft

Sierra City is the primary supply station for people headed to the **Sierra Buttes**, probably the closest thing to the Alps you'll find in California without hoisting a backpack. There's a vast network of trails, including access to the famous Pacific Crest Trail, which is ideal for backpacking and casual hikes. Get the *Lakes Basin, Downieville – Sierra City* map ($2) from the **Sierra Country Store** (☎ 530-862-1181; Hwy 49; ⌚ 9am-7pm; wi-fi), which welcomes Pacific Crest Trail refugees with its Laundromat and deli. The town has a useful website (www.sierracity.com).

Sierra City's local museum, the **Kentucky Mine** (☎ 530-862-1310; adult/child $7/3.50; ⌚ 10am-4pm Wed-Sun Jun-Aug), has tours of a gold mine and stamp mill, just north of town.

To reach the Buttes, and many lakes and streams nearby, take Gold Lake Hwy north from Hwy 49 at Bassetts, 9 miles northeast of Sierra City. An excellent hiking trail leads 1.5 miles to **Haskell Peak** (8107ft), where you can see from the Sierra Buttes right to Mt Shasta and beyond. To reach the trailhead, turn right from Gold Lake Hwy at Haskell Peak Rd (Forest Rd 9) and follow it for 8.5 miles.

One of several US Forest Service (USFS) campgrounds recommended for camping north of Hwy 49, **Salmon Creek campground** (☎ 530-993-1410; tent & RV sites without hook-ups $18) is 2 miles north of Bassetts on Gold Lake Hwy. It has vault toilets, running water and first-come, first-served sites for RVs and tents, but no hook-ups.

Going east from Sierra City along Hwy 49 are Wild Plum, Sierra, Chapman Creek and Yuba Pass **USFS campgrounds** (☎ 530-993-1410; tent sites $18). They have vault toilets and running water (Sierra has river water only), and first-come, first-served sites. Wild Plum (47 sites) is the most scenic.

The 1862 **Old Sierra City Hotel** (☎ 530-862-1300; 212 Main St; r $55; ⌚ Jun-Oct) is cozy, with a welcoming bar and a wood-burning stove. Each of the simple four rooms has a private bathroom. On weekends it serves good fried-chicken lunches and dinners.

In the heart of Sierra City, the small **Buttes Resort** (☎ 530-862-1170, 800-991-1170; www.sierracity.com; 230 Main St; cabins $55-145) occupies a lovely

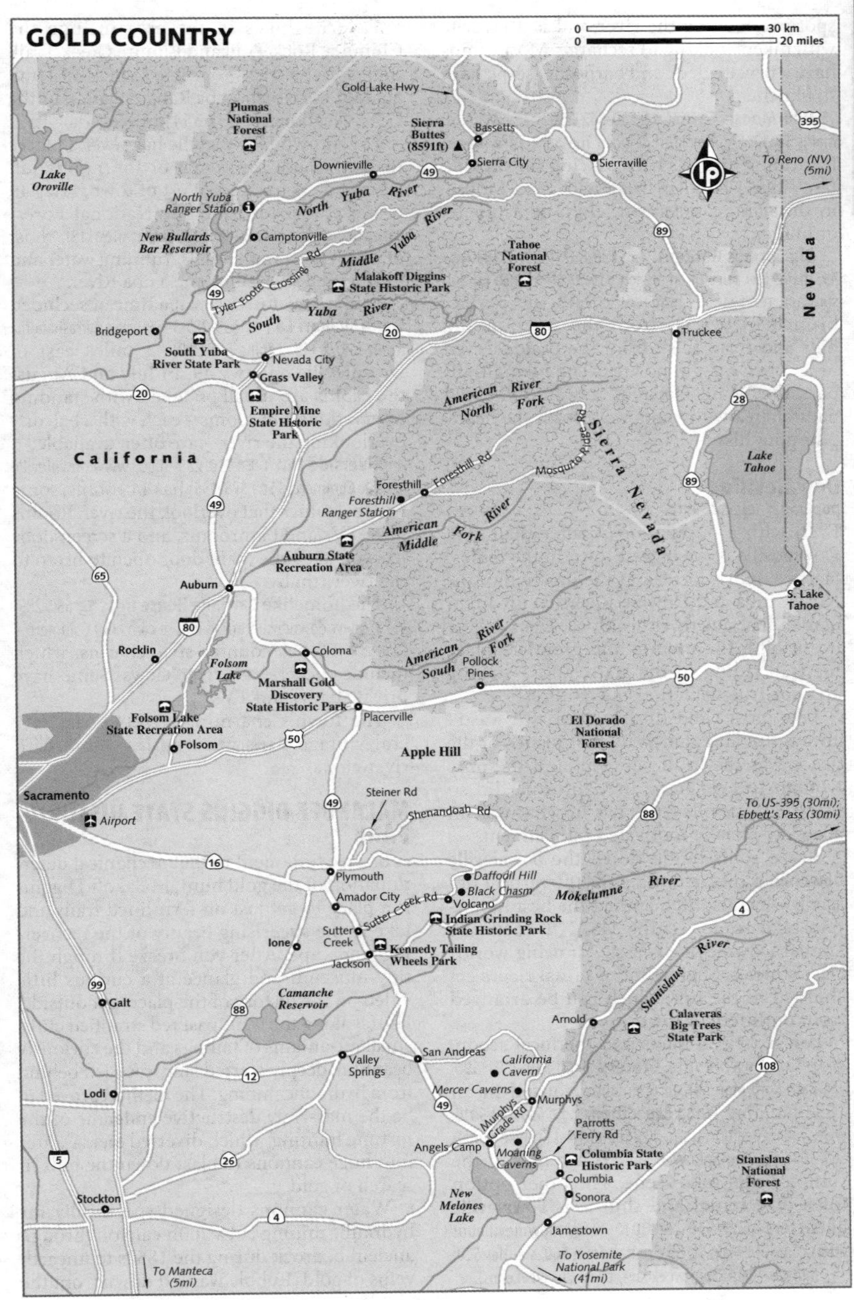
GOLD COUNTRY
0 30 km
0 20 miles
Gold Lake Hwy
Plumas National Forest
Sierra Buttes (8591ft)
Bassetts
Sierra City
Sierraville
Downieville
Lake Oroville
North Yuba Ranger Station
North Yuba River
To Reno (NV) (5mi)
New Bullards Bar Reservoir
Camptonville
Middle Yuba River
Tahoe National Forest
Tyler Foote Crossing Rd
Malakoff Diggins State Historic Park
South Yuba River
Nevada
Bridgeport
South Yuba River State Park
Truckee
Nevada City
Grass Valley
Empire Mine State Historic Park
American River North Fork
Sierra Nevada
Mosquito Ridge Rd
California
Foresthill Rd
Foresthill
Foresthill Ranger Station
Lake Tahoe
American River Middle Fork
Auburn State Recreation Area
Auburn
S. Lake Tahoe
Rocklin
Coloma
American River South Fork
Folsom Lake
Pollock Pines
Marshall Gold Discovery State Historic Park
Placerville
Folsom Lake State Recreation Area
El Dorado National Forest
Folsom
Apple Hill
Sacramento
Steiner Rd
Shenandoah Rd
Airport
To US-395 (30mi); Ebbett's Pass (30mi)
Plymouth
Daffodil Hill
Black Chasm
Mokelumne River
Amador City
Sutter Creek Rd
Volcano
Indian Grinding Rock State Historic Park
Sutter Creek
Ione
Kennedy Tailing Wheels Park
Jackson
Stanislaus River
Galt
Camanche Reservoir
Arnold
Calaveras Big Trees State Park
San Andreas
Valley Springs
California Cavern
Mercer Caverns
Lodi
Murphys
Murphys Grade Rd
Parrotts Ferry Rd
Angels Camp
Moaning Caverns
Columbia State Historic Park
Stanislaus National Forest
Columbia
New Melones Lake
Stockton
Sonora
Jamestown
To Yosemite National Park (41mi)
To Manteca (5mi)

spot overlooking the river and is a favorite with hikers looking to recharge. Most cabins have a private deck and barbecue, some have full kitchens.

Red Moose Cafe (☎ 530-862-1502; 224 Main St; mains $6-12; breakfast & lunch Tue-Sun) is a local institution and has been serving rib-sticking fare since 1940. Anything with 'Red Moose' in the name comes with chili, be it omelet or burger.

Big Springs Gardens (☎ 530-862-1333; 32163 Hwy 49; mains incl price of admission $35-37; lunch Fri-Sun summer, reservations required) offers the perfect brunch of berries from the surrounding hills and trout fresh from the pond, served in an open-air dining area. The hiking trails pass the 'Wild Garden,' a waterfall-laced natural area with views well worth the heart-pumping hike.

Downieville

pop 350 / elev 2899ft

Even with a population smaller than 400, Downieville is the biggest town in the remote Sierra County, located at the junction of the North Yuba and Downie Rivers. With a reputation that quietly rivals Moab, Utah (before it got big), the town is the premiere place for trail riding in the state, and a staging area for true wilderness adventures.

Like most Gold Rush survivors it wasn't always fun and games: its first justice of the peace was the local barkeep, and the only woman to ever hang in California did so from Downieville's gallows in what was an allegedly racially motivated punishment.

Brave souls bomb down the **Downieville Downhill**, a molar-rattling 5000ft vertical descent, which is rated among the best mountain-bike routes in the USA. It hosts the annual Downieville Classic, drawing world-class athletes. Slightly more casual riders get shuttled to the top, which can be arranged from outfitters in town.

For groceries, maps and the local scoop, stop at **Downieville Grocery** (☎ 530-289-3596; 8am-8pm Mon-Sat, to 6pm Sun), housed in an 1852 building. **Yuba Expeditions** (☎ 530-289-3010; www.yubaexpeditions.com; 105 Commercial St; bike rentals $65-100; 9am-5pm Wed-Mon) is a center of the summer trail-bike scene. The other option for a bike rental and shuttle is **Downieville Outfitters** (☎ 530-289-3010; www.downievilleoutfitters.com; 114 Main St; bike rentals from $60, shuttles $20; shuttles 10am, 2pm weekdays, every 2hr weekends).

Favorite hikes in the area include the Chimney Rock Trail and Empire Creek Trail. Both are a bit tricky to reach, so pick up a trail guide at the North Yuba Ranger Station or the USFS Headquarters (p334) in Nevada City.

Downtown Downieville has several places to stay where the rustle of the rapids lull weary bikers to sleep. West of town, Hwy 49 passes trailheads to Tahoe National Forest **campgrounds** (☎ 530-993-1410; tent sites $18), most of which have vault toilets, running water and unreserved sites along the Yuba River.

People stay for weeks at a time at secluded **Sierra Shangri-La** (☎ 530-289-3455; www.sierrashangrila.com; r $70-115, cabins $85-250), 3 miles east of Downieville on Hwy 49. In July and August the cabins are usually booked with standing reservations, but rooms – each with a balcony overlooking the river – are often available.

Riverside Inn (☎ 530-289-1000; www.downieville.us; 206 Commercial St; r $75-155) has 11 rooms, some with balconies that overlook the river. Rooms have TVs and bathrooms, and a screen door lets you keep the main door open to listen to the river run by.

The homelike **Carriage House Inn** (☎ 530-289-3573; www.downievillecarriagehouse.com; 110 Commercial St; r $55-100) has country-style charms, which include rockers and river views. Some have private baths and TVs.

The town's charming streets boast several vintage bars and eateries, some with river views.

MALAKOFF DIGGINS STATE HISTORIC PARK

A bizarre testament to the mechanical determination of the gold hunt, Malakoff Diggins is a place to get lost on fern-lined trails and take in the surprising beauty of the recovering landscape. After you breeze through the tidy museum and glance at a curious little video on the history of the place, get outside. Huff it along the trails past red stratified cliffs, small mountains of tailings and the curiously beautiful, deeply scarred landscape left behind from hydraulic mining. The method proved to be the massively destructive endgame of the fortune hunting, which diverted Sierra water into huge cannons to blast down the hills in search of gold.

Water cannons designed specifically for hydraulic mining cut a 200ft canyon through ancient bedrock during the 1850s to unearth veins of gold. Rubble washed down from the hillsides, and the tailings dropped back into the Yuba River. This often-toxic waste was filled with heavy metals, many of which remain in the Sacramento Valley floor. By the 1860s, 20ft mud glaciers blocked rivers and caused severe flooding each spring during the Sierra snowmelt. After a year of heated courtroom (and bar-room) debate between farmers and miners, the 1884 court case (known as the Sawyer Decision) makes a profoundly timely statement today: an abhorrently destructive, enormously profitable industry can be stopped for public good. North Bloomfield, the mining community at the center of Malakoff's operation, packed up the shingle shortly after, and what remains is an eerily quiet ghost town within the park's limits.

The **Park Headquarters and Museum** (☎ 530-265-2740; admission per vehicle $6; ⌚ 9am-5pm) offers tours at 1:30pm daily and the chance to see some impressive gold nuggets. The one-mile **Digging Loop Trail** is the quick way to get a glimpse of the deeply scarred moonscape. Grab a flashlight and find the side trail leading to the Hiller Tunnel; you can crouch along the 500ft tunnel with rushing water underfoot.

The park has primitive campsites, three moderately developed **campgrounds** (☎ 800-444-7275; www.parks.ca.gov; tent sites $15) and four converted very rustic old miners' cabins ($35), in which you'll need a sleeping pad and sleeping bag (maybe someone to keep you warm too, in the low season). The bathrooms are clean, but there are no showers.

You can reach Tyler Foote Crossing Rd, the turnoff for the park, 10 miles northwest of Nevada City on Hwy 49.

SOUTH YUBA RIVER STATE PARK

Icy swimming holes are fed by rushing, icy rapids in this 11,000-acre plot along the South Yuba River, a combination of state land and acres of land of federal jurisdiction. This area has a growing network of trails, including the wheelchair-accessible **Independence Trail**, which starts from the south side of the South Yuba River bridge on Hwy 49 and continues for a couple miles with canyon overlooks. June is the best time, when the rivers are rushing and the wildflowers are out.

The longest, single-span, wood-truss **covered bridge** in the USA, all 251ft of it, crosses the South Yuba River at Bridgeport (not to be confused with the Eastern Sierra town of the same name, p400). The bridge – built for private commercial use in 1862 – is at the end of a curvy 7-mile drive (westward off Hwy 49 on Pleasant Valley Rd). It's easy to spend a whole day hiking and swimming in this wild area, where crowds can be left behind with little effort. The Buttermilk Bend trail skirts the South Yuba for 1.4 miles, offering river access and wonderful wildflower-viewing around April.

Maps and park information are available from the **state park headquarters** (☎ 530-432-2546; ⌚ 11am-4pm) in Bridgeport, or from the Tahoe National Forest USFS Headquarters (p334) in Nevada City.

NEVADA CITY

pop 3000 / elev 2525ft

Maybe it's all those prayer flags, or new-agey Zen goodies that clutter the sandalwood-scented gift shops, but, like a yogi on top of a Pilates ball, Nevada City is all about *balance*. The city has the requisite Victorian Gold Rush tourist attractions – an elegantly restored town center, an informative local history museum, girlishly decorated bed and breakfasts by the dozen – and a proud contemporary identity, with a small but thriving independent arts and culture scene. Perch on a bar stool in any of the area watering holes and the person next to you might just as easily be a crusty old-timer, a sun-pink tourist or a mystical folk artist.

Spending a couple days here, you'll soak up distinctly rural NorCal culture – with theater companies, alternative film houses, bookstores and live music performances almost every night. Nevada City's streets, best navigated on foot, are jammed with pedestrians by day, especially in the summer. Broad St is the main drag, reached by the Broad St exit off Hwy 49/20. Just north of town on Hwy 49, look for dusty pull-outs at the trailheads to icy swimming holes. In December the blankets of snow and twinkling lights are something out of a storybook.

Information

Harmony Books (☎ 530-265-9564; 231 Broad St ⌚ 10am-6pm) For maps and travel guides, history books, bestsellers and magazines. The town is blessed with several other bookstores selling used and rare books.

Nevada City Chamber of Commerce (☎ 530-265-2692, 800-655-6569; www.nevadacitychamber.com; 132 Main St; ⌚ 9am-5pm Mon-Sat, 11am-4pm Sun) Ideally located at the east end of Commercial St, this has two welcome comforts for the traveler – an immaculate public toilet and expert local advice.

Tahoe National Forest USFS Headquarters (☎ 530-265-4531; 631 Coyote St; 8am-5pm Mon-Sat) A useful and friendly resource for trail and campground information, covering the area from here to Lake Tahoe. It sells topographical maps.

Sights & Activities

The main attraction is the town itself – its restored buildings, all brick and wrought-iron trimmings, wear their history proudly. There are curious (if pricey) boutiques, galleries and places for food and drink everywhere, all with exhaustive information about the town's history.

History buffs flock to the lacy **Firehouse Museum** (☎ 530-265-5468; www.nevadacountyhistory.org; 214 Main St; admission by donation; 1-4pm Fri-Sun, varies seasonally). Run by the Nevada Country Historical Society, the museum's shady interior smells of old wood and features an impressive collection from Chinese laborers who often built but seldom profited from the mines.

The **Nevada City Winery** (☎ 530-265-9463; 321 Spring St; 11am-5pm Mon-Sat, noon-5pm Sun) bottles two regional varietals, syrah and zinfandel, which you can savor while overlooking the production facility.

Sleeping

During weekends, Nevada City fills up with urban refugees who inevitably weigh themselves down with real-estate brochures. There are frilly B&Bs everywhere, but the cheapest options are the National Forest campgrounds, just outside of town in any direction.

Outside Inn (☎ 530-265-2233; www.outsideinn.com; 575 E Broad St; r $75-180;) This is an exceptionally friendly and fun motel, with 14 individually named and decorated rooms and a staff that loves the outdoors. Some rooms have a patio overlooking a small creek. It's a 10-minute walk from downtown.

Northern Queen Inn (☎ 530-265-3720; www.northernqueeninn.com; 400 Railroad Ave; r $99-154;) With a wide range of options – from basic queen rooms to two-story chalets – this hotel might be a bit dated, but that's more than made up for by the narrated narrow-gauge railroad rides through the historic cemetery. The cabins, with small kitchens, are the best deal.

Red Castle Historic Lodgings (☎ 530-265-5135; www.redcastleinn.com; 109 Prospect St; r $120-185;) In a city chock full of B&Bs this is the granddaddy of them all – the first in Nevada City and one of the oldest in the state. The historic building combines a Gothic Revival exterior with a well-appointed Victorian interior, surrounded by shady walking paths. The Garden Room is the most private.

Eating & Drinking

Café Mekka (☎ 530-478-1517; 237 Commercial St; meals $5-15; 8am-7pm Mon-Thu, to midnight Fri-Sun) Decorated in a style best described as 'whorehouse baroque,' this charmer serves coffee and beer through the day, along with sandwiches, pizzas and famous desserts. Listen for live folk music on some nights.

Ike's Quarter Cafe (☎ 530-265-6138; 401 Commercial St; meals $6-8 breakfast & lunch Wed-Mon) Ike's serves splendid Cajun fare with a sassy charm that leaves the blue hairs pink-cheeked. The creative menu features banana and pecan pancakes, jambalaya and more. The patio fountain is right out of the Garden District in New Orleans.

Citronee Bistro & Wine Bar (☎ 530-265-5697; 320 Broad St; mains $8-20; lunch Mon-Fri, dinner Mon-Sat) This small restaurant has a cheery charm backed by splendid examples of local art on the walls. The menu is comfort food, with highlights including pulled pork on flatbread and garlicky short ribs.

New Moon Café (☎ 530-265-6399; 230 York St; mains $13-20; lunch & dinner) Peter Selaya's regularly changing menu keeps an organic, local bent. If you visit during the peak of the summer keep to the aquatic theme by trying the wild, line-caught fish or seared duck, prepared with a French-Asian fusion.

Entertainment

Nevada City has yielded some excellent locals in recent years, including Joanna Newsom, a harp-playing singer songwriter whose elfin affectation and poetic writing rocketed her out of the edgy folk scene and onto a national stage. The Arts section of the *Union* newspaper comes out on Thursday, with a listing of what's going on around the area.

our pick **After The Gold Rush Records** (☎ 530-265-3090; 232 Commercial St) If you want to get the real skinny on the local happenings, head to this store, where there is a wall littered with flyers, a discriminating stock of vinyl LPs and good advice about where to find the party.

Nevada Theater (☎ 530-265-6161; 401 Broad St) This brick fortress is one of California's first theaters (1865) and has welcomed the likes of Jack London and Mark Twain to its stage. Now it's used for productions of the top-notch Foothill Theater Company (☎ 530-265-8587; www.foothillstheatre.com), as well as off-beat movie screenings.

Magic Theatre (☎ 530-265-8262; www.themagictheatrenc.com; 107 Argall Way) This fantastic theater screens a matchless line-up of unusual films and is about a mile south of downtown Nevada City. Enjoy bowls of fresh popcorn, coffee in real mugs and hot brownies at intermission.

Getting There & Away

The **Gold Country Stage** (☎ 530-477-0103; www.goldcountrystage.com) bus service links Nevada City with Grass Valley at least hourly from 7am to 5pm and serves the Amtrak station in Auburn several times a day ($1 to $5).

GRASS VALLEY

pop 11,000 / elev 2420ft

From the outside Grass Valley is the ugly utilitarian sister to Nevada City – where residents buy groceries, get oil changes and groom their pets – and its chain stores might as well be in Anywhere, USA. Once you get to know her though, by driving to the historic business district, the little gem at the center of the sprawl is another rich Gold Country downtown.

The mines in Grass Valley – some of the first shaft mines in the state – were hugely profitable, and the first to flaunt the benefits of lode mining techniques. Nearly 400 miles of shaft made up the Empire Mine, now a state park.

Grass Valley's main thoroughfares of Mill St and W Main St are the heart of the historic district, which boasts an old-time movie theater, cafés and bars. E Main St goes north to shopping centers and mini-malls, continuing north into Nevada City, while S Auburn St divides E and W Main St.

On Thursday nights in July and August, Mill St is closed to car traffic while farmstead food, arts and crafts and music entertain people in the street.

Information

Booktown Books (☎ 530-272-4655; 107 Bank St; 🕑 10am-6pm Mon-Thu, to 9pm Fri & Sat, 11am-4pm Sun) Hosts several used-book dealers under one roof.

Grass Valley/Nevada County Chamber of Commerce (☎ 530-272-8315; www.grassvalleychamber.com; 248 Mill St; 🕑 9am-5pm Mon-Fri) In the former Mill St home of enchantress Lola Montez. It has some very good maps and brochures. Be sure to pick up a copy of the historic walking-tour brochure.

Sights & Activities

The star of the downtown historic buildings is the **Nevada County Bank** (131 Mill St), which dates from 1917, when banks were built to look impenetrable.

Situated atop miles of mine shafts, **Empire Mine State Historic Park** (☎ 530-273-8522; 10791 E Empire St; admission $2; 🕑 9am-6pm Jun-Sep, 10am-5pm Oct-May) is the Gold Country's best-preserved gold quartz–mining operation – worth a solid half-day's exploration. From 1850 to 1956 the mines produced six million ounces of gold (about four billion modern dollars' worth). The mine yard is littered with massive mining equipment and buildings constructed from waste rock. There are docent-led tours and sunny hiking. There are plans to open the main mine shaft, next to the largest head frame (a structure that held the pulleys, which once hoisted the plunder up from underground) in the yard, for subterranean tours.

Around the side of the visitor center you'll find stately buildings that belonged to the Bourne family, who ran the mine. They did it in style too, apparent with the elegant country club, English manor home, gardener's house and rose garden. Take a guided tour; check the visitors center for schedules.

Hiking trails begin near the old stamp mill in the mine yard and pass abandoned mines and equipment. A trail map is available at the visitors center. The park is 2 miles east of Grass Valley via the Empire St exit off Hwy 49.

Grass Valley's **North Star Mining Museum** stands near where the largest Pelton waterwheel ever was made. The mine's 1895 stone powerhouse on the west bank of Wolf Creek, at Mill St's southern end, is now a **museum** (☎ 530-273-4255; donation requested; 🕑 10am-5pm May-Oct) with a small collection of Pelton waterwheels (and their prototypes), mining equipment and artifacts. A few shady, creekside tables behind the museum make nice picnic spots.

Sleeping & Eating

The quality of food here is proportional to how much you hunt for it: there are several good eateries and bars around downtown, and every imaginable chain lurks among the strip malls by the highway.

Holbrooke Hotel (☎ 530-273-1353, 800-933-7077; www.holbrooke.com; 212 W Main St; r $119-224;) The register in this 1862 hotel boasts the signatures of Mark Twain and Ulysses Grant and well-appointed rooms are named after other presidents who slept there. The bistro (mains $4 to $20) serves casual fare in the ornate dining room or on the shady patio. The bar has tables overlooking the Main St action.

Dorado Chocolates (☎ 530-272-6715; 104 E Main St; snacks $3; 10am-5pm Tue-Sat) Ken Kossoudji's handmade chocolates are made to savor slowly, and when the snow falls the hot chocolate is divine.

Cousin Jack Pasties (☎ 530-272-9230; 100 S Auburn St; meals $4-10; lunch & dinner) Cousin Jack has been serving flaky pasties – a meat-and-potato-stuffed pastry beloved by Cornish miners – for five generations.

Tofanelli's (☎ 530-272-1468; 302 W Main St; meals $8-22) Hugely popular with those locals in the know, this creative restaurant has everything from salads to hearty steaks with seasonal accents like summer squash ravioli. Portions are burly, prices are small and the patio is a treat.

Getting There & Away

The **Gold Country Stage** (☎ 530-477-0103; www.goldcountrystage.com) bus service links Nevada City with Grass Valley (adult/child $1/free, adult one-day pass $3, 30 minutes) at least hourly from 7am to 5pm.

AUBURN

pop 12,500 / elev 1255ft

Auburn might not be the most electrifying destination in the region, but its location off I-80 makes it an easy Gold Country detour for those rushing between the Bay Area and Lake Tahoe. A major stop on the Central Pacific's transcontinental route, Auburn is still busy with trains on the Union Pacific's main line to the east.

Sunny outdoor eating and antique hunting in the historic Old Town offer respite from the road, but navigate out of the narrow stone streets to get away from crowds of weekenders and there's as much flavor in the middle of town, along Lincoln Way. On Sunday, the Old Town hosts a traffic-jamming flea market, complete with live music and food stands.

Information

Auburn Area Chamber of Commerce (☎ 530-885-5616; www.auburnchamber.net; 601 Lincoln Way; 9am-5pm Mon-Fri) Housed in the old Southern Pacific railroad depot at the north end of Lincoln Way, it has lots of useful local info. There's a nearby monument to the first transcontinental railroad.

California Welcome Center (☎ 530-887-2111; www.visitplacer.com; 13411 Lincoln Way; 9am-3pm) Right off I-80 at the Foresthill exit; there is oodles of information for those entering the state from the east.

Sights & Activities

Placer County Museum (☎ 530-889-6500; 101 Maple St; admission free; 11am-4pm Tue-Sun), on the 1st floor of the monumental 1898 **Placer County Courthouse** (8am-5pm), has Native American artifacts and displays of Auburn's transportation heritage.

Those with a taste for exploring history should hit the **Gold Country Museum** (☎ 530-889-6500; 1273 High St; admission free; 11am-4pm Tue-Sun), toward the back of the fairgrounds, where you can walk through a reproduced mining tunnel. The **Bernhard Museum Complex** (☎ 530-888-6891; 291 Auburn-Folsom Rd; donation requested; 11am-4pm Tue-Sun), at the south end of High St, was built in 1851 as the Traveler's Rest Hotel. The museum has displays depicting the typical life of a 19th-century farm family, and at times volunteers in period garb ham it up.

Sleeping & Eating

Upper Lincoln Way toward the Chamber of Commerce has several restaurants popular with locals.

Power's Mansion (☎ 530-885-1166; www.powersmansioninn.com; 164 Cleveland St; r $160-250;) Built with a gold fortune in 1898, this B&B exudes the frilly, antique-loaded opulence you might expect from staying in 'Grandma's Room.' All 10 rooms are luxurious.

Ikedas (☎ 530-885-4243; 13500 Lincoln Way; meals $7-15; 8am-9pm) For many Californians, an I-80 journey is not complete without a stop at this small empire near Old Town. Sinking your teeth into anything from the menu of custom burgers, sandwiches and dreamy roadside fare will inspire groans of pleasure. The store area is a produce wonderland of treats grown in the region.

Monkey Cat Restaurant (☎ 530-888-8492; 805 Lincoln Way; meals $10-28) The smart decor accented by local artworks is the right setting for creative casual fare that ranges from unusual salads and huge burgers at lunch to steaks and seafood with fusion accents at dinner. It has a quiet patio.

Getting There & Away

Amtrak's *California Zephyr* stops in Auburn on its daily runs between the Bay Area and Chicago via Reno and Denver. The trip between Auburn and San Francisco takes just over 3 hours and costs $31. **Amtrak** (☎ 800-872-7245; www.capitolcorridor.org) also runs several buses a day linking Auburn with Sacramento ($11, one hour) where you can connect to Bay Area and Central Valley trains. There are usually two buses daily east to Reno (2½ hours).

The **Gold Country Stage** (☎ 530-477-0103; www.goldcountrystage.com) links Auburn with Grass Valley and Nevada City several times a day. You can catch this bus every two hours on weekdays between 6am and 5pm. Weekends have a slightly more limited schedule. Adult fare between the cities is $2 and the trip takes about 50 minutes.

AUBURN STATE RECREATION AREA

The deep gorges of this popular **park** (☎ 530-885-4527; www.parks.ca.gov, day use fee for some areas $5) were cut by the rushing waters of the North and Middle Forks of the **American River**, which converge below a bridge on Hwy 49, about 4 miles south of Auburn. In the early spring, when waters are high, this is immensely popular for white-water rafting, as the rivers offer a range of difficulty levels. Later in the summer the waters get a bit quieter, when it's great for sunning and swimming. Numerous trails in the area are shared by hikers, mountain-bikers and horses.

The best tour of the area is offered by **All-Outdoors California Whitewater Rafting** (☎ 800-247-2387; www.aorafting.com), a family-run outfit that was the first on the remote Middle Fork. It is one of the few to lead adventuresome two-day wilderness ventures that break up the trip with waterfall-lined hikes and historically significant sightseeing on the canyon. On the two-day trips they haul your camping gear and feed you. The burrito lunch might be worth the trip alone. All-Outdoors also operates excellent tours on other rivers throughout the area.

One of the most popular trails is the **Western States Trail**, which connects Auburn State Recreation Area to Folsom Lake State Recreation Area and Folsom Lake. It's the site of the Western States 100 Mile Endurance Run (for more information check the website at www.ws100.com).

The **Quarry Trail** takes a level path from Hwy 49, just south of the bridge, along the Middle Fork of the American. Several side trails go down to the river.

For camping, there are some basic sites on a sweeping bend of the Middle Fork at the blackberry-dotted **Ford's Bar**. It's accessible only by a 2-mile hike or half-day raft. A hike begins at the end of Ruck-A-Chucky Rd. Permits to this and other government-operated camping areas are available from **Foresthill Ranger Station** (☎ 530-367-2224; www.fs.fed.us; 22830 Foresthill Rd, Foresthill) for $15.

WHAT THE...?

Floating along any of the rivers in Gold Country, you're bound to pass someone still trying to get rich on the gold of the Sierras using a suction dredge – a floating contraption that sucks up rocks from the river bed and sorts the gold. Even though the dredging season is short and tightly regulated by the state, prospecting pays off – locals claim to average around $50,000 a year.

EL DORADO & AMADOR COUNTIES

In the heart of the pine- and oak-covered Sierra foothills, this is where gold was first discovered – Spanish-speaking settlers appropriately named El Dorado County after a mythical city of riches. Today, SUVs en route to South Lake Tahoe pull off of Hwy 50 to find a rolling hillside dotted with the historic towns, sun-soaked terraces and rocky soil of one of California's great underdog wine regions. If you make the stop, don't leave without toasting a glass of regional zinfandel, which, like the locals, is packed with earthy attitude and regional character. It's also worth the detour to pause a few minutes at the shore where a glint of gold caught James Marshall's eye and gave birth to the Golden State.

Traveling through much of the central part of Gold Country requires a car, as the public transportation is unreliable between the towns. The good news? This stretch of Hwy 49 makes an excellent road trip.

COLOMA

pop 1100 / elev 750ft

Coloma is the nearest town to Sutter's Mill (the site of California's first gold discovery) and Marshall Gold Discovery State Historic Park (right), and it's also a great launching pad for **rafting** operations, which fill nearly every storefront. The **South Fork of the American River** gets the most traffic, since it features exciting rapids, but is still manageable for beginners. Adrenaline junkies who have never rafted before should try the Middle Fork (p337).

Half-day rafting trips usually begin at the Chile Bar and end close to the state park. Full-day trips put in at the Coloma Bridge and take out at Salmon Falls, near Folsom Lake. The half-day options start in Class III rapids and are action-packed (full-day trips start out slowly, then build up to Class III as a climax). Full-day trips include a lavish lunch. The season usually runs from May to mid-October, depending on snow melts. Prices are generally lower on weekdays.

Whitewater Connection (☎ 530-622-6446, 800-336-7238; www.whitewaterconnection.com; half-day trips $89-109, full-day trips $109-129) is typical of the area's operators, with knowledgeable guides and excellent food.

Don't want to get wet? Watch people navigate the **Trouble Maker Rapids**, upstream from the bridge next to Sutter's Mill in the state park.

American River Resort (☎ 530-622-6700; www.americanriverresort.com; 6019 New River Rd; tent & RV sites $20-35, cabins $115-130; 🅿) is only a quarter mile off Hwy 49, just south of the state park. The site is more cushy than most other area campgrounds: there's a restaurant and bar, a playground, a pond and farm animals. The campsites are basic, but some are right on the river.

Another long-established riverside campground, **Coloma Resort** (☎ 530-621-2267; www.colomaresort.com; 6921 Mt Murphy Rd; tent & RV sites $40-45, tent cabins & on-site RV rentals $115-135; 🅿 wi-fi) comes with a full range of activities, playgrounds and every techie camper's dream: wi-fi.

The four-room **Coloma Country Inn** (☎ 530-622-6919; www.colomacountryinn.com; 345 High St; r $150-245; 💻 🅿) B&B is situated in a historic farmhouse and the hosts offer good advice about area rafting. If you're not in a rush, try the quiet cottage suite, where you can spend an afternoon floating on the pond.

Just north of Marshall Gold is **Coloma Club Cafe & Saloon** (☎ 530-626-6390; 7171 Hwy 49; 🕒 restaurant 6:30am-9pm, bar 10am-2am). The patio at this rowdy hangout comes alive with guides and river rats when the water is high. It also hosts occasional live music.

MARSHALL GOLD DISCOVERY STATE HISTORIC PARK

Compared to the stampede of gun-toting, hill-blasting, hell-raising settlers that populate tall tales along Hwy 49, the **Marshall Gold Discovery State Historic Park** (admission per car $5; 🕒 8am-sunset) is a place of bucolic tranquillity, with two tragic heroes in John Sutter and James Marshall. Sutter, who had a fort in Sacramento, partnered with Marshall to build a sawmill on a swift stretch of the American River in 1847. It was Marshall who discovered gold here on January 24, 1848, and though the men tried to keep their findings secret, it eventually brought a chaotic rush of prospectors from around the world. In one of the great tragic ironies of the Gold Rush, the men who made this discovery died nearly penniless.

The pastoral park is quietly befitting of this legacy, with a grassy area bordered on the east by the river. Follow a simple dirt path to the place along the bank where Marshall found gold and started the revolutionary birth of the 'Golden State.'

The park's quiet charms are mostly experienced outdoors, strolling past the carefully reconstructed mill and taking in the grounds. There's also a humble **Visitors Information Center & Museum** (☎ 530-622-3470; Bridge St; 🕒 10am-3pm) with a tidy shop where you can buy the kiddie kitsch from the frontier days.

On a hill overlooking the park is the **James Marshall Monument**, where he was buried in 1885, a ward of the state. You can drive a circuit but it's much better to meander the many trails around the park, past old mining artifacts and pioneer cemeteries.

Panning for gold is popular – you can pay $3.50 to pan at Bekeart's Gun Shop (across from the visitors center), and there is a decent café and plenty of places for picnics.

PLACERVILLE

pop 9650 / elev 1866ft

Placerville has always been a travelers' town: it was originally a destination for fortune

GOING FOR THE GOLD

California's Gold Rush started in 1848 when James Marshall was inspecting the both fatefully and poorly sited lumber mill he was building for John Sutter near present-day Coloma (opposite). He saw a sparkle in the mill's tailrace water and pulled out a nugget 'roughly half the size of a pea.' Marshall hightailed it to Sacramento and consulted Sutter, who tested the gold by methods described in an encyclopedia. But Sutter wanted to finish his mill so made a deal with his laborers, allowing them to keep any gold they found in their spare time if they kept working. Before long, word of the find leaked out.

Sam Brannan, for example, went to Coloma to investigate the rumors just a few months after Marshall's find. After finding 6oz of gold in one afternoon, he returned to San Francisco and paraded through the streets proclaiming, 'There's gold in the Sierra foothills!' Convinced there was money to be made, he bought every piece of mining equipment in the area – from handkerchiefs to shovels. When gold seekers needed equipment for their adventure, Brannan sold them goods at a 100% markup and was a rich man by the time the first folks hit the foothills.

By the time the mill's construction was finished in the spring of 1848, gold seekers had begun to arrive, the first wave coming from San Francisco. Only a few months later, San Francisco was almost depleted of able-bodied men, while towns near the 'diggins,' as the mines were called, swelled with thousands of people. News of the Gold Rush spread around the world, and by 1849 more than 60,000 people (who became widely known as '49ers) rushed to California. They were looking for the mother lode: the mythical big deposit that miners believed was the source of all the gold found in the streams and riverbeds.

Most prospectors didn't stick around after the initial diggings petered out. In 1859, when the Comstock Lode was found on the eastern side of the Sierra in Virginia City, Nevada, many left. Those who did stay signed on with large operations (such as the Empire Mine in Grass Valley) which were financed by businesses or private fortunes. Gold-extraction processes became increasingly complex and invasive, culminating in the practice of hydraulic mining, by which miners drained lakes and rivers to power their water cannons and blast away entire hillsides (see Malakoff Diggins State Historic Park, p332). People downstream who were inundated by the muck sued, and eventually the environmental cost was too great to justify staying in business.

hunters who reached California by following the South Fork of the American River. In 1857 the first stagecoach to cross the Sierra Nevada linked Placerville to Nevada's Carson Valley, which eventually became part of the nation's first transcontinental stagecoach route. Today, Placerville is a place to gas up and get a bite while traveling between Sacramento and Tahoe on Hwy 50. It has a thriving and well-preserved downtown with antique shops and character-filled bars, where local wags cherish the wild reputation of 'Hangtown' – a name earned when a handful of men swung from the gallows in the mid 1800s. (A reminder of this grisly frontier justice is marked by a dummy dangling from the second story of a dive bar downtown.) Among the many other awesome local legends is 'Snowshoe' John A Thompson, a postal carrier who carried some 80lbs of mail on skis from Placerville over the Sierra to Carson Valley during the winter.

Orientation & Information

Main St is the heart of downtown Placerville and runs parallel to Hwy 50 between Canal St and Cedar Ravine Rd. Hwy 49 meets Main St at the west edge of downtown.

Bookery (☎ 530-626-6454; 326 Main St; ⏰ 10am-5:30pm Mon-Thu, to 7pm Fri & Sat, 10am-4pm Sun) A great used-book store to stock up on vacation pulp.

El Dorado County Chamber of Commerce (☎ 530-621-5885, 800-457-6279; www.eldoradocounty.org; 542 Main St; ⏰ 9am-5pm Mon-Fri) Has decent maps and local information.

Placerville News Co (☎ 530-622-4510; www.pvillenews.com; 409 Main St; ⏰ 8am-7pm Mon-Sat, to 5:30pm Sun) This plank-floored shop has a wealth of maps, history and local interest books, newspapers and magazines.

Sights & Activities

Looking like a movie set, most buildings along Main St are false fronts and sturdy brick structures from the 1850s, dominated by the spindly **Bell Tower**, a relic from 1856 that once rallied volunteer firemen. The 1852 **Placerville**

Hardware (☎ 530-622-1151; 441 Main St), an anchor on Placerville's main drag, is the oldest continuously operating hardware store west of the Mississippi and one of many places along Main St to pick up a brochure for a self-guided tour of the town. The store has a smattering of Gold Country bric-a-brac but most of the goods that clutter the place are bona fide dry goods, like hammers and buckets, all unusually curious within the tight aisles.

As for museums, the best in Placerville is **Gold Bug Park** (☎ 530-642-5207; www.goldbugpark.org; 8:30am-5pm), about 1 mile north of town on Bedford Ave. The park stands over the site of four mining claims that yielded gold from 1849 to 1888; you can descend into the self-guided Gold Bug Mine, do some gold panning ($2) and explore the grounds and picnic area for free.

Placerville Historical Museum (☎ 530-626-0773; 524 Main St; admission free; noon-4pm Fri-Sun), inside the Fountain & Tallman Soda Works building, has a small collection of soda factory relics and old Placerville photographs.

El Dorado County Historical Museum (☎ 530-621-5865; 104 Placerville Dr; admission free; 10am-4pm Wed-Sat, noon-4pm Sun), on the El Dorado County Fairgrounds west of downtown (exit north on Placerville Dr from Hwy 50), is an extensive complex of restored buildings, mining equipment and re-created businesses.

Sleeping & Eating

Chain motels and fast-food places can be found at either end of the historic center of Placerville along Hwy 50.

Cary House Hotel (☎ 530-622-4271; www.caryhouse.com; 300 Main St; r from $80;) This historic hotel in downtown Placerville was once a bordello and is said to be haunted, though the modern rooms with tasteful period decor belie its rich history. Ask for a room at the back of the hotel overlooking the courtyard to avoid street noise, or for room 212, which is rumored to be a supernatural hangout.

Chichester-McKee House B&B (☎ 530-626-1882, 800-831-4008; 800 Spring St; r $110-130;) Built in 1892 by the head of the local lumber company, this B&B features wonderful wood insets, stained-glass windows and four elegant rooms. Brownies are served in the evening and a full breakfast is provided in the morning.

Combellack-Blair House B&B (☎ 530-622-3764; 3059 Cedar Ravine Rd; r $115-150) With three Victorian-style rooms and a lovely garden, this gingerbread-laced Queen Anne is on the National Register of Historic Places. If it looks like a scene from a Thomas Kincaid painting, that's because it is: the 'Bob Ross of Placerville' used it as a subject for his *'Victorian Christmas I.'*

Z-Pie (☎ 530-621-2626; 3182 Center St; mains $5-6; 11am-9pm daily) With its whimsical take on the all-American comfort food staple, this casual stop across from City Hall stuffs pot pies with a gourmet flourish (Steak cabernet! Thai chicken! Black bean chili and tofu!), which are washed down with California beers on tap.

Sweetie Pie's (☎ 530-642-0128; 577 Main St; mains $5-12; breakfast & lunch) Ski bunnies and bums fill this diner on the weekends en route to Tahoe slopes, filling up with egg dishes and top-notch homemade baked goods. Breakfast is its specialty, but it also does a capable lunch, with sandwiches and salads.

Cozmic Cafe (☎ 530-642-8481; 594 Main St; meals $6-10; breakfast, lunch & dinner) The menu is organic and boasts vegetarian and healthy fare backed by fresh smoothies. There's a good selection of microbrews and live music on weekends, when it is often open late.

Heyday Café (☎ 530-626-8097; 325 Main St; mains $9-19; lunch & dinner) Fresh, simple and well-executed, the menu here leans toward simple Italian comfort food, made all the more comfortable by the wood-and-brick interior.

Drinking

The wines of El Dorado County are rising in profile, and several tasting rooms dot the main street offering earthy, elegant zins of the region (see opposite for more on wineries). Placerville's bars, on the other hand, are akin to the neighborhood watering holes in the Midwest: they open around 6am, get an annual cleaning at Christmas and are great for people who want to chew the fat with a colorful cast of locals. Marked by vintage signs, the **Hangman Tree** (☎ 530-622-3878; 305 Main St) is built over the stump of the eponymous tree, while the **Liars' Bench** (☎ 530-622-0494; 255 Main St) is just a *bit* less shady, standing under a classic old martini sign that beckons after dark.

Getting There & Away

Amtrak (☎ 800-872-7245; www.capitolcorridor.org) runs three buses daily to Sacramento ($14, one hour 20 minutes) and South Lake Tahoe ($14, one hour). The **Placerville Transit Station** (2984 Mosquito Rd) is a charming covered bus stop with benches and restrooms; it's about half a mile from downtown, on the north side of Hwy 50.

AROUND PLACERVILLE

Apple Hill

In 1860 a miner planted a Rhode Island Greening apple tree on what is the present-day property of a family named Larsen. Thus began what is now the bountiful Apple Hill, a 20-sq-mile area east of Placerville and north of Hwy 50 where there are more than 60 orchards. Apple growers sell directly to the public, usually from August to December, and some let you pick your own. Other fruits are available during different seasons.

A decent map of Apple Hill is available at the **Apple Hill Visitors Center** (☎ 530-644-7692; www.applehill.com) in the Camino Hotel, near the Camino exit off Hwy 50.

Placerville Wineries

The region's high heat and rocky soil have produced some excellent wines, which frequently appear on California menus. Oenophiles could spend a long afternoon rambling through the welcoming vineyards of El Dorado Country alone (though a full weekend of tasting could be had if it was coupled with the adjoining Amador County). Details can be found at the **El Dorado Winery Association** (☎ 800-306-3956; www.eldoradowines.org) or the **Wine Smith** (☎ 530-622-0516; 346 Main St; 🕑 10am-6pm Tue-Thu & Sun, to 8pm Fri), a local shop with just about everything grown in the area.

Some noteworthy wineries, all north of Hwy 50, include **Lava Cap Winery** (☎ 530-621-0175; www.lavacap.com; 2221 Fruitridge Rd; 🕑 11am-5pm) and **Boeger Winery** (☎ 530-622-8094; www.boegerwinery.com; 1709 Carson Rd; 🕑 10am-5pm). Both have free tastings.

AMADOR COUNTY WINERIES

Amador County might be something of an underdog among California's winemaking regions, but a thriving circuit of family wineries, Gold Rush history and local characters make for excellent wine touring without a whiff of pretension. The region lays claim to the oldest zinfandel vines in the United States and the surrounding country has a lot in common with this celebrated variety – bold and richly colored, earthy and constantly surprising.

To begin the circuit of Amador wineries, leave Hwy 49 in Plymouth and follow Plymouth Shenandoah Rd, taking you through rows of vines basking in the heat. You'll see hill after rolling hill covered with rocky rows of neatly pruned vines, soaking up gallons of too-bright sun. Tastings at the family-operated wineries around the county have little in common with those in the Napa Valley – most hosts are welcoming and helpful, offering free tastes and information about their operations.

Maps are available at the wineries, and from the **Amador Vintners Association** (☎ 209-267-2297; www.amadorwine.com).

Recommended wineries:

Deaver Vineyards (☎ 209-245-5592; www.deavervineyard.com; 12455 Steiner Rd; 🕑 10:30am-4pm) A true family affair where nearly everyone's last name seems to match the one on the bottles.

Drytown Cellars (☎ 209-245-3400; www.drytowncellars.com; 16030 Hwy 49; 🕑 11am-5pm Fri-Sun) This is the most fun tasting room in Amador County, thanks to a gregarious host and an array of stunning reds.

Sobon Estate (☎ 209-245-6554; www.sobonwine.com; 14430 Shenandoah Rd; 🕑 10am-5pm) Founded in 1856, it's home to the Shenandoah Valley Museum featuring wine-related memorabilia.

Wildrotter (☎ 209-245-4455; www.wildrottervineyard.com; 19890 Shenandoah School Rd; 🕑 10am-5pm Fri-Sun, 11am-4pm Mon & Thu). This winery brought home prestigious honors for California's best red at a recent State Fair.

PLYMOUTH

pop 980 / elev 1083ft

The home base for exploring Amador County's wine region is Plymouth, where the region's Gold Rush history is evident in its original name, Pokerville. Few card sharks haunt the slumbering main street today; it wakes late when the tiny main street fills with the smell of barbecue, a few strolling tourists and the odd rumble of a motorcycle posse. In town, you'll likely spot the ruins of the **Plymouth Consolidated Mine**, which dug some $14 million in gold out of the ground below. For a casual lunch, try **Incahoots** (☎ 209-245-4455; 9486 Main St; mains $5-23; 🕑 lunch & dinner), a scruffy barbecue place with a roadhouse vibe where bikers, ranchers and wine drinkers pack rough-cut wooden tables. For something more refined – *much* more refined – book a table at **Taste** (☎ 209-245-3463; 9402 Main St, Plymouth; mains $31-50; 🕑 dinner), where excellent Amador wines are paired with a four-star menu of California fusions. Pull on the oversized fork-shaped door handle to be greeted by smells of fresh, seasonally changing dishes, all artfully presented.

AMADOR CITY

pop 270 / elev 620ft

Once home to the Keystone Mine – one of the most prolific gold producers in California – the town lay deserted from 1942 (when the mine closed) until the 1950s, when a family from Sacramento bought the dilapidated buildings and converted them into antique shops. The tiny brick box of the **Amador Whitney Museum** (☎ 209-267-0928; Main St; admission free; ⌚ noon-4pm Fri-Sun) has changing exhibits of local artworks.

Behind Amador City's old firehouse (the building with a bright red garage door and bell tower in front) is a stone arastra (a round, shallow pool with a turnstile in the middle used to crush rocks into gravel), once used here to grind gold-laced quartz. The arastra still works and is put to use during the Jose Amador Fiesta in late April.

The **Imperial Hotel** (☎ 209-267-9172, 800-242-5594; www.imperialamador.com; 14202 Main St; r $100-140;), built in 1879, is one of the area's most inventive updates to the typical antique-cluttered hotels, with sleek deco touches accenting the usual gingerbread flourish, a genteel bar and an excellent seasonally minded restaurant (dinner $20 to $30). On weekends during the summer, expect a two-night minimum.

SUTTER CREEK

pop 2350 / elev 1198ft

Perch on the balcony of one of the gracefully restored buildings on the Main St and view Sutter Creek, a gem of a Gold Country town with raised, arcaded sidewalks and high-balconied buildings with false fronts that are perfect examples of California's 19th-century architecture.

Begin the visit at volunteer-operated **Sutter Creek Visitor Center** (☎ 209-267-1344; www.suttercreek.org; 25 Eureka St; ⌚ hours vary) to collect a walking-tour map of town or an excellent, free driving-tour guide to local gold mines.

Sights & Activities

Next door to the visitor center, **Monteverde General Store** (☎ 209-267-5155; admission free; ⌚ 10am-3pm, with seasonal variations) is a trip back in time to when the general store was the center of the town's social and economic life, represented by the chairs that circle the potbelly stove and the detailed historic scale.

In its prime, Sutter Creek was Gold Country's main supply center. Three foundries operating in 1873 made pans and rock crushers. The **Knight Foundry** (☎ 209-267-0201; 81 Eureka St) operated until 1996 as the last water-powered foundry and machine shop in the US. You can still see the workings of the foundry, and on some days volunteers can explain how everything worked while they toil to put the foundry back into production.

One of several excellent Gold Country arts groups, the **Sutter Creek Theatre** (☎ 877-547-6518; www.suttercreektheater.com; 44 Main St) has a nearly 100-year-long history of presenting live drama, films and other cultural events.

Sleeping & Eating

Sutter Creek Inn (☎ 209-267-5606; www.suttercreekinn.com; 75 Main St; r $90-195;) The 17 rooms and cottages here vary in decor and amenities (antiques, fireplaces, patios) but all have private bathrooms. Guests can snooze in the hammock by the gardens or sprawl out on the large lawn, which is dotted with comfy chairs for curling up in with a book. Of course it's jammed with knickknacks, including a spectacular collection of cow-shaped coffee creamers.

Eureka Street Inn (☎ 209-267-5500; www.eurekastreetinn.com; 55 Eureka St; r $110-130;) Each of the four rooms in this 1914 home has different decor. Once the home of a wealthy stagecoach operator, the inn is on a quiet street close to everything and serves a good breakfast.

Foxes Inn (☎ 209-267-5882; www.foxesinn.com; 77 Main St; r incl breakfast $160-210;) Foxes has seven plush rooms with refrigerators and bathrobes, lovely gardens and a sunny piano room. Breakfasts are inspired and there are free beverages throughout the day.

Sutter Creek Coffee Roasting Co (☎ 209-267-5550; 20 Eureka St; meals $4-7; ⌚ breakfast & lunch) This café's patio is a local social hub with hair-raising coffee.

Tommy's Cafe (☎ 209-267-0500; 40 Hanford St; meals $5-9; ⌚ breakfast, lunch & dinner Fri & Sat;) A real star in a galaxy of them, this eponymous place serves classic fare ranging from eggs Benedict to prime rib dinners. There's a sunny little patio.

The **Saturday farmers market** (⌚ 8-11am Jun-Oct) is a good place to sample the bounteous delights of this fertile region.

VOLCANO

pop 100 / elev 2053ft

One of the many fading plaques in Volcano accurately calls it a place of 'quiet history,' and even though the little L-shaped village on the bank of Sutter Creek yielded tons of gold and a Civil War battle, today it slumbers away in remote solitude. Now only a scattering of greening bronze monuments attest to Volcano's lively past.

Large sandstone rocks line Sutter Creek, which skirts the center of town. The rocks, now flanked by picnic tables, were blasted from surrounding hills by a hydraulic process before being scraped clean of gold-bearing dirt. The process had dire environmental consequences, but at its peak miners were getting rich, making nearly $100 a day.

The winding 12-mile drive from Sutter Creek is along lovely Sutter Creek Rd.

Sights & Activities

Between mid-March and mid-April, **Daffodil Hill**, 2 miles northeast of Volcano, is blanketed with more than 300,000 daffodils. The McLaughlin and Ryan families have operated the hilltop farm since 1887 and keep hyacinths, tulips, violets, lilacs and the occasional peacock among the daffodils. The hill is open daily when the flowers are in bloom. There's no fee, but donations toward next year's planting are accepted.

Indian Grinding Rock State Historic Park (☎ 209-296-7488; Pine Grove-Volcano Rd; admission per vehicle $6), 2 miles southwest of Volcano, is a sacred area for the local Miwok people. There's a limestone outcrop that's covered with petroglyphs – 363 originals and a few modern additions – and over 1000 mortar holes called *chaw'ses* used for grinding acorns into meal. Near the rock are impressive replica Miwok structures and the **Regional Indian Museum** (🕒 11am-3pm Mon-Fri, 10am-4pm Sat & Sun), which has displays about northern Miwok culture and leads tours of the park on weekends.

On weekends between April and November, the highly regarded **Volcano Theatre Company** (☎ 209-223-4663; www.volcanotheatre.org; adult/child $14/9) produces live dramas in the restored Cobblestone Theater.

Black Chasm (☎ 888-762-2837; www.caverntours.com; 15701 Pioneer Volcano Rd; adult/child $12/6; 🕒 9am-4pm), a quarter of a mile east of Volcano, has the whiff of a tourist trap, but one look at the helictite crystals – rare, sparkling white formations that look like enlarged snowflakes – makes the crowd more sufferable. The tour guides are all experienced cavers.

Sleeping & Eating

St George Hotel (☎ 209-296-4458; www.stgeorgehotel.com; 16104 Main St; r $80-190) Up the crooked stairs of this charming, creaky hotel are 20 rooms which vary in size and amenity. However, all are refreshingly free from excessive laciness, and open to comfortable sitting areas and balconies. The restaurant (open for dinner Thursday to Sunday, brunch Sunday) has a menu anchored by steak, but the best place to hang out is in the accompanying bar, where the local concoction of 'Moose Milk' (a whisky- and dairy-based inebriant) is worthy of the bartender's playful warning.

Volcano Union Inn (☎ 209-296-7711; www.volcanounioninn.com; 21375 Consolation St; r $90-170; 💻) All kinds of ghosts haunt the modest rooms here. The bar is folksy inside and opens to a big patio. The dining is more casual, especially on Sunday when meals are served family-style around a communal table (reservations required).

The beautiful **campground** (tent/RV sites $15/20) at Indian Grinding Rock State Historic Park has fresh water, plumbing and 23 unreserved sites set among the trees, with tent sites and hookups for RVs.

JACKSON

pop 4000 / elev 1200ft

Jackson has some historic buildings and a small downtown, but it ain't much to look at; standing at the junction of Hwy 49 and Hwy 88 it's probably the least attractive Gold Rush hub.

Hwy 88 turns east from Hwy 49 here and heads over the Sierra near the Kirkwood ski resort (see p356). The **Amador County Chamber of Commerce** (☎ 209-223-0350; 125 Peek St; 🕒 9am-4pm Mon-Fri), on the corner of Hwys 49 and 88, has enough brochures to fill several recycling bins.

Perched on a hill overlooking downtown, the **Amador County Museum** (☎ 209-223-6386; 225 Church St; donation requested; 🕒 10am-4pm Wed-Sun), two blocks north of Main St, celebrates Gold Country history and has some cool models of working mines.

One mile from downtown Jackson via North Main St, **Kennedy Tailing Wheels Park** doesn't look like much at first glance, but the four iron and wood wheels, 58ft in diameter (they look like fallen carnival rides), transported tailings from the Eureka Mine over two low hills and are marvelous examples of engineering and craftsmanship. Be sure to climb to the top of the hill behind the wheels to see the impounding dam.

Somewhat undiscovered **Mokelumne Hill**, which lies 7 miles south of Jackson just off Hwy 49, was settled by French trappers in the early 1840s. It's a good place to see historic buildings without the common glut of antique stores and gift shops.

Jackson's cheap and chain motels are on the outskirts of town along Hwys 49 and 88.

National Hotel (☎ 209-223-0500; fax 223-4845; 2 Water St; r $75-195) Jackson's historic hotel, though the rooms, which are decorated with themed flair from pop icons, don't jive with the historic facade. The rooms are worn, and there's plenty of sound from the nearby highway and locals who gather on the bar's balcony below, so light sleepers should look elsewhere.

Best Western Amador Inn (☎ 209-223-0211; www.bestwestern.com; 200 S Hwy 49; r $75-105;) This large, recently renovated inn is close to downtown and has 118 spacious, comfortable rooms, some with fireplaces.

Mel's and Faye's Diner (☎ 209-223-0853; 205 N Hwy 49; meals $5-12; breakfast, lunch & dinner) is a local institution near Hwy 88. It serves up excellent diner fare that includes breakfasts that could feed a small family, classic burgers (try the chili-soaked 'Miner') and – to balance the divine grease binge – a decent salad bar.

Getting There & Away

Placer Country runs its (fairly pathetic) bus system out of Jackson, but good luck catching it – the buses are few and far between. The only way to reliably travel through this area is with a car.

CALAVERAS COUNTY & SOUTH GOLD COUNTRY

The southern region of Gold Country is hot as blazes in the summer, when cruising through its historic Gold Rush hubs will demand more than one stop for ice cream. The tall tales of yesteryear come alive here through the region's infamous former residents: author Mark Twain, who got his start writing about a jumping contest in Calaveras County, and Joaquin Murrieta, a Robin Hood figure who somehow seems to have frequented every old bar and hotel in the area.

SAN ANDREAS

pop 2300 / elev 1008ft

San Andreas, the seat of Calaveras County, has utilitarian businesses concentrated on Hwy 49. The old town along N Main St is noteworthy for its county courthouse housing an art gallery, restored jail and jail yard where notorious stagecoach robber Black Bart awaited trial. Also here is the **Calaveras County Historical Museum Complex** (☎ 209-754-1058; 30 N Main St; adult/child $3/1; 10am-4pm), which has one of the area's most engaging history displays and a native-plant garden.

In Cave City, 8 miles east of San Andreas (take Mountain Ranch Rd to Cave City Rd), is the **California Cavern** (☎ 209-736-2708; www.caverntours.com; adult/child $12/6; 10am-5pm Jun-Sep, 10am-4pm Sat & Sun Oct-May), which John Muir described as 'graceful flowing folds deeply placketed like stiff silken drapery.' Regular tours take 60 to 90 minutes. For $130 you can try a Middle Earth Expedition, which lasts five hours and includes serious spelunking.

ANGELS CAMP

pop 2900 / elev 1379ft

On the southern stretch of Hwy 49 one figure looms over all others: literary giant Mark Twain, who got his first big break with the story of *The Celebrated Jumping Frog of Calaveras County*, written and set in Angels Camp. There are differing claims as to when or where Twain heard this tale, but Angels Camp makes the most of it; hosting the **Jumping Frog Jubilee** the third weekend in May (in conjunction with the county fair) and **Mark Twain Days** over the Fourth of July weekend. There are gentlemanly Twain impersonators, statues and dozens of bronze frogs embedded in the sidewalk of Main St commiserating amphibious champions of the past 80 years. Look for the plaque for Rosie the Riveter, who set an impressive 21ft record in 1986.

Even though Twain is the town's favorite ambassador, it was booming well before he arrived, after being founded by George Angel in 1849 as a service center for surrounding mines. Hard-rock mining peaked in the 1890s, when 200 stamp mills worked around the clock. Remains of the last mine are visible in

DETOUR: CALAVERAS BIG TREES STATE PARK

From Angels Camp, Hwy 4 ascends into the High Sierra, eventually cresting at Ebbetts Pass (8730ft) and then descending to junctions with Hwys 89 and 395. Along the way the road passes through the workmanlike town of Arnold, which has a few cafés and motels strung along the roadside. But the real reason for taking Hwy 4 is 2 miles east of Arnold and 20 miles east of Murphys: a chance to commune with the largest living things on the planet.

Calaveras Big Trees State Park (☎ 209-795-2334; admission per vehicle $6) is home to giant sequoia redwood trees. Reaching as high as 325ft and with trunk diameters up to 33ft, these leftovers from the Mesozoic era are thought to weigh upwards of 3000 tons, or close to 20 blue whales.

The redwood giants are distributed in two large groves, one of which is easily seen from the **North Grove Big Trees Trail**, a 1.5-mile self-guided loop, near the entrance, where the air is fresh with pine and rich soil. A 4-mile trail that branches off from the self-guided loop climbs out of the North Grove, crosses a ridge and descends 1500ft to the Stanislaus River.

It's possible to find giant trees throughout the park's 6000 acres, though the largest are in fairly remote locations. The **visitors center** (🕑 9am-4pm) can offer maps and lots of good advice on the miles of trails. It also has good exhibits about the trees and how a few dedicated individuals fought for decades to save them from becoming so many thousands of picnic tables.

Camping is popular and **reservations** (☎ 800-444-7275; www.parks.ca.gov; tent sites $15-25) are essential. North Grove Campground is near the park entrance; less crowded is Oak Hollow Campground, 4 miles further on the park's main road. Most atmospheric are the hike-in environmental sites.

Utica Park at the west end of Main St. Today the town is an attractive mix of buildings from the Gold Rush to art-deco periods.

With a great collection of photographs, relics and tons of rusty farm and transportation equipment (including a horse-drawn hearse), the **Angels Camp Museum and Carriage House** (☎ 209-736-2963; 753 S Main St; 🕑 10am-3pm Mar-Dec), set on 3 acres, tells of the area's mining heyday.

Calaveras County Visitors Bureau (☎ 209-736-0049; www.gocalaveras.com; 1192 S Main St; 🕑 9am-5pm Mon-Sat, 11am-3pm Sun) has a walking and driving tour of Angels Camp, history books and lots more information for your trip.

Across from the museum, **Gold Country Inn** (☎ 209-736-4611, 800-851-4944; www.goldcountryinnangelscamp.com; 720 S Main St; r $50-120; ❄) has great rates and 40 modern, comfy rooms, many with refrigerators.

The simple decor at local favorite **Crusco's** (☎ 209-736-1440; 1240 S Main St; mains $14-17; 🕑 lunch & dinner) belies a serious Italian menu. Each year the owners travel to Italy in search of new recipes and bring home treats like polenta Castellana (creamy corn meal with garlic and parsley).

Getting There & Away

Calaveras Transit (☎ 209-754-4450; www.calaverastransit.com) operates the most reliable public transportation system in the region from the **Government Center** (891 Mountain Ranch Rd) in downtown San Andreas. You can use it to connect to Angels Camp ($1.50, 30 minutes, several times daily) and other surrounding towns. Take the bus to Lodi ($3, 45 minutes, several times daily), where you can connect through Amtrak and Greyhound to Sacramento.

MURPHYS

pop 3400 / elev 2171ft

With its white picket fences and old world charm, Murphys is one of the most picturesque towns along the southern stretch of Gold Country, befitting its nickname as 'Queen of the Sierra.' It lies 8 miles east of Hwy 49 on Murphys Grade Rd, and is named for Daniel and John Murphy, who founded a trading post and mining operation on Murphy Creek in 1848, in conjunction with the local Maidu people. John was apparently very friendly with the tribe and eventually married the chief's daughter. The town's Main St is refined with boutiques and galleries and good strolling.

Sights & Activities

Even more than frogs, wine touring is a consistent draw in Calaveras County, and even though there are a couple boutique wineries located right in town, the best are just out of town. The **Ironstone Vineyards** (☎ 209-728-1251; www.ironstonevineyards.com; 1894 Six Mile Rd;

JOAQUIN MURRIETA: AVENGER OR TERRORIST?

In a land where tall tales tower, none casts a darker shadow than that of Joaquin Murrieta, the rakish immigrant miner long celebrated as the Robin Hood of the Gold Rush, whose inscrutable portrait gazes out from a tin type (an early method of photography) at the Murphys Old Timers Museum (below). Stories of the bloodthirsty Murrieta are as ubiquitous as they are incongruous: he was born in either Sonora, Mexico or Quillota, Chile and, after immigrating to California seeking gold in 1850, he became either a treacherous villain of the lawless West or a folk hero who avenged the intense racial persecution of Mexicans in Gold Country. In the soft focus of historical hindsight, the fiery wrath of Joaquin Murrieta – real or not – has forged Gold Country's most intriguing antihero.

A consolidation of 'Once upon a time' stories reads something like this: Murrieta and his brother had a claim near Hangtown (now known, somewhat blandly, as Placerville). After some luck they refused to pay a newly established 'foreign miners tax' that the state legislature adopted in response to the overwhelming success of experienced Mexican and Chileno prospectors. To force Murrieta off his claim, a mob of jealous Anglo miners whipped Murrieta and raped his young wife. With no recourse in the racist justice system, Murrieta formed a posse to kill assaulters and turned to a life of banditry that left a trail of slashed throats and purloined gold. His band of highwaymen, known as the Five Joaquins, terrorized the countryside between 1850 and 1853.

Under Governor John Bigler, the state legislature offered a large reward for Murrieta, and a Texas bounty hunter named Harry Love hunted him with the newly formed California State Rangers. In July of 1853 Love produced a jar containing the severed head of a man he claimed was Murrieta and the namesake appendage of Murrieta's cohort, Three Fingered Jack. Love toured cities of Northern California charging audiences $1 to see the head but, even in death, Murrieta's legend grew: a woman claiming to be his sister said the head was not her brother's and sightings of the bandit continued long after his alleged death. Joaquin Murrieta was celebrated as a peoples' hero by many Latin Americans who were enraged by the oppressive, racist laws of the Gold Rush which are largely unmentioned today, and his legend is a centerpiece of Gold Rush folklore.

10am-5pm) has a natural spring waterfall, a mechanical pipe organ, frequent exhibits by local artists, and blossoming grounds. The large winery is particularly distinct for its family-friendly atmosphere, a deli and a museum which displays the world's largest crystalline gold leaf specimen (it weighs 44lb and was found in Jamestown in 1992). While crowds are frequent, the wine-tasting room is spacious. Ironstone is 1 mile south of town via Six Mile Rd, and other wineries cluster nearby.

Located 2 miles west of Murphys, off Sheep Ranch Rd, **Stevenot Winery** (209-728-0638; 2690 San Domingo Rd; 10am-5pm) comes a close second in popularity. Its amphitheatre hosts **Theatre Under the Stars** (866-463-8659; www.sierratickets.com; Thu-Sat Jun-Sep), a well-regarded drama series.

The name of the **Murphys Old Timers Museum** (209-728-1160; donation requested; 11am-4pm Fri-Sun) is a good hint that this place approaches history with a whimsical touch. Housed in an 1856 building, it holds a photograph of so-called Mexican Robin Hood, Joaquin Murrieta (above), and the excellent 'Wall of Relative Ovation.' Guided **tours** leave from the museum every Saturday at 10:30am.

Sleeping & Eating

Most accommodations in Murphys are top-end B&Bs. Check nearby Angels Camp or Arnold for cheaper alternatives.

Murphys Historic Hotel & Lodge (209-728-3444, 800-532-7684; www.murphyshotel.com; 457 Main St; r $69-125) Dating back to either 1855 or 1856 (you have your pick of plaques out front), Murphys anchors Main St and is the best place to stay in town. A must-stop on the Twain tour of the area (he was a guest here, as was the bandit Black Bart), the original structure is a little rough around the edges, but has a bar that blends locals and 1850s decor. The dining room's menu (mains $8 to $35) goes deep into game dishes like elk and wild boar.

Murphys Inn Motel (209-728-1818, 888-796-1800; www.centralsierralodging.com; 76 Main St; r $75-105;) Just off Hwy 4, half a mile from the center of town, this option has clean and modern motel rooms with a small pool.

Victoria Inn (☎ 209-728-8933; www.victoriainn-murphys.com; 402 Main St; r $125-310) This newly built B&B is thankfully free of lacy clutter, with well-appointed common spaces and claw-foot tubs. There's a long veranda where you can enjoy good tapas and wines from the long list at the bar (mains $6 to $12; noon to 10pm Wednesday to Sunday).

Alchemy Market & Wine Bar (☎ 209-728-0700; 191 Main St; meals $7-15; 🕑 11am-7pm Sun-Thu, 7am-8pm Fri & Sat) Arrange a fancy picnic and this upscale food store and deli will make you an excellent sandwich. The adjoining wine bar has a small fusion menu you can enjoy on the patio.

Grounds (☎ 209-728-8663; 402 Main St; meals $8-24; 🕑 breakfast & lunch daily, dinner Wed-Sun) Grounds does everything competently – expert breakfast foods, a roster of light lunch mains and weekend dinners of steaks and fresh fish. The herbal ice tea and fresh vegetarian options are key when the temperatures rise.

V Restaurant (☎ 209-728-0107; 402 Main St; mains $10-25; 🕑 lunch & dinner Wed-Sun) Mediterranean small and large plates punch up the menu at Murphys' most elegant dinner spot, where excellent tapas (deep-fried anchovy-stuffed olives!) are joined by creative cocktails and a smart wine list.

COLUMBIA STATE HISTORIC PARK

More than any other place in Gold Country, Columbia blurs the lines between present and past with a carefully preserved Gold Rush town – complete with volunteers in authentic dress – at the center of a modern community. In 1850 Columbia was founded over the 'Gem of the Southern Mines,' and the center of the town (which was taken over by the state parks system) looks almost exactly as it did then. The authenticity of the old Main St is only shaken a bit by the sugared fragrance of the fudge and the occasional play-acting '49er who forgets to remove his digital watch. On the fringe of these blocks are homes and businesses that blend in so well that it becomes hard to tell what's park and what's not.

The blacksmith's shop, theater, old hotels and authentic bar are a carefully framed window into history, completed by gold panning and breezy picnic spots.

Looking rather like dinosaur bones, limestone and granite boulders are noticeable around town. These were washed out of the surrounding hills by hydraulic mining and scraped clean by prospectors. There's a fascinating explanation of this technique at the renovated **Columbia Museum** (☎ 209-532-4301; cnr Main & State Sts; admission free; 🕑 10am-4:30pm). For information and snacks, stop at the friendly **Columbia Mercantile** (☎ 209-532-7511; cnr Main & Jackson Sts; 🕑 9am-6pm), which also has a wide variety of groceries.

After most shops and attractions close around 5pm, you can have the atmospheric town to yourself, which makes staying here an attractive option.

Among the many elegant hotel restorations in the area, the **City Hotel** (☎ 209-532-1479; www.cityhotel.com; r $125-145; ⊠) is the most thoughtful, and is attentively operated by students of Columbia College's Culinary Arts Program. Rooms overlook a shady stretch of street and open to lovely sitting rooms. The **dining room** (mains $12-25; 🕑 dinner Wed-Sun) serves seasonal items presented with French technique, after which you can retire to the adjoining What Cheer Saloon.

Fallon Hotel (☎ 209-532-1470; www.cityhotel.com; cnr Washington St & Broadway; r $90-145; ⊠) is just as refined and has wider options. It also hosts the most professional theater troupe in the region, the **Sierra Repertory Theatre** (☎ 209-532-3120; www.sierrarep.org), who mix chestnuts of the stage *(Romeo & Juliet, South Pacific)* with popular reviews.

SONORA

pop 5500 / elev 1796ft

Settled in 1848 by miners from Sonora, Mexico, this town was once a cosmopolitan center of commerce and culture with parks, elaborate saloons and the Southern Mines' largest concentration of gamblers, drunkards and gold. Racial unrest drove the Mexican settlers out and their European immigrant replacements got rich on the Big Bonanza Mine, where Sonora High School now stands. That mine yielded 12 tons of gold in two years (including a 28lb nugget).

Today, people en route to Yosemite National Park use it as a staging area, wandering though its pubs for refreshment or grabbing quick eats at the chain restaurants and stores that have cropped up on its periphery. Fortunately, the historic center is well preserved (so much so that it's a frequent backdrop in films, including *Unforgiven* and *Back to The Future III*).

Orientation & Information

Two highways cross the Sierra Nevada east of Sonora and connect with Hwy 395 in the

Eastern Sierra: Hwy 108 via Sonora Pass and Hwy 120 via Tioga Pass. Note that the section of Hwy 120 traveling through Yosemite National Park is only open in summer (see the boxed text, p379).

The center of downtown Sonora is the T-shaped intersection of Washington and Stockton Sts, with Washington the main thoroughfare. There are boutiques, shops, cafés, bars and more.

Sierra Nevada Adventure Company (☎ 209-532-5621; 173 S Washington St; 9am-6pm Sun-Thu, to 7pm Fri & Sat) For maps, equipment rental and sales and friendly advice from guides with a passionate knowledge of the area.

Tuolumne County Visitors Bureau (☎ 209-533-4420; www.tcvb.com; 542 Stockton St; 9am-6pm Jun-Sep, 9am-6pm Mon-Sat Oct-May) More so than many other brochure-jammed chamber of commerce joints, the staff here offers helpful trip planning throughout Gold Country. It also covers Yosemite National Park and Stanislaus National Forest up in the Sierras on Hwy 108.

Sights & Activities

In the former 1857 Tuolumne County Jail, the **Tuolumne County Museum** (☎ 209-532-1317; 158 W Bradford St; admission free; 10am-4pm), two blocks west of Washington St, is an interesting museum with a fortune's worth of gold on display.

Among the historic structures is the wood-and-adobe **Snugg House** (cnr S Stewart & Theall Sts), which was built in 1857 by a freed slave. Residential neighborhoods, off the north end of Washington St, are lined with restored Victorians, and the spooky old **cemetery** at the west end of Jackson St has many graves from that era. **St James Episcopal Church** (N Washington St), a local landmark north of Elkin St, has been in continuous use since it was built in 1860 and is now simply called the 'Red Church.'

If you're looking to get out of town, try a short hike through the oaks on the newly developed **Dragoon Gulch Trail**, which can be found just northwest of the main drag on Alpine Lane.

Sonora is also a base for white-water rafting: the Tuolumne River is known for Class IV rapids and its population of golden eagles and red-tailed hawks, while the Stanislaus River is more accessible and better for novices. **Sierra Mac River Trips** (☎ 209-532-1327; www.sierramac.com; trips from $195) and All-Outdoors California Whitewater Rafting (p337) both have good reputations and run trips of one day or more.

Sleeping & Eating

Gunn House Hotel (☎ 209-532-3421; www.gunnhousehotel.com; 286 S Washington St; r $69-106;) The Sarno family operates a lovely B&B in a central location. The rooms are clean and well appointed and there's a breezy veranda, shady trees and a poolside breakfast.

Sonora Days Inn (☎ 209-532-2400; www.sonoradaysinn.com; 160 S Washington St; r $70-100;) Though taken over by a chain, this 1896 structure is Sonora's oldest hotel. The Spanish arches along the street have more character than the rooms, which are modern. There's a rooftop pool and modern motel addition.

Bradford Place Inn (☎ 209-532-2400; www.bradfordplaceinn.com; 56 W Bradford St; r $130-245;) Gorgeous gardens and inviting porch seats surround this four-room B&B, which emphasizes green living. With a two-person claw-foot tub, the Bradford Suite is the definitive elaborate, romantic B&B experience.

Miner's Shack (☎ 209-532-5252; 157 S Washington St; meals $5-7; breakfast & lunch Mon-Thu, breakfast, lunch & dinner Fri & Sat;) A classic Sierra coffee shop where locals gather at counter seats to talk politics. Wood paneling and animal heads adorn the walls and the eggs are made to utter perfection. The omelets are *killer*. Actually, so are all of the breakfasts.

our pick **Diamondback Grill** (☎ 209-532-6661; 110 S Washington St; meals $6-10; lunch & dinner) With exposed brick and modern fixtures, the fresh menu and contemporary details at this café are a reprieve from occasionally overbearing Victorian frill. Sandwiches dominate the menu (the salmon and mozzarella eggplant are both excellent) and everything is homemade, but for the freshest fare try one of the six (count 'em – six!) daily specials scrawled on the chalkboard.

Banny's Café (☎ 209-209-533-4709; 83 S Stewart St; mains $12-18; lunch & dinner Mon-Sat, dinner Sun) This charming café has clean lines and a seasonal eclectic Mediterranean menu. The wine list is reasonable and highlights many of the area's best vintages.

The downtown **Saturday farmers market** (8am-noon May-Oct) is renowned for its rich selection of regional bounty.

Entertainment

The free and widely available weekend supplement of the *Union Democrat* comes out on Friday and lists movies, music, performance art and events for Tuolumne County.

Iron Horse Lounge (☎ 209-532-4482; 97 S Washington St) The most elaborate of the traditional old taverns in the center; bottles glitter like gold on the backlit bar.

Sierra Repertory Theatre (☎ 209-532-3120; www.sierrarep.com; 13891 Hwy 108; tickets $15-22) In East Sonora, close to the Junction Shopping Center, is the same critically acclaimed company that performs in the Fallon Hotel in Columbia.

Getting There & Away

Bus service to Sonora, the major town in the region, ended in 2005. Hwy 108 is the main access road and it links up with I-5, 55 miles west near Stockton. An entrance to Yosemite National Park (p376) is 60 scenic miles south on Hwy 120. Many Yosemite visitors stay in the Sonora area.

JAMESTOWN

pop 600 / elev 1405ft

Perhaps the most Disneyland of all Gold Country towns, Jamestown is 3 miles south of Sonora, just south of the Hwy 49/108 junction. It was founded around the time of Tuolumne County's first gold strike in 1848 and has suffered the ups and downs of the region's roller-coaster development: economic boosts in 1897, when railroad struck here; the 1920s, when it became the construction headquarters for dams on the Stanislaus and Tuolumne Rivers; and recently, with its renovation into a (slightly gaudy) tourist magnet. A renumbering scheme for Main St has only partially caught on, thus the mixture of two- and five-digit numbers. It's really only a few blocks long.

Five blocks south of Main St, **Railtown 1897 State Historic Park** (☎ 209-984-3953; 5th Ave; admission $2; 🕑 9:30am-4:30pm) – a 26-acre collection of trains and railroad equipment – is the little sister to the huge rail museum in Sacramento, though the surrounding hills have made it the backdrop for countless films and TV shows including *High Noon*. On weekends and holidays you can ride the narrow-gauge railroad that once transported ore, lumber and miners. It's the best train ride in Gold Country, with the air spiced with creosote, campfire and pine, and a route of fresh views. The state-operated park includes a restored station, engine house and bookstore.

Gold Prospecting Adventures (☎ 209-984-4653; www.goldprospecting.com; 18170 Main St) has a range of gold-finding outings involving pans, sluices and more that start at $30. It even offers a three-day college-accredited gold-prospecting course ($595).

Jamestown has some inexpensive cafés and historic hotels on Main St. On weekends, book in advance. If you're heading into the **Stanislaus National Forest**, get permits and information at the **Mi-Wuk Ranger District Office** (24695 State Highway 108; ☎ 209-586-3234).

The nine rooms in the 1859 **National Hotel** (☎ 209-984-3446; www.national-hotel.com; 77 Main St; r from $140 with seasonal variations; ⊠ 💻) feature period-era brass beds and lacy curtains, plus access to the 1880 'soaking room' where you can splash around in a claw-foot tub with a friend. Both the restaurant and saloon on-site are quality; the menu at the former swings between light lunch fare and dinners with a continental bent.

Though many locals may claim **Willow Steakhouse** (☎ 209-984-3998; cnr Main & Willow Sts; mains $13-22; 🕑 lunch & dinner Mon-Sat, lunch Sun) is haunted (a number of mine tragedies and murders happened on the site), this popular old watering hole has a dining room that features cheese fondue with all of its meals.

Sierra Nevada

With fierce granite mountains standing watch over high-altitude lakes, the eastern spine of California throws up an exquisite topographical barrier from north to south. When the Sierra Nevada and White Mountain ranges finally drop back down to earth at the basin of Nevada and Death Valley, almost a dozen peaks have topped out over 14,000ft.

An outdoor adventurer's wonderland, the region's a year-round pageant of snow sports, white-water rafting, hiking, biking, backpacking and rock climbing. Skiers and snow boarders explore the hushed pine-tree slopes and suicidal chutes hovering over the glittering blue expanse of Lake Tahoe, or stop to catch their breath as they ascend the southern giant of Mammoth Mountain.

In the majestic national parks of Yosemite and Sequoia and Kings Canyon, visitors will be humbled by the enduring groves of solemn giant sequoias, the ancient rock formations and valleys, and the omnipresent opportunity to see bears and other wildlife.

At the close of the day, you can sooth your soul in a piece of hot-springs heaven, or by the fire of a woodsy 19th-century lodge. Though not a particularly cosmopolitan section of the state, here you'll find plenty of excellent food and entertainment options, especially in South Lake Tahoe, Mammoth Lakes and nearby Reno.

History unfolds here at varying rates of speed: the timelessness of the physical landscape; the presence of its first people, Native American tribes who still call it home; the decomposing ghost towns left behind by California's early white settlers and miners. And now you. Tread lightly.

HIGHLIGHTS

- **Wettest eyeful** Marvel at the springtime waterfall gush at Yosemite National Park (p376).
- **Top stroll to feel small** Gaze heavenward through the celestial sequoia canopies of Sequoia & Kings Canyon National Parks (p391).
- **Most exhilarating downtown transport** Run the rapids at Reno's Truckee River Whitewater Park (p373) by kayak.
- **Most dazzling blue views** Survey the shimmering expanse of blue Lake Tahoe from atop its many ski resorts (opposite).
- **Best Wild West backdrop** Amble around the evocative ghost town of Bodie (p402).

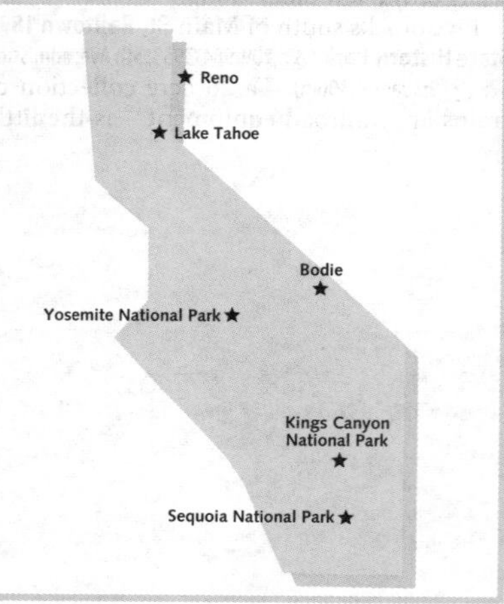

LAKE TAHOE

Shimmering softly in myriad shades of blue and green, Lake Tahoe, which straddles the California–Nevada state line, is one of the most beautiful lakes in the USA and also its second deepest with an average depth of 1000ft. The largest alpine lake in North America, and at 6225ft, it is one of the highest lakes in the country; driving around the lakeshore's 72 miles would give you quite a workout behind the wheel, but also reward you with spellbinding scenery. Generally speaking, the north shore is quiet and upscale, the west shore rugged and old-timey, the east shore undeveloped, and the south shore busy and a tad tacky with aging motels and gaudy casinos.

The sun shines on Tahoe three out of four days in the year, making it ideal for outdoor pursuits of all stripes. Swimming, boating, kayaking, windsurfing and other water-based activities are all popular, as are hiking and camping among the horned peaks around the lake. Winter brings bundles of snow, perfect for hitting the slopes at more than a dozen ski resorts.

Unfortunately, the news isn't all good: the lake is gradually losing its famous clarity. Development, erosion, runoff and air pollution reduce visibility by about 1.5ft every year. Steps are underway to stop this decline, but the challenge is enormous and the future remains murky.

TAHOE SKI AREAS

Lake Tahoe has phenomenal skiing, with thousands of acres of the white stuff beckoning at more than a dozen resorts. These complexes range from the giant, jet-set slopes of Squaw Valley and Heavenly to no less enticing insider playgrounds like Sugar Bowl and Homewood. Tahoe's simply got a hill for everybody, kids to kamikazes. Ski season generally runs November to April, although it can start as early as October with the last storm whipping through in June.

All resorts have ski schools, equipment rental and other facilities as well; check their websites for snow conditions and weather reports. Many also operate shuttle buses.

> **FAST FACTS**
>
> **Population of Reno** 205,300
>
> **Average temperature low/high in Reno** Jan 20/45°F, Jul 48/88°F
>
> **Reno to Truckee** 35 miles, 30 minutes
>
> **Truckee to San Francisco** 185 miles, three to four hours
>
> **Truckee to South Lake Tahoe/Stateline, NV** 40 miles, 1¼ hours
>
> **Reno to Las Vegas** 450 miles, eight hours

Information

Between late fall and early spring, bring snow chains in case a storm rolls in.

California Department of Transportation (Caltrans; ☎ 800-427-7623; www.dot.ca.gov) California road conditions.

Nevada Department of Transportation (NDOT; ☎ 877-687-6237, 511 within Nevada; www.nevadadot.com/traveler/roads) Nevada road conditions.

Sliding on the Cheap (www.slidingonthecheap.com) Personal website listing discounts and bargains on Tahoe lift tickets.

Ski Lake Tahoe (www.skilaketahoe.com) Portal for the seven big resorts, with deals covering all.

Activities

DOWNHILL SKIING & SNOWBOARDING

Truckee & Donner Summit

Sugar Bowl (☎ 530-426-9000; www.sugarbowl.com; Soda Springs/Norden exit off I-80; adult/teen $60/50; 9am-4pm) Cofounded by Walt Disney in 1939, this is one of the oldest ski resorts in the Sierra and a miniature Squaw Valley in terms of variety of terrain, including plenty of exhilarating gullies and chutes. Views are stellar on sunny days, but conditions go downhill pretty quickly, so to speak, during stormy weather. Stats: 12 lifts, 1500 vertical feet, 84 runs. Three miles east of I-80.

Northstar-at-Tahoe (☎ 530-562-1010, 800-466-6784; www.northstarattahoe.com; Hwy 267; adult/child/teen $74/28/64; 8:30am-4pm) An easy 6 miles south of I-80, this hugely popular resort has great intermediate terrain, although advanced and expert skiers can look for challenges on the back of the mountain. Continuing additions to the slick Village Plaza are making it look a lot more like amenity-rich Squaw. Its relatively sheltered location makes it the second-best choice after Homewood (p353) when it's snowing. Weekends get superbusy. Stats: 17 lifts, 2280 vertical feet, 83 runs.

Boreal (☎ 530-426-3666; www.borealski.com; Boreal/Castle off I-80; adult/child day $44/12, night $25/12; 9am-9pm) Boreal is fun for newbies and

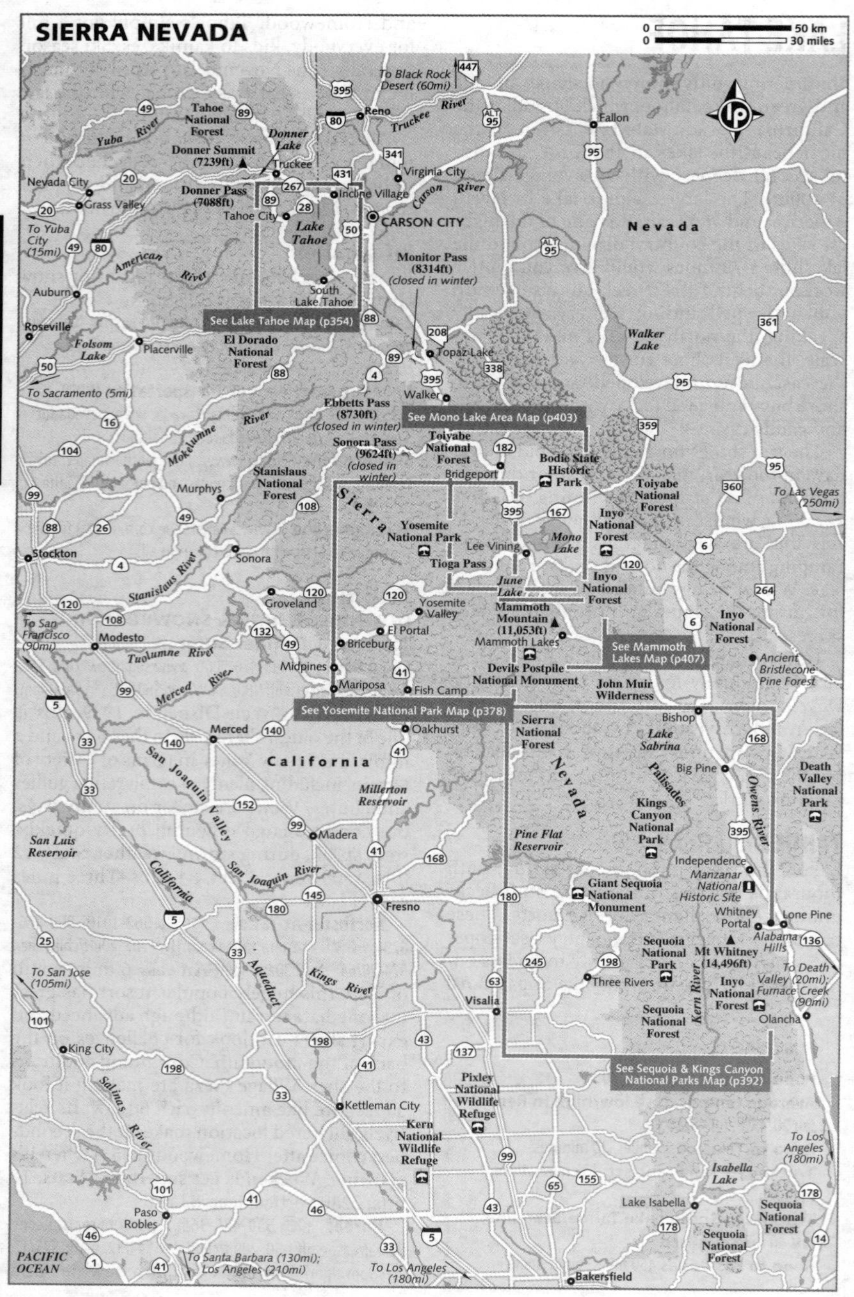
SIERRA NEVADA
0 50 km
0 30 miles
To Black Rock Desert (60mi)
Reno
Truckee River
Fallon
Tahoe National Forest
Yuba River
Donner Lake
Donner Summit (7239ft)
Truckee
Nevada City
Grass Valley
Donner Pass (7088ft)
Incline Village
Virginia City
Carson River
Tahoe City
Lake Tahoe
CARSON CITY
Nevada
To Yuba City (15mi)
American River
Monitor Pass (8314ft) (closed in winter)
Auburn
South Lake Tahoe
See Lake Tahoe Map (p354)
Roseville
Folsom Lake
Placerville
El Dorado National Forest
Topaz Lake
Walker Lake
To Sacramento (5mi)
Walker
Ebbetts Pass (8730ft) (closed in winter)
See Mono Lake Area Map (p403)
Mokelumne River
Sonora Pass (9624ft) (closed in winter)
Toiyabe National Forest
Bridgeport
Bodie State Historic Park
Stanislaus National Forest
Toiyabe National Forest
Murphys
Sierra
Yosemite National Park
Mono Lake
Inyo National Forest
To Las Vegas (250mi)
Lee Vining
Stockton
Sonora
Tioga Pass
Stanislaus River
June Lake
Inyo National Forest
Groveland
Yosemite Valley
Mammoth Mountain (11,053ft)
Inyo National Forest
To San Francisco (90mi)
Modesto
El Portal
Mammoth Lakes
See Mammoth Lakes Map (p407)
Tuolumne River
Briceburg
Devils Postpile National Monument
Ancient Bristlecone Pine Forest
Midpines
Merced River
Mariposa
Fish Camp
John Muir Wilderness
See Yosemite National Park Map (p378)
Oakhurst
Sierra National Forest
Bishop
Merced
Lake Sabrina
California
San Joaquin Valley
Nevada
Palisades
Big Pine
Death Valley National Park
Millerton Reservoir
Kings Canyon National Park
Owens River
San Luis Reservoir
Madera
Pine Flat Reservoir
Independence
California
San Joaquin River
Manzanar National Historic Site
Giant Sequoia National Monument
Fresno
Whitney Portal
Lone Pine
Alabama Hills
To San Jose (105mi)
Aqueduct
Sequoia National Park
Mt Whitney (14,496ft)
Kings River
Three Rivers
Inyo National Forest
To Death Valley (20mi); Furnace Creek (90mi)
Visalia
Sequoia National Forest
Kern River
Olancha
King City
See Sequoia & Kings Canyon National Parks Map (p392)
Pixley National Wildlife Refuge
Salinas River
Kettleman City
Kern National Wildlife Refuge
To Los Angeles (180mi)
Isabella Lake
Lake Isabella
Sequoia National Forest
Paso Robles
Sequoia National Forest
PACIFIC OCEAN
To Santa Barbara (130mi); Los Angeles (210mi)
To Los Angeles (180mi)
Bakersfield

intermediate skiers, and is traditionally the first resort to open in the Tahoe area. For boarders, there are eight terrain parks – the most among Tahoe resorts – plus a competition-level 450ft superpipe. Boreal is the only area resort besides Squaw that offers night skiing. Stats: nine lifts, 500 vertical feet, 41 runs.

Soda Springs (☎ 530-426-3901; www.skisodasprings.com; Soda Springs/Norden exit off I-80; adult/child/teen $28/15/20, tubing $20; 9am-4pm) This cute little resort is a winner with kids. They can snowtube, ride around in pint-sized snowmobiles or try the Kids X Park. Stats: four lifts, 650 vertical feet, 16 runs.

Donner Ski Ranch (☎ 530-426-3635; www.donnerskiranch.com; Soda Springs/Norden exit off I-80; adult/child/teen $38/10/30; 9am-4pm) Generations of skiers have enjoyed this itty-bitty family-owned resort. It's a great place to teach your kids how to ski or for beginners to build their skills. Prices drop midweek. Stats: six lifts, 750 vertical feet, 52 runs. It's 3.5 miles east of I-80 on Donner Pass Rd.

Tahoe Donner (☎ 530-587-9444; www.skitahoedonner.com; Donner State Park exit off I-80; adult/child $35/15; 9am-4pm) Small, low-key and low-tech, Tahoe Donner is a darling resort with family-friendly beginner and intermediate runs only. Stats: three lifts, 600 vertical feet, 14 runs.

Tahoe City

Squaw Valley USA (☎ 530-583-6985, 888-736-9740; www.squaw.com; off Hwy 89; adult/child/teen $73/10/55; 9am-9pm Mon-Fri, 8:30am-9pm Sat & Sun) Few ski hounds can resist the siren call of this mega-sized, world-class, see-and-be-seen resort that hosted the 1960 Winter Olympic Games. Hardcore skiers thrill to white-knuckle cornices, chutes and bowls, while beginners can practice their turns in a separate area on the upper mountain. Stats: 34 lifts, 2850 vertical feet, over 170 runs. Squaw Valley is 5 miles northwest of Tahoe City.

Alpine Meadows (☎ 530-583-4232, 800-441-4423; www.skialpine.com; off Hwy 89; adult/child/teen $58/15/49; 9am-4pm; wi-fi) Alpine is a no-nonsense resort without the fancy village, attitude or crowds. It gets more snow than neighboring Squaw and its open-boundary policy makes it the most backcountry-friendly around. Boarders can jib down the mountain in a terrain park designed by Eric Rosenwald. Also look for the adorable – and supersmart – ski patrol dogs. Stats: 13 lifts, 1802 vertical feet, 100 runs. It's 6 miles northwest of Tahoe City.

Homewood (☎ 530-525-2992, 877-525-7669; www.skihomewood.com; Hwy 89; adult/child/teen Fri-Sun $53/10/35, adult Mon-Thu $39; 9am-4pm) Larger than it looks from the road, this gem 5 miles south of Tahoe City proves that bigger isn't always better. Locals and in-the-know visitors cherish the awesome lake views, laid-back ambience, smaller crowds, tree-lined slopes and open bowls (including the excellent but expert 'Quail Face'). Families love the wide, gentle slopes. This is also the best place to ski during stormy weather, and a new high-speed quad gets things moving. Stats: eight lifts, 1650 vertical feet, 60 runs.

South Lake Tahoe

Heavenly (☎ 775-586-7000, 800-432-8365; www.skiheavenly.com; cnr Wildwood & Saddle; adult/child $78/39; 9am-4pm Mon-Fri, 8:30am-4pm Sat & Sun) The 'mother' of all Tahoe mountains boasts the most acreage, the longest run and the biggest vertical drop in the western USA. Follow the sun by skiing on the Nevada side in the morning, moving to the California side in the afternoon. Views of the lake and the high desert are heavenly indeed. New features include two groomed tree skiing runs and a regraded Skyline Trail that won't strand snowboarders. Stats: 30 lifts, 3500 vertical feet, 94 runs.

Kirkwood (☎ 209-258-6000, 877-547-5966; www.kirkwood.com; Hwy 88; adult/child/teen $69/14/56; 9am-4pm) Off-the-beaten-path Kirkwood, set in a high-elevation valley, gets great snow and holds it longer than any other Tahoe resort. It has stellar tree-skiing, gullies and chutes, and is the only Tahoe resort with backcountry runs accessible by snowcats. Novice out-of-bounds skiers should check out the backcountry safety-skills clinics. Stats: 14 lifts, 2000 vertical feet, 68 runs. It's 35 miles southwest of South Lake Tahoe via Hwy 89.

Sierra-at-Tahoe (☎ 530-659-7453; www.sierraattahoe.com; Hwy 50; adult/child/teen $65/16/55; 9am-4pm Mon-Fri, 8:30am-4pm Sat & Sun) Sierra, 12 miles southwest of South Lake Tahoe, is snowboarding central with six raging terrain parks and a 17ft-high superpipe. A great beginners' run meanders gently for 2.5 miles from the summit, but there are also gnarly steeps and chutes for speed demons. Stats: 12 lifts, 2212 vertical feet, 46 runs.

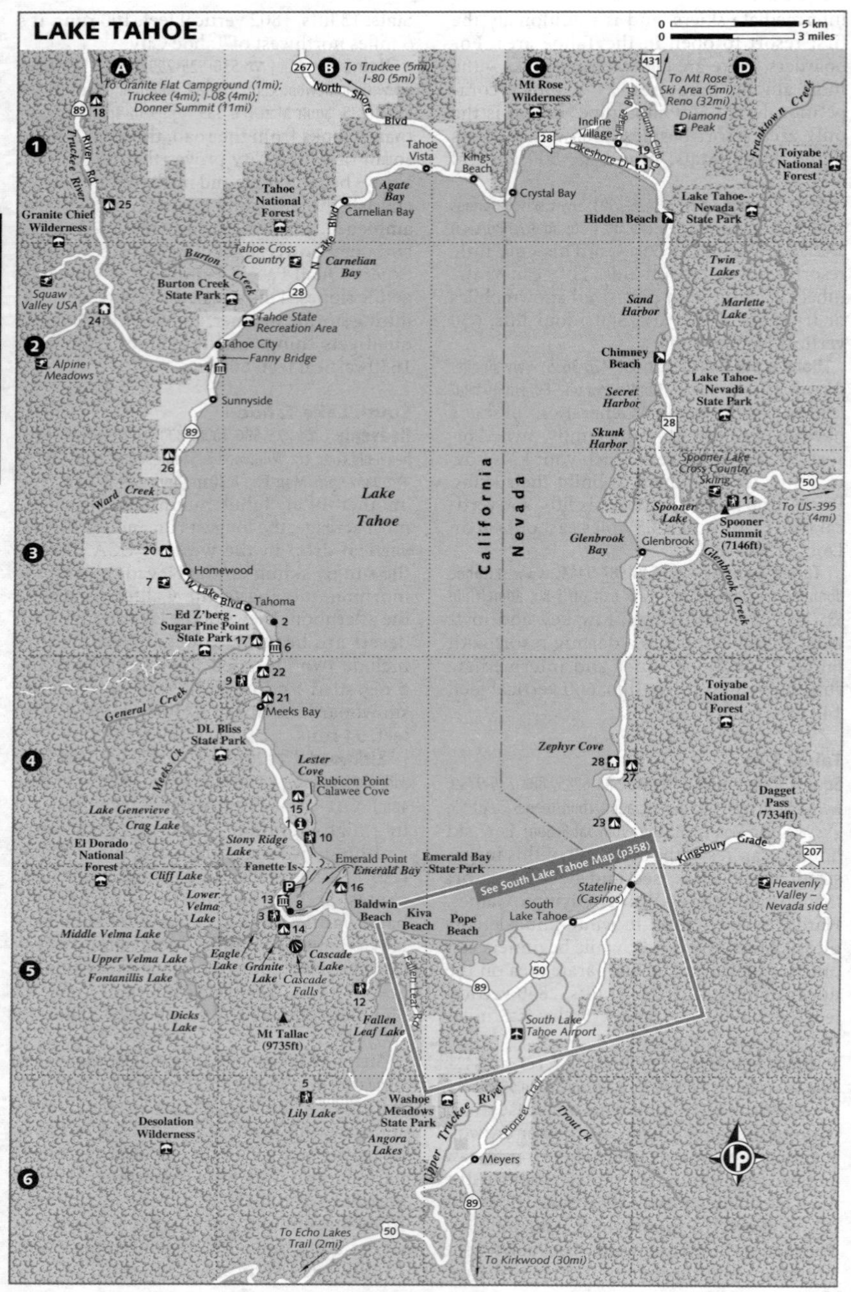
LAKE TAHOE
To Granite Flat Campground (1mi); Truckee (4mi); I-08 (4mi); Donner Summit (11mi)
To Truckee (5mi); I-80 (5mi)
North Shore Blvd
Mt Rose Wilderness
To Mt Rose Ski Area (5mi); Reno (32mi)
Diamond Peak
Incline Village
Lakeshore Dr
Tahoe Vista
Kings Beach
Crystal Bay
Agate Bay
Carnelian Bay
Tahoe National Forest
Granite Chief Wilderness
Toiyabe National Forest
Lake Tahoe-Nevada State Park
Hidden Beach
Tahoe Cross Country
Burton Creek
Burton Creek State Park
Squaw Valley USA
Tahoe State Recreation Area
Tahoe City
Fanny Bridge
Alpine Meadows
Sunnyside
Twin Lakes
Marlette Lake
Sand Harbor
Chimney Beach
Secret Harbor
Skunk Harbor
Ward Creek
Lake Tahoe
California
Nevada
Spooner Lake Cross Country Skiing
Spooner Lake
Spooner Summit (7146ft)
To US-395 (4mi)
Glenbrook Bay
Glenbrook
Glenbrook Creek
Homewood
W Lake Blvd
Tahoma
Ed Z'berg - Sugar Pine Point State Park
General Creek
Meeks Bay
DL Bliss State Park
Meeks Ck
Lester Cove
Rubicon Point
Calawee Cove
Zephyr Cove
Dagget Pass (7334ft)
Lake Genevieve
Crag Lake
El Dorado National Forest
Stony Ridge Lake
Cliff Lake
Fanette Is
Emerald Point
Emerald Bay
Emerald Bay State Park
Kingsbury Grade
See South Lake Tahoe Map (p358)
Stateline (Casinos)
Heavenly Valley - Nevada side
Lower Velma Lake
Middle Velma Lake
Baldwin Beach
Kiva Beach
Pope Beach
South Lake Tahoe
Upper Velma Lake
Fontanillis Lake
Eagle Lake
Granite Lake
Cascade Lake
Cascade Falls
Fallen Leaf Rd
Dicks Lake
Mt Tallac (9735ft)
Fallen Leaf Lake
South Lake Tahoe Airport
Lily Lake
Washoe Meadows State Park
Upper Truckee River
Pioneer Trail
Trout Ck
Desolation Wilderness
Angora Lakes
Meyers
To Echo Lakes Trail (2mi)
To Kirkwood (30mi)

Nevada

Diamond Peak (☎ 775-832-1177; www.diamondpeak.com; 1210 Ski Way, Incline Village; adult/child/teen $48/18/38; 9am-4pm) This midsize mountain is a good place to learn, but experts might get bored quickly. Boarders can romp around the Snowbomb SuperPark. From the top you'll have a 360-degree panorama of desert, peaks and lake. Stats: six lifts, 1840 vertical feet, 31 runs.

Mt Rose (☎ 775-849-0704, 800-754-7673; www.skirose.com; 22222 Mt Rose Hwy/Hwy 431; adult/child/teen $64/17/44; 9am-4pm) Mt Rose has Tahoe's highest base elevation (8260ft) and offers good snow conditions well into spring. The newer expert terrain (the Chutes) delivers some screamers along its north-facing steeps. Crowds aren't too bad, but the mountain's exposure means it gets hammered in a storm. Stats: eight lifts, 1800 vertical feet, 60 runs.

CROSS-COUNTRY SKIING

Royal Gorge (☎ 530-426-3871; www.royalgorge.com; Soda Springs/Norden exit off I-80; adult/child Sat & Sun $29/16, Mon-Fri $25/15; 9am-5pm Mon-Fri, 8:30am-5pm Sat & Sun) Cross-country aficionados won't want to pass up a spin around North America's largest resort with its mind-boggling 308km of groomed track crisscrossing some 9000 acres of terrain on 90 trails. It has great skating lanes and diagonal stride tracks and also welcomes telemark skiers and snowshoeing fans. Consider overnighting at one of its two cozy lodges.

Spooner Lake (☎ 775-749-5349; www.spoonerlake.com; adult/child/teen $21/free/10; 9am-5pm) This area, near the junction of Hwys 28 & 50 in Nevada, offers some of the prettiest trails – some around the lake, some through aspen and pine forest, and some through high country with fabulous views. Altogether there are 80km for all levels of expertise and fitness.

Camp Richardson Resort (☎ 530-542-6584; www.camprichardson.com; 1900 Jameson Beach Rd; adult/child $19/12) At this woodsy resort with 35km of groomed track you can ski lakeside or head for the solitude of the Desolation Wilderness (p361). Locals turn out in droves for the Full Moon Ski & Snowshoe Parties, which kick off at the Beacon Bar & Grill (p360).

Tahoe Donner (☎ 530-587-9484; www.tdxc.com; 11509 Northwoods Blvd; adult/child $22/free; 8:30am-5pm, night skiing 5-7pm Wed) Occupying 4800 acres of forest north of Truckee, this is lovely and varied terrain with 114km of groomed tracks covering three track systems and 48 trails. The most beautiful area is the secluded Euer Valley, where a warming hut serves foods on weekends. A 2.5km loop stays open for night skiing.

Clair Tappaan Lodge (☎ 530-426-3632; 19940 Donner Pass Rd; lodge guest/visitor free/$7; 9am-5pm) You can ski right out the door if you're staying at this rustic mountain lodge (p368) on Donner Summit, near Truckee. Its 12km of groomed and tracked trails are great for beginners and intermediate skiers and connect to miles of backcountry skiing.

Tahoe Cross Country (☎ 530-583-5475; www.tahoexc.org; 925 Country Club Dr; adult/10-17yr $21/17; 8:30am-5pm; wi-fi) Run by the nonprofit Tahoe Cross Country Ski Education Association, this center, 3 miles north of Tahoe City, has 65km of groomed tracks (17 trails) winding through lovely forest. Dogs are allowed on two trails. Ask about the free skate clinics.

Northstar-at-Tahoe (☎ 530-562-1010; www.northstarattahoe.com; Hwy 267; adult/child $25/13; 8:30am-5pm) This resort, 6 miles south of I-80, has a highly regarded Nordic and telemark school, making it a great choice for novices. A package

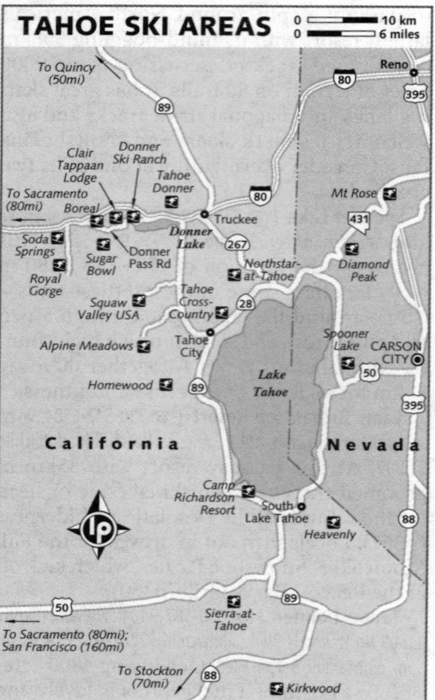

including the trail fee, ski rental and a group lesson is $65. Afterwards you can explore the 40km of groomed trails.

Kirkwood (☎ 209-258-7248; www.kirkwood.com; adult/child under 10 $22/free; 🕑 9am-4pm) Definitely not a jogging trail, Kirkwood's cross-country network has sections that are very challenging and where you can actually gain some elevation. Groomed track stretches for 50 miles, and views from the higher slopes are phenomenal. Dogs are welcome on one ridgeline loop.

SOUTH LAKE TAHOE & STATELINE

pop 27,700 / elev 6254ft

The most developed section around the lake, South Lake Tahoe is a commercial strip bordering the lake and framed by picture-perfect snowy mountains. At the foot of the world-class Heavenly resort and bustling with casinos across the Nevada border in Stateline, this southern area boasts the most tourist infrastructure, drawing visitors looking for lots of lodging and restaurant options, easy access to wintertime mountain runs and 24-hour gambling.

In the summer of 2007, a quick-moving wildfire burned over 3000 acres just south of town.

Orientation

The main east–west thoroughfare is a 5-mile stretch of Hwy 50 called Lake Tahoe Blvd. Most hotels and businesses cluster around the California–Nevada state line and Heavenly Village. Casinos are located in Stateline, which is officially a separate city. All addresses are in South Lake Tahoe unless otherwise noted. West of town, Hwy 50 runs into Hwy 89 at the 'Y' junction. Heavy snowfall sometimes closes Hwy 89 north of the Tallac Historic Site. The section of Hwy 89 between South Lake Tahoe and Emerald Bay, to the west, is also known as Emerald Bay Rd.

Traffic along Hwy 50 gets jammed around noon and 5pm Monday to Friday but winter Sunday afternoons (when skiers head back down the mountain) are the worst. An alternate route through town is Pioneer Trail, which branches east off the Hwy 89/50 junction (south of the 'Y') and reconnects with Hwy 50 at Stateline.

Information

Alpen Sierra Coffee Company (☎ 530-544-7740; 3940 Lake Tahoe Blvd; 🕑 6am-7pm) Coffee shop with free wi-fi and a computer; large selection of organic and fair-trade brews.

Barton Memorial Hospital (☎ 530-541-3420; 2170 South Ave; 🕑 24hr)

Explore Tahoe (☎ 530-542-2908; 4114 Lake Tahoe Blvd, Stateline; 🕑 9am-5pm) Interpretive exhibits and recreational info; site of Stateline Transit Center.

Lake Tahoe Basin Management Unit (☎ 530-543-2600; 35 College Dr; 🕑 8am-4:30pm Mon-Fri) Wilderness permits.

Lake Tahoe Visitors Authority (☎ 800-288-2463; www.bluelaketahoe.com); Stateline (☎ 775-588-4591; 169 Hwy 50; 🕑 9am-5pm); South Lake Tahoe (☎ 530-541-5255; 3066 Lake Tahoe Blvd; 🕑 9am-5pm)

South Lake Tahoe Library (☎ 530-573-3185; 1000 Rufus Allen Blvd; 🕑 Tue-Sat)

USFS Taylor Creek Visitors Center (☎ 530-543-2674; Hwy 89; 🕑 8am-5:30pm mid-Jun–Sep, to 4:30pm Oct) Outdoor information and wilderness permits. It's 3 miles north of the 'Y' junction.

Sights

CASINOS

The siren song of blackjack and slot machines lures the masses across the state line to Nevada. It's no Vegas, but there are plenty of ways to help you part with your paycheck. The main casinos are the **MontBleu**, **Harrah's**, **Horizon** and **Harvey's**, each with live entertainment, multiple restaurants and bars. See p360 for details.

HEAVENLY GONDOLA

Soar to the top of the world as you ride this **gondola** (Heavenly Village; adult/child/teen/senior $30/20/26/26; 9am-4pm Mon-Fri, 8:30am-4pm Sat & Sun winter), which sweeps you from Heavenly Village some 2.4 miles up the mountain in 12 minutes for panoramic views of the entire Tahoe Basin, the Desolation Wilderness and Carson Valley. At the top, a new **zip line** (per trip $30; 10am-3pm) lets you fly through the air for a heady 3100ft.

TALLAC HISTORIC SITE

Three miles north of 'Y', tucked within a pine grove bordering a wide, sandy beach, the **Tallac Historic Site** (530-541-5227; Hwy 89) sits on the grounds of the former Tallac Resort, a super-swish vacation retreat for California high society around the turn of the 20th century.

The **Tallac Museum** (donation requested; 11am-4pm mid-Jun–mid-Sep), inside the Baldwin Estate, has exhibits on the history of the resort and its founder, Elias 'Lucky' Baldwin. There's also the 1894 **Pope Estate**, now used for art exhibits and open for guided tours ($5). The boathouse of the grand **Valhalla Estate** now functions as a theater and concert venue. Other buildings contain a cultural arts store and an art gallery.

The forested grounds serve as a community arts hub and, in summer, host concerts and other events, most notably the three-decade-old **Valhalla Festival of Arts & Music** (530-541-4975; www.valhallatahoe.com; late May-Sep).

LAKE TAHOE HISTORICAL SOCIETY MUSEUM

A small though interesting **museum** (530-541-5458; 3058 Lake Tahoe Blvd; adult/discount $2/1; 10am-3pm Thu-Mon Jun-Aug), it displays items from Tahoe's pioneer past. The modest exhibits include resort artifacts, Washoe Indian baskets and a 150-year-old pipe organ.

Activities

For ski resorts in and around South Lake Tahoe, see p351.

HIKING

Three major trailheads provide easy access to the evocatively named Desolation Wilderness (p361): Echo Lakes (south of town; off Map p354); Glen Alpine (near Lily Lake south of Fallen Leaf Lake; Map p354); and Tallac (near the northwestern end of Fallen Leaf Lake; Map p354). The latter two lead to the peak of Mt Tallac (9735ft), a strenuous 10- to 12-mile day hike. Wilderness permits are required.

SWIMMING

El Dorado Beach is a free public beach in town, just off Lake Tahoe Blvd. The nicest beaches, though, are Pope, Kiva and Baldwin along Emerald Bay Rd (Hwy 89), west and east of the Tallac Historic Site, each with picnic tables and barbecues. Fallen Leaf Lake, where scenes from *The Bodyguard* with Kevin Costner were filmed, is also good for swimming.

BOATING

Ski Run Boat Company (530-544-0200; 900 Ski Run Blvd), at the Ski Run Marina, and **Tahoe Keys Boat & Charter Rentals** (530-544-8888; 2435 Venice Dr), at the Tahoe Keys Marina, both rent powerboats, pontoons and sailboats (from $90 per hour), as well as kayaks, canoes and paddleboats (from $22 per hour). Boat rentals are also available at Camp Richardson (p359) and Zephyr Cove Resort & Marina (p359).

CYCLING & MOUNTAIN-BIKING

The **South Lake Tahoe Bike Path** is a level and leisurely ride suitable for anyone. It heads west from El Dorado Beach (above), eventually connecting with the **Pope-Baldwin Bike Path** to Camp Richardson, the Tallac Historic Site and the Stream Profile Chamber (p359).

For expert mountain-bikers, the classic **Mr Toad's Wild Ride**, with its steep downhill sections and banked turns, should prove sufficiently challenging. Intermediate riders should steer towards the mostly single-track **Powerline Trail**, which traverses ravines and creeks. Anyone with good lungs might try the **Angora Lakes Trail**, which is steep but technically easy and rewards you with sweeping views of Mt Tallac and Fallen Leaf Lake.

Anderson's Bike Rental (530-541-0500; 645 Emerald Bay Rd/Hwy 89), about 1.5 miles north of the 'Y,' rents bikes with helmets.

Local visitors centers carry an excellent Lake Tahoe bike route map.

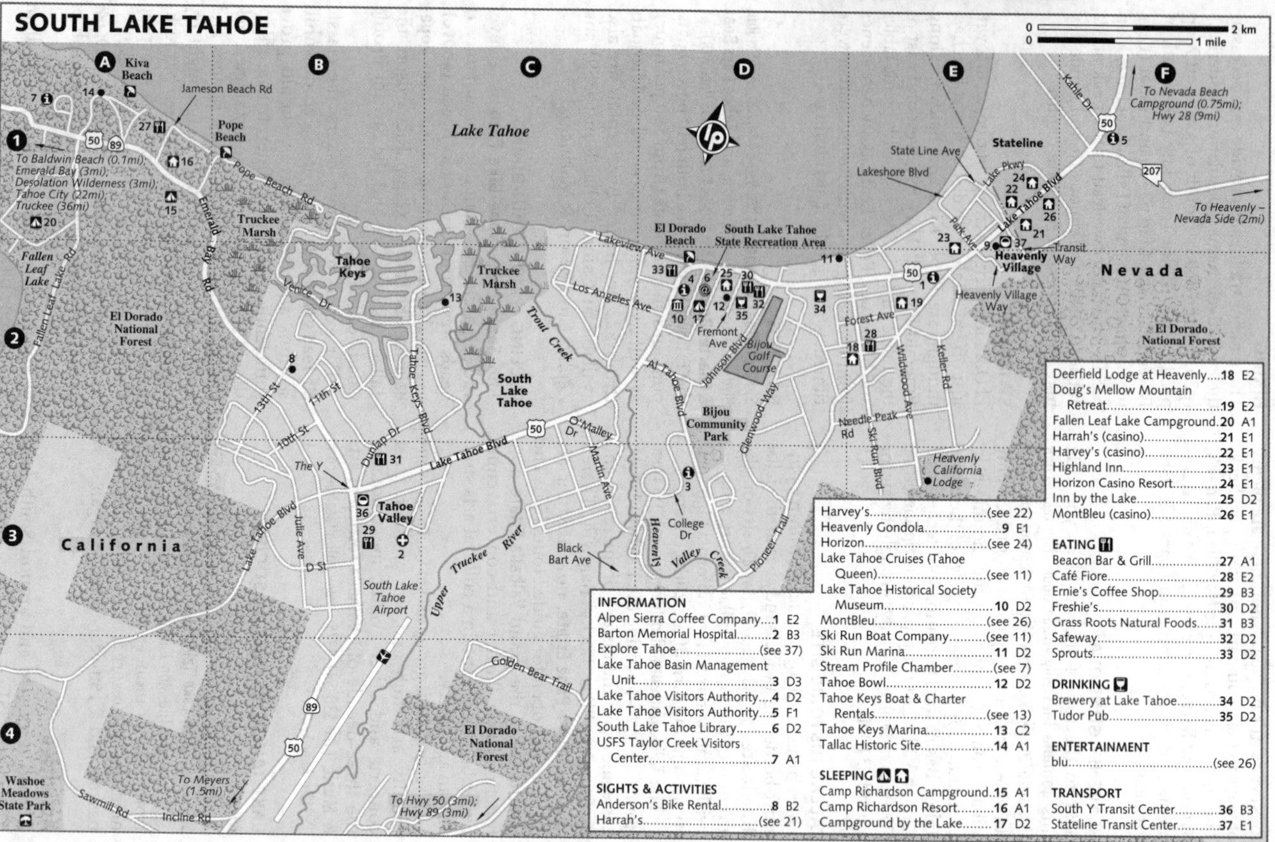
SOUTH LAKE TAHOE
INFORMATION
Alpen Sierra Coffee Company 1 E2
Barton Memorial Hospital 2 B3
Explore Tahoe (see 37)
Lake Tahoe Basin Management Unit 3 D3
Lake Tahoe Visitors Authority 4 D2
Lake Tahoe Visitors Authority 5 F1
South Lake Tahoe Library 6 D2
USFS Taylor Creek Visitors Center 7 A1
SIGHTS & ACTIVITIES
Anderson's Bike Rental 8 B2
Harrah's (see 21)
Harvey's (see 22)
Heavenly Gondola 9 E1
Horizon (see 24)
Lake Tahoe Cruises (Tahoe Queen) (see 11)
Lake Tahoe Historical Society Museum 10 D2
MontBleu (see 26)
Ski Run Boat Company (see 11)
Ski Run Marina 11 D2
Stream Profile Chamber (see 7)
Tahoe Bowl 12 D2
Tahoe Keys Boat & Charter Rentals (see 13)
Tahoe Keys Marina 13 C2
Tallac Historic Site 14 A1
SLEEPING
Camp Richardson Campground 15 A1
Camp Richardson Resort 16 A1
Campground by the Lake 17 D2
Deerfield Lodge at Heavenly 18 E2
Doug's Mellow Mountain Retreat 19 E2
Fallen Leaf Lake Campground 20 A1
Harrah's (casino) 21 E1
Harvey's (casino) 22 E1
Highland Inn 23 E1
Horizon Casino Resort 24 E1
Inn by the Lake 25 D2
MontBleu (casino) 26 E1
EATING
Beacon Bar & Grill 27 A1
Café Fiore 28 E2
Ernie's Coffee Shop 29 B3
Freshie's 30 D2
Grass Roots Natural Foods 31 B3
Safeway 32 D2
Sprouts 33 D2
DRINKING
Brewery at Lake Tahoe 34 D2
Tudor Pub 35 D2
ENTERTAINMENT
blu (see 26)
TRANSPORT
South Y Transit Center 36 B3
Stateline Transit Center 37 E1
Lake Tahoe
California
Nevada
South Lake Tahoe
Stateline
Tahoe Keys
Tahoe Valley
Truckee Marsh
Heavenly Village
El Dorado National Forest
South Lake Tahoe State Recreation Area
Bijou Community Park
Bijou Golf Course
El Dorado Beach
Pope Beach
Kiva Beach
Fallen Leaf Lake
Washoe Meadows State Park
South Lake Tahoe Airport
Heavenly California Lodge
To Nevada Beach Campground (0.75mi); Hwy 28 (9mi)
To Heavenly – Nevada Side (2mi)
To Baldwin Beach (0.1mi); Emerald Bay (3mi); Desolation Wilderness (3mi); Tahoe City (22mi); Truckee (36mi)
To Hwy 50 (3mi); Hwy 89 (3mi)
To Meyers (1.5mi)
Emerald Bay Rd
Lake Tahoe Blvd
Tahoe Keys Blvd
Ski Run Blvd
Pioneer Trail
Upper Truckee River
Trout Creek
Heavenly Valley Creek
The Y
2 km
1 mile

South Lake Tahoe for Children

For yucky-weather days or to tire out the tots by bedtime, the **Tahoe Bowl** (☎ 530-544-3700; 1030 Fremont Ave; game per person $2-5, shoe rental $3; 🕑 2-11pm summer, 11am-11pm winter) is a fun and family-friendly haunt with 16 bowling lanes and a pocket-sized pizza parlor.

A submerged glass structure in a teeming creek, the **Stream Profile Chamber** at the Taylor Creek Visitors Center (p356) lets you check out what plants and fish live below the waterline. The best time to visit is in October during the Kokanee salmon run, when the brilliant red beauties arrive to spawn.

Tours

Two paddle wheelers operated by **Lake Tahoe Cruises** (☎ 530-543-6191, 800-238-2463; www.zephyrcove.com) ply the 'big blue' year-round with a variety of food and sightseeing cruises, including a narrated two-hour trip to Emerald Bay (p361). The *Tahoe Queen* (adult/child/senior $46/20/43) leaves from the Ski Run Marina, right in South Lake Tahoe, while the MS *Dixie II* (adult/child/senior $41/20/38) is based at the Zephyr Cove Resort & Marina (Map p354).

A popular winter option is the ski shuttle to Squaw Valley ($114), which includes a coach trip to the slopes, an all-day lift ticket and a leisurely après-ski party cruise, with live music, back to South Lake Tahoe.

Sleeping

South Lake Tahoe has a bazillion lodging choices suitable for all budgets. Lodging options line Lake Tahoe Blvd (Hwy 50) between Stateline and Ski Run Blvd. Further west, closer to the 'Y,' are various budget motels ranging from barely adequate to inexcusable. Prices listed here are for peak season (generally winter or summer). Some properties may impose minimum rental periods.

BUDGET

Fallen Leaf Lake Campground (☎ info 530-544-0426, reservations 877-444-6777; www.recreation.gov; Fallen Leaf Lake Rd; tent & RV sites $25; 🕑 mid-May–mid-Oct) Near the north shore of stunning Fallen Leaf Lake, this is one of the biggest and most popular campgrounds, with 205 sites. No RV hookups.

Doug's Mellow Mountain Retreat (☎ 530-544-8065; hostelguy@hotmail.com; 3787 Forest Ave; dm $25) The shag carpeting and very lived-in living spaces at this funky 15-bed hostel will either float your boat or give you pause. A private home in a residential neighborhood, it's a laid-back place to chill and meet fellow travelers, with kitchen and laundry facilities available.

Camp Richardson Resort (☎ 530-541-1801, 800-544-1801; www.camprichardson.com; 1900 Jameson Beach Rd; tent sites from $25, RV sites with partial/full hookups from $27/35, r $95-180, cabins $110-250; 🕑 camping May–mid-Oct) A world removed from the downtown strip-mall aesthetic, this sprawling resort is a busy place with lodging options ranging from camping (213 tent-only lakeside and forest sites and a separate area for 110 RVs) to beachside hotel rooms. There's also a full-service marina and a great lakeside restaurant, the Beacon Bar & Grill. To get going, cruise the paved bike trail that runs by the resort (rentals available) and in winter you can cross-country ski right out the door. Wi-fi in lobby.

Zephyr Cove Resort & Marina (Map p354; ☎ 775-588-4907, 800-238-2463; www.zephyrcove.com; 760 Hwy 50; tent sites $29-40, RV sites with hookups $65, cabins from $169; 🕑 camping May-Sep) On the Nevada side, about 4 miles north of Stateline, this is another family-oriented lakeside resort with historic cabins scattered among the pines and similar facilities as Camp Richardson (93 paved RV sites, plus 10 drive-in and 47 walk-in tent sites deeper into the forest). The MS *Dixie II* cruise departs from the marina.

Campground by the Lake (☎ 530-542-6096; www.recreationintahoe.com/campground; 1150 Rufus Allen Blvd; tent sites $23, RV sites without/with electric hookups $23/31; 🕑 Apr-Oct; wi-fi) Highway noise can be an irritant, though proximity to the local pool and ice rink make this woodsy in-town campground a decent choice.

Nevada Beach Campground (☎ info 775-588-5562, reservations 877-444-6777; www.recreation.gov; off Hwy 50, Nevada; tent & RV sites $25-29; 🕑 mid-May–mid-Oct) Bed down on a carpet of pine needles in this pleasant beachfront campground with 54 sites amid Jeffrey pine.

Highland Inn (☎ 530-544-3862; www.highlandlaketahoe.com; 3979 Lake Tahoe Boulevard; r Mon-Fri/Sat & Sun from $59/149; wi-fi) Budget-conscious stylemongers will enjoy this older motel remodeled with contemporary flair. Bright white walls show off artsy prints, and light wood floors, comfy comforters and new plasma TVs make it an altogether pleasant place to lay your head.

MIDRANGE

At the high-rise casino complexes, prices rise and fall like your luck at the slot machines. Season, day of the week and type of room are key. In winter ask about special ski-and-stay packages.

Horizon Casino Resort (☎ 775-588-6211, 800-648-3322; www.horizoncasino.com; 50 Hwy 50, Stateline; r Mon-Fri $50-90, Sat & Sun $200-260;) Diehard Elvis fans can stay in the special suite where the star once boozed and snoozed at this otherwise fairly generic property. Distinctive touches include Tahoe's largest outdoor pool, a huge game arcade and a multiplex movie theater. Wi-fi in lobby.

MontBleu (☎ 775-588-3515, 888-829-7630; www.montbleuresort.com; 55 Hwy 50, Stateline; r $90-240; wi-fi) The public areas now sport a cheery modern boutique decor, but ornate rooms with hedonistic Jacuzzi tubs and a lavish indoor pool accented by a rockscape and waterfalls remind you that this was once Caesars. Catch top-flight entertainers at the theater.

Harrah's (☎ 775-588-6611, 800-427-7247; www.harrahslaketahoe.com; 15 Hwy 50, Stateline; r $99-209; wi-fi) Clad in an oddly tasteful forest-green facade, this is a glitzy contender. Even the standard rooms are spacious and have two (!) bathrooms, each featuring a small TV and telephone. For easy-on-the-eyes views, snag a window table at one of the upper-floor restaurants.

Harvey's (☎ 775-588-2411, 800-745-4320; www.harrahs.com/casinos/harveys-lake-tahoe/hotel-casino; 18 Hwy 50, Stateline; r $109-239;) Harvey's was South Lake Tahoe's first casino, and with 740 rooms, is also its biggest. Lake Tower rooms have fancy marble bathrooms and oodles of space.

Inn by the Lake (☎ 530-542-0330, 800-877-1466; www.innbythelake.com; 3300 Lake Tahoe Blvd; r incl breakfast $148-238; wi-fi) Heaps of bed pillows and standard kitchenettes are just a few of the homey in-room amenities found here, and the bilevel outdoor hot tub and free cruiser bicycle and snowshoe rentals are pretty nifty, too. Rooms are somewhat nondescript yet spotless and comfortable. Those in back are cheaper and quieter, but you'll miss the lake views.

Deerfield Lodge at Heavenly (☎ 888-757-3337; www.tahoedeerfieldlodge.com; 1200 Ski Run Blvd; r/ste incl breakfast $229/329; wi-fi) A small boutique hotel close to Heavenly's California Lodge, all 12 rooms here have a patio or balcony facing out over the green courtyard, kitchenettes, and amusing coat racks crafted from skis and snowboards. Afternoon wine and snacks are complimentary, and barbecue grills are put out in summer.

Eating

For late-night cravings, each of the four big casinos has a 24-hour coffee shop or diner.

Sprouts (☎ 530-541-6969; 3123 Harrison Ave; mains $6-8; 8am-9pm) The cheerful chatter of friendly folks greets you at this energetic and mostly organic natural-foods café that gets extra kudos for its smoothies. The eclectic menu will have you noshing happily on healthy, satisfying soups, rice bowls and sandwiches.

Ernie's Coffee Shop (☎ 530-541-2161; 1207 Hwy 50; mains $7-10; 6am-2pm) A sun-filled local institution, it dishes out filling four-egg omelets, hearty biscuits with gravy and bottomless cups of locally roasted coffee. Toddlers can happily munch the ears off the Mickey Mouse pancake.

Beacon Bar & Grill (☎ 530-541-0630; Camp Richardson Resort, 1900 Jameson Beach Rd; mains lunch $10-13, dinner $23-34; lunch & dinner) Enjoy Lake Tahoe as a front yard, tasty meals and a big wooden deck where bands rock in summer. Try its signature Rum Runner cocktail.

Freshie's (☎ 530-542-3630; 3330 Lake Tahoe Blvd; mains $13-22; lunch & dinner) This local mainstay has exotic Hawaiian looks. From vegans to steak-lovers, nobody should have a problem finding a favorite on the extensive menu: most of the produce is local and organic, and the fish tacos are the best in town.

Café Fiore (☎ 530-541-2908; 1169 Ski Run Blvd; mains $16-31; dinner) Upscale Italian without pretension, this tiny eatery pairs delectable pasta, seafood and meats with an award-winning 300-vintage wine list. Locals and visitors swoon over its rack of lamb, homemade white-chocolate ice cream and near-perfect garlic bread. With only seven tables (13 in summer), reservations are essential.

Self-caterers can stock up at **Grass Roots Natural Foods** (☎ 530-541-7788; 2040 Dunlap Dr) or at **Safeway** (☎ 530-542-7740; 1020 Johnson Blvd).

Drinking & Entertainment

Brewery at Lake Tahoe (☎ 530-544-2739; 3542 Lake Tahoe Blvd) A crazy-popular brewpub pumping its signature Bad Ass Ale into grateful patrons; its restaurant has dynamite barbecue and awesome crab cakes to boot.

DARTING AROUND DESOLATION WILDERNESS

This compact **wilderness area** (Map p354; www.fs.fed.us/r5/eldorado/wild/deso), sculpted by powerful glaciers eons ago, spreads south and west of Lake Tahoe and is the most popular in the Sierra Nevada. It's a 100-sq-mile wonderland of polished granite peaks, deep-blue alpine lakes, glacier-carved valleys and pine forests that thin quickly at the higher elevations. In late spring and summer, wildflowers nudge out from between the rocks.

All this splendor makes for some exquisite backcountry exploration. Six major trailheads provide access from the Lake Tahoe side: Glen Alpine, Tallac, Echo Lakes (the southernmost trailhead), Bayview, Eagle Falls and Meeks Bay. Tallac and Eagle Falls get the most traffic, but solitude comes quickly once you've scampered past the day hikers.

Wilderness permits are required year-round for both day and overnight explorations. Day hikers can self-register at the trailheads, but overnight permits must be picked up at the USFS Taylor Creek Visitor Center or the Lake Tahoe Basin Management Unit, both in South Lake Tahoe (p356). Permits cost $5 per person for one night and $10 per person for two or more nights.

Quotas are in effect from late May to late September. Half of the permits may be reserved for $5 by calling ☎ 530-647-5415 after the third Thursday in April; the other half are available on a first-arrival basis on the day of entry.

Bearproof canisters are compulsory in some areas. Also bring bug repellent as the mosquitoes can be merciless. Wood fires are a no-no, but portable stoves are OK.

Tudor Pub (☎ 530-541-6603; 1041 Fremont Ave) With Boddingtons on tap, fish-and-chips on the menu and a dart board on the wall, this dark and bustling pub wouldn't look out of place in Lancashire.

blu (☎ 775-586-2000; MontBleu casino, 15 Hwy 50, Stateline) With booths and beds stocked with furry pillows, this Top 40 and techno dance club draws a young party crowd that enjoys getting an in-house body painting.

Getting There & Around

South Lake Tahoe's two main transportation hubs are the South Y Transit Center, just south of the 'Y,' and the Stateline Transit Center in Heavenly Village. Amtrak Thruway buses to Sacramento stop at both locations daily ($33, 2½ hours), but can only be boarded in conjunction with a train ticket.

South Tahoe Express (☎ 866-898-2463; www.southtahoeexpress.com; one way/round-trip $24/43) runs 11 daily buses from area casinos to the Reno/Tahoe International Airport; the journey takes at least 1½ hours.

BlueGO (☎ 530-541-7149; www.bluego.org) local buses operate year-round from 6am to 1am daily, stopping all along Hwy 50 between the South Y Transit Center and Stateline. Rides cost $1.75. BlueGO also operates casino shuttles ($1.75) and a reservable on-demand shuttle with services to anywhere within South Lake Tahoe ($3).

From mid-June to early September, BlueGO's Nifty Fifty Trolley barrels along two loop routes between 9am and 7pm: from the Stateline Transit Center to Zephyr Cove and from the 'Y' to Camp Richardson, with onward connections to Emerald Bay. A day pass costs $5. In winter, BlueGO provides free and frequent shuttle service to all Heavenly base operations every 20 to 30 minutes from stops along Hwy 50.

Amtrak (☎ 800-872-7245; www.amtrak.com) has bus service between Sacramento and South Lake Tahoe (2½ hours), though tickets must be purchased as part of a train journey.

WESTERN SHORE

Lake Tahoe's densely forested western shore, between Emerald Bay and Tahoe City, is blissfully free of major development. Hwy 89 sinuously wends past gorgeous state parks with swimming beaches, easy trails, pine-shaded campgrounds and fanciful historic mansions. Several trailheads access the rugged splendor of the Desolation Wilderness. Note that campgrounds and many businesses here close between November and May, and Hwy 89 often closes for plowing with heavy snowfall.

Emerald Bay State Park

Sheer granite cliffs and a jagged shoreline hem in glacier-carved **Emerald Bay** (☎ 530-541-3030; www.parks.ca.gov; day-use fee $6; ⏲ late May-Sep), a teardrop cove that will get you digging for your camera. Its most captivating aspect is the water, which changes from cloverleaf green to light jade depending on the angle of the sun.

SIGHTS

There are plenty of pullouts along Hwy 89, including one at **Inspiration Point**. Just to the south of here, the road shoulder evaporates on both sides of a steep drop-off, revealing a perfect panoramic view of Emerald Bay to the north and Cascade Lake to the south.

The mesmerizing blue-green waters frame the impeccably placed **Fannette Island**. This uninhabited granite speck, the only island in Lake Tahoe, holds the vandalized remains of a tiny 1920s house formerly used as a 'tea house' for heiress Lora Knight, who would occasionally motorboat guests to the island from **Vikingsholm Castle** (tours adult/child $5/3; 10am-4pm late May-Sep), her Scandinavian-style mansion on the bay. The focal point of the state park, Vikingsholm Castle is a rare example of ancient Scandinavian-style architecture in these parts. Completed in 1929, it has trippy design elements aplenty, including sod-covered roofs that sprout wildflowers in late spring. The mansion is reached by a steep 1-mile trail, which also leads to a visitors center.

Visitors can reach the island by boat from July through December; Canadian geese take up residence during the rest of the year. The nearest boat rentals are in Meeks Bay (opposite) and South Lake Tahoe (p357). From the latter you can also catch a narrated bay cruise (p359).

ACTIVITIES

Two trailheads lead from Emerald Bay into the Desolation Wilderness (see the boxed text, p361). Starting at the Eagle Falls parking lot ($5), the **Eagle Falls Trail** travels one steep mile to Eagle Lake, crossing by Eagle Falls along the way. This scenic short hike often gets choked with visitors, but crowds thin out immediately beyond the lake as the trail continues to the Tahoe Rim Trail and Velma, Dicks and Fontanillis Lakes.

The **Tahoe Rim Trail** (☎ 775-298-0012; www.tahoerimtrail.org) wraps 165 miles around the lofty ridges and mountaintops of the Lake Tahoe Basin. Hikers, equestrians and – in some sections – mountain-bikers can enjoy inspirational views of the lake and the snowcapped Sierra Nevada while tracing the footsteps of early pioneers, Basque shepherds and the Washoe people. The drone of car traffic can be an occasional nuisance.

From the Bayview Trailhead at the back of the Bayview Campground, it's a steep 1-mile climb to glacial **Granite Lake** at the foot of Maggies Peaks. The less ambitious might want to opt for the easy to moderate 1.5-mile round-trip to **Cascade Falls**.

Vikingsholm Castle serves as the southern terminus of the famous Rubicon Trail (see below).

SLEEPING

Bayview Campground (tent & RV sites $15; Jun-Sep) This rustic USFS campground has 13 first-arrival sites and vault toilets, but its potable water supplies are often exhausted in July. It's off Hwy 89 across from Inspiration Point.

Eagle Point Campground (☎ 530-525-7277, 800-444-7275; www.reserveamerica.com; tent & RV sites $20-25; mid-Jun–early Sep) Perched on the tip of Eagle Point, this campground has flush toilets, hot pay showers, beach access and views of the bay.

DL Bliss State Park

Emerald Bay State Park spills over into **DL Bliss State Park** (☎ 530-525-7277; www.parks.ca.gov; day-use fee $6; late May-Sep), which has the western shore's nicest beaches at Lester Cove and Calawee Cove. A short nature trail leads to the **Balancing Rock**, a 130-ton chunk of granite perched on a rocky pedestal. Pick up information from the **visitors center** (8am-5pm) by the park entrance.

Near Calawee Cove is the trailhead of the scenic **Rubicon Trail**, which ribbons along the lakeshore for 4.5 mostly gentle miles to Vikingsholm Castle in Emerald Bay State Park. It leads past an old lighthouse and small coves for taking a cooling dip, treating you to great views along the way.

If you don't want to backtrack, you'll need to arrange for a vehicle to be parked at Emerald Bay as there is no public transportation between the two parks. Also note that it's another steep 1 mile up from the castle to the parking lot on Hwy 89.

The small parking lot at Calawee Cove usually fills up by 10am, in which case it's a 2-mile walk from the park entrance to the beach. Or ask at the ranger station by the entrance for closer access points to the Rubicon Trail.

SNOWSHOEING UNDER THE STARS

A crisp quiet night with a blazing glow across the lake. What could be more magical than a snowshoe tour under a full moon? Reserve ahead, as ramblings at these locations are very popular:

- **Ed Z'Berg–Sugar Pine Point State Park** (below)
- **Northstar-at-Tahoe** (p351)
- **Kirkwood** (p356)
- **Squaw Valley USA** (p353)

The park's **campground** (☎ 800-444-7275; www.reserveamerica.com; tent & RV sites $25-35; 🕑 Jun–mid-Sep) has 168 sites, including some supercoveted spots near the beach, along with flush toilets and hot pay showers.

Meeks Bay

pop 150

This sleek, shallow bay with a wide sweep of shoreline has warm water by Tahoe standards and is fringed by a beautiful, but busy, sandy beach. There's a trailhead for the Desolation Wilderness on the west side of the highway, a few hundred feet north of the fire station. From here a moderate, nicely shaded path parallels Meeks Creek on its way to swimmable Lake Genevieve (4.5 miles) and other Desolation Wilderness ponds.

Meeks Bay Campground (☎ 877-444-6777; www.recreation.gov; tent & RV sites $20; 🕑 mid-May–Oct) has 38 sites along the beach and flush toilets. For showers head to the adjacent Washoe-operated **Meeks Bay Resort** (☎ 530-525-6946, 877-326-3357; www.meeksbayresort.com; 7941 Emerald Bay Rd; tent site $25, RV site with full hookups $45, 2-/6-person cabins $200/375; 🕑 May-Oct), which offers various lodging options plus kayak and boat rentals. Minimum stays apply for cabins.

Ed Z'berg-Sugar Pine Point State Park

Ten miles south of Tahoe City, this **state park** (☎ 530-525-7982; www.parks.ca.gov; day-use fee $6) occupies a promontory blanketed by a fragrant mix of pine, juniper, aspen and fir. It has a swimming beach, hiking trails, abundant fishing in General Creek and, in winter, 20km of groomed cross-country trails. A paved bike path travels north to Tahoe City and Squaw Valley.

Nonnatural sights include the modest 1860 **cabin** of William 'General' Phipps, an early Tahoe settler, and the considerably grander 1903 Queen Anne–style **Hellman-Ehrman Mansion** (tours adult/child $5/3; 🕑 11am-4pm late May-Sep). Guided tours take in the richly detailed interior, including marble fireplaces, leaded-glass windows and period furnishings. This elegant lakefront house is also known as Pine Lodge.

The secluded **General Creek campground** (☎ 800-444-7275; www.reserveamerica.com; tent & RV sites $20-25; 🕑 year-round) has 175 fairly spacious, pine-shaded sites, plus flush toilets and hot pay showers.

Tahoma

pop 1065

Tahoma has a post office as well as number of places to stay and eat

Cute but not too kitschy, the red cabins of **Tahoma Meadows B&B Cottages** (☎ 530-525-1553, 866-525-1533; www.tahomameadows.com; 6821 W Lake Blvd; cottages incl breakfast $95-250, with kitchen $145-350; wi-fi) dot a pine grove. Each has classy country decor, thick down comforters, a small TV and bathrooms with clawfoot tubs. Be prepared for a big stuffed animal waiting on your bed and an in-room journal to record your impressions.

The lakeside **Chamber's Landing** (☎ 530-525-7262; 6300 W Lake Blvd; mains $20-37; 🕑 Jun-Sep) serves up fancy Mediterranean cuisine, but the biggest crowds descend for drinks and appetizers in the all-day bar, especially during Happy Hour (5pm to 7pm). Try a 'Chamber's Punch,' the signature cocktail.

The **PDQ Market** (☎ 530-525-7411; 🕑 6:30am-10pm) has groceries and a deli.

Homewood

pop 280

Popular with summertime boaters and wintertime skiers and snowboarders at Homewood Mountain (p353), Homewood also provides good backcountry ski access to Desolation Wilderness via Black Canyon (marked from Hwy 89). **West Shore Sports** (☎ 530-525-9920; 5395 W Lake Blvd) is a good spot for bike, kayak and snow-sports rentals.

The nearest campground is the nine-site, tent-only **Kaspian Campground** (☎ 877-444-6777; www.recreation.gov; tent sites $15-17; 🕑 late May-Sep), with flush toilets. It's around 1.5 miles north of Homewood.

Oriental rugs and Arts and Crafts decor give the luxurious new six-room **West Shore Café & Inn** (☎ 530-525-5200; www.westshorecafe.com; 5160 W Lake Blvd; r/ste incl breakfast from $275/550; wi-fi) a classic, aged feel, and the lake's so close you feel like you could dive in. Suites are decadent, with a fireplace, balcony and two bathrooms. In the restaurant, (dinner mains $32 to $55; open lunch and dinner summer, dinner only rest of year) chef Jayson Poe whips up French and California cuisine using local produce. It's across the street from Homewood Mountain.

Stop in for chicken fried steak, the ski patrol special, or some excellent French toast, bacon burgers or shakes at **Old Tahoe Café** (☎ 530-525-5437; 5335 W Lake Blvd; mains $7-11; 7am-2pm summer & winter, 8am-2pm fall & spring). A cheery yellow and blue diner, it's popular with skiers and summertime boaters, who tie up at the marina across the street.

Sunnyside

Sunnyside is a blink-and-you've-missed-it hamlet with two great restaurants.

For breakfast, head to the **Fire Sign Café** (☎ 530-583-0871; 1785 W Lake Blvd; mains under $10; 7am-3pm) for good omelets, pancakes, fresh pastries and other carbo-bombs.

Sunnyside Steakhouse & Lodge (☎ 530-583-7200; www.sunnysideresort.com; 1850 W Lake Blvd; mains lunch $11-14, dinner $24-35; wi-fi) offers classic and innovative takes on steak and seafood in its fine dining room (reservations required). In summer you'll probably have more fun doing lunch – or drinks with its signature zucchini sticks – on the huge lakefront deck. The 23 rooms with lake views ooze Old Tahoe flair (room including breakfast $135 to $335).

To work it off, rent a bicycle from **Cyclepaths** (☎ 530-581-1171; 1785 W Lake Blvd), where you can get the scoop on all sorts of local outdoor information.

TAHOE CITY

pop 1760 / elev 6240ft

The north shore's commercial hub, Tahoe City straddles the junction of Hwys 89 and 28 and is handy for grabbing food supplies and renting less expensive snow gear. It's also the closest lake town to Squaw Valley USA (p353). N Lake Blvd, the main drag, has all the outfitters, boutiques and restaurants you might need.

Information

Bookshelf (☎ 530-581-1900; 760 N Lake Blvd, Boatworks Mall) Great indie bookstore.

Tahoe City Library (☎ 530-583-3382; 740 N Lake Blvd; Tue-Sat) Free internet.

Visitors center (☎ 530-581-6900, 800-824-6348; 380 N Lake Blvd; 9am-5pm) Next to the fire station.

Sights

Just south of the Hwy 89/28 junction, the Truckee River flows through floodgates and passes beneath **Fanny Bridge**, cutely named for the most prominent feature of people leaning over the railings to look at fish – their fanny (or rear end). In a reconstructed log cabin nearby, the **Gatekeeper's Museum** (☎ 530-583-1762; 130 W Lake Blvd/Hwy 89; adult/child/senior $3/1/2; 11am-5pm Wed-Sun May–mid-Jun & Sep, daily mid-Jun–Aug, 11am-3pm Sat & Sun Oct-Apr) has a great collection of Tahoe memorabilia, and, in a new wing, an exquisite array of Native American baskets. A few blocks east and now used as a gift shop, the 1908 **Watson Cabin** (☎ 530-583-1762; 560 N Lake Tahoe Blvd; noon-4pm Jun-Aug) is one of the town's oldest buildings.

Activities

Though not an outstanding swimming area, **Commons Beach** is a small, attractive park with sandy and grassy areas as well as picnic benches, barbecues, and a climbing rock and playground for kids.

Hikers should explore the fabulous trails of the **Granite Chief Wilderness** north and west of Tahoe City. For maps and trailhead directions, stop by the visitors center or the outfitters listed at the end of this section. Recommended day hikes include the moderately strenuous **Five Lakes Trail** (round-trip 5 miles) and the easy trek to **Paige Meadows** (leading on to the Tahoe Rim Trail). Paige Meadows is also good terrain for novice mountain-bikers and for snowshoeing. Wilderness permits are not required, even for overnight trips, but campfire permits are needed for gas stoves or wood fires.

The paved 6-mile **Truckee River Bike Trail** runs between Tahoe City and Squaw Valley. It's easy, but expect crowds on summer weekends.

The Truckee River itself is gentle and wide as it flows northwest from the lake – perfect for novice rafters who like to drag a six-pack behind the boat. **Truckee River Raft Rentals** (☎ 530-583-0123; 185 River Rd; adult/child $35/30; 8:30am-3:30pm Jun-Sep) rents rafts for the 5-mile float from Tahoe City to the River

Ranch Lodge, including transportation back to town. For more challenging white-water runs, see p367.

Good outfitters:

Porters of Tahoe City (☎ 530-583-2314; 501 N Lake Blvd)

Tahoe City Bikes (☎ 530-581-5861; 690 N Lake Blvd) Bike rentals.

Tahoe Dave's (☎ 530-583-6415; www.tahoedaves.com; 590 N Lake Tahoe Blvd) Additional branches at Squaw Valley, Kings Beach and Truckee; rentals can be returned to any shop.

Sleeping

Mother Nature's Inn (☎ 530-581-4278, 800-558-4278; www.mothernaturesinn.com; 551 N Lake Blvd; r $65-150) Right in town behind the Cabin Fever knick-knack boutique, this good-value option offers quiet motel-style rooms with a tidy country look, fridges, eclectic furniture and comfy pillow-top mattresses. Some rooms are pet-friendly.

Pepper Tree Inn (☎ 530-583-3711, 800-624-8590; www.peppertreetahoe.com; 645 N Lake Blvd; r Mon-Fri $107-152, Sat & Sun $152-197; wi-fi) The tallest building in town – you can't miss this somberly painted establishment with birds'-eye lake views. Comfortable modern rooms have microwave, fridge and coffeemaker, with top-floor rooms most in demand.

River Ranch Lodge (☎ 530-583-4264, 866-991-9912; www.riverranchlodge.com; Hwy 89 at Alpine Meadows Rd; r incl breakfast $115-200) Drift off to dreamland as the Truckee River tumbles below your window at this delightful inn. Rooms bulge with character and feature either elegant antiques or classy lodgepole-pine furniture, and upstairs rooms have splendid balconies.

For camping head north to the three USFS campgrounds off Hwy 89 (p368) or 2 miles south to **William Kent Campground** (☎ 877-444-6777; www.recreation.gov; tent & RV sites $20; mid-May–mid-Oct), where the 94 nicely shaded, but cramped, sites often fill up. Amenities include flush toilets and beach access.

Eating

Stony Ridge Uncommon Kitchen (☎ 530-583-3663; 505 W Lake Blvd; dishes $7-10; 11am-7pm Mon-Fri, 9am-6pm Sat & Sun; V) Tucked away in the New Moon Natural Foods store, this deli concocts scrumptious ethnic food to go, all packaged in biodegradable and compostable containers. Try the Thai salad with organic greens and spicy peanut sauce, or the hand-rolled sushi.

Sol y Lago (☎ 530-583-0358; 760 N Lake Blvd; tapas $8-11, mains $12-27; lunch summer, dinner year-round) Feast on tapas and Latin cocktails in a romantic solarium dining room with a dynamite lake view, and save room for some rich *tres leches* cake. Upstairs at the Boatworks Mall.

River Ranch Lodge (☎ 530-583-4264; Hwy 89 at Alpine Meadows Rd; mains lunch $11-14, dinner $20-32) This riverside place is a popular stop, drawing rafters and bikers to its patio for festive summer barbecue lunches. Dinner is a meat-heavy gourmet affair, with rotating standouts like filet mignon and roasted duck.

Also recommended:

Syd's Bagelry (☎ 530-583-2666; 550 N Lake Blvd; bagels $1-3.50, sandwiches $5-7; 6am-6pm winter, to 9pm summer; wi-fi) A central spot serving bagels and fair-trade coffee, plus smoothies and fresh homemade soups (often vegan) made with organic produce.

Rosie's Cafe (☎ 530-583-8504; 571 N Lake Blvd; breakfast & lunch $8-12, dinner $14-18; 7:30am-9pm) Decorated with shiny bikes, antique skis and lots of pointy antlers, this quirky place serves breakfast until 2:30pm.

Getting There & Around

With the sauciest damn acronym and very reliable service, **Tahoe Area Rapid Transit** (TART; ☎ 530-550-1212, 800-736-6365; www.laketahoetransit.com; approx 6:30am-6:30pm) operates buses along the northern shore as far as Incline Village, south along the western shore to Sugar Pine Point State Park (June through September only) and to Truckee via Hwy 89. Tickets cost $1.50 each or $3.50 for an all-day pass.

From June to early September, TART also operates Tahoe Trolley, a free local bus service that does loops within Tahoe City and another that runs between Crystal Bay and Tahoe Vista.

SQUAW VALLEY USA

The nirvana of the north shore, Squaw Valley USA was host to the 1960 Olympic Winter Games and still ranks among the world's top ski resorts (also see p353). The stunning setting amid granite peaks, though, makes it a superb destination in any season. The village at the mountain base is about a 15- to 20-minute drive from Tahoe City or Truckee via Hwy 89 (turn off at Squaw Valley Rd).

Much of the action centers on 8200ft **High Camp**, reached by a dizzying cable car ($20), which has an outdoor **ice-skating rink** (with/without cable-car ride incl skates $26/10) and a heated outdoor **swimming lagoon** (with/without cable-car ride $27/12;

SIERRA NEVADA

Mar–mid-Sep). Your cable-car ticket also includes admission to the **Olympic Museum**, which relives magic moments from 1960. Discounts are available for children, teens and seniors, and prices go down after 5pm.

Several hiking trails radiate out from High Camp, or try the lovely, moderate **Shirley Lake Trail** (round-trip 5 miles), which follows a sprightly creek to waterfalls, granite boulders and abundant wildflowers. It starts at the mountain base, near the end of Squaw Peak Rd, behind the cable-car building.

Fun activities down below include a ropes course, a climbing wall ($14) and a Sky Jump (a bungee trampoline), all operated by the **Squaw Valley Adventure Center** (530-583-7673; www.squawadventure.com). Tee up at the 18-hole, par 71, Scottish-style links **Resort at Squaw Creek Golf Course** (800-327-3353; greens fee $110-115).

For lodging information, call **central reservations** (800-545-4350). The nicest accommodation is **PlumpJack Squaw Valley Inn** (530-583-1576, 800-323-7666; www.plumpjack.com; 1920 Squaw Valley Rd; r incl breakfast summer $169-199, winter Mon-Fri/Sat & Sun from $249/349; wi-fi), an artsy, almost whimsical boutique hotel in the village. Each room has mountain views and comfort factors like plush terry-cloth robes. The elegant restaurant (dinner mains $21 to $30; open lunch and dinner, breakfast for guests), with its crisp linens and charcoal banquettes, serves masterful Mediterranean cuisine and great wines.

For a social bite after shedding your bindings, **Le Chamois** (pizzas from $10; 11am-7pm Mon-Fri, to 8pm Sat & Sun), right between the cable-car building and the rental shop, is a slopeside favorite. Slide on over to devour pizza and beer with eye-pleasing mountain views.

Other good food spots:

Sierra Sunrise Biscuit Company (mains $7-9; 8am–cable-car closing) Fresh-baked buttermilk 'biskwiches' make great breakfasts or snacks at this to-go counter in the cable-car building.

Mamasake (530-584-0110; mains $10-17; noon-10pm-ish) In the village, try sushi rolls at shellacked futuristic tables; $5 hand roll and beer special during happy hour (3pm to 5pm).

TRUCKEE & DONNER LAKE

pop 15,700 / elev 5840ft

Cradled by mountains and the Tahoe National Forest, Truckee is a thriving town steeped in Old West history. It was put on the map by the railroad, grew rich on logging and ice harvesting, and even had its brush with Hollywood during the 1924 filming of Charlie Chaplin's *The Gold Rush*. Today tourism fills much of the city's coffers, thanks to a well-preserved historical downtown and its proximity to Lake Tahoe and world-class ski resorts.

West of Truckee, 3-mile-long Donner Lake is a busy recreational hub. The Donner Party (see boxed text, opposite) camped nearby during the fateful winter of 1846. Donner Summit, further west, has six downhill and cross-country ski resorts.

Orientation

Truckee straddles the I-80 and is connected to northern Lake Tahoe via Hwy 89 to Tahoe City and Hwy 267 to Kings Beach. Hwy 267 dead-ends in Truckee's historic and gentrified downtown, also known as Commercial Row. Lined by restaurants, shops and the Amtrak train depot, it is essentially one long block of the town's main drag of Donner Pass Rd, and you must pay for street parking. Most services, gas stations and outfitters are in the modern town about 1.5 miles west along Donner Pass Rd, near the junction with Hwy 89. Brockway Rd begins south of the river across from the visitors center. Donner Memorial State Park and Donner Lake are about another 2 miles further west.

Information

Tahoe Forest Hospital (530-587-6011; cnr Donner Pass Rd & Pine Ave; 24hr) Emergency room.

USFS Ranger Station (530-587-3558; 9646 Donner Pass Rd; 8am-5pm Mon-Sat) Keeps shorter winter hours.

Visitors center (530-587-2757, 866-443-2027; www.truckee.com; 10065 Donner Pass Rd; internet access per 15min $3; 9am-6pm) Inside the Amtrak train depot; free walking-tour maps.

Sights

HISTORIC TRUCKEE

The aura of the Old West still lingers over Truckee's teensy historic downtown, where railroad workers and lumberjacks once milled about in raucous saloons, bawdy brothels and shady gambling halls. Most of the late-19th-century buildings now contain restaurants and upscale boutiques. The **Old Jail** (530-582-0893; cnr Jiboom & Spring Sts; suggested donation $2; 11am-4pm Sat & Sun late May-early Sep), in use until the 1960s, is filled with relics from the wild days of yore, and George

THE DONNER PARTY

In the 19th century, tens of thousands of people migrated west along the Overland Trail with dreams of a better life in California. Among them was the ill-fated Donner Party.

When the families of George and Jacob Donner and their friend James Reed departed Springfield, Illinois, in April 1846 with six wagons and a herd of livestock, they intended to make the arduous journey as comfortable as possible. But the going was slow and, when other pioneers told them about an alternate trail that would save 200 miles, they jumped at the chance.

However, there was no road for the wagons in the Wasatch Mountains, and most of the livestock succumbed under the merciless heat of the barren 80-mile Great Salt Lake Desert. Arguments and fights broke out. James Reed killed a man, was kicked out of the group and left to trundle off to California alone. By the time the party reached the eastern foot of the Sierra Nevada, near present-day Reno, morale and food supplies ran dangerously low. To restore energies and provisions, they decided to rest for a week.

But an exceptionally fierce winter came early, quickly rendering Donner Pass impassable and forcing the pioneers to build basic shelter near Donner Lake. They had food to last a month and the fervent hope that the weather would clear by then. It didn't.

Snow fell for weeks, reaching a depth of 22ft. Hunting and fishing became impossible. In mid-December a small group of people made a desperate attempt to cross the pass. They quickly became disoriented and had to ride out a three-day storm that killed four of them. One month later, less than half of the original 15 staggered into Sutter's Fort near Sacramento, having survived on one deer and their dead friends.

By the time the first rescue party arrived at Donner Lake in late February, the trapped pioneers were still surviving – barely – on boiled ox hides. But when the second rescue party, led by the banished James Reed, made it through in March, evidence of cannibalism was everywhere. Journals and reports tell of 'half-crazed people living in absolute filth, with naked, half-eaten bodies strewn about the cabins.' Many were too weak to travel. When the last rescue party arrived in mid-April, only a sole survivor, Lewis Keseberg, was there to greet them. The rescuers found George Donner's body cleansed and wrapped in a sheet, but no sign of Tasmen Donner, George's wife. Keseberg admitted to surviving on the flesh of those who had died, but denied charges that he had killed Tasmen for fresh meat. He spent the rest of his life trying to clear his name. In the end, only 47 of the 89 members of the Donner Party survived. They settled in California, their lives forever changed by the harrowing winter at Donner Lake.

SIERRA NEVADA

'Machine Gun' Kelly was reportedly once held here for shoplifting at a local store.

DONNER LAKE

Warmer than Lake Tahoe, tree-lined Donner Lake is great for swimming, boating, fishing (license required), waterskiing and windsurfing. **West End Beach** (adult/child $3/2) is popular with families for its volleyball, basketball, snack stand and roped-off swimming area.

On the lake's eastern end, **Donner Memorial State Park** (☎ 530-582-7892; www.parks.ca.gov; vehicle fee $6) occupies one of three sites where the Donner Party got trapped (see boxed text, above). Though its history is gruesome, the park is lovely and has a nice campground (p368), a sandy beach with picnic tables, hiking trails and, in winter, cross-country ski trails.

The vehicle fee includes admission to the excellent **Emigrant Trail Museum** (☎ 530-582-7892; admission $6; 9am-4pm, longer hr possible Jun-Aug), which has exhibits and a 25-minute film reenacting the Donner Party's horrific plight, and is slated for a major revamping soon. Outside, the **Pioneer Monument** has a 22ft pedestal – the exact depth of the snow that fateful winter. A short trail leads to a memorial at one family's cabin site.

Activities

Truckee is a great base for outdoor explorations in the Tahoe National Forest, especially in the Donner Summit area. One popular hike is to the top of 8243ft **Mt Judah** (4.5 miles, moderate) for awesome views of Donner Lake and the surrounding peaks. A longer and more strenuous ridge-crest hike links Donner Pass and Squaw Valley (15.5 miles, moderate to difficult) skirting the base of four prominent peaks. The TART bus takes you back to the trailhead.

Truckee is close to eight downhill and four cross-country ski resorts (p351).

Donner Summit is a major rock-climbing mecca, with over 300 traditional and sport climbing routes. To learn the ropes, so to speak, try **Alpine Skills International** (☎ 530-582-9170; www.alpineskills.com; 11400 Donner Pass Rd).

From roughly June to September, **Tributary Whitewater Tours** (☎ 530-346-6812, 800-672-3846; www.whitewatertours.com; half-day Mon-Fri/Sat & Sun $69/79) operates a thrilling 7-mile, half-day rafting run on the Truckee River from Boca to Floriston (about 6 miles northeast of Truckee off the I-80) on Class III+ rapids.

For guided high-Sierra adventures, contact **Tahoe Adventure Company** (☎ 530-913-9212, 866-830-6125; www.tahoeadventurecompany.com; tours per person from $85). Staff members know the backcountry inside out and can customize any outing to your interest and skill level, from kayaking, hiking, mountain-biking, rock climbing or any combination thereof. Tours also introduce you to the area's natural and human history and its geology, flora and fauna.

Local outfitters:

Back Country (☎ 530-582-0909; www.thebackcountry.com; 11400 Donner Pass Rd) Good climbing and backcountry ski gear.

Porters Sports (☎ 530-587-1500; 11391 Deerfield Dr, Crossroads Center mall)

Sports Exchange (☎ 530-582-4510; 10095 W River St) Big climbing gym and deals on used equipment.

Sleeping

Donner Memorial State Park (☎ 530-582-7894, reservations 800-444-7275; www.reserveamerica.com; tent & RV sites $20-25; Jun-Sep) This park has 154 campsites with water, flush toilets and hot pay showers.

Clair Tappaan Lodge (☎ 530-426-3632, 800-629-6775; www.sierraclub.org/outings/lodges/ctl; 19940 Donner Pass Rd; dm members/nonmembers Easter-late Nov $46/51, Dec-Easter $55/60;) About a mile west of Sugar Bowl, this cozy Sierra Club–owned rustic mountain lodge puts you near major ski resorts and has space for 140 people in dorms and family rooms. Rates include family-style meals, but you're expected to do small chores and bring your own sleeping bag, towel and swimsuit (for the hot tub!). In winter you can cross-country ski right out the door and careen down the sledding hill out back. Cross-country ski and snowshoe rentals run $15 per day.

Truckee Hotel (☎ 530-587-4444, 800-659-6921; www.thetruckeehotel.com; 10007 Bridge St; r incl breakfast $79-139, with bath $129-209; wi-fi) Tucked behind an atmospheric front arcade, Truckee's most historic abode has welcomed weary travelers since 1873. It's fully restored but still gives you that total Victorian immersion. Expect some train noise.

Inn at Truckee (☎ 530-587-8888, 888-773-6888; www.innattruckee.com; 11506 Deerfield Dr; r incl breakfast $80-105 spring, $145-155 winter; wi-fi) Dependable, good-value option with nice Jacuzzi and sauna; off Hwy 89 just north of Squaw.

River Street Inn (☎ 530-550-9290; www.riverstreetinntruckee.com; 10009 E River St; r Mon-Fri/Sat & Sun incl breakfast $115/155) This sweet 1885 inn in Truckee's historic downtown has 11 rooms that blend nostalgia (clawfoot tubs) with modern comforts (TV/VCR, down comforter). Meet fellow guests during breakfast in the loungy common room, and bring earplugs to dull the occasional train noise.

our pick **Cedar House Sport Hotel** (☎ 530-582-5655; www.cedarhousesporthotel.com; 10918 Brockway Rd; r incl breakfast Mon-Fri/Sat & Sun from $160/190; wi-fi) A new environmentally conscious contemporary boutique hotel aimed at getting folks out into nature, it boasts countertops made from recycled paper, 'rain chains' that redistribute water from the green roof garden to landscaped areas, low-flow plumbing and in-room recycling, but doesn't skimp on good robes, pillow-top mattresses and a hot tub. A dining facility and greenhouse are in the works.

Along Hwy 89 are three riverside **USFS campgrounds** (☎ 877-444-6777; www.recreation.gov; tent & RV sites $18-20; May-Sep): Granite Flat, Goose Meadow and Silver Creek. All have potable water and vault toilets.

Eating & Drinking

Joe Coffee (☎ 530-550-8222; Jiboom near Spring St; mains $6-9; 6am-6pm, shorter winter hours; wi-fi) Acid-orange molded chairs and upbeat tunes set the backdrop for this cheerful café run by culinary school grads. Everything's made daily from scratch (mostly with organic ingredients), like the tantalizing breakfast burritos, flaky crust quiche and 'Thankful Turkey' sandwiches with cranberry cream cheese and walnut bread. It's next to the Old Jail.

Squeeze Inn (☎ 530-587-9814; 10060 Donner Pass Rd; mains under $12; 7am-2pm) Across from the

Amtrak station, this snug locals' favorite dishes up breakfasts big enough to feed a lumberjack. Over 60 varieties of humungous omelets are served in this funky place crammed with silly tchotchkes, and colorful handwritten notes plaster the walls.

Moody's (☎ 530-587-8688; 10007 Bridge St; mains lunch $12-14, dinner $22-30) With its sophisticated supper-club looks and live jazz (Thursday to Saturday), this gourmet restaurant in the Truckee Hotel oozes surprisingly urbane flair. Only the freshest organic ingredients make it into the perfectly pitched concoctions. Wednesday night is a big draw, featuring a Niman Ranch meatballs special ($18) and a superpopular reggae/dancehall DJ set starting at 8pm.

Fifty Fifty Brewing Co. (☎ 530-587-2337; 11197 Brockway Rd) Inhale the aroma of toasting grains at this brand-new brewpub near Hwy 267. Try the popular Donner Party Porter with some upscale pub grub or just a huge plate of nachos.

Getting There & Around

Greyhound has daily buses to Reno ($14.50, one hour), Sacramento ($31, 2½ hours) and San Francisco ($35, five to six hours). Buses stop at the train depot, as do Amtrak Thruway buses and the daily *California Zephyr* train to Emeryville/San Francisco ($42, 6½ to seven hours), Reno ($13, 1½ hours) and Sacramento ($39, 4½ hours).

The **Truckee Trolley** (☎ 530-587-7451; one way/all day $2/4; 🕑 9am-5pm Mon-Sat) connects the train depot hourly with Donner Lake. During ski season, it serves Sugar Bowl.

For Tahoe City and the northern or western shore, hop on the TART bus (p365) at the train depot. Tickets are $1.50 or $3.50 for a day pass.

Though the Truckee Tahoe Airport has no commercial service, a new shuttle service runs between Truckee and Reno, the closest airport (see p376).

NORTHERN SHORE

Heading northeast of Tahoe City, Hwy 28 takes you to a string of cute, low-key towns, many on superb sandy beaches, with reasonably priced motels and hotels. It rolls into Nevada at Crystal Bay and continues south along the eastern shore. The **North Lake Tahoe Visitors' Bureaus** (☎ 888-434-1262; www.gotahoenorth.com) can help get you oriented.

Tahoe Vista

pop 1670 / elev 6232ft

Tahoe Vista has more public beaches (six) than any other lake town, and includes small but pretty **Moon Dune Beach**, with firepits and picnic tables across from the Rustic Cottages, and the **Tahoe Vista Recreation Area**, with a small grassy area and marina. **North Tahoe Regional Park**, at the northern end of National St, has hiking, biking, cross-country ski trails and nice picnic facilities.

A cluster of about 20 little storybook houses in the pines, with nametags fashioned from hand saws, **Rustic Cottages** (☎ 530-546-3523, 888-778-7842; www.rusticcottages.com; 7449 N Lake Blvd; cabins incl breakfast $74-219; wi-fi) sports beautiful wrought-iron beds and a bevy of modern amenities, and most cabins have full kitchens. Other perks: waffles and homemade muffins at breakfast, and free popcorn, movies and cookies.

A large timeshare apartment complex spanning both sides of the main road, the **Tahoe Sands Resort** (☎ 530-546-2592, 888-546-7575; www.tahoesandsresort.com; 6610 N Lake Blvd; studio/1-bedroom/2-bedroom from $129/149/169; wi-fi) has a variety of well-kept lakefront and mountainside room options, plus free evening childcare and kids' activities on Thursdays during the summer. Studios have a fold-up Murphy bed plus a sofa bed, and larger one-bedrooms have porches and breakfast nooks.

Spindleshanks (☎ 530-546-2191; 6873 N Lake Blvd; mains $12-28; 🕑 dinner) looks just like an all-American country cabin, but has a chef with international inspiration (and an excellent wine bar). Ginger lemongrass chicken shares a menu with grilled ribs, filet mignon, griddled salmon and Louisiana-style gumbo with 'riding dirty' rice.

A lakeshore hot spot, **Gar Woods Grille & Pier** (☎ 530-546-3366; 5000 N Lake Blvd; mains lunch $12-18, dinner $20-35; 🕑 lunch & brunch Sun summer, dinner year-round) pays tribute to the era of classic wooden boats. Come for grilled anything and a Wet Woody cocktail, best slurped watching the sunset from the lake-view deck.

Also recommended:

Old Post Office (☎ 530-546-3205; 5245 N Lake Blvd; mains under $10; 🕑 6:30am-2pm) Scrumptious breakfasts.

Sancho's (☎ 530-546-7744; 7019 N Lake Blvd; mains $5-9; 🕑 10am-9pm) Grab a big fat burrito or an order of *huaraches* (griddled bean- and meat-filled tortillas) in this brilliantly painted *taqueria* (Mexican fast-food restaurant).

Kings Beach

pop 4000 / elev 6280ft

The utilitarian character of Kings Beach belies the fact that it has some of the area's best restaurants. The town is one of the more ethnically diverse lakeshore communities with a large Latino population, many of whom work in the tourism industry around Lake Tahoe. In summer much of the action focuses on **Kings Beach State Recreation Area**, a 700ft-long beach that often gets deluged with sun-seekers. There's a nice kids' play structure, and concessions rent kayaks, jet skis and paddleboats.

Jason's Beachside Grille (☎ 530-546-3315; 8338 N Lake Blvd; mains lunch $6-10, dinner $8-20) has a fun lake-view deck and unpretentious American fare, like coconut halibut and smoked chicken pasta alongside an abundant salad bar. On colder days, the red-velvet sofas orbiting a sunken fireplace are the coziest.

Come early (especially on weekends) or join the queue at the **Log Cabin Café** (☎ 530-546-7109; 8692 N Lake Blvd; mains $9-15; 🕑 7am-2pm) for the North Shore's best breakfast. Eggs benedict, whole-wheat pancakes with hot fresh fruit and cranberry-orange waffles are just a few highlights from the huge menu.

Next to the Safeway supermarket is **Lanza's** (☎ 530-546-2434; 7739 N Lake Blvd; mains $11-20; 🕑 dinner), a beloved Italian trattoria where a tantalizing aroma of garlic, rosemary and 'secret' spices perfumes the air. Dinners include salad and bread. Look for the owner's sepia-colored family photos in the entranceway.

Local dive bar **Tradewinds Cocktail Lounge** (☎ 530-546-2497; 8545 N Lake Blvd) looks a bit rough round the edges, but the beer's cheap, the locals are friendly and you can often catch live music ranging from bluegrass to punk.

Crystal Bay

Crossing into Nevada, the neon starts to flash and the casinos pant over your hard-earned cash. The gambling palaces here are older establishments, like the historic **Cal-Neva Resort** (☎ 775-832-4000, 800-225-6382; www.calnevaresort.com; 2 Stateline Rd; r $70-110, 2-bedroom chalets $200-250; ❄ 🚭 wi-fi). It literally straddles the California–Nevada border and has a colorful history involving ghosts, mobsters and Frank Sinatra, who once owned the joint. Ask about the tunnel tours. New owners are poised to pump millions of dollars into a top-to-bottom renovation, which might return the property to its onetime glory.

On the main drag of Hwy 28 and also a few skips over the state line, the **Tahoe Biltmore Lodge & Casino** (☎ 775-831-0660, 800-245-8667; www.tahoebiltmore.com; 5 Hwy 28; r from $60; 🚭 wi-fi), plays up its longevity with classic Tahoe photographs in modernized rooms, though the radiators give away the building's age. For grill food day or night, chow down under the mirrored ceilings and artificial forest of the 24-hour café (mains $8 to $13).

EASTERN SHORE

Lake Tahoe's eastern shore lies entirely within Nevada. Much of it is relatively undeveloped thanks largely to George Whittell, an eccentric San Franciscan playboy who owned much of the land, including 27 miles of shoreline. Upon his death in 1969, most of it was deeded to the US Forest Service, and you can visit Whittell's massive mansion, **Thunderbird Lodge** (☎ 775-832-8750, 800-468-2463; www.thunderbirdlodge.org; land/water approach tours $39/110; 🕑 Tue-Thu Jun–mid-Sep, reservations required), where he spent summers with his pet lion, Bill. Tours include a trip down a 600ft tunnel to the Card House where George used to play poker with Howard Hughes and other famous recluses. The only way to get to the lodge is by shuttle bus or catamaran cruise.

The lodge is near one of Lake Tahoe's ritziest communities, **Incline Village**, the gateway to the Diamond Peak ski resort (p355) and home of the ultradeluxe **Hyatt Regency Lake Tahoe** (☎ 775-832-1234, 800-633-7313; www.laketahoe.hyatt.com; 111 Country Club Dr; r from $355; ❄ 💻 ♿ wi-fi), where the spa is bigger than the casino. Decorated like a Arts and Crafts–style mountain lodge, every room – public or private – speaks of refinement. The outdoor pool, heated to a tepid 82°F year-round, is delightful after a day on the slopes. For dinner, cross the road for a meal at the sumptuous many-hearthed **Lone Eagle Grille** (mains $27-44), or sip a divine orange-flavored margarita as you sidle up to the outdoor fire pit overlooking the hotel's private beach.

In addition to maps and information, the town's **visitors bureau** (☎ 775-832-1606, 800-468-2463; www.gotahoenorth.com; 696 Tahoe Blvd; 🕑 8am-5pm Mon-Fri, 10am-4pm Sat & Sun) has free wi-fi and coffee.

A short drive north of the lake, via Hwy 431 (Mt Rose Hwy), **Mt Rose Wilderness** offers miles of unspoiled terrain. Take the Timberline Rd, Galena Creek County

Park or Mt Rose Summit exits. A well-trodden trail leads to the summit of Mt Rose (10,776ft). No wilderness permits are required. The Mt Rose ski area (p355) is also nearby.

Back on the lake, one of George Whittell's legacies is **Lake Tahoe-Nevada State Park** (☎ 775-831-0494; http://parks.nv.gov/lt.htm), which has beaches, lakes and miles of trails. The highlight here is beautiful **Sand Harbor**, where two sand spits have formed a shallow bay with brilliant, warm turquoise water and white, boulder-strewn beaches. It gets busy. At the park's southern end, near the Hwy 50/Hwy 28 junction, **Spooner Lake** is popular for catch-and-release fishing, picnicking and cross-country skiing (p355).

Spooner Lake is also the start of the famous 15-mile **Flume Trail**, a holy grail for experienced mountain-bikers. From the trail's end near Incline Village you can either backtrack via Hwy 28 or board a shuttle bus ($12.50) at Hidden Beach. Bikes are available at the trailhead from **Flume Trail Mountain Bikes** (☎ 775-749-5349; www.flumetrail.com; per day from $40).

RENO

pop 194,000 / elev 4500ft

A soothingly schizophrenic city of big-time gambling and top-notch outdoor adventures, Reno resists pigeonholing. 'The Biggest Little City in the World' has something to raise the pulse of adrenaline junkies, hardcore gamblers and city people craving easy access to wide open spaces. In the past, the bulk of Reno's visitors flocked to its smorgasbord of casinos, but the construction of a white-water park has raised the interest of kayakers and daredevil surfers.

ORIENTATION

Downtown's N Virginia St, with most of the casinos, is wedged between the I-80 and the Truckee River. South of the river it continues as S Virginia St for several miles of motels, malls and yet more casinos. Back downtown, W 4th St is the main east–west thoroughfare. The Arts District is west of Virginia St; California Ave and 1st St are the most happening. Sparks, which is technically a separate city, is about 4 miles east of downtown Reno via I-80.

INFORMATION

A staffed **information center** (🕑 7:30am-midnight) sits near the baggage claim at Reno-Tahoe Airport.

Downtown post office (50 S Virginia St)

Dreamer's Coffee House (☎ 775-322-8040; 17 S Virginia St; per 15min $2; 🕑 7am-8pm or 9pm) Loungy place with free wi-fi with purchase, great coffees and sandwiches, and art produced by residents of the Riverside Artist Lofts upstairs.

National Council on Problem Gambling (☎ 800-522-4700; 🕑 24hr)

Reno-Sparks Convention & Visitors Authority (☎ 775-827-7600, 800-367-7366; www.visitrenotahoe.com; 2nd fl, Reno Town Mall, 4001 S Virginia St; 🕑 8am-5pm Mon-Fri)

Renown Regional Medical Center (☎ 775-982-4100; 1155 Mill St; 🕑 24hr) Emergency room.

Sundance Bookstore (☎ 775-786-1188; 1155 W 4th St) Great indie bookstore.

SIGHTS

The casinos mentioned here are all open 24 hours. Circus Circus, Eldorado and Silver Legacy are connected by a skywalk.

Virginia St

North Virginia St is casino central with one neon-festooned behemoth after another. Approaching the strip from the north, the first big casino is **Circus Circus** (☎ 775-329-0711; 500 N Sierra St), easily the most family-friendly of the bunch. Free circus acts entertain kids beneath the giant, candy-striped big top, which also harbors a gazillion carnival games.

Next up is the Victorian-themed **Silver Legacy** (☎ 775-325-7401; 407 N Virginia St), easily recognized by its bulbous white landmark dome sheltering a giant mock mining rig underneath a massive sky painting that periodically erupts into a fairly tame sound-and-light spectacle.

A bit further on, the **Eldorado** (☎ 775-786-5700; 345 N Virginia St) has a kitschy Fountain of Fortune – featuring Neptune and nymphets (OK, angels) – that probably has Italian sculptor Bernini spinning in his grave.

South of here, across the train trench, you can rub a Blarney Stone for good luck before heading inside **Fitzgerald's** (☎ 775-785-3300; 255 N Virginia St), an older yet buzzy 351-room property with a silly 'lucky leprechaun' theme and the cheapest buffet in town. It's right next to the landmark **Reno Arch**, built in 1926 to commemorate the completion of the first transcontinental highway in North America. The

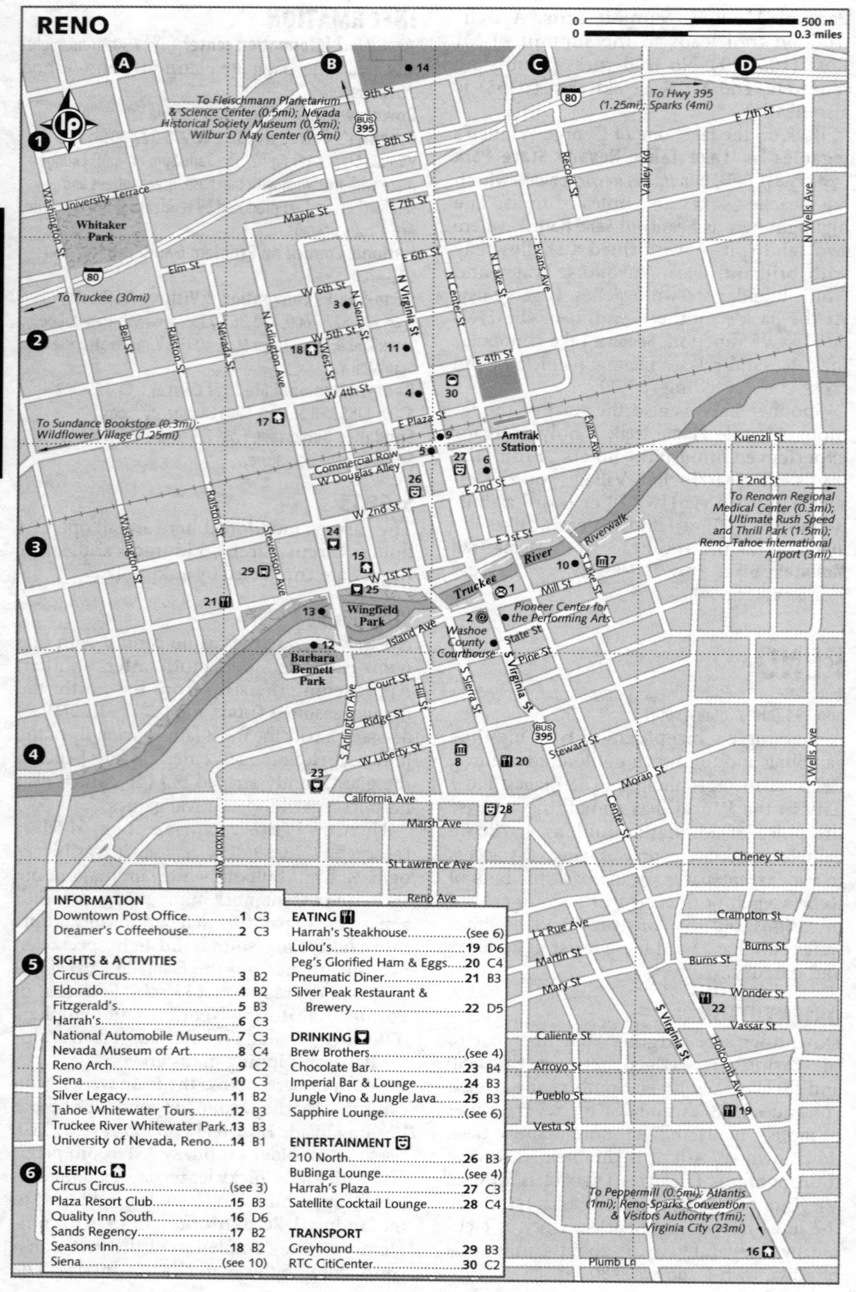

INFORMATION
Downtown Post Office.............1 C3
Dreamer's Coffeehouse............2 C3

SIGHTS & ACTIVITIES
Circus Circus..........................3 B2
Eldorado...................................4 B2
Fitzgerald's..............................5 B3
Harrah's....................................6 C3
National Automobile Museum....7 C3
Nevada Museum of Art..............8 C4
Reno Arch.................................9 C2
Siena.......................................10 C3
Silver Legacy............................11 B2
Tahoe Whitewater Tours..........12 B3
Truckee River Whitewater Park..13 B3
University of Nevada, Reno......14 B1

SLEEPING
Circus Circus..........................(see 3)
Plaza Resort Club....................15 B3
Quality Inn South.....................16 D6
Sands Regency.........................17 B2
Seasons Inn..............................18 B2
Siena.......................................(see 10)

EATING
Harrah's Steakhouse................(see 6)
Lulou's.....................................19 D6
Peg's Glorified Ham & Eggs.....20 C4
Pneumatic Diner.......................21 B3
Silver Peak Restaurant & Brewery....22 D5

DRINKING
Brew Brothers.........................(see 4)
Chocolate Bar..........................23 B4
Imperial Bar & Lounge.............24 B3
Jungle Vino & Jungle Java........25 B3
Sapphire Lounge......................(see 6)

ENTERTAINMENT
210 North.................................26 B3
BuBinga Lounge.......................(see 4)
Harrah's Plaza..........................27 C3
Satellite Cocktail Lounge..........28 C4

TRANSPORT
Greyhound................................29 B3
RTC CitiCenter.........................30 C2

original has since been replaced twice (the last time in 1987) but still proclaims Reno as being the 'Biggest Little City in the World.'

Nearby is **Harrah's** (☎ 775-786-3232; 219 N Center St), founded by Nevada gambling pioneer William Harrah in 1946 and still one of the biggest and most popular casinos in town. From about mid-May to September, live bands get the crowd hopping several nights weekly at Harrah's Plaza facing Virginia St.

Just a block east is Reno's ritziest hotel-casino, the Tuscan-themed **Siena** (☎ 775-337-6260; 1 S Lake St), which has a full spa as well as Enoteca, a comfy jazz bar.

About 2 miles south of downtown are two of Reno's biggest hotels. The **Peppermill** (☎ 775-826-2121; 2707 S Virginia St) dazzles with a new 17-story tower, and at the nearby **Atlantis** (☎ 775-825-4700; 3800 S Virginia St), you can gamble in a trippy tropical setting of indoor waterfalls, tiki huts and palm trees. Its atrium-like Sky Terrace is a rare smoke-free area.

National Automobile Museum

Stylized street scenes illustrate a century's worth of automobile history at this engaging **car museum** (☎ 775-333-9300; www.automuseum.org; 10 Lake St; adult/child/senior $10/4/8; 9:30am-5:30pm Mon-Sat, 10am-4pm Sun;). The collection is enormous and impressive, with one-of-a-kind vehicles including James Dean's 1949 Mercury from *Rebel Without a Cause*, a 1938 Phantom Corsair and a 24-karat gold-plated DeLorean, and rotating exhibits bringing in all kinds of souped-up or fabulously retro rides.

Nevada Museum of Art

In a sparkling building inspired by the geologic formations of the Black Rock Desert north of town, this **art museum** (☎ 775-329-3333; www.nevadaart.org; 160 W Liberty St; adult/child/student & senior $10/1/8; 10am-5pm Tue, Wed, Fri-Sun, 10am-8pm Thu; wi-fi) has been a major spark plug in the revitalization of downtown Reno. A floating staircase leads to galleries showcasing images related to the American West and temporary exhibits. Great café for postcultural refueling.

University of Nevada, Reno

Pop into the flying saucer–shaped **Fleischmann Planetarium & Science Center** (☎ 775-784-4811; http://planetarium.unr.nevada.edu; 1650 N Virginia St; admission free; 10:30am-8pm Sun-Thu, to 9pm Fri & Sat), a pint-sized but updated facility that offers a window on the universe during star shows and feature presentations (adult/child $6/4). Call for show times. Nearby is the **Nevada Historical Society Museum** (☎ 775-688-1190; 1650 N Virginia St; admission $3; 10am-5pm Mon-Sat), which includes interesting permanent exhibits on neon signs, local Native American culture and – something you don't often see as a museum theme – the presence of the federal government.

Wilbur D May Center

Wilbur May (1898–1982) was a rich traveler, adventurer, pilot, big-game hunter, rancher and philanthropist, who spent his latter years in Reno. This **museum** (☎ 775-785-5961; www.maycenter.com; 1595 N Sierra St, Rancho San Rafael Park; adult/child $7/6; variable) has exhibits on May's life and displays of the many artifacts, oddities and trophies he collected (or shot) during his travels. There's a shrunken head from South America, Eskimo scrimshaw and horse sculptures from the Chinese Tang dynasty. The museum is surrounded by 12 acres of gardens and a children's fun park.

ACTIVITIES

A major milestone in Reno's renaissance was the 2004 opening of the **Truckee River Whitewater Park** (admission free; year-round). Mere steps from the casinos, its Class II and III rapids are gentle enough for kids riding inner tubes, yet sufficiently challenging for professional freestyle kayakers. Two courses wrap around Wingfield Park, a small river island that hosts free concerts in summertime. **Tahoe Whitewater Tours** (☎ 775-787-5000; 400 Island Ave) rents kayaks.

The **Ultimate Rush Speed and Thrill Park** (☎ 775-786-7005; www.ultimaterushpark.com; cnr Hwy 395 & Glendale Ave) is a real scream indeed. Strap in on the Sling-shot ride ($25) and get bungeed into the stratosphere at speeds surpassing 70 miles per hour. It's next to the Grand Sierra Resort.

Reno is a 30- to 60-minute drive from Tahoe ski resorts (p351). Many hotels and casinos offer special stay and ski packages. Call the visitors center or check individual websites.

FESTIVALS & EVENTS

Reno River Festival (☎ 775-788-2131; www.renoriverfestival.com) The world's top freestyle kayakers compete in a mad paddling dash through Whitewater Park in mid-May.

Tour de Nez (☎ 775-348-6673; www.tourdenez.com) Called the 'coolest bike race in America,' the Tour de Nez brings together pros and amateurs for three days of races and partying in mid-June.

GREAT BALLS OF FIRE!

For one week at the end of August, **Burning Man** (www.burningman.com; admission $210-295) explodes onto the sunbaked Black Rock Desert, and Nevada sprouts a third major population center – Black Rock City. An experiential art party (and alternative universe) that climaxes in the immolation of a towering stick figure, Burning Man is a whirlwind of outlandish theme camps, dust-caked bicycles, bizarre bartering, costume-enhanced nudity and a general relinquishment of inhibitions. And when the last wig-wearing Burner heads home, volunteers make sure to leave no trace, picking up every last hot pink sequin.

Artown (www.renoisartown.com) During July, this festival puts on hundreds of visual and performing arts events across town, with both local and international talent.

Hot August Nights (☎ 775-356-1956; www.hotaugustnights.net) Catch the *American Graffiti* vibe during this seven-day celebration of hot rods and rock and roll in early August. Hotel rates skyrocket to their peak.

SLEEPING

Lodging rates vary widely depending on the day of the week, the season, the week's activities and the type of room. Sunday through Thursday are generally the best; Friday is somewhat more expensive and Saturday can be as much as triple the midweek rate. If your dates are flexible, many casinos have rate calendars so you can easily see which nights are the best bargain. The figures provided here are a loose guide.

Circus Circus (☎ 775-329-0711, 800-648-5010; www.circusreno.com; 500 N Sierra St; r Mon-Fri/Sat & Sun from $40/70; wi-fi) Standard rooms are sheathed in garish pinks and blues at this kid-friendly property. Some are in the separate Sky Tower, reached via a short tram ride from the main casino. A new 'Hound Hotel' (with video camera) lets you bring the pooch.

our pick Sands Regency (☎ 775-348-2200, 866-386-7829; www.sandsregency.com; 345 N Arlington Ave; r $40-140; wi-fi) With some of the largest standard digs in town, rooms here are decked out in a cheerful tropical palette of upbeat blues, reds and greens – a visual relief from standard-issue motel decor. The 17th-floor gym and Jacuzzi are perfectly positioned to capture your eyes with drop-dead panoramic mountain views.

Wildflower Village (☎ 775-747-8848; www.wildflowervillage.com; 4395 W 4th St; r $50-75, B&B $100;) Perhaps more of a state of mind than a motel, this artists colony on the edge of town has a tumbledown yet creative vibe. Individual murals decorate the facade of each room, and you can hear the freight trains rumble on by.

Seasons Inn (☎ 775-322-6000, 800-322-8588; www.seasonsinn.com; 495 West St; r Mon-Fri/Sat & Sun $59/89; wi-fi) A modest newer downtown motel a block off the Virginia St strip, it's dwarfed by glitzy high-rise towers and mega-resort casinos, and has ample rooms. A decent respite for visitors who want to gamble and then slip away from the action at night. Pets welcome.

Peppermill (☎ 775-826-2121, 866-821-9996; www.peppermillreno.com; 2707 S Virginia St; tower r Mon-Fri/Sat & Sun from $59/90; wi-fi) Banking its future on Vegas-style opulence, the popular Peppermill has added a brand-new 600-room tower with Tuscan-themed suites and is redesigning most of its public areas. Older rooms unintentionally ride the retro wave with a cool turquoise-and-black color scheme. The three sparkling pools are dreamy.

Quality Inn South (☎ 775-329-1001, 800-626-1900; www.qualityinn.com; 1885 S Virginia St; r $75-85; wi-fi) A tranquil choice along S Virginia St, this place has spacious and immaculate rooms with a balcony or patio overlooking the pool or nicely landscaped grounds. Rates include a discount coupon for breakfast at the on-site restaurant.

Siena (☎ 775-337-6260, 877-743-6233; www.sienareno.com; 1 Lake St; r from $100; wi-fi) Tuscany inspired this smooth newcomer, a sophisticated boutique hotel-casino complete with campanile (tower) overlooking the river. Instead of the usual casino frenzy, you'll find lots of stress-melting options, including a serene spa.

Plaza Resort Club (☎ 775-786-2200, 800-628-5974; www.plazaresortclub.com; 121 West St; r from $120; wi-fi) A small and classy nongaming timeshare, it feels like a deluxe apartment building. Standard rooms have oodles of traditionally decorated living space, as well as a sofa bed and dining table, and the larger Regal rooms have whirlpool tubs and full kitchens. A sky-lit indoor pool and a rooftop whirlpool spa look out over the neon-crazy city and a small upstairs lounge serves complimentary morning coffee and pastries.

EATING

Reno's dining scene goes far beyond the casinos.

Pneumatic Diner (☎ 775-786-8888; 2nd fl, 501 W 1st St; dishes $6-8; 11am-10pm Mon-Thu, 11am-11pm Fri, 9am-11pm Sat, 8am-10pm Sun; V) Consume a garden of vegetarian delights under salvaged neon lights. This groovy little place near the river has meatless and vegan comfort food and desserts to tickle your inner two-year-old, like the ice-cream laden Cookie Bomb. It's attached to the Truckee Lodge; use the Ralson St entrance.

Peg's Glorified Ham & Eggs (☎ 775-329-2600; 420 S Sierra St; dishes $7-10; 6:30am-2pm) Locally regarded as the best breakfast in town, Peg's offers tasty grill food that's not too greasy. It's the perfect place to sit outside and read the Sunday paper while munching on an overstuffed omelet. Crayons and color-in placemats are available by the door.

Silver Peak Restaurant & Brewery (☎ 775-324-1864; 124 Wonder St; mains lunch $8-10, dinner $9-22; 11am-midnight) Casual and pretense-free, this place hums with the chatter of happy locals settling in for a night of microbrews and great eats, from wild mushroom pizza to asparagus ravioli and grilled salmon.

Harrah's Steakhouse (☎ 775-788-2929; 219 N Center St; dinner mains $25-38; 11am-2:30pm & 5-9:30pm Mon-Fri, 5-10:30pm Sat & Sun) This elegant restaurant has amazing service and a romantic atmosphere – think roses, linen and low lighting. The recipient of numerous local awards for fine dining, it serves the requisite big juicy steaks along with other meat and seafood options.

Lulou's (☎ 775-329-9979; 1470 S Virginia St; mains $34-38; dinner Tue-Sat) This arty gourmet eatery is a surprise find on this otherwise drab strip. Bold canvases brighten brick walls, and a tantalizing mélange of aromas wafts from the open kitchen where chefs fuss over Eurasian concoctions. Reservations essential.

DRINKING

Jungle Java & Jungle Vino (☎ 775-329-4484; 246 W 1st St; 6am-midnight; wi-fi) A side-by-side coffee shop and wine bar with a cool mosaic floor and an internet café all rolled into one. The café serves breakfast bagels and lunchtime sandwiches ($6), and the wine bar has a movie night and a weekly wine tasting. Why would you ever leave?

Chocolate Bar (☎ 775-337-1122; 475 S Arlington Ave; 11:30am-midnight) This sinfully delicious hot spot enjoys most-favorite status with Reno scenesters for its wicked chocolate-themed drinks (both virgin and alcohol-infused), awesome desserts and big-city-cool decor.

Imperial Bar & Lounge (☎ 775-324-6399; 150 N Arlington Ave; dishes $9-14; 4pm-2am Thu-Sat, to midnight Sun-Wed) A newer watering hole inhabiting a relic of the past, this building was once an old bank, and in the middle of the wood floor you can see cement where the vault once stood. Sandwiches and pizzas go with 16 beers on tap and a buzzing weekend scene.

More watering holes:

Sapphire Lounge (☎ 775-786-3232; 219 N Center St; Tue-Sat) A slice of New York sophistication at Harrah's, with DJs and karaoke nights.

Brew Brothers (☎ 775-786-5700; 345 N Virginia St) Nightly bands, eight custom microbrews and tasty grub ($7 to $14) at the Eldorado.

ENTERTAINMENT

The free weekly *Reno News & Review* (www.newsreview.com) is your best source for listings.

BuBinga Lounge (☎ 775-786-5700; 345 N Virginia St; men/women $20/10; from 9pm Tue & Thu-Sat) At Reno's sexiest dance club, inside the Eldorado, DJs pull in the eye-candy crowd with a pulsating mix of house and hip-hop. After you've sweated it out on the crammed dance floor, you can chill in one of the two bars.

Satellite Cocktail Lounge (☎ 775-786-3536; 188 California Ave; Tue-Sun) A fixture on the local nightlife scene, this artsy bar and live small-to-midsized music venue is a good bet for weekend indie rock, hip-hop and pop shows or DJ dance nights. Sink into a booth and check out some local art or spread out on the sizeable patio.

210 North (☎ 775-786-6210; www.210north.com; 210 N Sierra St; before 10pm free, cover $5-20; Thu-Sat) When Reno wants to flaunt it, they end up here. A pulsing-hot dance club and downtempo lounge that would feel right at home in Vegas, this is the glam spot for throwing your moves. Trip out to the mesmerizing LED chandelier in the Divinity Lounge.

The casinos put on free lounge and cabaret acts that range from the enjoyable to the ridiculous. Some also have big showrooms where you can take in rock bands, magic shows or golden-throated stalwarts such as Tony Bennett.

DETOUR: VIRGINIA CITY

Virginia City, about 23 miles south of Reno, was the site of the legendary Comstock Lode, a massive silver bonanza that began in 1859 and stands as one of the world's richest strikes. Some of the silver barons went on to become major players in California history, among them Leland Stanford of university fame and Bank of California founder William Ralston. Much of San Francisco was built with the treasure dug up from the soil beneath Virginia City.

At its peak, it had over 30,000 residents and, as befits a mining town, was a wild and raucous place. A young local newspaper writer captured the shenanigans in a book called *Roughing It*, published under his pen name Mark Twain. A National Historic Landmark since 1961, Virginia City draws big crowds in search of Old West icons and lore. Though it sometimes has the feel of a frontier theme park, it's still a fun place to while away a few hours.

On the main drag, 'C' St, you'll find the **visitors center** (☎ 775-847-4386; www.virginiacity-nv.org; 86 S 'C' St; 🕑 10am-4pm) and vintage buildings restored into wacky saloons, cheesy souvenir shops and small museums ranging from hokey to intriguing.

To get a feel for mining life, take a tour of the **Chollar Mine** (☎ 775-847-0155; F St; adult/child $7/2; 🕑 1-4pm May-Oct), and see the inner workings of a mine that extracted gold and silver until WWII.

The historic **Chollar Mansion B&B** (☎ 775-847-9777, 877-246-5527; www.chollarmansion.com; 565 S D St; r incl full breakfast $135) used to be the town mine office. It's now filled with antiques and the views seem to go on forever.

The drive to Virginia City from Reno offers great views of the mountain. Take Hwy 395 south for about 10 miles, then Hwy 341 east for 13 miles.

GETTING THERE & AWAY

About 5 miles southeast of downtown, **Reno-Tahoe International Airport** (RNO; ☎ 775-328-6870; www.renoairport.com) has free wi-fi and is served by most major airlines. The new **North Lake Tahoe Express** (☎ 866-216-5222; www.northlaketahoeexpress.com) operates a shuttle ($35, six to seven daily, 3:30am to midnight) to and from the Reno airport to multiple North Shore Lake Tahoe locations including Truckee, Squaw Valley and Incline Village. Reserve in advance.

Greyhound (☎ 775-322-2970; 155 Stevenson St) has daily nonstop services to Truckee ($14.50, one hour), San Francisco ($33, five to seven hours) and Sacramento ($23, 2¾ to 3½ hours).

Reno is a stop on the *California Zephyr* route operated by **Amtrak** (☎ 775-329-8638, 800-872-7245; 280 N Center St). Westbound trains stop at Truckee ($13, one hour), Sacramento ($42, five hours) and Emeryville/San Francisco ($46, 7½ hours).

GETTING AROUND

A **taxi** (☎ 775-355-5555) between the airport and downtown Reno costs about $18, but most casinos offer frequent free shuttles for their guests (and don't ask to see reservations). For longer trips hop aboard **RTC Ride buses** (☎ 775-348-7433; www.rtcwashoe.com; per ride/all day $1.75/4). Most routes converge at the RTC CitiCenter downtown. Useful routes include bus 1 for S Virginia St, bus 11 for Sparks and bus 14 for the airport. The free Sierra Spirit bus loops around all major downtown landmarks – including the casinos and the university – every 10 minutes from 7am to 9pm daily.

YOSEMITE NATIONAL PARK

The jaw-dropping head-turner of America's national parks, Yosemite (yo-*sem*-it-tee) garners the devotion of all who enter. From the waterfall-striped granite walls buttressing emerald green Yosemite Valley to the skyscraping giant sequoias catapulting into the air at Mariposa Grove, you feel a sense of awe and reverence that so much natural beauty exists in one place. It is a Unesco World Heritage Site that makes even Switzerland look like God's practice run. As far as we can tell, America's third-oldest national park has only one downside: the impact of the 3.5 million visitors annually who wend their way here. But lift your eyes ever so slightly above the crowds and you'll feel your heart instantly moved by unrivalled splendors. The haughty profile of Half Dome, the hulking presence of El Capitan, the drenching mists of Yosemite Falls, the gemstone lakes of the high country's subalpine wilderness and Hetch Hetchy's pristine pathways.

HISTORY

The Ahwahneechee, a group of Miwok and Paiute peoples, lived in the Yosemite area for 4000 years before a group of pioneers, most likely led by legendary explorer Joseph Rutherford Walker, came through in 1833. During the Gold Rush era, conflict between the miners and native tribes escalated to the point where a military expedition (the Mariposa Battalion) was dispatched in 1851 to punish the Ahwahneechee, eventually forcing the capitulation of Chief Tenaya and his tribe later that year.

Tales of thunderous waterfalls and towering stone columns followed the Mariposa Battalion out of Yosemite and soon spread into the public's awareness. In 1855 San Francisco entrepreneur James Hutchings organized the first tourist party to the valley. Published accounts of his trip, in which he extolled the area's untarnished beauty, prompted others to follow and it wasn't long before inns and roads began springing up. Alarmed by this development, conservationists petitioned Congress to protect the area – with success. In 1864 President Abraham Lincoln signed the Yosemite Grant, which eventually ceded Yosemite Valley and the Mariposa Grove of Giant Sequoias to California as a state park. This landmark decision paved the way for a national park system of which Yosemite became a part in 1890, thanks to efforts led by pioneering conservationist John Muir.

Yosemite's popularity as a tourist destination continued to soar throughout the 20th century and, by the mid-1970s, traffic and congestion draped the valley in a smoggy haze. The General Management Plan (GMP) developed in 1980 to alleviate this and other problems ran into numerous challenges and delays. Despite many improvements, it still hasn't been fully implemented, at least in part because of federal funding cuts. Ultimately, the powers that be must balance the needs of visitors with the preservation of the natural beauty that draws them to Yosemite in the first place.

ORIENTATION

There are four main entrances: South Entrance (Hwy 41), Arch Rock (Hwy 140), Big Oak Flat (Hwy 120 W) and Tioga Pass (Hwy 120 E). Hwy 120 traverses the park as Tioga Rd, connecting Yosemite Valley with the Eastern Sierra.

Visitor activity concentrates in Yosemite Valley, especially in Yosemite Village, which has the main visitors center, a post office, a museum, eateries and other services. Curry Village is another hub. Notably less busy, Tuolumne (too-*ahl*-uh-*mee*) Meadows, towards the eastern end of Tioga Rd, primarily draws hikers, backpackers and climbers. Wawona, the park's southern focal point, also has a good infrastructure. In the northwestern corner, Hetch Hetchy gets the smallest number of visitors and has no services whatsoever.

Gas up year-round at Wawona and Crane Flat inside the park or at El Portal on Hwy 140 just outside its boundaries. In summer, gas is also sold at Tuolumne Meadows. The gas stations usually close after dark but you can always pay at the pump with a credit card.

WHEN TO GO

It's quite simple: from June to September, the entire park is accessible, all visitor facilities are open and everything from backcountry campgrounds to ice-cream stands are at maximum capacity. This is also when it's hardest – though not impossible – to evade the crush of humanity.

Crowds are smallest in winter but road closures (most notably of Tioga Rd, see p379, but also of Glacier Point Rd beyond Badger Pass Ski Area) mean that activity is concentrated in the valley and on Badger Pass. Visitor facilities are scaled down to a bare minimum and most campgrounds are closed and other lodging options limited. Note that 'winter' in Yosemite starts with the first heavy snowfall, which can be as early as October, and often lasts until May.

Spring is a particularly excellent time to visit Yosemite, because in May and June, the park's waterfalls – fed by the snowmelt – are gushing and spectacular. Late August to October bring fewer people, and fall brings an enchanting rainbow of foliage and crisp, clear weather. Waterfalls, however, have usually dried up to a trickle by that time.

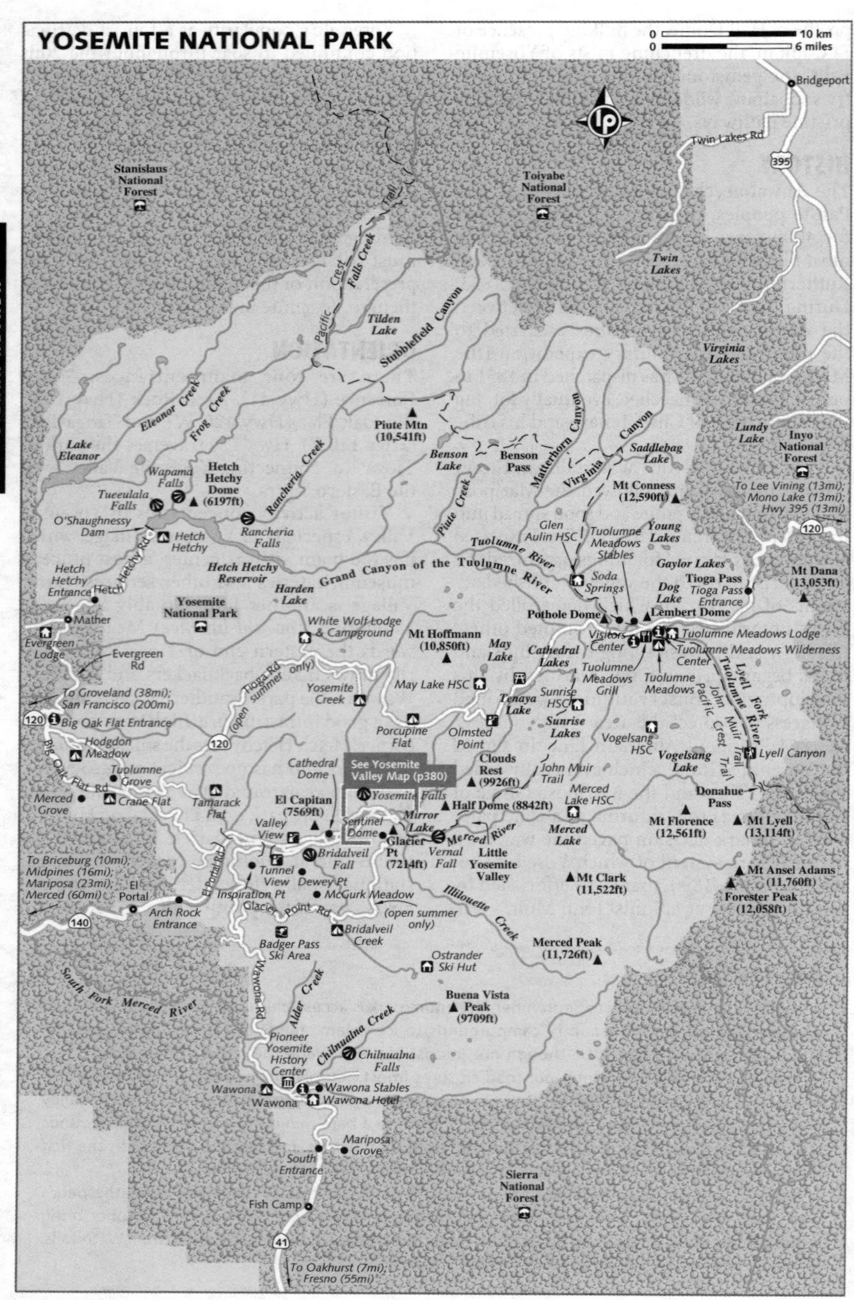
YOSEMITE NATIONAL PARK
10 km
6 miles
Bridgeport
Twin Lakes Rd
395
Stanislaus National Forest
Toiyabe National Forest
Twin Lakes
Trail
Pacific Crest
Falls Creek
Tilden Lake
Stubblefield Canyon
Virginia Lakes
Eleanor Creek
Frog Creek
Piute Mtn (10,541ft)
Matterhorn Canyon
Virginia Canyon
Lundy Lake
Inyo National Forest
Lake Eleanor
Rancheria Creek
Benson Lake
Benson Pass
Saddlebag Lake
Wapama Falls
Hetch Hetchy Dome (6197ft)
Mt Conness (12,590ft)
Tueeulala Falls
To Lee Vining (13mi); Mono Lake (13mi); Hwy 395 (13mi)
O'Shaughnessy Dam
Rancheria Falls
Piute Creek
Glen Aulin HSC
Tuolumne Meadows Stables
Young Lakes
120
Hetch Hetchy
Hetchy Rd
Tuolumne River
Hetch Hetchy Reservoir
Grand Canyon of the Tuolumne River
Gaylor Lakes
Mt Dana (13,053ft)
Hetch Hetchy Entrance
Hetch
Harden Lake
Soda Springs
Dog Lake
Tioga Pass
Tioga Pass Entrance
Yosemite National Park
Pothole Dome
Lembert Dome
Mather
White Wolf Lodge & Campground
Visitors Center
Tuolumne Meadows Lodge
Evergreen Lodge
Mt Hoffmann (10,850ft)
May Lake
Cathedral Lakes
Tuolumne Meadows Wilderness Center
Evergreen Rd
Tuolumne Meadows Grill
Tuolumne Meadows
Lyell Fork Tuolumne River
Tioga Rd (open summer only)
Yosemite Creek
May Lake HSC
Sunrise HSC
Tenaya Lake
John Muir Trail
Pacific Crest Trail
To Groveland (38mi); San Francisco (200mi)
120
Big Oak Flat Entrance
Porcupine Flat
Olmsted Point
Sunrise Lakes
Vogelsang HSC
120
Lyell Canyon
Hodgdon Meadow
Big Oak Flat Rd
Clouds Rest (9926ft)
John Muir Trail
Vogelsang Lake
Cathedral Dome
See Yosemite Valley Map (p380)
Tuolumne Grove
Merced Grove
Crane Flat
Tamarack Flat
Yosemite Falls
Merced Lake HSC
Donahue Pass
El Capitan (7569ft)
Half Dome (8842ft)
Mt Florence (12,561ft)
Mt Lyell (13,114ft)
Valley View
Sentinel Dome
Mirror Lake
Merced River
Merced Lake
Glacier Pt (7214ft)
Vernal Fall
Little Yosemite Valley
Bridalveil Fall
To Briceburg (10mi); Midpines (16mi); Mariposa (23mi); Merced (60mi)
Tunnel View
Dewey Pt
Mt Ansel Adams (11,760ft)
El Portal Rd
Mt Clark (11,522ft)
Forester Peak (12,058ft)
El Portal
Inspiration Pt
McGurk Meadow
Illilouette Creek
Arch Rock Entrance
Glacier Point Rd
(open summer only)
140
Bridalveil Creek
Badger Pass Ski Area
Merced Peak (11,726ft)
Ostrander Ski Hut
South Fork Merced River
Wawona Rd
Alder Creek
Buena Vista Peak (9709ft)
Chilnualna Creek
Pioneer Yosemite History Center
Chilnualna Falls
Wawona
Wawona Stables
Wawona
Wawona Hotel
Mariposa Grove
South Entrance
Sierra National Forest
Fish Camp
41
To Oakhurst (7mi); Fresno (55mi)

IMPASSABLE TIOGA PASS

Hwy 120, the main route into Yosemite National Park from the Eastern Sierra, climbs through Tioga Pass, the highest pass in the Sierra at 9945ft. On most maps of California, you'll find a parenthetical remark – 'closed in winter' – printed on the map near the pass. While true, this statement is also misleading. Tioga Rd is usually closed from the first heavy snowfall in October to May, June or even July! If you're planning a trip through Tioga Pass in spring, you're likely to be out of luck. According to official park policy, the earliest date the road will be plowed is 15 April, yet the pass has been open in April only once since 1980. Other mountain roads further north, such as Hwys 108, 4 and 88/89, may also be closed for heavy snow, albeit only temporarily. Call ☎ 800-427-7623 for road and weather conditions.

INFORMATION

Yosemite's entrance fee is $20 per vehicle or $10 for those on bicycle or foot and is valid for seven consecutive days. Upon entering the park, you'll receive an NPS map, an illustrated booklet and, most importantly, a copy of the biweekly *Yosemite Today* newspaper, which includes an activity schedule and current opening hours of all facilities.

For recorded park information, campground availability and road and weather conditions, call ☎ 209-372-0200.

Bookstores

Yosemite Association Bookstore (Map p380; ☎ 209-379-2648; www.yosemitestore.com; Yosemite Valley Visitors Center) Best selection of books about Yosemite and the Sierra.

Internet Access

Degnan's Café (Map p380; Yosemite Village; per min 25¢) Pay terminals in this café adjacent to Degnan's Deli.

Public library (Map p380; ☎ 209-372-4552; Girls' Club Bldg, Yosemite Valley; access free; vary)

Yosemite Lodgeat the Falls (Yosemite Valley; per min 25¢) Terminals are in the lobby. Wi-fi costs $6 per day.

Internet Resources

Yosemite Association (www.yosemite.org) Information and educational programs offered by the nonprofit park support organization.

Yosemite National Park (www.nps.gov/yose) Official Yosemite National Park Service site with the most comprehensive and current information.

Yosemite Park (www.yosemitepark.com) Online home of DNC Parks & Resorts, Yosemite's main concessionaire. Has lots of practical information and a lodging reservations function.

Laundry & Showers

Soap up year-round at Curry Village and seasonally at the Tuolumne Meadows Lodge, White Wolf Lodge and Housekeeping Camp. The latter also has a coin-op laundry.

Medical Services

Yosemite Dental Clinic (☎ 209-372-4200; Ahwahnee Dr, Yosemite Valley) Twenty-four hour service available.

Yosemite Medical Clinic (☎ 209-372-4637; Ahwahnee Dr, Yosemite Valley) Twenty-four hour service available.

Money

There is no bank, but the stores in Yosemite Village, Curry Village and Wawowa all have ATMs, as does the Yosemite Lodge at the Falls.

Post

The main post office is in Yosemite Village, but Wawona and the Yosemite Lodge at the Falls also have year-round services. Seasonal branches operate in Curry Village and Tuolumne Meadows.

Telephone

There are pay phones at every developed location throughout the park. Cell-phone reception is sketchy, depending on your location.

Tourist Information

Extended summer hours may apply.

Big Oak Flat Information Station (Map p378; ☎ 209-379-1899; 8am-5pm Apr-Oct) Issues wilderness permits.

Tuolumne Meadows Visitor Center (Map p378; ☎ 209-372-0263; 9am-5pm late spring-early fall)

Tuolumne Meadows Wilderness Center (Map p378; ☎ 209-372-0309; 8am-5pm, extended hr Jul & Aug) Issues wilderness permits.

Wawona Information Station (Map p378; ☎ 209-375-9531; 8:30am-5pm late May-early Oct) Issues wilderness permits.

Yosemite Valley Visitors Center (Map p380; ☎ 209-372-0299; Yosemite Village; 9am-5pm year-round)

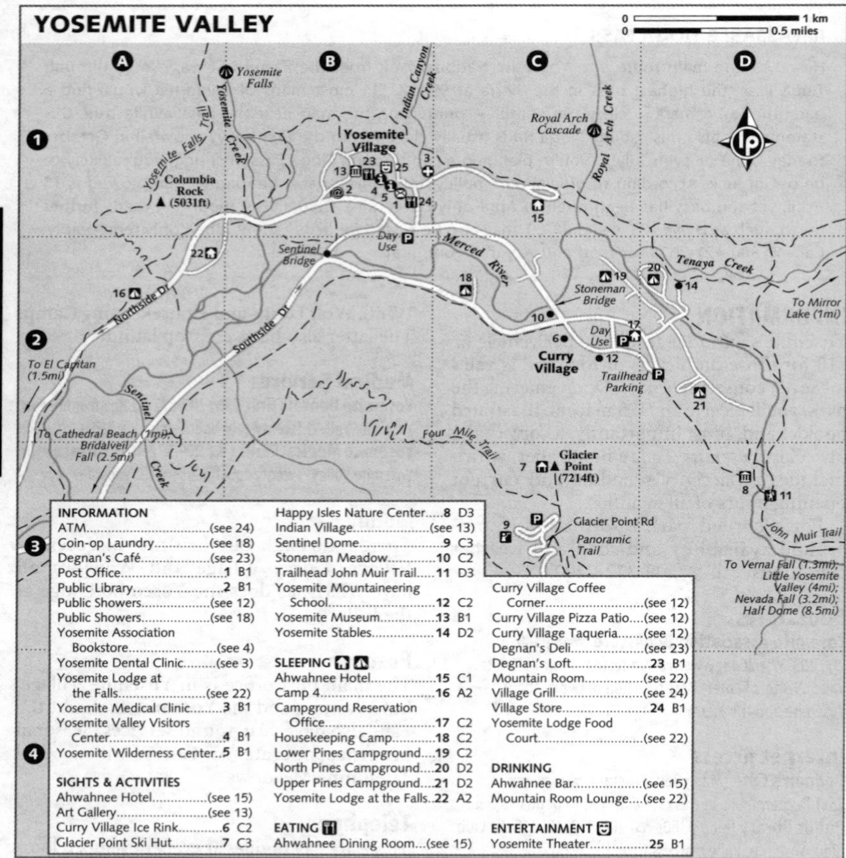

The main office with exhibits and free film screenings of *Spirit of Yosemite*.

Yosemite Wilderness Center (Map p380; ☎ 209-372-0745; Yosemite Village; 🕑 8am-5pm May-Sep) Wilderness permits, maps and backcountry advice.

DANGERS & ANNOYANCES

Yosemite is prime black bear habitat. To find out how to protect the bears and yourself from each other, see the boxed text, p70. Mosquitoes can be pesky in summer, so bug spray's not a bad idea. And please don't feed those squirrels. They may look cute but they've got a nasty bite.

Found cell-phone reception? Well, no one's come here to hear you yakking, so keep it down or turn it off.

SIGHTS

Yosemite Valley

The park's crown jewel, spectacular meadow-carpeted Yosemite Valley stretches 7 miles long, bisected by the rippling Merced River and hemmed in by some of the most majestic chunks of granite nature has wrought anywhere on earth. The most famous are, of course, the monumental 7569ft **El Capitan** (El Cap; Map p378), one of the world's largest monoliths and a magnet for rock climbers, and 8842ft **Half Dome** (Map p378), the park's spiritual centerpiece, whose rounded granite pate forms an unmistakable silhouette. You'll have great views of both from **Valley View** (Map p378) on the valley floor, but for the classic photo op head up Hwy 41 to **Tunnel**

View (Map p378), which boasts a new viewing area. With a little sweat you'll have even better postcard panoramas – sans the crowds – from the **Inspiration Point Trail** (2.6-mile round-trip), which starts at the tunnel.

Yosemite's waterfalls mesmerize even the most jaded traveler, especially when the spring runoff turns them into thunderous cataracts. Most are reduced to a mere trickle by late summer. **Yosemite Falls** (Map p380) is considered the tallest in North America, dropping 2425ft in three tiers. A slick new wheelchair-accessible trail leads to the bottom of this cascade or, if you prefer solitude and different perspectives, you can also clamber up **Yosemite Falls Trail**, which puts you atop the falls after a grueling 3.4 miles. No less impressive are nearby **Bridalveil Fall** (Map p378) and others scattered throughout the valley.

Any aspiring Ansel Adams should lug their camera gear along the 1-mile paved trail to **Mirror Lake** (Map p378) early or late in the day to catch the ever-shifting reflection of Half Dome in the still waters. The lake all but dries up by late summer.

South of here, where the Merced River courses around two small islands, lies **Happy Isles**, a popular area for picnics, swimming and strolls. It also marks the start of the John Muir Trail and Mist Trail to several waterfalls and Half Dome. The **Happy Isles Nature Center** (Map p380; admission free; May-Sep) keeps kids' attention with cool interactive exhibits.

Places of cultural interest in the valley include the **Yosemite Museum** (Map p380; ☎ 209-372-0200; admission free; 9am-4:30pm, closed for lunch), which has Miwok and Paiute artifacts, including woven baskets, beaded buckskin dresses and dance capes made from feathers. There's also an **art gallery** (Map p380) and, behind the museum, a reconstructed **Indian village** (Map p380) c 1870. A self-guided interpretive trail winds past pounding stones, an acorn granary, a ceremonial roundhouse and a conical bark house.

About a quarter-mile east of Yosemite Village, the **Ahwahnee Hotel** (Map p380; also see p387) is a graceful blend of rustic mountain retreat and elegant mansion dating back to 1927. You don't need to be a guest to come have a gawk and a wander. Built from local granite, pine and cedar, the building is splendidly decorated with leaded glass, sculpted tiles, Native American rugs and Turkish kilims. You can enjoy a meal in the baronial dining room or a casual drink in the piano bar. Around Christmas, the Ahwahnee hosts the **Bracebridge Dinner** (☎ 801-559-5000; per person $348), sort of a combination banquet and Renaissance *faire*. Book early.

Glacier Point

A lofty 3200ft above the valley floor, 7214ft Glacier Point (Map p380) presents one of the park's most eye-popping vistas and practically puts you at eye level with Half Dome. To the left of Half Dome lies U-shaped, glacially carved Tenaya Canyon, while below you'll see Vernal and Nevada Falls. Glacier Point is about an hour's drive from Yosemite Valley via Glacier Point Rd off Hwy 41. Along the road, hiking trails lead to other spectacular viewpoints, such as **Dewey Point** (Map p378) and **Sentinel Dome** (Map p378). You can also hike up from the valley floor to Glacier Point via the thigh-burning **Four Mile Trail** (Map p380). If you've driven up to Glacier Point and want to get away from the madding crowd, hiking down the Four Mile Trail for a bit will net you comparative solitude and more breathtaking views. Another way to get here is on the Glacier Point Hikers' Bus (p388). Many hikers take the bus one way and hike the other.

Tioga Road & Tuolumne Meadows

Tioga Road (Hwy 120 E), the only road to traverse the park, travels through 56 miles of superb high country at elevations ranging from 6200ft at Crane Flat to 9945ft at Tioga Pass. Heavy snowfall keeps it closed from about November until May. Beautiful views await after many a bend in the road, the most impressive being **Olmsted Point** (Map p380), where you can gawp all the way down Tenaya Canyon to the backside of Half Dome. Above the canyon's east side looms the aptly named 9926ft **Clouds Rest** (Map p380). Continuing east on Tioga Rd soon drops you at **Tenaya Lake** (Map p380), a placid blue basin framed by pines and granite cliffs.

Beyond here, about 55 miles from Yosemite Valley, 8600ft **Tuolumne Meadows** (Map p380) is the largest subalpine meadow in the Sierra. It provides a dazzling contrast to the valley, with its lush open fields, clear blue lakes, ragged granite peaks and domes, and cooler temperatures. If you come during July or August, you'll find a painter's palette worth of wildflowers decorating the shaggy meadows.

Tuolumne is far less crowded than the valley, though the area around the campground, lodge store and visitors center does get busy, especially on weekends. Some hiking trails, such as the one to Dog Lake, are also well traveled. Remember that the altitude makes breathing a lot harder than in the valley, and nights can get nippy, so pack warm clothes.

The **main meadow** is about 2.5 miles long and lies on the north side of Tioga Rd between Lembert Dome and **Pothole Dome** (Map p380). The 200ft scramble to the top of the latter – preferably at sunset – gives you great views of the meadow. An interpretive trail leads from the stables to muddy **Soda Springs** (Map p380), where carbonated water bubbles up in red-tinted pools. The nearby **Parsons Memorial Lodge** has a few displays.

Hikers and climbers will find a paradise of options around Tuolumne Meadows, which is also the gateway to the High Sierra Camps (p386).

The Tuolumne Meadows Tour & Hikers' Bus (p388) makes the trip along Tioga Rd once daily in each direction, and can be used for one-way hikes. There's also a free Tuolumne Meadows Shuttle (p388), which travels between the Tuolumne Meadows Lodge and Olmsted Point, including a stop at Tenaya Lake.

Wawona

Wawona, about 27 miles south of Yosemite Valley, is the park's historical center, but the main lure really is the **Mariposa Grove of Giant Sequoias** (Map p378), the biggest and most impressive cluster of big trees in Yosemite. The star of the show – and what everyone comes to see – is the **Grizzly Giant**, a behemoth that sprang to life some 2700 years ago, or about the time the ancient Greeks held the first Olympic Games. You can't miss it – it's a half-mile walk along a well-worn path starting near the parking lot. Beyond here, crowds begin to thin out a bit, although for more solitude you should arrive early in the morning or after 6pm. Also nearby is the walk-through **California Tunnel Tree**, which continues to survive despite having its heart hacked out in 1895.

In the upper grove you'll find the **Fallen Wawona Tunnel Tree**, the famous drive-through tree that toppled over in 1969. For scenic views, take a 1-mile (round-trip) amble from the fallen tree to **Wawona Point**. Also in the upper grove is the **Mariposa Grove Museum** (⌚ 10am-4pm May-Sep), with displays about sequoia ecology. The full hike from the parking lot to the upper grove is about 2.5 miles.

Parking can be very limited, so come early or late, or take the free shuttle bus from the Wawona Store or the park entrance. The grove can also be explored on a one-hour **guided tour** (tour adult $25; ⌚ usually May-Sep) aboard a noisy open-air tram leaving from the parking lot.

In Wawona itself, about 6 miles north of the grove, take in the manicured grounds of the elegant Wawona Hotel (p387) and cross a covered bridge to the rustic **Pioneer Yosemite History Center** (Map p378; admission free; ⌚ 24hr), where some of the park's oldest buildings were relocated. It also features stagecoaches that brought early tourists to Yosemite, and offers short rides ($3).

Hetch Hetchy

In the park's northwestern corner, Hetch Hetchy (which is Miwok for 'place of tall grass') gets the least amount of traffic yet sports waterfalls and granite cliffs that rival its famous counterparts in Yosemite Valley. The main difference is that Hetch Hetchy Valley is now filled with water, following a long political and environmental battle in the early 20th century. It's a lovely, quiet spot and well worth the 40-mile drive from Yosemite Valley, especially if you're tired of the avalanche of humanity rolling through that area.

The 8-mile long Hetch Hetchy Reservoir, its placid surface reflecting clouds and cliffs, stretches behind **O'Shaughnessy Dam** (Map p378), site of a parking lot and trailheads. An easy 5.4-mile (round-trip) trail leads to the spectacular **Tueeulala** (*twee*-lala) and **Wapama Falls** (Map p378), which each plummet more than 1000ft over fractured granite walls on the north shore of the reservoir. **Hetch Hetchy Dome** (Map p378) rises up in the distance. This hike is best in spring, when temperatures are moderate and wildflowers poke out everywhere. Bring bug spray and keep an eye out for rattlesnakes, especially in summer.

There are no visitors services at Hetch Hetchy. The road is only open during daylight hours; specifics are posted at the Evergreen Rd turnoff. After hours the gate is locked in keeping with regulations set forth by the Department of Homeland Security, which considers O'Shaughnessy Dam a terrorist target.

ACTIVITIES

Hiking

Over 800 miles of hiking trails tempt trekkers of all abilities. Take an easy half-mile stroll on the valley floor; venture out all day on a quest for viewpoints, waterfalls and lakes or go wilderness camping in the remote outer reaches of the backcountry.

Some of the park's most popular hikes start right in Yosemite Valley, including, the most famous of all, to the top of **Half Dome** (Map p378; 17-mile round-trip). It follows a section of the John Muir Trail and is strenuous, difficult and best tackled in two days with an overnight in Little Yosemite Valley. Reaching the top can only be done after rangers have installed fixed cables. Depending on snow conditions, this may occur as early as late May or as late as July, and the cables usually come down in mid-October. During Saturdays and holiday weekends, human logjams form on the cables and the route becomes a bit more nerve-wracking as hikers must 'share the road.' The less ambitious or physically fit will still have a ball following the same trail as far as **Vernal Fall** (2.6-mile round-trip), the top of **Nevada Fall** (6.5-mile round-trip) or idyllic **Little Yosemite Valley** (Map p378; 8-mile round-trip). The **Four Mile Trail** (Map p380) to Glacier Point, which is actually a 9.2-mile round-trip, is a strenuous but satisfying climb to a glorious viewpoint (also see p381).

If you've got the kids in tow, nice and easy destinations include **Mirror Lake** (Map p378; 2-mile round-trip, 4.5 miles via the Tenaya Canyon Loop) in the valley, the **McGurk Meadow** (Map p378; 1.6-mile round-trip) trail on Glacier Point Rd, which has a historic log cabin to romp around in, and the trails meandering beneath the big trees of the **Mariposa Grove** (Map p378) in Wawona.

Also in the Wawona area is one of the park's prettiest (and often overlooked) hikes to **Chilnualna Falls** (Map p378; 8.6-mile round-trip). Best done between April and June, it follows a cascading creek to the top of the falls, starting gently, then hitting you with some grinding switchbacks before sort of leveling out again.

The highest concentration of hikes lies in the high country of Tuolumne Meadows, which is only open in summer. A popular choice here is the hike to **Dog Lake** (Map p378; 2.8-mile round-trip), but it gets busy. You can also trek along a relatively flat part of the John Muir Trail into lovely **Lyell Canyon** (Map p378; 17.6-mile round-trip if going all the way), following the Lyell Fork of the Tuolumne River.

Shedding the high-season crowds is easiest when you set foot into Yosemite's backcountry wilderness. Start by identifying a route that matches your schedule, skill and fitness level. Then secure a wilderness permit, which is free but mandatory for overnight trips. To prevent tent cities sprouting in the woods, a quota system limits the number of people leaving from each trailhead each day. For trips between mid-May and mid-September around 60% of the quota may be reserved for a $5 fee by phone (☎ 209-372-0740) or online (www.nps.gov/yose/wilderness/permits.htm) from 24 weeks to two days before your trip. The remainder are distributed by the office closest to the trailhead (on a first-come, first-served basis no earlier than 24 hours before your planned hike) at Yosemite Valley Wilderness Center, Tuolumne Meadows Wilderness Center, the information stations at Wawona and Big Oak Flat and the Hetch Hetchy Entrance. Reservations are not available from October to April, but you'll still need to get a permit.

At night you must be sure to store all scented items in bear-resistant containers, which may be rented for $5 per trip at the wilderness and visitors centers. For locations and details, check www.nps.gov/yose/planyourvisit/bearcanrentals.htm.

Backpacks, tents and other equipment can be rented at the **Yosemite Mountaineering School** (Map p380; ☎ 209-372-8344; www.yosemitemountaineering.com; Curry Village Mountain Sport Shop; trips incl food & equipment per day per person 1/2/3/4 or more people $256/160/138/133; 🕐 8:30am-noon & 1-5pm). The school also offers two-day Learn to Backpack trips for novices and three- and four-day guided backpacking trips, which are great for inexperienced and solo travelers. The cost depends on the number of people in your group. In summer, the school operates a branch from Tuolumne Meadows.

Rock Climbing

With its sheer spires, polished domes and soaring monoliths, Yosemite is rock-climbing nirvana. The main climbing season runs from April to October. Most climbers, including some legendary stars, stay at Camp 4 (p386) near El Cap, especially in spring and fall. In summer, another base camp springs up at

Tuolumne Meadows Campground (p386). Climbers looking for partners post notices on bulletin boards at either campground.

Yosemite Mountaineering School offers top-flight instruction for novice to advanced rock hounds, plus guided climbs and equipment rental. All-day beginners classes are $117 per person if the group size is at least three people, more if there are fewer.

The meadow across from El Capitan and the northeastern end of Tenaya Lake (off Tioga Rd) are good for watching climbers dangle from granite (binoculars are needed for a really good view). Look for the haul bags first – they're bigger, more colorful and move around more than the climbers, making them easier to spot.

Cycling

Mountain-biking isn't permitted within the park, but biking along the 12 miles of paved trails is a popular and environmentally friendly way of exploring the valley. See p388 for rental information.

Swimming

On a hot summer day, nothing beats a dip in the gentle **Merced River**, though if chilly water doesn't float your boat, you can always pay to play in the outdoor swimming pools at Curry Village and Yosemite Lodge (adult/child $5/4). With a sandy beach, Tenaya Lake is a frigid but interesting option, though White Wolf's Harden Lake evaporates to a balmy temperature by mid-summer.

Horseback Riding

Yosemite Stables (trips 2hr/half-/full day $59/79/119) Tuolumne Meadows (Map p378; ☎ 209-372-8427); Wawona (☎ 209-375-6502); Yosemite Valley (Map p380; ☎ 209-372-8348) runs guided trips to such scenic locales as Mirror Lake, the Chilnualna Falls and the Mariposa Grove of Giant Sequoias from three bases. The season runs from May to October, although this varies slightly by location. No experience is needed for the two-hour and half-day rides, but reservations are advised, especially at the Yosemite Valley stables.

Rafting

From around late May to July, floating the **Merced River** from Stoneman Meadow, near Curry Village, to Sentinel Bridge is a leisurely way to soak up Yosemite Valley views. Six-person **raft rentals** (☎ 209-372-8319; per person $26) for the 3-mile trip are available at Curry Village and include equipment and a shuttle ride back to the rental kiosk. Or bring your own and pay $3.25 for the shuttle ride.

River rats are also attracted to the fierce **Tuolumne River**, a classic Class IV run that plunges and thunders through boulder gardens and cascades. Both Oars and Zephyr Whitewater Expeditions (p389) run a variety of trips.

Winter Sports

The white coat of winter opens up a different set of things to do, as the valley becomes a quiet, frosty world of snow-draped evergreens, ice-coated lakes and vivid vistas of gleaming white mountains sparkling against blue skies. Winter tends to arrive in full force by mid-November and whimper out in early April. Most of the action converges on the family-friendly **Badger Pass Ski Area** (Map p378; ☎ 209-372-8430; www.badgerpass.com; lift ticket adult/child $40/15), one of California's oldest ski resorts, the gentle slopes of which are perfect for families and beginning skiers and snowboarders. It's about 22 miles from the valley on Glacier Point Rd. There are five chairlifts, 800 vertical feet and 10 runs, a full-service lodge, equipment rental ($24 to $35 for a full set of gear) and the excellent **Yosemite Ski School** (☎ 209-372-8432), where generations of novices have learned how to get down a hill safely (group lessons from $28).

Cross-country skiers can explore 350 miles of skiable trails and roads, including 90 miles of marked trails and 25 miles of machine-groomed track near Badger Pass. The scenic but grueling trail to Glacier Point – 21-mile round-trip – also starts from here. More trails are at Crane Flat and the Mariposa Grove. The nongroomed trails can also be explored with snowshoes.

TOP FIVE SPOTS FOR TOTS

- Feel small among the giants at Mariposa Grove (p382)
- Raft down the Merced River (right)
- Touch, listen and explore the exhibits at the Happy Isles Nature Center (p381)
- Earn a Junior Ranger badge (p714)
- Cycle Yosemite Valley or watch it go by from a bike trailer (above)

The **Badger Pass Cross-Country Center & Ski School** (☎ 209-372-8444) offers beginners' packages ($31), guided tours (from $45) and equipment rentals ($22). The center also runs overnight trips to **Glacier Point Ski Hut** (Map p380), a rustic stone and log cabin. Rates, including meals, are $192/110 guided/self-guided for one night or $288/220 for two nights.

More experienced skiers can trek 10 miles out to the **Ostrander Ski Hut** (Map p378; ☎ 209-379-2646; www.ostranderhut.com) on Ostrander Lake, operated by the Yosemite Association. It is staffed all winter and open to backcountry skiers and snowshoers for $30 to $45 per person, per night. See website for details.

Another delightful winter activity is taking a spin on the outdoor **Curry Village ice rink** (Map p380; ☎ 209-372-8341; per session $8, rental skates $3; 🕑 Nov-Mar), where you'll be skating under the watchful eye of Half Dome.

A free shuttle bus connects the valley and Badger Pass. Roads in the valley are plowed, and Hwys 41, 120 and 140 are usually kept open, conditions permitting. The Tioga Rd (Hwy 120 E), though, closes with the first snowfall (see boxed text, p379). Be sure to bring snow chains with you, as prices for them double once you hit the foothills.

TOP FIVE THINGS TO DO IN WINTER

- Snowshoeing among the giants of Mariposa Grove (p382)
- Ice-skating at Curry Village (left)
- Taking an overnight cross-country skiing trip to Glacier Point Ski Hut (left)
- Feasting like royalty at the Bracebridge Dinner (p381) in the Ahwahnee Hotel
- Toasting s'mores in the Mountain Room Lounge (p388)

TOURS

First-timers often appreciate the two-hour **Valley Floor Tour** (per adult/child $25/13; 🕑 year-round), which covers the valley highlights. For other tour options stop at the tour and activity desks at Yosemite Lodge, Curry Village or Yosemite Village, call ☎ 209-372-1240 or check www.yosemi tepark.com.

The Yosemite Mountaineering School (p383) offers guided hikes and cross-country ski trips.

SLEEPING

All noncamping reservations within the park are handled by **DNC Parks & Resorts** (☎ 801-559-5000; www.yosemitepark.com) and can be made up to 366 days in advance; they are absolutely critical from May to early September. Rates – and demand – drop from October to April.

Budget

Competition for campsites is fierce from May to September, when arriving without a reservation and hoping for the best is tantamount to getting someone to lug your Barcalounger up Half Dome. Even first-come, first-served campgrounds tend to fill by noon, especially on weekends and around holidays. **Reservations** (☎ 518-885-3639, 877-444-6777; www.recreation.gov) are accepted up to five months in advance, beginning the 15th of each month.

Without a booking, your only chance is to hightail it to an open first-come, first-served campground or proceed to one of four campground reservation offices: try to get there before they open at 8am, put your name on a waiting list and then hope for a cancellation or early departure. Return when the ranger tells you (usually 3pm) and if you hear your name, consider yourself very lucky indeed. There are offices in Yosemite Valley, Wawona, the Big Oak Flat Entrance and Tuolumne Meadows. The latter three are only open seasonally.

All campgrounds have flush toilets, except for Tamarack Flat, Yosemite Creek and Porcupine Flat, which have vault toilets and no potable water. Those at higher elevations get chilly at night, even in summer, so pack accordingly. The Yosemite Mountaineering School (p383) rents camping gear.

If you hold a wilderness permit, you may spend the nights before and after your trip in the backpacker campgrounds at Tuolumne Meadows, Hetch Hetchy, White Wolf and behind North Pines in Yosemite Valley. The cost is $5 per person, per night and reservations aren't necessary.

Housekeeping Camp (Map p380; Yosemite Valley; units $74; 🕑 Apr-Oct) This cluster of 266 cabins, each walled in by concrete on three sides and lidded by a canvas roof, is crammed and noisy, but the setting along the Merced River has its merits. Each unit sleeps up to four and has electricity, light, a table and chairs, and a covered patio with picnic tables.

HIGH SIERRA CAMPS

In the backcountry near Tuolumne Meadows, the exceptionally popular High Sierra Camps provide shelter and sustenance to hikers who'd rather not carry food or a tent. The camps – called Vogelsang, Merced Lake, Sunrise, May Lake and Glen Aulin – are set 6 miles to 10 miles apart along a loop trail. They consist of dormitory-style canvas tent cabins with beds, blankets or comforters, plus showers and a central dining tent. Guests bring their own sheets and towels. The rate is $136 per adult, per night, including breakfast and dinner. Organized hiking or saddle trips led by ranger naturalists are also available (from $825).

A short season (roughly late June to September) and high demand require a lottery for reservations. Applications may be requested in the fall (☎ 801-559-4909; www.yosemitepark.com) and must be submitted before mid-December. Dates vary year to year, so check the website for updates. If you don't have a reservation, call after April 1 to check for cancellations.

SIERRA NEVADA

Tuolumne Meadows Lodge (Map p378; Tioga Rd; tent cabins $89; 🕑 mid-Jun–mid-Sep) In the high country, about 55 miles from the valley, this option attracts hikers to its 69 canvas tent cabins with four beds, a wood-burning stove and candles (no electricity). It's much less crowded than Housekeeping Camp. Breakfast and dinner are available.

White Wolf Lodge (Map p378; Tioga Rd; tent cabins $82, cabins with bath $96; 🕑 mid-Jun–mid-Sep) This complex enjoys its own little world a mile up a spur road, away from the hubbub and traffic of Hwy 120 and the Valley. There are 24 spartan four-bedded tent cabins and four very in-demand hard-walled cabins that feel like rustic motel rooms. The generator cuts out at 11pm, so you'll need a flashlight until early morning. There's also a dining room and a tiny counter-service store.

Opening dates for seasonal campgrounds vary slightly each year.

Bridalveil Creek (Map p378; Glacier Point Rd; tent & RV sites $14; 🕑 Jul-early Sep) Quieter than the valley campgrounds with 110 sites at 7200ft.

Camp 4 (Map p380; Yosemite Valley; per person $5; 🕑 year-round) Walk-in campground at 4000ft popular with climbers; sites are shared.

Crane Flat (Map p378; Big Oak Flat Rd; tent & RV sites $20; 🕑 Jun-Sep) Large family campground, at 6192 ft, with 166 sites; some loops are first-come, first-served.

Hodgdon Meadow (Map p378; Big Oak Flat Rd; tent & RV sites $14-20; 🕑 year-round) Utilitarian and crowded 105-site campground at 4872ft; reservations required May to September.

Lower Pines (Map p380; Yosemite Valley; tent & RV sites $20; 🕑 Mar-Oct) Crammed and noisy with 60 sites at 4000ft; reservations required.

North Pines (Map p380; Yosemite Valley; tent & RV sites $20; 🕑 Apr-Sep) A bit off the beaten path (4000ft) with 81 sites near Mirror Lake; reservations required.

Porcupine Flat (Map p378; Tioga Rd; tent & RV sites $10; 🕑 Jul-Sep) Primitive 52-site area, at 8100ft; some sites near the road.

Tamarack Flat (Map p378; Tioga Rd; tent sites $10; 🕑 Jun-early Sep) Quiet, secluded, primitive at 6315ft; the 52 sites are a rough 3-mile drive off Tioga Rd.

Tuolumne Meadows (Map p378; Tioga Rd; tent & RV sites $20; 🕑 Jul-Sep) Biggest campground in the park (8600ft) with 304 fairly well-spaced sites.

Upper Pines (Map p380; Yosemite Valley; tent & RV sites $20; 🕑 year-round) Busy, busy, busy – and big (238 sites, 4000ft); reservations required.

Wawona (Map p378; Wawona; tent & RV sites $14-20; 🕑 year-round) Idyllic riverside setting at 4000ft with 93 spaces; reservations required May to September.

White Wolf (Map p378; Tioga Rd; tent & RV sites $14; 🕑 Jul-early Sep) Attractive setting at 8000ft, but the 74 sites are fairly boxed in.

Yosemite Creek (Map p378; Tioga Rd; tent sites $10; 🕑 Jul-early Sep) Most secluded and quiet campground (7659ft), reached via a rough 4.5-mile road; 40 sites.

Midrange

Curry Village (Map p380; Yosemite Valley; canvas cabins $89-92, cabins with/without bath $130/97, r $147-160; ♿) Founded in 1899 as a summer camp, Curry has hundreds of units squished tightly together beneath towering evergreens. The canvas cabins are basically glorified tents, so for more comfort, quiet and privacy get one of the cozy wood cabins, which have bedspreads, drapes and vintage posters. There are also 18 attractive motel-style rooms in the Stoneman House, including a loft suite sleeping up to six.

Yosemite Lodge at the Falls (Map p380; Yosemite Valley; r $147-192; 💻 ♿ wi-fi) Situated a short walk from Yosemite Falls, this multibuilding complex gets a thumbs up for its centrality, wide range of eateries, lively bar, big pool and other handy amenities. Rooms are fairly generic; the nicest are the upstairs units with beamed ceilings and Native American touches. All have cable TV, a telephone and, mostly, great panoramas unfolding from your patio or balcony.

Wawona Hotel (Map p378; Wawona; r with/without bath $196/128; mid-Mar–Nov & Dec holidays;) This National Historic Landmark, dating from 1879, is a collection of six graceful, white-washed New England–style buildings flanked by wide porches. The 104 rooms – with no TV or phone – come with Victorian-style furniture and other period items, and about half the rooms share bathrooms, with nice robes provided for the walk there. The grounds are lovely, with a spacious lawn dotted with Adirondack chairs.

Evergreen Lodge (Map p378; 209-379-2606, 800-935-6343; www.evergreenlodge.com; 33160 Evergreen Rd; cabins $159-285; Feb-Dec;) While technically not inside the park, the woodsy Evergreen Lodge, near the Hetch Hetchy Entrance about 7 miles north of Hwy 120, is worth mentioning. Rustic cabins have private porches but no phone or TV. For entertainment, you can swap tales with fellow guests in the lounge, restaurant or during staff-led outdoor activities, many of them family-oriented. Wi-fi in recreation building.

Ahwahnee Hotel (Map p380; Yosemite Valley; r from $449; wi-fi) The crème de la crème of Yosemite's lodging, this sumptuous historic property dazzles with soaring ceilings, Turkish kilims lining the hallways and atmospheric lounges with mammoth stone fireplaces. It's the gold standard for upscale lodges, though if you're not blessed with bullion, you can still soak up the ambience during afternoon tea, a drink in the bar or a gourmet meal.

EATING

You can find food options for all budgets and palates within the park, from greasy slabs of fast food to swanky cuts of top-notch steak.

Bringing in or buying your own food in the park saves money but remember that you *must* remove it all from your car (or backpack or bicycle) and store it overnight in a bear box or canister. The Village Store in Yosemite Village has the best selection (including toiletries, health-food items and some organic produce), while stores at Curry Village, Wawona, Tuolumne Meadows, Housekeeping Camp and the Yosemite Lodge are more limited.

Curry Village Pizza Patio (Map p380; Curry Village; pizza $7-17; year-round) Enjoy tasty pizza at this buzzing eatery that becomes a chatty après-hike hangout in the late afternoon.

Yosemite Lodge Food Court (Map p380; Yosemite Lodge at the Falls; mains under $10; year-round) This self-service restaurant serves breakfast, lunch and dinner. Make your selection at several tummy-filling stations serving pastas, burgers, hot sandwiches and other fare that holds up well under heat lamps, then proceed to the cashier and find a table inside or on the patio.

Degnan's Loft (Map p380; Yosemite Village; pizza $6-21; Apr-Oct) Head upstairs to this convivial place with high-beamed ceilings and a many-sided fireplace, and kick back under the dangling lift chair for decent salads, lasagna and pizza.

Curry Village Dining Pavilion (Map p380; Curry Village; breakfast $10, dinner $12; Apr-Nov) Although the cafeteria-style setting has all the charm of a train-station waiting room, the all-you-can-eat breakfast and dinner buffets are great for families, gluttons and the undecided.

Wawona Hotel Dining Room (Map p378; 209-375-1425; Wawona Hotel; breakfast & lunch $10-16, dinner $18-33; mid-Mar–Nov & Dec holidays) Beautiful sequoia-painted lamps light this old-fashioned white-tablecloth dining room, and the Victorian detail makes it an enchanting place to have an upscale (though somewhat overpriced) meal. 'Tasteful, casual attire' is the rule for dinner dress, and there's a barbecue on the lawn every Saturday during summer. The Wawona's wide, white porch makes a snazzy destination for evening cocktails, and in the lobby, listen for veteran pianist Tom Bopp.

Ahwahnee Dining Room (Map p380; 209-372-1489; Ahwahnee Hotel; mains breakfast & lunch $13-21, dinner $30-50; year-round) The formal ambience (mind your manners) may not be for everybody, but few would not be awed by the sumptuous decor, soaring beamed ceiling and palatial chandeliers. The menu is constantly in flux, but most dishes have perfect pitch and are beautifully presented. There's a dress code at dinner, but otherwise shorts and sneakers are OK. Sunday brunch ($39, 7am to 3pm) is amazing.

Mountain Room (Map p380; 209-372-1274; Yosemite Lodge; mains $16-30; dinner year-round) With a killer view of Yosemite Falls, the window tables at this casual and elegant contemporary steakhouse are a hot commodity. The chefs at the lodge whip up some of the best meals in the park, with flat-iron steak and locally caught mountain trout wooing diners under a rotating display of nature photographs.

Other refueling stops:

Curry Village Coffee Corner (Map p380; ⌚ mid-spring–fall) For a coffee jolt or sugar fix.

Curry Village Taqueria (Map p380; snacks $3-8; ⌚ spring-fall) Tacos and burritos on a deck near the parking area.

Tuolumne Meadows Grill (Map p378; mains $4-8; ⌚ Jun–mid-Sep) Scarf down burgers and grill items at the outdoor picnic tables.

Village Grill (Map p380; Yosemite Village; items $5-9; ⌚ Apr-Oct) Fight the chipmunks for your burgers and fries alfresco.

Degnan's Deli (Map p380; Yosemite Village; sandwiches $6) Made-to-order sandwiches, breakfast items and snack foods.

DRINKING

No one will mistake Yosemite for nightlife central, but there are some nice spots to relax with a cabernet, cocktail or cold beer. Outside the park, the Yosemite Bug Rustic Mountain Resort (p390) and the Evergreen Lodge (p387) both have lively lounges.

Mountain Room Lounge (Map p380; Yosemite Lodge, Yosemite Valley) Catch up on the latest sports news while knocking back draft brews at this large bar that buzzes in wintertime. Order a s'mores kit (graham crackers, chocolate squares and marshmallows) to roast in the open-pit fireplace.

Ahwahnee Bar (Map p380; Ahwahnee Hotel, Yosemite Valley) The perfect way to experience the Ahwahnee without dipping too deep into your pockets; settle in for a drink at this cozy bar, complete with pianist. Appetizers and light meals provide sustenance ($9 to $23).

ENTERTAINMENT

Yosemite Theater (Yosemite Village, West Auditorium; adult/child $8/4) The fascinating life and philosophy of John Muir is brought to the stage by actor Lee Stetson several times weekly. His wife, Connie, does a humorous yet poignant program portraying a 19th-century pioneer woman, and Park Ranger Shelton Johnson re-creates the experiences of a Buffalo Soldier (see the boxed text, p399). There are also special children's shows.

Other activities scheduled year-round include campfire programs, children's photo walks, twilight strolls, night-sky watching, ranger talks and slide shows, while the tavern at the Evergreen Lodge (p387) has live bands some weekends. Scan *Yosemite Today* for full details.

GETTING THERE & AWAY

Yosemite is accessible year-round from the west (via Hwys 120 W and 140) and south (Hwy 41), and in summer also from the east (via Hwy 120 E). Roads are plowed in winter, but snow chains may be required at any time. In 2006 a mammoth rockslide buried part of Hwy 140, 6 miles west of the park, and rerouted traffic is restricted to vehicles under 45ft.

Yosemite is one of the few national parks that can be reached by public transportation relatively easily. Greyhound buses and Amtrak trains serve Merced west of the park, where they are met by buses operated by **Yosemite Area Regional Transportation System** (Yarts; ☎ 209-388-9589, 877-989-2787; www.yarts.com). Buses travel to Yosemite Valley along Hwy 140 several times daily year-round stopping along the way. In summer, another Yarts route runs from Mammoth Lakes (p406) along Hwy 120 East via the Tioga Pass. Tickets to Yosemite Valley are $13 ($10 child and senior; three hours) one way from Merced and $15 ($10 child and senior; four hours) for Mammoth Lakes, less if boarding in between. They include the park entrance fee, making them a super bargain.

GETTING AROUND

Bicycle

Bicycling is an ideal way to take in Yosemite Valley. You can rent a wide-handled cruiser (per hour/day $9.50/25.50) or a bike with an attached child trailer (per hour/day $16/50.50) at the Yosemite Lodge at the Falls or Curry Village.

Car

The speed limit is 45mph, except in Yosemite Valley, where it drops to 35mph. Roadside signs with red bears mark the many spots where bears have been killed by motorists, so think before you hit the accelerator. Glacier Point and Tioga Rds are closed in winter.

Public Transportation

The free, air-conditioned Yosemite Valley Shuttle Bus is a comfortable and comparatively efficient way of traveling around the park. Buses operate year-round at frequent intervals and stop at 21 numbered locations, including parking lots, campgrounds, trailheads and lodges. For a route map, see *Yosemite Today*.

Free buses also operate between Wawona and the Mariposa Grove (spring to fall), and Yosemite Valley and Badger Pass (winter only). The Tuolumne Meadows Shuttle runs between Tuolumne Lodge and Olmsted Point in Tuolumne Meadows (usually mid-June to early September).

Two fee-based hikers' buses also travel from Yosemite Valley. For trailheads along Tioga Rd, catch the **Tuolumne Meadows Tour & Hikers' Bus** (☎ 209-372-1240; Jul-early Sep), which runs once daily in each direction. Fares depend on distance traveled; the trip to Tuolumne Meadows costs $14.50/23 one way/round-trip. The **Glacier Point Hikers' Bus** (☎ 209-372-1240; one way/return $25/41; mid-May–Oct) is good for hikers as well as for people reluctant to drive up the long, windy road themselves. Reservations are required.

YOSEMITE GATEWAYS

FISH CAMP

pop 600 / elev 4300ft

Fish Camp, just south of the park on Hwy 41, is more of a bend in the road, but it does have some good lodging options as well as the ever-popular **Sugar Pine Railroad** (☎ 559-683-7273; www.ymsprr.com; rides adult/child $17.50/8.75; Mar-Oct;), a historical steam train that chugs through the woods on a 4-mile loop.

Next door, the friendly **Narrow Gauge Inn** (☎ 559-683-7720, 888-644-9050; www.narrowgaugeinn.com; 48571 Hwy 41; r incl breakfast Nov-Mar $79-109, Apr-Oct $120-195; wi-fi) is a beautiful and supremely comfortable 26-room inn with a hot tub, small bar, and one of the finest restaurants around (mains $19 to $38, open for dinner Wednesday to Sunday, April to October). Each tastefully appointed room features unique decor and a pleasant deck facing the trees and mountains, and some rooms were recently remodeled with flat-screen TVs.

One of the least expensive indoor options in town, the **White Chief Mountain Lodge** (☎ 559-683-5444; www.whitechiefmtnlodge.com; 7776 White Chief Mountain Rd; r $100-110) is a year-round 1950s-era motel with simple, standard kitchenette rooms and a restaurant on the grounds. It's located a few hundred yards east of Hwy 41; watch for the sign and go up the little wooded country road.

The USFS **Summerdale Campground** (☎ 877-444-6677; www.recreation.gov; tent & RV sites $19-21; May-Sep) has 28 well-dispersed sites along Big Creek.

OAKHURST

pop 13,500 / elev 2400ft

At the junction of Hwys 41 and 49, about 15 miles south of the park entrance, Oakhurst functions primarily as a service town. This is your last chance to stock up on reasonably priced groceries, camping supplies, gasoline and bug spray.

Right in the center of town, the 60-unit **Oakhurst Lodge** (☎ 559-683-4417, 800-655-6343; www.oklodge.com; 40302 Hwy 41; r $70-110; wi-fi) presents a fine no-frills budget motel option, with quiet, clean kitchenette rooms.

A former ranch dating back to 1875, the **Sierra Sky Ranch** (☎ 559-683-8040; www.sierraskyranch.com; 50552 Rd 632; r $135-155; wi-fi) has numerous outdoor activities available on 14 attractive acres. The homespun rooms are phone-free and pet-friendly, with double doors that open onto shady verandas. The rambling and beautiful old lodge features a restaurant (dinner only) and a rustic saloon.

MERCED RIVER CANYON

The approach to Yosemite via Hwy 140 is one of the most scenic, especially the section that meanders through Merced River Canyon. The springtime runoff makes this a spectacular spot for **river rafting**, with many miles of class III and IV rapids. Outfitters include **Zephyr Whitewater Expeditions** (☎ 209-532-6249, 800-431-3636; www.zrafting.com) and **Oars** (☎ 800-346-6277; www.oars.com). Half-day trips start at $100.

MARIPOSA

pop 1400 / elev 2000ft

About halfway between Merced and Yosemite Valley, at the junction of Hwys 140 and 49, Mariposa (Spanish for 'butterfly') is the largest and most interesting town near the park. Established as a mining and railroad town during the Gold Rush, it has the oldest courthouse in continuous use (since 1854) west of the Mississippi and a friendly feel.

At the junction of Hwy 49s and 140 is the info-laden **Mariposa County Visitor Center** (☎ 209-966-7081, 866-425-3366; www.homeofyosemite.com; 5158

Hwy 41; 7am-8pm Mon-Sat, 8am-5pm Sun summer, 8am-5pm Mon-Sat winter), which has friendly staff and racks of brochures.

Rock hounds should drive to the Mariposa County Fairgrounds, 2 miles south of town on Hwy 49, to see the 13-pound 'Fricot Nugget' – the largest crystalized gold specimen from the California Gold Rush era – and other gems and machinery at the **California State Mining & Mineral Museum** (209-742-7625; admission $3; 10am-6pm May-Sep, 10am-4pm Wed-Mon Oct-Apr). An exhibit on glow-in-the-dark minerals is also very cool.

Beautifully spruced up with a bold splash of psychedelic purple and dusty orange paint, **River Rock Inn** (966-5793, 800-627-8439; www.riverrockncafe.com; 4993 7th St; r incl breakfast $69-92;) claims to be the oldest motel in town. Rooms done up in artsy earth tones have TVs but no phones, and calming ceiling fans resemble lily pads. A block removed from Hwy 140 on a quiet side street, it features a small courtyard deck and deli café, with live acoustic music on weekend evenings in summer.

More of a generic motel, the simple, well-kept and friendly **Mariposa Lodge** (209-966-3607, 800-966-8819; www.mariposalodge.com; 5052 Hwy 140; r $109-129; wi-fi) sports clean, quiet rooms (with TV and phone) and friendly staff. It earns pluses for the good-sized rooms and for the blooming flowers that border the grounds.

The best restaurant in town is **Savoury's** (209-966-7677; 5027 Hwy 140; mains $15-28), whose food and walled-in courtyard will mentally transport you to Italy. It's tiny, so reservations are recommended.

MIDPINES

pop 980 / elev 2400ft

The highlight of this almost nonexistent town is the folksy **Yosemite Bug Rustic Mountain Resort** (209-966-6666, 866-826-7108; www.yosemitebug.com; dm $23, tent cabins $35-55, r $75-135, cabins with shared bath $65-85; wi-fi), tucked away on a forested hillside about 25 miles from the park. It's more like a convivial mountain retreat than a hostel: at night, a United Nations of friendly folks of all ages share stories, music and inexpensive meals in the woodsy café-lounge before retreating to whatever bed their money can buy – a dorm bunk, a tent cabin, a private room with shared facilities or a uniquely decorated cabin with private bathroom. Dorm dwellers have access to a communal kitchen, and the resort now has a spa just down the road with a hot tub, yoga lessons and massages available. The Yarts bus stops a quarter mile up the driveway, and the resort's Bug Bus tours offer a range of hiking trips (including overnights) to Yosemite.

BRICEBURG

Some 20 miles outside the park, right where the Merced River meets Hwy 140, Briceburg consists of a **visitors center** (209-379-9414, 916-985-4474; 1-6pm Fri, 9am-6pm Sat & Sun mid-Apr–Aug) and three primitive Bureau of Land Management (BLM) campgrounds ($10) with a to-die-for location right on the river. To reach them, you cross a beautiful 1920s wooden suspension bridge, so long trailers and large RVs are not recommended.

EL PORTAL

pop 1000 / elev 2100ft

Right outside the Arch Rock Entrance, and primarily inhabited by park employees, El Portal makes a convenient Yosemite base.

Primarily an inexpensive private campground, **Indian Flat RV Park** (209-379-2339, www.indianflatrvpark.com; 9988 Hwy 140; tent sites $20-30, RV sites $35-40, tent cabins $59, cottages $109;) has a number of interesting housing options, including two pretty stone cottages with air-conditioning. It's right on the way to the park, and nonguests can pay to shower.

Less than 2 miles from the park entrance, the modern complex of **Yosemite View Lodge** (209-379-2681, 800-321-5261; www.yosemiteresorts.us; 11166 Hwy 140; r $159-189, ste $219-439;) embraces hot tubs, restaurants and four pools. The nicest of its 336 rooms feature kitchenettes, gas fireplaces and views of the Merced River. Souped-up 'majestic suites' are massive, with crazy-opulent bathrooms featuring waterfall showers and plasma TV entertainment centers.

GROVELAND

pop 1500 / elev 2800ft

From the Big Oak Flat Entrance, it's 22 miles to Groveland, an adorable town with restored Gold Rush–era buildings.

A friendly 10-room 1918 confection with beds adorned in patchwork quilts, the **Hotel Charlotte** (209-962-7872, 800-961-7799; www.hotelcharlotte.com; 18736 Hwy 120; r incl breakfast $109-169; wi-fi) keeps the vintage flair alive. The

SIERRA NEVADA

cute café (mains $11 to $20) does creative things with chicken.

Across the street from the Hotel Charlotte, the historic **Groveland Hotel** (☎ 209-962-4000, 800-273-3314; www.groveland.com; 18767 Main St; r incl breakfast $145-285; wi-fi) dates from 1850 and now houses a saloon with Gold Rush flair, an upscale restaurant (mains $21 to $36) and 17 bright, lovingly decorated rooms with wraparound verandas.

SEQUOIA & KINGS CANYON NATIONAL PARKS

The twin parks of Sequoia and Kings Canyon dazzle with superlatives, though they're often overshadowed by Yosemite, their smaller neighbor to the north. With towering forests of giant sequoias containing some of the largest trees in the world, and the mighty Kings River careening through the depths of Kings Canyon, one of the deepest chasms in the country, the parks are lesser-visited jewels where it's easier to find quiet and solitude. Throw in opportunities for cave spelunking, rock climbing and backcountry hiking through granite-carved Sierra landscapes, and backdoor access to Mt Whitney, the tallest peak in the lower 48 states, and you have all the ingredients for one of the best parks in the country.

In 1890 Sequoia became the second national park in the USA (after Yellowstone). A few days later, the 4 sq miles around Grant Grove were declared Grant Grove National Park and, in 1940, absorbed into the newly created Kings Canyon National Park. In 2000, to protect additional sequoia groves, vast tracts of land in the surrounding national forest became the Giant Sequoia National Monument. The Bush administration subsequently attempted to open up the area to commercial logging, but a 2006 court ruling thwarted these plans for the time being.

The two parks, although distinct, are operated as one unit with a single admission (valid for seven consecutive days) of $20 per carload or $10 for individuals arriving on bicycle or foot. For 24-hour recorded information, call ☎ 559-565-3341 or visit www.nps.gov/seki, the parks' comprehensive website. At either entrance station, you'll receive an NPS map and a copy of the parks' *The Guide* newspaper with information on seasonal activities, camping and special programs, including those in the surrounding national forests and the Giant Sequoia National Monument.

Gas is available at Hume Lake and Stony Creek Lodge, both on forest land. Most cell phones do not work in this area.

Dangers & Annoyances

Air pollution wafting up from the Central Valley Sequoia and Kings Canyon often thwarts long-range visibility, and people with respiratory problems should check with a visitors center about current pollution levels. Black bears are common and proper food storage is always required. Heed park instructions on wildlife procedures and read the 'Bear Necessities' boxed text, p70.

KINGS CANYON NATIONAL PARK

With a dramatic cleft deeper than the Grand Canyon, Kings Canyon offers true adventure to those who crave seemingly endless trails, rushing streams and gargantuan rock formations. The camping, backcountry exploring and climbing here are all superb, with opportunities for surveying giant sequoias, gushing waterfalls, an exquisite cavern and a scenic driving road.

Orientation

Kings Canyon National Park has two developed areas with markets, lodging, showers and visitor information. Grant Grove Village is only 4 miles past the Big Stump Entrance (in the park's west), while Cedar Grove Village is 31 miles east at the bottom of the canyon. The two are separated by the Giant Sequoia National Monument and are linked by Kings Canyon Scenic Byway/Hwy 180.

Information

The gift shops at Grant Grove Village and the Cedar Grove market have ATMs. The post office is in Grant Grove Village.

Cedar Grove Visitor Center (☎ 559-565-3793; 9am-5pm late May-Sep) For tourist information.

Grant Grove Visitor Center (☎ 559-565-4307; 8am-8pm mid-Jun–Sep, 9am-4:30pm Oct–mid-Jun) Has exhibits, maps and wilderness permits.

Roads End Ranger Station (7am-3pm) Six miles east of Cedar Grove Village. Issues wilderness permits and sells topo maps and trail guides.

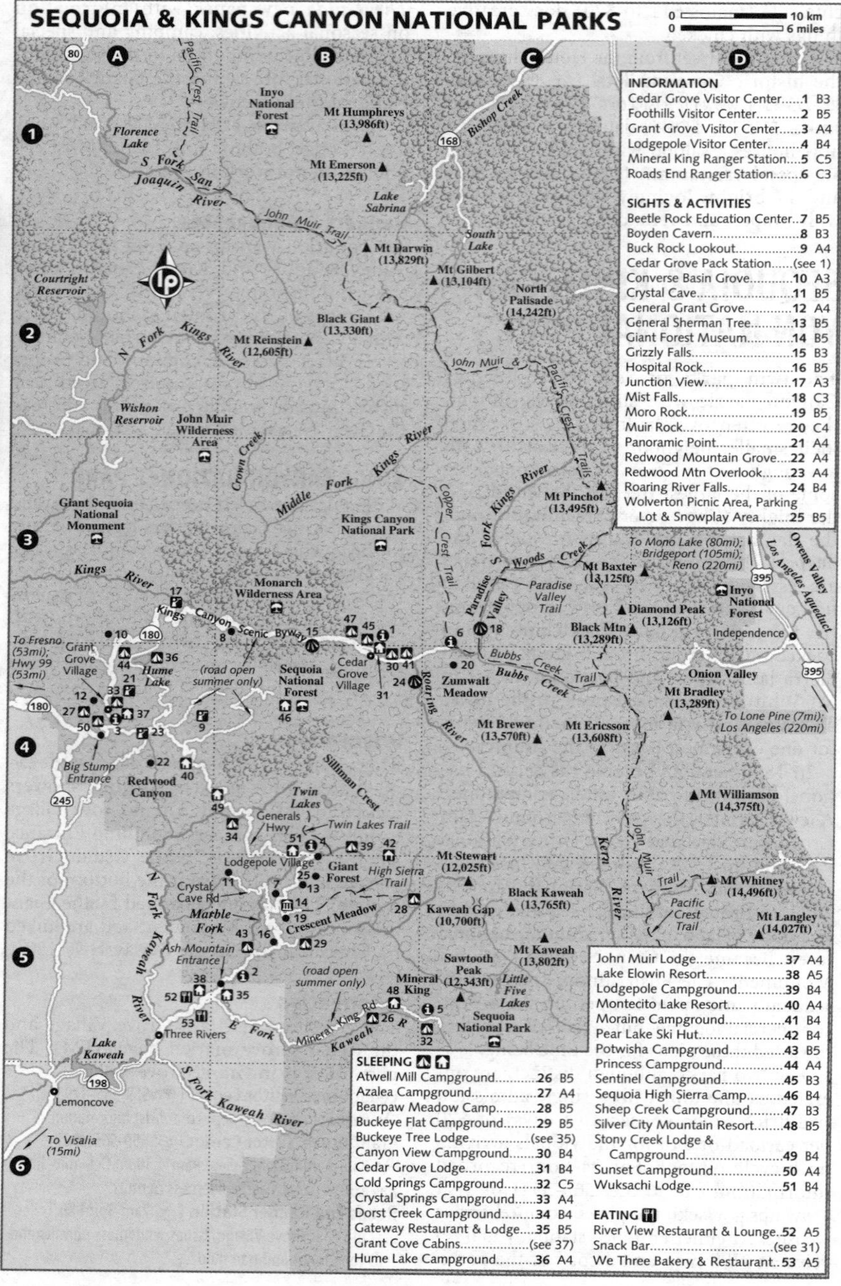
SEQUOIA & KINGS CANYON NATIONAL PARKS
0 10 km
0 6 miles
INFORMATION
Cedar Grove Visitor Center......1 B3
Foothills Visitor Center............2 B5
Grant Grove Visitor Center......3 A4
Lodgepole Visitor Center.........4 B4
Mineral King Ranger Station....5 C5
Roads End Ranger Station.......6 C3
SIGHTS & ACTIVITIES
Beetle Rock Education Center..7 B5
Boyden Cavern.........................8 B3
Buck Rock Lookout...................9 A4
Cedar Grove Pack Station......(see 1)
Converse Basin Grove............10 A3
Crystal Cave............................11 B5
General Grant Grove..............12 A4
General Sherman Tree............13 B5
Giant Forest Museum..............14 B5
Grizzly Falls............................15 B3
Hospital Rock..........................16 B5
Junction View..........................17 A3
Mist Falls.................................18 C3
Moro Rock................................19 B5
Muir Rock.................................20 C4
Panoramic Point......................21 A4
Redwood Mountain Grove......22 A4
Redwood Mtn Overlook..........23 A4
Roaring River Falls..................24 B4
Wolverton Picnic Area, Parking Lot & Snowplay Area.........25 B5
SLEEPING
Atwell Mill Campground...........26 B5
Azalea Campground.................27 A4
Bearpaw Meadow Camp...........28 B5
Buckeye Flat Campground........29 B5
Buckeye Tree Lodge................(see 35)
Canyon View Campground........30 B4
Cedar Grove Lodge..................31 B4
Cold Springs Campground.........32 C5
Crystal Springs Campground......33 A4
Dorst Creek Campground..........34 B4
Gateway Restaurant & Lodge....35 B5
Grant Cove Cabins..................(see 37)
Hume Lake Campground...........36 A4
John Muir Lodge.......................37 A4
Lake Elowin Resort....................38 A5
Lodgepole Campground.............39 B4
Montecito Lake Resort...............40 A4
Moraine Campground.................41 B4
Pear Lake Ski Hut......................42 B4
Potwisha Campground...............43 B5
Princess Campground................44 A4
Sentinel Campground................45 B3
Sequoia High Sierra Camp.........46 B4
Sheep Creek Campground.........47 B3
Silver City Mountain Resort........48 B5
Stony Creek Lodge & Campground...........49 B4
Sunset Campground...................50 A4
Wuksachi Lodge........................51 B4
EATING
River View Restaurant & Lounge..52 A5
Snack Bar.................................(see 31)
We Three Bakery & Restaurant..53 A5
Inyo National Forest
Mt Humphreys (13,986ft)
Mt Emerson (13,225ft)
Lake Sabrina
Bishop Creek
South Lake
Mt Darwin (13,829ft)
Mt Gilbert (13,104ft)
North Palisade (14,242ft)
Black Giant (13,330ft)
Mt Reinstein (12,605ft)
Florence Lake
S Fork San Joaquin River
John Muir Trail
Pacific Crest Trail
Courtright Reservoir
N Fork Kings River
Wishon Reservoir
John Muir Wilderness Area
Crown Creek
Middle Fork Kings River
Copper Creek Trail
John Muir & Pacific Crest Trails
Mt Pinchot (13,495ft)
S Fork Kings River
Giant Sequoia National Monument
Kings Canyon National Park
Woods Creek
Mt Baxter (13,125ft)
To Mono Lake (80mi); Bridgeport (105mi); Reno (220mi)
Owens Valley
Los Angeles Aqueduct
Inyo National Forest
Independence
Kings River
Monarch Wilderness Area
Kings Canyon Scenic Byway
Paradise Valley
Paradise Valley Trail
Diamond Peak (13,126ft)
Black Mtn (13,289ft)
To Fresno (53mi); Hwy 99 (53mi)
Grant Grove Village
Hume Lake
(road open summer only)
Sequoia National Forest
Cedar Grove Village
Zumwalt Meadow
Roaring River
Bubbs Creek
Bubbs Creek Trail
Onion Valley
Mt Bradley (13,289ft)
To Lone Pine (7mi); Los Angeles (220mi)
Mt Brewer (13,570ft)
Mt Ericsson (13,608ft)
Big Stump Entrance
Redwood Canyon
Silliman Crest
Twin Lakes
Twin Lakes Trail
Generals Hwy
Mt Williamson (14,375ft)
Lodgepole Village
Giant Forest
High Sierra Trail
Mt Stewart (12,025ft)
Crystal Cave Rd
Marble Fork
N Fork Kaweah River
Crescent Meadow
Kaweah Gap (10,700ft)
Black Kaweah (13,765ft)
Kern River
Mt Whitney (14,496ft)
Mt Langley (14,027ft)
Ash Mountain Entrance
Mt Kaweah (13,802ft)
Sawtooth Peak (12,343ft)
Little Five Lakes
Mineral King
Mineral King Rd
E Fork Kaweah R
Sequoia National Park
Three Rivers
Lake Kaweah
Lemoncove
S Fork Kaweah River
To Visalia (15mi)

Sights & Activities

GENERAL GRANT GROVE

The magnificence of this sequoia grove was recognized in 1890 when Congress designated it General Grant National Park, and in 1940 it became part of the newly created Kings Canyon National Park. The paved half-mile **General Grant Tree Trail** is an interpretive walk that visits a number of mature sequoias, including the 27-story **General Grant Tree**. This giant holds triple honors as the world's third-largest living tree, a memorial to US soldiers killed in war and as the nation's Christmas tree. The nearby **Fallen Monarch**, a massive, fire-hollowed trunk that you can walk through, has been a cabin, hotel, saloon and stables for US Cavalry horses.

PANORAMIC POINT

For a breathtaking view, head up 2.3 miles on supersteep Panoramic Point Rd (trailers and RVs not recommended). Steep canyons and the snowcapped peaks of the rugged ridge known as the Great Western Divide unfold below you. Snow closes the road to vehicles but not to cross-country skis.

KINGS CANYON SCENIC BYWAY (HIGHWAY 180)

The 31-mile rollercoaster road connecting Grant Grove and Cedar Grove ranks among the most dazzling in all of California. It winds past the **Converse Basin Grove**, which once contained the world's largest grove of mature sequoias until loggers turned it into a sequoia cemetery in the 1880s. A half-mile loop trail leads to the **Chicago Stump**, the remains of the tree that was cut down, sectioned and reassembled for the 1893 World Columbian Exposition in Chicago. Skeptical Easterners, thinking it was put together from several trees, called it the 'California hoax.' North of here, a second side road goes to **Stump Meadow**, where stumps and fallen logs make good picnic platforms, and to the **Boole Tree Trail**, a 2.5-mile loop to the only 'monarch' left to live.

Kings Canyon Scenic Byway soon begins its jaw-dropping descent into the canyon, serpentining past chiseled rock walls, some tinged by green moss and red iron minerals, others decorated by waterfalls. Turnouts provide superb views, especially at **Junction View**.

Eventually the road runs parallel with the gushing Kings River, its thunderous roar ricocheting off granite cliffs soaring as high as 8000ft, making Kings Canyon deeper than even the Grand Canyon. Stop at **Boyden Cavern** (☎ 559-338-0959; adult/child $12.50/7.50; 🕑 10am-5pm Jun-Sep, 11am-4pm Apr-May & Oct-Nov) for a tour of its whimsical formations. While beautiful, they are smaller and less impressive than Crystal Cave (p396) in Sequoia National Park, but no advance tickets are required. About 5 miles further east, **Grizzly Falls** can be torrential or drizzly, depending on the time of year.

On your return trip, consider a detour via **Hume Lake**, created in 1908 as a dam for logging operations and now offering boating, swimming and fishing. Facilities include a small market and a gas station.

CEDAR GROVE VILLAGE & ROADS END

At Cedar Grove Village a simple lodge and snack bar provide the last outpost of civilization before the rugged grandeur of the backcountry. Pretty spots around here include **Roaring River Falls**, where water whips down a sculpted rock channel before tumbling into a churning pool, and the 1.5-mile **Zumwalt Meadow Loop**, an easy nature trail around a verdant green meadow bordered by river and granite canyon. A short walk from Roads End,

WILDERNESS PERMITS: SEQUOIA AND KINGS CANYON NATIONAL PARKS

With 850 miles of marked trails, the parks are a backpacker's dream. Cedar Grove and Mineral King offer the best backcountry access. Trails are usually open by mid- to late May.

For overnight backcountry trips you'll need a wilderness permit ($15 per group), which is subject to a quota system in summer. About 75% of spaces can be reserved, the rest are available in person on a first-come, first-served basis. Reservations can be made from March 1 until two weeks before your trip. For details see www.nps.gov/seki/planyourvisit/wilderness.htm. There's also a dedicated wilderness desk at the **Lodgepole Visitor Center** (☎ 559-565-4408).

All ranger stations and visitors centers carry topo maps and hiking guides. Note that you need to store your food in park-approved bearproof canisters, which can be rented at markets and visitors centers (from $5 per trip).

Muir Rock is a large flat river boulder where John Muir often gave talks during Sierra Club field trips. The rock now bears his name, and the lazy river setting explodes with gleeful swimmers in summer.

The trail to **Mist Falls** (8-mile round-trip) is an easy to moderate hike to one of the park's larger waterfalls. The first 2 miles are fairly exposed, so start early to avoid the midday heat. Continuing past Mist Falls, it eventually connects with the John Muir/Pacific Crest Trail to form the 42-mile **Rae Lakes Loop**, the most popular long-distance trek in Kings Canyon National Park (wilderness permit required, see p400).

For guided horse trips, both day and overnight, check with **Cedar Grove Pack Station** (☎ 559-565-3464).

REDWOOD CANYON

South of Grant Grove Village, more than 15,000 sequoias cluster in this secluded and pristine corner of the park, making it the world's largest such grove. Relatively inaccessible, this area lets you enjoy the majesty of the giants away from the crowds on several moderate-to-strenuous trails. The trailhead is at the end of an unsigned, 2-mile bumpy dirt road across from the Hume Lake/Quail Flat sign on Generals Hwy, about 6 miles south of the village. If you want to pitch a tent, pick up a free permit from the Grant Grove Visitor Center.

Sleeping

Unless noted, all campsites are first-come, first-served. Showers are available at Grant Grove Village and Cedar Grove Village. The latter also has laundry facilities.

Cedar Grove's Sentinel campground, next to the village area, is open whenever Hwy 180 is open; Sheep Creek, Canyon View (tent only) and Moraine are opened as overflow when needed. These campgrounds are usually the last to fill up on busy summer weekends and are also good bets early and late in the season thanks to their comparatively low elevation (4600ft). All have flush toilets and $18 sites. Other facilities in the village don't start operating until mid-May.

Potential campers should also keep in mind that there are great free uncrowded and undeveloped campgrounds off Big Meadows Rd in the Sequoia National Forest. They're some of the only empty campsites in the Sierra Nevada during peak summer season. Also, free roadside camping is allowed in the forest, but no campfires without a permit (available from the Grant Grove Visitor Center).

Princess (☎ 877-444-6777; www.recreation.gov; Giant Sequoia National Monument; tent & RV sites $17; ⌚ May-Sep) About 6 miles north of Grant Grove, with vault toilets and 90 reservable sites; evocative sequoia stumps at the registration area.

Azalea (tent & RV sites $18; ⌚ year-round) Flush toilets, 110 sites; the nicest sites border a meadow. Close to Grant Grove Village (elevation 6500ft).

Crystal Springs (tent & RV sites $18; ⌚ late May–mid-Sep) Fifty wooded, well-spaced sites with flush toilets; the smallest campground in the Grant Grove area and generally very quiet.

Sunset (tent & RV sites $18; ⌚ late May–mid-Sep) Flush toilets, 157 sites, some overlooking the western foothills and the Central Valley. Close to Grant Grove Village.

Hume Lake (☎ 877-444-6777; www.recreation.gov; Hume Lake Rd, Giant Sequoia National Monument; tent & RV sites $19; ⌚ May-Sep) Flush toilets, 74 reservable sites; on the lake's northern shore about 10 miles northeast of Grant Grove.

Grant Grove Cabins (☎ 559-335-5500, 866-522-6966; www.sequoia-kingscanyon.com; Grant Grove Village; tent cabins $62-77, cabins with private bath $129-140,

GIANT SEQUOIAS: KINGS OF THE FOREST

In California you can stand under the world's oldest trees (in the Ancient Bristlecone Pine Forest, p413) and its tallest (the coastal redwoods in Redwood National Park, p292), but the record for biggest in terms of volume belongs to the giant sequoias *(Sequoiadendron giganteum)*. They grow only on the Sierra's western slope and are most abundant in Sequoia and Kings Canyon and Yosemite National Parks. John Muir called them 'Nature's forest masterpiece' and anyone who's ever craned their neck to take in their soaring vastness has done so with the awe usually reserved for Gothic cathedrals. Trees can grow to 300ft tall and 40ft in diameter with bark over 2ft thick. The Giant Forest Museum (p396) in Sequoia National Park has excellent exhibits about their fascinating history and ecology.

without bath $77-91) Set amid colossal sugar pines, 50-some cabins range from the decrepit tent-top shacks in 'Tent City' to the rustic yet comfortable heated duplexes (a few of which are wheelchair accessible) with electricity and private bathrooms. For loud lovebirds, number 9 – nicknamed the 'Honeymoon Cabin' – is the lone hard-sided cabin with a queen bed and no attached neighbors. The heated cabins are the only ones open year-round.

Cedar Grove Lodge (☎ 559-335-5500, 866-522-6966; www.sequoia-kingscanyon.com; Cedar Grove Village; r $119-135; May-Oct; wi-fi) The only indoor sleeping option in the canyon offers 21 motel-meets-lodge accommodations, some with kitchenettes. Decor isn't a strong point – the hallways tend toward dingy, the basic bathrooms are cramped and the bedspreads scream frumpy. Try to score one of the three ground-floor rooms with shady furnished patios with spiffy river views. All rooms have phones but no TVs.

John Muir Lodge (☎ 559-335-5500, 866-522-6966; www.sequoia-kingscanyon.com; Grant Grove Village; r $170-180) An atmospheric wooden building lined with historic old black-and-white photographs, this newer hotel is a comfortable place to lay your head and still feel like you're in the forest. Wide porches have wooden rocking chairs, and the homespun rooms contain rough-hewn wood furniture with bark trim, rustic wood headboards and patchwork bedspreads. There's a big stone fireplace for chilly nights, as well as a handy stash of board games. Open year-round; the rates halve in winter.

Eating

Grant Grove Restaurant (☎ 559-335-5500; mains breakfast & lunch $5-9, dinner $9-22; year-round;) More of a diner than a restaurant. Most visitors eat here, and there can be a wait at times. There's a breakfast, lunch sandwiches and filling all-American dinners. Vegetarians can always find at least one non-rabbit-food option, and children get their own menu as well.

The markets in Grant Grove Village and Cedar Grove Village have a limited selection of groceries.

Also worth noting:

Snack bar (☎ 559-565-0100; Cedar Grove Lodge; breakfast & lunch $2.50-8, dinner $10-17; May-early Oct) This basic grill is all about burgers, hot dogs, fried chicken, pork chops, and other hot and greasy fare.

DETOUR: BUCK ROCK LOOKOUT

Built in 1923, this active **fire lookout** (www.buckrock.org; 9:30am-6pm approx Jul-Oct) is one of the finest restored watchtowers you could ever hope to visit. Staffed in fire season, its 172 stairs lead to a dollhouse-sized wooden cab on a dramatic 8500ft granite rise with panoramic bird's-eye forest views. To reach it from General Hwy, go about 1 mile north of the Montecito Lake Resort and then east onto Big Meadows Rd (FS road 14S11). At approximately 2.5 miles, turn north on the signed dirt road (FS road 13S04) and follow signs another 3 miles to the lookout parking area.

Pizza parlor (pizza $7-25; 2-9pm summer, variable hours otherwise) Excellent crisp-crust pizzeria hidden off the back porch of the main Grant Grove restaurant; shows movies.

Getting There & Around

From the west, Kings Canyon Scenic Byway (Hwy 180) travels 53 miles east from Fresno to the Big Stump Entrance. Coming from the south, you're in for a long 46-mile drive through Sequoia National Park along sinuous Generals Hwy. Budget about two hours' driving time from the Ash Mountain Entrance to Grant Grove Village. The road to Cedar Grove Village is only open from around April or May until the first snowfall. For more on winter travel, see the boxed text, p397.

SEQUOIA NATIONAL PARK

Picture unzipping your tent flap and crawling out into a 'front yard' of trees as high as a 20-story building and as old as the Bible. Brew some coffee as you plan your day in this extraordinary park with its soul-sustaining forests and gigantic peaks soaring above 12,000ft.

Orientation

Nearly all of the park's star attractions are conveniently lined up along the Generals Hwy, which starts at the Ash Mountain Entrance and continues north into Kings Canyon. Tourist activity concentrates in the Giant Forest area and in Lodgepole Village, which has the most facilities, including a visitors center and market. The road to remote Mineral King veers off Hwy 198 in the town of Three Rivers, just south of the park's Ash Mountain Entrance. It is open from late May through October.

Information

Lodgepole Village has an ATM and a post office.

Foothills Visitor Center (☎ 559-565-3135; 🕑 8am-6pm Jun-Aug, to 4:30pm Sep-May) One mile north of Ash Mountain Entrance.

Lodgepole Visitor Center (☎ 559-565-4436; 🕑 7am-6pm late May-Aug, 7am-5pm Sep, 8am-4:30pm Oct, closed Nov–mid-May) Maps, information, exhibits, Crystal Cave tickets and wilderness permits (7am to 11am and noon-3:45pm).

Mineral King Ranger Station (☎ 559-565-3768; 🕑 8am-4pm Jun–mid-Sep) Twenty-four miles east of Generals Hwy; wilderness permits and campground availability info.

Sights & Activities

GIANT FOREST

Named by John Muir in 1875, this area is the top destination in the parks, and about 2 miles south of Lodgepole Village. By volume, the largest living tree on earth, the massive **General Sherman Tree** rockets 275ft to the sky. Pay your respects via a short descent from the Wolverton Rd parking lot, or join the **Congress Trail**, a paved 2-mile pathway that takes in General Sherman and other notable named trees, including the **Washington Tree**, the world's second biggest, and the see-through **Telescope Tree**. To lose the crowds, set off on the 5-mile **Trail of the Sequoias**, which puts you into the heart of the forest.

For a primer on the intriguing ecology, fire cycle and history of the 'big trees', drop in at the excellent **Giant Forest Museum** (☎ 559-565-4480; admission free; 🕑 9am-7pm summer, to 6pm spring & fall, to 4pm winter), then follow up your visit with a spin around the paved (and wheelchair-accessible) 1.2-mile interpretive **Big Trees Trail**, which starts right from the museum parking lot.

Bugs, bones and artificial animal scat are just some of the cool things children get to play with at the **Beetle Rock Education Center** (☎ 559-565-4480; admission free; 🕑 10am-4pm summer; 👶). A bright and cheerful cabin with activity stations galore, here inquisitive kiddos can scan bugs with digital microscopes, touch a taxidermied bobcat, put on a puppet show and paint ecology posters. Tents are set up for inside play, and binoculars lure youngsters out back for spotting animals.

Open in the warmer months, Crescent Meadow Rd heads east from the museum for 3 miles to **Crescent Meadow**, a relaxing picnic spot, especially in spring when it's ablaze with wildflowers. Several short hikes start from here, including the 1-mile trail to **Tharp's Log**, where the area's first white settler spent summers in a fallen tree. The road also passes **Moro Rock**, a landmark granite dome whose top can be reached via a quarter-mile carved staircase for breathtaking views of the Great Western Divide, a chain of mountains running north to south through the center of Sequoia National Park.

CRYSTAL CAVE

Discovered in 1918 by two fishermen, **Crystal Cave** (☎ 559-565-3759; www.sequoiahistory.org; Crystal Cave Rd; adult/child/senior $11/6/10; 🕑 tours 11am-4pm mid-May–Oct) was carved by an underground river and has formations estimated to be 10,000 years old. Stalactites hang like daggers from the ceiling, and milky white marble formations take the shape of ethereal curtains, domes, columns and shields. The 45-minute tour covers a half-mile of chambers. Longer tours ($19) and all-day, off-trail spelunking explorations ($129) are also available.

Tickets are *only* sold at the Lodgepole and Foothills visitors centers and *not* at the cave. Allow about one hour to get to the cave entrance, which is a half-mile walk from the parking lot at the end of a twisty 7-mile road; the turnoff is about 3 miles south of the Giant Forest. Bring a sweater or light jacket, as it's a huddle-for-warmth 48°F inside.

FOOTHILLS

From the Ash Mountain Entrance in Three Rivers, the Generals Hwy ascends steeply through this southern section of Sequoia National Park. With an average elevation of about 2000ft, the Foothills are much drier and warmer than the rest of the park. **Hiking** here is best in spring when the air is still cool and wildflowers put on a colorful show. Summers are buggy and muggy, but fall again brings moderate temperatures and lush foliage.

The Potwisha people lived in this area until the early 1900s, relying primarily on acorn meal. Pictographs and grinding holes

WINTER FUN

In winter, a thick blanket of snow drapes over trees and meadows, the pace of activity slows in the parks and a hush falls over the roads and trails. Note that snow often closes Generals Hwy between Grant Grove and Giant Forest and that tire chains may be required at any time. These can usually be rented near the park entrances, although you're not supposed to put them on rental cars. For up-to-date road conditions call ☎ 559-565-3341 or check www.nps.gov/seki.

Snowshoeing and **cross-country skiing** are both hugely popular activities with about 40 miles of marked but ungroomed trails crisscrossing the Grant Grove and Giant Forest areas. Trail maps are available at the visitors centers, and on weekends rangers lead free guided tours. Tree-marked trails connect with those in the Giant Sequoia National Monument and the 50 miles of groomed terrain maintained by the private **Montecito Lake Resort** (☎ 559-565-3388, 800-227-9900; www.mslodge.com; 8000 Generals Hwy; day pass incl lunch $30). Equipment rentals are available at Grant Grove Village, the Wuksachi Lodge and the Montecito Lake Resort. There are also **snow-play areas** near Columbine and Big Stump in the Grant Grove region, and at the Wolverton Picnic Area & Parking Lot.

In winter, cross-country skiers with reservations can stay in one of the 10 bunks at **Pear Lake Ski Hut** (☎ 559-565-3759; www.sequoiahistory.org; dm $26; mid-Dec–Apr), a 1940-era pine-and-granite building run by the Sequoia Natural History Association. You'll be oh-so-glad to see it after the strenuous 6-mile cross-country ski or snowshoe trek from Wolverton Meadow. Reservations are assigned by lottery in November. Call or check the website for details.

See p393 for winter activities at Kings Canyon National Park.

SIERRA NEVADA

still grace the **Hospital Rock** picnic area, once a Potwisha village site. **Swimming holes** abound along the Marble Fork of the Kaweah River, especially near Potwisha Campground (p398). Be careful, though – the currents can be deadly, especially when the river is swollen from the spring runoff.

MINERAL KING

A scenic, subalpine valley at 7500ft, Mineral King is Sequoia's backpacking mecca and a good place to find solitude. Gorgeous and gigantic, its glacially sculpted valley is ringed by massive mountains, including the jagged 12,343ft Sawtooth Peak. The area is reached via a slinky, steep and narrow 25-mile road not suitable for RVs or speed demons. Plan on spending the night unless you don't mind driving three hours round-trip.

Hiking anywhere from here involves a steep climb out of the valley along strenuous trails, so be aware of the altitude, even on short hikes. Enjoyable day hikes go to Crystal, Monarch, Mosquito and Eagle Lakes. For long trips, locals recommend the **Little Five Lakes** and, further along the High Sierra Trail, **Kaweah Gap**, surrounded by the sawtooth Black Kaweah, Mt Stewart and Eagle Scout Peak – all above 12,000ft.

From the 1860s to 1890s, Mineral King witnessed heavy silver mining and lumber activity. There are remnants of old shafts and stamp mills, though it takes some exploring to find them. A proposal by the Walt Disney Corporation to develop the area into a massive ski resort was thwarted when Congress annexed it to the national park in 1978. The website of the **Mineral King Preservation Society** (www.mineralking.org) has all kinds of info on the area, including its rustic and still-occupied historic mining cabins.

In spring and early summer, hordes of hungry marmots terrorize parked cars at Mineral King, chewing on radiator hoses, belts and wiring of vehicles to get the salt they crave after their winter hibernation. If you're thinking of going hiking during that time, you'd be a fool not to protect your car by wrapping the underside with chicken wire or a diaper-like tarp.

Sleeping & Eating

The market at Lodgepole Village is the best stocked in either park, but basic supplies are also available at the small store in Stony Creek Lodge (closed in winter).

ALONG GENERALS HWY

A handful of campgrounds line the highway and rarely fill up, although space may get tight on holiday weekends. Those in the Foothills area are best in spring and fall when the higher elevations are still chilly, but they get hot and buggy in summer. Unless noted, sites are available on a first-come, first-served basis. Free dispersed camping is possible in the Giant Sequoia National Monument. Stop by a visitors center or ranger station for details or a fire permit. Lodgepole Village and Stony Creek Lodge have pay showers.

Stony Creek (☎ 877-444-6777; www.recreation.gov; tent & RV sites $17-19; ⏲ late May-Oct) USFS-operated with 49 comfortable wooded sites, including some right on the creek, and flush toilets. Smaller, primitive Upper Stony Creek campground is across the street but not reservable.

Lodgepole (☎ 877-444-6777; www.recreation.gov; tent & RV sites $18-20; ⏲ year-round) Closest to the Giant Forest area with 214 closely packed sites and flush toilets; fills quickly because of proximity to Lodgepole Village amenities.

Buckeye Flat (tent sites $18; ⏲ late Apr-Sep) In the Foothills area, in an open stand of oaks about 6 miles north of the Ash Mountain Entrance; 28 tent-only sites and flush toilets. Can be somewhat rowdy.

Potwisha (tent & RV sites $18; ⏲ year-round) Also in the Foothills, and blazing in summertime, it's 3 miles from the Ash Mountain Entrance, with 42 sites, flush toilets and a pay phone.

Dorst Creek (☎ 877-444-6777; www.recreation.gov; tent & RV sites $20; ⏲ late May-early Sep) Big and busy campground with 204 sites and flush toilets; quieter back sites are tent-only.

Stony Creek Lodge (☎ 559-335-5500, 866-522-6966; www.sequoia-kingscanyon.com; r $140-180; ⏲ mid-May–mid-Oct; wi-fi) About halfway between Grant Grove Village and Giant Forest, this lodge has a big river-rock fireplace in its lobby and 11 aging but folksy motel rooms with telephone but no TV.

Wuksachi Lodge (☎ 559-565-4070, 866-807-3598; www.visitsequoia.com; r May-Sep $141-231, Oct-Apr $91-161; ⏲ year-round; wi-fi) Six miles north of Giant Forest, the modern Wuksachi is the most upscale lodging and dining option in the parks. Spacious rooms, all with TV and telephone, come in three sizes and are in three buildings a short walk from the main lodge, with a restaurant open for all meals (dinner mains $16 to $33). It serves delicious fare with a healthy bent, including several choices for vegetarians, as well as decadent desserts. Guests can join free yoga classes on Friday and Saturday mornings.

Sequoia High Sierra Camp (☎ 866-654-2877; www.sequoiahighsierracamp.com; s/d room without bath incl all meals $250/300; ⏲ mid-Jun–early Oct) Hike a mile in for gourmet meals and comfy beds in the high country at this luxury tent-cabin oasis at 8200ft. Opened in 2006, this off-the-grid and all-inclusive resort is nirvana for active, sociable people who don't think 'luxury camping' is an oxymoron. A rare plot of private land in the thick of the national forest, it's a great base for hiking, and the camp does a twice-weekly shuttle from Cedar Grove for one-way hikes to Kings Canyon.

Watchtower Deli & Snack Bar (Lodgepole Village; meals $3-10; ⏲ deli 11am-6pm, snack bar 8am-7:45pm) The snack bar serves less expensive fast-food breakfasts, burgers, pizza and hot dogs, while the deli doles out healthier prepared fare like deli salads and focaccia sandwiches.

BACKCOUNTRY

Bearpaw Meadow Camp (☎ 866-807-3598; www.visitsequoia.com; double occupancy per person $175; ⏲ mid-Jun–early Sep) About 11.5 miles east of the Giant Forest on the High Sierra Trail, this tent hotel is ideal for exploring the backcountry without lugging your own camping gear. Rates include showers, dinner and breakfast, as well as bedding and towels. Bookings start at 7am on January 2 and sell out almost immediately, though you should always check for cancellations.

MINERAL KING AREA

Silver City Mountain Resort (☎ 559-561-3223; www.silvercityresort.com; cabins $100-150, chalets $250-395; ⏲ late May-Oct; 👪) The only food and lodging option in Mineral King, this rustic family-run and family-friendly place has everything from cute and cozy 1950s-era cabins to large new holiday chalets. For kids, there's a Ping-Pong table, play structure with swings and nearby ponds to splash around in. Resources are limited, so all guests must bring their own linens and towels. Most of the cabins don't have electricity, and the property's generator shuts off at 10pm. Its restaurant (mains $5 to $12; open 8am to 8pm Thursday to Monday) serves delicious homemade pies and simple fare on wooden picnic tables under the trees. It's located 3 miles west of the ranger station.

Mineral King's two pretty campgrounds, **Atwell Mill** (tent sites $12; ⏲ late May-Oct) and **Cold Springs** (tent sites $12; ⏲ late May-Oct) often fill up

THE BUFFALO SOLDIERS

After the creation of the national parks in 1890, the US Army was called in to safeguard these new natural resources. In the summer of 1903, troops from the 9th Cavalry – one of four well-respected (though segregated) African American regiments, known as the 'Buffalo Soldiers' – were sent to patrol here and in Yosemite. In Sequoia and what was then General Grant National Park, the troops had an impressively productive summer – building roads, creating a trail system and setting a high precedent as stewards of the land.

The troops were commanded by Captain (later Colonel) Charles Young. At the time, Young was the only African American captain in the Army; his post as Acting Superintendent made him the first black superintendent of a national park.

on summer weekends. Pay showers available at the Silver City Mountain Resort.

THREE RIVERS

Just south of the Ash Mountain Entrance of Sequoia National Park and named for the nearby convergence of three forks of the Kaweah River, Three Rivers is a friendly small town populated by retirees and artsy newcomers. Stretched out along Hwy 198 (here called Sierra Dr), it's sparsely lined with motels, stores, galleries, cafés and restaurants.

Gateway Restaurant & Lodge (☎ 559-561-4133; www.gateway-sequoia.com; 45978 Sierra Dr; mains lunch $11-17, dinner $21-35; wi-fi) The most upscale restaurant in town, the Gateway has indoor and outdoor dining areas with dynamite river views and well-prepared meals. Lunch is mostly burgers and sandwiches, but dinner goes gourmet with dishes like chicken masala and trout almondine. The lodge has five institutional cinder-block motel rooms (midweek/weekend $99/135), but rooms 6 and 7 are in a different league, with sweeping river-view decks and tons more space.

Buckeye Tree Lodge (☎ 559-561-5900; www.buckeyetree.com; 46000 Sierra Dr; r $79-143; wi-fi) Sit out on your grassy back patio or balcony perch and watch the river ease through a maze of boulders. Modern white-brick motel rooms, some with kitchenettes, feel airy and bright.

We Three Bakery & Restaurant (☎ 559-561-4761; 43368 Sierra Dr; mains $6-9; 7am-2:30pm Wed-Mon; wi-fi) Tasty pastries, chunky French toast and good coffee lure in the breakfast crowd, and both hot and cold sandwiches on blindingly bright Fiestaware make We Three a fun lunch spot as well. A few vegetarian options grace the menu, including a tofu scramble. In summer, diners can eat outside under a shady oak patio.

Also recommended:

Lake Elowin Resort (☎ 559-561-3460; www.lake-elowin.com; 43840 Dineley Dr; cabin $120-300;) A secluded and lushly landscaped camp with private lake that's popular with families; well-stocked kitchen/kitchenette in every cabin and free canoeing.

River View Restaurant & Lounge (☎ 559-561-2211; 42323 Sierra Dr; lunch $6-9, dinner $12-26) Colorful honky-tonk with great back patio; live music Fridays and Saturdays.

Getting There & Around

Coming from the south, Hwy 198 runs north from Visalia through Three Rivers past Mineral King Rd to the Ash Mountain Entrance. Beyond here the road continues as the Generals Hwy, a narrow and windy road snaking all the way into Kings Canyon National Park where it joins the Kings Canyon Scenic Byway (Hwy 180) near the western Big Stump Entrance. Vehicles over 22ft long may have trouble negotiating the steep road with its many hairpin curves, although they are not prohibited from trying. For winter travel, see the boxed text, p397. Budget about one hour to drive from the entrance to the Giant Forest/Lodgepole area and another hour from there to Grant Grove Village in Kings Canyon.

From the town of Visalia, visitors to Sequoia National Park can catch the handy **Sequoia Shuttle** (☎ 877-287-4453; www.sequoiashuttle.com; late May-early Sep), which has five daily departures to the Giant Forest Museum. A $15 round-trip fare includes the park entry fee, and reservations are required.

In 2007 Sequoia National Park debuted a new free summertime shuttle system. From a hub at the Giant Forest Museum, two shuttle routes connect Wuksachi Lodge, Lodgepole, the Sherman Tree and its upper parking lot, Moro Rock and Crescent Meadow. Schedules are posted at stops, and buses arrive at very frequent intervals.

EASTERN SIERRA

Cloud-dappled hills and sun-streaked mountaintops dabbed with snow typify the landscape of the Eastern Sierra, where slashing peaks – many over 14,000ft – rush abruptly upward from the arid expanses of the Great Basin and Mojave deserts. It's a dramatic juxtaposition that makes for a potent cocktail of scenery. Pine forests, lush meadows, ice-blue lakes, simmering hot springs and glacier-gouged canyons are only some of the fabulous beauty you'll find in this region.

The Eastern Sierra Scenic Byway, officially known as Hwy 395, runs the entire length of the range. Turnoffs dead-ending at the foot of the mountains deliver you to pristine wilderness and countless trails, including the famous Pacific Crest Trail, John Muir Trail and main Mt Whitney Trail. The most important portals are the towns of Bridgeport, Mammoth Lakes and Bishop. Note that in winter, when traffic thins, many facilities are closed.

Getting There & Around

The Eastern Sierra is easiest to explore under your own steam, although it is possible to access the area by public transportation. Buses operated by **Eastern Sierra Transit Authority** (☎ 800-922-1930; www.easternsierratransitauthority.com) make round-trips between Bishop and Reno ($48, five to six hours) on Monday, Tuesday, Thursday and Friday, and between Mammoth Lakes and Ridgecrest ($31.50, 3½ to four hours) on Monday, Wednesday and Friday, stopping at all towns in between. Fares depend on distance; one-way tickets from Reno to Mammoth cost $42 (four to five hours). Reservations are recommended.

It also operates a bus service three times daily on +s (and one the first Saturday of the month) between Bishop and Lone Pine ($6) and from Bishop to Mammoth Lakes twice daily Monday through Saturday ($7).

BRIDGEPORT

pop 850 / elev 6500ft

Barely three blocks long and set amid open high valley and in view of the high peaks of Sawtooth Ridge, Bridgeport flaunts classic western flair with charming old storefronts and a homey ambience. Most everything shuts down or cuts back hours for the brutal winters, but the rest of the year the town is a magnet for anglers, hikers, climbers and hot-spring devotees. Stop by the **Bridgeport Ranger Station & Visitor Center** (☎ 760-932-7070; www.fs.fed.us/r4/htnf; Hwy 395; 🕑 8am-4:30pm daily Jul & Aug, 8am-4:30pm Mon-Fri Sep-Jun) for maps, information and Hoover Wilderness permits (below).

Sights & Activities

The gavel has been dropped since 1880 at the **Mono County Courthouse** (🕑 9am-5pm Mon-Fri), an all-white Italianate dreamboat surrounded by a gracious lawn framed by a wrought-iron fence. Two blocks away, in an schoolhouse of the same age, the **Mono County Museum** (☎ 760-932-5281; Emigrant St; adult/child $2/1; 🕑 10am-4pm Mon-Sat, noon-4pm Sun Jun-Sep) has mining artifacts on display from all the local ghost towns, plus a room of fine Paiute baskets.

A bit south of town, **Travertine Hot Spring** is the place to watch a panoramic Sierra sunset from the bliss of three hot pools set amid chiseled rock formations. To get there, turn east on Jack Sawyer Rd just before the ranger station, then follow the dirt road uphill for about 1 mile.

If you're trolling for trout, try the **Bridgeport Reservoir** and the **East Walker River**. For information and outdoor gear, stop by **Ken's Sporting**

WILDERNESS PERMITS: EASTERN SIERRA

Free wilderness permits for overnight camping are required year-round in the Ansel Adams, John Muir, Golden Trout and Hoover Wilderness areas. For the first three, trailhead quotas are in effect from May to October. About 60% of the quota may be reserved for a $5 fee by telephone, fax and mail from the **Inyo National Forest Wilderness Permit Office** (☎ 760-873-2483; fax 760-873-2484; Suite 200, 351 Pacu Lane, Bishop, CA 93514). From November to April, you can pick up permits at any ranger station mentioned in this section. If you find the station closed, look for self-issue permits outside the office. Regulations change on occasion, so call ☎ 760-873-2485 or check www.fs.fed.us/r5/inyo/passes for the latest.

Hoover Wilderness (www.fs.fed.us/r4/htnf/passes/hoover_permits.shtml), in boundaries of the Humboldt-Toiyabe National Forest, has similar permit requirements as Inyo. Check the website for details.

HIGHWAY 395: BRIDGEPORT TO RENO

North of Bridgeport, Hwy 395 barrels on through narrow **Walker Canyon**, paralleling a 10-mile stretch of the West Walker River, a designated Wild and Scenic River, which enjoys legendary status among trout fishers. The road eventually spills out into the fertile Antelope Valley, where the little western town of Walker has a few cheap motels and eateries.

A few miles further north, the Walker River empties into **Topaz Lake**, which straddles the California–Nevada border. It's open for all sorts of water sports but is really best known for its exceptionally long fishing season (January to September).

Beyond here, **Carson City**, the Nevada state capital, warrants a stop for a stroll around its pretty downtown, with some nice old buildings and the imposing capitol building. From here it's another 30 miles to Reno.

If you're headed for Tahoe, leave Hwy 395 just south of Topaz Lake and head into the mountains on incredibly scenic Hwy 89, which eventually merges with Hwy 50.

Goods (☎ 760-932-7707; www.kenssport.com; 258 Main St; 🕑 8am-6pm Sun-Thu, 8am-7pm Fri & Sat, closed Sun & Mon mid-Nov–mid-Apr).

Sleeping & Eating

Bodie Victorian Hotel (☎ 760-932-7020; www.bodievictorianhotel.com; 85 Main St; r $40-79; 🕑 May-Oct) Blink your eyes and go back to the 1800s in this curious building transplanted from Bodie (p402) that's completely furnished with antiques and rumored to be haunted. The bold Victorian wallpaper and striking bordello accoutrements more than make up for the slightly run-down feel. It doesn't accept reservations; poke your head inside the Sportsmen's Inn next door to rustle up an employee.

Redwood Motel (☎ 760-932-7060, 888-932-3292; www.redwoodmotel.net; 425 Main St; d from $79; 🕑 Apr-Oct; wi-fi) A bucking bronco, an ox in a Hawaiian shirt and other wacky farm animal sculptures provide a cheerful welcome to this little motel. Rooms are spotless and your dog-friendly host is superhelpful in dispensing local area tips.

Hays Street Café (☎ 760-932-7141; 21 Hays St; mains under $10; 🕑 6am-2pm May-Oct, 7am-1pm Nov-Apr) On the south end of town, this country-style place with striped curtains prides itself on its many homemade items, including its pancake batter, biscuits and gravy, and cinnamon rolls as big as bricks.

Pop's Galley (☎ 760-932-1172; 247 Main St; mains $6-9; 🕑 11am-9pm Mon-Sat, noon-9pm Sun) This casual eating joint prepares finger-lickin' fish and chips. Sit inside with a view of the mountains or outside for front-row seats on Main St.

TWIN LAKES

Eager anglers line the shoreline of Twin Lakes, a gorgeous duo of basins cradled by the fittingly named Sawtooth Ridge. The area's famous for its fishing – especially since some lucky guy bagged the state's largest ever brown trout here in 1987 (it weighed in at a hefty 26lbs). Lower Twin is quieter, while Upper Twin allows boating and waterskiing. Other activities include mountain-biking and, of course, hiking in the Hoover Wilderness and on into the eastern, lake-riddled reaches of Yosemite National Park. The main trailhead is at the end of Twin Lakes Rd just past Annett's Mono Village; weekly overnight parking is $10 per vehicle.

Twin Lakes Rd (Rte 420) runs through pastures and foothills for about 10 miles before reaching Lower Twin Lake.

A slippery stroll down a loose hillside brings you to secluded **Buckeye Hot Spring**, but it can get crowded. The water emerges piping hot from atop a steep hillside and cools quickly as it trickles down into several rock pools right by the side of lively Buckeye Creek, which is handy for taking a cooling dip. One pool is partially tucked into a small cave made from a rock overhang. Clothing is optional.

To get there, turn right onto the graded dirt road just past Doc & Al's Resort, cross the bridge at Buckeye Creek, then turn right at the sign for Buckeye Campground. Go uphill until you see a flat parking area on your right. The pools are down the hillside.

West of the springs, at a bridge spanning Buckeye Creek, a road goes 2 miles to **Buckeye Campground** (tent & RV sites $13; 🕑 May–mid-Oct), with tables, fire grates, potable water and toilets. You can also camp for free in undeveloped spots along Buckeye Creek on both sides of the bridge.

Honeymoon Flat, Robinson Creek, Paha, Crags and Lower Twin Lakes are all **USFS campgrounds** (☎ 800-444-7275; www.recreation.gov; tent & RV sites $13-15; ⏲ usually mid-May–Sep) set among Jeffrey pine and sagebrush along Robinson Creek and Lower Twin Lake. All have flush toilets except for Honeymoon Flat, which has vault toilets.

Twin Lakes Rd dead-ends at **Annett's Mono Village** (☎ 760-932-7071; www.monovillage.com; tent sites $15, RV sites with hookups $24, r from $65; ⏲ late Apr-Oct), a huge and rather chaotic tumbledown resort on Upper Twin Lake. It has cheap but cramped lodging, though we love the kitschy low-ceilinged café (mains $7 to $14) studded with taxidermied fish. Wi-fi available in the café.

BODIE STATE HISTORIC PARK

For a time warp back to the Gold Rush era, swing by **Bodie** (☎ 760-647-6445; www.parks.ca.gov; Hwy 270; adult/child $3/1; ⏲ 8am-7pm Jun-Aug, 9am-4pm Sep-May), one of the West's most authentic and best-preserved ghost towns. Gold was first discovered here in 1859, and within 20 years the place grew from a rough mining camp to an even rougher boomtown with a population of 10,000 and a reputation for unbridled lawlessness. Fights and murders took place almost daily, the violence no doubt fueled by liquor dispensed in the town's 65 saloons, some of which did double duty as brothels, gambling halls or opium dens. The hills disgorged some $35 million worth of gold and silver in the 1870s and '80s, but when production plummeted, so did the population and eventually the town was abandoned to the elements.

About 200 weather-beaten buildings still sit frozen in time in this cold, barren and windswept valley. Peering through dusty windows you'll see stocked stores, furnished homes, a schoolhouse with desks and books, and workshops filled with tools. The jail is still there, as are the fire station, churches, a bank vault and many other buildings. The former Miners' Union Hall now houses a **museum** and **visitors center** (⏲ 8am-7pm daily Jun-Aug, variable hours Sep-Oct & May). Rangers conduct free general tours daily at 10:15am and 3:15pm. In summertime, they also offer hourly tours of the stamp mill (adult/child $7/3).

Bodie is about 13 miles east of Hwy 395 via Rte 270; the last 3 miles are unpaved. Although the park is open year-round, the road is usually closed in winter and early spring, so you'd have to don snowshoes or cross-country skis to get there.

VIRGINIA LAKES & LUNDY LAKE

South of Bridgeport, Hwy 395 gradually arrives at its highest point, **Conway Summit** (8148ft), where you'll be whipping out your camera to capture the awe-inspiring panorama of Mono Lake, backed by the Mono Craters, backed by June and Mammoth Mountains.

Also at the top is the turnout for Virginia Lakes Rd, which parallels Virginia Creek for about 6 miles to a cluster of lakes flanked by **Dunderberg Peak** (12,374ft) and **Black Mountain** (11,797ft). A trailhead at the end of the road gives access to the Hoover Wilderness and the Pacific Crest Trail. The trail continues down Cold Canyon through to Yosemite National Park. Check with the folks at the 1923 **Virginia Lakes Resort** (☎ 760-647-6484; www.virginialakesresort.com; cabins per week from $614; ⏲ usually mid-May–mid-Oct) for maps and tips about specific trails. The resort itself has snug cabins, a café and a general store that sells fishing tackle and licenses. Cabins sleep two to 12 people and are subject to a three- or seven-night minimum rental.

There's also the option of camping at **Trumbull Lake Campground** (☎ 800-444-7275; www.recreation.gov; tent & RV sites $15; ⏲ mid-Jun–mid-Oct). The shady sites here are located among lodgepole pines. Nearby, **Virginia Lakes Pack Station** (☎ 760-937-0326; www.virginialakes.com) offers horseback trips.

After Conway Summit, Hwy 395 twists down steeply into the Mono Basin. Before reaching Mono Lake, Lundy Lake Rd meanders west of the highway for about 5 miles to **Lundy Lake**. This is a gorgeous spot, especially in spring when wildflowers carpet the canyon along Mill Creek, or in fall when it is brightened by colorful foliage. Before reaching the lake, the road skirts first-come, first-served **Lundy Canyon Campground** (tent sites $8-12; ⏲ mid-April–Nov), with vault toilets but no water.

At the end of the lake, the funky old **Lundy Lake Resort** (☎ 626-309-0415; tent sites $15, cabins $85-120; ⏲ late Apr-Sep) sits on the site of an 1880s mining town. You can stay in ramshackle cabins with shared facilities, nicer ones with bathrooms and a handful of campsites. There's a small store and boat rentals.

Past the resort, a good dirt road leads into **Lundy Canyon** where it dead-ends at the trailhead for Hoover Wilderness. A moderate 1.5-mile hike follows Mill Creek to the 200ft-high Lundy Falls. Ambitious types can continue on via Lundy Pass to Saddlebag Lake.

MONO LAKE

North America's second-oldest lake is a quiet and mysterious expanse of deep blue water whose glassy surface reflects jagged Sierra peaks, young volcanic cones and the unearthly tufa (*too*-fah) towers that make Mono Lake so distinctive. Jutting from the water like drip sand castles, the tufas form when calcium bubbles up from subterranean springs and combines with the carbonate in the alkaline lake waters.

In *Roughing It*, Mark Twain described Mono Lake as California's 'dead sea.' Hardly. The brackish water teems with buzzing alkali flies and brine shrimp, both considered delicacies by dozens of migratory bird species that return here year after year. So do about 85% of the state's nesting population of California gulls, which takes over the lake's volcanic islands from April to August. Mono Lake has been at the heart of an environmental controversy (see boxed text, p404).

Orientation

Hwy 395 skirts the western bank of Mono Lake, rolling into the support town of Lee Vining, where you can eat, sleep, gas up (for a pretty penny) and catch Hwy 120 to Yosemite National Park (summer only; see the boxed text p379).

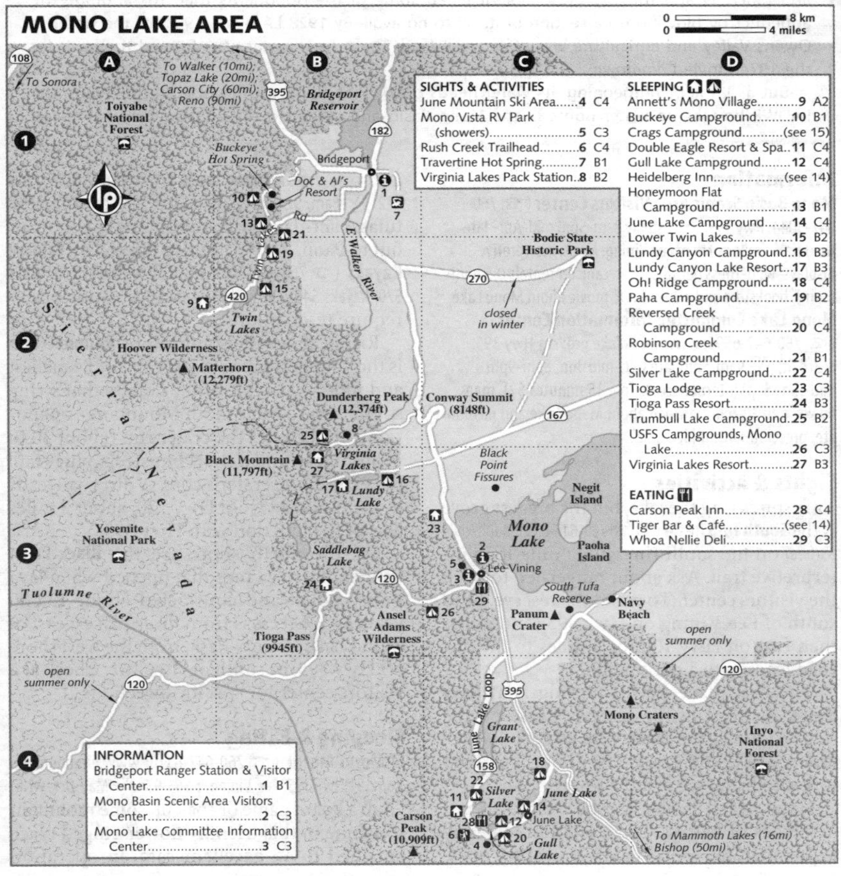

WATER FOR A THIRSTY GIANT: A TALE OF TWO LAKES

Los Angeles may be 250 miles away, but its history and fate are closely linked with that of the Eastern Sierra. When LA's population surged around the turn of the 20th century, it became clear that groundwater levels would soon be inadequate to meet the city's needs, let alone sustain future growth. Water had to be imported, and Fred Eaton, a former LA mayor, and William Mulholland, head of the LA Department of Water & Power (LADWP), knew just how and where to get it: by aqueduct from the Owens Valley, which receives enormous runoff from the Sierra Nevada.

The fact that the Owens Valley itself was settled by farmers who needed the water for irrigation didn't bother either of the two men. Nor did it cause qualms in the least with the federal government, which actively supported the city's less-than-ethical maneuvering in acquiring land and securing water rights in the valley area. Voters gave Mulholland the $24.5 million he needed to build the aqueduct and work began in 1908. An amazing feat of engineering – crossing barren desert as well as rugged mountain terrain – the aqueduct opened to great fanfare on November 5, 1913. The Owens Valley, though, would never be the same.

With most of its inflows diverted, Owens Lake, which once had been 30ft deep and an important stopover for migrating waterfowl, quickly shriveled up. A bitter feud between local farmers and ranchers and the city grew violent when some of the opponents tried to sabotage the aqueduct by blowing up a section of it. All to no avail. By 1928 LA owned 90% of the water in Owens Valley and agriculture was effectively dead. These early water wars formed the basis for the 1974 movie *Chinatown*.

But as LA kept burgeoning, its water needs grew right along with its size. In the 1930s, the LADWP bought up water rights in the Mono Basin and extended the aqueduct by 105 miles,

Information

Mono Basin Scenic Area Visitors Center (☎ 760-647-3044; Hwy 395; ⏲ usually 8am-5pm mid-Apr–late Nov) Half a mile north of Lee Vining. Maps, interpretive displays, wilderness permits, bear-canister rentals ($5 minimum), bookstore and a 20-minute movie about Mono Lake.

Mono Lake Committee Information Center (☎ 760-647-6595; www.monolake.org; cnr Hwy 395 & 3rd St; ⏲ 9am-5pm late Oct–mid-Jun, 8am-9pm mid-Jun–Sep) Internet access (per 15 minutes $2), maps, books, free 30-minute video about Mono Lake and passionate, preservation-minded staff.

Sights & Activities

Tufa spires ring the lake, but the biggest grove is the **South Tufa Reserve** (☎ 760-647-6331; adult/child $3/free) on the south rim with a mile-long interpretive trail. Ask about ranger-led tours at the visitors center. To get to the reserve, head south of Lee Vining on Hwy 395 for 6 miles, then east on Hwy 120 for 5 miles to the dirt road leading to a parking lot.

The best place for swimming is at **Navy Beach**, just east of the reserve. Rinse off the salt residue at the **Mono Vista RV Park** (Hwy 395; showers $2.50; ⏲ 9am-6pm) in Lee Vining, but don't forget to bring soap and a towel.

Navy Beach is also the best place to put in canoes or kayaks. From late June to early September, the Mono Lake Committee operates one-hour **canoe tours** (☎ 760-647-6595; tours $22; ⏲ 8am, 9:30am & 11am Sat & Sun) around the tufas. Half-day kayak tours along the shore or out to Paoha Island are also offered by **Caldera Kayaks** (☎ 760-934-1691; www.calderakayak.com; tours $70, kayaks $40; ⏲ mid-May–mid-Oct). Both places require reservations.

Rising above the south shore, **Panum Crater** is the youngest (about 640 years old), smallest and most accessible of the craters that string south toward Mammoth Mountain. A panoramic trail circles the crater rim (about 30 to 45 minutes), and a short but steep 'plug trail' puts you at the crater's core. A dirt road leads to the trailhead from Hwy 120, about 3 miles east of the junction with Hwy 395.

On the north shore are the **Black Point Fissures**, narrow crags that opened when lava mass cooled and contracted about 13,000 years ago. Access is from three places: east of Mono Lake County Park, from the west shore off Hwy 395, or south of Hwy 167. Check at a visitors center for specific directions.

Sleeping & Eating

El Mono Motel (☎ 760-647-6310; www.elmonomotel.com; 51 Hwy 395, Lee Vining; r $65-95; ⏲ May-Oct; wi-fi) Grab a board game or soak up some mountain sunshine in this friendly flower-ringed place attached to an excellent café. In operation diverting four of the five streams feeding into Mono Lake. Not surprisingly, the lake's water volume dropped significantly, doubling its salinity and posing a major threat to its ecological balance.

In 1976 environmentalist David Gaines began to study the concerns surrounding the lake's depletion and found that, if left untouched, it would totally dry up within about 20 years. To avert this certain disaster, he formed the Mono Lake Committee in 1978 and enlisted the help of the National Audubon Society. Years of lobbying and legal action followed, but eventually the committee succeeded. In 1994 the California State Water Resources Control Board mandated the LADWP to substantially reduce its diversions and allow the lake level to rise by 20ft. In August 2008 its surface stood at 6383ft, still about 8ft short of the goal.

The Owens Lake, meanwhile, was not as lucky. It remains a mostly barren lakebed that's the site of alkali dust storms, which are especially harmful to people with respiratory problems. However, a plan finalized in 1999 shallow flooded 30 sq miles of the lake (out of 100), and by 2006, this had largely remediated the dust storms and re-created an important habitat for waterfowl.

In 1997 the LADWP had agreed to restore a 62-mile stretch of the Lower Owens River by 2003. When both this deadline and a two-year extension were ignored, a county judge swung into action in July of 2005, imposing stiff daily fines and other sanctions, threatening to cut off a second aqueduct built in 1970. But by July of 2007, the flows were in compliance, though a controversy still lingered over the management plan.

The judge's threats certainly could have hurt LA: in an average year, the city still gets about 50% of its water supply via the LA aqueducts from the Eastern Sierra. The remainder is siphoned from the Sacramento and San Joaquin Rivers via the California Aqueduct and the Colorado River via the Colorado River Aqueduct; only about 15% comes from local LA water sources.

since 1927, and often booked solid, each of its 11 simple rooms is unique, decorated with vibrant and colorful art and fabrics.

Tioga Lodge (☎ 760-647-6423; www.tiogalodgeatmonolake.com; r $99-159; ⌚ May-Oct; wi-fi) About 2 miles north of Lee Vining, this cluster of cheery cabins has verandas overlooking Mono Lake. The buildings housing a three-menu restaurant (mains breakfast $8 to $10, dinner $10 to $25) and the registration office were moved here from Bodie in 1897.

Tioga Pass Resort (www.tiogapassresort.com; Hwy 120; r $115, cabins $185-230; ⌚ May–mid-Oct) Founded in 1914 and located 2 miles east of Tioga Pass, it attracts a fiercely loyal clientele to its basic and cozy cabins beside Lee Vining Creek. The thimble-sized café (mains $8 to $18) serves excellent fare all day long at a few tables and a broken horseshoe counter, with a house pastry chef concocting dozens of freshly desserts daily. Reserve lodging via email.

Whoa Nellie Deli (☎ 760-647-1088; near junction of Hwys 120 & 395, Lee Vining; mains $8-19; ⌚ 7am-9pm mid-May–Oct) Great food in a gas station? Come on… No, really, you gotta try this amazing kitchen where chef Matt 'Tioga' Toomey feeds delicious fish tacos, wild buffalo meatloaf and other tasty morsels to locals and clued-in passersby.

The closest developed camping is at a handful of first-come, first-served **USFS campgrounds** (www.fs.fed.us/r5/inyo/recreation/campgrounds.shtml#mono; tent & RV sites $14-17) along Tioga Rd (Hwy 120) in the direction of Yosemite, most with vault toilets and stream water.

JUNE LAKE LOOP

Under the shadow of massive Carson Peak (10,909ft), the 14-mile June Lake Loop meanders through a picture-perfect horseshoe canyon past the relaxed resort town of June Lake and four sparkling, fish-rich lakes: Grant, Silver, Gull and June. It's especially scenic in fall when the basin is ablaze with golden aspens. Catch the loop (Hwy 158) a few miles south of Lee Vining.

Activities

June Lake is backed by the Ansel Adams Wilderness, which runs into Yosemite National Park. Rush Creek Trailhead has a day-use parking lot, posted maps and self-registration permits. Gem and Agnew Lakes make spectacular day hikes, while Thousand Island and Emerald Lake (both on the Pacific Crest/John Muir Trail) are stunning overnight destinations.

Boat and tackle rentals, as well as fishing licenses, are available at five marinas. One of the most established outfitters is **Ernie's Tackle & Ski Shop** (☎ 760-648-7756; 2604 Hwy 158) in June Lake village.

Winter fun concentrates in the **June Mountain Ski Area** (☎ 760-648-7733, 888-586-3686; www.junemountain.com; lift tickets adult/child $60/30), which is smaller and less crowded than nearby Mammoth Mountain (p408) and perfect for beginner and intermediate skiers. Some 35 trails crisscross 500 acres of terrain served by eight lifts, including two high-speed quads. Boarders can get their adrenaline flowing at three terrain parks with a kick-ass superpipe.

Sleeping & Eating

Heidelberg Inn (☎ 760-648-7718, reservations 800-438-6493; www.extraholidays.com; 1-bedroom $122-209, 2-bedroom $160-283) Step into the hushed lobby and feel the history of this 80-year-old lodge where movie stars, including Clark Gable and Ingrid Bergman, once stayed. Slip past the mammoth four-sided volcanic rock fireplace and ascend tree-bark-lined stairs to the modern apartments, many with kitchenettes and some with June Lake views.

Double Eagle Resort & Spa (☎ 760-648-7004; www.doubleeagleresort.com; 5587 Hwy 158; r incl breakfast $229, cabins $364; wi-fi) A mighty swanky spot for these parts, the resort specializes in fishing and pampering. The sleek log cabins and balconied hotel rooms here lack no comfort, while worries disappear at the elegant spa. Its restaurant (breakfast and lunch mains $7 to $12, dinner $16 to $33) exudes rustic elegance, with cozy booths, a high ceiling and a huge fireplace.

Tiger Bar & Café (☎ 760-648-7551; 2620 Hwy 158; mains $7-16) After a day on slopes or trails, people gather at the long bar or around the pool table of this no-nonsense, no-attitude kind of place. The kitchen feeds all appetites with burgers, salads, tacos and other tasty grub, including homemade fries.

Carson Peak Inn (☎ 760-648-7575; Hwy 158 btwn Gull & Silver Lakes; meals $18-34; dinner) Inside a cozy house with fireplace, this well-regarded restaurant is much beloved for its tasty old-time indulgences, such as beef brochette, pan-fried trout and chopped sirloin steak. Portions sizes can be ordered for regular or 'hearty' appetites.

June Lake, Oh! Ridge, Silver Lake, Gull Lake and Reversed Creek are all **USFS campgrounds** (☎ 800-444-7275; www.recreation.gov; tent & RV sites $18; mid-Apr–Oct). The first three campgrounds accept reservations, and Silver Lake has gorgeous mountain views.

MAMMOTH LAKES

pop 7400 / elev 7800ft

A small mountain resort town endowed with larger-than-life scenery – active outdoorsy folks worship at the base of its dizzying 11,053ft Mammoth Mountain. Everlasting powder clings to these slopes, and when the snow finally fades, the area's an outdoor wonderland of mountain-bike trails, excellent fishing, endless alpine hiking and blissful hidden spots for hot-spring soaking. The Eastern Sierra's commercial hub and a four-season resort, outdoorsy Mammoth is backed by a ridgeline of jutting peaks, ringed by clusters of crystalline alpine lakes and enshrouded by the dense Inyo National Forest. And if you venture out, you'll find stunning and surprisingly crowd-free wilderness areas.

Orientation

Mammoth Lakes is 3 miles off Hwy 395 via Hwy 203, which turns into Main St after the first traffic light. At the second light it turns right and continues as Minaret Rd, going past the Village at Mammoth and gaining elevation on the way to the Mammoth mountain Ski Area and the shuttle bus to Reds Meadow/Devils Postpile. Continue straight at the second light for Mammoth Lakes Basin via Lake Mary Rd (closed in winter).

Information

The **Mammoth Lakes Visitors Bureau** (☎ 760-934-2712, 888-466-2666; www.visitmammoth.com; 8am-5pm) and the **Mammoth Lakes Ranger Station** (☎ 760-924-5500; www.fs.fed.us/r5/inyo; 8am-5pm) share a building on the north side of Hwy 203. This one-stop information center issues wilderness permits, helps find accommodations and campgrounds, and provides road and trail condition updates. From May through October, when trail quotas are in effect, walk-in wilderness permits are released at 11am the day beforehand; permits are self-issue the rest of the year.

Booky Joint (☎ 760-934-5023; 437 Old Mammoth Rd) Inside the Minaret Village Mall.

Looney Bean (☎ 760-934-1345; Gateway Mall, 26 Old Mammoth Rd; per 15min $2; 6am-7pm Sun-Thu, to 10pm Fri & Sat) Computers and wi-fi.

Main post office (3330 Main St) Just past the Chevron gas station.

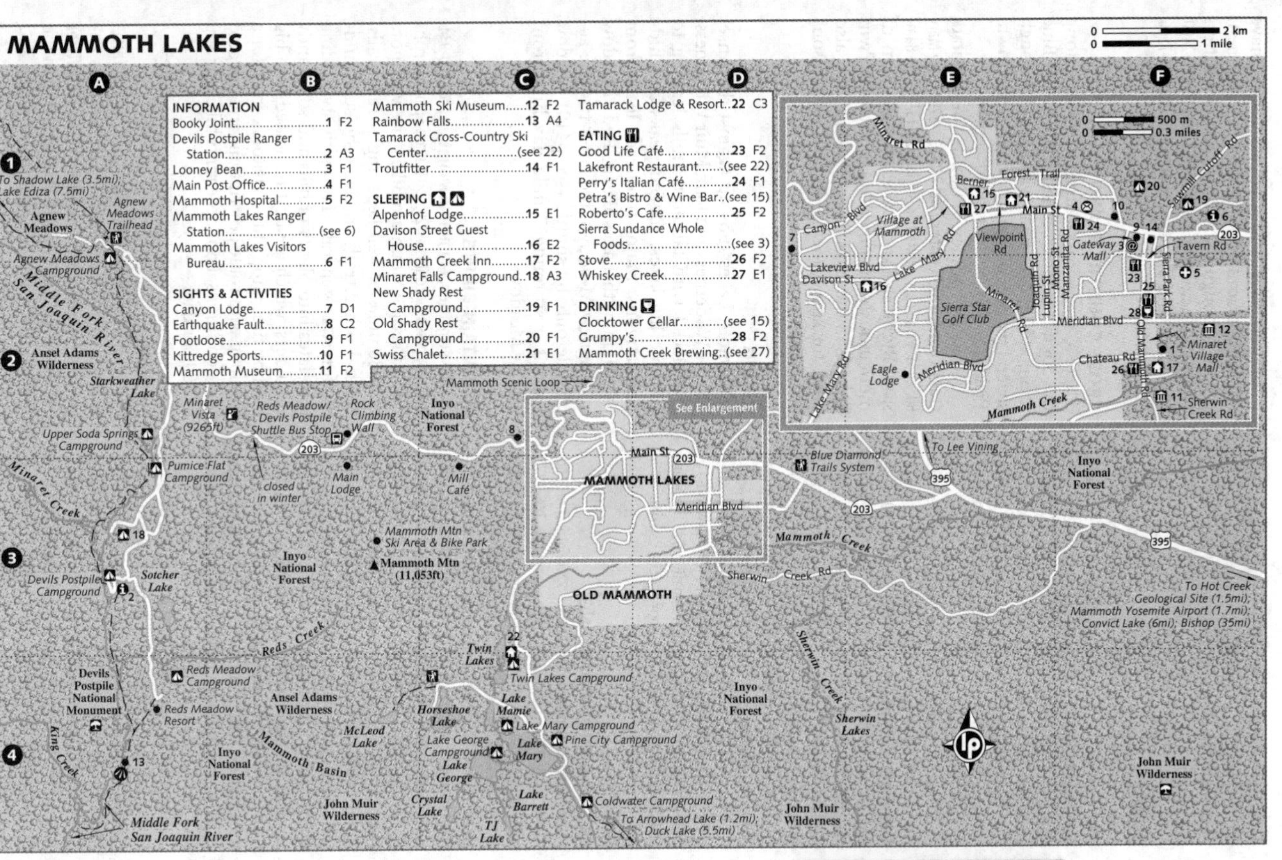

SIERRA NEVADA

Mammoth Hospital (☎ 760-934-3311; 85 Sierra Park Rd; 🕑 24hr) Emergency room.
Mammoth Times (www.mammothtimes.com) Free weekly tabloid.

Sights

On Minaret Rd about 1 mile west of the Mammoth Scenic Loop, detour to gape at **Earthquake Fault**, a sinuous fissure half a mile long and gouging a crevice up to 20ft deep into the earth. Ice and snow often linger at the bottom until late summer, and Native Americans and early settlers used it to store perishable food.

Possessing the world's largest collection of ski art, the sparkling and contemporary **Mammoth Ski Museum** (☎ 760-934-6592; 100 College Parkway; adult/child $5/3; 🕑 noon-5pm Wed-Sun) shines an artistic light on the sport with its great collection of vintage posters, photographs, paintings and pins. The small theater presents historical films, lectures and other events, and also has exhibits about local ski history.

For another walk down memory lane, stop by the little **Mammoth Museum** (☎ 760-934-6918; 5489 Sherwin Creek Rd; suggested donation $2; 🕑 10am-5:30pm Jun-Sep), inside a historic log cabin.

Activities

SKIING & SNOWBOARDING

Mammoth Mountain Ski Area (☎ information 760-934-0745, 800-626-6684, 24hr snow report 888-766-9778; www.mammothmountain.com; lift tickets adult/senior & child $80/40) is still a true skiers' and snowboarders' dream resort, where playing hard and having fun are more important than anything else. Sunny skies, reliable snow (the season generally runs from November to June) and over 3500 acres of fantastic tree-line and open-bowl skiing prove to be a potent cocktail. At the top you'll be dealing with some gnarly, nearly vertical chutes. The other stats are just as impressive: 3100 vertical feet, 150 trails, 29 lifts (including 10 quads). Boarders, meanwhile, will find world-class challenges in three terrain parks with intense superpipes and urban-style jibs.

Five hubs are at the base of the mountain: Main Lodge, Canyon Lodge, the Mountain Center (in the Village), Eagle Lodge and the Mill Café, each with ticket offices and parking lots. Free ski shuttles pick up throughout town. Alternatively, hop on the new Village Gondola that whisks you up to Canyon Lodge – the base of several chair lifts – in six minutes.

Main Lodge and Canyon Lodge have ski schools and state-of-the-art equipment rental, although prices are lower at outfitters in town, including **Footloose** (☎ 760-934-2400; 3043 Main St) and **Kittredge Sports** (☎ 760-934-7566; 3218 Main St).

CROSS-COUNTRY SKIING

There's free cross-country skiing along the 30km of nongroomed trails of the Blue Diamond Trails System, which winds through several patches of scenic forest around town. Pick up a map at the visitors center.

A nicer if pricier option is the **Tamarack Cross-Country Ski Center** (☎ 760-934-5293; Lake Mary Rd; all-day trail pass adult/child/senior $25/13/19; 🕑 8am-5pm). Right at Twin Lakes, it has 45km of meticulously groomed track around Twin Lakes and the lakes basin. The terrain is also great for snowshoeing. Rentals and lessons are available.

HIKING

Mammoth Lakes rubs up against the Ansel Adams Wilderness and John Muir Wilderness, both laced with fabulous trails leading to shimmering lakes, rugged peaks and hidden canyons. Major trailheads leave from the Mammoth Lakes Basin, Reds Meadow and Agnew Meadows; the latter two are accessible only by shuttle (see p410). Shadow Lake is a stunning 7-mile day hike from Agnew Meadows.

MOUNTAIN-BIKING

Come summer, **Mammoth Mountain** (☎ 760-934-0706; day pass adult/child $39/20; 🕑 8:30am-6pm) morphs into a massive Mountain Bike Park with more than 80 miles of well-kept single-track trails. Several other trails traverse the surrounding forest. In general, Mammoth-style riding translates into plenty of hills and soft, sandy shoulders, which are best navigated with big knobby tires. Stop at the visitors center for a free map with route descriptions and updated trail conditions. Footloose rents bikes for $40 to $60 per day.

FISHING

From the last Saturday in April, the Mammoth area lakes exert their lure to trout anglers from near and far. Check out **Troutfitter** (☎ 760-934-2517; cnr Hwy 203 & Old Mammoth Rd) in the Shell Mart Center for equipment rental and fishing licenses.

Sleeping

BUDGET

About 15 USFS campgrounds are scattered in and around Mammoth Lakes, all with flush toilets but no showers. Most are open from mid-June to mid-September, weather permitting. Most sites are available on a first-come, first-served basis and cost $16 to $19. Note that nights get chilly at these elevations, even in July. Stop by the Mammoth Lake Visitors Center for a full list of campgrounds and public shower locations.

You can also camp for free on National Forest land unless posted otherwise. The visitors center/ranger station has a map showing which areas are closed to dispersed camping, and also issues free but mandatory fire permits.

Davison Street Guest House (☎ 760-924-2188, reservations 619-544-9093, 858-755-8648; www.mammoth-guest.com; 19 Davison St; dm $35-44, r $71-123) An A-frame hostel on a quiet residential street. You can whip up entire meals in the stocked kitchen and enjoy mountain views from the living room with fireplace or sun deck. It sleeps up to 26 people in five rooms. There's self-registration in case the manager isn't around, and in summer it's possible to never actually see an employee.

Swiss Chalet (☎ 760-934-2403, 800-937-9477; www.mammoth-swisschalet.com; 3776 Viewpoint Rd; r $90-125) An older motel perched just off the main road, this charming two-story lodge has friendly owners and simply decorated rooms, with painted furniture, comfy beds, fridge, TV and telephone. Rooms have screen doors in front and back to catch summer breezes. After a day on the trails or slopes, wind down in the hot tub or sauna, both with superb mountain views.

Some of the nicest campgrounds are in the lakes basin around Twin Lakes, Lake Mary and Lake George, with well-spaced sites in a pine forest and along crackling creeks. Less picturesque but close to town, **New Shady Rest** and **Old Shady Rest** (☎ 877-444-6777; www.recreation.gov; tent & RV sites $18) are two sprawling options right behind the visitors bureau/ranger station. New Shady is usually the first to open.

MIDRANGE

Mammoth B&Bs and inns rarely sell out during midweek, when rates tend to be lower. During ski season, reservations are a good idea on weekends and essential during holidays. Many properties offer ski and stay packages.

Alpenhof Lodge (☎ 760-934-6330, 800-828-0371; www.alpenhof-lodge.com; 6080 Minaret Rd; r $155-185; wi-fi) This Euro-flavored inn is a snowball's toss away from the new Village and has fairly nondescript yet comfortable rooms in various sizes, including some with gas fireplace or balcony.

Tamarack Lodge & Resort (☎ 760-934-2442, 800-237-6879; www.tamaracklodge.com; Lakes Loop Rd, Twin Lakes; lodge r $99-169, cabins $169-549; wi-fi) A charming year-round resort on the shore of Lower Twin Lake. In business since 1924, the cozy lodge includes a fireplace, bar, excellent restaurant, 11 rustic rooms and 34 cabins. The cabins range from very simple to simply deluxe, and come with full kitchen, telephone, private bath, porch and wood-burning stove. Some can sleep up to nine people.

Mammoth Creek Inn (☎ 760-934-6162, 800-466-7000; www.mammothcreekinn.com; 663 Old Mammoth Rd; r $110-165, with kitchen $154-298; wi-fi) It's amenities galore at this pretty inn at the end of a commercial strip, with down comforters, fluffy terry robes and VCRs in the rooms, as well as a sauna, a hot tub and lots of cozy common areas. The best rooms overlook the majestic Sherwin Mountains, and some have full kitchens.

Condos are proliferating faster than rabbits on Viagra in Mammoth. They may work out cheaper than other types of lodging, especially if you're traveling as a group or staying a week or longer. Booking agencies include the following:

Central Reservations of Mammoth (☎ 760-934-8816, 800-321-3261; www.mammothlakes.com)

Mammoth Reservation Bureau (☎ 760-934-2528, 800-462-5571; www.mammothvacations.com)

Eating

Roberto's Café (☎ 760-934-3667; 271 Old Mammoth Rd; mains $7-15; 11am-10pm) Serving Mammoth's hands-down best Mexican food and a selection of more than 30 tequilas, this fun restaurant is usually bustling. Locals pack the outdoor deck to look out on a beautiful wildflower garden, or quaff margaritas in the tropical-themed upstairs cantina.

Good Life Café (☎ 760-934-1734; Mammoth Mall, 126 Old Mammoth Rd; mains $8-10; 6:30am-3pm) Healthy food, generously filled veggie wraps and big bowls of salad make this a perennially popular place. The front patio area is blissful for a long brunch on a warm day.

Petra's Bistro & Wine Bar (☎ 760-934-3500; 6080 Minaret Rd; mains $14-32; dinner Tue-Sun) Settle in here for seasonal California cuisine and wines recommended by the three staff sommeliers. In wintertime, the best seats in the house are the cozy fireside couches. Start the evening with a cheese course and choose from 28 wines available by the glass or 240 vintages by the bottle.

Whiskey Creek (☎ 760-934-2555; cnr Minaret Rd & Main St; mains $17-31; dinner) Consistently good food, sweeping mountain views and friendly, unobtrusive service get our vote any time. The steaks are excellent, as are the salmon-crab cakes and the artichoke-spinach dip.

Lakefront Restaurant (☎ 760-934-3534; Lakes Loop Rd, Twin Lakes; mains $23-32; lunch summer, dinner year-round, closed Tue & Wed in fall & spring) For a splurge, the Tamarack Lodge has an intimate and romantic dining room overlooking Twin Lakes. The chef crafts French-California specialties like elk medallions au poivre and heirloom tomatoes with Basque cheese, and the staff are superbly friendly. Reservations recommended.

Sierra Sundance Whole Foods (☎ 760-934-8122; 26 Old Mammoth Rd) Self-catering vegetarians can stock up on organic produce, bulk foods and tofu at this small store.

Other good eats:

Stove (☎ 760-934-2821; 644 Old Mammoth Rd; meals $7-18; 6:30am-2pm & 5-9pm) Great coffee and carbs.

Perry's Italian Café (☎ 760-934-6521; 3399 Main St; mains $10-26; 7am-10pm) Scrumptious pizza, calzone, pasta and salads.

Drinking

Clocktower Cellar (☎ 760-934-6330; 6080 Minaret Rd) In the winter especially, locals throng this half-hidden basement of the Alpenhof Lodge. The ceiling is tiled with a swirl of bottle caps, and it stocks 31 beers on tap – especially German brews – and about 50 bottled varieties.

Grumpy's (☎ 760-934-8587; 361 Old Mammoth Rd; dishes $10-12; 11am-2am) Mammoth's original party place still lures a lively crowd with its antler chandeliers, scores of TVs, pool tables and tried-and-true belly-fillers (good burgers).

Mammoth Creek Brewing (☎ 760-934-2555; cnr Minaret Rd & Main St; 5-9pm summer, 4-9pm winter) Upstairs at Whiskey Creek; it's a popular and noisy hangout with a pool table and large-screen TVs, with the decibels rising during the early evening happy hour. It serves beers brewed on-site as well as fancy pub grub.

Getting There & Away

Once daily round-trip bus service between Mammoth and Yosemite Valley (one way $30, four hours) is run by **Yarts** (☎ 209-388-9589, 877-989-2787; www.yarts.com) on Saturdays and Sundays in June and September, and daily from July through August.

To the horror of some and the delight of others, daily winter-season flights from Los Angeles to Mammoth's updated airport (called Mammoth Yosemite) began in 2008 on **Horizon Air** (www.alask aair.com).

AROUND MAMMOTH LAKES

Reds Meadow

One of the beautiful and varied landscapes near Mammoth is the Reds Meadow valley west of Mammoth Mountain. Drive on Hwy 203 as far as **Minaret Vista** for eye-popping views (best at sunset) of the Ritter Range, the serrated Minarets and the remote reaches of Yosemite National Park.

To minimize impact, the road is closed to private vehicles beyond here unless you are camping, have lodge reservations or are disabled. An access fee (per adult/child $7/4, maximum $20 per car) is good for three days, and pays your passage for unlimited rides on the mandatory shuttle bus. It leaves from the Gondola Building near the Main Lodge at least half-hourly between 7:15am and 7pm (last bus out leaves Devils Postpile at 7:45pm). The bus stops at trailheads, viewpoints and campgrounds before completing the one-way trip to Reds Meadow in about 45 minutes.

The most fascinating attraction here is the surreal volcanic formation of **Devils Postpile National Monument**. The 60ft curtains of near-vertical, six-sided basalt columns formed when rivers of molten lava slowed, cooled and cracked with perplexing symmetry. This honeycomb design is best appreciated from atop the columns, reached by a short trail. The columns are an easy, half-mile hike from the **Devil's Postpile Ranger Station** (☎ 760-934-2289; www.nps.gov/depo; 9am-5pm).

From the monument, a 2-mile hike passing through fire-scarred forest leads to the spectacular **Rainbow Falls**, where the San Joaquin River gushes over a 101ft basalt cliff. Chances of actually seeing a rainbow forming in the billowing mist are greatest at midday. The falls can also be reached on an easy 1.5-mile walk from the Reds Meadow area, which is carpeted in wildflowers in early summer and also has a café, store, campground and pack station.

Minaret Rd provides access to six campgrounds along the San Joaquin River. Campers can drive in but must still pay the access fee. Tranquil willow-shaded **Minaret Falls Campground** (tent & RV sites $16) is a popular fishing spot where the best riverside sites have views of its namesake cascade.

The Reds Meadow Rd is only accessible from about June until September, weather permitting.

Hot Creek Geological Site

For a graphic view of the area's geothermal power, journey a few miles south of Mammoth to where chilly Mammoth Creek blends with hot springs and continues its journey as Hot Creek. It eventually enters a small gorge and forms a series of steaming, bubbling cauldrons with water shimmering in shades of blue and green reminiscent of the tropics. Until recently, soakers reveled in the blissful but somewhat scary temperate zones where the hot springs mixed with frigid creek water. But in 2006 a significant increase in geothermal activity began sending violent geysers of boiling water into the air, and the site is off-limits for swimming until the danger of getting your goose cooked has subsided.

Turn off Hwy 395 about 5 miles south of town and follow signs to the Hot Creek Fish Hatchery. From here, it's another 2 miles on gravel road to the parking area, from where it's a short trek down into the canyon and to the creek.

Convict Lake

Located just southeast of Mammoth, Convict Lake is one of the area's prettiest lakes, with emerald water embraced by massive peaks. A trek along the gentle trail skirting the lake, through aspen and cottonwood trees, is great if you're still adjusting to the altitude. A trailhead on the southeastern shore gives access to Genevieve, Edith, Dorothy and Mildred Lakes in the John Muir Wilderness. To reach the lake, turn south from Hwy 395 on Convict Lake Rd (across from the Mammoth airport) and go 2 miles.

In 1871 Convict Lake was the site of a bloody shoot-out between a band of escaped convicts and a posse that had given chase. Posse leader, Sheriff Robert Morrison, was killed during the gunfight and the taller peak, Mt Morrison (12,268ft), was later named in his honor. The bad guys got away only to be apprehended later near Bishop.

The **campground** (☎ 877-444-6777; www.recreation.gov; tent & RV sites $18; ⌚ mid-Apr–Oct) has flush toilets and nicely terraced sites. Otherwise your only option is **Convict Lake Resort** (☎ 760-934-3800, 800-992-2260; www.convictlake.com; cabins from $139), whose 29 cabins with kitchens sleep from two to 34 and range from rustic to ritzy. Foodies with deep pockets flock to the elegant restaurant (☎ 760-934-3803, lunch mains $9 to $14, dinner mains $20 to $50), which many consider the best within a 100-mile radius.

BISHOP

pop 3570 / elev 4140ft

Many people think of Bishop as a place to refuel their car and their tummy, and given the abundance of gas stations, fast-food outlets and supermarkets, who can blame them? The truth is that this little western-flavored town is surrounded by awesome nature where you can wear yourself out with world-class rock climbing, fishing and hiking. The area is especially lovely in fall when dropping temperatures cloak aspen, willow and cottonwood in myriad glowing shades.

Orientation

Bishop's main street is full of motels, restaurants, coffeehouses, gas stations, small malls and outfitters, as well as a good bookstore, a tiny movie theater and a casino. Line St heads into the mountains as Hwy 168.

Information

Bishop Area Visitors Bureau (☎ 760-873-8405; www.bishopvisitor.com; 690 N Main St; ⌚ 10am-5pm Mon-Fri, to 4pm Sat & Sun).

Bishop Library (☎ 760-873-5115; 210 Academy) Free internet access.

Spellbinder Books (☎ 760-873-4511; 124 S Main St) Great indie bookstore with attached café.

White Mountain Ranger Station (☎ 760-873-2500; 798 N Main St; ⌚ 8am-5pm daily May-Oct, Mon-Fri rest of year) Wilderness permits, trail and campground information for the entire area.

Sights

To see the Sierra on display in all its majesty, pop into the **Mountain Light Gallery** (☎ 760-873-7700; 106 S Main St; admission free; ⌚ 10am-6pm Sun-Thu, to 8pm Fri & Sat), which displays and sells many of Galen Rowell's most magical photos taken in the mountains and elsewhere.

Railroad and Old West aficionados should make the 6-mile detour north on Hwy 6 to the **Laws Railroad Museum** (☎ 760-873-5950; www.lawsmuseum.org; requested donation $5; 10am-4pm;). It re-creates the village of Laws, an important stop on the route of the *Slim Princess*, a narrow-gauge train that hauled freight and passengers across the Owens Valley for nearly 80 years. The original 1883 train depot is here, as are a post office, a schoolhouse and other rickety old buildings. Many contain funky and eclectic displays (dolls, bottles, fire equipment, antique stoves etc) from the pioneer days.

Activities

Bishop is prime **bouldering** and **rock climbing** territory with terrain to match any level of fitness, experience and climbing style. The main areas are the granite Buttermilk Country west of town on Buttermilk Rd, and the stark Volcanic Tablelands and Owens River Valley to the north. For details, consult with the staff at **Wilson's Eastside Sports** (☎ 760-873-7520; 224 N Main St), which rents equipment and sells maps and guidebooks. The tablelands are also great for Native American petroglyph-spotting.

Hikers will want to head to the high country by following Line St (Hwy 168) west along Bishop Creek Canyon past Buttermilk Country and on to several lakes, including Lake Sabrina and South Lake. Trailheads lead into the John Muir Wilderness and on into Kings Canyon National Park. Check with the White Mountain Ranger Station (p411) for suggestions, maps and wilderness permits for overnight stays. **Fishing** is good in all lakes but North Lake is the least crowded.

About 8 miles south of Bishop is **Keough's Hot Springs** (☎ 760-872-4670; 800 Keough Hot Springs Rd; adult/concession $8/6; 11am-7pm Wed-Mon, longer summer hrs), a historic institutional-green outdoor pool (dating from 1919) that's filled with bathwater-warm water from local mineral springs and doused with spray at one end. A smaller and sheltered 106°F soaking pool sits beside it.

Sleeping

Bishop has plenty of roadside motels with unexciting rooms from $60. For a little more style and comfort, try the following places.

Chalfant House (☎ 760-872-1790, 800-641-2996; www.chalfanthouse.com; 213 Academy; r incl breakfast $80-105) Lace curtains and Victorian accents swirl through the six rooms of this restored historic home. Originally built by the editor and publisher of Owens Valley's first newspaper, some of the rooms are named after Chalfant family members.

Joseph House Inn Bed & Breakfast (☎ 760-872-3389; www.josephhouseinn.com; 376 W Yaney St; r incl full breakfast $143-178; closed Jan; wi-fi) A beautiful restored ranch-style home, it has a patio overlooking a tranquil 3-acre garden, and five nicely furnished rooms, some with fireplaces, all with TV and VCR. Guests enjoy a complimentary gourmet breakfast and afternoon wine and cheese.

The closest **USFS campgrounds** (tent & RV sites $19; May-Sep), all but one first-come, first-served, are between 9 miles and 15 miles west of town on Bishop Creek along Hwy 168, at elevations between 7500ft and 9000ft. Shower at Keough's Hot Springs or in town at the **Wash Tub** (☎ 760-873-6627; 236 N Warren St; 7am-10pm), where you can wash your smalls while playing air hockey.

Eating

Looney Bean (☎ 760-872-2326; 399 N Main St; pastries $3; 6am-8pm Sun & Mon-Thu, to 10pm Fri & Sat; wi-fi) The combination of really fine coffee, a comfortable modern space and free wi-fi guarantee the popularity of this central café. It carries some organic brews, and lots of tasty scones and pastries for snacking.

Erick Schat's Bakkerÿ (☎ 760-873-7156; 763 N Main St; sandwiches $4-8; 6am-6pm Sun-Thu, to 7pm Fri) A much-hyped tourist mecca filled to the rafters with racks of fresh bread, it has been making the signature shepherd bread and other baked goodies since 1938. The bakery also features a popular sandwich bar.

Jack's Restaurant & Bakery (☎ 760-872-7971; 437 N Main St; mains $6-18; 6am-9pm) In business since 1946, Jack's stocks a full menu of filling, inexpensive comfort food like meatloaf and chicken fried steak, as well as hearty breakfasts and creamy cakes. Guess which of the mounted fish are real.

Whiskey Creek (☎ 760-873-7174; 524 N Main St; mains $12-29) During the summertime, take your pick between the somewhat saccharine country dining room of floral curtains and captain's chairs or the mist-sprayed patio. The menu has comfort food like meatloaf and pork chops, and a smattering of seafood and pastas.

BIG PINE

pop 1350 / elev 3985ft

This blink-and-you-missed-it town has a few motels and basic eateries. It mainly functions as a launch pad for the Ancient Bristlecone Pine Forest (see the boxed text, below) and to the granite **Palisades** in the John Muir Wilderness, a rugged cluster of peaks including six above 14,000ft. Stretching beneath the pinnacles is **Palisades Glacier**, the southernmost in the USA and the largest in the Sierra. Stop by the **visitors center** (☎ 760-938-2114; www.bigpine.com; 128 S Main St; 🕓 10am-5:30pm Tue-Sat) for maps and information about the entire area.

To get to the trailhead, turn onto Glacier Lodge Rd (Crocker Ave in town), which follows trout-rich Big Pine Creek up **Big Pine Canyon** 10 miles west into a bowl-shaped valley. The strenuous 9-mile hike to Palisade Glacier via the North Fork Trail skirts several lakes – turned a milky turquoise color by glacial run-off – and a stone cabin built by horror-film actor Lon Chaney in 1925.

Glacier Lodge Rd passes by a trio of **USFS campgrounds** (☎ 877-444-6777; www.recreation.gov; tent & RV sites $18; 🕓 May–mid-Oct) – Big Pine Creek, Sage Flat and Upper Sage Flat. Showers are available for $4 at **Glacier Lodge** (☎ 760-938-2837; www.jewelofthesierra.com; tent & RV sites $35, cabins $110; 🕓 mid-Apr–mid-Nov), a bunch of rustic cabins with kitchens and a two-night minimum stay in July and August; it was one of the earliest Sierra getaways when built in 1917.

INDEPENDENCE

pop 580 / elev 3925ft

This sleepy highway town has been a county seat since 1866 and is home to the **Eastern California Museum** (☎ 760-878-0364; 155 N Grant St; donation requested; 🕓 10am-5pm Wed-Mon). It contains one of the most complete collections of Paiute and Shoshone baskets in the country, as well as artifacts from the Manzanar relocation camp (see boxed text, p414) and historic photographs of primitively equipped local rock climbers scaling Sierra peaks, including Mt Whitney.

West of town via Onion Valley Rd (Market St in town), pretty **Onion Valley** harbors the trailhead for the **Kearsarge Pass** (10-mile round-trip), an old Paiute trade route. This is also the quickest eastside access to the Pacific Crest Trail and Kings Canyon National Park.

SIERRA NEVADA

DETOUR: ANCIENT BRISTLECONE PINE FOREST

For encounters with some of the earth's oldest living things, plan at least a half-day trip to the **Ancient Bristlecone Pine Forest**. These gnarled, otherworldly-looking trees thrive above 10,000ft on the slopes of the seemingly inhospitable White Mountains, a parched and stark range that once stood even higher than the Sierra. The oldest tree – called Methuselah – is estimated to be over 4700 years, beating even the Great Sphinx of Giza by about two centuries.

To reach the groves, take Hwy 168 east 13 miles from Big Pine to White Mountain Rd, then turn left (north) and climb the curvy road 10 miles to **Schulman Grove**, named for the scientist who first discovered the trees' biblical age in the 1950s. There's a **visitors center** (☎ information 760-873-2500; www.fs.fed.us/r5/inyo/recreation/bristlecone/index.shtml; 🕓 10am-5pm late May-Oct) and access to self-guided trails. The entire trip should take about one hour. White Mountain Rd is usually closed from November to April. It's nicest in August when wildflowers sneak out through the rough soil.

A second grove, the **Patriarch Grove,** is dramatically set within an open bowl and reached via a 12-mile graded dirt road. Four miles further on you'll find a locked gate, which is the departure point for day hikes to the **White Mountain Peak** – at 14,246ft it's the third-highest mountain in California and only 250ft lower than Mt Whitney. The round-trip is about 14 miles via an abandoned road, soon passing through the Barcroft High Altitude Research Station, and some ride the route on mountain bikes. The easiest 14er in California, the nontechnical and marmot-laden route winds above the tree line, though naturally, high elevation makes the going tough. Allow plenty of time, bring at least two quarts of water per person. For maps and details, stop at the White Mountain Ranger Station (p411) in Bishop.

For altitude adjustment, spend a night at the undeveloped **Grandview Campground** (donation $3) at 8600ft. It has awesome views, but no water.

CAMP OF INFAMY

On December 7, 1941, Japanese war planes bombed Pearl Harbor, a day that, according to President Roosevelt, would forever live in infamy. The sneak attack plunged the US into WWII and fanned the flames of racial prejudice that had been fomenting against Japanese Americans for decades. Amid fears of sabotage and espionage, bigotry grew into full-blown hysteria, prompting Roosevelt to sign Executive Order 9066 in February 1942; another day that lives in infamy. The act stated that all West Coast Japanese – most of them American-born citizens – were to be rounded up and moved to relocation camps.

Manzanar was the first of 10 such camps, built among pear and apple orchards in the dusty Owens Valley near Independence. Between 1942 and 1945 up to 10,000 men, women and children lived crammed into makeshift barracks pounded by fierce winds and the blistering desert sun and enclosed by barbed wire patrolled by military police.

After the war the camp was leveled and its dark history remained buried beneath the dust for decades. Recognition remained elusive until 1973 when the site was given landmark status; in 1992 it was designated a national historic site and in 2004 a long-awaited interpretive center opened. The last Saturday every April, former internees and their descendants make a pilgrimage (www.manzanarcommittee.org) to honor family members who died here, keeping alive the memory of this national tragedy. For a vivid and haunting account of what life was like at the camp, read Jean Wakatsuki Houston's classic *Farewell to Manzanar*.

Another trail goes to Golden Trout Lake, but it's strenuous and poorly marked. A herd of California bighorn sheep lives south of Onion Valley around Shepherd Pass.

Onion Valley has a couple of **campgrounds** (☎ 877-444-6777; www.recreation.gov; tent & RV sites $13; ⌚ May-Sep) along Independence Creek. A fleet of homey, worn armchairs welcomes guests to the historic **Winnedumah Hotel** (☎ 760-878-2040; www.winnedumah.com; 211 N Edwards St; r with/without bath incl breakfast $85/75; wi-fi), a 1927 country-style inn that was popular with Hollywood celebs when the cameras were rolling in the Alabama Hills near Lone Pine.

Inexplicably located in a town otherwise inhabited by greasy spoon diners, **Still Life Café** (☎ 760-878-2555; 135 S Edward St; mains lunch $8-14, dinner $20-30; ⌚ usually lunch & dinner Thu-Sun), a French gourmet bistro, pops out like an orchid in a salt flat. Escargot, duck-liver mousse, steak au poivre and other French delectables are served with Gallic charm in this bright, artistic dining room.

MANZANAR NATIONAL HISTORIC SITE

A stark wooden guard tower alerts drivers to one of the darkest chapters in US history, which unfolded on a barren and windy sweep of land some 5 miles south of Independence. Little remains of the infamous war concentration camp, a dusty sq mile where more than 10,000 people of Japanese ancestry were corralled during WWII following the attack on Pearl Harbor (see boxed text, above). The camp's lone remaining building, the former high-school auditorium, houses a superb **interpretive center** (☎ 760-878-2194; www.nps.gov/manz; admission free; ⌚ 9am-4:30pm Nov-Mar, to 5:30pm Apr-Oct). A visit here is one of the historical highlights of the state and should not be missed.

Watch the 20-minute documentary, then explore the thought-provoking exhibits that chronicle the stories of the families who languished here yet built a vibrant community. Afterwards, take a self-guided 3.2-mile driving tour around the grounds, which takes you past vestiges of buildings and gardens as well as the haunting camp cemetery.

LONE PINE

pop 1700 / elev 3700ft

A tiny town, Lone Pine is the gateway to big things, most notably Mt Whitney (14,496ft), the loftiest peak in the contiguous USA, and Hollywood. In the 1920s cinematographers discovered the nearby Alabama Hills were a picture-perfect movie set for Westerns, and stars from Gary Cooper to Gregory Peck could often be spotted swaggering about town.

Orientation & Information

A few basic motels, restaurants and stores flank Hwy 395 (Main St in town). Whitney Portal Rd heads west at the lone stoplight, while Hwy 136 to Death Valley veers away about 2 miles south of town.

Eastern Sierra InterAgency Visitor Center (☎ 760-876-6222; www.fs.fed.us/r5/inyo; 8am-5pm, extended summer hrs) USFS information central for the Sierra, Death Valley and Mt Whitney; about 1.5 miles south of town at the junction of Hwys 395 and 136.

Lone Pine Chamber of Commerce (☎ 760-876-4444; www.lonepinechamber.com; 120 S Main St; 8:30am-4:30pm Mon-Fri)

Sights & Activities

MOUNT WHITNEY

West of Lone Pine, the jagged incisors of the Sierra surge skyward in all their raw and fierce glory. Cradled by scores of smaller pinnacles, Mt Whitney is a bit hard to pick out from Hwy 395, so for the best views, take a drive along Whitney Portal Rd through the Alabama Hills. As you get a fix on this majestic megalith, remember that the country's lowest point is only 80 miles (as the crow flies) east of here: Badwater (p683) in Death Valley. Climbing to Mt Whitney's summit is among the most popular hikes in the entire country (see boxed text, below).

ALABAMA HILLS

Located on Whitney Portal Rd, the warm colors and rounded contours of the Alabama Hills stand in contrast to the jagged snowy Sierras

CLIMBING MOUNT WHITNEY

The mystique of Mt Whitney captures the imagination, and conquering its hulking bulk becomes a sort of obsession for many. The main Mt Whitney Trail (the easiest and busiest one) leaves from Whitney Portal, about 13 miles west of Lone Pine via the Whitney Portal Rd (closed in winter), and climbs about 6000ft over 11 miles. It's a superstrenuous, really, *really* long walk that'll wear out even experienced mountaineers, but doesn't require technical skills if attempted in summer or early fall. Earlier or later in the season, you'll likely need an ice axe and crampons.

Many people in good physical condition make it to the top, although only superbly conditioned, previously acclimatized hikers should attempt this as a day hike. Breathing becomes difficult at these elevations and altitude sickness is a common problem. Rangers recommend spending a night or two camping at the trailhead and another at one of the two camps along the route: Outpost Camp at 3.5 miles or Trail Camp at 6 miles up the trail.

When considering an ascent, do your homework. A recommended guide is *Climbing Mt Whitney* by Walt Wheelock and Wynne Benti. When you pick up your permit and Waste Alleviation & Gelling (WAG) bags at the Eastern Sierra Interagency Visitor Center in Lone Pine, get the latest scoop about weather and trail conditions.

Whitney Portal has two attractive campgrounds tucked into a pine forest along Lone Pine Creek: **Whitney Portal** (☎ 877-444-6777; www.recreation.gov; tent sites $16; May–mid-Oct), about half a mile from the trailhead, with 43 lovely terraced sites, chemical flush toilets and potable water; and the 10-site first-come, first-served **Whitney Trailhead** (tent sites $8; May–mid-Oct), which has a one-night maximum and the same facilities. If they're full, consider the 43-site **Lone Pine Campground** (☎ 877-444-6777; www.recreation.gov; tent & RV sites $14; mid-Apr–Oct), about 7 miles east of the trailhead off Whitney Portal Rd. The **Whitney Portal Store** (www.whitneyportalstore.com) sells groceries and snacks, and rents bear-resistant food containers. It also has public showers and a café with hot meals. Its excellent website is a comprehensive starting point for Whitney research.

The biggest obstacle in getting to the peak may be to obtain a wilderness permit (per person $15), which is required for all overnight trips and for day hikes past Lone Pine Lake (about 2.8 miles from the trailhead). A quota system limits daily access to 60 overnight and 100 day hikers from May through October. Because of the huge demand, permits are distributed via a lottery. You must *mail* your application to the **Mt Whitney Lottery** (c/o Wilderness Permit Office, 351 Pacu Lane, Suite 200, Bishop, CA 93514) anytime in February. Click on 'Mt Whitney' at www.fs.fed.us/r5/inyo for full details and application forms.

Want to avoid the hassle of getting a permit for the main Mt Whitney Trail? Consider ascending this popular pinnacle from the west, using the backdoor route from Sequoia & Kings Canyon National Parks. It takes about four to six days from Crescent Meadow via the High Sierra Trail to the John Muir Trail – with no Whitney Zone permit required – and wilderness permits are much easier to secure. See p400 for park permit information.

just behind. The setting for countless ride-'em-out movies and the popular *Lone Ranger* TV series, the stunning orange rock formations are a beautiful place to experience sunrise or sunset. You can drive, walk or mountain-bike along dirt roads rambling through the boulders, and along Tuttle and Lone Pine creeks. A number of graceful rock arches are within easy hiking distance of the roads. Head west on Whitney Portal Rd and either turn left at Tuttle Creek Rd, after a half-mile, or north on Movie Rd, after about 3 miles. Pick up maps at the Lone Pine Chamber of Commerce.

Other Sights & Activities

You can see the names of movie stars scratched into the walls of the **Indian Trading Post** (137 Main St) and view exhibits in the small **Movie Room** (126 Main St). Over 450 movies have been shot in the area, and the new **Museum of Lone Pine Film History** (☎ 760-876-9909; www.lonepinefilmhistorymuseum.org; 701 S Main St; admission $5; 🕑 10am-6pm Mon-Wed, to 7pm Thu-Sat, to 4pm Sun) contains exhibits of paraphernalia from locally set films. Don't miss the 7pm screenings in its theater every Thursday and Friday.

Sleeping & Eating

Tuttle Creek Campground (tent & RV sites $5; 🕑 Mar-Oct) Take your pick from 85 first-come, first-served BLM sites off the Whitney Portal Rd. There's not much shade and no potable water, but Sierra and Alabama Hills views abound. Go 3.5 miles on Whitney Portal Rd, then 1.5 miles south on Horseshoe Meadow Road and follow signs to the campground.

Dow Hotel & Dow Villa Motel (☎ 760-876-5521, 800-824-9317; www.dowvillamotel.com; 310 S Main St; hotel r with/without bath $62/44, motel r $94-142; wi-fi) John Wayne and Errol Flynn are among the stars who have stayed at this venerable hotel. Built in 1922, the place has been restored but retains much of its rustic charm. The rooms in the newer motel section are more comfortable and bright, but also more generic.

High Sierra Café (☎ 760-876-5796; 446 S Main St; breakfast & lunch mains under $10, dinner mains $9-19; 🕑 24hr) The food won't knock your socks off, but this coffee shop is one of the only places along Hwy 395 that feeds hungry travelers 24/7.

Seasons (☎ 760-876-8927; 206 N Main St; mains $16-28; 🕑 dinner daily Apr-Oct, Tue-Sun Nov-Mar) Another place that hits the spot with hungry hikers, Seasons has everything you fantasized about the last time you choked down freeze-dried rations. Sauteed trout, roasted duck, filet mignon and plates of carb-replenishing pasta will revitalize your appetite, and nice and naughty desserts will leave you purring.

Central Valley

For most travelers going through California, the Central Valley is a blur of green and a few truck stops between LA and San Francisco. But those who are curious enough to take the slow road instead will find a study of California's opposites. Instead of the exhilarating bustle and jammed freeways of Los Angeles, tractors troll past cow-dotted fields on its two-lane byways; instead of the Bay Area's progressive peaceniks and foggy skies, there are blazing hot fields worked by conservative-leaning farmers. In place of the dramatic granite faces of the Sierras or the sparkling sunsets of the Pacific are arid planes that stretch into the horizon, interrupted only by grain elevators or rows of power lines. This is what some call the *other* California.

This 400-mile-long green strip in the center of the state is known as the greatest garden in the world. It's divided into two regions: the Sacramento Valley in the north and the San Joaquin Valley in the south. The migrant workers who tend that garden have made *español* the unofficial language of the region, but there are pockets where you'll hear Southern twang left over from the generation of Dust Bowl farmers who first rushed the fields, and the slacker drawl of the NorCal thrill-seekers who rush its hills for outdoor adventure.

HIGHLIGHTS

- **California Stories** Exploring California's other history at the California Museum for History, Women & Arts (p421) in Sacramento.
- **Jiving Buckaroos** Line dancing with sharp-dressed cowboys and -girls at Buck Owens' Crystal Palace club in Bakersfield (p440)
- **Fair Games** Petting the livestock and eating a deep-fried Snickers at the sprawling California State Fair (p422).
- **Best Lazy Drive** Driving the gently sweeping levee roads of the Sacramento River Delta (p426)
- **Big Toy Trains** Riding the choo-choo at the California State Railroad Museum (p421).
- **Best Afternoon Underground** Exploring Fresno's confounding Forestiere Underground Gardens (p437).
- **College Town River Cruise** Tubing though the icy waters that run though Chico (p431).
- **Fruit from the Source** Pulling over at the fruit stands of the San Joaquin Valley along historic Hwy 99 (p434)

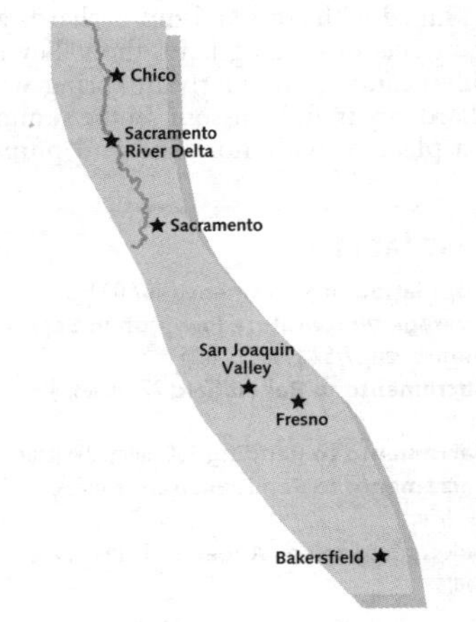

GETTING THERE & AROUND

The main routes through this part of California are Hwy 99 and I-5. I-80 meets Hwy 99 in Sacramento, and I-5 meets Hwy 99 south of Bakersfield. Amtrak also intersects the state with two lines – the *San Joaquins* route through the Central Valley and the *Pacific Surfliner* between the Central Coast and San Diego (see p738 for more information). The *San Jaoquins* service stops in just about every town covered here. **Greyhound** (☎ 800-229-9424) stops in all of the Central Valley towns and cities covered in this chapter. Trips between Sacramento and Bakersfield take about 6½ hours and cost around $50.

The Central Valley has lots of long, straight byways for those making the trip on bikes, and the **American River Parkway** (p422) is a veritable bicyclobahn for commuters between downtown Sacramento and Auburn.

SACRAMENTO VALLEY

The labyrinth of waterways that makes up the Sacramento–San Joaquin River Delta feeds the San Francisco Bay and divides the Central Valley in half, with the Sacramento Valley in the north and the San Joaquin Valley in the south. The Sacramento River, California's largest, rushes out of the northern mountains from Shasta Lake before hitting the valley basin above Red Bluff. Then, it snakes south across grassy plains and orchards before lazily skirting the state capital, fanning across the delta and draining into the San Francisco Bay. Lined with fruit and nut orchards and huge tracts of grazing land, the valley is a subtle beauty, particularly in spring when orchards are in full blossom. In the summer, it's a place of wide horizons and punishing, relentless sunshine; the skies go gray in fall, when they are decorated with the Vs of migratory birds.

Travelers going through the valley are often on their way to or from some other destination – the Bay Area, Gold Country or Lake Tahoe being the popular neighbors – but the shady streets, gardens and stately marble buildings of Sacramento and the inviting college town of Davis warrant exploring.

FAST FACTS

Population of Sacramento 407,000
Average temperature low/high in Sacramento Jan 37/52°F, Jul 55/87°F
Sacramento to Bakersfield 277 miles, 4½ hours
Sacramento to Redding 160 miles, 2½ hours
Sacramento to San Francisco 88 miles, 1½ hours
Bakersfield to Los Angeles 112 miles, 2 hours

SACRAMENTO

pop 407,000 / elev 52ft

Sacramento has become a city of head-scratching anomalies. It's a former cow town that gets choked with rush-hour traffic, with the polished sedans of state legislators idling next to muddy half-ton pickup trucks. It claims stunning racial diversity, yet its neighborhoods are homogenous pockets of single ethnicities. Square in the middle of the sweltering valley, Sacramento's downtown is couched by the confluence of two cool rivers – the American and the Sacramento – and its streets are shushed by the leaves of huge oaks. Its sprawling suburbanization has recently turned around, placing lofts and up-scale eateries next to abandoned midcentury shops in Midtown – an area called 'the Grid' for its uniformly square streets.

If you find yourself jammed on the roads that bypass Sacramento, jump off the highway for scoops at one of the city's vintage ice-cream parlors, or spend the evening in one of its elegantly preserved movie houses or welcoming dive bars, where newcomers are welcomed with cheap drinks and sent off with slaps on the back.

The people of 'Sac' are an unpretentious lot, and have fostered small but thriving arts and nightlife scenes. They beam with pride about Second Saturday, the monthly Midtown gallery crawl that is emblematic of the city's cultural awakening. The summer is best: fat-tired cruisers meander around the Grid, people crack cold ones and chat with neighbors on the porches of high-water Victorians (built to resist the flooding rivers in the years before they were levied), and farmers markets dot the downtown parks every day of the week.

Remember not to bruise feelings of locals by comparing Sacramento to the Bay Area – their perspective on the bigger, prettier kid-sister city is colored with an underdog's dismissiveness. After you spend a few hours

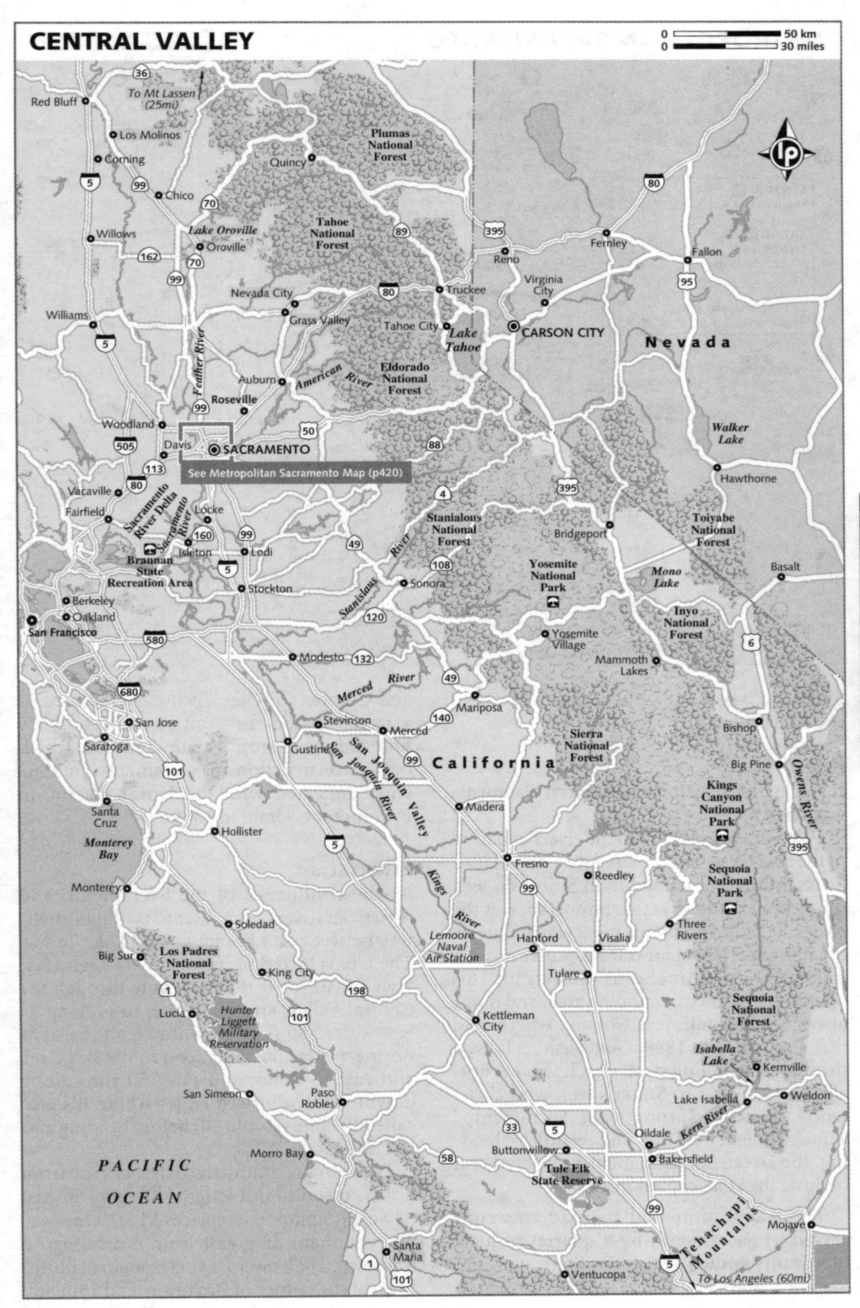
CENTRAL VALLEY
0 50 km
0 30 miles
To Mt Lassen (25mi)
Red Bluff
Los Molinos
Corning
Chico
Plumas National Forest
Quincy
Lake Oroville
Oroville
Willows
Tahoe National Forest
Nevada City
Grass Valley
Truckee
Reno
Fernley
Fallon
Virginia City
CARSON CITY
Tahoe City
Lake Tahoe
Nevada
Williams
Feather River
Auburn
American River
Eldorado National Forest
Roseville
Woodland
Davis
SACRAMENTO
See Metropolitan Sacramento Map (p420)
Walker Lake
Hawthorne
Vacaville
Fairfield
Sacramento River Delta
Sacramento River
Locke
Isleton
Brannan State Recreation Area
Lodi
Stockton
Stanialous National Forest
Bridgeport
Toiyabe National Forest
Yosemite National Park
Mono Lake
Basalt
Sonora
Stanislaus River
Berkeley
Oakland
San Francisco
Inyo National Forest
Yosemite Village
Mammoth Lakes
Modesto
Merced River
Mariposa
San Jose
Stevinson
Merced
Saratoga
Gustine
San Joaquin Valley
San Joaquin River
California
Sierra National Forest
Bishop
Big Pine
Owens River
Kings Canyon National Park
Santa Cruz
Monterey Bay
Hollister
Madera
Fresno
Reedley
Sequoia National Park
Monterey
Kings River
Soledad
Three Rivers
Lemoore Naval Air Station
Hanford
Visalia
Big Sur
Los Padres National Forest
King City
Tulare
Lucia
Hunter Liggett Military Reservation
Kettleman City
Sequoia National Forest
Isabella Lake
Kernville
San Simeon
Paso Robles
Lake Isabella
Weldon
Oildale
Kern River
Morro Bay
Buttonwillow
Bakersfield
PACIFIC OCEAN
Tule Elk State Reserve
Tehachapi Mountains
Mojave
Santa Maria
Ventucopa
To Los Angeles (60mi)
36
5
99
70
162
80
89
395
95
50
88
505
113
4
160
49
108
120
580
132
680
140
101
6
1
198
33
58
CENTRAL VALLEY

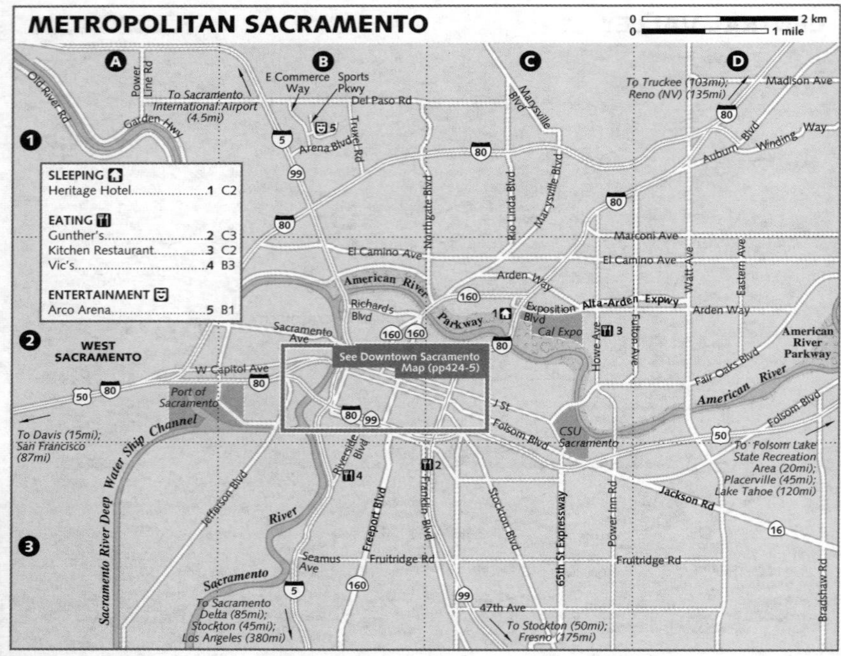

here, the Bay Area's bustle might start to seem jarring.

History

If you ask local historians, modern California was born here.

Paleo-era peoples fished the rivers and lived in the area for generations before a hot-headed Swiss immigrant named John Sutter showed up. Realizing the strategic importance of the rivers, he built an outpost here, which quickly became a safe haven for traders. Sutter raised a militia of Native Americans and extended his operations to the surrounding area, and it was at his lumber mill near Coloma where gold was discovered in 1848. Gold rushers flowed through the trading post, which was eventually handed over to Sutter's son, who christened the newly sprung town 'Sacramento.' Though plagued by fires and relentless flooding, the riverfront settlement prospered and became the state capital in 1850.

The transcontinental railroad was conceived in Sacramento by a quartet of local merchants known as the 'Big Four' – Leland Stanford, Mark Hopkins, Collis P Huntington and Charles Crocker – who are pictured in a fresco inside the Amtrak station. They founded the Central Pacific Railroad, which began construction in Sacramento in 1863 and connected with the Union Pacific in Promontory, Utah, in 1869.

Orientation

At the confluence of the Sacramento and American Rivers, Sacramento is roughly halfway between San Francisco and Lake Tahoe. The city is boxed in by four main highways: Hwy 99, which is the best route through the Central Valley, and I-5, which runs along its west side; I-80 skirts downtown on the city's northern edge, heading west to the Bay Area and east to Reno; and Hwy 50 runs along downtown's southern edge (where it's also called Business Route 80) before heading east to Lake Tahoe.

Downtown, numbered streets run from north to south and lettered streets run east to west (Capitol Ave replaces M St). One-way J St is a main drag east from downtown to Midtown. The Tower District is south of downtown at the corner of Broadway and 16th St.

Cal Expo, the site of the California State Fair every August, is east of I-80 from the Cal Expo exit.

Information

Beers Books Center (Map pp424-5; ☎ 916-442-9475; 915 S St; wi-fi) Cluttered and cozy, this is Sacramento's best bookstore, with a huge used selection and wi-fi.

Convention & Visitors Bureau (Map pp424-5; ☎ 916-264-7777; www.sacramentocvb.org; 1303 J St; 8am-5pm Mon-Fri) Local information, including event and bus schedules.

Old Sacramento Visitor Center (Map pp424-5; ☎ 916-442-7644; 1002 2nd St; 10am-5pm) Also has local information, including event and bus schedules.

Sights

CALIFORNIA STATE CAPITOL

The **California State Capitol** (Map pp424-5; ☎ 916-324-0333; cnr 10th & L Sts; 9am-5pm) is Sacramento's most recognizable structure. Built in the late 19th century, it underwent major reconstruction in the 1970s, and its marble halls offer a cool place for a stroll. There's a **bookstore** (9:30am-4pm Mon-Fri, 10:30am-4pm Sat & Sun) in the basement, but the real attraction is in the west wing, where there is a painting of a Hollywood action hero posing as a governor. Oh, wait a minute…

It could be argued that the 40 acres of garden surrounding the dome, **Capitol Park**, are better than the building itself. There are exotic trees from around the world, stern-looking statues of missionaries and a powerful Vietnam Memorial. A quieter war commemoration is the Civil War Memorial Grove, which was planted in 1897 with saplings from famous battlefields.

North of the Capitol is the **Governor's Mansion State Historic Park** (Map pp424-5; ☎ 916-323-3047; cnr 16th & H Sts; adult/child $4/2; 10am-5pm), built in 1877 and acquired by the state in 1903. No governor has lived in the house since Ronald Reagan moved out in the 1960s. Guided tours are given hourly from 10am to 4pm.

OLD SACRAMENTO

Though the art and culture of Midtown have challenged the conventional perception of Sacramento's visitors attractions as lackluster, this historic river port, adjacent to downtown, is the city's stalwart tourist draw. The pervasive scent of salt-water taffy and the somewhat garish restoration give Sacramento the vibe of a second-rate Frontierland, but it's good for a stroll on summer evenings, when boomers rumble though the brick streets on Harleys, and tourists and dolled-up legislative aides stroll the elevated sidewalks. It has California's largest concentration of buildings on the National Register of Historic Places (most of which now peddle Gold Rush trinkets and fudge) and a couple of quality attractions, but the restaurant scene is a bust – to eat and drink, head to Midtown.

At Old Sac's north end is the excellent **California State Railroad Museum** (Map pp424-5; ☎ 916-445-6645; www.csrmf.org; cnr 2nd & I Sts; adult/child $6/2; 10am-5pm), the largest of its kind in the US. It has an impressive collection of railcars, locomotives, toy models and memorabilia, and a fully outfitted Pullman sleeper and vintage diner cars to induce a joyful palsy in railroad enthusiasts. Tickets include entrance to the restored **Central Pacific Passenger Depot**, across the plaza from the museum entrance. On weekends from April to September, you can board a steam-powered passenger train from the depot (adult/child $8/3) for a 40-minute jaunt along the riverfront.

Next door to the railroad museum, the **Discovery Museum** (Map pp424-5; ☎ 916-264-7057; 101 I St; adult/child $5/3; 10am-5pm Jun-Aug, Tue-Sun Sep-May) has hands-on exhibits and Gold Rush displays for the kids.

CALIFORNIA MUSEUM FOR HISTORY, WOMEN & THE ARTS

our pick **California Museum for History, Women & the Arts** (Map pp424-5; ☎ 916-653-7524; 1020 O St; adult/child $7.50/5; 10am-5pm) A sleek contrast to Sacramento's traditional museum scene, this hip museum was a pet project of first lady Maria Shriver. Nary a dusty 19th-century relic lies in slumber among graceful modern

REQUIRED READING ON THE CENTRAL VALLEY

- *Where I Was From* (2003) – Joan Didion
- *The Grapes of Wrath* (1939) – John Steinbeck
- *The Other California* (1990) – Gerald Haslam
- *Proud to Be an Okie: Cultural Politics, Country Music, and Migration to Southern California* (2007) – Peter La Chapelle
- *Cadillac Desert* (1986) – Marc Reisner

exhibits, which tell an even-handed story of California's youth, by giving attention to typically underrepresented stories from the margins of history books. The excellent California Hall Of Fame – which honors everyone from Billie Jean King to Bill Gates – is worth the trip alone.

CROCKER ART MUSEUM

Housed in a pair of side-by-side Victorians, the **Crocker Art Museum** (Map pp424-5; ☎ 916-264-5423; 216 O St; adult/student $6/3, Sun morning free; 10am-5pm Tue-Sun, to 9pm Thu) is stunning as much for its outrageous stairways and beautiful tile floors as it is for its fine collection. There are some fine early California paintings and stellar drawings by European masters. The curatorial passion really comes through in its enthusiastic presentation of modern art.

SUTTER'S FORT STATE HISTORIC PARK

Sutter's Fort State Historic Park (Map pp424-5; ☎ 916-445-4422; cnr 27th & L Sts; adult/child $6/3; 10am-5pm), originally built by John Sutter, was once the only trace of white settlement for hundreds of miles – hard to tell by the housing developments that surround the park today. California history buffs should carve out a couple hours to stroll within its walls, where original furniture, equipment and a working ironsmith are straight out of the 1850s.

CALIFORNIA STATE INDIAN MUSEUM

It's with some irony that the humble structure of the **State Indian Museum** (Map pp424-5; ☎ 916-324-0971; 2618 K St; adult/child $2/free; 10am-5pm), sits across the park in the shadow of the turrets of Sutter's Fort. The fascinating pieces of Native American handicrafts – including immaculate weaving that once thrived in the area – were all but lost during the Gold Rush.

TOWER DISTRICT

South of Midtown, Tower District is dominated by **Tower Theatre** (Map pp424-5; ☎ 916-442-4700; 2508 Landpark Dr), a beautiful 1938 art-deco movie palace (see p425), which you'll probably spot on the way into town. From the theater, head east on Broadway to pass a stretch of the city's most eclectic and affordable ethnic eateries – including an excellent pair of side-by-side Thai restaurants. The **Tower Records** chain started in this building, and the original neon sign survives here, but the retailer itself closed its doors in 2006, a casualty of the digital music revolution.

Activities

The **American River Parkway** (Map p420), a 23-mile river system on the north bank of the American River, is surely Sacramento's most appealing geographic feature. It's one of the most extensive riparian habitats in the continental US, lined by a network of well-marked and -maintained trails and picnic areas. It's accessible from Old Sacramento by taking Front St north until it becomes Jiboom St and crosses the river, or by taking the Jiboom St exit off I-5/Hwy 99. The parkway includes a lovely bicycle and jogging path called the **Jedediah Smith National Recreation Trail**, which stretches over 30 miles from Old Sac to Folsom.

Sleeping

The capitol is a magnet for business travelers, so Sacramento doesn't suffer a lack of hotels – many of which sport good deals during the legislative break. Unless you're in town for the California State Fair or something else at Cal Expo, stay downtown or in Midtown, where there's plenty to do within walking distance. If you're into cheap and kitschy motor lodges of the 1950s, cross the river into West Sac and look for 'Motel Row' on Rte 40.

CALIFORNIA STATE FAIR

For the last two weeks in August, the **California State Fair** (☎ 916-263-3000; 1600 Exposition Blvd, Sacramento; adult/child $10/6) fills the Cal Expo with a small city of cows, candied apples and carnival rides. It's likely the only place on earth where you can plant a redwood tree, watch a pig give birth, ride a roller coaster, catch some barrel racing, taste exquisite Napa vintages and eat a deep-fried Snickers bar within an (admittedly exhausting) afternoon. Put on some comfy sneakers and pencil in two whole days, making time to see some of the auctions ($500 for a dozen eggs!) and the interactive exhibits run by the University of California, Davis. Try to book at room at the hotels near Cal Expo, which run regular shuttles to the event.

Folsom Lake State Recreation Area (off Map p420; ☎ 916-988-0205; www/www.parks.ca.gov; 7806 Folsom-Auburn Rd; tent & RV sites without/with hookups $15/34; office 6am-10pm summer, 7pm-7pm winter) Sacramento is a good staging area before going into the Sierras, and this campground, while hardly picturesque, is the best option for testing out your gear before heading into the mountains. It's not ideal – the rangers can be overbearing, the sites rocky and the lake overrun by powerboats, but the only other nearby camping is a KOA west of town on I-80.

Sacramento HI Hostel (Map pp424-5; ☎ 916-443-1691; www.norcalhostels.org/sac; 925 H St; dm $20-23, r $45-100; reception 7:30-9:30am & 5-10pm;) In a grand Victorian mansion, this hostel offers impressive trimmings at rock-bottom prices. It's within walking distance of the capitol, Old Sac and the train station. It attracts an international crowd and is a useful place to find rides to San Francisco and Lake Tahoe.

Heritage Hotel (Map p420; ☎ 916-929-7900; 1780 Tribute Rd; r $89-99;) If you have a car, this hotel close to Cal Expo is a good budget option. It looks like a fairly bland dormitory but is surrounded by lush gardens. Rooms are clean, quiet and spacious, and all have patios or balconies.

Delta King (Map pp424-5; ☎ 916-444-5464, 800-825-5464; www.deltaking.com; 100 Front St; r $89-164;) If you stay near Old Town, you can't beat the experience of sleeping aboard the *Delta King*, a docked 1927 paddlewheeler that lights up like a Christmas tree at night.

Amber House (Map pp424-5; ☎ 916-444-8085, 800-755-6526; www.amberhouse.com; 1315 22nd St; r $149-259;) This Dutch Colonial home in Midtown has been transformed into an elegant bed-and-breakfast, where rooms named for composers and writers come with Jacuzzi baths and fireplaces. Breakfast is served in the rooms – this is best enjoyed in Mozart, which boasts a private balcony.

Eating

Skip the overpriced fare in Old Sacramento or near the capitol and go to Midtown or the Tower District for higher-quality food at a lower price. A cruise up J St or Broadway will pass a number of hip, affordable restaurants where tables sprawl out onto the sidewalks in the summer.

our pick **La Bonne Soupe Cafe** (Map pp424-5; ☎ 916-492-9506; 920 8th St; $8-10; lunch Mon-Fri) Chef Daniel Pont assembles his divine sandwiches with such loving, affectionate care that the line of downtown lunchers snakes out the door. If you're in a hurry, skip it; Pont's humble lunch counter is focused on quality that predates drive-through haste. If you do have time, consider yourself lucky and ponder: smoky duck breast or apples and brie? Braised pork or smoked salmon? And the creamy soups made from scratch prove the restaurant's name is a painful understatement.

Andy Nguyen's (off Map pp424-5; ☎ 916-736-1157; 2007 Broadway; meals $8-16; lunch & dinner Mon-Sat, dinner Sun; V) This tranquil Buddhist Thai diner is the city's unrivaled vegetarian option, with steaming curries and hot pots. Fake meat dishes are artfully crafted (the 'chicken' leg has a little wooden bone).

Lucca (Map pp424-5; ☎ 916-669-5300; 1615 J St; meals $8-18) Within a stroll of the convention center is this quality Italian eatery. The escargot – wrapped in a buttery, flaky dough crust – is the way to start. After dinner, the music gets louder and a 30s see-and-be-seen set reaches for colorful bar drinks.

Zelda's Original Gourmet Pizza (Map pp424-5; ☎ 916-447-1400; 1415 21 St; mains $10-20; lunch Mon-Fri, dinner daily) Zelda's roughshod windowless exterior doesn't look like much, but through the doors of this Nixon-era pizza dive, a troupe of gruff veteran waitresses sling a magical, messy variation of doughy Chicago deep-dish. It can take a while to come out of the kitchen, so occupy yourself with cheap little glasses of Bud at the bar. And no, you can't get the dressing on the side.

Water Boy (Map pp424-5; ☎ 916-498-9891; 2000 Capitol Ave; mains $15-40; lunch Mon-Fri, dinner daily) The wicker and palms in the windowed dining room reflect the French colonial spin of the menu's California fusions. The seasonal menu soars from the briny oyster starter through the crispy skin of the poultry and smoky fresh catches. If it's too steep, look across the street for comfort food at Jack's Urban Eats.

our pick **Mulvany's Building and Loan** (Map pp424-5; ☎ 916-443-1189; 2726 Capitol Ave; mains $20-40; dinner Wed-Sun) With an obsessive flourish for seasonality, the menu here changes every single day. Patrick Mulvaney flutters between the kitchen and the dining room, offering delicate pasta dishes and buttery braised meats.

The Kitchen Restaurant (Map pp424-5; ☎ 916-568-7171; No 101, 2225 Hurley Way; prix-fixe dinner $125; dinner Wed-Sun) The cozy dining room of

husband-and-wife team Randall Selland and Nancy Zimmer is the pinnacle of Sacramento's foodie world. Their demonstration dinners focus on local, organic foods, immaculately prepared before your eyes. Book well in advance, and brace yourself.

Sacramento gets plenty hot in the summer, so cooling off with a refreshing milkshake or ice-cream cone is worth the drive from downtown. Both **Vic's** (Map p420; 3199 Riverside Blvd; shakes $4; 10am-9pm Mon-Sat, 11am-9pm Sun) and **Gunther's** (Map p420; 2801 Franklin Blvd; shakes $4; 10am-9:30pm Sun-Thurs, to 10pm Fri) are beautiful vintage soda fountains that make their own excellent ice cream. They're both south of Broadway and Hwy 50.

Drinking

Sacramento has a split personality when it comes to drinking – sleek upscale joints that serve a fruity rainbow of vodka drinks to dressed-up weekenders from the surrounding 'burbs, or sans-bullshit dive bars with vintage neons and a menu that begins and ends with a-shot-ana-beer. Both options dot the Midtown grid.

Temple Coffee House (Map pp424-5; ☎ 916-443-4960; 1014 10th St; 6am-11pm) The warm environs of this downtown coffee shop still imbibe the comfy feel of the bookstore that used to be in this space. Hip young patrons nurse organic free-trade coffee and chai while tapping at their wi-fi connected laptops.

58 Degrees and Holding Co (Map pp424-5; ☎ 916-442-5858; 1217 18th St) A huge selection of California reds and a refined bistro menu make this a favorite for young professional singles on the prowl.

Head Hunters (Map pp424-5; ☎ 916-492-2922; 1930 K St) Though there are wilder options within sight, start here before partying around the two-block radius of gay bars and clubs that locals coyly call 'Lavender Heights.' You might be back at the end of the night; the kitchen stays open into the wee hours.

Rubicon Brewing Company (Map pp424-5; ☎ 916-448-7032; 2004 Capitol Ave) These people take their hops *seriously*. Their heady selection is brewed on-site and crowned by Monkey Knife Fight Pale Ale, ideal to wash back platters of lip-tingling wings ($10 for one dozen).

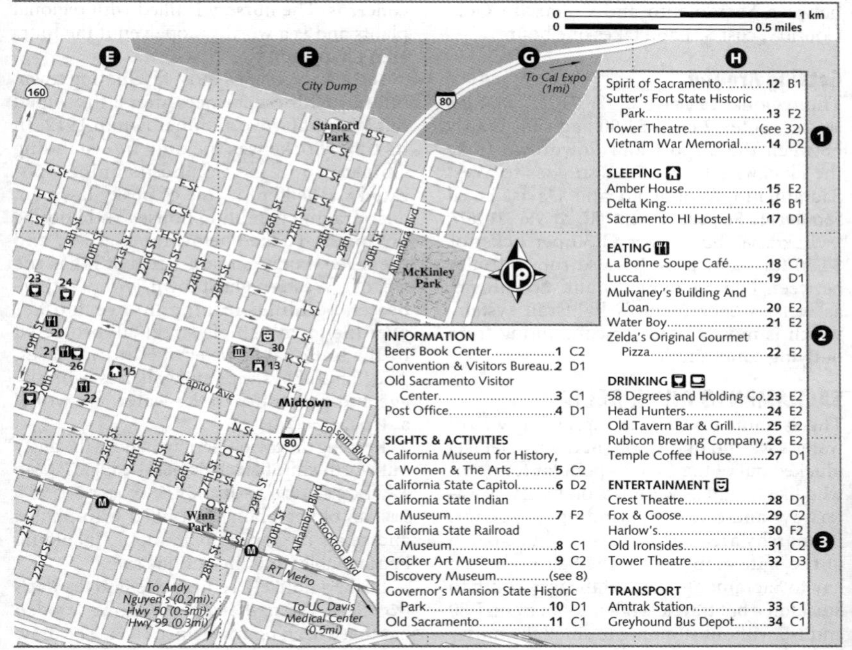

Old Tavern Bar & Grill (Map pp424-5; ☎ 916-444-5595; 1510 20th St) This friendly dive is a standout among Sacramento's many excellent workaday joints for their huge beer selection, tall pours and rowdy mix of tattooed bar hounds.

Entertainment

Pick up a copy of the free weekly **Sacramento News & Review** (www.newsandreview.com) for a list of current happenings around town.

Old Ironsides (Map pp424-5; ☎ 916-442-3504; 1901 10th St; cover $3-10) The tiny back room of this cool, somewhat crusty, venue hosts some of the best indie bands that come through town.

Harlow's (Map pp424-5; ☎ 916-444-3633; 2708 J St) A classy joint that's a solid bet for quality jazz, R&B and the occasional salsa or indie act…if you don't get lost on the potent martinis.

Fox & Goose (Map pp424-5; ☎ 916-443-8825; 1001 R St) This spacious, fern-filled warehouse-pub has good beer on tap and a jovial open-mic scene.

Tower Theatre (Map pp424-5; ☎ 916-442-4700; www.thetowertheatre.com; 2508 Landpark Dr) Classic, foreign and indie films screen at this historic movie house. Call to check if your film is showing on the main screen, rather than in a smaller side room.

Crest Theatre (Map pp424-5; ☎ 916-442-7378; www.thecrest.com; 1013 K St) Another classic old movie house that's been lovingly restored to its 1949 splendor, hosting indie and foreign films and the annual Trash Film Orgy.

Arco Arena (Map p420; ☎ information 916-928-6900, tickets 916-649-8497; 1 Sports Pkwy) The Kings, Sacramento's professional basketball (NBA) team, play home games at this arena from November to May. Ringling Bros and arena rockers pass through as well.

Getting There & Away

The small but busy **Sacramento International Airport** (☎ 916-929-5411; www.sacairports.org), 15 miles north of downtown off I-5, is serviced by all major airlines and offers some indirect flights to Europe.

Greyhound (Map pp424-5; ☎ 916-444-6858; cnr 7th & L Sts) stops near the capitol. Sacramento's **Amtrak Station** (Map pp424-5; cnr 5th & I Sts) is between downtown and Old Sac. Greyhound service between Sacramento and Colfax, in Gold Country, cost $21 and takes one hour.

Getting Around

The regional **Yolobus** (☎ 916-371-2877; www.yolobus.com) route 42 costs $1.50 and runs hourly between the airport and downtown (take the clockwise loop) and also goes to West Sacramento, Woodland and Davis. Local **Sacramento Regional Transit** (RT; ☎ 916-321-2877; www.sacrt.com) buses cost $1.50 per ticket or $3.50 for a day pass. RT also runs a trolley between Old Sacramento and downtown, as well as Sacramento's light-rail system, which is mostly used for commuting from outlying communities.

SACRAMENTO RIVER DELTA

The Sacramento Delta is a sprawling web of waterways and one-stoplight towns that feel plucked out of the 1930s – popular for locals who like to gun powerboats on its glassy waterways and cruise its winding levy roads. Its marshy area encompasses a huge patch of the state map – from the San Francisco bay to Sacramento, and all the way south to Stockton – but travelers often zoom by on I-80 and I-5 without stopping to smell the mossy Delta breeze blowing off the conflux of the Sacramento and San Joaquin Rivers, which drain into the San Francisco Bay. If you have the time to take the unhurried route between San Francisco and Sacramento, travel across the rusting iron bridges and gracefully winding roads of Hwy 160, which lazily makes its way through a region of lush wetlands, vast orchards and little towns with long histories.

In the 1930s the Bureau of Reclamation issued an aggressive water-redirection program – the Central Valley and California State Water Projects – that dammed California's major rivers and directed 75% of their supply through the Central Valley (for agricultural use) and Southern California. The siphoning has affected the Sacramento Delta, its wetlands and estuaries, and has been a source of environmental, ecological and political debate ever since. No one knows about this more than the folks at the Hartland Nursery, home of **Delta Ecotours** (☎ 916-775-4545; 13737 Grand Island Rd, Walnut Grove; admission free, tours adult/child $40/20; ⌚ Sat by appt). Led by Jeff Hart, the tours are ideal for land lubbers wanting to travel the channels and learn about the area's unique agricultural, environmental and historical concerns. The nursery is filled with regional plants and is a worthy stop even if the tours aren't happening

Locke is the delta's most fascinating town, built by Chinese farmers after a fire wiped out Walnut Grove's Chinatown in 1912. In its time, Locke was the only free-standing Chinatown in the US and its unincorporated status kept it free of pesky lawmen, encouraging gambling houses and bootleg gin joints. Tucked below the highway and the levee, Locke's main street still has the feel of a Western ghost town, with weather-beaten buildings leaning into each other over the town's single street, all protected by the National Register of Historic Places. The handful of shops and galleries, worn by age and proximity to the water, are worth a stroll.

Keeping the town's heritage alive is the dusty but worthwhile **Dai Loy Museum** (☎ 916-776-1661; www.locketown.com; admission $1.75; ⌚ noon-3pm Sat & Sun), an old gambling hall filled with photos and relics of gaming operations, including betting tables and the antique safe.

Locke's unlikely centerpiece is **Al the Wop's** (☎ 916-776-1800; meals $8-20), a creaking wooden bar that's been pouring since 1934. The draw isn't the food – the special is a peanut-butter-slathered hamburger – as much as it is the ambience. Below are creaking floorboards; above, the ceiling's covered in crusty dollar bills and more than one pair of erstwhile undies.

Hwy 160 passes through **Isleton**, so-called 'Crawdad Town USA,' whose main street is lined with shops, restaurants, bars and buildings hinting at the region's Chinese heritage. Isleton's Crawdad Festival, at the end of June, draws folks from all over the state, but you can slurp down the fresh little crayfish all year long at **Isleton Joe's** (☎ 916-776-1600; mains $6-16).

Further west on Hwy 160 you'll see signs for the **Delta Loop**, a drive that passes boater bars and marinas where you can rent something to take on the water. At the end, you come to the **Brannan State Recreation Area** (☎ 916-777-7701; tent/RV sites $11/25) a tidy state-run facility with boat-in, drive-in and walk-in campsites and picnic facilities galore.

DAVIS

pop 65,000

Davis, home to a University of California school, is a sunny college town where bikes outnumber cars two-to-one (it boasts more

CENTRAL VALLEY

bikes per capita than any other American city). With students comprising about half of the population, it's a progressive outpost amid the conservative farm towns of Sacramento Valley. Its vibrant café, pub and arts scene comes alive during the school year.

Dodging the bikes on a walk through downtown Davis you will pass a number of cute small businesses (the progressive city council has forbidden any store over 50,000 sq ft – sorry, Wal-Mart).

Orientation

I-80 skirts the south edge of town, and you can reach downtown via the Richards Blvd exit. University of California, Davis (UCD) is southwest of downtown, bordered by A St, 1st St and Russell Blvd. The campus' main entrances are accessed from I-80 via Old Davis Rd or from downtown via 3rd St. East of the campus, Hwy 113 heads north 10 miles to Woodland, where it intersects with I-5; another 28 miles north it connects with Hwy 99.

Information

The **Davis Conference and Visitor Bureau** (☎ 530-297-1900; www.davisvisitor.com; Suite 300, 105 E St; 8:30am-4:30pm Mon-Fri) has free maps and brochures. The exhaustive www.daviswiki.org is useful to peruse. The bookstore near downtown is the **Avid Reader** (☎ 530-758-4040; www.avidreaderbooks.com; 617 2nd St).

Sights & Activities

The impressive, purpose-built **Pence Gallery** (☎ 530-758-3370; 212 D St; noon-5pm Wed-Sun) exhibits contemporary California art and hosts lectures. **The Artery** (☎ 530-758-8330; 207 G St; 10am-6pm Mon-Thu & Sat, to 9pm Fri, noon-5pm Sun) gallery exhibits contemporary paintings and crafts (lots of pots).

For a short hike, there is a paved 2-mile trail through the peaceful **UC Davis Arboretum**. The university's **Equestrian Center** (☎ 530-752-2372; Equestrian Lane; rides 10am Sat) offers hour-long trail rides for $25; reservations required 48 hours ahead.

The **Davis farmers market** (cnr 4th & C Sts; 8am-noon Sat, 4.30-8.30pm Wed, 2-6pm Wed Oct-Mar) features food vendors, street performers and live bands.

Bicycling is popular here, probably because the only hill around is the bridge that crosses over the freeway. **Lake Berryessa**, around 30 miles west, is a favorite destination. See p428 for bike-rental information.

Sleeping

Davis ain't exactly a hotel town. Like most university towns, the rates are stable until during graduation or special campus events, when they rise high and sell out fast. Worse, the trains that roll though the middle of town will infuriate a light sleeper.

University Park Inn & Suites (☎ 530-756-0910; www.universityparkinn.com; 111 Richards Blvd; r $80-109;) Right off the highway and a short walk from campus and downtown, this independently operated hotel is not the Ritz, but is clean and has spacious suites.

Aggie Inn (☎ 530-756-0352; www.aggieinn.com; 245 1st St; r $85-127;) Across from UCD's east entrance, the Aggie is neat, modern and unassuming. The hotel has a Jacuzzi and offers free coffee and pastries.

Eating & Drinking

College students love to eat and drink cheap, and downtown has no short supply of lively ethnic eateries gunning for the student dollar.

Woodstocks (☎ 530-757-2525; 219 G St; slice $2.50, pizzas $15-20; lunch & dinner) Woodstocks has Davis' most popular pizza, which is also sold by the slice for lunch. In addition to cheap and meaty favorites, the menu also gets a touch more sophisticated with a variety of veggie and gourmet pies that come with a chewy wheat crust. Open until 2am Thursday to Saturday during school session.

Delta of Venus Coffeehouse & Pub (☎ 530-753-8630; 122b St; meals $5-10; breakfast, lunch & dinner; V) This converted Arts and Crafts bungalow has a very social shaded front patio. The chalkboard menu has breakfast items, salads, soups and sandwiches, including vegetarian and vegan options. At dinner time you can order jerk-seasoned Caribbean dishes and wash them down with a beer or wine. It comes alive with a hip folk scene at night.

Davis Noodle City (☎ 530-758-2288; D1, 129 E St; mains $5-10; lunch & dinner) Situated in the back of a courtyard behind Sophia's Thai Kitchen. The menu here has dishes from all over Asia, with homemade noodles and superb scallion pancakes. The pork-chop noodle soup – with thick noodles and slices of tender pork rubbed with Chinese five spice – is the best thing on the menu.

Redrum (☎ 530-756-2142; 978 Olive Dr; meals $5-10; 🕑 10am-midnight Mon-Sun) Formerly known as Murder Burger, Redrum is popular with students and travelers for fresh, made-to-order beef, turkey and ostrich burgers, thick espresso shakes and crispy curly fries. The ZOOM – a gnarled, deep-fried pile of zucchini, onion rings and mushrooms – is the menu must.

Entertainment

Major theater, music, dance and other performances take place at **Mondavi Center for the Performing Arts** (☎ 530-757-3199; www.mondaviarts.org; 1 Shields Ave), a state-of-the-art venue on the UCD campus. **Varsity Theatre** (☎ 530-759-8724; 616 2nd St) also stages performances. For tickets and information on shows at either the Varsity or the Mondavi Center, you can also call the **UC Davis Ticket Office** (☎ 530-752-1915, 866-823-2787).

Palm's Playhouse (www.palmsplayhouse.com), Davis' long-standing favorite live music venue, moved to the town of Winters, about 12 miles west of Davis. Shows now take place in the historic **Winters Opera House** (☎ 530-795-1825; 13 Main St). The old hall is a fantastic place to see acoustic, bluegrass, folk and rock shows.

CENTRAL VALLEY

Getting There & Away

Yolobus (☎ 530-666-2877; 🕑 5am-11pm) route 42 ($1.50) loops between Davis and the Sacramento airport. The route also connects Davis with Woodland and downtown Sacramento.

Davis' **Amtrak station** (☎ 530-758-4220; 840 2nd St) is on the southern edge of downtown. There are trains bound for Sacramento or San Francisco throughout the day. The fare to San Francisco is $23 and the trip takes about 2 hours.

Getting Around

When driving around – especially when you pull out from a parking space – be aware of bike traffic: it's the primary mode of transportation here. **Ken's Bike & Ski** (☎ 530-758-3223; 650 G St) rents basic bikes (from $14 per day) as well as serious road and mountain bikes.

If you're not biking, student-run **Unitrans** (☎ 530-752-2877; http://unitrans.ucdavis.edu; one-way fare $1; 🕑 7am-11.30pm Mon-Thu, to 7pm Fri, 9am-5pm Sat & Sun) shuttles people around town and campus. Many buses are red double-deckers.

OROVILLE

pop 14,400

Gold attracted the first settlers to Oroville and sawmills kept them here, but now the economy leans on the plastic-bag factory on the outskirts of town and the tourists who mill though the throng the antique stores. Oroville's population has boomed in recent years, with families fleeing the high-priced housing of the Bay Area. Oroville's most enduring attraction is an excellent museum left behind by a long-gone Chinese community.

Gold was discovered near here in 1848 by John Bidwell, and the booming little town took the name Ophir (Gold) City. Oroville was where Ishi, the last surviving member of the local Yahi tribe, was 'found' back in 1911 (p429).

Lake Oroville, a popular summertime destination, sits 9 miles northeast of town behind Oroville Dam, the largest earthen dam in the US. The surrounding Lake Oroville State Recreation Area attracts boaters, campers, swimmers, bicyclists, hikers and fishing folk. Oroville is also a gateway to the gorgeous Feather River Canyon and the rugged northern reaches of the Sierra Nevada.

Information

The **Oroville Area Chamber of Commerce** (☎ 530-538-2542, 800-655-4653; www.oroville-city.com; 1789 Montgomery St; 🕑 9am-4:30pm Mon-Fri) has information on local history and outdoor activities. The office of the US Forest Service (USFS) **Feather River Ranger District** (☎ 530-534-6500; 875 Mitchell Ave; 🕑 8am-4:30pm Mon-Fri) has maps and brochures. For road conditions, phone ☎ 800-427-7623.

Sights & Activities

By the levee, the **Chinese Temple** (☎ 530-538-2496; 1500 Broderick St; adult/child $2/free; 🕑 noon-4pm) is a compelling draw that exceeds expectations, a relatively quiet monument to the 10,000 Chinese people who once lived here. A 1907 flood wiped out Chinatown and many Chinese stayed to help rebuild the levee, but the devastation caused many others to move to established Chinese communities in the Bay Area or find other migrant work in the Central Valley. During the 19th century, theater troupes from China toured a circuit of Chinatowns in California and Oroville was the end of the line. The troupes often left their sets, costumes and puppets here before

LONE YAHI FOUND IN OROVILLE

In the early morning of August 29, 1911, a frantic barking of dogs woke the butchers sleeping inside a slaughterhouse outside Oroville. When they came out, they found their dogs holding a man at bay – a Native American clad only in a loincloth, who was starving, exhausted, afraid and spoke no English.

They called the sheriff, who took the man to the jail until something could be decided. Newspapers declared a 'wild man' had been discovered and people thronged in, hoping to see him. Local people came and tried to communicate with him in Maidu and Wintu, to no avail; his language was different from those of the surrounding tribes.

Professors Alfred L Kroeber and Thomas Talbot Waterman, anthropologists from the University of California, Berkeley, read the accounts in the news. Waterman took the train to Oroville and, using lists of vocabulary words of the Yana people who once lived in this region, discovered that the man belonged to the Yahi, the southernmost tribe of the Yana, who were believed to be extinct.

Waterman took 'Ishi,' meaning 'man' in the Yahi language, to the museum at the university, where he was cared for and brought back to health. Ishi spent his remaining years there, telling the anthropologists his life story and teaching them his tribal language, lore and ways.

Ishi's tribe had been virtually exterminated by settlers before he was born. In 1870, when he was a child, there were only 12 or 15 Yahi people left, hiding in remote areas in the foothills east of Red Bluff. By 1908 Ishi, his mother, sister and an old man were all who were left of the Yahi tribe. In that year the others died and Ishi was left alone. On March 25, 1916, Ishi died of tuberculosis at the university hospital and the Yahi disappeared forever.

In Oroville you can drive to the site where Ishi was found (east of town along Oro-Quincy Hwy at Oak Ave), though all that stands is a small monument. Part of the Lassen National Forest in the foothills east of Red Bluff, including Deer Creek and other areas where Ishi and the Yahi people lived, is now called the Ishi Wilderness. If you go to Berkeley, you can also see an exhibit on Ishi at the Phoebe Hearst Museum of Anthropology.

returning to China, which has left the temple with an unrivaled collection of 19th-century Chinese stage finery. The temple itself is a beautifully preserved building bursting with religious shrines, festival tapestries, ancient lion masks and furniture. To keep everything in context, take advantage of docent-led tours, which can take an hour.

From downtown, follow Oroville Dam Rd or Olive Hwy (Hwy 162) to the **Lake Oroville State Recreation Area**, home to many outdoor activities and the 770ft Oroville Dam. Completed in 1967, it's the tallest earthen dam in the US. The **Lake Oroville State Recreation Area Visitor Center** (☎ 530-538-2219; 917 Kelly Ridge Rd; 🕒 9am-5pm) has exhibits on the California State Water Project and local Native American history, plus a viewing tower and loads of recreational information.

The **Freeman Bicycle Trail** is a 41-mile off-road loop that takes cyclists to the top of Oroville Dam, then follows the Feather River back to the Thermalito Forebay and Afterbay storage reservoirs, east of Hwy 70. The ride is mostly flat, but the dam ascent is steep. Get a free map of the ride from the chamber of commerce. The **Forebay Aquatic Center** (☎ 530-624-6919; Garden Dr), just off Hwy 70, rents bikes for $7 per hour and a variety of equipment to get on the water.

The nearby **Oroville Wildlife Area**, along the Pacific Flyway, is a great place for bird-watching. Serious bird-watchers should also head to the **Sacramento National Wildlife Refuge** during winter, where the migratory waterfowl are a spectacular sight. The **visitors center** (☎ 530-934-2801; 752 County Rd, Willows; 🕒 7:30am-4pm Mon-Fri) is off I-5 near Willows; driving ($3) and walking trails are open daily.

The area surrounding Lake Oroville is full of hiking trails, and a favorite is the 7-mile round-trip walk to 640ft **Feather Falls**, which takes about four hours.

Hwys 162 and 70 head northeast from Oroville into the mountains and on to Quincy (p311). Hwy 70 snakes along the magnificent **Feather River Canyon**, an especially captivating drive during the fall.

Sleeping & Eating

A launching pad for outdoorsy trips, there's plenty of camping in the area, which you can arrange through the chamber of commerce, the USFS office or the Lake Oroville visitors center. A strip of decent budget motels lies on Feather River Blvd, east of Hwy 70 and south of Montgomery St.

Lake Oroville State Recreation Area (☎ 530-538-2219, 800-444-7275; www.parks.ca.gov; 917 Kelly Ridge Rd; tent/RV sites $15/35; wi-fi) The wi-fi might be the first clue that this isn't the most rustic choice, but there is a variety of sites. There are good primitive sites if you're willing to hike, and – perhaps the coolest feature of the park – floating campsites on platforms that are accessible only by boat.

Riverside Bed & Breakfast (☎ 530-533-1413; www.riversidebandb.com; 45 Cabana Dr; r $95-165;) With rustic trimmings, this B&B offers eight rooms right on the river's edge, drawing fly fishermen who aren't into roughing it. Some rooms are frillier than others, but many sport lovely views and Jacuzzis, and all have private bathrooms. It's along the Feather River west of Hwy 70.

Bidwell Canyon Marina (☎ 530-589-3165, 800-637-1767; www.gobidwell.com; 801 Bidwell Canyon Rd; 3-night weekends from $1000) Houseboats that sleep 10 to 16 people can be rented at this marina, on the south end of the lake. Rental availability and price depends on season and seasonal water levels, so advance planning is recommended.

Big Lem's BBQ (☎ 530-532-1000; 3017 Meyers St; lunch & dinner Tue-Sat) The sweet-potato pie and earthy, smoky ribs are something of a surprise in Oroville, as is Big Lem. To test his deep Southern pedigree, go for the crispy catfish plate.

Getting There & Away

Greyhound buses stop at **Tom's Sierra Chevron** (☎ 530-533-1333; cnr 5th Ave & Oro Dam Blvd), a few blocks east of Hwy 70. There are two buses daily between Oroville and Sacramento. The trip takes 1½ hours and costs $29.

CHICO

pop 64,400 / elev 230ft

With its huge population of students, Chico has the devil-may-care energy of a college kegger during the school year, and a lazy, lethargic hangover during the summertime. Its oak-shaded downtown and university attractions makes it one of Sacramento Valley's more attractive social and cultural hubs, where easygoing folks mingle late in the restaurants and bars, which open onto patios in the balmy summer evenings.

And though Chico wilts in the heat of the summer, the swimming holes in shady Bidwell Park take the edge off during the day, as does a tubing trip down the gentle Sacramento River. The fine pale ales produced at the Sierra Nevada Brewing Company, near downtown, are yet another of Chico's blessings.

Chico was established in 1860 by John Bidwell, who came to California in 1841 and was an illustrious early pioneer. In 1868, Bidwell and his wife, Annie Ellicott Kennedy, moved to the new mansion he had built, now the Bidwell Mansion State Historic Park. After John died in 1900, Annie continued as a philanthropist until her death in 1918.

Orientation & Information

Downtown is west of Hwy 99, easily reached via Hwy 32 (8th St). Main St and Broadway are the central downtown streets; from there, Park Ave stretches southward and the tree-lined Esplanade heads north.

Chico Chamber of Commerce & Visitor Center (☎ 530-891-5559, 800-852-8570; www.chicochamber.com; 300 Salem St; 9am-5pm Mon-Fri, 10am-3pm Sat) offers local information. For entertainment options, pick up the free weekly **Chico News & Review** (www.newsandreview.com), available in newspaper boxes and businesses downtown. **The Bookstore** (☎ 530-345-7441; 118 Main St) has a quality used selection.

Sights

Chico's most prominent landmark is **Bidwell Mansion State Historic Park** (☎ 530-895-6144; 525 Esplanade; adult/child $2/free; noon-5pm Wed-Fri, 10am-5pm Sat & Sun), the opulent Victorian home built for Chico's founders John and Annie Bidwell. The 26-room mansion was built between 1865 and 1868 and hosted many US presidents. Tours start every hour on the hour.

Though too big to officially qualify as a 'microbrewery,' the **Sierra Nevada Brewing Company** (☎ 530-893-3520; 1075 E 20th St) draws hordes of beer snobs to the birthplace of their nationally distributed Sierra Nevada Pale Ale and Schwarber, a Chico-only black ale. Free tours are given at 2:30pm daily, and continuously from noon to 3pm Saturday. There's also a pub and restaurant (see p432).

Ask for a free map of the **Chico State University** campus, or ask about campus events and tours, at the **CSU Information Center** (☎ 530-898-4636; cnr Chestnut & W 2nd Sts), on the main floor of Bell Memorial Union. The attractive campus is infused with sweet floral fragrances in spring, and there's a rose garden at its center.

The historic 1894 **Honey Run Covered Bridge** is straight out of *The Legend of Sleepy Hollow* – and an unusual type of bridge in this part of the country. Take the Skyway exit off Hwy 99 on the southern outskirts of Chico, head east and go left on Honey Run-Humbug Rd; the bridge is 5 miles along, in a small park.

Activities

Growing out of downtown, the 3670-acre **Bidwell Park** is the nation's third-largest municipal park. It stretches 10 miles northwest along Chico Creek with lush groves and miles of trails. The upper part of the park is fairly untamed, which is surprising to find smack dab in the middle of the city. Several classic movies have been shot here, including *The Adventures of Robin Hood* and parts of *Gone with the Wind.*

The park is full of hiking and mountain-biking trails and swimming spots, and has a nature center. You'll find pools at One-Mile and Five-Mile recreation areas and swimming holes (including Bear Hole, Salmon Hole and Brown Hole) in Upper Bidwell Park, north of Manzanita Ave. Don't be surprised if locals opt for birthday suits, not swimsuits.

In summer you'll want to cool off from the hike by **tubing** the Sacramento. Inner tubes can be rented at grocery stores and other shops along Nord Ave (Hwy 32) for around $6. Tubers enter at the Irvine Finch Launch Ramp on Hwy 32, a few miles west of Chico, and come out at the Washout, off River Rd.

Festivals & Events

With the students out of town, family-friendly outdoor events take over the town each summer. The **Thursday Night Market** fills several blocks of Broadway every Thursday evening from April to September. At City Plaza you'll find free **Friday Night Concerts** starting in May. **Shakespeare in the Park** (☎ 530-891-1382; www.ensembletheatreofchico.com; admission free), at Cedar Grove in lower Bidwell Park, runs from mid-July to the end of August.

Sleeping

There's an abundance of well-kept independent motels with sparkling swimming pools, some of them along the shady Esplanade north of downtown. Beware that Chico State's graduation and homecoming mania (in May and October, respectively) send prices through the roof.

Woodson Bridge State Recreation Area (☎ 530-839-2112, 800-444-7275; undeveloped/developed sites $9/25) This shaded campground, adjacent to a huge native riparian preserve, has 46 tent sites on the banks of the Sacramento River. It's about 25 miles north of Chico on Hwy 99, then west toward Corning.

Matador Motel (☎ 530-342-7543; 1934 Esplanade; r $47-51; ⊠ ⊠) This pleasant courtyard motel not far from downtown has simple rooms done up with old-fashioned Mission-style details. The buildings wrap around a beautiful tiled swimming pool shaded by palms.

Music Express Inn (☎ 530-891-9833; http://northvalley.net/musicexpress; 1091 El Monte Ave; r $61-125; ⊠) Guest rooms in this B&B are a bit too frilly but huge, and some have Jaccuzi tubs. A hearty breakfast is included.

The Grateful Bed (☎ 530-342-2464; www.thegratefulbed.net; 1462 Arcadian Ave; r $105-160; ⊠ ⊠) Well, obviously you're a bedhead if you stay here. Tucked in a residential neighborhood near downtown, it's a stately 1905 Victorian home. Some of the decor is trying too hard, but overall it's very comfortable. Breakfast is included.

our pick **Hotel Diamond** (☎ 866-993-3100; www.hoteldiamondchico.com; 220 W 4th St; r from $189; ⊠ ⊠) This whitewashed 1904 building is the most luxurious place to lay your head in Chico, with high-thread-count linens, valet laundry and room service of comfort foods in California-fusion style, like prawn-dressed macaroni and cheese. The Diamond Suite, with its balcony, original furnishings and spacious top-floor balcony is a-*maz*-ing.

For a budget choice smack in the middle of downtown, check out the **Vagabond Inn** (☎ 530-895-1323; 630 Main St; s/d $45/55; ⊠) and the nearby **Thunderbird Lodge** (☎ 530-343-7911; 715 Main St; r $45-60; ⊠). Both are a bit dog-eared but acceptable.

Eating

El Pasia Taco Truck (cnr 8th & Pine; mains $1.50-5; ⊠ lunch & dinner) Debate about which of Chico's taco trucks is the best can quickly lead to fisticuffs – but the smoky *carnitas* tacos are a broke college student's dream.

Celestino's Live from New York Pizza (☎ 530-896-1234; 101 Salem St; mains $3-7; 10:30am-10pm) One of the best imitations of 'real' New York pizza in Northern California, with a thin, chewy crust and rad themed variations like the meaty Godfather.

Tacos de Acapulco (☎ 530-892-8176; 429 Ivy St; meals $3-8; lunch & dinner) Your best bulk-up budget option is this *taquería* (taco joint) serving huge burritos to the tipsy 2am set.

Sins of Cortez (☎ 530-879-9200; 101 Salem St; mains $6-16; 7am-9pm) The service won't win awards for speed, but this local favorite draws a mob for its burly breakfast plates. Order anything with the homemade chorizo.

Sierra Nevada Taproom & Restaurant (☎ 530-345-2739; 1075 E 20th St; meals $8-15; lunch & dinner Tue-Sun) At the Sierra Nevada Brewery, this place is a genuine Chico destination. It has better-than-average pub food, superb fresh ales and lagers on tap, some not available anywhere else. The apple-malt pork loin is a standout.

Red Tavern (☎ 530-894-3463; 1250 Esplanade; dinner mains $15-24; dinner Mon-Sat) Slightly swanky, the Red Tavern is one of Chico's favorite fine-dining experiences, with a sophisticated menu that balances discriminatingly between Europe and Asia and uses local organic food.

5th Street Steakhouse (☎ 530-899-8075; 345 W 5th Street; mains $16-37; dinner Sun-Thurs, lunch & dinner Fri) This is the joint where college students take their visiting parents, featuring steaks tender enough to cut with a reproachful look, and occasional live jazz.

The year-round **outdoor farmers market** (cnr of Wall & E 2nd St; 7:30am-1pm Sat) draws from the plentiful surrounding valley.

Shubert's Ice Cream & Candy (178 E 7th St; 9.30am-10pm Mon-Fri, 11am-10pm Sat & Sun) is a beloved Chico landmark, having made delicious homemade ice cream and chocolates for more than 60 years.

Drinking

As you might have guessed from Chico's party-school rep, you're unlikely to go thirsty. There's a strip of bars on Main St if you want to go hopping.

Madison Bear Garden (☎ 530-891-1639; 316 W 2nd St; noon-2am) This whimsically decorated student hangout is housed in a spacious brick building. It's the place to chat to students over thick burgers and cool beers.

Panama Bar & Cafe (☎ 530-345-0601; 128 Broadway; 11am-10pm) The house specializes in variations of Long Island iced tea (most of which are priced around $3), so brace yourself. For a wild night out in Chico, the only way to consume more liquor would be with an IV drip.

Naked Lounge (☎ 530-895-0676; 118 2nd St; 10am-9pm Sun-Thu, to midnight Fri & Sat) With its dark-red, enveloping interior and expertly drawn espresso drinks, this is Chico's best place to get caffeinated.

Entertainment

LaSalle's (☎ 530-893-1891; 229 Broadway) This venue is open nightly for hip-hop, Top 40 and retro dance nights and live bands that play anything to pack people in – from reggae to hard rock.

Pageant Theatre (☎ 530-343-0663; 351 E 6th St) Screens international and alternative films. Monday is bargain night, with all seats just $2.50.

Chico Caberet (☎ 530-895-0245; www.chicocabaret.com; tickets $16) All fishnets and sass, this local theater troupe brings racy annual shows to Butte County theaters.

For theater, films, concerts, art exhibits and other cultural events at the CSU campus, contact the **CSU Box Office** (☎ 530-898-6333) or the **CSU Information Center** (☎ 530-898-4636) in the Bell Memorial Union.

Getting There & Around

Greyhound (☎ 530-343-8266) buses stop at the **Amtrak station** (cnr W 5th & Orange Sts). The train station is unattended so purchase tickets in advance from travel agents or on board from the conductor. Trips between Chico and Sacramento on the once-daily *Coast Starlight* line are $31(2½ hours). Amtrak also operates buses from the station multiple times daily for a similar fare.

B-Line (☎ 530-342-0221, 800-822-8145; www.bcag.org) handles all buses throughout Butte County, and can get you around Chico and down to Oroville (tickets $2, four times daily).

Bicycles can be rented from **Campus Bicycles** (☎ 530-345-2081; 330 Main St; mountain bikes half/full day $20/35).

RED BLUFF

pop 13,500 / elev 309ft

The smoldering streets of Red Bluff – one of California's hottest towns due to the hot air trap of the Shasta Cascades – are of marginal interest unto themselves, but looking to the mountain-dominated horizon offers a clue of the outdoor activities that bring most travelers through town. The agreeable tree-lined neighborhoods are full of restored 19th-century Victorian mansions and there are some historic storefronts in the business district.

Peter Lassen laid out the town site in 1847 and it grew into a key port along the Sacramento River. Now it's more of a pit stop on the way to the national park that bears his name and other points along on I-5.

Cowboy culture is alive and well here. Catch it in action the third weekend of April at the **Red Bluff Round-Up** (☎ 530-527-1000; www.redbluffroundup.com; tickets $10-19), a major rodeo event dating back to 1921, or in any of the dive bars where the jukeboxes are stocked with Nashville, and plenty of big-buckled cowboys belly up to the bar.

Orientation & Information

Downtown Red Bluff is on the west bank of the Sacramento River, just to the west of I-5. The town's main intersection is at Antelope Blvd and Main St. The historic Victorian neighborhood is west of Main St.

Heading south from downtown, Main St becomes a narrow, scenic stretch of historic Hwy 99W, which parallels I-5 and leads to the farm towns of Corning, Orland and Willows.

To get your bearings and a stack of brochures, go south of downtown to the small **Red Bluff-Tehama County Chamber of Commerce** (☎ 530-527-6220, 800-655-6225; 100 Main St; 🕑 8:30am-4pm Mon, to 5pm Tue-Thu, to 4:30pm Fri).

Sights & Activities

The **Kelly-Griggs House Museum** (☎ 530-527-1129; 311 Washington St; admission by donation; 🕑 1-4pm Thu-Sun) is the most impressive of Red Bluff's classical Victorian homes. It's dressed up with period exhibits. Dig the mannequins.

Set on a beautiful, shaded piece of land overlooking a languorous section of the Sacramento River, the **William B Ide Adobe State Historic Park** (☎ 530-529-8599; 21659 Adobe Rd; 🕑 sunrise-sunset) preserves the original adobe home and grounds of pioneer William B Ide, who 'fought' in the 1846 Bear Flag Revolt at Sonoma (p38) and was named president of the short-lived California Republic (though, even with the blacksmith shop and the gift shop, these are humble digs for a president). To get to the park, head about a mile north on Main St, turn east onto Adobe Rd and go another mile, following the signs.

The **Red Bluff Lake Recreation Area**, on the east bank of the Sacramento River, is a spacious park full of trees, birds and meadows. It offers numerous picnicking, swimming, hiking and camping opportunities and has interpretive trails, bicycle paths, boat ramps, a wildlife-viewing area with excellent bird-watching, a fish ladder (in operation between May and September) and a 2-acre native-plant garden. The **Sacramento River Discovery Center** (☎ 530-527-1196; 🕑 11am-4pm Tue-Sat) has kid-friendly displays about the river, questionable information about the benefits of cattle grazing and information on the Diversion Dam just outside its doors. From mid-May to mid-September, the dam diverts water into irrigation canals and in the process creates Red Bluff Lake, which is a popular swimming destination.

Sleeping & Eating

Motels are found beside I-5 and south of town along Main St, and the historic residential neighborhood has some bed-and-breakfasts. The restaurant scene isn't thrilling – a lot of cheap take-out Chinese, pizza and stick-to-the-ribs grub that's straight from a can.

Sycamore Grove Camping Area (☎ 530-824-5196; undeveloped/developed sites $16/$25) Beside the river in the Red Bluff Lake Recreation Area is this quiet, attractive USFS campground. Campsites are on a first-come, first-served basis. It also has a large group campground, Camp Discovery, where cabins are available (reservations required).

Travel Lodge (☎ 530-527-6020; 38 Antelope Blvd; s/d $59/65; ❄ 🏊) It's not just a chain, but an exemplary and well-preserved example of 1960s motorists accommodation. Rooms are large and clean, and the grounds around the pool are well kept.

Jeter Victorian Inn (☎ 530-527-7574; www.jetervictorianinn.com; 1107 Jefferson St; r $95-160; ❄) Just east of the business district, Jeter is a massive 1881 Victorian building surrounded by ancient trees. It has five rooms and a separate cottage.

Thai House (☎ 530-529-1217; 248 S Main St; mains $5-14 🕑 lunch & dinner) This is a remarkably good Thai restaurant, with excellent curries and tom yum soup. If you roll into town late, you'll thank the heavens for it.

Entertainment

Hal's Eat 'Em Up (☎ 530-529-0173; 158 Main St) If the heat is raging, grab a root-beer float from Hal's, a drive-in just south of downtown.

Getting There & Away

The **Greyhound station** (☎ 530-527-0434; 22825 Antelope Blvd) is east of town at the corner of Hwy 36 E.

SAN JOAQUIN VALLEY

The southern half of California's Central Valley – named for the San Joaquin River – sprawls from Stockton to the turbine-covered Tehachapi Mountains, southeast of Bakersfield. Everything stretches to the horizon in straight lines – railroad tracks, two-lane blacktop and long irrigation channels. Through the elaborate politics and machinery of water management, this once-arid region ranks among the most agriculturally productive places in the world, though the profits often go to agribusiness shareholders, not the increasingly displaced family farmer. While some of the tiny towns scattering the region, such as Gustine and Reedley, retain a classic Main St Americana feel, many have adopted the Latino culture of the enormous immigrant work force that harvests these fields in unaccounted numbers. Many other towns are paved over with housing developments that are populated by families escaping the oppressive housing prices of the Bay Area.

Today the San Joaquin Valley is beguiling for both travelers and locals, where intense heat and dubious reminders of history and progress are evident through tract houses and rusting tractors, scrawling spray-painted gang signs and the arching spray of irrigation systems.

It's also a place of seismic, often contentious, development. Housing prices in the coastal cities have sprawled eastward to pave over half a million acres in the last decade. Where there were once cattle ranches and vineyards are now the nostalgically named developments of American anyplace: a big-box shopping complex named Indian Ranch, a tidy row of McMansions named Vineyard Estates.

To sink your teeth into the region, skip I-5 and travel on Hwy 99 – a road with nearly as long a history as the famous Route 66. It'll be hot – very hot – so put the windows down and crank up the twangy traditional country or the booming traditional *norteño* (an accordion-driven genre of folk music imported from Mexico) that dominate the radio. If you have the time, exit often for bushels of the freshest produce on earth and brushes with California's nearly forgotten past.

Many of the following towns are excellent launching points for Yosemite National Park, and Hwy 99 is lined with classic affordable motor lodges and hotel chains.

LODI

pop 63,362

Although Lodi used to be the 'Watermelon capital of the world,' today, wine rules this patch of the valley. Breezes from the Sacramento River Delta soothe the area's hot vineyards, where more zinfandel grapes are grown than anywhere else in the world. Some particularly old vines have been tended by the same families for over a century. Lodi's diverse soil is sometimes rocky, sometimes a fine sandy loam, giving its zins a range of distinctive characteristics.

Get your first taste of Lodi's powerful, sun-soaked zins at the **Lodi Wine & Visitor Center** (☎ 209-365-0621; www.lodiwine.com; 2545 W Turner Rd; tastings $5; 🕑 10am-5pm), where 100 local vintages are sold by the glass at the solid-wood tasting bar. They'll provide maps to wineries of the region. Another stop to sip the region's boutique wines and experimental labels by more famous names is the Italian-style **Vino Piazza**, where you can park the car, order a bistro lunch and amble between tasting rooms.

Given Lodi's love of the tipple, its no surprise that they have a slew of festivals dedicated to wine, including the **Grape & Harvest Festival** in September and **Zinfest** in May.

Lodi's **Micke Grove Regional Park and Zoo** (☎ 209-953-8840; www.mgzoo.com; admission $2; 2545 W Turner Rd; 🕑 10am-5pm; 🚼) is good stop for the seriously underage, with a water play area, hissing cockroaches and some barking sea lions. There's also a small children's amusement park, where rides cost a nominal extra fee.

STOCKTON

pop 289,927

Little Stockton looked down and out for a while there. What remained of its proud past as a major inland port was blighted by crime-ridden streets and crumbling facades. This not-so-distant past is evident in the city's outskirts, which are lined with slouching, sun-bleached houses, old doughnut shops, liquor stores and taco trucks – a sad fate for a major supply point for Gold Rushers, which was hit hard by a decline in its shipbuilding and commercial transportation industries. But the downtown and waterfront redevelopment is one of the valley's more promising turnarounds, warranting a short detour.

You'll know you've reached the good part of town when you see the modern white edifice of the **Weber Point Events Center** (221 Center St), standing in the middle of a grassy park looking rather like a pile of sailboats. The events center is where much of the action is, with the huge Asparagus Festival in April, a series of open-air concerts, and fountains where squealing children cool off during summer break. Nearby is the beautiful new **Banner Island Ballpark** (☎ 209-644-1900; www.stocktonports.com; 404 W Freemont St), where the minor-league Stockton Seals play baseball (April to September). Also near is the **Haggin Museum** (☎ 209-940-6300; www.hagginmuseum.org; 1201 N Pershing Ave; tickets $5; 🕑 1:30am-5pm Wed-Sun), which has an excellent collection of American landscape paintings as well as an Egyptian mummy.

Just across the channel is the Greater Stockton Chamber of Commerce's **Department of Tourism** (☎ 209-547-2770; www.visitstockton.org; Suite 220, 445 W Weber Ave; 🕑 9am-5pm Mon-Fri), with complete information about the goings on in town.

Get lunch a few blocks north at **Manny's California Fresh Café** (☎ 209-463-6415; 1612 Pacific Ave; mains $6-15; 🕑 10am-9:45pm), where rotisserie meats and fried-chicken sandwiches burst with flavor. It's at the edge of the **Miracle Mile** district (a developing shopping stretch on Pacific Ave, north of downtown).

MODESTO

pop 205,721

Cruising was banned in Modesto in 1993, but the town still touts itself as the 'cruising capital of the world.' That notoriety stems mostly from hometown boy George Lucas' 1973 film *American Graffiti*. You'll still see hot rods and flashy wheels around town, but they won't be clogging thoroughfares on Friday night. The Ernest & Julio Gallo Winery, makers of America's best-selling jug wines, is among the town's biggest businesses. Old oaks arch over the city's attractive streets and you can eat well in the compact downtown. This is a good spot for getting off the dusty highway.

Downtown sits just east of Hwy 99 (avoid the area west of the freeway), centering on 10th and J Sts. From downtown, Yosemite Blvd (Hwy 132) runs east toward Yosemite National Park.

Many historic buildings have survived revitalization, including the 1934 **State Theatre** (☎ 209-527-4697; 1307 J St), which hosts films and live music, and the old **SP depot**, a Mission-style beauty. The famous **Modesto Arch**, on the corner of 9th and I Sts, erected in 1912, stands at what was once the city's main entry point (see p436). Classic car shows are held in 'Graffiti Month' (June); for details, call the **chamber of commerce** (☎ 209-577-5757; 1114 J St; 🕑 8:30am-5pm Mon-Fri).

A&W Drive-In (☎ 209-522-7700; cnr 14th & G Sts; mains $3-9, 🕑 10am-10pm) is a vintage burger stand (part of a chain founded in nearby Lodi) filled with poodle-skirt corniness, though roller-skating carhops, classic cars and ties to *American Graffiti* move a lot of root beer. (George Lucas supposedly cruised here as a youth.)

TULE FOG

Radiation or tule (*too*-lee) fog causes dozens of collisions each year on San Joaquin Valley roads, including Hwy 99 and I-5. As thick as the proverbial pea soup, the fog limits visibility to about 10ft, making driving nearly impossible. The fog is thickest from November to February, when cold mountain air settles on the warm valley floor and condenses into fog as the ground cools at night. The fog often lifts for a few hours during the afternoon, just long enough for the ground to warm back up and thus perpetuate the cycle.

Call **Caltrans** (☎ 800-427-7623) to check road conditions before traveling. If you end up on a fog-covered road, drive with your low beams on, keep a good distance from the car in front of you, stay at a constant speed, avoid sudden stops and never try to pass other cars.

WHAT THE...?

The old arch that made Modesto famous tells a traveler what the four main tenets of the town are. The slogan, 'Water, Wealth, Contentment, Health,' resulted from a local contest held prior to the construction of the arch. It is a pithy little poem and is as true today as when the arch went up in 1912. Interestingly, the slogan gracing the arch didn't actually win the contest. Judges chose the folksy, if less eloquent, slogan 'Nobody's Got Modesto's Goat' but were overruled by the city government.

Tresetti's World Caffe (☎ 209-572-2990; 927 11th St; mains $6-27; ⏰ lunch & dinner) Modesto's most romantic white-tablecloth spot offers a menu with Cal-Med leanings, and allows diners to choose from hundreds of bottles of wine in an accompanying shop.

With juggling bartenders in referee garb and big screens everywhere, **Hero's** (☎ 209-524-2337; 821 L St; mains $6-27; ⏰ lunch & dinner) isn't breaking ground with its atmosphere, but they do have all the varieties of St Stan's excellent microbrew on tap. This is one of the oldest in California, and is brewed and packaged on site.

MERCED

pop 69,800

You can jog over to Yosemite from many of the small towns in this part of the valley, but this is the most convenient staging area, right on Hwy 140. The machine of progress has not been kind to Merced, and it suffers more than its share of strip malls, but at its core there are tree-lined streets, historic Victorian homes and a magnificent 1875 courthouse. The downtown business district is a work-in-progress, with 1930s movie theaters, antique stores and a few casual eateries undergoing constant renovation.

Merced is right in the midst of a population makeover, thanks to the newest University of California campus, opened in 2005. UC Merced's first freshman class numbered just 1000 students, but the school continues to grow with a diverse student body, which will dramatically shape the city.

Downtown Merced is east of Hwy 99 along Main St, between R St and Martin Luther King Jr Way. The **California Welcome Center** (☎ 209-384-2791, 800-446-5353; 710 W 16th St), adjacent to the bus depot, has local maps and information on Merced and Yosemite.

The big attraction is the **Castle Air Museum** (☎ 209-723-2178; 5050 Santa Fe Dr; adult/child $8/6; ⏰ 10am-4pm) in Atwater, about 6 miles northwest of Merced. A squadron of restored military aircraft from WWII, the Korean War and the Vietnam War sit eerily dormant across from a large hangar. Even conscientious objectors stand agape at these streamlined beauties.

In a grand old Colonial-style mansion, **Hooper House Bear Creek Inn** (☎ 209-723-3991; www.hooperhouse.com; 575 W North Bear Creek Dr; r $95-135; ❄) is a leisurely retreat. Rooms are large, beautifully furnished and have private bathrooms. A full breakfast is included, which you can have sent to your room.

The eight-bed, family-style **HI Merced Home Hostel** (☎ 209-725-0407; dm $15-18; ⏰ reception 5:30-10pm) is in the home of longtime Merced residents who know tons about Yosemite. The hostel fills quickly, especially during summer weekends. Beds must be reserved in advance; call between 5:30pm and 10pm. The hostel doesn't give out its address but it will pick up and drop off guests at the bus and train stations.

The **Branding Iron** (☎ 209-722-1822; 640 W 16th St; lunch mains $9-11, dinner mains $17-25; ⏰ lunch Mon-Fri, dinner daily) roadhouse, a favorite of ranchers in the area, has been spruced up a bit for the tour buses, but folks dig the hearty steak platters and Western atmosphere. Presiding over the dining room is 'Old Blue,' a massive stuffed bull's head from a local dairy farm.

Yarts (☎ 209-388-9589, 877-989-2787; www.yarts.com) buses depart four times daily for Yosemite Valley from several Merced locations, including the **Merced Transpo Center** (cnr 16th & N Sts) and the **Amtrak station** (cnr 24th & K Sts). The trip takes about 2½ hours and stops include Mariposa, Midpines and the Yosemite Bug Lodge & Hostel. Round-trip adult/child tickets cost $25/18 and include the park entrance fee (quite a bargain!). **Greyhound** (710 W 16th St) also operates from the Transpo Center. There's also space on the Yarts buses for bicycles, but space is limited, so show up early.

FRESNO

pop 486,171 / elev 296ft

Bulging like a blister in the arid center of the state, Fresno is the biggest city in the San

Joaquin Valley by far. The old brick warehouses lining the Santa Fe railroad tracks are an impressive sight, as are the many historic downtown buildings, such as the 1894 Fresno Water Tower and the 1928 Pantages (Warnors) Theatre. These compete for attention with newer structures, including the sprawling Convention Center and the modern ballpark, Chukchansi Park, for Fresno's Triple-A baseball team, the Grizzlies.

The biggest surprise Fresno throws a traveler's way is the Tower District, which boasts the only active alternative-culture neighborhood between Sacramento and Los Angeles. North of downtown, the Tower District has book and record stores, music clubs and a handful of stylish restaurants.

Like many valley towns, Fresno's huge diversity comes from Mexican, Basque and Chinese communities, which have been here for decades. More recently thousands of Hmong people have put down roots in the area. The longstanding Armenian community is most famously represented by author and playwright William Saroyan, who was born, lived and died in this city he loved dearly.

Orientation & Information

Downtown lies between Divisadero St, Hwy 41 and Hwy 99. Two miles north, the Tower District sits around the corner of E Olive Ave and N Fulton Ave.

Fresno Convention & Visitors Bureau (☎ 559-237-0988, 800-788-0836; www.fresnocvb.org; cnr Fresno & O Sts; 10am-4pm Mon-Fri, 11am-3pm Sat) is inside the Fresno Water Tower.

Sights & Activities

If you see only one thing in Fresno, make it the **Forestiere Underground Gardens** (☎ 559-271-0734; www.undergroundgardens.info; 5021 W Shaw Ave; adult/child $12/7; tours 11am-2pm hourly Thu-Fri, 10am, 11am, noon, 1:30pm & 2:30pm Sat & Sun), two blocks east of Hwy 99. The gardens are the singular result of Sicilian immigrant Baldasare Forestiere, who dug out some 70 acres beneath the hardpan soil to plant citrus trees, starting in 1906. With a unique skylight system, he created a beautiful subterranean space for commercial crops and his own living quarters. The tunnel system includes bedrooms, a library, patios, grottos and a fish pond, and is now a historic landmark. This utterly fantastical accomplishment took Forestiere some 40 years to complete. He died in 1946.

Fresno's **Tower District** began as a shopping mecca during the 1920s, gaining its name after the **Tower Theatre** (☎ 559-485-9050; www.towertheaterfresno.com; 815 E Olive Ave), a beautiful art-deco movie house that opened in 1939. The theater is now used as a center for the performing arts (see p438). Surrounding it are bookstores, shops, high-end restaurants and coffeehouses, which cater to Fresno's gay and alternative communities. This is the city's best neighborhood for browsing and kicking back with an iced latte – even if the hipster quotient is tiny by comparison to that of, say, San Francisco's Mission District.

The **Fresno Art Museum** (☎ 559-441-4221; www.fresnoartmuseum.org; 2233 N 1st St; adult/student $4/2, Tue admission free; 11am-5pm Fri-Wed, to 8pm Thu), in Radio Park, has rotating exhibits of contemporary art – including work by local artists – that are among the most intriguing in the valley.

A favorite with children, the recently renovated **Fresno Metropolitan Museum of Art & Science** (☎ 559-441-1444; www.fresnomet.org; 1515 Van Ness Ave; adult/child under 2yr/child 3-12yr/students & seniors $9/free/5/7; 10am-6pm Fri-Wed, to 8pm Thu;) has hands-on science exhibits, Native American crafts, a large collection of antique puzzles and a William Saroyan gallery. The museum's holdings also include a large collection of Ansel Adams photographs. After major renovations, hours and fees are in flux, so be sure to confirm via phone before visiting.

On Olive Ave just east of Hwy 99, large and shady **Roeding Park** (per vehicle $3) is home to the small **Chaffee Zoological Gardens** (☎ 559-498-2671; www.fresnochaffeezoo.com; adult/child $7/3.50; 9am-4pm;). Adjacent to it are **Storyland** (☎ 559-264-2235; adult/child $4/3; 10am-5:30pm Sat & Sun, with seasonal variations;), a kitschy children's fairy-tale world dating from 1962, and **Playland** (adult/child $5/3.50;), which has kiddie rides and games.

Sleeping & Eating

Fresno has room to grow when it comes to world-class accommodations, but those using it as a launch pad for visiting Sequoia and Kings Canyon National Parks have plenty of options, either in slightly weathered mid-century structures on Hwy 99, a cluster of chains near the airport or a couple of high-rise offerings downtown.

Piccadilly Inn Shaw (☎ 559-226-3850; www.picadillyinn.com; 2305 W Shaw Ave; r $119-179;)

This is Fresno's nicest option, with a lovely pool, big rooms and tons of amenities. Ask for a room with a fireplace to cuddle by in winter. If they are full, try one of their other properties in town: Piccadilly Inn University, the Piccadilly Inn Express and the Piccadilly Inn Airport.

Sam's Italian Deli & Market (☎ 559-229-9346; 2415 N First St; mains $5-9; 🕑 8:30am-6pm Mon-Sat) This Italian market and deli is the real deal, stacking up the 'New Yorker' pastrami and some mean prosciutto and mozzarella.

Grand Marie's Chicken Pie Shop (☎ 559-237-5042; 2861 E Olive Ave; mains $5-12; 🕑 breakfast & lunch daily, dinner Mon-Sat) With a ladle of gravy and a flaky crust, the beautiful chicken-stuffed pies at this Tower District stalwart bear no resemblance to the frozen, soggy mess of your childhood. Breakfast is also supreme thanks to buttery biscuits.

Irene's Cafe (☎ 559-237-9919; 747 E Olive Ave; mains $10-15; 🕑 8am-9pm; 🕑 breakfast, lunch & dinner) In the hip Tower District, Irene's is popular for its chicken-fried steaks (made with Angus beef), whopping 9oz burgers and veggie burgers. Its trendy atmosphere comes off as friendly rather than hip, and the place does three meals a day.

Chef's Table at the Elbow Room (☎ 559-227-3200; 731 W San Jose Ave; mains $17-40; 🕑 dinner Tue-Sat) The most elegant option in Fresno can get a bit stuffy unless you retire to the patio to toss around the bocce balls. Earthy pheasant and wild-mushroom cannelloni gets things started on the menu of Mediterranean fusions. The wine list is as thick as a stack of bibles.

Entertainment

In the center of Fresno's hippest neighborhood, it's hard to miss the neon phallus of the **Tower Theatre for the Performing Arts** (☎ 559-485-9050; 815 E Olive Ave), a stunning deco palace that opens its stage to touring rock and jazz acts and ballet, and seasonal cultural events.

Getting There & Around

Greyhound (☎ 559-268-1829; 1033 Broadway) stops downtown near the new ballpark. One-way trips to or from Los Angeles are $29. One way between Fresno and San Francisco are $29.50 (5 hours, five daily). The local **Fresno Area Express** (FAX; ☎ 559-488-1122; one-way fare $1) has daily bus services to the Tower District (bus 22 or 26) and Forestiere Underground Gardens (bus 20, transfer to bus 9) from the downtown transit center at Van Ness Ave and Fresno St.

Just east of the center of town is the Fresno Yosemite International Airport, a dreary if serviceable two-runway strip surrounded by chain hotels. The 'Yosemite' and 'International' elements of the name are generous – it's a two-hour drive to the interior of the park and the only air service outside the States services Mexico City.

FESTAS FOR THE BULLS

Bullfighting has been illegal in the USA since 1957, but there are exceptions to the rule. When Portuguese communities in the Central Valley have *festas* (religious festivals) they are permitted to stage bloodless bullfights. The *festas* are huge events, attracting as many as 25,000 Portuguese Americans, and the bullfights are generally the climax of several days of parades, food, music and beauty contests.

Portuguese fishermen and farmers, mostly from the Azores, began settling in California during the late 19th century. The communities grew, especially in the Central Valley, with steady immigration continuing until very recently. Many people in the valley still speak Portuguese fluently and attend the *festas* that are held up and down the state.

Festas typically honor religious icons such as St Anthony or Our Lady of Fátima. But they are largely cultural events. Candlelight processions, folk dancing, blessing of the cows, performances of *pezinho* songs (sad melodies with a lilting violin accompaniment) and eating until you feel like a plump sausage are all part of the experience. The *festa* queen contests are taken very seriously by the contestants.

Festas are held throughout the summer, with major events in Hanford, Gustine (along Hwy 33, north of the junction of I-5 and Hwy 152) and Stevinson (east of Gustine). They're not well publicized and the relevant websites that go up are often temporary. The only reliable thing to do is search 'festas california' and see what comes up in English.

VISALIA

pop 96,900 / elev 331ft

Its agricultural prosperity and the well-maintained downtown make Visalia one of the valley's nicest places to stay en route to Sequoia and Kings Canyon National Parks or the Sierra Peaks, which are visible in the distance on clear days. Bypassed a century ago by the railroad, the city is 5 miles east of Hwy 99, along Hwy 198. Its downtown has great old buildings and is a popular place to stroll, day or night.

Sights & Activities

The original Victorian and Arts and Crafts–style homes in Visalia are architectural gems worth viewing on foot. Get information about a self-guided walking tour from the **Visalia Chamber of Commerce & Visitors Center** (☎ 559-734-5876, 877-847-2542; www.visaliatourism.com; 720 W Mineral King Ave; 8:30am-5pm Mon-Fri). The tour leads north of Main St on both N Willis and Encina Sts.

About 7 miles east of Visalia is **Kaweah Oak Reserve**, home to 324 acres of valley oak trees, which once stretched from the Sierras to (long-gone) Tulare Lake in the valley. Nice for a short hike, it's also a rare glimpse into the valley's past before the orchards and vineyards took over. From Hwy 198, turn north onto Rd 182; the park is about a half-mile along on your left.

South of downtown on Hwy 63 (Mooney Blvd), shaded **Mooney Grove Park** is home to the **Tulare County Museum** (☎ 559-733-6616; park entry $5, museum free; 10am-4pm Mon, Thu & Fri, 1-4pm Sat & Sun), a musty treasure trove of pioneer and Native American memorabilia.

The gloriously restored 1930 **Fox Theatre** (☎ box office 559-625-1369; cnr W Main & Encina Sts) hosts assorted concerts and special events.

Sleeping & Eating

There are tons of dining options in the middle of town. If you want to follow your nose just wander down Main St between Floral and Bridge Sts.

Spalding House (☎ 559-739-7877; www.thespaldinghouse.com; 631 N Encina St; r $85-95;) This B&B has three classy suites, each with an antique bed, a sitting room and a modern bathroom. The full-on breakfasts will get you going in the morning, and you can tinkle at the 1923 Steinway piano in the parlor all evening.

our pick **Brewbaker's Brewing Company** (☎ 559-627-2739; 219 E Main St; mains $6-12; lunch & dinner) If you can handle the wait in this busy brewpub, Brewbaker's microbrews are a reward, particularly the smooth flagship Sequoia Red. If you go for a few pints of the chocolaty Possum Porter, you'll need to soak it up with well-executed pub food.

Getting There & Away

Amtrak (☎ 559-582-5236) shuttles connect with the station in Hanford by reservation only. From Hanford riders can connect to all other Amtrak routes in the state, including the *San Joaquins* north to Sacramento ($29, four hours, two direct services daily) or south to Bakersfield ($15, 1½ hours, six trains daily).

BAKERSFIELD

pop 261,000 / elev 408ft

Nearing Bakersfield, the landscape is dotted with evidence of California's *other* gold rush: rusting rigs alongside the route continue to burrow into Southern California's vast oil fields. Oil was discovered here in the late 1800s, and Kern County, the southernmost county on Hwy 99, still pumps more than some OPEC countries. In the 1930s the oil attracted a stream of 'Okies' – farmers who migrated out of the dusty Great Plains – to work the derricks (see p441). The children of these tough-as-nails roughnecks minted the 'Bakersfield Sound' in the mid-1950s, with heroes Buck Owens and Merle Haggard waving a defiant middle finger to the silky Nashville establishment (see p440 for a Bakersfield roadtrip soundtrack).

As Bakersfield tries to become all sophisticated like some of its valley neighbors, it has an uneasy relationship with the rhinestone-studded country pluckers of its past. Much of the twangy Bakersfield sound went to the grave with Buck Owens, who passed in 2006.

Though some parts of town are rather shabby, downtown is a surprisingly upbeat mix of restored buildings, county offices, restaurants and antique shops, such as the **Five and Dime** (☎ 661-323-8048; cnr 19th & K Sts; 10am-5pm Mon-Sat, noon-5pm Sun) inside an original Woolworth's building. The 1930 **Fox Theater** hosts regular performances and the still-impressive **Padre Hotel**, a historical landmark, is struggling to find an owner. Near the freeway, Buck Owens' multi-million-dollar **Crystal**

KINGS OF BAKERSFIELD SOUND

Driving down Hwy 99 requires getting on a first-name basis with Bakersfield's two drawling titans: Merle and Buck. Masters of twanging Telecasters and hayseed heartbreak, they're country kings of the Central Valley.

- *I'm Gonna Break Every Heart I Can* – Merle Haggard
- *I've Got A Tiger by the Tail* – Buck Owens
- *Okie from Muskogee* – Merle Haggard
- *Second Fiddle* – Buck Owens
- *The Bottle Let Me Down* – Merle Haggard
- *Under Your Spell Again* – Buck Owens
- *Swinging Doors* – Merle Haggard
- *The Streets of Bakersfield* – Buck Owens and Dwight Yoakam

Palace is a neon triumph, where cowboys and cowgirls in well-polished boots still pack in to see A-list country stars and drink big beers.

Orientation & Information

The Kern River flows along Bakersfield's northern edge, separating it from its blue-collar neighbor, Oildale, and a host of oil fields. Truxtun and Chester Aves are the main downtown thoroughfares.

The **Greater Bakersfield Convention & Visitors Bureau** (☎ 661-325-5051; www.bakersfieldcvb.org; 515 Truxtun Ave; 8:30am-5pm Mon-Fri) carries maps and loads of brochures.

Sights

Old Town Kern, located east of downtown around Baker and Sumner Sts, though currently suffering from a bit of neglect, was once a vibrant and bustling centre. It certainly makes for an interesting view into the region's decaying past. The **Bakersfield Historic Preservation Commission** (☎ 661-326-3765; www.bakersfieldcity.us/edcd/historic/walkingtours.htm) has put together walking tour brochures covering Old Town Kern as well as Bakersfield's historic downtown.

The **Kern County Museum & Lori Brock Children's Discovery Center** (☎ 661-852-5000; 3801 Chester Ave; adult/student $8/7; 10am-5pm Mon-Sat, noon-5pm Sun;), has a pioneer village with more than 50 restored and replicated buildings. The musty main structure has a large (fairly disturbing) display of the area's taxidermy wildlife. On the 2nd floor waits a collection of pristine memorabilia from Bakersfield's musical heyday.

A half-hour northeast of town is the **California Living Museum** (661-872-2256; 10500 Alfred Harrell Hwy; admission $6.50; 9am-5pm), a zoo and botanical gardens that have a menagerie of native plants and animals. Kids will squirm in the rattlesnake house.

Sleeping & Eating

Along the highway, chain motels have sprung up like weeds. Old-school budget motels line Union Ave heading south from Hwy 178, though some are a bit shady. Bakersfield is blessed with several traditional Basque restaurants, where food is served family-style in a series of courses including soup, salad, beans and thin slices of tangy beef tongue. All this comes *before* the main course, so you'd better be hungry. Mexican food is plentiful here, too.

Best Western Crystal Palace (☎ 661-327-9651, 800-424-4900; www.bestwestern.com; 2620 Buck Owens Blvd; r $80;) Just a stumble across the parking lot from Owens' night club, this Best Western is the choice for those who want to boot-scoot until the wee hours.

Wool Growers (☎ 661-327-9584; 620 E 19th St; mains $7-20; lunch & dinner Mon-Sat) Bakersfield's oldest Basque restaurant is a simple eating hall loaded with character. A fried chicken dinner will leave you full for a week.

Dewar's Candy Shop (☎ 661-332-0933; 1120 Eye St; mains $3-10; 11am-9pm Mon-Thu, to 10pm Fri & Sat) Perched on the pastel stools at the counter, families dig into homemade ice cream – dreamy flavors like lemon flake and cotton candy change seasonally – all made from ingredients from surrounding farms.

Entertainment

Buck Owens' Crystal Palace (☎ 661-328-7560; www.buckowens.com; 2800 Buck Owens Blvd) For fans of the city's great musical heritage, this is the first stop – hard to miss thanks to its huge neon sign in the shape of Buck's famous guitar, lit up in patriotic colours. Part music museum, part honky-tonk, part steakhouse, the Palace has a top-drawer country act on stage every night, and locals in meticulous western wear tear up the dance floor.

Ethel's Old Corral (☎ 661-871-4136; 4310 Alfred Harrell Hwy) On the outskirts of town, Ethel's is a humble reminder of twangy country, with live music Friday and Sunday nights.

Trout's & the Blackboard Stage (☎ 661-399-6700; 805 N Chester Ave at Decatur St) The legendary Trout's, in Oildale, is the only remaining honky-tonk in town, hobbling along after half a century as the most accurate testament to the hell-raisin' days gone by. Crowds pack the place and dance to the music of the great Red Simpson, a Bakersfield Sound songwriter who still pens the occasional hit.

Getting There & Around

From the **Amtrak station** (☎ 661-395-3175, 800-872-7245; 601 Truxtun Ave at S St) trains head north to Sacramento ($40, five hours, two direct trains daily) and Amtrak buses head to LA, but are only available in combination with a train ticket.

The **Greyhound** (☎ 661-327-5617, 800-229-9424; 1820 18th St) depot is downtown near the Padre Hotel.

Airport Bus of Bakersfield (☎ 800-858-5000, 805-395-0635; 2530 F St) runs a shuttle seven times daily between Bakersfield and LAX ($27, 2½ hours).

Golden Empire Transit (GET; ☎ 661-869-2438; basic fare 90¢) is the local bus system. Route 2 runs north on Chester Ave to the Kern County Museum and Oildale.

KERN RIVER AREA

A half-century ago the Kern River originated on the slopes of Mt Whitney and journeyed close to 170 miles before finally settling into Buena Vista Lake in the Central Valley. Now, after its wild ride from the high country – where the river drops an incredible 60ft per mile – it's dammed in several places and almost entirely tapped for agricultural use after hitting the valley floor. Its upper reaches, declared wild and scenic by the Secretary of the Interior, are a white-water enthusiast's, ahem, wet dream.

Hwy 178 follows the dramatic **Kern River Canyon**, making for a stunning drive through the lower reaches of Sequoia National Forest. East of the lake, Hwy 178 winds another 50 miles through a picturesque mixture of pine and Joshua trees before reaching Hwy 395.

Sights & Activities

The town of **Lake Isabella** is a strip of local businesses on the south end of the lake. Here Hwy 155 heads north, around the west side of the lake, to **Kernville**, a cute little town straddling the Kern River and *the* hub for rafting on the Kern. While the lake is popular for cooling off, note that the river's deceptively strong currents can be extremely dangerous.

The Upper Kern and Forks of the Kern (both sections of the river north of Kernville) yield Class IV and V rapids during spring runoff and offer some of the most awe-inspiring white-water trips in the country. You'll need experience before tackling these sections, though there are plenty more opportunities for novices. Below Lake Isabella, the Kern is tamer and steadier.

About six rafting companies operate out of Kernville; all offer competitive prices and run trips from May to August, depending on conditions. Excursions include popular one-hour

DETOUR: WEEDPATCH LABOR CAMP

In the years following the Depression, Kern County boasted California's highest proportion of poor white farm laborers from the South and the Great Plains. Called 'Okies' (whether they came from Oklahoma or not), they came with dreams of a new life in the fields and farms of the Golden State. The majority, though, found only migrant labor jobs and continued hardship.

Dating from 1935, this Farm Security Administration labor camp (the model for 'Weedpatch Camp' in *The Grapes of Wrath*) was one of about 16 in the US set up at the time to aid migrant workers – and it's the only one with any original buildings left. At the time of research, the original structures were undergoing restoration, and some of the camp's newer buildings were still occupied by poor farm workers. The camp is a fascinating vision into the past – and a wake-up call to the continuing dichotomy between corporate agribusiness and its still-dirt-poor migrant workforce. **Tours** (☎ 661-832-1299; donations accepted) require advance arrangement.

From Bakersfield, take Hwy 58 east to Weedpatch Hwy; head south for about 7 miles, past Lamont; then turn left on Sunset Blvd, driving another mile. The buildings (the sign reads 'Arvin Farm Labor Center') are on your right. Please respect the privacy of the residents. **Dust Bowl Days** (www.weedpatchcamp.com) is a celebration of Okie history held here each October.

runs ($25), day-long Lower Kern trips ($130 to $190) and multiday Forks of the Kern wilderness experiences ($600 to $920). Walk-ups are welcome and experience isn't necessary. Kids aged six and up can usually participate too. Companies include **Sierra South** (☎ 760-376-3745, 800-457-2082; www.sierrasouth.com; 11300 Kernville Rd), **Whitewater Voyages** (☎ 800-400-7238, 660-376-8806; www.whitewatervoyages.com) and **Mountain & River Adventures** (☎ 800-861-6553, 760-376-6553; www.mtnriver.com; 11113 Kernville Rd).

Sleeping

Lake Isabella has motels, but Kernville's a nicer location and rates here are still reasonable. Many of Kernville's motels have two-day minimum stays on weekends.

Whispering Pines Lodge (☎ 760-376-3733; www.kernvalley.com/whisperingpines; 13745 Sierra Way; r $149-299;) This secluded B&B, blending rustic character with luxurious comfort, is just north of town.

USFS campgrounds (☎ 877-444-6777; developed/undeveloped sites $12/16) These campgrounds line the 10-mile stretch between Lake Isabella and Kernville, and several more lie north of Kernville on Mtn 99. The **Kernville Ranger Station** (☎ 760-376-3781; 105 Whitney Rd; 8am-5pm summer, 8:30am-4:30pm Mon-Fri winter) has hiking and camping information, as well as maps and wilderness permits.

Central Coast

Too often forgotten or dismissed as 'flyover' country between San Francisco and Los Angeles, this stretch of coastal California is like a Japanese bento box packed with nearly everything you've come to California for: wild Pacific beaches, deep forests of redwood trees (the tallest on earth) where hot springs beckon, and rolling golden hills hiding fertile vineyards.

Begin in the north, where flower-power Santa Cruz stands as the ideological counterpoint to treacly charming Carmel, the gateway to the rugged wildlands of the Big Sur coast. Here Hwy 1 pulls out all the stops, scenery-wise. It's an epic journey snaking down to vainglorious Hearst Castle, passing lighthouses and the Piedras Blancas elephant seal colony.

Or start your explorations in the old whaling port of Monterey, then get better acquainted with California's agricultural heartland in Salinas, both places immortalized by Nobel Prize–winner John Steinbeck in his gritty 20th-century novels. Then follow inland Hwy 101, called El Camino Real (the King's Highway) by Spanish conquistadors and Franciscan friars, who built a chain of Catholic missions here starting in the late 18th century.

No matter which highway you take, you'll end up cruising through the laid-back college town of San Luis Obispo, surrounded by beach towns, where you can kayak, surf, camp, hike or watch wildlife to your heart's content. Spend a few days or a week on this fairy-tale coast – it'll always leave you wanting more.

HIGHLIGHTS

- **Wildest ride** Scream your head off aboard the Giant Dipper roller coaster on Santa Cruz Beach Boardwalk (p444)
- **Coolest rainy-day fun** Meet the aquatic denizens of the 'indoor ocean' at Monterey Bay Aquarium (p455)
- **Most heart-stopping scenic drive** Cruise Hwy 1, where the sky touches the sea at Big Sur (p465)
- **Biggest over-the-top attraction** Marvel in disbelief at the grandiosity of Hearst Castle (p472)
- **Best down-to-earth adventure** Explore novelist John Steinbeck's blue-collar world in the agricultural town of Salinas (p480)
- **Poshest getaway** Soak up the chic culture of whitewashed, red-tiled Santa Barbara (p495)

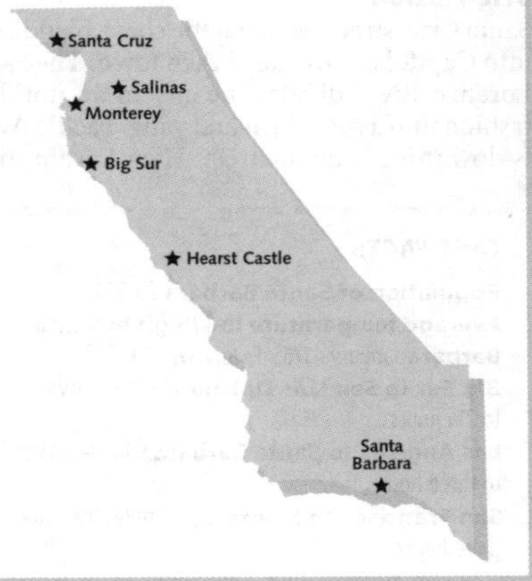

MONTEREY BAY

Anchored by Santa Cruz to the north and its namesake in the south, Monterey Bay is a remarkable place. It's teeming with richly varied marine life, lined with miles of often deserted beaches, and is home to towns full of character and idiosyncratic charm along its shore.

SANTA CRUZ

pop 56,950 / elev 14ft

Santa Cruz has marched to its own beat since long before the Beat Generation. It's counterculture central, a touchy-feely, new-agey city famous for its leftie-liberal politics and live-and-let-live ideology – except when it comes to dogs (rarely allowed off-leash), parking (meters run seven days a week) and Republicans (shot on sight). It's still cool to be a hippie or a stoner here (or better yet, both), although some far-out-looking freaks are really just slumming Silicon Valley millionaires underneath.

Santa Cruz is a crazy-fun city, with a vibrant but chaotic downtown. On the waterfront is the famous beach boardwalk, and in the hills redwood groves embrace the University of California, Santa Cruz (UCSC) campus. Plan to spend at least half a day in Santa Cruz, but to begin appreciating the aesthetic of jangly skirts and waist-length dreadlocks, stay longer and plunge headlong into the rich local brew of surfers, students, punks and more eccentric characters.

Orientation

Santa Cruz stretches along the coast, blending into Capitola, a low-key beach town. The San Lorenzo River divides the city in an untidy fashion into a sort of yin and yang. Pacific Ave is downtown's main street. Hwy 1 from the north leads into Mission St. Hwy 17, the main route from the Bay Area, turns into Ocean St. The university campus is uphill, about 2.5 miles northwest of downtown.

FAST FACTS

Population of Santa Barbara 89,550
Average temperature low/high in Santa Barbara January 41/65°F, July 57/77°F
Big Sur to San Luis Obispo 105 miles, two to 2½ hours
Los Angeles to Santa Barbara 95 miles, 1½ to three hours
San Francisco to Monterey 95 miles, two to three hours

Information

Bookshop Santa Cruz (Map p447; ☎ 831-423-0900; 1520 Pacific Ave; 🕑 9am-10pm Sun-Thu, 9am-11pm Fri & Sat) Vast selection of new books, a few used ones, popular and unusual magazines, and a café. Buy 'Keep Santa Cruz Weird' bumper stickers here.
FedEx Office (Map p447; ☎ 831-425-1177; 105 Laurel St; per min 20-30¢; 🕑 7am-11pm Mon-Fri, 9am-9pm Sat & Sun) High-speed internet workstations.
KPIG 107.5FM Plays the classic Santa Cruz soundtrack (think Bob Marley, Janis Joplin and Willie Nelson).
Santa Cruz County Conference & Visitors Council (Map p451; ☎ 831-425-1234; www.santacruz.org; 1211 Ocean St; 🕑 9am-5pm Mon-Fri, 10am-4pm Sat, 11am-3pm Sun) Free brochures, maps and internet access.

Sights

One of the best things to do in Santa Cruz is simply to stroll, shop and people-watch downtown on and around Pacific Ave. The beach is a 10-minute walk away.

SANTA CRUZ BEACH BOARDWALK

The 1907 **boardwalk** (Map p447; ☎ 831-423-5590; www.beachboardwalk.com; admission free, rides $2.25-4.50, all-day pass $30; 👶) is the West Coast's oldest beachfront amusement park. The boardwalk has a glorious old-school Americana vibe, with the smell of cotton candy mixing with the salt air, punctuated by the squeals of kids hanging upside down on carnival rides. Its most famous thrills include the half-mile-long Giant Dipper (a vintage 1924 wooden roller coaster) and the 1911 Looff carousel – both National Historic Landmarks. On Friday nights in summer, show up for free concerts by rock veterans you may have thought were already dead. For family-friendly train rides from the boardwalk up into the redwoods, see p451. The boardwalk usually opens at 11am; closing time varies.

MUNICIPAL WHARF

You can drive the length of the wharf (Map p447), where seafood restaurants, gift shops and barking sea lions compete for attention. A few shops rent fishing tackle and poles, if you're keen to join the local fishers along the wharf waiting patiently for a bite. The views here are first-rate.

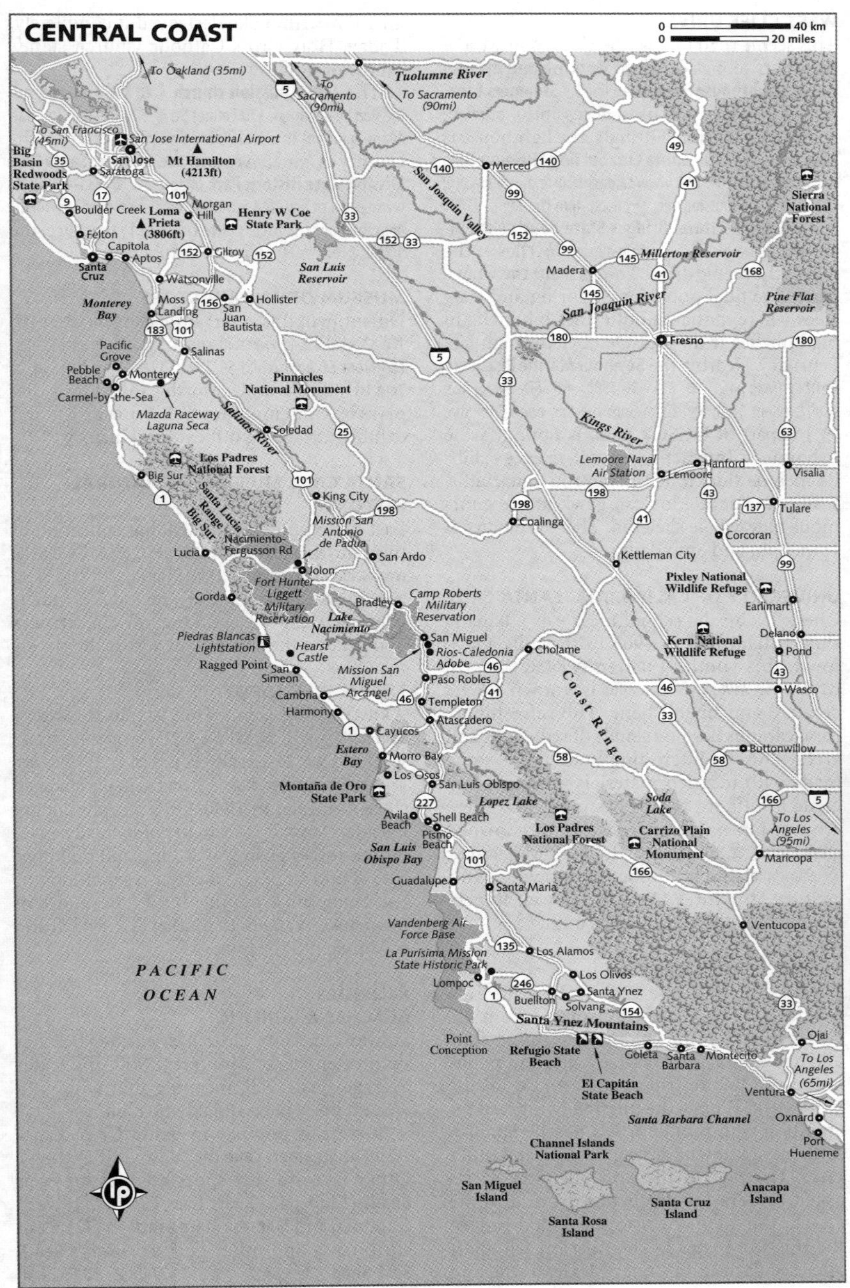
CENTRAL COAST
0 40 km
0 20 miles
To Oakland (35mi)
To Sacramento (90mi)
To Sacramento (90mi)
Tuolumne River
To San Francisco (45mi)
San Jose International Airport
San Jose
Mt Hamilton (4213ft)
Big Basin Redwoods State Park
Saratoga
Boulder Creek
Loma Prieta (3806ft)
Morgan Hill
Henry W Coe State Park
Felton
Capitola
Aptos
Santa Cruz
Gilroy
San Luis Reservoir
Watsonville
Monterey Bay
Moss Landing
San Juan Bautista
Hollister
Salinas
Pacific Grove
Pebble Beach
Monterey
Carmel-by-the-Sea
Mazda Raceway Laguna Seca
Pinnacles National Monument
Salinas River
Soledad
Los Padres National Forest
Big Sur
Santa Lucia Range
Big Sur
King City
Mission San Antonio de Padua
Nacimiento-Fergusson Rd
Lucia
Jolon
San Ardo
Fort Hunter Liggett Military Reservation
Gorda
Bradley
Camp Roberts Military Reservation
Lake Nacimiento
Piedras Blancas Lightstation
Hearst Castle
San Miguel
Rios-Caledonia Adobe
Ragged Point
San Simeon
Mission San Miguel Arcangel
Paso Robles
Cambria
Templeton
Harmony
Atascadero
Cayucos
Estero Bay
Morro Bay
Los Osos
Montaña de Oro State Park
San Luis Obispo
Lopez Lake
Avila Beach
Shell Beach
Pismo Beach
San Luis Obispo Bay
Los Padres National Forest
Guadalupe
Santa Maria
Vandenberg Air Force Base
La Purísima Mission State Historic Park
Los Alamos
Los Olivos
Lompoc
Buellton
Santa Ynez
Solvang
Santa Ynez Mountains
Point Conception
Refugio State Beach
El Capitán State Beach
Goleta
Santa Barbara
Montecito
PACIFIC OCEAN
Santa Barbara Channel
Channel Islands National Park
San Miguel Island
Santa Rosa Island
Santa Cruz Island
Anacapa Island
Merced
San Joaquin Valley
Madera
Millerton Reservoir
San Joaquin River
Sierra National Forest
Pine Flat Reservoir
Fresno
Kings River
Lemoore Naval Air Station
Lemoore
Hanford
Visalia
Tulare
Coalinga
Corcoran
Kettleman City
Pixley National Wildlife Refuge
Earlimart
Kern National Wildlife Refuge
Delano
Pond
Cholame
Coast Range
Wasco
Buttonwillow
Soda Lake
Carrizo Plain National Monument
To Los Angeles (95mi)
Maricopa
Ventucopa
Ojai
To Los Angeles (65mi)
Ventura
Oxnard
Port Hueneme
CENTRAL COAST

WEST CLIFF DRIVE

This scenic road follows the cliffs southwest of the wharf, alongside paved walking and cycling paths. **Lighthouse Point** overlooks **Steamers Lane**, one of the top – and most accessible – surfing spots in California. Fittingly, the lighthouse is home to the tiny **Santa Cruz Surfing Museum** (Map p451; ☎ 831-420-6289; www.santacruzsurfingmuseum.org; 701 W Cliff Dr; admission free; 🕑 noon-4pm Thu-Mon). Best for sunsets, **Natural Bridges State Beach** (☎ 831-423-4609; per vehicle $6; 🕑 8am-sunset; ♿) lies at the end of the scenic drive, 3 miles from the wharf. There are tidal pools for exploring and leafy trees where monarch butterflies hibernate in big bunches from mid-October through late February. Nearby, the **Seymour Marine Discovery Center** (Map p451; ☎ 831-459-3800; end of Delaware Ave; adult/student $6/4; 🕑 10am-5pm Tue-Sat, noon-5pm Sun; ♿) is part of UCSC's famous Long Marine Laboratory. Interactive natural-science exhibits include tidal touch pools and aquariums, while outside kiddos can gawk at the enormous blue-whale skeleton. There are tours at 1pm, 2pm and 3pm daily.

UNIVERSITY OF CALIFORNIA, SANTA CRUZ

Check it out: the school mascot is a banana slug! Established in 1965 in the hills above town, this youthful **university** (UCSC; Map p451; ☎ 831-459-2495; www.ucsc.edu) is known for its creative and liberal bent. The refreshingly rural campus has fine stands of redwoods and architecturally interesting buildings – some made with recycled materials – designed to blend in with the rolling pasture lands. There are two top-notch art galleries, a renowned **arboretum** (☎ 831-427-2998; 1156 High St; admission free; 🕑 9am-5pm) and a number of decaying 19th-century structures from the Cowell Ranch, upon which the campus was built.

MISSION SANTA CRUZ

Founded in 1791, the 12th of the California missions, Santa Cruz, was isolated from the comings and goings along El Camino Real and had only a small Native American population of Ohlone tribespeople to do all the hard work. Worse, the mission competed for attention with Branciforte, a nearby Spanish settlement known for its gambling and other vices. The devil finally won when the priests asked settlers for protection from a pirate attack: the good townsfolk decided to loot the mission instead. The mission fell apart after secularization under Mexican rule and an 1857 earthquake destroyed it completely. Today, Holy Cross Catholic Church stands on the original site.

The 1931 **mission church** (☎ 831-426-5686; admission by donation; 130 Emmet St; 🕑 10am-4pm Tue-Sat, 10am-2pm Sun) is a half-sized replica of the 18th-century original. Around the corner, **Santa Cruz Mission State Historic Park** (Map p451; ☎ 831-425-5849; www.parks.ca.gov; 144 School St; admission free; 🕑 10am-4pm Thu-Sun) includes one original structure, the 1791 Neary-Rodriguez Adobe.

MUSEUM OF ART & HISTORY

Downtown, this smart little **museum** (Map p447; ☎ 831-429-1964; www.santacruzmah.org; McPherson Center, 705 Front St; adult/child $5/2; 🕑 11am-5pm Tue-Sun, to 9pm 1st Fri of the month) is worth a look for its displays by contemporary California artists and exhibits exploring offbeat local history.

SANTA CRUZ MUSEUM OF NATURAL HISTORY

East of downtown, the wildlife collection at this pint-sized **museum** (Map p451; ☎ 831-420-6115; www.santacruzmuseums.org; 1305 E Cliff Dr; adult/child $2.50/free; 🕑 10am-5pm Tue-Sun; ♿) includes a touch-friendly tidepool showing off the critters living along the shore right across the street.

THE MYSTERY SPOT

A kitschy, old-fashioned tourist trap, the **Mystery Spot** (off Map p451; ☎ 831-423-8897; www.mysteryspot.com; 465 Mystery Spot Rd; admission $5, parking $5; 🕑 9am-7pm Jun-Aug, 9am-5pm Sep-May; ♿) has scarcely changed since it opened in 1940. On a steeply sloping hillside, compasses seem to point crazily, mysterious forces push you around and buildings lean at odd angles. Make tour reservations, or risk being stuck waiting. It's 3 miles north of town: take Water St to Market St, turn left and continue into the hills.

Activities

BEACHES & SURFING

Sun-kissed Santa Cruz has warmer beaches than often-foggy Monterey. Still, the water averages just 57°F, meaning that without a wetsuit body parts quickly turn blue.

Surfing is popular in Santa Cruz, especially at **Steamers Lane** off West Cliff Dr (left). Other favorite surf spots are **Pleasure Point Beach** (Map p451), on East Cliff Dr toward Capitola, and **Manresa State Beach** (p452). Rent surfboards and other gear at **Cowell's Beach Surf Shop** (Map p447; ☎ 831-427-2355; 30 Front St;

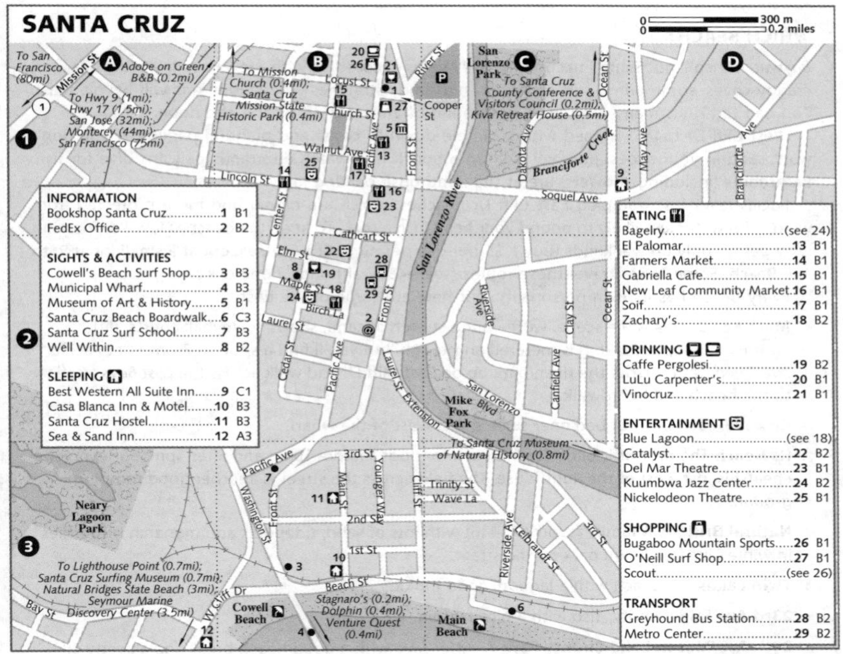

8am-5pm), where the veteran staff have heaps of local knowledge.

Wanna learn to surf? **Santa Cruz Surf School** (Map p447; ☎ 831-426-7072; www.santacruzsurfschool.com; 322 Pacific Ave) and **Richard Schmidt Surf School** (☎ 831-423-0928; www.richardschmidt.com) will have you standing and surfing the first day out. A two-hour group lesson costs from $80.

KAYAKING

Kayaking lets you discover the kelp beds, a favorite of sea otters, and the craggy coastline up close. **Venture Quest** (off Map p447; ☎ 831-427-2267; www.kayaksantacruz.com; Municipal Wharf) offers rentals, lessons and tours, as does **Kayak Connection** (Map p451; ☎ 831-479-1121; www.kayakconnection.com; Santa Cruz Harbor, 413 Lake Ave), which also operates at Elkhorn Slough (p452). Four-hour rentals cost from $30 (per day $45); lessons and tours run $25 to $75.

BOAT TRIPS

Whale-watching trips run from December to April, though there's plenty of marine life to see on a summer bay cruise, too. Fishing trips are also offered, usually with departures from the Municipal Wharf. **Stagnaro's** (off Map p447; ☎ 800-979-3370; www.stagnaros.com) is a longstanding tour operator, offering scenic cruises ($13), whale-watching tours ($39) and fishing trips (from $70).

SPAS

Santa Cruz has a surprising number of spas with private soaking tubs. Locals call 'em 'soak and pokes.' At sociable **Kiva Retreat House** (Map p451; ☎ 831-429-1142; www.kivaretreat.com; 702 Water St; noon-11pm Mon-Thu, noon-midnight Fri & Sat, 1:30-11pm Sun) a private outdoor tub for two rents for $28 to $40 per hour. Serene **Well Within** (Map p447; ☎ 831-458-9355; www.wellwithinspa.com; 417 Cedar St; 11am-midnight) has indoor and outdoor tubs at slightly lower prices. Both spas offer massage appointments.

Festivals & Events

Woodies on the Wharf (www.santacruzwoodies.com) A classic car show featuring vintage surf-style station wagons, held over the last weekend in June.

Shakespeare Santa Cruz (☎ 831-459-2121; www.shakespearesantacruz.org) Damn good productions of the Bard outdoors in a redwood grove during July and August.

WHICH BEACH?

Baywatch it isn't, but Santa Cruz does have 29 miles of coastline with a few Hawaii-worthy beaches, craggy coves, some primo surf spots and big sandy stretches where your kids will have a blast. Too bad fog ruins many a summer morning; it often burns off by the afternoon.

West Cliff Dr (p446) is lined with scramble-down-to coves and plentiful parking. If you don't want sand in your shoes, park yourself on a bench and watch enormous pelicans dive for fish. Bathrooms (including showers) are at the lighthouse parking lot.

Locals favor less-trampled East Cliff Dr beaches, which are bigger and more protected from wind, with water less likely to pound your head into a rock. To keep the beaches low-key, parking is by permit only on weekends (buy a $5-per-day permit at 9th Ave), except at a small lot at 26th Ave Beach. Some buses travel these routes (see p451), although none directly.

Every beach has its own personality, but here are some of the best:

- **Main Beach** This is *the* scene, with a huge stretch of sand, shops, volleyball courts and swarms of people. Parking is metered and tough, but you'll find a spot on Front St at Pacific Ave. Even better, cross the river, park up on East Cliff Dr and walk across the *Lost Boys* trestle to the beach and boardwalk.
- **Cowell Beach** Best for beginner surfers, just west of the wharf.
- **Its Beach** The only official off-leash beach for dogs (before 10am and after 4pm, but everyone cheats) is just west of the lighthouse. The field across the street is another good romping ground.
- **Natural Bridges** A family favorite (p446) with lots of sand, tidepools and monarch butterflies in winter. It's free if you park on the street.
- **Twin Lakes** Big beach with a lagoon, good for kids.
- **23rd Ave** Fairly empty, also with a nice lagoon.
- **26th Ave/Moran Lake County Park** A surfer fave with a good beach break and a pretty all-around sandy spot. There's a metered parking lot and bathrooms.

Also check out family-friendly Capitola (p452) and an enviable lineup of state beaches further south (p452).

Open Studio Art Tour (☎ 831-475-9600; www.ccscc.org) Visit local artists' creative workshops during three weekends in October.

Sleeping

Santa Cruz does not have not enough beds to satisfy demand: expect outrageous prices at peak times for nothing-special rooms. Choose places between downtown and the beach for easy foot access to both. If you're looking for a straightforward motel, check out Ocean St. Places near the boardwalk run the gamut from friendly to frightening.

Reserve ahead for state-park **campgrounds** (☎ reservations 800-444-7275; www.reserveamerica.com; tent & RV sites $25-35) at the beaches and in the mountains. Terrific spots include Henry Cowell Redwoods and Big Basin Redwoods State Parks in the Santa Cruz Mountains (p451); New Brighton State Beach (p452), near Capitola; and Manresa and Sunset State Beaches (p452), further south near Watsonville.

Santa Cruz Hostel (Map p447; ☎ 831-423-8304; www.hi-santacruz.org; 321 Main St; dm $20-28, r $45-90, all with shared bath; reception 8-11am & 5-10pm) A lovely hostel occupies the century-old Carmelita Cottages surrounded by flowering gardens. It's two blocks from the beach and five blocks from downtown. Bummer: there's an 11pm curfew and a three-night maximum stay. Make reservations.

Sunny Cove Motel Apartments (Map p451; ☎ 831-475-1741; 21610 E Cliff Dr; r $70-100;) It's nothing fancy, but this tidy little hideaway east of downtown is a staunch budget fave. Friendly, long-time Santa Cruzian owners rent retro beach-house units with kitchenettes. Outside is a small pool and barbecue area. Pet-friendly.

Best Western All Suite Inn (Map p447; ☎ 831-458-9898; www.bestwesterncalifornia.com; 500 Ocean St; r incl breakfast $139-269; wi-fi) Every room is a large-ish suite with a kitchenette, and sleeps up to four. The furniture is upscale-generic, but it's a safe choice for families or business travelers needing amenities. Several other chain motels stand nearby.

Redwood Croft (off Map p451; ☎ 831-458-1939; www.redwoodcroft.com; 275 Northwest Dr, Bonny Doon; r incl breakfast $145-230) Hidden in redwood groves, a 25-minute drive north of Santa Cruz, this welcoming B&B with old-fashioned charm has country-kitsch rooms with fireplaces, outdoor hot tubs, hammocks and a bouncy trampoline for kids. Dogs also welcome.

Adobe on Green B&B (off Map p447; ☎ 831-469-9866; www.adobeongreen.com; 103 Green St; r incl breakfast $159-219; wi-fi) Peace and quiet are the mantras here, just a three-block walk from Pacific Ave. The hosts are practically invisible, but their thoughtful touches are everywhere, from boutique-hotel amenities inside spacious, solar-powered rooms to organic-garden breakfast spreads.

Casa Blanca Inn & Motel (Map p447; ☎ 831-423-1570; www.casablanca-santacruz.com; 101 Main St; r $175-275) Built around a former mansion right near the wharf, this small hotel's quaint rooms have an odd mix of shabby-chic, white-wicker chairs and dark, Colonial-style beds and tables. Some have kitchens and fireplaces, and overlook the ocean.

Bella Notte (Map p451; ☎ 831-600-0001, 877-342-3552; 21305 E Cliff Dr; r $189-289; wi-fi) Aka 'The Inn at East Cliff,' this slate-gray roadside hotel east of the river, near Twin Lakes beach, has boutique-style rooms with high-thread-count linens, heated bathroom floors, flat-screen TVs and fireplaces.

Sea & Sand Inn (Map p447; ☎ 831-427-3400; www.santacruzmotels.com; 201 W Cliff Dr; r $189-399) A spiffy motel, the Sea & Sand is removed from the noisy boardwalk area and perched pleasantly on the cliff (fall asleep to braying sea lions!). Rooms are smallish, but have solid pine furniture; bathrooms need updating. It's pricey, but the ocean views are stellar.

Pleasure Point Inn (Map p451; ☎ 831-475-4657; www.pleasurepointinn.com; 23665 E Cliff Dr; r incl breakfast $250-295; wi-fi) Live out your fantasy of California beachfront living at this inn east of the river. Four clean-lined, contemporary rooms have hardwood floors, tiled bathrooms with Jacuzzi tubs, kitchenettes and private patios. Climb to the rooftop deck for drop-dead ocean views.

Eating

Alas, Santa Cruz' food scene lacks luster.

Emily's (Map p451; ☎ 831-429-9866; 1129 Mission St; items $2-7; 5:30am-6pm Mon-Fri, 6:30am-6pm Sat & Sun) Its motto is simply 'good things to eat,' and UCSC students couldn't agree more. Stop by for a fresh-baked cheese scone, plump muffin or delectable little fruit tart, or delight in a daily soup-and-salad combo on the shady creekside porch.

Bagelry (Map p447; ☎ 831-429-8049; 320a Cedar St; items $3-6; 6:30am-5:30pm Mon-Sat, 6:30am-4pm Sun) The bagels here are twice-cooked (boiled, then baked), and come with fantastic spreads, especially the hummus and egg salad. Check out the bulletin board for community goings-on.

Zachary's (Map p447; ☎ 831-427-0646; 819 Pacific Ave; mains $5-10; 7am-2:30pm Tue-Sun) At the brunch spot that locals don't want you to know about, brave the long line for huge portions of sourdough pancakes and blueberry cream-cheese coffee cake that'll keep you going all day. 'Mike's Mess' is the kitchen-sink standout.

El Palomar (Map p447; ☎ 831-425-7575; 1336 Pacific Ave; mains $7-22; 11am-11pm) Always packed and consistently good (if not great), El Palomar serves tasty Mexican staples – try the seviches – and fruity margaritas. The tortillas are made fresh by charming women in the covered courtyard.

Engfer Pizza Works (Map p451; ☎ 831-429-1856; 537 Seabright Ave; pizzas $8-23; 4-9:30pm Tue-Sun) Inside an old factory, wood-fired-oven pizzas are made with homemade dough and sauces – and love. The specialty 'no-name' pizza is like a giant salad on roasted bread. Play ping-pong and sip draft microbrews while you wait.

Dolphin (Map p447; ☎ 831-426-5830; 71a Municipal Wharf; mains $9-16; 8am-9pm) For fish on the wharf, you'll get the most bang for your buck at this unpretentious family-owned diner way out at the end of the pier. There's also a takeout window and picnic tables outside, great for parents with fidgety kids.

Gabriella Cafe (Map p447; ☎ 831-457-1677; 910 Cedar St; mains $12-30; lunch & dinner) Intimate and romantic, with tiny tables and twinkling lights, Gabriella's is a perfect date spot, with an outdoor garden for long, lingering California bistro lunches of seasonal, organic produce and sustainably raised meats. Dinners could be better, but if you're in love, who cares?

Soif (Map p447; ☎ 831-423-2020; www.soifwine.com; 105 Walnut Ave; mains $14-40; ⌚ lunch Wed-Sat, dinner daily) Part wine shop, part wine bar and restaurant, this is where food-savvy bon vivants gather for a heady selection of 50 international wines by the glass paired with a sophisticated, seasonally driven, small-plates, Cal-fusion menu. Expect mostly organic dishes like crostini with pumpkin-seed-encrusted goat cheese, and duck confit with blackberry *gastrique* (a thick reduction sauce made with fruit, sugar and wine).

If you're grazing, Pacific Ave downtown is lined with eateries. Cheaper multiethnic take-out joints line Mission St, near UCSC. Downtown, **New Leaf Community Market** (Map p447; ☎ 831-425-1793; 1134 Pacific Ave; ⌚ 9am-9pm) sells organic produce and groceries. For more organic produce and a taste of the local vibe, cruise by the **farmers market** (Map p447; ☎ 831-454-0566; cnr Lincoln & Center Sts; ⌚ 2:30-6:30pm Wed).

Drinking

Downtown Pacific Ave has prolific bars, hookah lounges and coffee shops.

Caffe Pergolesi (Map p447; ☎ 831-426-1775; 418 Cedar St; ⌚ 7am-11pm; wi-fi) Discuss conspiracy theories over strong coffee or beer at this way-popular landmark café in a historic house with a big streetside veranda.

LuLu Carpenter's (Map p447; ☎ 831-429-9804; 1545 Pacific Ave; ⌚ 7am-midnight; wi-fi) If you like to sip fresh-ground espresso and leafed teas while spreading out with the Sunday papers, visit this brick-walled café with casement windows and outdoor garden seating. Also at the Museum of Art & History (p446).

Vinocruz (Map p447; ☎ 831-426-8466; Abbott Sq, off Cooper St; ⌚ 11am-7pm Mon-Thu, 11am-8pm Fri & Sat, noon-6pm Sun) This airy, welcoming wine shop has a mod stainless-steel tasting bar with an ever-changing lineup of superior vintages made in the Santa Cruz Mountains. Hit the outdoor deck in summer.

Santa Cruz Mountain Brewing (Map p451; ☎ 831-425-4900; Swift Street Courtyard, 402 Ingalls St; ⌚ noon-10pm) Bold organic brews are poured at this chilled-out tasting bar and beer garden west of town off Mission St, near Natural Bridges State Beach. Oddest flavor? Olallieberry cream ale.

Entertainment

Free weeklies *Metro Santa Cruz* (www.metrosantacruz.com) and *Good Times* (www.gtweekly.com) cover the scene from Santa Cruz south to Monterey.

Catalyst (Map p447; ☎ 831-423-1338; www.catalystclub.com; 1011 Pacific Ave) Over the years, this major live-music venue has seen big-time national acts from Emmylou Harris to Nirvana play. When there's no music, the upstairs bar and pool room are still open.

Moe's Alley (Map p451; ☎ 831-479-1854; www.moesalley.com; 1535 Commercial Way; ⌚ 4pm-2am Tue-Sun) A small casual gathering place with live bands almost every night, from jazz and blues to reggae, salsa and acoustic world-music jams.

Kuumbwa Jazz Center (Map p447; ☎ 831-427-2227; www.kuumbwajazz.org; 320 Cedar St) Hosting jazz luminaries since 1975, Kuumbwa is for serious jazz cats who come for the big-name performers and intimate room.

Blue Lagoon (Map p447; ⌚ 831-423-7117; 923 Pacific Ave) Chicks invaded this gay dance club to escape the aggro stares of straight dudes, but the dudes soon followed, and now there's hardly a gay boy in sight. The crowd varies with the night's theme, ranging from comedy to hip hop to goth industrial.

Downtown, **Nickelodeon Theatre** (Map p447; ☎ 831-426-7500; www.thenick.com; 210 Lincoln St) shows indie and foreign films, while its sister, the landmark **Del Mar Theatre** (Map p447; ☎ 831-469-3220; 1124 Pacific Ave), shows art-house and midnight movies.

Shopping

Wander Pacific Ave and its side streets to find one-of-a-kind, locally owned boutiques (not just bong shops, we promise).

O'Neill Surf Shop (Map p447; ☎ 831-469-4377; 110 Cooper St) This is the mother ship for SC's own internationally popular brand of surf wear and gear. Also on the beach boardwalk (p444).

Bugaboo Mountain Sports (Map p447; ☎ 831-429-6300; 1521 Pacific Ave) Name-brand outdoor gear and clothing; owned by the same ecoconscious folks at **Scout** (Map p447; ☎ 831-427-3425; 1517 Pacific Ave), a cool women's activewear boutique that also sells handmade jewelry.

Donnelly Fine Chocolates (Map p451; ☎ 831-458-2414; 1509 Mission St) The Willy Wonka of Santa Cruz makes stratospherically priced chocolates on par with the big city. This guy is an alchemist! Try the cardamom truffles.

Getting There & Around

Santa Cruz is 75 miles south of San Francisco, via I-280 and Hwy 85 to Hwy 17, a fast-moving, often perilous route. Monterey is a 50-minute drive south of Santa Cruz via Hwy 1.

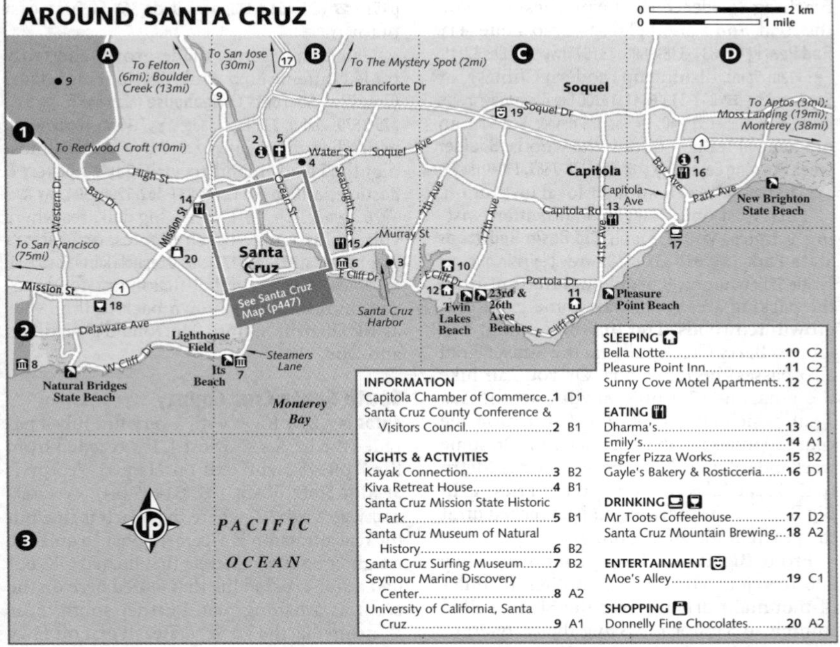

The **Greyhound bus station** (Map p447; ☎ 831-423-1800; 425 Front St), next to Metro Center, offers several daily runs to San Francisco ($13 to $17, 2½ to three hours), Salinas ($11 to $15, 65 minutes) and Los Angeles ($39 to $79, 8¾ to 10½ hours).

Santa Cruz Experience (☎ 831-419-2642) runs private shuttles to/from the airports at San Jose ($70) and San Francisco ($110); add $20 per extra passenger.

Santa Cruz Metro (☎ 831-425-8600; www.scmtd.com) runs frequent Hwy 17 express buses between Santa Cruz and San Jose's CalTrain/Amtrak station ($4, 50 minutes). Metro also operates extensive local and countywide bus services (tickets $1.50, day pass $4.50). Most routes converge on the **Metro Center** (Map p447), downtown between Pacific Ave and Front St.

Bus	Destination
3B	Mission St & Natural Bridges State Beach
7	Downtown, beach boardwalk & Lighthouse Field
35	Felton & Boulder Creek, limited service to Big Basin State Park
40 & 42	Davenport & North Coast beaches
69	Capitola

AROUND SANTA CRUZ

Santa Cruz Mountains

Between Santa Cruz and the Silicon Valley, winding Hwy 9 is a 35-mile backwoods byway through the Santa Cruz Mountains, passing tiny towns, vineyards (estate-bottled Pinot Noir is a specialty) and verdant redwood parks. Unlike on daredevil Hwy 17, the pace is slow, so budget at least a half-day for this detour. Most wineries are open on Saturday afternoons, with only a few open daily. Pick up a winery map at Vinocruz (opposite).

Heading north from Santa Cruz, it's 6 miles to Felton, passing through **Henry Cowell Redwoods State Park** (☎ 831-335-7077; per vehicle $6), which has miles of hiking trails through old-growth redwood groves along the San Lorenzo River. In Felton, **Roaring Camp Railroads** (☎ 831-335-4484; www.roaringcamp.com; Graham Hill Rd, off Mt Hermon Rd; adult/child from $20/14) operates narrow-gauge steam trains up into the redwoods and a standard-gauge train down to the Santa Cruz Beach Boardwalk (p444). On-site parking costs $7; train schedules vary.

Seven miles further north on Hwy 9, you'll pass through the village of Ben Lomond before reaching **Boulder Creek**, the prettiest town on the road, and a good place to grab a bite. Try **Red Pearl** (☎ 831-338-9800; 13151 Hwy 9; mains $7-15; ⏲ 11am-9pm), dishing up modern Chinese, or **Scopazzi's** (☎ 831-338-6441; 13300 Big Basin Way; mains lunch $8-17, dinner $24-40; ⏲ lunch & dinner Wed-Sun), an old-school Italian joint in the woods. **Boulder Creek Brewing Company** (☎ 831-338-7882; 13040 Hwy 9; ⏲ 11:30am-10:30pm) is another local institution.

Turn west onto Hwy 236 and, after twisting 9 miles, you'll reach **Big Basin Redwoods State Park** (☎ 831-338-8860; www.bigbasin.org; per vehicle $6), where a 0.6-mile nature trail from the parking area loops past some giant old-growth redwoods. The 10.5-mile round-trip loop to Berry Creek Falls via the Sunset Trail also passes the redwoods. Or you can hike the amazing 12.5-mile Skyline to the Sea Trail, which ends at Waddell Beach on the coast 20 miles north of Santa Cruz. On some weekends, if you check the Santa Cruz Metro (p451) schedules carefully, you can ride up to Big Basin in the morning and get picked up at the beach in the afternoon.

From Big Basin, loop around on Hwy 236 to rejoin Hwy 9. It's another 15 miles of mountain driving over the Skyline Blvd summit to Saratoga, passing the early-20th-century **Hakone Gardens** (☎ 408-741-4994; www.hakone.com; 2100 Big Basin Way; adult/child $5/3.50; ⏲ 10am-5pm Mon-Fri, 11am-5pm Sat & Sun), where walking paths lead past a traditional Japanese teahouse and tall bamboo groves.

CENTRAL COAST

Capitola

pop 9950 / elev 50ft

Five miles east of Santa Cruz, the little seaside town of Capitola, nestled quaintly between ocean bluffs, attracts affluent crowds less inclined to hold drum circles on the beach. Downtown is for strolling, with arty shops and touristy restaurants inside attractive houses. Streets can get crowded, and parking is a nightmare on weekends; in summer, try the parking lot behind City Hall, off Capitola Ave at Riverview Dr.

The **Capitola Chamber of Commerce** (Map p451; ☎ 831-475-6522; www.capitolachamber.com; Suite G, 716 Capitola Ave) has local tips, as well as info about mid-September's **Capitola Art & Wine Festival** and the famous **Begonia Festival** (☎ 831-476-3566), held over Labor Day weekend, with a flotilla of floral floats on Soquel Creek.

With blufftop campsites backed by Monterey pines, **New Brighton State Beach** (Map p451; ☎ 831-464-6330; per vehicle $6) is just east of town.

Catch an organic, shade-grown and fairly traded caffeine buzz while overlooking Soquel Creek at **Mr Toots Coffeehouse** (Map p451; ☎ 831-475-3679; 2nd fl, 231 Esplanade; ⏲ 7:30am-10pm; wi-fi), which has an art gallery and live music almost nightly. Head inland to visit **Gayle's Bakery & Rosticceria** (Map p451; ☎ 831-462-1200; 504 Bay Ave; ⏲ 6:30am-8:30pm; 👶), with a big deli area where you can assemble beach picnics, or **Dharma's** (Map p451; ☎ 831-462-1717; 4250 Capitola Rd; mains $5-11; ⏲ 8am-9pm; Ⓥ), a global-fusion fast-food vegetarian restaurant, known back in the 1980s as McDharma's, until McDonald's sued 'em and won.

South Santa Cruz County

Aptos is a tiny town with a very fun July 4 parade (the USA's shortest!). It's reached from the Aptos/Seacliff exit on Hwy 1. Nearby is **Seacliff State Beach** (☎ 831-685-6442; www.parks.ca.gov; per vehicle $6), where the beach is fine but the real attraction is a 'cement boat,' a quixotic freighter built of concrete that floated OK, but had a star-crossed life that ended here on the coast as a fishing pier. Further south, near Watsonville, the La Selva Beach exit off Hwy 1 leads to **Manresa State Beach** (☎ 831-761-1975; per vehicle $6) and **Sunset State Beach** (☎ 831-763-7062; per vehicle $6), where you might have miles of sand and surf all to yourself. All three state beaches have popular **campgrounds** (☎ reservations 800-444-7275; www.reserveamerica.com; tent & RV sites $25-35).

Moss Landing & Elkhorn Slough

Hwy 1 returns to the coast at Moss Landing, just south of the county line. There are interesting antiques shops, some good seafood and Mexican cafés, and a working fishing harbor – all in the unfortunate shadow of a power plant. **Sanctuary Cruises** (☎ 831-917-1046, tickets 800-979-3370; www.sanctuarycruises.com; tours adult/child from $40/30) operates year-round whale-watching and dolphin-spotting cruises led by experienced naturalists; the biodiesel boat tours last three to five hours.

A few miles further east, **Elkhorn Slough National Estuarine Research Reserve** (☎ 831-728-2822; www.elkhornslough.org; admission free, trail fee per adult $2.50; 1700 Elkhorn Rd, Watsonville; ⏲ 9am-5pm Wed-Sun) is popular with bird-watchers and hikers. Docent-led tours are offered at 10am and 1pm on Saturday and Sunday. Kayaking is a fan-

A GRAND CANYON UNDER THE SEA

Starting only a few hundred yards offshore from Moss Landing, the Monterey Canyon plummets to a depth of almost 10,000ft. A mile deep, this submarine canyon is about the same size as the Grand Canyon. Some scientists believe that, like the Grand Canyon, it also may have been carved by the Colorado River during ancient times. In summer the upwelling currents carry cold water from this deep canyon, sending a rich supply of nutrients up toward the surface level to feed the bay's diverse marine life. These frigid currents also account for the bay's lower water temperatures and the gloomy fog that often blankets the peninsula in summer.

tastic way to see the slough, though not on a windy day; contact Kayak Connection (p447) or Monterey Bay Kayaks (p458) for rentals and tours. **Elkhorn Slough Safari** (☎ 831-633-5555; www.elkhornslough.com; adult/child $32/24) takes photographers, bird-watchers and sea-otter fans on pontoon-boat nature tours.

MONTEREY

pop 30,200 / elev 60ft

Monterey, together with its laid-back neighbor Pacific Grove and posh Carmel to the south, form the Monterey Peninsula, a place most famous for its beauty, golf and art galleries. What draws many tourists to Monterey is its giant aquarium, overlooking the Monterey Bay National Marine Sanctuary, which protects dense kelp forests and a sublime variety of marine life. The city also possesses the most well-preserved evidence of the state's Spanish and Mexican periods, with many restored adobe buildings open for exploring. An afternoon's wander through the town's historic quarter promises to be more edifying than time spent in the tourist ghettos of Fisherman's Wharf and Cannery Row. A snorkeling excursion on the bay? Even better.

History

The Ohlone tribe, who had been on the peninsula since around 500 BC, may have spotted Spanish explorer Juan Rodríguez Cabrillo, the first European visitor, who sailed by in 1542. He was followed in 1602 by Sebastián Vizcaíno, who landed near the site of today's downtown Monterey and named it after his patron, the Count of Monte Rey.

A long hiatus followed before the Spanish returned in 1770 to establish Monterey as their first presidio in Alta (Upper) California. The expedition was led by conquistador Gaspar de Portolá and accompanied by Franciscan priest and mission founder Junípero Serra. A year later, Serra decided to separate church and state by moving the mission to Carmel, partly so that Native American neophytes would be further away from the corrupting influences of Spanish soldiers.

Monterey briefly became the capital of Alta California after Mexico broke from Spain in 1821. In this bustling international port, East Coast Yankees mixed with Russian fur traders and merchant seafarers carrying exotic goods from China. The stars and stripes were temporarily raised over Monterey in 1842 when Commodore Thomas Jones, hearing a rumor that war had been declared between Mexico and the USA, took the town. When war actually broke out in 1846, the American takeover signaled an abrupt change in the town's fortunes, for San Jose briefly became the state capital, and then the 1849 Gold Rush made everyone run for the Sierra Nevada foothills.

Monterey spent the next three decades as a forgotten backwater, eking out an existence from whaling. After railway entrepreneurs built a luxurious hotel, wealthy San Franciscans rediscovered Monterey as a vacation getaway. At the same time, fishermen began capitalizing on the rich marine life of the bay. By the 1930s, Cannery Row had made the port the 'Sardine Capital of the World,' but overfishing and climatic changes caused the industry's sudden collapse in the 1950s. More recently, locals have netted schools of tourists who visit Monterey in greater numbers each year.

Orientation & Information

Monterey's historic downtown is a compact area surrounding Alvarado St, which ends with Portola and Custom House plazas, near Fisherman's Wharf. This area is known as Old Monterey, as distinguished from Cannery Row, about a mile northwest. From Cannery Row, Lighthouse Ave segues west into Pacific Grove (p461).

Doctors on Duty (☎ 831-649-0770; 501 Lighthouse Ave; 8am-8pm Mon-Sat, 8am-6pm Sun) Walk-in, nonemergency medical clinic.

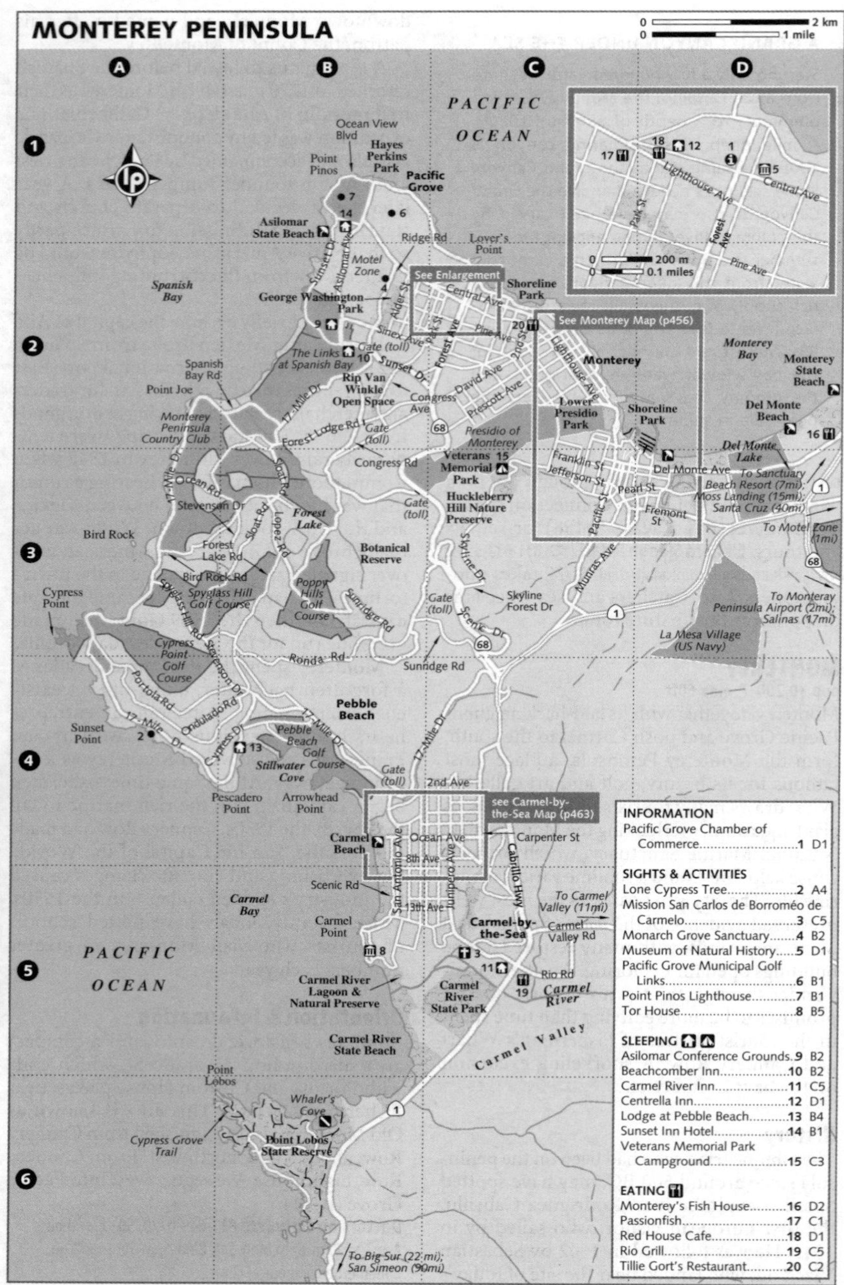

MONTEREY PENINSULA
0 2 km
0 1 mile
PACIFIC OCEAN
Ocean View Blvd
Point Pinos
Hayes Perkins Park
Pacific Grove
Asilomar State Beach
Sunset Dr
Asilomar Ave
Ridge Rd
Lover's Point
Motel Zone
Spanish Bay
George Washington Park
See Enlargement
Central Ave
Shoreline Park
Alder St
Park St
Forest Ave
Pine Ave
2nd St
Sinex Ave
The Links at Spanish Bay
Gate (toll)
Sunset Dr
Spanish Bay Rd
Point Joe
17-Mile Dr
Rip Van Winkle Open Space
Congress Ave
David Ave
Prescott Ave
Monterey Peninsula Country Club
Forest Lodge Rd
Gate (toll)
Presidio of Monterey
Congress Rd
Veterans Memorial Park
Sloat Rd
Ocean Rd
Stevenson Dr
Forest Lake
Huckleberry Hill Nature Preserve
Gate (toll)
Lopez Rd
Bird Rock
Forest Lake Rd
Botanical Reserve
Skyline Dr
Bird Rock Rd
Spyglass Hill Golf Course
Poppy Hills Golf Course
Sunridge Rd
Gate (toll)
Skyline Forest Dr
Cypress Point
Scenic Dr
Cypress Point Golf Course
Stevenson Dr
Ronda Rd
Sunridge Rd
Portola Rd
Onduldado Rd
Pebble Beach
Sunset Point
17-Mile Dr
Cypress Dr
Pebble Beach Golf Course
Stillwater Cove
Gate (toll)
2nd Ave
Pescadero Point
Arrowhead Point
see Carmel-by-the-Sea Map (p463)
Carmel Beach
Ocean Ave
Carpenter St
8th Ave
San Antonio Ave
Junipero Ave
Cabrillo Hwy
Scenic Rd
13th Ave
To Carmel Valley (11mi)
Carmel Bay
Carmel Point
Carmel-by-the-Sea
Carmel Valley Rd
PACIFIC OCEAN
Rio Rd
Carmel River
Carmel River Lagoon & Natural Preserve
Carmel River State Park
Carmel River State Beach
Carmel Valley
Point Lobos
Whaler's Cove
Cypress Grove Trail
Point Lobos State Reserve
To Big Sur (22 mi); San Simeon (90mi)
See Monterey Map (p456)
Monterey
Lighthouse Ave
Lower Presidio Park
Shoreline Park
Franklin St
Jefferson St
Del Monte Ave
Pearl St
Pacific St
Fremont St
Munras Ave
Monterey Bay
Monterey State Beach
Del Monte Beach
Del Monte Lake
To Sanctuary Beach Resort (7mi); Moss Landing (15mi); Santa Cruz (40mi)
To Motel Zone (1mi)
To Monteray Peninsula Airport (2mi); Salinas (17mi)
La Mesa Village (US Navy)
Lighthouse Ave
Central Ave
Park St
Forest Ave
Pine Ave
0 200 m
0 0.1 miles
INFORMATION
Pacific Grove Chamber of Commerce 1 D1
SIGHTS & ACTIVITIES
Lone Cypress Tree 2 A4
Mission San Carlos de Borroméo de Carmelo 3 C5
Monarch Grove Sanctuary 4 B2
Museum of Natural History 5 D1
Pacific Grove Municipal Golf Links 6 B1
Point Pinos Lighthouse 7 B1
Tor House 8 B5
SLEEPING
Asilomar Conference Grounds 9 B2
Beachcomber Inn 10 B2
Carmel River Inn 11 C5
Centrella Inn 12 D1
Lodge at Pebble Beach 13 B4
Sunset Inn Hotel 14 B1
Veterans Memorial Park Campground 15 C3
EATING
Monterey's Fish House 16 D2
Passionfish 17 C1
Red House Cafe 18 D1
Rio Grill 19 C5
Tillie Gort's Restaurant 20 C2

FedEx Office (☎ 831-373-2298; 799 Lighthouse Ave; per min 20-30¢; ⏰ 7am-10pm) High-speed internet workstations.
Monterey Bay Aquarium (☎ 831-648-4888; 886 Cannery Row) Has free public wi-fi.
Monterey County Visitors Center (☎ 888-221-1010; www.montereyinfo.org; 401 Camino El Estero; ⏰ 9am-5pm) Tourist brochures, maps and a free phone system for checking lodging availability.
Police (☎ 831-646-3914; 351 Madison St; ⏰ 24hr) For nonemergencies.
Post Office (☎ 800-275-8777) Main (565 Hartnell St; ⏰ 8:30am-5pm Mon-Fri, 10am-2pm Sat); Cannery Row (686 Lighthouse Ave; ⏰ 9:30am-12:30pm & 1-3pm Mon-Fri)

Sights

MONTEREY BAY AQUARIUM

Monterey's most mesmerizing experience is a visit to the ginormous **aquarium** (☎ 831-648-4888; www.montereybayaquarium.org; 886 Cannery Row; adult/child $25/16; ⏰ 10am-6pm, extended summer hours; 👪), built on the former site of the city's largest sardine cannery. All kinds of aquatic creatures are on proud display, from kid-tolerant sea stars and slimy sea slugs to animated sea otters and surprisingly nimble 800lb tuna. The aquarium is much more than an impressive collection of glass tanks – thoughtful placards underscore the bay's cultural and historical contexts.

Every minute, upwards of 2000 gallons of seawater are pumped into the three-story **kelp forest**, re-creating as closely as possible the natural conditions you see out the windows to the east. The large fish of prey are at their charismatic best during mealtimes; divers hand-feed at 11:30am and 4pm. More entertaining are the sea-otter-feeding sessions, at 10:30am, 1:30pm and 3:30pm. Otherwise, the otters can often be seen basking in the **Great Tide Pool** outside the aquarium, where they are readied for reintroduction to the wild.

Even new-agey music and the occasional infinity-mirror illusion don't detract from the astounding beauty of jellyfish in the **Drifter's Gallery**. To see fish – including hammerhead sharks – that outweigh you many times over, ponder the awesome **Outer Bay** tank. Throughout the aquarium there are **touch pools**, where you can get close to sea cucumbers, bat rays and various tidepool creatures. Small kids love the interactive, bilingual **Splash Zone**, where penguin feedings happen at 10:30am and 3pm.

A visit can easily become a full-day affair, so get your hand stamped so that you can break up the visit with lunch. To avoid long lines in summer and on weekends and holidays, buy **tickets** (☎ 831-648-4937, 800-756-3737) in advance via phone or online. Before you leave, pick up the wallet-sized Seafood Watch, a pocket dining guide to keeping fish and shellfish populations sustainable.

Metered on-street parking is limited, but pay lots and garages are plentiful.

MONTEREY STATE HISTORIC PARK

Old Monterey is home to an extraordinary assemblage of 19th-century brick and adobe buildings, administered as **Monterey State Historic Park** (☎ 831-649-7118; www.parks.ca.gov; admission free), all found along a 2-mile self-guided walking tour portentously called the **Path of History**. You can inspect dozens of buildings, many with charming gardens; expect some to be open while others aren't, according to a capricious schedule dictated by Governor Schwarzenegger's recent budget cuts.

Grab a free tour map and find out what's currently open at the park headquarters, inside the 1847 **Pacific House Museum** (☎ 831-649-7118; 20 Custom House Plaza; ⏰ 10am-4pm Fri-Wed, 10:30am-4pm Thu), which has in-depth exhibits covering the colorful, multicultural facets of state history. A free, docent-led, 45-minute tour of Old Monterey starts here, during which you'll pick up tidbits like how the roads of the town were once covered in crushed whalebones as protection from mud. There are also guided tours of some of the individual houses; ask for current schedules at park headquarters.

The following are just a few of the park's highlights, which also include an old whaling station, an 1850s mercantile shop, **California's first theatre** and the **Old Monterey Jail**, featured in John Steinbeck's novel *Tortilla Flat*.

Custom House

In 1822 newly independent Mexico ended the Spanish trade monopoly. At this time, it stipulated that any traders bringing goods to Alta California must first unload their cargoes at the **Custom House** (Custom House Plaza; ⏰ 10am-4pm Sat-Thu, 10:30am-4pm Fri) for duty to be assessed. Then in 1846 the American flag was raised over the Custom House, and *voilà!* – California was formally annexed from Mexico. Restored to its 1840s

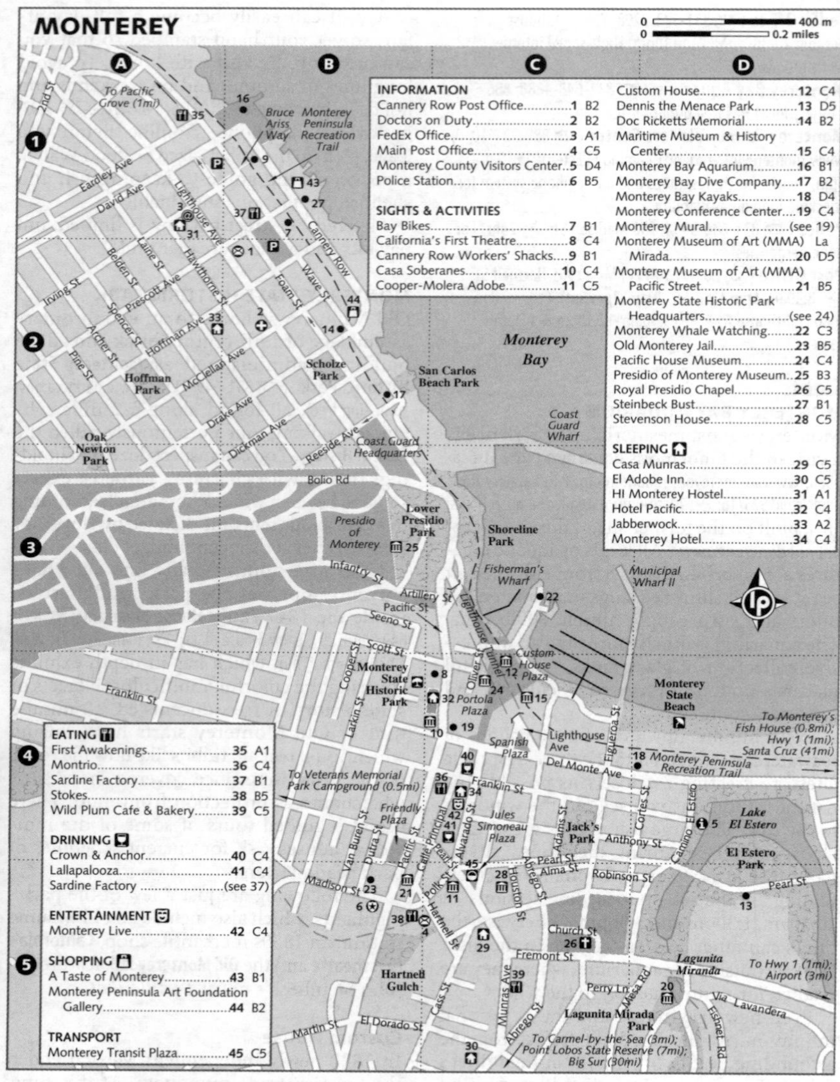

appearance, the house displays an exotic selection of goods that traders brought to exchange for California cowhides.

Casa Soberanes

A beautiful garden with meandering walkways paved with abalone shells, bottle glass and even whalebones fronts **Casa Soberanes** (336 Pacific St; hours vary), built in the 1840s during the late Mexican period. The interior is adorned with an eclectic mix of New England antiques, 19th-century goods imported on Chinese trading ships and modern Mexican folk art. Across Pacific St, the large and colorful **Monterey Mural** mosaic, on the Monterey Conference Center exterior, tells the city's history.

Stevenson House

Scottish writer Robert Louis Stevenson came to Monterey in 1879 to court his wife-to-be, Fanny Osbourne. This building, then the French Hotel, was where he stayed while reputedly devising his novel *Treasure Island*. The boarding-house rooms were pretty primitive, as Stevenson was still a penniless unknown. Today the **house** (530 Houston St; hours vary) displays a superb collection of Stevenson memorabilia.

Cooper-Molera Adobe

Starting in 1827, this stately **complex** (☎ 831-649-7111; 525 Polk St; 10am-4pm Mon-Sat, 1-4pm Sun) was built by John Rogers Cooper, a New England sea captain, and three generations of his family, who resided here until 1968. Over time, the adobe buildings were partitioned and expanded, gardens were added, and it was later willed to the National Trust, which ensures it has more regular opening hours than other places. The bookshop sells nostalgic toys and household goods; it's worth a stop.

MARITIME MUSEUM & HISTORY CENTER

Dive into local naval history, from the days of the early explorers to the 20th century, at this well-curated **museum** (☎ 831-372-2608; Stanton Center, 5 Custom House Plaza; admission free; 10am-5pm Tue-Sun). Highlights of the seafaring collection include the Fresnel lens from Point Sur Lightstation (p467), a ship-in-a-bottle collection and displays on Monterey's history, particularly the rise and rapid fall of the sardine business.

ROYAL PRESIDIO CHAPEL

Built of sandstone in 1794, this graceful **chapel** (☎ 831-373-2628; 500 Church St; admission by donation; 11am-noon & 1:15-3:15pm Fri, noon-2pm Sat, 1-3pm Sun, also 1:15-3:15pm 2nd & 4th Tue of the month), today called San Carlos Cathedral, is California's oldest continuously functioning church. The original 1770 mission church stood on this site before being moved to Carmel (see p464). Until the 1820s the presidio's fortified walls embraced pretty much the entire town. As Monterey expanded under Mexican rule, older buildings were gradually destroyed, eventually leaving behind this National Historic Landmark as the strongest reminder of the former Spanish colonial presence.

PRESIDIO OF MONTEREY MUSEUM

On the grounds of the original Spanish fort, this minor **museum** (☎ 831-646-3456; www.monterey.org; Bldg 113, Corporal Ewing Rd; admission free; 10am-1pm Mon, 10am-4pm Thu-Sat, 1-4pm Sun) is the place to learn about Monterey's history from a military perspective, covering the Native American, Mexican and American periods.

MONTEREY MUSEUM OF ART

With all of its art galleries, it's not surprising that Monterey has a respectable **art museum** (MMA; www.montereyart.org; adult/child $5/free; 11am-5pm Wed-Sat, 1-4pm Sun). You can visit both locations on the same ticket. **MMA Pacific Street** (☎ 831-372-5477; 559 Pacific St) is particularly strong in California contemporary art and modern landscape painters and photographers, including Ansel Adams and Edward Weston. **MMA La Mirada** (☎ 831-372-3689; 720 Via Mirada) inhabits a silent-film-star's villa, whose humble adobe origins are exquisitely concealed. With lovely rose and rhododendron gardens, it primarily displays selections from MMA's East Asian art collections.

CANNERY ROW

John Steinbeck's novel *Cannery Row* immortalized the sardine-canning business that Monterey lived on for the first half of the 20th century. Back in Steinbeck's day, it was a stinky, hardscrabble, working-class melting pot, which the novelist described as 'a poem, a stink, a grating noise, a quality of light, a tone, a habit, a nostalgia, a dream.' Sadly, there's precious little evidence of that era now. A bronze **bust** of the writer sits at the bottom of Prescott Ave, just steps from the unabashedly commercial experience his row has devolved into. Chockablock with chain restaurants and souvenir shops hawking saltwater taffy, there are only a few spots worth making time for, such as the **aquarium** (p455). Do check out the **Cannery Row Workers' Shacks** at the base of flowery Bruce Ariss Way, which have sobering explanations of the hard lives led by the Filipino, Japanese, Spanish and other immigrant laborers. A few blocks south, the **Doc Ricketts Memorial** (cnr Wave St & Drake Ave) marks the spot where the famous marine biologist and friend of Steinbeck died.

THE WHARVES

Like its larger namesake in San Francisco, **Fisherman's Wharf** is a tacky tourist trap at heart, and the jumping-off point for whale-watching expeditions and deep-sea fishing trips. On the flip side, the refreshingly authentic **Municipal**

Wharf II is a short walk east. There fishing boats bob and sway, painters work on their canvases, and seafood purveyors hawk fresh catches.

Activities

A must for fans of kick-ass playgrounds, **Dennis the Menace Park** (☎ 831-646-3860; 777 Pearl St; 10am-dusk, closed Tue Sep-May;) was the brainchild of Hank Ketcham, the creator of the classic comic strip. This ain't your standard dumbed-down playground, suffocated by too many Big Brother safety regulations. With lightning-fast slides, a hedge maze and towering climbing structures, even adults can't resist playing here.

WHALE-WATCHING

You can spot whales off the coast of Monterey year-round. The season for blue and humpback whales runs from late April to November, while gray whales pass by from mid-December to April. **Monterey Whale Watching** (☎ 831-372-2203, tickets 800-979-3370; www.montereywhalewatching.com; 96 Fisherman's Wharf; 2½hr tour adult/child $40/30) offers twice-daily departures. Operating out of Moss Landing, Sanctuary Cruises (p452) runs whale-watching trips on Monterey Bay in biodiesel vessels.

KAYAKING

Monterey Bay Kayaks (☎ 800-649-5357; www.montereybaykayaks.com; 693 Del Monte Ave; rentals per person per day from $30, tours adult/child from $50/30) rents equipment and offers weekend classes and natural-history tours, including full-moon paddles at Elkhorn Slough (p452).

DIVING & SNORKELING

Monterey Bay offers world-renowned diving and snorkeling, though the water is chilly. Excellent spots are off Lovers Point in Pacific Grove and at Point Lobos State Reserve (p464). Organize a scuba or snorkel trip at **Monterey Bay Dive Company** (☎ 831-656-0454; www.montereyscubadiving.com; 225 Cannery Row), which offers instruction and equipment rentals. Full standard dive outfits go for $80 per day; snorkel kits for $39 per day. Private guided tours cost from $59/89 for a one-/two-tank dive. They can also advise on snorkeling in the shallow inlets of the bay.

CYCLING & MOUNTAIN-BIKING

With stunning scenery and paved bike paths, cycling is a popular peninsula activity. Along a former railway line, the **Monterey Peninsula Recreational Trail** travels 18 car-free miles from Lovers Point in Pacific Grove along the waterfront, passing Cannery Row and downtown Monterey en route to Marina, north of town. Mountain-bikers head east to Fort Ord, which has 50 miles of single-track and fire roads; the **Sea Otter Classic** (☎ 800-218-8411; www.seaotterclassic.com) races take place there in April. Road-cycling enthusiasts with nerves of steel can make the round trip to Carmel along the **17-Mile Drive** (see the boxed text, p462).

For maps, rentals and advice, visit **Bay Bikes** (☎ 831-655-2453; www.baybikes.com; 585 Cannery Row; rentals per hr/day/week from $8/36/100).

Festivals & Events

AT&T Pebble Beach National Pro-Am (☎ 831-644-1533; www.attpbgolf.com) Famous golf tournament mixing pros and celebrities in late January or early February.

Marina International Festival of the Winds (www.marinafestival.com) Kite-flying, hang gliding and family-friendly fun on Mother's Day weekend in early May.

Artichoke Festival (☎ 831-633-2465; www.artichoke-festival.org) North of Monterey, Castroville's 'green' celebration features 3D 'agro art' sculptures, cooking demos, a farmers market and field tours in mid-May.

Red Bull US Grand Prix (☎ 831-648-5111; www.laguna-seca.com) The largest motorcycle race on the continent, at the Mazda Laguna Seca Raceway in late July.

Monterey Bay Strawberry Festival (☎ 831-724-3900; www.mbsf.com) Berry-licious pie-eating contests and live bands in Watsonville during mid-August.

Monterey County Fair (☎ 831-372-5863; www.montereycountyfair.com) Old-fashioned carnival fun, sand-sculpture and livestock competitions, cooking demos and live music at the fairgrounds in mid-August.

Concours d'Elegance (☎ 831-622-1700; www.pebblebeachconcours.net) Classic cars at Pebble Beach; mid-August.

Monterey Jazz Festival (☎ 831-373-3366; www.montereyjazzfestival.org) One of the world's longest-running jazz festivals (since 1954), held every September.

Monterey Wine Festival (☎ 800-422-0251; www.montereywine.com) Nonprofit wine-tasting shindig at the fairgrounds and aquarium in October.

Sleeping

Book ahead for summer visits; special events can also sell out the town in advance. Inexpensive chain motels are found south of downtown along Munras St and on N Fremont St, a couple of miles east of downtown, off Hwy 1. To avoid the tourist congestion and jacked-up prices of Cannery Row, also consider staying in Pacific Grove (p461).

Veterans Memorial Park Campground (Map p454; ☎ 831-646-3865; Veterans Memorial Park, off Skyline Dr; tent & RV sites $25-30, walk-ins $5) Tucked into the forest, this municipal campground has 40 well-kept, grassy, nonreservable sites near nature-preserve hiking trails. Amenities include hot showers, flush toilets, water and firepits, but no hookups. Three-night maximum stay.

HI Monterey Hostel (☎ 831-649-0375; www.montereyhostel.org; 778 Hawthorne St; dm $25-28, d $59-65; reception 8-10:30am & 5-10pm;) This well-run, basic hostel is just blocks from the aquarium and Cannery Row. Stuff yourself silly with breakfast pancakes, then gather on the outdoor barbecue patio for DIY dinners. Reservations strongly recommended. Take bus 1 from the Transit Plaza.

El Adobe Inn (☎ 831-372-5409; www.el-adobe-inn.com; 936 Munras Ave; r $75-125; wi-fi) This roadside motel offers basic accommodation with just a bit of charm. Rates include continental breakfast and use of a hot tub. It has a few cheapie motel neighbors as well, like the Super 8. Pet fee $15.

Monterey Hotel (☎ 831-375-3184, 800-727-0960; www.montereyhotel.com; 406 Alvarado St; r $119-309) Fresh off a centennial renovation, this 1904 hotel is in the heart of downtown. Its 64 Victorian-style rooms, which can be small and noisy, have old-world features like plantation shutters and hand-carved furniture. Book online for the lowest rates. Free wi-fi in common areas. Parking $5.

our pick **Sanctuary Beach Resort** (off Map p454; ☎ 831-883-9478, 877-944-3863; www.thesanctuarybeachresort.com; 3295 Dunes Dr, Marina; r $144-434; wi-fi) Be lulled to sleep by the surf at this low-lying retreat, hidden in the sand dunes north of Monterey. Townhouses harbor petite suites and rooms with gas fireplaces, kitchenettes and binoculars to borrow for whale-watching. The beach is off-limits because it's a recovering natural preserve, but there are plenty of nearby hiking trails. To further minimize the environmental impact, cars are not allowed in certain areas of the resort – but don't worry, because guests get an electric golf cart to tool around in.

Casa Munras (☎ 831-375-2411, 800-222-2446; www.hotelcasamunras.com; 700 Munras Ave; d $159-399; wi-fi) Built around an adobe hacienda once owned by a 19th-century Spanish colonial don, this historic downtown boutique hotel has chic modern rooms with lofty beds and some fireplaces. Splash in the heated outdoor pool, unwind at the tapas bar or take a sea-salt scrub in the tranquil spa. Pet-friendly.

Jabberwock (☎ 831-372-4777, 888-428-7253; www.jabberwockinn.com; 598 Laine St; r $169-299; wi-fi) High atop a hill and barely visible through a shroud of foliage, this 1911 Arts and Crafts house hums a playful *Alice in Wonderland* tune through its seven immaculate rooms – notice the book clock near the front door. Over a full gourmet breakfast, ask about the house's many salvaged architectural elements.

Hotel Pacific (☎ 831-373-5700, 800-554-5542; www.hotelpacific.com; 300 Pacific St; ste $185-409; wi-fi) This romantic small hotel offers green gardens, polished service and spacious suites outfitted with Spanish-style furniture, feather beds, large fireplaces, kitchenettes and private balconies or patios. Rates include continental breakfast and afternoon cheese and fruit.

Eating

Beyond Cannery Row, Lighthouse Ave is lined with budget-friendly, multiethnic eateries, from Japanese sushi to Hawaiian barbecue to Middle Eastern kebabs. Alternatively, you could keep going west to Pacific Grove (p461).

First Awakenings (☎ 831-372-1125; 125 Oceanview Blvd; mains $5-11; 7am-2pm Mon-Fri, 7am-2:30pm Sat & Sun;) Sweet and savory all-American breakfasts and lunches, plus bottomless pitchers of coffee, merrily weigh down outdoor tables at this hideaway café inside an outlet mall near the aquarium.

Wild Plum Cafe & Bakery (☎ 831-646-3109; 731 Munras Ave; mains $6-11; 7am-6:30pm Tue-Fri, 7am-5pm Mon & Sat;) Locals crowd into this friendly little sidewalk café for bountiful egg breakfasts, seasonal soups from scratch, and sandwiches on homemade bread with fillings like grilled chicken with roasted peppers, all made with lots of local, organic produce. Take-out box lunches available.

Monterey's Fish House (Map p454; ☎ 831-373-4647; 2114 Del Monte Ave, mains $12-35; lunch Mon-Fri, dinner daily) Watched over by photos of Sicilian fishermen, here you can dig into spanking-fresh seafood with an occasional Asian twist. Reservations are essential (it's *so* crowded), but Hawaiian shirts seem to be de rigueur for gentlemen. Try the barbecued oysters or, for those stout of heart, the Mexican squid steak.

Stokes (☎ 831-373-1110; 500 Hartnell St; mains $15-29; ⌚ dinner) Inside a beautifully restored old adobe furnished to evoke the Mexican era, a hit-or-miss Cal-Mediterranean menu focuses on rich, rustic flavors using local ingredients. Crab and steak are specialties but look for more complex and creative dishes too, using local, seasonal and often organic ingredients.

Montrio (☎ 831-648-8880; 414 Calle Principal; mains $15-30; ⌚ dinner;) Occupying a 1910 firehouse, Montrio looks dolled up with leather walls and iron trellises, but the tables have butcher paper and crayons for kids. The changeable menu mixes mostly organic fare with European bistro flair, often in tapas-sized portions.

Sardine Factory (☎ 831-373-3775; 701 Wave St; mains $20-47; ⌚ dinner) This 40-year-old institution prepares steaks and seafood, but its real strengths are its atmosphere and wine list. Each of the dining rooms is ornately and uniquely decorated, but the glass-domed conservatory is a fave. Still, it's overpriced. Consider ordering something simple off the tapas menu and a glass of wine at the bar instead.

Drinking & Entertainment

For comprehensive entertainment listings, pick up the free tabloid *Monterey County Weekly* (www.montereycountyweekly.com).

Crown & Anchor (☎ 831-649-6496; 150 W Franklin St) In the basement of this British pub, the first thing you'll notice is the red plaid carpeting. But these blokes know their way around a bar – there are plentiful single malts and draft beers, not to mention damn fine fish-and-chips.

Sardine Factory (☎ 831-373-3775; 701 Wave St) The legendary restaurant's lounge makes it worth venturing to Cannery Row after dark for the views, an exquisite selection of wines by the glass and live piano most nights.

Lallapalooza (☎ 831-645-9036; 474 Alvarado St) This hip resto-bar, with bold, splashy, contemporary art on the walls, is known for its selection of martinis, tequilas and Monterey County wines. It's most popular after work.

Monterey Live (☎ 831-375-5483; www.montereylive.org; 414 Alvarado St) This small historic adobe has become an intimate, low-ceilinged, cabaret-style theater where you can hear local blues, jazz and other varied talents, including comedians.

Shopping

Avoid the tourist traps on Cannery Row, although nearby antiques shops are worth browsing.

Monterey Peninsula Art Foundation Gallery (☎ 831-655-1267; 425 Cannery Row; ⌚ 11am-5pm) Just outside the tourist-shop danger zone, over two dozen local artists working in all media have banded together to sell their wares. A few can even be found painting away right outside.

A Taste of Monterey (☎ 831-646-5446; www.tastemonterey.com; tasting fee $10-15; 700 Cannery Row; ⌚ 11am-6pm) Tipple vintages from as far away as the Santa Lucia Highlands at this county wine shop, with thoughtful exhibits on barrel-making and cork production. The tasting room has panoramic sea-view windows.

Getting There & Around

Monterey is 120 miles south of San Francisco via Hwys 101 and 156, or a 50-minute drive from Santa Cruz via scenic Hwy 1.

About 4 miles southeast of downtown off Hwy 68, **Monterey Peninsula Airport** (MRY; ☎ 831-648-7000; www.montereyairport.com; Olmsted Rd) has flights with American Eagle (LAX), United (LAX and San Francisco) and Allegiant Air (Las Vegas). Major car-rental firms are at the airport.

Monterey/Salinas Airbus (☎ 831-373-7777; www.montereyairbus.com) links Monterey with airports in San Jose and San Francisco several times daily ($35 to $45).

If you don't fly or drive, getting to Monterey can be tricky. The best you can do is take a Greyhound bus or Amtrak train to Salinas (see p481), 20 miles east of Monterey, then catch a Monterey-Salinas Transit bus.

Monterey-Salinas Transit (MST; ☎ 831-899-2555, 888-678-2871; www.mst.org) operates local and regional buses. Routes converge at the **Monterey Transit Plaza** (cnr Pearl & Alvarado Sts). Fares start at $2 per ride (day pass $4.50) and rise depending on the distance covered.

Bus	Destination
1	Cannery Row & Pacific Grove
4 & 5	Carmel
20 & 21	Salinas
22	Big Sur via Carmel (weekends only Labor Day to Memorial Day)
24	Carmel Valley
55	San Jose via Gilroy

Between late May and early September, you can hop aboard the free Wave trolley bus that loops around downtown, Fisherman's Wharf and Cannery Row from 10am to 7pm Monday to Friday, and till 8pm on Saturday and Sunday.

PACIFIC GROVE

pop 15,300 / elev 125ft

Pacific Grove (aka PG) is a tranquil seaside community that began as a Methodist summer retreat in 1875 and maintained a quaint, holier-than-thou attitude until well into the 20th century – as California's last remaining 'dry' town, the selling of liquor was illegal here until 1969. Today, leafy streets lined by stately Victorian homes make a perfect respite from the Monterey-Carmel hubbub. In winter PG hosts swarms of monarch butterflies, which make their migratory homes in local pine groves.

PG's charmingly compact downtown, with its eclectic boutiques and antiques shops, centers on Lighthouse and Forest Aves. The **chamber of commerce** (Map p454; ☎ 831-373-3304, 800-656-6650; www.pacificgrove.org; cnr Central & Forest Aves; 9:30am-5pm Mon-Fri, 10am-3pm Sat) dispenses information.

Sights & Activities

Aptly named **Ocean View Blvd** affords views from Lover's Point west to Point Pinos, where the road becomes the appropriately named **Sunset Dr**, with numerous turnouts where you can enjoy the pounding surf, rocky outcrops and teeming tidepools. The entire route is great for walking or cycling; some think it surpasses the 17-Mile Dr (see the boxed text, p462) for beauty, and it's free.

On the tip of the Monterey Peninsula, at the northwestern end of Lighthouse Ave, humble-looking **Point Pinos Lighthouse** (Map p454; ☎ 831-648-5716; adult/child $2/1; 1-4pm Thu-Mon) is the oldest continuously operating lighthouse on the West Coast. It has been warning ships off this hazardous point since 1855. Inside are exhibits on its history and its failures – local shipwrecks. It's an excellent spot for whale-watching from December to April. The lighthouse grounds overlook the **Pacific Grove Municipal Golf Links** (Map p454; ☎ 831-648-5775; 77 Asilomar Ave; greens fees $20-45), where black-tailed deer freely range.

If you're in town during monarch season (roughly October to March), the best place to see them cluster by the millions is at the **Monarch Grove Sanctuary** (Map p454; ☎ 831-648-5716; Ridge Rd; admission free; dawn-dusk), a thicket of trees off Lighthouse Ave.

With a gray whale sculpture out front, PG's **Museum of Natural History** (Map p454; ☎ 831-648-5716; www.pgmuseum.org; 165 Forest Ave; admission free; 10am-5pm Tue-Sat;) has old-fashioned exhibits about Big Sur, Native American tribes, sea otters, coastal bird life and butterflies. It's often overrun by schoolkids.

Sleeping

Modest motels cluster at the western end of Lighthouse Ave. B&Bs have taken over many historic mansions around downtown and by the beach.

Asilomar Conference Grounds (Map p454; ☎ 831-372-8016, 866-654-2878; www.visitasilomar.com; 800 Asilomar Ave; d $105-195;) Sprawling over more than 100 acres of sand dunes and pine forests, this state-park conference center is a find. Skip ho-hum motel rooms for historic houses designed by early-20th-century architect Julia Morgan, where cozy, hardwood-floored rooms share a sociable fireplace lounge. Wi-fi in lobby.

Beachcomber Inn (Map p454; ☎ 831-373-4769; www.montereypeninsulainns.com; 1996 Sunset Dr; r $127-207;) It's hard to find a motel today run by such friendly folks, let alone one with such comfy beds. It's an easy stroll over to the beach, or you can borrow a bicycle for free; some rooms even have decks overlooking the dunes. Rates include an extended continental breakfast. The famous seafood restaurant next door (with different owners) is only so-so.

Sunset Inn Hotel (Map p454; ☎ 831-375-3529; www.gosunsetinn.com; 133 Asilomar Blvd; d $159-229) At this small motor lodge near the golf course and the beach, the attentive staff will check you into luxuriously redesigned rooms that have king-sized beds. Some are equipped with hot tubs and fireplaces. Wi-fi in common areas.

Centrella Inn (Map p454; ☎ 831-372-3372, 800-233-3372; www.centrellainn.com; 612 Central Ave; d $149-309; wi-fi) For a romantic night inside a Victorian seaside mansion, this turreted National Historic Landmark is dreamy, with enchanting gardens and a player piano. Some of the stately rooms have fireplaces, clawfoot tubs and kitchenettes. Rates include a gourmet breakfast buffet and afternoon refreshments.

Eating

Tillie Gort's Restaurant (Map p454; ☎ 831-373-0335; 111 Central Ave; mains $6-15; 11am-10pm; V) This 1960s veteran is still true to its hippie roots.

There are tons of vegetarian items on the menu, with global inspiration. Portions are hearty and the desserts are all-out decadent. It's not far from the aquarium.

Red House Cafe (Map p454; ☎ 831-643-1060; 662 Lighthouse Ave; mains $6-16; breakfast Sat & Sun, lunch & dinner Tue-Sun;) Always crowded with locals, this 1895 shingled house dishes up comfort food with delightful haute touches, from cinnamon-brioche French toast for breakfast to blue-cheese soufflés and grilled lamb at dinner. Exceptional European tea list.

our pick **Passionfish** (Map p454; ☎ 831-655-3311; www.passionfish.net; 701 Lighthouse Ave; mains $17-24; dinner) Fresh, sustainable seafood is served any number of inventive ways, like the Alaskan halibut with cilantro citrus sauce and garlic noodles. The menu also carries slow-cooked meats and locally grown vegetables. The earth-tone decor is spare, not distracting from the food, and tables are squeezed so close together that strangers may become fast friends. A pages-long wine list is priced at retail, and for tea lovers, there are twice as many Chinese teas as wines by the glass.

Getting There & Around

MST (p460) bus 1 shuttles between downtown Monterey, Cannery Row and Pacific Grove every half hour from 6:15am to 10:15pm daily.

CARMEL-BY-THE-SEA

pop 4040 / elev 200ft

The town's hyphenation distinguishes it from the inland Carmel Valley and the Carmel Highlands just south, but as everyone knows, there's really only one Carmel. Founded as a seaside resort in the 1880s, Carmel quickly attracted famous artists and writers, such as Sinclair Lewis and Jack London, and their hangers-on. The artistic flavor survives in

17-MILE DRIVE

Pacific Grove and Carmel are linked by the spectacularly scenic 17-Mile Dr, which meanders through Pebble Beach, a private resort and residential area that symbolizes the peninsula's jaw-dropping wealth. It's no chore staying within the 25mph limit – every curve in the road reveals another postcard vista, especially when wildflowers bloom. Expect to share the road with cyclists, some a bit wobbly on their wheels.

The drive is open sunrise to sunset, and entry is controlled by the **Pebble Beach Company** (☎ 831-647-7500; www.pebblebeach.com; per vehicle $9.25, bicycles free). Your entry fee can be applied as a discount on any minimum $25 food purchase you make later at restaurants in Pebble Beach. There are five gates; for the most scenic portion, enter the Pacific Grove Gate off Sunset Dr and exit at the Carmel Gate.

Using the map provided when you enter, you can easily pick out landmarks such as **Spanish Bay**, where explorer Gaspar de Portolá dropped anchor in 1769; treacherously rocky **Point Joe**, which in the past was often mistaken for the entrance to Monterey Bay and thus became the site of several shipwrecks; and **Bird Rock**, which is a bird and seal haven. The ostensible pièce de résistance of the drive is the **Lone Cypress**, the trademarked symbol of the Pebble Beach Company that perches on a seaward rock. The tree's already more than 250 years old, and is now reinforced with wire supports, which fortunately aren't that visible in photographs.

Besides the coast, the real attractions here are the world-famous **golf courses** such as Spyglass Hill, Cypress Point and, of course, Pebble Beach, where a celebrity and pro golf tournament (p458) happens in February. It's easy to picture Don Cheadle driving down the spectacular 18th hole for a victory.

The renowned **Lodge at Pebble Beach** (Map p454; ☎ 831-624-3811, 800-654-9300; www.pebblebeach.com; 1700 17-Mile Dr; r from $675; wi-fi) boasts a world-class spa, restaurants and extravagant shops where the most demanding of tastes are catered to. Even if you're not a trust-fund baby, you can still soak up the atmosphere in the art-filled public spaces and at the café.

Cycling 17-Mile Dr is enormously popular, but try to do it during the week, when traffic isn't as heavy. There's no shoulder on the road, so keep your wits about you. On weekends the flow of bikes goes primarily north to south. While not illegal, doing the ride from Carmel to Pacific Grove on weekends is discouraged, and is harder on drivers and cyclists alike. For rental shops in Monterey, see p458.

CENTRAL COAST

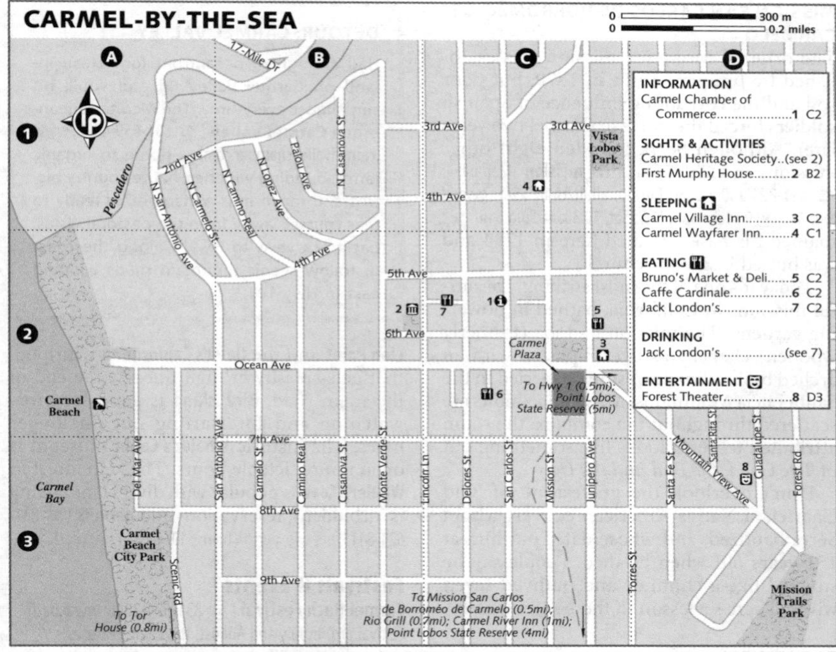

the more than 100 galleries that line the town's immaculate streets, but sky-high property values and the steady incursion of tour buses hungry to sample Carmel's much-vaunted quaintness have obliterated its salt-of-the-earth bohemia.

With impressive coastal real estate, upper-crust shops and borderline fanatical devotion to its canine citizens, Carmel glows with smugness. Local bylaws forbid neon signs and billboards. Fairy-tale Comstock cottages, with their characteristic stone chimneys and pitched gable roofs, dot the town. Even payphones, garbage cans and newspaper vending boxes are shingled. Buildings have no street numbers, so addresses always specify the street and nearest intersection. All this charm wears thin awfully fast, so once you've checked out Carmel's more idiosyncratic attractions, keep on moving.

Orientation & Information

Ocean Ave, an east–west road with tree-and-flower-filled medians, is the main strip, with most of the action near the intersection with San Carlos St. The **Carmel Chamber of Commerce** (☎ 831-624-2522, 800-550-4333; www.carmelcalifornia.org; San Carlos St; 🕑 10am-5pm), between 5th and 6th Aves, distributes maps and the *Carmel Gallery Guide*. The free weekly *Carmel Pine Cone* is packed with local personality and color – the police log is a comedy of manners.

Sights

One of the most pleasant things to do is to escape the shopping streets and stroll through the tree-lined neighborhoods on the lookout for domiciles charming and peculiar. The Hansel and Gretel houses at Torres St and Ocean Ave are just how you'd imagine them, and a home at 13th Ave and Monte Verde St is covered in bark. A wicked cool house in the shape of a ship, made from stone and salvaged ship parts, is near 6th Ave and Guadalupe St, three blocks east of Torres St. You can take a 90-minute walking tour guided by docents from the **Carmel Heritage Society** (☎ 831-624-4447; www.carmelheritage.org; tours $10; 🕑 tours 9:30am Sat). Tours leave from **First Murphy House** (Lincoln Lane at 6th Ave; 🕑 1-4pm Wed-Sun); reservations are required.

Often foggy, **Carmel Beach** is a beautiful crescent of white sand, where dogs excitedly run off-leash.

MISSION SAN CARLOS DE BORROMÉO DE CARMELO

The original Monterey mission was established by Junípero Serra in 1770, but poor soil and the corrupting influence of Spanish soldiers forced the move to Carmel two years later. Although Serra founded eight other missions in California, this **mission** (Map p454; ☎ 831-824-3600; 3080 Rio Rd; adult/child $5/1, guided tour $7; ⏲ 9:30am-5pm Mon-Sat, 10:30am-5pm Sun) remained his base. He died here in 1784 and was buried inside the church.

Today it's one of the most strikingly beautiful missions in California, bathed in flowering gardens. The mission's adobe (formerly wooden) chapel was later replaced with an arched basilica made of stone quarried in the Santa Lucia Mountains. Museum exhibits are scattered throughout the complex; the room attributed to Serra looks like something out of *The Good, the Bad and the Ugly*.

Don't overlook the gravestone of 'Old Gabriel,' a Native American convert whom Serra baptized, and whose dates put him at 151 years old when he died. People say he smoked like a chimney and outlived seven wives. There's a lesson in there somewhere.

TOR HOUSE

Even if you've never heard of the 20th-century poet Robinson Jeffers, a pilgrimage to the structures he built with his own hands – **Tor House** (Map p454; ☎ 831-624-1813; www.torhouse.org; 26304 Ocean View Ave; tours adult/student $7/2; ⏲ 10am-3pm Fri & Sat) and the Celtic-inspired Hawk Tower – offers fascinating insights into both the man and the ethos of Carmel he embodied. One of the portholes in the tower reputedly came from the wrecked ship that carried Napoleon from Elba. The only way to visit the property is to reserve space on a tour (children under 12 not allowed), although the tower can be glimpsed from the street.

POINT LOBOS STATE RESERVE

About 4 miles south of Carmel along Hwy 1, this **nature preserve** (Map p454; ☎ 831-624-4909; http://pt-lobos.parks.state.ca.us; per vehicle $10; ⏲ 8am-½hr after sunset; ♿) has a dramatically rocky coastline. It takes its name from the Punta de los Lobos Marinos (Point of the Sea Wolves), named by the Spanish for the howls of the resident sea lions. The full perimeter hike is about 6 miles, but several short walks take in wild scenery. Favorite destinations include **Sea Lion Point** and the **Devil's Cauldron**, a whirlpool that gets splashy at high tide. At the end of the main road, **Bird Island** is good for birdwatching and for starting out on longer hikes. The historic **Whaler's Cabin** museum is open unpredictable hours. The kelp forest in **Whaler's Cove** is popular with divers (snorkeling is forbidden); reservations and **permits** (☎ 831-624-8413; per two-person team $10) are required.

> **DETOUR: CARMEL VALLEY**
>
> Had enough of oceanfront fog? Head inland on Carmel Valley Rd and you'll hit sun almost every time. The Mediterranean-esque **Carmel Valley** (☎ 831-659-4000; www.carmelvalleychamber.com) is home to organic farms, budding wineries, haute country bistros and ranch inns. When you're ready to tear yourself away from the pastoral vistas, backtrack west to Hwy 1 along the coast or follow scenic mountain roads winding east to Hwy 101.

Festivals & Events

Carmel Bach Festival (☎ 831-624-2046; www.bachfestival.org) In July and August, this event features performances at different venues around town.

TomatoFest (☎ 800-965-4827; www.tomatofest.com) Over 350 heirloom tomato varieties and a 'salsa showcase' held in the neighboring Carmel Valley in mid-September.

Sleeping

Boutique hotels and B&Bs fill up quickly, especially in summer. Expect a two-night minimum stay on weekends. If you're on a budget, sleep in Monterey (p458). Campers can drive south into Big Sur (p470).

Carmel Village Inn (☎ 831-624-3864, 800-346-3864; www.carmelvillageinn.com; cnr Ocean & Junípero Aves; d $130-250; wi-fi) With cheerful flowers decorating its exterior, this centrally located motel across from Devendorf Park has pleasant rooms, some with fireplaces, and nightly quiet hours.

Carmel Wayfarer Inn (☎ 831-624-2711, 800-533-2711; www.carmelwayfarerinn.com; cnr 4th Ave & Mission St; d incl breakfast $149-179; wi-fi) At this 1929 apartment complex, none of the charming courtyard rooms or suites is the same. Some have delightfully retro kitchens and glorious sunset views. Rates include afternoon wine-and-cheese tastings and a help-yourself cookie jar. Dogs OK.

Carmel River Inn (Map p454; ☎ 831-624-1575, 800-966-6490; www.carmelriverinn.com; 26600 Oliver Rd; d $159-299; wi-fi) Tucked off Hwy 1, south of the mission, this peaceful garden retreat rents white-picket-fenced honeymooner and family cottages, many with fireplaces and kitchenettes, and simpler country-inn rooms. Pet fee $20.

Eating & Drinking

Carmel's restaurant scene is more about old-world sidewalk atmosphere than sustenance. Most places open early for breakfast, and stop serving dinner before 9pm.

Caffe Cardinale (☎ 831-626-2095; off Ocean Ave; items $2-8; 7am-5pm) Gets rave reviews for its rich, freshly roasted coffee, but also does baked goods, soups and panini sandwiches. It's hidden in an alley, between San Carlos and Dolores Sts.

Bruno's Market & Deli (☎ 831-624-3821; cnr 6th & Junípero Aves; mains $5-8; 7am-8pm) The best grocery store, Bruno's has daily barbecue specials and a superb deli for creating picnics. It also stocks Sparky's root beer from Pacific Grove.

Rio Grill (Map p454; ☎ 831-625-5436; 101 Crossroads Blvd; mains $9-26; 11:30am-10pm Sun-Thu, 11:30am-11pm Fri & Sat;) At this jazzy bistro, local ingredients find their destiny in flavorful Southwestern, Southern and Italian dishes. The fire-roasted artichokes and oakwood-smoked baby back ribs will have you licking your fingers. Exit Hwy 1 at the stoplight at Rio Rd, head east (inland) and turn right into the Crossroads Shopping Center.

Jack London's (☎ 831-624-2336; Su Vecino Court, Dolores St; mains $10-27; 11:30am-11pm Mon-Fri, 11:30am-midnight Sat & Sun) A Carmel institution since 1973, this joint pairs upscale pub grub with snarling service, but at least it's open late. Knock back a few drinks with the caddies from Pebble Beach next to the crackling fireplace. It's between 5th and 6th Aves.

Entertainment

Musicals, drama, comedies and film screenings take place at the **Forest Theater** (☎ 831-626-1681; www.foresttheaterguild.org; cnr Mountain View Ave & Guadalupe St; tickets $6-25; Apr-Jul), a 1910 outdoor performance venue anchored by enormous firepits.

Getting There & Around

Carmel is 5 miles south of Monterey via Hwy 1. There's free unlimited parking at **Vista Lobos Park** (cnr 3rd Ave and Junípero Ave).

Monterey-Salinas Transit (MST; ☎ 831-899-2555, 888-678-2871; www.mst.org) buses 4 and 5 connect north to Monterey about every 15 minutes; bus 4 continues south to the mission every half hour. Bus 22 passes through en route to and from Big Sur three times daily from late May to early September, and twice daily on Saturday and Sunday only the rest of the year. Fares start at $2, depending on the distance covered.

BIG SUR & HIGHWAY 1 SOUTH

On this 125-mile stretch of Hwy 1, you'll snake south along the unbelievably picturesque coast until it joins with Hwy 101 at San Luis Obispo. Driving along this narrow two-lane highway is slow going. Allow about three hours to cover the distance, much more if you want to explore coastal state parks. Traveling Hwy 1 after dark is perilous and futile, because you'll miss out on the seascapes. Day or night, watch out for cyclists.

BIG SUR

Big Sur is more a state of mind than a place you can pinpoint on a map. There are no traffic lights, banks or strip malls, and when the sun goes down, the moon and the stars are the only streetlights – if summer's dense fog hasn't extinguished them. Much ink has been spilled extolling the raw beauty and energy of this precious piece of land shoehorned between the Santa Lucia Range and the Pacific Ocean, but nothing quite prepares you for your first glimpse of the craggy, unspoiled coastline, adorned only with Mother Nature's palette.

In the 1950s and '60s, Big Sur – so named by Spanish settlers living in Carmel, who referred to the wilderness as *el país grande del sur* (the big country to the south) – became a favorite retreat for artists and writers, including Henry Miller and Beat Generation visionaries Jack Kerouac and Lawrence Ferlinghetti. It still attracts new-agey mystics, self-professed artists, latter-day hippies and eccentric types, as well as city slickers seeking to disengage from their cell phones and reflect deeply on this emerald-green edge of the continent. As

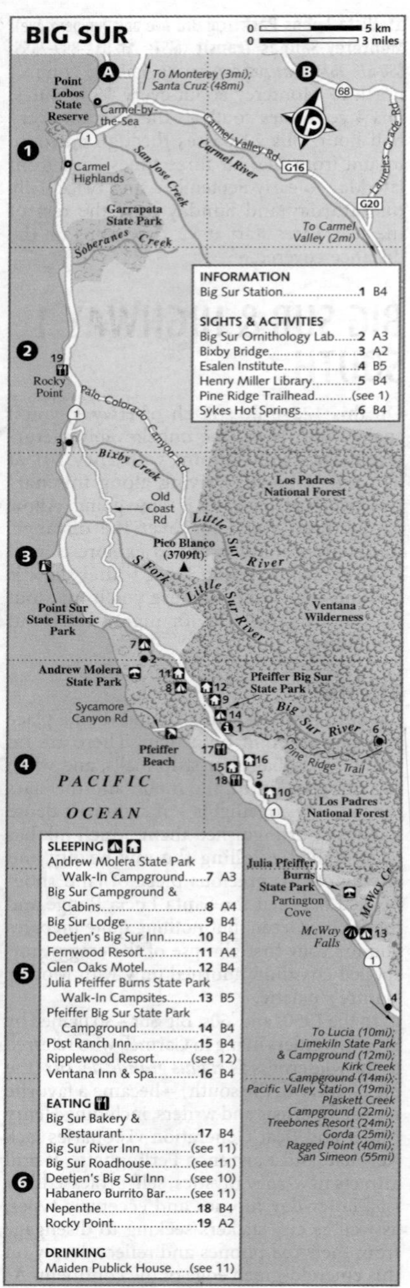

you travel through here, you'll notice that Big Sur is slowly recovering from massive fires that swept through the Ventana Wilderness in 2008.

Orientation & Information

Visitors often wander into businesses along Hwy 1 and ask, 'How much further to Big Sur?' In fact, there is no town of Big Sur as such, though you may see the name on maps. Commercial activity is concentrated along the stretch between Andrew Molera State Park and Pfeiffer Big Sur State Park. Sometimes called 'the Village,' this is where you'll find many of the restaurants, shops and lodging, and the post office.

Pick up the free annual *Big Sur Guide* published by the **Big Sur Chamber of Commerce** (☎ 831-667-2100; www.bigsurcalifornia.org; 🕑 9am-1pm). Just south of Pfeiffer Big Sur State Park, the ranger-staffed **Big Sur Station** (☎ 831-667-2315; Hwy 1; 🕑 8am-4:30pm) has information and maps for state parks, the Los Padres National Forest and Ventana Wilderness. South of the Nacimiento-Fergusson Rd turnoff, the USDA Forest Service (USFS) **Pacific Valley Station** (☎ 805-927-4211; Hwy 1; 🕑 8am-4:30pm) has limited visitor information.

Road and emergency services here are distant – in Monterey to the north or Cambria in the south. Fill up the tank beforehand, and be careful.

Sights & Activities

These are listed north to south. If you pay the entrance fee for one state park, you get in free to any others that day. Most parks are open a half-hour before sunrise until a half-hour after sunset, but campgrounds allow 24-hour access.

BIXBY BRIDGE

About 13 miles south of Carmel, this much photographed Big Sur landmark spans Rainbow Canyon and, at over 260ft, is one of the world's highest single-span bridges. Completed in 1932, it was built by prisoners eager to lop time off their sentences. There's a photo op pull-off just north of the bridge. Don't be tricked into thinking that Rocky Creek Bridge, just north of Bixby, is the real deal.

Before the Bixby Bridge was constructed, travelers had to trek 14 miles inland on what's now called the **Old Coast Road**, which heads off

CALIFORNIA'S COMEBACK CONDORS

When it comes to endangered species, one of the state's biggest success stories is the California condor. This gigantic, prehistoric bird has a 10ft wingspan used to fly great distances in search of carrion. It's easily recognized by its naked pink head and large white patches on each wing.

So rare did this big bird become that in 1987 there were only 27 left, which were all removed from the wild to special captive-breeding facilities. Before the fires of summer 2008 there were 332 condors, with increasing numbers released back into the wilds of California, where it is hoped that they will begin breeding. Pinnacles National Monument (p481) and the Big Sur coast both offer excellent opportunities to view this majestic bird.

At Andrew Molera State Park, the Ventana Wilderness Society operates the **Big Sur Ornithology Lab** (☎ 831-624-1202; www.ventanaws.org; sunrise-noon Tue-Sat Apr-Oct) out of a small shed, where the public is welcome to watch naturalists at work carrying out bird-banding and long-term species monitoring programs. Call to check opening hours between November and March.

east from the bridge's northern side, reconnecting with Hwy 1 opposite Andrew Molera State Park. This route is usually navigable with a 4WD vehicle.

POINT SUR STATE HISTORIC PARK

Just over 6 miles south of Bixby Bridge, Point Sur rises like a green velvet fortress. This imposing volcanic rock looks like an island, but is actually connected to land by a sandbar. Atop the rock is the 1889 stone-built **Point Sur Lightstation** (☎ 831-625-4419; www.pointsur.org; tours adult/child $8/4), which operated until 1974. Ocean views and tales of the lighthouse keepers' family lives are engrossing. Reservations are not accepted for the three-hour guided tours. Meet at the locked gate on Hwy 1, a quarter-mile north of the naval facility, at 10am or 2pm Saturday or 10am Sunday year-round. Tours also depart at 10am and 2pm on Wednesday between April and October, when monthly full-moon tours are also available. Call ahead to confirm tour schedules.

ANDREW MOLERA STATE PARK

Named after the Salinas farmer who first planted artichokes in California, this oft-overlooked **park** (☎ 831-667-2315; www.parks.ca.gov; per vehicle $8) enjoys a remote and wild setting, lots of wildlife and great beachcombing. You might even spot endangered California condors circling overhead.

The first-come, first-served, **walk-in campground** (tent sites $10), a 10-minute walk from the parking lot, has firepits, vault toilets and drinking water, but no ocean views. From the campground, a gentle quarter-mile trail leads past the 1861 redwood **Cooper Cabin**, Big Sur's oldest building, to a beautiful beach where the Big Sur River runs into the ocean. Back at the parking lot, more trails head out to the beach and along ocean bluffs. **Molera Horseback Tours** (☎ 831-625-5486, 800-942-5486; http://molerahorsebacktours.com) offers a variety of guided trail rides ($40 to $70); novices are welcome.

PFEIFFER BIG SUR STATE PARK

Named after Big Sur's first European settlers, who arrived in 1869, **Pfeiffer Big Sur State Park** (☎ 831-667-2315; www.parks.ca.gov; per vehicle $8) is the largest state park in Big Sur. Hiking trails loop through redwood groves and head into the adjacent Ventana Wilderness. The most popular trail – to 60ft-high **Pfeiffer Falls**, a delicate cascade hidden in the forest that runs from December to May – is only a 1.4-mile round-trip walk.

Built in the 1930s by the Civilian Conservation Corps (CCC), the rustic **Big Sur Lodge** (p470) has a restaurant, an espresso bar and a general store selling a few camping supplies, groceries and ice-cream treats. Beside the Big Sur River, the gigantic 218-site **campground** (☎ reservations 800-444-7275; www.reserveamerica.com; tent & RV sites $25-35) lies in a redwood valley; facilities include showers and laundry. Summer crowds are the only drawback.

PFEIFFER BEACH

Just west of Pfeiffer Big Sur State Park, this phenomenal, crescent-shaped and dog-friendly **beach** (☎ 831-667-2315; per vehicle $5; 9am-8pm) is known for its huge double rock formation, through which waves crash with life-affirming power. It's often windy, and the surf is too dangerous for swimming. But dig down into the wet sand – it's purple! That's because manganese garnet washes down from the craggy hillsides above. To get here from Hwy 1, make a sharp right onto Sycamore Canyon Rd, marked by a small brown sign that says 'narrow road' at the top. The turnoff is about a quarter-mile south of Big Sur Station.

HENRY MILLER LIBRARY

'It was here in Big Sur I first learned to say Amen!' wrote Henry Miller, a Big Sur denizen for 17 years, in *Big Sur and the Oranges of Hieronymus Bosch*. More of a living memorial, alt-cultural venue and bookshop, this **library** (☎ 831-667-2574; www.henrymiller.org; admission by donation; 11am-6pm Wed-Mon;) was never Miller's home. The house belonged to Miller's friend, painter Emil White, until his death and is now run by a nonprofit group. Inside are all of Miller's written works, many of his paintings and a collection of Big Sur and Beat Generation material, including copies of the top 100 books Miller claimed most influenced him. Stop by to browse and hang out on the front deck. Check the website for upcoming events. The library is a quarter-mile south of Nepenthe restaurant.

PARTINGTON COVE

From the west side of Hwy 1, a poorly marked, steep, dirt trail descends half a mile along Partington Creek to Partington Cove, named for a settler who built the first dock here in the 1880s. Originally, the cove was used for loading freight; during Prohibition it was an alleged landing spot for bootleggers. This is a beautiful hidden part of Big Sur, offering incredible vistas, picnic spots and creekside swimming. On the hike down to the cove, you'll cross a cool bridge and go through an even cooler tunnel. The water in the cove is unbelievably aqua and within it grow incredible kelp forests. There's no real beach access, but you can scamper on the rocks and look for tidepools as waves splash ominously. Look for the trailhead turnoff inside a large hairpin turn on Hwy 1, 8 miles south of Nepenthe restaurant or 2 miles north of Julia Pfeiffer Burns State Park.

CENTRAL COAST

JULIA PFEIFFER BURNS STATE PARK

Named for another Big Sur pioneer, this **park** (☎ 831-667-2315; www.parks.ca.gov; per vehicle $8) hugs both sides of Hwy 1. At the park entrance, on the east side of the highway, you'll find shady, forested picnic grounds along McWay Creek. The 4.5-mile **Ewoldsen Trail** offers views of the ocean and the Santa Lucia Range.

The highlight is California's only coastal waterfall, **McWay Falls**, which drops 80ft straight into the sea – or onto the beach, depending on the tide. This is the classic Big Sur postcard shot, with tree-topped rocks jutting above a golden, crescent-shaped beach next to swirling blue pools and crashing white surf. To reach the truly spectacular viewpoint, take the short Overlook Trail west from the parking lot and cross beneath Hwy 1. From the viewpoint benches, you may spot migrating gray whales between December and April. Nearby, two **walk-in campsites** (☎ reservations 800-444-7275; www.reserveamerica.com; tent sites $15-20) sit on an ocean bluff shaded by cypress trees. Camper registration is at Pfeiffer Big Sur State Park campground, 12 miles north.

ESALEN INSTITUTE

Marked only by a lighted sign reading 'Esalen Institute, By Reservation Only,' the **Esalen Institute** (☎ 831-667-3000; www.esalen.org) is like a new-agey, hippie camp for adults. Workshops deal with anything 'relating to our greater human capacity,' from shapeshifting to higher levels of consciousness to training for urban yogis. Things have changed a lot since Hunter S Thompson was the gun-toting caretaker here in the '60s.

The famous Esalen **baths** (☎ 831-667-3047; admission $20; baths 1-3am, reservations accepted 8am-7:45pm) are fed by a natural hot spring and sit on a ledge above the ocean. Dollars to donuts you'll never take another dip that compares panorama-wise with the one here, especially on stormy winter nights. Only two small outdoor pools perch directly over the waves, so once you've stripped down and taken a lightning-fast shower, head outside immediately to score the best views – otherwise, you'll be stuck with a tepid, no-view pool or a rickety bathtub. Clothing-optional 'nightly bathing' is open to the public by reservation only. Fees must be paid by credit card.

Esalen is 11 miles south of Nepenthe restaurant and 10 miles north of Lucia.

LIMEKILN STATE PARK

Two miles south of Lucia, this petite **park** (☎ 831-667-2403; per vehicle $6; 8am-sunset) gets its name from the four remaining lime kilns originally built here in the 1870s and '80s to smelt quarried limestone into powder, a

GO WILD IN BIG SUR

The 167,000-acre **Ventana Wilderness** (☎ 831-423-3191; www.ventanawild.org) is the Big Sur backcountry. It lies within the northern part of Los Padres National Forest, which straddles the Santa Lucia Range and runs parallel to the coast for its entire length. Most of the wilderness is covered with oak and chaparral, though canyons cut by the Big Sur and Little Sur Rivers support virgin stands of coast redwoods. The endemic Santa Lucia fir grows in rocky outcroppings above 4500ft.

Partly reopened after devastating wildfires in summer 2008, the wilderness remains popular with adventurous hikers and backpackers. A favorite destination is **Sykes Hot Springs**, natural 100°F mineral pools framed by redwoods. It's a moderately strenuous 10-mile one-way hike along the Pine Ridge Trail from Big Sur Station, where you can get a free campfire permit. Don't expect solitude at the springs during peak season (April to September).

key ingredient in cement used to construct buildings in Monterey and San Francisco. Pioneers chopped down the steep canyon's old-growth redwood forests to fuel the kilns' fires. A half-mile trail through a new redwood grove leads to the historic site, while another short hike reaches a gorgeous 100ft-high waterfall. A 24-hour **campground** (☎ reservations 800-444-7275; www.reserveamerica.com; tent & RV sites $25) sits by the park entrance, tucked under a bridge next to the ocean; it has flush toilets and showers.

SOUTH TO RAGGED POINT

The tortuously winding 40-mile stretch of Hwy 1 south to San Simeon is even more sparsely populated, rugged and remote. Most of what you'll see on this stretch is Los Padres National Forest land. Make sure you've got at least enough gas in the tank to reach Gorda, 20 miles south of Lucia.

Two miles south of Limekiln State Park, 43-site **Kirk Creek Campground** (☎ 805-434-1996, reservations 877-444-6777; www.campone.com, www.recreation.gov; walk-ins $5, tent & RV sites $25) is a national-forest facility on a beautiful bluff above the ocean; it has flush toilets and water, but no showers. Further south, Hwy 1 intersects with backcountry **Nacimiento-Fergusson Road**, which cuts over the mountains to Hwy 101 after about 45 miles. You can stop off en route at **Mission San Antonio de Padua** (p481).

South of Pacific Valley Station is the turnoff to **Sand Dollar Beach Picnic Area** (☎ 805-927-4211; per vehicle $5; ⌚ 9am-8pm), from where it's a five-minute walk down to southern Big Sur's longest sandy beach. Further south is USFS **Plaskett Creek Campground** (☎ 805-434-1996; www.campone.com; tent & RV sites $22), with 43 first-come, first-served spacious sites in a grassy area shaded by Monterey pine and cypress trees; it has flush toilets but no showers.

Just south of Plaskett Creek is the most scenic stretch of southern Big Sur. In 1971, in the waters of **Jade Cove**, three divers recovered a 9000lb jade boulder that measured 8ft long and was valued at $180,000. People still comb the beach today. The best time to find jade, which is black or blue-green and looks dull until you dip it in water, is during low tide or after a big storm. Keep an eye out for hang gliders flying in for a dramatic landing on the beach, too.

Next up is **Gorda**, named for an offshore outcropping resembling a fat lady. It now serves as a beacon for tourists looking for snacks and a gas station. If you have any sunlight left, keep trucking down the highway to **Salmon Creek Falls**, which usually runs from December through May. Tucked up a forested canyon, the double-drop waterfall can be glimpsed from the hairpin turn on Hwy 1 (roadside parking can be crowded), but that's missing the point. Take the 10-minute walk up to the falls to splash around in the pools, where kids shriek and dogs happily yip and yap.

Your last – or first – taste of Big Sur rocky grandeur comes at **Ragged Point**, a craggy cliff outcropping with fabulous views of the coastline in both directions, about 15 miles north of Hearst Castle. Originally part of the Hearst empire, it's now taken over by a sprawling, ho-hum resort. From this point south, the land grows increasingly wind-swept as Hwy 1 rolls gently down to the water's edge.

Sleeping

With few exceptions, Big Sur's lodgings do not have TVs and rarely have telephones. This is where you come to escape the world. There aren't a lot of rooms overall, so demand often exceeds supply and prices can be outrageous. During summer and on weekends, reservations are essential, whether for lodge rooms or campsites.

BUDGET

There's developed and walk-in camping at four of Big Sur's state parks: Andrew Molera State Park (p467), Pfeiffer Big Sur State Park (p467), Julia Pfeiffer Burns State Park (p468) and Limekiln State Park (p469). There are also developed and primitive USFS campgrounds further south (see p469). For private deluxe camping, call ahead to Treebones Resort (right) or the Ventana Inn & Spa (right).

Fernwood Resort (☎ 831-667-2422; www.fernwoodbigsur.com; tent/RV sites $35/45, tent cabins $60, motel d $99-160) It's not flashy, but this touristy complex has better-value basic rooms than other roadside motels in Big Sur. The friendly family also offers shady riverside campsites and summer-camp-style tent cabins.

Big Sur Campground & Cabins (☎ 831-667-2322; www.bigsurcamp.com; 47000 Hwy 1; tent sites $38-48, RV sites with full hookups $48-58, cabins $95-345) Popular with RVs, this well-run private campground right on the Big Sur River has 79 campsites, along with small tent and housekeeping cabins (pet fee $15), all shaded by redwoods. There are hot showers, a coin-op laundry, a playground and a general store.

Deetjen's Big Sur Inn (☎ 831-667-2377; www.deetjens.com; 48865 Hwy 1; d $80-200) Nestled among redwoods and wisteria, this creekside conglomeration of rustic, thin-walled rooms and cottages was built by Norwegian immigrant Helmuth Deetjen in the 1930s. Some are warmed by wood-burning fireplaces, while cheaper ones share a bathroom.

Ripplewood Resort (☎ 831-667-2242; www.ripplewoodresort.com; 46840 Hwy 1; cabins $115-195) Ripplewood has struck a blow for fiscal equality by having the same rates year-round. Cabins vary in details: all have kitchens and private bathrooms; some have fireplaces. The riverside cabins – like Nos 1 and 2 – are quiet and surrounded by redwoods, but the hillside ones can be noisy.

MIDRANGE

Bigger price tags don't necessarily buy you more amenities.

Glen Oaks Motel (☎ 831-667-2105; www.glenoaksbigsur.com; Hwy 1; d $155-225; wi-fi) Woodsy chic has never looked or felt as comfy as at this 1950s redwood-and-adobe motor lodge, where snug rooms with gas fireplaces have been dramatically transformed by hip San Francisco aesthetics and ecoconscious design elements.

Treebones Resort (☎ 877-424-4787; www.treebonesresort.com; 71895 Hwy 1; d $155-235; 🏊 👶) Don't let the word 'resort' throw you. Yes, it's got an ocean-view hot tub, heated pool and massage treatments. But yurts with polished pine floors, quilt-covered beds, sink vanities and redwood decks are actually like 'glamping' with little privacy. Bathrooms and showers are a short stroll away. Rates include a make-your-own waffle breakfast. Look for a tiny sign just north of Gorda, off Willow Creek Rd.

Lucia Lodge (☎ 831-667-2391, 866-424-4787; www.lucialodge.com; 62400 Hwy 1, Lucia; d $175-275) You'll feel the solitude of Big Sur back before the coastal highway was finished at this small, isolated place perched above the sea. It has a restaurant and lounge with an outdoor deck – some of the rooms and cabins share the same dreamy views.

Big Sur Lodge (☎ 831-667-3100, 800-424-4787; www.bigsurlodge.com; 47225 Hwy 1; d $199-359; 🏊) What you're really paying for is a peaceful location, right inside Pfeiffer Big Sur State Park. Pretty rustic cottages each have a deck or balcony looking onto redwoods; pricier ones also have kitchens and wood-burning fireplaces.

TOP END

High-end resorts are at odds with Big Sur's hippie-alternative vibe, but the following places manage to inject a little soul into their luxury.

Ventana Inn & Spa (☎ 831-667-2331, 800-628-6500; www.ventanainn.com; 48123 Hwy 1; d $500-1450; 🏊 wi-fi) Serene, romantic Ventana caters to honeymooning couples and paparazzi-fleeing celebs, who pad from yoga class to the Japanese baths and clothing-optional pool, or maybe hole up all day next to the wood-burning fireplace in their villa or ocean-view cottage. The restaurant, Cielo, has lofty views.

Post Ranch Inn (☎ 831-667-2200, 800-527-2200; www.postranchinn.com; Hwy 1; d $550-2185) The last word in luxurious coastal getaways, the legendary Post Ranch pampers guests with accommodations featuring slate spa tubs, fireplaces, private decks and walking sticks for coastal hikes. Ocean-facing rooms celebrate the sea, while the treehouses without views have a bit of sway. One sour note: snooty, standoffish staff.

Eating

Like Big Sur lodgings, eateries are often overpriced and overbooked.

Big Sur Bakery & Restaurant (☎ 831-667-0520; 47540 Hwy 1; snacks from $4, mains $14-36; bakery from 8am daily, restaurant lunch & dinner Tue-Sun) Behind the Shell station, this warmly lit house has menus that change with the seasons. Wood-fired pizzas share space with more refined dishes like wild salmon and succotash. Fronted by a pretty patio, the bakery pours Big Sur's most expensive coffee.

Habanero Burrito Bar (☎ 831-667-2700; Hwy 1; mains $4-6; 11am-7pm;) Beside the Big Sur River Inn, this made-to-order burrito and deli-wrap counter also serves real-fruit smoothies. It's at the back of a well-stocked general store for camping supplies.

Big Sur River Inn (☎ 831-667-2700; Hwy 1; mains breakfast & lunch $7-18, dinner $18-37; breakfast, lunch & dinner) This inn has a woodsy old supper club with a deck overlooking the creek teeming with throaty frogs. The food is classic American, with breakfast being the best deal.

Deetjen's Big Sur Inn (☎ 831-667-2377; 48865 Hwy 1; mains breakfast $8-12, dinner $12-32; breakfast & dinner) This quaint yesteryear lodge has a cozy, candle-lit dining room serving up steaks, cassoulets and other hearty country fare from a daily changing menu, primarily sourced from organic local produce, hormone-free meat and sustainable seafood.

Big Sur Roadhouse (☎ 831-667-2264; Hwy 1; mains $12-25; dinner Wed-Mon;) Run by talented chefs who once worked at the hoity-toity Post Ranch Inn, this Latin-flavored roadhouse fairly glows from the corner fireplace and copper-top bar. At riverside tables out back you can fork into hearty adobo-marinated skirt steak or barbecue chicken with sweet-potato puree.

our pick Nepenthe (☎ 831-667-2345; Hwy 1; mains $12-36; 11:30am-10pm;) Nepenthe comes from a Greek word meaning 'isle of no sorrow,' and indeed, it's hard to feel blue while sitting on its glorious clifftop terrace. The California bistro cuisine, while tasty (try the renowned Ambrosia burger), is secondary to the views and Nepenthe's history (Orson Welles and Rita Hayworth bought the place in 1944). Downstairs, Café Kevah (dishes $7 to $15; open 9am to 4pm March to December) serves light brunches and also has ocean views.

Rocky Point (☎ 831-624-2933; 36700 Hwy 1; mains breakfast & lunch $13-23, dinner $23-45; breakfast, lunch & dinner) Just 10 miles south of Carmel, the country-club atmosphere at this clifftop restaurant doesn't detract from a dizzying ocean-view terrace, where Bloody Marys and appetizers are served all day. Otherwise, stick to classic sandwiches and steaks on the restaurant's seriously old-school menu.

Drinking

Maiden Publick House (☎ 831-667-2355) Near the Big Sur River Inn, it has a respectable beer bible and motley musicians jamming on weekends.

Getting There & Around

Big Sur is best explored by car, since you'll be itching to stop frequently to take in the rugged beauty and vistas that reveal themselves after every hairpin turn. Even if your driving skills are up to the dizzying hills and switchbacks along Hwy 1, others aren't: expect to average about 35mph along the route. Parts of the highway are battle-scarred, evidence of the continual struggle to keep it open after landslides and washouts.

MST bus 22 ($4.50, 1¼ hours) travels from Monterey via Carmel as far south as Nepenthe restaurant three times daily between late May and early September, and twice daily on Saturdays and Sundays only the rest of the year. Buses are equipped with bike racks.

PIEDRAS BLANCAS LIGHTSTATION

Although many lighthouses still stand on the California coast, none offer such a historically evocative seascape. Federally designated an outstanding natural area, the jutting, rugged grounds of this 1875 **lighthouse** (www.piedrasblancas.org) – one of the tallest on the West Coast – have been replanted with colorful native vegetation. Picturesquely, everything looks much the way it did when the first lighthouse keepers helped ships find safe harbor at the whaling station at San Simeon Bay.

Free weekday tours (donations requested) currently meet at 9:45am on Tuesdays and Thursdays at the old Piedras Blancas Motel, about 1.5 miles north of the lightstation; call ahead to confirm schedules. Reservations are required for the monthly **living-history tours** (☎ 805-927-6811; adult/child $15/free; tours 10am & 1pm 3rd Sat of the month), where docents in Victorian period dress guide you around the

ENORMOUS E-SEALS

The glories of Hearst Castle now have some weighty competition: elephant seals (known locally as 'e-seals'). They can weigh over two tons – about the same as the SUVs whizzing by on Hwy 1. Nearly extinct by the 1880s, elephant seals have made a remarkable comeback along California's coast.

Until the late 1990s, the only place to see these beasts was at heavily protected **Año Nuevo State Reserve** (p193), north of Santa Cruz. But a new colony of elephant seals now hangs around near Piedras Blancas, including at a well-marked vista point 4.8 miles north of Hearst Castle, where interpretative panels and blue-jacketed docents from the **Friends of the Elephant Seal** (☎ 805-924-1628; www.elephantseal.org) society demystify the behavior of these humongous mammals.

During peak winter season, upwards of 12,000 seals seek shelter in the coves and beaches along this stretch of coast. Always observe them from a safe distance and do not approach or otherwise harass these unpredictable, truly wild animals, who move faster on the sand than humans can.

On sunny days the seals usually 'lie around like banana slugs,' in the words of one docent. Watching the seals snooze on the beach, you'd never guess that they regularly dive deeper (nearly a mile) and longer (over an hour) than any other mammal. The behemoth bulls engage in mock – and sometimes real – combat, all the while making odd guttural grunts, while their harems of females and young pups look on.

Here's a quick seasonal viewing guide:

- **November and December** Bull seals arrive at the beach, followed by juveniles and mature females already pregnant from last winter's breeding season.
- **January to March** Pregnant seals give birth, peaking in February; once delivered, the females mate with the waiting and rather anxious males, who then depart for feeding migrations.
- **April to May** Females wean pups and leave to feed, too; pups teach themselves how to swim and eventually leave as well.
- **June to October** Seals of all ages return to molt, with females arriving in early summer and males in late summer and early fall. Seals of all ages return briefly to molt, with females seen in early summer and males in late summer and early fall.

Curious to learn more? Stop by the **Coastal Discovery Center** (opposite) near Hearst Castle.

CENTRAL COAST

property while chatting about the marine wildlife and both the Native American and maritime history of this lonely, windswept coastal spot. Book by phone (reservations accepted 9am to 4pm weekdays) or in person at the National Geographic Theater inside Hearst Castle (opposite). The latter is also the meeting place and departure point for tour buses up to the point and back.

HEARST CASTLE

The most important thing to know about William Randolph Hearst (1863–1951) is that he did not live like *Citizen Kane*. Not that Hearst wasn't bombastic, conniving and larger than life, but the moody recluse of the movie he was definitely not. Hearst also didn't call his 165-room monstrosity a castle, preferring its official name, La Cuesta Encantada (the Enchanted Hill), or more often calling it simply 'the ranch.' From the 1920s into the '40s, Hearst and his longtime mistress Marion Davies (Hearst's wife refused to grant him a divorce) adored entertaining here, and it saw a steady stream of the era's biggest movers and shakers. Invitations were highly coveted, but Hearst had his quirks – he despised drunkenness, and guests were forbidden to speak of death.

Hearst Castle is a wondrous, historic (Winston Churchill penned anti-Nazi essays here in the 1930s), over-the-top homage to material excess perched high on a hill, and a visit is a must. Architect Julia Morgan based the main building, Casa Grande, on the design of a Spanish cathedral, and over decades catered to Hearst's every design whim, deftly integrating the spoils of his fabled European shopping sprees (ancient artifacts, monasteries etc) into the whole. The estate sprawls across acres of lushly landscaped gardens, accentuated by shimmering pools and fountains, statues from ancient Greece and Moorish Spain and the ruins of what was in Hearst's day the world's largest private zoo.

Like Hearst's construction budget, the castle will devour as much of your time as you let it. To see anything of this **state historic monument** (☎ general info 805-927-2020, reservations 800-444-4445; www.hearstcastle.com; tours adult/child from $20/10), you have to take a tour. For much of the year, reservations are absolutely necessary. In peak summer months and for special living-history evening and holiday tours, book tours at least a week or two in advance.

Tours start daily at 8:20am, with the last leaving at 3:20pm (later in summer). There are four main tours; for each you depart from the visitors center and take a 10-minute bus ride up the hill. No matter how many tours you go on, you have to make the up-and-down bus journey each time. Each tour lasts about 1¾ hours, and every tour includes the highlight Neptune and Roman pools. The docents are almost preternaturally knowledgeable – just try and stump 'em. Best of all are the evening sunset and Christmas holiday tours, featuring living-history reenactors who escort visitors back in time to the castle's 1930s heyday.

Facilities at the visitors center (there's no eating or drinking on the hilltop) are geared for industrial-sized mobs of visitors. It's better to grab lunch in nearby Cambria (p474). Before you leave the castle, take a moment to visit the often-overlooked museum area in the far back of the visitors center: it's worth it. The five-story-high **National Geographic Theater**, displaying 17th-century tapestries in the lobby, shows a 40-minute historical film (admission included with tour tickets) about the castle and the Hearst family.

Dress with plenty of layers: gloomy fog at the sea-level visitors center can turn into sunny skies at the castle's hilltop location, and vice versa. Getting to Hearst Castle without your own wheels can be a challenge. RTA bus 12 makes two or three daily round trips from San Luis Obispo to Hearst Castle ($2.50, two hours) via Morro Bay, Cayucos and Cambria.

SAN SIMEON & AROUND

pop 440 / elev 60ft

San Simeon began life as a whaling station in 1852. Shoreline whaling was practiced to catch gray whales migrating between Alaskan feeding grounds and birthing waters in Baja California. Sea otters were also hunted by Russian fur traders here. In 1865 Senator George Hearst purchased 45,000 acres of ranch land and established an oceanfront settlement on the western side of Hwy 1, across from today's entrance to Hearst Castle. Designed by architect Julia Morgan, these historic houses are now home to employees of the Hearst Corporation's 80,000-acre cattle ranch, which practices sustainable farming. **Sebastian's general store** sells water, snacks and beach gear.

Also just opposite the castle entrance, **William Randolph Hearst Memorial State Beach** (☎ 805-927-2020; admission free; www.parks.ca.gov; dawn-dusk) has a pleasant sandy stretch with rock outcroppings, kelp forests, a rickety wooden pier (fishing permitted) and picnic areas with barbecue grills. On the beach, **Sea for Yourself Kayak Tours** (☎ 805-927-1787, 800-717-5225; www.kayakcambria.com) rents kayaks (from $20 per hour), wetsuits, bodyboards and surfboards, weather permitting; ask about lessons and tours. Near the state-beach entrance, the **Coastal Discovery Center** (☎ 805-927-6575; admission free; 11am-5pm Fri-Sun mid-Mar–Oct, 10am-4pm Fri-Sun Nov–mid-Mar;), cooperatively run by the Monterey Bay National Marine Sanctuary and California State Parks, has educational displays about this unique meeting point of land and sea, including a talking artificial tidepool that kids can touch, real-life videos of deep-sea diving and a WWII-era shipwreck just offshore, and the lowdown on the Piedras Blancas elephant seal colony (see the boxed text, opposite).

A few miles south of the original whaling station, just outside the Hearst Corporation's property, the modern town of San Simeon is nothing more than a strip of unexciting motels and restaurants. There are better places to stay in Cambria (p474) or the beach towns of Estero Bay (p475).

Five miles south of the castle, **San Simeon State Park** has two very popular **campgrounds** (☎ 805-927-2035, reservations 800-444-7275; www.reserveamerica.com; tent & RV sites $15-25): San Simeon Creek, with hot showers and flush toilets; and undeveloped Washburn, located along a dirt road. Water is available at both.

CAMBRIA

pop 6500 / elev 65ft

With a whopping dose of natural beauty, the coastal idyll of Cambria is a lone pearl cast along the coast. Just like at nearby Hearst

WHAT THE...?

Fans of the crazy and curious should make a beeline for **Nitt-Witt Ridge** (☎ 805-927-2690; 881 Hillcrest Dr; tours adult/child $10/5), a three-story house built entirely out of recycled materials – from abalone shells to beer cans, ceramic tiles to toilet seats. This 'palace of junk' is the creation of Arthur Harold Beal (aka Captain Nit Wit, aka Der Tinkerpaw) and was hand-built over a period of 51 years. Call ahead to arrange tours.

Castle, money is no object in this well-heeled retirement community, whose motto 'Pines by the Sea' is affixed to the back of BMWs that toodle around 'the village.'

Cambria has three distinct parts: the tourist-choked East Village, a half-mile from Hwy 1, where antiques shops, art galleries and coffeehouses line Main St; the newer West Village, further west along Main St, where you'll find the **chamber of commerce** (☎ 805-927-3624; www.cambriachamber.org; 767 Main St; 9am-5pm Mon-Fri, noon-4pm Sat & Sun); and motel-lined Moonstone Beach, off Hwy 1. Although the beach's eponymous milky-white moonstones are long gone, it still attracts romantics with its oceanfront boardwalk and truly picturesque rocky shoreline. For more solitude, take the Windsor Rd exit off Hwy 1 and drive down to where the road dead-ends; from there, a 2-mile round-trip blufftop hiking trail leads across serene East West Ranch.

A 10-minute drive south of Cambria, past the Hwy 46 turnoff to Paso Robles' wine country, tiny **Harmony** is a slice of rural Americana, with a hillside winery and an 1865 creamery now housing local artists' workshops.

CENTRAL COAST

Sleeping

Cambria's choicest lodgings line Moonstone Beach Dr, while quaint B&Bs cluster around the village.

Bridge Street Inn (☎ 805-927-7653; www.bridgestreetinncambria.com; 4314 Bridge St; dm $22-25, r $50-70; wi-fi) Inside a 19th-century parsonage, this B&B-esque hostel has character, charm and a communal kitchen, but the shabby-chic rooms have thin walls. It's small, so reserve by calling ahead between 5pm and 9pm daily.

Bluebird Inn (☎ 805-927-4634, 800-552-5434; www.bluebirdmotel.com; 1880 Main St; d $70-220) With peaceful gardens, this friendly East Village motel has basic rooms, some with fireplaces and private balconies overlooking a creek. It's a reliable budget-conscious choice. Wi-fi in lobby.

Blue Dolphin Inn (☎ 805-927-3300, 800-222-9157; www.cambriainns.com; 6470 Moonstone Beach Dr; d incl breakfast $109-239; wi-fi) This gray, two-story, slat-sided building may not look as upscale as other oceanfront motels, but inside the cozy rooms have fireplaces, pillowtop mattresses and rich-feeling linens. Pet fee $25.

our pick **Fogcatcher Inn** (☎ 805-927-1400, 800-425-4121; www.fogcatcherinn.com; 6400 Moonstone Beach Dr; d incl breakfast $149-389; wi-fi) Motels along Moonstone Beach Dr are nearly identical, but this one is a standout for its courteous staff and handy hot tub. Faux English Tudor–style cottages harbor luxurious modern rooms, some with fireplaces and full ocean views.

Also recommended:

McCall Farm Bed & Breakfast (☎ 805-927-3140; www.mccallfarm.com; 6250 Santa Rosa Creek Rd; r $125-155) Restful 1895 farmhouse with just two cheery, antique-decorated rooms.

Cambria Shores Inn (☎ 805-927-8644, 800-433-9179; www.cambriashores.com; 6276 Moonstone Beach Dr; r $149-269; wi-fi) Small motel offering pampering amenities for pets (surcharge $15), including a welcome doggie basket.

Eating & Drinking

You can easily walk between several restaurants in the East Village. Rustic farm stands line Santa Rosa Creek Rd, a 15-minute drive east of Cambria via Main St.

Lily's Coffeehouse (☎ 805-927-7259; 2028 Main St; items $1-8; 8:30am-5pm Wed-Mon; wi-fi) A community gathering spot, Francophilic Lily's has a peaceful front garden patio and brews robust coffees and teas. Drop in on Saturday between 11am and 4pm for made-to-order crepes.

Linn's Easy as Pie Cafe (☎ 805-924-3050; 4251 Bridge St; mains $4-10; 11am-8pm;) If you don't have time to visit Linn's Fruit Bin, the original farm store out on Santa Rosa Creek Rd, you can still fork into their famous olallieberry pies and preserves at this take-out counter with a sunny patio in the East Village.

Indigo Moon (☎ 805-927-2911; 1940 Main St; mains lunch $6-12, dinner $12-25; 11am-4am daily, dinner Wed-Sun) Inside this artisan cheese and wine shop, breezy bistro tables complement market-fresh salads, toasty sandwiches and crunchy sweet-potato fries. Local luminaries gossip over lunch on the back patio.

Robin's (☎ 805-927-5007; 4095 Burton Dr; lunch mains $10-15, dinner $15-25; 11am-4:30pm Mon-Sat, 11am-3pm Sun, dinner daily) Reliable Robin's has been whipping up fresh, internationally inspired fare using local ingredients for more than two decades. Dine inside the cozy house or out on the wisteria-draped patio.

Wild Ginger (☎ 805-927-1001; 2380 Main St; mains $12-17; lunch & dinner Fri-Wed; V) This bright and cheery chef-owned café serves up garden-fresh, pan-Asian fare, perfectly seasoned and presented, plus housemade sorbets in exotic flavors like pomegranate and pineapple-coconut. Expect a wait.

Getting There & Around

RTA bus 12 makes two to four daily round trips from San Luis Obispo ($2, 1¾ hours) via Morro Bay and Cayucos, passing through Cambria via Main St and Moonstone Beach Dr. The free 'Otter Bus' trolley loops around Moonstone Beach Dr through the East and West Villages between 9am and 6pm from Friday to Monday (also Thursdays in summer).

ESTERO BAY

Estero Bay is a long, shallow bay with Cayucos at its northern end and Montaña de Oro State Park at its southern end. Between them, Morro Bay is a deep inlet separated from the ocean by a 5-mile-long sand spit. Overshadowed by power-plant smokestacks, Morro Rock is the bay's navigational landmark. Along this humble, working-class stretch of coast are fantastic opportunities for kayaking, surfing, hiking and camping, all within easy reach of San Luis Obispo, where Hwy 1 meets Hwy 101 just further south.

Cayucos

pop 2990 / elev 60ft

The main drag of amiable, slow-paced Cayucos calls to mind an Old West frontier town, while a block to the west, surf's up. Ocean Ave, which parallels Hwy 1, is the main street, lined with historic storefronts and hotels, eateries and antiques shops. At the town's north end, fronting a broad white-sand beach, is a long pier favored by fishers; it's also a sheltered spot for beginner surfers. Near the pier, **Cayucos Surf Company** (☎ 805-995-1000; www.surfcompany.com; 95 Cayucos Dr; hr vary) sells and rents surfboards (full day $20), wetsuits and bodyboards; half-day surfing lessons cost $50.

SLEEPING & EATING

Cayucos doesn't lack for motels or beachfront inns, most high-priced compared with Morro Bay (see p477).

Seaside Motel (☎ 805-995-3809, 800-549-0900; www.seasidemotel.com; 42 S Ocean Ave; d $70-155; wi-fi) Expect a warm welcome from the hands-on owners of this vintage motel. Country-kitsch rooms may be on the small side, but some have kitchenettes. Cross your fingers for quiet neighbors.

Cypress Tree Motel (☎ 805-995-3917; www.cypresstreemotel.com; 125 S Ocean Ave; d $77-117; wi-fi) This retro motor court has lovingly cared-for, but kinda hokey theme rooms, from 'Nautical Nellie,' where a net of seashells is suspended above the bed, to the 'Wild, Wild West,' where the bed is covered in an old-fashioned quilt.

Cayucos Beach Inn (☎ 805-995-2828, 800-482-0555; www.cayucosbeachinn.com; 333 S Ocean Ave; d incl breakfast $145-215) A remarkably pet-friendly motel, where even the doors have special peepholes for your canine. Otherwise, standard rooms may be nothing special, but there are invitingly grassy picnic areas and barbecue grills out front. Pet fee $10.

Cass House (☎ 805-995-3669; www.casshouseinn.com; 222 N Ocean Ave; d incl breakfast $175-375; wi-fi) Inside a renovated 1867 Victorian inn, opposite a gas station, five truly luxurious rooms await, some claiming ocean-view terraces and fireplaces. All have plush beds, flat-screen TVs and tasteful accents. Reservations are advised for the chef-driven French restaurant (three-/four-course prix-fixe dinner $48/56).

Ruddell's Smokehouse (☎ 805-995-5028; 101 D St; mains $4-10; 11am-6pm) 'Smoker Jim' transforms fresh-off-the-boat seafood into succulently smoked slabs, while fish tacos come slathered in a unique apple-celery relish. Squeeze yourself in the door to place your order, then scarf it down at an outside table (pets OK).

Sea Shanty (☎ 805-995-3272; 296 S Ocean Ave; mains $6-25; 8am-9pm, to 10pm Jun-Aug) At this family diner, where a bazillion baseball caps hang from the ceiling, just-OK fish-and-chips take a back seat to killer desserts – try the strawberry shortcake or 'Rocky Mountain High Pie.'

Hoppe's Bistro & Wine Bar (☎ 805-995-1006; 78 N Ocean Ave; mains lunch $8-36, dinner $14-60; 11am-10pm Wed-Sun) This kitschy but romantic classic features fresh seafood on its still-respectable seasonal menu, including incredible red-abalone

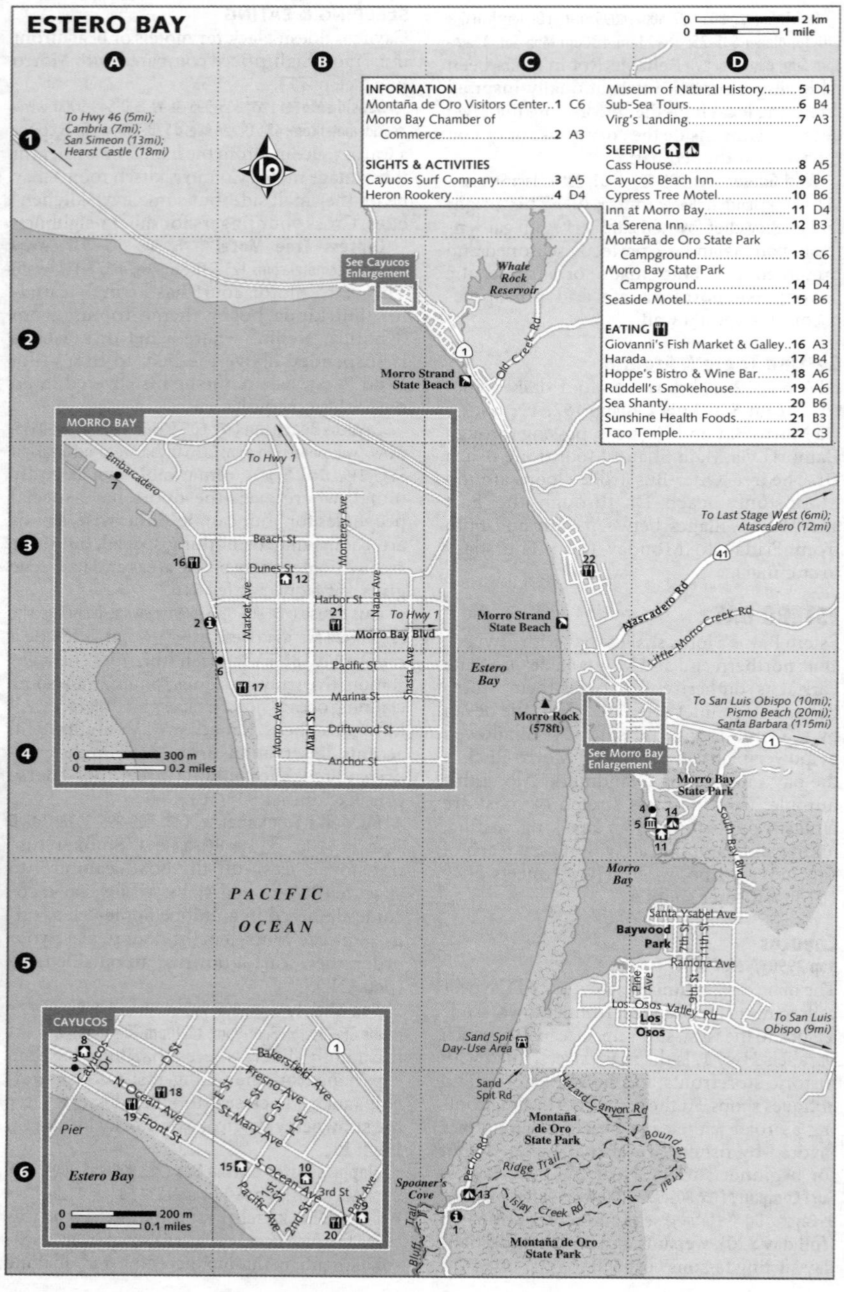
ESTERO BAY
0 2 km
0 1 mile
A
B
C
D
1
2
3
4
5
6
INFORMATION
Montaña de Oro Visitors Center..1 C6
Morro Bay Chamber of Commerce..2 A3
SIGHTS & ACTIVITIES
Cayucos Surf Company..3 A5
Heron Rookery..4 D4
Museum of Natural History..5 D4
Sub-Sea Tours..6 B4
Virg's Landing..7 A3
SLEEPING
Cass House..8 A5
Cayucos Beach Inn..9 B6
Cypress Tree Motel..10 B6
Inn at Morro Bay..11 D4
La Serena Inn..12 B3
Montaña de Oro State Park Campground..13 C6
Morro Bay State Park Campground..14 D4
Seaside Motel..15 B6
EATING
Giovanni's Fish Market & Galley..16 A3
Harada..17 B4
Hoppe's Bistro & Wine Bar..18 A6
Ruddell's Smokehouse..19 A6
Sea Shanty..20 B6
Sunshine Health Foods..21 B3
Taco Temple..22 C3
To Hwy 46 (5mi); Cambria (7mi); San Simeon (13mi); Hearst Castle (18mi)
See Cayucos Enlargement
Whale Rock Reservoir
Old Creek Rd
Morro Strand State Beach
To Last Stage West (6mi); Atascadero (12mi)
Atascadero Rd
Little Morro Creek Rd
Estero Bay
Morro Rock (578ft)
See Morro Bay Enlargement
To San Luis Obispo (10mi); Pismo Beach (20mi); Santa Barbara (115mi)
Morro Bay State Park
South Bay Blvd
Morro Bay
Santa Ysabel Ave
Baywood Park
7th St
11th St
Ramona Ave
Pine Ave
9th St
Los Osos Valley Rd
Los Osos
To San Luis Obispo (9mi)
Sand Spit Day-Use Area
Sand Spit Rd
Hazard Canyon Rd
Montaña de Oro State Park
Boundary Trail
Ridge Trail
Pecho Rd
Spooner's Cove
Islay Creek Rd
Bluff Trail
PACIFIC OCEAN
MORRO BAY
Embarcadero
To Hwy 1
Beach St
Dunes St
Monterey Ave
Harbor St
Napa Ave
Market Ave
To Hwy 1
Morro Bay Blvd
Pacific St
Shasta Ave
Marina St
Morro Ave
Main St
Driftwood St
Anchor St
0 300 m
0 0.2 miles
CAYUCOS
Cayucos Dr
D St
Bakersfield Ave
Fresno Ave
E St
F St
G St
H St
N Ocean Ave
St Mary Ave
Front St
Pier
Estero Bay
S Ocean Ave
1st St
2nd St
3rd St
Park Ave
Pacific Ave
0 200 m
0 0.1 miles

CENTRAL COAST

dishes. The sommelier knows local Paso Robles and Edna Valley wines.

GETTING THERE & AWAY

From San Luis Obispo, RTA bus 12 travels two to four times per day along Hwy 1 to Cayucos ($1.75, 1¼ hours) via Morro Bay, continuing north to Cambria ($1.25, 30 minutes) and Hearst Castle ($1.75, 45 minutes).

Morro Bay

pop 10,500 / elev 100ft

Home to a commercial fishing fleet, Morro Bay's biggest claim to fame is Morro Rock, a volcanic peak jutting dramatically from the ocean floor. It's one of the Nine Sisters, a 21-million-year-old chain of rocks stretching south to San Luis Obispo. Morro Bay's less boast-worthy landmark comes courtesy of the power plant, which threw up three cigarette-shaped smokestacks on the north side of town.

Leading south from Morro Rock is the Embarcadero, a small waterfront boulevard jam-packed with seafood eateries and souvenir shops. It's also the launching area for boat tours. The **chamber of commerce** (☎ 805-772-4467, 800-231-0592; www.morrobay.org; 845 Embarcadero; 9am-5pm Mon-Fri, 10am-4pm Sat) is in the thick of things. Three blocks uphill, Main St is the less tourist-driven part of town.

SIGHTS & ACTIVITIES

The town harbors extraordinary natural riches, worth a day's exploration.

Chumash tribespeople are the only people legally allowed to climb **Morro Rock**, as it's the protected nesting ground of peregrine falcons. You can laze at the small beach on the rock's north side, but you can't drive all the way around – instead, rent a kayak. The bay itself is a giant estuary inhabited by two dozen other threatened and endangered species, including brown pelicans, snowy plovers and sea otters.

For views of kelp forests and schools of fish, take a spin on a semisubmersible with **Sub-Sea Tours** (☎ 805-772-9463; www.subseatours.com; 699 Embarcadero; tours adult/child from $14/7, kayak rental 2/24hr $12/24; rentals 10am-5pm, sub tours 11am-4pm;); call ahead for reservations, especially in summer. Other places on the Embarcadero offer kayak rentals and whale-watching tours (adult/child from $30/20). If paddling out on your own, be aware of the tide schedules. Ideally, you'll want to ride the tide out and then back in; winds are calmest in the mornings. Salty dogs ready for a little sportfishing can book with **Virg's Landing** (☎ 805-772-1222, 800-762-5263; www.morrobaysportfishing.com; 1215 Embarcadero; tours $59-235).

South of the Embarcadero, **Morro Bay State Park** (☎ 805-772-2560; www.parks.ca.gov; admission free; sunrise-sunset) incorporates an 18-hole golf course and a marina with kayak rentals. **Central Coast Outdoors** (☎ 805-528-1080, 888-873-5610; www.centralcoastoutdoors.com; tours $65) arranges kayak tours (including full-moon trips) that launch from here, as well as guided hikes along the coast. At the state park's **Museum of Natural History** (☎ 805-772-2694; adult/child $2/free; 10am-5pm;), which has panoramic bay-view windows, cool interactive exhibits geared toward kids demonstrate how the forces of nature affect us all. Docents are often available to show visitors the wildlife mounts at the back of the museum. North of the museum is a eucalyptus grove with one of the last remaining great blue heron rookeries in California. Every January, bird-watchers flock together for the **Morro Bay Bird Festival** (☎ 805-275-4143, 866-464-5105; www.morrobaybirdfestival.org; 4-day pass $65), during which over 200 species can be spotted along the Pacific Flyway on this stretch of coast.

SLEEPING

Motels cluster along Harbor and Main Sts, off Hwy 1.

Morro Bay State Park Campground (☎ 805-772-7434, reservations ☎ 800-444-7275; www.reserveamerica.com; tent & RV sites without/with hookups $25/34) About 2 miles south of town, 135 woodsy sites are fringed by eucalyptus and cypress trees. There are fire rings, showers and trails leading to the beach.

La Serena Inn (☎ 805-772-5665; www.laserenainn.com; 990 Morro Ave; d $79-269; wi-fi) All of the large, immaculately kept rooms at this three-story hotel have microwaves and minifridges, and if you're lucky, private balconies with views of Morro Rock. You can hear the gentle clank-clank of boats in the harbor below.

Inn at Morro Bay (☎ 805-772-5651; www.innatmorrobay.com; 60 State Park Rd; d $149-279;) Inside the state park, this two-story waterfront lodge with brick-paved pathways delivers tranquility. Most of the rooms are comfortable, furnished with feather beds and gas fireplaces to ward off coastal fog, but avoid the motel-style petite queens.

EATING & DRINKING

Predictable seafood places line the Embarcadero.

Sunshine Health Foods (☎ 805-772-7873; 415 Morro Bay Blvd; mains $5-11; 11am-5:30pm Mon-Fri, 10:30am-5pm Sat; V) Has a mostly organic café serving karma-cleansing grub like tempeh tacos and blueberry smoothies.

Taco Temple (☎ 805-772-4965; 2680 Main St; mains $5-11; 11am-8pm Mon & Wed-Sat, to 8:30pm Sun) Nevermind the frontage road location (south of San Jacinto St): show up for huge helpings of Cal-Mex fusion flavor. At the next table, there might be fishers talking about the good ole' days or a group of starving surfers. Try one of the specials – they deserve the name. Cash only.

Giovanni's Fish Market & Galley (☎ 805-772-2123; 1001 Front St; mains $6-10; 9am-6pm) This family-run place on the Embarcadero is a classic California seafood shack. Folks line up for the fish-and-chips and killer garlic fries. Inside there's a market with all the fixin's for a beach barbecue or picnic.

our pick **Last Stage West** (☎ 805-461-1393; www.laststagewest.net; 15050 Morro Rd, Atascadero; mains $6-28; lunch & dinner Tue-Sun) At this Old West roadhouse and indie live-music venue, say 'Howdy, pardner!' to smoked tri-tip barbecue, slow-cooked pork ribs and ribeye steak. While you're waiting for dinner, step out back to feed the koi. To find the roadhouse, watch out for the wagon wheel along Hwy 41, about 10 miles northeast of Hwy 1 in Morro Bay, or 6 miles west of Hwy 101.

Harada (☎ 805-772-1410; 630 Embarcadero; mains lunch $14-19, dinner $23-35; lunch & dinner) Even sushi snobs from LA have to agree: this authentic Japanese restaurant serves up outstanding hot and cold dishes, with a few tasty concessions to California fusion tastes. Worthy of a Kurosawa movie set, this mini faux-Japanese castle is a serene upstairs retreat from the crushing Embarcadero crowds

GETTING THERE & AROUND

From San Luis Obispo, RTA bus 12 travels hourly along Hwy 1 to Morro Bay ($1.50, one hour). Two to four daily runs continue north to Cayucos ($1.25, 15 minutes), Cambria ($1.50, 45 minutes) and Hearst Castle ($2, one hour). In summer, a trolley (single ride 50¢, all-day pass $2) frequently loops around the waterfront and downtown, operating varying hours from Friday through Monday.

Montaña de Oro State Park

In spring the hills are blanketed by bright poppies, wild mustard and other wildflowers, giving this **state park** (☎ 805-772-7434; www.parks.ca.gov; Pecho Rd, Los Osos; admission free; sunrise-sunset) its Spanish name, meaning 'mountain of gold.' Incredibly windy coastal bluffs are a favorite spot for hiking, mountain-biking and horseback riding. The northern half of the park features sand dunes and an ancient marine terrace visible due to seismic uplifting. **Spooner's Cove**, once used by smugglers, is now a beautiful sandy beach and picnic area. If you go tidepooling, only touch the marine creatures such as sea stars, limpets and crabs with the back of one hand to avoid disturbing them, and never remove them from their aquatic homes. You can hike along the beach and the grassy ocean bluffs, or drive uphill past the visitors center to the start of the 7-mile loop trail tackling **Valencia and Oats Peaks**.

Tucked into a small canyon by the visitors center, an undeveloped **campground** (☎ reservations 800-444-7275; www.reserveamerica.com; tent & RV sites $11-15) has pleasantly cool sites with fire rings, vault toilets and drinking water. There are environmental walk-in sites, too.

The park boundary is 7 miles southwest of Hwy 1; exit at South Bay Blvd, then follow the signs through Los Osos. From Hwy 101 south of San Luis Obispo, exit at Los Osos Valley Rd and drive about 12 miles northwest.

HIGHWAY 101

Riding inland along Hwy 101 is a quicker way to travel between the Bay Area and Southern California. Although it lacks the striking scenery of coastal Hwy 1, the historic El Camino Real (the King's Highway), established by Spanish conquistadors and missionaries, has a beauty of its own, ranging from the fertile fields of Salinas (immortalized by John Steinbeck) to the oak-dappled green and golden hills of San Luis Obispo and beyond. Along the way are ghostly missions, the jaw-dropping Pinnacles National Monument and many excellent wineries, especially around Paso Robles and in the Santa Maria and Santa Ynez Valleys north of Santa Barbara. Greyhound buses

TOP FIVE REGIONAL FOOD FESTIVALS

- Castroville's **Artichoke Festival** (p458) – mid-May
- **Gilroy Garlic Festival** (below) – late July
- Watsonville's **Monterey Bay Strawberry Festival** (p458) – mid-August
- Carmel Valley's **TomatoFest** (p464) – mid-September
- Carpinteria's **Avocado Festival** (p499) – early October

and Amtrak trains travel along Hwy 101, the latter on the *Coast Starlight* route (p738).

GILROY

pop 48,550 / elev 200ft

Thirty miles south of San Jose, the self-proclaimed 'garlic capital of the world' puts on the overthronged **Gilroy Garlic Festival** (☎ 408-842-1625; http://gilroygarlicfestival.com) on the last full weekend in July. We can tell you from experience that eating mostly mediocre chow in the blazing hot sun is not much fun.

Unusual **Gilroy Gardens** (☎ 408-840-7100; www.gilroygardens.org; adult/child 3-6yr $43/33; daily Jun-Aug, Sat & Sun only Apr-May & Sep-Nov;) is a nonprofit family theme park focused on food and plants rather than cartoon characters. You've got to really love flowers, fruit and veggies, though. Opening hours vary.

Heading east on Hwy 152 toward I-5, **Casa de Fruta** (☎ 408-842-7282; www.casadefruta.com; 10021 Pacheco Pass Hwy, Hollister; admission free, rides from $2.50;) is a commercialized farm stand with some hokey, old-fashioned fun for tots, like carousel rides and choo-choo trains. Call for opening hours.

SAN JUAN BAUTISTA

pop 1730 / elev 220ft

In atmospheric old San Juan Bautista, where you can practically hear the whispers of the past, California's 15th mission is fronted by the only original Spanish plaza remaining in the state. The town has plenty of attractive historic buildings along 3rd St, mostly antiques shops and petite garden restaurants and cafés. Hark! That cock you hear crowing is one of the town's roosters, which are allowed by tradition to stroll the streets at will.

Founded in 1797, **Mission San Juan Bautista** (☎ 831-623-4528; www.oldmissionsjb.org; 406 2nd St; adult/child $4/2; 9:30am-4:30pm) has the largest church among California's original 21 missions. Since it was unknowingly built directly atop the San Andreas Fault, the mission has been rocked by earthquakes. Bells hanging in the tower today include chimes that were salvaged after the 1906 San Francisco earthquake toppled the original mission. Parts of Alfred Hitchcock's thriller *Vertigo* were shot here, although the bell tower in the climactic scene is just a special effect – sorry. Below the cemetery, a section of El Camino Real can be seen. This Spanish colonial road, built to link the missions, was the state's first. In many places Hwy 101 still follows the original route.

Buildings around the old Spanish plaza, between Washington and Mariposa Sts, are part of **San Juan Bautista State Historic Park** (☎ 831-623-4526; www.parks.ca.gov; 2nd St; adult/child $2/free; 10am-4:30pm). The large plaza stables hint at San Juan Bautista in its heyday as a stagecoach stop in the 1860s. The railroad quickly bypassed the town in 1876, and it has been a sleepy backwater ever since. Across the street is the 1858 **Plaza Hotel**, which started life as a single-story adobe building, and now houses a little historical museum. Next door, the **Castro-Breen Adobe** belonged to Mexican general José Maria Castro, who led a successful revolt against an unpopular governor, and in 1848 was bought by the Breen family, survivors of the Donner Party disaster (see the boxed text, p367).

Eleven miles south of town, **Fremont Peak State Park** (☎ 831-623-4255; San Juan Canyon Rd; per vehicle $4; 8am-30min after sunset) has a pretty, but primitive, 20-site **campground** (tent & RV sites $15) shaded by oak trees on a hilltop with distant views of Monterey Bay. Equipped with a 30in telescope, the park's **astronomical observatory** (☎ 831-623-2465;) is usually open to the public on moonless Saturday nights between April and October, starting at 8pm.

In town, **La Poblanita** (☎ 831-623-2161; 313 3rd St; mains $8-22; 9am-9pm Mon-Wed, 6:30am-9pm Thu, 6:30am-10pm Fri & Sat, 7:30am-1pm Sun) is the most reliable of a long lineup of touristy Mexican eateries; try the mole sauce and *chiles rellenos* (stuffed peppers). At **San Juan Bakery** (☎ 831-623-4570; 319 3rd St; snacks $2-4; 7:30am-5pm), pick up fresh loaves of cinnamon bread to sustain you during the drive south to San Luis Obispo. Get there early, as they often sell out.

San Juan Bautista is on Hwy 156, a 3-mile detour east of Hwy 101, south of Gilroy en route to Monterey or Salinas. Further south,

Hwy 101 enters the sun-dappled eucalyptus grove that James Stewart and Kim Novak drove through in *Vertigo*.

SALINAS

pop 148,350 / elev 41ft

Best known as the birthplace of John Steinbeck and nicknamed the 'Salad Bowl of the World,' Salinas is a working-class agricultural center with down-and-out, even mean streets. It makes a strong contrast with the affluence of the Monterey Peninsula, a fact of life that helped shape Steinbeck's novel *East of Eden*. The historic center stretches out along Main St, punctuated by the National Steinbeck Center at its northern end.

Pick up information and maps at the **Salinas Visitors Center** (☎ 831-424-7611; www.salinaschamber.com; 119 E Alisal St; 🕙 8am-5pm Mon-Fri), four blocks east of Main St.

Sights & Activities

The impressive **National Steinbeck Center** (☎ 831-796-3833; www.steinbeck.org; 1 Main St; adult/child $11/6; 🕙 10am-5pm; 🚸) will enthrall almost anyone, even if you don't know a lick about Salinas' Nobel Prize–winning native son, John Steinbeck (1902–68), whose literary explorations were influenced and inspired by the people who settled here from all over the world. Interactive exhibits chronicle the writer's life and works in an engaging way. Gems include Rocinante, the customized camper in which Steinbeck traveled around America while researching *Travels with Charley*. Take a moment and listen to his Nobel acceptance speech; it's grace and power combined. The center also includes the **Rabobank Agricultural Museum**, which takes visitors on a journey through the modern agricultural industry, from water to pesticides to transportation – trust us, it's way more interesting than it sounds.

Steinbeck was born and spent much of his boyhood in what is now **Steinbeck House** (132 Central Ave), three blocks west of the center. It's now a twee lunch **café** (☎ 831-424-2735; mains $10-12; 🕙 11:30am-2pm Tue-Sat). We're not sure he'd approve. Steinbeck is buried in the Hamilton family plot at the **Garden of Memories Cemetery** (cnr Abbott St & Romie Lane), less than two miles south of the center.

The Farm (☎ 831-455-2575; www.thefarm-salinasvalley.com; admission free, tours adult/child from $8/6; 🕙 9am-5pm Mon-Sat 10 Mar-20 Dec, to 6pm in summer) offers educational 45-minute walking tours of its mostly organic fields, usually at 1pm on Tuesdays and Thursdays. During the tour, watch for the giant-sized sculptures of farm workers by local artist John Cerney, also seen along Hwy 101 as you drive through the valley. The Farm is off Hwy 68 at Spreckels Rd, 4 miles southwest of Hwy 101; take the Sanborn Rd exit. **Ag Venture Tours** (☎ 831-384-7686; www.whps.com/agtours; half-/full-day minivan tours from $60/80) takes a more in-depth look at commercial farm fields and vineyards.

Festivals & Events

California Rodeo Salinas (☎ 831-775-3100; www.carodeo.com) Starts on the third Thursday of July.

Steinbeck Festival (☎ 831-775-4724; www.steinbeck.org) This four-day festival in August features films, lectures, guided tours, music and dancing.

California International Airshow (☎ 831-754-1983; www.salinasairshow.com) Held in September or October.

Sleeping

Salinas has plenty of budget motels, making it a less-expensive base from which to explore the Monterey Peninsula. Many are off Hwy 101, including at the Market St exit, where there are numerous chains, including an always-popular In-N-Out Burger.

Laurel Inn (☎ 831-449-2474, 800-354-9831; www.laurelinnmotel.com; 801 W Laurel Dr, off Hwy 101; r $60-100; wi-fi) A decent choice if chains don't do it for you, this sprawling, family-owned place has predictable motel rooms that are nevertheless spacious. There's a swimming pool, hot tub and dry sauna for relaxing.

Best Western Salinas Valley Inn & Suites (☎ 831-751-6411; www.bestwestern.com; 187 Kern St, off Hwy 101; r incl breakfast $89-299; wi-fi) As posh as you can get next to the freeway (take the Market St exit), the newer, more tasteful rooms here are great for extended stays. There's an outdoor pool, hot tub, exercise room and self-service laundry. The nearby Best Western Salinas Monterey Hotel, however, is not recommended.

Eating & Drinking

Monterey Coast Brewing (☎ 831-758-2337; 165 Main St; mains $8-25; 🕙 11am-9pm) A two-minute walk from the Steinbeck Center, this microbrewery is a welcome sign of life downtown. Chow down on enormous ranch burgers, fried calamari and flourless chocolate cake. A nine-beer tasting sampler costs under 10 bucks.

Hullaballoo (☎ 831-757-3663; 228 Main St; mains $8-25; 11:30am-9pm Mon-Thu, 11:30am-10pm Fri, 4-10pm Sat, 4-9pm Sun) There's a lively, artistic feel here, and a seasonally changing menu billed as 'bold American cooking' that features local produce – including awesome salads, of course. Bargain-priced daily lunch and three-course dinner specials are popular with locals. So's the bar.

Salinas Valley Fish House (☎ 831-775-0175; 172 Main St; mains $14-22; lunch Mon-Fri, dinner daily) An inland sister restaurant to the famed Monterey's Fish House (p459), this friendly place – where the staff all know locals' names by heart – really delivers, from barbecued oysters to blackened salmon and seafood ravioli.

Shopping

A Taste of Monterey (☎ 831-751-1980; www.tastemonterey.com; tasting fee $5; 127 Main St; 11am-5pm Mon-Thu, 11am-6pm Fri & Sat, 11am-4pm Sun) Downtown, this place lets you sample local wines and hands out Hwy 101 vineyard maps.

Getting There & Away

The **Greyhound bus station** (☎ 831-424-4418; cnr Gabilan & Salinas Sts) offers several daily runs to Santa Cruz ($11 to $15, 65 minutes), and along Hwy 101 north to San Francisco ($22 to $30, four hours) and south to Santa Barbara ($40 to $51, 5¼ hours).

From the **train station** (cnr Station Pl & Railroad Ave), Amtrak has daily service on the Seattle–LA *Coast Starlight*, stopping in Paso Robles ($18 to $29, two hours), San Luis Obispo ($22 to $37, three hours) and Santa Barbara ($38 to $59, 6½ hours). Several daily Thruway buses connect with regional trains in San Jose (see p189).

From the Salinas Transit Center, one block west of the Steinbeck Center and two blocks south of the Amtrak station, **Monterey-Salinas Transit** (MST; ☎ 831-424-7695, 888-678-2871; www.mst.org) buses 20 and 21 makes the 55-minute run to Monterey every 30 to 60 minutes daily.

PINNACLES NATIONAL MONUMENT

Named for the towering spires that rise abruptly out of the chaparral-covered hills east of Salinas Valley, this off-the-beaten-path **park** (☎ 831-389-4485; www.nps.gov/pinn; per vehicle $5; east entrance 24hr, west entrance 7:30am-8pm) protects the remains of an ancient volcano. A study in stunning geological drama, its craggy monoliths, sheer-walled canyons and twisting caves are the result of millions of years of erosion. The best times to visit are spring and fall; the heat of summer is too extreme.

The namesake rock formations divide the park. For the less-developed west entrance, exit Hwy 101 at Soledad and follow Hwy 146 northeast 14 miles. The east entrance is accessed via lonely Hwy 25 in San Benito County, southeast of Hollister and northeast of King City. There is no road connecting the two sides of the park, but you can hike across in about an hour. Information, maps, books and bottled water are available on the east side, from the visitors center inside the campground store.

Besides rock climbing (for info on routes, surf to www.pinnacles.org), the park's biggest attractions are its two talus caves, formed by piles of boulders. **Balconies Cave** is always open for exploration. Scrambling through it is not an exercise recommended for claustrophobes, as it's pitch-black inside, making a flashlight essential. Be prepared to get lost a bit, too. The cave is on a 2-mile hiking loop from the west entrance. Nearer the east entrance, **Bear Gulch Cave** is closed seasonally, so as not to disturb a resident colony of Townsend's big-eared bats.

To really appreciate Pinnacles' stark beauty, you need to hike. Moderate loops of varying lengths and difficulty ascend into the **High Peaks** and include some thrillingly narrow clifftop sections. In the early morning or late afternoon, you may spot endangered California condors flying overhead. Rangers lead full-moon and dark-sky hikes, as well as guided bat-viewing and star-gazing programs, on select Friday and Saturday nights from spring to fall. Reservations are required; call ☎ 831-389-4485.

On the park's east side, the popular **campground** (☎ reservations 877-444-6777; www.recreation.gov; tent/RV sites with hookups $23/36;) has some shady sites, plus water, barbecue pits and a seasonal outdoor pool.

MISSION SAN ANTONIO DE PADUA

Remote, tranquil and evocative, this **mission** (☎ 831-385-4478; www.missionsanantonio.net; Mission Rd, Jolon; adult/child $5/3; 9am-5pm) sits in the middle of Fort Hunter Liggett Military Reservation. It was founded in 1771 by Franciscan priest Junípero Serra. Built with Native American labor, the church has been restored to its 1813 appearance, with a wooden pulpit, canopied altar and decorative flourishes on whitewashed walls. A creaky door leads to a cloistered garden anchored by a fountain. The museum has a small collection of such utilitarian items as an olive press and a weaving loom once used in the mission's workshops. Around the grounds, you can inspect the remains of a grist mill and irrigation system with aqueducts.

It's seldom crowded, and you may have this vast site all to yourself. Pick up a visitor's pass from a military checkpoint on the way in; bring photo ID and proof of your vehicle's registration. From the north, take the Jolon Rd exit off Hwy 101 before King City and follow Jolon Rd (County Rte G14) about 18 miles south to Mission Rd. From the south, take the Jolon Rd (County Rte G18) exit off Hwy 101 and drive 22 miles northwest to Mission Rd. You can also reach the mission from Big Sur and Hwy 1, about 28 miles away via rugged Nacimiento-Fergusson Rd.

SAN MIGUEL

pop 1500 / elev 640ft

San Miguel is a small farming town right off Hwy 101, where life seems to have remained almost unchanged for decades. **Mission San Miguel Arcángel** (☎ 805-467-3256; www.missionsanmiguel.org; 775 Mission St; suggested donation family/individual $5/2; 9:30am-4:30pm) suffered heartbreaking damage during the 2003 Paso Robles earthquake. Previously it was one of the most accessible and authentic of the California missions. While repairs are underway, the museum, living quarters, gardens and other areas remain open. The enormous cactus out front was planted around the same time as the mission was built in 1818.

Just south of the mission is the **Rios-Caledonia Adobe** (☎ 805-467-3357; www.rios-caledoniaadobe.org; 700 S Mission St; admission by donation; 11am-4pm Fri-Sun), which stands on mission property that Mexican Governor Pio Pico illegally sold to Petronillo Rios in 1846. Using Chumash labor, Rios built the two-story adobe as a ranch headquarters and hacienda for his family, later turning it into a roadhouse on the stagecoach route between Los Angeles and San Francisco.

Inside a retro converted gas station, **Sam's Coffee Station** (☎ 805-467-2100; 1199 Mission St; items $2-6; 6am-2:30pm Mon-Thu, 6am-7pm Fri-Sun) vends live-wire espresso drinks, delicious sandwiches and whopping good brownies to keep you going strong, plus barbecued pork ribs, chicken and steak on weekend evenings.

PASO ROBLES

pop 29,000 / elev 721ft

Thirty minutes north of San Luis Obispo, Paso Robles is the heart of an agricultural region where grapes are now the biggest moneymaking crop. Several dozen wineries along Hwy 46 produce a brave new world of more-than-respectable bottles. The Mediterranean climate is yielding another bounty, too: there's a fledging olive-oil industry.

Historic downtown Paso Robles centers on Park and 12th Sts, where boutique shops and wine-tasting rooms await. The **chamber of commerce** (☎ 805-238-0506; www.pasoroblechamber.com; 1225 Park St; 8:30am-5pm Mon-Fri, 10am-2pm Sat & Sun) has winery maps and information.

Wineries & Tasting Rooms

You could spend days wandering the back roads off Hwy 46, both east and west of Hwy 101. Most vineyards have tasting rooms (tasting fees typically around $5) and a few offer tours. For anything else you might want to know, ask the **Paso Robles Wine Country Alliance** (☎ 800-549-9463; www.pasowine.com).

Some of our favorite wineries:

Castoro Cellars (☎ 805-238-0725; www.castorocellars.com; 1315 N Bethel Rd, off W Hwy 46; 10am-5:30pm) Husband-and-wife team produces 'dam fine wine' (the mascot is a beaver, get it?), including from custom-crushed and organic grapes.

Clautiere Vineyard (☎ 805-237-3789; www.clautierevineyard.com; 1340 Penman Springs Rd, off E Hwy 46; noon-5pm) Don't let the fantastical tasting room, where you can try on Dr Seuss-ian hats, fool you: serious Rhône-style blends will delight connoisseurs.

Eberle Winery (☎ 805-238-9607; www.eberlewinery.com; 3810 E Hwy 46; 10am-5pm Oct-Mar, 10am-6pm Apr-Sep) Offers lofty vineyard views, bocce ball courts and daily tours of its wine caves.

our pick Tobin James (☎ 805-239-2204; www.tobinjames.com; 8950 Union Rd, off E Hwy 46; 10am-6pm) Boisterous Old West saloon pours bold reds, including an outlaw 'Ballistic' zinfandel and 'Liquid Love' late-harvest dessert wine. No tasting fee.

York Mountain Winery (☎ 805-238-3925; www.yorkmountainwinery.com; 7505 York Mountain Rd, off W Hwy 46; 11am-4pm) The region's oldest winery (since 1882) has a log-cabin tasting room and award-winning pinot noirs.

Zenaida Cellars (☎ 866-936-5638; 1550 W Hwy 46; 11am-5pm) Rustic tasting room that's simply Zen for sampling estate zins and the signature 'Fire Sign' blend. Overnight vineyard accommodations available.

Festivals & Events

Wine festivals (www.pasowine.com) Wine buffs should show up for April's Zinfandel Festival, the Wine Festival in May or the Harvest Wine Weekend in October.

California Mid-State Fair (☎ 805-238-3565; www.midstatefair.com; adult/child $8/5) In late July and early August, this is a huge draw, with live rock concerts, farm exhibits, carnival rides and a rodeo.

Sleeping

Chain motels and hotels line Hwy 101, while B&Bs are scattered among the vineyards in the wine country (browse listings at www.pasowine.com).

Melody Ranch Motel (☎ 805-238-3911, 800-909-3911; 939 Spring St; r $48-70;) There's just one story and only 19 basic rooms at this small, family-owned, 1950s motor court downtown, but that translates into small prices at this budgetary friend. Take comfort in the tiny outdoor pool.

Wild Coyote Estate Winery (☎ 805-610-1311; www.wildcoyote.biz; 3775 Adelaida Rd; d incl breakfast $225-275;) Steal yourself away among the vineyards, where romantic adobe-walled casitas echo the Southwest and a complimentary bottle of wine awaits by a kiva-style fireplace. There's an outdoor hot tub and barbecue grills.

Hotel Cheval (☎ 805-226-9995, 866-522-6999; www.hotelcheval.com; 1021 Pine St; r $225-425; wi-fi) Cocoon with your lover inside an art-splashed aerie at this boutique hotel downtown. A dozen stylish, modern rooms all come with California king beds, spa-worthy amenities and plantation shutters. Some have gas fireplaces and sun decks with teak furniture. Staff can be snobby.

Also recommended:

Paso Robles Inn (☎ 805-238-2660, 800-676-1713; www.pasoroblesinn.com; 1103 Spring St; r $95-265;) Rustic 19th-century downtown hotel with a mineral hot-springs pool. Wi-fi in lobby.

Courtyard Marriott (☎ 805-239-9700, 888-236-2427; www.marriott.com; 120 S Vine St, off Hwy 101; r $129-289; wi-fi) Top-notch business hotel with immaculate rooms and full amenities.

Eating & Drinking

Restaurants, cafés and bars surround downtown's grassy central square, off Spring St between 11th and 12th Sts.

Vinoteca (☎ 805-227-7154; 835 12th St; shared plates $3-23; 4-9pm Sun & Mon, 4-10pm Tue-Thu, 4-11pm Fri & Sat) This romantic wine bar with cushy sofas will send you soaring with its wine flights (a series of typically three tasting-sized pours), artisan cheese plates and tapas-style hors d'oeuvres. Local winemakers often host Wednesday evening tasting events.

our pick **Artisan** (☎ 805-237-8084; 1401 Park St; mains lunch $12-20, dinner $21-30; 11am-10pm Mon-Sat, 10am-10pm Sun) Ecoconscious chef Chris Kobayashi often ducks out of the kitchen just to make sure you're loving his impeccable contemporary renditions of modern American cuisine, featuring sustainably farmed meats and wild-caught seafood. Expect long waits, though.

Villa Creek (☎ 805-238-3000; 1144 Pine St; mains $20-40; dinner) Perch casually at the wine bar or dine like a don in the formal restaurant, which marries early Spanish-colonial mission cooking traditions with sustainable, organic ingredients, as seen in shepherd's plates of artisan cheese, sausages and olives, or rancho-style cassoulet with duck.

DETOUR: CHOLAME

In Cholame, about 25 miles east of Paso Robles via Hwy 46, there's a **monument** near the spot where *Rebel Without a Cause* star James Dean fatally crashed his Porsche on September 30, 1955, at the age of 24. Ironically, the actor had recently filmed a public-safety campaign TV spot, in which he said, 'The road is no place to race your car. It's real murder. Remember, drive safely. The life you save might be mine.' Look for the shiny silver memorial wrapped around an oak tree outside the Jack Ranch Cafe, which has old photographs and movie-star memorabilia inside.

Getting There & Away

Greyhound has several daily routes along Hwy 101 from Paso's downtown **bus and train station** (☎ 805-238-1242; 800 Pine St). Amtrak has daily service on the *Coast Starlight*, heading north to Salinas ($18 to $29, two hours) and south to Santa Barbara ($20 to $31, 4½ hours). Several daily Thruway buses link to regional trains in San Luis Obispo (p487), Santa Barbara (p503) and San Jose (p189).

From San Luis Obispo, RTA bus 9 travels north to Paso Robles ($2, 70 minutes) several times daily from Monday to Friday, with three or four daily services on weekends.

SAN LUIS OBISPO

pop 44,450 / elev 234ft

Almost halfway between LA and San Francisco, and inland from the coast, San Luis Obispo (aka SLO) is a lively yet low-key town with an enviably high quality of life and *mucho* community spirit. With no must-see attractions, it might not seem to warrant high ranking on your itinerary, but its proximity to beaches, state parks and Hearst Castle (40 miles north on Hwy 1) make it a convenient hub. It's also one of those small cities that doles out urban pleasures and rural charm in equal measure – to wit: drive-throughs are illegal downtown. California Polytechnic State University (aka Cal Poly) students inject a healthy dose of hubbub into the city's streets, pubs and cafés throughout the school year. Nestled at the base of the Santa Lucia foothills, SLO is also just a grape's throw from thriving Edna Valley wineries, known for their crisp chardonnays and subtle syrahs.

Orientation & Information

SLO's compact downtown is bisected by the main one-way arteries of Higuera St and Marsh St, which run parallel to each other. San Luis Obispo Creek, once used to irrigate mission orchards, flows through downtown alongside Higuera St. Many banks are off Marsh St, near the main post office. Most student-filled cafés, including Linnaea's (p486), offer free wi-fi.

Chamber of commerce (☎ 805-781-2777; www.visitslo.com; 1039 Chorro St; 🕑 10am-5pm Sun-Wed, 10am-7pm Thu-Sat) Free maps and information.

FedEx Office (☎ 805-543-3363; 1127 Chorro St; per min 20-30¢; 🕑 7:30am-10pm Mon-Fri, 10am-6pm Sat & Sun) High-speed internet workstations.

Sierra Vista Regional Medical Center (☎ 805-546-7600; 1010 Murray Ave, off N Santa Rosa St; 🕑 emergency room 24hr) Across Hwy 1 from an urgent-care walk-in clinic.

Sights

SLO's minor attractions cluster around **Mission Plaza**, a shady oasis with restored adobe buildings and fountains overlooking the creek. Look for the Moon Tree, a coast redwood grown from a seed that journeyed on board Apollo 14's lunar mission.

Those satisfyingly reverberatory bells you'll hear are emanating from **Mission San Luis Obispo de Tolosa** (☎ 805-543-6850; www.missionsanluisobispo.org; suggested donation $3; 🕑 9am-4pm), still an active parish. The fifth California mission, it was established in 1772 and named for a 13th-century French saint. Nicknamed the 'Prince of the Missions,' its modest church has an unusual L-shape and whitewashed walls depicting Stations of the Cross. An adjacent building contains an old-fashioned museum about daily life during the Chumash and Spanish periods.

For an overview of local history, check out the **San Luis Obispo County Historical Museum** (☎ 805-543-0638; www.slochs.org; 696 Monterey St; admission free; 🕑 10am-4pm Wed-Sun), housed in a 1905 Carnegie Library. Nearby, the creek is lined with shady trails and public art, leading to the **San Luis Obispo Art Center** (☎ 805-543-8562; www.sloartcenter.org; 1010 Broad St; admission free; 🕑 11am-5pm Wed-Mon), which showcases local artists and traveling exhibitions from around California.

SLO's weirdest sight is **Bubblegum Alley**, off the 700 block of Higuera St. It's colorfully plastered with thousands of wads of ABC gum. Watch where you step.

Activities

There are good hikes around SLO, many starting from Poly Canyon Rd on the Cal Poly campus. Hiking maps and parking info are available at the booth on the right as you enter campus.

The most popular local trail summits **Bishop Peak** (1546ft), the tallest of the Nine Sisters, a chain of volcanic peaks. The 2.2-mile one-way trail starts in a grove of live oaks (watch out for poison oak, too) and heads along rocky, exposed switchbacks. Scramble up boulders at the top for panoramic bay views. To get to the trailhead, drive northwest from downtown on Santa Rosa St (Hwy 1), turn left onto Highland Dr, then right onto Patricia Dr; after a half-mile look for three black posts with a trailhead sign on your left.

More varied hikes are found in nearby Montaña de Oro State Park (p478).

Sleeping

Motels cluster along the northeastern end of Monterey St near Hwy 101, and on Santa Rosa St, off the Hwy 101 exit connecting to Hwy 1.

HI Hostel Obispo (☎ 805-544-4678; www.hostelobispo.com; 1617 Santa Rosa St; dm $22-25, r $45-75; 🕑 closed 10am-4:30pm; 💻) On a lovely tree-lined street, this solar-empowered, avocado-colored hostel inhabits a cozy Victorian, which gives it a bit

CENTRAL COAST

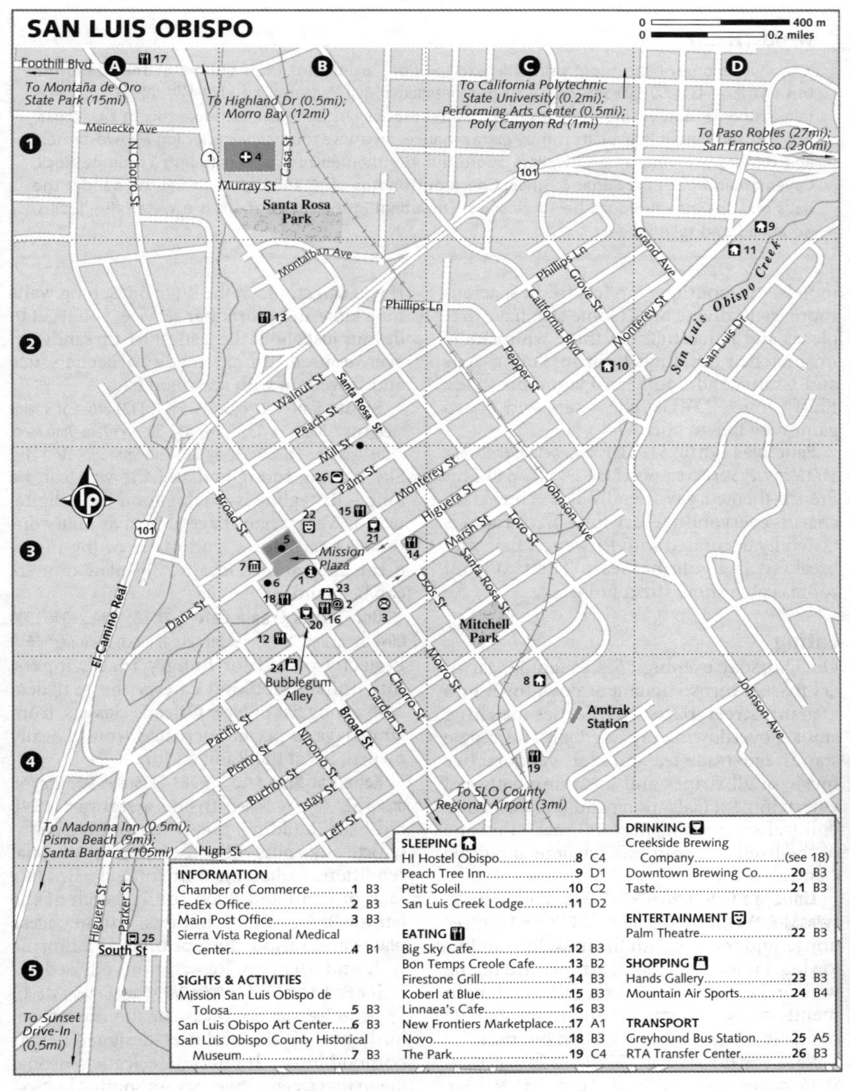

of a B&B feel. Amenities include a kitchen, games room, garden patio and bike rentals ($10 per day). For breakfast there are often sourdough pancakes. No credit cards.

Peach Tree Inn (☎ 805-543-3170, 800-227-6396; www.peachtreeinn.com; 2001 Monterey St; r incl breakfast $79-170; wi-fi) The friendly, folksy motel rooms here look inviting, especially those right by the creek or with rocking chairs on wooden porches overlooking grassy lawns, eucalyptus trees and rose gardens. Rates include a hearty breakfast with homemade breads.

San Luis Creek Lodge (☎ 805-541-1122, 800-593-0333; www.sanluiscreeklodge.com; 1941 Monterey St; r incl breakfast $130-250; wi-fi) Although it rubs shoulders a little too closely with neighboring

WHAT THE...?

'Oh, my!' is one of the more printable exclamations overheard from visitors at the **Madonna Inn** (☎ 805-543-3000, 800-543-9666; www.madonnainn.com; 100 Madonna Rd; r $179-449;), a fairy-tale-ish confection visible from Hwy 101. You'd expect outrageous kitsch like this in Las Vegas, not SLO, but here it is, in all its campy extravagance. Japanese tourists, vacationing Midwesterners and hip, irony-loving urban dwellers adore the 109 themed rooms – including Yosemite Rock, Caveman and hot-pink Sugar & Spice. Check out photos of all the rooms online, or wander the halls and spy into the ones being cleaned. The urinal in the men's room is a waterfall – ladies, go ahead and take a peek.

motels, this boutique inn has fresh, spacious rooms with divine beds (some also have fireplaces and jetted tubs) in three whimsically mismatched buildings built in Tudor, Arts and Crafts, and Southern Plantation styles. Fluffy robes, DVDs, chess sets and board games are free to borrow.

Petit Soleil (☎ 805-549-0321; www.petitsoleilslo.com; 1473 Monterey St; r incl breakfast $159-299; wi-fi) This French-themed, gay-friendly 'bed et breakfast' charms everyone at every turn. Each room is tastefully decorated with Provençal flair, and breakfast is a gourmet feast. The two front rooms catch some street noise.

Eating

On Thursday evenings, SLO's famous farmers market turns Higuera St downtown into a giant street party. Barbecues belching smoke, overflowing organic fruit and veggie stands, fair-trade tea and craft vendors, live music of all stripes and lotsa unintentional entertainment (salvation peddlers, wackadoo political signature collectors) make this one of the liveliest evenings anywhere along the Central Coast.

Linnaea's Cafe (☎ 805-541-5888; 1110 Garden St; mains $4-8; 6:30am-10pm; wi-fi) SLO's first coffeehouse, and the one with the most fervent following, Linnaea's has local art splashed on the walls and live music on weekends. Weeknight menus carry a theme (waffle night, tamale night etc). There's a tiny garden out back.

Novo (☎ 805-543-3986; 726 Higuera St; small plates $5-16, dinner mains $15-22; 11am-10pm Mon-Sat, 10am-10pm Sun) Airy Novo crafts hit-or-miss Mediterranean, Brazilian and Asian-inspired tapas, with an eye toward freshness and presentation. Doll yourself up, choose one of dozens of international beers, wines or sakes, and savor the view from the creekside deck.

Firestone Grill (☎ 805-783-1001; 1001 Higuera St; mains $6-10; 11am-10pm Sun-Thu, 11am-11pm Fri & Sat) If you can stomach the huge lines, long waits for a table and sports-bar service, you'll get to devour just about the tastiest tri-tip sandwich ever, doused in homemade barbecue sauce and served up with seasoned fries.

Big Sky Cafe (☎ 805-545-5401; 1121 Broad St; mains breakfast & lunch $6-13, dinner $13-20; 7am-9pm Mon, 7am-10pm Tue-Fri, 8am-10pm Sat, 8am-9pm Sun; V) Big Sky is a big room, and still the wait can be long – its tagline is 'analog food for a digital world.' Vegetarians have almost as many options as carnivores, and many of the ingredients are sourced locally. Big-plate dinners can be bland.

Bon Temps Creole Cafe (☎ 805-544-2100; 1000 Olive St; mains $8-17; breakfast, lunch & dinner;) Perfectly placed for hungry road-trippers, this unlikely looking café is the real deal with a long list of New Orleans classics, from jambalaya to pecan-encrusted trout. Locally owned, it's at the Ramada Inn.

Koberl at Blue (☎ 805-783-1135; 998 Monterey St; mains $22-48; dinner) Inside a stalwart 1898 red-brick building, this wine-country bistro effortlessly spins off contemporary seasonal renditions of haute continental classics like rack of lamb and duck confit. Perch at the bar for Bloody Mary shooters, artisan cheese plates and serious European and California wine and beer lists. Reservations advised.

The Park (☎ 805-545-0000; 1819 Osos St; mains $18-37; dinner Tue-Sun) Southeast of the downtown hurly-burly is this architect-designed neighborhood bistro. It offers an eclectic seasonal menu that freely ranges across South America, Asia, Africa and Europe to present creative dishes like sweet-potato soup with lime oil, or spicy grilled quail. Reservations are recommended.

Detour to **New Frontiers Marketplace** (☎ 805-785-0194; 896 E Foothill Blvd; 8am-9pm Mon-Fri, 8am-8pm Sat, 9am-8pm Sun) for organic groceries and take-out deli picnic lunches.

Drinking

Downtown streets are littered with college-student-jammed bars and clubs. When we visited, the new **Creekside Brewing Company** (805-542-9804; www.creeksidebrewing.com; 1040 Broad St) was due to open soon.

Downtown Brewing Co (☎ 805-543-1843; 1119 Garden St) This study in rafters and exposed brick has plenty of homemade beers to go with its decent pub grub. Downstairs, you'll find DJs or live music from local bands with names like 'The Phenomenauts' most nights. Catch four-buck pitchers on Tuesday nights.

Taste (☎ 805-269-8279; www.taste-slo.com; 1003 Osos St; 11am-9pm Mon-Sat, 11am-5pm Sun) At this high-ceilinged cooperative wine-tasting room, take the Enomatic wine-dispensing system for a spin with a Riedel tasting glass in hand, then pick up an Edna Valley winery map and go straight to the source tomorrow.

Entertainment

Palm Theatre (☎ 805-541-5161; www.thepalmtheatre.com; 817 Palm St; adult/concession $7.50/5) In SLO's blink-and-you'll-miss-it Chinatown, this small-scale art-house cinema shows foreign and indie flicks. It also happens to be the USA's first solar-powered cinema. All seats are $5 before 5pm daily and on Monday nights.

our pick **Sunset Drive-In** (☎ 805-544-4475; 255 Elks Lane; adult/child $6/2;) Recline your seat, put your feet up on the dash and munch on bottomless bags of popcorn at this classic Americana drive-in. Sticking around for the second feature (usually a B-list Hollywood blockbuster) won't cost you extra. It's off Hwy 101, near the Madonna Rd exit. From downtown SLO, take Higuera St south to Elks Lane.

Performing Arts Center (PAC; ☎ 805-756-2787, 888-233-2787; http://pacslo.org; 1 Grand Ave) On the Cal Poly campus, this state-of-the-art theater is SLO's main cultural venue, presenting a varied schedule of concerts, theater, dance recitals and other shows. Event parking costs $6.

Shopping

Higuera and Marsh Sts downtown, plus the cross streets in between, are stuffed full of indie boutiques. Take a wander to find something surprisingly wonderful.

Hands Gallery (☎ 805-543-1921; www.handsgallery.com; 777 Higuera St; 10am-6pm Mon-Wed, 10am-9pm Thu, 10am-8pm Fri & Sat, 11am-5pm Sun) This brightly lit gallery sells fine contemporary craftwork by local artisans, including jewelry, fiber arts, metal sculptures, ceramics and vibrant blown glass for gifts or souvenirs.

Mountain Air Sports (☎ 805-543-1676; 667 Marsh St; 10am-6pm Mon-Wed, Fri & Sat, 10am-8pm Thu, 11am-4pm Sun) This local independent outfitter is one of the only camping and outdoor-activity supply shop from Monterey to Santa Barbara. Pick up campstove fuel, top-name active clothing, hiking boots and rock-climbing shoes here.

Getting There & Away

Off Broad St, three miles southeast of downtown, **SLO County Regional Airport** (SBP; www.sloairport.com; ☎ 805-781-2025) offers commuter flights with American Eagle (Los Angeles) and United Express (LA and San Francisco). There's free wi-fi in the terminal.

The **Greyhound bus station** (☎ 805-543-2121; 150 South St), a mile southwest of downtown, has several daily buses along Hwy 101 south to Los Angeles ($31 to $41, 4½ to 5½ hours) via Santa Barbara ($21 to $26, 2¼ hours) and north to San Francisco ($44 to $51, 5½ to seven hours).

Amtrak's daily Seattle–LA *Coast Starlight* and twice-daily SLO–San Diego *Pacific Surfliner* stop at SLO's **train station** (1011 Railroad Ave). Both connect south to Santa Barbara ($19 to $29, 2½ to three hours) and Los Angeles ($30 to $36, 5½ hours), while only the former heads north to Salinas ($22 to $37, three hours). Several daily Thruway buses link to regional trains in San Jose (p189) and Santa Barbara (p503).

San Luis Obispo's **Regional Transit Authority** (RTA; ☎ 805-541-2228; www.slorta.org) operates frequent daily buses (with limited weekend services) across the region (one-way fares $1 to $2.75). All buses are equipped with bike racks. Lines converge on downtown's **transfer center** (cnr Palm & Osos Sts).

Bus	Destination
9	Paso Robles, San Miguel
10	Pismo Beach, Arroyo Grande
12	Morro Bay, Cayucos, Cambria, San Simeon & Hearst Castle

Getting Around

Downtown is compact enough for walking. On-street parking is metered. **SLO Transit** (☎ 805-541-2877; www.slocity.org) runs local city buses and the downtown trolley (25¢), which loops around every 15 to 20 minutes from 3:30pm to 9pm Thursday, from noon to

DETOUR: CARRIZO PLAIN NATIONAL MONUMENT

Hidden in far eastern San Luis Obispo County, **Carrizo Plain National Monument** (☎ 661-391-6000; www.ca.blm.gov/bakersfield; admission free; 🕑 24hr) is a geological wonderland, where you can walk or drive atop the San Andreas Fault. It's also an undisturbed wildlife preserve that protects such endangered species as the California condor, tule elk, pronghorn antelope and San Joaquin kit fox. Pick up 4WD and hiking maps at the **Goodwin Education Center** (☎ 805-475-2131; 🕑 9am-4pm Thu-Sun Dec-May), past the dazzling white salt flats of Soda Lake, near the trailhead for Painted Rock, which has Native American pictographs. Carrizo Plain is 60 winding miles east of Hwy 101 via Hwy 58 from Santa Margarita (north of SLO), or 55 miles west of the I-5 freeway via Hwy 58 and the California Valley. Free first-come, first-served camping is available at two primitive Bureau of Land Management campgrounds.

9pm Friday and Saturday, and from noon to 5:30pm Sunday.

AVILA BEACH

pop 840 / elev 69ft

Quaint, sunny Avila (*ah*-vi-la) Beach has had a rough shake. In the late 1980s it was discovered that for decades pipes from the nearby Unocal refinery and port had been leaking into the soil, contaminating it with a toxic soup of petroleum products. In 1992 a massive oil spill that occurred while a tanker was being loaded by the beach only added to the misery – and decimated sea otter populations. In 1999 Unocal began a legal settlement that involved tearing down the town and carting off the beach. Crowds have been lured back by a freshly built seafront commercial district with restaurants, shops and cafés.

Sights & Activities

West of Hwy 101, Avila Beach Dr passes through a glen of sycamore trees. At **Avila Valley Barn** (☎ 805-595-2810; www.avilavalleybarn.com; 560 Avila Beach Dr; 🕑 9am-6pm daily Jun-Oct, 9am-5pm Thu-Mon Nov-May; 👶), a fruit stand and pick-your-own berry farm, you can park alongside the sheep and goat pens, lick an ice-cream cone, then grab a basket and walk out into the fields for jammy olallieberries (May and June), peaches and nectarines (July), apples (August and September) and pumpkins (October).

After all that hard work, it's time for a luxuriant soak at **Sycamore Mineral Springs** (☎ 805-595-7302, 800-234-5831; www.sycamoresprings.com; 1215 Avila Beach Dr; hot-tub rentals per person per hr $12.50-15; 🕑 7am-midnight Mon-Thu, 7am-2am Fri-Sun), where private redwood hot tubs are discreetly laddered up a woodsy hillside. Call for reservations, as they're often booked. For those less flush with cash, **Avila Hot Springs** (☎ 805-595-2359; www.avilahotsprings.com; 250 Avila Beach Dr; adult/child $10/8; 🕑 7:30am-10pm; 👶), back east closer to Hwy 101, has a slightly sulfuric, lukewarm swimming pool with a pretty cool tube slide.

Two miles west of downtown Avila Beach, **Port San Luis** is a working fishing harbor. The barking of sea lions accompanies you as you stroll **Harford Pier**, one of the most authentic fishing piers on the coast. If you'd like to try your luck, **Patriot Sportfishing** (☎ 805-595-7200, 800-714-3474; www.patriotsportfishing.com; Harford Pier, off Avila Beach Dr; tours adult/child from $48/33) organizes deep-sea fishing trips, as well as whale-spotting tours from December to April. To paddle out among the sea otters and seals, talk to **Central Coast Kayaks** (☎ 805-773-3500; www.centralcoastkayaks.com; 1879 Shell Beach Rd, Shell Beach; rentals per hr single/double $15/20, 2hr tours $60).

Just getting to **Point San Luis Lighthouse** (☎ 805-546-4904; www.sanluislighthouse.org; admission by donation), surrounded by a nuclear power plant, is an adventure. The only way to reach the lighthouse is via a rocky, crumbling, 3.5-mile round-trip trail, open only for guided hikes led by Pacific Gas & Electric docents. Meet up by the pier at the fisherman's memorial at 8:30am any Saturday, as long as it's not raining; call ☎ 805-541-8735 to confirm schedules. Children under nine years are not allowed. Bring lots of water and expect to return around noon or 1pm.

Sleeping

At Port San Luis, first-come, first-served roadside **campsites** (without/with hookups $25/40) with ocean views are reserved for RVs only. At Avila Hot Springs (left), the crowded **campground** (tent & RV sites without/with hookups $30/45) has hot showers, flush toilets and discounted hot-springs admission.

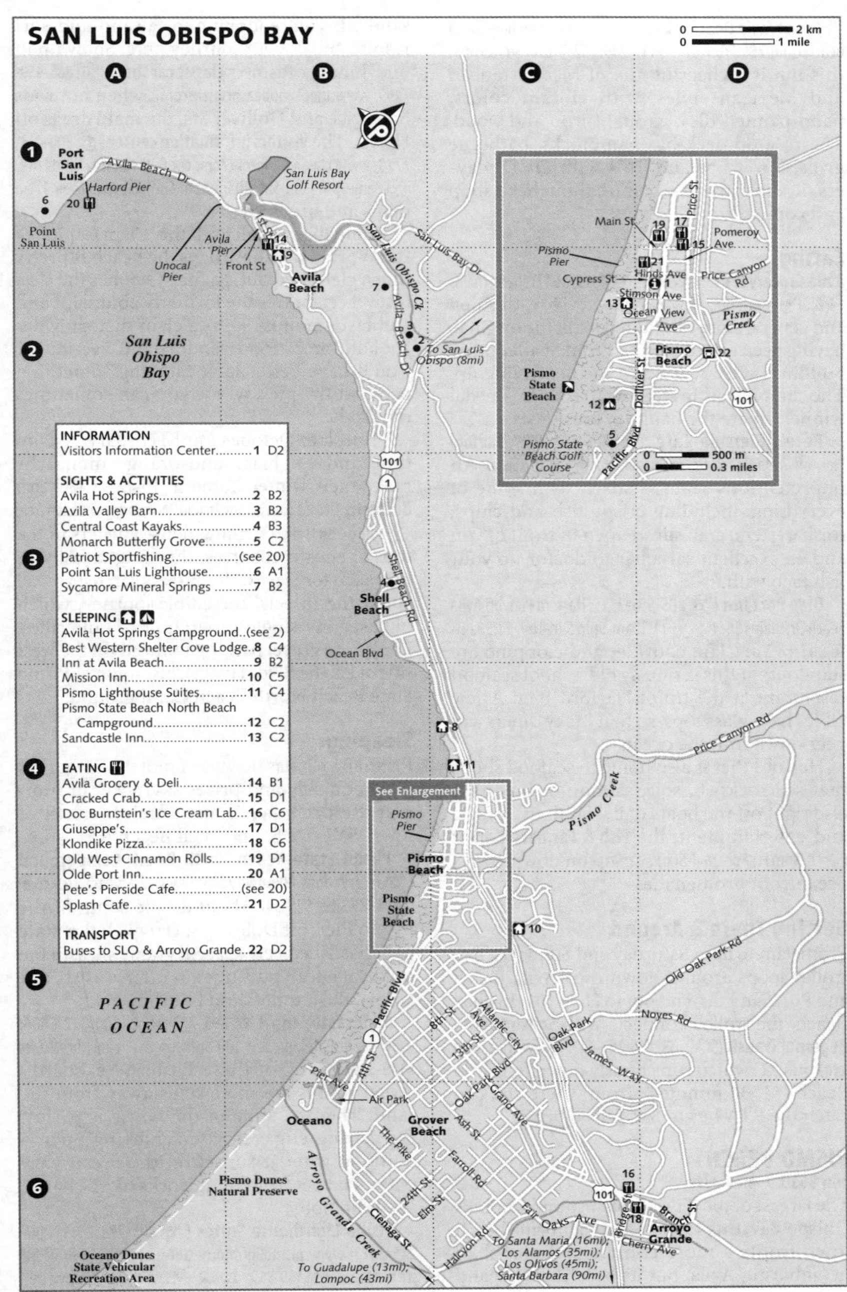
SAN LUIS OBISPO BAY
0 2 km
0 1 mile
Port San Luis
Avila Beach Dr
Harford Pier
Point San Luis
San Luis Bay Golf Resort
Avila Pier
Unocal Pier
Front St
1st St
Avila Beach
San Luis Obispo Ck
San Luis Bay Dr
Avila Beach Dr
To San Luis Obispo (8mi)
San Luis Obispo Bay
Shell Beach Rd
Shell Beach
Ocean Blvd
See Enlargement
Pismo Pier
Pismo Beach
Pismo State Beach
Price Canyon Rd
Pismo Creek
Main St
Price St
Pomeroy Ave
Hinds Ave
Cypress St
Stimson Ave
Ocean View Ave
Dolliver St
Pacific Blvd
Pismo State Beach Golf Course
0 500 m
0 0.3 miles
PACIFIC OCEAN
Old Oak Park Rd
Noyes Rd
Oak Park Blvd
James Way
Atlantic City Ave
8th St
13th St
Grand Ave
Ash St
Pier Ave
4th St
Air Park
Oceano
Grover Beach
The Pike
Farroll Rd
24th St
Elm St
Fair Oaks Ave
Bridge St
Branch St
Cherry Ave
Arroyo Grande
Arroyo Grande Creek
Clenaga St
Halcyon Rd
Pismo Dunes Natural Preserve
Oceano Dunes State Vehicular Recreation Area
To Guadalupe (13mi); Lompoc (43mi)
To Santa Maria (16mi); Los Alamos (35mi); Los Olivos (45mi); Santa Barbara (90mi)
INFORMATION
Visitors Information Center.........1 D2
SIGHTS & ACTIVITIES
Avila Hot Springs.........2 B2
Avila Valley Barn.........3 B2
Central Coast Kayaks.........4 B3
Monarch Butterfly Grove.........5 C2
Patriot Sportfishing.........(see 20)
Point San Luis Lighthouse.........6 A1
Sycamore Mineral Springs.........7 B2
SLEEPING
Avila Hot Springs Campground..(see 2)
Best Western Shelter Cove Lodge..8 C4
Inn at Avila Beach.........9 B2
Mission Inn.........10 C5
Pismo Lighthouse Suites.........11 C4
Pismo State Beach North Beach Campground.........12 C2
Sandcastle Inn.........13 C2
EATING
Avila Grocery & Deli.........14 B1
Cracked Crab.........15 D1
Doc Burnstein's Ice Cream Lab...16 C6
Giuseppe's.........17 D1
Klondike Pizza.........18 C6
Old West Cinnamon Rolls.........19 D1
Olde Port Inn.........20 A1
Pete's Pierside Cafe.........(see 20)
Splash Cafe.........21 D2
TRANSPORT
Buses to SLO & Arroyo Grande..22 D2

CENTRAL COAST

Inn at Avila Beach (☎ 805-595-2300; www.hotelsavilabeach.com; 256 Front St; r $119-289; 💻) Downtown, this inn is a cheerful mix of Mediterranean and Mexican styles, with vibrant colors, hand-painted tiles, wrought iron and wood. The rooftop deck has hammocks, barbecue grills, a wet bar and TVs with DVD players. Rooms span the gamut, though, so shop and compare.

Eating

Avila Grocery & Deli (☎ 805-627-1575; 354 Front St; mains $4-8; 🕑 7am-7pm; 🚸) A real survivor, this deli and general store's building is still the original, having been towed back to Front St after other buildings were razed and the beach dug up. The chipotle tri-tip steak wrap is a gold-medal winner; so are the bang-up breakfasts.

Pete's Pierside Cafe (☎ 805-595-7627; Harford Pier, off Avila Beach Dr; mains $4-16; 🕑 11am-5pm) An unpretentious seafood shack with some of everything, including crispy fish-and-chips, fresh oysters, crab sliced open in front of you and an excellent salsa bar to doctor up your fish taco with.

Olde Port Inn (☎ 805-595-2515; Harford Pier, off Avila Beach Dr; mains $6-46; 🕑 11:30am-9pm Sun-Thu, 11:30am-10pm Fri & Sat) Clam chowder and cioppino are standouts at this seriously old-school seafood restaurant at the tip of Harford Pier. A few tables have glass tops, so that lucky diners can peer down into the ocean.

Harford Pier is also home to seafood shops that sell rockfish, sole, salmon or anything else right off the boats daily. With live music and entertainment, the **Fish & Farmers Market** (🕑 4-8pm Fri Apr–mid-Sep) sets up on downtown's oceanfront promenade.

Getting There & Around

From 9am to 6pm Saturday and Sunday, a free trolley loops around downtown Avila Beach and Port San Luis, and out to Hwy 101. In Shell Beach, the trolley connects with **South County Regional Transit** (SCAT; ☎ 805-781-4472; www.scattransit.org) bus 21, which runs hourly down to Pismo Beach ($1, 30 minutes), from where you can catch the RTA bus to San Luis Obispo.

PISMO BEACH

pop 8620 / elev 33ft

The largest of the 'Five Cities' around San Luis Obispo Bay, this 1950s-retro California beach town fronts a more commercial pier than neighboring Avila, but its beach is wide and sandy. If you're looking for a sand-and-surf respite, break your journey here. Show up in mid-June for Pismo's **classic car show** (☎ 866-450-7469; www.thepismobeachclassic.com), when hot rods line Price and Dolliver Sts, the main drags off Hwy 1. The **visitors information center** (☎ 800-443-7778; www.classiccalifornia.com; cnr Dolliver St & Hinds Ave; 🕑 9am-5pm Mon-Sat, 10am-4pm Sun) dispenses free maps and brochures.

Pismo likes to call itself the 'Clam Capital of the World,' but these days the beach is pretty much clammed out. In mid-October the **Clam Festival** celebrates the formerly abundant and still tasty mollusk with a clam dig, chowder cookoff, more food vendors and live music. You'll have better luck catching something fishy off the pier, where you can sometimes rent rods.

From late October until February, tens of thousands of black-and-orange monarchs make their winter home in Pismo's **Monarch Butterfly Grove** (www.monarchbutterfly.org; admission free; 🕑 sunrise-sunset). Forming dense clusters in the tops of eucalyptus trees, they might easily be mistaken for leaves. Volunteers can tell you all about the insects' incredible journey, which outlasts any single generation of butterflies. Look for a gravel parking pull-out on the west side of Pacific Blvd (Hwy 1), just south of Pismo State Beach North Beach Campground.

Sleeping

Pismo Beach has dozens of motels, but rooms fill up quickly and prices skyrocket in summer. Resort hotels roost on cliffs north of town via Price St and Shell Beach Rd.

Pismo State Beach North Beach Campground (☎ reservations 800-444-7275; www.reserveamerica.com; tent & RV sites $25-34) About a mile south of the Pismo Pier, off Dolliver St (Hwy 1), this state park has 103 nicely spaced, grassy sites, in the shade of eucalyptus trees. It offers easy beach access, flush toilets and hot showers.

Sandcastle Inn (☎ 805-773-2422, 800-822-6606; www.sandcastleinn.com; 100 Stimson Ave; r incl breakfast $159-309) Many of these Eastern Seaboard–styled rooms are mere steps away from the sand. The best suite in the house is perfect for getting engaged after cracking open a bottle of wine at sunset on the ocean-view patio – take it from us, it works like a charm. Wi-fi in lobby.

Pismo Lighthouse Suites (☎ 805-773-2411, 800-245-2411; www.pismolighthousesuites.com; 2411 Price St; ste incl breakfast $189-369; 🏊 🏋 🚸 wi-fi) With everything a vacationing family needs – in-room Nintendo, a life-sized outdoor chessboard, a putting green, table tennis, badminton courts and a fitness center – this contemporary all-suites hotel can be hard to tear yourself away from. Ask about late checkout (usually $30).

Also recommended:

Mission Inn (☎ 805-773-6020, 866-773-6020; www.missioninnpismobeach.com; 601 James Way; r incl breakfast $139-239;) Reasonable rates and stylish, oversized rooms, but it's distant from the beach. It's off Hwy 101; exit at Five Cities Dr.

Best Western Shelter Cove Lodge (☎ 805-773-3511, 800-848-1434; www.bwsheltercove.com; 2651 Price St; r incl breakfast $144-334; wi-fi) It's all about the views at this cliffside motel with a heated pool.

Eating

Old West Cinnamon Rolls (☎ 805-773-1428; 861 Dolliver St; items $3-5; 6:30am-5:30pm) Wakey-wakey at this gobsmacking bakery, which brews decent coffee too.

Splash Cafe (☎ 805-773-4653; 197 Pomeroy Ave; mains $3-10; 8am-9pm;) Lines go out the door and wrap around this boisterous hole-in-the-wall, which makes award-winning clam chowder – in a sourdough bread bowl, naturally – and a long lineup of grilled and fried briny delights. It's open shorter hours in winter.

our pick **Cracked Crab** (☎ 805-773-2722; 751 Price St; mains $9-48; 11am-9pm Sun-Thu, 11am-10pm Fri & Sat;) Fresh seafood is the staple at this super-casual, family-owned grill. When the famous bucket o' seafood, full of flying bits of fish, Cajun sausage, red potatoes and cob corn, gets dumped on your butcher-paper-covered table, make sure you're wearing one of those silly-looking plastic bibs.

Giuseppe's (☎ 805-773-2870; 891 Price St; mains $12-28; lunch Mon-Fri, dinner daily) Occasionally outstanding Southern Italian fare is served at this lively, date-worthy *cucina*, which brims with the owner's personality – check out the lineup of Vespas in front. Safe bets are wood-fired pizzas and traditional pastas like spicy prawn spaghettini. Expect a long wait (no reservations).

Getting There & Around

RTA bus 10 links the outlet mall at Pismo Beach with San Luis Obispo ($1.25, 30 minutes) and Arroyo Grande ($1.25, 10 minutes) hourly on weekdays, less often on weekends. It also runs local buses ($1) between all five bayside cities for acronym-challenged **South County Regional Transit** (SCAT; ☎ 805-781-4472; www.scattransit.org).

ARROYO GRANDE

pop 16,550 / elev 114ft

A small town with a quaint swinging bridge, Arroyo Grande is just off Hwy 101, southeast of Pismo Beach. Near the famous bridge, a small collection of restored late-19th- and early-20th-century **historical buildings** (☎ 805-473-5077; www.southcountyhistory.org; admission free; most buildings noon-3pm Sat, 1-4pm Sun) have exhibits on local farming history.

It's a delight just to stroll along the main street past antiques shops, charming boutiques and **Doc Burnstein's Ice Cream Lab** (☎ 805-474-4068; 114 W Branch St; items $3-8; 11am-9:30pm Sun-Thu, 11am-10:30pm Fri & Sat;), which scoops up fantastical flavors like petite-sirah sorbet and the 'Elvis Special' (peanut butter with banana swirls). Live ice-cream lab shows start at 7pm sharp on Wednesday, with competitions to concoct the wildest flavor of the week. Overlooking the creek, Alaskan-run **Klondike Pizza** (☎ 805-481-5288; 104 Bridge St; pizzas $12-25; 11am-9pm Sun-Thu, 11am-10pm Fri & Sat;) is littered with peanut shells and has checkers and other board games to play while you wait for your reindeer-sausage pie. You can hum along with a kazoo during the twice-monthly Saturday-night sing-alongs.

From San Luis Obispo, RTA bus 10 via Pismo Beach stops in downtown Arroyo Grande ($1.50, 30 minutes), as does the hourly SCAT bus 21 to/from Pismo Beach ($1, 15 minutes).

GUADALUPE

Hwy 1 ends its brief relationship with Hwy 101 just south of Pismo Beach, as it veers off toward the coast. About 20 miles further south, you almost expect to have to dodge Old West tumbleweeds as you drive into the one-road agricultural town of Guadalupe.

In 1923 a huge Hollywood crew came here for the filming of the silent version of the *Ten Commandments* on the Guadalupe Dunes by the ocean. Enormous Egyptian sets were constructed in the sands, complete with huge sphinxes and more. Afterward, director Cecil B DeMille saved money by leaving the magnificent sets – albeit ones constructed of hay, plaster and paint – in place and simply burying them in the sand. Over the following decades knowledge of the exact location of the vast sets was lost. In 1983 film and archaeology buffs started looking for the 'Lost City of DeMille.' Several artifacts have been found and locations of main structures pinpointed. You can see some of the recovered pieces in town at the **Dunes Visitor Center** (☎ 805-343-2455; www.dunescenter.org; 1055 Guadalupe St; admission by donation; 🕑 10am-4pm Wed-Sun), which has exhibits about the ecology of the largest coastal dunes on the continent and about the Dunites, mystical folks who called the dunes home during the 1930s. You can get loads more information on the excavations at www.lostcitydemille.com. More recently, scenes from *Hidalgo* (2004) and *Pirates of the Caribbean: At World's End* (2007) were filmed here.

The dunes preserve is about 5 miles west of town via Hwy 166.

LOS ALAMOS

pop 1300 / elev 575ft

Midway between San Luis Obispo and Santa Barbara, this affable one-horse town is just off Hwy 101. Chat with the wine-making family behind the vines at **Bedford Thompson** (☎ 805-344-2107; www.bedfordthompsonwinery.com; 448 Bell St; 🕑 11am-5pm), a downtown tasting room. Fresh-baked pizzas, some with tasty house-made sausage or grilled peaches grown in nearby orchards, are sold at all-natural **Full of Life Flatbread** (☎ 805-344-4400; 225 Bell St; mains $8-12; 🕑 5-10pm Fri & Sat), which also makes fresh salads and brownie s'mores, and pours local microbrews and wines by the glass. If the town's quaint charms tempt you to linger, check into the Victorian-esque B&B inside the 1880 **Union Hotel** (☎ 805-344-2744; www.unionhotelvictmansion.com; 362 Bell St; r with shared/private bath $135/165), which has an Old West saloon serving root beer and espresso (no alcohol, sorry).

CENTRAL COAST

SANTA BARBARA AREA

Frankly put, this area is damn pleasant to putter around. Chic, Mediterranean-style Santa Barbara anchors the region, with a divinely cinematic wine country to the north, the unspoiled Channel Islands National Park to the south and quirky enclaves like new-agey Ojai to the east. Alternatively, don't even leave the oceans beaches – plenty of people don't.

LA PURÍSIMA MISSION STATE HISTORIC PARK

Around 3 miles northeast of Hwy 1 and the old town of Lompoc, which lies embedded in commercial flower fields, this pastoral valley **mission** (☎ 805-733-3713; www.lapurisimamission.org; per vehicle $4; 🕑 9am-5pm) was completely restored in the 1930s by the CCC. Today it's one of the most evocative of California's 21 original missions. Its buildings are fully intact and furnished as they were during the Spanish colonial era. The mission fields still support livestock, and outdoor gardens are planted with medicinal plants and trees once used by Chumash tribespeople. Surrounding the mission are miles of hiking and equestrian trails. The mission is about 15 miles west of Hwy 101 via Hwy 246; look for the turnoff to Purisima Rd on the north side of the highway and follow it for about a mile.

SANTA BARBARA WINE COUNTRY

Though large-scale winemaking has only been happening here since the 1980s, Santa Barbara's climate has always been perfect for growing grapes. Nearer the coast in the Santa Maria and Santa Ynez Valleys, pinot noir – a particularly fragile grape – flourishes in the fog. Further inland, sun-loving Rhône varietals like syrah and mourvédre thrive. The 2004 indie hit movie *Sideways* was filmed throughout the region, and it was both a blessing and a curse: it brought local wineries acclaim and huge crowds, but also pushed this down-to-earth wine region toward hoity-toity Napa style, complete with sky-high tasting fees, tour buses, limos and the like. That said, it's still a delight to wander around, as the rolling countryside unfurls to reveal not only wineries, but also lavender farms, epicurean eateries and peaceful overnight retreats.

Orientation & Information

The wine country is northwest of Santa Barbara; you can get there in under an hour via Hwy 101 or shorter, more scenic Hwy 154 (San Marcos Pass Rd). Highly trafficked Hwy 246 runs east–west across the bottom of the Santa Ynez Valley, passing the strip malls of Buellton, kitschy Danish-esque Solvang (where it's called Mission Dr) and the farm town of Santa Ynez. North–south backroads that pass by wineries include Alamo Pintado Rd, between Hwy 246 and Los Olivos; Refugio Rd, intersecting Hwy 246; and Foxen Canyon Rd, north of Los Olivos. The **Santa Barbara**

HIDDEN BEACHES OFF HIGHWAY 1

West of Lompoc lie some truly wild Pacific beaches worth the trouble of visiting.

Pristine **Ocean Beach County Park** (☎ 805-934-6123; www.sbparks.org; 8am-sunset) and **Surf Beach**, with its remote Amtrak train stop, are really one beach beside Vandenberg Air Force Base. During the 13-mile drive west of Lompoc on Ocean Ave, you'll pass mysterious-looking structures supporting spy and commercial satellite launches. The dunes are untrammeled and interpretive signs explain the estuary's ecology. Because endangered snowy plovers nest here, vast areas of the beach are usually closed from March to September.

Five miles south of Lompoc on Hwy 1, look for Jalama Rd. Its 14 miles of twisting tarmac traverse ranch and farmlands en route to **Jalama Beach County Park** (☎ 805-736-6316; www.jalamabeach.com; per vehicle/dog $8/3;). Utterly isolated, it's home to a crazily popular **campground** (☎ 805-736-3504; tent & RV sites without/with hookups $20/30). There are no reservations, so look for the 'campground full' sign, back at Hwy 1, to save yourself the drive; otherwise, arrive before 8am to get on the waiting list for a site.

County Vintners' Association (☎ 805-688-0881; www.sbcountywines.com) publishes a touring map, available online and at winery tasting rooms and the **Solvang Conference & Visitors Bureau** (☎ 805-688-6144, 800-468-6765; http://solvangusa.com; 1511 Mission Dr, Solvang; 10am-4pm).

Sights & Activities

WINERIES & TASTING ROOMS

Dozens of wineries are found inside the triangle formed by Hwys 154, 246 and 101; tasting fees average $10. The beautiful **Foxen Canyon Wine Trail** (www.foxencanyonwinetrail.com) runs north from Hwy 154 from west of Los Olivos into the rural Santa Maria Valley.

Some of our favorite wineries:

Beckmen (☎ 805-688-8664; www.beckmenvineyards.com; 2670 Ontiveros Rd, Los Olivos; 11am-5pm) Crafts Purisima Mountain estate-grown Rhône varietals, both white and red, including a rare cuvée.

Fess Parker (☎ 805-688-1545; www.fessparker.com; 6200 Foxen Canyon Rd, Los Olivos; 10am-5pm) Pinot noir and syrah specialist owned by a 1950s TV star who once played Davy Crockett and Daniel Boone (that's why raccoon-tail hats are etched on tasting glasses).

our pick **Foxen** (☎ 805-937-4251; www.foxenvineyard.com; 7200 Foxen Canyon Rd, Santa Maria; 11am-4pm) Rustic, farm-style tasting room with a corrugated-metal roof, where you can sample priceless pinot noir and syrah.

Gainey (☎ 805-688-0558; www.gaineyvineyard.com; 3950 E Hwy 246, Santa Ynez; 10am-5pm) 'Limited Selection' bottlings garner raves, especially the pinot noir. Vineyard tours at 11am, 1pm, 2pm and 3pm daily.

Kalyra (☎ 805-693-8864; www.kalyrawinery.com; 343 Refugio Rd, Santa Ynez; 11am-5pm Mon-Fri, 10am-5pm Sat & Sun) Australian surfer produces a unique shiraz-cabernet-sauvignon blend in bottles with Aboriginal art-inspired labels.

Los Olivos Tasting Room (☎ 805-688-7406; www.losolivoswines.com; 2905 Grand Ave, Los Olivos; 11am-5:30pm) Independent tasting room inside an 1887 general store, which stocks prized California vintages you can't taste anywhere else.

Melville (☎ 805-735-7030; www.melvillewinery.com; 5185 E Hwy 246, Lompoc; 11am-4pm) Cult winemaker in the Santa Rita Hills, west of Hwy 101, for crafts pinot noir, syrah and chardonnay.

Rideau (☎ 805-688-0717; www.rideauvineyard.com; 1562 Alamo Pintado Rd, Solvang; 11am-5pm) Focuses purely on Rhône varietals, offering N'awlins-style hospitality inside a 19th-century adobe house.

Rancho Sisquoc (☎ 805-934-4332; www.ranchosisquoc.com; 6600 Foxen Canyon Rd, Santa Maria; 10am-5pm) For a heady mix of Bordeaux, Burgundian and Tuscan varietals, visit this early 1900s ranch (*sisquoc* means 'gathering place' in Chumash).

Sunstone (☎ 805-688-9463; www.sunstonewinery.com; 125 Refugio Rd, Santa Ynez; 10am-4:30pm) You'd swear you were in Provence at this 18th-century stone farmhouse. The organic, family-run estate most famously makes Eros, a merlot meritage.

Zaca Mesa (☎ 805-688-9339; www.zacamesa.com; 6905 Foxen Canyon Rd, Santa Maria; 10am-4pm, to 5pm Fri & Sat in summer) A venerable player known for Rhône varietals, plus an oversized outdoor chessboard and walking trails.

AROUND THE WINE COUNTRY TOWNS

In 1911 bona fide Danes did indeed found **Solvang** – and start a folk school for the preservation of Danish heritage – but the intervening decades have seen 'Sunny Fields' sell out hard. Grumpy families and charmed blue-hairs plod down Copenhagen Dr, where overpriced trinket shops lurk behind faux-Scandinavian facades. The **Elverhøj Museum** (☎ 805-686-1211; www.elverhoj.org; 1624 Elverhoy Way; adult/child $3/free;

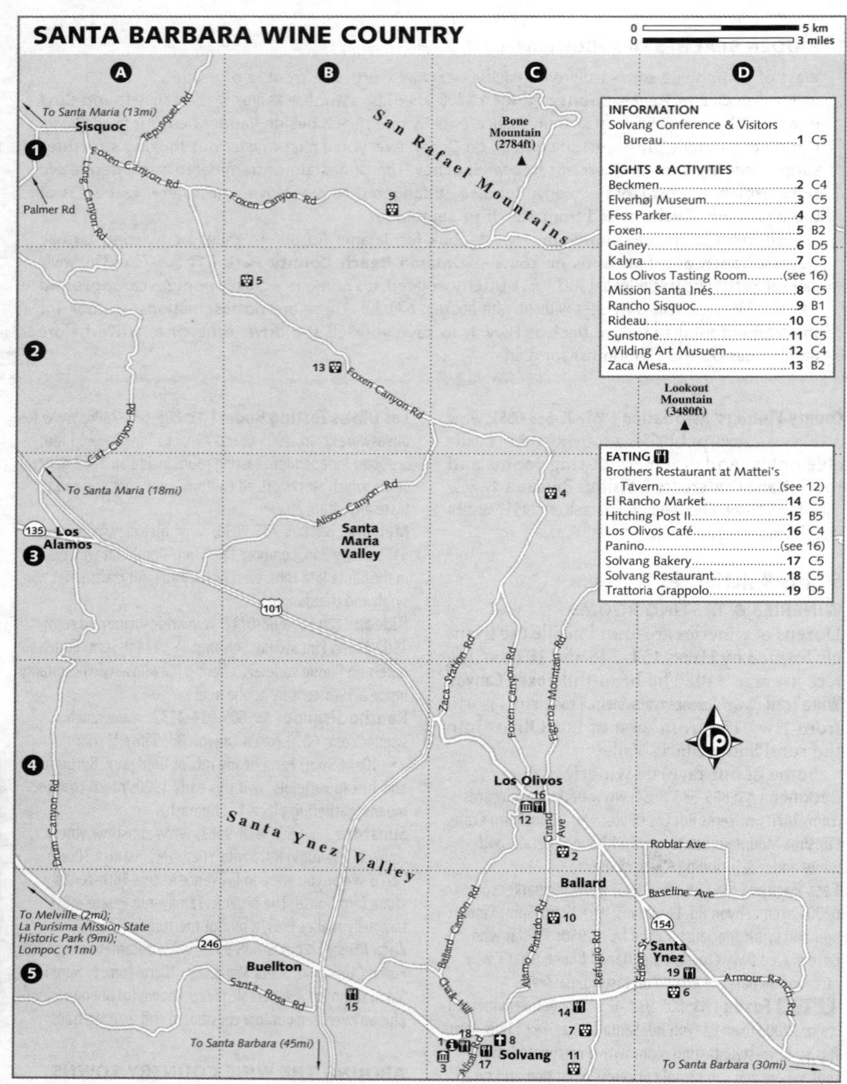

(🕑 1-4pm Wed & Thu, noon-4pm Fri-Sun) covers real Danish life in the area. Pretty **Mission Santa Inés** (☎ 805-688-4815; 1760 Mission Dr; adult/child $4/free; 🕑 9am-4:30pm) saw an 1824 Chumash revolt against Spanish colonial cruelty.

The tiny main streets of **Los Olivos** are lined with tasting rooms, wine-country boutiques and art galleries. Nearby, the petite **Wilding Art Museum** (☎ 805-688-1082; 2329 Jonata St; adult/child $2/free; 🕑 11am-5pm Wed-Sun) presents singular wilderness-themed art exhibitions inside a historic farmhouse.

Tours

Santa Barbara Wine Country Cycling Tours (☎ 888-557-8687; www.winecountrycycling.com; half-/full-day rentals $35/45, tours from $90/135) Bicycle tours depart Santa Ynez and stop at wineries; weekend packages available.

Sustainable Vine Wine Tours (☎ 805-698-3911; www.sustainablevine.com; 6hr tour incl lunch $115) Ride a biodiesel shuttle to visit wineries that implement organic and biodynamic agricultural practices. Don't fear: the wines are top-notch.

Sleeping & Eating

Avoid the price-gouging entirely by taking a day trip from Santa Barbara. Otherwise, at the junction of Hwys 101 and 246, Buellton has many motels and hotels. Solvang, 3 miles east along Hwy 246, has many more motels, but don't expect any bargains there either, especially not on weekends. More genteel towns like Santa Ynez offer more luxurious B&B inns.

El Rancho Market (☎ 805-688-4300; 2886 Mission Dr, Solvang; deli items $4-10; 6am-10pm) The place to stop if you want to fill a picnic basket (not to mention escape windmills and clogs), this supermarket is known for its fantastic deli case, barbecue takeout, bargain wine room and espresso bar.

Solvang Restaurant (☎ 805-688-4645; 1672 Copenhagen Dr, Solvang; mains $6-15; 6am-4pm Mon-Fri, 6am-5pm Sat & Sun summer, 6am-3pm Mon-Fri, 6am-5pm Sat & Sun rest of year;) Delivers good food and cheer, serving *aebleskiver* (ball-like pancakes dusted with powdered sugar), Danish meatballs and sausage sandwiches, and more typical diner fare.

Panino (☎ 805-688-9304; 2900 Grand Ave, Los Olivos; mains $8-10; 11am-4pm; V) Offers nine different kinds of veggie sandwiches as well as special creations, such as curried chicken, and fresh salads. Order at the counter, then grab an umbrella table outside on the sidewalk. Also in Solvang.

Los Olivos Café (☎ 805-688-7265; 2879 Grand Ave, Los Olivos; mains $11-25; 11:30am-10pm) With white canopies and a wisteria-covered trellis, this romantic Cal-Mediterranean wine bistro that featured in *Sideways* swirls up a casual-chic ambience. The menu gets mixed marks; try the mid-afternoon antipasto platters.

Trattoria Grappolo (☎ 805-688-6899; 3687 Sagunto St, Santa Ynez; mains lunch $13-17, dinner $17-30; lunch Tue-Sun, dinner daily) A local Italian favorite where the chefs hail from Tuscany, here you can casually feast beneath murals of the old country on rustic pastas, crispy pizzas, grilled seafood and lamb chops.

our pick **Brothers Restaurant at Mattei's Tavern** (☎ 805-688-4820; 2350 Railway Ave, Los Olivos; mains $18-44; dinner) You half expect a stagecoach to come thundering up in time for dinner at this vintage 1886 stagecoach stop and tavern. Unwind with wine in the fireplace lounge, then sit down at a checkered-tablecloth table for big bold country flavors, from spicy dry-rubbed steaks to grilled pork chops. Reservations advised.

Hitching Post II (☎ 805-688-0676; 406 E Hwy 246, Buellton; mains $20-48; dinner) You'll be hard-pressed to find better steaks and chops than at this legendary, old-guard country steakhouse, which serves locally raised meats and makes its own pinot noir (which is damn good, by the way). Reservations essential.

Solvang's bakeries prove an irresistible draw, but most aren't especially good. Tasty **Solvang Bakery** (☎ 805-688-4939; 460 Alisal Rd, Solvang; items $2-5; 7am-6pm) is a smiling exception, vending apple strudels and iced almond butter rings.

SANTA BARBARA

pop 89,550 / elev 50ft

Just a 90-minute drive north of Los Angeles, Santa Barbara basks smugly in its near-perfection. Tucked between the Santa Ynez Mountains and the ocean, the city's red-tile roofs, white stucco buildings, Spanish mission and Mediterranean vibe have long given credence to its claim to the title of 'the American Riviera.' It's blessed with almost freakishly good weather, a stunning masterpiece of a courthouse and a vibrant downtown. No one can deny the appeal of the public beaches that line the city from tip to toe – just ignore those pesky oil derricks out to sea.

History

For thousands of years before the arrival of the Spanish, the Chumash people thrived here, setting up canoe trading routes between the mainland and the Channel Islands. In 1542 explorer Juan Rodríguez Cabrillo sailed into the channel, claimed the area for Spain, then sailed off to winter – and eventually die – on one of the nearby islands.

The Chumash had little reason for concern until the permanent return of the Spanish in the late 1700s, when priests and soldiers arrived to establish military outposts and to convert the tribe to Christianity. The Spaniards forced the Chumash to construct the missions and presidios and to provide subsequent labor. Many Native Americans changed their diet and clothing, and contracted fatal European diseases.

The Spanish weren't the last of the settlers. Easterners began arriving en masse with the 1849 Gold Rush, and by the late 1890s the city was an established vacation spot for the wealthy. After a massive earthquake in 1925, tough laws required the town to be rebuilt in its now characteristic faux-Mediterranean style with palm trees.

Orientation

Santa Barbara's coast faces south, not west, an important fact to remember when navigating. Downtown is laid out on a grid. Its main artery is State St, which runs roughly north–south and divides the east side from the west side. Lower State St (south of Ortega St) has plenty of college dive bars, while upper State St has most of the precious boutiques and museums. Cabrillo Blvd hugs the coastline and turns into Coast Village Rd as it enters the eastern suburb of Montecito. The University of California, Santa Barbara (UCSB) campus lies west in Isla Vista, and most students live around campus or in neighboring Goleta (go-*lee*-ta).

Information

Many coffee shops downtown and near the waterfront offer wi-fi, sometimes for free.

FedEx Office (Map p500; ☎ 805-966-1114; 1030 State St; per min 20-30¢; 7am-10pm Mon-Thu, 7am-9pm Fri, 9am-7pm Sat, 10am-5pm Sun) High-speed internet workstations.

Pacific Travelers Supply (Map p500; ☎ 805-963-4438; 12 W Anapamu St; 10am-7pm) Sells guidebooks, maps and miscellaneous travel accessories.

Post office (Map p500; ☎ 800-275-8777; 836 Anacapa St; 8:30am-6pm Mon-Fri, 9am-2pm Sat) Full-service.

Santa Barbara Cottage Hospital (Map pp498-9; ☎ 805-682-7111; cnr Pueblo & Bath Sts; 24hr) Emergency room.

Santa Barbara Public Library (Map p500; ☎ 805-962-7653; 40 E Anapamu St; 10am-8pm Mon-Thu, 10am-5:30pm Fri & Sat, 1-5pm Sun) Free internet access.

Santa Barbara Visitors Center (Map p500; ☎ 805-965-3021; www.santabarbaraca.com; 1 Garden St; 9am-5pm Mon-Sat, 10am-5pm Sun) Helpful staff provide maps, brochures and information.

CENTRAL COAST

Sights

THE WATERFRONT

At its southern end, State St runs into **Stearns Wharf** (Map p500; www.stearnswharf.org), once owned in part by Jimmy Cagney. Built in 1872, the wharf is the oldest one continuously operating on the West Coast. The first 90 minutes of parking are free with validation from a souvenir or snack shop.

On the wharf, the family-friendly **Ty Warner Sea Center** (Map p500; ☎ 805-962-2526; www.sbnature.org/seacenter; adult/child $8/5; 10am-5pm;) has captivating hands-on exhibits and touch pools (the warty-looking sea cucumber actually feels like velvet). The coolest exhibit is the crawl tunnel through a 1500-gallon surge tank.

Kids will also get a kick out of the **Santa Barbara Maritime Museum** (Map p500; ☎ 805-962-8404; www.sbmm.org; 113 Harbor Way; adult/child $7/4, 3rd Thu of the month free; 10am-6pm Thu-Tue Jun-Aug, 10am-5pm Thu-Tue Sep-May;), southwest of the wharf by the yacht harbor. The two-level museum celebrates the town's briny history with memorabilia, hands-on and virtual-reality exhibits, and a movie theater.

MISSION SANTA BARBARA

The 'Queen of the Missions,' **Mission Santa Barbara** (Map pp498-9; ☎ 805-682-4713; www.sbmission.org; 2201 Laguna St; adult/child $5/1; 9am-5pm), was established on December 4, 1786, as the 10th California mission. Occupied by Catholic priests ever since, it escaped Mexico's policy of forced secularization. Today the mission functions as a Franciscan friary as well as a parish church and historical museum. The 1820 stone church has Chumash artwork and beautiful cloisters. The imposing Doric facade, an homage to a chapel in ancient Rome, is topped by twin bell towers. Behind the mission is an extensive cemetery (look for the skull carvings over the doorway), with 4000 Chumash graves and the elaborate mausoleums of early settlers.

SANTA BARBARA COUNTY COURTHOUSE

Built in Spanish-Moorish Revival style, the magnificent 1929 **courthouse** (Map p500; ☎ 805-962-6464; 1100 Anacapa St; admission free; 8:30am-4:45pm Mon-Fri, 10am-4:45pm Sat & Sun) features hand-painted ceilings, wrought-iron chandeliers and tiles from Tunisia and Spain. Step inside the 2nd-floor mural room depicting Spanish colonial history, then climb the bell tower for arched panoramas of the city, ocean and mountains. Docent-led tours (donations welcomed) are offered at 2pm Monday through Saturday and at 10:30am Monday, Tuesday and Friday.

SANTA BARBARA HISTORICAL MUSEUM

Embracing a romantic cloistered adobe courtyard, this hidden **museum** (Map p500; ☎ 805-966-1601; www.santabarbaramuseum.com; 136 E De La Guerra St; admission free, donation requested; ⏲ 10am-5pm Tue-Sat, noon-5pm Sun) has an endlessly fascinating collection of local memorabilia, ranging from simply beautiful, like Chumash woven baskets and colonial-era textiles, to intriguing, such as the intricately carved coffer that once belonged to Junípero Serra. You can also learn about the city's involvement in toppling the last Chinese monarchy, among other interesting footnotes in local history.

SANTA BARBARA BOTANIC GARDEN

After visiting the mission, take a soul-satisfying jaunt around this 65-acre **botanic garden** (Map pp498-9; ☎ 805-682-4726; www.sbbg.org; 1212 Mission Canyon Rd; adult/child $8/4; ⏲ 9am-6pm Mar-Oct, 9am-5pm Nov-Feb; 🚸), devoted to California's native flora. About 5.5 miles of trails meander through cacti, redwoods and wildflowers past the old mission dam and aqueduct, built by the Chumash. Guided tours are given at 11am on Saturday and Sunday and at 2pm daily. Ask for a 'Family Discovery Sheet' from the staffed info kiosk. Leashed dogs welcome.

SANTA BARBARA MUSEUM OF ART

This diverting little **museum** (Map p500; ☎ 805-963-4364; www.sbma.net; 1130 State St; adult/child $9/6, Sun free; ⏲ 11am-5pm Tue-Sun; 🚸) specializes in contemporary California artists, as well as big-name modern masters (think Dalí and Picasso), Asian art, 20th-century photography and classical sculpture. There's an interactive children's gallery, museum store and café.

EL PRESIDIO DE SANTA BARBARA STATE HISTORIC PARK

Founded in 1782 to protect missions between San Diego and Monterey, this **fort** (Map p500; ☎ 805-965-0093; www.sbthp.org; 123 E Cañon Perdido St; adult/child $5/free; ⏲ 10:30am-4:30pm) was Spain's last military stronghold in Alta California. Today it harbors some of the city's oldest structures, which seem to be in constant need of propping up and restoring. Stop by the well-restored chapel, its interior radiant with kaleidoscopic color. Tickets also include admission to the **Casa de la Guerra Historic House Museum** (Map p500; ☎ 805-966-6961; www.sbthp.org; 15 E De La Guerra St; ⏲ noon-4pm Thu-Sun), a 19th-century colonial adobe displaying Spanish-American heritage exhibits.

CHUMASH PAINTED CAVE STATE HISTORIC PARK

This tiny, off-the-beaten-path **historic site** (☎ 805-733-3713; www.parks.ca.gov; ⏲ dawn-dusk) shelters pictographs painted by the Chumash tribespeople between 400 and 2,000 years ago. The cave is protected from more graffiti by a metal screen, so a flashlight is helpful for getting a good look. Look for the turnoff to Painted Cave Rd, off Hwy 154 below San Marcos Summit, about 6 miles northwest of Hwy 101. The final 2-mile stretch of road is extremely narrow, rough and steep; it's not accessible by RVs or trucks with trailers. Only keen amateur anthropologists will find this detour worth the trip.

Activities

BEACHES

The long sandy stretch between Stearns Wharf and suburban Montecito is **East Beach** (Map pp498–9), Santa Barbara's largest and most crowded. At its east end, near the Biltmore hotel, Armani swimsuits and Gucci sunglasses abound at chic, but narrow **Butterfly Beach**.

Between Stearns Wharf and the harbor, **West Beach** (Map p500) is popular with tourists. Here you'll find **Los Baños del Mar** (Map p500; ☎ 805-966-6110; 401 Shoreline Dr; admission $5; 🚸), a municipal outdoor pool complex good for recreational and lap swimming (call for opening hours). On the other side of the harbor, **Leadbetter Beach** (Map p500) is the spot for beginning surfers and windsurfers. Climbing the stairs on the west end takes you to **Shoreline Park** (Map pp498–9), with picnic tables and awesome kite flying.

West of Santa Barbara, near the junction of Cliff Dr and Las Positas Rd, family-friendly **Hendry's Beach** (Map pp498–9), officially Arroyo Burro Beach County Park, has free parking. Above the beach is **Douglas Family Preserve**, offering cliffside romps for dogs.

About 12 miles south of Santa Barbara, calm **Carpinteria State Beach** (off Map pp498-9; ☎ 805-968-1033; www.parks.ca.gov; per vehicle $8; ⏲ 7am-sunset; 🚸) is great for swimming, wading and tidepooling. A 20-mile drive west of Santa Barbara, off Hwy 101, **Refugio State Beach** (off Map pp498-9; ☎ 805-968-1033; per vehicle $8; ⏲ 8am-sunset) is a popular surf spot, while **El Capitán State Beach** (off Map pp498-9;

CENTRAL COAST

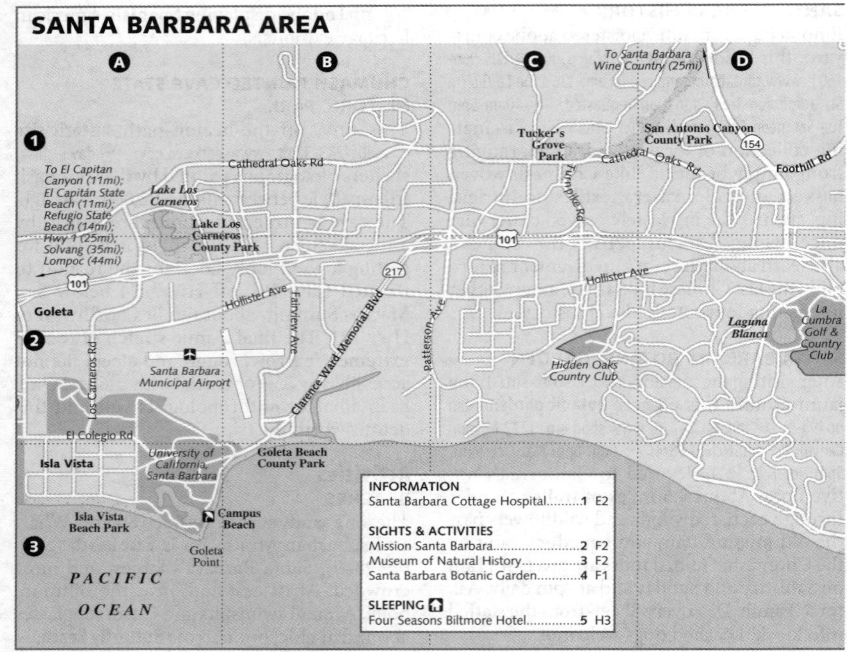

(☎ 805-968-1033; per vehicle $8; 🕒 8am-sunset; ♿), perched on low bluffs 3 miles east, is popular with families.

WHALE-WATCHING

Condor Express (Map p500; ☎ 805-882-0088, 888-779-4425; www.condorcruises.com; 301 W Cabrillo Blvd; tours adult/child from $48/28) runs year-round narrated whale-watching tours, including out to the Channel Islands, aboard a catamaran.

For more trips to the Channel Islands, see p505.

KAYAKING & SAILING

Kayakers can paddle the calm waters of the harbor or the coves of the Gaviota coast, or hitch a ride out to the Channel Islands for more solitude and sea caves. **Santa Barbara Adventure Co** (☎ 805-898-0671, 888-773-3239; www.sbadventureco.com; day tours $35-120) leads guided kayaking tours focused on marine ecology; ask about stargazing floats.

Santa Barbara Sailing Center (Map p500; ☎ 805-962-2826, 800-350-9090; www.sbsail.com; 133 Harbor Way; 🕒 9am-6pm May-Sep, 9am-5pm Oct-Apr) rents kayaks (from $10 per hour). Learn how to sail (20-hour course from $385) or kick back on a sunset cocktail cruise (from $20).

SURFING

Santa Barbara's proximity to the wind-breaking Channel Islands makes it a good spot to learn how to ride the waves. **Rincon Point** (off Map pp498–9) in Carpinteria has long, glassy, point-break waves; **Leadbetter Point** (Map p500) and **Goleta Beach** (Map pp498–9) are best for beginners. Unless you're a novice, conditions are too mellow in summer; swells kick back up in winter.

Learn to surf with **Santa Barbara Adventure Co** (☎ 805-452-0671, 888-773-3239; www.sbadventureco.com). A four-hour lesson including equipment rental and lunch costs $110.

CYCLING & IN-LINE SKATING

The Cabrillo Blvd **beachfront bike path** runs for 3 miles along the water between Andrée Clark Bird Refuge and Leadbetter Beach; **Goleta Bikeway** continues west to UCSB. The **Santa Barbara Bicycle Coalition** (www.sbbike.org) has more printable self-guided tours online. **Wheel Fun** (Map p500; ☎ 805-966-2282; www.wheelfunrentals.com; 23

CENTRAL COAST

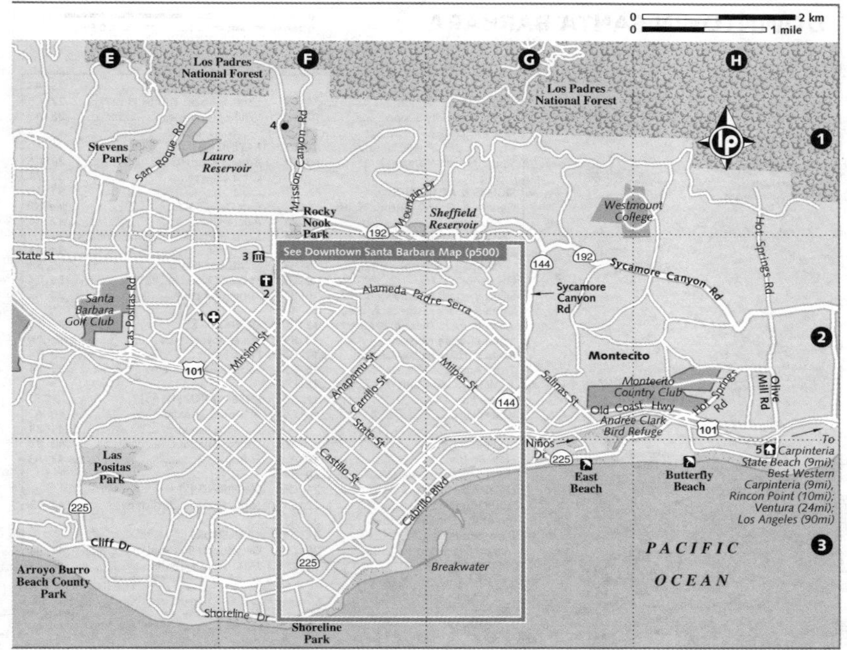

E Cabrillo Blvd & 22 State St; 8am-8pm) rents bicycles (from $8 per hour) and in-line skates.

Tours

The biodiesel-fueled **Santa Barbara Trolley** (805-965-0353; www.sbtrolley.com; adult/child $19/8) makes a hop-on, hop-off narrated loop around Stearns Wharf, the courthouse, the botanical garden and the mission every 30 minutes. One-way tickets are valid all day from 10am to 4pm, and include a free harbor cruise and discount coupons for various attractions.

Festivals & Events

On the first Thursday evening of each month, many downtown art galleries, museums and theaters come alive for a big street party, featuring live entertainment.

Santa Barbara International Film Festival (805-963-0023; www.sbfilmfestival.org) Film buffs arrive in droves from mid-January through early February for screenings of independent US and foreign films.

Summer Solstice Parade (805-965-3396; www.solsticeparade.com) Wildly popular – and just plain wild – performance-art parade in late June.

Old Spanish Fiesta Days (805-962-8101; www.oldspanishdays-fiesta.org) The city gets packed in early August for this long-running but slightly overrated heritage festival.

Avocado Festival (805-684-0038; www.avofest.com) In nearby Carpinteria, you get free admission to witness the world's largest guacamole vat in early October.

Sleeping

Don't just show up at the last minute and expect to find a cheap room, especially on weekends.

BUDGET

Fairly affordable motels cluster along upper State St, near Las Positas Rd.

Less than a 30-minute drive from Santa Barbara, Carpinteria, Refugio and El Capitán state beaches (p497) offer jam-packed **campgrounds** (reservations 800-444-7275; www.reserveamerica.com; tent & RV sites without/with hookups from $25/$34). Amenities include flush toilets, hot showers, barbecues and picnic tables.

Santa Barbara Tourist Hostel (Map p500; 805-963-0154; www.sbhostel.com; 134 Chapala St; dm $30, r $79-95; wi-fi) Traveling strangers, evening trains and a rowdy bar just steps from your door – it's either the perfect country-and-western

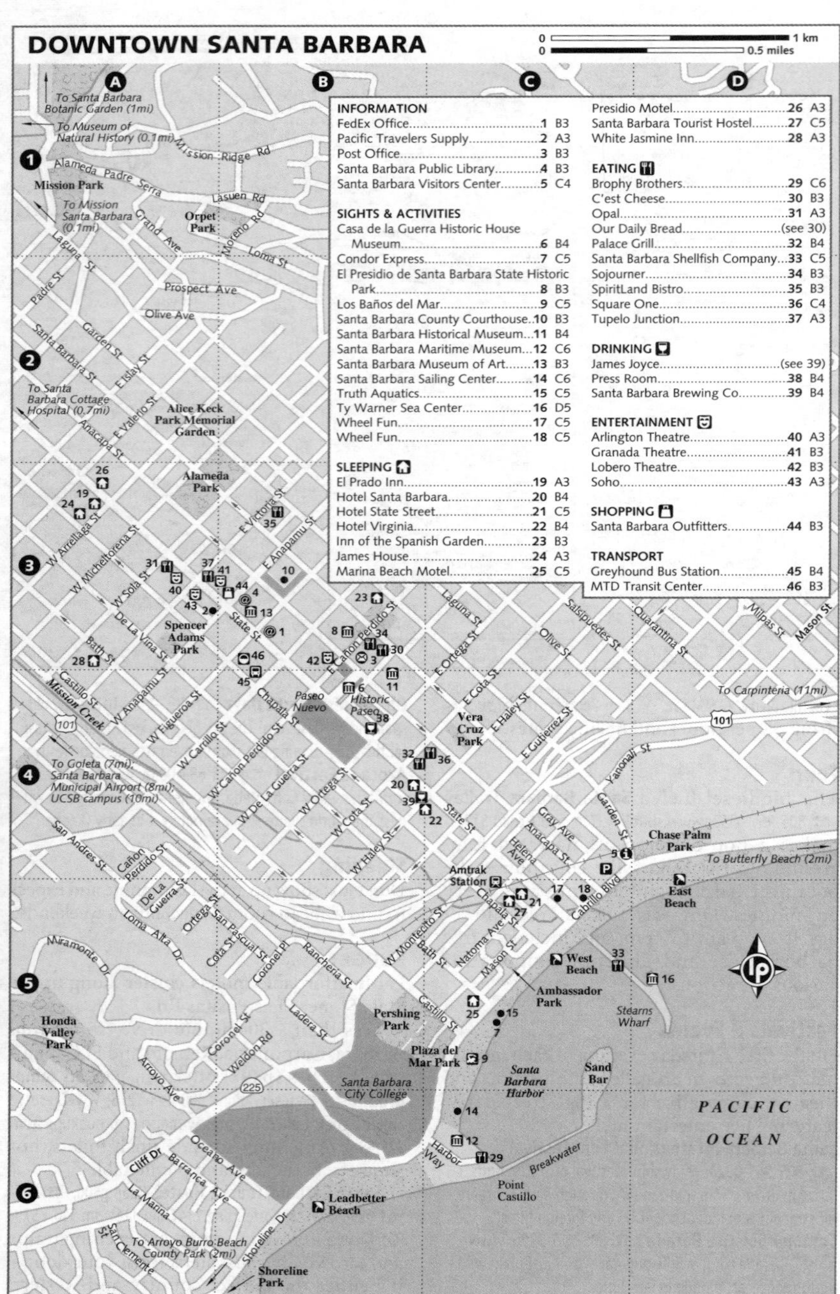
DOWNTOWN SANTA BARBARA
0 1 km
0 0.5 miles
A
B
C
D
1
2
3
4
5
6
INFORMATION
FedEx Office 1 B3
Pacific Travelers Supply 2 A3
Post Office 3 B3
Santa Barbara Public Library 4 B3
Santa Barbara Visitors Center 5 C4
SIGHTS & ACTIVITIES
Casa de la Guerra Historic House Museum 6 B4
Condor Express 7 C5
El Presidio de Santa Barbara State Historic Park 8 B3
Los Baños del Mar 9 C5
Santa Barbara County Courthouse 10 B3
Santa Barbara Historical Museum 11 B4
Santa Barbara Maritime Museum 12 C6
Santa Barbara Museum of Art 13 B3
Santa Barbara Sailing Center 14 C6
Truth Aquatics 15 C5
Ty Warner Sea Center 16 D5
Wheel Fun 17 C5
Wheel Fun 18 C5
SLEEPING
El Prado Inn 19 A3
Hotel Santa Barbara 20 B4
Hotel State Street 21 C5
Hotel Virginia 22 B4
Inn of the Spanish Garden 23 B3
James House 24 A3
Marina Beach Motel 25 C5
Presidio Motel 26 A3
Santa Barbara Tourist Hostel 27 C5
White Jasmine Inn 28 A3
EATING
Brophy Brothers 29 C6
C'est Cheese 30 B3
Opal 31 A3
Our Daily Bread (see 30)
Palace Grill 32 B4
Santa Barbara Shellfish Company 33 C5
Sojourner 34 B3
SpiritLand Bistro 35 B3
Square One 36 C4
Tupelo Junction 37 A3
DRINKING
James Joyce (see 39)
Press Room 38 B4
Santa Barbara Brewing Co. 39 B4
ENTERTAINMENT
Arlington Theatre 40 A3
Granada Theatre 41 B3
Lobero Theatre 42 B3
Soho 43 A3
SHOPPING
Santa Barbara Outfitters 44 B3
TRANSPORT
Greyhound Bus Station 45 B4
MTD Transit Center 46 B3
To Santa Barbara Botanic Garden (1mi)
To Museum of Natural History (0.1mi)
Mission Ridge Rd
Alameda Padre Serra
Mission Park
To Mission Santa Barbara (0.1mi)
Lasuen Rd
Orpet Park
Grand Ave
Moreno Rd
Loma St
Laguna St
Padre St
Prospect Ave
Olive Ave
Garden St
Santa Barbara St
E Islay St
To Santa Barbara Cottage Hospital (0.7mi)
E Valerio St
Anacapa St
Alice Keck Park Memorial Garden
Alameda Park
E Victoria St
E Anapamu St
W Arrellaga St
W Micheltorena St
W Sola St
State St
De La Vina St
Spencer Adams Park
Bath St
Castillo St
Mission Creek
W Anapamu St
W Figueroa St
W Carrillo St
Chapala St
Paseo Nuevo
Historic Paseo
E Cañon Perdido St
E Ortega St
E Cota St
E Haley St
E Gutierrez St
Vera Cruz Park
Laguna St
Salsipuedes St
Olive St
Quarantina St
Milpas St
Mason St
To Carpinteria (11mi)
101
Yanonali St
To Goleta (7mi); Santa Barbara Municipal Airport (8mi); UCSB campus (10mi)
W Cañon Perdido St
W De La Guerra St
W Ortega St
W Cota St
W Haley St
Garden St
Gray Ave
Anacapa St
Helena Ave
Chase Palm Park
To Butterfly Beach (2mi)
San Andres St
Cañon Perdido St
De La Guerra St
Amtrak Station
Cabrillo Blvd
East Beach
Loma Alta Dr
Ortega St
San Pascual St
Cota St
Coronel Pl
Rancheria St
W Montecito St
Bath St
Natoma Ave
Mason St
West Beach
Ambassador Park
Miramonte Dr
Castillo St
Ladera St
Pershing Park
Stearns Wharf
Honda Valley Park
Coronel St
Weldon Rd
Plaza del Mar Park
Santa Barbara Harbor
Sand Bar
Arroyo Ave
225
Santa Barbara City College
PACIFIC OCEAN
Cliff Dr
Oceano Ave
Barranca Ave
Harbor Way
Breakwater
Point Castillo
La Marina
Leadbetter Beach
San Clemente St
To Arroyo Burro Beach County Park (2mi)
Shoreline Dr
Shoreline Park
CENTRAL COAST

SANTA BARBARA FOR KIDS

- **Ty Warner Sea Center** (p496) See a 70ft whale, play with hands-on exhibits and feel the sea critters that live in the touch pool.
- **Santa Barbara Maritime Museum** (p496) Peer through a periscope, reel in a virtual fish or check out the gorgeous model ships.
- **Museum of Natural History** (Map pp498-9; ☎ 805-682-4711; www.sbnature.org; 2559 Puesta del Sol Rd; adult/child $10/6; ⏰ 10am-5pm) Giant skeletons and a pitch-dark planetarium captivate kids' imaginations.
- **Santa Barbara Botanic Garden** (p497) Lush gardens with colorful blooms, prickly cacti and gentle strolling paths.
- **Arroyo Burro Beach** (aka Hendry's Beach; p497) Wide sandy beach, away from the tourists, popular with local families.

song or this low-slung bungalow, which feels like a grungy college dorm, next to the Amtrak station (bring earplugs).

Hotel State Street (Map p500; ☎ 805-966-6586; www.hotelstatestreet.net; 121 State St; r with shared bath $70-100; wi-fi) Despite the whimsical origami cranes hanging from the lobby ceiling, this hostel-esque hotel has a slightly institutional feel. Many rooms have a sink and TV, but no phone. It's only two blocks to the beach, and even closer to the noisy railroad tracks.

Best Western Carpinteria (off Map pp498-9; ☎ 805-684-0473, 800-780-7234; www.bestwestern.com; 4558 Carpinteria Ave, Carpinteria; d $95-189; wi-fi) This Spanish-style motel has wooden balconies and a palm-tree-shaded courtyard. It's near Carpinteria State Beach. All in all, this BW is much more restful than your run-of-the-mill roadside motel.

Presidio Motel (Map p500; ☎ 805-963-1355; www.thepresidiomotel.com; 1620 State St; r $110-190; wi-fi) Presidio is to lodging what H&M is to shopping: a cheap, trendy alternative. Just north of downtown along superbusy State St, its crisp, modern rooms break the Super 8 mold – wonderful beds, high ceilings and art splashed on the walls. Free cruiser bikes to borrow.

Marina Beach Motel (Map p500; ☎ 805-963-9311, 877-627-4621; www.marinabeachmotel.com; 21 Bath St; r $119-284; wi-fi) This old-fashioned, one-story motor lodge has been done up inside and made bright; some comfy rooms have kitchenettes. There's free bike use. Pet fee $15.

MIDRANGE

There's a school of upscale motels in the residential blocks behind West Beach.

our pick El Capitan Canyon (off Map pp498-9; ☎ 805-685-3887, 866-352-2729; www.elcapitancanyon.com; 11560 Calle Real, off Hwy 101; safari tents $145, cabins $225-350; wi-fi) Enjoy the great outdoors by day, and 'safari tents' by night. Or glamp it up in a creekside cedar cabin with a top-quality mattress, high-thread-count sheets and a kitchenette. Both tents and cabins have outdoor firepits and picnic tables. The resort is sandwiched between the Santa Ynez mountains and El Capitán State Beach, a 30-minute drive west of Santa Barbara. No cars are allowed tentside, so it feels like a walk-in campground.

White Jasmine Inn (Map p500; ☎ 805-966-0589; http://glenboroughinn.com; 1327 Bath St; r $149-289) A 10-minute walk west of State St, this B&B has bright, cheerful ambience. Whether you sleep in the Arts and Crafts bungalow or the Victorian cottage, all of the cozy, sound-insulated rooms have gas fireplaces, and some have spa tubs. The art-nouveau suite, with its private Jacuzzi terrace, is a honeymooners' fave.

El Prado Inn (Map p500; ☎ 805-966-0807, 800-669-8979; www.elprado.com; 1601 State St; r $155-215; wi-fi) North of downtown, family-run El Prado has a 1960s mod exterior, above-average, spacious motel rooms and a large heated pool. Notice the cool oversized aerial photo of Santa Barbara in the lobby.

Hotel Santa Barbara (Map p500; ☎ 805-957-9300, 800-549-9869; www.hotelsantabarbara.com; 533 State St; r $170-230; wi-fi) As unpretentiously sophisticated as its namesake city, this 1925 hotel has airy rooms where rattan and light woods mix with Mediterranean tones – kind of like Provence meets the beach. It's perfectly located.

Hotel Virginia (Map p500; ☎ 805-963-9757, 800-549-1700; www.hotelvirginia.com; 17 W Haley St; r incl breakfast $175-235; wi-fi) This early-20th-century hotel downplays its Holiday Inn Express affiliation. It has heaps of character, starting in the tile-filled lobby with fountain, and tidy rooms with upgrades like flat-screen TVs and CD players.

The **Santa Barbara Hotel Group** (☎ 805-687-5511, 888-726-3972; www.sbhotels.com; d $149-235; wi-fi) has a small collection of upscale motels by the waterfront or north of downtown. See the website for locations.

TOP END

Inn of the Spanish Garden (Map p500; ☎ 805-564-4700, 866-564-4700; http://spanishgardeninn.com; 915 Garden St; r & ste incl breakfast $259-515; wi-fi) At this small Spanish Revival–style hotel, two dozen romantic rooms and suites have balconies and patios overlooking a gracious fountain courtyard, while palm trees surround an outdoor lap pool. Beds have luxurious linens, bathrooms feature decadent oversized soaking tubs and concierge service is top-notch.

Also recommended:

James House (Map p500; ☎ 805-569-5853; www.jameshousesantabarbara.com; 1632 Chapala St; r incl breakfast $259-289; wi-fi) For a traditional B&B experience, revel in this hospitable Queen Anne Victorian.

Four Seasons Biltmore Hotel (Map pp498-9; ☎ 805-969-2261, 800-332-3442; www.fourseasons.com/santabarbara; 1260 Channel Dr; r from $600; wi-fi) At Santa Barbara's iconic beachfront resort, ocean-view suites exude 1920s chic.

Eating

Sojourner (Map p500; ☎ 805-965-7922; 134 E Cañon Perdido St; mains $7-13; 11am-11pm Mon-Sat, 11am-10pm Sun; V) This granola-flavored favorite has been doing its all-natural, mostly meatless magic since 1978 and infuses each dish with a unique twist. The chilied tempeh tacos and gingered tofu wonton pillows are delish.

Palace Grill (Map p500; ☎ 805-963-5000; 8 E Cota St; mains lunch $8-15, dinner $16-30; 11:30am-3pm daily, 5:30-10pm Sun-Thu, 5:30-11pm Fri & Sat) With all the exuberance of Mardi Gras, this N'awlins grill dishes up delectable baskets of housemade biscuits and breads – ask the kindly host for the recipe – followed by ginormous plates of jambalaya, blackened catfish and pecan chicken.

Santa Barbara Shellfish Company (Map p500; ☎ 805-966-6676; 230 Stearns Wharf; mains $8-20; 11am-9pm) 'From sea to skillet to plate' best describes this wharf-top crab shack that's more of a counter joint. Great lobster bisque, ocean views and the same owners for 25 years.

Brophy Brothers (Map p500; ☎ 805-966-4418; 119 Harbor Way; mains $8-20; 11am-10pm Sun-Thu, 11am-11pm Fri & Sat) The seafood at this always-bustling harbor hangout is so fresh that you half expect it to leap straight out of the ocean. The upstairs deck is awesome at sunset.

Opal (Map p500; ☎ 805-966-9676; 1325 State St; mains lunch $9-13, dinner $13-30; 11:30am-2:30pm Mon-Sat, 5-10pm Sun-Thu, 5-11pm Fri & Sat) An elegant sidewalk bistro, this gem draws city sophisticates for its seasonal creations and trusty standbys, like chili-encrusted steak or grilled pork loin with figs. The discerning California and European wine list is top-notch.

SpiritLand Bistro (Map p500; ☎ 805-966-7759; 230 E Victoria St; mains lunch $10-14, dinner $15-27, 3-course veg/nonveg dinner menu $35/44; 11:30am-9pm Mon, Wed, Thu & Sun, 11:30am-10pm Fri & Sat; V) Although execution is uneven, this side-street café inside a Victorian house is a charmer, with its cornucopia of vegetarian, vegan and raw-foods dishes. The seasonal, international menu can feature anything from Caribbean sweet-potato fritters to Thai curry.

Tupelo Junction (Map p500; ☎ 805-899-3100; 1218 State St; mains $12-33; 8am-2pm & 5-9pm) Southern-style comfort food is the specialty here. Busiest at breakfast, this sunny café offers fresh takes on good ol' standards like cinnamon-apple beignets. Later in the day, choose between gouda mac and cheese, fried-chicken salad and creole-buttered shrimp and grits.

Square One (Map p500; ☎ 805-965-4565; 14 E Cota St; mains $14-38, prix fixe veg/nonveg $65/75, incl wine pairings $90/100; dinner Tue-Sun) The chef's postmodern menu reaches stratospheric heights of inventiveness, piquing even jaded palates with the likes of grapefruit gelée and avocado mousse laid atop seafood. There's roasted game and Kobe steaks, too, and the sculpted desserts are sweetly challenging.

Saturdays there's a **downtown farmers market** (☎ 805-962-5354; cnr Santa Barbara & Cota Sts; 8:30am-12:30pm Sat), which also takes place on Tuesday afternoons along the 500 and 600 blocks of State St. To fill a picnic basket for the beach, stop in at **C'est Cheese** (Map p500; ☎ 805-965-0318; 825 Santa Barbara St; 10am-7pm Mon-Fri, 8am-6pm Sat) and **Our Daily Bread** (Map p500; ☎ 805-966-3894; 831 Santa Barbara St; 6am-5:30pm Mon-Fri, 7am-4pm Sat).

Drinking

Santa Barbara's after-dark scene revolves around college-age bars on lower State St. Saturday nights here are rowdy.

Santa Barbara Brewing Co (Map p500; ☎ 805-730-1040; 501 State St) Find plenty of microbrews on tap, including a killer Rincon Red ale made with Munch malts and Oregon hops. There's a long menu of pub grub, too. The pool tables and game room are out back.

James Joyce (Map p500; ☎ 805-962-2688; 513 State St) With peanut shells heaped on the carpet, this vaguely Irish pub is always a boisterous place for a pint. There's live music almost nightly, with Dixieland jazz on Saturdays.

Press Room (Map p500; ☎ 805-936-8121; 15 E Ortega St) This unpretentious pub attracts locals, Brooks Institute photography students and a slew of European travelers. There's no better place to watch footie, stuff the jukebox and be abused by the British bartender.

Entertainment

Nightclubs on lower State St change names and formats on a whim. The free weekly *Santa Barbara Independent* (www.independent.com) has complete listings and reviews. The daily *Santa Barbara News-Press* (www.newspress.com) publishes *Scene,* an arts and entertainment supplement, on Fridays.

Soho (Map p500; ☎ 805-962-7776; www.sohosb.com; 1221 State St; cover $10-20) An unpretentious brick room above a McDonald's, with live bands nightly; styles range from blues to funk to rock.

Arlington Theatre (Map p500; ☎ 805-963-4408; www.thearlingtontheatre.com; 1317 State St) This 1931 mission-style movie palace has a Spanish courtyard and a gorgeous ceiling spangled with stars. It's a splendid place to see a concert, dance recital or Broadway-style musical.

Lobero Theatre (Map p500; ☎ 805-963-0761; www.lobero.com; 33 E Cañon Perdido St) One of California's oldest theaters, it presents modern dance, chamber music, and jazz and world-music concerts.

Granada Theatre (Map p500; ☎ 805-899-2222; www.granadasb.org; 1216 State St) This beautifully restored 1930s Spanish Moorish–style theater is home to Santa Barbara's symphony, opera and ballet.

Shopping

Santa Barbara Outfitters (Map p500; ☎ 805-564-1007; 1200 State St; 🕑 10am-8pm Mon-Sat, 11am-6pm Sun). Stop by this locally owned outdoor-equipment and clothing store for all your active-lifestyle needs, from tents to kayaks to rock-climbing shoes. Expert staff also lead guided outdoor-activity tours.

Getting There & Away

If you use public transportation to get to Santa Barbara, you're eligible for discounts at select hotels, plus a nice swag bag of coupons for various activities and attractions, courtesy of **Santa Barbara Car Free** (www.santabarbaracarfree.org).

Ten miles west of downtown off Hwy 101, small **Santa Barbara Municipal Airport** (SBA; Map pp498-9; ☎ 805-967-7111; www.flysba.com; 500 Fowler Rd) is served by Allegiant Air (Las Vegas), American Eagle (LA), United Express (LA, San Francisco and San Jose) and US Airways (Las Vegas). Major car-rental firms are found here.

Santa Barbara Airbus (☎ 805-964-7759, 800-423-1618; www.santabarbaraairbus.com) shuttles between Los Angeles International Airport (LAX) and Santa Barbara (one way/round trip $48/90, 2½ to three hours), making stops in Carpinteria and Goleta.

The **Greyhound bus station** (Map p500; ☎ 805-965-7551; 34 W Carrillo St) has several daily services along Hwy 101 south to Los Angeles ($14 to $18, 2¼ to three hours) and north to San Francisco ($42 to $59, 7¾ to ten hours) via San Luis Obispo ($21 to $26, 2¼ hours).

The beautifully restored Amtrak **train station** (Map p500; 209 State St) is a stop on the daily Seattle–LA *Coast Starlight.* Frequent *Pacific Surfliner* regional trains head south to LA ($16 to $25, 2¾ to 3¼ hours) and San Diego ($32 to $37, 5½ to six hours), and twice daily north to San Luis Obispo ($19 to $29, 2½ to three hours). Frequent Thruway buses head north along Hwy 101 to San Jose via SLO.

Santa Barbara is bisected by Hwy 101; to reach downtown, take the Garden St or Cabrillo Blvd exits. Parking on the street or in any of 10 municipal lots is free for the first 75 minutes; each extra hour or part thereof costs $1.50.

Getting Around

Buses operated by **Santa Barbara Metropolitan Transit District** (MTD; ☎ 805-963-3366; www.sbmtd.gov; single ride $1.25) travel across the city and to nearby communities. The **MTD Transit Center** (Map p500; 1020 Chapala St) has details on routes and schedules.

Bus	Destination
11	State St, UCSB, Airport
20	Carpinteria
22	Mission, Botanic Garden (weekends only)

MTD's Downtown Shuttle (25¢, every 10 to 30 minutes from 9am to 6pm, to 10pm Friday and Saturday in summer) runs along State St to Stearns Wharf. Its Waterfront Shuttle (25¢, every 15 to 30 minutes from 10am to 6pm) travels along the waterfront between Stearns Wharf, Harbor Way and the zoo. The biodiesel-fueled, bright-yellow Lil' Toot water taxi (one way adult/child $4/1, every half-hour from noon to 6pm) shuttles between Stearns Wharf and the harbor.

CHANNEL ISLANDS NATIONAL PARK

An eight-island chain lying off the Southern California coast, the Channel Islands are named for the troughs separating them from the mainland. Originally inhabited by Chumash tribespeople (who were forced to move to mainland missions by 1830), the islands were later owned by sheep ranchers and the US Navy until conservation efforts began in the mid-1970s. Four of these islands, along with tiny Santa Barbara Island further south, now comprise this national park. Rich with unique flora and fauna species, tidepools and kelp forests, the islands have earned the (not entirely deserved) nickname 'California's Galapagos.' They offer rugged opportunities for camping, hiking, kayaking and scuba diving. In spring, wildflowers bloom; winter is best for wildlife watching. Watersports may be best in fall, when the ocean is calmest and reaches temperatures of up to 70°F. Peak summer season is bone-dry.

Information

At the far end of Ventura Harbor, off Harbor Blvd southwest of Hwy 101, the **National Park Service (NPS) visitors center** (☎ 805-658-5730; www.nps.gov/chis; 1901 Spinnaker Dr, Ventura; 8:30am-5pm;) is a one-stop shop for books, maps and trip-planning information. You can also learn about the islands' diverse natural and human history here, and there's a lookout from where you can see the islands on a clear day.

Sights & Activities

If you're short on time, **Anacapa Island**, which is actually three separate islets, gives a memorable introduction to the islands' ecology. Boats dock on the East Island and after a short climb you'll find 2 miles of trails offering fantastic views of island flora, a historic lighthouse, and the rocky Middle and West Islands. Kayaking, diving, tidepooling and seal-watching are popular activities here. After checking out the small museum at the visitors center, ask about ranger-led programs. In summer, scuba divers with video cameras occasionally broadcast live images to TV monitors you can watch.

The western side of **Santa Cruz Island**, which is the largest island in the park, is owned by the Nature Conservancy and can only be accessed with a special permit. But the 24% of the eastern side of the island near Scorpion Beach, managed by the NPS, packs a wallop. It's perfect for anyone looking for an action-packed camping trip. Here you can swim, snorkel, scuba dive and kayak. There are excellent hikes, too, including a 2-mile loop to Cavern Point – ocean views don't get much better than this.

Gorgeous white-sand beaches and a chance to spot nearly 200 bird species and the endemic island fox are highlights of **Santa Rosa Island**, where seals and sea lions haul out. Hiking trails through the grasslands and along beaches abound, but high winds typically make swimming, diving and kayaking tough for everyone but experts.

San Miguel Island – the most remote of the four northern islands – offers solitude and a wilderness experience, but it's often shrouded in fog and is very windy. Attractions include a ghostly caliche forest, made of the calcium carbonate castings of trees, and pinniped colonies that haul out at Point Bennett at various times of year.

Only 1 sq mile in size, isolated **Santa Barbara Island** is home to northern elephant seals. It's also a thriving playground for seabirds and marine wildlife. Ask at the visitors center here about the best spots for diving, snorkeling, kayaking and hiking.

Sleeping

All five islands have primitive year-round **campgrounds** (☎ reservations 877-444-6777; www.recreation.gov; tent sites $15) with pit toilets and picnic tables. Water is only available on Santa Cruz and Santa Rosa Islands. Campers must pack everything in and out, including trash. Because of fire danger, campfires are not allowed, but enclosed campstoves are OK. Be prepared to carry your gear 0.5 to 1.5 miles uphill from the boat landing area. Before boarding your boat, you'll need to show proof of camping reservations, but don't reserve campsites until you've booked transportation to the islands first.

Getting There & Away

The only way to get to the islands is by boat or plane. Organized tours usually require a minimum number of participants and can be canceled anytime due to surf and weather conditions. Reservations are recommended for weekend, holiday and summer trips, and advance payment is required.

Near the NPS visitors center at Ventura Harbor, **Island Packers** (☎ 805-642-1393; www.islandpackers.com; 1691 Spinnaker Dr, Ventura) is the only operator that provides regularly scheduled ferry service to the islands for campers (round trip adult/child from $58/42). It also runs whale-watching and wildlife cruises (from $28/19), guided day trips (from $45/28) and multiday activity tours. Some boats depart from Oxnard.

Truth Aquatics (Map p500; ☎ 805-962-1127; www.truthaquatics.com; 301 W Cabrillo Blvd, Santa Barbara) offers similar tours to Island Packers, but caters mostly to divers and kayakers.

Channel Islands Aviation (☎ 805-987-1301; www.flycia.com; half-day tours adult/child $160/135) runs half-day beach excursions, surf-fishing trips and shuttle flights to Santa Rosa Island, departing from Camarillo and Santa Barbara airports.

VENTURA

pop 106,750 / elev 100ft

The primary departure point for Channel Islands trips, Ventura is not the most enchanting coastal city, but it has its scruffy charms, especially in the historic downtown corridor along Main St, north of Hwy 101. There you'll find a terrific assortment of antiques, vintage and secondhand thrift shops, and the **Ventura Visitors & Convention Bureau** (☎ 805-648-2075, 800-483-6214; www.ventura-usa.com; 101 S California St; 8:30am-5pm Mon-Fri, 9am-5pm Sat, 10am-4pm Sun).

The town's Spanish colonial roots are evidenced by **Mission San Buenaventura** (☎ 805-643-4318; www.sanbuenaventuramission.org; 211 E Main St; suggested donation adult/child $2/50¢; 10am-5pm Mon-Fri, 9am-5pm Sat, 10am-4pm Sun), the last California mission founded by Junípero Serra in 1782. A stroll around this petite parish church, a short walk west of California St, is a tranquil experience, leading through a small museum, past statues of saints, centuries-old religious paintings and unusual wooden mission bells, and around a garden courtyard.

The mission's original foundations and Native American artifacts are on display at the nearby **Albinger Archaeological Museum** (☎ 805-648-5823; 113 E Main St; admission free; 10am-4pm Wed-Sun). South of Main St, the storefront **Museum of Ventura County** (☎ 805-653-0323; www.venturamuseum.org; 89 S California St; admission free; 11am-6pm Tue-Thu, Sat & Sun, to 8pm Fri) has an eclectic mix of historical and cultural exhibits, from Chumash basketry to contemporary California art.

Two blocks east of California St, **Mary's Secret Garden** (☎ 805-641-3663; 100 S Fir St; mains $5-12; 11am-4pm Tue & Wed, 11am-9:30pm Thu-Sat; V) is an internationally spiced vegan haven that crafts fresh juices, smoothies and out-of-this-world cakes. Just off California St, **Brooks** (☎ 805-652-7070; 545 E Thompson Blvd; mains lunch $12-25, dinner $22-38; lunch Thu & Fri, dinner Tue-Sun) restaurant serves high-flying New American cuisine like cornmeal-fried oysters, jalapeño cheddar grits and Maytag blue cheesecake with seasonal berries.

Right downtown, casual **Anacapa Brew Pub** (☎ 805-643-2337; 472 E Main St; mains $9-20; 5-9pm Mon, 11:30am-midnight Tue-Sun) crafts its own microbrews and makes a fine pulled-pork sandwich. At the end of a brick-lined passageway, **Zoey's Café** (☎ 805-652-1137; www.zoeyscafe.com; 451 E Main St) showcases live acts weekly – mostly bluegrass, acoustic folk and comedy – inside a cozy, indie coffeehouse.

Ventura's unstaffed **Amtrak station** (cnr Harbor Blvd & Figueroa St) has several daily trains north to Santa Barbara ($11 to $15, 40 minutes) and south to Los Angeles ($17 to $23, two hours). **Vista** (☎ 805-642-1591; www.goventura.org) runs several daily Coastal Express buses between Ventura and Santa Barbara ($2, one to 1¼ hours), stopping in Carpinteria.

DETOUR: OJAI

About 35 miles east of Santa Barbara via Hwys 101 and 150, or 15 miles inland from Ventura off Hwy 33, **Ojai** (pronounced *oh*-hi, meaning 'moon' to the Chumash) is a town that has long drawn artists and new-agers. It's famous for the 'Pink Moment,' a rosy glow that emanates from its mountains at sunset. Many have been taken by this fetching place, including Frank Capra, who had Ojai Valley represent mythical Shangri-La in his 1937 movie *Lost Horizon*. For more information, contact the **Ojai Valley Chamber of Commerce** (☎ 805-646-8126; www.ojaichamber.org; 201 S Signal St; 9am-noon & 1-4pm Mon-Fri).

Los Angeles

Ride your beach bike beneath the Santa Monica Pier one midday, and you'll see stars. Beneath the amusement park above are not the stars of the heavens or stars of stage or screen, but pinpoints of light streaming through the wooden slats and beams, reflected on the concrete below. Beneath the bustle, there's order and – dare we say it? – serenity.

Not the LA you were expecting? That's just one of the surprises in store. In America's second city and largest county, the unexpected is everyday.

The entertainment industry touches every corner of this vast metropolis, and your waitress today might be a starlet next year. Beaches and gyms abound, but so do ethnic spas where you can get whacked with sticks. LA's famous for celebrity chefs, but fusion cuisine and a UN of cooking have pushed Americans' perception of food for generations. Arts and architecture? Here's where Wright, Greene & Greene and Gehry innovated forms first viewed as quizzical and now iconic. Music? Domingo to The Doors to Dr Dre.

One thing you won't need are your preconceptions: smog, traffic, celebrity murders and plastic culture (and bosoms). So sorry, but so wrong, and so waiting for you to explore.

HIGHLIGHTS

- **Easiest Way to Get into Showbiz** Go behind the scenes on a studio tour (p529)
- **Top Venues for Culture Vultures** Visit world-famous venues such as the Walt Disney Concert Hall (p524), Los Angeles County Museum of Art (p533) or the Getty Center (p536)
- **Best Place for a Drive** Go hot-rodding along the breathtaking Pacific Coast Hwy to Malibu (p536), preferably on a sunny summer's day with the top down
- **Tastiest World Cuisine** Discover the perfect taco, shrimp dumpling or Korean barbecue at one of thousands of ethnic restaurants (p552)
- **Most Historic and Diverse** Take a trip around the world and back in time in Downtown LA (p523)
- **Best Outdoor Music Venue** Enjoy a picnic and a concert under the stars at the venerable Hollywood Bowl (p564)
- **Most Muscle-bound Beach** Bask with the bronzed, buff, bicyclists, 'bladers and buskers in Venice (p537)
- **Best Place to Take a Hike** Explore LA's 'wild' side on a trek through the Santa Monica Mountains (p543)
- **Best Stars and Bars** Mingle with the beau monde in a hip Hollywood bar or club (p560)

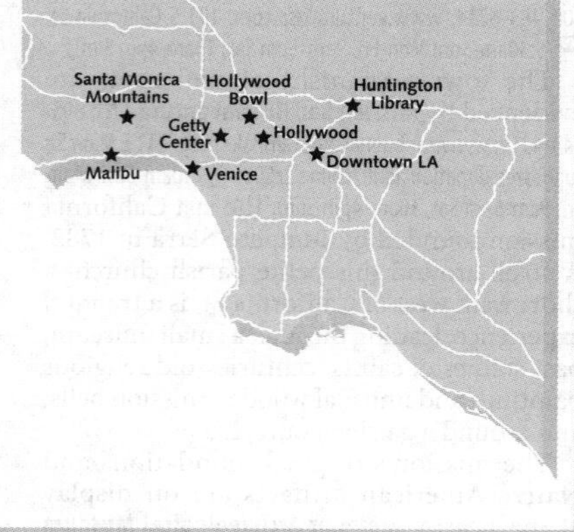

HISTORY

Los Angeles' human history began as early as 6000 BC, when the Gabrieleño and Chumash peoples occupied the region. Their hunter-gatherer existence ended in the late 18th century with the arrival of Spanish missionaries and pioneers, led by Padre Junípero Serra. Known as El Pueblo de la Reina de Los Angeles (the Village of the Queen of the Angels), the first civilian settlement became a thriving farming community but remained an isolated outpost for decades.

After Spain lost its hold on the territory to Mexico in 1821, many of that nation's citizens looked to California to quench their thirst for private land. By the mid-1830s the missions had been secularized and their land divvied up into free land grants by Mexican governors, thus giving birth to the rancho (cattle ranch) system.

At the time of the Mexican-American War (1846–48), American soldiers encountered some resistance from General Andrés Pico and other Mexican commanders, but eventually LA came under US rule along with the rest of California. The city was incorporated on April 4, 1850.

A series of seminal events caused LA's population to swell to two million by 1930: the collapse of the Northern California Gold Rush in the 1850s, the arrival of the transcontinental railroad in the 1870s, the birth of the citrus industry in the late 1800s, the discovery of oil in 1892, the launch of the port of LA in 1907, the birth of the movie industry in 1908 and the opening of the LA Aqueduct in 1913.

Aside from motion pictures, few industries have had as strong an impact on LA as aviation. During WWI, the Lockheed brothers and Donald Douglas established aircraft manufacturing plants here. Two decades later, the aviation industry – helped along by billions of federal dollars for military contracts – helped to lift LA out of the Great Depression. Defense contracts continued to be a driving force behind the city's economy through the end of the Cold War. The 10th Summer Olympic Games, held here in 1932, marked LA's coming of age as a world city (10th St was renamed Olympic Blvd in their honor).

After WWII, a deluge of new residents, drawn by reasonably priced housing (particularly in the San Fernando Valley), seemingly boundless opportunity and reliably fabulous weather, shaped LA into the megalopolis of today. The city grew from 1.5 million in 1950 to over three million in 1980, surpassing Chicago as America's second city. Culturally too, LA's freewheeling, free-thinking, free-living lifestyle defined the American consciousness of the 1960s and '70s, a boom culminating in a second Summer Olympics held here in 1984.

LA's growth was not without its problems, including suburban sprawl and air pollution, though smog levels have fallen annually since records have been kept. Major riots in 1965 and 1992 created distrust between the city's police department and various ethnic groups, although in 2002 the arrival of a new police chief, William Bratton of New York, seemed to stabilize the situation. Violent crime has dropped significantly on his watch and, despite isolated incidents of police brutality, he has earned the respect of most constituencies. In May 2005 Angelenos elected Antonio Villaraigosa, the city's first mayor of Latino descent since 1872.

In the new millennium, traffic, a struggling public education system and a fluctuating real-estate market are among the problems that continue to cloud LA's sunny skies. But with a strong and diverse economy, falling pollution levels, low unemployment and decreasing crime rate, overall morale remains high.

FAST FACTS

Population LA County 10.3 million (2007)
Population of Los Angeles 4.2 million (2007)
Average temperature low/high Jan 47/66°F, July 62/82°F
LA to Disneyland 26 miles
LA to San Diego 120 miles
LA to Palm Springs 110 miles
LA to Santa Barbara 95 miles
LA to Las Vegas 270 miles

ORIENTATION

Los Angeles may be vast and amorphous, but the areas of visitor interest are fairly well defined. About 12 miles inland, Downtown LA is the region's hub, combining great architecture and museums with global-village pizzazz thanks to such enclaves as Chinatown, Little Tokyo and El Pueblo de Los Angeles. Northwest of Downtown, there's sprawling Hollywood with its hip 'hoods of Los Feliz and Silver Lake. West Hollywood is LA's center of urban chic and the gay and lesbian community, while Long Beach, at six o'clock from Downtown, is a bustling port with big city sophistication. Most TV and movie studios are actually north of Hollywood in the San Fernando Valley, and to its east Pasadena feels like an All-American small town writ large.

South of Hollywood, Mid-City's main draw is Museum Row, while further west are ritzy Beverly Hills and the Westside communities of Westwood, home to the University of California (UCLA); mansion-studded Bel Air; and Brentwood with the hilltop Getty Center. Of the beach towns, Santa Monica is the most tourist- and pedestrian-friendly; others include swish-but-low-key Malibu and bohemian Venice.

Famously, the car is LA's prescribed mode of transportation, but the more central neighborhoods (except for West Hollywood and Silver Lake) are quite well served by light-rail and a rather stylish subway system. Bus transport is available for destinations south and west of Hollywood, but a car will speed your way.

For information on traveling to and from Los Angeles International Airport (LAX), see p569.

Maps

If you don't have a GPS, a good map is as essential in LA as sunscreen. For navigating within specific neighborhoods, the maps in this book should be sufficient. Otherwise, pick up a street map at gas stations, bookstores, convenience stores, supermarkets, tourist offices or branches of the **American Automobile Association** (AAA; ☎ 800-874-7532; www.aaa.com).

For serious urban trekkers, the phone-book-sized street atlas by the Thomas Bros company is a point of reference for every Angeleno.

INFORMATION

Bookstores

Outlets of Barnes & Noble and Borders abound throughout LA; check the Yellow Pages. Here are our favorite indie bookstores:

A Different Light (Map pp516-17; ☎ 310-854-6601; 8853 Santa Monica Blvd, West Hollywood; 🕒 11am-10pm) LA's bastion of queer literature, nonfiction and magazines.

Bodhi Tree (Map pp516-17; ☎ 310-659-1733, 800-825-9798; 8585 Melrose Ave, West Hollywood; 🕒 10am-11pm) Celebrity-heavy dispensary of new and used spiritual tomes, soulful music and aura-enhancing incense. Psychic readings, too.

Book Soup (Map pp516-17; ☎ 310-659-3110; 8818 W Sunset Blvd, West Hollywood; 🕒 9am-9pm) Solid selection of entertainment and fiction. Also great people-watching (high celeb quotient) and big-name book signings.

Distant Lands (Map pp510-11; ☎ 626-449-3220; 56 S Raymond Ave, Pasadena; 🕒 10:30am-8pm Mon-Thu, to 9pm Fri & Sat, 11am-6pm Sun) Treasure chest of travel books, guides and gadgets, including luggage and daypacks.

Equator (Map pp520-1; ☎ 310-399-5544; 1103 Abbot Kinney Blvd, Venice; 🕒 11am-10pm Tue-Thu, to 11pm Fri & Sat, to 5pm Sun) Rare and collectible books about art, surf culture, black studies, drugs and crime, and other assorted offbeat subjects inside a gallery-style store.

Traveler's Bookcase (Map pp516-17; ☎ 323-655-0575; 8375 W 3rd St, Mid-City; 🕒 10am-7pm Mon-Sat, 11am-5pm Sun) Just what it says.

Vroman's (Map pp510-11; ☎ 626-449-5320; 695 E Colorado Blvd, Pasadena; 9am-9pm Mon-Thu, to 10pm Fri & Sat, 10am-9pm Sun) Southern California's oldest bookstore (since 1894) and a favorite with local literati.

Emergency

Emergency number (☎ 911) For police, fire or ambulance service.

Rape & Battering Hotline (☎ 800-656-4673)

Internet Access

Along with books, **public libraries** (☎ 213-228-7272; www.lapl.org) also offer limited free internet access. For branches, call or log on to

FREEWAY LOGIC

Sooner or later you will find yourself on one of LA's freeways, and a little preparation goes a long way. Freeways have both a number and a name corresponding to where they're headed from Downtown LA. I-10, for instance, is called the Santa Monica Fwy west of Downtown and the San Bernardino Fwy east of it. I-5 heading north is the Golden State Fwy; heading south it's the Santa Ana Fwy. And I-110 is both the Pasadena Fwy and the Harbor Fwy. I-405, which avoids Downtown, is the San Diego Fwy everywhere. That said, Angelenos tend to call freeways by the number with 'the' in front of it (eg 'Sorry I'm late, dude. The 10 was a friggin' beast!').

TICKETS TO SAVINGS

The **Go Los Angeles Card** (☎ 866-652-3053; www.golosangelescard.com; adult/child 1 day $55/50, 2 day $90/70, 3 day $160/120, 5 day $200/150, 7 day $220/170) covers admission to as many of the 40 leading sights and attractions (such as Universal Studios, p539; the Museum of Contemporary Art, p532; and the Aquarium of the Pacific, p538) as you can cram in, plus discounts at shops, restaurants and services. Multiday cards may be used on nonconsecutive days during a 14-day period.

If you're sticking to Hollywood, the **Hollywood CityPass** (www.citypass.com; adult/child 3-9yr $50/39) coupon booklet offers one-time admission to a Red Line walking tour (p545), the Hollywood Museum (p528) or Kodak Theatre (p528), a narrated bus tour of movie stars' homes with Starline Tours (p545) and more, at savings of about 40% off full admission. The roster of venues changes periodically; check the website.

the website. For wi-fi locations, check www.jiwire.com. The Coffee Bean & Tea Leaf, LA's answer to Starbucks, offers free wi-fi in its branches. Visit coffeebean.com, or phone ☎ 800-832-5323 for locations.

Internet Resources

Daily Candy (www.dailycandy.com) Little bites from the stylish LA scene.
Discover Los Angeles (www.visitlosangeles.info) Website of LA Inc, the Los Angeles Convention and Visitors Bureau.
Eater LA (www.eaterla.com) Smart restaurant blog.
Experience LA (www.experiencela.com) Excellent cultural calendar packed with useful public transportation maps and trips.
Gridskipper (www.gridskipper.com/travel/los-angeles) Urban travel guide to the useful, offbeat, naughty and nice.
The Guide (http://theguide.latimes.com) Arts, dining and entertainment listings from the *LA Times*.
LA Almanac (www.laalmanac.com) All the facts and figures at your fingertips.
LA.com (www.la.com) Hip guide to shopping, dining, nightlife and events.
Thrillist (www.thrillist.com) A Daily Candy for guys.

Media

For entertainment listings magazines, see p561.

KCRW 89.9 fm (www.kcrw.org) Santa Monica–based National Public Radio (NPR) station with cutting-edge music and well-chosen public affairs programming.
KPCC 89.3 fm (www.kpcc.org) Pasadena-based NPR station with NPR network programming and intelligent local talk shows.
KPFK 90.7 fm (www.kpfk.org) Part of the left-leaning Pacific radio network; news and talk.
LA Weekly (www.laweekly.com) Free alternative news and listings magazine.
Los Angeles Magazine (www.losangelesmagazine.com) Glossy lifestyle monthly with useful restaurant guide.
Los Angeles Times (www.latimes.com) The west's leading daily and winner of dozens of Pulitzer Prizes. Embattled but still useful.

Medical Services

Cedars-Sinai Medical Center (Map pp516-17; ☎ 310-423-5000; 8700 Beverly Blvd, West Hollywood; 24hr emergency room)
Rite-Aid pharmacies (☎ 800-748-3243) Call for the branch nearest you (some are open 24 hours).
UCLA Medical Center (Map pp518-19; ☎ 310-825-9111; 10833 Le Conte Ave, Westwood; 24hr emergency room)
Venice Family Clinic (Map pp520-1; ☎ 310-392-8630; 604 Rose Ave, Venice) For general health concerns, with payment on a sliding scale according to your means.
Women's Clinic (Map pp518-19; ☎ 310-203-8899; Suite 500, 9911 W Pico Blvd, Century City) Fees are calculated on a sliding scale according to your capacity to pay.

Money

American Express (Map pp516-17; ☎ 310-659-1682; 8493 W 3rd St, West Hollywood; 9am-6pm Mon-Fri, 10am-3pm Sat)
TravelEx (☎ 800-287-7362) West Hollywood (Map pp516-17; 8901 Santa Monica Blvd, West Hollywood; 9:30am-5pm Mon-Fri); Beverly Hills (Map pp518-19; 9595 Wilshire Blvd, Beverly Hills; 9:30am-5:30pm Mon-Fri)

Post

You're never far from a post office in LA. Call ☎ 800-275-8777 or visit www.usps.com for the nearest branch.

Telephone

LA County is covered by 10 area codes (some shared with neighboring counties); this chapter gives the area code for all telephone numbers.

(Continued on page 523)

GREATER LOS ANGELES

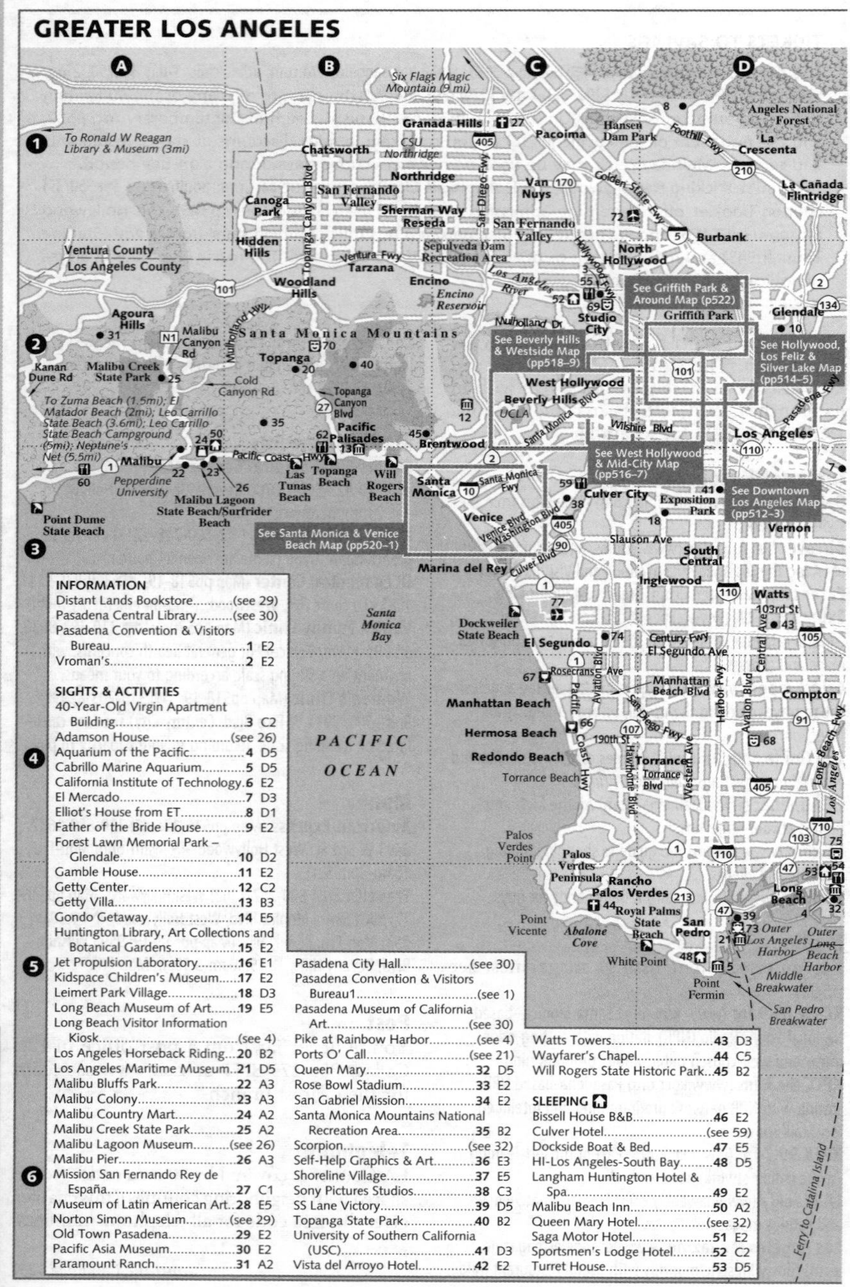

INFORMATION
Distant Lands Bookstore..........(see 29)
Pasadena Central Library..........(see 30)
Pasadena Convention & Visitors Bureau..........1 E2
Vroman's..........2 E2

SIGHTS & ACTIVITIES
40-Year-Old Virgin Apartment Building..........3 C2
Adamson House..........(see 26)
Aquarium of the Pacific..........4 D5
Cabrillo Marine Aquarium..........5 D5
California Institute of Technology..........6 E2
El Mercado..........7 D3
Elliot's House from ET..........8 D1
Father of the Bride House..........9 E2
Forest Lawn Memorial Park – Glendale..........10 D2
Gamble House..........11 E2
Getty Center..........12 C2
Getty Villa..........13 B3
Gondo Getaway..........14 E5
Huntington Library, Art Collections and Botanical Gardens..........15 E2
Jet Propulsion Laboratory..........16 E1
Kidspace Children's Museum..........17 E2
Leimert Park Village..........18 D3
Long Beach Museum of Art..........19 E5
Long Beach Visitor Information Kiosk..........(see 4)
Los Angeles Horseback Riding..........20 B2
Los Angeles Maritime Museum..........21 D5
Malibu Bluffs Park..........22 A3
Malibu Colony..........23 A3
Malibu Country Mart..........24 A2
Malibu Creek State Park..........25 A2
Malibu Lagoon Museum..........(see 26)
Malibu Pier..........26 A3
Mission San Fernando Rey de España..........27 C1
Museum of Latin American Art..........28 E5
Norton Simon Museum..........(see 29)
Old Town Pasadena..........29 E2
Pacific Asia Museum..........30 E2
Paramount Ranch..........31 A2
Pasadena City Hall..........(see 30)
Pasadena Convention & Visitors Bureau1..........(see 1)
Pasadena Museum of California Art..........(see 30)
Pike at Rainbow Harbor..........(see 4)
Ports O' Call..........(see 21)
Queen Mary..........32 D5
Rose Bowl Stadium..........33 E2
San Gabriel Mission..........34 E2
Santa Monica Mountains National Recreation Area..........35 B2
Scorpion..........(see 32)
Self-Help Graphics & Art..........36 E3
Shoreline Village..........37 E5
Sony Pictures Studios..........38 C3
SS Lane Victory..........39 D5
Topanga State Park..........40 B2
University of Southern California (USC)..........41 D3
Vista del Arroyo Hotel..........42 E2
Watts Towers..........43 D3
Wayfarer's Chapel..........44 C5
Will Rogers State Historic Park..........45 B2

SLEEPING
Bissell House B&B..........46 E2
Culver Hotel..........(see 59)
Dockside Boat & Bed..........47 E5
HI-Los Angeles-South Bay..........48 D5
Langham Huntington Hotel & Spa..........49 E2
Malibu Beach Inn..........50 A2
Queen Mary Hotel..........(see 32)
Saga Motor Hotel..........51 E2
Sportsmen's Lodge Hotel..........52 C2
Turret House..........53 D5

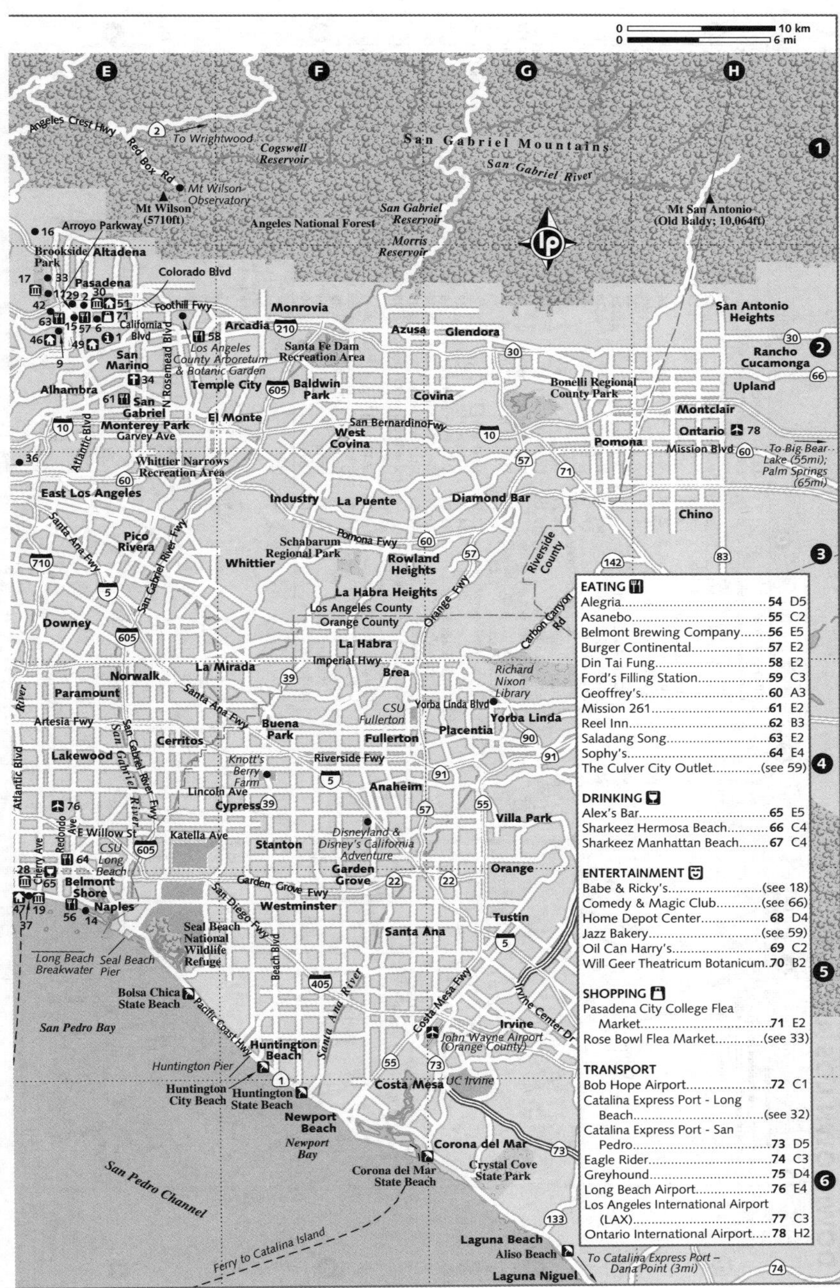
0 10 km
0 6 mi
E
F
G
H
1
2
3
4
5
6
Angeles Crest Hwy
To Wrightwood
Red Box Rd
Cogswell Reservoir
San Gabriel Mountains
San Gabriel River
Mt Wilson Observatory
Mt Wilson (5710ft)
San Gabriel Reservoir
Angeles National Forest
Morris Reservoir
Mt San Antonio (Old Baldy; 10,064ft)
Arroyo Parkway
Brookside Park
Altadena
Pasadena
Colorado Blvd
Foothill Fwy
California Blvd
Los Angeles County Arboretum & Botanic Garden
N Rosemead Blvd
Monrovia
Arcadia
Azusa
Glendora
San Antonio Heights
Rancho Cucamonga
Upland
Santa Fe Dam Recreation Area
San Marino
Alhambra
Temple City
Baldwin Park
Covina
Bonelli Regional County Park
Montclair
San Gabriel
El Monte
Monterey Park
Garvey Ave
San Bernardino Fwy
West Covina
Ontario
Pomona
Mission Blvd
To Big Bear Lake (55mi); Palm Springs (65mi)
Atlantic Blvd
Whittier Narrows Recreation Area
East Los Angeles
Industry
La Puente
Diamond Bar
Chino
Santa Ana Fwy
Pico Rivera
San Gabriel River Fwy
Schabarum Regional Park
Pomona Fwy
Rowland Heights
Whittier
Riverside County
La Habra Heights
Los Angeles County
Orange County
Orange Fwy
Carbon Canyon Rd
Downey
La Habra
Imperial Hwy
Richard Nixon Library
La Mirada
Norwalk
Brea
Paramount
Yorba Linda Blvd
Yorba Linda
CSU Fullerton
Artesia Fwy
Buena Park
Fullerton
Placentia
Cerritos
Lakewood
Knott's Berry Farm
Riverside Fwy
Anaheim
Lincoln Ave
Cypress
Villa Park
Redondo Ave
E Willow St
Katella Ave
Disneyland & Disney's California Adventure
Stanton
Cherry Ave
CSU Long Beach
Garden Grove
Orange
Belmont Shore
Garden Grove Fwy
Naples
Westminster
San Diego Fwy
Tustin
Seal Beach National Wildlife Refuge
Santa Ana
Beach Blvd
Long Beach Breakwater
Seal Beach Pier
Bolsa Chica State Beach
Pacific Coast Hwy
Santa Ana River
Costa Mesa Fwy
Irvine Center Dr
San Pedro Bay
Irvine
John Wayne Airport (Orange County)
Huntington Beach
Huntington Pier
Costa Mesa
UC Irvine
Huntington City Beach
Huntington State Beach
Newport Beach
Newport Bay
Corona del Mar
Crystal Cove State Park
Corona del Mar State Beach
San Pedro Channel
Laguna Beach
Aliso Beach
Ferry to Catalina Island
To Catalina Express Port – Dana Point (3mi)
Laguna Niguel

EATING
Alegria.....54 D5
Asanebo.....55 C2
Belmont Brewing Company.....56 E5
Burger Continental.....57 E2
Din Tai Fung.....58 E2
Ford's Filling Station.....59 C3
Geoffrey's.....60 A3
Mission 261.....61 E2
Reel Inn.....62 B3
Saladang Song.....63 E2
Sophy's.....64 E4
The Culver City Outlet.....(see 59)

DRINKING
Alex's Bar.....65 E5
Sharkeez Hermosa Beach.....66 C4
Sharkeez Manhattan Beach.....67 C4

ENTERTAINMENT
Babe & Ricky's.....(see 18)
Comedy & Magic Club.....(see 66)
Home Depot Center.....68 D4
Jazz Bakery.....(see 59)
Oil Can Harry's.....69 C2
Will Geer Theatricum Botanicum.....70 B2

SHOPPING
Pasadena City College Flea Market.....71 E2
Rose Bowl Flea Market.....(see 33)

TRANSPORT
Bob Hope Airport.....72 C1
Catalina Express Port - Long Beach.....(see 32)
Catalina Express Port - San Pedro.....73 D5
Eagle Rider.....74 C3
Greyhound.....75 D4
Long Beach Airport.....76 E4
Los Angeles International Airport (LAX).....77 C3
Ontario International Airport.....78 H2

LOS ANGELES

DOWNTOWN LOS ANGELES

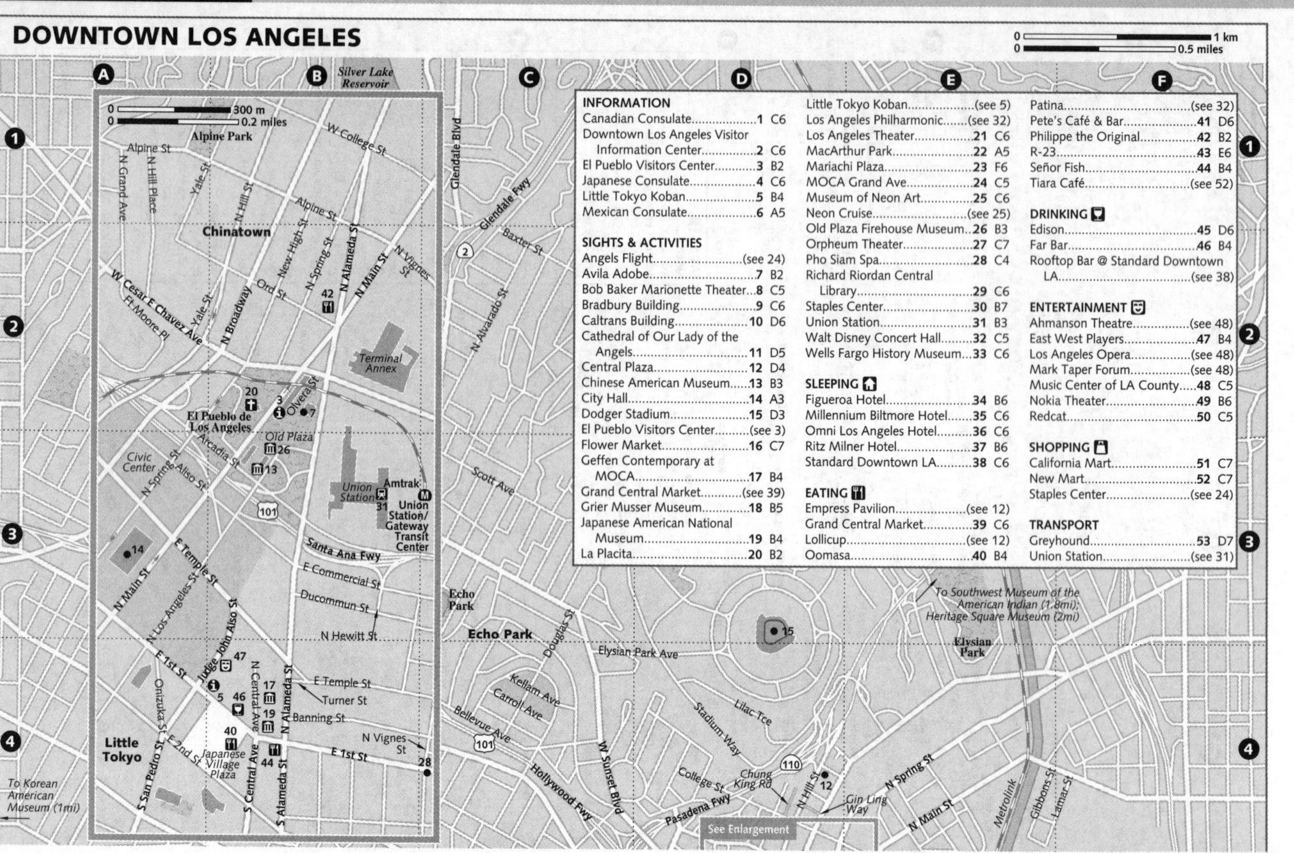
0 1 km
0 0.5 miles
0 300 m
0 0.2 miles
INFORMATION
Canadian Consulate.....1 C6
Downtown Los Angeles Visitor Information Center.....2 C6
El Pueblo Visitors Center.....3 B2
Japanese Consulate.....4 C6
Little Tokyo Koban.....5 B4
Mexican Consulate.....6 A5
SIGHTS & ACTIVITIES
Angels Flight.....(see 24)
Avila Adobe.....7 B2
Bob Baker Marionette Theater.....8 C5
Bradbury Building.....9 C6
Caltrans Building.....10 D6
Cathedral of Our Lady of the Angels.....11 D5
Central Plaza.....12 D4
Chinese American Museum.....13 B3
City Hall.....14 A3
Dodger Stadium.....15 D3
El Pueblo Visitors Center.....(see 3)
Flower Market.....16 C7
Geffen Contemporary at MOCA.....17 B4
Grand Central Market.....(see 39)
Grier Musser Museum.....18 B5
Japanese American National Museum.....19 B4
La Placita.....20 B2
Little Tokyo Koban.....(see 5)
Los Angeles Philharmonic.....(see 32)
Los Angeles Theater.....21 C6
MacArthur Park.....22 A5
Mariachi Plaza.....23 F6
MOCA Grand Ave.....24 C5
Museum of Neon Art.....25 C6
Neon Cruise.....(see 25)
Old Plaza Firehouse Museum.....26 B3
Orpheum Theater.....27 C7
Pho Siam Spa.....28 C4
Richard Riordan Central Library.....29 C6
Staples Center.....30 B7
Union Station.....31 B3
Walt Disney Concert Hall.....32 C5
Wells Fargo History Museum.....33 C6
SLEEPING
Figueroa Hotel.....34 B6
Millennium Biltmore Hotel.....35 C6
Omni Los Angeles Hotel.....36 C6
Ritz Milner Hotel.....37 B6
Standard Downtown LA.....38 C6
EATING
Empress Pavilion.....(see 12)
Grand Central Market.....39 C6
Lollicup.....(see 12)
Oomasa.....40 B4
Patina.....(see 32)
Pete's Café & Bar.....41 D6
Philippe the Original.....42 B2
R-23.....43 E6
Señor Fish.....44 B4
Tiara Café.....(see 52)
DRINKING
Edison.....45 D6
Far Bar.....46 B4
Rooftop Bar @ Standard Downtown LA.....(see 38)
ENTERTAINMENT
Ahmanson Theatre.....(see 48)
East West Players.....47 B4
Los Angeles Opera.....(see 48)
Mark Taper Forum.....(see 48)
Music Center of LA County.....48 C5
Nokia Theater.....49 B6
Redcat.....50 C5
SHOPPING
California Mart.....51 C7
New Mart.....52 C7
Staples Center.....(see 24)
TRANSPORT
Greyhound.....53 D7
Union Station.....(see 31)
Silver Lake Reservoir
Alpine Park
Chinatown
El Pueblo de Los Angeles
Old Plaza
Civic Center
Terminal Annex
Union Station
Amtrak
Union Station/Gateway Transit Center
Little Tokyo
Japanese Village Plaza
Echo Park
Elysian Park
To Southwest Museum of the American Indian (1.8mi); Heritage Square Museum (2mi)
To Korean American Museum (1mi)
See Enlargement
W College St
Alpine St
N Grand Ave
N Hill Place
Yale St
N Hill St
New High St
N Spring St
N Alameda St
N Main St
N Vignes St
Ord St
N Broadway
W Cesar E Chavez Ave
Ft Moore Pl
Olvera St
Arcadia St
Aliso St
Santa Ana Fwy
E Commercial St
Ducommun St
N Hewitt St
E Temple St
N Los Angeles St
Judge John Aiso St
E 1st St
Turner St
Banning St
N Central Ave
Onizuka St
E 2nd St
S San Pedro St
S Central Ave
S Alameda St
Glendale Blvd
Glendale Fwy
Baxter St
N Alvarado St
Scott Ave
Douglas St
Elysian Park Ave
Kellam Ave
Carroll Ave
Bellevue Ave
Hollywood Fwy
W Sunset Blvd
Stadium Way
Lilac Tce
College St
Chung King Rd
Pasadena Fwy
Gin Ling Way
Metrolink
Gibbons St
Lamar St

Los Angeles River
Chinatown
N Broadway
Civic Center
Civic Center/ Tom Bradley
Little Tokyo
Old Bank District
Boyle Heights
Arts District
Pershing Square
Financial District
Jewelry District
Fashion District
South Park
7th St/Metro Center
Westlake/ MacArthur Park
MacArthur Lake
Los Angeles Convention Center
Los Angeles Trade-Technical College
Mount St Mary's College
Metrolink Station
Santa Ana Fwy
Harbor Fwy
Santa Monica Fwy
Santa Ana Fwy
Metro Red Line
Metro Blue Line
Pico
Grand
San Pedro
S Alameda St
S Central Ave
S Santa Fe Ave
S Mission Rd
E Cesar E Chavez Ave
Mission St
W Temple St
W 1st St
W 2nd St
W 3rd St
W 4th St
W 5th St
W 6th St
W 7th St
W 8th St
W 9th St
W Olympic Blvd
W 11th St
W 12th St
W Pico Blvd
W 14th St
W Venice Blvd
W Washington Blvd
W Adams Blvd
W 23rd St
E Olympic Blvd
E 1st St
E 4th St
E 6th St
E 7th St
E 8th St
S Figueroa St
S Flower St
S Hope St
S Grand Ave
S Olive St
S Hill St
S Broadway
S Main St
S San Pedro St
Wilshire Blvd
S Alvarado St
Soto St
To East Los Angeles
To Koreatown Galleria and Chosun Galbee (1.5 mi)
To St Sophia Cathedral (1mi)
To Bullocks Wilshire Building (0.3mi); Ambassador Hotel (0.8mi); Wiltern Theatre (1.5mi)
To Watts Towers (6mi)
To University of Southern California (USC; 0.3mi); Exposition Park (Natural History Museum of Los Angeles County (0.8mi); California Science Center (0.8mi); California African American Museum; 0.8mi)

LOS ANGELES

HOLLYWOOD, LOS FELIZ & SILVER LAKE

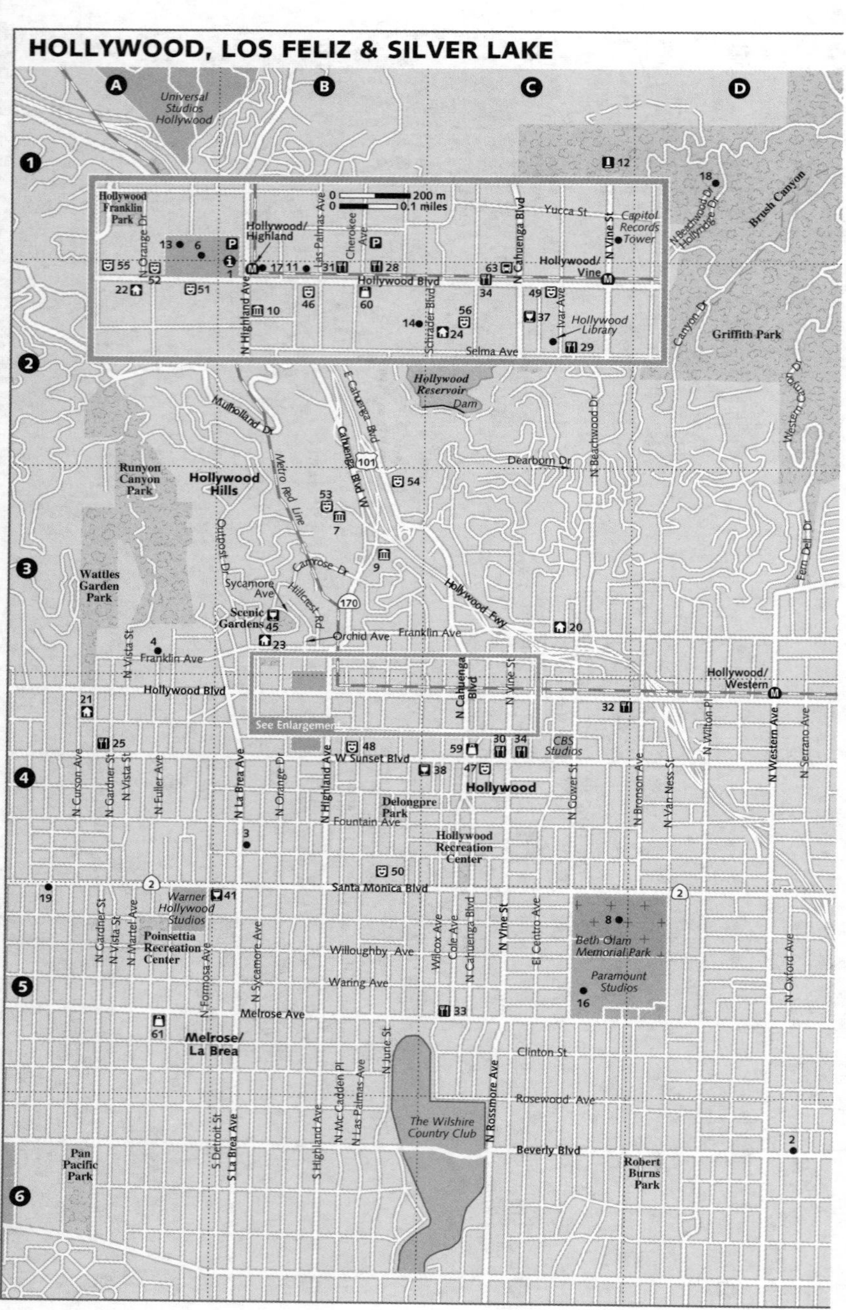

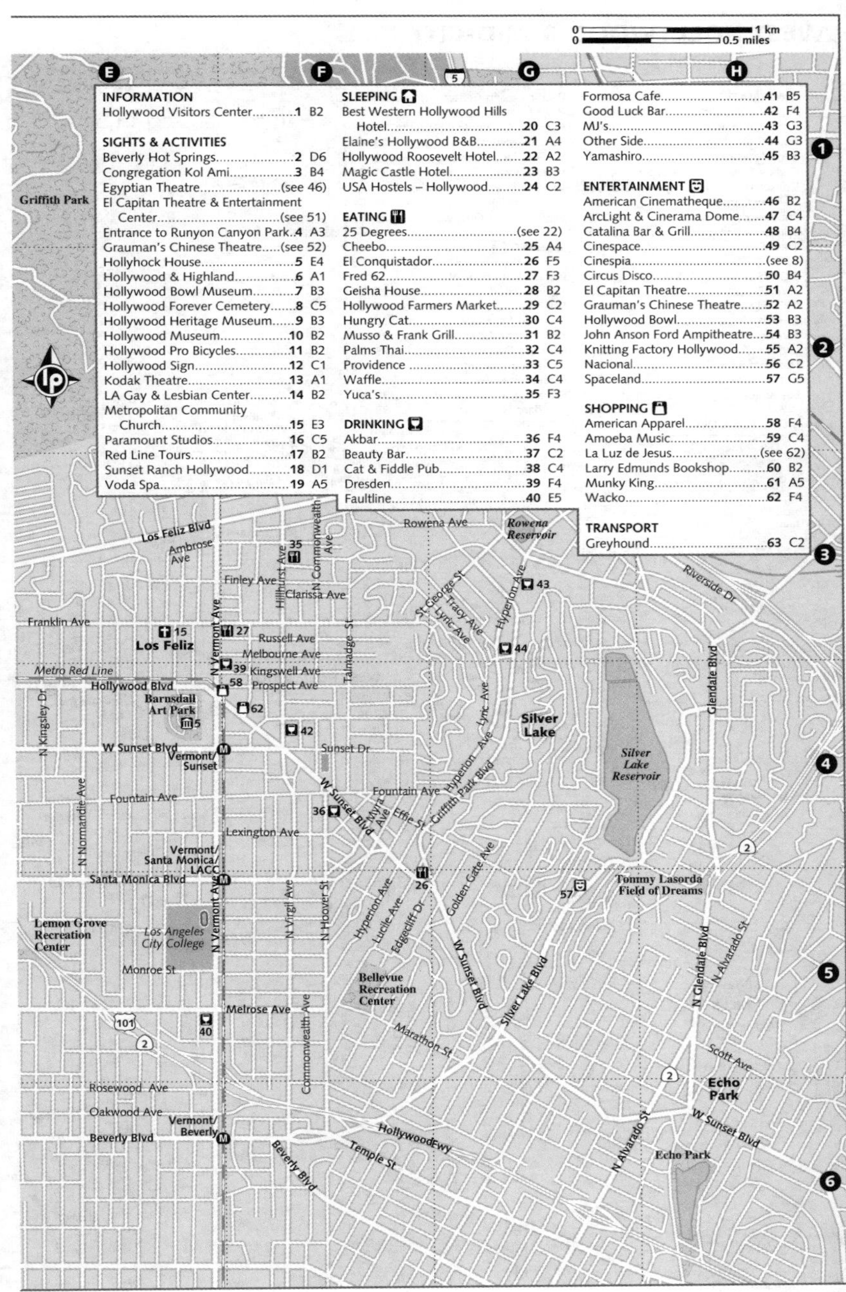
0 1 km
0 0.5 miles
INFORMATION
Hollywood Visitors Center....1 B2
SIGHTS & ACTIVITIES
Beverly Hot Springs....2 D6
Congregation Kol Ami....3 B4
Egyptian Theatre....(see 46)
El Capitan Theatre & Entertainment Center....(see 51)
Entrance to Runyon Canyon Park..4 A3
Grauman's Chinese Theatre....(see 52)
Hollyhock House....5 E4
Hollywood & Highland....6 A1
Hollywood Bowl Museum....7 B3
Hollywood Forever Cemetery....8 C5
Hollywood Heritage Museum....9 B3
Hollywood Museum....10 B2
Hollywood Pro Bicycles....11 B2
Hollywood Sign....12 C1
Kodak Theatre....13 A1
LA Gay & Lesbian Center....14 B2
Metropolitan Community Church....15 E3
Paramount Studios....16 C5
Red Line Tours....17 B2
Sunset Ranch Hollywood....18 D1
Voda Spa....19 A5
SLEEPING
Best Western Hollywood Hills Hotel....20 C3
Elaine's Hollywood B&B....21 A4
Hollywood Roosevelt Hotel....22 A2
Magic Castle Hotel....23 B3
USA Hostels – Hollywood....24 C2
EATING
25 Degrees....(see 22)
Cheebo....25 A4
El Conquistador....26 F5
Fred 62....27 F3
Geisha House....28 B2
Hollywood Farmers Market....29 C2
Hungry Cat....30 C4
Musso & Frank Grill....31 B2
Palms Thai....32 C4
Providence....33 C5
Waffle....34 C4
Yuca's....35 F3
DRINKING
Akbar....36 F4
Beauty Bar....37 C2
Cat & Fiddle Pub....38 C4
Dresden....39 F4
Faultline....40 E5
Formosa Cafe....41 B5
Good Luck Bar....42 F4
MJ's....43 G3
Other Side....44 G3
Yamashiro....45 B3
ENTERTAINMENT
American Cinematheque....46 B2
ArcLight & Cinerama Dome....47 C4
Catalina Bar & Grill....48 B4
Cinespace....49 C2
Cinespia....(see 8)
Circus Disco....50 B4
El Capitan Theatre....51 A2
Grauman's Chinese Theatre....52 A2
Hollywood Bowl....53 B3
John Anson Ford Ampitheatre....54 B3
Knitting Factory Hollywood....55 A2
Nacional....56 C2
Spaceland....57 G5
SHOPPING
American Apparel....58 F4
Amoeba Music....59 C4
La Luz de Jesus....(see 62)
Larry Edmunds Bookshop....60 B2
Munky King....61 A5
Wacko....62 F4
TRANSPORT
Greyhound....63 C2
Griffith Park
Los Feliz Blvd
Ambrose Ave
Rowena Ave
Rowena Reservoir
Riverside Dr
Franklin Ave
Los Feliz
Metro Red Line
Hollywood Blvd
Barnsdall Art Park
W Sunset Blvd
Vermont/ Sunset
Silver Lake
Silver Lake Reservoir
Fountain Ave
Lexington Ave
Vermont/ Santa Monica/ LACC
Santa Monica Blvd
Lemon Grove Recreation Center
Los Angeles City College
Monroe St
Melrose Ave
Bellevue Recreation Center
Tommy Lasorda Field of Dreams
Marathon St
Rosewood Ave
Oakwood Ave
Vermont/ Beverly
Beverly Blvd
Hollywood Fwy
Temple St
Echo Park
Scott Ave
Glendale Blvd
N Alvarado St
Silver Lake Blvd
Hyperion Ave
Griffith Park Blvd
N Vermont Ave
N Normandie Ave
N Kingsley Dr
N Virgil Ave
N Hoover St
Commonwealth Ave
Golden Gate Ave
Sunset Dr
Talmadge St
Hillhurst Ave
N Commonwealth Ave
Finley Ave
Clarissa Ave
Russell Ave
Melbourne Ave
Kingswell Ave
Prospect Ave

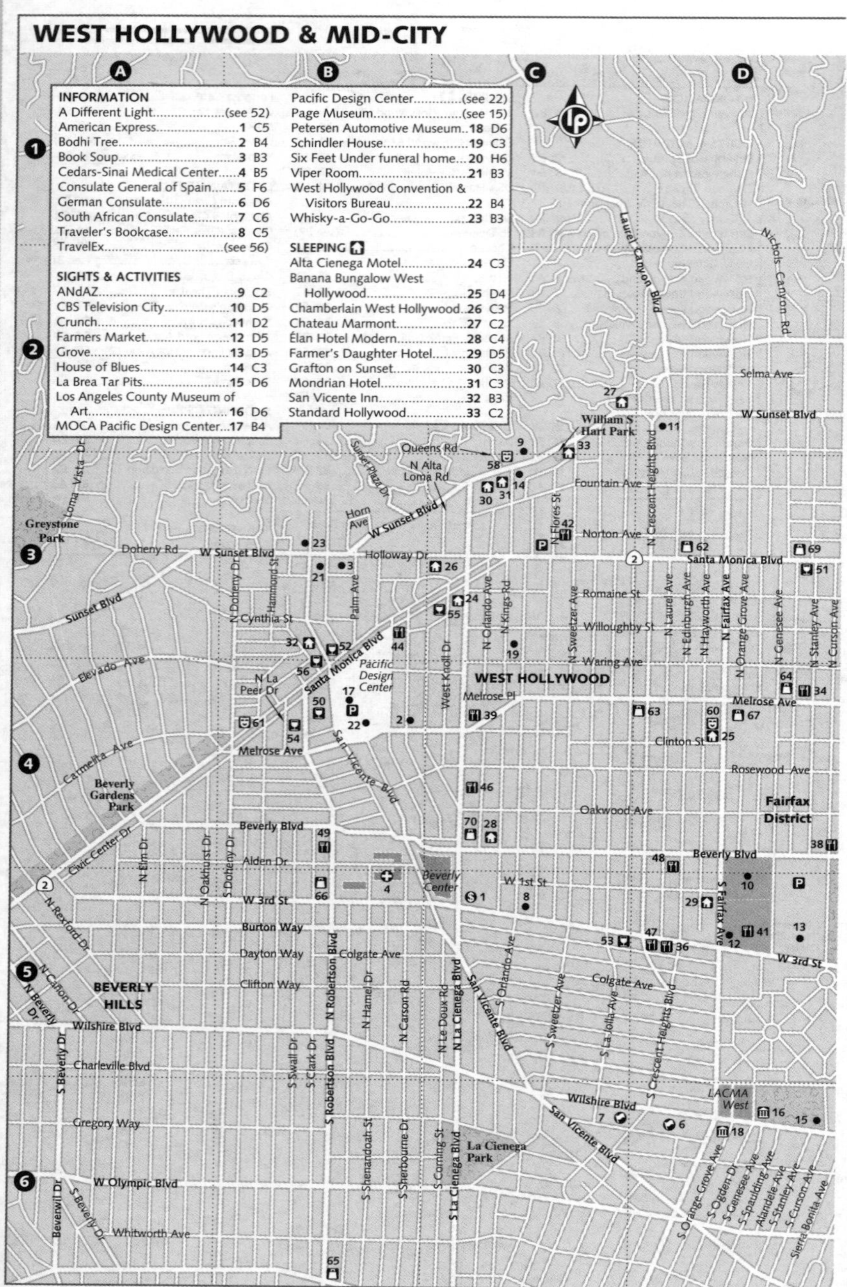
WEST HOLLYWOOD & MID-CITY
INFORMATION
A Different Light....................(see 52)
American Express....................1 C5
Bodhi Tree....................2 B4
Book Soup....................3 B3
Cedars-Sinai Medical Center....................4 B5
Consulate General of Spain....................5 F6
German Consulate....................6 D6
South African Consulate....................7 C6
Traveler's Bookcase....................8 C5
TravelEx....................(see 56)
SIGHTS & ACTIVITIES
ANdAZ....................9 C2
CBS Television City....................10 D5
Crunch....................11 D2
Farmers Market....................12 D5
Grove....................13 D5
House of Blues....................14 C3
La Brea Tar Pits....................15 D6
Los Angeles County Museum of Art....................16 D6
MOCA Pacific Design Center....................17 B4
Pacific Design Center....................(see 22)
Page Museum....................(see 15)
Petersen Automotive Museum....................18 D6
Schindler House....................19 C3
Six Feet Under funeral home....................20 H6
Viper Room....................21 B3
West Hollywood Convention & Visitors Bureau....................22 B4
Whisky-a-Go-Go....................23 B3
SLEEPING
Alta Cienega Motel....................24 C3
Banana Bungalow West Hollywood....................25 D4
Chamberlain West Hollywood....................26 C3
Chateau Marmont....................27 C2
Élan Hotel Modern....................28 C4
Farmer's Daughter Hotel....................29 D5
Grafton on Sunset....................30 C3
Mondrian Hotel....................31 C3
San Vicente Inn....................32 B3
Standard Hollywood....................33 C2
WEST HOLLYWOOD
BEVERLY HILLS
Fairfax District
Greystone Park
Beverly Gardens Park
William S Hart Park
La Cienega Park
Pacific Design Center
Beverly Center
LACMA West
W Sunset Blvd
Santa Monica Blvd
Melrose Ave
Beverly Blvd
W 3rd St
Wilshire Blvd
W Olympic Blvd
Laurel Canyon Blvd
Nichols Canyon Rd
San Vicente Blvd
N La Cienega Blvd
S La Cienega Blvd
N Fairfax Ave
S Fairfax Ave
N Robertson Blvd
S Robertson Blvd
Fountain Ave
Norton Ave
Romaine St
Willoughby St
Waring Ave
Melrose Pl
Clinton St
Rosewood Ave
Oakwood Ave
W 1st St
Burton Way
Dayton Way
Clifton Way
Colgate Ave
Charleville Blvd
Gregory Way
Whitworth Ave
Selma Ave
Holloway Dr
Doheny Rd
Sunset Blvd
Elevado Ave
Carmelita Ave
Civic Center Dr
Alden Dr
N Crescent Heights Blvd
S Crescent Heights Blvd
Queens Rd
N Alta Loma Rd
Sunset Plaza Dr
Horn Ave
N La Peer Dr
N Cynthia St

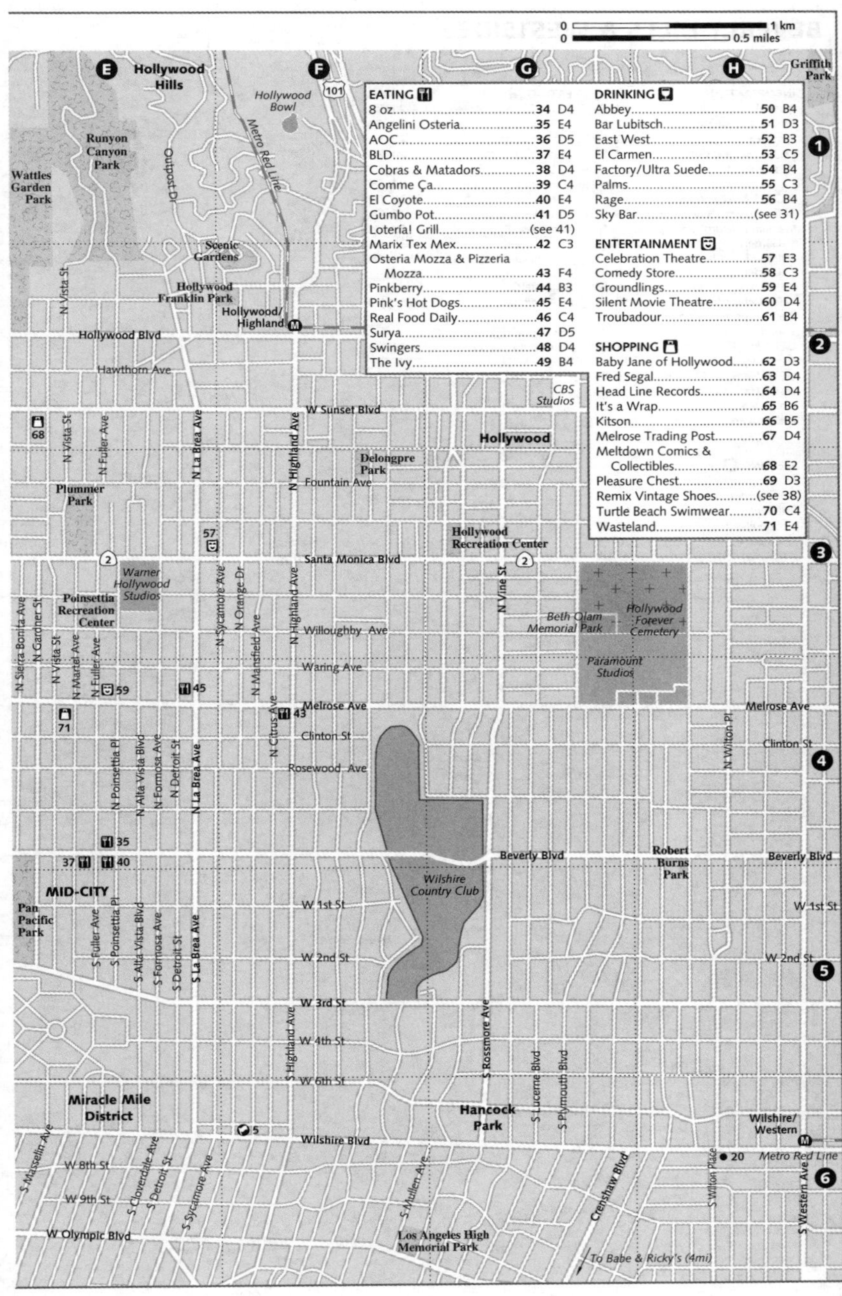
0 1 km
0 0.5 miles
E
F
G
H
1
2
3
4
5
6
EATING
8 oz. 34 D4
Angelini Osteria 35 E4
AOC 36 D5
BLD 37 E4
Cobras & Matadors 38 D4
Comme Ça 39 C4
El Coyote 40 E4
Gumbo Pot 41 D5
Lotería! Grill (see 41)
Marix Tex Mex 42 C3
Osteria Mozza & Pizzeria Mozza 43 F4
Pinkberry 44 B3
Pink's Hot Dogs 45 E4
Real Food Daily 46 C4
Surya 47 D5
Swingers 48 D4
The Ivy 49 B4
DRINKING
Abbey 50 B4
Bar Lubitsch 51 D3
East West 52 B3
El Carmen 53 C5
Factory/Ultra Suede 54 B4
Palms 55 C3
Rage 56 B4
Sky Bar (see 31)
ENTERTAINMENT
Celebration Theatre 57 E3
Comedy Store 58 C3
Groundlings 59 E4
Silent Movie Theatre 60 D4
Troubadour 61 B4
SHOPPING
Baby Jane of Hollywood 62 D3
Fred Segal 63 D4
Head Line Records 64 D4
It's a Wrap 65 B6
Kitson 66 B5
Melrose Trading Post 67 D4
Meltdown Comics & Collectibles 68 E2
Pleasure Chest 69 D3
Remix Vintage Shoes (see 38)
Turtle Beach Swimwear 70 C4
Wasteland 71 E4
Hollywood Hills
Hollywood Bowl
101
Griffith Park
Runyon Canyon Park
Wattles Garden Park
Outpost Dr
Metro Red Line
Scenic Gardens
N Vista St
Hollywood Franklin Park
Hollywood/Highland
Hollywood Blvd
Hawthorn Ave
CBS Studios
W Sunset Blvd
Hollywood
N Fuller Ave
N La Brea Ave
N Highland Ave
Delongpre Park
Fountain Ave
Plummer Park
Hollywood Recreation Center
Santa Monica Blvd
2
Warner Hollywood Studios
Poinsettia Recreation Center
N Sycamore Ave
N Orange Dr
N Vine St
Beth Olam Memorial Park
Hollywood Forever Cemetery
N Sierra Bonita Ave
N Gardner St
N Martel Ave
N Mansfield Ave
Willoughby Ave
Waring Ave
Paramount Studios
Melrose Ave
N Citrus Ave
Clinton St
Rosewood Ave
N Wilton Pl
N Poinsettia Pl
N Alta Vista Blvd
N Formosa Ave
N Detroit St
Beverly Blvd
Robert Burns Park
MID-CITY
Wilshire Country Club
Pan Pacific Park
W 1st St
S Fuller Ave
S Poinsettia Pl
S Alta Vista Blvd
S Formosa Ave
S Detroit St
S La Brea Ave
W 2nd St
W 3rd St
S Highland Ave
W 4th St
S Rossmore Ave
W 6th St
S Lucerne Blvd
S Plymouth Blvd
Miracle Mile District
Hancock Park
Wilshire/Western
Wilshire Blvd
S Masselin Ave
W 8th St
W 9th St
S Cloverdale Ave
S Sycamore Ave
S Mullen Ave
Crenshaw Blvd
S Wilton Place
S Western Ave
Metro Red Line
W Olympic Blvd
Los Angeles High Memorial Park
To Babe & Ricky's (4mi)

BEVERLY HILLS & WESTSIDE

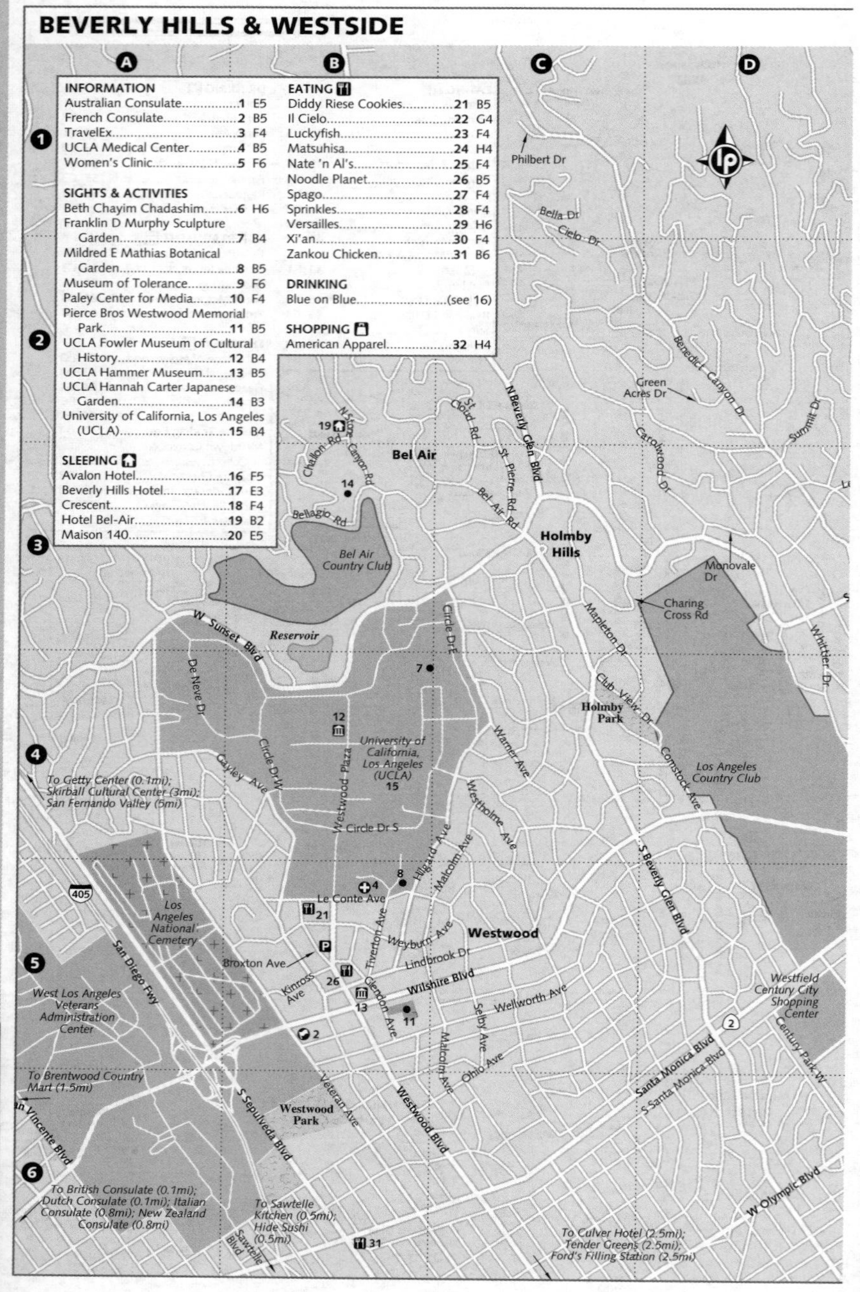

LOS ANGELES

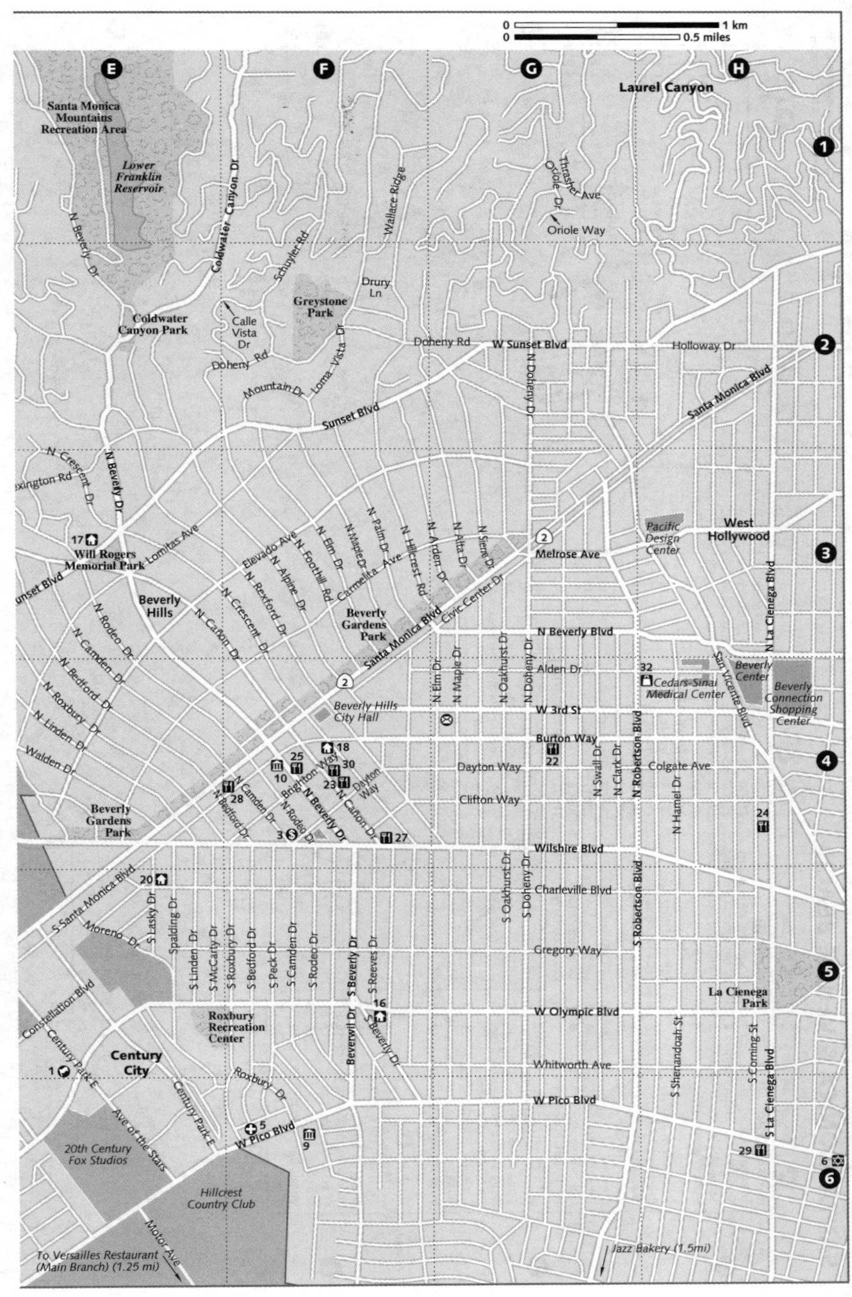
0 1 km
0 0.5 miles
E
F
G
H
Laurel Canyon
Santa Monica Mountains Recreation Area
Lower Franklin Reservoir
Coldwater Canyon Dr
Wallace Ridge
Thrasher Ave
Oriole Dr
Oriole Way
N Beverly Dr
Schuyler Rd
Drury Ln
Greystone Park
Coldwater Canyon Park
Calle Vista Dr
Doheny Rd
W Sunset Blvd
N Doheny Dr
Holloway Dr
Loma Vista Dr
Mountain Dr
Sunset Blvd
Santa Monica Blvd
N Crescent Dr
Lexington Rd
Pacific Design Center
West Hollywood
Melrose Ave
17
Will Rogers Memorial Park
Lomitas Ave
Elevado Ave
N Elm Dr
N Maple Dr
N Palm Dr
N Hillcrest Rd
N Arden Dr
N Alta Dr
N Sierra Dr
Carmelita Ave
N Alpine Dr
N Foothill Rd
N Rexford Dr
N Crescent Dr
Civic Center Dr
Beverly Hills
Beverly Gardens Park
N Cañon Dr
N Rodeo Dr
N Camden Dr
N Bedford Dr
N Roxbury Dr
N Linden Dr
Walden Dr
N Beverly Blvd
N La Cienega Blvd
Alden Dr
32
Cedars-Sinai Medical Center
Beverly Center
Beverly Connection Shopping Center
San Vicente Blvd
N Oakhurst Dr
N Doheny Dr
N Elm Dr
N Maple Dr
Beverly Hills City Hall
W 3rd St
N Robertson Blvd
Burton Way
18
25
30
10
23
22
Brighton Way
Dayton Way
Colgate Ave
Clifton Way
N Swall Dr
N Clark Dr
N Hamel Dr
28
N Camden Dr
N Bedford Dr
N Rodeo Dr
N Beverly Dr
N Cañon Dr
3
27
24
Beverly Gardens Park
Wilshire Blvd
20
S Santa Monica Blvd
Charleville Blvd
S Oakhurst Dr
S Doheny Dr
Moreno Dr
S Lasky Dr
Spalding Dr
S Linden Dr
S McCarty Dr
S Roxbury Dr
S Bedford Dr
S Peck Dr
S Camden Dr
S Rodeo Dr
S Beverly Dr
S Reeves Dr
Gregory Way
S Robertson Blvd
La Cienega Park
Constellation Blvd
16
W Olympic Blvd
Roxbury Recreation Center
Beverwil Dr
S Beverly Dr
Century City
Century Park E
Whitworth Ave
S Shenandoah St
S Corning St
S La Cienega Blvd
1
Roxbury Dr
Century Park E
W Pico Blvd
Ave of the Stars
5
W Pico Blvd
9
29
6
20th Century Fox Studios
Hillcrest Country Club
Motor Ave
To Versailles Restaurant (Main Branch) (1.25 mi)
Jazz Bakery (1.5mi)
1
2
3
4
5
6

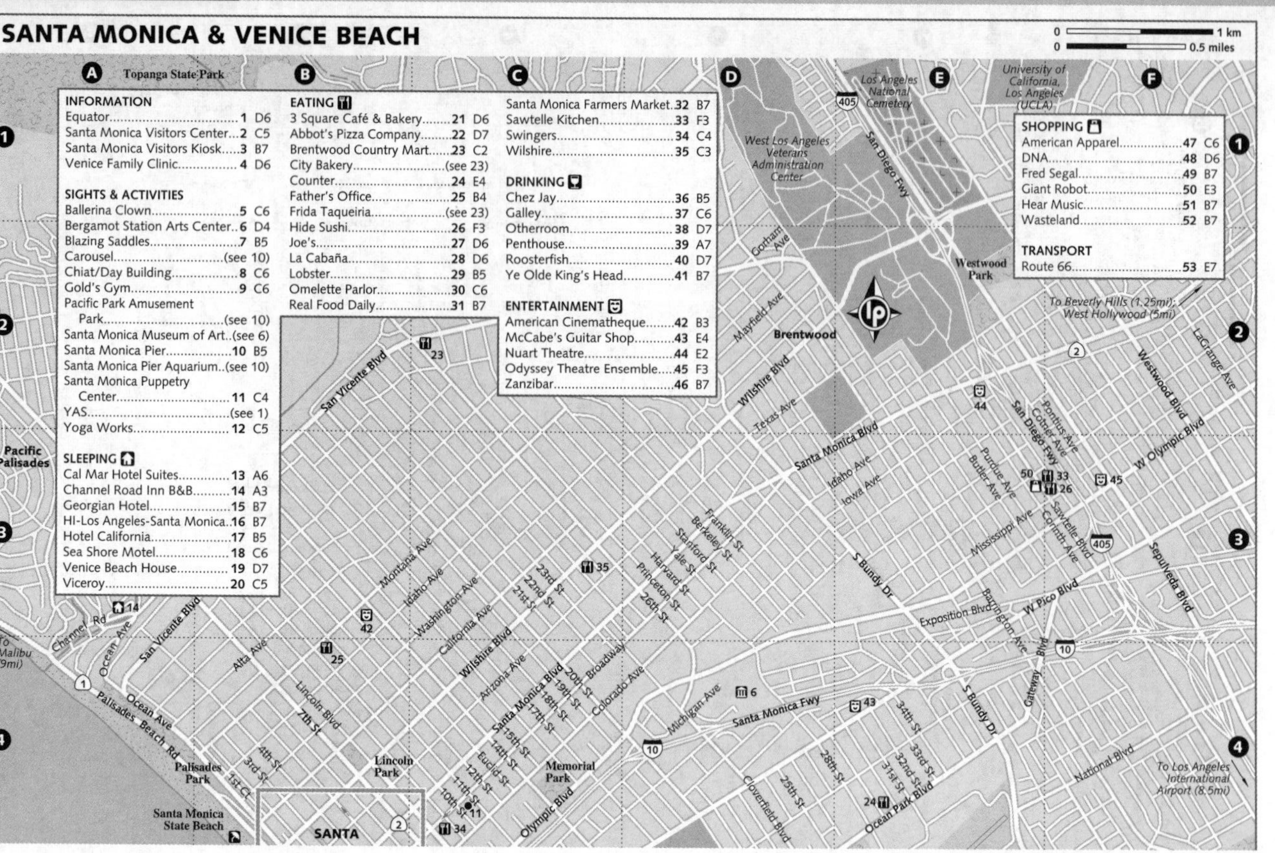
SANTA MONICA & VENICE BEACH
0 1 km
0 0.5 miles
INFORMATION
Equator 1 D6
Santa Monica Visitors Center 2 C5
Santa Monica Visitors Kiosk 3 B7
Venice Family Clinic 4 D6
SIGHTS & ACTIVITIES
Ballerina Clown 5 C6
Bergamot Station Arts Center 6 D4
Blazing Saddles 7 B5
Carousel (see 10)
Chiat/Day Building 8 C6
Gold's Gym 9 C6
Pacific Park Amusement Park (see 10)
Santa Monica Museum of Art (see 6)
Santa Monica Pier 10 B5
Santa Monica Pier Aquarium (see 10)
Santa Monica Puppetry Center 11 C4
YAS (see 1)
Yoga Works 12 C5
SLEEPING
Cal Mar Hotel Suites 13 A6
Channel Road Inn B&B 14 A3
Georgian Hotel 15 B7
HI-Los Angeles-Santa Monica 16 B7
Hotel California 17 B5
Sea Shore Motel 18 C6
Venice Beach House 19 D7
Viceroy 20 C5
EATING
3 Square Café & Bakery 21 D6
Abbot's Pizza Company 22 D7
Brentwood Country Mart 23 C2
City Bakery (see 23)
Counter 24 E4
Father's Office 25 B4
Frida Taqueiria (see 23)
Hide Sushi 26 F3
Joe's 27 D6
La Cabaña 28 D6
Lobster 29 B5
Omelette Parlor 30 C6
Real Food Daily 31 B7
Santa Monica Farmers Market 32 B7
Sawtelle Kitchen 33 F3
Swingers 34 C4
Wilshire 35 C3
DRINKING
Chez Jay 36 B5
Galley 37 C6
Otherroom 38 D7
Penthouse 39 A7
Roosterfish 40 D7
Ye Olde King's Head 41 B7
ENTERTAINMENT
American Cinematheque 42 B3
McCabe's Guitar Shop 43 E4
Nuart Theatre 44 E2
Odyssey Theatre Ensemble 45 F3
Zanzibar 46 B7
SHOPPING
American Apparel 47 C6
DNA 48 D6
Fred Segal 49 B7
Giant Robot 50 E3
Hear Music 51 B7
Wasteland 52 B7
TRANSPORT
Route 66 53 E7
Topanga State Park
Pacific Palisades
Los Angeles National Cemetery
University of California, Los Angeles (UCLA)
West Los Angeles Veterans Administration Center
Westwood Park
Brentwood
To Beverly Hills (1.25mi); West Hollywood (5mi)
To Malibu (9mi)
To Los Angeles International Airport (8.5mi)
Palisades Park
Lincoln Park
Memorial Park
Santa Monica State Beach
SANTA
San Diego Fwy
Santa Monica Fwy
Wilshire Blvd
Santa Monica Blvd
San Vicente Blvd
Ocean Ave
Palisades Beach Rd
Lincoln Blvd
Olympic Blvd
W Olympic Blvd
W Pico Blvd
S Bundy Dr
Sepulveda Blvd
Westwood Blvd
Exposition Blvd
Ocean Park Blvd
Cloverfield Blvd
National Blvd
Colorado Ave
Broadway
Montana Ave
Channel Rd

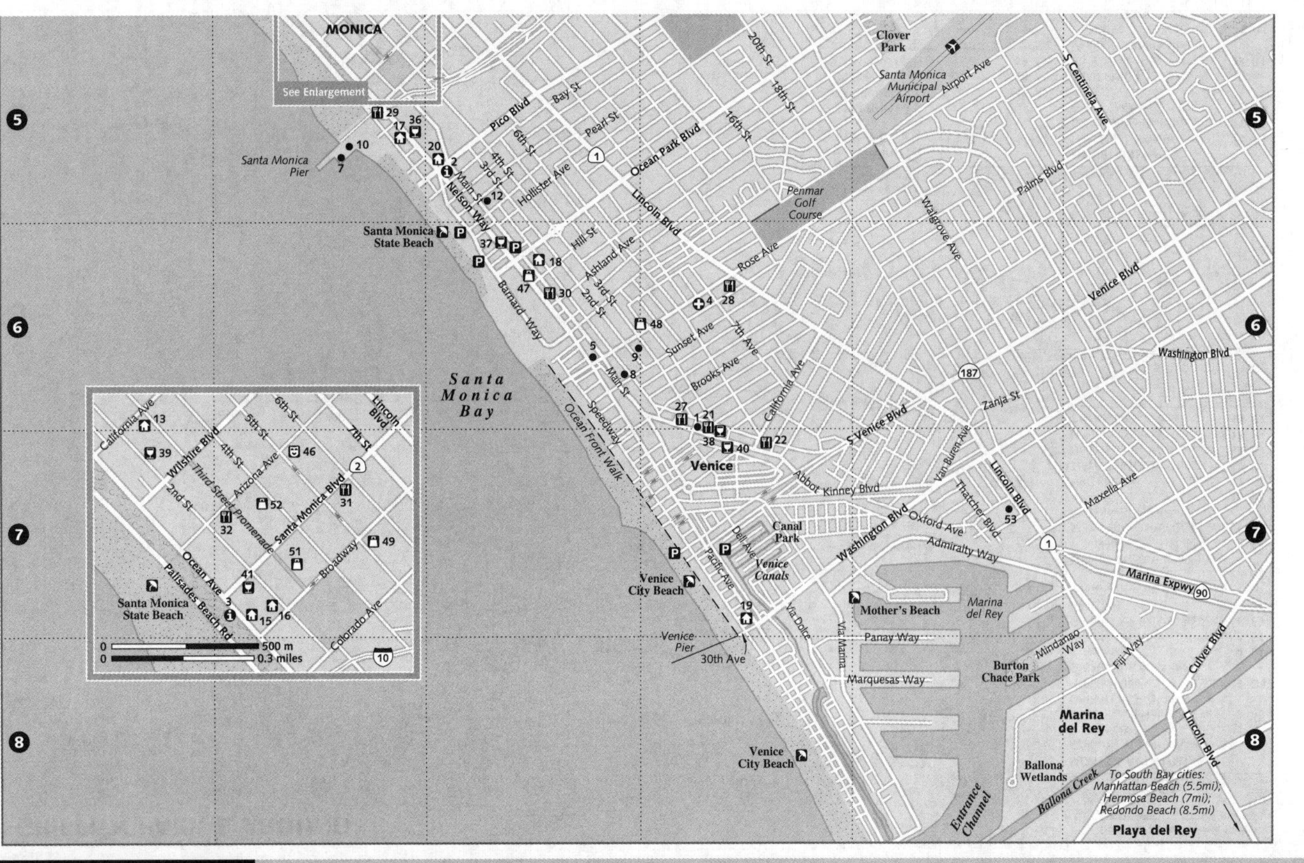
MONICA
See Enlargement
Santa Monica Pier
Clover Park
Santa Monica Municipal Airport
Airport Ave
S Centinela Ave
Palms Blvd
Walgrove Ave
Venice Blvd
Washington Blvd
Penmar Golf Course
20th St
18th St
16th St
Pico Blvd
Bay St
Pearl St
Ocean Park Blvd
Lincoln Blvd
6th St
4th St
3rd St
Hollister Ave
Main St
Nelson Way
Santa Monica State Beach
Hill St
Ashland Ave
3rd St
2nd St
Barnard Way
Rose Ave
Sunset Ave
7th Ave
Brooks Ave
California Ave
Main St
Speedway
Ocean Front Walk
Santa Monica Bay
S Venice Blvd
Zanja St
Van Buren Ave
Venice
Abbot Kinney Blvd
Thatcher Blvd
Lincoln Blvd
Maxella Ave
Oxford Ave
Washington Blvd
Admiralty Way
Canal Park
Dell Ave
Venice Canals
Pacific Ave
Venice City Beach
Marina Expwy
Via Dolce
Via Marina
Mother's Beach
Marina del Rey
Panay Way
Venice Pier
30th Ave
Mindanao Way
Fiji Way
Culver Blvd
Burton Chace Park
Marquesas Way
Marina del Rey
Venice City Beach
Ballona Wetlands
Ballona Creek
Entrance Channel
To South Bay cities: Manhattan Beach (5.5mi); Hermosa Beach (7mi); Redondo Beach (8.5mi)
Playa del Rey
California Ave
Lincoln Blvd
6th St
5th St
7th St
Wilshire Blvd
4th St
Arizona Ave
Third Street Promenade
2nd St
Santa Monica Blvd
Broadway
Ocean Ave
Palisades Beach Rd
Santa Monica State Beach
Colorado Ave
500 m
0.3 miles
LOS ANGELES

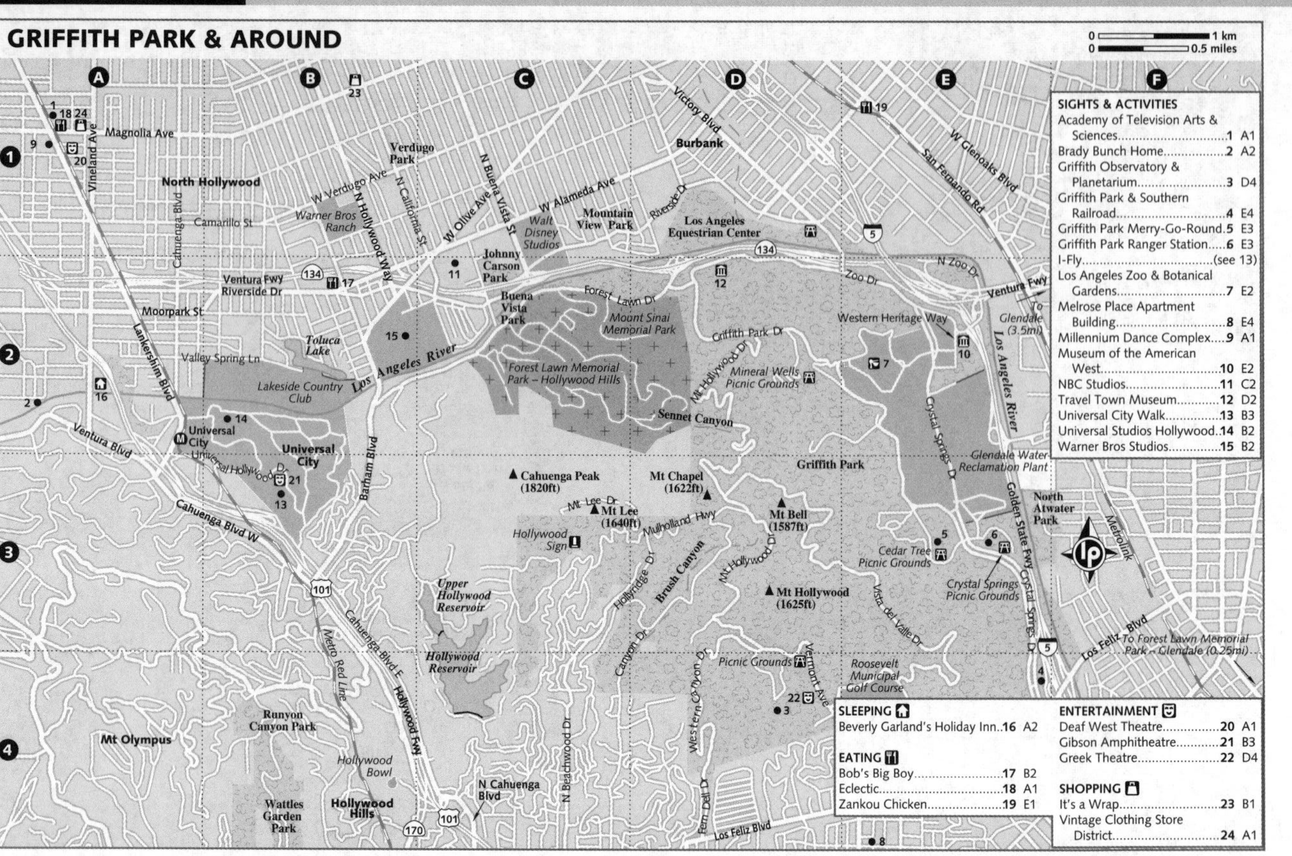
GRIFFITH PARK & AROUND
0 1 km
0 0.5 miles
SIGHTS & ACTIVITIES
Academy of Television Arts & Sciences....1 A1
Brady Bunch Home....2 A2
Griffith Observatory & Planetarium....3 D4
Griffith Park & Southern Railroad....4 E4
Griffith Park Merry-Go-Round....5 E3
Griffith Park Ranger Station....6 E3
I-Fly....(see 13)
Los Angeles Zoo & Botanical Gardens....7 E2
Melrose Place Apartment Building....8 E4
Millennium Dance Complex....9 A1
Museum of the American West....10 E2
NBC Studios....11 C2
Travel Town Museum....12 D2
Universal City Walk....13 B3
Universal Studios Hollywood....14 B2
Warner Bros Studios....15 B2
SLEEPING
Beverly Garland's Holiday Inn....16 A2
EATING
Bob's Big Boy....17 B2
Eclectic....18 A1
Zankou Chicken....19 E1
ENTERTAINMENT
Deaf West Theatre....20 A1
Gibson Amphitheatre....21 B3
Greek Theatre....22 D4
SHOPPING
It's a Wrap....23 B1
Vintage Clothing Store District....24 A1
North Hollywood
Burbank
Griffith Park
Los Angeles River
Universal City
Toluca Lake
Lakeside Country Club
Warner Bros Ranch
Walt Disney Studios
Johnny Carson Park
Buena Vista Park
Verdugo Park
Mountain View Park
Los Angeles Equestrian Center
Forest Lawn Memorial Park – Hollywood Hills
Mount Sinai Memorial Park
Sennet Canyon
Cahuenga Peak (1820ft)
Mt Lee (1640ft)
Mt Chapel (1622ft)
Mt Bell (1587ft)
Mt Hollywood (1625ft)
Hollywood Sign
Upper Hollywood Reservoir
Hollywood Reservoir
Brush Canyon
Mineral Wells Picnic Grounds
Cedar Tree Picnic Grounds
Crystal Springs Picnic Grounds
Picnic Grounds
Roosevelt Municipal Golf Course
North Atwater Park
Glendale Water Reclamation Plant
Hollywood Bowl
Hollywood Hills
Runyon Canyon Park
Wattles Garden Park
Mt Olympus
Metrolink
Metro Red Line
Golden State Fwy
Hollywood Fwy
Ventura Fwy
To Glendale (3.5mi)
To Forest Lawn Memorial Park – Glendale (0.25mi)
Los Feliz Blvd
Vermont Ave
Lankershim Blvd
Ventura Blvd
Cahuenga Blvd W
Cahuenga Blvd E
N Cahuenga Blvd
Barham Blvd
Mulholland Hwy
Western Canyon Dr
Crystal Springs Dr
Zoo Dr
N Zoo Dr
Western Heritage Way
Griffith Park Dr
Forest Lawn Dr
Victory Blvd
San Fernando Rd
W Glenoaks Blvd
N Hollywood Way
N Buena Vista St
W Olive Ave
W Alameda Ave
W Verdugo Ave
N California St
Riverside Dr
Ventura Fwy Riverside Dr
Moorpark St
Valley Spring Ln
Camarillo St
Cahuenga Blvd
Vineland Ave
Magnolia Ave
N Beachwood Dr
Fern Dell Dr

(Continued from page 509)

You must dial 1 plus the area code before the final seven digits, even when calling within the same area code.

Tourist Information

Downtown Los Angeles Visitor Information Center (Map pp512-13; ☎ 213-689-8822; www.visitlosangeles.info; 685 S Figueroa St, Downtown; 8:30am-5pm Mon-Fri)
Hollywood Visitors Center (Map pp514-15; ☎ 323-467-6412; Hollywood & Highland, 6801 Hollywood Blvd, Hollywood; 10am-10pm Mon-Sat, to 7pm Sun)
Santa Monica Visitors Center (Map pp520-1; ☎ 310-393-7593; www.santamonica.com; 1920 Main St, Santa Monica; 9am-6pm)
Santa Monica Visitors Kiosk (Map pp520-1; 1400 Ocean Ave, Santa Monica; 10am-5pm Jun-Aug, to 4pm Sep-May)

DANGERS & ANNOYANCES

Despite what you see in the movies, walking around LA is generally safe. Common-sense rules apply: a dark alley anywhere on earth is probably not the safest place to be. That said, extra caution should be exercised in East LA, Compton, South LA and Watts, sections long plagued by gangs and drugs. Stay away from these areas after dark. Hollywood and Venice have also been associated with seediness and danger after dark, but the crime rate is falling as they become gentrified. Crime rates are lowest in Westside communities such as Westwood and Beverly Hills, as well as in the beach towns (except Venice) and Pasadena.

Downtown is home to numerous homeless folks, especially on Skid Row, an area roughly bounded by 3rd, Alameda, 7th and Main Sts. Surprisingly, Santa Monica is too, though they usually avoid you if you avoid them.

SIGHTS

Downtown & Around

Downtown is LA's historic core, hub of commerce, government and culture with a big C. But for much of the last few decades the area languished as a no-man's land, particularly after dark and on weekends.

While Downtown still doesn't have the 24-hour energy of other big cities, there's something big afoot here: it's a budding arts district with edgy galleries, stylish lofts reclaimed from aging office buildings, and new quirky bars and restaurants, not to mention such headline-grabbing architecture as Frank Gehry's Walt Disney Concert Hall, longstanding ethnic neighborhoods and a booming entertainment area around Staples Center arena.

Downtown is easily reached by subway or bus and then explored on foot or by DASH minibuses (p570). Parking is cheapest around Little Tokyo and in Chinatown (about $4 or $5 all day).

EL PUEBLO DE LOS ANGELES & AROUND

Compact, colorful and car-free, this state historic park commemorates LA's founding and preserves the city's oldest buildings, most notably the 1818 **Avila Adobe** (Map pp512-13; ☎ 213-628-1274; E-10 Olvera St; admission free; 10am-3pm). It's right on **Olvera St**, a block-long, Mexican-flavored brick alley where you can browse for tacky souvenirs, feast on tacos and *tortas* (sandwiches), and peruse Chicano art.

Pick up a free self-guided tour pamphlet at the **El Pueblo Visitors Center** (Map pp512-13; ☎ 213-628-1274; Sepulveda House, Olvera St; 10am-3pm), or join a free guided tour leaving from the **Old Plaza Firehouse Museum** at 10am, 11am and noon Tuesday to Saturday.

Olvera St spills over into the **Old Plaza**, the Pueblo's central square with a pretty wrought-iron bandstand. Families stroll, couples kiss and everyone seeks shade beneath the grand old Australian Moreton Bay fig trees here. Across the street, the little church affectionately known as **La Placita** (Our Lady Queen of Angels Church; Map pp512-13; ☎ 213-629-3101; 535 N Main St; 8am-8pm) dates from 1822 and is a sentimental favorite with LA's Latino community. Peek inside for a look at the gold-festooned altar and painted ceiling.

Southeast of the plaza looms the soaring tower of **Union Station** (Map pp512-13; 800 N Alameda St), built in 1939, the last of the grand railroad stations in the USA. It's a glamorous exercise in Spanish-Mission and art deco, and has a waiting room easily the size of a football field with the loftiness of a cathedral. The station has appeared in dozens of movies, including *Guilty by Suspicion, Blade Runner, The Way We Were* and *Catch Me if You Can.*

The terminal stands on the spot of LA's original Chinatown, whose residents were relocated a few blocks north, along Broadway and Hill St. Today, the 'new' **Chinatown** is still a cultural and social hub of LA's Chinese-Americans. In recent years, artists and hipsters have moved in to open galleries and eclectic stores in the historic **Central Plaza** (Map pp512-13;

N Broadway), in the 900 block between Broadway and Hill St, and on nearby Chung King Rd.

The history of LA's Chinese-Americans is engagingly commemorated in the **Chinese American Museum** (Map pp512-13; ☎ 213-485-8567; www.camla.org; 425 N Los Angeles St; adult/student/senior $3/2/2; 10am-3pm Tue-Sun), further south in El Pueblo. It's in the 1890 Garnier Building, once the original Chinatown's unofficial 'city hall.'

DODGER STADIUM

Just north of Chinatown sits this beloved, 56,000-seat **baseball park** (Map pp512-13; ☎ 866-363-4377; losangeles.dodgers.mlb.com; 1000 Elysian Park Ave; tour adult/child 4-14yr/senior $15/10/10; tours 10am & 11:30am except during day games), home of the Los Angeles Dodgers (see p565). Go during a game, or a public tour (advance tickets recommended) of up to 90 minutes will take you to the press box, dugout, field, Dugout Club and training center.

CIVIC CENTER AREA

The ziggurat-style crown of LA's 1928 **City Hall** (Map pp512-13; ☎ 213-978-1995; 200 N Spring St; admission free; 8am-5pm Mon-Fri) makes it the long-time icon of the Civic Center, south of El Pueblo across US-101 (Hollywood Fwy). City Hall cameoed as the Daily Planet Building in the *Superman* TV series, got blown to bits in the 1953 sci-fi thriller *War of the Worlds* and was on the police sergeant's badge on the opening credits of *Dragnet*. In clear skies, you'll have great views from the wraparound Observation Deck. Call ahead for information on guided tours.

Heading south on Main St from City Hall, you'll see the Civic Center's newest icon, the **Caltrans Building** (Map pp512-13; ☎ 213-897-3656; 100 S Main St; admission free), as locals call the headquarters of District 7 of the California Department of Transportation. Santa Monica–based architect Thom Mayne won the 2005 Pritzker Prize, the Oscar of architecture, for this futuristic design. The neon stripes on the facade recall head- and tail-lights whizzing along a freeway, and the windows open or close depending on the outside temperature and angle of the sun.

CATHEDRAL OF OUR LADY OF THE ANGELS

Downtown's new **cathedral** (Map pp512-13; ☎ 213-680-5200; www.olacathedral.org; 555 W Temple St; 6:30am-6pm Mon-Fri, 9am-6pm Sat, 7am-6pm Sun, free tours 1pm Mon-Fri) is a monumental work completed by Spanish architect José Rafael Moneo in 2002. Behind its austere ochre mantle awaits a vast hall of worship filled with plenty of original art (note the contemporary tapestries of saints by John Nava) and soft light filtering in through milky, alabaster windows. Gregory Peck is buried in the mausoleum. The cathedral store sells self-guided tour booklets ($2.50). Unless you're coming for Mass, weekday parking is expensive ($3.50 per 15 minutes, $16.50 maximum, until 4pm), but there's usually metered street parking nearby.

GRAND AVENUE CULTURAL CORRIDOR

Grand Avenue, on the northern edge of the Civic Center district, is being touted as the epicenter of Downtown revitalization and brims with architectural landmarks, museums and even a few good restaurants.

Walt Disney Concert Hall

The undisputed centerpiece along Grand Ave is this sparkling **concert venue** (Map pp512-13; ☎ 323-850-2000; www.laphil.com; 111 S Grand Ave). Designed by Frank Gehry, the concert hall is a gravity-defying sculpture of curving and billowing stainless-steel walls that conjure visions of a ship adrift in a cosmic sea. The auditorium, meanwhile, feels like the inside of a finely crafted instrument, a cello perhaps, clad in walls of smooth Douglas fir. Check the website for details of free guided and audio tours. Disney Hall is the home of the Los Angeles Philharmonic (see p564), which used to play at the Dorothy Chandler Pavilion at the Music Center of LA County, one block north of here.

MOCA Grand Avenue

A bit south of Disney Hall, this much-touted **museum** (Map pp512-13; ☎ 213-626-6222; www.moca-la.org; 250 S Grand Ave; adult/child/student/senior $10/free/5/5, 5-8pm Thu free; 11am-5pm Mon & Fri, to 8pm Thu, to 6pm Sat & Sun) is a delicacy for contemporary art fans. Besides headline-grabbing special exhibits, it presents all the heavy hitters of the art world working from the 1940s to the present – from Andy Warhol to Cy Twombly. It's in a building by Arata Isozaki that many consider his masterpiece. There are two other branches of MOCA, the Geffen Contemporary at MOCA (opposite) in Little Tokyo and the MOCA Pacific Design Center (p532) in West Hollywood. The same ticket is valid for both

Downtown branches, and admission is free to the West Hollywood branch.

MOCA is shadowed by the glistening towers of **California Plaza**, a vast office complex that hosts the **Grand Performances** (www.grandperformances.org), one of the best free summer outdoor-performance series in town.

On the plaza's southeastern side is **Angels Flight**, a historic funicular that was briefly revived in 1996 only to be mothballed five years later after a derailed car left one person dead and others injured. There are stairs down to Hill St and the wonderful **Grand Central Market** (see p552), although you may have to hopscotch around a few homeless folks to get there.

Wells Fargo History Museum

Continuing south along Grand Ave is this small but intriguing **museum** (Map pp512-13; ☎ 213-253-7166; www.wellsfargohistory.com; 333 S Grand Ave; admission free; ⏰ 9am-5pm Mon-Fri), which relives the Gold Rush era with an original Concord stagecoach, a 100oz gold nugget and a 19th-century bank office.

Richard Riordan Central Library

Who says Angelenos don't read? The main branch of the city's **public library** (Map pp512-13; ☎ 213-228-7000; www.lapl.org; 630 W 5th St; ⏰ 10am-8pm Mon-Thu, to 6pm Fri & Sat, 1-5pm Sun, free tours 12:30pm Mon-Fri, 11am & 2pm Sat, 2pm Sun) is pretty spectacular. It's worth a browse for the 1922 architecture, designed by Bertram Goodhue in quasi-Egyptian style, and the soaring modern wing, which was added in 1993 along with the **Maguire Gardens**, a small and tranquil park of sinuous walkways, pools, fountains and whimsical artwork. Oh yes, and you can check email, read magazines and newspapers, browse the stacks, view the latest exhibits at the excellent Getty Gallery or the Photography Gallery, or grab a bite in the cafeteria.

Pershing Square & Around

A short stroll southwest of City Hall drops you right into Downtown's historic core, anchored by Pershing Square, LA's oldest public park (1866), and flanked on its north by the grand old **Millennium Biltmore Hotel** (p547).

Southwest of Pershing Sq, along Hill St, gold and diamonds are the main currency in the **Jewelry District**. For dazzling architecture, head one block northeast to Broadway, where the 1893 **Bradbury Building** (Map pp512-13; ☎ 213-626-1893; 304 S Broadway; admission free; ⏰ 9am-6pm Mon-Fri, to 5pm Sat & Sun) is the crown jewel. Its red brick facade conceals a light-flooded, galleried atrium that has starred in many movies, most famously *Blade Runner*. Across the street, the colorful and frenzied **Grand Central Market** (Map pp512-13; ☎ 213-624-2378; 317 S Broadway; ⏰ 9am-6pm) is great for a browse or a snack (see p552).

Until eclipsed by Hollywood in the mid-1920s, Broadway was LA's entertainment hub, with no fewer than a dozen **historic movie theaters** built in a riot of styles, from beaux arts to East Indian to Spanish Gothic. Their architectural and historic significance earned them a spot on the National Register of Historic Places. Standouts include the 1931 **Los Angeles Theater** (Map pp512-13; 615 S Broadway), where Charlie Chaplin's *City Lights* premiered, and the 1926 **Orpheum Theater** (Map pp512-13; 842 S Broadway), which more recently has hosted *American Idol* auditions. Most of the time, the theaters are closed to the public, so the best way to see them is by joining one of the excellent tours offered by the LA Conservancy (see p545). The Conservancy also presents 'Last Remaining Seats,' a film series of Hollywood classics, in these theaters.

A couple blocks east of Broadway, centered around 4th and Main Sts, is the **Old Bank District**, a series of early-20th-century office buildings and, later, flophouse hotels which have been recently turned into lofts and apartments for Downtown's newest residents.

LITTLE TOKYO

Little Tokyo is the Japanese counterpart of Chinatown, a contemporary but attractive mix of traditional gardens, Buddhist temples, outdoor shopping malls and sushi bars. Stop into the **Little Tokyo Koban** (Map pp512-13; ☎ 213-613-1911; 307 E 1st St; ⏰ 10am-6pm Mon-Sat) visitors center for maps and information. The **Japanese American National Museum** (Map pp512-13; ☎ 213-625-0414; www.janm.org; 369 E 1st St; adult/child/student/senior $8/free/4/5, 5-8pm Thu free; ⏰ 10am-5pm Fri-Wed, to 8pm Thu) brims with objects of work and worship, photographs, art and even a uniform worn by *Star Trek* actor (and Japanese-American) George Takei. Special focus is given to the painful chapter of the WWII internment camps (see p414).

Just north of here, the **Geffen Contemporary at MOCA** (Map pp512-13; ☎ 213-626-6222; www.moca-la.org; 152 N Central Ave; adult/child/student/senior $10/free/5/5, Thu free; ⏰ 11am-5pm Mon & Fri, to 8pm Thu, to 6pm Sat

& Sun) is an outpost of MOCA Grand Avenue (see p524), housed in a former warehouse. It presents mostly large-scale installations.

In the gritty, industrial section southeast of Little Tokyo, an increasingly lively **Arts District** is emerging ever so slowly. It draws a young and adventurous crowd, who live and work in makeshift studios above abandoned warehouses and small factories. There's enough of them here to support a growing number of cafés, restaurants and shops. Just off the corner of 4th and Main, the **Museum of Neon Art** (MONA; Map pp512-13; ☎ 213-489-9918; www.neonmona.org; 136 W 4th St; adult/child/student/senior $7/free/5/5; 🕑 11am-5pm Wed-Sat, noon-5pm Sun) is a cool gallery highlighting neon, electric and kinetic art, including a serenely smiling *Mona Lisa*.

SOUTH PARK

In the southwestern corner of Downtown, South Park isn't a park but an emerging neighborhood bordering the Staples Center arena, the LA Convention Center and the new entertainment hub under construction called **LA Live**. City planners and developers are betting the farm that this $1.7 billion megaproject will polevault Downtown LA onto the map of must-go destinations for both locals and visitors.

The area got its first jolt in 1999 with the opening of the **Staples Center** (Map pp512-13; ☎ 213-742-7340; www.staplescenter.com; 1111 S Figueroa St), a saucer-shaped sports and entertainment arena with all the high-tech trappings. It's home turf for the Los Angeles Lakers, Clippers and Sparks basketball teams, the Kings ice hockey team and the Avengers indoor football team. When major headliners – Justin Timberlake or Barbra Streisand the next time she comes back out of retirement – are in town, they'll most likely perform at Staples. Parking is $20.

The anchor of LA Live is the 7100-seat Nokia Theatre (see p562), which hosts awards shows and major spectacles. When LA Live is completed, there will also be a huge live-music club, a megaplex movie theater, a dozen restaurants and a 54-story hotel tower shared by Marriott and the Ritz-Carlton.

Heading east on Olympic Blvd takes you into the heart of the **Fashion District** (see the boxed text, p566), a 90-block nirvana for bargain hunters, even if shopping around here is more Middle Eastern bazaar than Rodeo Dr. The vast selection of samples, knockoffs and original designs will make your head spin.

Nearby, LA's **flower market** (Map pp512-13; ☎ 213-627-3696; Wall St; Mon-Fri $2, Sat $1; 🕑 8am-noon Mon, Wed & Fri, 6am-noon Tue, Thu & Sat), between 7th and 8th Sts, is the largest in the country and dates back to 1913.

KOREATOWN

Koreatown is a cacophonous, amorphous and steadily expanding area, hundreds of square blocks west of Downtown.

Despite the large proportion of residents and businesses here that are ethnic Korean, most of the sights have nothing to do with Korean culture, the lone exception being the **Korean American Museum** (off Map pp512-13; ☎ 213-388-4229; www.kamuseum.org; 4th fl, 3727 W 6th St; admission free; 🕑 11am-6pm Wed-Fri, to 3pm Sat). If you have a strong interest in historic and contemporary Korean culture, a short drive west of Koreatown is the **Korean Cultural Center** (Map pp516-17; ☎ 323-936-7641; www.kccla.org; 5505 Wilshire Blvd, Los Angeles; admission free; 🕑 9am-5pm Mon-Fri, to 6pm Sat), with a museum and art gallery, a library, a film archive and a screening room.

Wilshire Blvd is K-town's main east–west artery. Coming from Downtown, your first stop is **MacArthur Park** (Map pp512–13), an expanse of green that's gone from gritty to pretty following a recent refurbishment, though it should still be avoided after dark.

Fans of Victoriana will get their fill at the nearby **Grier Musser Museum** (Map pp512-13; ☎ 213-413-1814; www.griermussermuseum.com; 403 S Bonnie Brae St; adult/child/student/senior $10/5/7/7; 🕑 noon-4pm Wed-Sat by appointment; Ⓟ), an immaculately restored turn-of-the-20th-century Queen Anne villa that's stuffed with period antiques and knickknacks.

Further west, a couple of delicacies for art deco buffs await: the 1929 **Bullocks Wilshire Building** (off Map pp512-13; ☎ 213-738-8240; www.swlaw.edu/bullockswilshire; 3050 Wilshire Blvd), a former department store and now a law school; and the **Wiltern Theatre** (off Map pp512-13; 3790 Wilshire Blvd), an elegant music venue that tends to feature alt-rock bands. In between is the site of the 1922 **Ambassador Hotel** (off Map pp512-13; 3400 Wilshire Blvd), where Robert F Kennedy was assassinated in 1968; after much controversy the hotel itself was torn down to make way for a new school.

In southern Koreatown, the Greek Orthodox **St Sophia Cathedral** (off Map pp512-13; ☎ 323-737-2424; www.stsophia.org; 1324 S Normandie Ave; 🕑 10am-4pm Tue-Fri, to 2pm Sat, 12:30-2:30pm Sun) is so lavishly decorated it inspires comparison to a giant's treasure chest, spilling over with gold, crystal and jewels. Sunday service is at 10am.

EXPOSITION PARK

A couple of miles to the south of Downtown, the family-friendly Exposition Park started as an agricultural fairground in 1872 and now contains three fine museums, a lovely **Rose Garden** (admission free; 9am-sunset mid-Mar–Dec) and the 1923 **Los Angeles Memorial Coliseum**. The latter hosted the 1932 and 1984 Summer Olympic Games, the 1959 baseball World Series and two Super Bowls.

The **University of Southern California** (USC; Map pp510-11; 213-740-5371, tours 213-740-6605; www.usc.edu; 3535 S Figueroa St), which counts George Lucas, John Wayne and Neil Armstrong among its alumni, is just north of Exposition Park.

The DASH bus 'F' (p570) from Downtown serves Exposition Park. There's parking ($6) on Figueroa at 39th St.

Natural History Museum of Los Angeles County

Take a spin around the world and back in time at this popular **museum** (NHM; off Map pp512-13; 213-763-3466; www.nhm.org; 900 Exposition Blvd; adult/child/student/senior $9/2/6.50/6.50; 9:30am-5pm Mon-Fri, 10am-5pm Sat & Sun;), inside a baronial building in Exposition Park's northwest corner (if it looks familiar, it stood in for Columbia University in the first *Spider-Man* movie). There is usually some special exhibit going on, but the permanent halls are also well worth a spin. Crowd-pleasers include stuffed African elephants and the giant megamouth, one of the world's rarest sharks. Historical exhibits include prized Navajo textiles, baskets and jewelry in the **Hall of Native American Cultures**. The **Gem & Mineral Hall**, meanwhile, is a glittering spectacle with a walk-through gem tunnel and more gold than any other such collection in the US. Kids love the hands-on **Discovery Center** and the **Insect Zoo** with its tarantulas, hissing cockroaches and other creepy-crawlies. Note, though, that the dinosaur hall is closed for renovation until 2011.

California Science Center

If your memories of school science make you groan, then a visit to this imaginative multimedia **museum** (off Map pp512-13; 213-744-7400; www.casciencectr.org; 700 State Dr; admission free; 10am-5pm;) should convince you that, gee, science *can* be fun. There's absolutely nothing stuffy about this place, where you can watch baby chicks hatch in an incubator, and you'll have plenty of buttons to push, lights to switch on and knobs to pull. During the school year, the center usually crawls with school kids on weekday mornings, so plan accordingly if you want a little more quiet.

Of the three main exhibition areas, **World of Life** focuses mostly on the human body. You can 'hop on' a red blood cell for a computer fly-through of the circulatory system, ask Gertie how long your colon really is and meet Tess, a giant techno-doll billed as '50ft of brains, beauty and biology.'

Virtual-reality games, high-tech simulations, laser animation and other gizmos and gadgets await in the **Creative World** exhibit, which zooms in on the tools and devices humans have invented in order to facilitate communication, transportation and construction.

In an adjacent building, spirits will soar in the **Air & Space Gallery** (off Map pp512-13; 10am-1pm Mon-Fri, 11am-4pm Sat & Sun), where exhibits include the pioneering 1902 Wright Glider and the Soviet-made *Sputnik*, the first human-made object to orbit the earth in 1957.

The adjacent **IMAX** (p561) theater is a good place to relax and wind down at the end of an action-filled day.

California African American Museum

This acclaimed **museum** (off Map pp512-13; 213-744-7432; www.caamuseum.org; 600 State Dr; admission free; 10am-4pm Wed-Sat) does an excellent job documenting African and African American art and history, especially as it pertains to California and other western states. An active lecture and performance schedule brings together the community and those wanting to gain a deeper understanding of what it means to be black in America.

SOUTH LOS ANGELES

The area south of Exposition Park was long known as South Central, a name that quietly went away after the 1992 riots that had their epicenter here. Gangs, drugs, poverty, crime and drive-by shootings are just a few of the negative images – not entirely undeserved – associated with this district. This is too bad because South Central (named for Central Ave, which runs through it) was once a proud and prosperous heart of LA's African American community. The upscale shops and restaurants of **Leimert Park Village** (luh-*murt*) reflect this heritage, particularly around the intersection of Degnan and 43rd Sts.

South LA's beacon of pride, the **Watts Towers** (Map pp510-11; ☎ 213-847-4646; 1765 E 107th St; adult/under 12yr/13-19yr/senior $7/free/3/3; tours 11am-3pm Fri, 10:30am-3pm Sat, 12:30-3pm Sun) rank among the world's greatest monuments of folk art. Italian immigrant Simon Rodia spent 33 years (from 1921 to 1954) cobbling together this whimsical free-form sculpture from a motley assortment of found objects – from green 7-Up bottles to sea shells, rocks to pottery.

EAST LOS ANGELES

Beyond the concrete gulch of the Los Angeles River lies a sprawling neighborhood that's home to the largest concentration of Mexicans outside of Mexico, plus thousands of Latinos from Central and, to a lesser extent, South America. Life in the barrio is tough but lively. People shop in streets lined with *panaderías* (bakeries), *tiendas* (convenience stores) and stores selling *botánicas* (herbal cures). Brightly colored murals adorn many of the facades, but behind the color, life can be pretty grim. Unemployment is high, incomes are low, and gang violence and poor schools are ubiquitous.

There are no major tourist sights here, although **Boyle Heights**, the neighborhood closest to Downtown LA, features a few worthwhile stops. At **Mariachi Plaza** (Map pp512-13; cnr Boyle Ave & E 1st St), traditional Mexican musicians dressed in fanciful suits and wide-brimmed hats mill beneath wall-sized murals, waiting to be hired for restaurant or social events. A bit further east, **El Mercado** (Map pp510-11; 3425 E 1st St) is a wonderfully boisterous indoor market, where locals stock up on tortilla presses, pig bellies and toys. The upstairs restaurants here are often packed, especially when there's live music.

North of here is one of LA's major Latino arts centers, **Self-Help Graphics & Art** (Map pp510-11; ☎ 323-881-6444; www.selfhelpgraphics.com; 3802 Cesar E Chavez Ave; admission free; 10am-4pm Tue-Sat), whose colorful facade is a mosaic of pottery and glass shards. The center was founded by a Franciscan nun in 1973 and has been nurturing and promoting Latino art ever since. The galleries and gift shops are well worth checking out.

Hollywood, Los Feliz & Silver Lake

Aging movie stars know that a facelift can quickly pump up a drooping career, and the same has been done with the legendary **Hollywood Blvd** (Map pp514–15), preened and spruced up in recent years. Though it still hasn't recaptured its Golden Age glamour (1920s–1940s), much of its late-20th-century seediness is gone.

Historic movie palaces bask in restored glory, Metro Rail's Red Line makes access easy, some of LA's hottest bars and nightclubs have sprung up here, and even 'Oscar' has found a permanent home in the Kodak Theatre, part of the vast shopping and entertainment complex called Hollywood & Highland.

The most interesting mile runs between La Brea Ave and Vine St, along the **Hollywood Walk of Fame**, which honors more than 2000 celebrities with brass stars embedded in the sidewalk. For interesting historical tidbits about local landmarks, keep an eye out for the sign markers along here, or join a guided walking tour operated by Red Line Tours (p545).

Following Hollywood Blvd east beyond Hwy 101 (Hollywood Fwy) takes you to the neighborhoods of **Los Feliz** (los *fee*-liss) and **Silver Lake**, both boho-chic enclaves with offbeat shopping, funky bars and a hopping cuisine scene.

The Metro Red Line (p569) serves central Hollywood (Hollywood/Highland and Hollywood/Vine stations) and Los Feliz (Vermont/Sunset station) from Downtown LA and the San Fernando Valley. Pay-parking lots abound in the side streets. The Hollywood & Highland parking garage charges $2 for four hours with validation (no purchase necessary) from any merchant within the mall or the Hollywood Visitors Center.

HOLLYWOOD BOULEVARD

Even the most jaded visitor may feel a thrill in the famous forecourt of the 1927 **Grauman's Chinese Theatre** (Map pp514-15; ☎ 323-464-6266; 6925 Hollywood Blvd), where generations of screen legends have left their imprints in cement: feet, hands, a protruding proboscis (that would be Jimmy Durante) and even magic wands (the young stars of the *Harry Potter* films). Actors dressed as Superman, Marilyn Monroe

BEHIND THE CURTAIN

Did you know it takes a week to shoot a half-hour sitcom? Or that you rarely see ceilings on TV because the space is filled with lights and lamps? You'll learn these and other fascinating nuggets about the world of film and TV production while touring a working studio. Action is slowest (and star-sighting potential lowest) during 'hiatus' (May to August). Reservations recommended; bring photo ID.

Paramount Studios (Map pp514-15; ☎ 323-956-1777; 5555 Melrose Ave, Hollywood; tours $35; ⌚ Mon-Fri) The only remaining studio in Hollywood proper runs two-hour tram tours of its historic lot, by reservation only. Group size is limited to eight per tram, giving you ample opportunity to pepper your guide with questions. No two tours are alike, as guides don't follow a set script and access to stages varies daily, but they might include the sets of *Dr Phil* or *Nip/Tuck*. Minimum age 12.

Sony Pictures Studios (Map pp510-11; ☎ 323-520-8687; www.sonypicturesstudiostours.com; 10202 W Washington Blvd, Culver City; tour $28; ⌚ tours 9:30am, 10:30am, 12:30pm, 1:30pm & 2:30pm Mon-Fri; P) This two-hour walking tour includes possible visits to the sound stages where *Men in Black, Spider-Man, Charlie's Angels* and other blockbusters were filmed. Munchkins hopped along the Yellow Brick Rd in the *Wizard of Oz*, filmed when this was the venerable MGM studio. You might even pop in on the set of *Jeopardy*. Minimum age 12.

Warner Bros Studios (Map p522; ☎ 818-972-8687; www.wbstudiotour.com; 3400 Riverside Dr, Burbank; tours $45; ⌚ 8:30am-4pm Mon-Fri) This 2¼-hour tour offers the most fun yet authentic look behind the scenes. It kicks off with a video of WB's greatest hits (*Rebel Without a Cause, Harry Potter* etc) before you travel by mini-tram to sound stages, backlot sets and technical departments, including costumes and set building. The studio museum is a treasure trove of props and memorabilia, including Hogwarts' famous Sorting Hat. Tours leave roughly every half-hour. Minimum age eight; longer hours March to September. Parking $5.

and the like are usually on hand to pose for photos (for tips).

The anchor for the boulevard's rebirth is next door: **Hollywood & Highland** (Map pp514-15; ☎ 323-467-6412; www.hollywoodandhighland.com; 6801 Hollywood Blvd; admission free; ⌚ shops 10am-10pm Mon-Sat, to 7pm Sun), a multistory mall marrying kitsch and commerce. Its focal point is **Babylon Court**, anchored by a preposterous triumphal arch (inspired by DW Griffith's 1916 movie *Intolerance*) that frames views of the Hollywood Sign.

Hollywood & Highland includes the **Kodak Theatre** (Map pp514-15; ☎ 323-308-6363; www.kodaktheatre.com; adult/child/senior $15/10/10; ⌚ 10:30am-4pm Jun-Aug, to 2:30pm Sep-May), which hosts the Academy Awards and other star-studded events. Pricey 30-minute tours take you inside the auditorium, the VIP room and past an actual Oscar statuette. The first Academy Awards ceremony was held diagonally across the street in the 1927 Hollywood Roosevelt Hotel (see p548).

Other classic movie palaces here include the flamboyant 1926 **El Capitan Theatre** (Map pp514-15; ☎ 323-467-7674; 6838 Hollywood Blvd) and the 1922 **Egyptian Theatre** (Map pp514-15; ☎ 323-466-3456; www.egyptiantheatre.com; 6712 Hollywood Blvd), now the home of the nonprofit American Cinematheque (see p561).

Another way to time-travel through Hollywood history is by perusing the props, costumes, photos, posters, scripts and memorabilia at the **Hollywood Museum** (Map pp514-15; ☎ 323-464-7776; www.thehollywoodmuseum.com; 1660 N Highland Ave; adult/child/senior $15/12/12; ⌚ 10am-5pm Wed-Sun), a veritable shrine to the stars – from Chaplin to DiCaprio. The basement holds Hannibal Lecter's original jail cell from the movie *Silence of the Lambs*.

HOLLYWOOD SIGN

LA's most recognizable landmark first appeared atop its hillside perch in 1923 as an advertising gimmick for a real-estate development called Hollywood Land. Each letter is 50ft tall and made of sheet metal. It's illegal to hike up to the sign, but there are many places where you can catch good views, including Hollywood & Highland (opposite), Griffith Park (p530) and the top of Beachwood Dr (Map pp514–15).

HOLLYWOOD BOWL & AROUND

Summer concerts at the **Hollywood Bowl** (Map pp514-15; ☎ 323-850-2000; www.hollywoodbowl.com; 2301 N Highland Ave; ⌚ late Jun-Sep) have been a great LA tradition since 1922. This 18,000-seat hillside amphitheater is the summer home of the LA Philharmonic (p564), and is also host to big-name rock, jazz and blues acts. Many concertgoers come early to enjoy a pre-show picnic on the parklike grounds or in their seats (alcohol is allowed). For insight into the bowl's storied history, visit the **Hollywood Bowl Museum** (Map pp514-15; ☎ 323-850-2058; www.hollywoodbowl.com/event/museum.cfm; 2301 N Highland Ave; admission free; 🕒 10am-8pm Tue-Sat, 4-7pm Sun Jul–mid-Sep, 10am-5pm Tue-Fri mid-Sep–Jun).

South of here, across from the Bowl, is the **Hollywood Heritage Museum** (Map pp514-15; ☎ 323-874-2276; 2100 N Highland Ave; adult/child/senior $5/1/3; 🕒 noon-4pm Thu-Sun). It's inside the horse barn used by the movie pioneer Cecil B DeMille in 1913 and 1914 to shoot *The Squaw Man*, Hollywood's first feature-length film. Inside are exhibits on early filmmaking, including costumes, projectors and cameras, as well as a replica of DeMille's office.

HOLLYWOOD FOREVER CEMETERY

Next to Paramount Studios, this **cemetery** (Map pp514-15; ☎ 323-469-1181; www.hollywoodforever.com; 6000 Santa Monica Blvd; 🕒 8am-6pm May-Sep, to 5pm Oct-Mar) is crowded with famous 'immortals,' including Rudolph Valentino, Tyrone Power, Jayne Mansfield and Cecil B DeMille. Pick up a map ($5) at the flower shop (🕒 9am-5pm) near the entrance. See p561 for details of **film screenings** here. No, really.

HOLLYHOCK HOUSE

An early masterpiece by Frank Lloyd Wright, this **house** (Map pp514-15; ☎ 323-644-6269; www.hollyhockhouse.net; 4800 Hollywood Blvd; tours adult/child/student $7/free/3; 🕒 hourly tours 12:30-3:30pm Wed-Sun; Ⓟ) marks the famous architect's first attempt at creating an indoor-outdoor living space in harmony with LA's sunny climate, a style he later referred to as California Romanza. Admission is by tour only. The house is inside the Barnsdall Art Park, where the Municipal Art Gallery sells tour tickets and screens documentaries about the restoration.

Griffith Park

A gift to the city in 1896 by mining mogul Griffith J Griffith, **Griffith Park** (Map p522; ☎ 323-913-4688; admission free; 🕒 6am-10pm, trails 6am-dusk; Ⓟ) is a wonderful playground with facilities for all age levels and interests. At five times the size of New York's Central Park, it is one of the country's largest urban green spaces and embraces an outdoor theater, the city zoo, an observatory, two museums, golf courses, tennis courts, playgrounds, bridle paths, 53 miles of hiking trails, Batman's caves and even the Hollywood Sign.

In May 2007 a devastating fire roared across the park's chaparral-cloaked hillsides, charring about 850 acres – or one quarter of the park – but most of the damage was away from the facilities, which remain open. These includes the richly festooned 1926 **Griffith Park Merry-Go-Round** (Map p522; ☎ 323-665-3051; Park Center; rides $1; 🕒 11am-5pm daily May-Sep, 11am-5pm Sat & Sun Oct-Apr; 👶), with beautifully carved and painted horses sporting real horse-hair tails. Your (inner) five-year-old can climb aboard the vintage railcars and steam locomotives of the **Travel Town Museum** (Map p522; ☎ 323-662-5874; 5200 W Zoo Dr; admission free; 🕒 10am-5pm Mon-Fri, to 6pm Sat & Sun; 👶). Or, south of here, ride the **Griffith Park & Southern Railroad** (Map p522; ☎ 323-664-6903; 4400 Crystal Springs Dr; tickets $2.50; 🕒 10am-4:30pm Mon-Fri, to 5pm Sat & Sun; 👶), a miniature train chugging through a re-created old Western town and a Native American village.

Access to the park is easiest via the Griffith Park Dr or Zoo Dr exits off I-5 (Golden State Fwy). Parking is plentiful and free. For information and maps, stop by the **Griffith Park Ranger Station** (Map p522; ☎ 323-665-5188; 4730 Crystal Springs Dr).

GRIFFITH OBSERVATORY & PLANETARIUM

After four years and $93 million, this landmark 1935 **observatory** (Map p522; ☎ 213-473-0800; www.griffithobservatory.org; 2800 Observatory Rd; admission free, planetarium shows adult/child/student & senior $7/3/5; 🕒 noon-10pm Tue-Fri, 10am-10pm Sat & Sun; 👶) reopened in 2006 and now boasts the world's most advanced star projector in its planetarium – phone or check the website for show times.

In the lower level is the Big Picture, a 150ft floor-to-ceiling digital image of a sliver of the universe bursting with galaxies, stars and lurking dark matter. For more tangible thrills, weigh yourself on nine planetary scales (weight-watchers should go for Mercury), generate your own earthquake or head to the rooftop to peek through the refracting and solar telescopes housed in the smaller domes. From here, sweeping views of the Hollywood Hills and the gleaming city below are just as spectacular, especially at sunset.

The observatory has starred in many movies, most famously *Rebel Without a Cause* with James Dean. Have your picture snapped

HOLLYWOOD ON HOLLYWOOD

Hollywood likes nothing better than to see itself on screen. Self-indulgent? Maybe, but often highly entertaining. To wit, our own subjective list of 10 classics about Hollywood that every cinephile should know:

- *Sunset Boulevard* (1950) – The ultimate Hollywood story. Gloria Swanson plays Norma Desmond, a washed-up silent-film star pining for her return, and William Holden plays the screenwriter she hires to make that happen.
- *Singin' in the Rain* (1952) – Exuberant musical fairy tale about love in the time of talkies, starring Gene Kelly, Debbie Reynolds and Donald O'Connor.
- *What Ever Happened to Baby Jane?* (1962) – The best catfight film. Eh-verrr. Bette Davis and Joan Crawford play sisters and washed-up actresses in a feast of jealousy, rage and mind games.
- *Silent Movie* (1976) – Screwball comedy from Mel Brooks about a director trying to revive a movie studio by producing the first silent film in decades. *Silent Movie* is also a silent movie… except for one well-placed word.
- *Postcards from the Edge* (1990) – Mike Nichols directs Shirley MacLaine and Meryl Streep as a mom and daughter pair dealing with stardom's seamy underbelly.
- *Barton Fink* (1991) – John Turturro and John Goodman have a battle of wits over how to write a screenplay in this dark comedy by the Coen brothers.
- *The Player* (1992) – In arguably the most accessible film by legendary director Robert Altman, Tim Robbins plays a studio executive who takes his power too far and has to cover for it.
- *Ed Wood* (1994) – Tim Burton directs Johnny Depp as perhaps the worst director in history, famous for cross-dressing in pink angora.
- *Swimming with Sharks* (1994) – Kevin Spacey plays a Hollywood agent with no soul. Is there any other kind?
- *Get Shorty* (1995) – In Barry Sonnenfeld's comedy based on the Elmore Leonard novel, John Travolta plays a mafioso who gets entangled in Hollywood and wonders which industry has fewer scruples.

beside the actor's bust with the Hollywood Sign caught neatly in the background.

LOS ANGELES ZOO & BOTANICAL GARDENS

With its 1200 finned, feathered and furry friends, the **LA Zoo** (Map p522; ☎ 323-644-4200; www.lazoo.org; 5333 Zoo Dr; adult/child/senior $12/7/9; ⏲ 10am-5pm; P ♿) enthralls the little ones. What began in 1912 as a refuge for retired circus animals is also a botanical garden. Crowd-pleasers include meerkats, swinging gibbons, frolicking sea lions, posturing chimpanzees, cuddly koalas and, according to the zoo's director, anything currently defecating. Tots gravitate toward **Adventure Island**, with its petting zoo and hands-on play stations, as well as the brand-new **Children's Discovery Center**.

MUSEUM OF THE AMERICAN WEST

This delightful **museum** (Map p522; ☎ 323-667-2000; www.autrynationalcenter.org; 4700 Western Heritage Way; adult/child/student/senior $9/3/5/5, free 2nd Tue each month; ⏲ 10am-5pm Tue-Sun, to 8pm Thu Jun-Aug; P ♿) offers the mother lode of knowledge on how the West was won. Its 10 galleries engagingly combine scholarship and showmanship, and are a veritable gold mine of Old West memorabilia.

Inquire here also about its sister museum, the **Southwest Museum of the American Indian** (off Map pp512-13; ☎ 323-221-2164; www.southwestmuseum.org; 234 Museum Dr), LA's first museum and one of the largest collections of Native American artifacts. It was undergoing renovation as we went to press and may have reopened by the time you read this. It's north of Downtown LA, off the 110 (Pasadena) Fwy.

West Hollywood

West Hollywood (WeHo) is an independent city that packs more personality into its 1.9 sq miles than most larger neighborhoods. It is the heart of gay and lesbian life in LA (see p546), the center of Southern California's design community and the adopted home of about 6000 immigrants from the former Soviet Union who've turned eastern WeHo into 'little Russia.' LA's fabled nightlife mecca, the Sunset Strip, is its main artery.

Street parking is heavily restricted (our favorite WeHo T-shirt slogan: 'So many men, so little parking'), but the structure at 8383 Santa Monica Blvd offers two hours of free parking in the daytime ($3 flat fee after 6pm). WeHo is also served by the DASH bus (p570).

SUNSET STRIP

The famed Sunset Strip – Sunset Blvd between Laurel Canyon Blvd and Doheny Dr – has been a favorite nighttime playground since the 1920s. The **Chateau Marmont** (p549) and clubs such as Ciro's (now the **Comedy Store**; p565), Mocambo and the Trocadero (both now defunct) were favorite hangouts for Hollywood high society, from Bogart to Bacall, Monroe to Sinatra. The 1960s saw the opening of **Whisky-a-Go-Go** (Map pp516-17; ☎ 310-652-4202; 8901 W Sunset Blvd), America's first discotheque, the birthplace of go-go dancing and a launch pad for The Doors, who were the club's house band in 1966. Nearby is the **ANdAZ** (Map pp516-17; ☎ 323-656-1234; 8401 W Sunset Blvd), which, in its previous incarnation as the Hyatt Hotel, earned the moniker 'Riot House' during the 1970s, when it was the hotel of choice for Led Zeppelin and other raucous rock royalty. At one time, the band rented six floors and raced motorcycles in the hallways.

Today the strip is still nightlife central, although it's lost much of its cutting edge. It's a visual cacophony dominated by billboards and giant advertising banners draped across building facades. More recent places include the **House of Blues**; the jet-set **Mondrian Hotel** (p549), home of the **Sky Bar** (p561), still trendy after a decade and a half; and the **Viper Room**, until recently owned by Johnny Depp, where Tommy Lee attacked a paparazzo and, in 1993, actor River Phoenix overdosed.

PACIFIC DESIGN CENTER & AROUND

South of Sunset Strip, near the western end of trendy boutique-lined **Melrose Ave**, is the architecturally striking **Pacific Design Center** (PDC; Map pp516-17; ☎ 310-657-0800; 8687 Melrose Ave), with around 130 trade-only showrooms and the **West Hollywood Convention & Visitors Bureau** (Map pp516-17; ☎ 310-289-2525; www.visitwesthollywood.com; 🕓 8:30am-5:30pm Mon-Fri) on the mezzanine level. Outside, in a small pavilion, the **MOCA Pacific Design Center** (MOCA; Map pp516-17; ☎ 213-626-6222; www.moca-la.org; admission free; 🕓 11am-5pm Tue, Wed & Fri, to 8pm Thu, to 6pm Sat & Sun) presents rotating exhibits that tend to revolve around architecture and design themes. The surrounding **Avenues of Art & Design** invite strolling, people-watching and gallery hopping.

SCHINDLER HOUSE

The former **home and studio** (Map pp516-17; ☎ 323-651-1510; www.makcenter.com; 835 N Kings Rd; adult/student/senior $7/6/6, 4-6pm Fri free; 🕓 11am-6pm Wed-Sun) of Vienna-born architect Rudolph Schindler (1887–1953) is an excellent introduction to the modernist style that came to dominate Southern California. It's hard to imagine now, but its open floor plan, flat roof and glass sliding doors were considered avant-garde back in the 1920s. Today it's mostly a research center with lectures and cultural events.

Mid-City

Mid-City encompasses an amorphous area east of West Hollywood, south of Hollywood, west of Koreatown and north of I-10 (Santa Monica Fwy). A historic farmers market and a row of top-notch museums are its main attractions. There's plenty of street parking and validated parking at the Farmers Market and the adjacent Grove shopping mall. The main sights are served by DASH buses on the Fairfax route (p570).

FARMERS MARKET

Apples to zucchinis, you'll find these and then some at the landmark **Farmers Market** (Map pp516-17; ☎ 323-933-9211; www.farmersmarketla.com; 6333 W 3rd St; admission free; 🕓 9am-9pm Mon-Fri, to 8pm Sat, 10am-7pm Sun), in business since 1934. It's a fun, family-friendly place for a browse, snack or a spot of people-watching.

Though it's no longer a farmers market in the folks-in-overalls-selling-produce-off-trucks sense (see boxed text, p557, for other suggestions), it remains a casual, fun, kid-friendly spot for browsing, snacking and people watching.

Note that many restaurants here are open beyond Farmers Market hours. Next door there's the **Grove** (Map pp516-17; ☎ 323-900-8080; www.thegrovela.com; 189 The Grove Dr), an attractive outdoor shopping mall built around a central plaza with a musical fountain and a free trolley to take you back and forth.

North of the mall is **CBS Television City** (Map pp516-17; ☎ 323-575-2624; www.cbs.com; 7800 Beverly Blvd), where game shows, talk shows, soap operas and other programs are taped, often before a live audience. See the boxed text, p539, for ticketing information, or drop by the **CBS ticket office** (🕑 9am-5pm Mon-Fri) or the farmers market office (near the clock tower on the market's north side) for free tickets.

LOS ANGELES COUNTY MUSEUM OF ART

Huge, compelling and global, **LACMA** (Map pp516-17; ☎ 323-857-6000; www.lacma.org; 5905 Wilshire Blvd; adult/child under 17yr/student/senior $12/free/8/8, 'pay what you wish' after 5pm, free 2nd Tue each month; 🕑 noon-8pm Mon, Tue & Thu, to 9pm Fri, 11am-8pm Sat & Sun) is one of the country's top art museums and the largest in the western US. A major revamp masterminded by Renzo Piano and completed in 2008 brought a new entry pavilion and the three-story **Broad Contemporary Art Museum** (B-CAM to its friends), which presents part of the personal collection of local real-estate developer/philanthropist Eli Broad and his wife Edythe, including seminal pieces by Jeff Koons, Roy Lichtenstein and Andy Warhol and two gigantic works in rusted steel by Richard Serra on the ground floor.

The rest of the museum brims with several millennia worth of paintings, sculpture and decorative arts from around the world. Feast your eyes on works by Rembrandt, Cézanne or Magritte; marvel at ancient pottery from China, Turkey or Iran; and see photographs by Ansel Adams or Henri Cartier-Bresson. The jewel box of a Japanese pavilion is another LACMA standout, and there are often headline-grabbing touring exhibits. Check the museum's website or the listings magazines (p561) for film screenings, concerts and guided tours. Parking is $7.

LA BREA TAR PITS & PAGE MUSEUM

Between 40,000 and 10,000 years ago, saber-toothed cats, mammoths, dire wolves and other extinct critters prowled the land that is now LA. If you've seen *Ice Age,* this cast of characters may sound familiar, and here you can see where they met their maker after becoming trapped in gooey crude oil bubbling up from deep below what's now Wilshire Blvd. It all makes the La Brea Tar Pits one of the world's most fecund and famous fossil sites. Fossils are on display at the **Page Museum** (Map pp516-17; ☎ 323-934-7243; www.tarpits.org; 5801 Wilshire Blvd; adult/child 5-12yr/student/senior $7/2/4.50/4.50, free 1st Tue each month; 🕑 9:30am-5pm Mon-Fri, 10am-5pm Sat & Sun; 🚸). Parking is $6.

PETERSEN AUTOMOTIVE MUSEUM

LA's love affair with the automobile is celebrated at this fun **museum** (Map pp516-17; ☎ 323-930-2277; www.petersen.org; 6060 Wilshire Blvd; adult/child/student/senior $10/3/5/5; 🕑 10am-6pm Tue-Sun; 🅿 🚸). Even pedestrians will enjoy the walk-through LA streetscape that reveals the city as the birthplace of gas stations, billboards, strip malls, drive-in restaurants and drive-in movie theaters. Upstairs it's cars galore, from vintage wheels to hot rods, presented in changing exhibits. On the 3rd floor, a 'Discovery Center' playfully teaches kids about science by way of the automobile. Parking is $8.

Beverly Hills & Westside

The mere mention of Beverly Hills conjures up images of fame and wealth, reinforced ad nauseam by film and TV. Fact is, the reality is not so different from the myth. Stylish and sophisticated, this city is indeed where the well-heeled frolic. Opulent mansions flank manicured grounds on palm-lined avenues, especially north of **Sunset Blvd**, while legendary **Rodeo Drive** is three solid blocks of style for the Prada and Gucci brigade.

All that said, these days Beverly Hills' wealth is actually mostly new-money, brought here by immigrants from Iran who've been settling here since the fall of the Shah some 30 years ago. About 25% of the 35,000 residents are of Iranian descent, which has spawned the moniker 'Tehrangeles.' In March 2007 the city elected its first Iranian-born mayor, Jimmy Delshad.

If you're into stargazing, you can follow the little tour in this book (see the boxed text, p534), take a guided bus tour (p545) or hope to spy a famous face at such hot spots as Spago (p557) or Nate 'n Al's (p556).

Several city-owned parking lots and garages, including the one at 9510 Brighton Way near Rodeo Dr, offer two hours of free parking.

West of Beverly Hills to the Santa Monica city line, the well-to-do LA neighborhoods Brentwood and Bel Air, as well as Westwood, home of UCLA, and the separate city Culver City, are collectively referred to as the

STAR STRUCK: LONELY PLANET'S GUIDE TO THE STARS' HOMES *Andrea Schulte-Peevers*

Star-chasing isn't usually our style, but even we admit that visiting LA just wouldn't be the same without any celestial navigation. So here's our own gossipy tour of the stars' homes, custom-made just for you (Map pp518–19). Expect plenty of tall hedges and security cameras, and don't trespass. This trip will allow you to indulge your inner paparazzo in about 60 minutes, 90 minutes tops.

Rev up your engine and head to the Sunset Strip, then climb up Kings Rd to No 1467 and get ready to be a 'Paris-ite.' Yup, this is where everybody's favorite ex-jailbird, **Paris Hilton**, leads her 'simple life.' From the street at least, the house is surprisingly modest and almost as beige and bland as the hotel chain she'll one day inherit.

Double back down to Sunset, turn right and right again on Doheny Dr, where **Halle Berry** is having a 'Monster's Ball' at No 1164, previously owned by *Malcolm in the Middle* star Frankie Muniz. All you can see through the tall Old Mexico gate are some parked cars and flowers. Berry's almost next-door neighbor **Winona Ryder** hides behind a tall, thick hedge at No 1320, but perhaps some paparazzi have snipped a hole in the foliage so you can at least see her front yard.

Up, up and up you continue on Doheny, into the 'bird streets.' Hook a right on Oriole Dr and a left on Oriole Way. From this hilltop perch **Leonardo DiCaprio** must feel quite literally like the 'king of the world' at his modernist pad at No 9045. It's the one at the end of the cul-de-sac, but only the top portion is visible. Leo also owns the adjacent lot but got sued in 2007 for allegedly infringing upon a neighbor's property when building a basketball court for himself.

Backtrack to Oriole Dr, then turn right on Thrasher Ave. On your right, at No 9000 just before the road veers to the left, is the 1962 concrete cube that DiCaprio buddy **Tobey Maguire** unloaded for a cool $10.8 million in May 2007, more than triple what he paid for it back in 2002. Nice move, Spidey! **Megan Mullally** (Karen on *Will & Grace*) lives right next door; **Keanu Reeves** is behind the metal fence and marble portal of No 9024; and **Courtney Love** used to live at No 8936.

Back down to Sunset you go, then it's right on Doheny Rd. See that big white residential high-rise? That's the celeb-studded Sierra Towers (9255 Doheny Rd), where **Matthew Perry** owns a

Westside. For tours of Sony Pictures Studios in Culver City, see the boxed text, p529.

PALEY CENTER FOR MEDIA

Fancy watching the pilot of *Bonanza* or *Star Trek*? How about the moon landing? Or maybe the pilot of *Ugly Betty*? These and thousands more classic broadcasts dating back to 1918 are only a mouse click away in this sparkling **radio and television museum** (Map pp518-19; ☎ 310-786-1000; www.mtr.org; 465 N Beverly Dr; suggested donation adult/child/student/senior $10/5/8/8; ⏰ noon-5pm Wed-Sun), formerly the Museum of Television and Radio. View or listen to your selections while seated at private consoles. The museum also presents daily screenings in its auditorium, seminars and the occasional live broadcast. Pick up a schedule at the information desk or call ☎ 310-786-1025.

MUSEUM OF TOLERANCE

This **museum** (Map pp518-19; ☎ 310-553-8403; www.museumoftolerance.com; 9786 W Pico Blvd; adult/child/student/senior $13/10/11/11; ⏰ 11am-6:30pm Mon-Thu, to 3:30pm Fri, to 7:30pm Sun; Ⓟ) uses interactive technology to make visitors confront racism and bigotry. It's quite effective. Given that the museum is at the Simon Wiesenthal Center, named for the famous Nazi-hunter, there's a particular focus on the Nazi Holocaust, and as such it may not be appropriate for children under 12. Last entry is 2½ hours before closing.

A separate exhibit called 'Finding Our Families, Finding Ourselves' (appropriate for all ages) explores what it means to be an American and follows the personal histories of several celebrities, including musician Carlos Santana, poet Maya Angelou, skater Michelle Kwan and Dodgers' manager Joe Torre.

UNIVERSITY OF CALIFORNIA, LOS ANGELES

Westwood is practically synonymous with **UCLA** (Map pp518-19; ☎ 310-825-4321, tour reservations 310-825-8764; www.ucla.edu; 405 Hilgard Ave), the alma mater of Francis Ford Coppola, James Dean, Jim Morrison and several Nobel Prize laureates. Free student-led tours are offered at 10:30am and 1:30pm Monday to Friday (reservations required), although tours are not required to visit the campus.

condo on the 22nd floor and **Elton John** shelled out about $2.5 million for his unit two floors below. Views from up there are also enjoyed by **Cher** but no longer by **Lindsay Lohan**, who sold hers in 2007.

Turn right on Hillcrest Rd to catch a glimpse of **Jennifer Aniston**'s home at the end of the driveway at No 1004. We're not sure, but we think it's one of those places up on the hill. We do know that it's a six-bedroom 1970s house designed by modernist architect Hal Levitt, famous for gray and black marble floors, and that she snapped it up for a measly $13.5 million.

When Jen gets lonely, she has only a short walk to BFF **Courteney Cox** and her hubby **David Arquette**, who are at 1012 Wallace Ridge. You can get there by doubling back on Hillcrest, turning right on Drury Lane, right again on Loma Vista Dr and again right on Wallace Ridge. It's the first house on the right, with the velvety grass and the palm trees.

Turn around, go left on Doheny, right on Sierra Dr, right on Sunset and left on Hillcrest Rd where you can get a good look at **Larry King**'s house at No 707. From here it's right on Elevado Ave, right again on Palm Dr where America's most (in)famous Brit, **Simon Cowell**, paid $8 million to live at No 717. See those trees and the big hedge north across Sunset? Somewhere behind there is **Madonna**'s shack (9425 Sunset Blvd). The lady sure values her privacy.

And so do **Tom Cruise** and **Katie Holmes**, who forked over $30.5 million for a giant mansion at 1111 Calle Vista Dr. To get there, turn left on Sunset, right on Foothill Rd (which becomes Doheny Rd), then left on Calle Vista and it's the second compound on your left. The house itself is at the end of a long driveway and there's just a black iron gate to gawk at. It's a 13,000-sq-ft mansion with seven bedrooms, nine bathrooms and a pool; use your imagination. Then go back to Sunset, right and right again on Alpine Dr, where the Cruises used to make do with the mega-shack at No 918. Not much to see there either.

OK, last chance to snap pictures, and it's a good one. You can see plenty of **Dr Phil**'s pretty Mediterranean-style villa at 1008 Lexington Rd. It has a tiled roof, lots of flowers, a Rapunzel tower and, at about 11,000 sq ft, is a lot bigger than it looks. That's it – show's over.

The **UCLA Fowler Museum of Cultural History** (Map pp518-19; ☎ 310-825-4361; www.fowler.ucla.edu; admission free; ⏰ noon-5pm Wed & Fri-Sun, noon-8pm Thu) presents a rich variety of arts, crafts and artifacts from non-Western cultures. Garden retreats include the sprawling **Franklin D Murphy Sculpture Garden**, which has dozens of works by Rodin, Moore, Calder and other American and European artists; the tranquil **Mildred E Mathias Botanical Garden** (Map pp518–19); and also the secluded **UCLA Hannah Carter Japanese Garden** (Map pp518-19; ☎ 310-825-4574; www.japanesegarden.ucla.edu; 10619 Bellagio Rd; admission free; ⏰ 10am-3pm Tue, Wed & Fri, reservations required).

UCLA HAMMER MUSEUM

South of the campus, in Westwood Village, this museum started as a mere vanity project for its main benefactor, the late oil tycoon Armand Hammer (1898–1990), but has since graduated to an increasingly well-respected contemporary and avant-garde art **museum** (Map pp518-19; ☎ 310-443-7000; www.hammer.ucla.edu; 10899 Wilshire Blvd; adult/child/student/senior $5/free/free/3, Thu free; ⏰ 11am-7pm Tue, Wed, Fri & Sat, to 9pm Thu, to 5pm Sun; Ⓟ). A selection from Hammer's collection of impressionists, postimpressionists and Old Masters is usually on view alongside changing exhibitions. There's also a nice courtyard café.

PIERCE BROS WESTWOOD MEMORIAL PARK

This small and star-studded **cemetery** (Map pp518-19; ☎ 310-474-1570; 1218 Glendon Ave; admission free; ⏰ 8am-sunset) is a bit hard to find – from Wilshire Blvd, turn south onto Glendon Ave and look for the driveway immediately to your left. Marilyn Monroe is buried in an above-ground crypt next to an empty one reserved for Playboy owner Hugh Hefner. She's in good company for also planted here (in the ground) are Natalie Wood, Burt Lancaster, Walter Matthau, Jack Lemmon, Roy Orbison and numerous other film and music legends.

SAWTELLE BLVD

Can't make it all the way to Little Tokyo? The smaller Japanese neighborhood around Sawtelle Blvd (off Map pp518–19), between Olympic and Santa Monica Blvds and just west of I-405, is sometimes called **Little Osaka**, after Japan's second city. It's easy to spend an hour or two browsing shops selling *manga,* Japanese trinkets and housewares, going 'hmm?' in the groceries and, of course, enjoying the restaurants (see p556). The largest concentration is within a few blocks north of Olympic Blvd; there's street and lot parking available.

GETTY CENTER

In the Santa Monica Mountains, high above the 405 Fwy, the billion-dollar **Getty Center** (off Map pp518-19; ☎ 310-440-7300; www.getty.edu; 1200 Getty Center Dr; admission free; 10am-6pm Tue-Thu & Sun, to 9pm Fri & Sat;) presents triple delights: a stellar art collection (Renaissance to David Hockney), the cutting-edge architecture of Richard Meier and the visual splendor of the seasonally changing gardens by Robert Irwin. On clear days, you can add breathtaking views of the city and ocean to the list. Even getting up to the 110-acre 'campus' aboard a driverless tram is fun.

The paintings collection is strongest when it comes to pre-20th-century Europeans, including famous canvases by Van Gogh, Monet, Rembrandt and Titian. Tours, lectures and interactive technology, including audioguides ($5), make the art accessible to all. Visit in the late afternoon after the crowds have thinned, and you can watch the sunset while enjoying a picnic or a snack from a kiosk or the self-service café. Also check the Getty's cultural events calendar, which includes fabulous concerts, lectures and films (all free).

Metro bus 761 stops at the Getty. If arriving by car, parking is $10.

SKIRBALL CULTURAL CENTER

Although the focus of this large facility in the Sepulveda Pass is on the Jewish experience, the **Skirball** (off Map pp518-19; ☎ 310-440-4500, tickets 877-722-4849; www.skirball.org; 2701 N Sepulveda Blvd; adult/child 2-12yr/student/senior $10/5/7/7, Thu free; noon-5pm Tue, Wed & Fri, to 9pm Thu, 10am-5pm Sat & Sun, closed major Jewish holidays; P) has something for people of any or no creed.

The preschool set can board the gigantic wooden **Noah's Ark** by noted architect Moshe Safdie, an indoor playground inhabited by imaginative creatures made from car mats, couch springs, metal strainers and other recycled items. Entry to Noah's Ark is by timed tickets which also cover museum admission; advance reservations are recommended, especially during school holidays. Allow 60 to 90 minutes to see it.

Grown-ups will gravitate to the permanent exhibit, an engagingly presented view of 4000 years of history, traditions, trials and triumphs of the Jewish people. There are exhibits on Jewish holidays, a replica mosaic floor from an ancient Galilee synagogue and a copy of Hitler's racist rant *Mein Kampf.*

A busy event schedule features celebrities, Hollywood moguls and thinkers in panel discussions, lectures, readings and performances. Big crowds also turn out for the free outdoor world music summer concert series. Zeidler's Café (mains $6 to $10) serves tasty, kosher (meatless) California fare.

Malibu

Although the drive out doesn't look terribly posh, Malibu has been synonymous with celebrities since the early 1930s, when money troubles forced landowner May Rindge to lease out property to her Hollywood friends. Clara Bow and Barbara Stanwyck were the first to stake out their turf in what became known as the **Malibu Colony** (Map pp510–11). Privacy-seeking celebs, including Tom Hanks and Barbra Streisand, Leo, Britney and Jennifer, still own or rent homes in this gated, well-policed neighborhood.

What's the attraction? The spectacular 27-mile stretch of the Pacific Coast Hwy, where the Santa Monica Mountains plunge into the ocean. There are some fine beaches, including **Las Tunas**, **Point Dume**, **Zuma** and **Surfrider**, the last a world-famous surf spot. Rising behind Malibu is **Malibu Creek State Park**, part of the Santa Monica Mountains National Recreation Area and laced with hiking trails (see p543). For good bird's-eye views, head a little up the coast to **Malibu Bluffs Park** (Map pp510–11).

Malibu has no real center, but you'll find the greatest concentration of restaurants and shops near the century-old **Malibu Pier** (Map pp510–11). The most likely star-spotting venue is the villagelike shopping center **Malibu Country Mart** (Map pp510-11; 3835 Cross Creek Rd).

Malibu's star cultural attraction is the **Getty Villa** (Map pp510-11; ☎ 310-440-7300; www.getty.edu; 17985 Pacific Coast Hwy; admission free; 10am-5pm Thu-Mon), which reopened in 2006 following a massive eight-year revamp. The complex showcases the Getty's precious Greek, Roman and Etruscan antiquities, centered around a stunning replica of the Roman Villa dei Papiri, with views down to the ocean. The rest of the Getty's collection can be seen at the hilltop Getty Center (left).

Admission is by timed ticket, available online or by phone. Parking is $10.

Other Malibu cultural sights include the **Adamson House** (Map pp510-11; ☎ 310-456-8432; www.adamsonhouse.org; 23200 Pacific Coast Hwy; adult/child $5/2; 11am-3pm Wed-Sat), a beautiful Spanish-Moorish villa lavishly decorated with locally made hand-painted tiles (last admission is 2pm). The grounds also house the **Malibu Lagoon Museum** (admission free; 11am-3pm Wed-Sat), which covers local history.

Santa Monica

Seaside Santa Monica is one of the most agreeable cities in LA, with a century-old pier, pedestrian-friendly downtown, miles of wide, sandy beaches and excellent shopping and dining. Once quaint and slightly wacky, it has evolved into a manicured beach town with cosmopolitan flair and famously lefty politics. For visitors, Santa Monica is a central, safe and fun base for exploring LA. Stop by either the visitors center or kiosk (see p523) for maps and information. Parking is free for two hours at several downtown public parking garages on 2nd and 4th Sts between Broadway and Wilshire Blvd ($3 after 6pm).

The city's most recognizable landmark is the **Santa Monica Pier** (Map pp520-1; ☎ 310-458-8900; www.santamonicapier.org; admission free, unlimited rides under/over 42in tall $11/22; 24hr;), the oldest amusement pier in California (1908). It has plenty of kid-friendly diversions, including a historic **carousel** (it appeared in the movie *The Sting*) and the small **Pacific Park** amusement park with a solar-powered Ferris wheel, a quaint roller coaster and other rides each costing between $2.50 and $5 without an unlimited ride pass.

Below the pier, the local environmental organization Heal the Bay runs the small **Santa Monica Pier Aquarium** (Map pp520-1; ☎ 310-393-6149; admission by donation, suggested/minimum $5/2, child under 12yr free; 2-6pm Tue-Fri, 12:30-6pm Sat & Sun). Kids can have close encounters with jellyfish, small sharks and other critters residing in Santa Monica Bay.

Meandering right by the pier is the **South Bay Bicycle Trail** (p543), a paved bicycle and walking path. Bike or in-line skate rentals are available on the pier and at beachside kiosks.

A couple of blocks inland, the car-free **Third Street Promenade** – located between Wilshire Blvd and Broadway – is a great place for a stroll, a bite, a movie, a shopping spree and lots of free street entertainment, from balalaika-strumming hipsters to hip-hop dancers.

Fans of avant-garde art should continue inland for about 2.5 miles to the **Bergamot Station Arts Center** (Map pp520-1; 2525 Michigan Ave, enter from Cloverfield Blvd; 10am-6pm Tue-Sat; P), home to more than 30 galleries, shops, a café and the progressive **Santa Monica Museum of Art** (Map pp520-1; ☎ 310-586-6488; www.smmoa.org; admission by donation; 11am-6pm Tue-Sat).

Other Santa Monica neighborhoods suitable for strolling, shopping and dining are the chichi shopping enclave of **Montana Ave** in the city's northern section and **Main St** on the southern end of town, near the border with Venice. Main St is connected to Downtown by the electric Tide Shuttle (50¢ per ride).

Venice

If aliens landed on Venice's famous **Ocean Front Walk** (Map pp520-1; Venice Pier to Rose Ave; 24hr), they'd probably blend right into the human zoo of wannabe Schwarzeneggers, Speedo-clad 'snake man' and roller-skating Sikh minstrel. Known locally as Venice Boardwalk, this is the place to get your hair braided, skin tattooed or aura adjusted. It's a freak show that must be seen to be believed, preferably on a hot summer's weekend when the scene is at its most surreal, though the Boardwalk takes on a less savory character after dusk.

Venice was created in 1905 by eccentric tobacco heir Abbot Kinney as an amusement park, called 'Venice of America,' complete with a Ferris wheel, water ride and Italian *gondolieri* who poled visitors around canals. Most of the waterways vanished beneath roads later on, but some have been restored and are now flanked by flower-festooned villas. The **Venice Canal Walk** threads through this idyllic neighborhood, easily accessed from either Venice or Washington Blvds.

Kinney may have been a little kooky but he unwittingly set the trend for 20th-century Venice, California. Counterculture royalty such as beatniks Lawrence Lipton and Stuart Perkoff and uberhippie Jim Morrison made their homes here at one time. Today, Venice is still a cauldron of creativity, peopled by karmically correct new-agers, eternal hippies, cool-conscious musicians and even a few celebs, including Dennis Hopper, Anjelica Huston, Mira Sorvino and Julia Roberts.

Galleries, studios and public art abound, much of it with a predictably bizarre bent.

Cases in point: Jonathan Borofsky's tutu-clad **Ballerina Clown** (Map pp520-1; Rose Ave & Main St) and Frank Gehry's **Chiat/Day Building** (Map pp520-1; 340 Main St), fronted by a three-story-tall pair of binoculars, and now occupied by the effects house Digital Domain.

A fun place for a stroll is the mile-long stretch of **Abbot Kinney Blvd** between Venice Blvd and Main St. It's chockablock with boutiques, galleries, bars and restaurants.

South Bay & Palos Verdes

South of LAX, Santa Monica Bay is lined by a trio of all-American beach towns – **Manhattan Beach**, **Hermosa Beach** and **Redondo Beach** – with a distinctive laid-back vibe. Pricey, if not lavish, homes come all the way down to the gorgeous white beach, which is the prime attraction here and paralleled by the **South Bay Bicycle Trail** (p543).

The beaches run straight into the **Palos Verdes Peninsula**, a rocky precipice that's home to some of the richest and most exclusive communities in the LA area. A drive along Palos Verdes Dr takes you along some spectacular rugged coastline with sublime views of the ocean and Catalina Island. A worthwhile stop is at the 1949 **Wayfarers Chapel** (Map pp510-11; ☎ 310-377-1650; www.wayfarerschapel.org; 5755 Palos Verdes Dr S; admission free; 8am-5pm), an enchanting modernist hillside structure surrounded by mature redwood trees and gardens. The work of Lloyd Wright (Frank's son), it is almost entirely made of glass and is one of LA's most popular spots for weddings.

San Pedro

San Pedro is a slow-paced harbor community on the edge of Worldport LA, the third-busiest container port after Singapore and Hong Kong. Nearly all the local sights are along the waterfront and served by the electric Red Car trolley from Friday to Monday (all-day fare $1).

For a salty introduction to the region, visit the **Los Angeles Maritime Museum** (Map pp510-11; ☎ 310-548-7618; www.lamaritimemuseum.org; Berth 84; adult/child/senior $3/1/1; 10am-5pm Tue-Sat, noon-5pm Sun), which tells the story of the city's relationship with the sea and displays some great ship models, figureheads and navigational equipment. If you like to clamber around old ships, head a mile north to **SS Lane Victory** (Map pp510-11; ☎ 310-519-9545; www.lanevictory.org; Berth 94; adult/child $3/1; 9am-3pm), an immaculately restored WWII-era cargo ship. Just south of the Maritime Museum is the touristy village of **Ports O' Call**, where you can grab a bite, hop on a port cruise or join a whale-watching trip.

A short drive south takes you to the **Cabrillo Marine Aquarium** (Map pp510-11; ☎ 310-548-7562; www.cabrilloaq.org; 3720 Stephen White Dr; admission by donation, suggested adult/child $5/1; noon-5pm Tue-Fri, 10am-5pm Sat & Sun), home to a parade of local oceanic denizens.

Long Beach

Long Beach, on the border with Orange County, has come a long way from its working-class oil and navy days, but gentrification hasn't completely spoiled its relaxed, small-town atmosphere. Much of the action in its compact downtown centers on southern **Pine Ave**, bubbling with restaurants, nightclubs and bars. About 3 miles east of here are the upscale neighborhoods of Belmont Shore and canal-laced Naples, which can be explored via hour-long cruises aboard authentic gondolas with **Gondo Getaway** (Map pp510-11; ☎ 562-433-9595; www.gondo.net; 5437 E Ocean Blvd; per couple $75, each additional person $20), carrying up to six passengers.

Downtown Long Beach is the southern terminus of the Metro Blue Line. A shuttle service, called **Passport** (90¢, free within Downtown), serves all major places of interest on four routes. A **Long Beach Visitor Information Kiosk** (Map pp510-11; ☎ 562-436-3645, 800-452-7829; www.visitlongbeach.com; 10am-5pm Jun-Sep, to 4pm Fri-Sun Oct-May) is right outside the Aquarium of the Pacific.

AQUARIUM OF THE PACIFIC & AROUND

One of the largest watery zoos in the country, the **Aquarium of the Pacific** (Map pp510-11; ☎ 562-590-3100; www.aquariumofpacific.org; 100 Aquarium Way; adult/child/senior $21/12/16; 9am-6pm;) is a joyful, high-tech romp through an intriguing underwater world. Its 12,500 creatures hail from tepid Baja California, the frigid northern Pacific, the coral reefs of the tropics and the kelp forests in local waters. You can pet small sharks, observe the antics of sea otters or be charmed by drifting sea dragons. Parking is $7.

At the nearby **Pike at Rainbow Harbor** development, diversions include an antique carousel, a fancy multiplex movie theater, a GameWorks arcade and chain restaurants galore. Further east is **Shoreline Village**, another shopping-and-dining complex.

YOUR 15 MINUTES OF FAME

Come on, haven't you always dreamed of seeing your silly mug on TV? Well, LA has a way of making dreams come true, but you have to do your homework before coming to town. Here are some leads to get you started.

Sitcoms and game shows usually tape between August and March before live audiences. To nab free tickets, check with **TV Tickets** (www.tvtix.com) or **Audiences Unlimited** (☎ 818-753-3470; www.tvtickets.com). The latter also has a booth in the Entertainment Center at Universal Studios Hollywood (below). For tickets to the *Tonight Show* at **NBC Studios** (Map p522; ☎ 818-840-3537; 3000 W Alameda Ave, Burbank), call or check www.nbc.com/nbc/footer/Tickets.shtml. Tickets may also be available to *Jimmy Kimmel Live,* which conveniently tapes at the **El Capitan Entertainment Center** (Map pp514-15; ☎ 800-866-5466 or www.1iota.com; 6840 Hollywood Blvd, Hollywood). If you don't have tickets, you may still be able to sneak in just before the 6pm taping. Just ask one of the ushers outside the theater (if they don't ask you first!). Most shows have a minimum age of 18.

Although many game shows tape in LA, the chances of actually becoming a contestant are greatest on *The Price is Right,* at **CBS** (Map pp516-17; ☎ 323-575-2624; 7800 Beverly Blvd, Mid-City). Check www.cbs.com/daytime/price for ticket details.

QUEEN MARY

Long Beach's flagship attraction is this elegant – and supposedly haunted – British **ocean liner** (Map pp510-11; ☎ 562-435-3511; www.queenmary.com; 1126 Queens Hwy; adult/child/senior $25/13/22; ⏰ 10am-6pm). Larger and more luxurious than even the *Titanic,* the *Queen Mary* transported royals, dignitaries, immigrants and troops during its 1001 Atlantic crossings between 1936 and 1964. In Long Beach since 1967, it is now a hotel and tourist attraction. Parking is $12.

The basic admission includes a self-guided tour covering 12 (!) decks, as well as the half-hour, tongue-in-cheek 'Ghosts and Legends' special-effects tour. Other tours are available.

Moored next to the *Queen Mary* is the **Scorpion** (adult/child/senior $11/10/10), an authentic Soviet submarine where you can clamber around the claustrophobic interior.

MUSEUMS

In Long Beach's fledgling East Village Arts District, the **Museum of Latin American Art** (Map pp510-11; ☎ 562-437-1689; www.molaa.org; 628 Alamitos Ave; adult/child/student/senior $7.50/free/5/5, Fri free; ⏰ 11:30am-7pm Tue-Fri, 11am-7pm Sat, 11am-6pm Sun) is the only museum in the western USA to exclusively showcase contemporary Latin American art, and it's quietly become one of the best in California. The permanent collection highlights spirituality and landscapes, and there are often first-rate special exhibits.

Sitting pretty on a waterfront bluff, the **Long Beach Museum of Art** (Map pp510-11; ☎ 562-439-2119; www.lbma.org; 2300 E Ocean Blvd; adult/child/student/senior $7/free/6/6, Fri free; ⏰ 11am-5pm Tue, Wed & Fri-Sun, to 8pm Thu) presents changing exhibitions mostly drawn from its collection of American decorative arts, California modernism, contemporary art (including video) and early-20th-century European art.

San Fernando Valley

The sprawling grid of suburbia known simply as 'the Valley' is home to most of the major movie studios, which makes it prime hunting grounds for 'industry' fans. It's also the world capital of the porn movie industry (sorry, studio tours not available). Car culture was basically invented here, and the Valley takes credit for giving birth not only to the mini-mall but also to the drive-in movie theater, the drive-in bank and, of course, the drive-in restaurant. More recently, an arts district in North Hollywood (NoHo) has given the Valley a hip, artsy side.

Note that temperatures here are often 15–20°F higher – and pollution levels worse – than in areas further south.

UNIVERSAL STUDIOS HOLLYWOOD & CITY WALK

One of the world's oldest continuously operating movie studios, Universal Studios Hollywood also operates this **theme park** (Map p522; ☎ 818-622-3801; www.universalstudioshollywood.com; 100 Universal City Plaza, Universal City; admission over/under 48in $67/57), with an entertaining mix of movie-themed rides and high-octane live action shows. If you're more interested in a serious studio tour, see the boxed text, p529.

AS SEEN ON TV

If driving through LA gives you a sense of déjà vu, chances are your eyes are not deceiving you. Here are some locations featured in the movies and on TV.

Remember, though, that these are private homes, so show proper respect and *never* disturb the residents.

- Elliot's house from *ET* – 7121 Lonzo St, Burbank (Map pp510–11)
- The *Brady Bunch* home – 11222 Dilling St, North Hollywood (Map p522)
- Doc Brown's house from *Back to the Future* – Gamble House, Pasadena (p542)
- Home of Steve Martin and family in *Father of the Bride* – 843 S El Molino Ave, Pasadena (Map pp510–11)
- *Melrose Place* apartment building – 4616 Greenwood Pl, Los Feliz
- *Six Feet Under* funeral home – on Wilton Ave, just south of Wilshire Blvd, Hollywood (pp516–17)
- Andy's apartment building in *The 40-Year-Old Virgin* – on Moorpark just east of Laurel Canyon in Studio City (Map pp510–11)

Try to budget a full day, especially in summer, as lines can easily take 45 minutes for top attractions. To beat the crowds, get there before the gates open or invest in the Front of Line Pass ($139) or the deluxe guided VIP Experience ($199). Some rides have minimum height requirements and most are not suitable for preschoolers if they're easily spooked.

First-timers should head straight for the 45-minute narrated **Studio Tour** aboard a rickety tram that takes you past working soundstages to outdoor sets used in *Jurassic Park, Psycho* and *King Kong,* as well as working sets like *Desperate Housewives,* when there's no filming. Also prepare to visit *The Mummy*'s tunnel, and survive a shark attack and an 8.3-magnitude earthquake. It's hokey but fun and a favorite of generations of visitors.

Of Universal's thrill rides, top billing goes to the new **Simpsons Ride**, a bang-you-over-the-head and rather twisted motion-simulated romp 'designed' by Krusty the Klown. **Jurassic Park** is a gentle float through a prehistoric jungle with a rather 'raptor-ous' ending – staff ratchets up the water levels in summer, and you can expect to get drenched here. **Revenge of the Mummy** has 'em screaming on an indoor roller coaster through 'Imhotep's Tomb' that at one point has you going backwards. The **Adventures of Curious George** is tailored to the younger set, with dozens of ways to splash in the water (bring a change of clothes) and a rather cool 'ball room.'

Of the live shows, the **Special Effects Stages** give you the studio's best glimpse into real movie-making (including green-screening, sound and creatures), and the **Animal Actors Stage** showcases Hollywood's furriest luminaries. The movie may have bombed, but the **Water World** show is a runaway hit, with mind-boggling stunts that include giant fireballs and a crash-landing seaplane.

Snack food and drinks are available throughout the park, although there's a lot more choice at the adjacent **Universal City Walk**, an unabashedly commercial (yet also entertaining) fantasy promenade of restaurants, shops, bars and entertainment venues. Get your hand stamped if you'd like to return to the park.

For a thrill ride outside the theme park, **I-Fly** (Map p522; ☎ 818-985-4359; www.iflyhollywood.com; Universal Studios City Walk, Universal City; 1/2 flights $40/60; 🕑 10am-11pm Sun-Thu, 11am-11:30pm Fri & Sat) is a vertical wind tunnel where you can experience the sensation of sky-diving surrounded by gawking passersby at Universal City Walk. After a video introduction to basic techniques and commands, instructors suit you up and guide you to your 'flight.' It ain't cheap, but it's cheaper than a real sky dive.

FOREST LAWN MEMORIAL PARK – GLENDALE

Often cheekily called the 'country club for the dead,' this humongous hillside **cemetery** (Map pp510-11; ☎ 818-241-4151; www.forestlawn.com; 1712 S Glendale Ave, Glendale; admission free; 🕑 8am-6pm late Jun-late Sep, to 5pm late Sep-late Jun) is the final resting place of Clark Gable, Carole Lombard, Jimmy Stewart, Walt Disney and numerous other Hollywood legends, though many celebrity gravesites are off limits and staff discourage star-seeking. Still, it's worth a visit for the repro art about the grounds, including Michelangelo's *David* and a stained-glass rendition of Da Vinci's *Last Supper*. Despite the obvious kitsch factor, a visit here is fascinating, if only to catch a glimpse of the death culture so powerfully satirized in Evelyn Waugh's novel *The Loved One* (1948).

NOHO ARTS DISTRICT

At the end of the Metro Red Line, **North Hollywood** (NoHo) was a down-on-its-heels neighborhood of artists until a public-private redevelopment project decided to capitalize on the strengths of the local population. Now it boasts 21 stage theaters in one square mile, and a burgeoning community of art galleries, restaurants, gyms and vintage clothing stores around them. Most of the theaters are 'Equity waiver houses,' 99 seats or fewer where members (some quite famous) of the Actors' Equity union can perform at below regular wages. Some Broadway producers come here to try out productions before taking them to New York, including the Tony-winning *Big River*, signed and sung by players at Deaf West Theatre, based here (see p564). Visit www.nohoartsdistrict.com to find out what's on.

You might start at the **Academy of Television Arts & Sciences** (Map p522; ☎ 818-754-2000; www.emmys.tv; 5200 Lankershim Blvd, North Hollywood; admission free), where **Hall of Fame Plaza** busts with busts and life-size bronzes of TV legends (Johnny Carson, Bill Cosby, Lucille Ball and more) and a giant, gleaming Emmy award. **Millennium Dance Complex** (Map p522; ☎ 818-753-5081; www.millenniumdancecomplex.com; 5113 Lankershim Blvd, North Hollywood; classes from $15) trains many of the world's top hip-hop dancers and is open to the public. The vintage clothing stores (many with celebrity clients) are on Magnolia Ave east of Lankershim Blvd.

The best times to visit NoHo are late afternoon through early evening, Thursday through Sunday, when the streets are buzzing with activity around the theaters.

MISSION SAN FERNANDO REY DE ESPAÑA

This historic Spanish **mission** (Map pp510-11; ☎ 818-361-0186; 15151 San Fernando Mission Rd, Mission Hills; adult/child/senior $4/3/3; ⌚ 9am-4:30pm) was the second built in the LA area (after the one in San Gabriel, p543). The highlight is the 1822 convent, built with 4ft-thick adobe walls and Romanesque arches. Inside is an elaborate baroque altarpiece from Spain, and a small museum chronicling the mission's history. It's in the far northern Valley, near where I-405 and Hwy 118 meet.

RONALD W REAGAN LIBRARY & MUSEUM

When Ronald Reagan, the country's 40th president, died on June 5, 2004, at age 93, he was buried in the shadow of his **presidential library** (off Map pp510-11; ☎ 800-998-7641; www.reaganlibrary.net; 40 Presidential Dr, Simi Valley; adult/child 13-19yr/senior $7/2/5; ⌚ 10am-5pm) in the western Valley, just across the Ventura county line from LA. Love him or hate him, the exhibits here are fascinating, spanning from his childhood in Dixon, Illinois, through his early days in radio and acting and stint as governor of California, through his presidency (1980–88). Some highlights: re-creations of the Oval Office and the Cabinet Room, gifts from heads of state, a nuclear cruise missile and a graffiti-covered chunk of the Berlin Wall.

Pasadena & San Gabriel Valley

Resting below the lofty San Gabriel Mountains, Pasadena is a genteel city with old-time mansions, superb Arts and Crafts architecture and fine-art museums. Every New Year's Day, it is thrust into the national spotlight during the **Rose Parade** (p545).

The main fun zone is **Old Town Pasadena**, a bustling 20-block shopping and entertainment district in handsomely restored historic Spanish colonial buildings along Colorado Blvd west of Arroyo Pkwy. Pick up information at the **Pasadena Convention & Visitors Bureau** (Map pp510-11; ☎ 626-795-9311, 800-307-7977; www.pasadenacal.com; 171 S Los Robles Ave; ⌚ 8am-5pm Mon-Fri, 10am-4pm Sat).

While Pasadena has an old-money, white-shoe vibe, the suburban communities of the San Gabriel Valley to the east have a distinctly Asian flavor thanks to waves of immigrants, largely from China, in recent decades.

Pasadena and the San Gabriel Valley are served by the Metro Gold Line (p569) from Downtown LA. Pasadena ARTS buses (fare 50¢) plough around the city on seven different routes.

NORTON SIMON MUSEUM

Rodin's *The Thinker* outside this exquisite **museum** (Map pp510-11; ☎ 626-449-6840; www.nortonsimon.org; 411 W Colorado Blvd; adult/child under 18yr & student/senior $8/free/4; ⌚ noon-6pm Wed-Mon, to 9pm Fri; Ⓟ)

is only a mind-teasing overture to the full symphony of art awaiting behind its doors. Norton Simon (1907–93) was an entrepreneur with the Midas touch and a collector with a passion for Western art. He amassed a respectable assortment of all the household names, from Rembrandt to Renoir, Raphael to Van Gogh, Botticelli to Picasso. The basement holds a sampling of Simon's secondary fancy: Indian and Southeast Asian sculpture. Western sculpture graces the gorgeous garden designed in the tradition of Monet's at Giverny, France. Audioguides rent for $3.

GAMBLE HOUSE

A masterpiece of Arts and Crafts architecture, the **Gamble House** (Map pp510-11; ☎ 626-793-3334; www.gamblehouse.org; 4 Westmoreland Pl; adult/child/student/senior $8/free/5/5; ⏲ noon-3pm Thu-Sun; P) was created in 1908 by the style's prime practitioners, Charles and Henry Greene. One-hour tours give you close-ups of the beautiful woodwork, the iridescent stained glass and romantic design features such as outdoor sleeping porches. The house starred as the home of mad scientist Doc Brown (Christopher Lloyd) in the three *Back to the Future* movies.

Other Greene & Greene homes, including **Charles Greene's private residence** (368 Arroyo Tce), line nearby Arroyo Tce and Grand Ave. Pick up a self-guided walking tour pamphlet at the Gamble House bookstore.

ROSE BOWL STADIUM & BROOKSIDE PARK

One of LA's most venerable landmarks, the 1922 **Rose Bowl Stadium** (Map pp510-11; ☎ 626-577-3100; www.rosebowlstadium.com; 1001 Rose Bowl Dr) can seat up to 93,000 spectators and, every New Year's Day, hosts the famed Rose Bowl Game between two top-ranked college football teams. At other times, concerts, special events and a huge monthly **flea market** (see p567) bring in the crowds.

The Rose Bowl is surrounded by **Brookside Park**, a broadening of the Arroyo Seco, a now-dry riverbed that runs from the San Gabriel Mountains to Downtown LA. It's a nice spot for hiking, cycling and picnicking. South of the stadium is the **Kidspace Children's Museum** (see p545), and beyond are the gracefully arched 1913 **Colorado St Bridge** and the former **Vista del Arroyo Hotel** (Map pp510-11; ☎ 626-441-2797; 125 S Grand Ave), a grand 1903 structure that now houses the Ninth Circuit Court of Appeals.

PASADENA CIVIC CENTER AREA

Pasadena's Civic Center, built in the 1920s, is a reflection of the great wealth and civic pride that have governed this city since its early days. Highlights include the Spanish Renaissance–style **City Hall** (Map pp510-11; 100 N Garfield Ave) and the **Central Library** (Map pp510-11; 285 E Walnut St).

A block east, in a Chinese-style mansion, the **Pacific Asia Museum** (Map pp510-11; ☎ 626-449-2742; www.pacificasiamuseum.org; 46 N Los Robles Ave; adult/student/senior $7/5/5; ⏲ 10am-6pm Wed-Sun) showcases five millennia worth of art and artifacts from Asia and the Pacific arranged around a koi pond. Just around the corner is the **Pasadena Museum of California Art** (Map pp510-11; ☎ 626-568-3665; www.pmcaonline.org; 490 E Union St; adult/child/student/senior $6/free/4/4; ⏲ noon-5pm Wed-Sun), where exhibits focus on art, architecture and design created by California artists from 1850 to today.

CALIFORNIA INSTITUTE OF TECHNOLOGY

With 29 Nobel laureates among its faculty or alumni, it's no wonder that **Caltech** (Map pp510-11; ☎ 626-395-6341; www.caltech.edu; 551 S Hill Ave) is regarded with awe in academic circles (yes, Albert Einstein slept here). Free campus tours leave from the **visitors center** (355 S Holliston Ave), which also distributes free self-guided tour maps. Tour hours vary; call for information.

The Caltech-operated **Jet Propulsion Laboratory** (JPL; ☎ 818-354-9314; www.jpl.nasa.gov), NASA's main center for robotic exploration of the solar system, is about 3.5 miles north of here. Click 'Public Services' on the website for information about tours, by appointment.

HUNTINGTON LIBRARY, ART COLLECTIONS AND BOTANICAL GARDENS

Urban LA feels a world away at this rarefied **country estate** (Map pp510-11; ☎ 626-405-2100; www.huntington.org; 1151 Oxford Rd; adult/child/student/senior $15/6/10/12, adult/senior Sat, Sun & Mon holidays $20/15); ⏲ noon-4:30pm Mon & Wed-Fri, 10:30am-4:30pm Sat & Sun early Sep-late May, 10:30am-4:30pm Wed-Mon late May-early Sep; P), which was once owned by railroad tycoon Henry Huntington. Don't miss the Japanese Garden, the Desert Garden and the 1455 Gutenberg Bible in the library. The art gallery focuses mainly on 18th-century British and French paintings, and counts Thomas Gainsborough's famous *Blue Boy* among its most prized possessions. Admission is free the first Thursday of each month, but free tickets must be reserved weeks in advance.

The classic way to cap off a visit to the Huntington is with afternoon tea in the **Rose Garden Tea Room** (☎ reservations 626-683-8131; adult/child $25/12.50). Next door there's a more casual café. Picnicking is not allowed.

HERITAGE SQUARE MUSEUM

Eight Victorian beauties dating from 1865 to 1914 were saved from the wrecking ball in the late 1960s and literally airlifted to this villagelike **outdoor museum** (off Map pp512-13; ☎ 626-449-0193; www.heritagesquare.org; 3800 Homer St; adult/child/senior $10/5/8; 🕑 noon-5pm Fri-Sun Apr-Oct, 11:30am-4:30pm Fri-Sun Nov-Mar), just off the Ave 43 exit of I-110 (Pasadena Fwy). Highlights of the museum include the Italianate **Perry House**, the Queen Anne/Eastlake-style **Hale House** and the quirky Longfellow Hastings **Octagon House**. The grounds are open for self-guided tours. Tours of the interiors run on the hour from noon to 3pm on Saturday and Sunday.

SAN GABRIEL MISSION

About 3 miles southeast of central Pasadena, the city of San Gabriel is home to the fourth **mission** (Map pp510-11; ☎ 626-457-3035; www.sangabrielmission.org; 428 S Mission Dr, San Gabriel; adult/child 6-17yr/senior $5/3/4; 🕑 9am-4:30pm; Ⓟ) in the chain of 21 built in California. It was from here in 1781 that a group of settlers set out to found El Pueblo de Los Angeles (p523), the beginning of LA. The church (1805) is a sturdy stone structure with numerous Spanish-Moorish design accents, a copper baptismal font, an altar made in Mexico City in 1790 and carved statues of saints. Wandering the pretty grounds takes you past the cemetery, original soap and tallow vats, and fountains. The **museum** contains bibles, religious robes and Native American artifacts.

ACTIVITIES

Cycling & In-line Skating

Anyone who's ever watched a tourism story about LA on TV (or the opening of *Three's Company*) knows about skating or riding on the **South Bay Bicycle Trail**. This paved path parallels the beach for 22 miles, from just north of Santa Monica to Torrance, with a detour around the yacht harbor at Marina del Rey. Mountain-bikers will find the **Santa Monica Mountains** a suitably challenging playground. You'll find lots of good information at www.labikepaths.com.

There are numerous bike-rental places throughout town, especially along the beaches. Prices range from about $6 to $10 per hour and $10 to $30 per day (more for high-tech mountain bikes).

Blazing Saddles (Map pp520-1; ☎ 310-393-9778; Santa Monica Pier, Santa Monica)

Hollywood Pro Bicycles (Map pp514-15; ☎ 323-466-5890; www.hollywoodprobicycles.com; 6731 Hollywood Blvd, Hollywood)

Gyms & Yoga

Many midrange and practically all top-end hotels have fitness centers, but try the following for exercise classes or a fully fledged workout:

Crunch (Map pp516-17; ☎ 323-654-4550; www.crunch.com; 8000 W Sunset Blvd, West Hollywood; per day $25; 🕑 5am-11pm Mon-Thu, to 10pm Fri, 8am-8pm Sat & Sun) High-tech gym with cutting-edge classes such as Disco Yoga and Cycle Karaoke.

Gold's Gym (Map pp520-1; ☎ 310-392-6004; www.goldsgym.com; 360 Hampton Dr, Venice; per day/week $20/70; 🕑 4am-midnight Mon-Fri, 5am-11pm Sat & Sun) Pump it up at Ahnold's old gym.

YAS (Map pp520-1; ☎ 310-396-6993; www.go2yas.com; 1101 Abbot Kinney Blvd, Venice; per class $16) YAS stands for 'yoga and spinning' and you can get either or both; the yin and yang of workouts combines 30 minutes of each. There's also yoga for athletes. Hours vary.

Yoga Works (Map pp520-1; ☎ 310-393-5150; www.yogaworks.com; 2215 Main St, Santa Monica; per class $20; 🕑 6am-9pm Mon-Fri, 7am-9pm Sat & Sun) Popular place for doing the plough or sun salutation.

Hiking

LA has a wealth of trails surprisingly close to the city, for instant getaways that may make you forget you're in the nation's second largest metropolis.

For a quick ramble, head to **Griffith Park** (p530) or **Runyon Canyon** (Map pp514-15; www.runyon-canyon.com), both just a hop, skip and jump from frenzied Hollywood Blvd. The latter is a favorite playground of hip and fitness-obsessed locals and their dogs, which roam mostly off-leash. You'll have fine views of the Hollywood Sign, the city and, on clear days, all the way to the beach. Runyon's southern trailhead is at the end of Fuller St, off Franklin Ave.

Runyon Canyon is on the eastern edge of the 150,000-acre **Santa Monica Mountains National Recreation Area** (Map pp510-11; ☎ 805-370-2301; www.nps.gov/samo). This hilly, tree- and chaparral-covered park follows the outline of Santa

TOP FIVE LA BEACHES

- **El Matador** (off Map pp510-11) Small beach hideaway hemmed in by battered rock cliffs and strewn with giant boulders. Wild surf; not suitable for children. Clothing optional (unofficially).
- **Zuma** (off Map pp510-11) Gorgeous 2-mile-long ribbon of sand with good water quality, excellent swimming and body surfing, and lots of tight bodies.
- **Malibu Lagoon/Surfrider** (Map pp510-11) Legendary surf beach with superb swells and extended rides. Water quality is only so-so. The lagoon is great for bird-watching.
- **Santa Monica** (Map pp520-1) Extra-wide, hugely popular beach that's packed on weekends with families escaping the inland heat. Besides sand and ocean, attractions include the Santa Monica Pier (p537) and the paved shoreline path for strolling, in-line skating and cycling.
- **Venice** (Map pp520-1) LA's most outlandish beach thanks to the Venice Boardwalk (p537), with its nonstop parade of friends and freaks. Drum circle in the sand on Sundays.

Monica Bay from just north of Santa Monica all the way north across the Ventura county line to Point Mugu. The 65-mile **Backbone Trail** covers its entire length, but there are many scenic shorter hikes, especially in **Will Rogers State Historic Park** (Map pp510–11), **Topanga State Park** (Map pp510–11) and **Malibu Creek State Park** (Map pp510–11). The latter has a great trail leading to the set of the hit TV series *M*A*S*H,* where an old Jeep and other leftover relics rust serenely in the sunshine. The trailhead is in the park's main parking lot on Malibu Canyon Rd, which is called Las Virgenes Rd if coming from Hwy 101 (Hollywood Fwy). Parking is $8. Malibu Creek also harbors the **Paramount Ranch** (Map pp510-11; ☎ 818-735-0896; Cornell Rd; ⏰ 8am-sunset), a historic movie ranch that has been used in countless features and TV shows. To get there, catch Cornell Rd off Kanan Dume Dr or Mulholland Hwy. For more ideas, consult the Santa Monica Mountains Conservancy (www.lamountains.com).

Horseback Riding

Leave the urban sprawl behind on the forested bridle trails of Griffith Park or Topanga Canyon. All rides are accompanied by an experienced equestrian wrangler. Rates vary, and a 20% tip is customary.

Los Angeles Horseback Riding (Map pp510-11; ☎ 818-591-2032; www.losangeleshorsebackriding.com; 2661 Old Topanga Canyon Rd, Topanga Canyon) Sunset, day and full-moon rides along the Santa Monica Mountains Backbone Trail with fabulous views all around. Western-style only, group size limited to six people, reservations required.

Sunset Ranch Hollywood (Map pp514-15; ☎ 323-469-5450; www.sunsetranchhollywood.com; 3400 Beachwood Dr, Hollywood) Guided tours, including popular Friday-night dinner rides.

Spas

You'll have no problem finding chichi day spas throughout LA – the top hotels all have them – but there are other stand-alone spas that reflect the city's ethnic riches.

In the Russian enclave of eastern West Hollywood, **Voda** (Map pp514-15; ☎ 323-654-4411; www.vodaspa.com; 7700 Santa Monica Blvd, West Hollywood; treatments from $25; ⏰ 9am-midnight Mon-Fri, 7am-midnight Sat & Sun) offers *banyas* as a signature treatment, involving hot-stone saunas and a cold plunge pool. *Platza* involves vigorous massage and whacking with a *venik,* a water-soaked bundle of birch, oak and eucalyptus. Some days are single-sex only, and swimsuits are required on other days.

Natural hot spring baths fed by an artesian well are a feature at **Beverly Hot Springs** (Map pp514-15; ☎ 323-734-7000; www.beverlyhotsprings.com; 308 N Oxford St, Koreatown; admission $30, treatments from $40; ⏰ 9:30am-9pm). The alkaline waters are slick and sheeny, a perfect yang to the yin of treatments such as a take-no-prisoners body scrub – what feels like the bristly sponge from hell invades every surface, nook and crevice, but it feels heaven-sent afterwards. So the place is showing its age; think of it as a trip to a bygone Korea.

Thai **Pho Siam Spa** (Map pp512-13; ☎ 310-652-2250; www.phosiam.com; 1525 Pizarro St, Echo Park; massage from $25; ⏰ 9am-10:30pm Mon-Fri, 8am-5pm Sat, 9am-5pm Sun) walks all over you. Literally. Family-owned, friendly and superclean, Pho Siam specializes in 'no pain, no gain' Thai massage – imagine a sports massage on (herbal) steroids, traditionally performed on mats on the floor.

Swimming & Surfing

LA pretty much defines beach culture, yet many visitors are surprised that the Pacific is generally pretty chilly; in colder months you'll definitely want a wet suit. Water temperatures become tolerable by late spring and peak at about 70°F in August and September. Water quality varies; for updated conditions check the 'Beach Report Card' at www.healthebay.org.

Surfing novices can expect to pay about $70 to $120 for a two-hour private lesson or $40 to $60 for a group lesson, including board and wet suit. Contact these schools for details:

Learn to Surf LA (☎ 310-663-2479; www.learntosurfla.com)

Malibu Long Boards (☎ 310-467-6898; www.malibulongboards.com)

Surf Academy (☎ 310-372-2790; www.surfacademy.org)

LOS ANGELES FOR CHILDREN

LA is a dream vacation for kids. Many museums and attractions have special kid-oriented exhibits, activities and workshops, but the excellent **Kidspace Children's Museum** (Map pp510-11; ☎ 626-449-9144; www.kidspacemuseum.org; 480 N Arroyo Blvd, Pasadena; admission $8; 9:30am-5pm daily Jun-Aug, Tue-Sun Sep-May; P), with hands-on exhibits, outdoor areas and gardens for exploring, is dedicated specifically to the younger set.

Kids love animals, of course, making the sprawling **Los Angeles Zoo** (p531) in family-friendly Griffith Park a sure winner. South of here, dinosaur fans gravitate to the **Natural History Museum of LA County** (p527), while budding scientists can have a field day next door at the **California Science Center** (p527) and inspect an *Ice Age*'s worth of fossils at the **Page Museum near the La Brea Tar Pits** (p533). Fabulously creative animals made of salvaged materials can be found at the Noah's Ark exhibit at the **Skirball Cultural Center** (p536).

Along the coast, the **Santa Monica Pier** (p537) has carnival rides and a small aquarium, but for a full marine immersion head south to the **Aquarium of the Pacific** (p538) in Long Beach, where you can even pet baby sharks. The latter city also has the grand **Queen Mary** (p539), where teens might get a kick out of the ghost tours.

The littlest kids won't get much out of the big amusement parks – and may actually be scared by the rides and effects at Universal and Magic Mountain, but check with the El Capitan Theatre (p562) in Hollywood; if one of Disney's big blockbuster animated films is playing, the screening may well be preceded by a live stage show. The adorable singing and dancing marionettes at **Bob Baker Marionette Theater** (Map pp512-13; ☎ 213-250-9995; www.bobbakermarionettes.com; 1345 W 1st St; tickets $15; 10:30am Tue-Sat, 2:30pm Sat & Sun; P), near Downtown, have enthralled generations of Angelenos (reservations required). A similarly magical experience awaits at **Santa Monica Puppetry Center** (Map pp520-1; ☎ 310-656-0483; www.puppetmagic.com; 1014 Broadway, Santa Monica; tickets $7.50; shows 2pm Wed, Sat & Sun, 10am Tue & Thu).

Many hotels can provide referrals to reliable, qualified babysitter services.

TOURS

Architecture Tours (☎ 323-464-7866; www.architecturetoursla.com; tours from $68) Tool around town taking in styles from Tudor to Gehry.

Esotouric (☎ 323-223-2767; www.esotouric.com; bus tours $58) Literary-minded Angelenos and highbrow hipsters flock to Esotouric's smartly narrated romps through the LA of Charles Bukowski, Raymond Chandler and famous criminals.

Hornblower Cruises (☎ 310-301-6000; www.hornblower.com; cruises $28-75) Brunch, cocktail and dinner cruises depart from Marina del Rey.

Los Angeles Conservancy (☎ 213-623-2489; www.laconservancy.org; tours $10) Thematic walking tours with an architectural focus, mostly in Downtown LA (reservations required).

Neon Cruise (Map pp512-13; ☎ 213-489-9918; www.neonmona.org; 136 W 4th St, Downtown; tours $55) Board an open-top double-decker bus for a glide though the city's vintage neon, sponsored by MONA, the Museum of Neon Art (p525).

Red Line Tours (Map pp514-15; ☎ 323-402-1074; www.redlinetours.com; 6773 Hollywood Blvd, Hollywood; adult/child/student/senior $20/15/18/18) 'Edutaining' walking tours of Hollywood and Downtown using headsets that cut out traffic noise (reservations suggested).

Starline Tours (☎ 323-463-333, 800-959-3131; www.starlinetours.com; tours from $35) Your basic narrated bus tours of the city, stars' homes and theme parks.

FESTIVALS & EVENTS

LA has a packed calendar of annual festivals and special events. We've only got space for the all-time blockbusters. For more ideas download the **LA Festival Calendar** (www.culturela.org); click on 'Events.'

Awards nights such as the Oscars, Grammys or Emmys are always a to-do. While some visitors make a point to go star-gazing, most

GAY & LESBIAN LOS ANGELES

LA has long been one of the country's gayest cities. The *Advocate* magazine, PFLAG (Parents and Friends of Lesbians and Gays) and America's first gay church and synagogue all started here, and today gays and lesbians can be found in just about any segment of society: entertainment, politics, business and actor/waiter/models. When the California Supreme Court legalized same-sex marriage in the state in May 2008, couples married in LA by the thousands, and when voters amended the California constitution six months later to take that right away, Angelenos – gay, straight and otherwise – protested by the thousands.

The rainbow flag flies especially proudly in 'Boystown,' along Santa Monica Blvd in West Hollywood (WeHo). Dozens of high-energy bars, cafés, restaurants, gyms and clubs flank this strip, busy all the time but especially Thursday through Sunday. Most places cater to gay men and a smaller quotient of lesbian or 'mixed' places. Beauty reigns supreme here and the intimidation factor can be high unless you're buff, bronzed and styled…or a 'fag hag.'

Elsewhere, the gay scenes are considerably more laid-back. Silver Lake, LA's original gay enclave, has evolved from largely leather and Levi's to encompass everyone from cute hipsters of all ethnicities to an older contingent. Long Beach also has a significant gay neighborhood, and there's a smattering of gay nightspots in the San Fernando Valley and Venice. For suggestions on nightlife, see the boxed text, p562.

Except for the hard-core places, most of LA's gay venues get their share of opposite-sex and straight visitors; some actually arrive on their own for the utter fabulousness of the venues, abundant eye candy and, for women in gay bars at least, nonthreatening atmosphere. Within the

locals know them as an excuse to stay away from the venues and avoid traffic.

Tournament of Roses Parade (☎ 626-449-4100; www.tournamentofroses.com) Every inch of every float along Pasadena's Colorado Blvd is covered in some sort of plant or seed. The Rose Bowl football game usually follows. January 1.

Pasadena Doo Dah Parade (☎ 626-205-4029; www.pasadenadoodahparade.info) On the Sunday of the Martin Luther King Jr Day holiday weekend (mid-January), this wacky parody of the Rose Parade marches along Colorado Blvd in Pasadena.

Chinese New Year (☎ 213-680-0243, 213-617-0396) Colorful Dragon Parade, plus free entertainment, fireworks, food, games, carnival rides and other traditional revels in the heart of Chinatown during late January or early February.

Toyota Grand Prix of Long Beach (☎ 888-827-7333; www.longbeachgp.com) A week-long auto-racing spectacle in mid-April drawing world-class drivers.

Fiesta Broadway (☎ 310-914-0015; www.fiestabroadway.la) Huge Cinco de Mayo street fair along historic Broadway in Downtown on the last Sunday in April, with performances by Latino stars.

Central Avenue Jazz Festival (www.culturela.org) In late July, this festival celebrates the period from the 1920s to the '50s when Central Ave was a hotbed of West Coast jazz; music, food, arts and crafts.

Sunset Junction Street Fair (☎ 323-661-7771; www.sunsetjunction.org) Late-August street party celebrating Silver Lake's culture and counterculture with grub, libations and edgy bands.

Los Angeles County Fair (☎ 909-623-3111; www.fairplex.com) Carnival rides, livestock exhibits and live country entertainment in Pomona, in eastern LA County, in mid- to late September.

West Hollywood Halloween Carnival (☎ 323-848-6400; www.visitwesthollywood.com) Rambunctious street fair with eccentric, and occasionally X-rated, costumes along Santa Monica Blvd. October 31.

Griffith Park Light Festival (☎ 323-913-4688; www.laparks.org) Walk through this mile-long stretch of various holiday-themed light displays from 5pm to 10pm in December (check ahead for exact nights).

SLEEPING

When picking a neighborhood for your stay in LA, think about what type of experience you want. For beach life, base yourself in Santa Monica or Venice, which are fairly close to LAX, while a stay in posh Beverly Hills is certain to impress folks back home. Urban explorers will find plenty of hot spots and nightlife in West Hollywood and Hollywood; Hollywood also has easy access to the Metro Red Line. Downtown offers history, architecture and transit, and it's increasingly interesting after dark. The San Fernando Valley is well situated for visitors to the studios, while Long Beach is handy for forays to Disneyland and Orange County.

Some bargains notwithstanding, hotel rates in Los Angeles are higher than in other parts gay community this new trend meets with – shall we say – a diversity of opinions, but given the historic discrimination against gays, few are willing to tell others they can't be there.

If nightlife isn't your scene, the gay community has plenty of ways to meet, greet and engage. **Will Rogers Beach** ('Ginger Rogers' to her friends) in Santa Monica is LA's unofficial gay beach. Outdoor activities include the running club **Frontrunners** (www.lafrontrunners.com) and the hiking club **Great Outdoors** (www.greatoutdoorsla.com). **Metropolitan Community Church** (Map pp514-15; ☎ 323-669-3434; www.mccla.org; 4953 Franklin Ave, Hollywood) and the synagogues **Beth Chayim Chadashim** (off Map pp518-19; ☎ 323-931-7023; www.bcc-la.org; 6000 Pico Blvd, Los Angeles) and **Congregation Kol Ami** (Map pp514-15; ☎ 323-606-0996; www.kol-ami.org; 1200 N La Brea Ave, West Hollywood) all cater specifically to the LGBT community.

The **LA Gay & Lesbian Center** (Map pp514-15; ☎ 323-993-7400; www.laglc.org; 1625 Schrader Blvd, Hollywood; 9am-8pm Mon-Fri, to 1pm Sat) is a one-stop service and health agency. Freebie magazines (such as *Frontiers* and *IN Los Angeles*) containing up-to-date listings and news about the community are available in gay and gay-friendly venues around town, and the website www.westhollywood.com has comprehensive listings throughout LA County.

The festival season kicks off in late May with the **Long Beach Pride Celebration** (www.longbeachpride.com), which basically serves as the warm-up for **LA Pride** (www.lapride.org), a three-day festival in mid-June with nonstop partying and a parade down Santa Monica Blvd. A few months later, on **Halloween** (October 31), the same street morphs into a veritable freak show bringing together tens of thousands of fancifully – and often erotically – costumed revelers of all sexual persuasions. For further information for gay and lesbian travelers, see p718.

of California. Expect to pay between $125 and $225 a night for a midrange room. We've listed peak rates, so prices should drop in the low season. The lodging tax is 12% to 14% on top of rates, unless otherwise noted. Parking at many hotels is in the $20 to $30 range; hotels with free parking are noted with P.

Downtown

BUDGET

Ritz Milner Hotel (Map pp512-13; ☎ 213-627-6981, 800-827-0411; www.milner-hotels.com; 813 S Flower St; r incl breakfast $99-119) 'A bed and a bath for a buck and a half' was the advertising slogan of this mini-chain, family-owned since 1918. The tab is still cheap, but don't get delusions of that other 'Ritz.' Still, the entire place has had a fairly recent date with a paint bucket and a designer, so it's definitely a solid, central and safe cheapie choice with a cool retro pub downstairs.

MIDRANGE

Omni Los Angeles Hotel (Map pp512-13; ☎ 213-617-3300, 800-843-6664; www.omnihotels.com; 25 S Olive St; r $110-210) Modern and efficient, the Omni puts you within steps of major Downtown cultural hubs. Rooms are spacious and amenity-laden but can't quite shake that generic business-hotel feel. The rooftop pool, however, is a mighty fine unwinding spot indeed. Weekend rates sometimes drop below $100 (check the website).

Figueroa Hotel (Map pp512-13; ☎ 213-627-8971, 800-421-9092; www.figueroahotel.com; 939 S Figueroa St; r $134-174, ste $195-245; wi-fi) This historic charmer near LA Live welcomes guests with a striking, Spanish-style lobby leading to a relaxing pool and outdoor bar. The Moroccan-themed rooms are nice but not all are equal, so check out a few before picking your favorite.

our pick **Standard Downtown LA** (Map pp512-13; ☎ 213-892-8080; www.standardhotel.com; 550 S Flower St; r from $140; wi-fi) So LA it's almost a cliché, this hotel – cleverly converted from an old office building – goes after the same young, hip and shag-happy crowd as its Sunset Strip sister, Standard Hollywood (p548). Rooms feature platform beds and peek-through showers, and the rooftop pool bar (p560) has one of the city's most intense party scenes.

TOP END

Millennium Biltmore Hotel (Map pp512-13; ☎ 213-624-1011, 800-245-8673; www.thebiltmore.com; 506 S Grand Ave; r $160-360, ste from $460) Drenched in tradition and gold leaf, this palatial hotel has bedded stars, presidents and royalty in modestly sized but gold-and-blue-hued rooms with all the trappings, although some are surprisingly small. The gorgeous art-deco health club takes the work out of workout. There's free wi-fi in the lobby.

Hollywood

BUDGET

USA Hostels – Hollywood (Map pp514-15; ☎ 323-462-3777, 800-524-6783; www.usahostels.com; 1624 Schrader Blvd; incl tax dm $24-38, r $68-95; wi-fi) Energetic, well run and central to the Hollywood party circuit, this hostel is a convivial spot with lots of freebies, including linen, pancake breakfast and all-day coffee and tea. Dorms have attached bathrooms and lockers for each guest. Making new friends is easy during staff-organized barbecues, comedy nights and tours or while microwaving your pizza in the big, recently spruced-up kitchen.

Elaine's Hollywood B&B (Map pp514-15; ☎ 323-850-0766; www.elaineshollywoodbedandbreakfast.com; 1616 N Sierra Bonita Ave; r incl tax & breakfast from $80) A great find if you're not the type in need of buckets of privacy, this B&B comprises just two rooms in a lovingly restored 1910 bungalow on a quiet street, yet it's smack-dab in Hollywood. Your outgoing hosts Avik and Elaine speak several languages, make a mean breakfast and will happily help you plan your day. Cash only.

MIDRANGE

Magic Castle Hotel (Map pp514-15; ☎ 323-851-0800, 800-741-4915; www.magiccastlehotel.com; 7025 Franklin Ave; r $130-240; P) Walls are thin, but otherwise this mostly revamped stand-by around a courtyard is a fine base, with contemporary furniture, attractive art and such deluxe touches as comfy bathrobes and fancy bath amenities. Days start with freshly baked goods and gourmet coffee on your balcony (some rooms) or by the pool. Ask about access to the namesake private club for magicians.

Best Western Hollywood Hills Hotel (Map pp514-15; ☎ 323-464-5181, 800-287-1700; www.bestwestern.com; 6141 Franklin Ave; r $150-225, children under 17yr free; wi-fi) A central location, cleanliness and accommodating staff are among the winning attributes of this family-run hotel; that said, not all rooms are equal here. For more space and quiet get a room – all with fridge and microwave – in the back facing the sparkling tiled pool. The attached coffee shop is a hipster spot that's open until 3am.

Hollywood Hills Hotel (Map pp514-15; ☎ 323-874-5089, 800-741-4915; www.hollywoodhillshotel.com; 1999 N Sycamore Ave; r incl breakfast $160-240; P) The Magic Castle Hotel (left) also operates this hotel a short walk away, with city views, a curvy pool guarded by a pagoda, and roomy digs with balcony and kitchen.

TOP END

Hollywood Roosevelt Hotel (Map pp514-15; ☎ 323-466-7000, 800-950-7667; www.hollywoodroosevelt.com; 7000 Hollywood Blvd; r $200-400; wi-fi) The current darling of the Hollywood in-crowd, this venerable old hotel has seen its share of elite players since the first Academy Awards were held here in 1929. It pairs a palatial Spanish lobby with rooms sporting a sleek Asian contemporary look. Marilyn Monroe shot her first commercial by the pool.

West Hollywood & Mid-City

BUDGET

Banana Bungalow West Hollywood (Map pp516-17; ☎ 323-655-2002, 877-666-2002; www.bananabungalow.com; 603 N Fairfax Ave; incl tax & breakfast dm $25-30, d/tr/q $89/104/119; P wi-fi) Mod decor, a hip location and small dorms with private baths are among the assets of this convivial hostel, which also has plenty of space for lounging and socializing. There's a café but no kitchen. Inquire about limited, free pickup from LAX.

Alta Cienega Motel (Map pp516-17; ☎ 310-652-5797; www.altacienegamotel.com; 1005 N La Cienega Blvd; r incl breakfast $65-74; P wi-fi) Nothing distinguishes this basic motel from dozens of others in town, yet for Doors fans it's a place of pilgrimage: the 'Lizard King,' Jim Morrison, himself boozed and snoozed in room No 32 back in the late 1960s.

MIDRANGE

San Vicente Inn (Map pp516-17; ☎ 310-854-6915, 800-577-6915; www.thesanvicenteinn.com; 845 N San Vicente Blvd; r $89-219; P wi-fi) LA's main guesthouse for gay men is in the heart of Boystown. Rooms and cottages overlook a tropical garden and frolicking zones include a hot tub, sauna, pool and sundeck.

Standard Hollywood (Map pp516-17; ☎ 323-650-9090; www.standardhotel.com; 8300 W Sunset Blvd; r $150-275; wi-fi) This hipster haven seems stuck in perpetual party mode, so don't come here for a quiet night's sleep. Surprises abound, including a model in a glass box behind the front desk, a pool fringed by blue Astroturf, a barber who doubles as a tattoo artist, and condoms in the minibar. At night the lobby morphs into a chic club lounge.

Farmer's Daughter Hotel (Map pp516-17; ☎ 323-937-3930, 800-334-1658; www.farmersdaughterhotel.com; 115 S Fairfax Ave; r $160-250; wi-fi) This LA fixture sports a cheeky 'urban cowboy' look, complete with denim bedspreads and rocking chairs. The hotel's Tart restaurant serves Americana with a twist, and staff run a clinic for hopefuls on the *Price is Right* game show, filmed across the street at CBS TV City.

Élan Hotel Modern (Map pp516-17; ☎ 323-658-6663, 888-611-0398; www.elanhotel.com; 8435 Beverly Blvd; r incl breakfast $195-260; wi-fi) Primo location, bland facade and rooms with surprising panache, near the Beverly Center for shopping and restaurants. The rooms, decked out in mellow natural tones, all sport plenty of beyond-standard-issue amenities, including Egyptian cotton sheets, goose-down comforters and fancy bath accoutrements. Ample breakfast, small fitness room.

TOP END

Grafton on Sunset (Map pp516-17; ☎ 323-654-4600, 800-821-3660; www.graftononsunset.com; 8462 W Sunset Blvd; r $120-280, ste $350-600, children under 18yr free; wi-fi) We like this charismatic boutique hotel on the Sunset Strip for its pleasing feng shui aesthetic, enormous swimming pool and stylish rooms. Plus, you're within a whisker of the strip's high-velocity club scene (ask the concierge about VIP access). The on-site Balboa steak house is popular with nonguests as well.

Chamberlain West Hollywood (Map pp516-17; ☎ 310-657-7400, 800-201-9652; www.chamberlainwesthollywood.com; 1000 Westmount Dr; r $260-290; wi-fi) This sassy lifestyle hotel scores points with trendy, design-minded travelers. The 112 gadget-filled studios and suites are draped in icy blues and dusky grays, and come with gas fireplace, balcony and sumptuous bedding – perfect after a night of cavorting on the nearby Sunset Strip. Nice rooftop pool, too.

our pick **Chateau Marmont** (Map pp516-17; ☎ 323-656-1010, 800-242-8328; www.chateaumarmont.com; 8221 W Sunset Blvd; r $350-785; P wi-fi) Its French-flavored indulgence may look dated, but this faux castle has long lured A-listers with its five-star mystique and legendary discretion. Howard Hughes used to spy on bikini beauties from the same balcony suite that today is Bono's favorite. The garden cottages are the most romantic, but the superstitious might want to steer clear of No 2 where John Belushi set his final speedball in 1982.

Mondrian Hotel (Map pp516-17; ☎ 323-650-8999, 800-525-8029; www.mondrianhotel.com; 8440 W Sunset Blvd; r from $445; wi-fi) Like gates to heaven, two giant doors but no marquee signal your arrival at this beacon for the rich and beautiful. The Philippe Starck–designed public spaces – the sleek lobby, the restaurant, the open-air Sky Bar (p561), the sexy swimming pool – are like stages where the auditioning never stops. Even the valets look like Armani models.

Beverly Hills & Westside

MIDRANGE

Culver Hotel (Map pp510-11; ☎ 310-838-7963, 888-328-5837; www.culverhotel.com; 9400 Culver Blvd, Culver City; r $150-325, children free; P wi-fi) The selling point here is history. Opened in 1924, the Culver is where the Munchkins stayed while filming the *Wizard of Oz*, and rooms befit those times, though some feel, well, historic too. New and edgy is just out the door, though, amid the excellent eating, culture and galleries in hip and happening downtown Culver City.

Crescent (Map pp518-19; ☎ 310-247-0505; www.crescentbh.com; 403 N Crescent Dr, Beverly Hills; r from $175; wi-fi) This mod hot spot has a buzzing lobby-lounge-bar (ask for a room on the 2nd floor and in back if you'll be bothered by noise), plus a stylish indoor-outdoor restaurant. Rooms tend to be on the small side but flat-screen TV and iPods are welcome hipster touches.

our pick **Maison 140** (Map pp518-19; ☎ 310-281-4000, 800-432-5444; www.maison140.com; 140 S Lasky Dr, Beverly Hills; r from $220; wi-fi) This sensuous gem in the former home of silent-movie siren Lillian Gish cleverly marries French frivolity and Asian understatement in rooms that skimp on size but not on luxury. Rates include an evening wine reception, a small fitness facility and pool privileges at the top-end Avalon (below).

TOP END

Avalon Hotel (Map pp518-19; ☎ 310-277-5221, 800-535-4715; www.avalonbeverlyhills.com; 9400 W Olympic Blvd, Beverly Hills; r $280-410; wi-fi) Mid-Century cool meets amenities fit for the new millennium at this hipper-than-thou boutique hotel. Rooms vamp it up with vintage Nelson bubble lamps and Eames cabinets, and the pool is as curvaceous as Marilyn Monroe, who once lived in this former apartment building. The Blue on Blue restaurant-bar (p560) is on-site.

our pick **Hotel Bel-Air** (Map pp518-19; ☎ 310-472-1211, 800-648-4097; www.hotelbelair.com; 701 N Stone Canyon Rd, West LA; r from $425; wi-fi) Direct your urge to splurge toward this peaceful hideaway where every detail speaks of refinement and discretion is key. Rooms, each with private entrance and classy French country furnishings, are hugged by romantic gardens where white swans preen. If the price tag is too steep, come for afternoon tea or drinks in the fireplace bar.

Beverly Hills Hotel (Map pp518-19; ☎ 310-276-2251, 800-283-8885; www.thebeverlyhillshotel.com; 9641 Sunset Blvd, Beverly Hills; r from $515; wi-fi) The legendary Pink Palace from 1912, set back from Beverly Hills parkland, oozes opulence and historical charm. The pool deck is classic, the grounds lush, and the Polo Lounge remains a clubby lunch spot for the well heeled and well dressed. Rooms are comparably Old World, with gold accents and marble tiles.

Malibu

Leo Carrillo State Beach Campground (off Map pp510-11; ☎ 800-444-7275; www.reserveamerica.com; 35000 W Pacific Coast Hwy; tent & RV sites $20-25) This shady, kid-friendly site, around 28 miles northwest of Santa Monica, gets busy in summer, so book early, especially on weekends. It has 135 sites, flush toilets and coin-operated hot showers. A long sandy beach, offshore kelp beds and tide pools are all great places for exploring.

Malibu Beach Inn (Map pp510-11; ☎ 310-456-6444; www.malibubeachinn.com; 22878 Pacific Coast Hwy; r from $325, ste from $725; wi-fi) If you want to live like a billionaire, stay with one. Hollywood mogul David Geffen has plunked megabucks (chump change to him) into giving this intimate hacienda the deluxe treatment. It's right near his private house on Carbon Beach and has 47 superdeluxe ocean-facing rooms sheathed in soothing browns and outfitted with fireplaces, a handpicked wine selection and Dean & Deluca gourmet goodies.

Santa Monica & Venice

BUDGET

HI-Los Angeles-Santa Monica (Map pp520-1; ☎ 310-393-9913, 800-909-4776, ext 137; www.lahostels.org; 1436 2nd St, Santa Monica; members/nonmembers dm incl tax $39/41, r with shared bathroom $82/88; wi-fi) This 260-bed hostel is in an architecturally interesting building that's just received a $2 million makeover, but it's the location – between the beach and Third Street Promenade – that really makes it. Rates include sheets, but not breakfast, though there are dozens of restaurants steps away.

Sea Shore Motel (Map pp520-1; ☎ 310-392-2787; www.seashoremotel.com; 2637 Main St, Santa Monica; r from $105, ste from $150; P wi-fi) Amid the funky shops and fun restaurants of Main St and a block from the beach, this family-owned motel is one of a dying breed: a clean, budget-priced option, even if traffic noise may stop it from being some visitors' cup of tea. The Spanish-tiled rooms are attractive enough, but the lofty suites (sleeping up to six) with full kitchens and balconies are killer.

MIDRANGE

Venice Beach House (Map pp520-1; ☎ 310-823-1966; www.venicebeachhouse.com; 15 30th Ave, Venice; r without bath $145, with bath $190-225; P wi-fi) A block from the beach, this ivy-draped B&B in a 1911 Arts and Crafts bungalow (listed on the National Register of Historic Places) is a welcoming old-California retreat with nine cozy rooms. The romantically inclined should book the James Peasgood room with its lofty wood ceiling and double Jacuzzi.

Cal Mar Hotel Suites (Map pp520-1; ☎ 310-395-5555, 800-776-6007; www.calmarhotel.com; 220 California Ave, Santa Monica; ste $160-200; P) The place may look hopelessly stuck in the disco decade, but who's to complain if a moderate tariff buys you a large suite with kitchen and a super-central yet quiet location? It's a great choice for families and anyone in need of plenty of elbow room. The heated pool in its neat tropical setting comes in handy if the ocean's too cold for a swim.

Channel Road Inn B&B (Map pp520-1; ☎ 310-459-1920; www.channelroadinn.com; 219 W Channel Rd, Santa Monica; r incl breakfast $195-450; P) Upscale and romantic, this B&B has sumptuous, amenity-laden rooms facing either the ocean or the lovely garden. Breakfasts are gourmet affairs, and the afternoon tea and evening wine and cheese gatherings provide ample opportunity to mingle with fellow guests. Bicycles for taking a spin along the beach are available for free.

Hotel California (Map pp520-1; ☎ 310-393-2363, 800-571-0000; www.hotelca.com; 1670 Ocean Ave, Santa Monica; r incl breakfast from $209; wi-fi) No, it's not the place the Eagles sang about – *that's* on a dark desert highway and *this* is just steps from the ocean. Still, this 1940s inn has a sense of place: beach-dude vibe, walkways lined with local flora, and compact rooms with surfboard art.

But you're really paying for the location (and continental breakfast), at a fraction of the hotels down the block. No air-con, but ocean breezes usually suffice.

TOP END

Georgian Hotel (Map pp520-1; ☎ 310-395-9945, 800-538-8147; www.georgianhotel.com; 1415 Ocean Ave, Santa Monica; r from $267; wi-fi) This eye-catching art-deco landmark with its snug veranda for breakfast and sunset lounging has decor so *Great Gatsby*–esque that wearing a straw boater wouldn't feel out of place. The rooms, decked out in soothing earth tones, are surprisingly modern. The baked French toast for breakfast or lunch in the Verandah restaurant is worth writing home about.

Viceroy (Map pp520-1; ☎ 310-260-7500, 800-622-8711; www.viceroysantamonica.com; 1819 Ocean Ave, Santa Monica; r from $390; wi-fi) Ignore the high-rise eyesore exterior and plunge headlong into this fabulous outpost one block from the beach. It's a showcase for *Top Design*'s Kelly Wearstler's 'Hollywood Regency' decor, with a color palette from dolphin gray to mamba green. All the usual hot-spot trappings are here, from poolside cabanas to Italian designer linens, plus a bar and chic restaurant.

San Pedro & Long Beach

BUDGET

HI-Los Angeles-South Bay (Map pp510-11; ☎ 310-831-8109, 800-909-4776; www.lahostels.org; 3601 S Gaffey St, No 613, San Pedro; dm $22, d member/nonmember $51/57; May-Sep; P wi-fi) You'll enjoy sweeping Pacific views from this bluff-top hostel with its nifty muraled walls, from African jungle to American jazz. The facilities include a big kitchen, a TV room and a guest laundry. Contact the hostel if you're planning to arrive by public transportation.

MIDRANGE

Turret House (Map pp510-11; ☎ 562-624-1991, 888-488-7738; www.turrethouse.com; 556 Chestnut Ave, Long Beach; r incl breakfast $99-135) Owners Brian and Jeff (and their adorable dogs) have poured their hearts and cash into turning this little B&B into an oasis of charm. The stately Victorian has five cozy rooms, each with fireplace, TV and bathroom with clawfoot tub. Rates include passes to a nearby gym, and there's a hot tub on the premises.

Queen Mary Hotel (Map pp510-11; ☎ 562-435-3511; www.queenmary.com; 1126 Queens Hwy, Long Beach; r $119-269; wi-fi) This grand ocean liner time-warps you back to a slower-paced era. The 1st-class staterooms have been nicely refurbished and brim with original art-deco details (avoid the cheapest ones, which are on the inside). Larger suites (from $360) combine two to three staterooms. Rates include admission to guided tours (see p539).

TOP END

Dockside Boat & Bed (Map pp510-11; ☎ 562-436-3111, 800-436-2574; www.boatandbed.com; Dock 5, Rainbow Harbor, Long Beach; r incl tax & breakfast $200-325; wi-fi) Let the waves rock you to sleep as you snuggle up aboard of selection of motor yachts. Boats are moored close to downtown Long Beach and they enjoy views of the *Queen Mary*. Breakfast is delivered directly to your vessel.

San Fernando Valley

Sportsmen's Lodge Hotel (Map pp510-11; ☎ 818-769-4700, 800-821-8511; www.slhotel.com; 12825 Ventura Blvd, Studio City; r $169-199; wi-fi) At this longstanding favorite in the Valley on a 6-acre campus too authentically 1962 to be called 'retro,' 190 reasonably proportioned rooms, mostly in a five-story building, encircle palms, pines and a pool. It's set way back from busy Ventura Blvd, but you're close to the sushi shops and steps from the funky boutiques, and there's shuttle service to Universal Studios.

Beverly Garland's Holiday Inn (Map p522; ☎ 818-980-8000, 800-476-9981; www.beverlygarland.com; 4222 Vineland Ave, North Hollywood; r $189-219; wi-fi) Owner and actress Beverly Garland oversees this sprawling and nicely landscaped property with seven-story towers and Mission-style accents (it's on El Camino Real). It's close to Universal Studios (free shuttles) and has its own pool, sauna and tennis courts, and a fitness room with equipment not found at many more expensive hotels. Families should ask about the kids' suites.

Pasadena

BUDGET

Saga Motor Hotel (Map pp510-11; ☎ 626-795-0431, 800-793-7242; www.thesagamotorhotel.com; 1633 E Colorado Blvd; r incl breakfast $92-98; P wi-fi) One of the best bets on Pasadena's 'motel row' on historic Route 66, this well-kept vintage inn (built in 1957) has comfortable, spotless rooms. The nicest are near the good-sized pool orbited by plenty of chaises and chairs for soaking up the SoCal sunshine. Extra-large units available for families.

MIDRANGE

Bissell House B&B (Map pp510-11; ☎ 626-441-3535, 800-441-3530; www.bissellhouse.com; 201 S Orange Grove Blvd; r incl tax & breakfast $195-350; P wi-fi) Sumptuous antiques, sparkling hardwood floors and a crackling fireplace make this romantic, six-room 1887 Victorian B&B on 'Millionaire's Row' a bastion of warmth and hospitality. If you don't like flowery decor, book the Prince Albert room. The Garden Room comes with a Jacuzzi for two.

TOP END

Langham Huntington Hotel & Spa (Map pp510-11; ☎ 626-568-3900; www.pasadena.langhamhotels.com; 1401 S Oak Knoll Ave; r from $269; wi-fi) If it weren't for the palm trees, you'd half expect this ultraposh hostelry (until recently a Ritz-Carlton property) to be a French country estate complete with rambling gardens, a huge pool and even a covered picture bridge. Rooms are lavishly dressed in regal reds or blues. Sunday champagne brunch ($75) is a pricey but memorable buffet treat.

EATING

LA's culinary scene is one of the world's most vibrant and eclectic, and Angelenos are hip to it. You'll have no trouble finding high-profile restaurants helmed by celebrity chefs, whipping up farmers-market-fresh Continental-California fare. But ethnic neighborhoods covering huge swaths also mean authentic international cooking. Among Angelenos, dinner might just as easily be burritos or *bulgogi* (marinated, grilled Korean beef), dim sum, sushi or tapas. No less than Ruth Reichl (editor of *Gourmet* magazine and former restaurant critic for the *Los Angeles Times*) has said that LA's real culinary treasure is its ethnic restaurants. With 140 nationalities in LA, we can only scratch the surface.

Reservations are recommended for dinner, especially at top-end places.

Downtown

BUDGET

Grand Central Market (Map pp512-13; ☎ 213-624-2378; www.grandcentralsquare.com; 317 S Broadway; meals $2-10; 9am-6pm) This historic indoor market is perfect for sopping up Downtown's mélange of ethnicities, languages and cuisines. Just wander along the aisles and pick a place that looks good, or head straight to Maria's Pescado Frito for great fish tacos and seviche tostadas; Kabab and More for charbroiled kebabs and tangy humus; or China Café for sinus-clearing chicken soup or heaping plates of chow mein.

Philippe the Original (Map pp512-13; ☎ 213-628-3781; www.philippes.com; 1001 N Alameda St; dishes $2.50-10; 6am-10pm; P) From cops to couples and families, they all flock to this legendary 'home of the French dip sandwich,' dating back to 1908 at the edge of Chinatown. Do as millions have done before you and order your choice of meat on a crusty roll dipped in au jus, and hunker down at the tables on the sawdust-covered floor. Coffee is just 9¢ (and that's no misprint). Cash only.

Señor Fish (Map pp512-13; ☎ 213-625-0566; 422 E 1st St; mains $4-12; lunch & dinner) It may be in Little Tokyo, but the fish tacos here are like a trip to Ensenada in Baja California. It's an arty space with big windows, counter service and fountain drinks…and a cut above, especially the scallop burritos, fried shrimp, seviche and, for land-lubbers, pork carnitas. *¡Ay!*

Koreatown Galleria (off Map pp512-13; ☎ 323-733-6000; www.koreatowngalleria.com; cnr Olympic Blvd & Western Ave; lunch & dinner; P) K-town's three-story mall has a food court on the top floor with stalls specializing in *soon dubu* (spicy tofu stew) to *tonkatsu* (fried pork cutlet) and soups that Koreans swear cure hangovers. Or pick up takeout at the supermarket downstairs. Work it off browsing for toys, chic car accessories and traditional bedding.

MIDRANGE

Empress Pavilion (Map pp512-13; ☎ 213-617-9898; 3rd fl, Bamboo Plaza, 988 N Hill St; dim sum per plate $2-5, dinner $20-25; 9am-10pm; P) Other Chinatown places do dim sum, but regulars swear by this Hong Kong–style banquet hall with seating for a small village (500 people, to be exact). Dumplings, wontons, pot stickers, spring rolls, barbecued pork and other delicacies just fly off the carts wheeled right to your table by a small army of servers.

Tiara Café (Map pp512-13; ☎ 213-623-3663; 127 E 9th St; sandwiches $8-11, mains $14-16; 11:30am-3pm; P) Pretty in pink and with a high ceiling, this Fashion District lunch spot feeds designers, sales clerks and frenzied bargain hunters with healthy, organic fare that can be calibrated to meet vegan and vegetarian needs. The salads

BERRY, BOBA AND CUPCAKE

These may sound like the nicknames of the latest, cutest boy band, but actually they're sweet treats as popular among Angelenos as the Jonas Brothers are among schoolgirls.

'Berry' is LA shorthand for frozen yogurt. It started with **Pinkberry** (www.pinkberry.com), the LA-born minichain that does for fro-yo what *Queer Eye* did for straight guys: turn it from workaday to fabulous. Pinkberry's stylish interiors are filled with Philippe Starck furniture. Yogurt comes in tangy 'original' or green tea flavors, which take on additional complexity when topped with fresh fruit (mango, kiwi etc) or cereals including Cap'n Crunch. Pinkberry started in West Hollywood (Map pp516-17; ☎ 310-659-8285; 868 Huntley Dr, West Hollywood) and has proven so popular that a raft of other 'berry' and other fruit-monikered shops (eg Red Mango) have opened up.

Boba is black pearls of tapioca, best found at the bottom of large plastic cups filled with tea (iced, sweetened milk tea is the standard). Sip them through a wide straw – it's kinda cool eating and drinking at the same time. Boba originated in Taiwan and, like much local Chinese culture, arrived in LA via the San Gabriel Valley. **Lollicup** (www.lollicup.com) has locations in key neighborhoods, such as **Chinatown** (Map pp512-13; ☎ 213-687-8283; 988 N Hill St, Downtown).

'Cupcake' sounds like what it is, but in LA these diminutive desserts are way beyond birthday party treats. Beverly Hills' **Sprinkles** (☎ 310-274-8765; 9635 Little Santa Monica Blvd, Beverly Hills) started the trend, and customers line out the door for flavors like red velvet, black & white and about two dozen others that rotate daily. They're color-coded, stylish and very presentable.

are fresh and abundant, and the sandwiches are custom-made. Carbo-phobes should try the rice-paper-wrapped versions.

Oomasa (Map pp512-13; ☎ 213-623-9048; 100 Japanese Village Plaza; mains lunch $9-13, dinner $10-20; 🕑 11:30am-12:30am Wed-Sun) This long-standing Little Tokyo sushi shop, with its giant horseshoe-shaped bar, is a haven for sushi purists. From dark-red tuna to marbled salmon, it's all superfresh, expertly cut (if a bit on the chintzy side), affordably priced and best enjoyed while snuggled into one of the old-timey booths.

Pete's Café & Bar (Map pp512-13; ☎ 213-617-1000; www.petescafe.com; 400 S Main St; mains lunch $8-17, dinner $9-26; 🕑 11:30am-2am) *The* late-night hot spot in the Old Bank District, Pete's has a classic interior and is alive with loft dwellers, politicos, journos and artists. The menu is modern American feel-good food, including a mean burger doused in fontina and tomato aioli. Come on, be extra bad and get a side of killer blue-cheese fries. Food's served till closing time.

Chosun Galbee (off Map pp512-13; ☎ 323-734-3330; 3300 Olympic Blvd; mains $12-24; 🕑 11am-11pm) Great for Korean barbecue virgins. On request, staff will help you cook meat on a grill set into your table, preferably on the trendy-looking bamboo-accented concrete and metal patio. *Galbee* (short rib cubes), *bulgogi* (beef slices) and *dak bulgogi* (chicken) are marinated in tangy soy-sesame sauce. *Panchan* (side dishes, included in the price) are varied and excellent: marinated veggies, salads and *kimchi*, Korea's national dish of spicy pickled cabbage.

TOP END

Patina (Map pp512-13; ☎ 213-972-3331; 141 S Grand Ave; mains lunch $18-30, dinner $33-40; 🕑 lunch Mon-Fri, dinner daily; Ⓟ) The flagship restaurant of culinary wunderkind Joachim Splichal is in stunning digs at the Walt Disney Concert Hall (p524). Tantalize your tongue with such unique compositions as blue-crab mango cannelloni or Peking duck with caramelized Belgian endives. Or go all out and order the chef's menu (lunch/dinner $50/100).

R-23 (Map pp512-13; ☎ 213-687-7178; 923 E 2nd St; mains lunch $10-15, dinner $40-60; 🕑 lunch Mon-Fri, dinner daily) Hidden in the gritty Arts District east of Little Tokyo, R-23 is a fantasy come true for serious sushi aficionados. Not even the bold art and bizarre Frank Gehry–designed corrugated-cardboard chairs can distract from the exquisite and ultrafresh piscine treats prepared by a team of sushi masters. Green-tea cheesecake makes for a fitting finish.

Hollywood, Los Feliz & Silver Lake

BUDGET

Yuca's (Map pp514-15; ☎ 323-662-1214; www.yucasla.com; 2056 Hillhurst Ave, Los Feliz; mains $1.50-4.25; 🕑 11am-6pm Mon-Sat; Ⓟ) Fresh ingredients, clever spicing and rock-bottom prices are what keep business constant at this tiny Mexican stand with a few parking-lot tables – and won it a James Beard award. Burritos, tacos and *tortas* all fly nonstop through the service window. Grab a cold one at the liquor store next door and dig in.

Waffle (Map pp514-15; ☎ 323-465-6901; www.thewaffle.us; 6255 Sunset Blvd, Hollywood; mains $9-12; 6:30am-2:30am Sun-Thu, to 4:30am Fri & Sat) After a night out clubbing, do you really feel like filling yourself with garbage? Us too. But here the 21st-century diner food – corn-meal-jalapeño waffles with grilled chicken, carrot cake waffles, mac and cheese, samiches, heaping salads – is organic and locally sourced so it's (almost) good for you. Bonus: short but well-chosen wine list.

Fred 62 (Map pp514-15; ☎ 323-667-0062; 1850 N Vermont Ave, Los Feliz; mains $5-14; 24hr) Polyethnic sandwiches, salads and noodles for young guns on small budgets in the Los Feliz hipster haven.

MIDRANGE

Cheebo (Map pp514-15; ☎ 323-850-7070; 7533 W Sunset Blvd, Hollywood; breakfast & lunch $7-16, dinner $10-23; 8am-11:30pm; wi-fi) This cheap and cheerful hipster joint is the go-to place for yummy organic pizzas topped creatively (sausage and fennel) and delivered piping hot on wooden boards. Regulars are partial to the 'porkwich,' a winning combo of slow-roasted pork doused with Manchego cheese, and 'da bomb,' a killer chocolate soufflé.

25 Degrees (Map pp514-15; ☎ 323-785-7244; 7000 Hollywood Blvd, Hollywood; burgers $12; breakfast, lunch & dinner) As if there weren't enough reasons to visit the Hollywood Roosevelt Hotel (p548), this rock 'n' roll burger joint is as gourmet as it is juicy. Dress your burger with top-notch cheeses from burrata to Point Reyes blue, and bag the ketchup for sauces like garlic aioli or tarragon remoulade. Who says rockers have to settle for bad food?

El Conquistador (Map pp514-15; ☎ 323-666-5136; www.elconquistadorrestaurant.com; 3701 W Sunset Blvd, Silver Lake; mains $9-16.50; lunch Tue-Sun, dinner daily) This wonderfully campy Mexican cantina is perfect for launching yourself into a night on the razzle. The margaritas are potent, so be sure to fill your belly with tasty nachos, *chiles rellenos* (stuffed peppers, usually with cheese, but anything goes) and quesadillas to sustain your stamina through the night.

Palms Thai (Map pp514-15; ☎ 323-462-5073; www.palmsthai.com; 5900 Hollywood Blvd, Hollywood; mains $6-19; 11am-2am) A steady stream of Thai families, tattooed scenesters and cops happily mingle here in Thai Town, while an (actually quite good) Elvis impersonator entertains. Dismiss it as a gimmick at your own risk, because the food's fab. The huge menu has all the usual favorites, but you'll be amazed what can be done with frog, quail and jellyfish.

Hungry Cat (Map pp514-15; ☎ 323-462-2155; www.thehungrycat.com; 1535 N Vine St, Hollywood; mains $14-22; dinner daily, brunch Sun) This kitty is small, sleek and hides out in the trendy Sunset & Vine complex (behind Schwab's). It fancies fresh seafood and will have you purring for such dishes as the tangy chorizo and clam stew, the hunky lobster roll or the portly crab cakes. Purists might prefer a portion of meaty peel-and-eat shrimp from the raw bar.

TOP END

Musso & Frank Grill (Map pp514-15; ☎ 323-467-7788; 6667 Hollywood Blvd, Hollywood; mains $12-35; lunch & dinner Tue-Sat) Hollywood history hangs thickly in the air at the boulevard's oldest eatery. Waiters balance platters of steaks, chops, grilled liver and other dishes harking back to the days when cholesterol wasn't part of our vocabulary. For breakfast, which is served all day, try the signature flannel cakes (thin pancakes; $6). Service is smooth, and so are the martinis.

Providence (Map pp514-15; ☎ 323-460-4170; 5955 Melrose Ave, Hollywood; mains lunch $25-38, dinner $35-48; lunch Fri, dinner daily) Michael Cimarusti's gourmet creations will definitely take your tastebuds on a wild ride. Foie gras parfait? Sea urchin with truffles? To truly sample the master's talents, sign up for the nine-course tasting menu ($105, with wine $150).

Geisha House (Map pp514-15; ☎ 323-460-6300; www.dolcegroup.com/geisha; 6633 Hollywood Blvd, Hollywood; most dishes $9-22; 6pm-2am) In a word: a scene. Nothing's been quite the same on Hollywood Blvd since Ashton Kutcher and pals opened this slick *izakaya*. Look for small plates – sushi, grills, noodles and more – served with a heaping dollop of style. Multiple rooms and levels mean that everyone watches each other; dress to impress.

West Hollywood & Mid-City

BUDGET

Pink's Hot Dogs (Map pp516-17; ☎ 323-931-4223; 709 N La Brea Ave, Mid-City; dishes $2.85-6.35; 9:30am-2am

Sun-Thu, to 3am Fri & Sat) Look for the long queue at the corner of Melrose and La Brea.

Swingers (Map pp516-17; ☎ 323-653-5858; 8020 Beverly Blvd; dishes $4-10; 6:30am-4am) If you're after Americana with a dollop of Hollywood, this diner is the genuine article. Its red plastic booths often fill with kool kids combating hunger pangs or hangovers. Servers in fishnet stockings and a certain, shall we say, sassy charm balance heaping platters of energy-restoring goodies while Little Richard makes the jukebox hop. Also at 802 Broadway, Santa Monica (Map pp520–1; ☎ 310-393-9793; 7am to 2am Sunday to Wednesday, open till 3am Thursday to Saturday).

8 oz (Map pp516-17; ☎ 323-852-0008; www.8ozburgerbar.com; 7661 Melrose Ave, Mid-City; mains $8-10; 6pm-midnight Mon-Sat) You'd expect a burger joint next to a Melrose Ave tattoo parlor to have a hipster factor, but the gourmet grub…score! Get yours with heirloom tomato ketchup and escarole or a side of fried cheese curds. On the short rib grilled cheese, the meat seems to melt away before the cheese does.

Gumbo Pot (Map pp516-17; ☎ 323-933-0358; 6333 W 3rd St, Mid-City; mains $6-11) A favorite belly-filling station in the farmers market, where the Southern food is fingerlickin' good. The farmers market itself is a great spot for a casual meal any time of day, especially if the rug rats are tagging along.

Lotería! Grill (Map pp516-17; ☎ 323-930-2211; 6333 W 3rd St, Mid-City; mains $7-11) If you've got a hankering for handmade, gourmet Mexican, there's no better place than this farmers market grill.

El Coyote (Map pp516-17; ☎ 323-939-2255; www.elcoyotecafe.com; 7312 Beverly Blvd, Mid-City; mains $5-13; lunch & dinner) It's always fiesta time at this red-boothed, been-there-forever kitsch-filled cantina, where stiff margaritas pretty much guarantee a cheap buzz even if the food is so-so (stick to fresh-made dishes like fajitas). Frilly-skirted waitresses are sweet and sassy. Celebrity trivia: Sharon Tate ate her last meal here before being murdered by Charles Manson's mad posse.

MIDRANGE

Cobras & Matadors (Map pp516-17; ☎ 323-932-6178; 7615 Beverly Blvd, Mid-City; tapas $5-19; dinner) Tables at this trendy tapas bar are squished together as tight as lovers, but scoring one can still be a tall order. Bacon-wrapped dates, cod fritters and roasted artichoke hearts with Serrano ham are just part of the attraction. Pick up a bottle of vino at the shop next door, and corkage is waived.

Surya (Map pp516-17; ☎ 323-653-5151; 8048 W 3rd St, Mid-City; mains $10-17; lunch Mon-Fri, dinner daily) Curries are like culinary poetry at this upscale Indian restaurant dedicated to Surya, the Hindu god of the sun, which might explain the saffron-colored walls. Friendly waitstaff will happily help you navigate the menu, although your bill should always include an order of steamy naan and anything out of the tandoor (clay oven).

Marix Tex Mex (Map pp516-17; ☎ 323-656-8800; 1108 N Flores St, West Hollywood; mains $9-19; 11:30am-11pm) It should be stamped on airline tickets: every gay or lesbian visitor to WeHo has to go here at least once. Many an evening on Santa Monica Blvd has begun flirting on Marix's patios over kick-ass margaritas, plus great fish tacos, fajitas, chipotle chicken sandwiches and other Mex faves.

Angelini Osteria (Map pp516-17; ☎ 323-297-0070; www.angeliniosteria.com; 7313 Beverly Blvd, Mid-City; mains $10-34; lunch Tue-Fri, dinner Tue-Sun) The conversation flows as freely as the wine at this convivial eatery, whose eclectic clientele share a passion for great Italian food with owner-chef Gino Angelini. Choose from soulful risottos, piquant pastas and delightful lamb chops. Price tags to match all budgets.

BLD (Map pp516-17; ☎ 310-930-9744; www.bldrestaurant.com; 7450 Beverly Blvd, Mid-City; mains $14-22; breakfast, lunch & dinner) Chef Neal Fraser, the first to win on the *Iron Chef* TV series, prepares solid American cooking at this open bistro. It's about the ingredients, sourced locally wherever possible: shaved rib-eye for the Philly cheese steak, Cuban-style pork sandwich, and 'construct your own' entrees with a protein, starch etc. Smart wine selection.

TOP END

AOC (Map pp516-17; ☎ 323-653-6359; 8022 W 3rd St, Mid-City; dishes $4-14; dinner) The small-plate menu at this stomping ground of the rich, lithe and silicone-enhanced will have you noshing happily on sweaty cheeses, homemade charcuterie and such richly nuanced morsels as braised pork cheeks. Huge list of wines by the glass.

Osteria Mozza & Pizzeria Mozza (Map pp516-17; ☎ 323-297-0100; www.mozza-la.com; 6602 Melrose Ave, Mid-City; mains Osteria $17-29, Pizzeria $10-18; lunch & dinner) Even a month ahead of time you'll be lucky to get a reservation at LA's hottest

Italian eatery, run by celebrity chefs Mario Batali and Nancy Silverton. Two restaurants share the same building: top-notch ingredients blend in harmony at the Osteria, and precision-made pizzas are baked before your eyes at the Pizzeria (☎ 323-297-0101, 641 N Highland Ave). Mozzarella bar, anyone?

Comme Ça (Map pp516-17; ☎ 323-782-1178; www.commecarestaurant.com; 8479 Melrose Ave, West Hollywood; mains breakfast $8-14, lunch $12-25, dinner $19-28; 8am-midnight) 'Bistro cooking' way understates the case at this vibrant, all-day Francophile eatery. Look for *croque madame, moules frites,* a cheese bar and a raw bar, all from Michelin-starred chef David Myers. Plus there's old-world bartending; the Penicillin cocktail will cure what ails you with scotch, ginger, lemon and honey.

The Ivy (Map pp516-17; ☎ 310-274-8303; 113 N Robertson Blvd, West Hollywood; mains $20-38; 11:30am-11pm Mon-Fri, 11am-11pm Sat, 10am-11pm Sun) The picket-fenced patio and rustic cottage may not look posh but never mind – the Ivy is *the* power lunch spot in town. Chances of catching A-lister babes choke on a carrot stick or studio execs discussing sequels over the lobster omelet are excellent if you're willing to put up with the self-conscious servers and steep bill. Desserts are outstanding.

Beverly Hills & Westside

BUDGET

Diddy Riese Cookies (Map pp518-19; ☎ 310-208-0448; www.diddyriese.com; 926 Broxton Ave, Westwood; cookies 35¢) No night out in Westwood is complete without Diddy's bargain-priced ice-cream sandwiches ($1.50), made with your choice of fresh-baked cookies and over a dozen ice-cream flavors.

Noodle Planet (Map pp518-19; ☎ 310-208-0777; www.noodleplanet.com; 1118 Westwood Blvd, Westwood; mains $7-9; 11am-11pm Sun-Thu, to 1am Fri & Sat) Students know what's cheap and good, and hordes of the UCLA variety hunker over steaming serves of noodles from all across Asia: Japanese udon, Chinese lo mein, Vietnamese pho and more. Atmosphere: contempo-cafeteria. Service: indifferent, but at these prices…

Frida Taqueria (Map pp520-1; ☎ 310-395-9666; www.fridarestaurant.com; Brentwood Country Mart, 225 S 26th St, West LA; mains $6-10; 11am-7pm) Frida Taqueria serves famous *moles* and *aguas frescas* (fresh fruit drinks) and righteous lobster tacos ($13). It's one of a small but fine selection of eateries and other shops at the barnlike Brentwood Country Mart, on the chichi border of Brentwood and Santa Monica.

City Bakery (Map pp520-1; ☎ 310-656-3040; www.thecitybakery.com; Brentwood Country Mart, 225 S 26th St, West LA; baked goods $2-4, takeout $12 per pound; 7:30am-7pm Mon-Sat, 8am-6pm Sun) An import all the way from New York at Brentwood Country Mart, with spin-the-globe takeout by the pound, gleaming pastries and hot chocolate so thick it's sold by the shot.

Hide Sushi (off Map pp518-19; ☎ 310-477-7242; 2040 Sawtelle Blvd, West LA; mains $8-14; 11:30am-9pm Tue-Sat, to 8pm Sun) Sushi bars come and go, but Hide (*hee*-day) is the longstanding fave on Sawtelle. Look for lots of combos including tempura and teriyaki, and lines out the door on weekend evenings. Cash only.

Versailles (☎ 310-558-3168; www.versaillescuban.com; 10319 Venice Blvd, Culver City; mains $8-14; lunch & dinner; P) There's nothing fancy about this country-style Cuban eatery, but that barely matters when the garlic sauce (served with everything from roast chicken to fish) is so celestial. Many dishes come with rice, beans and fried plantains. Also at 1415 S La Cienega Blvd in West LA (Map pp518–19; ☎ 310-289-0392).

Tender Greens (Map pp518-19; ☎ 310-842-8300; www.tendergreensfood.com; 9523 Culver Blvd, Culver City; dishes $10; 11:30am-9pm Sun-Thu, to 10pm Fri & Sat; V) Herbivore or meathead, your tastebuds will be doing somersaults when treated to the carefully composed salads, tossed up as you move down the (usually considerable) line. The ahi tuna nicoise and grilled flatiron steak are fabulous, and the chicken soup's soul-restoring. The greens, meats and other ingredients are sourced from local providers.

MIDRANGE

Nate 'n Al's (Map pp518-19; ☎ 310-274-0101; www.natenal.com; 414 N Beverly Dr, Beverly Hills; most mains $9-17; 7am-9pm) Dapper seniors, chatty girlfriends, busy execs and even Larry King have kept this New York–style deli busy since 1945. The huge menu brims with what may quite possibly be the best pastrami on rye, lox and bagels and chicken soup this side of Manhattan.

Sawtelle Kitchen (off Map pp518-19; ☎ 310-473-2222; 2024 Sawtelle Blvd, West LA; mains $10-16; lunch & dinner Mon-Sat) This contempo dining room with sizable, informal outdoor patio gives standard Western dishes an eccentric Japanese twist, mostly with success. Pasta is paired with pollock caviar and daikon sprouts, the pork chops are drizzled with olive-ginger

LA'S FABULOUS FARMERS MARKETS

In a city as big as LA, it's easy to forget that California is America's most productive agricultural state. Nearby farmers, top-name chefs and locavore home-cooks come together at dozens of certified farmers markets; somewhere in the county there's a farmers market every day of the week. Here are just some standouts; for more, visit www.farmernet.com.

Hollywood (Map pp514-15; ☎ 323-463-3171; cnr Ivar & Selma Aves, Hollywood; 8am-1pm Sun) Some 90 farmers set up stalls alongside vendors of prepared foods including Mexican, Caribbean and espresso. Artisans and street musicians round out the experience.

Santa Monica (Map pp520-1; www.smgov.net/farmers_market; cnr Arizona Ave & 2nd St, Santa Monica; 8:30am-1:30pm Wed & 8:30am-1pm Sat) Cream of the crop. Serious gourmets gather over superfresh everyday produce and exotica from Asian vegetables to heirloom tomatoes, herbs and lotions and potions made from them, raw cheeses and organically raised meat. Go on Wednesdays for the highest chef quotient.

sauce, and the yams deep-fried and served with plum mayo.

Luckyfish (Map pp518-19; ☎ 310-274-9800; www.luckyfishsushi.com; 338 N Cañon Dr, Beverly Hills; sushi $3.50-7.50; lunch Mon-Sat, dinner daily) Domo arigato, Mr Roboto indeed. Luckyfish serves sushi on a high-tech *kaiten* (conveyor belt) alongside other Japanese standards like edamame, potato croquettes and miso black cod. Plates are color-coded to prices – just pull them off the conveyor as they go by – and embedded with computer chips that let the conveyor know when they can no longer be served (though we've never seen a plate last that long).

Xi'an (Map pp518-19; ☎ 310-275-3345; www.xian90210.com; 362 N Cañon Dr, Beverly Hills; mains $10-18; lunch Mon-Sat, dinner daily) This bustling and stylish eatery lets health- and waist-conscious Beverly Hillsters dip into a pool of mostly low-fat exotic dishes such as black peppercorn chicken and poached cod in black bean sauce. Local ingredients are used whenever possible, but MSG is a no-no.

Ford's Filling Station (Map pp510-11; ☎ 310-202-1470; www.fordsfillingstation.net; 9531 Culver Blvd, Culver City; mains lunch $14-17, dinner $14-32; lunch & dinner) The 'Ford' in question is Ben Ford (son of Harrison) and he'll fill you up in his lively gastropub favored by a chatty crowd. Flatbreads are topped with white shrimp or Serrano ham (one of many charcuterie selections), the fish and chips have the lightness of tempura, and the vegetarian polenta cake is a symphony of textures and flavors. It's a bit noisy, but hey, it's LA.

TOP END

Il Cielo (Map pp518-19; ☎ 310-276-9990; www.ilcielo.com; 9018 Burton Way, Beverly Hills; mains lunch $11-26, dinner $22-43; lunch & dinner Mon-Sat) Candles, chianti and a courtyard table under the stars are all you need for a romantic night out with your significant other at this classy yet cozy *ristorante*. The food is solid, and the attentive waitstaff and the setting ensure an unforgettable night.

Matsuhisa (Map pp518-19; ☎ 310-659-9639; 129 N La Cienega Blvd, Beverly Hills; mains $18-38) Chef Nobu Matsuhisa has gone on to conquer the world with Nobu restaurants in major food capitals. The legend began here on La Cienega's Restaurant Row. There's always something fresh and innovative alongside old standbys like lobster seviche and sushi adorned with cilantro and jalapeño.

Spago (Map pp518-19; ☎ 310-385-0880; www.wolfgangpuck.com;176 N Cañon Dr, Beverly Hills; mains lunch $19-36, dinner $36-53; lunch Mon-Sat, dinner daily) Wolfgang Puck practically defined California cuisine for SoCal, and his flagship emporium has long been tops for A-list celebrity-spotting and fancy eating. Try to score a table on the lovely patio and prepare your taste buds to do cartwheels as chef Lee Hefter keeps up the good work, giving pork chops, porcini, pasta and Wolfgang's famous pizzas the gourmet treatment. Even dessert is worth the hip-expanding indulgence. Reservations essential.

Malibu

Reel Inn (Map pp510-11; ☎ 310-456-8221; 18661 Pacific Coast Hwy; meals $10-32; lunch & dinner; P) Across PCH from the ocean, this shambling shack with counter service and patio serves up fish and seafood for any budget and many styles, including grilled, fried or Cajun. The coleslaw, potatoes and Cajun rice (included in most meals) have fans from Harley riders to beach bums and families. It's an easy detour from Topanga State Park or the Getty Villa (p536).

Geoffrey's (Map pp510-11; ☎ 310-457-1519; 27400 Pacific Coast Hwy; mains lunch $14-24, dinner $18-36; P) This posh player in northern Malibu possesses just the right mix of assets to ensure it'll never go out of style: the Pacific Ocean as a front yard, nicely executed Cal-Asian cuisine, and a regular clutch of celebrity patrons. In short, it's the perfect date spot, especially at night when romance rules.

Santa Monica & Venice

Santa Monica's Third Street Promenade and Main St, as well as Abbot Kinney Blvd in Venice, are all happy hunting grounds for browsing. The promenade in particular has many budget options.

BUDGET

The Counter (Map pp520-1; ☎ 310-399-8383; www.thecounterburger.com; 2901 Ocean Park Blvd, Santa Monica; burgers from $6.50; lunch & dinner; P) Let your creativity fly at this postmodern patty-and-bun joint, where you can build your own gourmet burger by choosing your favorite bread, cheese, topping and sauce. The basket of fries – a steal at just $2 – easily feeds two or three.

Omelette Parlor (Map pp520-1; ☎ 310-399-7892; 2732 Main St, Santa Monica; mains $6-12; 6am-2:30pm Mon-Fri, to 4pm Sat & Sun) An institution since before Main St was fashionable, festooned with black-and-whites of old Santa Monica, a soundtrack of oldies and an airy courtyard out back. Breakfast may last you to dinner, with big-as-your-head omelets and famous waffles. Service is low-key and friendly.

Abbot's Pizza Company (Map pp520-1; ☎ 310-396-7334; 1407 Abbot Kinney Blvd, Venice; slices from $3, pizzas from $10.50; 11am-11pm) Join the leagues of surfers, students and urbanites at this little walk-in joint for its addictive bagel-crust pizzas. Go classic with pepperoni and sausage or gourmet with wild mushroom, barbecue chicken or olive pesto.

MIDRANGE

La Cabaña (Map pp520-1; ☎ 310-392-6161; www.lacabanavenice.com; 738 Rose Ave, Venice; mains $8-17; 11am-3am) It may be on a nondescript corner, but there's always a party in this cozy Mexican cottage with lots of dark nooks and crannies, busy open grills for roasting tortillas and a brick patio (smoking allowed). The food's good but pretty standard, but the margaritas are not: friendly servers will let you linger until you've sopped up the last delicious drop.

Real Food Daily (Map pp520-1; ☎ 310-451-7544; www.realfood.com; 514 Santa Monica Blvd, Santa Monica; mains $10-14; lunch & dinner; V) Are you tempted by tempeh? Salivating for seitan? Vegan cooking queen Ann Gentry sure knows how to give these meat substitutes the gourmet treatment. Start things off with lentil-walnut pâté, move on to the vegan club sandwich with Caesar salad, then finish up with a rich tofu cheesecake.

3 Square Café & Bakery (Map pp520-1; ☎ 310-399-6504; www.rockenwagner.com; 1121 Abbot Kinney Blvd, Venice; mains lunch $8-13, dinner $15-19; 8am-9:30pm) Chef Hans Röckenwagner is a local culinary luminary, and newbies and loyalists devour his famous pretzel burgers, schnitzel, gourmet sandwiches and apple pancakes at his minimalist café. Next door, shelves at the bakery (open 7am to 6pm) are piled high with rustic breads and fruity tarts.

Father's Office (Map pp520-1; ☎ 310-393-2337; www.fathersoffice.com; 1018 Montana Ave, Santa Monica; tapas from $4, mains $12-16; 5pm-1am Mon-Thu, 4pm-2am Fri, noon-2am Sat, noon-midnight Sun) This elbow-to-elbow pub packs 'em in for LA's chic-est burger: a dry-aged beef number dressed in smoky bacon, sweet caramelized onion and an ingenious combo of Gruyère and blue cheese. Pair it with fries served in a mini shopping cart and a mug of handcrafted brew chosen from three dozen on tap. Downside: service can be snooty. Also at 3229 Helms Ave, Culver City (Map pp516–17; ☎ 310-736-2224).

TOP END

The Lobster (Map pp520-1; ☎ 310-458-9294; www.thelobster.com; 1602 Ocean Ave, Santa Monica; mains $12-38; 11:30am-10pm Sun-Thu, to 11pm Fri & Sat) The ocean views by the entrance to Santa Monica Pier impress as much as the food at this slick and lively seafood shrine. It's always packed to the gills thanks to dock-fresh ingredients and Allyson Thurber's innovative seasonal cooking. Impress your server by ordering a side of the off-menu truffle parmesan fries, and make sure you try the rich chocolate banana bread pudding or feathery panna cotta.

Joe's (Map pp520-1; ☎ 310-399-5811; www.joesrestaurant.com; 1023 Abbot Kinney Blvd, Venice; mains lunch $13-18, dinner $26-30, 4/5-course menus $60/75; lunch Tue-Sun, dinner daily) Like a good wine, this charmingly unpretentious restaurant only seems to get better with age, with a new Michelin star to prove it. Owner-chef Joe Miller consistently serves great and gimmick-free seasonal Cal-French food. Choicest tables are out on the patio with its waterfall fountain. Three-course lunch menus are a steal at $18.

Wilshire (Map pp520-1; ☎ 310-458-9294; www.wilshirerestaurant.com; 2454 Wilshire Blvd, Santa Monica; mains lunch $14-27 dinner $24-27; 11:30am-10pm Sun-Thu, to 11pm Fri & Sat) The candle-festooned bar and glam interior and tiered terrace by designer Thomas Schoos are your entry to contemporary California cuisine for the smart set: duck pot pie, kurobuta pork chop, braised short ribs, pan-roasted salmon. At dinnertime, look for wood-grilled steaks (from $26). For dessert: chocolate pudding cake.

Long Beach

Sophy's (Map pp510-11; ☎ 562-494-1763; 3240 E Pacific Coast Hwy, Long Beach; mains $6-14; 9am-10pm) North Long Beach is America's largest Cambodian community, and this newly expanded restaurant is a great place to sample its cuisine, like a cross between Thai and Vietnamese. Standouts include *such koh ngeat* (beef jerky), beef *lok lak* (in lime and black pepper sauce) and *chanpu* (stir-fried noodles with crabmeat). Service alternates between busy and the warmth of a Southeast Asian sun.

Belmont Brewing Company (Map pp510-11; ☎ 562-433-3891; www.belmontbrewing.com; 25 39th Place, Long Beach; mains $12-22) This bustling brewpub has a great outdoor deck (overlooking the Belmont Pier – perfect for watching sunsets), handcrafted brews and a well-priced menu that goes far beyond pub grub. You can even go *haute* with such dishes as seafood Leo, a fishy bonanza packaged in filo pastry.

Alegria (Map pp510-11; ☎ 562-436-3388; www.alegriacocinalatina.com; 115 Pine Ave, Long Beach; tapas $7-11, mains $14-22) Long Beach's busy Pine Ave nightlife district, trippy, technicolor mosaic floor, trompe l'oeil murals and an eccentric art-nouveau bar form an appropriately spirited backdrop to Alegria's vivid Latino cuisine. The tapas menu is great for grazers and the paella a feast for both eyes and stomach. There's even live flamenco some nights.

San Fernando Valley

Bob's Big Boy (Map p522; ☎ 818-843-9334; www.bigboy.com; 4211 Riverside Dr, Burbank; mains $6-9; 24hr; P) This 1950s coffee shop is a classic for its design and has been doing comfort food (patty melts, half-pound burgers, mac and cheese, great fries and shakes) since way before it became fashionable again. A short drive from Warner Bros.

Zankou Chicken (Map p522; ☎ 818-238-0414; 1001 N San Fernando Rd, Burbank; mains $6-10; 10am-11pm) Lip-smacking Armenian-style rotisserie chicken, best paired with vampire-repellent garlic sauce. Also in Westwood at 1716 Sepulveda Blvd (Map pp518–19, ☎ 310-444-0550).

Asanebo (Map pp510-11; ☎ 818-760-3348; 11941 Ventura Blvd, Studio City; dishes $3-21; lunch Tue-Fri, dinner Tue-Sun) Ventura Blvd in Studio City is Sushi Row, which locals will tell you has the highest concentration of sushi restaurants in America. But Asanebo stands out and has a Michelin star to prove it. Try halibut sashimi with fresh truffle, kanpachi with miso and Serrano chilies, and sparkling renditions of even humble dishes like eggplant with ground chicken. Service, too, is sweet.

Eclectic (Map p522; ☎ 818-760-2233; www.eclecticwinebarandgrille.com; 5156 Lankershim Blvd, North Hollywood; mains $8-32; lunch Sun-Fri, dinner daily) An anchor of NoHo's Arts District (p541), this loft-style space is as diverse as its name suggests (though trends Italian) with pastas and pizzas to BLTs and rack of lamb. It's best, though, for people-watching after a show, when the casts come in and hold court.

Pasadena & San Gabriel Valley

Pasadena boasts a lively restaurant scene, particularly in Old Town, but it's well worth heading east to the San Gabriel Valley communities of Monterey Park, Alhambra and San Gabriel for some of the finest Chinese cooking this side of the Pacific.

Din Tai Fung (Map pp510-11; ☎ 626-588-1666; www.dintaifungusa.com; 1108 S Baldwin Ave, Arcadia; dumpling plates $5-9; lunch & dinner; P) LA outpost of Taiwan's most venerable house of dumplings, served in steamers. The specialty here is soup dumplings (little steamed packets filled with meat and broth) – lift it into your spoon and poke it with your chopstick to release the luscious liquid. Expect a line.

Burger Continental (Map pp510-11; ☎ 626-792-6634; www.burgercontinental.com; 535 S Lake Ave, Pasadena; breakfast/lunch buffet $6/9, all-you-can-eat Sunday brunch adult/child $19/10, mains $5-20; breakfast, lunch & dinner; P) What sounds like a patty-and-bun joint is in reality Pasadena's most beloved Middle Eastern nosh spot. Nibble on classic hummus, dig into sizzling kebab dinners or go adventurous with the Moon of Tunis platter (chicken, gyros and shrimp in filo). Live bands and belly dancers provide candy for ears and eyes. Great patio.

Saladang Song (Map pp510-11; ☎ 626-793-5200; 383 S Fair Oaks Ave, Pasadena; mains $8-20; ⏰ breakfast, lunch & dinner) Soaring concrete walls with artsy, cut-out steel insets hem in the outdoor dining room of this modern Thai temple. Even simple curries become extraordinary at Saladang Song, while the unusual breakfast soups offer a nice change from the standard eggs-and-bacon routine.

Mission 261 (Map pp510-11; ☎ 626-588-1666; 261 S Mission Dr, San Gabriel; dim sum each $2-8, dinner $11-40; ⏰ dim sum 10:30am-3pm Mon-Fri, 9am-3pm Sat & Sun, dinner daily; Ⓟ) Inside a century-old adobe near the San Gabriel Mission (p543), this elegantly proportioned place is the holy grail of dim sum, many fashioned into artistic shapes. No carts here; order by filling out a form on your table. Dinner is for adventurers – think braised goose and sea cucumber stew, or the obscene-looking geoduck clam.

DRINKING

Hollywood has been legendary sipping territory since even before the Rat Pack days. Nowadays bartenders get as creative as they were back then, even if your taste is Budweiser. Hollywood Blvd and the Sunset Strip are classic bar-hopping grounds, but there's plenty of good drinking going on in the beach cities and Downtown as well.

Downtown

Edison (Map pp512-13; ☎ 213-613-0000; 108 W 2nd St; ⏰ 5pm-2am Wed-Fri, 6pm-2am Sat) *Metropolis* meets *Blade Runner* at this industrial-chic basement boîte, where you'll be sipping mojitos surrounded by turbines and other machinery back from its days as a boiler room. Don't worry, it's all tarted up nicely with cocoa leather couches and three cavernous bars. No athletic wear, flip-flops or baggy jeans. It's off Harlem Alley.

Far Bar (Map pp512-13; ☎ 213-617-9990; 347 E 1st St; ⏰ 5pm-midnight Mon-Wed, to 2am Thu-Sun) For less of a scene, walk down the long, narrow alley (that's the far part) to the chill bar part, where twinkling lights arch over the open-air courtyard. You might not know that it's in Little Tokyo were it not for the Sapporo beer and the vittles you can order when the next door restaurant is open.

Rooftop Bar @ Standard Downtown LA (Map pp512-13; ☎ 213-892-8080; 550 S Flower St; ⏰ noon-1:30am) The scene at this outdoor lounge, swimming in a sea of skyscrapers, is libidinous, intense and more than a bit surreal. There are vibrating waterbed pods for lounging, hot-bod servers and a pool for cooling off if it all gets too steamy. Velvet rope on weekends.

Hollywood, Los Feliz & Silver Lake

Formosa Cafe (Map pp514-15; ☎ 323-850-9050; 7156 Santa Monica Blvd, Hollywood) Bogie and Bacall used to knock 'em back at this watering hole, and today you can use all that nostalgia to soak up mai tais and martinis.

Dresden (Map pp514-15; ☎ 323-665-4294; 1760 N Vermont Ave, Los Feliz; 4pm-1:30am Mon-Sat, to midnight Sun) If Formosa had Bogie and Bacall, Dresden has the songster duo Marty & Elaine, who've been there for almost as long. They're an institution (watch them perform 'Muskrat Love') – you saw them singing 'Stayin' Alive' in *Swingers*.

Good Luck Bar (Map pp514-15; ☎ 323-666-3524; 1514 Hillhurst Ave, Los Feliz; 7pm-2am Mon-Fri, 8pm-2am Sat & Sun) The clientele is cool, the jukebox loud and the drinks are seductively strong at this cultish watering hole decked out in Chinese opium-den carmine red. The baby-blue Yee Mee Loo and Chinese herb-based whiskey are popular choices.

Yamashiro (Map pp514-15; ☎ 323-466-5125; 1999 N Sycamore Ave, Hollywood; 5pm-midnight Sun-Thu, to 1am Fri & Sat) Sure, this landmark Japanese palace is also a restaurant, but we think the classy bar is simply the perfect spot for romantic tête-à-têtes, with the entire city glittering below.

Cat & Fiddle Pub (Map pp514-15; ☎ 323-468-3800; 6530 W Sunset Blvd, Hollywood; ⏰ 11:30am-2am) Order up a pint, grab an outdoor table in the fountain courtyard and enjoy Sunday twilight jazz radio broadcasts at this ever-popular pub, a favorite among expat Brits.

Beauty Bar (Map pp514-15; ☎ 323-464-7676; 1638 N Cahuenga Blvd, Hollywood; ⏰ 9am-2am Sun-Wed, 6pm-2am Thu-Sat) This pint-sized cocktail bar is decorated with hair-salon paraphernalia from the Kennedy era. Sip your martini, get your nails done or peruse the hip crowd while sitting in a swivel chair beneath a plastic hair dryer.

West Hollywood, Beverly Hills & Westside

WeHo is the epicenter of LA's gay scene (see the boxed text, p562), but there's a cluster of other venues frequented by hipsters of all sorts.

Bar Lubitsch (Map pp516-17; ☎ 323-850-9050; 7702 Santa Monica Blvd, West Hollywood; 🕑 6pm-2am Sun-Thu, 7pm-2am Fri & Sat) Quaff an absinthe martini, Moscow mule or Molotov cocktail (vodka and apple juice on the rocks, served on fire, naturally) at this Soviet-chic bar amid the Russian shops and groceries of eastern WeHo.

Blue on Blue (Map pp518-19; ☎ 310-277-5221, 800-535-4715; www.avalonbeverlyhills.com; 9400 W Olympic Blvd, Beverly Hills) Trendy types sip their cosmos poolside at the restaurant-bar at the Avalon Hotel (p549). Cozy into a private cabana, and dip into the Elixir cocktail. It's almost good-for-you: cucumber-dill infused vodka, sweetened lime juice and white cranberry juice.

El Carmen (Map pp516-17; ☎ 323-852-1552; 8138 W 3rd St, Mid-City; 🕑 5pm-2am Mon-Fri, 7pm-2am Sat & Sun) Beneath mounted bull heads and *lucha libre* (Mexican wrestling) masks, this tequila temple dispenses with the food (mostly tacos) on the first page of the menu, leaving the other seven pages to cocktails, based on over 100 tequilas. Industry-heavy crowd.

Sky Bar (Map pp516-17; ☎ 323-848-6025; 8440 W Sunset Blvd, West Hollywood) The poolside bar at the Mondrian Hotel (p549) has made a virtue out of snobbery. Unless you're exceptionally pretty, rich or are staying at the hotel, chances are relatively slim that you'll be imbibing expensive drinks (from plastic cups no less, because of the pool) with the ultimate in-crowd.

Santa Monica & Venice

Ye Olde King's Head (Map pp520-1; ☎ 310-451-1402; 116 Santa Monica Blvd, Santa Monica; 🕑 9am-10pm Mon-Thu, to midnight Fri, 8am-midnight Sat, 8am-10pm Sun) This is the unofficial headquarters of the Westside's big British expat community, complete with darts, soccer, er, football on TV and the best fish and chips in town.

Otherroom (Map pp520-1; ☎ 310-396-6230; 1201 Abbot Kinney Blvd, Venice; 🕑 5pm-2am) Dark, loud and industrial, this loftlike lounge screams 'Soho transplant' but is actually a laid-back lair for local lovelies, artists and professionals. Only beer and wine are served, but the selection is tops and handpicked; sometimes the crowd is too.

Penthouse (Map pp520-1; ☎ 310-393-8080; 1111 2nd St, Santa Monica; 🕑 2:30pm-1am) Atop Santa Monica's Huntley Hotel, designer Thomas Schoos' mod silver bar, retracting roof and sheer curtains for (semi-) privacy accent views that are awe-inspiring as the sun sets over the ocean, and merely fab thereafter. The Cucumber Squeeze sounds like salad in a glass: cucumber, basil and lemon juice. Oh, plus sake and vodka.

For bars that ooze history, pop into **Chez Jay** (Map pp520-1; ☎ 310-395-1741; 1657 Ocean Ave, Santa Monica; 🕑 3pm-1am Mon, noon-1am Tue-Fri, 9am-1am Sat & Sun) or the **Galley** (Map pp520-1; ☎ 310-452-1934; 2442 Main St, Santa Monica; 🕑 5pm-1am Mon-Sat, 1pm-1am Sun), both classic watering holes with campy nautical themes.

South Bay & Long Beach

South Bay, particularly Manhattan and Hermosa Beaches, comes alive after dark, with crowds filling the local watering holes.

Alex's Bar (Map pp510-11; ☎ 562-434-8292; 2913 E Anaheim St, Long Beach) This punk hole is as alternative as it gets in Long Beach. Cheap drinks, free wireless internet access with purchase and occasional live bands. Enter from the back.

The action is wild and wacky at the twin 'Animal Houses by the sea' called **Aloha Sharkeez** (Map pp510-11; ☎ 310-374-7823; 52 Pier Ave, Hermosa Beach) and **Baja Sharkeez** (Map pp510-11; ☎ 310-545-6563; 3801 Highland Ave, Manhattan Beach). It's a nonstop frat party where potent libations, frequent drink specials and an abundance of bare skin help fan the party.

ENTERTAINMENT

LA's nightlife is lively, progressive and multifaceted. You can hobnob with hipsters at a trendy dance club, groove to experimental sounds in an underground bar, skate along the cutting edge at a multimedia event in an abandoned warehouse or treat your ears to a concert by the LA Philharmonic. Mainstream, offbeat and fringe theater and performance art all thrive, as do the comedy clubs. Seeing a movie, not surprisingly, has become a deluxe event, with stadium-style multiplex theaters offering giant screens, total surround-sound and comfy leather seats.

The freebie *LA Weekly* and the *Los Angeles Times* Calendar section are your best sources for plugging into the local scene. Buy your tickets at the box office or through **Ticketmaster** (☎ 213-480-3232; www.ticketmaster.com). Half-price tickets to many shows are sold online by **LAStageTIX** (www.theatrela.org).

Cinemas

Moviegoing is serious business in LA; it's not uncommon for viewers to sit through the end

OUT & ABOUT IN LA

West Hollywood is LA's most sizzling gay and lesbian party zone, but there are plenty of happening places to be found in Silver Lake and beyond. Here are some of our favorites:

WeHo

Abbey (Map pp516-17; ☎ 310-289-8410; www.abbeyfoodandbar.com; 692 N Robertson Blvd; mains $9-13; 🕑 8am-2am, breakfast to 2pm) From its origins as a humble coffeehouse, the Abbey has grown into WeHo's coolest, most fun and most varied bar-restaurant. There are so many flavored martinis you'd think Abbey invented them, plus a full menu of pub grub and desserts (yes, they still serve coffee). Take your pick from many spaces, which range from an outdoor patio (superflirty on warm weekend afternoons) to a Goth-mod lounge, a chill room and a private divan.

East West (Map pp516-17; ☎ 310-360-6186; www.eastwestlounge.com; 801 Larrabee St) Finally, WeHo has an intimate, mod lounge worthy of the mod hotties who live here. Prices aren't cheap, but the drink menu is creative (there's a whole list of champagne cocktails), plus bottle service available. Lots of big windows and sidewalk seating allow you to watch the busy street life, too.

Factory/Ultra Suede (Map pp516-17; ☎ 310-659-4551; www.factorynightclubla.com; 652 La Peer Dr) This giant double club has an edgy New York feel and sports different stripes nightly. On Friday night, the Girl Bar (at the Factory) is the preferred playground of fashion-forward femmes, while male hot bods strut their stuff on Saturdays. Music-wise, anything goes here as long as it's got a good beat.

Palms (Map pp516-17; ☎ 310-652-6188; www.thepalmsbar.com; 8572 Santa Monica Blvd) This scene staple has been keeping lesbians happy for over three decades and even gets the occasional celebrity drop-in, as in Melissa Etheridge or Ellen DeGeneres. Check the website for frequent special events.

Rage (Map pp516-17; ☎ 310-652-7055; 8911 Santa Monica Blvd; 🕑 11:30am-2am) This pulsating double-decker bar and dance club for boy pals has a rotating roster of DJs spinning house, R&B, hip-hop, funk and other sounds. There's no cover for Monday's Alternative Night, while 18+ Tuesdays bring in the younger set.

credits, out of respect for friends and neighbors. Venues listed here are as noteworthy for their atmosphere as for their projection facilities. Movie ticket prices run between $10 and $15, a little less before 6pm. Tickets for most theaters can be booked online or through **Moviefone** (☎ from any LA area code 777-3456).

American Cinematheque (☎ 323-466-3456; www.americancinematheque.com) Hollywood (Map pp514-15; Egyptian Theatre, 6712 Hollywood Blvd); Santa Monica (Map pp520-1; Aero Theatre, 1328 Montana Ave) Eclectic film fare from around the world for serious cinephiles, often followed by chats with the actors or director.

ArcLight (Map pp514-15; ☎ 323-464-4226; www.arclightcinemas.com; 6360 W Sunset Blvd, Hollywood) Pick your flick from the airport-style 'departure board' at this ultramodern multiplex. Bonus: no commercials before the film (only trailers). The ArcLight also encompasses the landmark geodesic Cinerama Dome.

California Science Center IMAX (off Map pp512-13; ☎ 323-724-3623; www.californiasciencecenter.org; 700 State Dr, Exposition Park; adult/child/student/senior $7.50/4.50/5.50/5.50; ♿) Nature-themed films for the entire family.

Cinespia (Map pp514-15; www.cemeteryscreenings.com; 6000 Santa Monica Blvd, Hollywood; 🕑 Sat & Sun May-Oct) Screenings 'to-die-for,' projected on the wall of the mausoleum at Hollywood Forever Cemetery (p530). Bring a picnic and cocktails (yes, alcohol is allowed!) to watch classics with a hipster crowd. A DJ spins until showtime.

El Capitan Theatre (Map pp514-15; ☎ 323-347-7674; 6838 Hollywood Blvd, Hollywood; ♿) Lavish historic theater showing mostly first-run Disney movies, occasionally preceded by live show extravaganzas; phone ahead.

Grauman's Chinese Theatre (Map pp514-15; ☎ 323-464-8111; 6925 Hollywood Blvd, Hollywood) Bona fide tourist attraction and industry favorite for glitzy movie premieres.

Nuart Theatre (Map pp520-1; ☎ 310-478-6379; www.landmarktheaters.com; 11272 Santa Monica Blvd, West LA) The best in offbeat and cult flicks, including the camp classic, *The Rocky Horror Picture Show,* every Saturday at midnight. Near Westwood.

Silent Movie Theatre (Map pp516-17; ☎ 323-655-2520; www.silentmovietheatre.com; 611 N Fairfax Ave, Mid-City) 'Silents are golden' at this unique theater where screenings are accompanied by live music.

Live Music

Big-name acts appear at numerous venues around town, including the **Staples Center** (Map pp512-13; ☎ 213-742-7340; www.staplescenter.com; 1111 S Figueroa St, Downtown); next door at the **Nokia Theatre** (Map pp512-13; ☎ 213-763-6030; www.nokiatheatrelive.com; 1111 S Figueroa St, Downtown); the **Gibson Amphitheatre** (Map p522; ☎ 818-622-4440; www.hob

Silver Lake

Akbar (Map pp514-15; ☎ 323-665-6810; www.akbarsilverlake.com; 4356 W Sunset Blvd) Best jukebox in town, Casbah-style atmosphere and a great mix of people that's been known to change from hour to hour – gay, straight, on the fence or just hip, but not too-hip-for-you. Some nights, the back room turns into a dance floor; other nights you can watch comedy or do crafts.

Faultline (Map pp514-15; ☎ 323-660-0889; 4216 Melrose Ave; 6pm-2am Tue-Fri, 2pm-2am Sat & Sun) This indoor-outdoor venue is party central for manly men – there's nary a twink in sight. Take off your shirt and head to the beer bust on Sunday afternoon (it's an institution). Be sure to get there early or expect to settle in for a long wait.

MJ's (Map pp514-15; ☎ 323-660-1503; www.mjsbar.com; 2810 Hyperion Ave) Popular contempo hangout with a mix of dance nights, 'porn star of the week' and cruising. Attracts a younger but diverse crowd.

Other Side (Map pp514-15; ☎ 323-661-0618; www.flyingleapcafe.com; 2538 Hyperion Ave) Piano bar where the crowd skews older and you can actually hear yourself talk. On Friday nights, pianist James Lent swings with a bevy of crooners so talented you'll wonder where they all hide the rest of the week.

Other Neighborhoods

Oil Can Harry's (Map pp510-11; ☎ 818-760-9749; www.oilcanharrysla.com; 11502 Ventura Blvd, Studio City; Tue & Thu-Sat) If you've never been country-and-western dancing, you'll be surprised at just how sexy it can be, and Oil Can's is the place to do it, three nights a week. On Tuesdays, Thursdays and Fridays, it even offers lessons for the uninitiated. Saturday night is retro disco.

Roosterfish (Map pp520-1; ☎ 310-392-2123; www.roosterfishbar.com; 1302 Abbot Kinney Blvd, Venice; 11am-2am) The Westside's last gay bar standing is a friendly, reasonably priced, been-there-forever kind of place that's still current and cool. Strike up new friendships while playing pool or shooting electronic darts. Friday nights are busiest, or the Sunday afternoon barbecue brings in the locals.

.com; 100 Universal City Plaza, Universal City; P), next to Universal Studios Hollywood; the historic **Wiltern Theater** (off Map pp512-13; ☎ 380-5005; 3790 Wilshire Blvd), near Downtown; and, in summer, the Hollywood Bowl (p564) and the **Greek Theatre** (Map p522; ☎ 323-665-1927; www.greektheatrela.com; 2700 N Vermont Ave, Griffith Park; P). For world music, check out what's playing at the intimate outdoor **John Anson Ford Amphitheatre** (Map p529; ☎ 323-461-3673; 2580 E Cahuenga Blvd, Hollywood; May-Oct; P).

Following are some of our favorite live-music clubs. Cover charges vary widely – some gigs are free, but most average between $5 and $10. Unless noted, venues are open nightly and only open to those 21 or older. Also check the listings mags for free concerts playing at Amoeba Music (p567).

Knitting Factory Hollywood (Map pp514-15; ☎ 323-463-0204; www.la.knittingfactory.com; 7021 Hollywood Blvd, Hollywood) This bastion of indie bands welcomes patrons of all ages and offers up top-notch world music, progressive jazz and other alterna-sounds. Headliners take the main stage, the rest make do with the intimate AlterKnit Lounge.

Troubadour (Map pp516-17; ☎ 310-276-6168; www.troubadour.com; 9081 Santa Monica Blvd, West Hollywood; Mon-Sat) The Troub did its part in catapulting the Eagles and Tom Waits to stardom, and it's still a great place to catch tomorrow's headliners. The all-ages policy ensures a mixed crowd that's refreshingly low on attitude. Mondays are free.

Spaceland (Map pp514-15; ☎ 323-661-4380; www.clubspaceland.com; 1717 Silver Lake Blvd, Silver Lake) Mostly local alt-rock, indie, skate-punk and electrotrash bands take the stage here in the hopes of making it big. Beck and the Eels played some of their early gigs here.

Catalina Bar & Grill (Map pp514-15; ☎ 323-466-2210; www.catalinajazzclub.com; 6725 W Sunset Blvd, Hollywood; cover $10-18, plus dinner or 2 drinks; Tue-Sun) LA's premier jazz club has a top-notch booking policy, which has included heavies like the Marsalis brothers.

Jazz Bakery (Map pp510-11; ☎ 310-271-9039; www.jazzbakery.org; 3233 Helms Ave, Culver City; cover $15-30) Nonprofit jazz joint in the Helms Bakery, regularly pulling in such headliners as Mark Murphy and Steve Lacy alongside top local talent, performing for a serious and respectful crowd; don't even think about whispering, eating or leaving your cell phone on.

McCabe's Guitar Shop (☎ 310-828-4403; www.mccabes.com; 3101 Pico Blvd, Santa Monica) This mecca of musicianship sells guitars and other instruments, and the likes of Jackson Browne, Liz Phair and Phranc perform live in the postage-stamp-sized back room.

Babe & Ricky's (Map pp510-11; ☎ 323-295-9112; www.bluesbar.com; 4339 Leimert Blvd, Leimert Park) Mama Laura has presided over LA's oldest blues club for nearly four decades. The Monday-night jam session, with free food, often brings the house down.

Nightclubs

If you want all your clichés about Los Angeles confirmed, look no further than a nightclub in Hollywood or West Hollywood. Come armed with a hot bod, a healthy attitude or a fat wallet in order to impress the armoire-sized goons presiding over the velvet rope. Clubs in other neighborhoods are considerably more laid-back, but most require you to be at least 21 (bring picture ID). Cover ranges from $5 to $20. Doors are usually open from 9pm to 2am.

Cinespace (Map pp514-15; ☎ 323-817-3456; www.cinespace.info; 6356 Hollywood Blvd, Hollywood) DJ-to-the-stars Steve Aoki has a Tuesday residency at this upstairs playground of skinny jeansters who favored eyeliner long before certain pirates made it fashionable. The dinner-and-a-movie nights (Thursday to Saturday) are perfect if you're not into switching venues halfway through the evening.

Nacional (Map pp514-15; ☎ 323-962-7712; 1645 Wilcox Ave, Hollywood; Tue-Sat; P) Another entry in Hollywood's growing cadre of megaclubs, this one has a seductive prerevolution-Cuba theme with fiery mood lighting and loungy Bauhaus-style furniture. A picky door policy keeps out any weekend warriors that don't fit the profile (whatever that may be).

Circus Disco (Map pp514-15; ☎ 323-462-1291; www.circusdisco.com; 6655 Santa Monica Blvd, Hollywood) It's quite literally a 'seven-ring circus' on Saturday nights when DJs spin mostly hip-hop and Latin in – count them – seven separate rooms in this ginormous warehouse. Strapping gay boyz sweat it out on the dance floor on Tuesday and Friday nights, but there's always the patio for cooling off.

Zanzibar (Map pp520-1; ☎ 310-451-2221; www.zanzibarlive.com; 1301 5th St, Santa Monica) DJs Jason Bentley and Garth Trinidad of radio KCRW (p509) are among the spinmeisters working their turntable magic (deep house, dubbed-out funk, retro jazz) at this lounge with a sultry Indian/African vibe. The shape-shifting global lineup goes from Arabic to Latin to African depending on the night. The crowd is just as multiculti. Show up early to avoid the inevitable line.

Performance Arts

Los Angeles Philharmonic (Map pp512-13; ☎ 323-850-2000; www.laphil.org; 111 S Grand Ave, Downtown; tickets $15-120) Conductor Esa Pekka-Salonen will soon pass the baton to Venezuelan phenom Gustavo Dudamel, and by all indications he's leaving the world-class LA Phil in excellent hands. Catch them at Frank Gehry's amazing Walt Disney Concert Hall from October to June (see p524).

Hollywood Bowl (Map pp514-15; ☎ 323-850-2000; www.hollywoodbowl.com; 2301 N Highland Ave, Hollywood; tickets $1-105; late Jun-Sep) One of those quintessential LA summer experiences, this historic natural amphitheater is the summer home of the LA Phil (above) and also a stellar place to catch big-name rock, jazz, blues and pop acts. Do as the locals do and come early for a preshow picnic (alcohol is allowed).

Los Angeles Opera (Map pp512-13; ☎ 213-972-8001; www.laopera.com; Dorothy Chandler Pavilion, Music Center of LA County, 135 N Grand Ave, Downtown; tickets $30-190) Star tenor Plácido Domingo presides over the LA Opera, whose productions range from real crowd-pleasers to rarely performed esoteric works.

Redcat (Map pp512-13; ☎ 213-237-2800; www.redcat.org; 631 W 2nd St, Downtown) Part of the Walt Disney Concert Hall complex, this venue presents a global feast of avant-garde and experimental theater, performance art, dance, readings, film and video.

Theater

Believe it or not, there are more live theaters in LA than in New York. Venues range from a thousand-plus seats down to 99-seat-or-less 'Equity waiver' houses, so named because actors can showcase themselves or new works free of the rules of the Actors' Equity union. Here are some of the leaders:

Mark Taper Forum (Map pp512-13; ☎ 213-628-2772; www.taperahmanson.com; Music Center of LA County, 135 N Grand Ave, Downtown) The Taper is the home base of the Center Theatre Group, one of SoCal's leading resident ensembles. It has developed numerous new plays, most famously Tony Kushner's *Angels in America*. Ask about public rush tickets ($12).

Actors' Gang Theatre (Map pp518-19; ☎ 310-838-4264; www.theactorsgang.com; Ivy Substation, 9070 Venice Blvd, Culver City) The 'Gang' was founded in 1981 by Tim Robbins and his fellow renegade UCLA acting-school grads. Its daring and offbeat reinterpretations of classic plays have a loyal following, although it's the bold new works pulled from ensemble workshops that make this socially mindful troupe one to watch.

East West Players (Map pp512-13; ☎ 213-625-4397; www.eastwestplayers.org; 120 N Judge John Aiso St, Little Tokyo; tickets $23-38) Founded in 1965, this pioneering Asian-American ensemble presents modern classics as well as premieres by local playwrights. Alumni have gone on to win Tony, Emmy and Academy awards.

Will Geer Theatricum Botanicum (Map pp510-11; ☎ 310-455-3723; www.theatricum.com; 1419 N Topanga Canyon Blvd, Topanga; tickets $11-25; Jun-Oct; P) This magical natural outdoor amphitheatre was founded by Will Geer (TV's Grandpa Walton) and takes on Shakespeare, Dylan Thomas, Tennessee Williams and other American and European writers.

Other thespian venues:

Ahmanson Theatre (Map pp512-13; ☎ 213-628-2772; www.taperahmanson.com; Music Center of LA County, 135 N Grand Ave, Downtown; tickets $20-80) Mostly big-time Broadway-style musicals and visiting blockbusters.

Odyssey Theatre Ensemble (Map pp520-1; ☎ 310-477-2055; www.odysseytheatre.com; 2055 S Sepulveda Blvd; tickets $20-25; P) Well-respected ensemble presenting new work and updated classics in three 99-seat theaters under one roof, near Westwood.

Deaf West Theatre (Map p522; ☎ 818-762-2773; www.deafwest.org; 5112 Lankershim Blvd, North Hollywood) Hearing-impaired actors perform classic and contemporary plays in sign language with voice interpretation and/or supertitles.

Celebration Theatre (Map pp516-17; ☎ 323-957-1884; www.celebrationtheatre.com; 7051 Santa Monica Blvd, West Hollywood) One of the nation's leading producers of gay and lesbian plays, winning dozens of awards.

Comedy

Little surprise that LA is one of the world's comedy capitals. Comedy clubs often fill up, so make reservations or show up early for decent seats. At clubs serving full menus, the best seats are reserved for dinner patrons. If you're not eating, many clubs require a two-drink minimum order on top of the cover charge (usually $10 to $20). Except where noted, you must be 21 or older to get in.

Comedy & Magic Club (Map pp510-11; ☎ 310-372-1193; www.comedyandmagicclub.com; 1018 Hermosa Ave, Hermosa Beach) Best known as the place where Jay Leno tests out his *Tonight Show* shtick most Sunday nights. Reservations required and patrons must be 18 years old.

Groundlings (Map pp516-17; ☎ 323-934-4747; www.groundlings.com; 7307 Melrose Ave, Mid-City) This improv school and company launched the careers of Lisa Kudrow, Jon Lovitz, Will Ferrell and other top talent. Improv night on Thursday brings together the main company, alumni and surprise guests. All ages.

Comedy Store (Map pp516-17; ☎ 323-656-6225; www.thecomedystore.com; 8433 W Sunset Blvd, West Hollywood) From Chris Tucker to Whoopi Goldberg, there's hardly a famous comic alive that has not at some point performed at this classic, which was a gangster hangout in an earlier life.

Sports

BASEBALL

Since moving here from Brooklyn in 1958, the **LA Dodgers** (www.dodgers.com) have become synonymous with LA baseball. The team plays from April to October at Dodger Stadium (p524).

BASKETBALL

They may have lost some of their hustle, but the **LA Lakers** (www.nba.com/lakers) still pack 'em into the sparkling **Staples Center** (Map pp512-13; ☎ 213-742-7340; www.staplescenter.com; 1111 S Figueroa St, Downtown), which is also home to the city's second men's NBA team, the historically mediocre **LA Clippers** (www.nba.com/clippers), and the considerably more successful women's team, the **LA Sparks** (www.wnba.com/sparks). The WNBA season (late May to August) follows the regular men's NBA season (October to April). Lakers tickets are hardest to come by and are mostly sold through **Ticketmaster** (☎ 213-480-3232; www.ticketmaster.com).

ICE HOCKEY

The **LA Kings** (www.lakings.com) play in the National Hockey League (NHL), whose regular season runs from October to April, followed by the play-offs. Home games take place at Staples Center (see above).

SOCCER

The arrival of David (and Victoria) Beckham to Major League Soccer's **LA Galaxy** (www.lagalaxy.com) was supposed to spike attendance at the

LA'S FASHION DISTRICT DEMYSTIFIED

Nordstrom's semiannual sale? Barney's warehouse blowout? These are mere child's play to serious bargain shoppers, who save their best game for Downtown LA's **Fashion District** (Map pp512-13; ☎ 213-488-1153; www.fashiondistrict.org), a frantic, 90-block trove of stores, stalls and showrooms where discount shopping is an Olympian sport. Basically, the district is subdivided into specialty areas:

Designer knockoffs (Santee & New Alleys) Enter on 11th St between Maple Ave and Santee St.
Children (Wall St) Between 12th St and Pico Blvd.
Jewelry and accessories (Santee St) Between Olympic Blvd and 11th St.
Men and bridal (Los Angeles St) Between 7th and 9th Sts.
Textiles (8th St) Between Santee and Wall Sts.
Women (Los Angeles St) Between Olympic and Pico Blvds; also at 11th St between Los Angeles and San Julian Sts.

Shops with signs reading 'Wholesale Only' or *'Mayoreo'* are off-limits to the public. Haggling is OK, but don't expect more than 10% or 20% off, and most vendors accept only cash. Refunds or exchanges are rare, so choose carefully; many items are 'seconds,' meaning they're slightly flawed. Most stores don't have dressing rooms. Hours are generally 9am to 5pm Monday to Saturday; many stores are closed on Sunday except on Santee Alley.

On the last Friday of the month (except during trade shows or around holidays; call to confirm), you can snap up amazing deals when dozens of designer showrooms open to the public for 'sample sales.' Sales take place from 9am to 3pm in and around the **New Mart** (Map pp512-13; ☎ 213-627-0671; 127 E 9th St, Downtown), which specializes in contemporary and young designers, and the **California Mart** (Map pp512-13; ☎ 213-630-3600; 110 E 9th St, Downtown), one of the largest apparel marts in the country, with 1500 showrooms.

game, but injuries and lackluster performance has tempered that success. Still, *fútból* definitely enjoys a passionate following among LA's Latino population. In 2005 the **Club Deportivo Chivas USA** (http://chivas.usa.mlsnet.com/MLS/cdc) joined the fray. Teams play from April to October in the slick new **Home Depot Center** (Map pp510-11; 18400 Avalon Blvd), in the southern LA suburb of Carson (take the Avalon exit off I-405).

SHOPPING

Fashion-forward fashionistas (and paparazzi) flock to Robertson Blvd (between N Beverly Blvd and W 3rd St) or Melrose Ave (between San Vicente and La Brea) in West Hollywood, while bargain hunters haunt Downtown's Fashion District (see the boxed text, above). If money is no object, Beverly Hills beckons with international couture, jewelry and antiques, especially along Rodeo Dr, which is ground central for groovy tunes, while east of here Silver Lake has cool kitsch and collectibles, especially around Sunset Junction (Hollywood and Sunset Blvds). Santa Monica has good boutique shopping on Tony Montana Ave and eclectic Main St, while the chain store brigade (Gap to Sephora) has taken over Third Street Promenade. In nearby Venice, you'll find cheap and crazy knickknacks along the Venice Boardwalk, although locals prefer Abbot Kinney Blvd with its fun mix of art, fashion and new-age emporiums.

Fashion

LA teems with shopping malls for everyday wear and large chain shops, and Melrose Ave between Fairfax and La Brea Avenues has been a fun and funky stroll for youth fashion for over a generation. There are vintage shops throughout town, including a large concentration in North Hollywood, on Magnolia Ave east of Lankershim Blvd.

Fred Segal West Hollywood (Map pp516-17; ☎ 323-651-4129; 8100 Melrose Ave; P); Santa Monica (Map pp520-1; ☎ 310-458-9940; 500 Broadway; P) Cameron and Gwyneth are among the stars kitted out at this kingpin of LA fashion boutiques, where you can also stock up on beauty products, sunglasses, gifts and other essentials.

Kitson (Map pp516-17; ☎ 310-859-2652; 115 S Robertson Blvd, West Hollywood) If you like to stay ahead of the fashion curve, pop into this hip haven chock-full of tomorrow's outfits and accessories, many of them by local labels. It's a major stop for celebs on a shopping prowl.

Wasteland Mid-City (Map pp516-17; ☎ 323-653-3028; 7428 Melrose Ave); Santa Monica (Map pp520-1; ☎ 310-395-2620; 1338 4th St) This warehouse-sized space has glamour gowns, velvet suits and other vintage outfits going back to the '40s, plus rows of racks packed with contemporary styles, all in great condition.

DNA (Map pp520-1; ☎ 310-399-0341; 411 Rose Ave, Venice; P) Tiny DNA is jam-packed with a small but choice assortment of hip garb for men and women, much of it with stylish European flair, by both local and national designers.

American Apparel (www.americanapparel.net) AA's stylish logo-free T-shirts, tank tops, skirts and shorts – available in bold popsicle colors – are made right here in LA in a sweatshop-free facility. Check the website for a branch near you – there are several, including at Santa Monica, Los Feliz and Beverly Hills.

Remix Vintage Shoes (Map pp516-17; ☎ 323-936-6210; 7605 Beverly Blvd, Mid-City) This handsome store is stocked with never-worn vintage footwear from the 1920s to the '70s. If you need a pair of wingtips or wedgies to complete your retro look, this is the place to go.

Turtle Beach Swimwear (Map pp516-17; ☎ 310-652-6039; 320 N La Cienega Blvd, West Hollywood) This little shop will have you looking good poolside with its big selection of mix-and-match tops and bottoms. Tankinis to push-ups, thongs to boy shorts in nylon, cotton, velvet, crochet – you name it, it's here.

Flea Markets

Rose Bowl Flea Market (Map pp510-11; Rose Bowl, 1001 Rose Bowl Dr, Pasadena; admission $7-20; 5am-4:30pm 2nd Sun of the month) This is the mother of all flea markets, with over 2200 vendors. True pros show up at 5am (when admission is $20), flashlight in hand, to ferret out the best stuff.

Pasadena City College Flea Market (Map pp510-11; 1570 E Colorado Blvd, Pasadena; admission free; 8am-3pm 1st Sun of the month) With over 450 vendors, this market has plenty in store for treasure hunters and is more manageable than the Rose Bowl. The music section is legendary.

Melrose Trading Post (Map pp516-17; 7850 Melrose Ave, West Hollywood; admission $2; 8am-6pm Sun; P) Small but choice, this market at Fairfax High School has up to 200 purveyors feeding the current retro frenzy with funky and often quite bizarre stuff – from '40s glamour gowns to mermaid swizzle sticks.

Music

Amoeba Music (Map pp514-15; ☎ 323-245-6400; www.amoeba.com; 6400 W Sunset Blvd, Hollywood; 10:30am-10pm Mon-Sat, 11am-9pm Sun; P) San Francisco Amoeba has made a big splash in Hollywood – our friends call it 'Hot-moeba.' All-star staff and listening stations help you sort through over half a million new and used CDs, DVDs, videos and vinyl, and there are free in-store live shows.

Head Line Records (Map pp516-17; ☎ 323-655-2125; www.headlinerecords.com; 7706 Melrose Ave, Mid-City; noon-8pm) The ultimate source for punk and hardcore.

Hear Music (Map pp520-1; ☎ 310-319-9527; 1429 Third St Promenade, Santa Monica; 8am-11pm Sun-Thu, to 12:30am Fri & Sat) This former indie store is now in cahoots with Starbucks but still specializes in choice grown-up sounds – from electronica to blues, world music to jazz.

Quirky

Wacko/La Luz de Jesus (Map pp514-15; ☎ 323-663-0122; 4633 Hollywood Blvd, Silver Lake; 11am-7pm Mon-Wed, to 9pm Thu-Sat, noon-6pm Sun) Billy Shire's emporium of camp and kitsch has been a fun browse for over three decades. Pick up hula-girl swizzle sticks, a Frida Kahlo mesh bag, an inflatable globe or other, well, wacky stuff. In back is La Luz de Jesus, one of LA's top lowbrow art galleries.

Munky King (Map pp516-17; ☎ 323-938-0091; 7308 Melrose Ave, Hollywood; noon-8pm) This toy temple with a twist specializes in independent designer playthings from around the world, including Ugly Dolls, urban vinyl toys from Hong Kong and Kubricks from Japan.

Giant Robot (Map pp520-1; ☎ 310-478-1819; 2015 Sawtelle Blvd, West LA; 11:30am-8pm Mon-Sat, noon-7pm Sun). For Japanese toys, similar to the selection sold at Munky King. Start here and venture on to the nearby Japanese groceries, bakeries and restaurants.

Meltdown Comics & Collectibles (Map pp516-17; ☎ 323-851-7283; www.meltcomics.com; 7522 W Sunset Blvd, West Hollywood; 11am-10pm) LA's coolest comics store beckons with indie and mainstream books, from Japanese manga to graphic novels by Daniel Clowes of *Ghost World* fame. The Baby Melt department stocks rad stuff for kids.

Pleasure Chest (Map pp516-17; ☎ 323-650-1022; 7733 Santa Monica Blvd, West Hollywood; 10am-midnight Sun-Wed, to 1am Thu, to 2am Fri & Sat; P) This kingdom of kinkiness is filled with sexual hardware

TINSELTOWN TREASURES

So you've stood in Tom Cruise's footsteps at Grauman's Chinese Theatre, dined at the table at Spago once occupied by Britney Spears and seen Ashton Kutcher in the flesh during a taping of the *Tonight Show*. To keep the tinsel glittering for a bit longer, pick up a souvenir from one of these stores, all of which stock a bit more than plastic Oscar statuettes and Hollywood Sign fridge magnets.

It's a Wrap (Map p522; ☎ 818-567-7366; 3315 W Magnolia Ave, Burbank) Tank tops to tuxedos worn by actors, extras and cameos working on TV or movies and sold at steep discounts. Another branch is located at 1164 S Robertson Blvd, Los Angeles.

Larry Edmunds Bookshop (Map pp514-15; ☎ 323-463-3273; 6644 Hollywood Blvd, Hollywood) Longtime purveyor of scripts, posters, stills and books about movies, theater and TV.

Baby Jane of Hollywood (Map pp516-17; ☎ 323-848-7080; 7985 Santa Monica Blvd, West Hollywood; noon-8pm; P) The go-to place for famous autographs, vintage movie posters or even topless pictures of Dame Julie Andrews.

catering to every conceivable fantasy and fetish, though more of the naughty than the nice variety.

GETTING THERE & AWAY

Air

The main gateway to LA is **Los Angeles International Airport** (LAX; Map pp510-11; ☎ 310-646-5252; www.lawa.org; 1 World Way, Los Angeles), located right on the coast between Venice and the South Bay city of Manhattan Beach. Its eight terminals are built around a horseshoe-shaped bi-level traffic loop. Ticketing and check-in desks are on the upper (departure) level, while baggage-claim areas are on the lower (arrival) level. The hub for most international airlines is the Tom Bradley International Terminal.

Free shuttles to other terminals and hotels stop outside each terminal on the lower level. A free minibus for the mobility-impaired can be ordered by calling ☎ 310-646-6402.

Locals love **Bob Hope Airport** (BUR; Map pp510-11; ☎ 818-840-8840, 800-835-9287; www.bobhopeairport.com; 2627 N Hollywood Way, Burbank), which many still call Burbank Airport, in the San Fernando Valley. It has delightful art-deco style, easy-to-use terminals and proximity to Hollywood, Downtown or Pasadena.

To the south, on the border with Orange County, **Long Beach Airport** (LGB; Map pp510-11; ☎ 562-570-2600; www.longbeach.gov/airport; 4100 Donald Douglas Dr, Long Beach) is convenient for Disneyland. Another regional landing base is **Ontario International Airport** (ONT; Map pp510-11; ☎ 909-937-2700; www.lawa.org/ont; 2900 E Airport Dr, Ontario), approximately 35 miles east of Downtown LA.

Bus

LA's hub for **Greyhound** (Map pp512-13; ☎ 213-629-8401, 800-231-2222; 1716 E 7th St) is in an unsavory part of Downtown, so avoid arriving after dark. Bus 18 makes the 10-minute trip to the 7th St metro station with onward service across town, including Metro Rail's Red Line to Hollywood. Some northbound buses stop at the terminal in **Hollywood** (Map pp514-15; ☎ 323-466-6381; 1715 N Cahuenga Blvd), and a few southbound buses also pass through **Long Beach** (Map pp510-11; ☎ 562-218-3011; 1498 Long Beach Blvd).

Greyhound buses serve San Diego at least hourly ($17, 2¼ to four hours) and there are up to eight buses to/from Santa Barbara ($14, 2¼ to three hours). Services to/from San Francisco run almost hourly ($45.50, 7½ to 12½ hours). There are also frequent departures to Anaheim ($14, one hour). For general information about Greyhound travel, see p731 and p732.

Car & Motorcycle

All the major international car-rental agencies have branches at airports and throughout Los Angeles (see p735 for central reservation numbers). If you haven't prebooked, use the courtesy phones in the arrival areas at LAX. Offices and lots are outside the airport, but each company provides free shuttles to take you there.

For Harley rentals, check **Eagle Rider** (Map pp510-11; ☎ 310-536-6777; www.eaglerider.com; 11860 S La Cienega Blvd, Hawthorne; 9am-5pm) or **Route 66** (Map pp520-1; ☎ 310-578-0112, 888-434-4473; 4161 Lincoln Blvd, Marina del Rey; 9am-6pm Tue-Sat, 10am-5pm Sun & Mon). Rates start from $135 to $195 a day, with discounts for longer rentals.

Train

Amtrak trains roll into Downtown's historic **Union Station** (Map pp512-13; ☎ 800-872-7245; 800 N Alameda St) from across California and the country. The *Pacific Surfliner* travels daily to San Diego ($34, 2¾ hours), Santa Barbara ($25, 2¾ to 3¼ hours) and San Luis Obispo ($36, 5½ hours). See p738 for full details.

GETTING AROUND

To/From the Airports

LOS ANGELES INTERNATIONAL AIRPORT

Door-to-door shuttles, such as those operated by **Prime Time** (☎ 800-473-3743; www.primetimeshuttle.com) and **Super Shuttle** (☎ 310-782-6600; www.supershuttle.com), leave from the lower level of all terminals. Typical fares to Santa Monica, Hollywood or Downtown are $21, $26 and $16, respectively. Practically all airport-area hotels and some hostels have arrangements with shuttle companies for free or discounted pick-ups. **Coach America** (☎ 714-978-8855; www.grayline.com) travels hourly or half-hourly from LAX to the main Disneyland resorts for $20 one way or $30 round-trip.

Curbside dispatchers will summon a taxi for you. There's a flat fare of $46.50 to Downtown LA, and fares average $25 to Santa Monica, $35 to Hollywood and up to $85 to Disneyland. There is a $2.50 surcharge for taxis departing LAX.

Flyaway Buses (☎ 866-435-9529; www.lawa.org/flyaway; adult/child $4/2) depart LAX terminals every 30 minutes from about 5am to midnight, to Westwood, Van Nuys and Union Station in Downtown LA.

Public transportation is slower and less convenient but cheaper. From outside any terminal, catch a free shuttle bus to parking lot C, from where it is a walk of under a minute to the LAX Transit Center, the hub for buses serving all of LA. You can also take shuttle bus G to Aviation Station and the Metro Green Line light rail, from where you can connect to the Blue Line and Downtown LA. Trip planning help is available at ☎ 800-266-6883 or www.metro.net.

Popular routes (trip times given are approximate and depend on traffic):

Downtown Metro Buses 42a or 439 West ($1.25, 1½ hours)
Hollywood Metro bus 42a West to Overhill/La Brea, transfer to Metro bus 212 North ($2.50, 1½ hours)
Venice & Santa Monica Big Blue Bus 3 (75¢, 30 to 50 minutes)

BOB HOPE AIRPORT

For door-to-door shuttle companies, see the LAX information (left). Typical shuttle fares are Hollywood $24, Downtown $26 and Pasadena $24. Cabs charge about $20, $30 and $40, respectively. Metro Bus 163 South goes to Hollywood (30 minutes), while Downtown is served by Metro Bus 94 South (one hour).

LONG BEACH AIRPORT

See the LAX information for shuttle services (left), which cost $35 to the Disneyland area, $40 to Downtown LA and $29 to Manhattan Beach. Cabs cost $45, $65 and $40, respectively. Long Beach Transit Bus 111 South makes the trip to the Transit Mall in downtown Long Beach in about 45 minutes. From here you can catch the Metro Blue Line to Downtown LA and points beyond.

Bicycle

Most buses have bike racks and bikes ride for free, although you must securely load and unload it yourself. Bikes are also allowed on Metro Rail trains except during rush hour (6:30am to 8:30am and 4:30pm to 6:30pm, weekdays). For rental places, see p543.

Car & Motorcycle

Unless time is no factor – or money is extremely tight – it makes sense to drive yourself, despite some of the worst traffic in the country. Avoid rush hour (7am to 9am and 3:30pm to 6pm).

Parking at motels and cheaper hotels is usually free (free parking is noted with Ⓟ), while fancier ones charge anywhere from $8 to $25. Valet parking at nicer restaurants and hotels is common, with charges from $1 to $10 or more at fancy clubs. It is customary to tip the valet $1 per car when it is returned.

For local parking suggestions, see the introductions to individual neighborhoods.

Public Transportation

METRO

LA's main public transportation agency is **Metro** (☎ 800-266-6883; www.metro.net), which operates about 200 bus lines as well as four subway/light-rail lines:

Red Line Downtown LA's Union Station to North Hollywood, via central Hollywood and Universal Studios.
Blue Line Downtown to Long Beach.
Gold Line Union Station to Pasadena.
Green Line Norwalk to Redondo Beach (and near LAX).

Tickets cost $1.25 per boarding or $5/17 per day/week pass with unlimited rides. Bus drivers sell single tickets and day passes (exact fare required), while train tickets are available from vending machines at each station. Phone or click for trip planning help.

BUS

Some neighborhoods are served by local **DASH minibuses** (☎ your area code +808-2273; www.ladottransit.com). Here are some of the useful routes (fare per boarding 25¢):

Beachwood Canyon Route Useful for close-ups of the Hollywood Sign, runs from Hollywood/Vine Metro station up Beachwood Dr.

Downtown Routes Six separate routes, hitting all the hot spots, including Chinatown, City Hall, Little Tokyo, the Financial District and Exposition Park.

Fairfax Route Makes a loop taking in the Beverly Center mall, the Pacific Design Center, the farmers market, LACMA and other museums on the Miracle Mile.

Hollywood/West Hollywood Route Connects Hollywood & Highland with the Beverly Center along Sunset Blvd (including Sunset Strip) and La Cienega Blvd.

Santa Monica–based **Big Blue Bus** (☎ 310-451-5444; www.bigbluebus.com) serves much of western LA, including Santa Monica, Venice, Westwood and LAX (75¢). Its express bus 10 runs from Santa Monica to Downtown LA ($1.75).

Taxi

Except for those taxis lined up outside airports, train stations, bus stations and major hotels, it's best to ring for a cab. Fares are metered: $2.85 at flag fall plus $2.70 per mile. Taxis serving the airport accept credit cards, though sometimes grudgingly. Some recommended companies:

Checker (☎ 800-300-5007)
Independent (☎ 800-521-8294)
Yellow Cab (☎ 800-200-1085)

AROUND LOS ANGELES

CATALINA ISLAND

pop 3650

Mediterranean-flavored Catalina Island is a popular getaway for harried Angelenos, even if it sinks under the weight of day-trippers in summer. Stay overnight, though, and feel the ambience go from frantic to romantic.

Part of the Channel Islands (p504), Catalina has a unique ecosystem and history. Until the late 19th century it went through phases as a hangout for sea-otter poachers, smugglers and Union soldiers. Chewing-gum magnate William Wrigley Jr (1861–1932) purchased it in 1919 and brought his baseball team, the Chicago Cubs, here for spring training. In 1924 bison were imported for the shooting of a western *(The Vanishing American)*; today their descendants form a managed herd of about 200. Most of the island's interior of sun-baked hillsides, valleys and canyons is owned by the Santa Catalina Island Conservancy, which ensures that most of it remains free of development, though open for visitors. In 2007 a fire burned some 4750 acres, sparing most of the island and its habitats.

Orientation

Nearly all tourist activity concentrates in the pint-sized port town of Avalon, where a yacht-studded harbor hems in a tiny downtown with shops, hotels and restaurants. The only other settlement is remote Two Harbors in the backcountry, which has a general store, dive and kayak center, snack bar and lodge.

Information

Catalina Visitors Bureau (☎ 310-510-1520; www.catalina.com; Green Pier, Avalon)

Public library (☎ 310-510-1050; 1-7pm Tue-Thu, 11am-5pm Fri & Sat; internet access)

US Bank (Crescent Ave & Metropole St) Has 24-hour ATM.

Sights

Avalon's most recognizable landmark is the art deco **Casino** (☎ 310-510-0179; 1 Casino Way), which dates from 1929 and has great murals, a theater with a twinkling domed ceiling and a famous ballroom upstairs, which can be seen only via an amusing one-hour tour ($14.50). Tour tickets also include admission to the **Catalina Island Museum** (☎ 310-510-2414; www.catalinamuseum.org; 1 Casino Way; adult/child/senior $5/2/4; 10am-4pm daily Apr-Dec, 10am-4pm Fri-Wed Jan-Mar), which has modest exhibits about milestones in the island's history, including its role during WWII and the Chicago Cubs era.

About 1.5 miles inland from Avalon harbor is the peaceful **Wrigley Memorial & Botanical Garden** (☎ 310-510-2595; 1400 Avalon Canyon Rd; adult/child $5/free; 8am-5pm), which has sweeping views, handmade local tiles and impressive gardens of cacti, succulents and plants unique to the island.

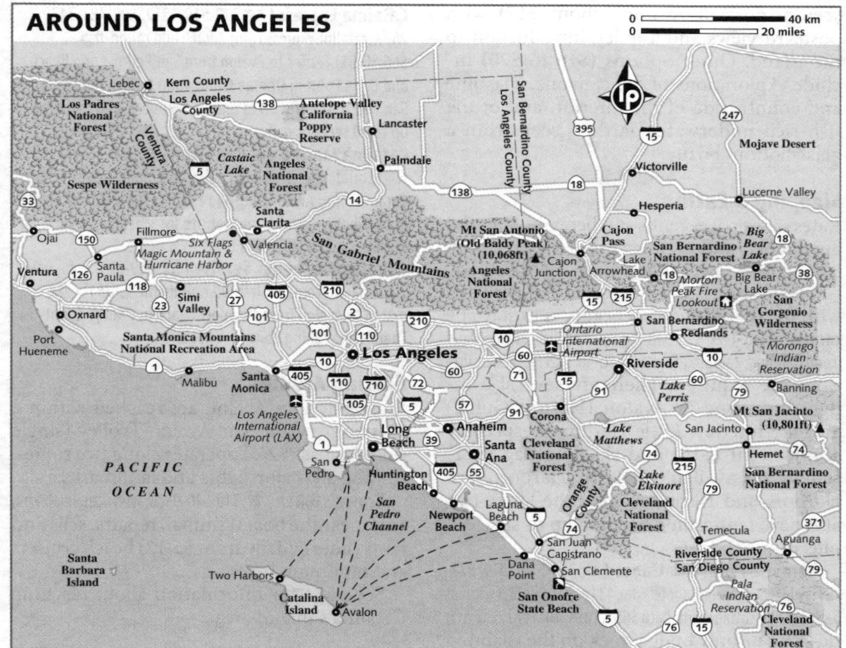

Catalina's hilly interior is a protected **nature preserve** and may only be explored on foot or mountain bike (see below), or on an organized tour (see right). Although the landscape appears barren, it actually teems with plant life and animals, and there are memorable views of the rugged coast and sandy coves. If you're lucky, you'll even run into the resident herd of bison.

Activities

HIKING & MOUNTAIN-BIKING

Escape Avalon's crowds by hitting the trails. The trailheads closest to town are above Hermit Gulch campground and behind the Wrigley Memorial. Pick up maps and compulsory permits at the **Catalina Island Conservancy** (☎ 310-510-2595; www.catalinaconservancy.org; 125 Claressa St; biking/hiking permit $20/free; ⏲ 8:30am-3:30pm). Permits are also available at Two Harbors and the airport.

To reach the protected backcountry, hop on the **Airport Shuttle** (☎ 310-510-0143; adult/child round-trip $20/15; up to 6 daily) or **Safari Bus** (☎ 310-510-4205; tickets $6.50-26; ⏲ mid-Jun–early Sep). The hilltop airport is a popular starting point as you're hiking back downhill virtually the whole time. Both companies require advance reservations. There's very little shade, so bring a hat, sunscreen and plenty of water.

WATER SPORTS

Avalon's sliver of a beach along Crescent Ave gets packed, and it's not much better at palm-tree-lined **Descanso Beach** (admission $2), a beach club with a bar and restaurant that's a short walk north of the Casino. Nearby, though, is some of SoCal's finest kayaking. **Descanso Beach Ocean Sports** (☎ 310-510-1226; www.kayakcatalinaisland.com; rentals from hr/day $16/48) rents snorkeling gear and kayaks, and also runs guided kayaking tours and kayak camping trips.

There's good **snorkeling** at Lovers' Cove and at Casino Point Marine Park, an actual marine reserve that's also the best shore dive. Rent gear at any of these locations or on Green Pier.

Tours

Discovery Tours (☎ 310-510-2500; www.visitcatalinaisland.com) and **Catalina Adventure Tours** (☎ 310-510-2888; www.catalinaadventuretours.com) both offer scenic tours of Avalon (about $17) with postcard views and a quick introduction to the island. Other options ($16 to $70) include explorations of the canyons, coastline and countryside of the interior, and of the fish-rich underwater gardens seen from a glass-bottom boat.

Sleeping & Eating

Rates soar on weekends and between May and September, and at other times they're about 30% to 60% lower than what's listed below.

The best way to get up close and personal with the island's natural beauty is to stay at a **campground** (☎ 310-510-8368; www.visitcatalinaisland.com/camping; camping fees adult/child $12/6); reservations are required. There are several campgrounds, one in Avalon (Hermit Gulch) and the interior; Little Harbor is especially scenic. Tent ($16) and sleeping bag ($11) rentals are available at Little Harbor, Two Harbors and Hermit Gulch; the latter two also have tent cabins sleeping up to six ($57, plus camping fee).

Hermosa Hotel & Cottages (☎ 310-510-1010, 877-453-1313; www.hermosahotel.com; 131 Metropole St; r without bath $45-75, cottage with bath $65-170) Central, clean, tidy – your only budget pick on the island.

Villa Portofino (☎ 310-510-0555, 800-346-2326, 888-510-0555; www.hotelvillaportofino.com; 111 Crescent Ave; r $140-390;) Comfortable and elegant with gas fireplaces and bay-view sundeck, and fancy Italian dining.

La Paloma & Las Flores (☎ 310-510-0737, 800-310-1505; www.lapalomalasflores.com; 328 Sunny Lane; cottage $160-240, r $190-250; wi-fi) Choose from Old Catalina cottages or newer rooms with two-person spas and balconies.

Casino Dock Café (☎ 310-510-2755; 1 Casino Way; dishes $5-10; 7:30am-6pm Apr-Nov) Casual waterfront hangout, good for a beer and a simple meal.

The Cottage (☎ 310-510-0726; 603 Crescent Ave; breakfast & lunch $6-13, dinner $10-23; breakfast & lunch daily, dinner Wed-Sun) Huge breakfasts, sandwiches and American, Italian and Mexican favorites, in a setting of stained glass and cut glass.

Catalina Country Club Restaurant (☎ 310-510-7404; 1 Country Club Dr; mains lunch $8-12, dinner $20-35) Fine dining on creative California fusion.

Getting There & Away

The following companies operate ferries to Avalon and Two Harbors. Reservations are recommended in summer.

Catalina Express (☎ 310-519-1212, 800-481-3470; www.catalinaexpress.com; adult/child round-trip $66.50/51) Ferries to Avalon from San Pedro, Long Beach and Dana Point in Orange County and to Two Harbors from San Pedro. The trip takes one to 1½ hours, and there are up to 30 services daily.

Catalina Marina del Rey Flyer (☎ 310-305-7250; www.catalinaferries.com; adult/child round-trip $75/56) Catamaran to Avalon and Two Harbors from Marina del Rey in LA. Phone or check the website for schedules, which vary seasonally. The trip takes one to 1½ hours.

Catalina Passenger Service (☎ 949-673-5245; www.catalinainfo.com; adult/child round-trip $68/51) Catamaran to Avalon from Newport Beach in Orange County. There's one sailing daily (1¼ hours).

Getting Around

Most places in Avalon are reached within a 10-minute walk. The Avalon Trolley (single ride/day pass $2/6) operates along two routes, passing all major sights and landmarks.

Brown's Bikes (☎ 310-510-0986; www.catalinabiking.com), near the boat terminal, repairs, sells and rents (hourly/daily from $5/12) beach cruisers and mountain bikes.

See p571 for information about reaching Catalina's inland areas.

SIX FLAGS MAGIC MOUNTAIN & HURRICANE HARBOR

Velocity rules at **Six Flags Magic Mountain** (☎ 661-255-4111, 818-367-5965; www.sixflags.com/parks/magicmountain; 26101 Magic Mountain Pkwy, Valencia; adult/child under 4ft $60/30; from 10am daily Apr-early Sep, Sat & Sun only mid-Sep–Mar, closing times vary from 6pm-midnight), where you can go up, down and inside-out faster and in more baffling ways than anywhere besides a space shuttle.

The ever-growing arsenal of rides, shows and attractions (themed for Warner Bros films such as *Batman*) includes 14 roller-coasters likely to scare the bejeezus out of most of us. **Tatsu** is billed as the world's tallest (263ft drop), fastest and longest coaster. The aptly named **Scream** goes through seven loops, including a zero-gravity roll and a dive loop with you sitting – feet dangling – in a floorless car. If you've got a stomach of steel (we don't), don't miss **X2**, where you ride in cars that spin around themselves while hurtling forward and plummeting all at once.

Children under 4ft are not allowed on many of the fiercest rides. In summer, you might take them instead right next door to **Six Flags Hurricane Harbor** (☎ 661-255-4100, 818-367-5965; www

.sixflags.com/parks/hurricaneharborla; 26101 Magic Mountain Pkwy; adult/child under 4ft $30/21; from 10am daily Jun-Aug, Sat & Sun only May & Sep;), a jungle-themed water park where they can keep cool frolicking in fanciful lagoons and churning wave pools, plunging down wicked speed slides or getting pummeled on rafting rides with action rated from 'mild' to 'max.'

Combination tickets to both parks cost $70 (no discounts) and can be used on the same day or on separate days.

The parks are about 30 miles north of LA, right off the Magic Mountain Pkwy exit off I-5 (Golden State Fwy). If you don't have your own vehicle, it's easiest to join an organized tour. Just look for flyers in your hotel.

BIG BEAR LAKE

pop 6,700 / elev 6570ft

Big Bear Lake and the towns in its surrounding valley (total population 21,000) are a family-friendly, four-season playground, drawing ski bums and boarders in winter, and hikers, mountain-bikers and water-sports enthusiasts the rest of the year. About 110 miles northeast of LA, it's a quick and popular getaway for people from across the Southland and even Las Vegas.

Big Bear is on the scenic **Rim of the World Drive** (Hwys 18 and 38), a panorama-filled road that climbs, curves and meanders through the **San Bernardino National Forest** for about 87 miles from the town of San Bernardino. Past Big Bear it plunges back down through canyons and chaparral to Redlands. Views are spectacular on clear days and downright depressing on smoggy ones, but the gentle curvature of the route east of Big Bear Lake and Redlands makes it the best drive. The forest is hugely popular with weekend warriors, but from Monday to Thursday you'll often have trails and facilities to yourself, and can also benefit from lower accommodation prices.

Orientation

Most of Big Bear Lake is sandwiched between the lake's south shore and the mountains. The main thoroughfare is Big Bear Blvd (Hwy 18), which is lined by motels, cabins and other businesses. It skirts the pedestrian-friendly 'Village,' which has cutesy shops, restaurants and the visitor center (Big Bear Lake Resort Association). The ski resorts are east of the Village. North Shore Blvd (Hwy 38) is quieter and provides access to campgrounds and hiking and mountain-biking trails.

Information

Drivers need to obtain a National Forest Adventure Pass if parking on forest land; see p73 for details. Passes are available at the Big Bear Discovery Center (below).

INTERNET ACCESS

Public library (909-866-5571; 41930 Garstin Rd; 5-9:30pm Mon-Thu, 5-11pm Fri, 10:30am-11pm Sat & Sun) Free wi-fi available.

MEDICAL SERVICES

Bear Mountain Family Medicine/Urgent Care (909-878-3696; 41949 Big Bear Blvd)

POST

Post office (cnr Big Bear Lake & Pine Knot Dr)

TOURIST INFORMATION

Big Bear Discovery Center (909-382-2790; www.bigbeardiscoverycenter.com; North Shore Dr, Fawnskin; 8am-6pm May-Oct, to 4:30pm Nov-Apr) Operated in cooperation with the US Forest Service, the center offers outdoor information, exhibits and guided tours.

Big Bear Lake Resort Association (909-866-7000, 800-424-4232; www.bigbear.com; 630 Bartlett Rd; 8am-5pm daily, call center to 6pm Mon-Fri, 9am-5pm Sat & Sun) Maps, information and room reservations.

Activities

HIKING

In summer, people trade their ski boots for hiking boots and hit the forest trails. If you only have time for one short hike, make it the **Castle Rock Trail**, which is 2.4-mile round-trip and offers superb views. The first half-mile is pretty steep but the trail flattens out somewhat after that. The trailhead is off Hwy 18 on the western end of the lake. Also popular is the moderate **Cougar Crest Trail** (5 miles round-trip), starting near the Discovery Center, which links up with the **Pacific Crest Trail** (PCT) after about 2 miles and offers views of the lake and Holcomb Valley. Most people continue eastward for another half-mile to the top of **Bertha Peak** (8502ft) for a 360-degree view of Bear Valley, Holcomb Valley and the Mojave Desert.

MOUNTAIN-BIKING

Big Bear is a mountain-biking mecca, with over 100 miles of trails for cross-country adventure. It hosts several pro and amateur races each year. A good place to get your feet in gear is along the aptly named 9-mile **Grandview Loop**, which starts at the top of Snow Summit, easily reached via the **Scenic Sky Chair** (one way/round-trip/day pass $7/10/20). One of the best single-track rides is the intermediate 13-mile **Grout Bay Trail**, which starts on the north shore. For more experienced bikers, Delamar Mountain, Holcomb Valley and Van Dusen Canyon off Hwy 38 are popular destinations. **Bear Valley Bikes** (☎ 909-866-8000; 40298 Big Bear Blvd; half-/full day from $25/35), near the Alpine Slide (see below), is a good rental place.

SKIING

With an 8000ft ridge rising above the lake's southern side, Big Bear usually gets snow between mid-December and March or April, and has two ski mountains with the same parent: **Bear Mountain** (☎ 909-585-2519; www.bearmountain.com) and **Snow Summit** (☎ 909-866-5766; www.snowsummit.com), both off Hwy 18. Bear Mountain, the higher of the two, has a vertical drop of 1665ft (1200ft at Snow Summit), and is an all-mountain freestyle park, while Snow Summit focuses on traditional downhill skiing. Altogether the mountains are laced by over 60 runs and served by 24 lifts, including four high-speed quads. An adult lift ticket costs half-/full day $40/51 Monday to Friday, $54/64 on Saturday and Sunday. One ticket buys access to both resorts, which are linked by a free shuttle. Complete ski and boot rentals range from $15 to $40.

WATER SPORTS

In summer, Big Bear Lake provides a cool respite from the heat. **Swim Beach**, near the Village, has lifeguards and is popular with families. For a bit more privacy, rent a boat, kayak or waverunner and get out on the water. A pretty destination is **Boulder Bay** near the lake's western end. Rentals are available at several marinas, including **Holloway's** (☎ 909-866-5706; www.bigbearboating.com; 398 Edgemoor Rd), about 1 mile west of the Village.

The lake teems with fish, but catching them is not always easy. Those bent on success should sign up with **Cantrell Guide Service** (☎ 909-585-4017), which guarantees a catch – or your money back. You'll need a fishing license, available at sporting stores around town, and there's a three-hour minimum for boat hire (per hour $75).

Great for families is the **Alpine Slide** (☎ 909-866-4626; www.alpineslidebigbear.com; Big Bear Blvd), a small fun park with a water slide, a wheeled downhill bobsled ride, a go-cart track and a miniature golf course.

Tours

Take a 20-mile self-guided tour through the Holcomb Valley, the site of Southern California's biggest Gold Rush in the early 1860s on the Gold Fever Trail. The dirt road is negotiable by mountain bikes and practically all vehicles. Budget two to four hours, stops included. The Big Bear Discovery Center (p573) has a free pamphlet describing 12 sites of interest along this route.

For guided adventures, **Off-Road Adventures** (☎ 909-585-1036; www.offroadadventure.com) offers tours to a variety of landscapes.

Another fun backcountry destination is Butler Peak a mountain top crowned by a historic fire lookout tower, from where you have tremendous panoramic views. You'll need a mountain bike or high-clearance vehicle to get there, or join a guided tour ($30) offered by the Discovery Center (9am to noon on Saturday).

Between late December and March, a flock of bald eagles makes Big Bear their winter home. The Discovery Center **Eagle Tour** (🕑 9am-noon Sat late Dec–mid-Mar; $30) combines an educational slide program with an eagle-spotting outing.

Sleeping

Expect rates to be highest in the winter peak and lowest in summer. Big Bear Lake Resort Association books accommodations for $20 per reservation.

Big Bear has five **US Forest Service campgrounds** (USFS; ☎ 800-444-6777; www.recreation.gov): Pine Knot, Serrano, Hanna Flat, Big Pine Flat and Holcomb Valley. All but the latter have potable water and flush toilets, and are open from spring until fall (exact times vary each year). Serrano, near the Discovery Center, is the biggest campground. Except for Pine Knot, all are on the north shore.

Big Bear Hostel (☎ 909-866-8900; www.bigbearhostel.com; 527 Knickerbocker Rd; dm $24-30, r from $40; P 💻 wi-fi) Grayson, a mountain-biker/snowboarder enthusiast and a fount of local info, oversees this 49-bed inn. Furnishings and bedding are standard-issue – but hey, it's a hostel – and there's a deck for lounging with views of the lake. Linens are provided, though BYOT (towel).

Castlewood Theme Cottages (☎ 909-866-2720; www.castlewoodcottages.com; 547 Main St; r $49-319; P 💻 wi-fi) Bored with bland motel rooms? Your fantasies can go wild in these well-crafted, clean and amazingly detailed cabins, complete with Jacuzzi tubs and costumes. Let your inner Tarzan roar, fancy yourselves Robin and Marian or Antony and Cleopatra, or cavort amongst woodland fairy-folk or an indoor waterfall. It's cheesy, wacky and, oddly, fun. Kids are not allowed.

Grey Squirrel Resort (☎ 909-866-4335, 800-381-5569; www.greysquirrel.com; 39372 Big Bear Blvd; r $94-218; P 💻 wi-fi) On the main road into town, amid pines, this delightful throwback, built in 1927, has an assortment of classic mountain cabins named for woodland creatures and sleeping two to 14. All have a kitchen and the nicest come with a fireplace, sundeck and Jacuzzi.

Northwoods Resort (☎ 909-866-3121, 800-866-3121; www.northwoodsresort.com; 40650 Village Dr; r $100-215; P 💻 wi-fi) 'Resort' may be a bit overblown, but this 148-room inn is your best bet in town for mod-cons. Timber beams in the hallways like in an old mine shaft lead you to motel-style rooms, where walls are surprisingly thin. The large pool is heated year-round. The restaurant (mains lunch $9 to $13, dinner $14 to $30) has lots of palate-pleasers and nice tables on the pond-adjacent patio.

Knickerbocker Mansion (☎ 909-878-9190, 800-388-4179; www.knickerbockermansion.com; 869 Knickerbocker Rd; r $125-240; P 💻 wi-fi) Secluded from the tourist fray of Big Bear Lake's village, innkeepers Thomas and Stanley have poured their hearts into this ornate B&B with nine rooms and two suites inside a hand-built 1920s log home and a converted carriage house. Breakfasts are to-die-for, and fine dinners are served on Fridays and Saturdays (make reservations).

Eating & Drinking

Grizzly Manor Cafe (☎ 909-866-6226; 41268 Big Bear Blvd; mains $3-8.50; 🕑 6am-2pm Mon-Fri, 7am-2pm Sat & Sun) You'll feel like you've stepped into a backwoods sitcom at this buzzy locals' hangout, about a quarter mile east of the Village, where the breakfasts are bear-sized (look for pancakes bigger than the plate), the staff irreverent, the walls covered with whacky stickers and the prices small. No lunch served on weekends.

Desi's (☎ 909-866-3374; 40766 Village Dr; desserts $5-6; 🕑 lunch & dinner) A new, small but comfy pub, Desi's serves desserts you usually have to go to a state fair to try: deep fried Twinkies and such.

Himalayan Restaurant (☎ 909-878-3068; 672 Pine Knot Ave; mains $7-14; 🕑 10:30am-9pm Sun-Thu, to 10pm Sat & Sun; V) This new, homestyle spot serves authentic dishes from Nepal and India, with some from Tibet for good measure. Momo (Tibetan dumplings) are a refreshing start, while chicken soup is thick with garlic, onion and tomato, and tandoori chicken and chicken saag (with pureed spinach) are also popular.

B's Backyard Bar-B-Que (☎ 909-866-5400; 350 Alden Rd; mains $7-25; 🕑 lunch & dinner) Bring your pooch or your sweetie and quaff beers overlooking the lake at B's bar. There's a separate building for smokehouse favorites (brisket, baby back ribs etc), which you can also order at the bar. Opinions vary about the vittles, but the scenery is primo, especially at sunset.

Peppercorn Grille (☎ 909-866-5405; 553 Pine Knot Ave; mains $12-34; 🕑 lunch & dinner) Though we might have made different decorating choices (floral wrought-iron chandeliers?), locals and visitors alike swear by the Italian-inspired American fare for a fancy meal in the Village: brick-oven baked pizzas, a dozen or so pastas, chicken breast stuffed with artichoke and spinach, steak, lobster and homemade desserts like tiramisu.

Self-caterers can stock up at **Vons** (42170 Big Bear Blvd) and **Stater Bros** (42171 Big Bear Blvd), across from each other near the lake's eastern end. For fresh produce, your best bet is **Forest Farms** (41078 Big Bear Blvd), about 0.25 miles east of the Village.

Getting There & Away

Big Bear is most easily reached from I-10 via I-210 and CA-330, which starts in Highland and intersects with CA-18 in Running Springs. If you don't like serpentine mountain roads, pick up CA-38 near Redlands, which is longer but relatively easy on the queasy.

Mountain Area Regional Transit Authority (MARTA; ☎ 909-878-5200; www.marta.cc) buses connect Big Bear with the Greyhound bus station in San Bernardino ($7) a couple of times daily Monday to Saturday. On weekends and holidays, it also operates a trolley around town (single ride/day pass $1/3).

Amtrak offers one daily train between LA and San Bernardino (from $13, 1¾ hours). There are frequent buses from LA's Greyhound Station (p568) to San Bernardino, ($12, from about 1½ hours).

Orange County

Who best symbolizes Orange County? Is it Rick Warren, pastor of the 20,000-member Saddleback Church, who hosted a faith-minded Q&A with the presidential candidates in 2008? Or maybe it's fashion maven Lauren Conrad, former star of MTV's *Laguna Beach*, now sprung from her coastal perch and spreading her sunny beach-chic across the land. Or maybe it's Mickey Mouse, Anaheim's favorite commercial kingpin, set to launch a $1.1 billion revamp of Disneyland's sidekick, Disney's California Adventure.

Or maybe it's none of the above. Three million people live in the OC, where 34 independent cities jostle for attention within the county's 789 sq miles. This huge swath of real estate stretches south from Los Angeles to San Diego, and there's more to the populace than evangelical Christians, flighty fashionistas and one cartoon mouse. Consider the burgeoning communities of Little Saigon and Santa Ana, where Vietnamese and Latino immigrants seek the American dream. There's friendly Seal Beach, where mom-and-pop store owners welcome visitors to their strollable, small-town Main St. And we can't forget the surfers, who've banded with ecowarriors recently to save the beaches – as well as the choicest surf spots.

What does this mean for you? Make the most of Mickey's hospitality, the 42 miles of shimmering coast and the world-class shopping malls, but take time to get off the beaten path to see what makes Orange County residents thrive. And while the cynical among you might still conclude that most OC locals are slaves to money, style and marketing – there are lots of Beamers and big box mansions – the more charitable might say that they're all just winners in the hands of a happy God.

HIGHLIGHTS

- **Top Disney Day** Waving at Mickey during the Disneyland Parade of Dreams (p581) then relaxing on a comfy couch in the stunning lobby of the Grand Californian (p583)
- **Surf and Sand** Building a beach bonfire at Huntington State Beach (p588), just south of the Huntington Beach Pier.
- **Classic Diner** Slurping a frothy date shake at Ruby's Crystal Cove Shake Shack (p592), near a gorgeous stretch of the Pacific Coast Hwy.
- **Feel the Earth Move** Holding tight during a 6.9 earthquake inside the Shake Shack at the Discovery Science Center (p586) in Santa Ana.
- **Natural Beauty** Watching the sun dip below the horizon from Heisler Park in Laguna Beach (p594).

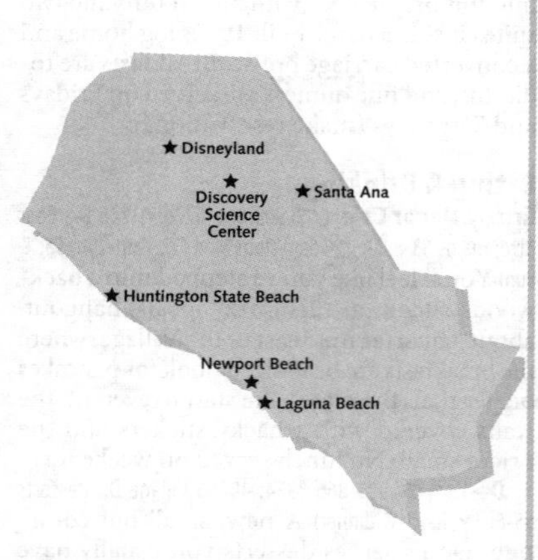

Getting There & Around

AIR

If you're heading to Disneyland or the Orange County beaches, avoid always-busy Los Angeles International Airport (LAX) by flying in to the easy-to-navigate **John Wayne Airport** (SNA; ☎ 949-252-5200; 18601 Airport Way; www.ocair.com) in Santa Ana. The airport is 8 miles inland from Newport Beach, via Hwy 55, near the junction of I-405 (San Diego Fwy). Airlines serving Orange County include Alaska, American, Continental, Delta, Frontier, Northwest, Southwest, United and US Airways.

Long Beach Airport (LGB; ☎ 562-570-2600; 4100 Donald Douglas Dr; www.longbeach.gov/airport), to the north just across the county line, is a handy alternative.

From John Wayne Airport, Orange County bus 76 runs west to South Coast Plaza and Huntington Beach, and southeast to Fashion Island in Newport Beach. To get to Orange County from Long Beach Airport, take Long Beach bus 111 to the Long Beach Transit Center. Catch Orange County bus 60 to 7th and Channel and transfer to Orange County bus 1, which travels along the Orange County coast.

For information on shuttle services, see p584.

BUS

The **Orange County Transportation Authority** (OCTA; ☎ 714-636-7433; www.octa.net; info line 7am-8pm Mon-Fri, to 7pm Sat & Sun) runs county-wide bus service. Buses generally run from about 5am to 10pm weekdays, with hours usually shorter on weekends. The fare is $1.25 per ride or $3 for a day pass. Both types of tickets are sold onboard, and you'll need exact change. Look for OCTA bus system maps and schedules at train stations and online. To get schedule information by phone, call during the hours noted above; there is no after-hours automated phone service.

Although it would not be time efficient to explore all of Orange County by bus, hopping OCTA bus 1 – which runs along the coast between Long Beach and San Clemente – is a cheap and easy way to visit the county's oceanfront communities. Bus 1 runs about every half hour on weekdays (4:30am to 10pm) and every hour on weekends (5:30am to 7:20pm).

CAR

The easiest way to get around is by car, but avoid driving on the freeways during the morning and afternoon rush hours (7am to 10am and 3pm to 7pm).

TRAIN

Fullerton, Anaheim, Orange, Santa Ana, Irvine, Laguna Niguel, San Juan Capistrano and San Clemente are all served by Amtrak's *Pacific Surfliner* (p738).

A one-way trip from Los Angeles to Anaheim ($15) takes about 40 minutes, and the trip to San Juan Capistrano ($15) from LA is one hour and 20 minutes. From San Diego, it takes 1 hour and 20 minutes to get to San Juan Capistrano ($15), and two hours to get to Anaheim ($20). The *Pacific Surfliner* currently runs about every hour between 6am and 5pm weekdays and between 7am and 5pm on weekends.

> **FAST FACTS**
>
> **Population of Huntington Beach** 202,250
> **Average temperature low/high in Huntington Beach** Jan 40/67°F, Jul 54/77°F
> **Disneyland to Huntington Beach** 16 miles, 30 minutes
> **Hollywood to Disneyland** 34 miles, one to two hours
> **LAX to Disneyland** 35 miles, one to 1½ hours
> **Seal Beach to Laguna Beach** 30 miles, one hour

DISNEYLAND & ANAHEIM

pop 342,410

Mickey is one lucky mouse. Created by animator Walt Disney in 1928, he caught a ride on a multimedia juggernaut (film, TV, publishing, music, merchandising and theme parks) that's made him an international superstar. Plus, he lives in the Happiest Place on Earth, a slice of 'imagineered' hyperreality where the streets are always clean, the employees – called cast members – are always upbeat, and there's a parade every day of the year. It would be easy to hate the guy but since opening the doors to his Disneyland home in 1955, he's been a thoughtful host to millions of guests.

But there are grounds for discontent. Every ride seems to end in a gift store, prices

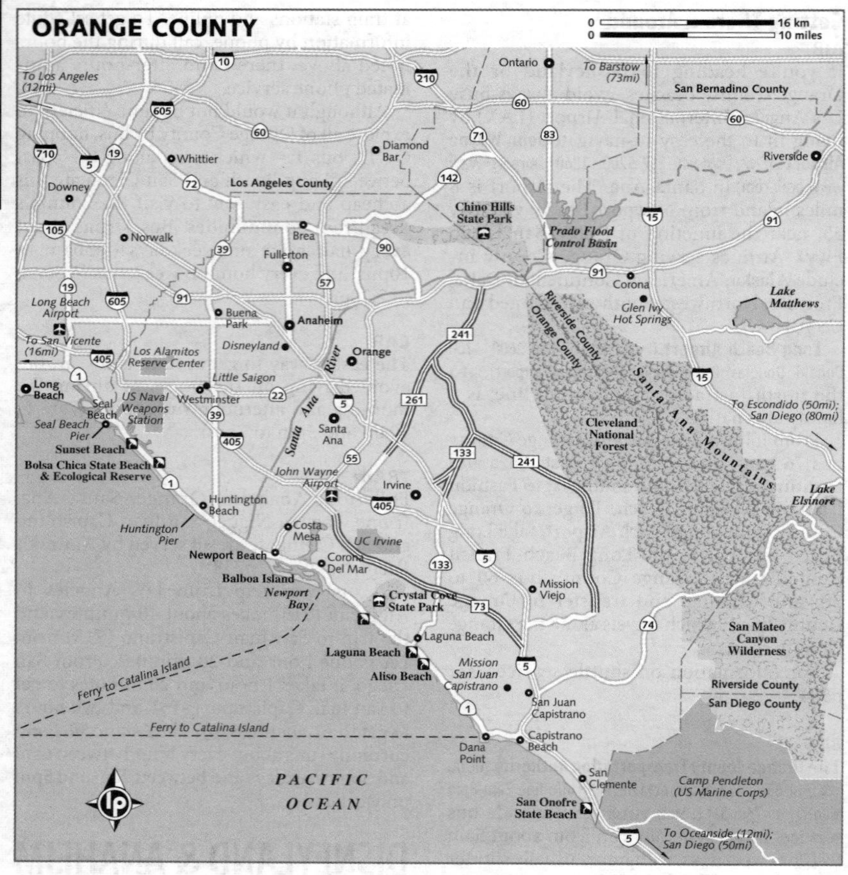

are high, and there are grumblings that management could do more to ensure affordable local housing for employees as well as cover health insurance for more workers at its three hotels.

But the parade marches on, and for the millions of kids and families who visit every year, Disneyland remains a magical experience.

HISTORY

In the 1990s Anaheim, the city surrounding Disneyland, undertook a staggering $4.2-billion revamp and expansion, cleaning up rundown stretches where hookers once roamed and establishing the first police force in the US devoted specifically to guarding tourists. The cornerstone of the five-year effort was the addition of a second theme park in February 2001, Disney's California Adventure (DCA). Adjacent to the original park, it pays tribute to the state's cultural history and its most famous landmarks. Also added was Downtown Disney, an outdoor pedestrian mall. The ensemble is called the Disneyland Resort.

Roads near the park have been widened, landscaped and given the lofty name 'the Anaheim Resort.' In 2008, Anaheim GardenWalk opened on Katella Ave within walking distance of the park. This outdoor mall, though lacking personality, brings a welcome, much-needed array of sit-down restaurants to the Disney-adjacent neighborhood.

INFORMATION

Medical Services

Western Medical Center Anaheim (☎ 714-533-6220; www.westernmedanaheim.com; 1025 S Anaheim Blvd; 🕑 24hr) Emergency Room available 24/7.

Tickets & Opening Hours

Both parks are open 365 days a year, but park hours depend on the marketing department's projected attendance numbers. You can access the **current calendar** (☎ recorded info 714-781-4565, live assistance 714-781-7290; www.disneyland.com) by phone or online. During peak season (mid-June to early September) Disneyland's hours are usually 8am to midnight. The rest of the year it's open from 10am to anytime between 8pm and 11pm. DCA closes at 9pm in summer, earlier in the low season.

One-day admission to *either* Disneyland or DCA costs $69 for adults and $59 for children aged three to nine. To visit *both* parks in one day costs $94/84 per adult/child. Multi-Day Park Hopper Tickets cost $143/123 for two days, $199/169 for three days, $224/194 for four days, and $244/214 for five days. Ticket prices increase annually, so check the website for the latest information or to buy tickets, where they may be discounted.

You can also purchase a Southern California CityPass for $259/219, which permits three-day admission to Disneyland and DCA as well as one-day admission to Universal Studios Hollywood, SeaWorld, and either the San Diego Zoo or the San Diego Zoo's Wild Animal Park.

For parking, see p585.

FASTPASS & SINGLE RIDERS

With a bit of preplanning, you can significantly cut your wait time for popular attractions. At the Fastpass ticket machine (located near the entrance to the ride) insert your ticket. You'll receive a slip of paper showing a window of time for boarding the ride. Show up within that window and join the Fastpass line. Note: you can only get one Fastpass at a time. If you're traveling solo, ask the greeter at the entrance to the ride if there's a single-rider line; you can often head to the front of the queue. Availability may depend on the crowd size.

Tourist Information

Anaheim Visitors Center (☎ 714-765-8888; www.anaheimoc.org; 800 W Katella Ave; 🕑 8am-5pm Mon-Fri) Just south of DCA at the Anaheim Convention Center. Offers information on county-wide lodging, dining and transportation. No public internet access. Best to walk here to avoid a parking fee of $10 per day.

SIGHTS & ACTIVITIES

Disneyland Park

In 2007, nearly 15 million guests pushed through the gates at the entrance to **Disneyland** (☎ recorded info 714-781-4565, live assistance 714-781-7290, switchboard 714-781-4565; www.disneyland.com; 1313 S Harbor Blvd), where a giant floral Mickey provides a perfectly bloomed welcome. The sign above the nearby archway leading to Main St, USA, reads 'Here you leave today and enter the world of yesterday, tomorrow and fantasy' – an apt but slightly skewed greeting that's indicative of the upbeat, slightly skewed 'reality' of the park itself. But it's a reality undeniably

DOING DISNEY RIGHT

Here are some tips to help you make the most of your visit:

- Plan on at least one day for each park, more if you want to go on all the rides. Lines are longest during summer and around major holidays. Generally, midweek is better than Friday, Saturday or Sunday, and arriving early in the day is best. If you really want to avoid crowds, come in spring, fall or right after Labor Day. Nobody's here in February.
- In summer bring a hat, suntan lotion, patience and – if cutting costs is important – bottled water. You're also allowed to bring in small food items like chips and cookies. There's a picnic area outside Disneyland to the left of the baggage check.
- Many rides have minimum age and height requirements; avoid tantrums by prepping the kids.
- When you arrive at the park, expect to have your bags searched for bombs and knives etc before passing through the turnstiles. Plan your time carefully. As you enter pick up a park map and show schedule to help prioritize.

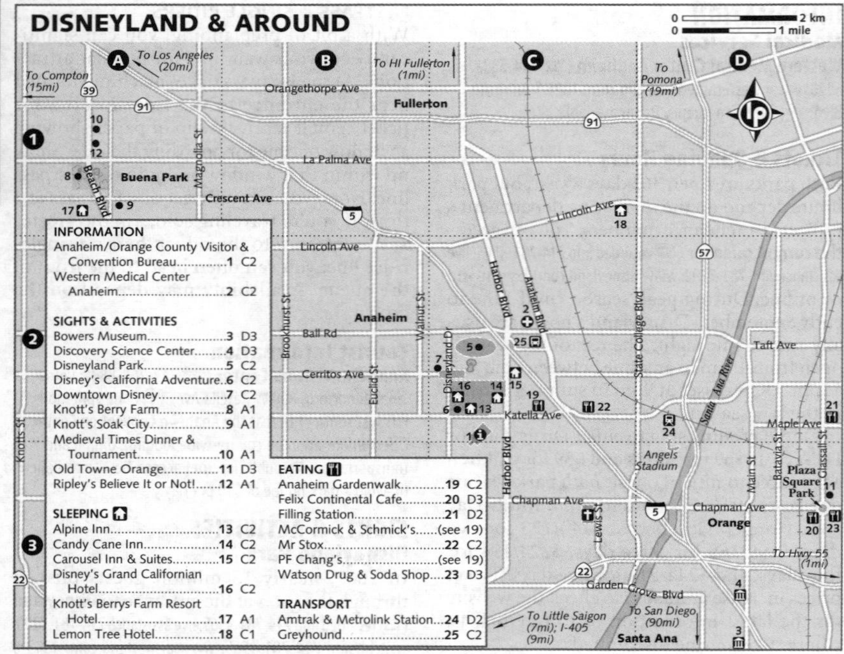

beloved by the millions of children who visit every year.

MAIN STREET, USA

Fashioned after Walt's hometown of Marceline, Missouri, bustling Main Street, USA resembles a classic turn-of-the-20th-century all-American town. It's an idyllic, relentlessly cheerful representation complete with barbershop quartet, penny arcades, ice-cream shops and a steam train.

If you're visiting on a special occasion, stop by City Hall to pick up oversized buttons celebrating birthdays, anniversaries and those 'Just Married.' There's also an Information Center here. Nearby there's a station for the **Disneyland Railroad**, a steam train that loops the park and stops at four different locations.

There's plenty of shopping along Main St, but you can save that for the evening as the stores remain open after the park's attractions close. Main St ends in the **Central Plaza**, the hub of the park from which the eight different lands (such as Frontierland and Tomorrowland) can be reached. **Sleeping Beauty Castle** lords over the plaza, its towers and turrets fashioned after Neuschwanstein, a Bavarian castle owned by Mad King Ludwig. One difference? The roof here was placed on backward.

Pay attention to the cool **optical illusion** along Main St. As you look from the entrance, up the street toward Sleeping Beauty Castle, everything looks big and far away. When you're at the castle looking back, everything looks closer and smaller. This effect is known as forced perspective, a technique used on Hollywood sets where buildings are constructed at a decreasing scale to create an illusion of height or depth.

TOMORROWLAND

The future looks different than imagineered in 1955, the year Tomorrowland opened, so in 1998 this 'land' was revamped to honor three timeless futurists: Jules Verne, HG Wells and Leonardo da Vinci. Rumble through an underwater earthquake and look for Nemo from inside a sub in the new $100-million **Finding Nemo Submarine Voyage**, which debuted in 2007. **Space Mountain**, one of the park's signature attractions and one of the best roller coasters in America, is still hurtling through complete darkness at frightening speeds nearby. The **monorail**, which travels a 2.5-mile round-trip route between Downtown Disney and the park, stops here. Sleek Mark VII monorails – the first upgrades in 21 years – breezed onto the tracks in 2008.

FANTASYLAND

Behind Sleeping Beauty Castle, Fantasyland is filled with characters from classic children's stories, such as Dumbo the Elephant and Peter Pan. Kids love whirling around the **Mad Tea Party** ride, while fans of old-school attractions enjoy **Mr Toad's Wild Ride**, a loopy jaunt through London in an open-air jalopy. As for the classic **It's a Small World** attraction, the public's response has long been ambivalent: 'That song is so annoying. And those kids are creepy. I just hope they never change it.' But change is afoot, and by 2009 – despite protests by purists – recognizable Disney characters will be interspersed among the international array of animatronic singing children.

FRONTIERLAND

In the wake of the successful *Pirates of the Caribbean* movies, Tom Sawyer Island – the only attraction in the park personally designed by Uncle Walt – was re-imagined as **Pirate's Lair on Tom Sawyer Island**, and now honors Tom in name only. After a raft ride to the island, guests wander amongst rowing pirates, cannibal cages, ghostly apparitions and buried treasure. Somewhere, Injun Joe is smiling. The rest of Frontierland gives a nod to the rip-roarin' Old West.

ADVENTURELAND

Adventureland loosely derives its style from Southeast Asia and Africa. The hands-down highlight is the jungle-themed **Indiana Jones Adventure**. Enormous Humvee-type vehicles lurch and jerk as they re-create stunts from the famous film trilogy. (Look closely at Indie during the ride: is he real or animatronic?) Nearby, little ones love climbing the stairways of **Tarzan's Treehouse**.

NEW ORLEANS SQUARE

New Orleans was Walt and his wife Lilian's favorite city, and he paid tribute to it by building this charming square. **Pirates of the Caribbean**, the longest ride in Disneyland (17 minutes) and the 'inspiration' for the movies, opened in 1967 and was the first addition to the original park. Real human skeletons from the UCLA Medical Center were used as props when the attraction first opened because the artificial versions didn't look real enough.

Today, you'll float through the subterranean haunts of tawdry pirates where artificial skeletons perch atop mounds of booty. At the **Haunted Mansion**, '999 happy haunts' – spirits and goblins, shades and ghosts – evanesce while you ride in the Doom Buggy through web-covered graveyards of dancing skeletons. The Disneyland Railroad stops at New Orleans Square.

CRITTER COUNTRY

Tucked behind the Haunted Mansion, Critter Country is home to both Winnie the Pooh and **Splash Mountain**, a flume ride through the story of Brer Rabbit and Brer Bear, based on the controversial film *Song of the South.* Right at the big descent, a camera snaps your picture. Some visitors lift their shirts, earning the ride the nickname 'Flash Mountain.' The photos are usually destroyed, but a few years ago some made their way to the internet.

SHOWS & PARADES

Verify all show times once you arrive in the park; also see p582 for events at DCA.

In summer look for **fireworks** above the park, nightly around 9:30pm. (During winter, snow falls after the fireworks; check schedules for locations.) Featuring an array of Disney characters dancing, waving and smiling their way down Main St, the **Parade of the Stars** occurs twice daily during the high season.

Fantasmic!, a seasonal outdoor extravaganza on Rivers of America across from New Orleans Square, may be the best show of all with its full-size ships, lasers and pyrotechnics. Arrive early to snag the best seats, which are down front by the water, or splurge and reserve balcony seating upstairs in New Orleans Square, which includes premium show seating, coffee and desserts. **Premium seating tickets** (☎ 714-781-4400; adult/child $59/49) can be reserved up to 30 days in advance. Ordinary seats are included in the price of park admission.

At the new **Princess Fantasy Faire** in Fantasyland, which occurs throughout the day, little princesses and knights can join the Royal Court and meet some of the Disney Princesses.

Disney's California Adventure

Disney's California Adventure, which sits just across the plaza from Disneyland, is devoted to California's history and its natural wonders. The park, open since 2001, covers more acres than Disneyland and feels less crowded. It also feels less magical, a vibe that's earned the park derogatory nicknames like Disney's Berry Farm and Mickey's Magic Mountain. Responding in grand style, the Disney honchos recently initiated a $1.1 billion building spree at DCA that's set to finish in 2012. The park will remain open during construction, rolling out over the next few years a state-of-the-art water show, a Little Mermaid ride and a Cars Land Theme area.

SUNSHINE PLAZA

The entrance to DCA was designed to look like an old-fashioned painted-collage postcard. As you pass through the turnstiles, note the gorgeous mosaics on either side of the entrance. One represents Northern California, the other Southern California. After passing under the Golden Gate Bridge, you'll arrive at Sunshine Plaza, where a 50ft-tall sun made of gold titanium 'shines' all the time (heliostats direct the rays of the real sun onto the Disney sun).

HOLLYWOOD PICTURES BACKLOT

With its soundstages, movable props and studio store, Hollywood Pictures Backlot is designed to look like the backlot of a Tinseltown studio. If you're early you'll have an unobstructed view of the forced-perspective **mural** at the end of the street, a sky-and-land backdrop that looks, at least in photographs, like the street keeps going. In the air-conditioned **Animation Building** you can have a live conversation with Crush, the animated sea turtle from Finding Nemo. The big attraction, though, is the 183ft-tall **Twilight Zone Tower of Terror**, a 13-story drop down an elevator chute in a haunted hotel – one eerily resembling the historic Hollywood Roosevelt Hotel in Los Angeles. From the upper levels of the ride you have stellar views of the Santa Ana mountains, if only for a few heart-pounding seconds.

A BUG'S LAND

Giant clover, rideable insects and oversized pieces of fake litter give kids a view of the world from a bug's perspective. Attractions here, which were designed in conjunction with Pixar Studios after its film *A Bug's Life,* include the 'irrigation systems' at **Bountiful Valley Farm**, where kids can splash around, and the 3-D **It's Tough to Be a Bug**. Hilarious and oddly touching, it packs some unexpected tactile surprises.

GOLDEN STATE

Broken into sections that recognize California's cultural achievements, the Golden State has several distinct areas. **Condor Flats**, a nod to the state's aerospace industry, features **Soarin' Over California**, a virtual hang-gliding ride using IMAX technology. Enjoy the light breeze as you soar, and keep your nostrils open for smells of the sea, orange groves and pine forests. **Grizzly River Run** takes you 'rafting' down a faux Sierra Nevada river; you *will* get wet so try it when it's warm.

PARADISE PIER

If you like rides, start at Paradise Pier, an amalgam of California's beachside amusement piers. The newest attraction is **Toy Story Mania**, a 3-D blast-and-shoot interactive journey through a carnival midway with Buzz, Woody and other characters from the movie *Toy Story*. The **California Screamin'** roller coaster occupies 10 acres and resembles an old wooden coaster, but it's got a smooth-as-silk steel track; the beginning of the ride feels like you're being shot out of a cannon. Awesome.

SHOWS & PARADES

The premier show at DCA is **Aladdin**, a 40-minute one-act musical extravaganza, based on the movie of the same name. It's in the Hyperion Theater on the Hollywood Studios Backlot. Arrive 30 to 60 minutes early to get good seats. Sit in the mezzanine for the best view of the flying carpet.

In the evening the **Electrical Parade** ends the day at DCA, with half a million tiny colored lights blinking on fabulous floats. If you're here in summer and have a Park Hopper ticket, first see the Electrical Parade then head to Disneyland to watch the fireworks.

Downtown Disney

This quarter-mile-long pedestrian mall feels longer than it is, mostly because it's packed with stores, restaurants, entertainment venues and, in summer, hordes of people. Most shops and restaurants are chains and there are very few stores with individual character. On summer evenings, musicians perform outside.

Short-term visitors can **self-park** at just off Disneyland Dr. It's free for three hours, plus two more hours with validation if you dine in Downtown Disney or see a movie – then rates jump to $6 for each additional hour, charged in 20-minute increments. Valet costs an additional $6 plus tip above the hourly rate.

SLEEPING

Anaheim gets most hotel business from Disneyland tourism, but the city is also a year-round convention destination. Room rates spike accordingly, so the rates below may fluctuate. Most properties offer packages combining lodging with tickets to Disneyland or other local attractions. Some run shuttles to the park. Prices listed are for standard double rooms during high season. Many hotels have family rooms that sleep up to six people.

For the full Disney experience, stay right at the **resort** (☎ reservations 714-956-6425, 800-225-2024; www.disneyland.com). One-night stays are expensive, but rates fluctuate almost daily. Also be aware that the Disney hotels are charging an additional daily resort fee of $14 per day, which covers parking, internet access and other amenities.

Budget

HI Fullerton (☎ 714-738-3721, 800-909-4776, ext 138; www.hiusa.org; 1700 N Harbor Blvd, Fullerton; dm members/nonmembers $24/27; Jun-Sep; wi-fi) About 5 miles north of Disneyland, this clean and friendly summer-only facility is inside a Mediterranean home with just 20 beds in three dorms (no private rooms). Free wireless access and kitchen facilities. The office closes at 11pm but 24-hour access is available. Bus 47 runs to the hostel from the Anaheim Greyhound station; from the Amtrak station, take bus 43. Call the hostel for details about where to disembark. Bus 43 will also get you to and from Disneyland.

Alpine Inn (☎ 714-535-2186, 800-772-4422; www.alpineinnanaheim.com; 715 W Katella Ave; r $59-189;) Connoisseurs of kitsch will love this snow-covered motel with its A-frame exterior and glistening 'icicles' – framed by palm trees of course. On the border of DCA, the inn has views of the Ferris wheel and is close to a shuttle stop. Rooms are on the older side but clean, and there are five family-friendly suites.

Lemon Tree Hotel (☎ 714-772-0200, 866-311-5595; www.hotelaaa.com; 1600 E Lincoln Ave; r $89-159; wi-fi) It's hard to be hip in Anaheim, but Aussie-owned Lemon Tree gives it a shot with a funky, upbeat charm. Rooms are decorated with faux-rustic, Mission-style flair – wrought-iron lamps, paintings of senoritas, chunky wooden furniture – and some have kitchens. Studios and apartments are available for longer stays. It's 2.5 miles and two left turns to Disneyland.

Midrange

Knott's Berry Farm Resort Hotel (☎ 714-995-1111, 866-752-2444; www.knottshotel.com; 7675 Crescent Av, r from $89-129; wi-fi) If your kids are fans of Charlie Brown and his gang, ask about the themed Camp Snoopy rooms. For an extra $45 to $50 per night, kids will be treated to *Peanuts*-themed decor and a goodnight visit from Snoopy himself. The hotel, which is adjacent to Knotts's Berry Farm, provides complimentary shuttle service to Disneyland. Parking costs $10 per day, and wi-fi costs $12 per day.

Candy Cane Inn (☎ 714-774-5284, 800-345-7057; www.candycaneinn.net; 1747 S Harbor Blvd; r $99-139; wi-fi) Bright bursts of flowers, tidy grounds and a cobblestone drive welcome guests to this cute motel, which is also adjacent to the main gate at Disneyland. Rooms have all the mod-cons, plus down comforters and plantation shutters. It's a top choice, and booking a year out is strongly advised.

Carousel Inn & Suites (☎ 714-758-0444, 800-854-6767; www.carouselinnandsuites.com; 1530 S Harbor Blvd; r $181, ste $191-320; wi-fi) Recently remodeled, this four-story motel makes an effort to look stylish, with upgraded furniture and pots of flowers hanging from the wrought-iron railings of its exterior corridors. The rooftop pool has great views of Disneyland's fireworks. Suites sleep four to eight people. Parking is $5, and wi-fi is $10.

Top End

our pick **Disney's Grand Californian Hotel** (☎ 714-635-2300; 1600 S Disneyland Dr; r $480-890;) Soaring timber beams rise majestically above the lobby of the six-story Grand Californian, a monument to the American Arts and Crafts movement and the top choice for lodging at Disneyland. Rooms have cushy amenities, such as triple-sheeted beds, and outside there's a redwood waterslide into the pool. At night kids can wind down with bedtime stories by the lobby's giant stone hearth. Even if you're not staying here, a brief respite in the lobby is a must (and totally acceptable). Don't be surprised to see several worn-out dads stealing a quick snooze in the comfy chairs. Enter from Downtown Disney or DCA.

EATING

For both parks, call **Disney Dining** (☎ 714-781-3463; 🕑 7am-9pm daily) if you need to make dining reservations, have dietary restrictions or want to inquire about character dining (Disney characters work the dining room and greet the kids). For a birthday, call to ask about decorate-your-own-cake parties and birthday meals (you'll need to order 48 hours ahead). Park maps use the red apple icon to indicate restaurants where you can find healthy foods and vegetarian options.

Disneyland Park

Besides the following sit-down options, each 'land' has several cafeteria-style options.

Blue Bayou (☎ 714-781-3463; New Orleans Sq; lunch mains $20-34, dinner mains $28-38; 🕑 lunch & dinner) Surrounded by the 'bayou' inside Pirates of the Caribbean, this place is famous for its Monte Cristo sandwiches at lunch and Creole and Cajun specialties at dinner. Make reservations. The children's menu for lunch and dinner is $8 to $13.

River Belle Terrace (☎ 714-781-3463; Frontierland; mains under $13; 🕑 10am-3pm Mon-Thu, 9am-9pm Fri-Sun) Kids love the Mickey Mouse pancakes at breakfast, served until 11:30am.

Disney's California Adventure

In addition to the following option, there is a good food court at Pacific Wharf.

Trattoria at Golden Vine Winery (☎ 714-781-3463; mains $5-15; 🕑 11am-6pm) DCA's best place for a relaxing sit-down lunch serves surprisingly inexpensive and wonderfully appetizing Italian pasta, salads and gourmet sandwiches.

Downtown Disney

La Brea Bakery (☎ 714-490-0233; breakfast mains $5-14, lunch & dinner mains $11-20; 🕑 breakfast, lunch & dinner) This branch of one of LA's top bakeries serves up great sandwiches and salads. Express items under $10.

Napa Rose (☎ reservations 714-956-6755; Disney's Grand Californian Hotel, 1600 S Disneyland Dr, Downtown Disney; mains $34-46, 4-course prix fixe $85, incl wine $130; 🕑 dinner) Disney's – and one of the OC's – finest restaurants occupies a soaring Arts and Crafts–style dining room overlooking DCA's Grizzly Peak. There's a special emphasis on pairing native ingredients with native wines. Splurge on the four-course meal. Reservations strongly recommended.

Anaheim

The 2008 opening of **Anaheim GardenWalk** (☎ 714-635-7400; www.anaheimgardenwalk.com; 321 W Katella Ave), an outdoor mall on Katella Ave one block east of Harbor Blvd, brought a welcome influx of sit-down eateries within walking distance of the park. Yes, it's heavy on chain restaurants, and it takes a long walk to get there, but dining options beyond downtown Disney are so scarce, we won't complain.

PF Chang's (☎ 714-507-2021; Suite 120, 321 W Katella Ave; lunch mains $8-12, dinner mains $13-17; 🕑 11am-11pm Sun-Thu, to midnight Fri & Sat) A terra-cotta-style warrior welcomes guests to this sleek, high-ceilinged outpost of the popular Asian chain. Lettuce wraps are always a hit with those watching their waistlines.

McCormick & Schmick's (☎ 714-535-9000; Suite 109, 321 W Katella Ave; lunch mains $10-16, most dinner mains $10-30; 🕑 lunch & dinner) In addition to a long list of daily fresh fish, the menu at this stylish seafood restaurant includes grilled chicken Caesar salad, pork sliders and pasta with beef bolognese.

Beyond GardenWalk, consider **Mr Stox** (☎ 714-634-2994; 1105 E Katella Ave; lunch mains $11-20, dinner mains $20-40; 🕑 lunch Mon-Fri, dinner daily). For country club ambience, settle into one of the oval booths and savor some of Anaheim's best Cal-American cooking. Mains include prime rib, duck and rack of lamb, plus a fair number of seafood and vegetarian options. Wear nice shoes and make reservations.

GETTING THERE & AWAY

Air

See p577 for information on air connections.

Southern California Gray Line/Coach America (☎ 714-978-8855, 800-828-6699; www.graylineanaheim.com) runs the Disneyland Resort Express between LAX and Disneyland-area hotels at least hourly (one way/round-trip to LAX $20/30). It also serves John Wayne Airport (SNA) in Santa Ana ($15/25).

Bus

Frequent departures are available with **Greyhound** (☎ 714-999-1256, 800-231-2222; 100 W Winston Rd) to/from downtown LA ($12, one hour) and to San Diego ($18, 2½ hours).

Car

The Anaheim Resort is just off I-5 on Harbor Blvd, about 30 miles south of downtown LA. The park is roughly bordered by Ball Rd, Disneyland Dr, Harbor Blvd and Katella Ave. Giant, easy-to-read overhead signs indicate which ramps you need to take for the theme parks, hotels or Anaheim's streets.

All-day parking costs $12. Enter the 'Mickey & Friends' parking structure from southbound Disneyland Dr at Ball Rd. (It's the largest parking structure in the world, with a capacity of 10,300 vehicles.) Take the tram to reach the parks; follow signs. The lots stay open one hour after the parks close.

The parking lots for Downtown Disney are reserved for shoppers and have a different rate structure: the first three hours are free, with an additional two more free hours if you have a validation from a table-service restaurant or the movie theater. After that it's $6 per hour, up to $30 a day. Downtown Disney also has valet parking for an additional $6, plus tip.

Train

In Anaheim, **Amtrak** trains (☎ 714-385-1448, 800-872-7245; 2150 E Katella Ave) pull in to the depot next to Angels Stadium. Tickets to/from LA's Union Station are $10 (40 minutes); to San Diego it's $20 (two hours).

GETTING AROUND

Bus

The bus company **Anaheim Resort Transit** (ART; ☎ 714-563-5287, 888-364-2787; www.rideart.org) provides frequent service between Disneyland and hotels in the immediate area, saving headaches parking and walking. An all-day pass costs $4 per adult and $1 for a child aged three to nine. You must buy the pass before boarding; pick one up at one of a dozen kiosks (exact cash or credit card) or online. If you hop on without a pass, you can pay $3 onboard for a one-way trip. Service starts one hour before Disneyland opens and ends half an hour after it closes.

Many hotels and motels have free shuttles to Disneyland and other area attractions.

Monorail

Take the monorail from Tomorrowland to the Disneyland Hotel, across from Downtown Disney, and save about 20 minutes of walking time. It's free if you've bought a park admission ticket.

AROUND DISNEYLAND

If the relentless cheeriness of Disneyland starts to grate on your nerves, there are several entertaining – even kitschy – alternatives within 5 miles of the park. Anaheim's streets are laid out in an easy-to-navigate grid, with most neighborhoods flowing seamlessly from one to another.

KNOTT'S BERRY FARM

They drop off kids by the busload at **Knott's** (☎ 714-220-5200; www.knotts.com; 8039 Beach Blvd, Buena Park; adult/child 3-11yr/senior $52/23/23; 🚼), the first theme park in America. Just 4 miles northwest of Anaheim off the I-5, Knott's is smaller and less frenetic than the Disneyland parks, but it can be fun, especially for roller-coaster fanatics, young teens and kids who love the *Peanuts* gang. Opening hours vary seasonally so call ahead or check online. Also check the website for the latest discounts; some can be substantial. Parking costs $10.

The park opened in 1940 when Mr Knott's boysenberries (a blackberry-raspberry hybrid) and Mrs Knott's fried-chicken dinners attracted crowds of local farmhands. Mr Knott built an imitation ghost town to keep them entertained. Eventually they hired local carnival rides and charged admission. Mrs Knott kept frying chicken but the rides and Old West buildings became the main attraction.

Today the park keeps the Old West theme alive with shows and demonstrations at Ghost Town, but it's the thrill rides that draw the crowds. Nearby, the suspended, inverted **Silver Bullet** screams through a corkscrew, a double spiral and an outside loop. From the ground, look up to see the dirty socks and bare feet of suspended riders who've removed their shoes. The **Xcelerator** is a '50s-themed roller coaster that blasts you from 0mph to 82mph in only 2.3 seconds. There's a hair-raising twist at the top. The newest roller coaster is 2008's not-too-scary **Pony Express**, in which riders climb onto the back of a 'roller-horse' for a 36-second simulated gallop around a figure-eight track. **Camp Snoopy** is a kiddie wonderland populated by the Peanuts characters and family-friendly rides.

In October Knott's hosts what is regarded as SoCal's best and scariest Halloween party. On select dates from late September to Halloween, the park closes at 5:30pm and reopens at 7pm as Knott's Scary Farm. Terrifying mazes and creepy shows – not to mention 1000 roaming monsters – keep things scary.

Next to Knott's is the affiliated water park **Knott's Soak City USA** (☎ 714-220-5200; www.knotts.com; adult/child 3-11yr & senior $30/20, after 3pm $20; 🕑 mid-May–Sep; 🚸).

MEDIEVAL TIMES DINNER & TOURNAMENT

Hear ye, hear ye! Gather ye clans and proceed forthwith to **Medieval Times** (☎ 714-521-4740; www.medievaltimes.com; 7662 Beach Blvd, Buena Park; adult/child $54/37; 🕑 daily, show times vary; 🚸) for an evening of feasting and performance in 12th-century style. Guests root for various knights as they joust, fence and show off their horsemanship (on real live Andalusian horses). Dinner is OK, roast chicken and spare ribs that you eat with your hands, but the show's the thing.

RIPLEY'S BELIEVE IT OR NOT!

Cannibals, deformities and the Last Supper designed out of toast: exactly what you'd expect from **Ripley's** (☎ 714-522-7045; www.ripleysbp.com; 7850 Beach Blvd, Buena Park; adult/child $14/10; 🕑 10am-6pm Mon-Fri, 9am-7pm Sat & Sun; 🚸), one block north of Knott's. Robert L Ripley was an adventurer, reporter and collector who traveled the globe in the 1920s and '30s in search of curiosities. Kids will rave or be scarred for life. At this Ripley's you'll find an unfortunate-looking shrunken head, about the size of a tennis ball, on the left as you exit the jungle corridor. Ick.

DISCOVERY SCIENCE CENTER

This fantastic **science center** (☎ 714-542-2823; www.discoverycube.org; 2500 N Main St, Santa Ana; adult/child/senior $13/10/12; 🕑 10am-6pm; 🚸) has more than 100 interactive displays in exhibit areas that include Dynamic Earth, The Body and Dino Quest. Step into the eye of a hurricane – you hair will get mussed – or grab a seat in the Shake Shack for a 6.9 quake. Heading south on the I-5 from Disneyland (about 5 miles), look for the 10-story cube seemingly balanced on one of its points.

BOWERS MUSEUM OF CULTURAL ART

When you're in town, visit the website for this Mission-style **museum** (☎ 714-567-3600; www.bowers.org; 2002 N Main St, Santa Ana; permanent collection adult/child, student & senior $12/9; 🕑 11am-4pm Tue-Sun) to check the traveling exhibits. The museum has a rich permanent collection of pre-Columbian, African, Oceanic and Native American art, but gets its biggest crowds with its tantalizing, high-quality special exhibits such as the recent appearance of several of China's famed terra-cotta warriors. Special exhibits require separate tickets, which have cost as much as $27 per adult; call ahead for prices.

ORANGE

pop 138,640 / elev 195ft

For a pleasant dose of small-town life complete with a wide selection of mom-and-pop restaurants and shops, drive 1.5 miles south on S Harbor Blvd then turn left on Chapman Ave, following it east about 3.5 miles to Old Towne Orange in the City of Orange. Old Towne was originally laid out by Alfred Chapman and Andrew Glassell who, in 1869, received the 1-square-mile piece of real estate in lieu of legal fees. Built around a pretty plaza at the intersection of Chapman Ave and Glassell Sts, it's the most concentrated collection of antiques shops in Orange County. Some dealers may try to pass off replicas as antiques: *caveat emptor*.

You can enjoy breakfast inside a former gas station at the **Filling Station** (☎ 714-289-9714; 201 N Glassell St; mains under $12; 🕑 breakfast & lunch), now serving gourmet scrambles and pancake sandwiches instead of unleaded. For lunch or dinner, nab a patio table at **Felix Continental Cafe** (☎ 714-633-5842; 36 Plaza Sq; lunch mains $5-12, dinner mains $7-14; 🕑 breakfast, lunch & dinner). This longtime favorite serves spiced-just-right Caribbean, Cuban and Spanish dishes, most accompanied by a hefty serving of black beans or rice. Disneyland's imagineered Main St, USA, will lose a little luster after you slurp a chocolate malt at the counter inside **Watson Drug & Soda Shop** (☎ 714-633-1050; 116 E Chapman Ave; 🕑 6:30am-9pm Mon-Sat, 8am-6pm Sun), a longtime diner and soda fountain.

LITTLE SAIGON

If you head a few miles southwest of Disneyland, you'll drive into the city of Westminster near the junction of I-405 and Hwy 22. Home to a large Vietnamese population, the community has carved out its own vibrant commercial district around the intersection of Bolsa and Brookhurst Aves. At its heart is the **Asian Garden Mall** (☎ 714-842-8018; 9200 Bolsa Ave), a behemoth of a structure packed with 400 ethnic boutiques, including herbalists and jade jewelers. One of the best casual eateries here is **Pho 79** (☎ 714-893-1883), on the lower level toward the mall's north entrance. It has a great variety of noodle and vegetable dishes and the *pho ga* (chicken noodle soup) is superb.

Another popular restaurant is **Brodard** (☎ 714-530-1744; 9892 Westminster Ave, Garden Grove; mains under $13; 8am-9pm, closed Tue) where half the fun is finding the place. The restaurant is known for its *nem nuong cuon*, rice paper wrapped tightly around a Spam-like pork paste and served with a light special sauce. It's oddly addictive. From Disneyland, follow Harbor Blvd south 3.5 miles. Turn right at W 17th St which becomes Westminister Ave. Cross Brookhurst Ave. At the mall on your left, drive behind the 99 Cent Store, and continue to the restaurant's red awning.

ORANGE COUNTY BEACHES

An inviting string of beaches and coastal communities lines Orange County's 42-mile coast, each of them boasting a distinctly different set of charms. The six major towns, starting with Seal Beach in the north, are linked by the Pacific Coast Hwy (PCH; Hwy 1) and grow increasingly scenic – and some may say ritzy – as you continue south.

From Seal Beach, PCH passes scruffy Sunset Beach, surfing-crazed Huntington Beach, ritzy Newport Beach and Corona del Mar before rolling into the cliff-and-cove-dotted artists' enclave of Laguna Beach. Just south, Dana Point draws the yacht crowd, while end-of-the-county San Vicente returns to the small-town vibe – and one awesome, border-hugging surf spot.

In summer, accommodations book up far in advance, prices rise and some properties impose minimum two- or three-night stays.

SEAL BEACH

pop 24,100

In the pageant for charming small towns, Seal Beach enjoys an unfair advantage over the competition: 1.5 miles of pristine beach glittering like an already won crown. And that's without mentioning its three-block Main St – a lineup of locally owned restaurants, mom-and-pop stores and indie coffeehouses that are refreshingly low on attitude and high on welcoming charm.

Main St spills into **Seal Beach Pier**, which extends 1885ft out over the ocean. The beach faces south here and, except for the off-shore oil rigs (which locals seem to easily tune out), it's very pleasant. The mild waves make it a great place to learn how to surf before heading to more challenging waves further south. Good thermal winds make the coast here a prime spot for kite-surfing. For surfing lessons, look for the marked van owned by **M&M Surfing School** (☎ 714-846-7873; www.mmsurfingschool.com; one day lesson $65-80) usually parked in the lot north of the pier. For kite-surfing instruction, try **Kitesurfari** (☎ 562-596-6451; www.kitesurfari; 452 Pacific Coast Hwy; two-day lesson $440).

The one hotel that's within walking distance of the beach is **Pacific Inn** (☎ 562-493-7501, 866-466-0300; www.pacificinn-sb.com; 600 Marina Dr; r $149-169; wi-fi). The property could use a little TLC, but the rooms do have down comforters and comfy mattresses. There's also a sunny central pool.

As for food, most of the restaurants on Main St are worthy of recommendation. In the morning, we suggest **Nick's Deli** (☎ 562-598-5072; 223 Main St; mains $5-7; breakfast & lunch) for the county's best breakfast burritos (they sell about one per minute). Everybody's favorite for fresh fish is **Walt's Wharf** (☎ 562-598-4433; 201 Main St; lunch mains $8-15, dinner mains $12-25; lunch & dinner). Some people even drive here from LA. Walt's gets packed on weekends, and you can't make reservations, but it's worth the long wait for the oak-fire-grilled seafood and steaks, served with delicious sauces.

HUNTINGTON BEACH

pop 202,250

Huntington Beach (HB) has been a surf mecca for nearly a century, starting in 1914 when Hawaiian-Irish surfing star George Freeth (brought to California by pioneer developer Henry Huntington) gave demonstrations of the exotic sport off the coast. In recent years, the beach's surfing image has been heavily marketed, with city fathers even getting a bit aggro (surfer slang for 'territorial') in their efforts to ensure HB's exclusive rights to the now-trademarked nickname 'Surf City, USA.' The moniker originally came from Jan and Dean's 1963 pop hit by the same name. But the sport is big business, with buyers for major retailers coming here to see what surfers are wearing and then marketing the look.

Recent uninspired development along Main St has left downtown with a vaguely antiseptic, prefab feel, but the bland facades are frequently enlivened by sidewalk-surfing skateboarders and inebriated barflies whooping it up from the street's numerous bars. Despite the soulless architecture, HB is still the quintessential place to celebrate the coastal SoCal lifestyle.

Huntington Beach Convention and Visitors Bureau (☎ 714-969-3492; www.surfcityusa.com; Suite 208, 301 Main St; 9am-5pm Mon-Fri) provides tourist maps and other information. In late July, the city hosts the **US Open of Surfing** (www.go211.com/usopenofsurfing/site6.html), a six-star competition drawing more than 600 surfers, 400,000 spectators and a minivillage of concerts, motocross demos and skater jams.

Sights & Activities

SURFING & BEACHES

Surfing in Huntington Beach is competitive. Control your longboard or draw the ire of territorial locals. Surf north of the pier. For lessons (and a bodyguard), consider **M&M Surfing School** (p587). To watch surfers in action, walk down to **Huntington City Beach** at the foot of the pier. Just south is **Huntington State Beach**, the place to build a beach bonfire. Buy wood at nearby concessionaires then stake out a concrete fire ring. Romp with your dog in the surf at **Dog Beach**, northwest of Goldenwest St.

INTERNATIONAL SURFING MUSEUM

A small but interesting collection of surf-related memorabilia can be found at this **museum** (☎ 714-960-3483; www.surfingmuseum.org; 411 Olive Ave; suggested donation $2; noon-5pm Mon-Fri, 11am-6pm Sat & Sun), off Main St. Exhibits chronicle the sport's history with photos, surfboards and surf music. The museum recently added a tiny theater that plays rotating surf movies, currently ranging from *Surf's Up* to *Endless Summer*. There's a small but interesting display about the filming of the latter, complete with the film's camera. Hours may vary slightly in winter.

BOLSA CHICA STATE ECOLOGICAL RESERVE

Just north of Huntington Beach, Pacific Coast Hwy looks out onto **Bolsa Chica State Ecological Reserve** (☎ 714-846-1114; sunrise to sunset). At first glance it may look rather desolate (especially with the few small oil wells scattered about), but this restored salt marsh is an environmental success story teeming with bird life. Its 1700 acres have been saved from numerous development projects over the years by a band of determined locals. A 1.5-mile loop trail starts from the parking lot on Pacific Coast Hwy. There's a small **interpretative center** (3842 Warner Ave; 9am-4pm Tue-Fri, 10am-3pm Sat & Sun) just north.

Sleeping

There aren't many budget option in HB, especially in summer when nothing-special motels hike their prices to ridiculous levels. If you want budget accommodation, head inland toward I-405.

Hotel Huntington Beach (☎ 714-891-0123, 877-891-0123; www.hotelhb.com; 7667 Center Ave; r $89-150; wi-fi) This eight-story hotel, which looks like an office building, is decidedly sans personality and a bit worn, but the rooms are clean and perfect for get-up-and-go travelers (the hotel's adjacent to I-405). The Jacuzzi is a perk.

Comfort Suites (☎ 714-841-1812, 800-714-4040; www.comfortsuites.com; 16301 Beach Blvd (Hwy 39); r $100-120; wi-fi) Hot breakfast items such as scrambled eggs and bacon or ham-and-cheese omelettes make this chain worth a mention. The rates are pretty reasonable for comfortable, if not particularly distinctive, rooms. Closer to I-405 than the beach.

Sun 'n Sands (☎ 714-536-2543, www.sunnsands.com; 1102 Pacific Coast Hwy; r $129-189, mini-ste $229-269; wi-fi) This mom-and-pop motel would cost well under $100 a night anywhere east of town, but its location across from the beach lets it get away with absurdly high rates. One nice touch is a small collection of sundries for sale in the lobby, ranging from potato chips to toothpaste and contact-lens solution. To note: it can get loud here at night.

Hilton Regency Huntington Beach Resort & Spa (☎ 714-845-8000, 800-445-8667; www.waterfrontbeachresort.hilton.com; 21100 Pacific Coast Hwy; r $289-329, ste from $499; wi-fi) The spacious poolside terrace is vaguely reminiscent of Vegas: a sprawling patio covered with lounge chairs and the indolent sun-worshippers who claim them. But then you see the backdrop that brings you home to SoCal: miles of golden sand and deep blue sea. Rooms are plush but tempered with a smart, beach-casual style. Use of hotel boogie boards, beach chairs and volleyballs is free, but wireless access isn't – it's $10 per day. Parking costs $24 per day.

Eating & Drinking

Sugar Shack (☎ 714-536-0355; 213 Main St; mains $5-8; ⏰ breakfast & lunch) The sidewalk patio is the place to sit at this Main St stalwart for some of HB's best people-watching. And if you're here really early, you might catch surfer dudes donning their wet suits. The $5 Breakfast Special comes with two pancakes, an egg, and bacon or sausage. Sign up for a table at the clipboard on the outside wall.

Chronic Tacos (☎ 714-960-0339; 328 11th St; mains under $7; ⏰ breakfast, lunch & dinner) For surfer haute cuisine, mosey into this sticker-covered shack and request a made-to-order Fatty Taco, then settle in for one of the best Mexican meals around. With the Dead playing on the stereo, a couple of surf bums chillin' by the pool tables, and chatty, laid-back staff, you might just never leave.

Park Bench Cafe (☎ 714-842-0775; 17732 Goldenwest St; breakfast mains $6-10, lunch mains $9-10; ⏰ breakfast & lunch; 🚸) A short drive east on Goldenwest St from PCH lands you at this shady outdoor café in Huntington Central Park. If you're traveling with Fido, he can order the Hound Dog Heaven patty off the dog menu.

Duke's (☎ 714-374-6446; 317 Pacific Coast Hwy; lunch mains $9-15, most dinner mains $20-30; ⏰ lunch Tue-Sat, dinner daily) It may be touristy, but this Hawaiian-themed restaurant – named after surfing legend Duke Kahanamoku – is also fun and offers up some of the best views around. Start things off with the poke-roll appetizer then pick your fish and seasoning from a long list of choices.

Good for a cheap bite on Main St is **Smokin' Mo's BBQ** (☎ 714-374-3033; 301 Main St; most mains $7-16; ⏰ 11am-9pm; 🚸), where you can spice up a towering minced-barbecue sandwich with messy coleslaw and four different sauces. For hearty Italian fare and waiters renowned for their physiques, drive a few miles north on PCH to Sunset Beach and look for the twinkling white lights of **Roman Cucina** (☎ 562-592-5552; 16595 Pacific Coast Hwy, cnr 20th St; mains $12-18; ⏰ dinner).

As for drinking, it's easy to find a bar in HB. Walk up Main St and you'll spot them all. Cavernous brewpub **Huntington Beach Beer Co** (☎ 714-960-5343; 2nd fl, 201 Main St) specializes in ales and has giant, stainless-steel kettles brewing it all the time. **Hurricanes Bar & Grill** (☎ 714-374-0500; 2nd fl, 200 Main St) can be described in two words: meat market. But then again, any strip of beach bars worth its margarita salt needs at least one.

NEWPORT BEACH

pop 84,218

Newport Beach has two things going for it: a superb stretch of coast and lots and lots of money. Its citizens, uniformly fresh-faced and sun-kissed, are the last word in resort wear. You'll be hard-pressed to find even one brooding, pimply-faced smoker in a too-large sweater. But otherwise…let's just say that if you judge the character of a city by the welcome you get from its visitors center, then Newport Beach might be ambivalent about your presence. Nary a road sign marks its location (though one is apparently on the way), it's tucked inside a poorly marked office complex, and only a handful of brochures are available there. Don't be surprised if you're greeted with, 'How did you find us?' Your best bet for information? Order the visitors guide from the website before arrival from the **Newport Beach Conference and Visitors' Center** (☎ 949-719-6100; www.newportbeach-cvb.com; Suite 120, 1200 Newport Center Dr; ⏰ 8am-5pm).

So why visit Newport? Because the local environment is particularly lovely. The city surrounds a pretty natural harbor that's one of the largest for pleasure craft in the US. Balboa Peninsula, which faces the harbor on one side and the open ocean on the other, is less ritzy than the rest of Newport, but its wide beaches are terrific. The shopping's pretty darn good too.

Sights & Activities

BALBOA PENINSULA

For a more down-to-earth vibe, follow Hwy 55 south onto Balboa Peninsula. Six miles-long and a quarter-mile wide, the peninsula is home to white-sand beaches, a number of hotels, seafood restaurants and stylish homes – and lots of surfers catching ocean-side waves. One of its most architecturally significant homes, the 1926 **Lovell House** (1242 W Ocean Front), sits beside the beach bike path. Designed by seminal modernist architect Rudolph Schindler, it was built using site-cast concrete frames and wood.

Hotels, restaurants and bars cluster around the peninsula's two piers: **Newport Pier**, near its western end, and **Balboa Pier**, at the eastern end. The oceanfront strip teems with

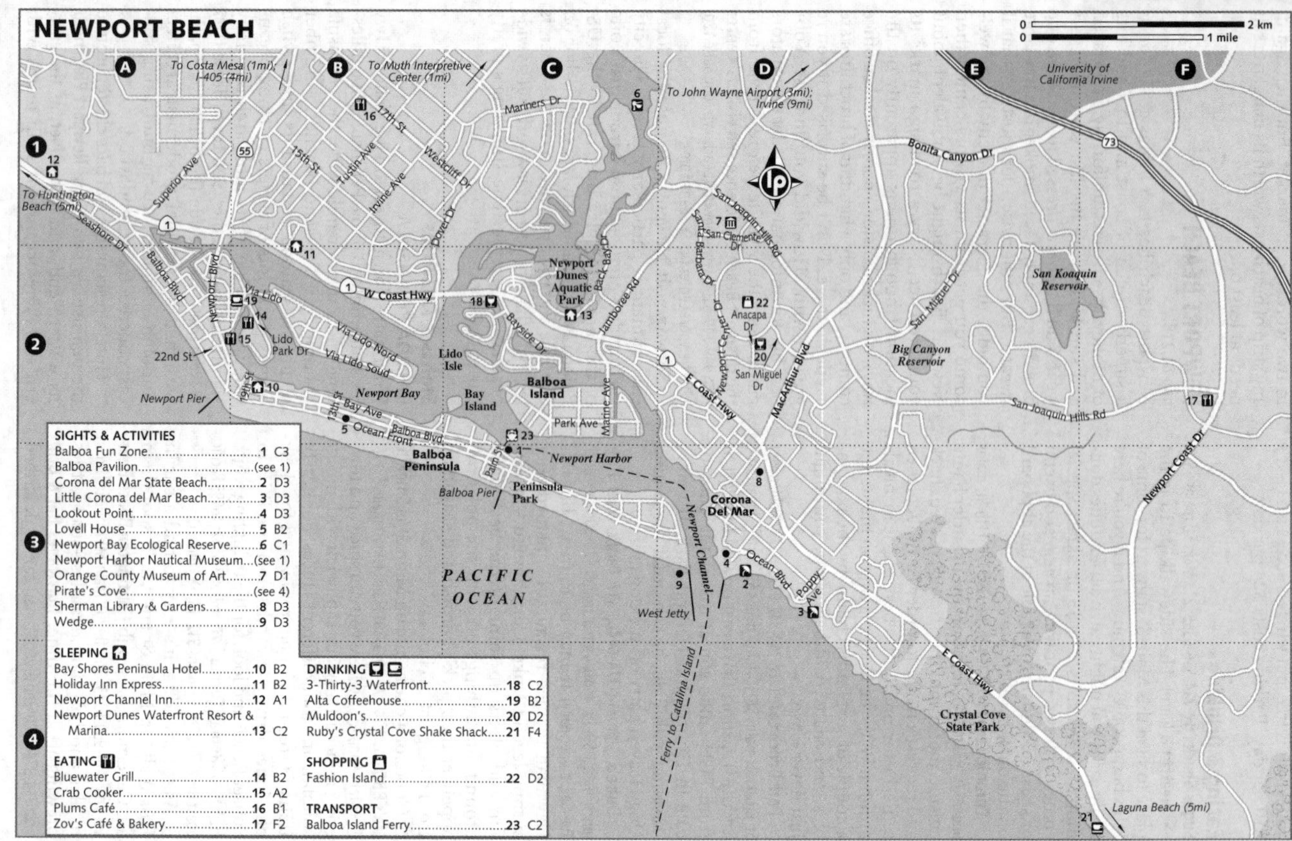
NEWPORT BEACH
0 2 km
0 1 mile
A
B
C
D
E
F
1
2
3
4
To Costa Mesa (1mi); I-405 (4mi)
To Muth Interpretive Center (1mi)
To John Wayne Airport (3mi); Irvine (9mi)
University of California Irvine
To Huntington Beach (5mi)
Laguna Beach (5mi)
Mariners Dr
17th St
15th St
Tustin Ave
Irvine Ave
Westcliff Dr
Dover Dr
Superior Ave
Seashore Dr
Balboa Blvd
Newport Blvd
Via Lido
Via Lido Nord
Via Lido Soud
Lido Park Dr
22nd St
19th St
13th St
Bay Ave
Ocean Front
W Coast Hwy
E Coast Hwy
Bayside Dr
Back Bay Dr
Jamboree Rd
Marine Ave
Park Ave
Palm St
San Joaquin Hills Rd
Santa Barbara Dr
San Clemente Dr
Newport Center Dr
Anacapa Dr
San Miguel Dr
MacArthur Blvd
Bonita Canyon Dr
Newport Coast Dr
Ocean Blvd
Poppy Ave
Newport Dunes Aquatic Park
Lido Isle
Bay Island
Balboa Island
Balboa Peninsula
Peninsula Park
Newport Bay
Newport Harbor
Newport Channel
Newport Pier
Balboa Pier
West Jetty
Ferry to Catalina Island
Corona Del Mar
San Koaquin Reservoir
Big Canyon Reservoir
Crystal Cove State Park
PACIFIC OCEAN
SIGHTS & ACTIVITIES
Balboa Fun Zone........1 C3
Balboa Pavilion........(see 1)
Corona del Mar State Beach........2 D3
Little Corona del Mar Beach........3 D3
Lookout Point........4 D3
Lovell House........5 B2
Newport Bay Ecological Reserve........6 C1
Newport Harbor Nautical Museum...(see 1)
Orange County Museum of Art........7 D1
Pirate's Cove........(see 4)
Sherman Library & Gardens........8 D3
Wedge........9 D3
SLEEPING
Bay Shores Peninsula Hotel........10 B2
Holiday Inn Express........11 B2
Newport Channel Inn........12 A1
Newport Dunes Waterfront Resort & Marina........13 C2
EATING
Bluewater Grill........14 B2
Crab Cooker........15 A2
Plums Café........16 B1
Zov's Café & Bakery........17 F2
DRINKING
3-Thirty-3 Waterfront........18 C2
Alta Coffeehouse........19 B2
Muldoon's........20 D2
Ruby's Crystal Cove Shake Shack.....21 F4
SHOPPING
Fashion Island........22 D2
TRANSPORT
Balboa Island Ferry........23 C2

beachgoers, and the people-ogling is great. Insider tip? Think twice before renting a four-wheeled surrey (it's like a family-sized bike) and pedaling the path between the Newport and Balboa piers; locals have been known to bombard them with water balloons.

Opposite the Balboa Pier on the harbor side of the peninsula, visitors can hop aboard the iconic Ferris wheel or take a spin on the carousel at the **Balboa Fun Zone** (www.thebalboafunzone.com; 603 E Bay Ave; 11am-6pm Sun-Thu, to 9pm Fri, to 10pm Sat), which has been around since 1936. The park's other attractions (arcade games, bumper cars) were recently dismantled to make room for the model ships and maritime memorabilia on display at the newly arrived **Newport Harbor Nautical Museum** (949-675-8915; www.nhnm.org; Balboa Fun Zone, 600 E Bay Ave; suggested donation $5; 10am-6pm Wed-Mon, with varied lunch closures), which moved from its former home on East Coast Hwy. The nearby **Balboa Pavilion**, a landmark dating from 1905, is beautifully illuminated at night.

At the very tip of the peninsula, by the West Jetty, the **Wedge** is a bodysurfing and knee-boarding spot famous for its perfectly hollow waves that can get up to 30ft high. Look for the small crowd watching the high-octane action from the shore. But beware venturing in yourself – the waves are shore-breakers and regularly smash bodysurfers against the sand like rag dolls.

BALBOA ISLAND

In the middle of the harbor sits the island that time forgot. Its streets are still largely lined with tightly clustered cottages built in the 1920s and '30s when this was a summer getaway from LA. The 1.5-mile promenade that circles the island makes a terrific car-free stroll or jog. The island is connected to the Fun Zone via a tiny car and passenger **ferry** (www.balboaislandferry.com; adult/child/car & driver $1/50¢/2; 6:30am-midnight Sun-Thu, to 2:30am Fri & Sat). It lands at Agate Ave, about 11 blocks west of Marine Ave, the main drag lined with cutesy stores and restaurants.

ORANGE COUNTY MUSEUM OF ART

Less than a mile from Fashion Island, this engaging **museum** (949-759-1122; www.ocma.net; 850 San Clemente Dr; adult/child under 12yr/student & senior $10/free/8; 11am-5pm Wed-Sun, to 8pm Thu) highlights California art and cutting-edge contemporary artists with exhibits rotating through its two large gallery areas every four to six months. There's also a sculpture garden, an eclectic gift shop and a theater screening classic, foreign and art-related films.

CORONA DEL MAR

This ritzy bedroom community, perched on the privileged eastern bluffs of the Newport Channel, has some of the best coastal views in SoCal. It also includes a high-end stretch of Pacific Coast Hwy, with trendy shops and restaurants, as well as **Corona del Mar State Beach** (949-644-3151; www.parks.ca.gov; 5am-10pm), which lies at the foot of rocky cliffs. Parking is $8 on weekdays, $10 on weekends. If you're early (or lucky) try to nab a free parking spot above the beach on Ocean Blvd.

Lookout Point sits above the beach along Ocean Blvd near Heliotrope Ave. Locals throw sunset cocktail parties here, though be discreet with your chardonnay: technically, open containers are illegal. Stairs lead to **Pirate's Cove**, which has a great, waveless beach and is great for families. Scenes from *Gilligan's Island* were shot here. A bit further east on Ocean Blvd is **Inspiration Point**, another nice spot to enjoy the view. Children love the tide pool just east at **Little Corona del Mar Beach**.

Corona del Mar's prize attraction is the compact **Sherman Library & Gardens** (949-673-2261; www.slgardens.org; 2647 E Coast Hwy; adult/child $3/1, Mon admission free; gardens 10:30am-4pm daily, library 9am-4:30pm Tue-Thu). The gardens are manicured, lush and bursting with color. The small, noncirculating research library holds a wealth of California historical documents, as well as paintings by early California landscape artists.

CRYSTAL COVE STATE PARK

Once you get past the parking lots ($10), it's easy to forget you're in a crowded metropolitan area at this state **beach** (949-494-3539; www.parks.ca.gov; Pacific Coast Hwy; 6am-sunset), where visitors are treated to 2000 acres of undeveloped woodlands and 3.5 miles of coastline. Everyone thought the hilltops were part of the state park too, until the Irvine Company, the actual landowner, bulldozed them to make room for McMansions that are the dream of many an OC resident. For a more discreet, short-term stay, reserve one of the park's inland campsites (it's a 3-mile hike each way) with **Reserve America** (800-444-7275; www.reserveamerica.com; tent sites $15).

NEWPORT BAY ECOLOGICAL RESERVE

Inland from the harbor, where run-off from the San Bernardino Mountains meets the sea, the brackish water of the Newport Bay Ecological Reserve supports more than 200 species of bird. This is one of the few estuaries in Southern California that has been preserved, and it's an important stopover on the Pacific Flyway (see the boxed text, p324). The **Muth Interpretive Center** (☎ 949-923-2290; www.ocparks.com/unbic; 2301 University Dr; ⏰ 10am-4pm Tue-Sun;), near Irvine Ave and just out of view of the parking lot, is made from sustainable materials. Inside, you'll find displays and information about the 752-acre reserve, as well as a kid-friendly activity room with a number of small, snake-and-spider-filled terraria. For guided tours with naturalists ($25 canoeing, $15 kayaking, free for walking) contact the **Newport Bay Naturalists & Friends** (☎ 949-640-6746; www.newportbay.org).

Sleeping

Rates drop by as much as 40% (or more) in winter. Those listed are for high season.

Newport Dunes Waterfront Resort & Marina (☎ 949-729-3863, 800-765-7661; www.newportdunes.com; 1131 Back Bay Dr; tent and RV sites with hookups from $64, cottages $135-$365; wi-fi) Welcome to RV heaven. Besides hookups, Newport Dunes has a pool, a spa, game rooms and a small beach on one of Newport's brackish lagoons. For those without a Winnebago, the tiny cottages are a good deal, especially in the low season. There are a few campsites. In the lobby, look for the concrete handprints of several cast members from the now-canceled show *The OC;* the memorial was booted from its former spot of glory at the visitors bureau.

our pick **Newport Channel Inn** (☎ 949-642-3030, 800-255-8614; www.newportchannelinn.com; 6030 W Coast Hwy; r $119-200; wi-fi) Cyclists love this two-story motel's proximity to the beach bike path, which is just across the street. Other perks include large rooms, a big common sundeck and genuinely friendly owners. The large A-framed room 219 sleeps up to seven. Top budget choice that works well for traveling groups.

Bay Shores Peninsula Hotel (☎ 949-675-3463, 800-222-6675; www.thebestinn.com; 1800 W Balboa Blvd; r from $400; wi-fi) *Endless Summer* surf murals. Fresh-baked cookies. Shelves of free movies. This three-story motel has a fun, beach-minded hospitality that makes the surfing lifestyle seem accessible – even if you're a middle-aged landlubber who's never touched a board in you're life. The hotel is pretty close to the beach, which accounts for the price.

For a good midrange chain, consider **Holiday Inn Express** (☎ 949-722-2999, 888-465-4329; www.ichotelsgroup.com; 2300 W Coast Hwy; r $190-219; wi-fi). Rooms have up-to-date furnishings and extras such a microwaves and refrigerators. Centrally located on PCH between major attractions.

Eating

Crab Cooker (☎ 949-673-0100; 2200 Newport Blvd; mains $6-30; ⏰ 11am-9pm Sun-Thu, to 10pm Fri & Sat, market opens 10am) Expect a wait at this always-busy fish joint, which serves great seafood and fresh crab on paper plates to an always-appreciative crowd in flip-flops and jeans. The delicious chowder is loaded with clams. If you're in a hurry, order your meal at the fish market counter to-go.

Plums Cafe (☎ 949-722-7568; Westport Plaza, 369 E 17th St; mains $8-15; ⏰ breakfast & lunch) With its exposed-brick walls and sleek decor, Plums will have you feeling ever-so-chic as you nibble hazelnut pancakes, Oregon pepper bacon, French-rolled omelets and other gourmet fare with a Pacific Northwest spin. Like most good eateries in Newport Beach, this one's tucked in a cookie-cutter strip mall.

Zov's Café & Bakery (☎ 949-760-9687; 21123 Newport Coast Dr; breakfast & lunch mains $8-15, dinner mains $10-23; ⏰ 8am-9pm Sun-Thu, to 10pm Fri & Sat) Bustling Zov's is the creation of local chef Zov Karamardian, renowned for her Mediterranean-style dishes prepared with California flair. From Moroccan salmon salads to grilled-lamb sandwiches to spinach-and-ricotta ravioli, it's all good. The milk-chocolate bomb should satisfy the cravings of most chocoholics. To get here, take a left off PCH at the lights at Newport Coast Dr after leaving Corona del Mar. Follow Newport Coast Dr 2 miles to Joaquin Hills. It's in the strip mall on your left.

Bluewater Grill (☎ 949-675-3474; 630 Lido Park Dr; most mains $10-25; ⏰ lunch & dinner) Sit on the wooden deck and watch the boats at this polished harborside restaurant/oyster bar, which serves incredibly fresh fish. Great for Bloody Marys and a leisurely lunch of seafood and coleslaw.

Drinking

Ruby's Crystal Cove Shake Shack (☎ 949-464-0100; 7703 E Coast Hwy; shakes under $5; ⏰ 10am-sunset) This

DETOUR: COSTA MESA SHOPPING

Newport Beach and Anaheim won't be kicking sand in the face of Costa Mesa any time soon. This land-locked suburb is home to **South Coast Plaza** (☎ 800-782-8888; www.southcoastplaza.com; 3333 Bristol St), a sprawling shopping complex that's home to 300 luxury stores – it attracts 25 million visitors a year and reports annual sales approaching $1.5 billion. Boutiques such as Chanel and Rolex do their part to keep the numbers high. Bigger stores include Saks Fifth Avenue, Nordstrom, Macy's and Crate & Barrel.

If this is too much mall for you, consider a visit to the **Lab** (☎ 714-966-6660; www.thelab.com; 2930 Bristol St), an ivy-covered, outdoor antimall where indie shoppers can sift through vintage clothing, trendy styles and eclectic tennis shoes. Vegans, tree-huggers and rock climbers may have more fun at the **Camp** (☎ 714-444-4267; www.thecampsite.com; 2937 Bristol St): one-stop shopping for outdoor-and-natural living needs with Adventure 16, Cycle Werks, a scuba shop and a Native Foods vegetarian eatery.

been-here-forever wooden milkshake stand is now owned by the Ruby's Diner chain, but the shakes and the ocean view are just as good as ever. Don't fear the date shake, it's dee-lish. Located just east of the Crystal Cove/Los Trancos entrance to the state park.

Alta Coffee House (☎ 949-675-0233; 506 31st St; 6am-11pm Mon-Thu, to midnight Fri & Sat, 7am-11pm Sun) Regulars hang their mug on the wall at this cozy coffee shop housed in an inviting bungalow.

Muldoon's (☎ 949-640-4110; 202 Newport Center Dr, Fashion Island; closed Mon) The SoCal Irish tradition continues at lively Muldoon's, which anchors a small strip mall across the street from Fashion Island.

3-Thirty-3 Waterfront (☎ 949-673-8464; 333 Bayside Dr) Perfect for a low-key happy hour with friends (try the gourmet sliders and fries), this stylish harborside lounge morphs into the stereotypical Newport 'scene' as the night rolls on – think Botoxed former beauties and over-tanned yachtsmen, all on a midnight prowl.

Shopping

A string of tiny boutiques lines Pacific Coast Hwy in Corona del Mar. On Balboa Island, Marine Ave is lined with unassuming (but not cheap) shops in a villagelike atmosphere.

Fashion Island (☎ 949-721-2000; 401 Newport Center Dr; 10am-9pm Mon-Fri, 9am-7pm Sat, 11am-6pm Sun) Sometimes referred to as Fascist Island, this chic mall has nearly 200 stores and is the draw here for serious shopping. Its breezy, Mediterranean-style walkways are lined with specialty stores, national chains, upscale kiosks, restaurants and the occasional koi pond and fountain. Anchor stores include Bloomingdales, Macy's and Neiman Marcus. There's a small indoor section, Atrium Court, with a Barnes & Noble.

Getting Around

OCTA bus 71 stops at the corner of Pacific Coast Hwy and Hwy 55, and goes south to Palm St beside the Balboa Pier. Bus 57 goes north to South Coast Plaza in Costa Mesa. Check current schedules at www.octa.net. Bus 71 departs every half hour during the week and every 40 minutes on weekends. The trip between Newport Pier and Balboa Pier is about eight minutes. Bus 57 runs about every 30 minutes daily from the Newport Transportation Center on San Nicolas Dr (near Fashion Island) to South Coast Plaza. The trip takes about 25 minutes.

Local fare is $1.25 per trip, cash only. It can be purchased from OCTA fareboxes or the bus driver – you'll need exact change. A one-day pass, available from the driver, is $3.

LAGUNA BEACH

pop 25,130

If you've ever wanted to step into a painting, a sunset stroll through Laguna Beach might be the next best thing. But hidden coves, romantic cliffs, azure waves and waterfront parks aren't the only aesthetic draw. Public sculptures, arts festivals and gallery nights imbue the city with an artistic sensibility you won't find elsewhere in SoCal. Most locals here, though wealthy, are also live-and-let-live, and there's a palpable artistic joie de vivre in the air that increases the sense of fun (the kids of MTV's *Laguna Beach* being the one troubling exception).

The city's natural beauty was a siren's call for San Francisco artist Norman St Clair, who discovered Laguna around 1910 and stayed on to paint its surf, cliffs and hills. His enthusiasm attracted other artists who, influenced by French impressionism, came to be known as the 'plein air' (open air) school.

Partly tucked into canyons and partly arrayed on oceanfront bluffs, Laguna is also a refreshing change from OC's beige-box architecture, with a combination of classic Arts and Crafts cabins and bold (if at times garish) modern homes. There's even a distinct downtown, known as the 'Village,' with shops, art galleries and restaurants.

While Laguna swells with tourists on summer weekends, there are plenty of uncrowded beaches once you move away from downtown and the adjacent Main Beach.

Orientation & Information

Laguna stretches for about 7 miles along Pacific Coast Hwy. Shops, restaurants and bars are concentrated along a quarter-mile stretch in the Village, along three parallel streets: Broadway, Ocean Ave and Forest Ave.

The staff at **Laguna Beach Visitors Center** (☎ 949-497-9229, 800-877-1115; www.lagunabeachinfo.org; 252 Broadway; 🕑 10am-4pm Mon-Fri) is very helpful, and one wall here is filled with maps, brochures, bus schedules and coupons. You can check your email for free for 15 minutes. There's also a new **satellite visitors center** (381 Forest Ave; 🕑 11am-5pm Mon-Fri, noon-4pm Sat & Sun). At the **Laguna Beach Library** (☎ 949-497-1733; www.ocpl.org; 363 Glenneyre St; 🕑 10am-8pm Mon-Wed, to 6pm Thu, 10am-5pm Fri & Sat), visitors can surf the internet at no charge for one hour per day.

Sights & Activities

LAGUNA ART MUSEUM

This breezy **museum** (☎ 949-494-8971; www.lagunaartmuseum.org; 307 Cliff Dr; adult/child under 12yr/student $10/free/8; 🕑 11am-5pm, free during First Thursdays Art Walk) has changing exhibits usually featuring one or two California artists, plus a permanent collection heavy on California landscapes, vintage photographs and works by early Laguna artists. The museum also makes an effort to support new artists.

The museum is a centrally located stop on the **First Thursdays Art Walk** (www.firstthursdaysartwalk.com; 🕑 6pm-9pm). During this convivial monthly event, numerous galleries open their doors for an evening of art, music and special exhibits.

BEACHES

With 30 public beaches and coves, Laguna is perfect for do-it-yourself exploring. Although many beaches are hidden from view by multi-million-dollar homes, a sharp eye will reveal one of the numerous stairways leading to the sand. Traveling south from the Village on PCH, pick an oceanside cross street and see what you can find.

Located at the western end of Broadway, **Main Beach** has volleyball and basketball courts, benches, tables and restrooms. It's also the best beach for swimming. Northwest of Main Beach, it's too rocky to surf; tide-pooling is best. (Tidepool etiquette: tread carefully and don't pick up any living thing that you find in the rocks.)

Just northwest of Main Beach, follow the path to the grassy, bluff-top **Heisler Park** for sweeping views of the craggy coves and deep blue sea. Bring your camera. Drop down below the park to **Diver's Cove**, a deep, protected inlet popular with snorkelers and, of course, divers. Northwest of town, **Crescent Bay** has big hollow waves good for bodysurfing, but parking is difficult here; try the bluffs atop the beach.

Tours

The visitors center has brochures detailing self-guided tours. *The Heritage Walking Companion* is a tour of the city's architecture with an emphasis on bungalows and cottages. The self-guided *Tour Laguna by Bus* gives a more general overview.

On the first Thursday of the month, downtown gets festive during the **First Thursdays Gallery Art Walk** (☎ 949-683-6871; www.firstthursdaysartwalk.com; admission free), which includes 40 local galleries and the Laguna Art Museum from 6pm to 9pm. Shuttles run from the museum to various clusters of galleries.

Sleeping

Most hotels in Laguna are on PCH, and traffic can be loud. If you're sensitive ask for a room away from the street or use earplugs. There are no budget lodgings in summer, but it's the best place in the OC for charming, noncorporate digs. Summer rates are listed. Come fall, they drop significantly.

Inn at Laguna Beach (☎ 949-497-9722, 800-544-4479; www.innatlagunabeach.com; 211 N Coast Hwy; r $129-599; 💻 🅿) This three-story white concrete hotel at the north end of Main Beach walks the fine

line between hip and homey, with personable finesse. All rooms have a fresh, clean look enhanced by French blinds and thick featherbeds. Some have balconies overlooking the water. Cookies and apple cider served at 5pm. Parking costs $14 per day.

America's Best Inn (☎ 949-494-6464, 877-363-7229; www.lagunabeachamericasbestinn.com; 1404 N Coast Hwy; $179-199; wifi) This easygoing, better-than-average budget hotel is located 1 mile northwest of the Village. Floral prints and big mirrors brighten average rooms, and each comes with a microwave and a fridge. This is a good place for big groups and is popular with on-the-cheap wedding parties in the fall.

our pick By the Sea Inn (☎ 949-497-6645, 800-297-0007; www.bytheseainn.com; 475 N Coast Hwy; r $250-379;) Be it good feng shui, friendly staff, comfy beds or proximity to the ocean, something just feels right at this 36-room inn. From the big green pillows on the bed and the flat screen TVs to the hardwood floors, the decor is a nice mix of new, comfy and clean. For a relaxing close to the day, settle in to the outdoor Jacuzzi with your honey as the sun drops over the ocean.

Casa Laguna Inn (☎ 949-494-2996, 800-233-0449; www.casalaguna.com; 2510 S Coast Hwy; r $280-400, ste $400-550; wi-fi) Laguna's B&B gem is built around a historic 1920s Mission-revival house surrounded by lush, manicured, mature plantings. Rooms are inside former artists' bungalows built in the 1930s and '40s; all have delicious beds, some have Jacuzzi tubs.

LAGUNA ART FESTIVALS

With a 6-acre canyon as its backdrop, Laguna's landmark event is the **Festival of the Arts** (☎ 949-494-1145; www.foapom.com; 650 Laguna Canyon Rd; adult/student & senior $7/4; ⏰ from 10am Jul & Aug), a two-month celebration of original artwork in almost all its forms. The 140 exhibiting artists – all approved pursuant to a juried selection process – display art ranging from paintings to handcrafted furniture to scrimshaw. Begun in the 1930s by local artists who needed to drum up buyers, the festival celebrated its 75th anniversary in 2008 and now attracts patrons and tourists from around the world. In addition to the art, there are free daily artists workshops, docent tours and live entertainment. For a slightly more indie-minded art show, look for the **Sawdust Art Festival** (☎ 949-494-3030; www.sawdustartfestival.org; 935 Laguna Canyon Rd; adult/child/senior $7/3/6; ⏰ 10am-10pm Jul & Aug) across the street.

The most thrilling part of the main festival is the **Pageant of the Masters** (☎ 949-497-6582, 800-487-3378; www.pageanttickets.com; admission $20-100), where human models blend seamlessly into re-creations of famous paintings. It began in 1933 as a sideshow to the main festival. Tickets generally go on sale around the beginning of December the previous year and sell out before the year ends. You may be able to snag last-minute cancellations at the gate. Nightly performances begin at 8:30pm.

There's a full breakfast, and evening wine and cheese. Delightful.

Eating

Taco Loco (☎ 949-497-1635; 640 S Coast Hwy; mains $2-12; ⏰ 11am-midnight Sun-Thu, to 2am Fri & Sat) Throw back Coronas at this sticker-covered sidewalk café, where taco fillers include grilled mahi-mahi, beef, pork, shrimp and veggies. Order at the counter then nab a spot on the sidewalk patio.

The Stand (☎ 949-494-8101; 238 Thalia St; mains under $10; ⏰ 7am-7pm; Ⓥ) This tiny tribute to vegetarian cuisine reflects what's best about Laguna living – it's friendly, unassuming and filled with indie spirit. The long menu includes hummus-and-guac sandwiches, sunflower-sprout salads and bean-and-rice burritos. For a snack try a smoothie or the corn-tortilla chips and salsa. Order at the counter next to Laguna Cyclery (in the red minibarn) and grab a spot on the wooden patio.

242 Café Fusion Sushi (☎ 949-494-2444; 242 N Coast Hwy; mains $6-19; ⏰ dinner) One of the only female sushi chefs in Orange County rolls and slices some of the Laguna's best sushi – and it's artfully presented, too. The place seats maybe 20 people, so expect a wait or come early. The yellowtail with spicy miso sauce and the Laguna Canyon roll are delicious. Make your life a little better.

Sapphire Laguna (949-715-9888; 1200 S Coast Hwy; lunch mains $14-17, dinner mains $20-32; ⏰ lunch & dinner) This stylish purveyor of global cuisine serves succulent specialties ranging from chicken pot pie to pan-seared barramundi. It also serves up some excellent views of the sea from its corner-side patio. The home-fired sage and rosemary sea salt potato chips are as addictive as their name is long. Come for dinner rather than lunch and make reservations.

Mozambique (949-715-7777; 1740 S Coast Hwy; lunch mains $9-15, dinner mains $15-44; ⏰ lunch Fri-Sun, dinner daily) New on the scene but already winning raves, this two-level ode to piripiri-spiced cuisine from southern Africa manages to have fun with its theme – see the parrot out front and the canopied lounge – while serving sophisticated, exotically spiced dishes that tickle your tastebuds as well as your sense of adventure. Dinner choices include piripiri chicken, lamb curry, and sausage on coriander polenta. Who knows? You might even see a *Desperate Housewives* cast member hiding out in the clubhousey 2nd-floor bar.

Drinking & Entertainment

K'ya (☎ 949-376-9718; 1287 S Coast Hwy) Laguna finally has a rooftop bar and locals are singing mojito hallelujahs. Perched atop the La Casa del Camino Hotel, the bar is noteworthy for its beautiful coastal views and friendly vibe. Follow the crowds through the hotel lobby and take the elevator to the top. As for mojitos, there are five on the cocktail menu, including mango and wild berry.

Las Brisas (☎ 949-497-5434; 361 Cliff Dr) Locals roll their eyes at the mere mention of this tourist-heavy spot, but out-of-towners flock here for a good reason: the blufftop view of the beach. Sip margaritas while you stare at the crashing waves from the glassed-in patio; the image of the coast will leave an indelible impression. Cocktail hour gets packed; make reservations.

Getting There & Around

To reach Laguna Beach from the I-405, take Hwy 133 (Laguna Canyon Rd) southwest. Laguna is served by OCTA bus 1, which runs along the coast from Long Beach to San Clemente.

Number one piece of advice? Bring lots of quarters to feed the meters. Laguna is hemmed in by steep canyons, and parking is a perpetual problem. In and around the Village you'll find a few outdoor change machines (there's one on Cliff Dr by Heisler Park). If you're spending the night, leave your car at the hotel and ride the local bus. Parking lots in the Village charge $10 to $15 or more per entry and fill up early during summer.

Laguna Beach Transit (☎ 949-497-0746; www.lagunabeachcity.net; 300 block of Broadway) has its central bus depot on Broadway, just north of the visitors center in the heart of the Village. It operates three routes at hourly intervals (approximately 7am to 6pm Monday to Friday, 9am to 6pm Saturday). Routes are color-coded and easy to follow but subject to change. For tourists, the most important route is the one that runs north–south along Pacific Coast Hwy. Pick up a brochure and schedule at your hotel or the visitors center. Rides cost 75¢. No Sunday service.

SAN JUAN CAPISTRANO

Famous for the swallows that annually return here from their winter migration on March 19th (though sometimes they arrive a bit early), San Juan Capistrano is also home to the 'jewel of the California missions.'

Located about 10 miles southeast and inland of Laguna Beach, the beautiful **Mission San Juan Capistrano** (☎ 949-234-1300; www.missionsjc.com; 31882 Camino Capistrano, cnr Ortega Hwy; adult/child/senior $9/5/8; 🕑 8:30am-5pm) was built around a series of 18th-century arcades, all of which enclose photogenic fountains and lush gardens. The charming Serra Chapel – whitewashed outside and decorated with vivid frescoes inside – is considered the oldest building in California. It's the only chapel still standing in which Padre Junípero Serra gave Mass. He founded the mission on November 1, 1776 and tended it personally for many years. Particularly moving are the remains of the Great Stone Church, almost completely destroyed by an earthquake in 1812 that killed 42 Native Americans worshipping inside. Plan to spend at least an hour looking around. The gift shop has a good collection of books on early California and mission history.

To celebrate the swallows' return from their South American sojourn, the city puts on the **Festival of the Swallows** every year. The birds nest in the walls of the mission until around October 23. They're best observed at feeding time, usually early in the morning and late afternoon to early evening.

One block west, next to the Capistrano train depot, is the **Los Rios Historic District**, a cutesy assemblage of cottage and adobes housing cafés and gift shops.

Eating

Ramos House Cafe (☎ 949-443-1342; 31752 Los Rios St; mains $11-16, weekend brunch per person $35; 🕑 breakfast & lunch Tue-Sun) Famous for earthy comfort food, the board-and-batten Ramos House is the best spot for breakfast or lunch near the mission. To find it, walk across the railroad tracks at the end of Verdugo St and turn right. Burlap tablecloths, passing trains and disconcertingly enthusiastic waitresses ('Oh my gosh, the duck hash is awesome!') add color.

Tea House on Los Rios (☎ 949-443-3914; 31731 Los Rios St; mains $14-19; 🕑 11am-5pm Wed-Fri, 10am-5pm Sat & Sun) Made for ladies who lunch – or sip tea. Think flower-covered trellis, a table-dotted porch and dainty settings. Groups may enjoy the Victorian Tea serving ($36), which includes champagne amid the finger sandwiches, scones and tea. For dudes who don't do tea, prime rib, shepherd's pie and beer are on the regular menu.

Entertainment

Coach House (☎ 949-496-8930; www.thecoachhouse.com; 33157 Camino Capistrano) A well-known entertainment venue featuring local and regional rock and alternative bands; expect a cover of $17 to $30 depending on who's playing. Recent guests have included the Young Dubliners, Toad the Wet Sprocket and Matthew Sweet.

Getting There & Away

From Laguna Beach, take OCTA bus 1 south to Ave Pico, then connect to bus 191/A in the direction of Mission Viejo, which drops you near the mission ($2.50, about one hour). OCTA Buses 1 and 191/A run about every 30 minutes on weekdays and every 60 minutes on weekends.

The Amtrak depot is one block south and west of the mission; it would be perfectly reasonable to arrive by train from LA or San Diego in time for lunch, visit the mission and be back in the city for dinner.

Drivers should exit I-5 at Ortega Hwy and head west for about a quarter of a mile.

DANA POINT & AROUND

Nineteenth-century adventurer Richard Dana called Dana Point 'the only romantic spot on the coast.' Nowadays its yacht-filled marinas don't inspire immediate thoughts of romance, but it is a pleasant place to wander if you enjoy maritime history and family-oriented attractions. Most of the action occurs around the man-made harbor on Dana Point Harbor Dr, just off PCH.

The kid-friendly **Ocean Institute** (☎ 949-496-2274; www.ocean-institute.org; 24200 Dana Pt Harbor Dr; basic admission adult/child $6.50/4.50, extra for cruises; ⏰ 10am-3pm Sat & Sun; 👪) includes replicas of historic tall ships, maritime-related exhibits and a floating research lab. Specific trips include a marine-wildlife cruise aboard the RV *Sea Explorer* (adult/child $35/22) and a Pyrate Adventure Sail – with a cast of pirates – on the 118ft *Spirit of Dana Point* tall ship. It's open on weekends.

Just as fun may be nearby **Doheny State Beach** (☎ 949-496-6172; www.parks.ca.gov, www.dohenystatebeach.org; ⏰ 6am-8pm Nov-Feb, to 10pm Mar-Oct; 👪 wi-fi), where you'll find picnic tables, grills, volleyball courts, a bike path and surf that's good for swimming, surfing, tide-pooling and diving. It's also the one place in Orange County that allows **beach camping** (☎ 800-444-7275, international callers 916-638-5883; www.reserveamerica.com; tent & RV sites $25-35). Day-use parking is $10.

Dedicated surfers won't mind the 1-mile hike to world-renowned **Trestles**, just south of the town of **San Clemente** and north of San Onofre State Beach, bordering the San Diego County line. It's a natural surfbreak that consistently churns out perfect waves. Check out www.surfrider.org for more information on the potential extension of a nearby toll road that could affect the waves. Exit at Los Christianos Rd off I-5.

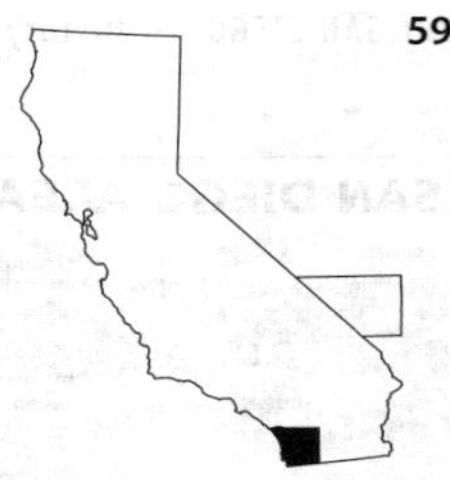

San Diego Area

There's a certain arrogance that comes with living on the SoCal coast, a breezy confidence that springs from the assumption that your life is just, well, *better* than everyone else's. No offense, bro. It just is. But as far as coastal snobs go, San Diegans are the ones we like the most. Whether it's a battle-tested docent sharing stories on the USS *Midway*, a La Jolla mom spilling secrets about kid-friendly beach spots, or a no-worries surf diva helping you catch a wave, folks here are a little more willing to share the good life than in counties further north. Heck, even the bouncers at the Gaslamp Quarter's 'velvet rope' clubs will give you the time of day – even if they won't let you in.

Stick around a day or two, and you'll feel a spring in your step, too. The only problem? With 70 miles of coastline, a near-perfect climate and loads of outdoor distractions, it's tough to decide where to start. Maritime history buffs can stroll the tall ships docked on the Embarcadero. Bikers and bladers can cop a suntan while gliding down Ocean Front Walk. Kayakers, scuba divers and tide-poolers can get their kicks in the coves and caves of La Jolla. And that's without mentioning the surf spots – from newbie-friendly shores to pro-only breaks stretching from Oceanside south to Imperial Beach.

Away from the surf, a re-energized Gaslamp Quarter is drawing stylish crowds with rooftop bars, hipster hotels, and baseball games with the Padres. Pandas, lions and killer whales wile away the day at world-famous zoos and marine habitats, while museums and gardens await exploration at the world's largest urban park. Horse races, New Age retreats and a theme park constructed from joinable blocks are only a short train ride north.

HIGHLIGHTS

- **Soothing Stroll** Wandering the museums and gardens at Balboa Park (p607).
- **Roof with a View** Sipping a martini on a rooftop bar in the Gaslamp Quarter (p603).
- **History Time** Wandering the 4-acre flight deck on the USS *Midway* at the Embarcadero (p607).
- **Animal Instincts** Coming face-to-face with the King of the Jungle at the San Diego's Zoo Wild Animal Park (p613) .
- **Water Sports** Kayaking to sea caves along the coast of La Jolla Cove (p626 and learning to surf off La Jolla shores (p625).
- **Serenity Now** Soaking up rays and ocean views from the Babcock & Story patio at the Hotel del Coronado (p616).
- **Chow's Up** Chowing down on fish tacos and juicy burgers in Ocean Beach (p633).

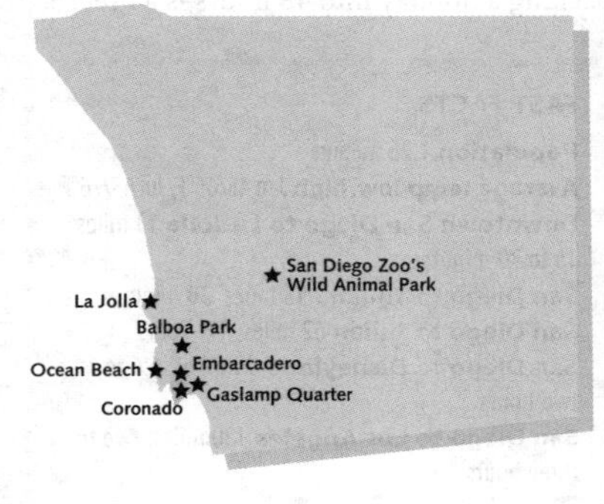

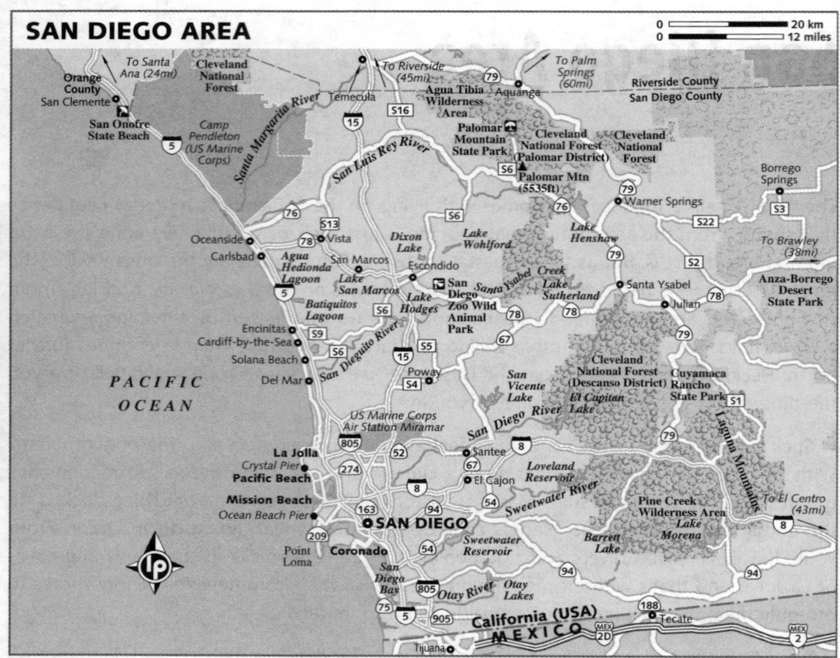

SAN DIEGO

pop 1.26 million

Most Americans work all year for a two-week vacation. San Diegans will tell you they work all week for a two-day vacation. And it's easy to see why. With a world-renowned zoo, eye-catching architecture, diverse museums, breezy rooftop lounges, and gorgeous beaches all within city limits (and a 15-mile drive) packing a holiday into 48 hours is a breeze.

FAST FACTS

Population 1.26 million

Average temp low/high Jan 48/65°F, Jul 65/76°F

Downtown San Diego to La Jolla 13 miles, 15 to 30 minutes

San Diego to Tijuana 18 miles, 30 minutes

San Diego to Julian 62 miles, 1½ hours

San Diego to Disneyland 94 miles, 1½ to two hours

San Diego to Los Angeles 120 miles, two to three hours

HISTORY

Evidence of human habitation in the region dates back to 18,000 BC. By the time the Spanish explorer Juan Rodriguez Cabrillo sailed into San Diego Bay in 1542 – the first European to do so – the region was divided peaceably between the Kumeyaay and Luisenõ/Juanenõ peoples. Their way of life continued undisturbed until Junípero Serra and Gaspar de Portolá arrived in 1769. They founded a mission and a military fort on the hill now known as the Presidio, making it the first permanent European settlement in California.

When the United States took California from Mexico in the 1840s, San Diego remained little more than a ramshackle village. But William Heath Davis, a San Francisco property speculator, knew there was a fortune to be made. In the 1850s, he bought 160 acres of bayfront property and erected prefabricated houses, a wharf and warehouses. 'Davis' Folly' eventually went bust, but only because he was ahead of his time. A decade later, another San Francisco speculator, Alonzo E Horton, snapped up almost 1000 waterfront acres and promoted the area as 'New Town.' This time, the idea stuck, making him a rich man.

The discovery of gold in the hills east of San Diego in 1869 pushed things along, and the ensuing rush brought the railroad here in 1884. A classic Wild West culture of saloons, gambling houses and brothels thrived along 5th St in the Gaslamp Quarter. When gold played out, the economy took a nosedive, and the city's population plummeted yet again.

When San Francisco hosted the successful Panama-Pacific International Exposition (1914), San Diego responded with its own Panama-California Exposition (1915–16), hoping to attract investment to a city with a deepwater port, a railroad hub and a perfect climate – but virtually no industry. To give San Diego a unique image, boosters built exhibition halls (see p607) in the romantic, Spanish colonial style that still defines much of the city today.

However, it was the bombing of Pearl Harbor in 1941 that made San Diego. The US Pacific Fleet needed a mainland home for its headquarters. The top brass quickly settled on San Diego, whose excellent deepwater port affords protection in almost all weather. The military literally reshaped the city, dredging the harbor, building landfill islands and constructing vast tracts of instant housing.

For San Diego, WWII was only the start of the boom, thanks largely to the continued military presence. However, the opening of the University of California campus in the 1960s heralded a new era, as students and faculty slowly drove a liberal wedge into the city's homogenous, flag-and-family culture. The university, especially strong in the sciences, has also become an incubator for the region's biotech sector.

ORIENTATION

San Diego may be the country's eighth-largest city, but it's surprisingly easy to navigate. Downtown is a compact grid of streets east of San Diego Bay and encompasses the Gaslamp Quarter, the Embarcadero and Little Italy. Within the city center, north–south avenues are numbered (1st, 2nd etc) while east–west streets in the Gaslamp Quarter and just north of Broadway are lettered (A, B, C etc). The airport, train station and Greyhound are all in or near downtown.

Balboa Park and the San Diego Zoo sit on a bluff northeast of downtown. At the northwest edge of the park are Uptown and Hillcrest, headquarters of the city's large gay and lesbian community. Northwest of Hillcrest is Old Town, site of San Diego's original settlement. Above Old Town, Presidio Hill and park overlook Mission Valley, now a freeway and a commercial corridor.

Coronado, the peninsula that guards San Diego Bay, is accessible from downtown by bridge or a short ferry. Across the mouth of the bay lies another, rockier peninsula, which comes to a dramatic end at Point Loma. Moving north up the coast, you arrive at Ocean Beach, a surfer's delight, followed by Mission Bay, with its parks and lagoons at the mouth of the San Diego River. Beyond Mission Bay and Beach lies Pacific Beach, which epitomizes the SoCal beach scene. Last up is La Jolla, an upscale seaside community and home of the University of California at San Diego (UCSD).

The region's main north–south highway is I-5, which parallels the coast from the Camp Pendleton Marine Corps Base in the north to the Mexican border at San Ysidro in the south. The I-8 runs east from Ocean Beach, through Mission Valley, past suburbs including El Cajon, and on to the Imperial Valley and, eventually, Arizona.

A good way to see it all in one day is with Old Town Trolley tours (p627).

INFORMATION

Bookstores

Chain bookstores are located in most malls.

Borders (Map pp604-5; ☎ 619-702-4200; www.borders.com; 668 6th Ave) Good selection of local interest books. There's also a coffee shop, and it offers wi-fi access through T-Mobile.

Le Travel Store (Map pp604-5; ☎ 619-544-0005; 745 4th Ave) Excellent selection of maps, travel guides and accessories. Helpful staff.

Emergency & Medical Services

Scripps Mercy Hospital (Map pp608-9; ☎ 619-294-8111; www.scripps.org; 4077 5th Ave; 24hr) Has a 24-hour emergency room.

Internet Access

All city-operated libraries provide free internet access (see p603); no library card is required. They also offer free wireless access. Check www.sandiego.gov/public-library to check various use policies. At Central Library downtown, call to make reservations one day

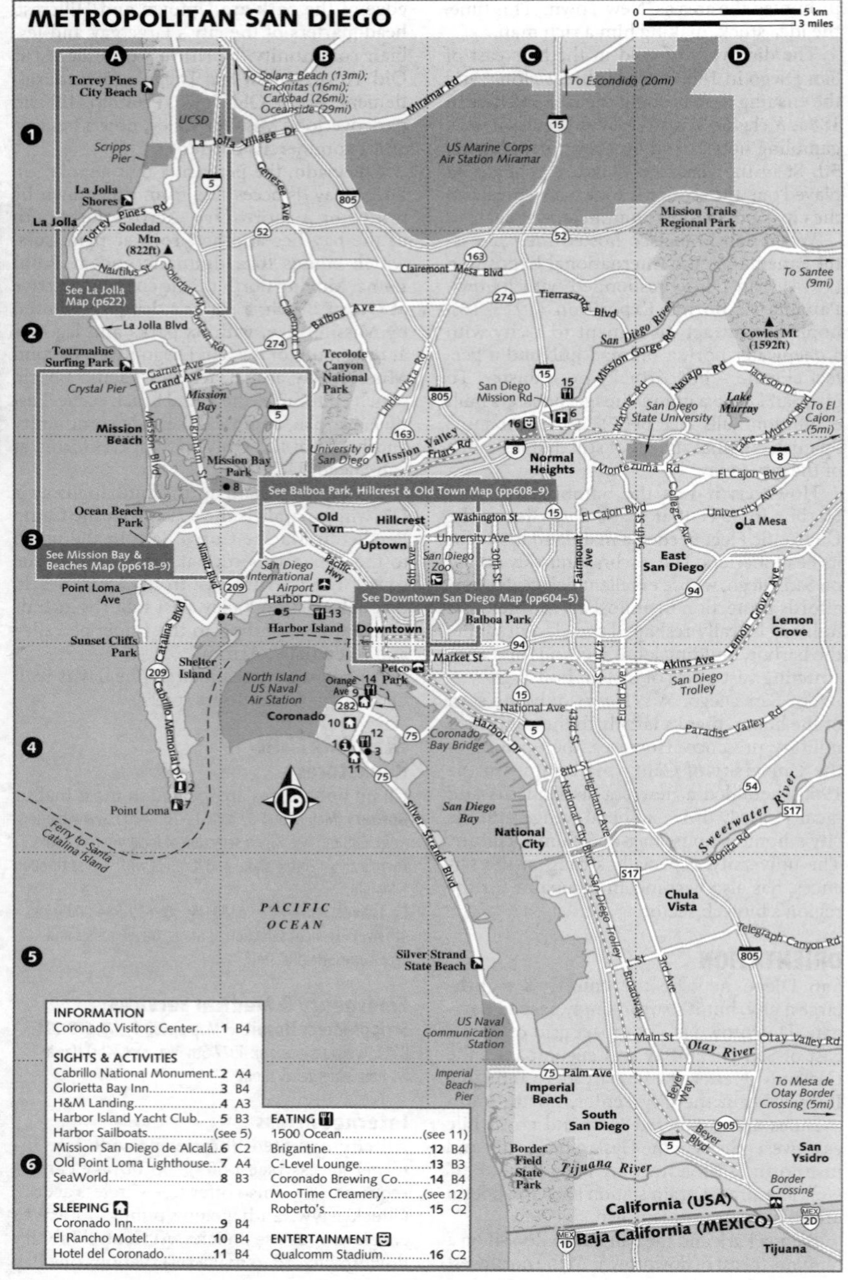
METROPOLITAN SAN DIEGO
0 5 km
0 3 miles
A
B
C
D
1
2
3
4
5
6
Torrey Pines City Beach
UCSD
Scripps Pier
La Jolla Village Dr
La Jolla Shores
La Jolla
Torrey Pines Rd
Soledad Mtn (822ft)
Nautilus St
Soledad Mountain Rd
See La Jolla Map (p622)
To Solana Beach (13mi); Encinitas (16mi); Carlsbad (26mi); Oceanside (29mi)
Miramar Rd
Genesee Ave
To Escondido (20mi)
US Marine Corps Air Station Miramar
Mission Trails Regional Park
Clairemont Mesa Blvd
To Santee (9mi)
Tierrasanta Blvd
San Diego River
Cowles Mt (1592ft)
Mission Gorge Rd
Balboa Ave
Clairemont Dr
La Jolla Blvd
Tourmaline Surfing Park
Garnet Ave
Grand Ave
Crystal Pier
Mission Bay
Mission Beach
Mission Blvd
Ingraham St
Tecolote Canyon National Park
Linda Vista Rd
San Diego Mission Rd
Navajo Rd
Jackson Dr
Lake Murray
San Diego State University
To El Cajon (5mi)
Waring Rd
Lake Murray Blvd
Mission Valley
Friars Rd
University of San Diego
Normal Heights
Montezuma Rd
El Cajon Blvd
Mission Bay Park
See Balboa Park, Hillcrest & Old Town Map (pp608–9)
Ocean Beach Park
Old Town
Hillcrest
Washington St
University Ave
La Mesa
Uptown
College Ave
54th St
Fairmount Ave
East San Diego
See Mission Bay & Beaches Map (pp618–9)
Nimitz Blvd
San Diego International Airport
Pacific Hwy
6th Ave
San Diego Zoo
30th St
Point Loma Ave
Harbor Dr
See Downtown San Diego Map (pp604–5)
Harbor Island
Downtown
Balboa Park
Lemon Grove Ave
Lemon Grove
Sunset Cliffs Park
Catalina Blvd
Shelter Island
Market St
Petco Park
Akins Ave
San Diego Trolley
North Island US Naval Air Station
Orange Ave
Coronado
National Ave
Euclid Ave
47th St
43rd St
Paradise Valley Rd
Cabrillo Memorial Dr
Coronado Bay Bridge
8th St
Highland Ave
Point Loma
Ferry to Santa Catalina Island
San Diego Bay
National City
National City Blvd
Sweetwater River
Bonita Rd
Silver Strand Blvd
San Diego Trolley
Chula Vista
PACIFIC OCEAN
Telegraph Canyon Rd
Silver Strand State Beach
L St
3rd Ave
Broadway
US Naval Communication Station
Main St
Otay River
Otay Valley Rd
Imperial Beach Pier
Palm Ave
Imperial Beach
To Mesa de Otay Border Crossing (5mi)
South San Diego
Beyer Way
Beyer Blvd
Border Field State Park
Tijuana River
San Ysidro
Border Crossing
California (USA)
Baja California (MEXICO)
Tijuana
INFORMATION
Coronado Visitors Center.......1 B4
SIGHTS & ACTIVITIES
Cabrillo National Monument..2 A4
Glorietta Bay Inn.......................3 B4
H&M Landing...........................4 A3
Harbor Island Yacht Club......5 B3
Harbor Sailboats.................(see 5)
Mission San Diego de Alcalá..6 C2
Old Point Loma Lighthouse...7 A4
SeaWorld...............................8 B3
SLEEPING
Coronado Inn..........................9 B4
El Rancho Motel....................10 B4
Hotel del Coronado..............11 B4
EATING
1500 Ocean......................(see 11)
Brigantine..............................12 B4
C-Level Lounge......................13 B3
Coronado Brewing Co...........14 B4
MooTime Creamery...........(see 12)
Roberto's...............................15 C2
ENTERTAINMENT
Qualcomm Stadium..............16 C2

in advance (☎ 619-236-5800) or use the 15-minute, no-reservation express terminals near the entrance.

Pay to log on at FedEx Kinko's copy stores throughout the city (www.fedex.com) or try **Babycakes** (Map pp608-9; ☎ 619-296-4173; 3766 5th Ave, Hillcrest; 7am-10pm Sun-Thu, to 11pm Fri & Sat). Formerly David's Coffeehouse, the café offers computer terminals and wi-fi in Hillcrest.

Left Luggage

Greyhound station (Map pp604-5; ☎ general 619-239-3266, 619-515-1100; 120 W Broadway) Luggage storage is $3 for first three to five hours with a $6 maximum the first day, then it's $8 per day.

Libraries

Central library (Map pp604-5; ☎ 619-236-5800; www.sandiego.gov/public-library; 820 E St; noon-8pm Mon & Wed, 9:30am-5:30pm Tue & Thu-Sat, 1-5pm Sun) About two blocks east of the Gaslamp Quarter. Check the website for branch locations.

Media

KPBS 89.5FM (www.kpbs.org) Public radio, high-quality news and information.

San Diego Reader (www.sandiegoreader.com) On Thursdays, look for this alt-weekly with the latest on the active music, art and theater scenes.

San Diego Union-Tribune (www.signonsandiego.com) The city's major daily.

Money

You'll find ATMs throughout San Diego.

Travelex (Map pp604-5; ☎ 619-235-0901; 177 Horton Plaza; 10am-7pm Mon-Fri, to 6pm Sat, 11am-4pm Sun) For foreign-currency exchange.

Post

For local post office locations, call ☎ 800-275-8777 or log on to www.us ps.com.

Downtown post office (Map pp604-5; ☎ 619-232-8612; 815 E St; 8:30am-5pm Mon-Fri) Self-service kiosks available when window closed.

Tourist Information

International Visitors Information Center (Map pp604-5; ☎ 619-236-1212; www.sandiego.org; W Broadway at Harbor Dr; 9am-5pm daily Jun-Aug, to 4pm Sep-May) The San Diego Convention & Visitors Bureau runs this well-stocked visitors center. Staff is multilingual. The visitors center is currently located across from Broadway Pier on Harbor Dr across from the Embarcadero but plans to relocate one block south by this book's publication. Call or email for the helpful information guide; look for discounts and packages on the website. There's a satellite booth in La Jolla on Hershel Ave near Prospect St.

Old Town State Historic Park Visitor Center (Map pp608-9; ☎ 619-220-5422; www.parks.ca.gov; 10am-5pm; P) For information about state parks in San Diego County, head to the Robinson-Rose House at the western end of the plaza in Old Town.

DANGERS & ANNOYANCES

Areas of interest to visitors are well defined and mostly within easy reach of downtown by foot or by public transportation. San Diego is fairly safe, though you should be cautious venturing east of 6th Ave in downtown, especially after dark. Hostile panhandling is the most common problem. Also steer clear of Balboa Park after dark.

SIGHTS

Downtown

With baseball fans flowing into Petco Park, scenesters cramming into Gaslamp Quarter nightclubs, kids scrambling into the New Children's Museum and maritime history buffs lining up outside the USS *Midway*, downtown feels like it just gulped a shot of Redbull. If you haven't visited in a few years, you're in for a surprise. San Diego is feeling a little, well, hip. It seems the opening of Petco Park baseball stadium in 2004 started a wave of development that still hasn't crested, and the energy here is palpable, especially on weekends.

Downtown lies east of the waterfront, and its skyline is dominated by office towers, condos and hotels. Just south of Broadway, running along 5th Ave, is the historic Gaslamp Quarter, the primary hub for shopping, dining and entertainment. New bars and restaurants are also popping up just north of Petco Park in edgy East Village. To the west lies the Embarcadero district, a nice spot for a bayfront jog or a stroll through historic sea-faring vessels. A short walk north lands you in Little Italy, where mom-and-pop eateries alternate with high-end design stores.

GASLAMP QUARTER

Soon after his arrival in San Diego in 1867, San Francisco speculator Alonzo Horton purchased 960 acres of land stretching south from Broadway to the waterfront and east to 15th St – for a grand total of $265. While respectable businesses went up along Broadway, the 5th Ave area became known as The Stingaree, a

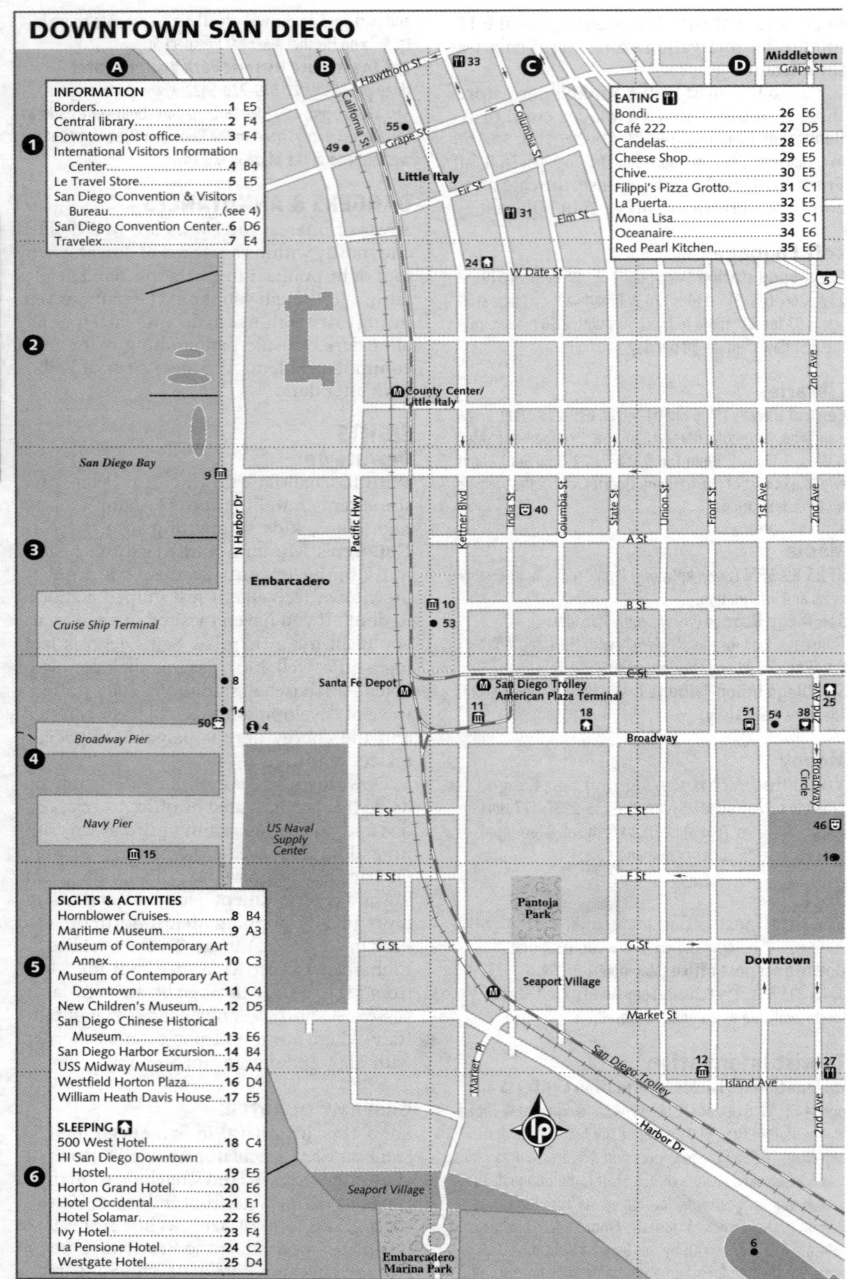
DOWNTOWN SAN DIEGO
INFORMATION
Borders....1 E5
Central library....2 F4
Downtown post office....3 F4
International Visitors Information Center....4 B4
Le Travel Store....5 E5
San Diego Convention & Visitors Bureau....(see 4)
San Diego Convention Center..6 D6
Travelex....7 E4
EATING
Bondi....26 E6
Café 222....27 D5
Candelas....28 E6
Cheese Shop....29 E5
Chive....30 E5
Filippi's Pizza Grotto....31 C1
La Puerta....32 E5
Mona Lisa....33 C1
Oceanaire....34 E6
Red Pearl Kitchen....35 E6
SIGHTS & ACTIVITIES
Hornblower Cruises....8 B4
Maritime Museum....9 A3
Museum of Contemporary Art Annex....10 C3
Museum of Contemporary Art Downtown....11 C4
New Children's Museum....12 D5
San Diego Chinese Historical Museum....13 E6
San Diego Harbor Excursion...14 B4
USS Midway Museum....15 A4
Westfield Horton Plaza....16 D4
William Heath Davis House....17 E5
SLEEPING
500 West Hotel....18 C4
HI San Diego Downtown Hostel....19 E5
Horton Grand Hotel....20 E6
Hotel Occidental....21 E1
Hotel Solamar....22 E6
Ivy Hotel....23 F4
La Pensione Hotel....24 C2
Westgate Hotel....25 D4
Middletown
Grape St
Hawthorn St
California St
Columbia St
Little Italy
Fir St
Elm St
W Date St
County Center/ Little Italy
San Diego Bay
N Harbor Dr
Pacific Hwy
Kettner Blvd
India St
State St
Union St
Front St
1st Ave
2nd Ave
A St
B St
C St
Embarcadero
Cruise Ship Terminal
Santa Fe Depot
San Diego Trolley American Plaza Terminal
Broadway
Broadway Pier
Broadway Circle
Navy Pier
US Naval Supply Center
E St
F St
G St
Pantoja Park
Seaport Village
Downtown
Market St
Market Pl
San Diego Trolley
Harbor Dr
Island Ave
Embarcadero Marina Park

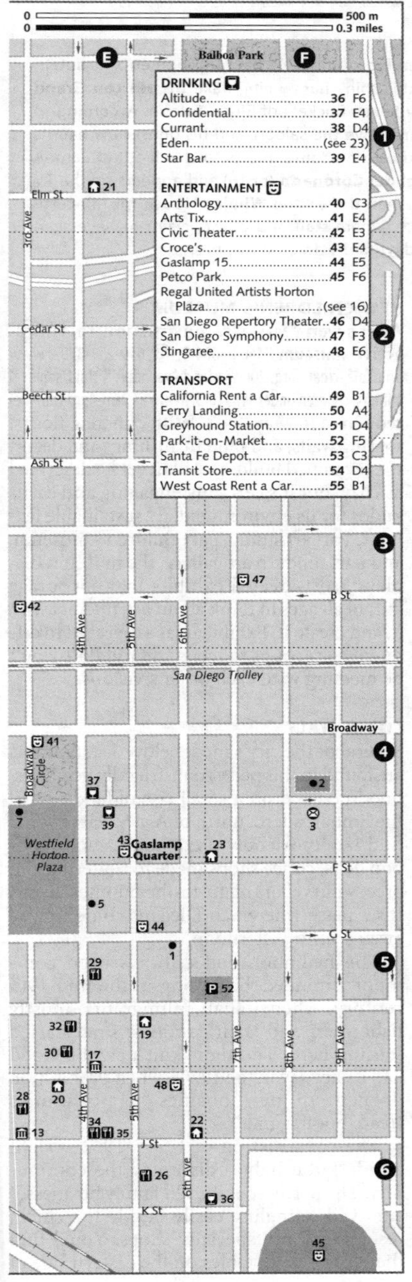

notorious red-light district filled with saloons, bordellos, gambling halls and opium dens.

By the 1960s it had declined to a skid row of flophouses and bars, but the neighborhood's very seediness made it so unattractive to developers that many of the older buildings survived when others around town were being razed. When developers turned their eyes toward the area in the early 1980s, preservationists organized to save the old brick and stone facades from the wrecking ball. The city stepped up, contributing trees, benches, wide brick sidewalks and replica 19th-century gas lamps. Restored buildings (built between the 1870s and the 1920s) became home to restaurants, bars, galleries, shops and theaters. The 16-acre area south of Broadway between 4th Ave and 6th Ave is designated a National Historic District and development is strictly controlled.

These days, the Gaslamp Quarter is enjoying a second, post-Petco wave of revitalization and growth, one characterized by a youthful, stylish energy. Upscale hotels and sleek restaurants are making ever-more-frequent debuts, while new rooftop bars and velvet-rope clubs are fending off (or creating) long lines of martini-craving scenesters. The neighborhood isn't a total hipster haven – yet – and a smattering of dive bars are working hard to keep things real.

For good parking rates, try the Park-it-on-Market lot on Market St between 6th Ave and 7th Ave, which costs $1 per hour up to 6pm, then it's a $3 flat fee until 3am.

There's a lot of history packed into the **William Heath Davis House** (Map pp604-5; ☎ 619-233-4692; www.gaslampquarter.org; 410 Island Ave; adult/senior $5/4; ⏲ 10am-6pm Tue-Sat, 9am-3pm Sun), one of about 10 prefabricated houses that Davis, San Diego's original real estate developer, had shipped here from Maine in 1850. Alonzo Horton lived here briefly, and the house has been moved twice. Today, at the corner of Island Ave and 4th Ave, it holds a small museum with 19th-century furnishings. Upstairs, look for the hidden prohibition-era still. At 11am each Saturday, the Gaslamp Quarter Historical Foundation offers a two-hour guided walking tour from here (adult/senior, student and military $10/8). Trolley tour bus tickets can be purchased at the museum.

For an insight into the city's Chinese history, check out the **San Diego Chinese Historical Museum** (Map pp604-5; ☎ 619-338-9888; www.sdchm.org;

SAN DIEGO – PORTAL TO HELL?

For such a sunny place, San Diego has an unnerving number of haunted homes and hotels. Do the ghosts know something we don't about this shiny happy city? Take the **Horton Grand Hotel** (p628), built on the site of the 19th-century Seven Buckets of Blood Saloon. According to hotel lore, a local troublemaker was shot in a room above the saloon, and his ghost now haunts the hotel's Room 309, playing tricks on maids and causing some guests to check out at 2am. A jilted woman allegedly walks the halls at the **Hotel del Coronado** (p616) and appears on the TV screen in the room where her heart was broken. Then there's the **Whaley House** (p614), certified haunted by the US Department of Commerce, where staff and guests claim to have seen apparitions, even in the daytime. Ghosts? In the daytime? I don't know, bro.

404 3rd Ave; admission $2; 10:30am-4pm Tue-Sat, noon-4pm Sun) in the heart of San Diego's former Chinatown. It occupies the attractive Chinese Mission Building, built in the 1920s, as well as a contemporary annex completed in 2004. Exhibits include a former warlord's 40-piece wood-carved bed – assembled without nails – as well as the ornate, ultratiny slippers worn by women with bound feet.

That uninviting megalith hulking at the western edge of the Gaslamp District is the **Westfield Horton Plaza** (Map pp604-5; ☎ 619-238-1596; 324 Horton Plaza; 10am-9pm Mon-Fri, 10am-8pm Sat, 11am-7pm Sun; P), a five-story mall designed by Los Angeles architect Jon Jerde, who also designed Universal City Walk. Inside, toy-town arches, post-modern balconies and an asymmetrical floor plan – all surrounding an open-air atrium – are reminiscent of an MC Escher drawing. Here you'll find a Nordstrom, Macy's and the usual retail suspects, including Abercrombie & Fitch, Banana Republic and J Jill. There's also a cinema complex and a food court. The main pedestrian entrance is on Broadway. Three hours free parking with validation.

MUSEUM OF CONTEMPORARY ART (MCA) DOWNTOWN

The downtown branch of the **MCA** (Map pp604-5; ☎ 858-454-3541; www.mcasd.org; 1100 & 1001 Kettner Blvd; adult/senior/25yr & under $10/5/free; 11am-5pm Fri-Mon & Wed, to 7pm Thu) dates from 1986, and is located next to the San Diego Trolley Stop. In 2007, the museum renovated a section of the San Diego's train station across the street, so there are now two downtown locations just steps apart. The original branch, open since the 1960s, is in La Jolla (p620). Tickets are valid for seven days in all locations. Downtown, there is discounted parking, with validation, at 501 West C St.

NEW CHILDREN'S MUSEUM

After seven years of reconstruction, this interactive **museum** (Map pp604-5; ☎ 619-233-8792; www.thinkplaycreate.org; 200 W Island Ave; adult & child/senior & military/children under 1yr $10/5/free; 9am-4pm Thu-Tue) reopened in May 2008. With concrete floors, soaring walls, and mod furnishings and decor, the revamped building will never be described as cozy, but it's certainly engaging and earns kudos for its environmentally sustainable features. Part art studio, part children's museum, and part modern art gallery, the museum displays artist-created exhibits that encourage kids of all ages to think about art, interact with it, and create it. Exhibit areas are geared to different age groups so teens and toddlers won't be messing with each other's visions.

LITTLE ITALY

Several of the city's most beloved restaurants are found in this pedestrian-friendly neighborhood perched on a small rise of land east of the Embarcadero, north of Ash St. Here you'll find family-friendly pizza joints, mom-and-pop delis, coffee shops made for loitering and breezy purveyors of up-to-the minute cuisine. It's a place where San Diegans come to wile away a sunny afternoon.

The neighborhood's always been community minded, beginning in the mid-19th century, when Italian immigrants, mostly fishermen and their families, first started settling here. The tight-knit neighborhood had its heyday in the 1920s, when Prohibition opened up new business opportunities (read 'bootlegging').

The construction of I-5 in 1962 – right beside Little Italy – disrupted the community. The hardiest of the old family businesses survived, mingling easily beside the chichi restaurants and specialty shops. You'll find the busiest patio tables on the eastern side of

India Street (Map pp604–5), a prime spot for a glass of Chianti.

Embarcadero

Heading west from downtown, cross the tram tracks to enter a 500yd-wide stretch of landfill that culminates with the Embarcadero. This wide pedestrian strip hugs the bay, offering breezy views of the water and an impressive line-up of ships and vessels, not to mention a few overpriced restaurants. It's also the launch point for the ferry to Coronado and several harbor cruises.

It's hard to miss the **Maritime Museum** (Map pp604-5; ☎ 619-234-9153; www.sdmaritime.org; 1492 N Harbor Dr; all 7 vessels adult/child 6-17yr/senior & military $14/8/11 ⌚ 9am-8pm, to 9pm Memorial Day to Labor Day), just north of Ash St. The 100ft masts of the square-rigger tall ship *Star of India* – one of seven vessels open to the public here – make the museum easy to find. Built on the Isle of Man and launched in 1863, the restored ship plied the England–India trade route, carried immigrants to New Zealand, became a trading ship based in Hawaii and, finally, worked the Alaskan salmon fisheries. Nowadays she's taken out once a year for a sail, making her the oldest active ship in the world.

Kids can learn the Pirate's Code at the small but engaging pirate's exhibit below deck on the HMS *Surprise*. For the highest wow-per-square-foot factor, squeeze into the museum's B-39 Soviet attack submarine. Take note: with its cramped quarters, knob-and-faucet-covered walls and small chamber-linking portholes, the sub is a claustrophobe's nightmare. If you do venture in, though, check out the torpedo tubes. In a last-ditch attempt to escape a crippled sub, sailors would blast from these tubes as human torpedoes.

A short walk south is the Embarcadero's heavyweight attraction, the **USS Midway** (Map pp604-5; ☎ 619-544-9600; www.midway.org; 910 N Harbor Dr; adult/child/senior & student $17/9/13; ⌚ 10am-5pm), which clocks in with a total weight of 69,000 tons. Commissioned in 1945, the ship is the Navy's longest-serving aircraft carrier, seeing action in Vietnam and the first Gulf War. It opened as a museum in 2004 and by 2007 had welcomed 3 million guests. An engaging self-guided audio tour – filled with first person accounts from former crewmen – takes visitors on a maze-like climb through the engine room, the brig, the galley and the 4-acre flight deck, where an impressive lineup of fighter jets – including an F-14 Tomcat – await up-close inspection. For an eagle-eye view of the flight deck and San Diego Bay, take the docent-led tour of the Island Superstructure, which includes stops in the bridge and flight control. Allow at least two hours for exploring and hit the flight deck attractions early to beat the crowds. Parking costs $5 to $10.

Continue south to **Seaport Village** (Map pp604-5; ☎ 619-235-4014; ⌚ 10am-10pm summer), which is neither a Seaport nor a Village. Filled with overpriced restaurants and knick-knack shops (if you need a coffee mug or T-shirt, come here), it's a nice place to relax, look at the water and catch an afternoon concert.

Walking southeast along the **Embarcadero Marina Park** – where there's a public fishing pier and an open-air amphitheater with free summer concerts – you'll see the 'sails' of the **San Diego Convention Center** (☎ 619-525-5000, www.sdccc.org; 111 W Harbor Dr). Designed by Canadian avant-garde architect Arthur Erickson, the building – which some say was inspired by an ocean liner – opened in 1989 and stretches for a half-mile. Parking here is normally $8 per day and $10 per day during events.

Balboa Park

In 1868 city planners, led by civic booster Alonzo Horton, set aside 1400 acres of scrubby hilltops and steep-sided arroyos (water-carved gullies) northeast of downtown for use as a park, the largest west of the Mississippi River at the time. Since then, Balboa Park – with the aid of tenacious supporters – has resisted developers' efforts to maximize its commercial potential and survived almost intact, losing only a bit of land to the highway and the Navy Hospital in the 1950s.

The park today holds strong at an impressive 1200 acres, preening on prime real estate just minutes from Hillcrest, downtown, the beaches and Mission Valley. It's an ideal place to see San Diegans at play – jogging, strolling, in-line skating, catching rays and playing catch. It's also a premier cultural center, with a cluster of theaters and museums arrayed along the extraordinary El Prado promenade. Nearby is a faithful reconstruction of Shakespeare's Old Globe theater, and a short walk north leads to the world-famous San Diego Zoo. The park is named after the Spanish conquistador believed to be the first European to see the Pacific Ocean.

BALBOA PARK, HILLCREST & OLD TOWN

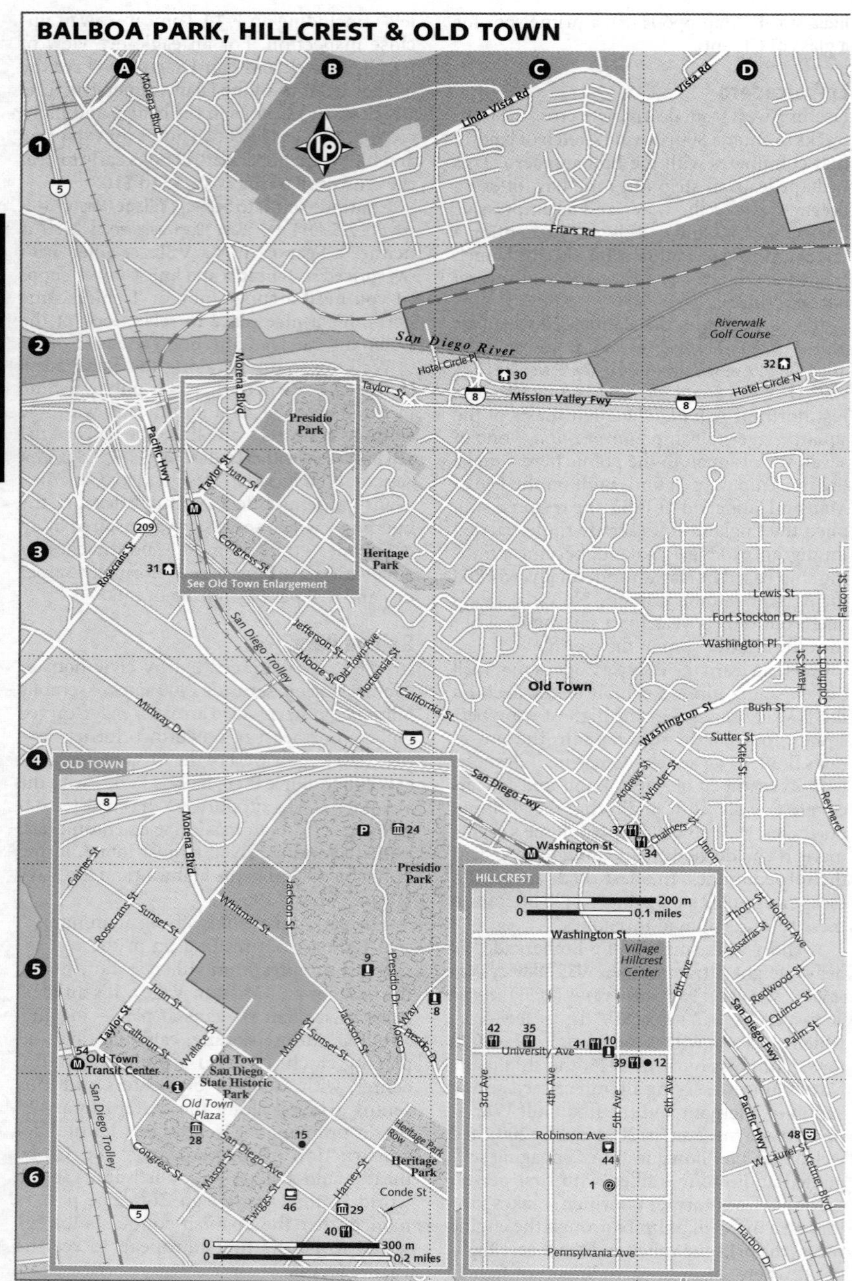

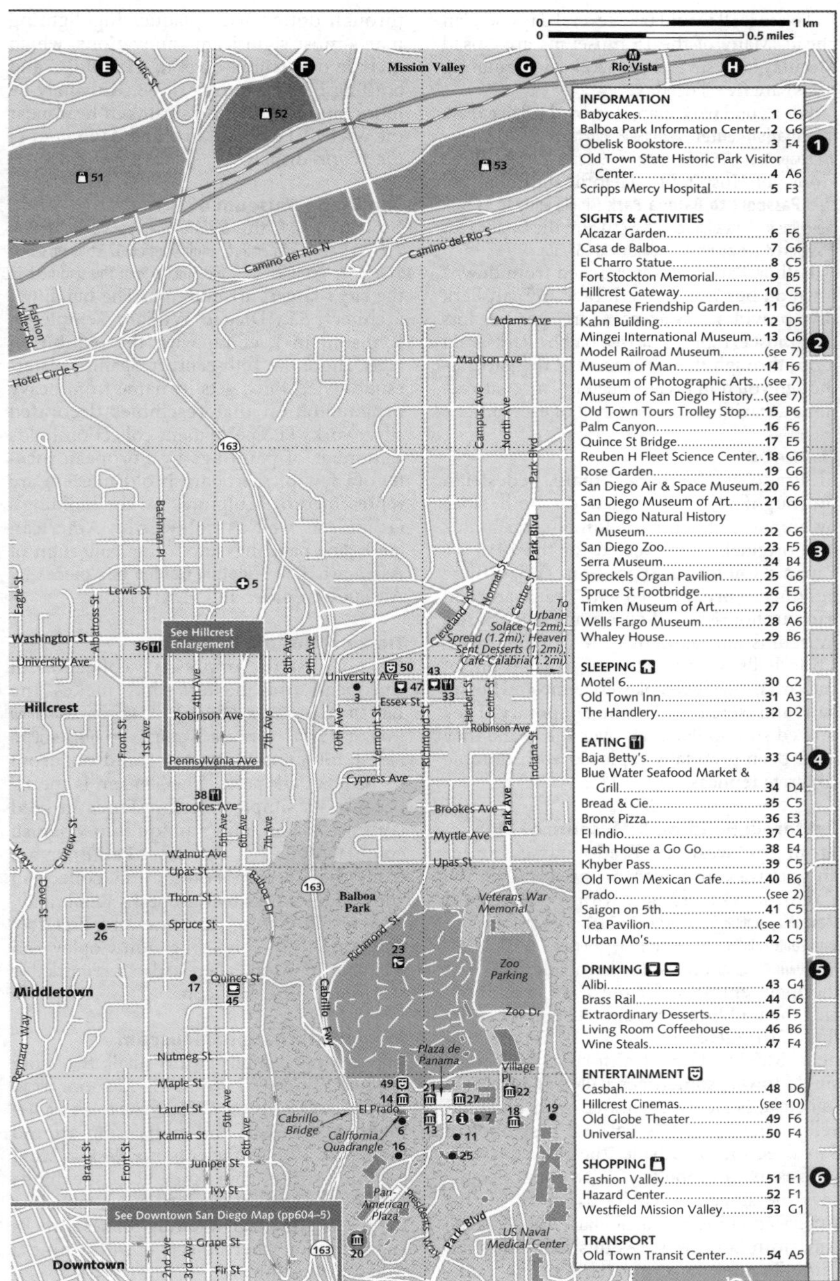
0 1 km
0 0.5 miles
Mission Valley
Rio Vista
E
F
G
H
Ulric St
Camino del Rio N
Camino del Rio S
Fashion Valley Rd
Hotel Circle S
Adams Ave
Madison Ave
Campus Ave
North Ave
Park Blvd
Bachman Pl
Lewis St
Eagle St
Albatross St
Washington St
University Ave
See Hillcrest Enlargement
4th Ave
Robinson Ave
Pennsylvania Ave
8th Ave
9th Ave
Normal St
Cleveland Ave
Centre St
To Urbane Solace (1.2mi); Spread (1.2mi); Heaven Sent Desserts (1.2mi); Café Calabria (1.2mi)
Essex St
Herbert St
Hillcrest
Front St
1st Ave
7th Ave
10th Ave
Vermont St
Richmond St
Robinson Ave
Indiana St
Cypress Ave
Brookes Ave
Park Ave
Myrtle Ave
Upas St
5th Ave
6th Ave
Walnut Ave
Curlew St
Dove St
Thorn St
Spruce St
Balboa Dr
Balboa Park
Veterans War Memorial
Richmond St
Quince St
Middletown
Reynard Way
Cabrillo Fwy
Zoo Parking
Zoo Dr
Nutmeg St
Maple St
Plaza de Panama
Village Pl
Laurel St
El Prado
Cabrillo Bridge
California Quadrangle
Kalmia St
Brant St
Juniper St
Ivy St
Pan-American Plaza
Presidents Way
Park Blvd
US Naval Medical Center
See Downtown San Diego Map (pp604–5)
Grape St
2nd Ave
3rd Ave
Fir St
Downtown
INFORMATION
Babycakes 1 C6
Balboa Park Information Center 2 G6
Obelisk Bookstore 3 F4
Old Town State Historic Park Visitor Center 4 A6
Scripps Mercy Hospital 5 F3
SIGHTS & ACTIVITIES
Alcazar Garden 6 F6
Casa de Balboa 7 G6
El Charro Statue 8 C5
Fort Stockton Memorial 9 B5
Hillcrest Gateway 10 C5
Japanese Friendship Garden 11 G6
Kahn Building 12 D5
Mingei International Museum 13 G6
Model Railroad Museum (see 7)
Museum of Man 14 F6
Museum of Photographic Arts (see 7)
Museum of San Diego History (see 7)
Old Town Tours Trolley Stop 15 B6
Palm Canyon 16 F6
Quince St Bridge 17 E5
Reuben H Fleet Science Center 18 G6
Rose Garden 19 G6
San Diego Air & Space Museum 20 F6
San Diego Museum of Art 21 G6
San Diego Natural History Museum 22 G6
San Diego Zoo 23 F5
Serra Museum 24 B4
Spreckels Organ Pavilion 25 G6
Spruce St Footbridge 26 E5
Timken Museum of Art 27 G6
Wells Fargo Museum 28 A6
Whaley House 29 B6
SLEEPING
Motel 6 30 C2
Old Town Inn 31 A3
The Handlery 32 D2
EATING
Baja Betty's 33 G4
Blue Water Seafood Market & Grill 34 D4
Bread & Cie 35 C5
Bronx Pizza 36 E3
El Indio 37 C4
Hash House a Go Go 38 E4
Khyber Pass 39 C5
Old Town Mexican Cafe 40 B6
Prado (see 2)
Saigon on 5th 41 C5
Tea Pavilion (see 11)
Urban Mo's 42 C5
DRINKING
Alibi 43 G4
Brass Rail 44 C6
Extraordinary Desserts 45 F5
Living Room Coffeehouse 46 B6
Wine Steals 47 F4
ENTERTAINMENT
Casbah 48 D6
Hillcrest Cinemas (see 10)
Old Globe Theater 49 F6
Universal 50 F4
SHOPPING
Fashion Valley 51 E1
Hazard Center 52 F1
Westfield Mission Valley 53 G1
TRANSPORT
Old Town Transit Center 54 A5

To see it all would take several days, so plan ahead. Many of the 15 museums are closed Monday, and several per week (on a rotating basis) are free Tuesday.

For a good park map, stop by the **Balboa Park Information Center** (Map pp608-9; ☎ 619-239-0512; www.balboapark.org; 1549 El Prado; 9:30am-4:30pm) in the House of Hospitality. Helpful staff here sell the **Passport to Balboa Park** (single entry to 13 park museums for 1 wk adult/child $39/21) and the **Combo Pass** (Passport & zoo admission adult/child $65/36).

Balboa Park is easily reached from downtown on bus 7 along Park Blvd. By car, Park Blvd provides easy access to free parking lots near most exhibits. The free Balboa Park Tram loops through the main areas of the park, although you don't really need it – most attractions are within an easy stroll of each other.

EL PRADO

El Prado is the park's main pedestrian thoroughfare, surrounded on both sides by romantic Spanish colonial-style buildings originally constructed for the 1915–16 Panama-California Exposition. Today, these buildings – ornamented with beaux-arts and baroque flourishes – house many of the park's museums and gardens. The original exposition halls were mostly constructed out of stucco, chicken wire, plaster, hemp and horsehair, and were meant to be temporary. They proved so popular that, over the years, they have been gradually replaced with durable concrete replicas.

California Building & Museum of Man

From the west, El Prado passes under an archway and into an area called the California Quadrangle, with the **Museum of Man** (Map pp608-9; ☎ 619-239-2001; www.museumofman.org; adult/child 3-12yr/youth 13-17yr/senior $10/5/7.50/7.50; 10am-4:30pm) on its northern side. This was the main entrance for the 1915 exposition, and the building was said to be inspired by the churrigueresque church of Tepotzotlán near Mexico City. California Building's single tower, sometimes called the **Tower of California**, is richly decorated with blue and yellow tiles, and has become a symbol of San Diego itself. Inside, the museum specializes in anthropology – 'it's about people' says the slogan – with a focus on Native American cultures, particularly those in the American Southwest. Adults will enjoy the Time Tunnel, an eye-catching blue walk-through dotted with plaques highlighting man's most significant innovations, which include domiciling dogs in 11,000 BC and bottling beer in Europe 1568. Kids may be more impressed by the shrunken head near the ancient Egyptian area and *Mummies of the World* display.

San Diego Museum of Art

Built in 1924, the **SDMA** (Map pp608-9; ☎ 619-232-7931; www.sdmart.org; adult/youth 6-17/student/senior $10/4/7/8; 10am-6pm Tue-Sun, to 9pm Thu summer) is the city's largest art museum. The building's architect, San Diegan William Templeton Johnson, in keeping with the exhibition halls, chose the 16th-century Spanish plateresque style, which gets its name from heavy ornamentation that resembles decorated silverwork. The permanent collection holds a number of paintings by European masters (a few of the Spanish old masters are represented by sculptures on the building's facade), as well as noteworthy American landscape paintings and a fine collection of Asian art. The **Sculpture Garden** has pieces by Alexander Calder and Henry Moore.

Timken Museum of Art

It's not just the impressive collection of European old masters that makes the **Timken** (Map pp608-9; ☎ 619-239-5548; www.timkenmuseum.org; 1500 El Prado; admission free; 10am-4:30pm Tue-Sat, 1:30-4:30pm Sun Oct-Aug) stand out from its Balboa Park peers. The Timken is special because its simple exterior stands in bold contrast to the park's ubiquitous Spanish colonial style. It's also free. Paintings are from the Putnam Foundation collection and include works by Europeans Rembrandt, Rubens, El Greco, Cézanne and Pissarro, and Americans John Singleton Copley and Eastman Johnson. There's also a remarkable selection of Russian icons.

Mingei International Museum

The rotating exhibits at this small, two-story **museum** (Map pp608-9; ☎ 619-239-0003; www.mingei.org; adult/youth 6-17/senior $7/4/5; 10am-4pm Tue-Sun) highlight folk arts and crafts from around the world. Stop by the entrance desk to see if anything strikes your fancy. Recent exhibits have been unexpectedly intriguing, including the recent American Viewing Stones – rocks suggestive of other objects – with Chinese woodblock prints.

Casa de Balboa

When fire destroyed the original Spanish colonial structure in 1978, the city rebuilt a faithful copy that included concrete decorations cast from pieces of the original. Today, the building houses three museums.

The engaging **Museum of Photographic Arts** (Map pp608-9; ☎ 619-238-7559; www.mopa.org; adult/child under 12/student/senior $6/free/4/4, 2nd Tue of month free; ⌚ 10am-5pm) clearly embraces its mission to collect and display 'the entire spectrum of the photographic medium,' with recent exhibits including Civil War daguerreotypes, flesh-minded MRI exposures and boldly colored prints of life in India. The museum has some 7000 photographs in its permanent collection, and the addition of a state-of-the-art theater has extended the museum's reach to film. Worth a stop.

The **Museum of San Diego History** (Map pp608-9; ☎ 619-232-6203; www.sandiegohistory.org; adult/youth 13-17/student & senior $5/2/4; ⌚ 10am-5pm Tue-Sun) traces the city's past from about 1848 on, with exhibits examining the miner's life, stagecoach travel and women's department-store fashion.

The rattle and hum of model trains chugging over miniature tracks is oddly soothing, but train buffs won't be snoozing at the **Model Railroad Museum** (☎ 619-696-0199; www.sdmrm.org; adult/child under 15/student/senior $6/free/3/5, 1st Tue of month free; ⌚ 10am-4pm Tue-Fri, 11am-5pm Sat & Sun), where miniature trains (historic and contemporary) traverse 24,000 sq ft of SoCal-mimicking track. The trains and tracks are maintained by local model train clubs. Wander to the back for engaging displays on women of the railroads and 'good' train robbers like the Wild Bunch – they never killed anybody.

Reuben H Fleet Science Center

The exhibits at this hands-on **science center** (Map pp608-9; ☎ 619-238-1233; www.rhfleet.org; adult/child 3-12/senior $8/6.75/6.75, with 1 IMAX film $12.50/9.75/9.75; ⌚ 9:30am-8pm Sat-Thu, to 9pm Fri) include the energy-focused So Watt! and the galaxy-minded Origins in Space, where colorful Hubble images of colliding galaxies are particularly mesmerizing. The place could use a little sprucing up – especially when compared to other SoCal science centers – but the kids don't seem to mind. The big draw is the 76ft 'tilted-dome' IMAX theater, with several different films daily. Scheduled to reopen after this book's publication following extensive renovations, the improved theater will have a seamless dome screen and a 16,000-watt digital surround-sound audio system. Wi-fi is available.

San Diego Natural History Museum

Seventy-five million years of SoCal fossils are the subject of the new permanent exhibit, Fossil Mysteries, which opened at the **museum** (Map pp608-9; ☎ 619-232-3821; www.sdnhm.org; adult/child/youth 13-17/senior $13/7/8/11; ⌚ 10am-5pm) in 2006. Evolution and extinction are key topics of discussion but kids jones for the bones (nudge to curators: put a few more on display), which range from composite skeletons of a dire wolf and a sabertooth cat to cool casts of albertosaurus and lambeosaurus dinosaurs that show both their skeletal frames and their exteriors. Twelve William Stout murals were commissioned by the museum to accompany the exhibit and set a properly awe-inspiring, prehistoric mood. A 2001 renovation of the original 1933 building designed by William Templeton Johnson includes beautiful new galleries and a giant-screen cinema devoted exclusively to the natural world. Be sure to see what's rotating through exhibition-wise. The museum drew record crowds with its recent Dead Sea Scrolls and A Day in Pompeii exhibitions.

SPRECKELS ORGAN PAVILION

South of Plaza de Panama, an extravagantly curved colonnade provides shelter for one of the world's largest **outdoor organs** (Map pp608–9). Donated by the Spreckels family of sugar fortune and fame, the pipe organ – which has more than 4500 pipes – came with the stipulation that San Diego must always have an official organist. Free concerts are held at 2pm every Sunday, and at 7:30pm Monday from mid-June through August.

SAN DIEGO AIR & SPACE MUSEUM

One look at the banged-up silver pod inside the rotunda of this **museum** (Map pp608-9; ☎ 619-234-8291; www.aerospacemuseum.org; adult/youth 3-11/student/senior $15/6/12/12; ⌚ 10am-4:30pm, to 5:30pm Jun-Aug), at the end of Pan American Plaza, and you'll be glad you chose not to become an astronaut. The pod, known as Gumdrop, is the Apollo 9 command module used in a 1969 mission to test the lunar module before the first moon landing. Exhibits here trace the history of aviation, providing plenty of close-up views of planes with dangerous names – Flying Tiger, Cobra and

Skyhawk – plus a few reproductions. Moon rocks and a space suit are also cool.

BALBOA PARK GARDENS

Balboa Park is home to nine gardens, most clustered just south of El Prado. The **Alcazar Garden**, a formal Spanish-style garden, is tucked in a courtyard across from the Old Globe, south of El Prado, while the **Palm Canyon**, which has more than 50 species of palms, is a short stroll south. For a tranquil stroll or a bit of meditation, the **Japanese Friendship Garden** (Map pp608-9; ☎ 619-232-2721; www.niwa.org; adult /student/senior $4/2.50/2.50 ⏲ 10am-4pm Tue-Sun, to 5pm Mon-Fri Jun-Aug), just north of Spreckels Organ Pavilion, is a convenient retreat. A short path winds past a koi pond, rippling water and the Exhibit House with a glass-walled meditation room overlooking the Zen Garden.

Free weekly **Offshoot Tours** (www.balboapark.org/info/tours.php, ⏲ 10am Sat Jan-Thanksgiving), which highlight the gardens and other attractions on a rotating basis, depart the Balboa Park Visitor Center.

SAN DIEGO ZOO

With its new Monkey Trails & Forest Tales exhibit, the **zoo** (Map pp608-9; ☎ 619-231-1515; www.sandiegozoo.org; adult/child 3-11 $24.50/16.50, with 35 min guided bus tour, express bus & aerial tram $34/24; ⏲ 9am-5pm, last admission at 4pm, to 9pm Jul & Aug, last admission at 8pm, to 6pm Sep, last admission 4pm; Ⓟ ⓕ) creatively continues its mission to protect animals and their habitats while educating visitors. This 3-acre, multilevel habitat is packed with energetic monkeys – which occasionally swing up to say hello face to face – and other exotic animals from tropical Asian and African forests. Informative, conservation-minded plaques dot lush, bamboo-lined walkways, offering slightly alarming updates on the status of these animals in the wild.

Located in the northern section of Balboa Park, the sprawling zoo holds more than 4000 animals representing more than 800 species, tucked here and there in 100 canyon-filled acres. It is not only the sheer size of its collection that makes this zoo special. Since its opening in 1916, the zoo has also pioneered ways to house and display animals that mimic their natural habitat, leading to a revolution in zoo design and, so the argument goes, to happier animals. In its efforts to re-create those habitats, the zoo has also become one of the country's great botanical gardens. Experts trick San Diego's near-desert climate to yield everything from bamboo to eucalyptus to Hawaiian koa. The plants don't just provide pleasant cover for cages and fences; many are grown specifically to feed the zoo's more finicky eaters.

There's a large, free parking lot off Park Blvd that starts filling fast right at opening time. Write down where you parked, it can be confusing at the end of the day. Bus 7 will get you there from downtown. If you would like to leave the zoo and return, staff will stamp your hand.

Perennial favorites **Polar Bear Plunge** and **Hippo River** wow crowds with up-close, underwater views of the animals through thick glass walls. Another hotspot is the **Panda Discovery Center**, where Bai Yun and Zhen Zhen gnaw on bamboo before adoring crowds. A live narrator shares facts about pandas at the outdoor viewing area here and, more importantly, keeps the line moving. To avoid the heaviest crowds – and they can border on oppressive – stop by early. That cacophony of barks and growls you hear just south of Scripps Aviary? It's kids at **Tiger River** pushing the 'roar, chuffle and growl' buttons near the tiger habitat and mimicking what they hear – much to the delight of the Malayan tigers who pace as far away as possible in their faux Asian rainforest.

Arboreal orangutans and siamangs peacefully coexist in **Absolutely Apes**, another re-creation of an Asian rain forest. And don't miss the vast **Scripps Aviary** and **Owens Rain Forest Aviary**, where carefully placed feeders (and remarkably fearless birds) allow for close-up viewing. To note: if you didn't like Hitchcock's *The Birds*, the aviaries might be a less than enjoyable experience. The koalas have proved so popular that Australians may be surprised to find them an unofficial symbol of San Diego. Less cuddly is the Komodo dragon in the reptile house, an Indonesian lizard that grows up to 10ft long.

The zoo has also expanded its entertainment and educational role in the community with the opening of a **children's zoo exhibit** (where youngsters can pet small critters) and outdoor theaters for animal shows. Both children and adults will enjoy the animal nursery, where you can see the zoo's newest arrivals.

If you're not in a hurry, take the 35-minute double-decker bus tour first thing in the morning to get oriented. You'll also pick up

DETOUR: SAN DIEGO ZOO WILD ANIMAL PARK

How close can you get to the animals at this 1800-acre **open-range zoo** (Map p600; ☎ 760-747-8702; www.wildanimalpark.org; 15500 San Pasquale Valley Rd, Escondido; adult/child 3-11 $28.50/17.50, incl tram $34/24; 9am-8pm mid-Jun–Aug & hols, 9am-4pm rest of year;) just 30 miles northeast of downtown? Consider this sign near the Lowlands Gorilla Habitat: 'In gorilla society prolonged eye contact is not only impolite, but it's considered a threat. Please respect the social signals of our gorillas and do not stare at them directly.' Seems we're so close we need to be reminded of our manners. But the sign is indicative of the experience here, where protecting and preserving wild animals and their habitats – while educating guests in a soft-handed manner – is the primary goal.

For a minisafari, hop aboard The Journey into Africa biodiesel tram for a drive through the world's second-largest continent. Sit on the left-hand side (a change from prior years) for slightly better views of the rhinos, giraffes, ostriches and other herbivores (by law, predators can't share space with prey). To enjoy close-up views of big cats, follow signs to the 33,000 sq ft Lion Camp and the Safari Walk Backcountry – and pray there's not a park-disrupting earthquake. Combination tickets with the San Diego Zoo are $60/43 per adult/child.

Kids will dig the **Roar & Snore** (☎ 619-718-3000; tents $89-209; seasonal) camping experience on a hilltop where families sleep in canvas tents overlooking the East African–style plains and their wild inhabitants.

The park is in Escondido. Take the freeway to the Vio Rancho Parkway exit, turn right and continue to San Pasqual Rd. Turn right and follow signs to the park. Parking costs $9. For bus information contact **North San Diego County Transit District** (☎ 619-233-3004, from northern San Diego 800-266-6883; www.gonctd.com).

intriguing facts about the animals – grizzlies can run the length of a football field in six seconds! Discount coupons are widely available from San Diego magazines, weekly newspapers, and hotels and information centers. A combined ticket for both the San Diego Zoo and the Wild Animal Park within a five-day period cost $60/43 per adult/child. Add Seaworld for $109/86.

It's wise to arrive early, as many of the animals are most active in the morning, and be prepared to do some walking – animals are scattered in canyons and on hilltops. The Skyfari cable car goes right across the park and can save you some walking time, though there may be a queue. From late June to early September, the zoo is open until 9pm and has special exhibits that focus on nocturnal creatures. Before your visit, check out the panda and polar bear cameras on the website.

Extensive facilities are provided for disabled visitors. Call ☎ 619-231-1515 ext 4526 for specifics.

Mission San Diego de Alcalá

Though the first California mission was established on Presidio Hill near Old Town, Padre Junípero Serra decided in 1773 to move upriver several miles, closer to a better water supply and more arable land. In 1784 the missionaries built a solid adobe and timber church, but it was destroyed by an earthquake in 1803. The church was promptly rebuilt, and at least some of it still stands on a slope overlooking Mission Valley. With the end of the mission system in the 1830s, the buildings were turned over to the Mexican government. The buildings were later used as US army barracks before falling into disrepair. Some accounts say that they were reduced to a facade and a few crumbling walls by the 1920s. Extensive reconstruction began in 1931, and the pretty white church and the buildings you see now are the result of the thorough restoration.

Inside, a bougainvillea-filled garden offers a tranquil spot for meditation, and nearby tile panels that depict the crucifixion are moving in their simplicity. In the museum, a glass case holds items unearthed at the site, ranging from old spectacles to buttons to medicine bottles. In fact, don't be surprised if you see an archaeologist sifting through the dirt just outside. Look for old photographs and artifacts set up beside their dig site – currently across from the visitors center – when they're working.

The **mission** (Map p602; ☎ 619-281-8449; www.missionsandiego.com; 10818 San Diego Mission Rd; adult/child/senior $3/2/2; 9am-5pm; P) is two blocks north of I-8 via the Mission Gorge Rd exit just east of I-15. After exiting, take a left just past Roberto's at San Diego Mission Rd (on the right it's called Twain Ave) and follow it to the mission. You can take the trolley to the Mission stop, walk two blocks north and turn right onto San Diego Mission Rd.

Old Town

In 1769 Padre Junípero Serra and Gaspar de Portola established the first Spanish settlement in California on **Presidio Hill**, overlooking the valley of the San Diego River. Spanish soldiers built adobe homes and started families at the southwestern base of the hill, and in 1821 the community, with 600 citizens, became the first official civilian Spanish settlement – called a pueblo – in California. It remained the city center until a devastating fire in 1872, after which the city's main body moved to the downtown.

Today, this area below Presidio Hill is called Old Town, and it presents life as it was between 1821 and 1872. Although it is neither very old (most of the buildings are reconstructions), nor exactly a town (more like a leafy suburb), it's a more-or-less faithful copy of San Diego's original nucleus, offering a pedestrian plaza surrounded by historic building, shops, a number of restaurants and cafes, and a good opportunity to explore San Diego's early days.

The **Old Town State Historic Park visitor center** (Map pp608-9; ☎ 619-220-5422; www.parks.ca.gov; Robinson-Rose House; 🕑 10am-6pm; P) is at the western end of the plaza. It houses memorabilia and books about the era as well as a diorama depicting the pueblo in 1872. If you're really interested in the historical background, take a guided tour, which leaves from the visitors center at 11am and 2pm. Wi-fi is available. A row of small, historical-looking buildings (only one is authentically old) line the southern border of the plaza and some house souvenir and gift shops. To see an original stagecoach and learn about Black Bart and stagecoach robberies, pop into the free **Wells Fargo Museum** (🕑 9am-5pm) inside the Colorado House, a former hotel. There's an ATM inside a rolltop desk.

We can't guarantee what you'll see at the **Whaley House** (Map pp608-9; ☎ 619-297-7511; www.whaleyhouse.org; 2476 San Diego Ave; adult/child/senior $6/4/5, after 5pm adult/child $10/5; 🕑 10am-10pm daily Jun-Aug, 10am-5pm Mon & Tue, 10am-10pm Thu-Sun Sep-May), a lovely Victorian home (and the city's oldest brick building) two blocks northeast of the Old Town perimeter. It's served as a courthouse, theater and private residence, but that's not the cool part. What's intriguing is that the house was *officially* certified as haunted by the US Department of Commerce. Guides here claim ghostly encounters occur even during the day, from observing figures with no faces to hearing talking behind them (when no one's there) to learning that a visitor's camera batteries have drained while in the house. Ask the informative guides to share their stories.

The walk from Old Town east along Mason St to the top of Presidio Hill rewards you with excellent views of San Diego Bay and Mission Valley – just don't depend on the most horribly marked trail in all of California to get you there! At the end of Mason St, if you obey the arrow pointing left, you'll follow a series of historic trail markers that *supposedly* end up at the Serra Museum. If you follow the arrow pointing up Presidio Hill, turn left at the dirt trail at the top and you might stumble upon the **Fort Stockton Memorial**. American forces occupied the hill in 1846, during the Mexican-American War, and named it for American commander Robert Stockton. A flagpole, cannon, some plaques and earthen walls form the memorial. If you turn right at the top of the hill, the path leads to Presidio Dr. Follow it to the **El Charro Statue**, a bicentennial gift to the city from Mexico depicting a Mexican cowboy on horseback. Nothing remains of the original Presidio structures.

The **Serra Museum** (Map pp608-9; ☎ 619-297-3258; www.sandiegohistory.org; 2727 Presidio Dr; adult/child/senior $5/4/2; 🕑 11am-3pm Tue-Fri, to 3pm Sat & Sun; P) is a Spanish colonial-style structure designed by William Templeton Johnson in 1929. The museum has a small but interesting collection of artifacts and pictures from the mission and rancho periods. We recommend driving here instead of following the god-forsaken trail.

The Old Town Transit Center, on the trolley line off Taylor St just east of Congress St at the western edge of Old Town, is a stop for the *Coaster* commuter train, the San Diego Trolley (blue and green lines) and buses. Old Town Trolley tours stop southeast of the plaza on Twiggs St.

Uptown & Hillcrest

Just east of Old Town, between Mission Valley to the north and downtown to the south, is Uptown. As you head north from downtown along the west side of Balboa Park, you arrive

GAY & LESBIAN SAN DIEGO

Interestingly, many historians trace the roots of San Diego's thriving gay community to the city's strong military presence. During WWII, amid the enforced intimacy of military life, gay men from around the country were suddenly able to create strong (if clandestine) social networks. After the war, many stayed.

In the late 1960s, a newly politicized gay community began to make the Hillcrest neighborhood its unofficial headquarters. Here you'll find the highest concentration of bars, restaurants, cafés and bookstores catering to lesbians and gays. The scene is generally more casual and friendly than in San Francisco and LA. For more complete listings and events, pick up the free *Gay and Lesbian Times*.

Bookstores

Obelisk Bookstore (Map pp608-9; ☎ 619- 297-4171; 1029 University Ave; 10am-10pm Mon-Fri, 11am-10pm Sun) Caters particularly to gay, lesbian, bisexual and transgender readers.

Bars

Baja Betty's (Map pp608-9; ☎ 619-269-8510; 1421 University Ave) Gay owned and straight friendly, this restaurant-bar is always a party with a just-back-from Margarita-ville vibe (and dozens of tequilas to take you back there) alongside dishes like Mexi-queen queso dip and You Go Grill swordfish tacos.

Brass Rail (Map pp608-9; ☎ 619-298-2233; 3796 5th Ave) The city's oldest gay bar has a different music style nightly, from Latin to African to Top 40.

Urban Mo's (Map pp608-9; ☎ 619-491-0400; 308 University Ave) Equal parts bar and restaurant, Mo's isn't particularly known for great food, service or prices, but it's popular nonetheless for its thumping Club Beats, casual vibe, dance floor and happy hours.

at a series of bluffs that, in the late 19th century, became San Diego's most fashionable neighborhood – only those who owned a horse-drawn carriage could afford to live here. Known as Bankers Hill after some of the wealthy residents, these upscale heights had unobstructed views of the bay and Point Loma before I-5 went up.

As you head northward toward Hillcrest consider a detour across the 375ft **Spruce Street Footbridge** (Map pp608–9). Note that the 1912 suspension bridge, built over a deep canyon between Front St and Brant St, wriggles beneath your feet. But don't worry; it was designed that way. The nearby **Quince Street Bridge**, between 4th Ave and 3rd Ave, is a wood-trestle structure built in 1905 and refurbished in 1988 after community activists vigorously protested its slated demolition.

Just up from the northwestern corner of Balboa Park, you hit **Hillcrest** (Map pp608–9), the heart of Uptown. The neighborhood began its life in the early 20th century as a modest middle-class suburb. Today, it's San Diego's most bohemian district, with a decidedly urban feel, despite the suburban visuals. It's also the headquarters of the city's gay and lesbian community. University Ave and 5th Ave are lined with coffeehouses, fashion-forward thrift shops and excellent restaurants in all price ranges.

For a tour, begin at the **Hillcrest Gateway** (Map pp608–9), which arches over University Ave at 5th Ave. On 5th Ave between University Ave and Washington St is the multiplex **Landmark Hillcrest Cinemas** (Map pp608–9) and lots of restaurants and shops. Go east on University Ave to see the 1919 **Kahn Building** (Map pp608–9) at No 535; it is an original Hillcrest commercial building with a kitschy facade. Then head south on 5th Ave to find a variety of café's, friendly gay bars, vintage clothing shops and independent bookstores, many with a good selection of nonmainstream publications.

Coronado

In 1885 Coronado Island wasn't much more that a scrappy patch of land sitting off the coast of what's now downtown San Diego. Home to jackrabbits and the occasional tycoon that rowed over to shoot them, Coronado was not a postcard-worthy destination. But what a difference three years makes. In February 1888, the Hotel del Coronado – at the time the largest hotel west of the Mississippi – welcomed its very

DETOUR: NORTH PARK

North Park, a gentrifying, Bohemian-light enclave just east of Hillcrest, is earning kudos for its restaurants. The big North Park sign at 30th and University Aves marks the center of the action. Gourmet southern comfort food is the draw at **Urban Solace** (☎ 619-295-6464; 3823 30th St; lunch mains $8-16, dinner mains $9-18; ⏰ lunch & dinner), recently named the city's best new restaurant by *San Diego Magazine*. The eatery draws hipster hordes to Sunday's Bluegrass Brunch with a bluegrass band pickin' tunes on the patio (note to solo diners: brunch gets crowded, so you may be packed off to the bar). Just west on University Ave is **Spread** (☎ 619-543-0406; 2879 University Ave; mains $13-15; ⏰ dinner Tue-Sat), a mod, all-vegetarian and vegan eatery preparing shareable small plates, and **Heaven Sent Desserts**, (☎ 619-793-4758; 3001 University Ave; ⏰ 11am-11pm Tue-Thu, to 11:30pm Fri & Sat, to 9:30pm Sun), where the tarts, tiramisus and chunky chocolate chip cookies are equally tempting. For a great indie coffeehouse, walk a block west to high-ceilinged **Café Calabria** (☎ 619-291-1759; 3933 30th St; ⏰ 6am-3pm Mon-Fri, 7am-3pm Sat & Sun), where burlap bales of coffee beans, easygoing staff, sunny patio tables, and a long list of coffee and teas equal one great spot for loitering.

first guests. Today, the hotel and its stunning surroundings are the primary reasons to visit this well-manicured community.

The city of **Coronado** (Map p602) is now connected to the mainland by the graceful 2.12-mile Coronado Bay Bridge (opened in 1969), as well as by a narrow spit of sand known as the Silver Strand, which runs south to Imperial Beach and connects Coronado to the mainland. The large North Island US Naval Air Station occupies a northern tip of the island.

The **Coronado Visitors Center** (Map p602; ☎ 619-437-8788; www.coronadovisitorcenter.com; 1100 Orange Ave; ⏰ 9am-5pm Mon-Fri, 10am-5pm Sat, 11am-4pm Sun) has information and conducts a walking tour ($12), starting from the **Glorietta Bay Inn** (Map p602; 1630 Glorietta Blvd), near Silver Strand Blvd, at 11am Tuesday, Thursday and Saturday. The 90-minute route takes in many of Coronado's most interesting sights.

A **shuttle** ($1 per trip) loops up and down Orange St between the ferry landing, Hotel del Coronado, and city hall.

ourpick **Hotel del Coronado** (1500 Orange Ave) This iconic hotel, familiar today with its white-washed exterior, red conical towers, cupolas and balconies, sprang from the vision of two of the aforementioned jackrabbit hunters, Elisha Babcock and HL Story, who bought the island for $110,000. They cooked up the idea of building a grand hotel as a gimmick to entice people to buy parcels of land on the island. Coronado land sales were a booming success and construction began on the hotel in 1887. Craftsmanship and innovation were strong points – the Del was the first hotel to have electric lights – as was sheer determination to finish it. The hotel had its grand opening, with 399 completed rooms, in February 1888 (although work on the property continued for two more years). Though the hotel was a success, Babcock and Story couldn't keep up with the bills and by 1900 millionaire John D Spreckels bankrolled the island into one of the most fashionable getaways on the west coast.

Guests have included 11 US presidents and world royalty – pictures are displayed in the history gallery downstairs from the lobby. The Hotel, affectionately known as The Del, achieved its widest exposure in the 1959 movie *Some Like It Hot*, which earned its lasting association with Marilyn Monroe. Today, the hotel still exudes a snappy, look-at-me exuberance that makes guests and day-trippers alike feel as though they've been invited to the jazziest party in town.

San Diego Harbor Excursion operates the hourly **Coronado Ferry** (☎ 619-234-4111; www.sdhe.com; per person one way $3.50; ⏰ 9am-9pm from Broadway Pier; ⏰ 9:30am-9:30pm from Coronado) shuttling between Broadway Pier on the Embarcadero to the ferry landing at the foot of Coronado's main drag, Orange Ave. Bring your bike for an extra 50¢. The company also operates an on-call **water taxi** (☎ 619-235-8294; www.sdhe.com; per person one way $7; ⏰ 3pm-10pm) serving Harbor Island, Shelter Island, Downtown and Coronado. Use the $1 per trip Coronado Shuttle to get around. Alternatively, bus 901 from downtown runs along Orange Ave to the Hotel Del Coronado. The Old Town Trolley tour stops in front of Mc P's Irish Pub, on Orange Ave at 11th St.

Point Loma

For spectacular views of downtown San Diego, Coronado, and San Diego Bay, take a half-day to visit **Cabrillo National Monument** (Map p602; ☎ 619-557-5450; www.nps.gov/cabr; per person/car $3/5; ⌚ 9am-5pm) on the southern tip of Point Loma, the handily placed peninsula that provides shelter to the bay. This hilltop monument is also the best place in San Diego to see the gray whale migration (January to March) from land. Historically, this is the spot where Portuguese conquistador Juan Rodriguez Cabrillo landed in 1542 – making him the first European to step on the United States' western shores. A small museum highlights his travels. The 1854 **Old Point Loma Lighthouse**, atop the point, is furnished with typical lighthouse furniture from the 1880s. Displays reveal the lonely, hard life (endless maintenance, sleepless nights) of the lighthouse keeper. Gearheads will want to check out the massive 5ft 2in 3rd Order Fresnel lens weighing 1985lb. On the ocean side of the point, drive or walk down to the **tide pools** to look for anemones and starfish.

Ocean Beach

In Ocean Beach, the beach bums and the restaurants are a little scruffier than those in coastal communities to the north. And the pier? It just doesn't seem to care that it's not all that photogenic. But therein lies the charm of this Bohemian neighborhood just south of I-8 and Mission Beach. You can get tattooed, shop for antiques, and walk into a restaurant shirtless and barefoot and nobody cares. You can also enjoy the best cheap eats in town and maybe grab a nice sunset or a little surfing. All with a minimum of surf-god pretension.

Newport Ave, which runs perpendicular from the beach, is the main drag, passing surf shops, bars, music stores, java joints, and used-clothing and secondhand furniture stores. The street ends a block from the half-mile-long **Ocean Beach Pier** (Map pp618–19), an excellent spot for fishing or a breath of fresh air.

Just north of the pier, near the end of Newport Ave, is the central beach scene, with volleyball courts and sunset barbecues. A bit further north is **Dog Beach** (Map pp618–19), where Fido can run unleashed around the marshy area where the San Diego River meets the sea. A few blocks south of the pier is **Sunset Cliffs Park**, a great spot to watch the sun dipping below the horizon.

There are good surf breaks at the cliffs and, to the south, off Point Loma. Under the pier, the brave slalom the pilings. If you're new to the area, beware of the rips and currents, which can be deadly.

Mission Bay

While San Diego is famous generally as a watersports mecca, the actual heart of the sailing, windsurfing and kayaking scene is Mission Bay, shimmering in sun-dappled glory at the end of the San Diego River just west of the I-5.

In the 18th century, the mouth of the river formed a shallow bay when the river flowed, and a marshy swamp when it didn't; the Spanish called it False Bay. After WWII, a combination of civic vision and coastal engineering turned the swamp into a 7 sq mile playground, with 27 miles of shoreline and 90 acres of public parks. With financing from public bonds and expertise from the Army Corps of Engineers, the river was channeled to the sea, the bay was dredged, and millions of tons of sludge were used to build islands, coves and peninsulas. A quarter of the land created has been leased to hotels, boatyards and other businesses, providing ongoing city revenue. Today, Mission Bay Park, at 4235 acres, is the largest man-made aquatic park in the US.

Don't be surprised if you find yourself yelling for Shamu during *Believe*, the 30-minute aquatic show that fills Shamu Stadium twice a day inside **SeaWorld** (Map pp618-19; ☎ 619-226-3901; www.seaworld.com; adult/child 3-9 $61/51; ⌚ 9am-11pm Jul–mid-Aug, reduced hr rest of year). We can't explain why, but there's something undeniably compelling about an 8000lb killer whale leaping into the air and splashing you with gallons of water.

SeaWorld, along with the zoo, is one of San Diego's most popular attractions, and Shamu has become an unofficial mascot for the city itself (not to be a spoilsport but, for the record, several killer whales here perform under the name Shamu). SeaWorld has a shamelessly commercial feel, but it's entertaining and, if you really concentrate, it can even be educational. Its popularity means you should plan on long waits for rides, shows and exhibits during peak seasons.

SeaWorld's claim to fame is its live shows, which feature trained dolphins, seals, sea lions and killer whales. **Believe** is the most visually spectacular program, and the one you won't

MISSION BAY & THE BEACHES

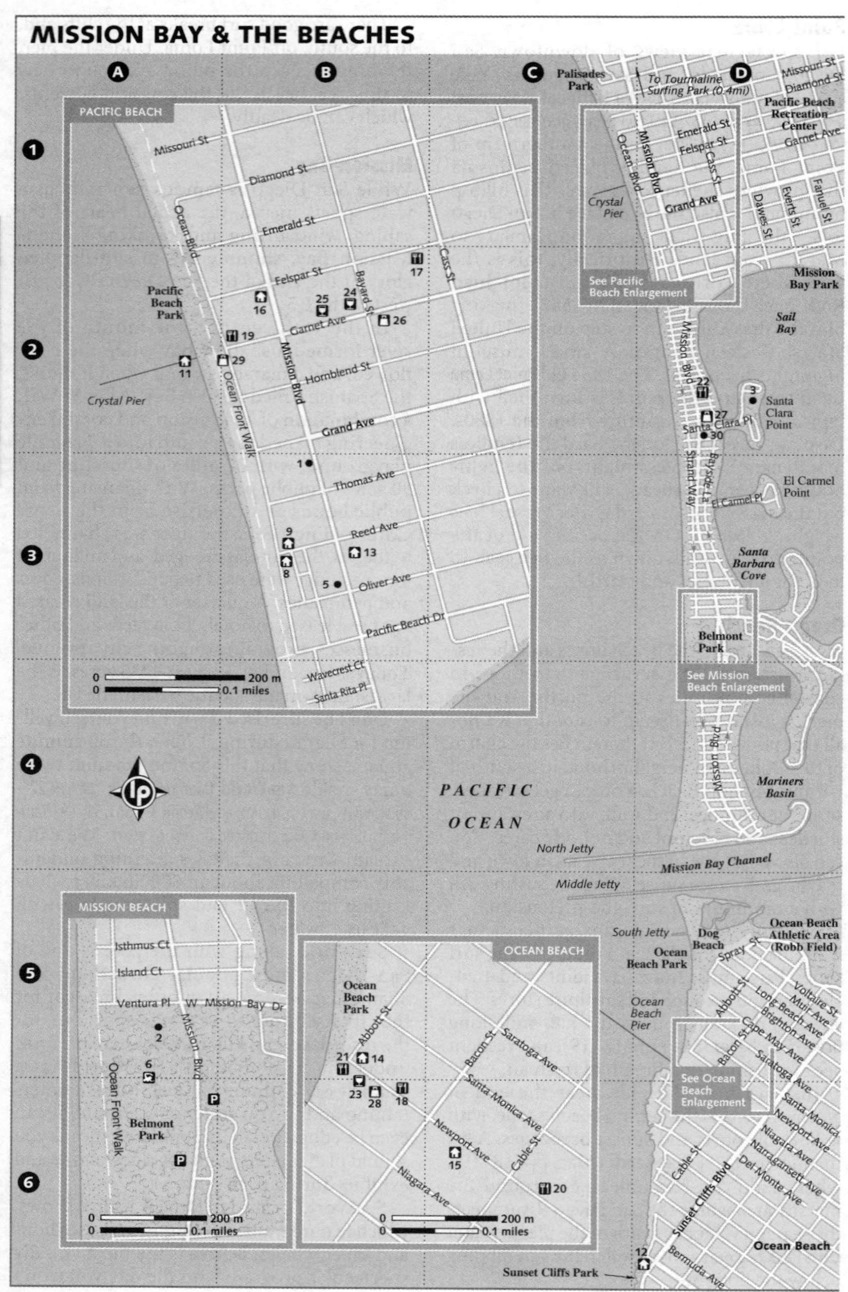

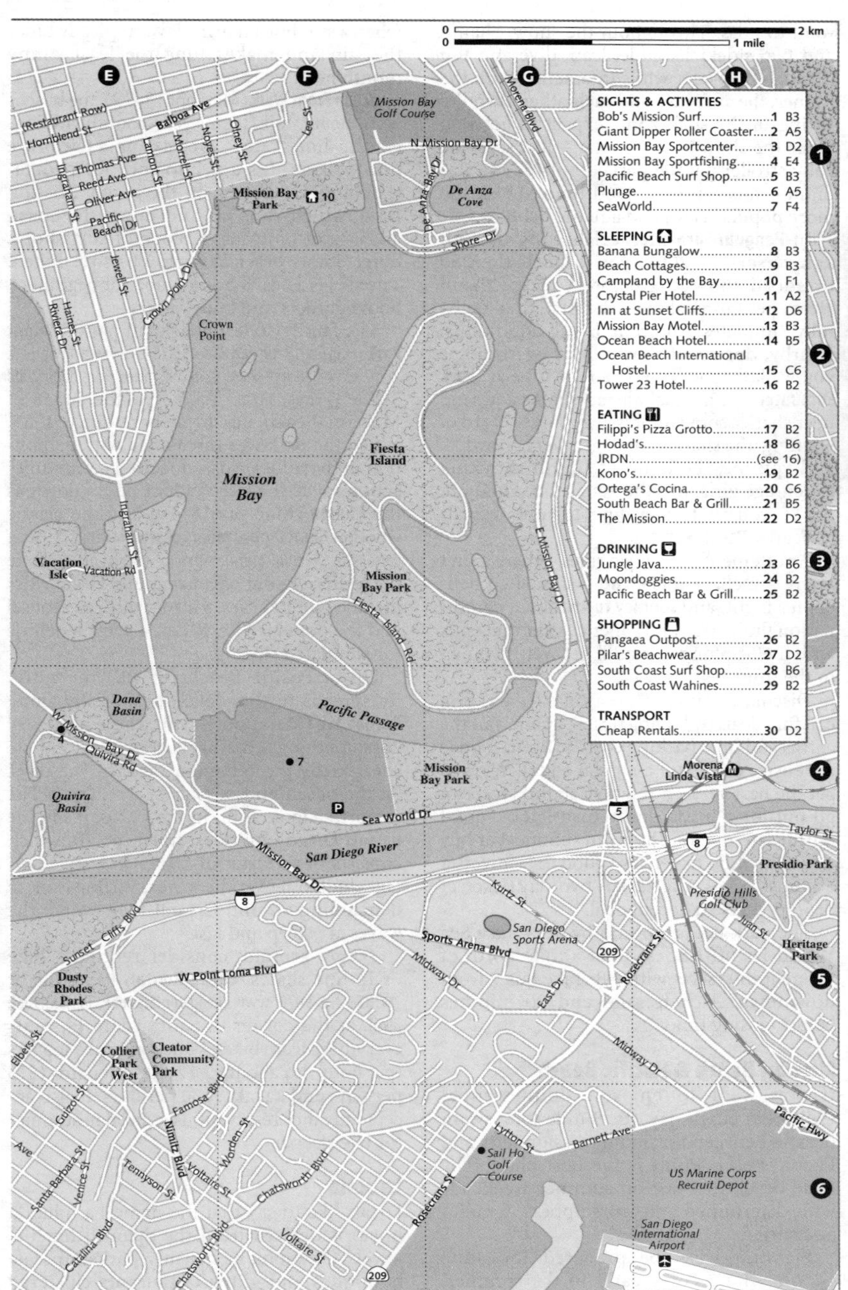
0 2 km
0 1 mile
E
F
G
H
1
2
3
4
5
6
SIGHTS & ACTIVITIES
Bob's Mission Surf....................1 B3
Giant Dipper Roller Coaster.....2 A5
Mission Bay Sportcenter..........3 D2
Mission Bay Sportfishing.........4 E4
Pacific Beach Surf Shop...........5 B3
Plunge....................................6 A5
SeaWorld.................................7 F4
SLEEPING
Banana Bungalow....................8 B3
Beach Cottages.......................9 B3
Campland by the Bay.............10 F1
Crystal Pier Hotel...................11 A2
Inn at Sunset Cliffs................12 D6
Mission Bay Motel..................13 B3
Ocean Beach Hotel.................14 B5
Ocean Beach International Hostel................15 C6
Tower 23 Hotel......................16 B2
EATING
Filippi's Pizza Grotto.............17 B2
Hodad's...................................18 B6
JRDN.................................(see 16)
Kono's.....................................19 B2
Ortega's Cocina......................20 C6
South Beach Bar & Grill.........21 B5
The Mission...........................22 D2
DRINKING
Jungle Java.............................23 B6
Moondoggies..........................24 B2
Pacific Beach Bar & Grill.......25 B2
SHOPPING
Pangaea Outpost....................26 B2
Pilar's Beachwear...................27 D2
South Coast Surf Shop...........28 B6
South Coast Wahines.............29 B2
TRANSPORT
Cheap Rentals........................30 D2
(Restaurant Row)
Hornblend St
Balboa Ave
Thomas Ave
Reed Ave
Oliver Ave
Pacific Beach Dr
Ingraham St
Lamont St
Morrell St
Noyes St
Olney St
Lee St
Jewell St
Crown Point Dr
Haines St
Riviera Dr
Mission Bay Golf Course
N Mission Bay Dr
Morena Blvd
De Anza Cove
De Anza Dr
Shore Dr
Mission Bay Park
10
Crown Point
Mission Bay
Fiesta Island
Vacation Isle
Vacation Rd
Mission Bay Park
Fiesta Island Rd
E Mission Bay Dr
Dana Basin
Pacific Passage
W Mission Bay Dr
Quivira Rd
4
7
Quivira Basin
Mission Bay Park
Morena Linda Vista
5
Sea World Dr
San Diego River
Mission Bay Dr
Taylor St
8
Presidio Park
Presidio Hills Golf Club
Kurtz St
Juan St
San Diego Sports Arena
Sports Arena Blvd
209
Rosecrans St
Heritage Park
Sunset Cliffs Blvd
W Point Loma Blvd
Midway Dr
East Dr
Dusty Rhodes Park
Elbers St
Collier Park West
Cleator Community Park
Midway Dr
Famosa Blvd
Guizot St
Worden St
Nimitz Blvd
Pacific Hwy
Lytton St
Barnett Ave
Sail Ho Golf Course
Ave
Santa Barbara St
Venice St
Tennyson St
Voltaire St
Chatsworth Blvd
US Marine Corps Recruit Depot
Rosecrans St
San Diego International Airport
Catalina Blvd
Chatsworth Blvd
Voltaire St
209

want to miss. Throughout the show, Shamu and two sidekicks glide, leap, dive and flip through the water while interacting with the trainer, the audience and each other. If you're sitting in the soak zone, expect to get wet. Since the show is so popular – just scan the baby stroller parade parked outside the stadium – this can be a good time to visit the more popular rides and aquatic habitats.

In **Penguin Encounter**, celebrating its 25th anniversary in 2008, you'll smell the 250 tuxedoed show-offs before you see them. Here, penguins share a habitat that faithfully simulates Antarctic living conditions. Nearby, dozens of sharks glide overhead as you walk through a 57ft acrylic tube at **Shark Encounter**. Species include reef sharks and sand tiger sharks, some impressively large. Word of warning: the shark habitat gets very crowded, and you may be tempted to lob shrieking tween-age girls into the aquarium. Hold off. For $5, you can feed sardines to honking seals at nearby **Pacific Point**.

Amusement park-style rides – there aren't many – include **Wild Arctic**, a simulated helicopter flight, and **Journey to Atlantis**, a combination flume ride and roller coaster that ends with a 60ft plunge – you'll get wet if you sit in the front seat.

Discount coupons are available, and you can find deals by buying tickets online, but the extras add up – parking costs $12 and food is expensive ($2.79 for a regular soda). Ways to get the best value: a re-entry stamp (you can go out for a break and return later – good during late-opening hours in summer) or buy a combination ticket, also good for Universal Studios (in Los Angeles). A two-day ticket, at $66/56, is also a decent deal.

The park is easy to find by car – take Sea World Dr off I-5 less than a mile north of where it intersects with I-8. Take bus 9 from downtown. Tickets sales end 90 minutes before closing time.

Mission Beach & Pacific Beach

If you want to enjoy a quintessential California beach day, the 3 mile-long swath of sand between the South Mission Jetty and Pacific Beach Point is the best place. The wide beach fills fast on summer weekends with determined sun-worshippers, families and surfers.

Planning-wise, be prepared for 'June Gloom' cloud cover early in the summer, when a stubborn marine layer typically hides the sun and makes June the least sunny month here.

Ocean Front Walk (Map pp618–19), the beachfront boardwalk, teems year-round with joggers, in-line skaters, cyclists and a few brave dog-walkers. It's a primo spot for people-watching. One block off the beach, Mission Blvd, which runs up and down the coast, consists of block after block of surf shops, burger joints, beach bars and '60s-style motels. The surf is a beach break, good for beginners, bodyboarders and bodysurfers.

The family-style amusement park **Belmont Park** (Map pp618-19; ☎ 858-488-1549; www.belmontpark.com; admission free, rides $2-6, unlimited rides adult/child $23/16; from 11am; P) in the heart of Mission Beach has been here since 1925. When the park was threatened with demolition in the mid-1990s, concerted community action saved the large indoor pool known as the **Plunge** (Map pp618–19) and the classic wooden **Giant Dipper roller coaster** (Map pp618-19; per person $6; from 11am), which might just shake the teeth right out of your mouth. Other rides include bumper cars, a tilt-a-whirl, a carousel and the popular FlowRider, a wave machine for simulated surfing.

Up in Pacific Beach (or PB) the activity spreads further inland, especially along **Garnet Ave** (Map pp618–19), where hordes of 20-somethings toss back brews and gobble cheap tacos. It gets hoppin' on Taco Tuesdays. At the ocean end of Garnet Ave, **Crystal Pier** is worth a look. Built in the 1920s, it's home to San Diego's quirkiest hotel (p630), which consists of a cluster of Cape Cod–style cottages built out over the waves. Surfing is more demanding around Crystal Pier, where the waves are steep and fast.

To get around, consider renting a bike or in-line skates. **Cheap Rentals** (Map pp618-19; ☎ 858-488-9070; www.cheap-rentals.com; 3689 Mission Blvd), at the corner of Santa Clara Pl, rents everything from bikes, skates and baby joggers (per hour/day about $5/12) to surfboards ($15 per day) and kayaks ($30 per day); it also accepts advance reservations, crucial in summer for late sleepers.

La Jolla

Locals like to say that the name La Jolla (la hoya) is derived from the Spanish for 'the jewel.' One look at the tidy parks, upscale boutiques and glitzy restaurants clustered downtown and the appropriateness of this explanation is immediately apparent. Some challenge this claim, however, saying that the indigenous people who lived in the area until the mid-19th century called it 'Mut la Hoya, la Hoya' – the place of many caves. It's this second explanation that's more intriguing to outdoor enthusiasts and fun-loving families because the sea caves, sandy coves and marine life here make it a fantastic place to kayak, dive, snorkel and tide-pool.

Technically part of San Diego, La Jolla feels like a world apart, both because of its radical affluence as well as its privileged location above San Diego's most photogenic stretch of coast. The community – generally stretching from Pacific Beach north past Torrey Pines to Del Mar – first became fashionable when Ellen Browning Scripps moved here in 1897. The newspaper heiress acquired much of the land along Prospect St, which she then donated to various community uses, including **Bishop's School** (Map p622; cnr Prospect St & La Jolla Blvd) and the **La Jolla Woman's Club** (Map p622; 715 Silverado St). She also hired Irving Gill to set the architectural tone – an elegant if unadorned Mediterranean style noted by its arches, colonnades, palm trees, red-tile roofs and pale stucco.

Bus 30 connects La Jolla to downtown via the Old Town Transit Center.

DOWNTOWN LA JOLLA

La Jolla Village, known locally as 'the Village,' sits atop a bluff lapped by the Pacific on three sides. There's little interaction between the compact downtown and the sea, although you can catch lovely glimpses of Pacific blue from a few of the fancy rooftop restaurants. The main thoroughfares, Prospect St and Girard Ave, are lined with boutiques, galleries and jewelry stores plus a fair number of chains (Talbots, Banana Republic, Armani Exchange).

To read news from around the world, stop by the **Athenaeum Music & Arts Library** (Map p622; ☎ 858-454-5872; www.ljathenaeum.org; 1008 Wall St; ⏲ 10am-5:30pm Tue-Sat, to 8:30pm Wed). Housed in a small but graceful Spanish renaissance structure near the intersection of Prospect St and Girard Ave, the library hosts small art exhibits and concerts. There's also a good selection of art and music books in the library plus a few used books (including current fiction) for sale.

The La Jolla branch of the small but excellent **Museum of Contemporary Art** (MCASD; Map p622; ☎ 858-454-3541; www.mcasd.org; 700 Prospect St; adult/senior/25yr & under $10/5/free; ⏲ 11am-5pm Fri-Tue, to 7pm Thu) shows world-class exhibitions that rotate every six months. Originally designed by Irving Gill in 1916 as the home of Ellen Browning Scripps, the building was renovated by Philadelphia's postmodern architect Robert Venturi. Overall, MCASD holds more than 4000 works of art created after 1950 in its collection. Inside, the Krichman Family Gallery offers a superb view of the ocean below. Outside, Nancy Rubin's *Pleasure Point* sculpture bursts with boats – from kayaks to canoes to paddleboards. Look for *Automatic Cities: The Architectural Imaginary in Contemporary Art* in late 2009 to early 2010. Tickets are good for one week at all three museum locations.

TOP FIVE BEACHES

- **Best for Beginner Surfers** La Jolla Shores (p623)
- **Best for Perfect SoCal Beach Day** Pacific Beach (opposite)
- **Best View** Coronado Beach behind Hotel Del (p616)
- **Best for Active Families** La Jolla Cove (below)
- **Best for Illegal Nude Sunbathing** Black's Beach (p623)

THE COAST

For a camera-worthy stroll, take the half-mile bluff-top path that winds above the shoreline a few blocks west of the Village. Near the path's western end is the **Children's Pool** (Map p622), off Coast Dr near Jenner Blvd. Here, a jetty funded by Ellen Browning Scripps protects the beach from big waves. Originally intended to give La Jolla's youth a safe place to frolic, the Children's Pool beach is now populated by sea lions, which you can view up close as they lounge on the shore (see boxed text, p623).

Continuing northeast, you'll reach Point La Jolla, at the path's eastern end, and **Ellen Browning Scripps Park** (Map p622), a tidy expanse of green lawns and palm trees. It's a great place to read, relax with your kids or watch the sunset. A short walk north leads to picnic tables and grills plus views of **La Jolla Cove** just below the path. This gem of a beach provides access to some of the best

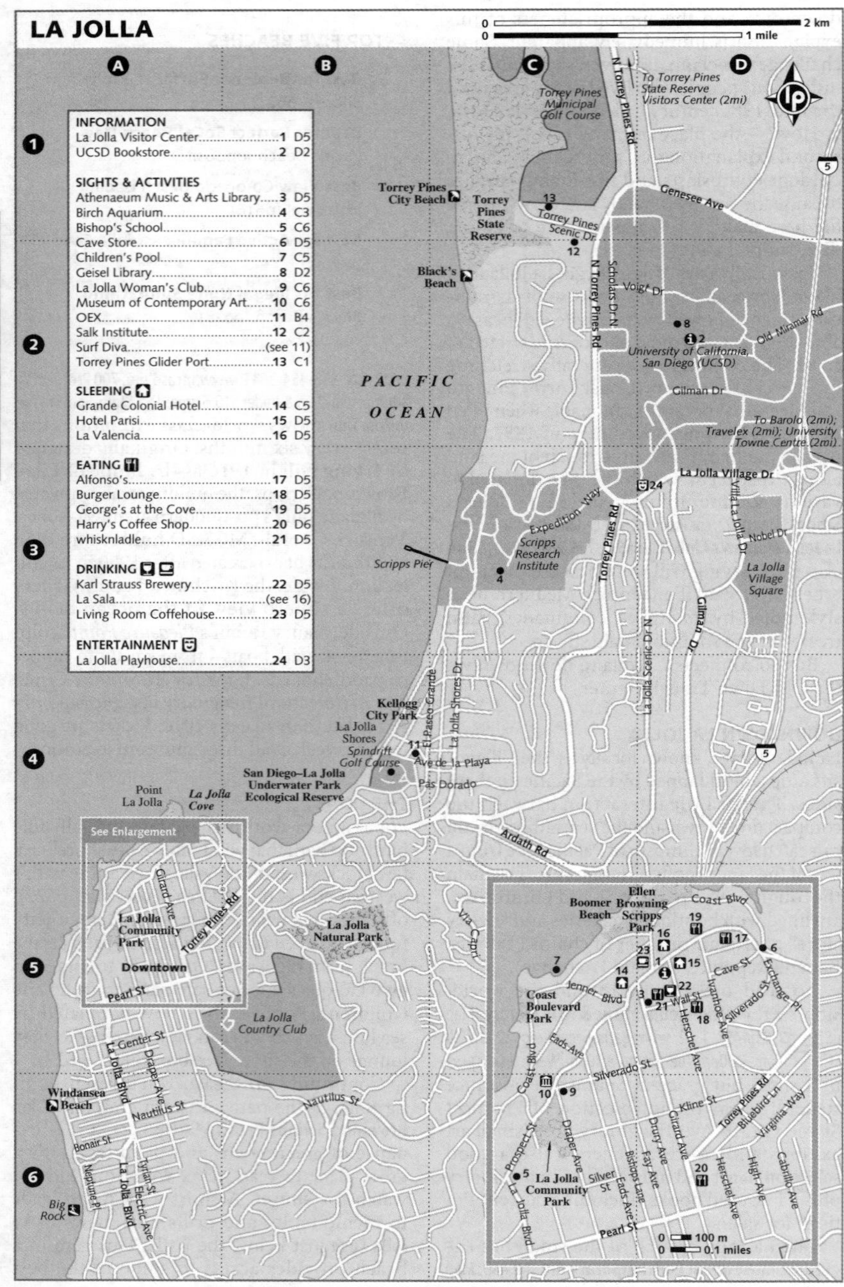
LA JOLLA
0 2 km
0 1 mile
INFORMATION
La Jolla Visitor Center 1 D5
UCSD Bookstore 2 D2
SIGHTS & ACTIVITIES
Athenaeum Music & Arts Library 3 D5
Birch Aquarium 4 C3
Bishop's School 5 C6
Cave Store 6 D5
Children's Pool 7 C5
Geisel Library 8 D2
La Jolla Woman's Club 9 C6
Museum of Contemporary Art 10 C6
OEX 11 B4
Salk Institute 12 C2
Surf Diva (see 11)
Torrey Pines Glider Port 13 C1
SLEEPING
Grande Colonial Hotel 14 C5
Hotel Parisi 15 D5
La Valencia 16 D5
EATING
Alfonso's 17 D5
Burger Lounge 18 D5
George's at the Cove 19 D5
Harry's Coffee Shop 20 D6
whisknladle 21 D5
DRINKING
Karl Strauss Brewery 22 D5
La Sala (see 16)
Living Room Coffeehouse 23 D5
ENTERTAINMENT
La Jolla Playhouse 24 D3
To Torrey Pines State Reserve Visitors Center (2mi)
Torrey Pines Municipal Golf Course
Torrey Pines City Beach
Torrey Pines State Reserve
Black's Beach
PACIFIC OCEAN
University of California, San Diego (UCSD)
To Barolo (2mi); Travelex (2mi); University Towne Centre (2mi)
Scripps Research Institute
Scripps Pier
La Jolla Village Square
Kellogg City Park
La Jolla Shores
Spindrift Golf Course
San Diego–La Jolla Underwater Park Ecological Reserve
Point La Jolla
La Jolla Cove
See Enlargement
La Jolla Community Park
Downtown
La Jolla Natural Park
La Jolla Country Club
Windansea Beach
Big Rock
Boomer Beach
Ellen Browning Scripps Park
Coast Boulevard Park
0 100 m
0 0.1 miles

SEALS VS SWIMMERS

The **Children's Pool** was created in the early 1930s when the state deeded the area to the city with the proviso that it be used as a public park and children's pool. As part of the arrangement, Ellen Browning Scripps paid for a protective 300ft seawall. Then came the seals, drawing tourists but gradually nudging out swimmers. Animal rights groups want to protect the cove as a rookery while some swimmers and divers want the seals – whose presence raises bacteria levels in the water to unsafe levels – removed. In 2005 the California Superior Court ruled that the seals had to go. The US Appeals Court refused to hear an appeal by animal activists in 2008, and the California Supreme Court has done the same. In sum, the seals are going to have to be removed, but activists keep up the fight, manning an information table near the pool's entrance.

snorkeling around; it's also popular with rough-water swimmers.

Look for the white buoys offshore from Point La Jolla north to Scripps Pier (visible to the north) that mark the **San Diego-La Jolla Underwater Park Ecological Reserve** (Map p622), a protected zone with a variety of marine life, kelp forests, reefs and canyons (see p625). Waves have carved caves into the sandstone cliffs east of the cove. For a spooky mini-adventure, continue walking north on Coast Dr until you reach the **Cave Store** (Map p622; ☎ 858-459-0746; 1325 Cave St; adult/child $4/3; ⏰ 10am-5pm). Here, 145 wooden steps descend a dank, man-made tunnel (completed in 1905) to the largest of the caves, Sunny Jim Cave. From its marine-ripe interior, you can watch kayakers paddling off-shore.

A popular, not-for-beginners surf spot is **Windansea Beach** (Map p622), 2 miles south of downtown (take La Jolla Blvd south and turn west on Nautilus St). Locals here can be aggressive toward outsiders. If you brave their ire, you'll find that the surf's consistent peak – a powerful reef break – works best at medium to low tide. Immediately south at **Big Rock**, at the foot of Palomar Ave, is California's version of Hawaii's Pipeline, which has steep, hollow tubes. The name comes from the large chunk of reef protruding just offshore – a great spot for tide pooling at low tide.

LA JOLLA SHORES

Called 'the Shores,' this area northeast of La Jolla Cove is where La Jolla's cliffs meet the wide, sandy beaches that stretch north to Del Mar. To reach the **beach** (Map p622), take La Jolla Shores Dr north from Torrey Pines Rd and turn west onto Ave de la Playa. The waves here are gentle enough for beginner surfers, and kayakers can launch from the shore without much problem.

Some of the best beaches in the county are north of the Shores in the southern section of **Torrey Pines State Reserve** (Map p622), which is west of the Salk Institute. At extreme low tides (about twice a year), you can walk from the Shores north to Del Mar along the beach. The **Torrey Pines Glider Port** (Map p622) at the end of Torrey Pines Scenic Dr, is the place for hang gliders and paragliders to launch themselves into the sea breezes that rise over the high cliffs. It's a beautiful sight – tandem flights are available if you can't resist trying it (p626). Below, **Black's Beach** (Map p622), is a storied clothing-optional venue – though bathing suits are technically required, most folks don't seem to know that; there's a gay section at the far (north) end.

Crowds swarmed the area for the historic, Tiger Woods–winning US Open golf tournament at **Torrey Pines Municipal Golf Course** (p622) in June 2008. Located just north of the glider port, Torrey Pines is only the second public course to ever host the event.

BIRCH AQUARIUM AT SCRIPPS

Marine scientists were working here as early as 1910 and, helped by donations from the ever-generous Scripps family, it has become one of the world's largest marine research institutions. It is now part of UCSD, and its pier is a local landmark.

Birch Aquarium (Map p622; ☎ 858-534-3474; www.aquarium.ucsd.edu; 2300 Exhibition Way; adult/youth 3-17/senior $11/7.50/9; ⏰ 9am-5pm; P ♿), off N Torrey Pines Rd, has brilliant displays about the marine sciences and marine life. The **Hall of Fishes** has more than 60 fish tanks simulating marine environments from the Pacific Northwest to the tropics of Mexico and the Caribbean. Divers feed leopard sharks, garibaldi, sea bass and eels in the 70,000-gallon kelp tank during half-hour shows on Tuesdays, Thursdays and weekends. Check the website for times. The 13,000-gallon shark tank holds white-tip and black-tip reef sharks and others native to tropical reef habitats. There's a small touch-tank tide pool in back. Adults may have the most fun listening to questions from curious kids. Recently heard? Everything from 'Why are the sardines swimming in circles?' to 'Do these fishes do anything?'

From downtown San Diego and La Jolla, take bus 30.

SALK INSTITUTE

Jonas Salk, the pioneer of polio prevention, founded the **Salk Institute** (Map p622; ☎ 858-453-4100 ext 1287; www.salk.edu; 10010 N Torrey Pines Rd; tours ⏰ noon-Mon, Wed, Fri, reservations required) in 1960 for biological and biomedical research. San Diego County donated 27 acres of land, the March of Dimes provided financial support and Louis Kahn designed the building. Completed in 1965, it is a masterpiece of modern architecture, with its classically proportioned travertine marble plaza and cubist, mirror-glass laboratory blocks framing a perfect view of the Pacific. The Salk Institute attracts the best scientists to work in a research-only environment. The facilities have been expanded, with new laboratories designed by Jack McAllister, a follower of Kahn's work. Free guided architectural tours are offered Mondays through Fridays at noon by reservation. For reservations, call or email tours@salk.edu. Bus 101 follows N Torrey Pines Rd from the University Town Center (UTC) transit center.

TORREY PINES STATE RESERVE

Birders, whale-watchers, hikers and those seeking great coastal views will want to amble through this tree-studded **reserve** (Map p622; ☎ 858-755-2063; www.torreypine.org; ⏰ 8am-sunset) that preserves the last mainland stands of the Torrey pine *(Pinus torreyana)*, a species adapted to sparse rainfall and sandy, stony soils that's only found here and on Santa Rosa Island in Channel Islands National Park. Steep sandstone gullies are eroded into wonderfully textured surfaces, and the views over the ocean and north to Oceanside are superb, especially at sunset. The reserve is on the Pacific Flyway, making it a popular pit stop for migrating birds.

The main access road, Torrey Pines Park Rd, off N Torrey Pines Rd (bus 101) at the reserve's northern end, winds its way up to a simple adobe – built as a lodge in 1922 by (drum roll) Ellen Browning Scripps – which is now a **visitors center** (⏰ 9am-6pm mid-March–Oct, to 4pm Nov–mid-Mar) – with displays on the local flora and fauna. Rangers lead nature walks from here at 10am and 2pm on weekends.

Parking is $8 per car, but admission is free if you enter on foot. Several walking trails wind through the reserve and down to the beach. For a good sampling of reserve highlights, plus good whale-watching spots, staff recommend the ⅔-mile Guy Fleming loop trail.

UNIVERSITY OF CALIFORNIA, SAN DIEGO

The 1200-acre campus of the University of California San Diego (UCSD) was established in 1960 and now enrolls more than 22,000 undergraduates. Known for its math and science programs, the respected university lies on rolling coastal hills in a park-like setting, with many tall and fragrant eucalyptus trees shading the campus. Its most distinctive structure is the space-agey **Geisel Library** (Map p622), a visually stunning upside-down pyramid of glass and concrete whose namesake, Theodor Geisel, is better known as Dr Seuss, creator of the *Cat in the Hat*. He and his wife, longtime residents of La Jolla, contributed substantially to the library. A collection of his drawings and books are displayed on the ground level in March.

For an engaging fusion of art and exercise, stroll the **Stuart Collection** of outdoor sculptures dotting the campus. Pick up the Stuart Collection brochure and map from the library's helpful information desk. From the eastern side of the library's second level, an allegorical snake created by artist Alexis Smith winds around a native California plant garden, past an enormous marble copy of John Milton's *Paradise Lost*. Other works include Niki de Saint Phalle's *Sun God*, Bruce Nauman's *Vices & Virtues* (which spells out seven of each in huge neon letters), and a forest containing poem-reciting and music-singing trees. Most installations are near the Geisel Library.

The **UCSD bookstore** (Map p622; ☎ 858-534-7323), located at the Price Center, has helpful staff and excellent stock that includes travel, religion, arts, sci-fi and California history. Inside the Mandell Weiss Center for the Performing Arts, the **La Jolla Playhouse** (Map p622; ☎ 858-550-1010; www.lajollaplayhouse.org) is known for high-quality productions.

The best access to campus is off La Jolla Village Dr or N Torrey Pines Rd (bus 30 from downtown). Pick up a campus map at Gilman Dr Visitor Center. Parking is free on weekends. During the week, look for a metered spot ($1 per hour) just north of the library.

ACTIVITIES

Surfing

San Diego has great surf spots for all skill levels, but the water can get crowded. Several spots, particularly Sunset Cliffs and Windansea, get especially territorial and you could get taunted unless you're an awesome surfer.

Fall brings the strong swells and offshore Santa Ana winds. In summer, swells come from the south and southwest, and in winter from the west and northwest. Spring brings more frequent onshore winds, but the surfing can still be good. For the latest beach, weather and surf reports, call ☎ 619-221-8824.

Beginners looking for classes and board rentals should try Mission or Pacific Beaches, where the waves are gentle. North of the Crystal Pier, Tourmaline Surfing Park is an especially good place to take your first strokes. Friendly **Pacific Beach Surf Shop** (Map pp618-19; ☎ 858-373-1138; www.pacificbeachsurfschool.com; 4150 Mission Blvd, Suite 161, Pacific Beach; 90-minute lesson per person $85) provides instruction through its Pacific Beach Surf School (lessons are cheaper for groups). It also rents wetsuits and both soft (foam) and hard (fiberglass) boards. Call ahead. Also check out **Bob's Mission Surf** (Map pp618-19; ☎ 858-483-8837; www.missionsurf.com; 4320 Mission Blvd, Pacific Beach). Soft boards rent for half-/full day $15/20, fiberglass boards $10/15 and wetsuits $6/10, with a discount if you rent board and wetsuit together.

In La Jolla, the wonderful women at **Surf Diva** (Map p622; ☎ 858-454-8273; www.surfdiva.com; 2160 Av de la Playa) offer two-day weekend workshops for gals of all ages ($165 per person) and private classes for gals and guys ($82.50 per hour per person, price decreases with added students). They take newbies into the easygoing waves at nearby La Jolla Shores.

The best surf breaks, from south to north, are at Imperial Beach (south of Coronado, especially in winter); Point Loma (reef breaks, which are less accessible but less crowded; best in winter); Sunset Cliffs in Ocean Beach (a bit territorial); Pacific Beach; Big Rock (California's Pipeline); Windansea (hot reef break, best at medium to low tide; locals can be territorial); La Jolla Shores (beach break, best in winter); and Black's Beach (a fast, powerful wave). In North County (Map p643), there are breaks at Cardiff State Beach, San Elijo State Beach, Swami's, Carlsbad State Beach and Oceanside.

Bodysurfing is good at Coronado, Mission Beach, Pacific Beach and La Jolla Shores.

Diving & Snorkeling

Divers will find kelp beds, shipwrecks (including the *Yukon*, a WWII destroyer) and deep canyons just off the coast of San Diego County. For current diving conditions, call ☎ 619-221-8824.

For some of the state's best and most accessible (no boat needed) diving and snorkeling, try **San Diego-La Jolla Underwater Park Ecological Reserve** (Map p622) just a few kicks from La Jolla Cove. With an average depth of 20ft, the 6000 acres of look-but-don't-touch underwater real estate are home to the bright orange garibaldi, California's protected state fish (there's a fine for poaching one). Further out, you'll see forests of giant California kelp (which can increase its length by up to 2ft per day) and the 100ft-deep La Jolla Canyon.

A number of commercial outfits teach scuba courses, sell or rent equipment, fill tanks and run boat trips to nearby wrecks and islands. In La Jolla, in walking distance to the ocean, **OEX** (Map p622; ☎ 858-454-6195; www.oeexpress.com; 2158 Av de la Playa) is a full-service PADI dive shop in La Jolla Shores that provides rentals, instruction, and guided shore and wreck trips. Mask and snorkel cost $10 per day, wetsuit $15 a day, or the full package for $30 a day. Scuba gear rental packages start at $50. OEX also has shops in Mission Beach and Point Loma. In La Jolla, near La Jolla Cove, also try the Cave Store (p623) for equipment rentals.

Fishing

If you're over 16 years of age, you'll need a state fishing license, except when fishing from an ocean pier (one/two/10 days $12.60/19.45/38.85). Call a recorded service on ☎ 619-465-3474 for fishing information. An ocean enhancement stamp ($4.45) is currently required for 10 day trips but not one or two day trips.

The most popular public fishing piers are Imperial Beach Municipal Pier, Embarcadero Fishing Pier at the Marina Park, Shelter Island

Fishing Pier, Ocean Beach Pier and Crystal Pier at Pacific Beach. The best time of year for pier fishing is from about April to October. Offshore catches can include barracuda, bass and yellowtail. In summer albacore is a special attraction.

For guided fishing try the following outfitters. Prices do not include license and tackle (about $10 to $12).

H&M Landing (Map p602; ☎ 619-222-1144; www.hmlanding.com; 2803 Emerson St) This outfit is on Shelter Island. Half-day trips just off the coast cost $42/32 per adult/child. See the website for full day-trip prices.

Mission Bay Sportfishing (Map pp618-19; ☎ 619-222-1164; www.islandiasportfishing.com; 1551 West Mission Bay Dr) Formerly Islandia Sportfishing, this outfitter offers half-day trips that cost adult/child and senior $40/30. See website for twilight and overnight trip prices.

Boating

Rent power and sailboats, sailboards, kayaks and Waverunners on Mission Bay. Try **Mission Bay Sportcenter** (Map pp618-19; ☎ 858-488-1004; www.missionbaysportcenter.com; 1010 Santa Clara Pl). A sailboat costs $18/54/65 per hour/four hours/full day and a single kayak is $13/39/44.

Ocean kayaking is a good way to see sealife and explore cliffs and caves inaccessible from land. **Family Kayak** (☎ 619-282-3520; www.familykayak.com) offers a guided tour of San Diego Bay (per adult/child $40/15) and lessons (from $55 per person). Call for details. It's easy to explore the caves and cliffs around La Jolla from the boat launch of **OEX** (Map p622; ☎ 858-454-6195; www.oeexpress.com; 2158 Av de la Playa; s/d 2hr kayak rental $28/45) in La Jolla Shores. It also guides tours.

Experienced sailors can charter yachts and sailboats for trips on San Diego Bay and out into the Pacific. You'll find the following charter companies on Harbor Islands (on the west side of San Diego Bay near the airport).

Harbor Island Yacht Club (Map p602; ☎ 619-291-7245, 800-553-7245; www.harboryc.com; 1880 Harbor Island Dr; rental 4hr $105-695, full-day $150-995)

Harbor Sailboats (Map p602; ☎ 619-291-9568, 800-854-6625; www.harborsailboats.com; 2040 Harbor Island Dr, Suite 104; rental half-day $75-105, full-day $150-1080)

Whale-Watching

From mid-December to late February, gray whales pass San Diego on their way south to Baja California and again in mid-March on their way back to Alaskan waters. Their 12,000-mile round-trip journey is the longest migration of any mammal on earth.

There's a bluff-top viewing area at Cabrillo National Monument (Map p602), the best place to observe the whales from land. You'll also find whale-related film and exhibits year-round and, seasonally, whale-centric ranger programs. Southwest of the Old Point Loma Lighthouse is a small glass-walled shelter, where you can watch the whales breach (bring binoculars). Further north, Torrey Pines State Reserve (p624) and La Jolla Cove (p621) are also good whale-watching spots.

Three-hour whale-watching boat trips are offered seasonally by **H&M Landing** (p625; trip per adult/youth 13-17/child $25/20/17.50). **Hornblower Cruises** (Map pp604-5; ☎ 619-725-8888; www.hornblower.com; tour per adult/child/senior $35/15/30) offers a seasonal 3½-hour tour.

Hang Gliding

Don't let age keep you from a tandem paraglide with an instructor at La Jolla's **Torrey Pines Glider Port** (Map p622; ☎ 858-452-9858; www.flytorrey.com; 2800 Torrey Pines Scenic Dr; tandem paraglider flights/hang glider flights per person $150/175). Instructors have lifted off with three-years-olds and 99-year-olds at this world-renowned gliding center by the sea, where most rides last between 20 and 25 minutes. The difference between paragliding and hang gliding? With paragliding, the instructor and passenger remain in a seated position under a soft 'wing,' while hang gliders fly in a prone position under a triangular wing.

Experienced pilots can fly here if they are USHGA members and/or have on them a temporary 30-day USGHA membership card.

HIKE TO CITYWIDE VIEWS

A popular trail leads to the top of 1592ft **Cowles Mountain** (www.mtpr.org) near San Diego State. On this two-hour summit bagger (3 miles round trip), you'll pass joggers, dog-walkers and moms with toddlers, all hoping to catch sweeping views that can stretch from La Jolla south to Coronado on a clear day. From I-8, take the College Ave north exit, following College Ave to Navajo Rd. Take a right onto Navajo Rd and drive almost 2 miles, turning left onto Goldcrest Dr then enter parking lot.

TOURS

Look for brochures with discounts or check online for deals.

Old Town Trolley Tours (☎ 619-298-8687, 800-868-7482; www.trolleytours.com; adult/child 4-12 per day $32/16; 9am-7pm, varies seasonally;) Not to be confused with the Metropolitan Transit System's rail trolleys, these open-air, hop-on-hop-off buses loop to the main attractions in and around downtown and in Coronado. Tickets for the orange-and-green trolleys are good for unlimited all-day travel. Tours run every 30 minutes.

San Diego Scenic Tours (☎ 858-273-8687; www.sandiegoscenictours.com; adult $30-60, child 3-11 $15-30) Leads half- and full-day bus tours around San Diego and Tijuana, some of which build in time to shop and dine. You can combine some tours with a harbor cruise.

Both **Hornblower Cruises** (Map pp604-5; ☎ 888-467-6256, 619-725-8888; www.hornblower.com) and **San Diego Harbor Excursion** (Map pp604-5; ☎ 800-442-7847, 619-234-4111; www.sdhe.com) operate boat tours of San Diego Harbor. One- and two-hour sightseeing tours (adult $20 to $25, child $10 to $12.50) leave from the Embarcadero (near the *Star of India*). Nightly dinner-dance cruises are about $67 to $94 per person and whale-watching excursions run in season.

FESTIVALS & EVENTS

For the most current list, contact the San Diego Convention & Visitors Bureau (Map pp604–5).

Kiwanis Ocean Beach Kite Festival (☎ 619-531-1527) Kite-making, decorating, flying and competitions at Ocean Beach on the first Saturday in March.

San Diego County Fair (☎ 858-755-1161; www.sdfair.com) Over 1.2 million attended this huge county fair in 2008, held from mid-June to July 4; features headline acts and hundreds of carnival rides and shows at the Del Mar Fairgrounds in Del Mar.

US Open Sandcastle Competition (☎ 619-424-6663; www.usopensandcastle.com) You won't believe what can be made out of sand at the amazing sandcastle-building competition held mid-July in Imperial Beach, south of Coronado.

Del Mar Horse Racing (☎ 858-755-1141; www.dmtc.com) The well-heeled bet on the horses at Del Mar Fairgrounds, 'where the turf meets the surf,' from mid-July to early September.

San Diego Gay Pride (☎ 619-297-7683; www.sdpride.org) The city's gay community celebrates in Hillcrest and Balboa Park at the end of July.

Comic-con International (☎ 619-491-2475; www.comic-con.org) America's largest event for collectors of comic, pop culture and movie memorabilia at the Sand Diego Convention Center. Late July.

Summerfest Chamber Music Festival (☎ 858-459-3728; www.ljcms.org) La Jolla hosts this three-week series in August.

San Diego Street Scene (www.street-scene.com) Downtown's East Village hosts this outdoor music festival, which featured 40 bands in 2008, including Beck, the New Pornographers and Vampire Weekend. Mid-September.

December Nights (☎ 619-239-0512; www.balboapark.org) Festival in Balboa Park includes crafts, carols and a candlelight parade in the park.

Harbor Parade of Lights (www.sdparadeoflights.org) More than 100 decorated, illuminated vessels float in procession on the harbor on two Sunday evenings in December.

SLEEPING

High-season summer tariffs for double-occupancy rooms are listed in this section; suites cost more. The prices drop significantly between September and June, often by 40% or more.

Budget

DOWNTOWN

Despite its recent popularity, downtown still has some great, quirky budget options. It's also where you'll find the bulk of the city's high-end palaces.

HI San Diego Downtown Hostel (Map pp604-5; ☎ 619-525-1531; www.sandiegohostels.org; 521 Market St; dm $19-27, r $47-85; wi-fi) Friendly, helpful staff coordinate lots of activities and tours at this bustling, mazelike hostel. Located in the heart of the Gaslamp Quarter, this former Victorian-era hotel is close to public transportation and nightlife. The rates include a pancake breakfast, good kitchen facilities, laundry room, lockers (bring your own lock) and 24-hour access. No air-con.

500 West Hotel (Map pp604-5; ☎ 619-234-5252, 866-315-4251; www.500westhotel.com; 500 W Broadway; s/d $89/109; wi-fi) Rooms are shoebox size and bathrooms down the hall inside this 1920s beauxarts YMCA building (there's still a Y gym in the basement), but budget-minded hipsters will dig the bright decor, flat-screen TVs, communal kitchen (or diner-style restaurant), and easy access to trolleys and Greyhound. Guests can use Y gym for $5 a day. No air-con.

La Pensione Hotel (Map pp604-5; ☎ 619-236-8000, 800-232-4683; www.lapensionehotel.com; 606 W Date St; r $95; P) At this four-story Little Italy hotel, rooms are built around a frescoed courtyard – a pleasant place to sip coffee from the adjacent

SAN DIEGO AREA

café. Queen-size beds fill smallish, but clean, rooms. There's complimentary parking under the building, but you may not need your car, as the hotel's within walking distance of many downtown attractions. A great bargain, but no air-con.

UPTOWN

Hotel Occidental (Map pp604-5; ☎ 619-232-1336, 800-205-9897; www.hoteloccidental-sandiego.com; 410 Elm St; r $79-139; wi-fi) Stylish, lean and a little exotic, Hotel Occidental is the European supermodel of San Diego's hotels – though her rates are a bit more pedestrian. Colorful pillows and San Diego Expo prints add a splash of color to the rooms, which come with kitchenettes, small TVs and in-room safes. Some rooms share bathrooms (individual and lockable) that are just down the hall. Simple continental breakfast. Parking is $10.

MISSION VALLEY

If downtown rates are too high, try one of the hotels – mostly chains – along Hotel Circle Dr in Mission Valley. For those not planning to spend much time in the room, the lack of charm may be outweighed by lower prices and proximity to the freeways.

Motel 6 (Map pp608-9; ☎ 619-296-1612; www.motel6.com; 2424 Hotel Circle N; r $90; P wi-fi) This branch of the national budget chain is clean, safe, and centrally located near the I-5, I-8, and Old Town. Wi-fi costs $2.99 a day.

CORONADO

El Rancho Motel (Map p602; ☎ 619-435-2251; www.elranchocoronado.com; 370 Orange Ave; r $120; P) Don't be put off by the vaguely low-rent name at this mom-and-pop, 10-room charmer. Pink and white flowers adorn a narrow courtyard tucked between two white-clapboard rows of rooms. Bright rooms, high ceilings and sparkling white bedding make the small-to-midsized rooms feel cozy, not cramped.

OCEAN BEACH

Ocean Beach (OB) is under the outbound flight path of jets departing from San Diego airport; pack earplugs.

Ocean Beach International Hostel (Map pp618-19; ☎ 619-223-7873; www.californiahostels.com; 4961 Newport Ave; dm incl breakfast $24; wi-fi) The cheapest option in the neighborhood is only a couple of blocks from the ocean; it's a fun place reserved for international travelers and educators, with bonfires, barbecues and free linens. There's eggs, toast and coffee for breakfast daily and dinner twice a week. Free transport to the hostel from San Diego Airport or the bus or train station via taxi, shuttle or express bus. No air-con.

Ocean Beach Hotel (Map pp618-19; ☎ 619-223-7191; www.obhotel.com; 5080 Newport Ave; r $100-150; P wi-fi) This three-story hotel is right across the street from the beach, and it's an easy walk to some of San Diego's best cheap eats. Rooms are small but clean, and a bougainvillea-draped courtyard adds a little pizzazz. All have refrigerators and microwaves. Pets welcome on 1st floor.

MISSION BAY & PACIFIC BEACH

Banana Bungalow (Map pp618-19; ☎ 858-273-3060; www.bananabungalow.com; 707 Reed Ave; dm/r $25/105; wi-fi) The Bungalow has a top beachfront location that's just a few blocks from the Garnet Ave bar scene. It's reasonably clean but pretty basic and can get crowded. A communal, made-for-keggers patio overlooks the boardwalk and Mission Beach. Breakfast included. No air-con.

Campland on the Bay (Map pp618-19; ☎ 858-581-4260; 800-422-9386; www.campland.com; 2211 Pacific Beach Dr; tent & RV sites $40-140, beachfront from $160; P wi-fi) The loneliest place at this kid-friendly campground is the video arcade, as all the kids are outside – biking, tossing frisbees or enjoying the water. The complex, with more than 40 acres fronting Mission Bay, also has a restaurant, two pools, a small grocery, a 124-slip marina, boating rentals and full RV hook-ups. The location is great, but the tent area can be pretty sorry – try to avoid the shadeless, dusty sites. Sites are reservable up to two years in advance, and cost depends on proximity to the water.

Midrange

DOWNTOWN

Horton Grand Hotel (Map pp604-5; ☎ 619-544-1886, 800-542-1886; www.hortongrand.com; 311 Island Ave; r $199-229; wi-fi) Victorian-era furniture and fixtures (including rooms with pull-chain toilets) mix easily with modern conveniences at this 132-room hotel, a restoration of two separate hotels dating from 1886 (one of which Wyatt Earp called home). Located in the Gaslamp Quarter, the Horton is popular with convention-goers who can walk to the convention center. Friendly staff will fill you in on the inn's history and resident ghost (p606). Suites have less Victoriana. Parking is $24 per day and wi-fi $9.95 per day.

OLD TOWN

You almost don't need a car if staying near Old Town, which has its own transit center served by trolleys (rail and tour), the Coaster and city buses.

Old Town Inn (Map pp608-9; ☎ 619-260-8024, 800-643-3025; www.oldtown-inn; 4444 Pacific Hwy; r $75-186; P wi-fi) Rooms look a bit dark when compared to those in the shiny hipster hotels downtown, but otherwise this simple, mission-style motel has a lot to recommend it. Centrally located off the I-5, it's an easy walk to Old Town and the Old Town Transit Center. Sturdy mattresses, an on-site laundry, and complimentary wi-fi, parking and continental breakfast round out the appeal. Some rooms have efficiencies (kitchenette and bath).

MISSION VALLEY

The Handlery (Map p602; ☎ 619-298-0511, 800-676-6567; www.handlery.com; 950 Hotel Circle N; r from $189; wi-fi) The family-owned Handlery has attractive furnishings (wooden armoires and writing desks), and there's a complimentary shuttle to area attractions. It's popular with runners in the Rock-n-Roll marathon in late spring. Parking costs $12 a day, and wi-fi is $10 a day.

CORONADO

Coronado Inn (Map p602; ☎ 619-435-4121, 800-598-6624; www.coronadoinn.com; 266 Orange Ave; r $179, with kitchen $269; P wi-fi) It feels like home – in a good way – at this tidy, motel-style property wrapped around a small parking lot on Orange Ave near the ferry. Relax among palm trees and brick walkways while enjoying afternoon lemonade and snacks from the lobby.

OCEAN BEACH

Inn at Sunset Cliffs (Map pp618-19; ☎ 619-222-7901, 866-786-2543; www.innatsunsetcliffs.com; 1370 Sunset Cliffs Blvd; r from $150; P wi-fi) Rooms surround a flower-bedecked courtyard that faces the sea at this bluff-top charmer perched at the southern end of Ocean Beach. Breezy rooms are compact, but some suites have full kitchens. With easygoing staff and the sound of surf crashing below, it's easy to see why some guests book month-long stays.

MISSION BAY & PACIFIC BEACH

Mission Bay Motel (Map pp618-19; ☎ 858-483-6440, 866-649-5828; www.missionbaymotel.com; 4221 Mission Blvd; r from $130; P) No air-con. No internet. Industrial carpets. But hey, it's clean and close to the beach.

Beach Cottages (Map pp618-19; ☎ 858-483-7440; www.beachcottages.com; 4255 Ocean Blvd; r $140-160, cottages from $295-335; P wi-fi) Celebrating its 60th birthday in 2008, this family-owned complex is great for families with restless kids. Ping-pong tables, shuffleboard courts and the adjacent beach should keep the under-12 crowd occupied for hours. There are plenty of motel rooms here, but booking one of the 17 cozy, 1940s-era beachfront cottages may be most economical – and fun – for groups. Reserve well in advance.

Tower23 Hotel (Map pp618-19; ☎ 866-869-3723; www.t23hotel.com; 4551 Ocean Blvd; r from $199; P wi-fi) For contemporary cool, try this modernist show place with minimalist decor, a teal-and-mint-blue color scheme and a sense of humor. But cool doesn't triumph over comfort – not with six pillows propped on every bed. There's no pool but you're right on the beach. Parking is $20 per day.

Top End

DOWNTOWN

Hotel Solamar (Map pp604-5; ☎ 619-819-9500, 877-230-0300; www.hotelsolamar.com; 435 6th Ave; r $229-349; wi-fi) Teetering on hipper-than-thou, this 235-room Gaslamp newcomer is saved by welcoming staff, ecoawareness that's above the norm and a hotel 'theme' of supporting the artist within. Polka-dot throws and leopard-print robes keep things quirky inside average-sized rooms decorated with blue-and-chocolate flair. There's a complimentary wine hour between 5pm and 6pm. Parking is $32 a day. Pets welcome.

Westgate Hotel (Map pp604-5; ☎ 619-238-1818, 800-522-1564; www.westgatehotel.com; 1055 2nd Ave; r from $245;) With its grand tapestries and ornate furniture, the sumptuous, chandeliered lobby is reminiscent of a grand European palace – just swanky enough to make you forget the unfortunate 1970s, office-tower shell. Large, 400-sq-ft rooms are equally deluxe, with imported European furniture, marble-tiled bathrooms and balconied views of the city. Parking is $27 per day.

Ivy Hotel (Map pp604-5; ☎ 619-814-1000, 877-489-4489; www.ivyhotel.com; 600 F St; r $279-379, ste from $479; wi-fi) What happens at the Ivy might not stay at the Ivy – not with nearby condo-dwellers training their eyes on this sultry new hotel, where stripper poles and glass-enclosed showers with bed views are a few of the decadent amenities. Other touches include personal butler service, Thai linens and pet-friendly rooms. Three nightclubs – including Eden, the city's largest rooftop bar – turn this A-lister into a thumping party zone on weekends. Parking is $30 a day.

CORONADO

Hotel del Coronado (Map p602; ☎ 619-435-6611, 800-468-3533; www.hoteldel.com; 1500 Orange Ave; r $380-750;) You probably don't *need* to take the antique elevator – complete with uniformed operator – to your 2nd-floor room but 'the Del' is so darn charming you won't want to miss a bit of its history. The 120-year old hotel combines tradition (p616), luxury and access to the city's most stunning beach. Amenities include two pools, a full-service spa, fitness center, shops, restaurants and manicured grounds. Note that half the accommodations are not in the main Victorian-era hotel, but in an adjacent seven-story building constructed in the 1970s. For a sense of place, book a room in the original hotel. Watch the fees, though. There's a $25 daily resort fee that includes use of the broadband in your room and access to the fitness center. Parking is $23 per day.

MISSION BAY & PACIFIC BEACH

Crystal Pier Hotel (Map pp618-19; ☎ 858-483-6983, 800-748-5894; www.crystalpier.com; 4500 Ocean Blvd; cottages summer $270-420, winter $225-355; P wi-fi) White clapboard cottages with flower boxes and blue shutters are the draw at this popular hotel, and not just because they're picturesque. The cottages – dating from 1936 – are special because they sit atop the pier itself, offering one-of-a-kind views of coast and sea. Newer, larger cottages sleep more people, but the older units are the best. Book eight to eleven months in advance for summer reservations. Minimum-stays requirements vary seasonally.

LA JOLLA

It's hard to find a cheap room here, even on weekdays off-season. The least expensive are on La Jolla Blvd, south of town. Longer stays yield lower rates.

Grande Colonial Hotel (Map p622; ☎ 858-454-2181, 888-530-5766; www.thegrandecolonial.com; 910 Prospect St; r $255-500, ste from $339; wi-fi) Warm colors, simple prints and classic furnishings set a conservative but sophisticated mood at the popular Grande Colonial, demure step-sister to the pink palace just down the road. There's been a hotel on the site for almost a century, and its central location makes it a perfect home base for exploring. Accommodating staff add to the ambiance. Parking is $18 a day.

La Valencia (Map p622; ☎ 858-454-0771, 800-451-0772; www.lavalencia.com; 1132 Prospect St; r $275-575, ste $600-1275; wi-fi) For Old Hollywood style, book at a room at this pink 1926 Mediterranean-style palace, where publicity stills of Lillian Gish and Greta Garbo line the hallways. The 116 rooms are compact – befitting the era – but they have modern conveniences and there are plenty of nooks and lounging areas to loll like an old-school celebrity. Even if you can't afford to sleep with the ghosts of Depression-era Hollywood, have a drink in La Sala, the elegant Spanish revival lounge. Parking is $20 a night.

Hotel Parisi (Map p622; ☎ 858-454-1511, 877-472-7474; www.hotelparisi.com; 1111 Prospect St; r $295-395, ste $495; wi-fi) This sumptuous boutique hotel is reminiscent of a high school prom queen, gorgeous, stylish and just friendly enough – though there's a hint of cooler-than-thou. But no mind, just put on your best airs and swoop in like you own the place – although you'll have to swoop to the 2nd floor to get to the lobby. The hotel is centrally located downtown, and rooms boast a sleek but comfortable contemporary style (think sand, russets and chocolate browns). Guests love the pillows. Parking is $15 a night.

EATING

San Diego has never been known for its culinary prowess or breadth of ethnic choices, but new restaurants and top chefs are stirring things up in the Gaslamp Quarter, La Jolla, and burgeoning neighborhoods like New Park and East Village.

Downtown & Embarcadero

It seems new restaurants are opening weekly in the Gaslamp Quarter, particularly in and around the trendy hotels surrounding nearby Petco Park. Many have bar scenes running well into the night. On weekends, make reservations or arrive early.

BUDGET

Cheese Shop (Map pp604-5; ☎ 619-232-2303; 627 4th Ave; mains $7-9; breakfast & lunch;) For a simple, filling lunch, try this old-fashioned luncheonette complete with long wooden counter, cozy booths and brick walls. The roasted pork loin sandwich with cheese and avocado hits the spot after a morning of sightseeing. Look for classics like corned beef hash for breakfast.

La Puerta (Map pp604-5; ☎ 619-696-3466; 560 4th Ave; mains $7-10; 11am-2:30am) Tossing back Coronas is always more fun inside the lair of a Mexican vampire. Or maybe it's Zorro's basement. Decide for yourself inside this dark, big-doored newcomer from the folks behind Confidential (p635). Small plates focus on thoughtfully prepared burritos, enchiladas and street tacos. For such a trendy spot, attitude is surprisingly nonexistent and the staff downright welcoming. Large booths work well for groups.

Café 222 (Map pp604-5; ☎ 619-236-9902; 222 Island Ave; mains $7-12; 7am-1:45pm;) Before heading to the New Children's Museum, load up on the renowned pumpkin waffles, orange pecan pancakes and egg scrambles at this popular breakfast joint (kids might enjoy the green eggs and spam). Small, but bright and airy, it's also a relaxing place to sip coffee and read the paper. Lunch is served, but we always go for breakfast.

Filippi's Pizza Grotto (Map pp604-5; ☎ 619-232-5094; 1747 India St; mains $7-17; lunch & dinner) Regularly lauded by locals for its pizza, this old-school Italian joint – think red-and-white checked tablecloths, tiny booths, small deli up front – often has a line out the door. Look for a second location in Pacific Beach at 962 Garnet St (Map pp618–19).

Mona Lisa (Map pp604-5; ☎ 619-234-4893; 2061 India St; lunch mains $7-9, dinner $12-15; lunch Mon-Sat, dinner daily) If you're heading to the Embarcadero or out of town and need picnic fixin's, order up at Mona Lisa's deli counter (grab a number, it's busy), then pick up wine and cheese from the adjoining, slightly cramped, specialty market. Try the prosciutto on a baguette. The adjacent restaurant is known for its hearty fare. Mmm, cannelloni.

MIDRANGE & TOP END

Bondi (Map pp604-5; ☎ 619-342-0212; 333 5th Ave; lunch mains $10-20, dinner $12-30; lunch & dinner) Australian rosewood, a steel baobab tree and a dining pod that rises above the floor are your backdrop for inventive cooking inspired by Down Under. Try the barbecued jumbo prawns, char-grilled rack of lamb and *wagyu* (Japanese beef) sliders washed down with select Aussie beers.

Red Pearl Kitchen (Map pp604-5; ☎ 619-231-1100; 440 J St; small dishes $7-20; dinner) Even dim sum looks sexy at this stylish pan-Asian gathering spot, where flickering lights, dark booths and a deep-red decor set a stylish yet convivial mood. Chattering hipsters share savory small plates that include pineapple kobe beef satay, steamed shrimp dumplings and Thai chili-glazed calamari. Don't miss the curried cauliflower.

C-Level Lounge (Map p602; ☎ 619-298-6802; 880 Harbor Island Dr; mains $11-25; lunch & dinner) The food is as aesthetically pleasing as the view at ever-pleasant C-Level Lounge, perched on a Harbor Island patio with sweeping vistas of the bay and downtown. Here, carefully crafted salads, sandwiches and light seafood fare are winning rave reviews. The uber-rich lobster and fontina BLT – dunked in lobster bisque – is a top choice, while the towering Hawaiian ahi tuna stack is perfect for a light lunch. Recommended.

Chive (Map pp604-5; ☎ 619-232-4483; 558 4th Ave; mains $7-35; dinner) For guilt-free nibbling and a glass of wine after a day of sightseeing, settle in on the chive-bordered patio at this stylishly spare Gaslamp stalwart. The short but varied Cal-Asian plates menu recently included Vietnamese meatballs, duck spring rolls and crab sliders. For sharing, try the lightly fried calamari salad. Great happy hour deals (Fat Tire $3, pineapple margarita $7).

Candelas (Map pp604-5; ☎ 619-702-4455; 416 3rd Ave; most mains $18-43; dinner) Come here to close the deal. Upscale 'rustic' decor, flattering lighting, attentive waiters and savory Mexican specialties – from beef tenderloin au gratin (with blue cheese) to jumbo prawns flamed with tequila – make Candelas one of downtown's most romantic dining experiences. Don't be surprised if someone pops the question at the adjacent table.

Oceanaire (Map pp604-5; ☎ 619-231-3140, 619-858-2277; 400 J St; most mains $20-39; dinner) Voted 2008's Best Seafood restaurant by readers, critics and editors in three separate polls by *San Diego Magazine*, this swanky dinner spot – styled like an art-deco ocean liner – fills early on weekends. 'Ultrafresh' halibut, snapper, mahi mahi and daily catches are prepared

EXCUSE ME WAITER, THERE'S A FISH IN THIS TORTILLA

The basics are always the same: a soft tortilla topped with fish, salsa, cabbage and special sauce. It's the preparation that makes San Diego's addition to the culinary lexicon – the fish taco – so interesting. Ralph Rubio, who founded his namesake fish-centric fast-food chain **Rubio's Fresh Mexican Grill** (www.rubios.com) in 1983, is credited with popularizing the dish. Who serves the city's best version? Perennial frontrunners include the piled-high bad boys at **South Beach Bar & Grill** (opposite) in Ocean Beach, where the lightly fried mahi mahi is the fish of choice. Then there are the uber-fresh grilled fish tacos at **Blue Water Seafood Market & Grill** (opposite) on India St. The deep-fried fish taco at longtime chain **Roberto's** (Map p602; www.robertos.us) is a corndog-sized piece of fried fish that is sure to ruin any diet. Minichain **Brigantine** (Map p602; ☎ 619-435-4166; 1333 Orange Ave) is also a list-topper. Less heralded but one of our favorites is the messy hunk of fried goodness at **El Indio** (below).

with seasonal flair. From the host to the bartenders, service is both welcoming and professional. The oyster bar gets elbow-to-elbow crowded on Fridays evenings.

Balboa Park

Prado (Map pp608-9; ☎ 619-557- 9441; 1549 El Prado; lunch mains $9-20, dinner $9-43; lunch daily, dinner Tue-Sun) Not just for ladies who lunch, this busy museum-district spot serves kobe burgers, wild mushroom risotto, and lobster and asparagus quiche to military men, office workers, dealmakers and weary tourists, all looking for a thoughtfully prepared meal and knowledgeable (but not always speedy) service. Red booths, bright tiles, a shaded patio and Mexican-inspired decor set a convivial mood.

Tea Pavilion (☎ 619-231-0048; mains under $10; 10:30am-3pm Mon, to 4pm Tue-Sun) Need a no-fuss meal or a moment to catch your breath? Enjoy a quick, not-too-spicy noodle bowl under an umbrella at this low-key eatery, next to the Japanese Garden. Or simply wind down with a cup of tea while appreciating the park's well-manicured grounds.

Old Town

Most Old Town eateries serve uninspired Mexican fare in contrived digs, although hearty servings, strong margaritas and outdoor seating can add up to a fun evening.

Old Town Mexican Cafe (Map pp608-9; ☎ 619-297-4330; 2489 San Diego Ave; most mains $3-14; 7am-11pm) Watch staff make some of the best tortillas in town – they're visible through the front window – at this hometown favorite. Wooden floors, green tables, bright banners and a big central bar set a festive tone. This place is perfect for slurping an Old Town margarita, grazing on crispy chips and chowing down on the famous *machacas* (shredded pork with onion). If not for the birds swooping low through the covered patio, this would've been a top recommendation.

Hillcrest & Mission Hills

You'll find lots of dining options in Hillcrest. Restaurants here tend to be more casual than downtown – and better value. For some of the city's best cheap eats, follow Washington St west from Hillcrest to India St (just before I-5) in Mission Hills.

El Indio (Map pp608-9; ☎ 619-299-0333; 3695 India St; mains $1-9; 8am-9pm; P) Don't be fooled by the fast food–style counter at this 60-year-old Mexican food stalwart. The staff is super friendly, the taquitos fresh and crispy (they were invented here), and the chips and salsa addictive – you can even get containers to go. Eat inside in the basic dining area or head across India St to umbrella-shaded picnic tables. Free parking in the lot beside the picnic tables. Look for the signs.

Bread & Cie (Map pp608-9; ☎ 619-683-9322; 350 University Ave; mains $2-10; 7am-7pm Mon-Fri, 7am-6pm Sat, 8am-6pm Sun;) A delightful sensory overload of aromatic fresh bread, chattering locals and pastry-filled trays awaits inside this bustling Hillcrest crossroads. Daily breads include black olive, walnut raisin, and jalapeno and cheese. Try the curried chicken salad at lunch.

Bronx Pizza (Map pp608-9; ☎ 619-291-3341; 111 Washington St; pizza slices from $2, mains $13-19; 11am-10pm Sun-Thu, until 11pm Sat & Sun) For a no-fuss, New York–style slice, order at the counter then check out the black-and-white photos of *The Sopranos*, Donald Trump and tough-guy boxers dotting the walls while you wait.

Lines can spill out the door (this is the best pizza in town), so be ready with your order and remember: no credit cards, no pineapple, no beer. But don't worry, the guys behind the counter aren't as gruff as they let on.

Blue Water Seafood Market & Grill (Map pp608-9; ☎ 619-497-0914; 3667 India St; mains $4-30; ⏰) Yeah, it's weak on decor, service can be slow and parking challenging, but the made-to-order fish tacos (go for mahi mahi) and the clam chowder (loaded with clams) make this blue-trimmed seafood shack worth the effort.

Hash House a Go Go (Map pp608-9; ☎ 619-298-4646; 3628 5th Ave; mains breakfast & lunch $8-15, dinner $14-36; ⏰ breakfast & lunch daily, dinner Tue-Sun) What is hash exactly? At this long-popular gathering spot it's a pile of breakfast potatoes tossed with meat or veggies and topped with two eggs. Sound decadent? Wait until you see the massive portions. Also vying for your attention are straight outta Carolina flapjacks, benedicts, and biscuits and gravy.

Khyber Pass (Map pp608-9; ☎ 619-294-7579; 523 University Ave; most mains $13-30; ⏰ 11:30am-10pm; V) Afghan tapestries and moody photos set the tone in this tall-ceilinged space, with adventuresome Afghan cooking. Never had it? Think Indian meets Middle Eastern, with yogurt curries, kabobs and stews.

For good Vietnamese, there's elegant but not overbearing **Saigon on Fifth** (Map pp608-9; ☎ 619-220-8828; 3900 5th Ave; mains $8-16; ⏰ 11am-midnight).

Coronado

MooTime Creamery (Map p602; ☎ 619-435-2422; 1025 Orange Ave; ice cream from $3.25; ⏰ 10am-11pm Sun-Thu, 11am-11pm Fri & Sat) Follow the trail of crumpled napkins to this upbeat ice-cream shop where peanut butter, Mexican chocolate and silly vanilla (is aqua-blue a natural color?) are a few of the homemade flavors. Cows, '50s music and a mess of toppings add to the fun.

Cornado Brewing Co (Map p602; ☎ 619-437-4452; 170 Orange Ave; mains $10-22; ⏰ lunch & dinner) The delicious house brew (the Pilsner-Style Coronado Golden) goes well with the pizzas, pastas, sandwiches and fries at this good-for-your-soul, bad-for-your-diet bar and grill near the ferry. Happy hour is between 2pm and 5pm Monday to Friday.

1500 Ocean (Map p602; ☎ 619-435-6611; Hotel del Coronado; 1500 Orange Ave; mains $28-45; ⏰ dinner) Bright marigolds border the veranda at the Del's most romantic restaurant, adding a cheerful splash of color to palm-framed views of the sea. Come here to flirt, propose, celebrate or simply revel in your good fortune. Look for rib-eye, duck confit, seared scallops and pork tenderloin among the nine mains.

Ocean Beach

OB is the place to go for the city's best cheap eats. Most places are on Newport Ave.

Hodad's (Map pp618-19; ☎ 619-224-4623; 5010 Newport Ave; mains $4-12; ⏰ lunch & dinner) If there was a glossy magazine called *Beach Bum Living*, then legendary Hodad's, with its surfboards-and-license-plates decor, communal wooden tables and baskets of burgers and fries, would score the very first cover. But it's not just the easygoing vibe that's behind that sidewalk-jostling line. It's the succulent burgers that many claim are the best in town. Add an order of fries for a buck and a quarter and you'll go home happy. No shirt, no shoes, no problem.

Ortega's Cocina (Map pp618-19; ☎ 619-222-4205; 4888 Newport Ave; mains $4-18; ⏰ breakfast, lunch & dinner) Tiny, family-run Ortega's is so popular that people queue for a spot at the counter. Seafood, *moles* and *tortas* (sandwiches) are the specialties but all its dishes are soulful and classic.

South Beach Bar & Grill (Map pp618-19; ☎ 619-226-4577; 5059 Newport Ave; mains $3-11; ⏰ lunch & dinner) Maybe it's the lightly fried mahi mahi. Or the kickin' white sauce. Or the layer of cabbage and salsa. Or maybe it's ingrediential teamwork. Whatever the secret, the fish tacos at this beachside bar and grill stand out in a city of awesome fish tacos. On Fridays, follow the noise to the nondescript building at the end of Newport Ave (it looks like an insurance company). Order your beer at the bar before settling in; waitresses don't do drink orders at this quirky but festive watering hole.

Mission Bay & Pacific Beach

You can eat well on a tight budget in these two coastal communities. Both have a young, mostly local scene; PB has the bulk of the restaurants, especially along Garnet Ave.

Kono's (Map pp618-19; ☎ 858-483-1669; 704 Garnet Ave; mains from $5; ⏰ breakfast & lunch) According to the girls at nearby Wahine's, the line at tiny Kono's, across from Crystal Pier, moves fast. And for $5 breakfast burritos and plates piled high with pancakes, bacon and eggs, who's complaining anyway?

The Mission (Map pp618-19; ☎ 858-488-9060; 3795 Mission Blvd; dishes $7-10; breakfast & lunch; V) Savor French toast or homemade cinnamon bread for breakfast or kick back with lunch specialties that include rosemary potatoes with sautéed tomatoes, salsa and eggs or the Chino-Latino ginger sesame tofu. Famously good coffee, too.

JRDN (Map pp618-19; ☎ 858-270-5736; Tower 23, 723 Feldspar St; breakfast mains $7-17, lunch $8-26, dinner $20-44; breakfast Sat & Sun, lunch & dinner daily) Sustainably farmed meats and seafood join local veggies for a plate-topping farmers market at chic, vowel-disdaining JRDN, where you can choose futuristic decor indoors or ocean views outdoors. Try dry scallops with crabmeat risotto, miso halibut and green-onion creamers (aka mashed potatoes).

La Jolla

La Jolla is a major haute-cuisine outpost, but there are some good budget options, too.

Harry's Coffee Shop (Map p622; ☎ 858-454-7381; 7545 Girard Ave; dishes $4-11; 6am-3pm) Classic coffee shop serving all-American fare with vinyl booths and a posse of regulars, from blue-haired socialites to sports celebs.

Burger Lounge (Map p622; ☎ 858-456-0196; 1101 Wall St; Girard Ave; dishes $6-8; 11am-9pm, to 10pm Fri & Sat) The minimalist interior is in direct contrast to the messiness of the burgers at this new patty-and-bun joint one block east of Girard Ave. In fact, these juicy numbers – made from organic, grass-fed beef – are best cut in half to prevent the whole thing squishing apart in your hands. Don't count calories, get the fresh-cut fries. It's all good.

Alfonso's (Map p622; ☎ 858-454-2232; 1251 Prospect St; lunch mains $9-11, dinner $8-26; 11am-11pm Mon-Sat, to 10pm Sun) Red and green decor, bright patchwork tablecloths and mariachi tunes keep things convivial on the chattering patio at this bustling Mexican joint where messy, plate-filling combos keep the masses happy.

our pick **whisknladle** (☎ 858-551-7575; 1044 Wall St; lunch mains $12-14, dinner $11-28; lunch & dinner) Just east of the Athenaeum, brand-new whisknladle is already earning kudos (Condé Nast Traveler's Hot Table 2008) for its carefully selected and seasoned 'slow food' – fresh fare simply prepared. The breezy covered patio is the main dining area, and there's only a small bar – and artsy wall of empty wine bottles – inside. The dinner menu includes spicy Catalan shrimp, Niman Ranch Hangar steak, and ricotta and Swiss chard ravioli. For lunch, try the oh-so-tender smoked chicken tossed with grapes, almonds, goat cheese and greens. You won't leave a crumb on the plate.

George's at the Cove (Map p622; ☎ 858-454-4244; 1250 Prospect St; mains $15-44; dinner) If you like your icons stylish, well-mannered and boasting terrific ocean views, then take your pick from the three dining areas at this perpetually praised landmark. For Chef Trey Foshee's top-ranking Euro-Cal cuisine (dry-aged strip steak, bacon-wrapped albacore), try George's California Modern, La Jolla's top special-occasion restaurant (mains $15 to $44). Step upstairs for lighter fare, open-air views and cheaper prices at the chic, green-and-orange-tiled Ocean Terrace ($16 to $24) where, on a recent visit, every diner seemed to be sipping George's Famous Soup with smoked chicken, broccoli and black beans. George's Bar shares Ocean Terrace's views and menu; it's just inside.

DRINKING

Cafés

Extraordinary Desserts (Map pp608-9; ☎ 619-294-2132; 2929 5th Ave, Hillcrest; 8:30am-11pm Mon-Thu, to midnight Fri, 10am-midnight Sat, 10am-11pm Sun) You know that one lady at work who says she gets fat just from looking at sweets? Don't bring her to Karen Krasne's treasure trove of stylishly decadent pastries (fruit-topped tarts, chunky and gooey cookies, thick cheesecakes) or she'll gain 100lbs just standing by the counter. Intimate couches are great for gabbing, sipping coffee, and sharing sweets.

Jungle Java (Map pp618-19 ☎ 619-224-0249; 5047 Newport Ave, Ocean Beach; 7am-9pm Sun-Thu, to 10pm Sat & Sun summer, varies winter) Funky, canopy-covered café and plant shop with easygoing owners and staff.

Living Room Coffeehouse (Map p622; ☎ 858-459-1187; 1010 Prospect St, La Jolla; 6am-midnight) This popular café serves sandwiches and has a great central position in the heart of the Village, which is perfect for meeting friends. There's a second location in Old Town (Map pp608–9; 2541 San Diego Ave).

Bars

Rooftop bars perched atop trendy hotels are the new, new thing in the Gaslamp Quarter, each boasting about its size, its views and its hipness. Downtown, demand seems to be outstripping capacity at the moment, so on weekends arrive a bit early (before 9pm) to nab a spot in the best nightclubs and more popular bars.

Many bars in Hillcrest are gay. For a complete list, check out *Buzz* and the *Gay & Lesbian Times*.

For Pacific Beach drinks, start walking east on Garnet Ave from the pier and you'll pass a seemingly endless line-up of beach bars. The street, especially on Taco Tuesdays with its cheap beers and tacos, attracts a younger crowd.

Altitude (Map pp604-5; ☎ 619-696-0234; 660 K St) The Marriott's rooftop bar is the best of the lot. It may have the de rigueur firepits and sleek decor, but unlike other open-air lounges, the vibe is friendly, not hipper-than-thou. Sightlines to Petco Park are superb.

Confidential (Map pp604-5; ☎ 619-696-8888; 901 4th Ave) White leather banquettes and smooth clean lines exude LA cool at this corner bar, which opened in 2006, raising the bar for the Gaslamp's second, youthful wave of stylish revitalization. The owners also run the swanky but slightly lower-key Currant Brasserie (140 W Broadway), one of the few bars in town serving absinthe.

Eden (Map pp604-5 ; ☎ 619-814-1000; 600 F St) There's naughtiness in the air at this sexy rooftop lounge where candlelight and cushions set the stage for, well, we wouldn't say romance. It purrs atop Ivy hotel, downtown's favorite adult playground.

Star Bar (Map pp604-5 ; ☎ 619-234-5575; 423 E St) Down-and-divey Star Bar: the place where dreams come to die.

Alibi (Map pp618-19; ☎ 619-295-0881; 1403 University Ave, Hillcrest) All the straight people in Hillcrest who go out drinking – young, old, rich or poor – pass through the doors of Alibi, earning it the nickname the 'Star Wars' bar.

our pick **Wine Steals** (Map pp608-9; ☎ 619-295-1188; 1243 University Ave) Gay, straight, not sure, who cares. This place gets elbow-to-elbow crowded with a stylish but laid-back crew that comes for the affordable wine tastings ($10 for a glass on Saturday nights with 20 tasting wines), cheese boards and wine-infused conviviality. Popular with small groups.

Moondoggies (Map pp618-19; ☎ 858-483-6550; 832 Garnet Ave, Pacific Beach) This orange-accented bar has a large patio, big-screen TVs, pool tables, good food and an extensive tap selection.

Pacific Beach Bar & Grill (Map pp618-19; ☎ 858-272-4745; 860 Garnet Ave, Pacific Beach) This classic attracts a young, party-hearty crowd to its long wooden tables, patios and big central bar. Sells $1.50 street tacos on Tuesdays.

La Sala (Map p622; ☎ 858-454-0771; La Valencia Hotel, 1132 Prospect St, La Jolla) For civilized cocktails or Sunday-afternoon Bloody Marys, visit the romantic, ocean-view lobby bar of La Valencia Hotel, which becomes a piano lounge on Friday and Saturday evenings.

Karl Strauss Brewery (Map p622; ☎ 858-551-2739; cnr Wall St & Herschel Ave, La Jolla) This microbrewery (with beer tanks right inside) offers six homebrews (including an amber light, IPA and wheat hefeweizen) and three that vary seasonally. It also has an inviting corner patio.

ENTERTAINMENT

The Thursday editions of the free weekly *San Diego Reader* and the Night & Day section of the San Diego *Union Tribune* list the latest movies, theater shows, gallery exhibits and music gigs in the area. From a kiosk outside Horton Plaza, **Arts Tix** (Map pp604-5; ☎ 619-497-5000; www.sandiegoperforms.com; cnr 3rd Ave & Broadway; 🕑 11am-6pm Tue-Thu, 10am-6pm Fri & Sat, 10am-5pm Sun) sells half-price tickets for same-day evening performances as well as discounts tickets to other events.

Nightclubs & Live Music

Anthology (Map pp604-5; ☎ 619-595-0300; www.anthologysd.com; 1337 India St) Watch live jazz over dinner and drinks at this swank supper club (with three floors of stage viewing options) that opened in 2007 just south of Little Italy. It books both up-and-comers and big-name performers. North of Downtown.

Casbah (Map pp604-5; ☎ 619-232-4355; www.casbahmusic.com; 2501 Kettner Blvd, Downtown) Liz Phair, Alanis Morisette and Ben Harper have all rocked the Casbah on their way up, and it's still a good place to catch tomorrow's headliners. Near Little Italy, it has couches, pinball machines, and dimly lit alcoves for nondancers.

Stingaree (Map pp604-5; ☎ 619-544-9500; www.stingsandiego.com; 454 6th Ave, Downtown) Arrive early on weekends, as the line can snake far down the sidewalk at San Diego's trendiest nightclub, where super-slinky decor is the backdrop. There's table service for your drinks and cabanas on the roof. Cover charges vary and can be expensive.

Universal (Map pp608-9; ☎ 619-692-1900; www.universalhillcrest.com; 1202 University Ave, Hillcrest) The newest and most buzzed-about dance club and lounge in Hillcrest, Universal is cool blue, invitingly mod and currently touting itself as omnisexual. Which means you can now get all dressed up and be rejected by both sexes.

Croce's Restaurant & Jazz Bar (Map pp604-5; ☎ 619-233-4355; www.croces.com; cnr 5th Ave & F St, Downtown) Ingrid Croce's tribute to her late husband Jim, this sizzling restaurant and club hosts great nightly jazz, blues and R&B performers.

Cinemas

Hillcrest Cinemas (Map pp608-9; ☎ 619-819-0236; www.landmarktheatres.com; 3965 5th Ave, Hillcrest) Regularly shows new art, foreign films and classics in the boxy, postmodern Village Hillcrest Center.

The main downtown cinemas, both showing current-release movies, are **Regal United Artists Horton Plaza** (Map pp604-5; ☎ 619-234-8602; Horton Plaza) and **Gaslamp 15** (Map pp604-5; ☎ 619-232-0400; 701 5th St).

Theater

There's a thriving theater culture in San Diego. Book tickets at the box office or with one of the agencies listed in the introduction to this section. Recommended venues:

La Jolla Playhouse (Map p622; ☎ 619-550-1010; www.lajollaplayhouse.com; UCSD) Classic and contemporary plays.

Old Globe Theatre (Map pp608-9; ☎ 619-234-5623; www.theoldglobe.org; Balboa Park; tickets $40-79) Three venues stage Shakespeare, classics and contemporary plays.

San Diego Repertory Theatre (Map pp604-5; ☎ 619-544-1000; www.sandiegorep.com; Lyceum Theatre, 79 Horton Plaza) Avant-garde, multicultural and a musical or two.

Classical Music & Opera

San Diego Opera (Map pp604-5; ☎ 619-533-7000; www.sdopera.com; Civic Theatre, cnr 3rd Ave & B St; tickets $29-200) This fine company presents high quality, eclectic programming under the direction of maestro Karen Keltner.

San Diego Symphony (Map pp604-5; ☎ 619-235-0804; www.sandiegosymphony.com; 750 B St; tickets $20-93) Nearly a century old, this accomplished symphony presents classical and family concerts at the Copley Symphony Hall. Starting in June, performances move to the Embarcadero Marina Park South for the lively outdoor Summer Pops season.

Sports

Petco Park (Map pp604-5; ☎ 619-795-5000, tickets 877-374-2784; www.padres.com; 100 Park Blvd; tickets $7-69) The San Diego Padres Major League Baseball team began the 2004 season in this new stadium in the middle of downtown San Diego. The season lasts from April to early October.

Qualcomm Stadium (Map p602; ☎ 619-280-2121; www.chargers.com; 9449 Friars Rd; tickets $54-98) The San Diego Chargers National Football League team plays here in Mission Valley (there's a trolley stop right in front). The season runs August through January.

SHOPPING

Souvenir hunters will find stuffed Shamus at SeaWorld, rubber snakes at the zoo or city history books at the Museum of San Diego History.

For general shopping downtown, **Westfield Horton Plaza Center** (☎ 619-239-8180; 324 Horton Plaza; 🕐 10am-9pm Mon-Fri, to 8pm Sat, 11am-7pm Sun) has the highest concentration of shops, most of them chain stores, with a multiscreen cinema, two live theaters and a variety of eateries.

The San Diego Trolley green line (or your car) takes you to each of three large malls in Mission Valley, visible just north of I-8 and bordering Hotel Circle. Furthest west is **Fashion Valley** (pp608-9 ☎ 619-688-9113; www.simon.com; 7007 Friars Rd; 🕐 10am-9pm Mon-Sat, 11am-7pm Sun), home to Tiffany & Co, Burberry, Louis Vuitton, Kiehl's, Restoration Hardware, and department stores Neiman Marcus, Saks Fifth Avenue, Macy's and Nordstrom.

Just east, **Westfield Mission Valley** (Map pp608-9; ☎ 619-296-6375; www.westfield.com/missionvalley; 1640 Camino del Rio N; 🕐 10am-9pm Mon-Sat, 11am-6pm Sun) houses upscale discount outlets, including Nordstrom Rack, as well as the Inflatable World mini-amusement parks for kids.

Hazard Center (Map pp608-9; www.hazardcenter.com; 7510-7610 Hazard Center Dr; 🕐 varies) is the smallest of the three but has a large Barnes & Noble bookstore.

The coastal communities run heavy with surf shops and bikini boutiques. Surf dudes staff the counter at **South Coast Surf Shop** (Map pp618-19; ☎ 619-223-7017; 5023 Newport Ave), a beach apparel and surf-gear shop in Ocean Beach that carries a good selection of Quiksilver, Hurley, Billabong and O'Neill for men and women. Surf chicks sell women's beachwear and accessories at sister store **South Coast Wahines** (Map pp618-19; ☎ 858-273-7600; 4500 Ocean Blvd) in Pacific Beach. For swimwear, women should head south to **Pilar's Beachwear** (Map pp618-19; ☎ 858-488-3056; 3745 Mission Blvd, Mission Beach), which has the latest styles in all sizes.

Beyond surf-related shops, you can do some antique shopping in consignment stores in the 4800–4900 blocks of Newport Ave, the main drag in Ocean Beach. For an awesome array of last minute gifts (and cool stuff for yourself), pop into **Pangaea Outpost** (Map pp618-19; ☎ 858-581-0555; 909 Garnet Ave) in Pacific Beach, where more than 60 miniboutiques and craft stores are clustered under one roof – think surf-baby tanks, hand-painted wine glasses and bright Oaxacan figurines. For jewels and couture, head to La Jolla Village.

GETTING THERE & AWAY

Air

Because of the limited length of runways, most flights into **San Diego International Airport-Lindbergh Field** (SAN; Map p602; ☎ 619-231-2100; www.san.org; 3225 N Harbor Dr) are domestic. The airport sits just 3 miles from downtown and plane-spotters will be thrilled watching planes come in over Balboa Park for landing. Coming from overseas, you'll likely change flights – and clear US Customs – at one of the major US gateway airports, such as LA, Chicago or Miami.

The standard one-way, nonstop fare between LA and San Diego was, at press time, running between $350 and $511. The flight from LA takes only about 35 minutes, but by the time you drive to the airport, check-in, clear security and board the flight you could have made the two-hour drive (except during rush hour) and saved a heck of a lot of cash. Include a stopover in Phoenix and the fare may go down to $160. To/from other US cities, flights to San Diego are generally as cheap as from LA. Most major US airlines serve San Diego, plus AeroMéxico and Air Canada.

Bus

Greyhound (Map pp604-5; ☎ 619-239-3266, 800-231-2226, Broadway Station ☎ 619-515-1100; www.greyhound.com; 120 W Broadway) serves San Diego from cities all over North America. The station has luggage lockers ($6 the first day then $8 per day) and telephones.

Buses depart frequently for LA; standard one-way/round-trip fare is $18/30 and from San Diego it takes about 2½ hours. There is a bus to Anaheim, the home of Disneyland, which runs five or six times per day for the same prices (and about the same trip duration).

Service between San Diego and San Francisco (one way/round-trip from $65/128, 11 to 13½ hours, six to eight daily) requires a transfer in LA. If traveling to Las Vegas, (one way/round-trip $50/97, nine to 11 hours, nine to 10 daily), most routes require a transfer in LA or San Bernardino.

Train

Amtrak (☎ 800-872-7245; www.amtrak.com) runs the Pacific Surfliner several times daily to Anaheim ($20, two hours), Los Angeles ($30, three hours) and Santa Barbara ($32, 5½ hours) from the historic **Santa Fe Depot** (Map pp604-5; 1050 Kettner Blvd).

GETTING AROUND

While many people get around by car (and the city's fairly easy to navigate), it's possible to enjoy an entire vacation here using buses, trolleys, and trains operated by the **Metropolitan Transit System** (MTS; ☎ 619-233-3004; www.sdcommute.com). The **Transit Store** (Map pp604-5; ☎ 619-234-1060; www.transit.511sd.com; 102 Broadway; 9am-5pm Mon-Fri) is one-stop shopping for route maps, tickets and one-/two-/three-/four-day regional Day Tripper passes ($5/9/12/15, also available at trolley stations). Day Tripper passes are good for unlimited trips on most MTS buses and trolley routes, and NCTD BREEZE buses.

To/From the Airport

Bus 992 (the *Flyer*; $2.25) runs at 10-to-15-minute intervals between the airport (stops between Terminal 1, 2 and the commuter terminal) and downtown, with stops along Broadway. Shuttle services (about $8 to $11 to downtown, $15 to $16 to Coronado) include **Super Shuttle** (☎ 800-974-8885; www.supershuttle.com) and **XPress Shuttle** (☎ 800-900-7433; www.xpressshuttle.com). Both are open 24 hours a day; make reservations a day or two ahead. A taxi to downtown from the airport costs $8 to $12.

Bicycle

Some areas around San Diego are great for biking, particularly Pacific Beach, Mission Beach, Mission Bay and Coronado.

All public buses are equipped with bike racks and will transport two-wheelers free. Inform the driver before boarding, then stow your bike on the rack on the tail end of the bus. For more information telephone ☎ 619-685-4900.

For rentals try Cheap Rentals (p620).

Boat

San Diego Harbor Excursion operates a **water taxi** (☎ 619-235-8294; www.sdhe.com; per person one way $7; 3pm-10pm) serving Harbor Island, Shelter Island, Downtown and Coronado. It also runs the hourly **Coronado Ferry** (☎ 619-234-4111; www.sdhe.com; person one way $3.50; 9am-9pm from Broadway Pier, 9:30am-9:30pm from Coronado) shuttling between Broadway Pier on the Embarcadero to the ferry landing at the northern end of Orange Ave.

Public Transportation

BUS

The MTS covers most of the metropolitan area, North County, La Jolla and the beaches. It's most convenient if you're staying downtown and not partying until the wee hours. Get a free *Regional Transit Map* from the Transit Store.

For route and fare information, call **MTS** (☎ 619-233-3004, 24hr recorded info 619-685-4900, in San Diego 511). Operators are available from 5:30am to 8:30pm Monday to Friday and 7am to 7pm Saturday and Sunday. For online route planning, visit www.sdcommute.com or www.sdm ts.com.

Fares are $2.25 for most trips; express routes cost $2.50. Exact fare is required on all buses; drivers cannot make change. Consider purchasing a day pass if you will be making numerous trips and transfers.

Useful routes to/from downtown:

Route No	Destination
3	Hillcrest, UCSD Medical Center
7	Balboa Park, Zoo
11	Hillcrest, Adams Ave Antique Row
30	Old Town, Pacific Beach, La Jolla, University Town Center
901	Coronado

Useful routes to/from Old Town:

Route No	Destination
8/9	Pacific Beach, SeaWorld
35	Ocean Beach

Car

All the big-name rental companies have desks at the airport, but lesser-known ones may be cheaper. Shop around – prices vary widely, even from day to day within the same company. All three terminals have courtesy phone banks with direct lines to a number of car-rental companies – you can call several and then get a courtesy bus to the company of your choice. Rates tend to be comparable to Los Angeles.

Check the company's policy before taking the car into Mexico.

For contact information for the big-name rental companies, see p735. Smaller, independent companies in Little Italy include **California Rent a Car** (Map pp604-5; ☎ 619-238-9999; 904 W Grape St) and **West Coast Rent a Car** (Map pp604-5; ☎ 619-544-0606; 834 W Grape St). The one-day rate for a midsize car is about $33 to $40.

Taxi

Fares are around $2.40 to start, and then are about $2.60 per mile. Some established companies:

American Cab (☎ 619-234-1111)
Orange Cab (☎ 619-291-3333; www.orangecabsandiego.com)
Yellow Cab (☎ 619-234-6161; www.driveu.com)

Train

Coaster commuter trains ($4.50 to $6) run from downtown's Santa Fe train depot (Map pp604–5) up the coast to North County, stopping in Solana Beach, Encinitas, Carlsbad and Oceanside. Before entering North County, it stops at the Old Town Transit Center and Sorrento Valley, where there are Coaster Connections throughout Torrey Pines. Buy self-validating tickets from Coaster stations. Machines accept cash, Visa, MasterCard and most debit cards, and they provide up to $10 in change for cash purchases.

There are 11 daily trains in each direction Monday to Friday; the first trains leave Oceanside at 5:18am and the Santa Fe depot at 6:33am; the last ones depart at 5:30pm and 6:46pm, respectively. On Saturday, there are four trains only, and no Sunday service unless there's a Padres home game.

For information, contact **North San Diego County Transit District** (☎ 619-233-3004, from North County 800-266-6883; www.gonctd.com) or check www.transit .511sd.com.

Trolley

San Diego's trolleys are an efficient, convenient and typically safe way to travel. They're also fun, especially for kids. The blue, orange and green routes are the city's three trolley lines. From downtown's transit center, located across the street from the Santa Fe Train Depot (see Map pp604–5), Blue Line trolleys head south to San Ysidro (last stop, just before Tijuana, Mexico) and north to Old Town Transit Center. The Green Line runs east through Mission Valley, past Fashion Valley to Qualcomm Stadium and Mission San Diego de Alcala. The Orange Line connects the Convention Center and Seaport Village with downtown, but otherwise it's more useful for commuters. There may be increased special event service during home Padres games at Petco Park and Chargers games at Qualcomm Stadium.

Trolleys run between about 4:15am and midnight at roughly 15-minute intervals during the day and half-hour intervals in the evening. The Blue Line continues limited almost-all-night service on Saturdays. Fares vary with distance but peak at $3 one way. Buy tickets at vending machines on station platforms; they are valid for two hours from the time of purchase. Machines give change up to $5. Compliance officers will jump aboard to check tickets and will write citations for those without a ticket.

On weekends, kids aged 12 and under can ride for free with each fare-paying adult.

NORTH COUNTY COAST

The North County Coast feels like summer camp: loads of outdoor activities, gorgeous natural surroundings and a laid-back approach to daily life. If there's a real emergency, the big city is less than an hour away.

'North County,' as locals call it, begins at pretty Del Mar, just north of La Jolla and Torrey Pines, and continues up the coast through Solana Beach, Encinitas and Carlsbad (home of Legoland) before hitting Oceanside, largely a bedroom community for Camp Pendleton Marine Base. The communities hug the shore and overlook fantastic beaches (with lots of good surf spots). They also offer a variety of unique attractions, including the Del Mar Racetrack, the Chopra Center and Legoland. It's also a good place to just relax on the beach.

As you drive north on Hwy 1, coastal cliffs and coves gradually give way to wide sandy shores. A constant companion is the railroad tracks, and though the trains can be distracting, they do make it easy to glide up here for a day trip. By car via I-5 in non-rush-hour traffic, Del Mar is only 20 to 30 minutes from San Diego, Oceanside 45 to 60 minutes.

Call or email the **San Diego North County Convention & Visitors Bureau** (☎ 760-745-4741, 800-848-3336; www.sandiegonorth.com; 360 N Escondido Blvd; 🕑 8:30am-5pm Mon-Fri) for a free visitors guide. On the website, look for discounts to Legoland and other attractions.

Getting There & Around

For the most scenic approach, take N Torrey Pines Rd to Del Mar. Driving north along the coast, S21 changes its name from Camino del Mar to Coast Hwy 101 to Old Hwy 101 to Carlsbad Blvd. If you're in a hurry or headed to Los Angeles, the parallel I-5 is quicker. Traffic can snarl everywhere during rush hour, however, as well as during race or fair season when heading toward the Del Mar Racetrack.

Bus 101 departs from University Towne Centre near La Jolla and follows the coastal road to Oceanside; for information call the **North County Transit District** (NCTD; ☎ 760-966-6500; www.gonctd.com). All NCTD buses and trains have bike racks. Greyhound buses stop at Oceanside and San Diego, but nowhere in between.

The NCTD also operates the *Coaster* commuter train, which originates at the Santa Fe Depot in downtown San Diego and travels north, stopping in Old Town, Solana Beach, Encinitas, Carlsbad and Oceanside. Train travel is an easy and convenient way to visit the north coast communities because most stations are right in town and close to the beach. The *Coaster* runs every 45 minutes Monday to Friday, starting at 6:30am in San Diego and 5:18am in Oceanside, and departs four times on Saturday. The fare is $4.50 to $6 one way, and tickets may be purchased with cash or credit card at ticket vending machines.

DEL MAR

pop 4500

North County's ritziest seaside suburb, Del Mar has good, if pricey, restaurants, high-end boutiques and a fabled horse-racing track that's also the site of the annual county fair in June. Downtown Del Mar (sometimes called 'the Village') extends for about a mile along Camino del Mar. 15th St crosses Camino del Mar at the tasteful Del Mar Plaza, the city's unofficial hub, where

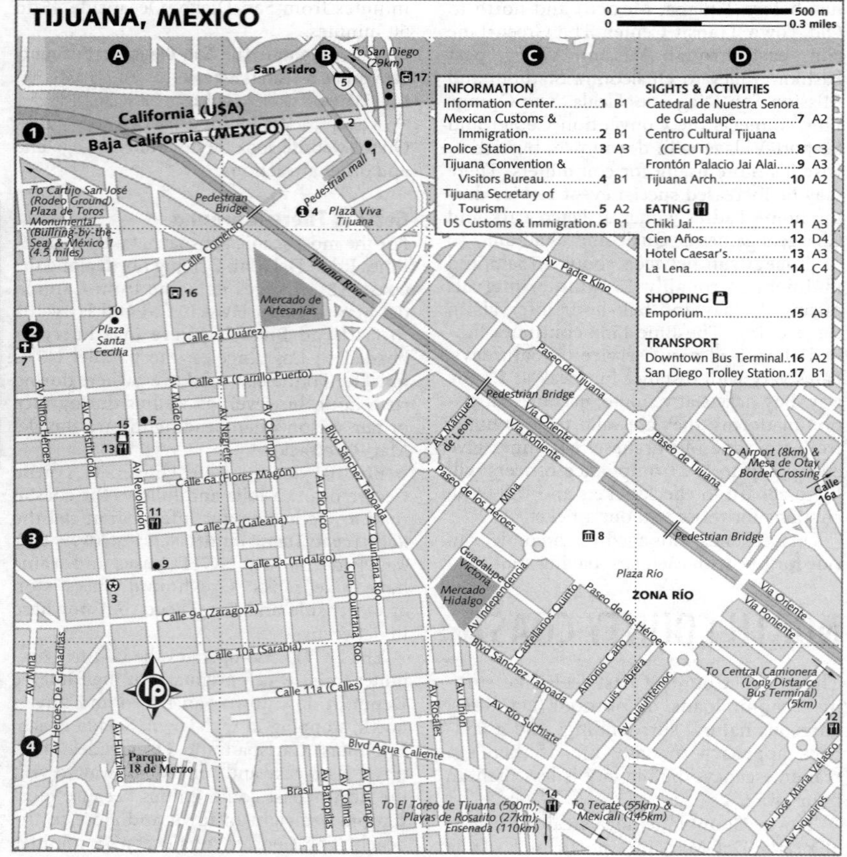

you'll find restaurants, shops and upper-level terraces that look out to sea.

Sights & Activities

At the beach end of 15th St **Seagrove Park** overlooks the ocean. Despite the occasional whooshing train on the adjacent train tracks, this little stretch of tidy beachfront lawn is a favorite gathering place for locals and a good spot for a picnic.

The **Del Mar Racetrack & Fairgrounds** (☎ 858-755-1141; www.dmtc.com; 2260 Jimmy Durante Blvd; admission $4-8) was founded in 1937 by a number of Hollywood luminaries, including Bing Crosby and Jimmy Durante. The lush gardens and pink, Mediterranean-style architecture are a visual delight. Get gussied up for the horse races, which run from mid-July to early-September.

Brightly colored hot-air balloons are a trademark of the Del Mar's northern skies. For a sunset flight, contact **California Dreamin'** (☎ 800-373-3359; www.californiadreamin.com; per person from $186).

The *Reader* (available in cafés and convenience stores) carries other balloon-company listings and frequently contains hot-air excursion discount coupons.

Sleeping

There are no real budget options available in Del Mar, at least in high season. Rates drop significantly outside summer and holiday weekends in the off-season.

TIJUANA, MEXICO

Times are tough in Tijuana. For years 'TJ' has been a cheap, convivial destination just south of the border, popular with hard-partying San Diegans, Angelenos and sailors. A recent spate of violent kidnappings and fatal shoot-outs, however, has turned once-bustling tourist areas into near ghost towns.

The government has taken steps to turn things around, but efforts haven't met with much success. Indeed, the heavy presence of armed soldiers clad in bulletproof vests tends to inspire fear, not confidence, in foreign guests. On the other hand, intrepid tourists who stay low-key (avoid flashy jewelry) will find fantastic dining experiences, great cultural attractions and an otherwise welcoming populace.

After descending from the pedestrian bridge at the border, stop by the San Ysidro Border crossing **visitor center** (☎ 011-52-664, 607-3097; www.tijuanaonline.org; 9am-6pm) for a map. Pass through the turnstile and follow the street just past the McDonald's toward the **Tijuana Arch**. After a 10-minute walk, you'll arrive at the blocks-long Av Revolution (La Revo). La Revo's once-raucous streets are decidedly light on revelers, although you'll still find plenty of souvenir shops, low-priced pharmacies and liquor stores. There's no need to change your money, as nearly all businesses accept US dollars. For a nice selection of arts and crafts – decorative mirrors, Oaxacan wood carvings, ceramics – without the hard sell, stop by **Emporium** (☎ 685-1342; Av Revolucion 1025). Nearby is the venerable but shop-worn **Hotel Caesar** (☎ 685-1606; Av Revolucion 827), where you can taste a Caesar salad at its birthplace.

For sightseeing, at the far end of Av Revolucion check out the striking **Fronton Palacio Jai Alai** (Av Revolucion), between Calle 7a and Calle 8a, which celebrated its 60th birthday in 2007. For decades this striking building hosted jai alai, a kind of hybrid between squash and lacrosse, which originated in the Basque Country in northern Spain. The building now hosts cultural events, including music and theater performances. Heading back north on Av Revolucion, rentable mariachi bands wait for work at the Plaza Santa Cecilia at the Calle 2a intersection. Just west is **Catedral de Nuestra Senora de Guadalupe** (cnr Av Ninos Heroes & Calle 2a), Tijuana's oldest church.

A short drive away is **Centro Cultural Tijuana** (CECUT; ☎ 687-9695; www.cecut.gob.mx; cnr Paseo de los Heroes & Av Independencia), a modern cultural center showcasing highbrow concerts, theater, readings, conferences and dance recitals. Inside the Centro Cultural the **Museo de las Californias** (☎ 664-687-9641/42; adult/child $2/1.50; 10am-6:30pm) provides an excellent history of Baja California from prehistoric times to the present, including the earliest Spanish expeditions, the mission period, the Treaty of Guadalupe Hidalgo, irrigation of the Colorado River and the advent of the railroad. Signage is in English.

For dining, try the paella at bright **Chiki Jai** (☎ 685-4955; Av Revolucion 1388). Thanks to its proximity to Fronton Palacio Jai Alai and its Spanish Basque seafood, this small, friendly eatery has been packed with patrons since 1947. For some of the most savory, tender beef in town, leave the tourist area for a short drive to **La Lena** (☎ 686-4752; Blvd Agua Caliente Blvd 11191, Col Aviacion; lunch & dinner), a midrange local favorite with tranquil views of the Tijuana Country Club golf course. Everything from the guacamole to the rice and beans to the tortillas is top-notch, but try the brick filet. For *alta cocina* (haute cuisine), **Cien Años** (☎ 634-7662; Av Jose Marai Velazco 1407; 8am-11pm) serves ancient Mexican recipes, some going back to the Aztecs and Mayans. No shorts, jeans or T-shirts.

An easy way to get to Tijuana is via the San Diego Trolley on the blue line, which runs from Old Town to downtown to San Ysidro ($3, about 30 minutes). From the Sam Ysidro stop, follow the pedestrian bridge mentioned above. You can also drive to the border, but it's better to leave your car on the US side. Traffic in Tijuana is frenetic, parking is competitive, and there will likely be a long wait to cross back into the States. If you do drive, buy daily Mexican car insurance at a US office on Via San Ysidro and Camino de la Plaza.

US citizens not planning to go past the border zone (ie beyond Ensenada, or 20km to 30km/12.4 miles to 18.6 miles of the border, depending on location), or planning to stay in the border zone more than 72 hours, don't need a visa. All visitors, however, must bring their passport and US visa (if needed) for re-entry to the US.

Clarion del Mar Inn (☎ 858-755-9765, 800-451-4515; www.delmarinn.com; 720 Camino del Mar; d $95, ste $110-160; P wi-fi) The floral prints, the Tudor exterior and the Victorian-style furnishings at Clarion del Mar don't exactly scream 'beach,' but this 81-room property is clean and has rooms that are slightly bigger than average, plus lots of counter space in the bathrooms. Continental breakfast is delivered to your room and afternoon tea is served in the library.

Best Western Stratford Inn (☎ 858-755-1501, 800-446-7229; www.Pacificahost.com; 710 Camino Del Mar; r $165-250; P wi-fi) The sprawling Stratford has large, handsome rooms, lots of wood in its construction, a spa and two heated pools. A few have kitchenettes and distant ocean views. If traveling with a group or big family, ask for two adjacent alcove rooms for more privacy and easy accessibility.

Eating

Pacifica Breeze Cafe (☎ 858-509-9147; 1555 Camino Del Mar; breakfast & lunch mains $8-10; breakfast & lunch) The name fits for this 2nd-floor patio bistro in Del Mar Plaza, where ocean views and light breezes accent a quintessentially SoCal menu. The light, guilt-free and ethnically diverse dishes on offer include blackened fish tacos, Thai chicken wraps and seared ahi nicoise salad.

Bully's (☎ 858-755-1660; 1404 Camino Del Mar; lunch mains $10-28, dinner $18-30; lunch & dinner) If your inner carnivore has been feeling a bit repressed in sushi-and-salad centric SoCal, let him out for a graze in this old-school chophouse, where the lights are dim, the booths deep red and the steaks never less than prime. The staff is downright accommodating, and solo diners seem to do just fine.

Jake's del Mar (☎ 858-755-2002; 1660 Coast Blvd; lunch mains $10-17, dinner $10-53; lunch Tue-Sun, dinner daily) Just north of Seagrove Park is ever-popular Jake's, exuding a clubby feel with its wood-planked ceiling, historic photos, and rich old guys enjoying seafood chowder, crusted sea bass, filets and lobster tail. Great views of kids and volleyball players on the beach. Families and couples dig the place, too.

To craft your own meal, try **Harvest Ranch Market** (☎ 858-847-0555; 1555 Camino Del Mar; 8am-9pm) in the Del Mar Plaza for high-quality groceries and sandwiches for the beach, and wine and beer for later. Check the sign outside for wine tasting times and costs.

SOLANA BEACH

pop 13,500

Solana Beach was the focus of atypically bad press in April 2008 when a wetsuit-clad swimmer died after a shark attack. Seas have been safe ever since, however, and things have returned to normal in this low-key community just north of Del Mar. Solana Beach may not be as posh as its neighbor, but it has good beaches as well as the **Cedros Design District** (Cedros Ave), a blocks-long avenue filled with home-furnishing stores, art and architecture studios, antiques shops and handcrafted-clothing boutiques. For camping and outdoor gear, stop by **Adventure 16** (☎ 858-755-7662; 143 S Cedros Ave).

Zinc Cafe (☎ 858-793-5436; 132 S Cedros Ave; mains $6-9; 7am-4pm Mon-Thu, to 5pm Fri-Sun; V) Order at the counter at all-veg café Zinc, which serves breakfasts, salads, vegetarian chili and pizza, then join yogaholics, crunchy surf dudes, and moms and babies on the shaded, sidewalk-adjacent patio.

Pizza Port (☎ 858-481-7332; 135 N Hwy 101) This branch of the popular local pizza chain is across the street from the train station.

Belly Up Tavern (☎ 858-481-8140; www.bellyup.com; 143 S Cedros Ave; tickets $5-40) This converted warehouse and bar draws regular crowds with consistently good bands, playing jazz to funk.

CARDIFF-BY-THE-SEA

pop 10,400

The stretch of restaurants, surf shops and new age–style businesses just north of Encinitas (and technically part of that city) on the Pacific Coast Hwy – called 'Cardiff' by locals – is known for its surfing and laid-back crowds.

Cardiff is also home to **San Elijo Lagoon** (☎ 760-436-3944; www.sanelijo.org), an ecological preserve (almost 1000 acres) popular with bird-watchers for herons, coots, terns, ducks, egrets and about 250 more species. Nearly 7 miles of trails lead through the area. The nature center, being rebuilt at press time, is at 2710 Manchester Ave. See the website for information about parking and nature walks on the second Saturday of the month.

At **Cardiff State Beach** (☎ 760-753-5091; www.parks.ca.gov; 7am-sunset), just south of Cardiff-by-the-Sea, the surf break on the reef is mostly popular with longboarders. Parking costs $8. A little further north, **San Elijo State Beach** has good winter waves.

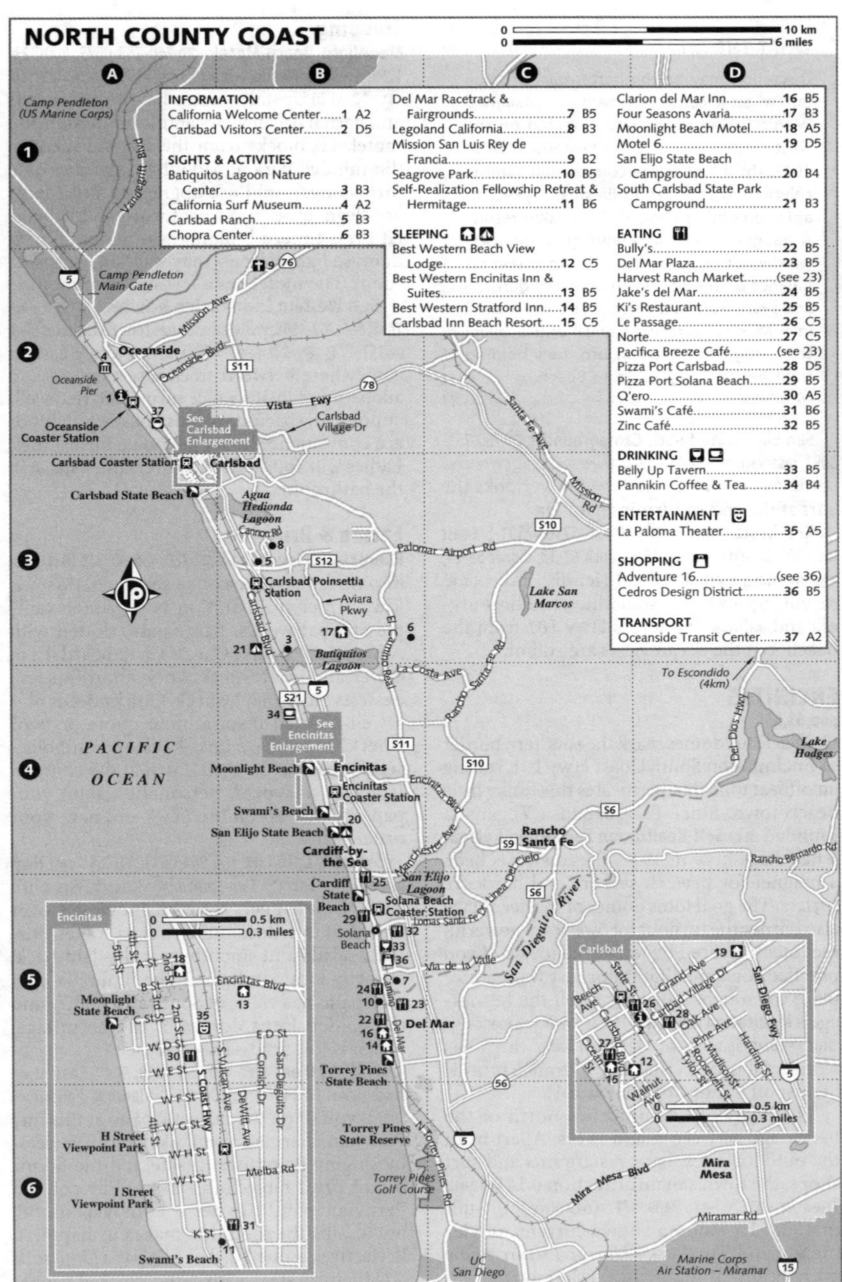

SAN DIEGO AREA

WHAT THE ...?

Discretion may be the better part of small talk when it comes to the much-maligned 'Magic Carpet Ride' statue erected on the west side of Hwy 101 at Chesterfield Dr in 2007. The intent was to commission a statue celebrating the surfing lifestyle – presumably something cool. The $120,000 result? A gangly young man with his arms awkwardly outstretched, trying to maintain his balance on the board. An object of derision and pranksters ever since, he's been draped in a Mexican wrestling mask and a bikini top. Judge for yourself, bro, he's holding tight beside San Elijo State Beach.

San Elijo State Beach Campground (☎ 760-753-5091, reservations 800-444-7275; www.parks.ca.gov, reserveamerica.com; tent/RV sites $26/39; wi-fi) Overlooks the surf at the end of Birmingham Dr.

Ki's Restaurant (☎ 760-436-5236; 2591 S Coast Hwy 101; breakfast mains $5-8, lunch $7-13, dinner $9-21; breakfast, lunch & dinner) Friendly indie café serving up awesome smoothies, healthy burgers and salads. It's across Hwy 101 from the beach, but the ocean views are still nice.

ENCINITAS

pop 63,850

Golden lotus domes mark the southern border of Encinitas on South Coast Hwy 101, setting an offbeat tone that permeates this funky little beach town. Since Paramahansa Yoganada founded his **Self-Realization Fellowship Retreat & Hermitage** here in 1937, the town has been a magnet for healers, seekers and hardcore surfers. The gold lotus domes of the hermitage also border the turnout for **Swami's**, a powerful reef break favored by territorial locals. If you practice yoga, meditation or just want a nice place to stretch your legs, stroll the hermitage's **Meditation Garden** (215 K St; www.yogananda-srf.org; 9am-5pm Tue-Sat, 11am-5pm Sun), which has wonderful ocean vistas; the entrance is on K St, just off South Coast Hwy 101.

The heart of Encinitas lies north of the hermitage between E and D Sts. Apart from the outdoor cafes, bars, restaurants and surf shops, the town's main attraction is **La Paloma Theater** (☎ 760-436-7469; 471 S Coast Hwy 101), built in 1928. La Paloma shows current movies nightly and *The Rocky Horror Picture Show* every Friday at midnight. Cash only.

Sleeping

Moonlight Beach Motel (☎ 760-753-0623, 800-323-1259; www.moonlightbeachmotel.com; 233 2nd St; r $125-160; P wi-fi) Upstairs rooms have private decks and partial ocean views at this mom-and-pop motel, 1½ blocks from the sea and the kiddie-minded park at Moonlight Beach. Some furnishings could use upgrading, but rooms are clean, quiet and have furnished kitchens. At press time, a building was going up next door, so light sleepers may want an oceanside room. The motel has a few smoking rooms.

Best Western Encinitas Inn & Suites (☎ 760-942-7455, 866-362-4648; www.bwencinitas.com; 85 Encinitas Blvd; r $157-174; P wi-fi) With an exterior caught somewhere between treehouse-modern and adobe-mission, it's a nice surprise to find well-appointed, spacious rooms boasting all modern conveniences and up-to-date furnishings. Ladies will appreciate lots of counter space in the bathroom.

Eating & Drinking

Pannikin Coffee & Tea (☎ 760-436-0033; 510 N Coast Hwy) As far as indie coffee shops go, this yellow former train station is a prime example of what works. Large patio dotted with Adirondack chairs? Check. Chalkboard list of coffee and teas? Check. Lots of muffins and desserts on display? Check. Quirky decor plus a well-planted inspirational quote or two? Check. In fact, we only have one quibble – service can get bogged down at the counter. If you're a Type-A personality, skim your paper, catch up on the news and have your order ready.

Swami's Café (☎ 760-944-0612; 1163 S Coast Hwy; mains under $10; 7am-5pm) Hunker down with surfers, new-agers and businessmen over breakfast burritos, multigrain pancakes, stir-fries, salads and smoothies at this laid-back, crunchy local landmark. The umbrella-covered patio has views of South Coast Hwy and the golden lotus domes of the hermitage, which is just across the street.

our pick **Q'ero** (☎ 760-753-9050; 564 S Coast Hwy; lunch mains $8-14, dinner $30-45; lunch & dinner Tue-Sun) If you sit on the sidewalk patio at this tiny Peruvian charmer, you'll likely hear passers-by singing its praises. Inside, red-tile floors, bright print tablecloths and boldly colored Peruvian paintings set a convivial mood, but ah, it's the food that makes us happiest. Perfectly seasoned dishes like papa *lomo saltado* (flatiron steak with garlic, cracked pepper and sautéed onions) and *aji gallina* (tender chicken in toasted walnut and chili sauce) bring out the best flavors of Peru. For lunch, try the lip-smacking *pachamanga* braised pork, a hefty portion that won't stay inside the oh-so-soft bun. And yes, 'slow food' aptly describes the cooking process, but it's well worth the wait. Make reservations for dinner.

CARLSBAD

pop 103,800

While Carlsbad may be known for Legoland, a theme park built on our love for joinable plastic blocks, it's the natural attractions here that may be the most stunning, from long, sandy beaches to a 50-acre flower field to a flora-and-fauna filled lagoon.

The community got its start when train service arrived in the 1880s, building up a solid four square block downtown rather than stretching along the highway like most North County towns. Early homesteader John Frazier, a former ship's captain, sank a well and found water with a high mineral content, supposedly identical to that of spa water in Karlsbad, Bohemia (now the Czech Republic). He built a grand spa hotel that prospered until the 1930s.

Carlsbad is bordered by I-5 and Carlsbad Blvd, which run north–south. You'll find many of the community's hotels and restaurants clustered on or near Carlsbad Village Dr, the east–west road connecting I-5 and Carlsbad Blvd.

If you're looking for Carlsbad Caverns, hop back on I-5. Those are in New Mexico.

Sights & Activities

LEGOLAND CALIFORNIA

Modeled loosely after the original in Denmark, **Legoland California** (☎ 760-918-5346; www.lego.com/legoland/california; 1 Legoland Dr; adult/child 3-12 $60/50; ⏰ 10am-5pm, varies by season; 👶) is a fantasy environment built on the backs of an army of joinable plastic building blocks. Geared toward younger kids, expect to spend most of the day here. Also, hold tight to your maps, the park is surprisingly hard to navigate, and you'll be passing plenty of confused-looking parents.

The newest themed area in the park is **Land of Adventure**, where a 16ft Pharaoh made from 300,000-plus Legos guards the new Lost Kingdom Adventure. Inside, families can laser-blast targets from a moving car. A longtime highlight includes **Miniland** (actually looking a bit worn in spots), where the skylines of major metropolitan cities have been spectacularly re-created entirely of Legos. The blinking lights and rah-rah of Mini-Las Vegas – don't miss the Lego wedding chapel and its happy Lego newlyweds – are especially entertaining. Elsewhere, many activities are geared specifically to kids, such as face painting, boat rides and scaled-down roller coasters.

Compared with some of the flashier, bigger parks nearby, like Disneyworld and SeaWorld, it's rather low-key and a bit less commercial – although there are plenty of opportunities to buy Legos.

From I-5, take the Legoland/Cannon Rd and follow the signs. From downtown Carlsbad or downtown San Diego, take the *Coaster* to the Carlsbad Village Station and hop on bus 344 straight to the park. Parking costs $10.

CARLSBAD RANCH

From early March to early May, nearly 50 acres of flower fields of **Carlsbad Ranch** (☎ 760-431-0352; http://visit.theflowerfields.com; 5704 Paseo del Norte; adult/senior/child $10/9/5; ⏰ 9am-6pm) come ablaze in a vibrant sea of carmine, saffron and snow-white ranunculus blossoms. The fields are two blocks east of I-5; take the Palomar Airport Rd exit, go east, then left on Paseo del Norte Rd.

BATIQUITOS LAGOON

One of the last remaining tidal wetlands in California, Batiquitos Lagoon separates Carlsbad from Encinitas. A self-guided tour lets you explore area plants, including the prickly pear cactus, coastal sage scrub and eucalyptus trees, as well as lagoon birds, such as the great blue heron and the snowy egret. To get to the **Nature Center** (☎ 760-931-0800; www.batiquitosfoundation.org; 7380 Gabbiano Ln; ⏰ 9am-12:30pm Mon-Fri, to 3pm Sat & Sun) follow Poinsettia Lane east past the I-5 turn and go right onto Batiquitos Dr, then turn right onto Gabbiano Lane, taking it to the end.

CHOPRA CENTER

This den of tranquility and personal empowerment offers free tea to those browsing several shelves of books by alternative-health guru Deepak Chopra and acolyte David Simon. The welcoming (but no-pressure)

DETOUR: TEMECULA

According to the menu at the Swing Inn Café, 'Temecula' was a Native American word meaning 'The Valley of Joy.' That label certainly holds true today, with tourists flocking here for weekends filled with wine tasting, gambling and a bit of Old West–style shopping.

Located in Riverside County 20 miles east of the Pacific, the area was a ranching outpost for Mission San Luis Rey in the 1820s, later becoming a stop along the Butterfield stagecoach line. But perhaps most interesting is the region's recent history. Marketing itself as a stylish wine country community, the town successfully lured newcomers with its small town charms. Perhaps too successfully. Temecula's population nearly doubled from 57,000 in 2000 to 101,000 in 2008.

Tourists come to wander five-block Front St, the heart of Old Town Temecula, where faux Old West facades front a line-up of restaurants, antique dealers and wine shops. This is motorcycle country, so don't be surprised to hear Harleys rumbling up behind you. For cheap diner-style eats check out the aforementioned **Swing Inn Cafe** (☎ 951-676-2321; 28676 Old Town Front St; ⏰ breakfast, lunch & dinner), where two eggs, two hotcakes and two strips of bacon will set you back six bucks. The hickory-smoked pork at nearby **Sweet Lumpy's BBQ** was voted best barbecue in the Inland Empire. (☎ 951-506-3747; 28464 Old Town Front St; mains $2-20; ⏰ 11am-8:30pm Tue-Fri, to 4pm Sat). As for Old Town shopping, you'll find flavored olive oils and free samples at **Temecula Olive Oil Company** (☎ 951-693-0607; 28653 Old Town Front St). Next door at **Temecula House of Jerky** (☎ 951-308-9232; 28655 Old Town Front St) look for ostrich, buffalo and venison jerky in addition to the usual teeth-pulling suspects.

Wine tasting is popular in the rolling hills about 10 minutes east of Old Town. **Wilson Creek** (☎ 951-699-9463; www.wilsoncreekwinery.com; 35960 Rancho California Rd; tastings $10; ⏰ 10am-5pm) makes almond champagne (infused with almond oil in the fermentation process) and a chocolate-infused port. Further afield, **Leonesse Cellars** (☎ 951-302-7601; www.leonessecellars.com; 38311 De Portola Rd; tastings $10; ⏰ 10am-5pm) offers award-winning Viognier and Melange des Reves, plus sweeping views from its Tutor-esque tower. For a tour, try **Grapeline Temecula** (☎ 888-894-6379; www.gogrape.com). To see Temecula by air, contact **California Dreamin'** (☎ 800-373-3359; www.californiadreamin.com) for an air balloon ride (from $168 per person).

Of course, you could just blow off the wine, jerky and balloons and head straight to California's largest casino, **Pechanga Resort & Casino** (☎ 877-711-2946; www.pechanga.com; 45000 Pechanga Pkwy) where your perception of the Valley of Joy may depend on the spin of the wheel.

center (☎ 760-494-1600; www.chopra.com; 2013 Costa del Mar Rd; ⏰ 6:30am-8pm Mon-Fri, 7:30am-6pm Sat & Sun), located on the lush grounds of La Costa Resort & Spa, offers Ayurveda-based programs and workshops (Perfect Health Program, Secrets of Enlightenment) as well as yoga classes and personal consultations.

Sleeping

South Carlsbad State Park Campground (☎ 760-438-3143, reservations 800-444-7275; www.parks.ca.gov; 7201 Carlsbad Blvd; tent & RV sites without hookups $25-35; wi-fi) Three miles south of downtown, this campground has 222 tent and RV sites and a bluff-top perch above the beach. Spots go fast; start calling seven months before your desired date.

Motel 6 (☎ 760-434-7135; www.motel6.com; 1006 Carlsbad Village Dr; r $76; P ⌘) For no-frills budget lodging not too far from the center of things, try this decent, freeway-adjacent branch of the national chain. It's pet-friendly, local calls are free, and there's a clean laundromat across the street. Wi-fi is $2.99 per day.

Best Western Beach View Lodge (☎ 760-729-1151; www.beachviewlodge.com; 3180 Carlsbad Blvd; d $167-185; P ⌘ wi-fi) An Arts and Crafts–style lobby with great ocean views welcomes guests to this small, friendly Best Western that's just across Hwy 101 (called Carlsbad Blvd here) from the beach. Three floors wrap around a small courtyard and pool. Tidy, occasionally tired, furnishings include pastel prints, sturdy mattresses and big mirrors, perfect for primping before…Legoland?

Carlsbad Inn Beach Resort (☎ 760-434-7020, 800-235-3939; www.carlsbadinn.com; 3075 Carlsbad Blvd; r from $240; ⌘ P) This faux-Tudor upper-end-tourist-class hotel and time-share property sits just across from the beach. The lobby is busy and there's a whiff of indifference in the air, but the inn's proximity to the ocean, Norte and downtown – as well as the twinkling white lights, which look welcoming at night – may balance out any negative perceptions.

Four Seasons Aviara (☎ 760-603-6800, 800-332-3442; www.fourseasons.com/aviara; 7100 Four Seasons Point; r from $415;) Cares drop away as you glide down Aviara's palm-lined drive, utterly perishing as you stroll into this flower-dotted bastion of customer service and style. Expect superb service, top-flight amenities, golf, tennis, a spa, children's activities and views of Batiquitos Lagoon. Check the website for a variety of packages. Overnight parking costs $29, and wi-fi is $10 per day.

Eating

Pizza Port (☎ 760-720-7007; 571 Carlsbad Village Dr; mains $7-20; 11am-10pm Sun-Thu, to midnight Fri & Sat;) Pizza Port is like the general store of yore, an easygoing hub where everybody seems to swing by at some point. The main draw inside this surfboard-adorned miniwarehouse are the thick, buttery, almost fluffy slices, ranging from standard pepperoni to 'anti-wimpy' gourmet pies (margherita, garlic veggie). The homebrewed beers are a plus. Even though things can get convivial, it's never out-of-hand and kids fit in with the mix. Recommended.

Norte (☎ 760-729-0903; 3003 Carlsbad Blvd; mains $9-15; lunch & dinner;) Get here early on weekends. The festive bar, patio and dining room fill fast with locals and tourists (it's also a good place for groups). Decor is classic 'cantina rah-rah' – wooden booths with green trim, a few beer flags, brightly covered patio umbrellas – but it's the big, messy plates of classic Mexican fare that keep the crowds really happy. It all looks good.

Le Passage (☎ 760-729-7097; 2961 State St; lunch mains $8-16, dinner $16-28; 7am-6pm) This welcoming country French bistro is a retreat from the ocean fray and a nice place to bump it up a notch (just a bit) from T-shirts and flip-flops. There's a rustic exposed-brick interior and cozy back patio – walk through the kitchen to get there – where guests can enjoy baked brie and lavender roasted chicken.

OCEANSIDE

pop 178,800

Just outside the giant Camp Pendleton Marine Base, Oceanside lacks the charm of Encinitas and Carlsbad, but the wide beaches and fine surf continue unabated. Amtrak, Greyhound, the *Coaster* and MTS buses stop at the **Oceanside Transit Center** (235 S Tremont St). Another crowd-getter is the **California Welcome Center** (☎ 760-721-1101, 800-350-7873; www.oceansidechamber.org, www.californiawelcomecenter.org; 928 N Coast Hwy; 9am-5pm), which has loads of brochures and coupons for local attractions, as well as maps and information about the San Diego area and the entire state.

Nearby, stretch your legs on the wooden **Oceanside Pier**, which extends 1942ft out to sea. Return to N Coast Hwy to see a history of surfing at the tiny **California Surf Museum** (☎ 760-721-6876; www.surfmuseum.org; 223 N Coast Hwy; admission donation; 10am-4pm Thu-Mon). Rotating exhibits have included a look at surfboard shapers, surf photographers and a surf-minded cartoonist.

Mission San Luis Rey de Francia (☎ 760-757-3651; www.sanluisrey.org; 4050 Mission Ave; adult/child/senior $6/4/5; 10am-4pm), lies 4 miles inland. Founded in 1798, it was the 18th of the 21 California missions and, as the largest California mission, was dubbed 'King of the Missions.' It was also the most successful in recruiting Native American converts. After the Mexican government secularized the missions, San Luis fell into ruin; only the adobe walls of the 1811 church are original. Inside, exhibits highlight work and life in the mission, with some original religious art and artifacts. Ruins of the *lavanderia* (the Luiseno Indian laundry) and mission soldiers' barracks are visible in front. From I-5, follow Hwy 76 about 4 miles east. The mission is on the left at the Rancho del Oro exit.

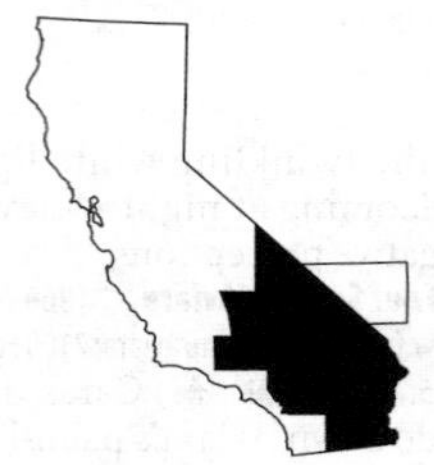

The Deserts

It's hard to believe, but over 25% of California is desert, from the lower Sonoran (aka Colorado) Desert that straddles the US-Mexico border, to the vast Mojave Desert, with its twisted forests of Joshua trees, 'singing' sand dunes and volcanic cinder cones. The Mojave is also home to the hellaciously hot Death Valley and the Rat Pack–era celeb playground of Palm Springs. Hidden fan-palm oases, rare wildlife such as bighorn sheep and desert tortoises, geological wonderlands of rocks and towering mountain summits are all protected by various national and state parks that deserve at least a week, if not a lifetime, of wandering.

For early Western explorers, such as conquistador Juan Bautista de Anza and frontier trailblazer Jedediah Smith, the desert was just a barrier to the California coast. Treasure-seeking miners also came and went, establishing now ghostly towns that died as the minerals played out, leaving their skeletons and stories scattered in the sand. Dust Bowl refugees with 'California or Bust' signs on their old jalopies braved desert crossings along Route 66 during the 1930s Great Depression. Military bases took over after WWII, when General Patton rolled tanks and trained troops in the Mojave. At high-tech aerospace testing grounds, the sound barrier was first broken by Chuck Yeager in 1947 – and records are still set here today.

Visit the deserts in spring when wildflowers bloom, or during the cooler fall months. In summer the crazy heat peaks above 120°F. Temperatures commonly drop below freezing on winter nights, when snow-covered Joshua trees, palms and cacti are not unheard of, even on the desert floor.

HIGHLIGHTS

- **Most vertiginous views** Ascend through five distinct life zones in under 15 minutes aboard the Palm Springs Aerial Tramway (p651)
- **Wildest history lesson** Poke around miners' ghost towns and hark to Old West pioneer disaster stories in Death Valley National Park (p680)
- **Coolest rock-and-roll adventure** Go boulder hopping around the 'Wonderland of Rocks' at Joshua Tree National Park (p664)
- **Most far-out trip** Hunt rare elephant trees and scramble around the wind caves of vast Anza-Borrego Desert State Park (p669)
- **Best place to find solitude** Hide out at Hole-in-the-Wall in the forgotten Mojave National Preserve (p678)

PALM SPRINGS & COACHELLA VALLEY

The Rat Pack is back, baby, or at least its hangout is. In the 1950s and '60s, Palm Springs, some 100 miles east of LA, was the swinging getaway of Sinatra, Elvis and dozens of other stars, partying the night away in Mid-Century Modern estate homes. Once the Rat Pack packed it in, the 300-sq-mile Coachella Valley swarmed with retirees in golf clothing. That is, until the mid-1990s, when a new generation fell in love with the city's retro-chic charms: steel-and-glass bungalows, boutique hotels with vintage decor and kidney-shaped pools, and piano bars serving perfect martinis. In today's PS, elderly denizens mix amicably with younger hipsters and an active gay and lesbian community. Around here, you can hike palm-oasis canyons or snowshoe high into the mountains (or both in the same day), hunt down Mid-Century Modern architecture, sample a date milkshake, tour a windmill or straddle a fault line.

HISTORY

For over 1000 years, Cahuilla (ka-*wee*-ya) tribespeople occupied canyons on the southwest edge of the Coachella Valley, where streams flowed from the San Jacinto Mountains. Early Spanish explorers called the hot springs where the city now stands *agua caliente* (hot water), which later was used to refer to the local Cahuilla band.

In 1876 the federal government divided the valley into a checkerboard. The Southern Pacific Railroad received odd-numbered sections, while the even-numbered sections were given to the Agua Caliente as their reservation. But boundaries were not established until the 1940s – and by then much of the Native American land had been built on. Some local tribes today are quite wealthy, because they own the valley's casinos.

The town of Indio, about 20 miles southeast of Palm Springs, began as a railway construction camp and its artesian water was tapped to irrigate crops. Date palms were imported from French-held Algeria in 1890 and have become the valley's major crop, along with citrus fruit and table grapes.

FAST FACTS

Population of Palm Springs 46,900

Average temperature low/high in Palm Springs January 43/70°F, July 76/108°F

Los Angeles to Palm Springs 110 miles, two to three hours

San Diego to Borrego Springs 95 miles, 1½ to two hours

San Francisco to Barstow 415 miles, 6½ to seven hours

ORIENTATION

At the northwest edge of the Coachella Valley, downtown Palm Springs is compact. Traffic goes south on Palm Canyon Dr (Hwy 111) and north on parallel Indian Canyon Dr. Tahquitz Canyon Way, dividing addresses north from south, heads east to Palm Springs' airport. Southeast of the city, Hwy 111 continues into commercial Cathedral City and tony 'Down Valley' towns – Rancho Mirage, Palm Desert, Indian Wells and La Quinta – which boast world-class golf resorts, ritzy shopping and aristocratic retirement homes. Visiting the valley, it's often quicker to take I-10, then cut over on roads named for Frank Sinatra, Bob Hope, Gerald Ford, Dinah Shore and the like, than to follow Hwy 111 through miles of suburbs and dozens of traffic lights.

INFORMATION

High season is October to April, but Palm Springs (population 46,900, elevation 487ft) stays reasonably busy even in summer, when hotel rates drop and temperatures spike above 100°F. Between June and August, many businesses keep shorter hours or even close, so call ahead to check.

Anderson Travel (Map p654; ☎ 760-325-2001; 700 E Tahquitz Canyon Way; 🕓 8:30am-5pm Mon-Fri) AmEx representative for foreign-currency exchange.

Desert Regional Medical Center (Map p654; ☎ 760-323-6511, emergency room 760-323-6251; 1150 N Indian Canyon Dr; 🕓 24hr)

Palm Springs Koffi (Map p654; ☎ 760-416-2244; 515 N Palm Canyon Dr; 🕓 5:30am-8pm) Free wi-fi.

Palm Springs Official Visitors Center (Map pp652-3; ☎ 760-778-8418, 800-347-7746; www.palm-springs.org; 2901 N Palm Canyon Dr; 🕓 9am-5pm) North of downtown, the city's main visitor center books hotels, offers specialty tourism guides (mobility-impaired, gay and lesbian, architecture etc) and sells maps. It's inside a 1965 Albert Frey–designed gas station with a landmark design.

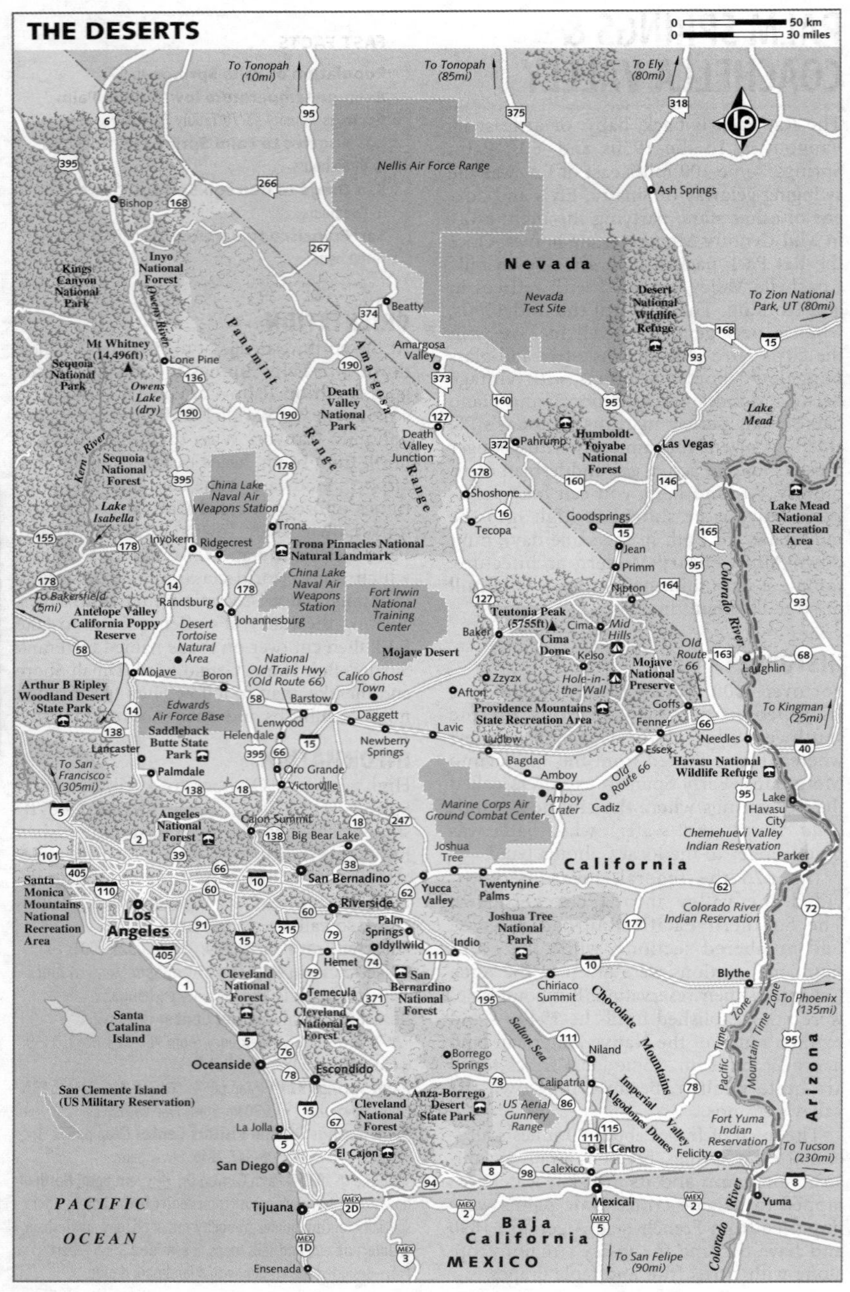
THE DESERTS
0 50 km
0 30 miles
To Tonopah (10mi)
To Tonopah (85mi)
To Ely (80mi)
Nellis Air Force Range
Ash Springs
Bishop
Nevada
Nevada Test Site
Desert National Wildlife Refuge
To Zion National Park, UT (80mi)
Kings Canyon National Park
Inyo National Forest
Owens River
Beatty
Panamint
Amargosa Valley
Mt Whitney (14,496ft)
Lone Pine
Sequoia National Park
Owens Lake (dry)
Death Valley National Park
Amargosa
Range
Death Valley Junction
Pahrump
Humboldt-Toiyabe National Forest
Las Vegas
Lake Mead
Kern River
Sequoia National Forest
China Lake Naval Air Weapons Station
Shoshone
Tecopa
Goodsprings
Lake Mead National Recreation Area
Lake Isabella
Trona
Jean
Inyokern
Ridgecrest
Trona Pinnacles National Natural Landmark
Primm
China Lake Naval Air Weapons Station
Colorado River
To Bakersfield (5mi)
Randsburg
Johannesburg
Fort Irwin National Training Center
Nipton
Antelope Valley California Poppy Reserve
Desert Tortoise Natural Area
Teutonia Peak (5755ft)
Baker
Cima
Mid Hills
Cima Dome
Kelso
Mojave Desert
Mojave National Preserve
Old Route 66
Laughlin
Mojave
Boron
National Old Trails Hwy (Old Route 66)
Calico Ghost Town
Zzyzx
Hole-in-the-Wall
Arthur B Ripley Woodland Desert State Park
Edwards Air Force Base
Barstow
Afton
Providence Mountains State Recreation Area
Goffs
To Kingman (25mi)
Lenwood
Daggett
Fenner
Saddleback Butte State Park
Helendale
Newberry Springs
Lavic
Ludlow
Needles
Lancaster
Essex
To San Francisco (305mi)
Palmdale
Oro Grande
Bagdad
Havasu National Wildlife Refuge
Victorville
Amboy
Old Route 66
Amboy Crater
Cadiz
Lake Havasu City
Angeles National Forest
Cajon Summit
Marine Corps Air Ground Combat Center
Chemehuevi Valley Indian Reservation
Big Bear Lake
Joshua Tree
Parker
California
Santa Monica Mountains National Recreation Area
San Bernadino
Yucca Valley
Twentynine Palms
Los Angeles
Riverside
Colorado River Indian Reservation
Palm Springs
Joshua Tree National Park
Idyllwild
Indio
Hemet
San Bernardino National Forest
Blythe
Cleveland National Forest
Temecula
Chiriaco Summit
Chocolate Mountains
To Phoenix (135mi)
Pacific Time Zone
Mountain Time Zone
Santa Catalina Island
Cleveland National Forest
Salton Sea
Niland
Oceanside
Borrego Springs
Escondido
Calipatria
Imperial Valley
Arizona
San Clemente Island (US Military Reservation)
Anza-Borrego Desert State Park
Cleveland National Forest
US Aerial Gunnery Range
Algodones Dunes
Fort Yuma Indian Reservation
La Jolla
El Cajon
El Centro
Felicity
To Tucson (230mi)
San Diego
Calexico
Yuma
PACIFIC OCEAN
Tijuana
Mexicali
Colorado River
Baja California
MEXICO
To San Felipe (90mi)
Ensenada

THE DESERTS

Palm Springs Police (☎ 760-323-8116) For non-emergency situations.

Palm Springs Post Office (Map p654; ☎ 800-275-8777; 333 E Amado Rd; 8am-5pm Mon-Fri, 9am-3pm Sat)

Palm Springs Public Library (Map p654; ☎ 760-322-7323; www.palmspringslibrary.org; 300 S Sunrise Way; 9am-8pm Mon & Tue, 9am-5:30pm Wed, Thu & Sat, 10am-5:30pm Fri) Free wi-fi and walk-in internet-access terminals.

SIGHTS

Many of the most fascinating attractions are not in downtown Palm Springs, but spread out across the Coachella Valley.

Palm Springs Aerial Tramway

A highlight of any Palm Springs getaway, this revolving **cable car** (Map pp652-3; ☎ 760-325-1391, 888-515-8726; www.pstramway.com; 1 Tramway Rd; round-trip adult/child $22.25/15.25, after 3pm $19.25/$12.25; departures 10am-8pm Mon-Fri, 8am-8pm Sat & Sun, last tram back down 9:45pm;) climbs nearly 6000 vertical feet through five different vegetation zones, from the Sonoran desert floor into the San Jacinto Mountains, in less than 15 minutes. It's 30°F to 40°F cooler as you step out into pine forests at the top, so bring warm clothing – the 2.5-mile ascent is said to be the temperature equivalent of driving from Mexico to Canada. It takes about three hours to park, ride the tram and take a leisurely stroll around the top.

The **Mountain Station** (8516ft), at the top of the tramway, has a bar, a cafeteria, an observation area and a theater that shows documentary films. The views from the restaurant are brilliant, but the food less so. Outside, check out the **Winter Adventure Center** (10am-4pm Thu, Fri & Mon, 8am-4pm Sat & Sun, snow conditions permitting) to rent snowshoes ($18) and purchase cross-country ski packages ($21) for both children and adults.

At **Mt San Jacinto State Park** (☎ 951-659-2607; www.parks.ca.gov) there are 54 miles of hiking trails, including a nontechnical route up San Jacinto Peak (10,834ft). Anyone heading into the backcountry (whether for overnight camping or even just for a few hours of hiking) must self-register for a wilderness permit at **Long Valley Ranger Station**, which is a 10-minute walk downhill from the Mountain Station. Before heading out, though, ask about trail conditions at the state park's visitors information center, inside the Mountain Station. Here you'll find books, maps and nature-themed gifts.

Living Desert Zoo & Gardens

This amazing, wide-open **zoo** (Map pp652-3; ☎ 760-346-5694; www.livingdesert.org; 47900 Portola Ave, Palm Desert; adult/child $12/7.50, in summer $9/5; 8am-1:30pm (last entry 1pm) mid-Jun–Aug, 9am-5pm (last entry 4pm) Sep–mid-Jun;) shows off a variety of desert plants and animals, along with exhibits on desert geology and Native American culture. Highlights include a walk-through wildlife hospital and an African-themed village with a fair-trade market and storytelling grove. Bring hiking shoes to explore miles of wilderness trails out back. Overnight 'Starry Safaris' are pitched at families.

The zoo is about a 30-minute drive southeast of Palm Springs.

Indian Canyons

Streams flowing from the San Jacinto Mountains sustain a rich variety of plants in oases around Palm Springs. Home to Native American communities for hundreds of years and now part of the Agua Caliente Indian Reservation, these **canyons** (Map pp652-3; ☎ 760-323-6018; www.indian-canyons.com; adult/child $8/4, incl 1½hr guided hike $11/6; 8am-5pm daily Oct-Jun, 8am-5pm Fri-Sun Jul-Sep) are a delight to hike, shaded by fan palms and surrounded by towering cliffs.

From downtown Palm Springs, head south on Palm Canyon Dr (continue straight when the main road turns east) for about 2 miles to the reservation entrance. From here, it's 3 miles up to the Trading Post, which sells hats, maps, water and knickknacks. Trail posts at the entrance to each canyon have maps and hiking info.

Closest to the entrance gate is **Andreas Canyon**, with a pleasant picnic area. Nearby are imposing rock formations where you can find Native American mortar holes, used for grinding seeds, and some rock art. The trail up the canyon is an easy walk. About a 20-minute walk south from Andreas Canyon is **Murray Canyon**, which can't be reached by road and is therefore less visited. It's a good place for bird-watching, and bighorn sheep might be seen on the slopes above the canyon. At the end of the winding access road is 15-mile-long **Palm Canyon**, the most extensive canyon, with hardier trails. In the morning, look for animal tracks in the sandy patches.

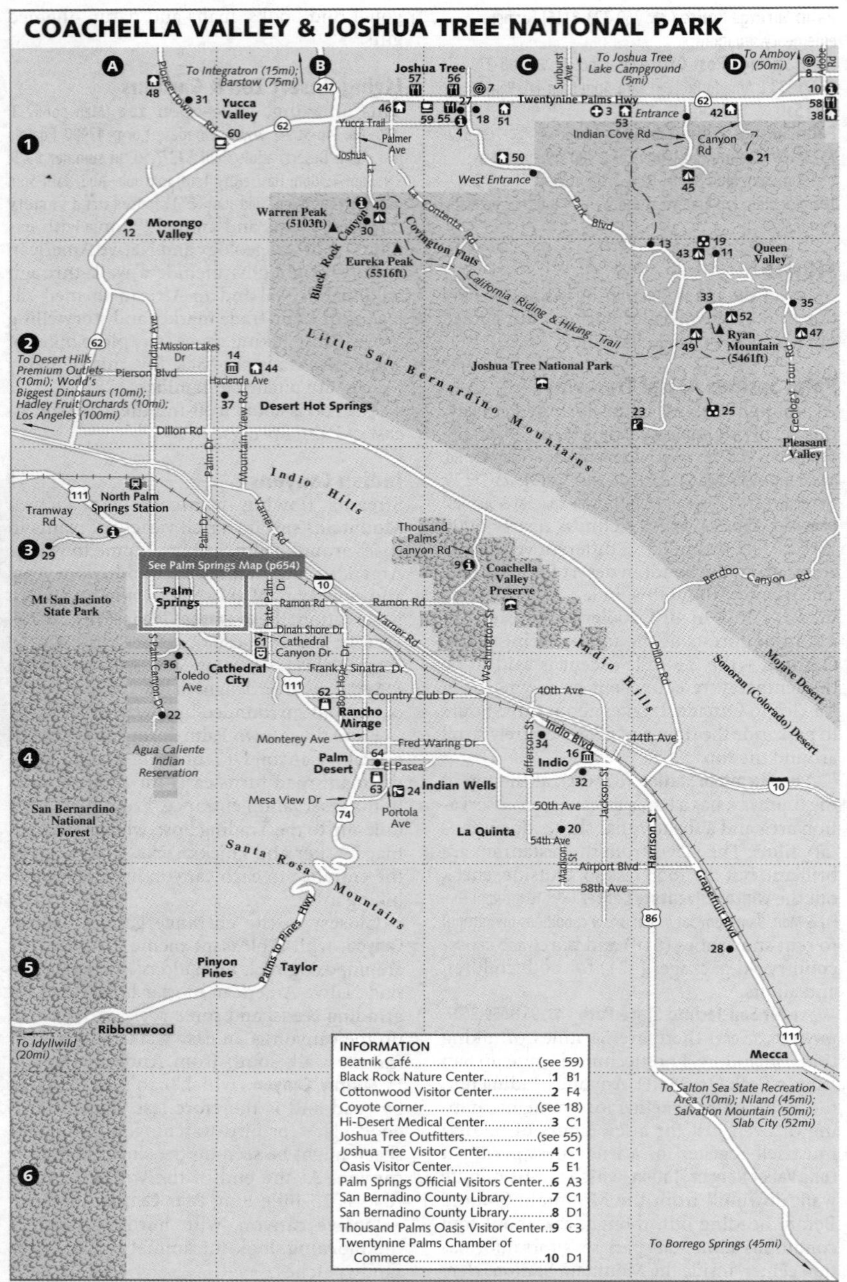
COACHELLA VALLEY & JOSHUA TREE NATIONAL PARK
To Integratron (15mi); Barstow (75mi)
Joshua Tree
To Joshua Tree Lake Campground (5mi)
To Amboy (50mi)
Yucca Valley
Twentynine Palms Hwy
Yucca Trail
Palmer Ave
Indian Cove Rd
Canyon Rd
West Entrance
Entrance
Warren Peak (5103ft)
Eureka Peak (5516ft)
Black Rock Canyon
La Contenta Rd
Covington Flats
California Riding & Hiking Trail
Park Blvd
Queen Valley
Ryan Mountain (5461ft)
Geology Tour Rd
Pleasant Valley
Morongo Valley
Pioneertown Rd
Little San Bernardino Mountains
Joshua Tree National Park
To Desert Hills Premium Outlets (10mi); World's Biggest Dinosaurs (10mi); Hadley Fruit Orchards (10mi); Los Angeles (100mi)
Mission Lakes Dr
Pierson Blvd
Hacienda Ave
Indian Ave
Desert Hot Springs
Dillon Rd
Palm Dr
Mountain View Rd
Indio Hills
North Palm Springs Station
Tramway Rd
Varner Rd
Thousand Palms Canyon Rd
Coachella Valley Preserve
Berdoo Canyon Rd
See Palm Springs Map (p654)
Mt San Jacinto State Park
Palm Springs
Ramon Rd
Date Palm Dr
Dinah Shore Dr
Cathedral Canyon Dr
Frank Sinatra Dr
Washington St
Dillon Rd
Mojave Desert
Sonoran (Colorado) Desert
S Palm Canyon Dr
Toledo Ave
Cathedral City
Bob Hope Dr
Country Club Dr
Rancho Mirage
40th Ave
44th Ave
Indio Blvd
Agua Caliente Indian Reservation
Monterey Ave
Fred Waring Dr
Palm Desert
El Paseo
Indian Wells
Indio
Jefferson St
Jackson St
Mesa View Dr
Portola Ave
50th Ave
San Bernardino National Forest
La Quinta
54th Ave
Madison St
Harrison St
Airport Blvd
58th Ave
Grapefruit Blvd
Santa Rosa Mountains
Palms to Pines Hwy
Pinyon Pines
Taylor
Ribbonwood
To Idyllwild (20mi)
Mecca
To Salton Sea State Recreation Area (10mi); Niland (45mi); Salvation Mountain (50mi); Slab City (52mi)
To Borrego Springs (45mi)
INFORMATION
Beatnik Café....(see 59)
Black Rock Nature Center....1 B1
Cottonwood Visitor Center....2 F4
Coyote Corner....(see 18)
Hi-Desert Medical Center....3 C1
Joshua Tree Outfitters....(see 55)
Joshua Tree Visitor Center....4 C1
Oasis Visitor Center....5 E1
Palm Springs Official Visitors Center...6 A3
San Bernadino County Library....7 C1
San Bernadino County Library....8 D1
Thousand Palms Oasis Visitor Center..9 C3
Twentynine Palms Chamber of Commerce....10 D1

THE DESERTS

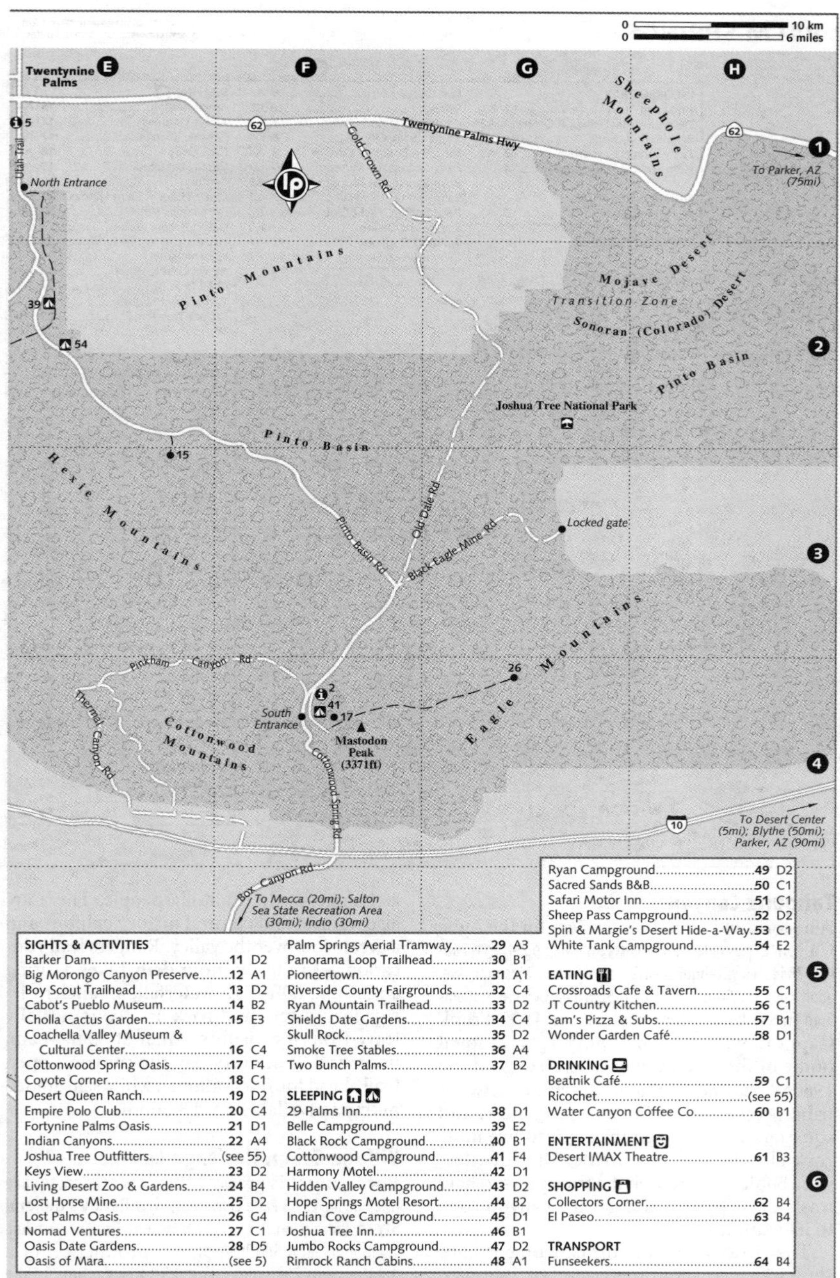
0 10 km
0 6 miles
E
F
G
H
Twentynine Palms
5
Utah Trail
North Entrance
62
Twentynine Palms Hwy
Gold Crown Rd
Sheephole Mountains
To Parker, AZ (75mi)
1
Pinto Mountains
39
54
Mojave Desert
Transition Zone
Sonoran (Colorado) Desert
2
Pinto Basin
Joshua Tree National Park
Pinto Basin
15
Hexie Mountains
Old Dale Rd
Pinto Basin Rd
Black Eagle Mine Rd
Locked gate
3
Eagle Mountains
Pinkham Canyon Rd
Thermal Canyon Rd
26
2
41
17
South Entrance
Cottonwood Mountains
Mastodon Peak (3371ft)
Cottonwood Spring Rd
4
10
To Desert Center (5mi); Blythe (50mi); Parker, AZ (90mi)
Box Canyon Rd
To Mecca (20mi); Salton Sea State Recreation Area (30mi); Indio (30mi)
5
6
SIGHTS & ACTIVITIES
Barker Dam 11 D2
Big Morongo Canyon Preserve 12 A1
Boy Scout Trailhead 13 D2
Cabot's Pueblo Museum 14 B2
Cholla Cactus Garden 15 E3
Coachella Valley Museum & Cultural Center 16 C4
Cottonwood Spring Oasis 17 F4
Coyote Corner 18 C1
Desert Queen Ranch 19 D2
Empire Polo Club 20 C4
Fortynine Palms Oasis 21 D1
Indian Canyons 22 A4
Joshua Tree Outfitters (see 55)
Keys View 23 D2
Living Desert Zoo & Gardens 24 B4
Lost Horse Mine 25 D2
Lost Palms Oasis 26 G4
Nomad Ventures 27 C1
Oasis Date Gardens 28 D5
Oasis of Mara (see 5)
Palm Springs Aerial Tramway 29 A3
Panorama Loop Trailhead 30 B1
Pioneertown 31 A1
Riverside County Fairgrounds 32 C4
Ryan Mountain Trailhead 33 D2
Shields Date Gardens 34 C4
Skull Rock 35 D2
Smoke Tree Stables 36 A4
Two Bunch Palms 37 B2
SLEEPING
29 Palms Inn 38 D1
Belle Campground 39 E2
Black Rock Campground 40 B1
Cottonwood Campground 41 F4
Harmony Motel 42 D1
Hidden Valley Campground 43 D2
Hope Springs Motel Resort 44 B2
Indian Cove Campground 45 D1
Joshua Tree Inn 46 B1
Jumbo Rocks Campground 47 D2
Rimrock Ranch Cabins 48 A1
Ryan Campground 49 D2
Sacred Sands B&B 50 C1
Safari Motor Inn 51 C1
Sheep Pass Campground 52 D2
Spin & Margie's Desert Hide-a-Way 53 C1
White Tank Campground 54 E2
EATING
Crossroads Cafe & Tavern 55 C1
JT Country Kitchen 56 C1
Sam's Pizza & Subs 57 B1
Wonder Garden Café 58 D1
DRINKING
Beatnik Café 59 C1
Ricochet (see 55)
Water Canyon Coffee Co 60 B1
ENTERTAINMENT
Desert IMAX Theatre 61 B3
SHOPPING
Collectors Corner 62 B4
El Paseo 63 B4
TRANSPORT
Funseekers 64 B4

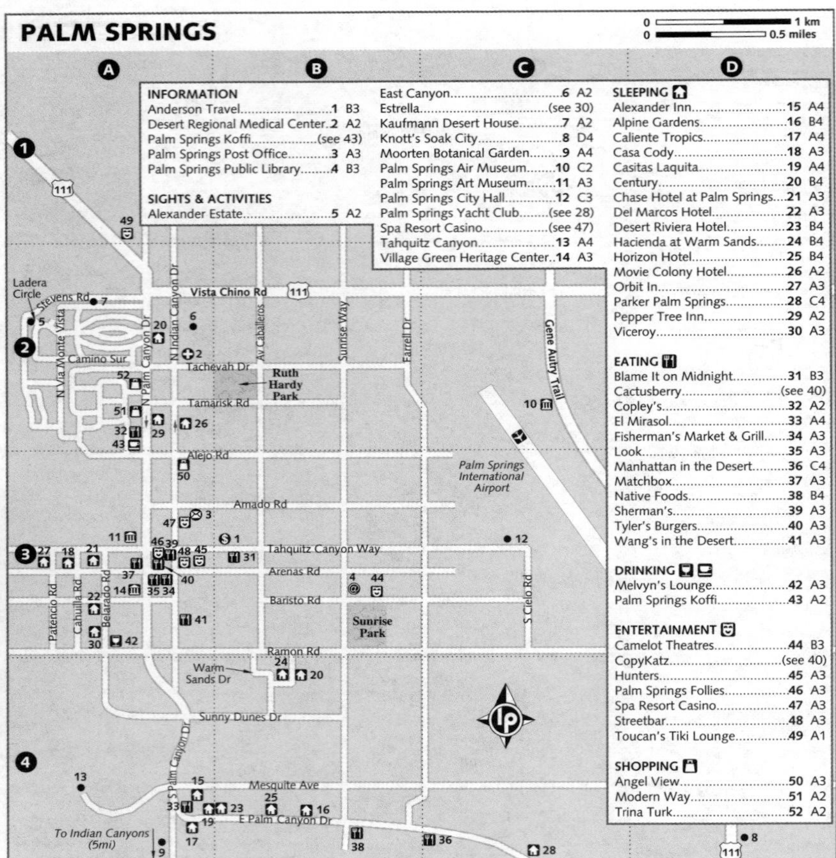

Tahquitz Canyon

A historic and sacred centerpiece for the Agua Caliente people, this **canyon** (Map p654; ☎ 760-416-7044; www.tahquitzcanyon.com; 500 W Mesquite Ave; adult/child $12.50/6; 7:30am-5pm daily Oct-Jun, 7:30am-5pm Fri-Sun Jul-Sep) featured in the 1937 Frank Capra movie *Lost Horizon*. The traditional home of the Agua Caliente ancestors, in the 1960s it became a point of contention between tribespeople, law-enforcement agencies and squatters who claimed the right to live in its rock alcoves and caves. After the squatters were booted out, it took the tribe years to haul trash, erase graffiti and get the canyon back to its natural state.

The visitors center at the canyon entrance shows a video about the legend of Tahquitz, a shaman of the Cahuilla people. There are also natural and cultural history exhibits and a great view over the valley. Rangers lead educational 2-mile, 2½-hour daily hikes, visiting a seasonal 60ft-high waterfall, an ancient irrigation system and rock art. Tours usually leave from the visitors center at 8am, 10am, noon and 2pm every day the canyon's open (call ahead for reservations), while self-guided hiking is available until 3:30pm.

Village Green Heritage Center

Bordering this grassy little downtown **square** (Map p654; 221 S Palm Canyon Dr) are **Ruddy's General Store** (admission 95¢; 10am-4pm Thu-Sun Oct-Jun, 10am-4pm Sat & Sun Jul-Sep), a reproduction of a 1930s general store; the 1884 **McCallum Adobe**

(☎ 760-323-8297; www.palmspringshistoricalsociety.com; admission $1; 10am-4pm Thu-Sat, noon-3pm Wed & Sun mid-Oct–May), a historical museum inhabiting Palm Springs' oldest building; and the **Agua Caliente Cultural Museum** (☎ 760-778-1079; www.accmuseum.org; admission free; 10am-5pm Wed-Sat, noon-5pm Sun mid-Sep–mid-May, 10am-5pm Fri & Sat, noon-5pm Sun mid-May–mid-Sep), which has exhibits on the tribe's history.

Palm Springs Art Museum

This lynchpin downtown **museum** (Map p654; ☎ 760-322-4800; www.psmuseum.org; 101 Museum Dr; adult/child $12.50/5, free 4-8pm Thu; 10am-5pm Tue, Wed & Fri-Sun, noon-8pm Thu) has a worthy mid-20th-century and contemporary art collection, with standout pieces of pre-Columbian and Native American art. Outside is a sculpture garden with desert plants. Recently, the quality of temporary exhibits has greatly improved, especially of photography and design. Check schedules of musical performances, films and lectures.

Palm Springs Air Museum

Adjacent to the airport, this **museum** (Map p654; ☎ 760-778-6262; www.palmspringsairmuseum.org; 745 N Gene Autry Trail; adult/child $10/5; 10am-5pm, last entry 4pm;) has an exceptional collection of WWII aircraft and flight memorabilia, a movie theater and occasional flying demonstrations.

Moorten Botanical Garden

This plant **collection** (Map p654; ☎ 760-327-6555; 1701 S Palm Canyon Dr; adult/child $3/1.50; 9am-4:30pm Mon, Tue & Thu-Sat, 10am-4pm Sun) packs some 3000 specimens of cacti, succulents and other desert flora into a small lot south of town. Founded in 1938, the garden became the life's passion of Chester 'Cactus Slim' Moorten, one of the original Keystone Cops, and his wife Patricia; today their son Clark, an expert on low-water vegetation, curates the garden.

Coachella Valley Preserve

You can wander atop the San Andreas Fault and wind through the Thousand Palms Oasis, passing dozens of native desert flora species along the way, at this **preserve** (Map pp652-3; ☎ 760-343-2733; http://coachellavalleypreserve.org; admission free; Thousand Palms Canyon Rd; sunrise-sunset Sep-Jun, 5am-10am Jul & Aug), which also protects the habitat of the endangered fringe-toed lizard. The Thousand Palms Oasis Visitor Center is a 25-minute drive east of downtown Palm Springs, north of I-10 (exit at Ramon Rd).

PALM SPRINGS MODERN

In the mid-20th century, a generation of architects – William F Cody, Albert Frey, Richard Neutra, E Stewart Williams, Donald Wexler, William Krisel and others – used Palm Springs as a modern design testing ground for innovative forms and building techniques that are now commonplace: long overhangs and flying roofs to protect from the sun, rail-thin supports, clerestory windows and easy transitions between indoors and out. Meanwhile, stars like Sinatra, Elvis, Liberace and their hip, stylin' 1960s Rat Pack–era contemporaries strove to outdo each other with their homes, fueling (and financing) an architectural revolution. In the mid-1990s, fashion photographers rediscovered these Mid-Century Modern architectural treasures, which led to a second boom, this time in restoration. Some of these gems have become hotels, including the Orbit In (p658), Del Marcos Hotel (p657) and Horizon Hotel (p658). Here are some more easily visible public buildings to get you started on a DIY tour:

- **Tramway Gas Station** – now Palm Springs' visitors center (p649)
- **Kaufmann Desert House** (Map p654; 470 W Vista Chino Rd)
- **Alexander Estate** (Map p654; ☎ 760-322-1192; www.elvishoneymoon.com; 1350 Ladera Circle; tours $25-35; tours 1pm Mon-Fri, by reservation Sat & Sun) Tour 'Elvis' Honeymoon Hideaway.'
- **Trina Turk** (p661)
- **Palm Springs City Hall** (Map p654; 3200 E Tahquitz Canyon Way)

For a more in-depth look, take a guided architectural tour (p657), or pick up *A Map of Palm Springs Modern* ($5), published by the **Palm Springs Modern Committee** (www.psmodcom.com) and also sold at the visitors center.

SPA ME, BABY

Palm Springs and 'Down Valley' towns have dozens of sumptuous spas. North of I-10, **Desert Hot Springs** (Map pp652-3; ☎ 760-329-6403; www.deserthotsprings.com) offers cheaper spa pools at newly hip-again hotels atop those namesake springs. Wherever you go, make reservations first.

- **East Canyon** (Map p654; ☎ 760-320-1928; www.eastcanyonps.com; 288 E Camino Monte Vista) Palm Springs' only exclusively gay spa.
- **Estrella** (Map p654; ☎ 760-320-4117; www.viceroypalmsprings.com; 415 S Belardo Rd) Swanky hotel spa for massages in poolside cabanas.
- **Palm Springs Yacht Club** (Map p654; ☎ 760-770-5000; www.theparkerpalmsprings.com; 4200 E Palm Canyon Dr) Ritzy, glitzy and a fave of society ladies and celebs.
- **Spa Resort Casino** (Map p654; ☎ 760-778-1772, 888-999-1995; www.sparesortcasino.com; 100 N Indian Canyon Dr) Try a 'taking of the waters' course through the valley's original hot springs.
- **Two Bunch Palms** (Map pp652-3; ☎ 760-329-8791; www.twobunchpalms.com; 67425 Two Bunch Palms Trail, Desert Hot Springs) Tim Robbins famously soaked in the mud baths here in *The Player*.

Cabot's Pueblo Museum

Inside a rambling 1913 adobe house built by Cabot Yerxa, a wealthy East Coaster who traded high society for the solitude of the desert, this quirky **museum** (Map pp652-3; ☎ 760-329-7610; www.cabotsmuseum.org; 67616 E Desert Ave, at Miracle Hill, Desert Hot Springs; tour adult/child $8/6; ⏲ usually 10am-3pm Sat Oct-May) displays Native American basketry and pottery, and a photo collection from Cabot's turn-of-the-century travels to Alaska. It's a fantastical story told at an eclectic venue. Call ahead to confirm tour schedules.

ACTIVITIES

Swimming

On a hot day, kids go nuts at **Knott's Soak City** (Map p654; ☎ 760-327-0499; www.knotts.com/soakcity/ps; 1500 S Gene Autry Trail; adult before/after 3pm $30/20, child $32; ⏲ mid-Mar–Sep; 🚸), a water park with an 800,000-gallon wave pool, towering water slides and tubes rides. Parking costs $8. Call for opening hours.

Golf

Golf is huge here, with more than 100 public, semiprivate, private and resort golf courses in the Coachella Valley (greens fees from $155). Some efforts are being made to reduce the million gallons of water per day used to irrigate the courses, but even so, it's far from ecofriendly in the desert. **Stand By Golf** (☎ 760-321-2665; www.standbygolf.com) books tee times for discounted same-day or next-day play at a few dozen courses around the valley.

Hiking, Skiing & Snowshoeing

For hiking in summer, and snowshoeing and cross-country skiing in winter, ride the **Palm Springs Aerial Tramway** (p651) up to Mt San Jacinto State Park. For snowshoeing tours, contact **Trail Discovery/Desert Safari Outdoor Guide Service** (☎ 760-325-4453; www.palmspringshiking.com; tours from $75), whose interpretive guides also lead moonlight hikes overlooking the Salton Sea (p668).

For desert hikes near downtown Palm Springs, check out **Indian Canyons** (p651) and **Tahquitz Canyon** (p654). More wilderness hikes, including along stretches of the Pacific Crest Trail, are accessible from the **Palms to Pines Highway** (see the boxed text, p663).

Horse Riding

Near Indian Canyons, **Smoke Tree Stables** (Map pp652-3; ☎ 760-327-1372; www.smoketreestables.com; 2500 S Toledo Ave; 1/2hr guided ride $40/80) arranges trail rides, from one-hour outings to all-day treks, for both novice and experienced riders. Make reservations.

TOURS

The *Palm Springs Map of the Stars' Homes* ($5), available at the visitors center, pinpoints the abodes of the city's rich and famous, but you usually won't glimpse much more than bougainvillea-covered walls.

Best of the Best Tours (☎ 760-320-1365; www.bestofthebesttours.com; tours adult/child from $20/10) If the gigantic windmills outside town have captivated your imagination, go behind the scenes (and hang onto your hat!). On bus tours of celebrity homes, catch up on the gossip and glamour of mid-20th-century Palm Springs.

Desert Adventures (☎ 760-340-2345, 888-440-5337; www.red-jeep.com; 3hr tour from $109) Natural history and Native American–themed jeep tours of the Joshua Tree backcountry and the shake-rattle-and-roll country of the San Andreas Fault.

Palm Springs Modern Tours (☎ 760-318-6118; psmoderntours@aol.com; 2½hr tour $65) The minivan tour pays special attention to the 1950s and '60s, when architects such as Albert Frey and Richard Neutra were major players on the scene.

FESTIVALS & EVENTS

Every Thursday evening in downtown Palm Springs, Palm Canyon Dr is closed to traffic for **Villagefest** (☎ 760-320-3781), with a farmers market, food vendors, live music, and arts and handicrafts booths. Ask the visitors center for an up-to-date calendar of annual events, including celebrity golf tournaments.

Palm Springs International Film Festival (☎ 760-322-2930; www.psfilmfest.org) Early January brings a Hollywood-star-studded film festival, showing more than 200 films from over 60 countries. There's a short-film festival in late August.

National Date Festival Held in February. See the boxed text, p659.

Modernism Week (www.modernismweek.com) In mid-February, a modernism art show, lectures, screenings and architecture tours revolve around the Palm Springs Art Museum (p655).

Desert Swing 'N Dixie Jazz Festival (☎ 760-333-7932; www.desertjazz.org; 1-/3-day tickets from $25/75) Three days of dancing and music in mid-March, sponsored by the Dixieland Jazz Society of the Desert.

Coachella Valley Music & Arts Festival (www.coachella.com; 1-/3-day tickets $91/272) In late April, Indio's Empire Polo Club (Map pp652–3) hosts one of the hottest music festivals of its kind, with acts ranging from hip indie no-names to Björk, Beck and Prince.

Stagecoach Festival (www.stagecoachfestival.com; 1-/3-day passes from $99/249) Also at Indio's Empire Polo Club, the weekend after Coachella, find a who's who of country-and-western and roots music, such as Shelby Lynne, Dwight Yoakam and the Judds.

SLEEPING

You'll find many 'inns' and 'lodges' around Palm Springs, where the word 'motel' seems to have a bad connotation. Many places serve continental breakfast of varying quality; a few have rooms with full or partial kitchens. Peak winter-season rates quoted here are steeply discounted during summer. 'Down Valley' accommodations mostly consist of golf, tennis and spa resorts and luxury hotels. You can often score good deals there or near the airport using online travel discounters like Hotwire.com.

Budget

Chain motels cluster at the south end of downtown Palm Springs and along I-10 heading east toward Indio. Campers head to Joshua Tree National Park (p666), about an hour's drive away, or into the backcountry of Mt San Jacinto State Park (p651), at the top of the tramway.

Alpine Gardens (Map p654; ☎ 760-323-2231, 888-299-7455; www.alpinegardens.com; 1586 E Palm Canyon Dr; d $70-155; wi-fi) All 10 rooms at this meticulously landscaped 1950s motel have redwood-beamed ceilings, mini refrigerators and slightly kitsch but still charming furnishings.

Caliente Tropics (Map p654; ☎ 760-327-1391, 800-658-6034; www.calientetropics.com; 411 E Palm Canyon Dr; d $75-250;) Although reception closes before midnight and security can be lacking, this classic Mid-Century Modern motel, where Elvis and Nancy Sinatra once lounged poolside, has nifty tiki-style, family-sized motel rooms. Wi-fi in lobby. Pet fee $15.

Del Marcos Hotel (Map p654; ☎ 760-325-6902, 800-676-1214; www.delmarcoshotel.com; 225 W Baristo Rd;

MORE POWER TO YA!

California is a massive consumer of fossil fuels, but it has also established some full-scale projects to exploit alternative energy sources. The desert regions offer not just abundantly strong sunshine, but also places for geothermal energy to be tapped and, most arrestingly, for those quixotic-looking windmills.

The wind generators are quite spectacular, with their blades the size of airplane wings, rotating on top of towers (some over 300ft tall) that turn to face the prevailing wind. Thousands of towers make up wind farms in San Gorgonio Pass near Palm Springs, Tehachapi Pass west of Mojave and Altamont Pass east of San Francisco. Statewide, 13,000 wind turbines generate just over 1% of California's electricity needs – but that's enough to power the city of San Francisco.

r $100-300; wi-fi) After suffering years of bad remodels, this 1947 gem finally looks like it should. Groovy tunes in the lobby usher you to a saltwater pool and ineffably chic rooms named for local architectural luminaries. Breakfast isn't provided, but you're right downtown.

Chase Hotel at Palm Springs (Map p654; 760-320-8866, 877-532-4273; www.chasehotelpalmsprings.com; 200 W Arenas Rd; d $119-209; wi-fi) A classic Mid-Century Modern motel complex with large open spaces, the Chase has immaculately kept, oversized rooms decorated with contemporary cool furnishings. It's great value, with friendly service and afternoon cookies.

Also recommended:

Pepper Tree Inn (Map p654; 760-318-9850, 866-887-8733; www.peppertreepalmsprings.com; 622 N Palm Canyon Dr; d $100-360; wi-fi) A Spanish-style hotel with modern rooms, just north of downtown.

Casa Cody (Map p654; 760-320-9346; www.casacody.com; 175 S Cahuilla Rd; d incl breakfast $100-410; wi-fi) Tucked behind billowing bougainvillea, this complex of adobe bungalows (some with kitchens and wood-burning fireplaces) once hosted Charlie Chaplin.

Midrange

Shelling out a little more may put you within walking distance of downtown.

our pick **Orbit In** (Map p654; 760-323-3585, 877-996-7248; www.orbitin.com; 562 W Arenas Rd; d incl breakfast $149-269; wi-fi) Swing back into the 1950s during the 'Orbitini' happy hour at this fabulously retro property, with high-end Mid-Century Modern furniture (Eames, Noguchi et al) around a quiet pool with a Jacuzzi and firepit. Throwback touches include LP record players (juxtaposed with plasma-screen TVs) and retro beach-cruiser bikes to borrow.

Horizon Hotel (Map p654; 760-323-1858, 800-377-7855; www.thehorizonhotel.com; 1050 E Palm Canyon Dr; r $175-440; wi-fi) Marilyn Monroe and Betty Grable once lounged by the poolside bar at this Mid-Century Modern gem built by architect William F Cody, who wasn't a fan of 90-degree angles. Pamper yourself with al-fresco showers, a chemical-free geometric swimming pool and private patios.

Also recommended:

Desert Riviera Hotel (Map p654; 760-327-5314; www.desertrivierahotel.com; 610 E Palm Canyon Dr; d $149-179; wi-fi) Hands-on management assures generous amenities at this poolside motel complex.

Movie Colony Hotel (Map p654; 760-320-6340, 888-953-5700; www.moviecolonyhotel.com; 726 N Indian Canyon Dr; d $189-329; wi-fi) Little luxuries make all the difference at this minimalist hideaway.

Hope Springs Motel Resort (Map pp652-3; 760-329-4003; www.hopespringsresort.com; 68075 Club Circle Dr, Desert Hot Springs; d from $195;) This modernist mecca made Desert Hot Springs cool again, with authentic period furniture and natural hot-springs pools.

Alexander Inn (Map p654; 760-327-4970; www.alexander-inn.com; 1425 S Via Soledad; d $215-265; wi-fi) Hushed villa oasis with four fully equipped kitchen suites.

Top End

If you're going to splash out in the deserts, Palm Springs is the place to do it.

Parker Palm Springs (Map p654; 760-770-5000, 800-543-4300; www.theparkerpalmsprings.com; 4200 E Palm Canyon Dr; d $345-3000; wi-fi) Featured in the Bravo TV series *Welcome to the Parker*, this posh full-service resort boasts whimsical decor by designer du jour Jonathan Adler. Drop by for a cocktail at Mister Parker's or a posh brunch at Norma's five-star coffee shop. The grounds boast hammocks, *petanque* and the Palm Springs Yacht Club spa (see the boxed text, p656).

Viceroy (Map p654; 760-320-4117, 800-237-3687; www.viceroypalmsprings.com; 415 S Belardo Rd; d $379-769; wi-fi) Wear a Pucci dress and blend right in at this 1960s-chic miniresort done up in black, white and lemon-yellow (think Austin Powers meets Givenchy). There's a full-service spa (Estrella; see the boxed text, p656), a fab but pricey Cal-French restaurant for a white-linen luncheon or swanky supper, and free town-cruiser bikes to borrow. Pet fee $85.

EATING

Palm Springs isn't what you'd call a 'foodie town' like LA; it's better known for fabulous cocktails than for dining. Still, downtown has pretty good eats, both on and off the main drag, Palm Canyon Dr. **Restaurant Week** (www.palmspringsrestaurantweek.com) features discounted prix-fixe menus in June.

Budget

Cactusberry (Map p654; 760-325-3228; 116 La Plaza; dishes $3-6; noon-10pm) PS' contribution to SoCal's frozen-yogurt craze serves it with biodegradable bowls and spoons, made from corn and potatoes, respectively.

Tyler's Burgers (Map p654; 760-325-2990; 149 S Indian Canyon Dr; dishes $4-8; 11am-4pm Mon-Sat;) The city's favorite burger stand has a maga-

THE DESERTS

WANNA DATE?

The Coachella Valley is the ideal place to find the date of your dreams – the kind that grows on trees, that is. Some 90% of US date production happens here, with dozens of permutations of shape, size and juiciness, and species with exotic-sounding names like halawy, deglet noor and golden zahidi.

Date orchards let you sample different varieties for free, an act of shameless but delicious self-promotion. A signature taste is the date shake: crushed dates mixed into a vanilla milk shake. They're much richer than they look!

Shields Date Gardens (Map pp652-3; ☎ 760-347-7768; 80-225 Hwy 111, Indio; 9am-5pm) continuously screens *The Romance and Sex Life of the Date,* with the chirpy 'Oh, *you!*' feel of a 1950s educational film. Between Indio and the Salton Sea, certified-organic **Oasis Date Gardens** (Map pp652-3; ☎ 800-827-8017; 59-111 Hwy 111, Thermal; 9am-4pm) is a more welcoming place to pick up medjool gift boxes and yummy date shakes. For a quick grab-and-go on your way to or from LA, there's **Hadley Fruit Orchards** (off Map pp652-3; ☎ 951-849-5255; www.hadleyfruitorchards.com; 48980 Seminole Dr, Cabazon; 9am-7pm Mon-Thu, 8am-8pm Fri-Sun), which claims to have invented trail mix.

For old-fashioned carnival fun, the **National Date Festival** (Map pp652-3; ☎ 800-811-3247; www.datefest.org; Riverside County Fairgrounds, 82503 Hwy 111, Indio; adult/child $8/6, parking $7;) features outrageous camel and ostrich races in February. Inside a 1920s adobe home, the modest **Coachella Valley Museum & Cultural Center** (Map pp652-3; ☎ 760-342-6651; 82616 Miles Ave, Indio; adult/child $3/1; 10am-4pm Thu-Sat, 1-4pm Sun Oct-May) explores the valley's date culture and pioneer history.

zine rack stocked with the *Robb Report*. It's at La Plaza, a drive-through shopping street downtown. Expect a wait.

Sherman's (Map p654; ☎ 760-325-1199; 401 E Tahquitz Canyon Way; mains $5-15; 7am-9pm;) With a sidewalk-facing terrace, this retro-looking downtown Jewish deli serves lox-and-bagel breakfasts and early-bird dinners. It's festooned with headshots of aficionados no less than Don Rickles.

our pick **Manhattan in the Desert** (Map p654; ☎ 760-322-3354; 2665 E Palm Canyon Dr; mains $6-18; 7am-9pm Sun-Thu, 7am-10pm Fri & Sat;) A swankier rival to Sherman's out in the suburbs, with an impressive deli counter. Simply massive slices of cake mirror the enormity of its mile-high pastrami sandwiches.

Fisherman's Market & Grill (Map p654; ☎ 760-327-1766; 235 S Indian Canyon Dr; mains $6-25; 11am-9pm Mon-Sat, noon-8pm Sun;) At this no-frills counter-service shack, the seafood is so fresh (for the desert, that is) you half expect to see fishing boats bobbing outside. Fish-and-chips is a classic, as are seafood combos with coleslaw.

El Mirasol (Map p654; ☎ 760-323-0721; 140 E Palm Canyon Dr; mains $7-19; 11am-10pm) There are showier Mexican places around town, but everyone ends up back at El Mirasol, with its rustic decor, copious margaritas and snappy dishes, from spinach enchiladas to chicken mole.

Native Foods (Map pp652-3; ☎ 760-416-0070; Smoke Tree Village, 1775 E Palm Canyon Dr; mains $8-15; 11:30am-9:30pm Mon-Sat; V) Seitan and soy are the order of the day at this LA import, which merits a special trip for a half dozen kinds of veggie burgers, Southwestern salads and sizzling-hot rice bowls to feed your soul, all served in a candlelit, natural-wood setting.

Midrange & Top End

Matchbox (Map p654; ☎ 760-778-6000; 2nd level, 155 S Palm Canyon Dr; mains $11-24; 5-11pm Sun-Thu, 5pm-1am Fri & Sat) A winner, with gourmet wood-oven-fired pizzas made from fresh dough, a plaza-view patio, and martini-and-cigar happy hours. California bistro classics are hit-or-miss.

Wang's in the Desert (Map p654; ☎ 760-325-9264; 424 S Indian Canyon Dr; mains $12-21; dinner) The menu may sound like standard-issue Chinese fusion, but the atmosphere is anything but. This mood-lit outpost, with indoor koi pond and giant cocktails, is a darling of the in-crowd. Come early or make reservations. Kiss, kiss.

Copley's (Map p654; ☎ 760-327-9555; 621 N Palm Canyon Dr; mains $25-35; dinner daily Jan–mid-May, dinner Tue-Sat mid-May–mid-Jul & late-Aug–Dec) After stints in the UK, Australia and Hawaii, chef Copley gets seriously inventive here on the former Cary Grant estate. Think mac-nut-crusted

GAY & LESBIAN PALM SPRINGS

Like 'Provincetown in the Desert,' or the 'Key West of the West,' PS is an outstanding LGBT vacation destination. Surf www.palmspringsgayinfo.com, then pick up the *Official Gay & Lesbian Visitors Guide* from the visitors center.

Festivals & Events

In early April, **Dinah Weekend** (www.thedinah.com, www.dinahshoreweekend.com) hosts lesbian comedy, pool parties, mixers and more during the Nabisco (ex–Dinah Shore) LPGA Golf Tournament. Over Easter weekend, the **White Party** (www.jeffreysanker.com) is one of the USA's biggest gay dance events. Show up in early November for **Palm Springs Pride** (www.pspride.org).

Sleeping

Gay lodging in Palm Springs, approximately 40 resorts in all, ranges from sleazy to sumptuous. Because they're small properties, many are conducive to finding companions for dinner, drinks, daytime activities or whatever. Budget-conscious travelers can try the Alpine Gardens inn (p657) or Caliente Tropics motel (p657).

Men's Resorts

Men's resorts are concentrated in the Warm Sands neighborhood, just southeast of downtown Palm Springs, or on San Lorenzo Rd, about a mile away. Most men's resorts are clothing-optional.

Hacienda at Warm Sands (Map p654; ☎ 760-327-8111, 800-359-2007; www.thehacienda.com; 586 Warm Sands Dr; r incl breakfast & lunch $149-399; wi-fi) With Indonesian teak and bamboo furnishings, the Hacienda raises the bar for luxury, starting with its pillow 'menu' and flawless landscaping. The genial innkeepers are never intrusive, always available. Bring your own lover.

Century (Map p654; ☎ 760-323-9966, 800-475-5188; www.centurypalmsprings.com; 598 Grenfall Rd; r incl breakfast $179-289; wi-fi) To stay gay and not give up that Mid-Century Modern vibe, make a beeline to the small Century, designed by William Alexander in 1955. It's furnished with pieces by Starck, Eames and Noguchi, and has a minimalist pool deck with serene mountain views. Plush bedding, catered breakfast and cocktails.

THE DESERTS

Scottish salmon and 'Oh My Lobster Pot Pie.' Make reservations and bring your sweetie.

DRINKING

Divey locals' bars and chic restaurants with late-night happy hours inhabit downtown Palm Springs.

Melvyn's Lounge (Map p654; ☎ 760-325-2323; Ingleside Inn, 200 W Ramon Rd; 10am-2am) Loll with a stiff martini at the bar while retired celebs and LA hipsters sway to torch singers backed by live combos at this old-guard standby, once a haunt of Sinatra. Sunday afternoon jazz is a long-standing tradition. Shine your shoes.

Palm Springs Koffi (Map p654; ☎ 760-416-2244; 515 N Palm Canyon Dr; 5:30am-8pm; wi-fi) Tucked among the art galleries on North Palm Canyon Dr, this coolly minimalist, indie java bar serves strong organic coffee.

ENTERTAINMENT

Palm Springs isn't exactly the hip party spot it once was when the Rat Pack ruled.

Casinos

Spa Resort Casino (Map p654; ☎ 888-999-1995; www.sparesortcasino.com; 401 E Amado Rd; 24hr) Empty your pockets at Palm Springs' original casino or any of the other Native American–owned gambling halls off I-10. Just remember, this ain't Vegas, baby.

Cinema

Camelot Theatres (Map p654; ☎ 760-325-6565; 2300 Baristo Rd; adult/child $9.50/7, before 2pm $7/6.50) The desert's premier art-house cinema for foreign and indie flicks has a full bar and café.

Desert IMAX Theatre (Map pp652-3; ☎ 760-324-7333; 68510 E Palm Canyon Dr, Cathedral City; tickets $9-11;) Big-screen Hollywood and 3D movies, as well as virtual-reality IMAX ridefilms, screen here.

Theater

Palm Springs Follies (Map p654; ☎ 760-327-0225; www.psfollies.com; 128 S Palm Canyon Dr; tickets $50-92; Nov-May) This Ziegfeld Follies–style revue includes

Women's Resorts

Lesbian resorts (fewer in number) are scattered throughout town.

Casitas Laquita (Map p654; ☎ 760-416-9999; www.casitaslaquita.com; 450 E Palm Canyon Dr; r $145-165, ste $185-350;) At this tranquil Southwestern compound, romantic rooms and suites all have kitchens and some have kiva-style fireplaces. Afternoon tapas and drinks are complimentary, as is continental breakfast. Free wi-fi poolside.

Eating

Every restaurant in central PS has a significant gay clientele, especially Wang's in the Desert (p659).

Look (Map p654; ☎ 760-778-3520; 139 E Andreas Rd; mains $8-23; 11am-9pm, bar to 1am) The real action is on the patio, not in the dining room with old Hollywood publicity stills. Standard California bistro cuisine, such as quesadillas, Cobb salad, sandwiches, burgers, is on offer, plus weekend brunch.

Blame it on Midnight (Map p654; ☎ 760-323-1200; 777 E Tahquitz Canyon Way; mains $13-33; 5pm-close) Undyingly popular but pretty subpar grills, salads and eclectic mains, with Vegas lounge-style entertainment most nights.

Entertainment

Arenas Rd, east of Indian Canyon Dr, is gay nightlife central. Park 'n' party.

Toucan's Tiki Lounge (Map p654; ☎ 760-416-7584; 2100 N Palm Canyon Dr) A couple of miles north of Arenas, this locals' hangout has something for everyone: tropical froufrou, bingo mavens, karaoke, drag revues, smoking patio and dance floor. It's packed on weekends.

Hunters (Map p654; ☎ 760-323-0700; 302 E Arenas Rd) Wildly diverse male clientele, lots of TV screens, a cruisy dance scene and pool tables.

Streetbar (Map p654; ☎ 760-320-1266; 244 E Arenas Rd) Congenial community mix of locals, long-time visitors and occasional drag performers. There's a cozy streetside patio for watching the crowds saunter by.

See also CopyKatz (below).

music, dancing, showgirls and comedy. The twist? Many of the performers are as old as the theater – all are over 50, some into their 80s. But this is no amateur hour: in their heyday, many of these old-timers hoofed it alongside Hollywood and Broadway's biggest, who occasionally guest-star.

CopyKatz (Map p654; ☎ 760-864-9293; www.copykatzps.com; 200 S Palm Canyon Dr; tickets $29-49; shows 8pm Tue-Sun) Energetic female-impersonator acts inspired by Barbra Streisand, Diana Ross, Bette Midler and, uh, Michael Jackson. Shows have more than just a gay following.

SHOPPING

Go art-gallery hopping in downtown Palm Springs along North Palm Canyon Dr.

Modern Way (Map p654; ☎ 760-320-5455; 745 N Palm Canyon Dr) The largest, oldest and most stylin' consignment shop for collectors of modern furniture.

Trina Turk (Map p654; ☎ 760-416-2856; 891 N Palm Canyon Dr) Find shagadelic resort-chic drag at Palm Springs' most unique clothing boutique, inside a 1960s Albert Frey–designed storefront.

Angel View (Map p654; ☎ 760-320-1733; 462 N Indian Canyon Dr) At Palm Springs' thrift-store chain of record, today's hipsters can buy clothes as cool as when they were first worn a generation or two ago.

Collectors Corner (Map pp652-3; ☎ 760-346-1012; 71280 Hwy 111, Rancho Mirage) Antiques, vintage clothing, jewelry and furniture draw enthusiastic shoppers from across the Coachella Valley, where well-heeled retirees, and their propensity to pass on to the next world, mean shelves are constantly replenished.

El Paseo (Map pp652-3; ☎ 877-735-7273; El Paseo, Palm Desert) For serious shopping, head to El Paseo, dubbed the Rodeo Dr of the desert. The street runs parallel to, and one block south of, Hwy 111 in Palm Desert, a 30-minute trip from Palm Springs. Opening hours vary.

WHAT THE...?

You may do a double-take when you see the giant T-Rex and apatosaurus north of I-10 in Cabazon. The **World's Biggest Dinosaurs** (off Map pp652-3; ☎ 951-922-8700; www.cabazondinosaurs.com; 50800 Seminole Dr, Cabazon; gift shop 10am-6:30pm daily, museum 10am-7pm Fri-Mon;) were created by Claude K Bell, a sculptor for Knott's Berry Farm, but are now owned by Christian creationists. Alongside the dino-swag you might find at other science museums, read about what the museum describes as the hoaxes and fallacies of evolution and Darwinism, biblical quotes purporting to refer to dinosaurs, and evidence dinosaurs and humans existed at the same time.

Desert Hills Premium Outlets (off Map pp652-3; ☎ 951-849-6641; 48400 Seminole Dr, Cabazon; 10am-8pm Sun-Thu, 10am-9pm Fri, 9am-9pm Sat) The offerings at this posh outlet mall range from Polo and Prada to department-store discounts like Off 5th and Barneys New York. It's off I-10 (exit at Fields Rd), 20 miles west of Palm Springs.

GETTING THERE & AWAY

Air

A 10-minute drive northeast of downtown, **Palm Springs International Airport** (PSP; Map p654; ☎ 760-318-3800; www.palmspringsairport.com; 3400 E Tahquitz Canyon Way) is served year-round by Alaska, American, Delta, Horizon, United and US Airways, and seasonally by Air Canada, Continental, Northwest and Sun Country. For airline information, see p727.

Bus

Greyhound (☎ 800-231-2222; www.greyhound.com) has a few daily buses to/from LA ($25 to $37, three hours). Buses depart from and arrive at Palm Springs' train station.

Car & Motorcycle

From LA, I-10 is the fastest route into and through the Coachella Valley. The trip here takes two to three hours.

Train

Amtrak (☎ 800-872-7245; www.amtrak.com) serves the unstaffed and kinda creepy North Palm Springs Station (Map pp652–3), about 5 miles north of downtown Palm Springs. *Sunset Limited* trains run to/from LA ($22 to $35, 2¾ hours) on Sundays, Wednesdays and Fridays (depart LA 2:30pm, depart Palm Springs 6:35am). Trains are often late.

GETTING AROUND

To/From the Airport

Unless your hotel provides airport transfers, take a taxi; figure at least $12 to downtown Palm Springs. SunLine bus 24 stops outside the airport.

Bicycle

Check if your hotel has loaner bicycles to get around town. **Funseekers** (Map pp652-3; ☎ 760-340-3861; www.palmdesertbikerentals.com; 73865 Hwy 111, Palm Desert; rentals per hr/day/week from $7/28/75, delivery & pick-up from $30) rents and sells bikes for city and mountain use, plus in-line skates, mopeds and even Segways.

Bus

Alternative-fuel-powered **SunLine** (☎ 760-343-3451, 800-347-8628; www.sunline.org; single ride/transfer $1/25¢), the local bus service, will take you around the valley, albeit slowly, from around 5am to 10pm. Route 111 follows Hwy 111 between Palm Springs and Palm Desert (one hour) and Indio (1½ hours). Buses have air-con, wheelchair lifts and a bicycle rack. Cash only (bring exact change).

Car

Though you can walk to most sights in downtown Palm Springs, you'll need a car to get around the valley. Major rental-car companies have airport desks.

AROUND PALM SPRINGS & COACHELLA VALLEY

JOSHUA TREE NATIONAL PARK

Joshua Tree National Park straddles the transition zone between the Colorado Desert and the higher, cooler Mojave Desert, where Joshua trees (actually tree-sized yuccas) grow. The trees were so named by Mormon settlers, who imagined the branches stretching up toward heaven like the arms of a biblical prophet. In spring they bloom dramatically with a profusion of creamy-

THE DESERTS

white blossoms. Lower down, the desert is characterized by cacti, particularly prickly green cholla, and ocotillos, whose octopus-like tentacles shoot out crimson flowers in spring. Wildflowers bloom at varying elevations between February and April. In winter it can snow at higher points, such as Keys View (5185ft).

The mystical quality of this stark, boulder-strewn landscape has inspired many artists, most famously the band U2, which named its 1987 album *The Joshua Tree.* The park's wonderfully shaped rocky outcroppings also draw world-class climbers, who know 'J-Tree' as the best place to climb in California. Kids and the young-at-heart alike love the chance to scramble up, down and around the giant boulders. Hikers seek out hidden, shady desert-fan-palm oases fed by natural springs and small streams, while mountain-bikers are hypnotized by the desert vistas seen from dirt 4WD roads.

Orientation

Twentynine Palms Hwy (Hwy 62) parallels the north side of the park, where you'll find the most attractions (including all of the Joshua trees), while I-10 borders the remote south side. Unless you're day-tripping from Palm Springs, base yourself in the towns of Joshua Tree, Twentynine Palms or Yucca Valley. All are basically stretches along Twentynine Palms Hwy, but Joshua Tree has more soul and is favored by artists. Twentynine Palms serves the nearby Marine Corps Air Ground Combat Center (the world's largest marine facility at 932 sq miles, or twice the footprint of the city of Los Angeles). Don't disparage US troops here, and don't freak out over the occasional kaboom. See the map on p654.

Information

Admission to **Joshua Tree National Park** (☎ 760-367-5500; www.nps.gov/jotr; 7-day entry pass per car/bicycle $15/5; 🕑 24hr) includes a map/brochure and the seasonal *Joshua Tree Guide*. The National Park Service (NPS) website has extensive information about nature walks, 4WD roads, stargazing, wildflower viewing and more. Check schedules of free ranger programs at the Oasis Visitor Center, where nature videos are shown between 11am and 3pm.

There are no facilities inside the park except restrooms, so gas up and bring food and plenty of water. The nearby towns of Joshua Tree (population 4210, elevation 3250ft), Twentynine Palms (population 14,800, elevation 2001ft) and Yucca Valley (population 16,900, elevation 3279ft) all have gas stations, post offices and banks with 24-hour ATMs. In the park, cell-phone coverage is almost nonexistent, but there's an emergency-only telephone at the Intersection Rock parking lot by Hidden Valley Campground.

INTERNET ACCESS

Beatnik Café (☎ 760-366-2090; 61597 Twentynine Palms Hwy, Joshua Tree; 15min/1hr $2/6; 🕑 9am-midnight Thu-Tue, 9am-2am Wed) Self-serve internet terminals (a bit temperamental – use at your own risk).

Coyote Corner (☎ 760-366-9683; 6535 Park Blvd, Joshua Tree; 🕑 9am-7pm) Free wi-fi for customers at this outdoor-activity supply shop.

Joshua Tree Outfitters (☎ 760-366-1848, 888-366-1848; 61707 Twentynine Palms Hwy, Joshua Tree; 🕑 usually 9am-5pm Thu-Tue) Complimentary free internet terminal, for customers only.

San Bernardino County Library Joshua Tree (☎ 760-366-8615; 6465 Park Blvd); Twentynine Palms (☎ 760-367-9519; 6078 Adobe Rd) Free walk-in internet access with a visitors' pass; call ahead for hours (closed Sunday).

THE DESERTS

DETOUR: PALMS TO PINES HIGHWAY

Coming from LA, the scenic Palms to Pines Hwy leaves I-10 west of Banning and heads into the San Jacinto Mountains via Hwys 243 and 74, eventually joining Hwy 111 west of Palm Springs. Along the way, stop at **Idyllwild** (☎ 951-659-3259, 888-659-3259; www.idyllwildchamber.com), an arts-and-music mountain community stuffed full of bakeries, cafés and art galleries. It's an outdoor gateway to hiking and mountain-biking trails and rock-climbing routes with think-twice names like 'The Vampire.' If you're headed to Temecula (see the boxed text, p646), leave the Palms to Pines Hwy behind south of Idyllwild and follow Hwy 79 west of Hemet. Take State St south, then Domengioni Pkwy west to the multimillion dollar **Western Center for Archaeology & Paleontology** (☎ 951-791-0033; www.westerncentermuseum.org; 2345 Searl Pkwy, Hemet; adult/child $8/6; 🕑 10am-5pm Tue-Sun; 👶), a kid-friendly museum that's a blast from the prehistoric past.

MEDICAL SERVICES

Hi-Desert Medical Center (☎ 760-366-3711; 6601 Whitefeather Rd, Joshua Tree; ⏱ emergency room 24hr)

TOURIST INFORMATION

Black Rock Nature Center (www.nps.gov/jotr; 9800 Black Rock Canyon Rd, south of Hwy 62; ⏱ 8am-4pm Sat-Thu, noon-8pm Fri Oct-May)
Cottonwood Visitor Center (www.nps.gov/jotr; Cottonwood Spring Rd, north of I-10; ⏱ 9am-3pm)
Joshua Tree Visitor Center (www.nps.gov/jotr; Park Blvd, south of Hwy 62, Joshua Tree; ⏱ 8am-5pm)
Oasis Visitor Center (www.nps.gov/jotr; National Park Blvd at Utah Trail, Twentynine Palms; ⏱ 8am-5pm)
Sun Runner (www.thesunrunner.com) Free arts-and-culture magazine loaded with helpful travel info.
Twentynine Palms Chamber of Commerce (☎ 760-367-3445; www.visit29.org; Suites C-D, 73660 Civic Center, Twentynine Palms; ⏱ 9am-5pm Mon-Fri, 9am-1pm Sat Sep-May, 9am-3pm Mon-Fri Jun-Aug) Comprehensive online guide to 'California's outback,' with photos.

Sights

Behind the Oasis Visitor Center, near the park's northern entrance, the natural **Oasis of Mara** has the original 29 palm trees for which the nearby town is named. They were planted by Serrano tribespeople, who named this 'the place of little springs and much grass.' The Pinto Mountain Fault, a small branch of the San Andreas, runs through the oasis, as does a 0.5-mile, wheelchair-accessible nature trail with labeled desert plants.

In the center of the park, the most whimsically dramatic conglomeration of rocks is known as the **Wonderland of Rocks**, where designated picnic areas, pull-offs and campgrounds give everyone a chance to clamber on the giant boulders. East of Queen Valley, travelers with 4WD vehicles or mountain bikes can detour onto **Geology Tour Road**, an 18-mile field trip down into and around Pleasant Valley, where the forces of erosion, earthquakes and ancient volcanoes combine. Pick up a self-guided tour brochure and ask about current road conditions at the Oasis Visitor Center first.

Joshua trees grow throughout the upper area of the park, including right along Park Blvd, but some of the biggest trees are found in **Covington Flats**, along a dirt road that ends with views of Palm Springs, the Morongo Basin and the mountains. Much more easily reached, about a 20-minute drive south of Park Blvd, **Keys View** overlooks the entire Coachella Valley and the San Bernardino Mountains. You can clearly observe the San Andreas fault system from here.

To see the natural transition from the high Mojave Desert to the low Colorado (Sonoran) Desert, wind along **Pinto Basin Road** down to Cottonwood Spring, a 30-mile drive from the Wonderland of Rocks. En route take a break at **Cholla Cactus Garden**, where a quarter-mile loop leads around waving ocotillo plants and jumping 'teddy bear' cholla. Most visitors give **Cottonwood Spring Oasis** only a passing glance, if they stop at all. But Cahuilla tribespeople depended on this natural spring, leaving behind *olla* (clay pots) and *morteros* (rocks used by Native Americans for grinding seeds) pounded into nearby rocks. Miners came searching for gold here in the late 19th century.

Anyone with the slightest interest in history and local lore should tour the **Desert Queen Ranch** (☎ reservations 760-367-5555; tour adult/child $5/2.50; ⏱ tours 10am & 1pm Sat & Sun Oct-May, call for weekday schedules). Here in Queen Valley, Russian immigrant William Keys started building a 160-acre homestead in 1917. Over the next 60 years, his family forged a full working ranch, school, store and workshop out of the harsh desert. Everything stands much as it did when Keys died in 1969. Reservations for the 1½-hour, half-mile walking tour are recommended by calling in advance or showing up the day before at the Oasis or Joshua Tree Visitor Center. If last-minute spaces are available, you can buy tickets (cash only, exact change required) just before the tour starts at the ranch gate. To get there, take the turnoff east of Hidden Valley Campground, turn left

OASIS HUNTING

Desert-fan-palm oases are rare, with just over 150 mapped across North America. California's desert fan palms, *Washingtonia filifera,* are often found growing along fault lines, where cracks in the earth's crust allow subterranean water to surface. Each tree can live for 80 or 90 years, grow up to 75ft tall and weigh up to 3 tons. To see the miraculous groves for yourself, drive to the **Oasis of Mara** (above) or **Cottonwood Spring Oasis** (right). Hikers who put in more effort can discover **Fortynine Palms Oasis** (opposite) or the even more remote and mysterious **Lost Palms Oasis** (opposite).

DETOUR: PIONEERTOWN

From Hwy 62 (Twentynine Palms Hwy) in the town of Yucca Valley, head 5 miles north along hilly Pioneertown Rd, and you'll drive straight into the past.

Pioneertown (www.pioneertown.com;) was built as a Hollywood movie backdrop in 1946, and has hardly changed since. On 'Mane St,' you can witness a 'real' Old West–style gunfight at 2:30pm on the second and last Sundays of the month from April to October, or go bowling at an old-fashioned bowling alley built for Roy Rogers that has an amazing collection of vintage pinball games.

Then scarf down plates of 'cue as live bands play at **Pappy & Harriet's Pioneertown Palace** (760-365-5956; www.pappyandharriets.com; 53688 Pioneertown Rd; mains $8-25; 11am-1am Thu-Sun, 5pm-midnight Mon), an authentic honky-tonk. Bed down where silver-screen stars of yesteryear slept at the **Pioneertown Motel** (760-365-4879; www.pioneertownmotel.com; 5040 Curtis Rd; r $75-95; wi-fi), where memorabilia-filled rooms have kitchenettes and satellite TV (but no phones).

at the Y-intersection and follow the dirt road out to the locked gate.

Activities

For kids, official **junior ranger program** activity books are available at park visitors centers. Fun for all ages, **star-viewing parties** are held monthly on the Saturday closest to the new moon at Hidden Valley Campground. The Joshua Tree National Park Association's **Desert Institute** (760-367-5535; www.joshuatree.org) arranges lectures, naturalist field trips, desert survival workshops, and art, science and cultural history classes for adults, including some courses taught by Native Americans.

HIKING

Leave the car behind to appreciate Joshua Tree's trippy lunar landscapes. Try to hike early or late in the day, to avoid the worst heat. To protect plants and the cryptobiotic soil crust that keeps the desert from blowing away, always stay on established trails.

Visitors centers provide maps and advice about a dozen short nature walks, which focus on different features of the park, and longer hiking trails. If you're short on time, amble along the 1.3-mile loop out to **Barker Dam**, which passes a little lake and a rock incised with Native American petroglyphs. Then stretch your legs on the 1.7-mile trail around **Skull Rock** and other cool boulder pile-ups in the Wonderland of Rocks.

To escape the crowds, take the 3-mile round-trip hike to **Fortynine Palms Oasis**, an up-and-down trail starting near Indian Cove, or the 7.2-mile fairly flat round-trip trek out to **Lost Palms Oasis**, in a remote canyon filled with desert fan palms, starting from Cottonwood Spring. The strenuous 4-mile round-trip climb to **Lost Horse Mine** (elevation 5278ft) visits the remains of an authentic Old West silver and gold mine that operated on the mountain until 1931. If views are what you're after, tackle the 3-mile round-trip ascent of nearby **Ryan Mountain** (5461ft); the 5.5-mile **Panorama Loop**, with a side trip up **Warren Peak** (5103ft), starting from Black Rock Campground; or the 3-mile round-trip from Cottonwood Spring up **Mastodon Peak** (3371ft), for vistas of the Salton Sea (p668).

Backpacking routes, like the 16-mile, out-and-back **Boy Scout Trail** and a 35-mile, one-way stretch of the **California Riding & Hiking Trail** (which passes by the Eureka Peak summit trail) present a challenge because of the need to carry so many gallons of water per person per day. No open fires are allowed in the park, so you'll have to bring a campstove and fuel, too. Overnight backcountry hikers must register (to aid in census-taking, fire safety and rescue efforts) at one of 13 backcountry boards located at trailhead parking lots throughout the park. Unregistered vehicles left overnight may be cited or towed.

ROCK CLIMBING

From boulders to cracks to multipitch faces, there are more than 8000 established routes, many accessed off Park Blvd. The longest climbs are not much more than 100ft or so, but there are many challenging technical routes, and most can be easily top-roped for training.

With a free, info-packed website, **Nomad Ventures** (760-366-4684; www.joshuatreevillage.com/515/515.htm; 61795 Twentynine Palms Hwy, Joshua Tree; 8am-6pm Mon-Thu, 8am-8pm Fri & Sat, 8am-7pm Sun) sells the latest, greatest rock-climbing gear and guidebooks. **Coyote Corner** (☎ 760-366-9683; www.joshuatreevillage.com/546/546.htm; 6535 Park Blvd, Joshua Tree; 9am-7pm) also sells climbing guides and gear, and lets you thumb through route diaries. If you're going bouldering, rent crash pads from **Joshua Tree Outfitters** (☎ 760-366-1848, 888-366-1848; www.joshuatreeoutfitters.com; 61707 Twentynine Palms Hwy, Joshua Tree; usually 9am-5pm Thu-Tue).

For a day or weekend of instruction or a private guided climb, contact **Uprising Adventure Guides** (☎ 888-254-6266; www.uprising.com; half-/full-day guided climb from $65/120).

MOUNTAIN-BIKING

All bicycles must keep to established paved and dirt roads, and are not allowed on hiking trails. Favorite mountain-biking routes include challenging **Pinkham Canyon Road**, starting from the Cottonwood Visitor Center, and the long-distance **Black Eagle Mine Road**, which start 6.5 miles further north. **Queen Valley** has a gentler set of trails with bike racks found along the way, so people can lock up their bikes and go hiking, but it's busy with cars, as is the bumpy, sandy and steep **Geology Tour Road**. There's a wide-open network of dirt roads at **Covington Flats**, where the biggest Joshua trees grow.

BIRD-WATCHING

More than 250 species have been spotted here, including such common desert birds as the roadrunner and dozens of winter migratory birds. Go bird-watching at **Barker Dam** or around natural oases (see the boxed text, p664).

Tucked into the Little San Bernardino Mountains, about a 25-minute drive west of Joshua Tree, **Big Morongo Canyon Preserve** (☎ 760-363-7190; www.bigmorongo.org; 11055 East Dr, Morongo Valley; admission free; 7:30am-sunset) encloses native riparian habitat where cottonwoods and willows grow. Even bighorn sheep are occasionally attracted to its watering holes. From the interpretive kiosk at the entrance, wooden boardwalks pleasantly meander through marshy woodlands.

Festivals & Events

Contact the Twentynine Palms Chamber of Commerce (p664) for current events info.

Joshua Tree Music Festival (☎ 877-327-6265; www.joshuatreemusicfestival.com; 2-day pass $60) Over a long weekend in May, this family-friendly indie-music fest grooves out at Joshua Tree Lake Campground. It's followed by a soulful roots celebration in mid-October.

Pioneer Days (☎ 760-367-3445; www.visit29.org; admission free) Twentynine Palms' Old West–themed carnival in mid-October has a rodeo, an arm-wrestling competition and wacky outhouse races.

Sleeping

There are no lodges in the park, only campgrounds. Twentynine Palms has the biggest selection of accommodations, but many are grotty no-tell motels (some geared more toward hourly than nightly rentals). More welcoming inns, B&Bs and vacation rentals are spread out around Joshua Tree. Chain motels and business hotels line Twentynine Palms Hwy, especially heading toward Yucca Valley.

BUDGET

Camping

There are nine **NPS campgrounds** (www.nps.gov/jotr; tent & RV sites $10-15) in the park. **Reservations** (☎ 877-444-6777; www.recreation.gov) are accepted for Black Rock and Cottonwood, which have shared-use water, flush toilets and dump stations. All other campgrounds are first-come, first-served, and have pit toilets, picnic tables and fireplaces. At peak times (eg when wildflowers bloom) all campsites fill by noon. In summer some campgrounds are closed.

Along Park Blvd, Jumbo Rocks has sheltered rock alcoves that act as perfect sunset-

WHAT THE...?

In the late 1940s, former aerospace engineer George van Tassel moved to the desert and began meditating near giant rocks. Allegedly designed with telepathic help from extraterrestrial beings, his wooden **Integratron** (☎ 760-364-3126; www.integratron.com; 2477 Belfield Blvd, Landers; sound baths $10-55, private tours from $60), sitting on a geomagnetic vortex northwest of Joshua Tree, was designed as a time machine, antigravity device and rejuvenation chamber. Judge for yourself by taking a personal tour or a sonic healing bath, in which crystal bowls are struck under the acoustically perfect dome (many visitors report an out-of-body experience). Check the website for special events like UFO symposiums. Visits are by appointment only.

THE DESERTS

and sunrise-viewing platforms. Belle and White Tank also have boulder-embracing views. Hidden Valley is always busy. Sheep Pass and Ryan are also centrally located campgrounds. Family-friendly Black Rock, outside Joshua Tree town, is good for camping novices; more remote Indian Cove also has 100-plus sites. Cottonwood, near the park's southern entrance, is popular with RVs.

Backcountry camping is permitted as long as it's 1 mile from the road and 500ft from any trail. Free self-registration is required at one of 13 backcountry boards throughout the park. Campfires are strictly forbidden.

Joshua Tree Outfitters (opposite) rents and sells camping gear. Coyote Corner (opposite) has coin-op showers and free water.

Motels

For more character and a restful atmosphere, Pioneertown Motel (see the boxed text, p665) is a hidden find.

Safari Motor Inn (☎ 760-366-1113, 866-313-1333; www.joshuatreemotel.com; 61959 Twentynine Palms Hwy, Joshua Tree; r $55-75; wi-fi) This elemental, international-tourist-friendly, two-story roadside motel may be nothing to write home about, but it's a short walk to eateries and outdoor outfitters. Most of the well-worn standard rooms have microwaves and mini refrigerators. Pets OK.

Harmony Motel (☎ 760-367-3351; www.harmonymotel.com; 71161 Twentynine Palms Hwy, Twentynine Palms; r $62-105;) It's a little arty, and a lot hippie-dippy. This extremely basic 1950s motel, where U2 once stayed, has a small pool and large rooms (some with kitchenettes, no TVs). Expect some traffic noise, especially in the cabin. Management can be ill-tempered.

Joshua Tree Inn (☎ 760-366-1188; www.joshuatreeinn.com; 61259 Twentynine Palms Hwy, Joshua Tree; r incl breakfast $85-175;) Alt-country pioneer and 1970s rock legend Gram Parsons overdosed in this large U-shaped motel; his fans still flock here to stay in Room 8. Other famous blast-from-the-past guests include Robert Plant, Keith Richards and Emmy-Lou Harris. Retro digs have beamed ceilings and country-kitsch furnishings. The communal area features a rock fireplace.

Also recommended:

29 Palms Inn (☎ 760-367-3505; www.29palmsinn.com; 73950 Inn Ave, Twentynine Palms; r & ste $95-340;) Oddball collection of rustic adobe-and-wood cabins, bungalows and houses, some pet-friendly. No phones.

Rimrock Ranch Cabins (☎ 760-228-1297; www.rimrockranchcabins.com; 50857 Burns Canyon Rd, Pioneertown; cabins $100-155;) Vintage 1940s cabins come with kitchens, plus a common stargazing patio. Pets OK.

MIDRANGE & TOP END

There's often a two-night minimum stay, especially on weekends.

our pick Spin & Margie's Desert Hide-a-Way (☎ 760-366-9124; www.deserthideaway.com; 6920-6923 Sunkist Rd, Joshua Tree; ste $125-160;) Boldly colorful, snappy-looking suites each have their own kitchen, TV/VCR and stereo at this delightful hacienda-style inn, where unusual design motifs include corrugated tin, old license plates and cartoon art. Knowledgeable, gregarious owners ensure a relaxed visit.

Desert Lily (☎ 760-366-4676, 877-887-7370; www.thedesertlily.com; PO Box 139, Joshua Tree; s/d incl breakfast $140/155, houses $165-275; Sep-Jun;) The thoughtful hosts at this Old West-meets-Southwest charmer offer two contemporary B&B rooms, a rustic-styled ranch bunkhouse and three private casitas – the adobe retreat has a full kitchen, satellite TV and French doors opening onto a barbecue patio. Well-behaved pets considered.

Sacred Sands B&B (☎ 760-424-6407; www.sacredsands.com; 63155 Quail Springs Rd, Joshua Tree; d incl breakfast $269-299; wi-fi) Just two luxurious suites, each with a private outdoor shower, hot tub, sundeck and sleeping terrace under the stars, make up this straw-bale-walled, gay-friendly desert retreat. Hospitable owners serve healthy gourmet breakfasts daily.

Eating

Yucca Valley is full of diners, coffee shops and family-style restaurants. For rib-sticking barbecue, burgers and live bands, detour to Pappy & Harriet's Pioneertown Palace (see the boxed text, p665).

our pick Crossroads Cafe & Tavern (☎ 760-366-5414; 61715 Twentynine Palms Hwy, Joshua Tree; mains $3-11; 6:30am-3pm Sun-Tue, 6:30am-8pm Thu-Sat; V) An eclectic-looking joint with a treehugger-friendly atmosphere, the much-loved Crossroads dishes up homemade breakfast hashes, fresh sandwiches, fruit smoothies and dragged-through-the-garden salads that make both omnivores and vegans happy.

Wonder Garden Café (☎ 760-367-2429; 73511 Twentynine Palms Hwy, Twentynine Palms; mains $4-8;

7:45am-3pm Mon-Sat;) Opposite a local supermarket, this laid-back natural-foods café lets you nosh on bagel sandwiches, vegetarian soups and sandwiches, fresh juice smoothies and popular ice-cream treats.

JT Country Kitchen (760-366-8988; 61768 Twentynine Palms Hwy, Joshua Tree; mains $4-10; 6am-3:30pm) This roadside shack serves down-home cookin': eggs, pancakes, biscuits with gravy, sandwiches and…what's this? Cambodian noodles and salads? Delish. Breakfast served all day.

Sam's Pizza & Subs (760-366-9511; 61380 Twentynine Palms Hwy, Joshua Tree; mains $8-11; 11am-8pm Mon-Thu, 11am-7pm Fri & Sat, 3-8pm Sun;) Pizza? Yeah, but cognoscenti come here for Indian dishes like chicken tikka masala and aloo gobi. Atmosphere: nil. Solution: takeout.

Drinking

Ricochet (760-366-1898; 61705 Twentynine Palms Hwy, Joshua Tree; Wed-Mon) Friendly lasses rule the roost at this espresso and juice bar, wine and beer shop, and recycled clothing store. Daily specials from the bakery and kitchen at the back sell out quickly. Diehard urbanites can buy the *New York Times* here. Call for opening hours.

Beatnik Café (760-366-2090; 61597 Twentynine Palms Hwy, Joshua Tree; 9am-midnight Thu-Tue, 9am-2am Wed;) At this trippy, youthful strip-mall coffeehouse with beat-up furniture, there's something happening almost every night: indie films, live music and, on Wednesdays, open mic.

Water Canyon Coffee Co (760-365-7771; 55844 Twentynine Palms Hwy, Yucca Valley; 7am-9pm Sun-Thu, 9am-10pm Fri & Sat; wi-fi) At the Hwy 62 turnoff for Pioneertown, hit this coffeehouse for richly roasted java, art and live acoustic sounds, usually on Tuesdays, Thursdays and Saturdays.

Shopping

Twentynine Palms Hwy is lined not just with dusty secondhand thrift shops, but also with vibrant arts-and-craft galleries. You can tour artists' galleries and workshops during the **Open Studio Tour** (760-366-2226; www.mbcac.org), held over two weekends in October. The non-profit **National Park Art Festival** (760-367-5500; www.joshuatree.org) shows desert-themed paintings, sculpture, photography, ceramics and jewelry in early April.

Getting There & Around

Rent a car in Palm Springs or LA. From LA, the trip takes two to three hours via I-10 then Hwy 62. From Palm Springs, it takes just an hour to reach the national park's west or south entrance. On the 15-mile stretch of Twentynine Palms Hwy between Joshua Tree and Twentynine Palms, people drive like maniacs, especially at night.

Morongo Basin Transit Authority (760-366-2395; www.mbtabus.com) runs local buses along Twentynine Palms Hwy (one-way fares $1 to $2, day pass $3) and limited services to Palm Springs (one way/round-trip $10/15). Many buses are equipped with bicycle racks, if you can bring a two-wheeled steed. Otherwise, you've got to drive everywhere inside the park (no shuttles).

SALTON SEA

It's a most unexpected sight: California's largest lake in the middle of its largest desert. The Salton Sea has a fascinating past, complicated present and uncertain future.

Geologists say that the Gulf of California once extended 150 miles further north to the present-day Coachella Valley, but millions of years' worth of rich silt flowing through the Colorado River gradually cut it off, leaving a sink behind. Native Americans cultivated crops for centuries here and fished beside Lake Cahuilla, which arose around AD 700. After Western pioneers arrived during California's Gold Rush, the lakebed became the site of salt mines. Once Western settlers realized the mineral-rich soil would make excellent farmland, Colorado River water was diverted into irrigation canals.

In 1905 the Colorado River flooded again, its water flowing uncontrolled into the Imperial Valley, and the Salton Sea was born. It took 18 months, 1500 workers and half a million tons of rock to put the river back on course, but with no natural outlet, the sea was here to stay. With its surface 220ft below sea level and its water 30% more salty than the Pacific Ocean, the sea today covers over 375 sq miles.

By the mid-20th century the Salton Sea was stocked with fish, including tilapia and corvina, and marketed as the 'California Riviera,' with vacation homes along its shores. The fish, in turn, attracted birds, and the sea remains a prime spot for bird-watching, including migratory and endangered species such as snow geese, eared grebes, ruddy ducks, white and brown pelicans, bald eagles and peregrine falcons.

THE DESERTS

WHAT THE…?

East of the Salton Sea, **Salvation Mountain** (www.salvationmountain.us) is a 100ft-high hill of concrete and hand-mixed adobe, covered with acrylic paint. With the motto 'God Never Fails,' it's the vision of folk artist Leonard Knight, who has been living behind his mountain since 1985. Turn off Hwy 111 at Niland, drive 5 miles east along Beal Rd and you can't miss it. Further along you'll find the entrance to **Slab City** (www.slabcity.org), an abandoned WWII-era barracks where 'snowbird' RVers, hippies and all kinds of genial freaks squat over the winter. Christopher McCandless (aka Alexander Supertramp) stayed here during his epic journey of self-discovery, as portrayed in the movie *Into the Wild*.

These days, if you've heard of the Salton Sea at all it's probably due to annual fish die-offs, which cause a rotting stench to permeate the beaches. The die-offs are due to phosphorous and nitrogen in runoff from farmland. The minerals cause algal blooms, and when the algae die they deprive the water – and fish – of oxygen. Even if farming were to stop tomorrow, there are still generations' worth of minerals in the soil, waiting to reach the sink.

One obvious solution would seem to be to cut off the water to the sea and let it die, but that carries its own dilemma. A dry Salton Sea would leave a dust bowl, with projections of a permanent dust cloud devastating air quality valleywide. The debate rages as ragged, rough-and-tumble communities try to eke out a living around the sea, as seen in the documentary film *Plagues and Pleasures on the Salton Sea* and the striking photos and essays of *Salt Dreams: Land and Water in Low-Down California*.

To see the sea for yourself, visit the **Salton Sea State Recreation Area** (☎ 760-393-3052; www.parks.ca.gov; day-use fee $6, campsites without/with hookups $17/23), about 25 miles south of Indio on the north shore. First-come, first-served Mecca Beach campground is a mile south of the visitors center. Further south, **Sonny Bono Salton Sea National Wildlife Refuge** (☎ 760-348-5278; http://saltonsea.fws.gov; 906 W Sinclair Rd, Calipatria; 🕑 sunrise-sunset, visitors center 7am-3:30pm Mon-Fri year-round, 8am-4:30pm Sat & Sun Oct-Mar), a migratory stopover and nesting spot for more than 400 species along the Pacific Flyway, is about 4 miles west of Hwy 111 between Niland and Calipatria.

ANZA-BORREGO DESERT STATE PARK

Enormous and little-developed, Anza-Borrego Desert State Park comprises almost a fifth of San Diego County and extends almost all the way to Mexico, making it the largest state park in the USA outside Alaska. It covers 640,000 acres – over 40% of the land in the California state park system. This untamed desert claims some of SoCal's most spectacular scenery and wildlife, with untrammeled backcountry byways to explore, all within easy reach of the retro-flavored resort town of Borrego Springs.

Human history here goes back more than 10,000 years, as recorded by Native American pictographs and petroglyphs. When Spanish explorer Juan Bautista de Anza passed through in the 1770s, pioneering a colonial trail from Mexico, he no doubt saw *borregos cimarrónes*, the Spanish term for the 1.5 million wild Peninsular bighorn sheep that once ranged as far south as Baja California. (Today only a few hundred of these animals survive, having been endangered by drought, disease, poaching and off-highway driving.) In the 1850s Anza-Borrego became a stop along the Butterfield stagecoach line, which delivered mail between St Louis and San Francisco.

Depending on winter rains, wildflowers bloom brilliantly, albeit briefly, in Anza-Borrego starting in late February, making a striking contrast to the subtle earth tones of the desert. Call the **Wildflower Hotline** (☎ 760-767-4684) for updates. Summers are extremely hot, hotter than in Joshua Tree National Park. The average daily maximum temperature in July is 107°F, but it can reach 125°F.

Orientation

Borrego Springs (population 2800, elevation 590ft) has a handful of restaurants and lodgings. On the outskirts of town, you'll find the state park visitors center and easy-to-reach sights, such as Borrego Palm Canyon and Fonts Point, that are fairly representative of the park as a whole. The Split Mountain area, east of Ocotillo Wells, is popular with off-highway vehicles (OHVs), but also contains interesting geology and spectacular wind

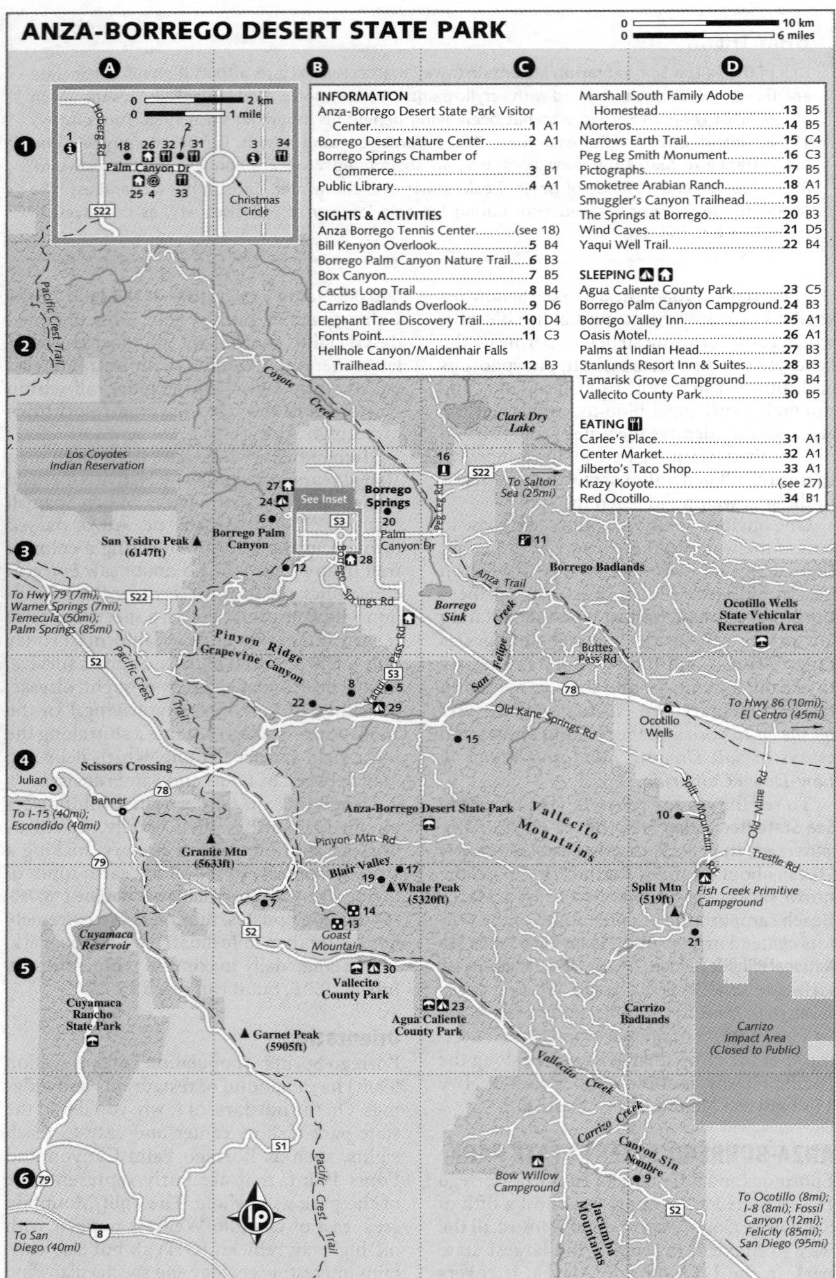
ANZA-BORREGO DESERT STATE PARK
INFORMATION
Anza-Borrego Desert State Park Visitor Center.....1 A1
Borrego Desert Nature Center.....2 A1
Borrego Springs Chamber of Commerce.....3 B1
Public Library.....4 A1
SIGHTS & ACTIVITIES
Anza Borrego Tennis Center.....(see 18)
Bill Kenyon Overlook.....5 B4
Borrego Palm Canyon Nature Trail.....6 B3
Box Canyon.....7 B5
Cactus Loop Trail.....8 B4
Carrizo Badlands Overlook.....9 D6
Elephant Tree Discovery Trail.....10 D4
Fonts Point.....11 C3
Hellhole Canyon/Maidenhair Falls Trailhead.....12 B3
Marshall South Family Adobe Homestead.....13 B5
Morteros.....14 B5
Narrows Earth Trail.....15 C4
Peg Leg Smith Monument.....16 C3
Pictographs.....17 B5
Smoketree Arabian Ranch.....18 A1
Smuggler's Canyon Trailhead.....19 B5
The Springs at Borrego.....20 B3
Wind Caves.....21 D5
Yaqui Well Trail.....22 B4
SLEEPING
Agua Caliente County Park.....23 C5
Borrego Palm Canyon Campground.....24 B3
Borrego Valley Inn.....25 A1
Oasis Motel.....26 A1
Palms at Indian Head.....27 B3
Stanlunds Resort Inn & Suites.....28 B3
Tamarisk Grove Campground.....29 B4
Vallecito County Park.....30 B5
EATING
Carlee's Place.....31 A1
Center Market.....32 A1
Jilberto's Taco Shop.....33 A1
Krazy Koyote.....(see 27)
Red Ocotillo.....34 B1
Palm Canyon Dr
Hoberg Rd
Christmas Circle
See Inset
Borrego Springs
Borrego Palm Canyon
San Ysidro Peak (6147ft)
Los Coyotes Indian Reservation
Coyote Creek
Clark Dry Lake
To Salton Sea (25mi)
Borrego Badlands
Borrego Sink
Anza Trail
Peg Leg Rd
Borrego Springs Rd
Yaqui Pass Rd
Pinyon Ridge
Grapevine Canyon
San Felipe Creek
Buttes Pass Rd
Ocotillo Wells State Vehicular Recreation Area
To Hwy 86 (10mi); El Centro (45mi)
Ocotillo Wells
Old Kane Springs Rd
To Hwy 79 (7mi); Warner Springs (7mi); Temecula (50mi); Palm Springs (85mi)
Pacific Crest Trail
Scissors Crossing
Julian
Banner
To I-15 (40mi); Escondido (40mi)
Granite Mtn (5633ft)
Anza-Borrego Desert State Park
Vallecito Mountains
Pinyon Mtn Rd
Blair Valley
Whale Peak (5320ft)
Goast Mountain
Split Mountain Rd
Old Mine Rd
Trestle Rd
Split Mtn (519ft)
Fish Creek Primitive Campground
Cuyamaca Reservoir
Vallecito County Park
Agua Caliente County Park
Cuyamaca Rancho State Park
Garnet Peak (5905ft)
Carrizo Badlands
Carrizo Impact Area (Closed to Public)
Vallecito Creek
Carrizo Creek
Canyon Sin Nombre
Bow Willow Campground
Jacumba Mountains
To Ocotillo (8mi); I-8 (8mi); Fossil Canyon (12mi); Felicity (85mi); San Diego (95mi)
To San Diego (40mi)

THE DESERTS

DESERT SURVIVAL 101

The desert is an unforgiving place with summertime temperatures up to 120°F, but if you take precautions you'll have nothing to fear. Here are some tips:

- **Water** Don't risk being stranded without it. Plan on drinking at least a gallon of water per day, double if you're hiking. Sports drinks high in sodium and potassium are also helpful. For info on heat exhaustion and heat stroke, see p742.
- **Your Vehicle** Fill up the gas tank whenever you can. An underinflated tire can overheat quickly. Watch the temperature gauge. If it starts to rise into the red zone, turn off the air-con, turn on the heater and roll down the windows. Or pull over, face the front of the car into the wind, carefully pop the hood and keep the car idling. If the engine gets hotter, shut it off immediately.
- **Hiking** Carry a compass and map, and know how to use them. GPS units are helpful, but batteries die and units can malfunction. Cell phones won't work in most areas. Carry a small mirror, matches and even flares to signal for help. A tent rainfly or groundsheet provides vital sun protection and increases your visibility. Also useful are a flashlight, a pocketknife, a first-aid kit, and extra food and water.
- **Flash Floods** Floods occur after heavy rains, even if the downpour is miles away. Don't park or camp in streambeds or washes. Check the weather forecast. If skies look threatening, don't start hiking into canyons from which you can't escape.
- **Mines** There are hundreds of abandoned mineral mines in the deserts. Watch out for holes, which are easy to fall into. Never enter old mines, as the shaft's supporting timbers usually have deteriorated and the air may contain poisonous gases.
- **Wildlife** Black widows, scorpions, rattlesnakes and centipedes are venomous but unlikely to attack. Obviously, cacti have spikes. Less obvious are their tiny barbs, which make the spikes difficult to extract. Bring strong tweezers or pliers, and avoid hiking in shorts.

caves. The desert's southernmost region is the least visited and, aside from Blair Valley, has few developed trails and facilities. Besides solitude, its attractions include historic sites and hot springs.

Information

You'll find ATMs, banks, gas stations, a post office and an urgent-care medical center in Borrego Springs, where cell phones usually work. The **public library** (☎ 760-767-5761; 571 Palm Canyon Dr, Borrego Springs; 9am-4pm Tue, Fri & Sat, noon-8pm Wed, 9am-6pm Thu) offers free walk-in internet access. The **chamber of commerce** (☎ 760-767-5555, 800-559-5524; www.borregosprings.org; 786 Palm Canyon Dr, Borrego Springs; 9am-4pm Mon-Fri) provides tourist information.

The **Borrego Desert Nature Center** (☎ 760-767-3098; www.california-desert.org; 652 Palm Canyon Dr, Borrego Springs; 9am-5pm daily Sep-Jun, 9am-3pm Fri & Sat Jul & Aug) is an excellent bookshop run by the Anza-Borrego Desert Natural History Association, which organizes tours, lectures, guided hikes and outdoor-skills courses. The **Anza-Borrego Foundation and Institute** (☎ 760-767-4063; www.theabf.org) also offers workshops, guest lectures, field trips and astronomy programs.

The excellent **Anza-Borrego Desert State Park Visitor Center** (☎ 760-767-4205; www.parks.ca.gov; 200 Palm Canyon Dr, Borrego Springs; 9am-5pm daily Oct-May, 9am-5pm Sat & Sun Jun-Sep) is built partly underground. From the parking lot, it looks like a low scrubby hill. Its stone walls blend beautifully with the mountain backdrop, while the interior has award-winning displays and audiovisual presentations. Park entry fees ($6 per vehicle per day) are required only for entering campgrounds, to access trails or to go picnicking.

The towns of Ocotillo Wells, Ocotillo and Julian (p674) also have gas stations.

Sights

Many of the most awesome sights are accessible only by dirt roads. To find out which roads require 4WD vehicles or are currently impassable, check the signboard inside the state park visitors center.

Northeast of Borrego Springs, where County Rte S22 takes a 90-degree turn east,

THE DESERTS

there's a pile of rocks just north of the road. This **monument** memorializes Thomas Long 'Peg Leg' Smith – mountain man, fur trapper, horse thief, con artist and Wild West legend – who passed through Borrego Springs in 1829 and allegedly picked up some rocks that were later found to be pure gold. Strangely, when he returned during the Gold Rush era, he was unable to find the lode. Nevertheless, he told lots of prospectors about it (often in exchange for a few drinks), and many came to search for the 'lost' gold and to add to the myths. On the first Saturday of April, the **Peg Leg Smith Liars Contest** is a hilarious event in which amateur liars compete in the Western tradition of telling tall tales. Anyone can enter, so long as the story is about gold and mining in the Southwest, is less than five minutes long and is anything but the truth.

East of Borrego Springs, a 4-mile dirt road, sometimes passable without 4WD, diverges south from County Rte S22 out to **Fonts Point**, a spectacular panorama over the Borrego Valley to the west and the Borrego Badlands to the south. You'll be amazed when the desert seemingly drops from beneath your feet. The turnoff, about 3.7 miles east of the monument, is easily missed. On the way back to town, take the dirt-road turnoff north to **Clark Dry Lake**, a bird habitat bordered by mesquite.

South of Hwy 78 at Ocotillo Wells, where you may see and hear OHVs, paved Split Mountain Rd passes the mile-long dirt road turnoff for the **Elephant Tree Discovery Trail**, a sandy 1.5-mile loop around these unusual and rare trees, whose stubby trunks and waving branches are thought to resemble elephants' legs and trunks. Related to frankincense and myrrh, these fragrant trees were thought not to exist in the Colorado Desert until a full-fledged hunt found them in 1937. Four miles further south along Split Mountain Rd is the dirt-road turnoff for Fish Creek primitive campground; another 4 miles brings you to **Split Mountain**, where a popular 4WD road goes right between 600ft-high walls created by earthquakes and erosion. At the southern end of this 2-mile-long gorge, steep trails lead up to delicate **wind caves** carved into sandstone outcroppings.

About 5 miles southeast of 'Scissors Crossing,' where County Rte S2 crosses Hwy 78, is the turnoff to **Blair Valley**, known for its *morteros* (rocks used by Native Americans for grinding seeds) on the former site of a Kumeyaay village. The valley and its hiking trailheads lie a few miles east of S2 along a dirt road. A steep 1-mile trail climbs **Ghost Mountain** to the remains of the 1930s adobe homestead built by desert recluse Marshall South and his family. Further east into the valley, past the *morteros* site, a boulder covered in Native American pictographs can be seen by walking about a mile along the **Smuggler's Canyon Trail**. Over on the north side of the valley, a monument at Foot and Walker Pass marks a difficult spot on the Butterfield Overland Stage Route, and in **Box Canyon** you can see the marks of wagons along the 19th-century pioneer Southern Emigrant Trail, also trod by the Mormon Battalion in 1847.

Further south along County Rte S2, you can wander around a replica of a historic stage station in the refreshing green valley of **Vallecito County Park** (☎ 760-765-1188; www.co.san-diego.ca.us/parks; 37349 County Rte S2; admission $2; 🕑 Sep-May). Four miles further down the road, take a hot-springs dip at **Agua Caliente County Park** (☎ 760-765-1188; www.co.san-diego.ca.us/parks; 39555 County Rte S2; admission $5; 🕑 8am-5:30pm Sep-May), which has indoor and outdoor pools. Continuing south on S2, you'll leave the crowds behind and pass dusty pull-offs for short hikes to palm oases, in addition to the spectacular **Carrizo Badlands Overlook**. If you make it all the way down to Ocotillo, drive a few miles north on dirt Shell Canyon Rd to see **Fossil Canyon.** As its name implies, fossils are commonly found there.

Activities

The park offers many more hiking trails and 4WD roads than just those described under Sights. It's also renowned for **stargazing** – sky charts are available at the visitors center.

HIKING

Free interpretive, self-guided hiking trail brochures are available at the visitors center, but not at trailheads.

Borrego Palm Canyon Nature Trail, a popular 3-mile loop trail that starts near the Borrego Palm Canyon Campground, passes a palm grove and waterfall, a delightful oasis in the dry, rocky countryside favored by bighorn sheep. The plucky **Maidenhair Falls Trail** starts from the Hellhole Canyon Trailhead, south of the visitors center on County Rte S22, and climbs 3 miles each way past several palm oases to a seasonal waterfall that supports bird life and a variety of plants.

South of Borrego Springs, a 1-mile loop starts from Yaqui Pass primitive campground and rolls out to the **Bill Kenyon Overlook**, with sprawling views of San Felipe Wash, the Pinyon Mountains and, on clear days, the Salton Sea (p668). Lower down, opposite Tamarisk Grove campground, are two nature walks: the 1-mile **Cactus Loop Trail** and the 1.6-mile **Yaqui Well Trail**. The latter has many labeled desert plants and passes a natural watering hole that attracts a rich variety of birds.

The 0.5-mile **Narrows Earth Trail**, about 4.5 miles east of Tamarisk Grove along Hwy 78, is an amateur geologist's walk in a fault zone. Look for low-lying, brilliant red chuparosa shrubs, which attract hummingbirds.

More hiking trails await in **Blair Valley**, described under Sights (opposite).

MOUNTAIN-BIKING

Over 500 miles of the park's dirt and paved roads (but never hiking trails) are open to bikes. Popular routes are Grapevine Canyon off Hwy 78 and Canyon Sin Nombre in the Carrizo Badlands. Flatter areas to take a spin around include Blair Valley and Split Mountain. Ask at the visitors center for more mountain-biking information.

GOLF

There are several championship golf courses around the Borrego Springs. **The Springs at Borrego** (☎ 760-767-0004, 866-330-0003; www.springsatborrego.com; 2255 DiGorgio Rd, Borrego Springs; greens fees $55) RV resort has a driving range and a nine-hole, par-36 course incorporating native desert vegetation.

TENNIS

Rent tennis courts and equipment at the **Anza Borrego Tennis Center** (☎ 760-767-0577; 286 Palm Canyon Dr, Borrego Springs; day pass adult/child $11/5.50). Opening hours vary.

HORSE RIDING

Catering mostly to groups, **Smoketree Arabian Ranch** (☎ 866-408-1812; www.smoketreearabianranch.com; 302 Palm Canyon Dr, Borrego Springs; 1¾hr tour $80, 4½hr tour incl lunch $250) also leads private guided rides on a working cattle ranch along the Pacific Crest Trail.

Sleeping

BUDGET

Camping

Camping is permitted anywhere in the park as long as you're off-road and not within 100yd of any water source. There are also several free primitive campgrounds in the park, which have pit toilets but no water. All campfires must be in metal containers. Gathering vegetation (dead or alive) is strictly prohibited.

Borrego Palm Canyon Campground (☎ reservations 800-444-7275; www.reserveamerica.com; tent & RV sites without/with hookups $20/29;) Near the visitors center, this campground has award-winning toilets, close-together campsites and an amphitheater with ranger programs on topics like astronomy and bats.

Tamarisk Grove Campground (☎ reservations 800-444-7275; www.reserveamerica.com; tent & RV sites $20) A dozen miles south of Borrego Springs, near Hwy 78, Tamarisk is smaller and quieter than Borrego Palm Canyon, and has more sheltering shade.

Also recommended:

Agua Caliente County Park (☎ reservations 858-565-3600, 877-565-3600; www.co.san-diego.ca.us/parks; 39555 County Rte S2; tent sites $15, RV sites with partial/full hookups $20/25; Sep-May) A better choice for sociable RVers, with natural hot-springs pools.

Vallecito County Park (☎ reservations 858-565-3600, 877-565-3600; www.co.san-diego.ca.us/parks; 37349 County Rte S2; tent & RV sites $15; Sep-May) Has more tent-friendly sites, in a cool, green valley refuge.

Motels

Oasis Motel (☎ 760-767-5409; www.oasisinnborrego.com; 366 Palm Canyon Dr, Borrego Springs; r $70-125; wi-fi) Standard-issue 1950s motel rooms, some with kitchens, and an outdoor barbecue.

Stanlunds Inn & Suites Resort (☎ 760-767-5501; www.stanlunds.com; 2771 Borrego Springs Rd, Borrego Springs; r $75-150; wi-fi) This convivial cinder-block motel has some kitchenettes, but no phones. Pet fee $10.

MIDRANGE

In summer, rates drop significantly and some places may close.

Palms at Indian Head (☎ 760-767-7788; www.thepalmsatindianhead.com; 2220 Hoberg Rd, Borrego Springs; r $129-229;) This tattered-around-the-edges Mid-Century Modern masterpiece has aerial views of the desert and an Olympic-sized swimming pool, where movie stars once frolicked. The atmosphere is pure Zen, but the

THE DESERTS

front desk is often deserted, often just when you need help fixing something that's broken in your room. Poolside bungalows have wood-burning fireplaces. No phones.

Borrego Valley Inn (☎ 760-767-0311, 800-333-5810; www.borregovalleyinn.com; 405 Palm Canyon Dr, Borrego Springs; r incl breakfast $200-280;) This petite, immaculately kept inn, filled with Southwestern artifacts and Native American weavings, is an intimate spa-resort, perfect for adults. One pool is clothing-optional. Most rooms have kitchenettes, but expect some traffic noise. The grounds are entirely nonsmoking. Wi-fi in the lounge.

Eating & Drinking

In summer many places keep shorter hours or close additional days.

Center Market (☎ 760-767-3311; 590 Palm Canyon Dr, Borrego Springs; 8:30am-6:30pm Mon-Sat, 8.30am-5pm Sun) The better of the town's two supermarkets also stocks camping supplies. It's across from the mall, which has mostly disappointing eateries.

Jilberto's Taco Shop (☎ 760-767-1008; 655 Palm Canyon Dr, Borrego Springs; mains $3-8; 7am-10pm Sun-Thu, 7am-11pm Fri & Sat) The cheapskate's fave, Jilberto's lacks both flavor and atmosphere, but it's not like you've got many other choices in town. So scarf your greasy tacos and shut up already. That's the attitude here.

our pick **Red Ocotillo** (☎ 760-767-7400; 818 Palm Canyon Dr, Borrego Springs; mains $6-15; 6am-9pm; V wi-fi) In an air-conditioned Quonset hut on the east side of town, this anonymous café (the sign simply says 'Eat') is a welcoming oasis. Fuel up on breakfast skillets, hulking sandwiches and bottomless cups of coffee. A pet-friendly patio is out back.

Carlee's Place (☎ 760-767-3262; 660 Palm Canyon Dr, Borrego Springs; mains $6-25; 11am-9pm) Even though the decor feels like it hasn't been updated since the 1970s, locals pick Carlee's, near Christmas Circle, for its burgers, pastas and steak dinners – the pool table, live music and karaoke are big draws, too.

Krazy Koyote (☎ 760-767-7788; Palms at Indian Head, 2220 Hoberg Rd, Borrego Springs; mains $12-36; dinner, closed summer) This chilled-out resort bar and grill serves its famous martinis and classics like chicken cordon bleu alongside inventive, fusion-spiced fare. The lounge atmosphere with boudoir-style lamps is more fabulous than the food. Service is unobtrusive.

Getting There & Around

From Palm Springs (1½ hours), take I-10 to Indio, then Hwy 86 south along the Salton Sea, turning west onto County Route S22. From LA (three hours) and Orange County (via Temecula), take I-15 south to CA Hwy 79 to County Rte 2 and County Rte 22; the final descent into Borrego Springs is head-spinning. From San Diego (two hours), take twisty Hwy 79 north from I-8 through Cuyamaca Rancho State Park, or follow the equally winding, even more scenic Sunrise Hwy (County Rte S1) north into Julian, then head east on Hwy 78 and north on County Rte S3 over Yaqui Pass into Borrego Springs.

JULIAN

pop 300 / elev 4235

For a cooler retreat, especially in summer, consider this small country town, famed for its apple pie. It was settled by Confederate soldiers after the Civil War, and flecks of gold were found in Coleman Creek in 1869, sparking a short-lived burst of speculation. More lasting riches were found in the fertile soil. Today apple orchards and equestrian ranches fill the countryside. For tourist information, contact the **chamber of commerce** (☎ 760-765-1857; www.julianca.com; 2129 Main St; 10am-4pm).

Be regaled with tales of the hardscrabble life of the town's early pioneers during an hour-long underground tour at **Eagle and High Peak Mine** (☎ 760-765-0036; end of C St; adult/child $10/5; 10am-2pm Mon-Fri, 10am-3pm Sat & Sun;). Along Hwy 78 outside town, family-owned orchards let you pick your own apples in September and October. Julian's apple harvest takes place in early autumn, but crowds descend year-round on its pint-sized main street, often jammed by motorcyclists out for a Sunday afternoon ride. False-fronted shops along the wooden sidewalks all claim to make the very best apple pie, cider, jams and jellies.

Julian Pie Company (☎ 760-765-2449; 2225 Main St; mains $3-15; 9am-5pm) churns out apple cider, cinnamon-dusted cider donuts and classic apple-filled pastries. For Old West atmosphere, stay at the historical landmark **Julian Gold Rush Hotel** (☎ 760-765-0201, 800-734-5854; www.julianhotel.com; 2032 Main St; r $130-210), a turn-of-the-20th-century B&B with antiques and a quaint honeymoon cottage. Outside town the countryside is filled with even more peaceful B&B retreats.

WHAT THE…?

Just west of the Arizona state line, the eccentric mayor of **Felicity** (☎ 760-572-0100; www.felicityusa.com; admission by donation; 15min tours available Thanksgiving-Easter) lets you tour the 'official center of the world,' as proclaimed in a children's fairy tale. At this bizarre desert landmark (officially a town, though it's just a few buildings), gawk at the spiral staircase from the Eiffel Tower (now surreally ascending to nowhere) and granite walls in the desert etched with eclectic scenes from world history. But it's a long way from civilization, that's for sure. Coming from the coast, take I-8 to exit 164, then backtrack west along the north frontage road for a mile or so.

Julian is a 40-minute drive southwest of Borrego Springs. Head south over Yaqui Pass on County Rte S3, then take curvy Hwy 78 west; Julian is 12 miles past Scissors Crossing. From San Diego, it's about an hour's drive: take I-8 east, then CA Hwy 79 north to Julian.

ROUTE 66

Never has a highway been so symbolic as Route 66, now bypassed by the modern interstate system. Snaking across the belly of America, it connected the prairie capital of Chicago with distant Los Angeles, starting in 1926. What novelist John Steinbeck called the 'Mother Road' came into its own during the Depression, when thousands of migrants escaped the Dust Bowl by slogging westward in beat-up old jalopies painted with 'California or Bust' signs, *Grapes of Wrath*–style. After WWII, Americans took their newfound wealth and convertible cars on the road to get their kicks on Route 66. As traffic along the USA's post-WWII interstate highway system boomed, many small towns along Route 66, with their neon-signed motor courts, diners and drive-ins, eventually went out of business. Every year another landmark goes up for sale, but more get rescued from ruin.

In California, Route 66 mostly follows the National Old Trails Hwy, which is prone to potholes and dangerous bumps. After running a gauntlet of Mojave Desert ghost towns, you'll motor through the railroad towns of Barstow and Victorville, cross over Cajon Summit and dive into the LA Basin, where crashing ocean waves await at the end of Santa Monica Pier. For Route 66 enthusiasts who want to drive every mile of the old highway, free turn-by-turn driving directions are available online at www.historic66.com. Also surf to www.cart66pf.org and www.route66ca.org for more historical background, photos and info about special events.

BARSTOW

pop 38,750 / elev 2106ft

At the junction of I-40 and I-15, nearly halfway between LA and Las Vegas, down-and-out Barstow has been a desert travelers' crossroads for centuries. In 1776 Spanish colonial priest Francisco Garcés caravanned through, and in the mid-19th century the Old Spanish Trail passed nearby, with pioneer settlers on the Mojave River selling supplies to California immigrants. Meanwhile, mines were founded in the hills outside town. Barstow, named after a railway executive, got going as a railroad junction after 1886. After 1926 it became a major rest stop for motorists along Route 66. Today it exists to serve nearby military bases, as well as being a charmless pit stop for travelers.

Information

Barstow Area Chamber of Commerce (☎ 760-256-8617; www.barstowchamber.com; 681 N 1st Ave; 10am-4pm Mon-Fri) At the train station, just north of downtown.

Barstow Community Hospital (☎ 760-256-1761; 555 S 7th Ave; emergency room 24hr)

Highway Radio (98.1FM, 99.8FM, 99.5FM) Mojave traffic and weather updates every half-hour.

Sights

Like an outdoor gallery, history-themed **murals** (www.mainstreetmurals.com) spruce up often empty and boarded-up buildings downtown, mostly along Main St between 1st and 6th Aves.

North of Main St, across the train tracks, is the beautifully restored **Casa Del Desierto** (681 N 1st Ave), a 1911 Harvey House designed by famed Western architect Mary Colter. It once provided hospitality to Santa Fe Railway travelers. Inside, poke around the **Route 66 'Mother Road' Museum** (☎ 760-255-1890; http://route66museum.org; admission by donation; 10am-4pm Fri-Sun Apr-Oct, 11am-4pm Fri-Sun Nov-Mar), full of black-and-white historical photographs and relics of everyday life along the historic highway. Route 66 driving guides, maps and books are sold in the gift shop. Next door, the humble **Western America Railroad Museum** (☎ 760-256-9276; www.barstowrailmuseum.org; admission by donation; 11am-4pm Fri-Sun) has memorabilia and a growing stock collection outside.

Back near I-15, stop by the kid-oriented, educational **Desert Discovery Center** (☎ 760-252-6060; www.discoverytrails.org; 831 Barstow Rd; admission free; 11am-4pm Tue-Sat) to see Old Woman Meteorite (6070lb), the second-largest ever found in the USA. Nearby, the musty **Mojave River Valley Museum** (☎ 760-256-5452; www.mojaveriver museum.org; 270 E Virginia Way; admission free; 11am-4pm) displays a few prehistoric fossils, and Native American baskets and projectile points.

East of town off I-15, **Calico Ghost Town** (☎ 760-254-2122, 800-862-2542; www.calicotown.com; Ghost Town Rd, Yermo; adult/child $6/3; 9am-5pm) is a shamelessly hokey Old West attraction, with reconstructed pioneer-era buildings amid the ruins of a late-19th-century silver mining town. You'll pay extra to go gold panning, tour the Maggie Mine, ride a narrow-gauge railway or see the 'mystery shack.' Old-timey heritage celebrations include Civil War reenactments and a bluegrass 'hootenanny.'

THE DESERTS

Sleeping & Eating

Only when the Mojave freezes over will there be no rooms left in Barstow. Check yourself into any of the dozens of well-worn budget motels along E Main St, many with doubles for $40 or less.

Oak Tree Inn (☎ 760-254-1148; www.oaktreeinn.com; 35450 Yermo Rd, Yermo; r incl breakfast $75-90; wi-fi) A better bargain than most places in Barstow, this comfy three-story motel with a heated outdoor pool is east of town off I-15 (exit Ghost Town Rd), on the opposite side of the highway from a KOA campground. Breakfast is served at the 1950s-style diner, also a 24-hour truck stop. Pets OK.

Texas Style BBQ (☎ 760-256-6222; 208 E Main St; mains $6-15; 11am-9pm Mon-Sat, noon-9pm Sun) Talk about hot! From the Lone Star state, this downhome take-out shack slow-cooks succulent beef brisket, tri-tip, pork ribs, chicken and spicy sausage with baked beans and potatoes, with sweet-potato pie for dessert.

Idle Spurs Steakhouse (☎ 760-256-8888; 690 Old Hwy 58; mains lunch $8-14, dinner $14-35; 11am-9pm Mon-Fri, 4-9pm Sat & Sun) In the saddle since 1950, this Western-themed spot ringed around an atrium and a full bar is a fave of locals and RVers. Get yer prime rib, London broil and shrimp cocktails here, folks.

Di Napoli's Firehouse (☎ 760-256-1094; 1358 E Main St; mains $8-15; 11am-9pm Mon-Sat) At a kitschy old-school Italian joint in a strip mall, friendly servers dish up big bowls of minestrone soup hearty enough to fuel an expedition, plus gigantic calzones, meatball pizzas and pastas, and classic chicken parmesan.

Hacienda La Colima (☎ 760-255-4200; 29836 Old Hwy 58; mains $8-21; dinner) Barstow definitely doesn't lack for Mexican joints, but it's worth going out of your way to this *muy auténtico* seafood grill and restaurant, where mariachi bands play on weekend nights. Try the *sopa azteca*, chicken topped with homemade mole sauce and 'crazy' octopus cocktails.

Entertainment

Skyline Drive-In (☎ 760-256-3333; 31175 Old Hwy 58; adult/child $6/2) One of the few drive-ins left in California, this 1960s movie theater shows double features nightly.

Getting There & Around

You'll need a car to get around Barstow and to drive Route 66. A few major car-rental agencies have in-town offices.

Frequent **Greyhound** (☎ 800-231-2222; www.greyhound.com) buses from LA ($30 to $40, 2½ to 5¼ hours), Las Vegas ($32 to $41, 2¾ hours) and Palm Springs ($31 to $44, four to 7½ hours) arrive at a **bus station** (☎ 760-256-8757; 1611 E Main St; 9am-6pm Mon-Sat, 7:30am-4:30pm Sun) east of downtown, near I-15.

Amtrak (☎ 800-872-7245; www.amtrak.com) trains stop at Barstow's historic **train station** (685 N 1st Ave). The *Southwest Chief* runs to/from LA ($27, 3¾ hours) daily (depart LA 6:45pm, depart Barstow 3:39am), stopping at San Bernardino and continuing east to Needles. There's no staffed ticket office. Trains are often late. Thruway buses to these and other destinations depart from the Greyhound station.

NEEDLES TO BARSTOW

Start at the Arizona border, where the Old Trails Arch Bridge carried the Joad family across the Colorado River in *The Grapes of Wrath*. West along I-40 is Needles, named after nearby mountain spires. Drive downtown on Front St, past the old mule-train wagon and 1920s Palm Motel alongside the railroad tracks, to **El Garces**, a 1908 Harvey House undergoing restorations. Head west on Broadway and left onto Needles Hwy, where vintage motels and diners still stand on the western edge of town.

Join I-40 westbound, exit at US 95, drive north for 6 miles, then at the railroad tracks turn west toward Goffs, where the 1914 Mission-style **Goffs Schoolhouse** (☎ 760-733-4482; www.mdhca.org; 37198 Lanfair Rd; admission by donation; usually 9am-4pm Sat & Sun) remains part of the best-preserved historic settlement in the Mojave Desert. Back on Goffs Rd, drive through Fenner, which has a high-priced gas station, to the south side of I-40. Keep following old Route 66 by turning right onto the National Old Trails Hwy, a potholed, crumbling backcountry stretch of the Mother Road that races through more ghostly desert towns, which were once perfectly named in backward alphabetical order. Only a few landmarks interrupt the limitless horizon, most famously **Roy's Motel & Cafe**, east of **Amboy Crater**, an almost perfectly symmetrical volcanic cinder cone, which you can scramble up the west side of (but don't attempt it in high winds or summer heat). Keep driving west, past haunting ruins spliced in among the majestic landscape.

In Ludlow, turn right onto Crucero Rd, pass under I-40, then turn left onto the northern frontage road. After several bumpy miles, turn left again at Lavic Rd. Cross back over I-40, then drive west on the National Old Trails Hwy to Newberry Springs, where the grizzled **Bagdad Café** (☎ 760-257-3101; 46548 National Old Trails Hwy; mains $5-10) roadhouse, renamed after the 1980s indie flick, collects notebooks of tourists' scribblings from around the world (opening hours vary).

The highway passes under I-40 again on its way through Daggett, site of the California inspection station once dreaded by Dust Bowl refugees. Pay your respects to early desert adventurers like Death Valley Scotty (see p684) at the crumbling historic **Stone Hotel**, then drive west to Nebo Rd, turning left to rejoin I-40 toward Barstow, and exiting at Main St.

BARSTOW TO LOS ANGELES

On the western outskirts of Barstow, Main St becomes the National Old Trails Hwy, curving southwest through Lenwood and Helendale. Beloved by Harley bikers, this rural stretch is like a scavenger hunt for Mother Road ruins, such as antique filling stations and tumble-down motor courts. Colorful as a box of crayons, **Elmer's Place** is a roadside folk-art collection of recycled glass bottles, telephone poles and railroad signs. In Oro Grande, singing cowboy Roy Rogers once imbibed at the **Iron Hog Saloon** (☎ 760-843-8004; 20848 National Old Trails Hwy), now a biker bar and barbecue shack.

Cross the Mojave River on a steel-truss bridge, following D St into downtown Victorville. Opposite the train station, the **California Route 66 Museum** (☎ 760-951-0436; www.califrt66museum.org; 16825 D St; donations welcome; 10am-4pm Thu-Mon, sometimes 11am-3pm Sun) has a mishmash of historical exhibits and art inside the old Red Rooster Cafe roadhouse. Turn right onto 7th St, driving past the county fairgrounds, home of the Route 66 Raceway.

Rejoin I-15 southbound over daunting Cajon Summit. Take the Oak Hill Rd exit to the **Summit Inn** (☎ 760-949-8688; 5960 Mariposa Rd, Oak Hills; mains $5-10; 6am-8pm Mon-Thu, 6am-9pm Fri & Sat), a 1950s truck stop with antique gas pumps, a retro jukebox and a lunch counter that serves ostrich burgers and date shakes. At Cleghorn, exit at Cajon Blvd and trundle south along an ancient section of the Mother Road, then get back on I-15 at Kenwood Ave. Keep heading south, moving over onto I-215, then exiting right away at Devore.

Follow Cajon Blvd south into San Bernardino, then detour east to the **First McDonald's Museum** (☎ 909-885-6324; 1398 N E St; admission by donation; 10am-5pm), which has interesting historic Route 66 exhibits. Nearby, the **Inland Empire 66ers** (☎ 909-888-9922; www.ie66ers.com; 280 S E St; tickets $6-9; Apr-Aug) play minor-league baseball at Arrowhead Park. Take 5th St west of downtown, curving slightly onto Foothill Blvd to find the **Wigwam Motel** (☎ 909-875-3005; www.wigwammotel.com; 2728 W Foothill Blvd, Rialto; r $65-80; wi-fi), with its kooky-looking concrete faux tipis dating from 1949.

Cruising through Fontana, birthplace of the notorious Hells Angels biker club, you'll see the now boarded-up **Giant Orange** (15395 Foothill Blvd), a 1920s juice stand of the kind that was once a fixture alongside SoCal's citrus groves. On the western outskirts of town are two retro steakhouses: the rustic **Sycamore Inn** (☎ 909-982-1104; 8318 Foothill Blvd; mains $19-48; dinner), dating from 1848; and the **Magic Lamp Inn** (☎ 909-981-8659; 8189 Foothill Blvd; mains $15-25; lunch Tue-Fri, dinner Tue-Sun), with a fabulous neon sign and dancing most evenings.

In Glendora, Route 66 diverts briefly onto Alosta Blvd. **The Hat** (☎ 626-857-0017; 611 W Rte 66; mains $3-8; ⏰ 10am-1am; 👶) has made piled-high pastrami sandwiches since 1951. Back on Foothill Blvd, wind west through Azusa to Duarte, which puts on a Route 66 parade every September, with boisterous marching bands, old-fashioned carnival games and a classic car show. The older alignment of Route 66 follows Foothill Blvd through Monrovia, where the Mayan Revival–style architecture of the **Aztec Hotel** (☎ 626-358-3231; 311 W Foothill Blvd) is worth a look.

Otherwise, stay on Huntington Dr westbound, passing under I-210 into Arcadia. The Marx Brothers' *A Day at the Races* was filmed at **Santa Anita Park** (☎ 626-574-7223, tour reservations 626-574-6677; www.santaanita.com; 285 W Huntington Dr; ⏰ live racing 26 Dec-20 Apr), where legendary thoroughbred Seabiscuit ran. During the live-racing season, free tram tours take you behind the scenes into the jockeys' room and training areas; reservations are required.

Veer right onto Colorado Pl, then go straight onto Colorado Blvd and drive west into Pasadena. With the motto 'timeless appeal with modern luxuries,' vintage **Saga Motor Hotel** (☎ 626-795-0431, 800-793-7242; www.thesagamotorhotel.com; 1633 E Colorado Blvd; r $92-108; wi-fi) still hands out quaint metal room keys to its guests. Stop off for an egg cream at the nostalgic soda fountain at the 1915 **Fair Oaks Pharmacy** (☎ 626-799-1414; 1526 Mission St; mains $4-8; ⏰ 9am-9pm Mon-Sat, 10am-7pm Sun; 👶) before braving traffic on the final stretch through Los Angeles.

Drive south on I-110 toward LA, exiting at Sunset Blvd. After a few miles driving west on Sunset Blvd, turn left onto Manzanita Blvd and cruise slowly west along Santa Monica Blvd, which eventually dead-ends at oceanfront Palisades Park. Here a plaque marks the terminus of Route 66, a short walk north of **Santa Monica Pier** (p537).

MOJAVE NATIONAL PRESERVE

Controversially created as part of the 1994 California Desert Protection Act, this lonely, windswept preserve contains 1.6 million acres of 'singing' sand dunes, Joshua trees, volcanic cinder cones, and the ruins of Native American, military and mining settlements. Solitude and serenity are the big draws, often with bighorn sheep, desert tortoises, jackrabbits and coyotes as your only companions. Daytime temperatures hover above 100°F during summer, then hang around 50°F in winter, when snowstorms are not unheard of. Strong winds will practically knock you over in spring and fall.

INFORMATION

Admission to the **Mojave National Preserve** (☎ 760-252-6100; www.nps.gov/moja; ⏰ 24hr) is free.

Highway Radio (98.1FM, 99.8FM, 99.5FM) Broadcasts Mojave traffic and weather updates every half-hour.

Hole-in-the-Wall Information Center (☎ 760-252-6104, 760-928-2572; ⏰ 9am-4pm Fri-Sun May-Sep, 9am-4pm Wed-Sun Oct-Apr) Seasonal ranger programs, basic backcountry information and road condition updates. It's about 20 miles north of I-40 via Essex Rd.

Kelso Depot Visitor Center (☎ 760-252-6108; Kelbaker Rd, Kelso; ⏰ 9am-5pm) Ranger-staffed information desk with a gift shop selling maps and books.

Nipton Trading Post (☎ 760-856-2335; 107355 Nipton Rd, Nipton; ⏰ 8am-6pm; wi-fi) Books, maps, groceries, water and 24-hour coin-op laundry.

SIGHTS & ACTIVITIES

You can spend an entire day or just a few hours driving around the preserve, taking in its sights and exploring some of them on foot.

Visible to the south from I-15, **Cima Dome** is a 1500ft hunk of granite spiked with volcanic cinder cones and crusty outcroppings of basalt left by lava. At one point the number of cones is so great that they're protected as **Cinder Cones National Natural Landmark**. This anciently charred landscape is best viewed from a distance. Alternatively, tackle the 4-mile round-trip hike up **Teutonia Peak** (5755ft), starting off Cima Rd, 6 miles north of Cima. The moderately strenuous trail wanders through the world's largest Joshua Tree forest.

On Black Canyon Rd, east of Kelso-Cima Rd via unpaved Cedar Canyon Rd, is the **Hole-in-the-Wall** formation. These vertical walls of rhyolite tuff (pronounced toof), which look like Swiss-cheese cliffs made of unpolished marble, are the result of a powerful prehistoric volcanic eruption that blasted rocks across the landscape. On the 0.5-mile Rings Trail, metal rings lead down through a narrow slot canyon, once used by Native Americans to escape 19th-century ranchers. Ask at the visitors

SLOW: DESERT TORTOISE X-ING

The Mojave is the abode of the desert tortoise, which can live for up to 80 years, munching on wildflowers and grasses. With its canteenlike bladder, it can go for up to a year without drinking. Using its strong hind legs, it burrows to escape the summer heat and freezing winter temperatures, and also to lay eggs. The sex of the hatchlings is determined by temperature: cooler for males, hotter for females.

Disease and shrinking habitat have decimated the desert tortoise population. They do like to rest in the shade under parked cars (take a quick look around before just driving away), and are often hit by high-speed, off-road drivers. If you see a tortoise in trouble, eg stranded in the middle of a road, call a ranger.

It's illegal to pick one up or even approach too closely, and for good reason: a frightened tortoise may urinate on a perceived attacker, possibly dying of dehydration before the next rains come.

center if **Wild Horse Canyon Road**, an incredibly scenic 9.5-mile backcountry drive up to Mid Hills, is currently passable.

The heart of the preserve is the palm-fringed **Kelso Depot Visitor Center**, inside a gracefully restored 1920s railway depot. Stop by to watch the 12-minute park orientation film and peruse in-depth museum exhibits that explore the multicultural and natural history of the desert, from Native American days to the arrival of the Union Pacific Railroad in 1905.

Three miles along a graded dirt road west of Kelbaker Rd, 7.5 miles south of Kelso Depot, the weathered **Kelso Dunes** rise 600ft high above the Devil's Playground. Like Death Valley's Eureka Dunes (see the boxed text, p685), these 'singing' dunes can produce a musical sound when sand slips down their faces – try running downhill to jump-start the unusual sound effects. The dunes are a 3-mile round-trip hike from the parking area.

To the east, the Providence Mountains are an impressive wall of rocky peaks. In Providence Mountains State Recreation Area, the **Mitchell Caverns** (☎ 760-928-2586; www.parks.ca.gov; adult/child $5/2; 🕑 tours 1:30pm daily, also 10am & 3pm Sat & Sun Sep-May) are known for their driplike formations called speleothems. Tours often sell out early, but reservations can only be made by mail at least three weeks in advance. Short nature hikes commence nearby. The caverns are 6 miles west of Essex Rd, and about 16 miles northwest of I-40.

Coming from Barstow, take the Afton Rd exit off I-15 and drive a graded gravel road for 3 miles to reach **Afton Canyon**, the terminus of the historic Mojave Rd. Or take the Zzyzx Rd exit, 6 miles west of Baker, and follow a washboard gravel road 4 miles down to **Soda Dry Lake**. On the site of a mid-20th-century mineral-springs spa resort run by Doc Springer, who wanted to name the road so that it sounded just like sleep, California State University's solar-powered **Desert Studies Center** (http://biology.fullerton.edu/dsc) offers all-inclusive weekend courses and field trips.

SLEEPING & EATING

Cheap motels and take-out restaurants in Baker, north of the preserve along I-15, are best avoided. Southeast of the preserve along Route 66, Needles (p676) has slightly better budget-saving options.

Providence Mountains State Recreation Area has a half-dozen first-come, first-served primitive campsites ($12), perched high above the desert floor. First-come, first-served sites with pit toilets and potable water are available at two small, developed **NPS campgrounds** (☎ 760-928-2572; www.nps.gov/moja; tent & RV sites

DETOUR: PIONEER SALOON

About 10 miles north of Stateline, NV, on I-15 is the gambling gulch of Jean. Turn off at Gold Strike casino hotel for the 7-mile trip west on NV 161 to Goodsprings and the **Pioneer Saloon** (☎ 702-874-9362; 310 W Spring St, Goodsprings; 🕑 11am-late), a little stamped-metal roadside shack built in 1913 (which makes it southern Nevada's oldest bar). Riddled with bullet holes, the saloon has a vintage cherrywood bar and movie-star memorabilia from the 1940s, when Clark Gable waited here for news about the plane crash that killed his wife, Carole Lombard, another Old Hollywood star.

THE MOJAVE PHONE BOOTH

If a phone rang in the middle of the Mojave Desert, and someone was around to answer it, does that mean it still exists? Sadly, no.

Called the loneliest phone booth in the world, there once was a bullet-hole-riddled payphone on Aiken Mine Rd, 15 miles from the nearest highway. It was marked on AAA maps only as 'Telephone.' After seeing it mentioned in a magazine, artist Godfrey Daniels became curious enough to call the phone booth every day until miner Lorene Caffee finally answered. He chronicled their 1997 conversation online (www.deuceofclubs.com/moj/mojave.htm).

The phone booth soon became a cult attraction. People from Vietnam to Germany would call the pay phone at all hours of the day or night. Burning Man festival-goers and other travelers would stop by just to answer the ringing phone. It even cameoed in an *X-Files* episode.

And then it disappeared. In 2000 PacBell and the National Park Service removed the phone booth. NPS Superintendent Mary Martin argued that all the traffic was damaging the environment. But to some, the phone booth symbolized a greater controversy over land-use rights in the Mojave National Preserve. Everyday folks had just lost out to the feds – again.

$12): Hole-in-the-Wall, surrounded by rocky desert landscape; and Mid Hills (no RVs), set among pine and juniper trees. Free camping is allowed off most unpaved roads (except Zzyzx Rd and around Kelso Dunes), as long as you're not within 200yd of a water source and don't build a campfire; ask for more details at visitor centers.

Primm Valley Resorts (☎ 800-386-7867; www.primmvalleyresorts.com; 31900 Las Vegas Blvd S, Primm, NV; r from $23; wi-fi) At the Nevada state line, next to an outlet shopping mall off I-15, these casino hotels are basic, but much better than motels in Baker. Family-friendly Buffalo Bill's is best, although Whiskey Pete's accepts pets ($15 fee). There are dozens of predictable dining options inside all three casino hotels: fast-food courts, all-you-can-eat buffets and 24-hour coffee shops.

Hotel Nipton (☎ 760-856-2335; www.nipton.com; 107355 Nipton Rd, Nipton; tent cabins d $70, hotel r with shared bath $80, all incl breakfast; reception 8am-6pm; wi-fi) In the northeastern corner of the preserve, this early-20th-century railroad town has all the peace you could ever ask for. Accommodations comprise a historic adobe hotel and tented cabins (equipped with electricity, fans, woodstoves and platform beds). Guests of both share a garden hot tub under the stars. Check in at the Nipton Trading Post.

Whistlestop Oasis (mains lunch $5-10, dinner $10-25) Next door to the Hotel Nipton, this place serves up scrumptious pork chops for dinner. There's just one cook in the kitchen, so pop open an ice-cold beer and shoot some stick while you wait. Opening hours vary.

GETTING THERE & AWAY

To reach the north side of the preserve, access roads are off I-15 between Barstow and Stateline, NV. The main exit is at Baker, about an hour's drive east of Barstow and 90 minutes from Las Vegas. Entrances to the south side of the preserve are off I-40, not far from Route 66.

DEATH VALLEY NATIONAL PARK

Death Valley National Park, the largest national park in the continental USA, covers an enormous area – more than 5000 sq miles – that includes other valleys and mountain ranges to the north. The name itself evokes all that is harsh, hot and hellish in the deserts of the imagination, a punishing, barren and lifeless place of Old Testament severity. But Death Valley is full of life. Inside this crazy-quilted geological playground, you'll find giant sand dunes, mosaic marbled canyons, boulders that appear to race across the sun-baked desert floor, extinct volcanic craters, palm-shaded oases and dozens of rare wildlife species that exist nowhere else in the world.

Death Valley is not a true valley – it's a basin formed by earthquakes. Extensive earthquake faulting and fracturing allows some of the oldest rocks to be visible on the earth's surface, when normally they would be hidden deep underground. Formed on an ancient seabed, these rock strata were bent, folded and cracked as converging tectonic plates

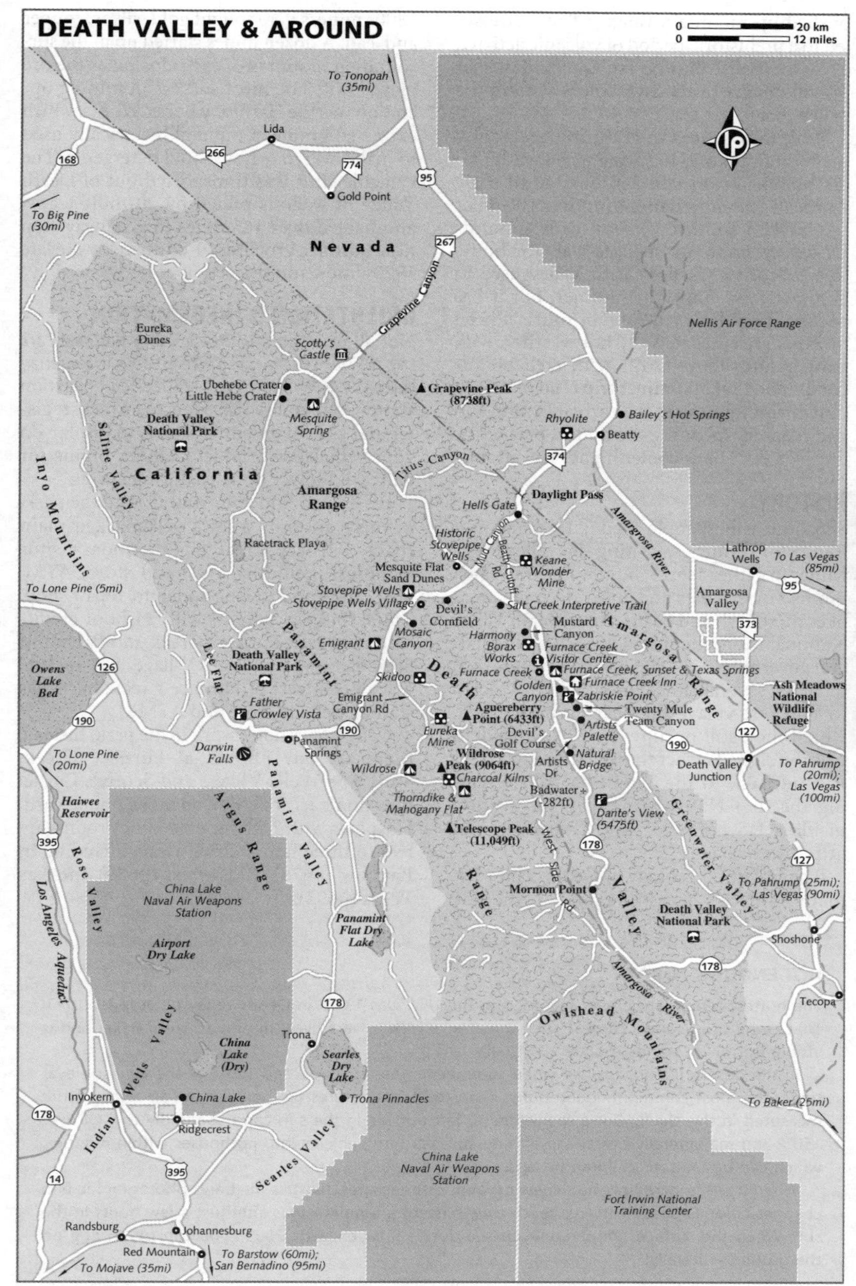
DEATH VALLEY & AROUND
0 20 km
0 12 miles
To Tonopah (35mi)
Lida
Gold Point
To Big Pine (30mi)
Nevada
Grapevine Canyon
Nellis Air Force Range
Eureka Dunes
Scotty's Castle
Ubehebe Crater
Little Hebe Crater
Grapevine Peak (8738ft)
Mesquite Spring
Death Valley National Park
Saline Valley
Rhyolite
Bailey's Hot Springs
Beatty
California
Titus Canyon
Inyo Mountains
Amargosa Range
Daylight Pass
Hells Gate
Mud Canyon
Beatty Cutoff Rd
Amargosa River
Racetrack Playa
Historic Stovepipe Wells
Keane Wonder Mine
Lathrop Wells
To Las Vegas (85mi)
Mesquite Flat Sand Dunes
To Lone Pine (5mi)
Stovepipe Wells
Stovepipe Wells Village
Devil's Cornfield
Salt Creek Interpretive Trail
Amargosa Valley
Mosaic Canyon
Mustard Canyon
Harmony Borax Works
Emigrant
Panamint
Lee Flat
Death Valley National Park
Furnace Creek Visitor Center
Owens Lake Bed
Furnace Creek
Furnace Creek, Sunset & Texas Springs
Skidoo
Death
Furnace Creek Inn
Golden Canyon
Zabriskie Point
Ash Meadows National Wildlife Refuge
Emigrant Canyon Rd
Father Crowley Vista
Agueereberry Point (6433ft)
Twenty Mule Team Canyon
Artists Palette
Amargosa Range
Eureka Mine
Devil's Golf Course
Panamint Springs
Darwin Falls
To Lone Pine (20mi)
Wildrose Peak (9064ft)
Artists Dr
Natural Bridge
Death Valley Junction
To Pahrump (20mi); Las Vegas (100mi)
Wildrose
Charcoal Kilns
Thorndike & Mahogany Flat
Badwater (-282ft)
Haiwee Reservoir
Argus Range
Panamint Valley
Dante's View (5475ft)
Greenwater Valley
Telescope Peak (11,049ft)
West Side Rd
Rose Valley
China Lake Naval Air Weapons Station
Range
Mormon Point
Valley
To Pahrump (25mi); Las Vegas (90mi)
Los Angeles Aqueduct
Airport Dry Lake
Death Valley National Park
Panamint Flat Dry Lake
Shoshone
Amargosa River
Tecopa
Owlshead Mountains
Wells Valley
China Lake (Dry)
Trona
Searles Dry Lake
Inyokern
China Lake
Trona Pinnacles
To Baker (25mi)
Indian
Ridgecrest
Searles Valley
China Lake Naval Air Weapons Station
Fort Irwin National Training Center
Randsburg
Johannesburg
Red Mountain
To Barstow (60mi); San Bernadino (95mi)
To Mojave (35mi)
168
266
774
95
267
374
373
126
190
127
178
395
14

THE DESERTS

pushed up mountain ranges. These stresses led to a prehistoric period of volcanic activity, explosively distributing ash and cinders that provide many of the rich colors seen in the valley today.

Peak tourist season is during the cooler winter months and in spring when wildflowers bloom. From late February until early April, all accommodations for over 100 miles are booked solid for weeks, campgrounds fill before noon and people wait for hours to see Scotty's Castle. Death Valley used to be practically empty in summer, but it has become popular with foreign tourists keen to experience hellaciously hot weather, with temperatures above 120°F. With a reliable air-conditioned car, a summer trip is possible, but only if you sightsee in the early morning and late evening, spending the hottest part of the day by a pool or at cooler higher elevations.

HISTORY

Shoshone tribespeople lived in the Panamint Range for centuries, visiting the valley every winter to gather acorns, hunt waterfowl, catch pupfish in marshes and cultivate small areas of corn, squash and beans. After Death Valley National Monument was created by the federal government in 1933, the tribe was forced to move several times, eventually restricted to a 40-acre village site near Furnace Creek, which they still occupy. In 2000 President Clinton signed an act transferring 7500 acres of land back to the Timbisha tribe, creating the first Native American reservation inside a US national park. Learn more at http://timbisha.org.

The fractured geology of Death Valley left many minerals accessible, and in the late 1800s miners here sought gold, silver, copper and lead. A dozen mines started up in the surrounding mountains, each closing as the ore played out. The most successful mining operation was the Harmony Borax Works, which extracted borate, a mineral historically used to make everyday household detergents. The valuable stuff was transported out of Death Valley in wagons pulled by 20-mule teams and hauled over 165 miles to a railway stop near Boron, a grueling 10-day trip. By the late 1920s, most mining activities had ceased.

ORIENTATION & INFORMATION

Not all entrances to **Death Valley National Park** (☎ 760-786-3241; www.nps.gov/deva; 7-day entry pass per car/bicycle $20/10; 24hr) have a staffed fee-collection station, but you're still expected to self-register and pay for an entry permit to display on your vehicle's windshield. Check online for daily wildflower updates during spring.

It's easy to find your way around the park, as there are only a few, well-marked main roads. Furnace Creek has the most visitor facilities, including a general store, ATM, post office, and towing and auto-repair shop. You'll find gas stations with 24-hour credit-card pumps at Furnace Creek and Panamint Springs. Stovepipe Wells Village, a 35-minute drive northwest of Furnace Creek, has a gas station, general store and ATM.

Cell phones don't work in the park. Instead, there are pay phones at Furnace Creek, Stovepipe Wells Village and Scotty's Castle; they don't accept coins, so buy a phone card. Hospitals with 24-hour emergency rooms are two to three hours' drive away, including in Barstow (p675), Ridgecrest (p689) and Las Vegas (p693).

HOT ENOUGH FOR YA?

The hottest temperature ever recorded in the USA was 134°F in Death Valley on July 10, 1913. That's why the 'World's Largest Thermometer,' which towers over the tiny town of Baker and is visible from I-15, stands exactly 134ft tall.

In the desert, it's no surprise when summer temperatures exceed 120°F at the lowest elevations. The most commonly quoted and reported temperatures are only for the air temperature measured in the shade. But a thermometer left outside in the sun can rise rapidly to well over 150°F and may literally burst. The blazing sun will turn vehicles into hothouses within minutes, which can be fatal for children or pets.

When it's this incredibly hot, chewing gum disintegrates, plastics melt and photographic film changes color. Exposed surfaces reach truly blistering temperatures after just a few hours in the sun. When the surface temperature on the desert floor exceeds 200°F, you can fry an egg on the ground – literally!

Death Valley Chamber of Commerce (www.deathvalleychamber.org) Comprehensive website, plus a small visitors center in Shoshone (p687).

Death Valley Natural History Association (☎ 800-478-8564; http://dvnha.org) Runs NPS visitors centers bookstores and occasionally organizes special events.

Furnace Creek Visitor Center (☎ 760-786-3200; Hwy 190, Furnace Creek; 🕑 9am-5pm) Sells books and maps, offers free informational handouts (available online) and screens a 15-minute slide show. Check schedules of ranger activities, given daily between November and March.

Scotty's Castle Visitor Center (☎ 760-786-2392; North Hwy; 🕑 9am-4:30pm summer, 8:30am-5pm rest of year) Has exhibits from the castle's museum-worthy collection.

SIGHTS

You really can't do it all in a day, even if you start out very early in the morning (always a good thing to do in the desert). A peaceful overnight stay inside or near the park ensures you'll catch a memorable sunset *and* sunrise. In summer, stick to paved roads (dirt roads can quickly overheat vehicles) and strictly limit your exertions (eg hiking).

Badwater & Furnace Creek

In a park filled with Mother Nature's oddities, the strangest place may be **Badwater**, officially the lowest elevation point in the Western Hemisphere (282ft below sea level). Here you can walk out onto a boardwalk over a constantly evaporating bed of salty, mineralized water that's otherworldly in its beauty. It's a 25-minute drive from Furnace Creek, at the southern end of the valley.

As you drive back north on Hwy 178, gaze west across the valley floor at the **Devil's Golf Course**, filled with lumps of crystallized salt. Further north is the **Artists Drive**, a one-way scenic loop that passes alluvial fans, where streams have left deposits at the mouths of side canyons, and the **Artists Palette** of colorful exposed minerals and volcanic ash.

Take a break at shady Furnace Creek Ranch. The **Borax Museum** (☎ 760-786-2345; admission free; 🕑 10am-5pm Oct-May) will tell you all about the once-valuable stuff, with a collection of pioneer-era stagecoaches and wagons out back. The Furnace Creek Visitor Center, with its small **museum** of natural and human history, is up the road. A short drive further north, a short interpretive trail leads in the footsteps of late-19th-century Chinese laborers and through the adobe ruins of **Harmony Borax Works**, where you can take a side trip through twisting **Mustard Canyon**.

At the end of the day, backtrack to **Dante's View** (5475ft). This panoramic vision of an inferno of badlands is gorgeously hued at sunset. En route, detour through **Twenty Mule Team Canyon**, a bone-rattling one-way driving and mountain-biking loop through an ancient lakebed that will make you feel like an ant. Heading back down toward the valley, it's a short walk out to **Zabriskie Point**, where you can scramble down into the eroded badlands.

Stovepipe Wells Village

En route from Furnace Creek to Stovepipe Wells, keep an eye out for a camera-icon sign and a roadside pull-off on your right, where you can walk out (as long as it's not too hot) into the Sahara-like **Mesquite Flat sand dunes**. Do this when the sun is low in the sky, which makes the dunes more photogenic, or on a full-moon night. On the other side of the road, look for the **Devil's Cornfield**, full of arrow weed clumps. Just west of **Stovepipe Wells Village**, the site of Death Valley's original 1920s tourist resort, a 3-mile gravel side road leads to **Mosaic Canyon**, where you can hike, then crawl through a polished marble slot canyon.

Further southwest, Emigrant Canyon Rd detours off Hwy 190, passing the turnoff to **Skidoo**, a mining ghost town that went bust and where the silent movie *Greed* was filmed in 1923. This turnoff travels along a graded high-clearance gravel road to jaw-dropping Sierra Nevada views. Emigrant Canyon Rd also passes the high-clearance dirt-road turnoff to **Eureka Mine**, beyond which vertiginous **Aguereberry Point** (6433ft) provides views back into Death Valley. Back on the main road, climb steeply over Emigrant Pass and through Wildrose Canyon to reach the **charcoal kilns**, a lineup of large, stone, beehive-shaped structures historically used by miners to make fuel for smelting silver and lead ore. The landscape is subalpine, with forests of piñon pine and juniper; it can be covered with snow, even in spring.

Back east of Stovepipe Wells, off Beatty Cutoff Rd, a 3-mile graded gravel road leads out to the **Keane Wonder Mine**, the ruins of which still feel like an Old West movie set. It's a short but stiff uphill hike from the road. Remember not to venture inside any mine shafts in and around the park, which can suddenly collapse without warning.

Scotty's Castle

Walter E Scott, alias 'Death Valley Scotty,' was the quintessential tall-tale teller who captivated people with his fanciful stories of gold. His most lucrative friendship was with Albert and Bessie Johnson, insurance magnates from Chicago. Despite knowing that Scotty was a freeloading liar, they bankrolled the construction of this elaborate Spanish-inspired villa. Restored to its 1930s appearance, the historic house has sheepskin drapes, carved California redwood, handmade tiles, elaborately wrought iron, woven Shoshone baskets and a bellowing pipe organ upstairs.

For the full story on **Scotty's Castle** (☎ 760-786-2392; adult/child $11/6; ⌚ grounds 7:30am-5:30pm summer, 7:30am-6pm rest of year, tours 9am-4:30pm summer, 8:30am-5pm rest of year), take one of the guided 'Living History' tours. More technically minded 'Underground Mysteries' tours, as well as guided visits to Scotty's cabin at Lower Vine Ranch, are available seasonally. All tickets are first-come, first-served, and there can be a long wait (or they may sell out completely). If you just want a glimpse of the place, Scotty's Castle Visitor Center exhibits bits and pieces of the past.

Scotty's Castle is a 90-minute drive north of Furnace Creek. Nearly 3000ft above sea level, and noticeably cooler than the valley floor, the castle's palm-shaded lawns make for a picturesque escape from the midday heat. Three miles west of the castle, turn off the main road to visit 770ft-deep **Ubehebe Crater**, formed by the explosive meeting of fiery magma and cool groundwater. Hikers can loop around its half-mile-wide rim and over to younger **Little Hebe Crater**.

Panamint Springs

In the remote western area of the park, Panamint Springs is a tiny enclave that not many tourists get to. It has incredible hidden gems, starting with **Father Crowley Vista**, which peers into Rainbow Canyon, created by lava flows and scattered with colorful volcanic cinders. In spring, DIY adventurers attempt the 2-mile graded gravel road, followed by a mile-long cross-country trek out to **Darwin Falls**, a natural-spring-fed cascade that plunges into a gorge, embraced by willows that attract migratory birds. You could also take roughshod Saline Valley Rd out to **Lee Flat**, where Joshua trees thrive.

ACTIVITIES

Families can pick up fun-for-all-ages **junior ranger program** activity books at the Furnace Creek Visitor Center, which has info-packed handouts on all kinds of activities, including hiking trails and mountain-biking routes. Cycling is allowed on all established paved and dirt roads, but never on trails.

Hiking

In addition to the interpretive trails and canyon walks described under Sights, there are many more trails here, from easy nature walks to tougher, mountain-goat climbs. Avoid hiking in summer, except on higher-elevation mountain trails, which may be snowed over in winter.

FACING DEATH IN THE VALLEY

A small band of pioneer '49ers first wandered into this valley after they separated from a larger emigrant group along the Old Spanish Trail, taking a sensible southern route to avoid crossing the Sierra Nevada in winter and repeating the Donner party disaster of 1846–47 (see the boxed text, p367).

Taking what they hoped would be a shortcut to the California goldfields, the small party struggled across the Nevada desert for a month before entering this valley from the east. Exhausted and running out of food and water, they arrived near Furnace Creek on Christmas Eve of 1849. They just couldn't get their broken-down wagons over the Panamint Range.

While most of the party sheltered near a water hole, two young men were sent to scout for a route west over the mountains. Only two families waited for the scouts, who eventually returned after 26 days in the wilderness. Near Stovepipe Wells, they all slaughtered their oxen, burned their wagons and walked out of the valley via what is now Emigrant Canyon.

As they left, one woman reputedly looked back and uttered the words 'Good-bye, death valley.' Ironically, the most life-threatening part of their journey – crossing the Mojave Desert plateau – was yet to come.

4WD TRACKS AROUND DEATH VALLEY

The mysterious **Racetrack Playa** is a 28-mile trip south of Ubehebe Crater, over a tire-shredding dirt road that requires 4WD. Two miles south of the rocky 'grandstand,' you can see large rocks that appear to have moved on their own across this mud flat, making long, faint tracks in the sunbaked surface. Scientific theories abound, but nothing has been proven.

Want more 4WD adventure? East of Ubehebe Crater, a graded dirt road heads 45 miles northwest, out past Crankshaft Junction (slow down, then turn left) and Hanging Canyon (hang another left) to **Eureka Dunes**, California's tallest. Rising almost 700ft out of a dry lakebed, some of the world's only 'singing' dunes sound deep bass notes during sandslides. An easier approach is from Big Pine (p413), from where it's 28 miles along a paved road, then 21 miles of roughly graded dirt.

If you exit Death Valley to the east via Hells Gate, climbing over Daylight Pass past the Nevada border, the turnoff to Leadfield ghost town is the start of a 27-mile, one-way road that drops ruggedly down through spectacular **Titus Canyon**, passing petroglyphs around Klare Spring, where bighorn sheep sometimes gather, to the floor of Death Valley. The road may be closed at any time. Without a 4WD vehicle, you can still reach the mouth of Titus Canyon from the west.

Inquire about weather and road conditions, pick up 4WD trail guides and buy topographic maps at the Furnace Creek Visitor Center.

On Hwy 190, just north of Beatty Cutoff Rd, is the half-mile **Salt Creek Interpretive Trail**; in late winter or early spring, rare pupfish splash in the stream alongside the boardwalk. A few miles south of Furnace Creek is **Golden Canyon**, where a self-guided interpretive trail winds for a mile up to the now-oxidized iron cliffs of **Red Cathedral**. With a good sense of orientation, you can keep going up to **Zabriskie Point**, for a hardy 4-mile round-trip. Before reaching Badwater, stretch your legs with a 1-mile round-trip walk to the **Natural Bridge**.

Off Wildrose Canyon Rd, starting by the charcoal kilns, **Wildrose Peak** (9064ft) is an 8.4-mile round-trip trail. The elevation gain is 2200ft, but you only have to hike halfway up to enjoy good views. The park's most demanding summit is **Telescope Peak** (11,049ft), with views that plummet down to the desert floor, which is two Grand Canyons deep! The 14-mile round-trip trail climbs 3000ft above Mahogany Flat, off upper Wildrose Canyon Rd. The last mile is a steep grade, so don't attempt it in winter unless you're an experienced climber equipped with ice axes and crampons. The last stretch of road to the trailhead requires a high-clearance (possibly 4WD) vehicle. Otherwise, start from the charcoal kilns, adding another 1.5 miles and another 2000ft of elevation change each way.

Golf

For novelty's sake, you can play a round at historic **Furnace Creek Golf Course** (☎ 760-786-2301; Hwy 190, Furnace Creek; greens fees $25-55; ⏰ mid-Oct–early May), the world's lowest-elevation course (18 holes, par 70), redesigned by Perry Dye in 1997. Players claim the below-sea-level setting helps them set personal records. Well, it can't hurt, right?

Horse Riding

At the ranch, **Furnace Creek Stables** (☎ 760-786-3339; Hwy 190, Furnace Creek; 1/2hr rides $45/65; ⏰ Oct-May) arranges three horseback rides daily, except during summer; monthly full-moon rides are best.

FESTIVALS & EVENTS

Badwater (www.badwater.com) Staged at the suicidal height of summer in mid-July, Badwater is a 135-mile ultramarathon from Badwater Basin up to Whitney Portal (p415).

Death Valley '49ers (www.deathvalley49ers.org) In early November, a historical encampment happens at Furnace Creek, featuring cowboy poetry, campfire sing-alongs, a gold-panning contest and a Western art show. Show up early to watch the pioneer wagons come thunderin' in.

SLEEPING

You'll find more campgrounds and basic motels in towns scattered around Death Valley (see p687).

There are nine **NPS campgrounds** (www.nps.gov/deva; tent & RV sites $12-18) inside the park. **Reservations** (☎ 877-444-6777; www.recreation.gov) are only accepted for Furnace Creek Campground arrivals between mid-October and mid-May. All other campgrounds are always first-come, first-served. At peak times (eg when spring wildflowers bloom), all campsites fill by noon.

In summer, it's too hot to camp on the valley floor. High-elevation campgrounds may get snowed in during winter.

Furnace Creek (crowded, little shade, mostly RVs), Mesquite Spring (an oasis near Scotty's Castle) and free Wildrose (higher in the Panamint Range, no RVs) campgrounds are open year-round. Stovepipe Wells and Sunset, near Furnace Creek, are roadside gravel parking lots, with plenty of RVs; Texas Springs, on a hillside above Furnace Creek, has more shade. Near Stovepipe Wells Village, year-round Emigrant campground has free, tent-only sites; it's cooler and has valley views, too. Higher in the Panamint Range are two free, tent-only campgrounds without water: Thorndike (7400ft) and Mahogany Flat (8200ft), usually open from March until November. You may need 4WD to reach them, especially during winter.

For backcountry camping, allowed only in some parts of the park, you must be at least 2 miles from the nearest developed area or paved road, and 200yd from any water source. Old mining areas are for day-use only. Stop by the Furnace Creek Visitor Center for more details and to pick up a free permit.

Stovepipe Wells Village (☎ 760-786-2387, reservations 303-297-2757, 800-236-7916; www.stovepipewells.com; Hwy 190, Stovepipe Wells Village; RV sites with hookups $23, r $75-115;) It may be just a roadside motel with a small pool, but it has more quirky character than Furnace Creek. Renovated motel rooms (no phones or TVs) are spacious, and definitely the valley's best bargain. Wi-fi in the lounge. Pets OK.

Furnace Creek Ranch (☎ 760-786-2345, reservations 303-297-2757, 800-236-7916; www.furnacecreekresort.com; Hwy 190, Furnace Creek; cabins $123-139, motel r $154-189;) Tailor-made for families, this dusty, Old West–style ranch is a short walk from the general store and restaurants. Not as peaceful as Stovepipe Wells Village, it has only ordinary cabins and motel rooms, but more facilities, such as a children's playground, tennis courts and a natural-spring-fed swimming pool. There's wi-fi outside the general store.

Furnace Creek Inn (☎ 760-786-2345, reservations 303-297-2757, 800-236-7916; www.furnacecreekresort.com; Hwy 190, Furnace Creek; r $305-410, ste $410-425; mid-Oct–mid-May;) At this elegant hilltop adobe hotel built in 1927, Mission-style buildings are spread among California-fan-palm-shaded garden terraces. Elemental, almost Zen-like rooms with cable TV are overpriced, but the serenity is priceless. There's a warm-springs outdoor swimming pool with jaw-dropping valley views, plus tennis courts.

EATING & DRINKING

Toll Road Restaurant (☎ 760-786-2387; Stovepipe Wells Village, Hwy 190; mains breakfast & lunch $5-10, dinner $11-25; breakfast, lunch & dinner;) Above-par cowboy cooking happens inside this ranch house with fireplace. Native American blankets and rickety wooden chairs and tables make it feel like the Old West. At dinner, expect beef brisket, an unlimited salad bar and key lime pie for dessert. Next door, the divey Bad Water Saloon (open 4:30pm to 11pm) has Skynyrd on the jukebox and a pool table.

Panamint Springs Resort (☎ 775-482-7680; www.deathvalley.com; Hwy 190, Panamint Springs; mains $5-20; breakfast, lunch & dinner; wi-fi) Barely inside the park's western boundary, a winding 30-mile drive southwest of Stovepipe Wells Village, this friendly outback café cooks up three square meals a day, with outdoor barbecues in summer. Crack open a microbrew and toast the panoramic views from the front porch.

Forty-Niner Cafe & Wrangler Steak House (☎ 760-786-2345; Furnace Creek Ranch, Hwy 190, Furnace Creek; mains $8-25; cafe 7am-9pm mid-Oct–mid-May, 11:30am-9pm mid-May–mid-Oct, steakhouse 5-9pm mid-Oct–mid-May, 6-9:30pm mid-May–mid-Oct;) There are often very long waits for only average American food, yet it's always crowded. Portions are huge at the café and more ambitious steakhouse, but avoid the buffet. The always-busy Corkscrew Saloon (open 11:30am to midnight) has all types of firewaters, pub grub like buffalo wings, custom-made pizzas and pool tables.

Furnace Creek Inn (☎ 760-786-2345; Hwy 190, Furnace Creek; mains lunch $12-18, dinner $22-37; lunch & dinner mid-Oct–mid-May) At the elegant inn atop the oasis, reserve a table in the formal dining room (strict dress code applies), or keep things casual at the sociable bar, where you can order from the same menu of so-so Southwestern fare like fried cactus and pork tamales. Afternoon tea and Sunday brunch are hoity-toity affairs. Sunset cocktails and decent wines are served on the outdoor patio.

Furnace Creek and Stovepipe Wells have general stores stocking basic groceries and camping supplies. Scotty's Castle has a **snack bar** (10am-5pm summer, 9:30am-5:30pm rest of year).

GETTING THERE & AROUND

Furnace Creek is 110 miles (two to 2½ hours) north of Baker, or 145 miles (2½ to three hours) northwest of Las Vegas. Driving into the valley from I-15 (California) or US Hwy 95 (Nevada) takes you past high-desert scenery that looks airflifted from Mongolia or Morocco. Driving out of the valley along CA Hwy 190 via Panamint Springs, an hour's drive from Lone Pine and US Hwy 395, is just as breathtaking, with the Sierra Nevada range splayed out before you. Gas is expensive in the park, so fill up your tank beforehand.

AROUND DEATH VALLEY NATIONAL PARK

Keep in mind that it's a long haul from any of the following tiny desert settlements into the park. Further-flung gateways include Baker, on I-15 further south, and Ridgecrest (p689) to the west; neither is recommended for overnight stays. Heading north, Lone Pine (p414) is a more charming overnight stop.

TECOPA

pop 99 / elev 1329ft

About an hour's drive north of Baker and I-15, on a short looping detour east of CA Hwy 127, this desert hot-springs settlement is named after a peace-making Paiute chief.

Open year-round, **Delight's Hot Springs Resort** (☎ 760-852-4343, 800-928-8808; www.delightshotspringsresort.com; 368 Tecopa Hot Springs Rd; admission to hot springs $10, RV sites with hookups $33, r $69, cabins $85-99) has private hot-springs bathhouses (two sans roofs) and a handful of 1930s cabins and motel rooms. At **Tecopa Hot Springs Resort** (☎ 760-852-4420; www.tecopahotsprings.org; 860 Tecopa Hot Springs Rd; admission to hot springs $8, campsites without/with hookups $16/25, r $45-75; 🕑 6am-10pm Oct-May), simple, sex-segregated bathhouses shelter therapeutic mineral springs, where tribal elders, snowbird RVers and curious tourists soak together. Its humble little bistro, **Pastels** (☎ 760-852-4307; mains $5-15; 🕑 usually 9am-9pm), has a friendly 'flexitarian' kitchen, where the chef's California fusion menu often made with organic ingredients is always changing, and the bread is house-baked fresh daily.

An equally restful respite, **Ranch House Inn and Hostel** (☎ 760-852-4580; www.ranchhouseinn.com; 2000 Old Spanish Trail Hwy; dm $22-25, d $58-148, all with shared baths; ❄) has sex-segregated dorms and private hostel rooms inside funky, air-conditioned roadside trailers, sharing a communal kitchen. At the inn on China Ranch, you can sleep inside a 1920s cottage or in romantic tipis with king-sized beds and firepits. Reservations are essential, even if that means just calling ahead from the road.

Just outside town, **China Ranch Date Farm** (☎ 760-852-4415; www.chinaranch.com; 🕑 9am-5pm) is a family-run venture by an oasis, where you can go hiking or bird-watching in the canyons. To get here, follow Old Spanish Trail Hwy east of Tecopa Hot Springs Rd, turn right on Furnace Creek Rd and follow the signs. Mmm, fresh-baked date bread.

SHOSHONE

pop 52 / elev 1569ft

Just a blip on the desert map, a 15-minute drive north of Tecopa, Shoshone is the last place to stop and stretch your legs en route to the park. Look for an old Chevy parked outside the **Shoshone Museum** (☎ 760-852-4524; admission by donation; 🕑 10am-4pm), which has some unusual desert history and geology exhibits. The **Death Valley Chamber of Commerce** (☎ 760-852-4524; www.deathvalleychamber.org; 🕑 10am-4pm) visitors center is also here.

Across the street, beside the general store and gas station, the 1950s **Shoshone Inn** (☎ 760-852-4335; www.shoshonevillage.com; Hwy 127; d $75-105; ❄ 🏊) has basic, broken-down motel rooms with TVs and phones (some kitchenettes), and a small warm-springs pool outside. **Shoshone RV Park** (☎ 760-852-4569; campsites with full hookups $25) is just north of town.

our pick Cafe C'est Si Bon (☎ 760-852-4307; 118 Hwy 127; items $2-8; 🕑 8am-4pm Fri-Wed; 🚸 V wi-fi) An always delightful, solar-powered place where the genial chef-owner makes a mean espresso, gourmet baked goods, and 'flexitarian' breakfasts and lunches (think homemade crepes and quiche). World music plays soothingly in the background, occasionally interrupted by the happy oinks of Pizza, the pet pig.

It's 55 miles from Furnace Creek to Shoshone via Death Valley Junction, but most folks elect to take the 75-mile scenic route through Badwater Basin instead.

BEATTY, NEVADA

pop 1000 / elev 3308ft

Just over 40 miles north of Furnace Creek, this historic Bullfrog mining district boomtown

LIFE AT DEATH VALLEY JUNCTION

Where Hwys 127 and 190 collide, about 30 miles east of Furnace Creek, stands the ghostly **Amargosa Opera House & Hotel** (☎ 775-852-4441; www.amargosaoperahouse.com; r $68-84;). Built by the Pacific Borax Company, this 1920s Mexican colonial-style courtyard building was revived by New York dancer Marta Becket after her car broke down nearby in 1967. Marta has painted a trompe l'oeil audience on the walls of the opera house, where she performs heartbreakingly corny **dance-and-mime shows** (adult/child $15/12; shows 8:15pm Sat Nov–mid-May), even though she's now over 80 years old. Reservations are required to stay in the eerie motel-style rooms, some with boudoir lamps and murals (no TVs or phones).

has certainly seen better days, but has a few rare sights worth crossing the state line for, plus it's a good place to get fuel and stock up on supplies. Everything is close to the main crossroads, including a bank and the **chamber of commerce** (☎ 775-553-2424, 866-736-3716; www.beattynevada.org; 119 Main St; 10am-2pm). The **public library** (☎ 775-553-2257; cnr N 4th & E Ward Sts; 10am-4pm Mon & Wed, noon-7pm Tue, 10am-noon Sat; wi-fi) offers free walk-in internet terminals. There's a 24-hour gas station next to the Stagecoach Casino.

Worth a stop is the microscopic **Beatty Museum** (☎ 775-553-2303; 417 Main St; admission by donation; 10am-4pm), where you can be impressed by artifacts from the Old West mining days. A few miles further west toward the park is the ghost town of **Rhyolite** (☎ 775-553-2967; www.rhyolitesite.com; NV Hwy 374; admission free; 24hr). Don't overlook the 1906 'bottle house' or the skeletal remains of a three-story bank. Also on-site is the bizarre **Goldwell Open Air Museum** (☎ 702-870-9946; www.goldwellmuseum.org; admission free; 24hr) of trippy installation art, begun by Belgian artist Albert Szukalski in 1984.

Five miles north of town, **Bailey's Hot Springs** (☎ 775-553-2395; US Hwy 95 N; admission to hot springs $6, tent/RV sites $15/18; pools 8am-8pm) has natural mineral-springs pools in two antique bathhouses inside a 1906 railroad depot. Roadside campsites are better suited to RVs than tent campers. It's past the sign for Angel's Ladies brothel.

Opposite the now-shuttered Exchange Club Casino, the **Sourdough Saloon** (☎ 775-553-2266; 106 Main St; pizza $8-16; noon-midnight) has nickel video poker, pool tables and pizza. A mile north of the crossroads, the decent, cookie-cutter **Motel 6** (☎ 775-553-9090; www.motel6.com; 550 US Hwy 95 N; r $53-59;) accepts pets. At the nearby **Stagecoach Hotel** (☎ 775-553-2419, 800-424-4946; 900 US Hwy 95 N; r $60-110; wi-fi), spruced-up rooms are bland (so are the casino's restaurants), but they're the comfiest in town.

UPPER MOJAVE DESERT

The Mojave Desert covers a vast region, from urban areas on the northern edge of LA County to the remote, sparsely populated country of the Mojave National Preserve (p678). The upper Mojave is a harsh land, with sporadic mining settlements and vast areas set aside for weapons and aerospace testing. Most of the traffic here consists of big rigs making their way between Bakersfield and Barstow on Hwy 58, and heading up to the Sierras on US Hwy 395 – these highways cross each other at Kramer Junction. But there are a few things out here worth stopping for, too.

LANCASTER-PALMDALE

pop 145,250 / elev 2355ft

The Antelope Valley is dead flat. It's difficult to see a valley, much less an antelope. But in spring, it's spectacularly carpeted with bright-orange fields of California poppies, like a vision out of *The Wizard of Oz*.

West of Lancaster, the **Antelope Valley California Poppy Reserve** (☎ 661-724-1180; www.parks.ca.gov; 15101 Lancaster Rd at 170th St W; per vehicle $5; sunrise-sunset) offers hillside walks among the wildflowers. To get there, take Hwy 14 south of Mojave for about 25 miles, exit at Ave I in Lancaster and drive 15 miles west, following the signs. Five miles further west, **Arthur B Ripley Desert Woodland State Park** (☎ 661-942-0662; Lancaster Rd at 210th St W; admission free; sunrise-sunset) has an untrammeled interpretive trail leading through precious stands of Joshua trees.

East of Lancaster, **Antelope Valley Indian Museum** (☎ 661-942-0662; http://avim.parks.ca.gov; Ave M) displays Native American artifacts from around California and across the Southwest. It was closed at the time of research (but due to open again in spring 2009); call for admission prices and opening hours. To get here from Hwy 14, travel east on Ave K or Palmdale Blvd and follow the signs. The museum is between 150th and 170th Sts E; look for a quirky Swiss-style chalet up among the boulders on the north side of Ave M. You can camp among Joshua trees and desert-tortoise habitat at nearby **Saddleback Butte State Park** (☎ 661-942-0662; 170th St E, south of Ave J; tent & RV sites $12).

Budget motels line the Sierra Hwy, east of downtown Lancaster and Hwy 14. The retro 1950s **Town House Motel** (☎ 661-942-1195, 800-227-0012; 44125 Sierra Hwy; r $70-80; wi-fi) has clean, simple rooms. Chain motels and hotels cluster further south near **LA/Palmdale Regional Airport** (☎ 661-266-7600; www.lawa.org/pmd). Downtown Lancaster's **Lemon Leaf Cafe** (☎ 661-942-6500; 653 W Lancaster Blvd; mains $6-12; 11am-9pm Mon-Thu & Sat, 11am-10pm Fri) is a culinary oasis, making market-fresh salads, grilled panini sandwiches and artisan cakes bursting with berries, citrus or chocolate.

MOJAVE

pop 3840 / elev 2757ft

Driving around Mojave town, you might mistake it for a huge international airport, but all those airliners are actually in storage, as the dry desert air minimizes deterioration. To the southeast, **Edwards Air Force Base** (☎ 661-277-3510; www.edwards.af.mil) is a flight-test facility for the US Air Force, NASA and civilian aircraft, and a training school for test pilots with the 'right stuff.' Chuck Yeager piloted the world's first supersonic flight here, and it was here the first space shuttles glided in after their missions. In 2004 SpaceShipOne became the first civilian aircraft to reach suborbital altitudes here – twice. Public tours of the on-base flight museum and NASA research center are usually given on the first and third Fridays of the month; for reservations, contact the public affairs office a few weeks in advance.

BORON

pop 2030 / elev 2355ft

Off Hwy 58, about midway between Mojave and Barstow, this tiny town got its start when rich deposits of borax were found underground here in 1927. Historically, this was where Death Valley's famous 20-mule teams had previously deposited their huge loads of borax, hauled from over 165 miles away, at a dusty, desert railway station.

Downtown, the low-budget **Twenty Mule Team Museum** (☎ 760-762-5810; www.20muleteammuseum.org; 26962 Twenty Mule Team Rd; admission by donation; 10am-4pm) reveals why this mineral you've probably never heard of is actually so valuable. It also has railroad memorabilia and naturalist displays of gems, wildflowers and wildlife such as the endangered desert tortoise. North of town at the modern mine, company-run **Borax Visitor Center** (☎ 760-762-7588; www.borax.com; Borax Rd, off Hwy 58; per car $2; 9am-5pm) has more technical displays for the scientifically minded.

Back downtown, the geeky **Saxon Aerospace Museum** (☎ 760-762-6600; www.saxonaerospacemuseum.org; 26922 Twenty Mule Team Rd; admission by donation; usually 10am-4pm) recounts milestones in experimental flight testing in the surrounding desert. Further east, autographed photos of astronauts and air-force test pilots hang on the walls of **Domingo's Mexican & Seafood Restaurant** (☎ 760-762-6266; 27075 Twenty Mule Team Rd; mains $6-18; 11am-10pm), always packed with lunchtime crowds from the nearby military base.

RIDGECREST

pop 26,000 / elev 2239ft

Ridgecrest exists only because of the million-acre China Lake US Naval Air Weapons Station along its eastern edge. You can stock up on information, gas and supplies here before heading to Death Valley, but it's not a pretty place.

US citizens can visit the **US Naval Museum of Armament & Technology** (☎ 760-939-3530; www.chinalakemuseum.org; admission free; usually 10am-4pm Mon-Sat) on the military base; getting a guest pass from the entrance gate requires photo ID. In town, at the Northern Mojave Visitor Center, the **Maturango Museum** (☎ 760-375-6900; www.maturango.org; 100 E Las Flores Ave, cnr China Lake Blvd; adult/child $5/free; 10am-5pm;) has elementary exhibits focusing on natural science, Native Americans and military technology. Bring

DETOUR: RANDSBURG

About 20 miles south of Ridgecrest off US Hwy 395, **Randsburg** (☎ 760-374-2285; www.randsburg.com) is a 'living ghost town,' where you can visit a tiny historical museum, antiques shops, a saloon and an opera house café (where old-timey melodramas are occasionally performed). You can even stay overnight in the yesteryear hotel, where you can hear the coyotes howling outside at night.

some apples and carrots to feed the frisky equines at **BLM Wild Horse & Burro Corral** (☎ 760-384-5765; www.blm.gov; Randsburg-Wash Rd; admission free; 🕑 7:30am-4pm Mon-Fri), 4 miles east of town off Ridgecrest Blvd (Hwy 178).

Detour further east to the **Trona Pinnacles National Natural Landmark**, an awesome national landmark, where tufa spires rise out of an ancient lakebed in an alien fashion. Déjà vu? You may have already seen this place in that '60s TV show *Lost in Space* or the movie *Star Trek V: The Final Frontier*. Look for the turnoff from Hwy 178, about 7.5 miles east of Trona–Red Mountain Rd. From there, it's another 5 miles along a rutted dirt road. About 15 miles further north on Hwy 178, the hardscrabble mining town of Trona hosts a fossickers' festival, **Gem-o-Rama** (☎ 760-372-5356), on the second weekend of October. You can drink with some odd characters at Trona's roadside saloon.

Stay overnight in Ridgecrest only if you have to. A half dozen chain motels, hotels and family-style eateries line China Lake Blvd, south of Inyokern Rd (Hwy 178). Further north on US Hwy 395 in the Sierra Nevada, Lone Pine (p414) is a much more scenic and inviting overnight stop.

Las Vegas

You know you're in Nevada when even the gas stations have slot machines.

Las Vegas demands a suspension of disbelief, so don't take it too seriously. A Bible-toting Elvis kisses a giddy couple who just pledged eternity in the Drive-Thru Chapel of Love. A blue-haired granny pumps quarters into a slot machine while chain-smoking and slugging watered-down gin and tonic. A porn star saunters by a nightclub's velvet rope. Blink, and you'll miss it. Sleep? Fuhgeddaboutit.

Vegas is the ultimate escape. Give it a few days, and it'll give you the world. Time is totally irrelevant here. There are no clocks inside casinos, just never-ending buffets, ever-flowing drinks and nonstop partying. The USA's fastest-growing metropolis and its megaresorts stand ready to cater to your every whim 24/7. It doesn't matter if you play the penny slots or drop a bankroll every night – the Strip is a thrill a minute. Welcome to fabulous Las Vegas, where everyone lives like the King.

But do what locals do. Admit Las Vegas has flaws – it's far from 'civilization,' it's sometimes seedy, and it's an unforgiving place when you're down and out – but love it anyway. Buy a drink for an over-the-hill showgirl who remembers smooching with Sinatra. Sit down next to a degenerate gambler and reminisce about when the Mob really ran things. Hang with hipsters and artists at the frayed, oh-so-funky edges of downtown.

And when you tire of the ding-ding-ding of the slot machines, find instant rejuvenation just outside the city limits. Not a highway leaves Las Vegas that doesn't pass through the awesome wind- and water-carved landscapes of the Mojave Desert.

HIGHLIGHTS

- **Best Place to Be Sinful** Even if gambling isn't your style, cut loose on the world-famous Strip (p694)
- **Most Awesome Place to Get High** Jump on adrenaline-pumping thrill rides atop the Stratosphere Tower (p698)
- **Best Place to Find Vintage Vegas** Stumble along the Fremont Street Experience (p698) in downtown's historic 'Glitter Gulch'
- **'Greenest' Spot in the Desert** Find the source of life in this desert valley at the Springs Preserve (p699)
- **Fastest way to work off 'buffet belly'** Scramble around Red Rock Canyon (p709) or Valley of Fire State Park (p710)

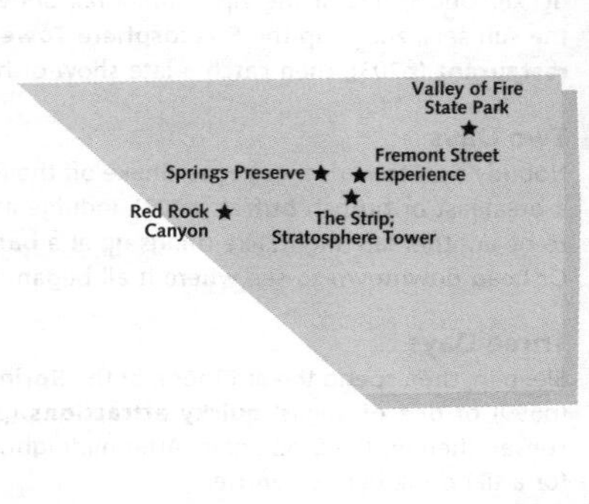

LAS VEGAS

pop 603,093 / elev 2030ft

HISTORY

Unlike the rest of the ruin-laden Southwest, this town has scant traces of early history. Southern Paiutes inhabited the valley around Las Vegas before the Spanish Trail blazed through this final area of the country to be encountered by Anglos.

In 1829 Rafael Rivera, a scout for a Mexican trading expedition, discovered a spring in this valley, after which it became known as *las vegas* (the meadows). Hell-bent on doing God's work in Native American country, Mormon missionaries arrived from Salt Lake City in 1855; their small fort was abandoned just two years later. After the Civil War, Octavius Decatur Gass transformed the fort into a flourishing ranch.

In 1905 the driving of a golden spike signaled the completion of a railroad linking Salt Lake City to Los Angeles. During two frenzied days, pioneers and real-estate speculators from LA bid for land. As the dust settled, the city was officially founded. Sin quickly took root in a downtown red-light district known as Block 16. Home to gambling, booze and prostitution, this row of saloons, with their makeshift 'cribs' (brothels) out back, survived Nevada's several bans on gambling and the supposedly 'dry' years of Prohibition. The federally sponsored Boulder (later Hoover) Dam project and the legalization of gambling in 1931 carried Las Vegas through the Great Depression that followed the stock-market crash of 1929. Lax divorce requirements, quickie weddings, legalized prostitution and championship boxing bouts proved money-making bets for the city. New Deal dollars for projects like Boulder Dam kept flowing into Southern Nevada's coffers right through WWII, which brought a huge air-force base to town.

In 1941 Thomas Hull opened the city's first casino hotel, El Rancho Vegas, along the two-lane Los Angeles highway that became eventually Las Vegas Blvd, aka 'the Strip.' Mobster Benjamin 'Bugsy' Siegel opened the glam Flamingo casino hotel in 1946. Big-name entertainers like Frank Sinatra and Liberace arrived at the same time as topless French showgirls in the early 1950s, when the Cold War era ushered in atomic-bomb blasts at the Nevada Test Site.

The high-profile purchase of the Desert Inn in 1966 by eccentric billionaire Howard Hughes gave the gambling industry a much-needed patina of legitimacy, paving the way for corporate-owned casinos in the late 1960s and early '70s. The 1990s experienced another building bonanza along the Strip. In 2005 the eponymous megaresort of casino impresario Steve Wynn opened as the city celebrated its centennial.

LAS VEGAS IN...

One Day

Cruise the **Strip** (p694), then hit the megaresorts for a taste of high-roller action. Ride the double-decker Deuce bus or the zippy monorail between casinos, with stops for **shopping** (p706). As the sun sets, zoom up the **Stratosphere Tower** (p698). After a catnap, dine at a celebrity chef's **restaurant** (p703), then catch a late show or hit the **clubs** (p706).

Two Days

Nobody's an early riser in Vegas. Shake off the Rabelaisian fete of the night before just in time for a breakfast or brunch **buffet** (p703). Indulge at a spa or chill poolside at your hotel – it's going to be another late night. Fire things up at a **bar** (p705) or an ultra lounge, then party until dawn. Or head downtown to see where it all began, near the **Fremont Street Experience** (p698).

Three Days

Sleep in, then spend the afternoon at the **Springs Preserve** (p699), the **Atomic Testing Museum** (p699) or one of Vegas' **quirky attractions** (p700). Roll west to **Red Rock Canyon** (p709) for sunset, then hit the Strip again. After midnight, drop by the Peppermill's **Fireside Lounge** (p705) for a tiki drink before sunrise.

ORIENTATION

Two interstate highways (I-15 and US Hwy 95) bisect the town. I-15 parallels the entire length of the Strip, a 4-mile stretch of Las Vegas Blvd, running from the Stratosphere Tower past the Luxor's landmark pyramid. Downtown sits at the far north end of Las Vegas Blvd, with the Fremont Street Experience streaking down the middle of Glitter Gulch.

More giant casino hotels are found east of the Strip along Paradise Rd, near the University of Nevada, Las Vegas (UNLV) campus; west of I-15, mostly facing Flamingo Rd; and east of downtown along the Boulder Hwy, which is the scenic route to Hoover Dam. The outlying metro area consists of mini-malls and sprawling suburbs, such as Henderson and Summerlin.

Disorientation is a constant risk, whether you're searching for your room, winding your way through a purposefully confusing casino, or just trying to remember where you parked the damn car. McCarran International Airport is southeast of the Strip off I-215; take a taxi or a shuttle. Greyhound buses arrive downtown at the Plaza. For local transportation, see p708.

FAST FACTS

Population 603,093

Average temps low/high Jan 28/60°F, Jul 68/107°F

Los Angeles to Las Vegas 270 miles, four to five hours

San Diego to Las Vegas 330 miles, 4½ to 5½ hours

San Francisco to Las Vegas 570 miles, nine to 10 hours

INFORMATION

Bookstores

Gamblers Book Shop (Map p694; ☎ 702-382-7555; 630 S 11th St; 🕑 9am-5pm Mon-Sat) Stocks almost every book ever written about Las Vegas.

Get Booked (Map p696; ☎ 702-737-7780; www.getbooked.com; 4640 S Paradise Rd; 🕑 10am-midnight Sun-Thu, to 2am Fri & Sat) In the gay-oriented Fruit Loop, east of the Strip (p701).

Emergency

Police, fire, ambulance	☎ 911
Police (nonemergency)	☎ 311
Rape Crisis Hotline	☎ 702-366-1640

Internet Access

High-speed internet access (either wired or wireless) in hotel rooms costs over $10 per 24 hours. Hotel business centers charge an arm and a leg for 24/7 internet access. Cheaper internet cafés hide inside Strip souvenir shops. The best wi-fi hotspots are off-Strip at the airport and Las Vegas Convention Center.

Internet Resources

Cheapo Vegas (www.cheapovegas.com) A hilarious cheapskate's guide.

Las Vegas Logue (www.lasvegaslogue.com) Celebrity gossip, breaking headlines and fresh reviews.

Only Vegas (www.visitlasvegas.com) The city's official tourism site.

Raw Vegas (www.rawvegas.tv) 24/7 programming, from daily news to reality vlogs (video blogs).

VEGAS.com (www.vegas.com) Encyclopedic info – watch out for advertorials.

Media

Published daily, the conservative *Las Vegas Review-Journal* (www.lvrj.com) includes Friday's Neon entertainment guide. Free alternative tabloid weeklies include *Las Vegas Weekly* (www.lasvegasweekly.com) and *Las Vegas CityLife* (www.lasvegascitylife.com). Free tourist magazines like *Las Vegas Magazine + Showbiz Weekly* and *What's On*, available in hotel rooms and at the airport, have valuable coupons.

Medical Services

Harmon Medical Center (Map p696; ☎ 702-796-1116; 150 E Harmon Ave; 🕑 24hr) Discounts for uninsured patients, courtesy vans and translation services.

University Medical Center (Map p694; ☎ 702-383-2000, emergency 702-383-2661; 1800 W Charleston Blvd; 🕑 24hr) Nevada's most advanced trauma center.

Walgreens The Strip (Map p696; ☎ 702-739-9645; 3765 Las Vegas Blvd S; 🕑 store & pharmacy 24hr) Downtown (Map p694; ☎ 702-385-1284; 495 Fremont St; 🕑 store 24hr, pharmacy 9am-5pm Mon-Sat & 10am-6pm Sun) Convenience store with a pharmacy that also sells over-the-counter medications.

Money

Every casino hotel has an ATM, as do most convenience stores. Fees imposed by casinos for foreign-currency exchange and ATM transactions are much higher than at banks.

American Express (Map p696; ☎ 702-739-8474; Fashion Show, 3200 Las Vegas Blvd S; 🕑 10am-9pm Mon-Fri, to 8pm

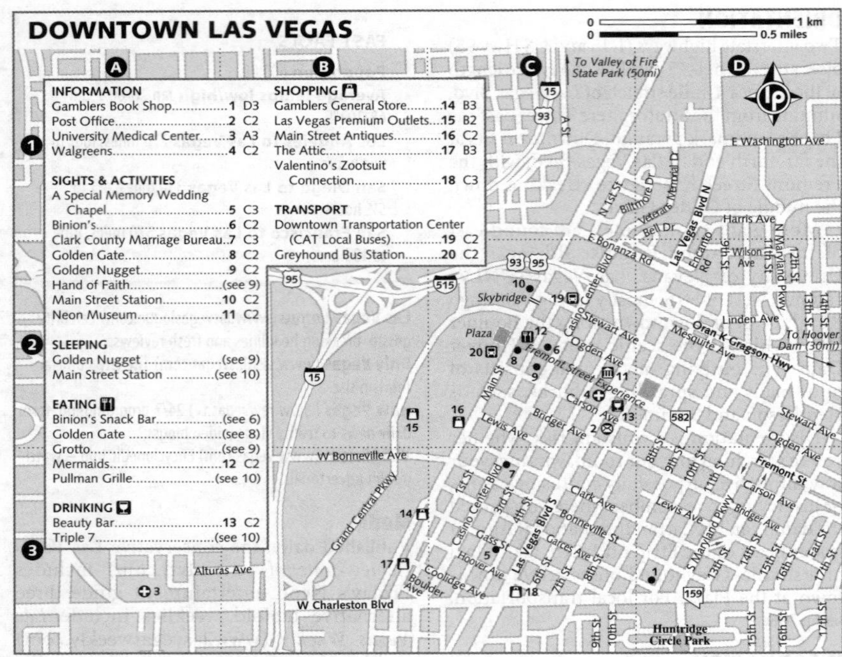

Sat, noon-6pm Sun) exchanges foreign currencies at competitive rates.

A 7.5% retail sales tax applies to most goods and services. A 9% hotel tax is added to all room rates.

Post

Convenient full-service **post offices** (☎ 800-275-8777; www.usps.com; 8:30am-5pm Mon-Fri):

Downtown (Map p694; 201 Las Vegas Blvd S)

Strip Station (Map p696; 3100 Industrial Rd)

Telephone

Using cell phones around casinos' race and sports books is strictly prohibited.

Tourist Information

Las Vegas Convention & Visitors Authority (LVCVA; Map p696; ☎ 702-892-7575, 877-847-4858; www.visitlasvegas.com; 3150 Paradise Rd; 8am-5pm, hotline 6am-9pm) The city's only official tourist-information center has a helpful hotline.

DANGERS & ANNOYANCES

The major tourist areas are safe. Las Vegas Blvd between downtown and the northern edge of the Strip is shady. Fremont St too far east of Las Vegas Blvd is also unsavory, even downright dangerous.

SIGHTS

Open for business 24/7/365 is the rule at casino hotels and megaresorts – many don't even bother with locks on their doors. Unless otherwise noted, admission is free.

The Strip

Las Vegas Blvd, aka the Strip, is always reinventing itself. Every megaresort is an attraction, with plenty on offer besides gambling. They're all on the double-decker Deuce bus line and offer free parking (self-service and valet; tip at least $2 for the latter). All are wheelchair-accessible.

CENTER STRIP

Here are the casino showpieces everyone comes to see, starting from the intersection of Las Vegas Blvd with Flamingo Rd.

Inspired by a lakeside Italian village, the **Bellagio** (Map p696; ☎ 702-693-7111; www.bellagio.com; 3600 Las Vegas Blvd S) is Vegas' opulent, if par-

LAS VEGAS

venu, pleasure palace. Dancing fountains put on a choreographed show every half hour or so until midnight for gawkers strolling the Strip. Beyond the hotel lobby, adorned with Dale Chihuly's sculpture of 2000 vibrant hand-blown glass flowers, the conservatory garden flaunts ostentatious floral arrangements installed by crane through a soaring 50ft-high ceiling. The **Bellagio Gallery of Fine Art** (☎ 702-693-7871, 877-957-9777; adult/child under 13yr/student/senior $15/free/10/12; 10am-6pm Sun-Thu, to 9pm Fri & Sat) hosts traveling museum-quality exhibitions.

Despite megabucks renovations, the kitschy, Greco-Roman fantasy land of **Caesars Palace** (Map p696; ☎ 702-731-7110; www.caesarspalace.com; 3570 Las Vegas Blvd S) is as quintessentially Vegas as ever. Bar girls still roam the gaming areas in skimpy togas, and out front are the same fountains daredevil Evil Knievel jumped on his motorcycle in 1967. Opposite, the Mafia-built **Flamingo** (Map p696; ☎ 702-733-3111; www.flamingolasvegas.com; 3555 Las Vegas Blvd S) was once the talk of the town; when it opened in 1946, even the janitors wore tuxedos. Its walk-through wildlife habitat comes alive with Chilean flamingos, exotic birds, ornamental koi and tropical plants.

The Polynesian-inspired **Mirage** (Map p696; ☎ 702-791-7111; www.mirage.com; 3400 Las Vegas Blvd S) is resplendent with a rainforest atrium, saltwater aquariums and a fiery faux volcano out front that erupts hourly after dark until midnight. Next door, swashbuckling **TI** (Treasure Island; Map p696; ☎ 702-894-7111; www.treasureisland.com; 3300 Las Vegas Blvd S) desperately tries to put the 'sin' back in 'casino' with its racy 'Sirens of TI' show, a hilarious mock sea battle of the sexes featuring sultry femme-fatale pirates dressed like lingerie models. With exploding pyrotechnics, the show's ships – a Spanish privateer and a British frigate – face off several times nightly.

Float away on **gondolas** (☎ 702-414-4300; indoor/outdoor ride per person $15/12.50) at the **Venetian** (Map p696; ☎ 702-414-1000; www.venetian.com; 3355 Las Vegas Blvd S), a small-scale replica of La Repubblica Serenissima di Venezia (Most Serene Republic of Venice), reputedly the home of the world's first casino. Outside by the mini Rialto Bridge is **Madame Tussauds Wax Museum** (Map p696; ☎ 702-862-7800; www.madametussauds.com; adult/child/senior & student $24/14/18; 10am-9pm Sun-Thu, to 10pm Fri & Sat), where you can play golf with Tiger Woods, sing like you're on *American Idol* or put on Playboy bunny ears to sit on Hugh Hefner's lap. Next door, the skyscraping Italianate **Palazzo** (Map p696; ☎ 702-607-7777; www.palazzolasvegas.com; 3325 Las Vegas Blvd S) claims the Strip's tallest high-rise tower. Across the street, casino impresario Steve Wynn's signature piece (literally, his name is signed across the top, punctuated

LAS VEGAS BY THE NUMBERS

- Metro-area population: 1.8 million
- Yearly visitors: more than 39 million
- Marriage licenses issued annually: 120,000
- Cost of a drink while you're betting: free
- Steak-and-eggs graveyard special: $5
- Miles of neon on the Strip: over 15,000
- Average visitor's gambling budget: $650
- Number of sunny days per year: over 300
- Height of the Stratosphere Tower: 1149ft
- Biggest slot-machine payout: almost $40 million

SIN CITY BY THE BOOK

With the exception of poker, all gambling pits the player against the house, which has the statistical edge. Over the long haul, you're guaranteed to lose everything you gamble. Some casinos offer introductory lessons in table games such as blackjack and craps. You can ask dealers for help and advice (eg what the strategy is for the blackjack hand you've just been dealt). If you're winning, it's polite to tip them.

State laws prohibit minors from being in gaming areas. The drinking and gambling legal age of 21 is strictly enforced (carry ID). Speaking of vices, prostitution is illegal in Las Vegas; the legal brothels are in more rural counties. Don't expect a romantic Old West bordello, though; some are just tattered double-wide trailers behind a barbed-wire fence on the side of a lonesome highway. For a real-life look behind the scenes, read Alexa Albert's *Brothel: Mustang Ranch and Its Women* or catch an episode of HBO's *Cathouse*.

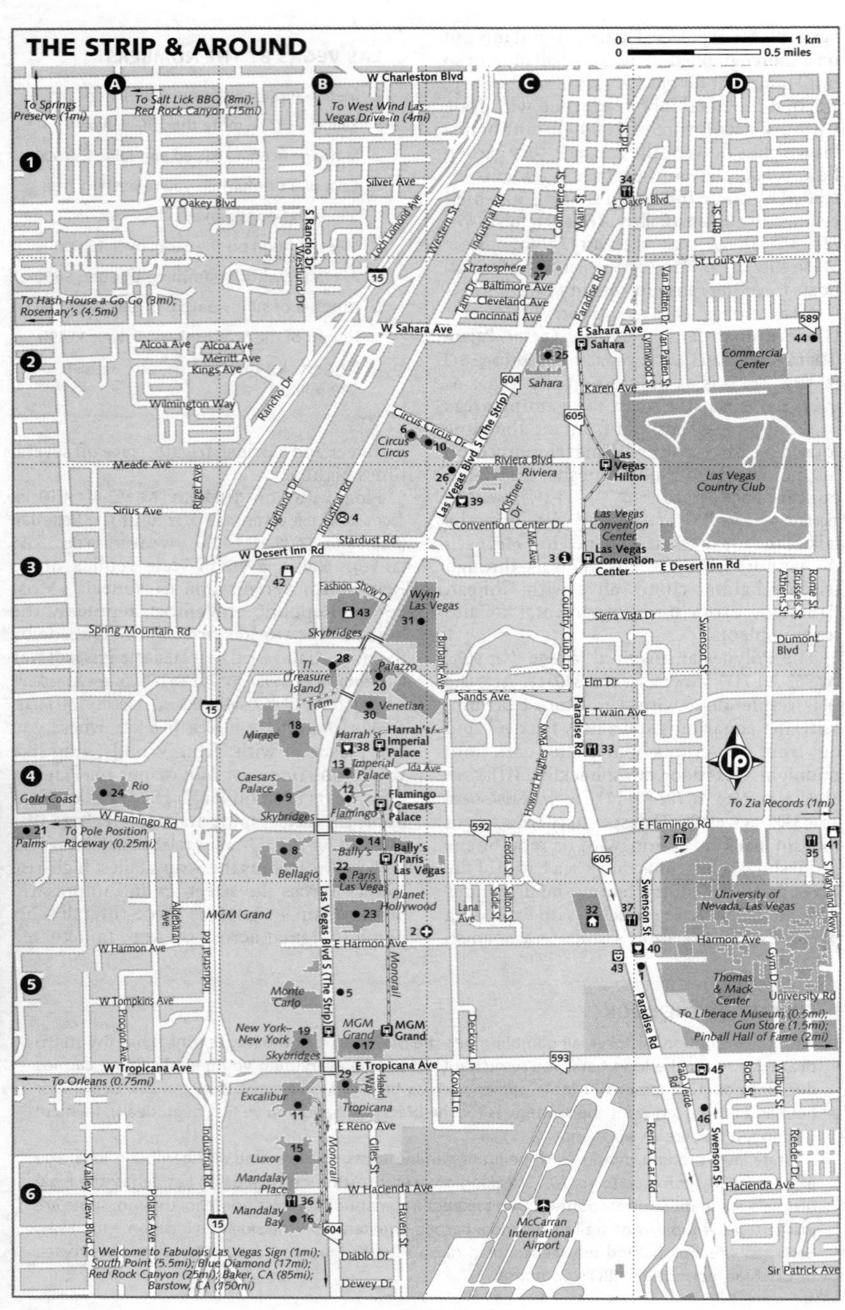
THE STRIP & AROUND
To Springs Preserve (1mi)
To Salt Lick BBQ (8mi); Red Rock Canyon (15mi)
To West Wind Las Vegas Drive-in (4mi)
To Hash House a Go Go (3mi); Rosemary's (4.5mi)
W Charleston Blvd
W Sahara Ave
W Desert Inn Rd
Spring Mountain Rd
W Flamingo Rd
W Tropicana Ave
E Tropicana Ave
E Flamingo Rd
E Desert Inn Rd
Stratosphere
Sahara
Circus Circus
Riviera
Las Vegas Hilton
Las Vegas Country Club
Las Vegas Convention Center
Wynn Las Vegas
TI (Treasure Island)
Palazzo
Venetian
Mirage
Caesars Palace
Rio
Gold Coast
Palms
Bellagio
Paris Las Vegas
Planet Hollywood
MGM Grand
Monte Carlo
New York–New York
Excalibur
Tropicana
Luxor
Mandalay Place
Mandalay Bay
McCarran International Airport
University of Nevada, Las Vegas
Thomas & Mack Center
To Zia Records (1mi)
To Pole Position Raceway (0.25mi)
To Orleans (0.75mi)
To Liberace Museum (0.5mi); Gun Store (1.5mi); Pinball Hall of Fame (2mi)
To Welcome to Fabulous Las Vegas Sign (1mi); South Point (5.5mi); Blue Diamond (17mi); Red Rock Canyon (25mi); Baker, CA (85mi); Barstow, CA (150mi)

INFORMATION
American Express (see 43)
Get Booked **1** D5
Harmon Medical Center **2** B5
Las Vegas Convention & Visitors Authority (LVCVA) **3** C3
Post Office **4** B3
Walgreens **5** B5

SIGHTS & ACTIVITIES
Adventuredome **6** B2
Atomic Testing Museum **7** D4
Bellagio **8** B4
Bellagio Gallery of Fine Art (see 8)
Caesars Palace **9** B4
Circus Circus **10** C2
Coney Island Emporium & Roller Coaster (see 19)
Eiffel Tower Experience (see 22)
Excalibur **11** B6
Flamingo **12** B4
Imperial Palace Dealertainers **13** B4
Jubilee! Backstage Tour **14** B4
Las Vegas Cyber Speedway (see 25)
Lion Habitat (see 17)
Luxor **15** B6
Madame Tussauds Wax Museum (see 30)
Mandalay Bay **16** B6
MGM Grand **17** B5
Mirage **18** B4
New York-New York **19** B5
Palazzo **20** B4
Palms Casino Hotel **21** A4
Paris Las Vegas **22** B4
Planet Hollywood **23** B5
Rio **24** A4
Sahara **25** C2
Shark Reef (see 16)
Slots A' Fun **26** C3
Speed (see 25)
Stratosphere Tower **27** C2
Stripper 101 (see 23)
TI (Treasure Island) **28** B3
Tropicana **29** B5
Venetian **30** B4
Venetian Gondolas (see 30)
Wynn Las Vegas **31** B3

SLEEPING
Circus Circus (see 10)
Hard Rock **32** C5
Luxor (see 15)
Mandalay Bay (see 16)
MGM Grand (see 17)
New York-New York (see 19)
Palms Place (see 21)
Palms (see 21)
Planet Hollywood (see 23)
Sahara (see 25)
THEhotel at Mandalay Bay (see 16)
TI (Treasure Island) (see 28)
Venetian (see 30)
Wynn Las Vegas (see 31)

EATING
Alex (see 31)
Alizé (see 21)
BLT Burger (see 18)
Cut (see 20)
Firefly **33** C4
Isla Mexican Kitchen (see 28)
Le Village Buffet (see 22)
Luv-It Frozen Custard **34** C1
Olives (see 8)
Origin India (see 37)
Payard Bistro (see 9)
Paymon's Mediterranean Café **35** D4
Restaurant Guy Savoy (see 9)
RM Seafood **36** B6
San-Toki Korean BBQ & Shabu Bar **37** C5
SushiSamba (see 20)
Terrace Point Café (see 31)
The Buffet (Bellagio) (see 8)
The Buffet (Wynn Las Vegas) (see 31)
Village Seafood Buffet (see 24)
Wolfgang Puck Bar & Grill (see 17)

DRINKING
Carnaval Court **38** B4
ESPN Zone (see 19)
Fireside Lounge **39** C3
Hofbräuhaus **40** D5
Mix (see 16)
Napoleon's (see 22)
New York-New York (see 19)
Nine Fine Irishmen (see 19)
Red Square (see 16)
Trader Vic's (see 23)

ENTERTAINMENT
Forty Deuce (see 36)
ghostbar (see 21)
House of Blues (see 16)
Krave (see 23)
Moon (see 21)
Pure (see 9)
Revolution Lounge (see 18)
Tao (see 30)
The Joint (see 32)
The Pearl (see 21)

SHOPPING
Buffalo Exchange **41** D4
Déjà Vu Love Boutique **42** B3
Fashion Show **43** B3
Forum Shops (see 9)
Grand Canal Shoppes (see 30)
Houdini's Magic Shop (see 9)
Miracle Mile Shops (see 23)

TRANSPORT
Las Vegas Harley-Davidson **44** D2
Megabus Station **45** D5
Rent-a-Vette **46** D6

by a period), **Wynn Las Vegas** (Map p696; ☎ 702-770-7100; www.wynnlasvegas.com; 3131 Las Vegas Blvd), stands on the old site of the 1950s-era Desert Inn. Its grandiose sequel, called Encore, rises just north.

Back south of the Flamingo, **Paris Las Vegas** (Map p696; ☎ 702-946-7000; www.parislasvegas.com; 3655 Las Vegas Blvd S) has an ersatz **Eiffel Tower Experience** (adult/child $10/7; 9:30am-12:30am, weather permitting) with a glass elevator and a dizzying observation deck for panoramic Strip views, day or night. Meanwhile, pimped-out **Planet Hollywood** (Map p696; ☎ 785-5555; www.planethollywoodresort.com; 3667 Las Vegas Blvd S) has stripped the old Aladdin casino hotel of its Middle Eastern fantasy; for fans of vintage Vegas, that feels like a crime.

SOUTH STRIP

The South Strip is attracting ever more of a crowd, especially to its after-dark haunts.

The minimegapolis of **New York-New York** (Map p696; ☎ 702-740-6969; www.nynyhotelcasino.com; 3790 Las Vegas Blvd S) features scaled-down replicas of the Big Apple's skyline, the Statue of Liberty and the Brooklyn Bridge, plus a bone-rattling **roller coaster** (ride $14, re-ride $7; 11am-11pm Sun-Thu, 10:30am-midnight Fri & Sat) inside the **Coney Island Emporium** (games from 50¢; 8am-midnight Sun-Thu, to 2am Fri & Sat;) video-game arcade (with bumper cars!).

The 'world's largest hotel' title belongs to the **MGM Grand** (Map p696; ☎ 702-891-1111; www.mgmgrand.com; 3799 Las Vegas Blvd S). Outside the entrance, it's impossible to miss the MGM's 100,000lb lion mascot surrounded by spritzing fountains. Other 'Maximum Vegas' attractions include a walk-through **lion habitat** (admission free; 11am-10pm;). Across the street, the **Tropicana** (Map p696; ☎ 702-739-2222; www.tropicanalv.com; 3801 Las Vegas Blvd S) has had more than half a century to sully its shine, lose its crowds

SPEAK LIKE A GAMBLING SAVANT

all in – to bet everything you've got
ante – a starting wager required to play table games
carpet joint – swanky old-school casino (as opposed to a gambling hall with sawdust-covered floors)
cooler – an unlucky gambler who makes everyone else lose, too
eye in the sky – high-tech casino surveillance systems
fold – to throw in your cards and stop betting
high roller – a gambler who bets big (aka 'whale')
let it ride – to roll over a winning wager into the next bet
low roller – a small-time gambler (eg penny slot machines)
marker – IOU credit-line debt owed to a casino
one-armed bandit – old-fashioned nickname for a slot machine
sucker bet – a gamble on nearly impossible odds
toke – a tip or gratuity

and go the way of the Sands – ashes to ashes, dust to dust. But miraculously, it just keeps hanging in there.

Dining and nightlife are big draws, but the standout attraction at **Mandalay Bay** (Map p696; ☎ 702-632-7777; www.mandalaybay.com; 3950 Las Vegas Blvd S) is the **Shark Reef** (adult/child $16/11, incl behind-the-scenes tour $24/19; ⏰ 10am-11pm, last entry 10pm; 👪), a gigantic walk-through aquarium that's home to over 2000 submarine beasties, including jellyfish, moray eels, stingrays and some of the world's last remaining golden crocodiles.

Named after Egypt's ancient city on the Nile, **Luxor** (Map p696; ☎ 702-262-4000; www.luxor.com; 3900 Las Vegas Blvd S) is guarded by a crouching sphinx. At the apex of a 30-story black-glass pyramid is the world's most powerful beacon, visible from space. With crayon-colored towers and a faux drawbridge, the medieval caricature of **Excalibur** (Map p696; ☎ 702-597-7777; www.excalibur.com; 3850 Las Vegas Blvd S) next door epitomizes tacky Vegas.

NORTH STRIP

The North Strip is where you'll find survivors from Vegas' swingin' heyday of the 1950s and early '60s, when the Mob ruled the roost and the Rat Pack defined hip.

The **Stratosphere Tower** (Map p696; ☎ 702-380-7777; www.stratospherehotel.com; 2000 Las Vegas Blvd S; elevator adult/concession $14/10, incl 3 thrill rides $28; 👪) has some of the highest thrill rides in the world (Insanity and Big Shot are your best bets). Also reached by America's fastest elevators are a revolving restaurant, a circular bar and indoor and outdoor viewing decks.

At the monorail station, the Moroccan-themed **Sahara** (Map p696; ☎ 702-737-2111; www.saharavegas.com; 2535 Las Vegas Blvd S) is one of the few old-Vegas carpet joints to have survived the megaresort onslaught. Jump on the Strip's best roller coaster, **Speed** (⏰ 2-10pm Thu-Mon), or virtually race a Formula One car at the **Las Vegas Cyber Speedway** (⏰ from 11am daily); each costs $10, or it's $21.95 for both.

Further south, **Circus Circus** (Map p696; ☎ 702-734-0410; www.circuscircus.com; 2880 Las Vegas Blvd S) is a very strange world. Trapeze artists, high-wire workers, jugglers and unicyclists perform above the casino floor every half hour until midnight. Its **Adventuredome** (Map p696; ☎ 702-794-3939, 866-456-8894; per ride $4-7, day pass $15-25; 👪) is packed with thrill rides and amusements. Next door, grab a few 75¢ beers and $1 half-pound hot dogs at **Slots A' Fun** (Map p696; ☎ 702-734-0410; 2890 Las Vegas Blvd S), then enjoy the laughable lounge acts.

Downtown

Known as Glitter Gulch, the city's original quarter attracts far fewer onlookers and is preferred by serious gamblers. The smoky, low-ceilinged Fremont St casinos are the city's oldest, and they've changed little over the years – which is the whole point. Most casinos offer free self-parking garages (maximum stay of a few hours) if your parking stub is validated inside at the casino cashier's cage (no gambling or purchase required).

FREMONT STREET EXPERIENCE

Always ready for a gamble, downtown boosters installed a 1400ft-long arched steel canopy along Fremont St, creating a five-block-long **pedestrian mall** (Map p694; ☎ 702-678-5600; www.vegasexperience.com; ⏰ shows hourly dusk-midnight) on Fremont Street, between Main St and Las Vegas Blvd. The cheesy light-and-sound show played out on a superbig Viva Vision screen enhanced by 12.5 million synchronized LEDs and 550,000 watts of concert-hall sound is enough to stop most people (particularly falling-down drunks) in their tracks.

CASINOS

You can easily stroll between almost a dozen gaming joints downtown. Gawk at the gigantic 61lb, 11oz **Hand of Faith**, the heftiest chunk of gold ever found, off the lobby of the luxe **Golden Nugget** (Map p694; ☎ 702-385-7111; www.goldennugget.com; 129 E Fremont St). Seriously old-school **Binion's** (Map p694; ☎ 702-382-1600; www.binions.com; 128 E Fremont St), opened as the Horseshoe in 1951, has a high-stakes poker room that became famous for its 'zero limit' betting policy. It was notorious Texan gambler Benny Binion who oversaw the transformation of Fremont St from a row of sawdust gambling halls into 'Glitter Gulch' with its classy carpet joints.

The **Golden Gate** (Map p694; ☎ 702-385-1906; www.goldengatecasino.net; 1 E Fremont St), an old-fashioned gambling hall, has stood on the corner of Fremont and Main Sts since 1906, just one year after this hard-scrabble railway town was founded. To the north, the neo-Victorian **Main Street Station** (Map p694; ☎ 702-387-1896; www.mainstreetcasino.com; 200 N Main St) displays an opulent collection of antiques, architectural artifacts and collectibles – pick up a free self-guiding brochure at the hotel's front desk. Just south of here is Buffalo Bill Cody's private railcar, which he used to travel the USA with his Wild West Show until his death in 1917.

NEON MUSEUM

This alfresco assemblage of vintage neon, with its genie lamps, glowing martini glasses and 1940s motel marquees, brightens up downtown, especially in the central courtyard of the Neonopolis and on cul-de-sacs north of the Fremont Street Experience. Although the permanent **museum** (Map p694; ☎ 702-387-6366; www.neonmuseum.org) is a work in progress, tours of the giant 'boneyard' of rescued signs north of downtown are available by appointment.

East of the Strip

During the atomic heyday of the 1950s, gamblers and tourists downtown watched as mushroom clouds rose behind Fremont Street, and the city even crowned a Miss Atomic Bomb. Learn more at the **Atomic Testing Museum** (Map p696; ☎ 702-794-5161; www.atomictestingmuseum.org; 755 E Flamingo Rd; adult/concession $10/7; ⏲ 9am-5pm Mon-Sat, 1-4pm Sun). Buy your tickets at the replica Nevada Test Site guard station, then watch a historical film inside the Ground Zero Theater, which mimics a concrete test bunker.

West of the Strip

SPRINGS PRESERVE

An ecoconscious achievement for the city, this fascinating **museum complex** (off Map p696; ☎ 702-822-7700; www.springspreserve.org; 333 S Valley View Blvd; adult/child/senior & student $19/11/17; ⏲ 10am-6pm; 🚼) weaves the natural and cultural history of Las Vegas into the OriGen Experience, then demonstrates a more sustainable future at the Desert Living Center. Walk the gardens and interpretive trails, nosh at chef Wolfgang Puck's ecocafé and pick up wildflower seed packets in the nature-themed gift shop. The Nevada State Museum should open here in 2009.

POLE POSITION RACEWAY

Dreamed up by NASCAR and Supercross racing champs, this Euro-style **raceway** (off Map p696; ☎ 702-227-7223; www.racep2r.com; 4175 S Arville St; race per adult/junior $25/22; ⏲ usually 11am-midnight) modeled on Formula 1 road courses boasts the fastest indoor go-karts in the USA, exciting for teen novices or adult speed freaks. Drivers must be over 48in tall.

LAS VEGAS FOR CHILDREN

Las Vegas only half-heartedly sells itself as a family vacation destination. Because the legal gambling age is 21, many casino hotels and resorts would rather you simply left the little ones at home. Some high-end casino hotels even prohibit strollers on their grounds.

POKER HOTSPOTS

With the rules of Texas Hold 'em a frequent conversation starter these days, it's obvious poker is the hottest game in town.

- **Wynn Las Vegas** (p697) Swim with sharks in Vegas' poshest poker room.
- **Venetian** (p695) Upscale poker room attracts high rollers and pros.
- **Binion's** (left) The cowboy gambling hall where the World Series of Poker (WSOP) began.
- **Golden Nugget** (left) A classy carpet joint with nonsmoking tables.
- **Rio** (Map p696; ☎ 702-777-7777; www.riolasvegas.com; 3700 W Flamingo Rd) Where the World Series of Poker finals tables happen.

MARRIAGES MADE IN…SIN CITY

There must be something magical about Las Vegas for lovers, since a blushing couple ties the knot every five minutes here. Maybe those 50-50 odds of a marriage lasting 'till death do us part' look pretty damn good after you've been gambling all night.

Before you get hitched, stop by the **Clark County Marriage Bureau** (Map p694; ☎ 702-671-0600; 201 Clark Ave; 🕑 8am-midnight) for a license ($55, cash only). After that, choices for the perfect spot to say 'I do' are endless. You'll pay from $200 for a basic wedding chapel service. Don't expect much ceremony, though: there's probably another couple, hearts bursting with love, in line right behind you.

Now, the good news. Most casinos have virtual-reality and video-game arcades, including **Circus Circus** (p698) and **New York-New York** (p697). Teens and adults alike will get a thrill atop the **Stratosphere Tower** (p698) or at **Pole Position Raceway** (p699).

Some shows welcome all-ages audiences, including a few Cirque du Soleil productions and magic acts. Kids can learn to do their own tricks at **Houdini's Magic Shop** (p707). Mandalay Bay's **Shark Reef** (p698) and the MGM Grand's **lion habitat** (p697) are entertaining. So are the **Pinball Hall of Fame** (right) and the old-fashioned **West Wind Las Vegas Drive-In** (p706), far off the Strip. For a 'green' multimedia museum, drop by the Springs Preserve (p699).

Surf to www.kidsinvegas.com for more advice and information.

ONLY IN LAS VEGAS

A Special Memory Wedding Chapel (Map p694; ☎ 702-384-2211, 800-962-7798; www.aspecialmemory.com; 800 S 4th St; 🕑 8am-10pm Sun-Thu, to midnight Fri & Sat) The drive-up window on Lovers Lane has a wedding menu board (breakfast packages cost from $55, plus a tip for the minister). A limo ride or an appearance by Elvis cost à la carte.

Gun Store (off Map p696; ☎ 702-454-1110; 2900 E Tropicana Ave; 🕑 9am-6:30pm) If you're just dying to fire off a submachine gun or feel the heft of a Beretta, a Colt or a Glock in your hot little hands, stop by this high-powered indoor training range. Tuesday is ladies day.

Imperial Palace Dealertainers (Map p696; ☎ 702-731-3311; www.imperialpalace.com; Imperial Palace, 3535 Las Vegas Blvd S; 🕑 shows every 15-30min noon-4am) Award-winning celebrity impersonators do double-duty as 'dealertainers,' jumping up from the blackjack tables to perform on the casino stage.

Liberace Museum (off Map p696; ☎ 702-798-5595; www.liberace.org; 1775 E Tropicana Ave; adult/child under 11yr/senior & student $12/free/10; 🕑 10am-5pm Tue-Sat, noon-4pm Sun, guided tours 11am Tue-Sat & 2pm Tue-Sun) For connoisseurs of bizarre extravagance, this creepy memorial museum is a must-do. A tribute to 'Mr Showmanship,' it houses the most flamboyant cars, outrageous costumes and ornate pianos you'll ever see.

Pinball Hall of Fame (Map p696; www.pinballmuseum.org; 3330 E Tropicana Ave at S Pecos Rd; most games 25-50¢; 🕑 11am-11pm Sun-Thu, to midnight Fri & Sat; ♿) Far east of the Strip, Tim Arnold lets you play his amazing 200-plus collection of vintage pinball, video-arcade and carnival game machines, dating from the 1950s to the '90s. Even better, profits go to charity.

Stripper 101 (Map p696; ☎ 702-260-7200; www.stripper101.com; Planet Hollywood, 3667 Las Vegas Blvd S; tickets from $40; 🕑 schedule varies) In a cabaret setting complete with strobe lights, cocktails and feather boas, these pole-dancing classes are a bachelorette must. Bring comfy workout clothes and a pair of high heels for practice.

'Welcome to Fabulous Las Vegas' Sign (Map p696; 5200 block of Las Vegas Blvd S; 🕑 24hr) South of the Strip, between Russell & Sunset Rds, the city's most iconic sign was designed by Betty Willis in 1959, with a flashing atomic-modern starburst at the top. Camera-happy daredevil tourists dash out onto the median for a souvenir photo op.

TOURS

It's easy enough to tour the Strip on your own, but these are some unique experiences. Check online for deep discounts.

Haunted Vegas Tours (☎ 702-737-5540, reservations 866-218-4935; www.hauntedvegastours.com; 2½hr show & tour $57; 🕑 9:30pm Sat-Thu) A campy sideshow begins the tell-all bus tour that visits the ghost of Bugsy at the Flamingo, creepy Liberace's café, the 'Motel of Death' and more. The 'Vegas Mob Tour' starts at 7pm.

Jubilee! Backstage Tour (☎ 702-967-4567; Bally's, 3645 Las Vegas Blvd S; 1hr tour $10-15; 🕑 11am Mon, Wed & Sat) Be astounded by technical trivia on a behind-the-scenes tour escorted by an actual performer from Vegas' long-running showgirl revue, *Jubilee!*.

Papillon Grand Canyon Helicopters (☎ 702-736-7243, 888-635-7272; www.papillon.com; McCarran Executive Terminal, 275 E Tropicana Ave) Flightseeing operator offers luxury Grand Canyon tours and 10-minute jetcopter flyovers of the Strip (from $69).

FESTIVALS & EVENTS

Contact the LVCVA (p694) for up-to-date information.

NASCAR Weekend (www.lvms.com) Over 140,000 fans descend on the Las Vegas Motor Speedway (Map p709) in mid-March.

Viva Las Vegas (www.vivalasvegas.net) Ultimate rockabilly weekend in early April with a va-va-voom burlesque competition and souped-up classic car show.

Clark County Fair & Rodeo (www.ccfair.com) Old-fashioned carnival fun, farm demonstrations and funnel cakes in Logandale, off I-15 northeast of Vegas, in mid-April.

Lei Day (www.alohavalley.com) Polynesian and Pacific Rim block party downtown in early May.

Helldorado Days (www.elkshelldorado.com) Dating from the 1930s, this historic May hoedown hosts barbecues, rodeo stunts, country fiddlers and an Old West frontier town.

World Series of Poker (www.worldseriesofpoker.com; late May-early Jul) High-stakes gamblers, casino dealers and celebrities match wits between late May and early July; free tournament viewing.

CineVegas (www.cinevegas.com) Sin City's premier independent film festival lights up the Palms casino hotel in mid-June.

Vegoose (www.vegoose.com) Over Halloween weekend, zany music-and-arts festival with live bands, performance art and costumed partying.

Aviation Nation (www.aviationnation.org) Top-gun military and civilian air show in mid-November at Nellis Air Force Base (Map p709).

National Finals Rodeo (www.nfrexperience.com) Ten days of steer wrestling and bull riding at UNLV's Thomas and Mack Center (Map p696) in mid-December.

SLEEPING

Rates fluctuate wildly here according to demand. Rooms typically cost half as much midweek than they do on weekends. Rates skyrocket during big conventions and major holidays. The slowest times of year are during summer and from Thanksgiving until late January, except around New Year's. The best deals can often be found on the hotels' own websites.

Whatever you do, don't arrive without a reservation. You'd be amazed how often every standard room in town is full. During the biggest annual events (left), even Laughlin (100 miles away) is booked solid. **TravelWorm** (www.travelworm.com) often has last-minute rooms available.

Nevada's casino-hotel rooms usually lack the amenities found at most nongaming motels in California (eg no coffee makers or minifridges, no free local or toll-free phone calls, no free internet access). But every hotel reviewed here provides free self-parking and at least one swimming pool.

The Strip

It's slim pickin's for budget hotels on the Strip, while many midrange places here would fall into the luxury bracket elsewhere. Impeccable service and 24/7 can-do concierge pampering are par for the course at top-end joints.

Sahara (Map p696; 702-737-2111, 866-382-8884; www.saharavegas.com; 2535 Las Vegas Blvd S; r $40-150; wi-fi) A delightfully tacky Moroccan theme pervades this 1950s-era casino hotel. It may not churn up much excitement, but the simple rooms are a bargain, especially the vintage-styled Tangiers Tower. Conveniently, it's on the monorail line.

Circus Circus (Map p696; 702-734-0410, 800-634-3450; www.circuscircus.com; 2880 Las Vegas Blvd S; r $40-150; wi-fi) Most of the nonsmoking rooms at this family favorite have love seats. Suites, like clowns, come in varying shapes and sizes. Some motel-style Manor rooms out back by the RV park have minifridges.

Luxor (Map p696; 702-262-4444, 877-386-4658; www.luxor.com; 3900 Las Vegas Blvd S; r $80-240; wi-fi) With vaguely art-deco Egyptian furnishings and marble bathrooms (no tubs), Luxor's pyramid

LAS VEGAS

GAY & LESBIAN LAS VEGAS

Queer Las Vegas exists, but it's largely unmapped. Public displays of same-sex affection aren't common or much appreciated by the moral majority in this conservative cowtown. Civil unions and same-sex marriages aren't recognized by the state of Nevada either.

'Alternative' megaclub **Kräve** (Map p696; 702-836-0830; Miracle Mile Shops, 3663 Las Vegas Blvd S; cover $20; 11pm-late Tue-Sun) is the Strip's only predominantly queer venue. The flamboyant Fruit Loop area, a mile east of the Strip along Paradise Rd, south of the Hard Rock (Map p696), is the epicenter of LGBT nightlife. To plug into the scene, pick up free monthly *QVegas* (www.qvegas.com) magazine at **Get Booked** (Map p696; 702-737-7780; www.getbooked.com; 4640 S Paradise Rd; 10am-midnight Sun-Thu, to 2am Fri & Sat).

rooms let you ride the bizarre elevators, called 'inclinators,' which travel at a 39-degree angle. Deluxe tower rooms often have better views.

New York-New York (Map p696; ☎ 702-740-6969, 888-815-4365; www.nynyhotelcasino.com; 3790 Las Vegas Blvd S; r $90-250; wi-fi) Sleek rooms have black-marble-topped sinks and comfy beds. The cheapest ones are rather tiny (just what one would expect in NYC), but loaded with class. Avoid noisy lower-level rooms facing the roller coaster.

MGM Grand (Map p696; ☎ 702-891-7777, 877-880-0880; www.mgmgrand.com; 3799 Las Vegas Blvd S; r $90-360, ste from $150; wi-fi) At the world's largest hotel, is bigger better? Maybe. Standard rooms have ho-hum Hollywood decor, but ultramodern West Wing rooms have walk-in showers built for two. Luxurious 'Signature Suites' come with kitchenettes and if you're lucky, step-out balconies.

Mandalay Bay (Map p696; ☎ 702-632-7777, 877-632-7800; www.mandalaybay.com; 3950 Las Vegas Blvd S; r $110-370; wi-fi) It's worth staying in these tasteful rooms just for the artificial beach and wave-pool complex outside. For more mod style, kick back with your entourage in the boutique THEhotel at Mandalay Bay (suites $150 to $490), where cosmo-chic suites come with wet bars, plasma-screen TVs, wi-fi and deep soaking tubs.

Venetian (Map p696; ☎ 702-414-1000, 877-883-6423; www.venetian.com; 3355 Las Vegas Blvd S; ste $200-680; wi-fi) Fronted by flowing canals and graceful arched bridges, the Venetian's 'standard' suites are anything but. In fact, they're among the Strip's most decadent, with oversized Italian marble baths and sunken living rooms, including in the concierge-level Venezia Tower and the next-door Palazzo.

Wynn Las Vegas (Map p696; ☎ 702-770-7100, 877-321-9966; www.wynnlasvegas.com; 3131 Las Vegas Blvd; r $299-439, ste from $450; wi-fi) If anything in Vegas is truly spectacular, this five-diamond destination is it. Resort rooms are huge, equipped with high-thread-count linens, flat-screen high-definition TVs, sofas with ottomans, oversized Turkish towels and all the little luxuries.

Also recommended:

Palazzo (Map p696; ☎ 866-263-3001; www.palazzolasvegas.com; 3265 Las Vegas Blvd S; ste $200-760; wi-fi) Newer suites at the Venetian's sister resort are just as sumptuous.

Planet Hollywood (Map p696; ☎ 702-785-5555, 866-517-3263; www.planethollywoodresort.com; 3667 Las Vegas Blvd S; r $90-410; wi-fi) With a rock-and-roll soundtrack, Planet Hollywood's Sheraton-run hotel offers oversized deluxe rooms draped in contemporary cool.

TI (Treasure Island; Map p696; ☎ 702-894-7111, 800-288-7206; www.treasureisland.com; 3300 Las Vegas Blvd S; r $90-260; wi-fi) Floor-to-ceiling windows make tiny rooms (with divine pillowtop beds) seem bigger, but those balconies are just props.

Downtown

Avoid rent-by-the-hour fleapits. Stay near the Fremont Street Experience (p698).

Main Street Station (Map p694; ☎ 702-387-1896, 800-713-8933; www.mainstreetcasino.com; 200 N Main St; r $40-115; wi-fi) As handsome as the antique-stuffed casino (p699), this gem of a hotel's tower is gussied up with tiled foyers, elegant Victorian sconces and marble-trimmed hallways. Bright, cheerful rooms have gilt mirrors and plantation shutters.

our pick **Golden Nugget** (Map p694; ☎ 702-385-7111, 800-846-5336; www.goldennugget.com; 129 E Fremont Street; r $59-179; wi-fi) This vintage Vegas jewel has newfound panache. Oversized standard rooms, with half-canopy beds and marble everywhere, are downtown's best. Outside by the swimming pool, a three-story water slide plunges through a 200,000-gallon shark tank.

East of the Strip

Don't get stuck at chain cheapies near the airport or the city's convention center.

Hard Rock (Map p696; ☎ 702-693-5544, 800-473-7625; www.hardrockhotel.com; 4455 Paradise Rd; r $109-450; wi-fi) Hip rooms inhabit this vainglorious shrine to rock and roll, which pulls in a sexy crowd from Southern California. French doors reveal expansive views to grace the stylish Euro-minimalist rooms. Too bad service can be half-assed. Seasonal swim-up blackjack and Tahitian-style cabanas await at the Beach Club.

West of the Strip

It's a short drive from the Strip to these popular casino hotels.

Orleans (off Map p696; ☎ 702-365-7111, 800-675-3267; www.orleanscasino.com; 4500 W Tropicana Ave; r $45-175; wi-fi) Hundreds of tastefully appointed French-provincial rooms are actually 450-sq-ft 'petite suites' with oversized tubs. On-site child care and the best bowling alley in town round out the family fun. Free Strip shuttle.

Palms (off Map p696; ☎ 702-942-7777, 866-942-7770; www.palms.com; 4321 W Flamingo Rd; r/ste from $69/139; wi-fi) is where Britney Spears spent her first wedding night. Request an upper-floor room to score a Strip view. Playpen suites are tailored for bachelor and bachelorette parties, or check into the condo high-rise **Palms Place** (Map p696; ☎ 702-932-7777, 866-942-7773; www.palmsplace.com; ste $159-749) and flaunt your VIP status in style, with a coed Turkish hammam and spa.

Greater Las Vegas

Most far off-Strip casino hotels are locals-only affairs.

South Point (off Map p696; ☎ 702-796-7111, 866-791-7626; www.southpointcasino.com; 9777 Las Vegas Blvd S; r $50-150; wi-fi) With rooms this huge and beds this divine, who needs a suite? Popular for its equestrian center, cineplex and bowling alley, South Point is a short drive from the Strip, near an outlet mall.

EATING

Celebrity chefs have taken up residence in nearly every casino, with the latest invasion from France. With so many star-struck tables to choose from, there are too many overhyped eating gambles. For penny-pinchers, every casino hotel has a 24-hour coffee shop.

The Strip

Casino restaurants alone could fill an entire guidebook; here are some of our favorites, but there are many, many more.

Luv-It Frozen Custard (Map p696; ☎ 702-384-6452; 505 E Oakey Blvd; items $2-5; 1-10pm Tue-Thu, to 11pm Fri & Sat;) Open since 1973, Luv-It's handmade custard concoctions are creamier than ice cream. Try a chocolate-dipped 'Luv Stick' bar or a superhero-sized sundae. Cash only.

BLT Burger (Map p696; ☎ 702-792-7888; www.bltburger.com; Mirage, 3400 Las Vegas Blvd S; mains $8-17; 11am-2am Sun & Tue-Wed, 10am-4am Mon & Thu-Sat;) French-trained NYC chef Laurent Tourondel grills up haute Black Angus beef, lamb and veggie burgers with all the trimmings, along with three dozen microbrews and liqueur-spiked 'adult' milkshakes, with peanut-buttery s'mores for dessert.

Terrace Point Café (Map p696; ☎ 702-248-3463; mains $8-25; Wynn Las Vegas, 3131 Las Vegas Blvd S; 24hr) Feel like a high roller as Wynn elevates the casino-coffee-shop concept to a whole new level, offering country-club-worthy atmosphere and a poolside patio. Whopping portions and prices will knock you out.

Isla Mexican Kitchen (Map p696; ☎ 702-894-7111; TI (Treasure Island), 3300 Las Vegas Blvd S; mains $13-27; 4pm-11pm Sun-Thu, to midnight Fri & Sat) Inventive Mexican-born chef Richard Sandoval creates a fusion of south-of-the-border tastes, like lobster spiked with serrano chilis and passion fruit. Call on Isla's tequila-bar goddess to lead you through the bounteous menu of agave elixirs.

Wolfgang Puck Bar & Grill (Map p696; ☎ 702-891-3000; MGM Grand, 3799 Las Vegas Blvd S; mains $13-37; 11:30am-10:30pm Sun-Thu, to 11:30pm Fri & Sat) California flair pervades this ultracontemporary bistro just off the casino floor. Truffled potato chips with blue cheese, skirt-steak skewers and ricotta gnocchi are as thrilling as the New World wine list.

Payard Bistro (Map p696; ☎ 702-731-7292; Caesars Palace, 3570 Las Vegas Blvd S; breakfast & lunch $16-25; 6:30am-3pm, patisserie till 11pm) Operated by third-generation chocolatier Françoise Payard, this exquisite French concoction offers an outrageously indulgent take-out pastry

BEST BELLY-BUSTING BUFFETS

When it comes to all-you-can-eat 'groaning boards,' the old adage 'you get what you pay for' was never truer: classier casino hotels have better buffets. Expect to pay $7 to $15 for breakfast, $15 to $20 for lunch (more for weekend champagne brunch) and $20 to $40 for dinner. Tip at least $1 per person, please.

- **Le Village Buffet** (Paris Las Vegas, p697)
- **Spice Market Buffet** (Planet Hollywood, p697)
- **The Buffet** (Bellagio, p694)
- **The Buffet** (Wynn Las Vegas, p697)
- **Village Seafood Buffet** (Map p696; ☎ 702-777-7777; Rio, 3700 W Flamingo Rd)

and espresso bar and perfectly executed bistro classics for breakfast and lunch.

Olives (Map p696; ☎ 702-693-8181; Bellagio, 3600 Las Vegas Blvd S; mains $16-52; ⏰ lunch & dinner) Bostonian chef Todd English pays homage to the life-giving fruit. Flatbread pizzas, housemade pastas and flame-licked meats get top billing, along with flamboyant desserts. Patio tables overlook Lake Como.

SushiSamba (Map p696; ☎ 702-607-0700; Shoppes at Palazzo, 3327 Las Vegas Blvd S; mains $23-46; ⏰ 11am-midnight Mon-Wed, to 1am Thu-Sat, 10am-midnight Sun, late-night menu until 4am daily) With the flouncy colors of Rio and martial-arts flicks digitally projected onto the walls, SushiSamba presents an ultrachic, sleek integration of Peruvian, Brazilian and Japanese cuisine. And whoa, the sake list is encyclopedic.

RM Seafood (Map p696; ☎ 702-632-9300; Mandalay Place, 3930 Las Vegas Blvd S; mains $27-62; ⏰ café lunch & dinner, restaurant dinner) From ecoconscious chef Rick Moonen, modern American seafood dishes, such as cajun popcorn and Maine lobster, come with comfort-food sides (like gourmet mac and cheese), a raw shellfish and sushi bar, and a 'biscuit bar' tossing savory salads.

Cut (Map p696; ☎ 702-607-6300; Shoppes at Palazzo, 3327 Las Vegas Blvd S; mains $40-140; ⏰ dinner) Peripatetic Wolfgang Puck is on fire – it's 1200°F in the broiler, to be exact. Modern earth-toned furnishings and silk flowers complement an innovative steakhouse menu, which doesn't hesitate to infuse Indian spices into Kobe beef or match Nebraska corn-fed steaks with spicy red Argentinean chimichurri sauce. Beautiful, modern furnishings.

Alex (Map p696; ☎ 702-770-3300; Wynn, 3131 Las Vegas Blvd S; prix fixe $140, tasting menu $195-235; ⏰ dinner) Award-winning chef Alessandro Stratta stretches his wings at this haute French Rivieran restaurant, with high-concept dishes like frog legs with garlic custard or roasted scallops with pink grapefruit, plus Asian influences. Desserts triumph. No casual attire.

Restaurant Guy Savoy (Map p696; ☎ 702-731-7286; Caesars Palace, 3570 Las Vegas Blvd S; tasting menu $190-290; ⏰ dinner Wed-Sun) If this three-star Michelin chef's high-flying modern French tasting menus would break the bank, just perch at the Bubble Bar for champagne by the glass and elegant appetizers, such as artichoke black-truffle soup. Dress to impress.

Downtown

Famous cheap eats on Fremont St include cheapo shrimp cocktails from the **Golden Gate** (Map p694; ☎ 702-385-1906; 1 E Fremont St; ⏰ 11am-2am), old-fashioned burgers from **Binion's Snack Bar** (Map p694; ☎ 702-382-1600; 128 E Fremont St; ⏰ 10am-10pm Sun-Thu, to midnight Fri & Sat), and deep-fried Oreos and Twinkies from Mardi Gras–style **Mermaids** (Map p694; ⏰ 24hr).

Grotto (Map p694; ☎ 702-385-7111; Golden Nugget, 129 E Fremont St; mains $13-30; ⏰ 11:30am-10:30pm Sun-Thu, to 11:30pm Fri & Sat, pizza bar until 1am daily) Gnocchi and osso bucco are the tenor of the old-world menu here. Wood-oven pizzas and a 200-bottle list of Italian wines are the stars. Sunny patio seats look out at the Nugget's shark-tank waterslide.

Pullman Grille (Map p694; ☎ 702-387-1896; Main Street Station, 200 N Main St; mains $23-41; ⏰ dinner Fri-Sun) The clubby Pullman features Black Angus beef and Pacific Rim seafood specialties amid gorgeous carved wood paneling. The centerpiece is a 1926 rail car, now a cigar lounge.

East of the Strip

our pick **Firefly** (Map p696; ☎ 702-369-3971; Citibank Plaza, 3900 Paradise Rd; small dishes $4-10, large dishes $11-20; ⏰ 11:30am-2am Sun-Thu, to 3am Fri & Sat) Firefly is always hopping. Shake hands with Spanish tradition as chorizo clams jostle alongside *patatas bravas* (fried potatoes in a spicy Spanish sauce). The backlit bar pours fruit-infused mojitos and sangria, while Latin turntablists perform some nights.

Paymon's Mediterranean Café (Map p696; ☎ 702-731-6030; 4147 S Maryland Pkwy; mains $8-19; ⏰ 11am-1am Sun-Thu, to 3am Fri & Sat; Ⓥ) Vegetarians savor the Middle Eastern baked eggplant with garlic, hummus and baba ghanoush, while carnivores fork into succulent rotisserie lamb, baked kibbe and hot gyros. Chill in the adjacent Hookah Lounge with a water pipe and a fig-flavored cocktail.

San-Toki Korean BBQ & Shabu Bar (Map p696; ☎ 702-732-8654; 4480 Paradise Rd; mains $8-25; ⏰ 5pm-4am) At this classy Korean barbecue joint opposite the Hard Rock, boisterous friends gather around DIY fondue-style hot pots, sizzling grills and potent bottles of *soju* (barley spirits).

Origin India (Map p696; ☎ 702-734-6342; 4480 Paradise Rd; dinner mains $13-26; ⏰ 11:30am-11:30pm; Ⓥ) An epic New World and European wine list is only a bonus when an imaginative Indian menu ranges across the subcontinent, dishing up centuries-old royal and Ayurvedic recipes to modern fusion tastes.

Hit the **Hard Rock** (Map p696; ☎ 702-693-5000; 4455 Paradise Rd) for top chefs' restaurants such as Nobu.

West of the Strip

Pan-Asian delights await in the strip malls of Chinatown, along Spring Mountain Rd.

Alizé (Map p696; ☎ 702-951-7000; Palms, 56th fl, 4321 W Flamingo Rd; mains $36-68; dinner) Local chef André Rochat's top-drawer gourmet room is named after the gentle French Mediterranean trade wind. Floor-to-ceiling views, haute French cuisine and a wine tower impress.

Greater Las Vegas

These are worth a special trip, or a stop en route to or from Red Rock Canyon (p709).

Salt Lick BBQ (off Map p696; ☎ 702-797-7535; 11011 W Charleston Blvd, at I-215, Red Rock; mains $11-25; 4-9pm Mon-Fri, 2-9pm Sat & Sun;) From the Lone Star State, this authentic 'cue joint gets a big thumbs-up for its slow-smoked pork ribs and succulent beef brisket with filling sides like smoked mac and cheese and coleslaw. Yee-haw!

Hash House A Go Go (off Map p696; ☎ 702-804-4646; 6800 W Sahara Ave; mains $12-27; 7:30am-2pm daily, dinner Mon-Sat;) This SoCal import's 'twisted farm food' has to be seen to be believed: pancakes as big as tractor tires, farm-worker-sized egg scrambles and housemade hashes that could knock over a cow.

Rosemary's (off Map p696; ☎ 702-869-2251; 8125 W Sahara Ave; dinner mains $30-42, 3-course prix-fixe dinner $55; lunch Mon-Fri, dinner daily) Words fail to describe the epicurean ecstasy you'll encounter here. Once you bite into heavenly offerings like Texas barbecue shrimp with Maytag blue-cheese slaw, you'll forget about the long drive from the Strip. Wine and beer pairings make each course sublime.

DRINKING

A lot of boozing in Las Vegas takes place while staring down slot machines. Casino booze is free as long as you're gambling, but tip your cocktail waitress at least $1 per drink.

Mix (Map p696; ☎ 702-632-9500; THEhotel at Mandalay Bay, 64th fl, 3950 Las Vegas Blvd S; cover after 10pm $25; 5pm-2am Sun-Thu, to 4am Fri & Sat) This is *the* place to grab sunset cocktails. The glassed-in elevator has amazing views, and that's even before you glimpse the mod interior design and the champagne bar.

LIGHT ME UP, BABY

A common complaint registered by Californians is that 'smoke-free' and 'Las Vegas' are rarely in the same sentence: there are ashtrays at every telephone, elevator and pool, in toilets and taxis. Token nonsmoking sections exist at some restaurants, and most hotels claim to offer nonsmoking rooms, but don't expect either to be free of a whiff (or much worse) of cigarettes.

our pick **Beauty Bar** (Map p694; ☎ 702-598-1965; 517 E Fremont St; cover up to $10; hr vary) At the salvaged innards of a 1950s New Jersey beauty salon, swill a cocktail while you get a manicure or chill out with the DJs and live bands. Around the corner is the Downtown Cocktail Room, a speakeasy lounge.

Trader Vic's (Map p696; ☎ 702-405-4700; Miracle Mile Shops, 3663 Las Vegas Blvd S; 11:30am-midnight Mon-Thu, 11am-midnight Fri-Sun) The legendary Polynesian tiki bar that most mixologists agree invented the mai tai has been reborn, with bamboo walls and zebra-print furnishings. Palm trees wave over a Strip-view patio, where DJs spin electronica.

Fireside Lounge (Map p696; ☎ 702-735-4177; Peppermill, 2985 Las Vegas Blvd S; 24hr) The Strip's most unlikely romantic hideaway is inside a retro coffee shop. Courting couples flock here for the sunken fire pit, cozy blue-velvet nooks and candy-colored tropical cocktails – sup a Scorpion.

Hofbräuhaus (Map p696; ☎ 702-853-2337; 4510 Paradise Rd; 11am-11pm Sun-Thu, to midnight Fri & Sat) Replicating the original in Munich, this beer hall and garden celebrates Oktoberfest all year with premium suds, big Bavarian pretzels, fair fräuleins and authentic oom-pah-pah bands nightly.

New York-New York (Map p696; ☎ 702-740-6969; 3790 Las Vegas Blvd S; hr vary) Find dueling pianos at the Bar at Times Square, perfectly poured pints and live Celtic tunes at Nine Fine Irishmen, big-screen sports TVs in the ESPN Zone, and rare American microbrews at Pour 24 upstairs.

Also recommended:

Carnaval Court (Map p696; ☎ 369-5000; outside Harrah's, 3475 Las Vegas Blvd S; noon-late) Flair bartenders juggle fire for raucous, spring-break crowds. Party on, dudes.

Napoleon's (Map p696; ☎ 702-946-7000; Paris Las Vegas, 3645 Las Vegas Blvd S; 4pm-2am) Whisk yourself off to 19th-century France, with over 100 types of bubbly, including vintage Dom Perignon.

Red Square (Map p696; ☎ 702-632-7407; Mandalay Bay, 3950 Las Vegas Blvd S; 5pm-2am) A headless Lenin and blood-red curtains, with vodka and caviar on a solid ice bar.

Triple 7 (Map p694; ☎ 702-387-1896; Main St Station, 200 N Main St; 24hr) Sports fans' fave spot for draft microbrews and huge plates of pub grub.

ENTERTAINMENT

Prostitution may be illegal, but there are plenty of strip clubs offering the illusion of sex on demand. Production stage shows are big business, too, from Cirque du Soleil spectaculars to cheesy celebrity-impersonator and topless-showgirl revues. Save money on shows at the Strip's same-day discount ticket booths at the Fashion Show mall, by the big Coca-Cola bottle north of the MGM Grand and downtown on Fremont St. Call **Ticketmaster** (☎ 702-474-4000; www.ticketmaster.com) for headliner concerts and major sports events.

Nightclubs & Ultra Lounges

Most dance clubs and ultra lounges (upscale bars with DJs, mixologists and occasionally celebrity events) are open from 10pm to 4am later in the week; cover charges vary, from $20 to $50. For Saturday after-hours parties, head to LGBT-friendly **Krâve** (p701).

Pure (Map p696; ☎ 702-731-7873; Caesars Palace, 3570 Las Vegas Blvd S) Crowds of fine young thangs lounge inside a labyrinth of rooms that make it feel like LA, especially now that the hot-hot-hot Pussycat Dolls Lounge has arrived. Strict dress code.

Tao (Map p696; ☎ 702-388-8588; Grand Canal Shoppes, Venetian, 3355 Las Vegas Blvd S) Modeled after the Asian-themed NYC club, here nearly naked go-go girls covered by strategically placed flowers splash in bathtubs. On the risqué dance floor, Paris Hilton lookalikes forgo enlightenment to bump and grind to earth-shaking hip-hop instead.

Moon (off Map p696; ☎ 702-942-6832; 53rd fl, Fantasy Tower, Palms, 4321 W Flamingo Rd) A short ride away from the Playboy Club casino via a glass-and-mirror elevator, this futuristic penthouse has a surreal moon roof that retracts to reveal the starry sky. The Palms' 55th-floor ultra lounge, ghostbar, also has 360-degree panoramas and sci-fi decor. Dress to kill.

our pick **Forty Deuce** (Map p696; ☎ 702-632-9442; www.fortydeuce.com; lower level, Mandalay Place, 3930 Las Vegas Blvd S) Ignore the crazy bachelorette antics and feast your eyes on the smoking-hot traditional burlesque acts backed up by a brassy three-piece jazz combo or rock-and-roll band. Shows start before midnight.

Revolution Lounge (Map p696; ☎ 702-692-8383; www.thebeatlesrevolutionlounge.com; Mirage, 3400 Las Vegas Blvd S) At Cirque du Soleil's psychedelic Beatles-themed ultra lounge, DJs spin everything from house, hip-hop, Brit pop and world music to mash-ups of classic rock and '80s new wave. The no-cover Abbey Road Bar opens at noon daily.

Live Music

House of Blues (Map p696; ☎ 702-632-7600; www.hob.com; Mandalay Bay, 3950 Las Vegas Blvd S; most tickets $15-100) Blues is the tip of the hog at this Mississippi Delta juke joint, where living legends and alt-rockers kick it. Seating is limited, so show up early if you want to take a load off.

Also recommended:

The Joint (Map p696; ☎ 702-693-5066; www.hardrockhotel.com; Hard Rock, 4455 Paradise Rd; most tickets $35-175) Standing-room-only concerts feel like private shows, even when Coldplay or the Beastie Boys are in town.

The Pearl (Map p696; ☎ 702-944-3200; www.palms.com; Palms, 4321 W Flamingo Rd; most tickets $25-150) Modern rock acts like Gwen Stefani and Morrissey have burned up the stage here, with most seats less than 120ft away.

Cinema

Check **Fandango** (☎ 800-326-3264; www.fandango.com) for more movie-theater locations, show times and tickets.

West Wind Las Vegas Drive-In (☎ 702-646-3565; 4150 W Carey Ave, east of N Rancho Dr; admission per adult/child $6.25/1;) One of Nevada's last remaining drive-ins screens up to five double features daily. Bring your buddies, grab a bucket of popcorn and put your feet up on the dashboard – ah, heaven. Gates open one hour before show time.

SHOPPING

The Strip has the high-octane shopping action, with upscale boutiques found inside casino-hotel resorts and mega-malls from the Fashion Show south to Mandalay Place.

Downtown is where you'll find gambling souvenirs, showgirl wigs and feather boas, plus antique, vintage and thrift stores. Cruise west of the Strip for XXX adult goods and trashy lingerie. Bordering the UNLV campus, east of the Strip, Maryland Pkwy is chock-a-block with hip bargain-basement shops.

Clothing

Buffalo Exchange (Map p696; ☎ 702-791-3960; 4110 S Maryland Pkwy; 🕑 10am-8pm Mon-Sat, 11am-7pm Sun) Trade in your nearly new garb for cash or credit at this secondhand chain. They've combed through the dingy thrift-store stuff and culled only the best designer duds and vintage fashions from the 1940s to the '80s.

The Attic (Map p694; ☎ 702-388-4088; 1018 S Main St; 🕑 10am-5pm Mon-Thu, to 6pm Fri, 11am-6pm Sat) A $1 'lifetime pass' is required to enter this vintage emporium, but it's worth it, even if you don't buy any of the fabulous hats, outrageous wigs or retro clubwear.

Valentino's Zootsuit Connection (Map p694; ☎ 702-383-9555; 906 S 6th St; 🕑 11am-5pm Mon-Sat) A sweet (and stylish!) husband-and-wife team outfits party-goers with custom swinging zootsuits, vintage cocktail dresses, Old Hollywood glamour gowns, fringed Western wear and felt fedoras.

Malls

Forum Shops (Map p696; ☎ 702-893-4800; Caesars Palace, 3500 Las Vegas Blvd S; 🕑 10am-11pm Sun-Thu, to midnight Fri & Sat) Franklins fly out of Fendi bags faster at Caesars' fanciful re-creation of an ancient Roman market, housing 160 catwalk-designer emporia. Get your souvenir photo taken inside a Ferrari at the Exotic Cars showroom.

Grand Canal Shoppes (Map p696; ☎ 702-414-4500; Venetian, 3377 Las Vegas Blvd S; 🕑 10am-11pm Sun-Thu, to midnight Fri & Sat) Living statues and mezzo-sopranos stroll along the cobblestone walkways of this Italianate indoor mall, winding past 85 upscale shops. The next-door Shoppes at Palazzo, anchored by Barneys New York, are more glam.

Miracle Mile Shops (Map p696; ☎ 888-800-8284; Planet Hollywood, 3663 Las Vegas Blvd S; 🕑 10am-11pm Sun-Thu, to midnight Fri & Sat) This sleekly redesigned mall is a staggering 1.5 miles long. Stand-outs are Bettie Page, for vintage-style clothing; Brit imports H&M and Ben Sherman; LA denim king True Religion; and Vegas' own rock-star boutique, Stash.

Las Vegas Premium Outlets (Map p694; ☎ 702-474-7500; 875 S Grand Central Pkwy; 🕑 10am-9pm Mon-Sat, to 8pm Sun) Vegas' most upscale outlet mall claims 120 high-end names like Armani Exchange, Dolce & Gabbana and Kenneth Cole, alongside more casual brands like Levi's.

Music

For bookstores, see p693.

Zia Records (☎ 702-735-4942; 4225 S Eastern Ave; 🕑 10am-midnight) Calling itself the 'last real record store,' here you can dig up a demo by Vegas' next breakout band (who needs The Killers anyway?). Live in-store performances happen on a stage with the warning sign 'No moshing allowed.'

Quirky

Gamblers General Store (Map p694; ☎ 702-382-9903; 800 S Main St; 🕑 9am-5pm) Fascinating gambling-supply store has it all, from cheapo souvenirs to authentic custom-made chips, roulette wheels and poker tables identical to those found in many casinos, plus Nevada's largest inventory of slot machines.

Main Street Antiques (Map p694; ☎ 702-382-1882; 500 S Main St; 🕑 9am-6pm) With over 40 different antique dealers, this one-stop retro extravaganza is the place to pick up vintage Vegas souvenirs. Keep an eye out for Rat Pack–era memorabilia.

Houdini's Magic Shop (Map p696; ☎ 702-798-4789; Forum Shops, Caesars Palace, 3500 Las Vegas Blvd S; 🕑 10am-11pm Sun-Thu, to midnight Fri & Sat; ♿) The legendary escape artist's legacy lives on at this minimuseum and shop packed with gags, pranks, magic tricks and 'zines. Magicians perform for wide-eyed crowds. Every purchase includes a free private lesson.

Déjà Vu Love Boutique (Map p696; ☎ 702-731-5652; 3275 Industrial Rd; 🕑 10am-4am) Next door to a strip club, this candy-colored sex shop stocks quick pick-me-ups like passion-fruit lube, a bouncy paddle or a very adult DVD.

GETTING THERE & AWAY

Air

Las Vegas has direct flights from most US cities, as well as some Canadian, European and Asian gateways. During peak periods (such as weekends and holidays), arriving via a package that includes airfare and a hotel might be the best deal.

Not far from the South Strip, **McCarran International Airport** (LAS; Map p696; ☎ 702-261-5211;

www.mccarran.com; 5757 Wayne Newton Blvd; wi-fi) has ATMs, a bank, a post office, a 24-hour fitness center, free wi-fi, tourist information and bad-odds slot machines. Most domestic airlines use Terminal 1; international, charter and some domestic flights use Terminal 2.

Bus

Downtown, **Greyhound** (Map p694; ☎ 702-384-9561; www.greyhound.com; 200 S Main St) runs long-distance buses to/from California. East of the Strip (take CAT bus 201), **Megabus** (Map p696; ☎ 877-462-6342; www.megabus.com; cnr E Tropicana Ave & S Swenson St) offers three daily buses to/from downtown LA (Union Station), taking 4½ to five hours each way; fares vary from $1.50 to $35, depending on how far in advance you book a seat.

Car & Motorcycle

The main highways are I-15 from California, and US 95, the chief north–south artery to Reno, 450 miles away (an eight-hour drive). US Hwy 93 leads southeast from downtown to Hoover Dam. I-215 passes McCarran Airport. On weekends and holidays, trip times to/from California (see p693) can double or even triple. Along I-15, Highway Radio (98.1FM, 99.5FM) broadcasts traffic and weather updates. For Nevada road conditions, call ☎ 877-687-6237.

It's way more expensive to rent a car in Las Vegas than in California. Booking ahead scores the best rates, with the airport being cheaper than downtown or the Strip. For rental-car companies, see p738. For something glamorous, ring **Rent-A-Vette** (Map p696; ☎ 702-736-2592, 800-372-1981; www.exoticcarrentalslasvegas.com; 5021 Swenson St). Corvettes and exotic convertibles fetch $200 or more per day. **Las Vegas Harley-Davidson** (Map p696; ☎ 877-571-7174; www.lvhd.com; 2605 S Eastern Ave) rents Harleys from $90 to $155 per day, including unlimited mileage.

GETTING AROUND

To/From the Airport

Taxi fares to Strip hotels (30 minutes in heavy traffic) run $15 to $20, or to downtown around $25, cash only. Fare gouging (long-hauling) through the airport connector tunnel is common; ask your driver to use surface streets instead.

Most airport shuttles operate 8am to midnight (some run 24 hours) and charge $6 per person to the Strip, $7.50 to downtown or off-Strip hotels. If you're traveling light, CAT bus 108 ($1.25, 40 to 55 minutes) heads downtown from the airport between 5am and 2am, stopping at the Las Vegas Convention Center, Hilton and Sahara monorail stations.

Car & Motorcycle

Traffic often snarls, especially during morning and afternoon rush hours and on weekend nights everywhere along the Strip. Tune to 970AM for traffic updates. If you've been drinking, **Designated Drivers** (☎ 702-456-7433; 🕑 24hr) will pick you up and drive your car back to your hotel; fees vary, depending on mileage.

Public Transportation

The zero-emissions **monorail** (☎ 702-699-8200; single-/two-ride ticket $5/9, 24/72hr pass $15/40; 🕑 7am-2am Mon-Thu, to 3am Fri & Sun) stops at the MGM Grand, Bally's/Paris, Flamingo/Caesars Palace, Harrah's/Imperial Palace, Las Vegas Convention Center, Las Vegas Hilton and Sahara stations. Multiride discounts are available.

Citizens Area Transit (CAT; ☎ 702-228-7433, 800-228-3911; 24hr pass $5; 🕑 most routes 5am-2am) operates dozens of local bus routes (one-way fare $1.25) and double-decker 'The Deuce' buses ($2), which run 24/7 along the Strip to/from downtown. Cash only; exact change required.

Free trams link the Mirage and TI (Treasure Island); and the Excalibur, Luxor and Mandalay Bay casino hotels. Free shuttle buses connect the Rio to the Strip (Harrah's, Bally's/Paris, Caesars Palace) every 30 minutes from 10am to 1am daily.

Taxi

It's illegal to hail a cab on the street. Taxi stands are found at casino hotels and malls. Fares (cash only) are metered. A 4.5-mile lift along the entire Strip runs $12 to $16 (plus tip), depending on traffic. Call **Yellow/Checker/Star** (☎ 702-873-2000).

AROUND LAS VEGAS

You don't have to venture all the way out to the Grand Canyon just to experience the natural glories of the US Southwest.

Most tours appeal to seniors who prefer to leave the driving to others. Free Strip hotel pick-ups/drop-offs are sometimes included in tour prices. Check online for serious discounts.

Adventure Las Vegas (☎ 888-867-6259; www.adventurelasvegas.com; tours $89-539; reservations 24hr) One-stop adventure shop for everything from horseback rides to Lake Mead kayaking.

Black Canyon River Adventures (☎ 702-294-1414, 800-455-3490; www.blackcanyonadventures.com; Hacienda Hotel & Casino, US 93, Boulder City; tours $51-119) Three-hour motor-assisted raft floats from Hoover Dam down the Colorado River, with stops for swimming and lunch.

Boulder City Outfitters (☎ 702-293-1190, 800-748-3702; www.bouldercityoutfitters.com; 1631 Industrial Rd, Boulder City; mountain-biking & hiking/kayaking tours $100/163, canoe & kayak rental per day $35-55, mountain-bike rental per half-/full-day from $25/40) Guided kayak tours launch from the base of Hoover Dam, with hot springs and waterfall stops. DIY shuttles available.

Pink Jeep Tours (☎ 702-895-6777, 888-900-4480; www.pinkjeeplasvegas.com; half-day tours $79-124, full-day tours $209-565) Small-group, naturalist-guided excursions to Hoover Dam, Red Rock Canyon, Valley of Fire, Mt Charleston and more; the Grand Canyon combo tour features short helicopter and pontoon-boat rides.

RED ROCK CANYON

The startling contrast between the artificial neon glow of Las Vegas and the awesome natural forces of this **national conservation area** (Map p709; ☎ 702-515-5350; www.redrockcanyonlv.org; per car $5; visitors center 8:30am-4:30pm, scenic loop 6am-5pm Nov-Feb, to 7pm Mar & Oct, to 8pm Apr-Sep) can't be exaggerated. Created about 65 million years ago, the canyon is more like a valley, with a steep, rugged, red-rock escarpment rising 3000ft on its western edge. It's especially impressive around sunrise or sunset.

A 13-mile, one-way scenic driving and cycling loop passes by the canyon's striking natural features and panoramic viewpoints. Rugged hiking trails lead to seasonal waterfalls, while the popular Willow Springs picnic area offers nature walks. Book ahead for horseback rides with **Cowboy Trail Rides** (☎ 702-387-2457; www.cowboytrailrides.com; tours $69-388;). En route from the Strip, you can rent mountain bikes (from $35 per day) at **McGhie's Bike Outpost** (☎ 702-875-4820; www.bikeoutpost.com; 16 Cottonwood Dr, Blue Diamond; guided tours per person $109-129); call for opening hours.

Nearby **Bonnie Springs** (☎ 702-875-4191; www.bonniesprings.com; 1 Gunfighter Lane, Blue Diamond; per

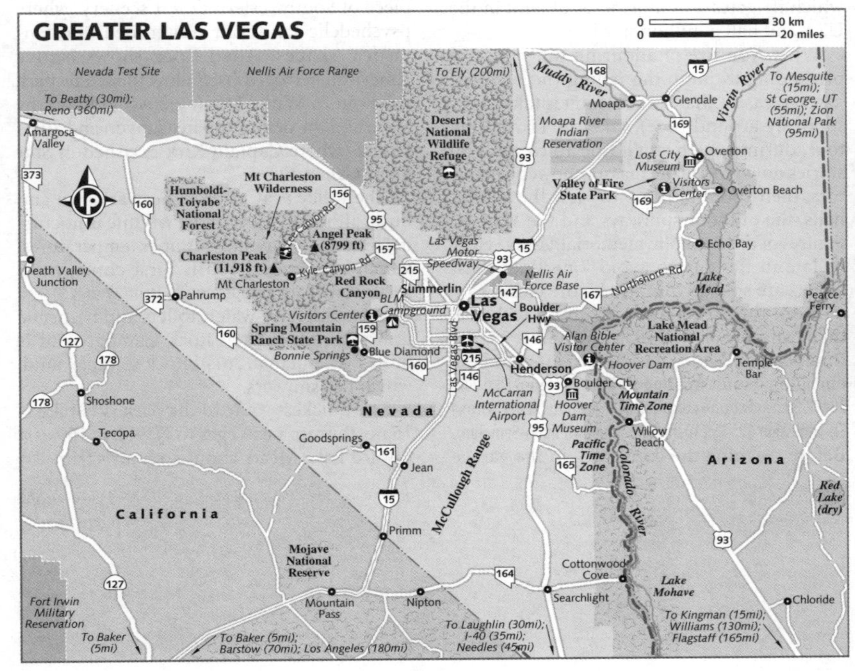

car $20; ⌚ 10:30am-5pm, to 6pm in summer; ♿), the scene of countless B-movie shoots, is a touristy sideshow for kiddies: Old West melodramas, simulated hangings and gunfights, miniature-train rides, a wax museum and a sad petting zoo.

About 2 miles east of the visitors center off NV Hwy 159 is a dusty Bureau of Land Management (BLM) **campground** (tents & RV sites $10; ⌚ Sep-May) offering first-come, first-serve sites with water and vault toilets (nonflush composting toilets).

From the Strip, it's a 30-minute journey. Take I-15 south, exit Blue Diamond Rd (NV Hwy 160) westbound, then veer right onto NV 159, which takes you back to Las Vegas via W Charleston Blvd.

HOOVER DAM

Once the world's tallest, **Hoover Dam** (Map p709; ☎ 702-494-2517; www.usbr.gov/lc/hooverdam; visitor center admission $8, tours $15-35; visitors center 9am-5pm, to 6pm in summer) is an engineering marvel, its imposing, graceful art-deco concrete curve filling a dramatic canyon. The dam was built primarily to control floods on the lower Colorado River, which irrigates a million acres of land in the USA and half a million in Mexico.

When you tire of admiring the view and pretending to jump the railing (no terrorist jokes, please – that sort of thing is taken *very* seriously around here), take the fascinating tour, during which you'll ride an elevator 50 stories down to see the massive power generators, then zoom back up to view the exhibit halls, the outdoor spillways and the Winged Figures of the Republic memorial. Arrive early or late in the day to avoid long lines. Last tickets are sold 45 minutes before closing.

From the Strip, take I-15 south to I-215, then continue on I-515/US Hwys 93 & 95 past Boulder City, which has motels, cafés and the engaging, hands-on **Hoover Dam Museum** (☎ 702-294-1988; www.bcmha.org; Boulder Dam Hotel, 1305 Arizona St; admission $2; ⌚ 10am-5pm Mon-Sat, noon-5pm Sun). Before reaching the dam, park in the garage ($7, cash only), or cross over the dam and the Arizona state line to perhaps find free roadside parking.

LAKE MEAD

Although lately the lake has been experiencing severe drought, this sprawling **national recreation area** (Map p709; ☎ 702-293-8906; www.nps.gov/lame; per car $5; ⌚ 24hr) has a scenic shoreline drive that passes hiking trails, beaches, marinas and bird-watching spots. Popular year-round activities include boat cruises, swimming, fishing, waterskiing and kayaking. Get oriented at the **Alan Bible Visitor Center** (☎ 702-293-8990; Lakeshore Scenic Dr; ⌚ 8:30am-4:30pm), a few miles west of Hoover Dam. North of Overton Beach, the **Lost City Museum** (☎ 702-397-2193; 721 S Moapa Valley Blvd, Overton; admission $3; ⌚ 8:30am-4:30pm) of Native American culture tells the story of Pueblo Grande de Nevada that existed here until 1150 AD.

VALLEY OF FIRE

West of Lake Mead, this **state park** (Map p709; ☎ 702-397-2088; http://parks.nv.gov/vf.htm; per car $6; ⌚ 24hr, visitors center 8:30am-4:30pm) is a masterpiece of Southwestern desert scenery, where psychedelic sandstone has eroded into fantastical shapes. Atlatl Rock shows Native American petroglyphs. Follow the scenic park road out to White Domes, passing Rainbow Vista and the detour to Fire Canyon and Silica Dome (where Captain Kirk perished in *Star Trek: Generations*).

The valley is at its most fiery at dawn and dusk, although most of the wildlife is nocturnal. Beware of daytime summer temperatures, which can exceed 100°F. First-come, first-serve **state park campgrounds** (tent/RV sites $14/24; ⌚ year-round) have water, toilets and barbecue grills. Primitive Arch Rock Campground is more peaceful than Atlatl Rock Campground, which has showers.

The quickest route to the park is to take I-15 north from Las Vegas to NV Hwy 169 east toward Lake Mead, about an hour's trip.

Directory

CONTENTS

ACCOMMODATIONS

California offers all kinds of overnight lodgings, from campgrounds, hostels and B&Bs to chain motels, big-city hotels and luxury oceanfront resorts. Accommodations in this book fall into one of three categories: budget (double-occupancy rooms starting under $125), midrange (starting over $125, up to $225) and top end (over $225). Prices listed in this book are for peak-season travel (typically summer) and, unless stated otherwise, don't include taxes.

Budget travelers will be checking in at campgrounds, hostels and basic motels and hotels. Midrange accommodations are generally the best value, and most of our reviews fall into this category. You can expect a clean, comfortable, decent-sized room with a private bathroom, cable TV, a telephone and often a coffeemaker, a microwave and a minifridge. Some midrange properties have outdoor swimming pools and hot tubs too. Top-end hotels offer resort-class amenities and, if you're lucky, a scenic location or historical ambience. Standard amenities include swimming pools, fitness rooms, business centers, concierge desks, even spas and high-caliber restaurants.

You can almost always save money on room rates midweek or in the low-season (usually winter). Membership of an automobile association (p733) or the American Association of Retired Persons (p717) may get you modest savings (usually 10%) at any time of the year. Also look out for freebie ad magazines packed with hotel discount coupons at gas stations, tourist offices and online at **Roomsaver.com** (www.roomsaver.com).

For deeper discounts, try booking online via the property's own website; these often have special internet rates, promotional deals and packages not available anywhere else. Also search for more deals using an online travel booking agency, such as **Expedia** (www.expedia.com), **Orbitz** (www.orbitz.com) or **Travelocity** (www.travelocity.com), or a travel discounter like **Priceline** (www.priceline.com) or **Hotwire** (www.hotwire.com). Another handy Web resource is **TripAdvisor**

PRACTICALITIES

- Major newspapers include the *Los Angeles Times, San Francisco Chronicle* and *Sacramento Bee*.
- Major TV networks are ABC, CBS, NBC, FOX and PBS (public broadcasting).
- Major cable TV channels are CNN (news), ESPN (sports), HBO (movies) and the Weather Channel.
- National Public Radio (NPR) is at the lower end of the FM dial.
- Electrical supply is 110V AC, 60Hz.
- The NTSC system (not compatible with PAL or SECAM) is used for videos.
- The imperial system is used for weights and measures, but road signs may be written in both kilometers and miles. For conversions, see the inside front cover.

BOOK YOUR STAY ONLINE

For more accommodation reviews and recommendations by Lonely Planet authors, check out the online booking service at www.lonelyplanet.com/hotels. You'll find the true, insider lowdown on the best places to stay. Reviews are thorough and independent. Best of all, you can book online.

(www.tripadvisor.com), which ranks user reviews of accommodations statewide.

Reservations are always a good idea year-round. They can be essential for travel during the busy summer months, especially July and August. Prices jump and rooms are scarce around holidays (p718), when you should expect minimum-stay requirements. For more advice about the best times to travel in California, see p23.

Where available we've listed toll-free reservations numbers in this book. If you book a reservation by phone, always get a confirmation number and ask about the cancellation policy before you give out your credit-card information. If you plan to arrive late in the evening, call ahead on the day of your stay to let them know. Hotels overbook, but if you've guaranteed the reservation with your credit card, they will accommodate you somewhere else and pick up the tab. If they don't, squawk.

Those properties with an internet-connected computer terminal available for guest use are designated with the internet icon (💻). More and more properties are offering free or fee-based wireless internet access (wi-fi). But advertising can be deceiving: sometimes a property's high-speed network may only be available in the lobby or other public areas, not in your room. If this matters to you, inquire when booking. For more tips on getting online in California, see p722.

In Southern California, nearly all lodgings have air-conditioning, but in Northern California and in coastal areas as far south as Santa Barbara, where it rarely gets hot, the opposite is true, and even fans may not be provided. Many lodgings are now exclusively nonsmoking. Where they exist, smoking rooms are often in less desirable locations and may be the last ones to be renovated. Owners may levy a hefty 'cleaning fee' (over $100) on guests who light up in specially designated nonsmoking rooms.

B&Bs

If you want an atmospheric, occasionally romantic alternative to impersonal motels and hotels, bed-and-breakfast inns typically inhabit fine old Victorian houses or other heritage buildings, bedecked with floral wallpaper and antique furnishings. People who like privacy may find the USA's B&Bs too intimate. Rates typically include a lavish home-cooked breakfast, but occasionally breakfast is not included (never mind what the name 'B&B' suggests). Amenities vary, but rooms with a TV and a telephone are the exception; the cheapest units share bathrooms. Most B&Bs require advance reservations, although some will accommodate the occasional drop-in guest. Smoking is generally prohibited and children are usually not welcome. Minimum-stay requirements are common, especially on weekends and during busy times. Many places belong to the **California Association of Bed & Breakfast Inns** (☎ 800-373-9251; www.cabbi.com).

Camping

In the Golden State, camping is so much more than just a cheap way to spend the night. The best sites in California will have you waking up on the beach, next to an alpine lake or underneath a canopy of redwoods. For the lowdown on camping, see p67.

Hostels

California currently has 21 hostels affiliated with **Hostelling International USA** (HI-USA; ☎ 301-495-1240, reservations 800-909-4776; www.hiusa.org), as well as a growing number of independent hostels, particularly in the cities. The latter have more relaxed rules and often no curfew. Indies also tend to have a more convivial vibe, with regular parties and organized events and activities. Some hostels include a light breakfast in their rates, arrange local tours or will pick up guests at transportation hubs. Some say they accept only international visitors (basically to keep out destitute locals), but Americans who look like travelers may be admitted, especially during slower months. A passport, a HI-USA membership card or an international plane ticket can help establish your credentials. Reservations are always a good idea, especially in peak season. Most hostels take bookings online and by phone, and some also via email. Many independent hostels belong to online booking services such as www.hostels.com, www.thehostelhandbook.com and www

THE CHAIN GANG

In this book we aim to highlight independently owned establishments – places designed to be remembered, not instantly forgotten. But these are too few to sustain travelers, so we also include the best choices among the chains. For more locations of chain hotels and motels, contact:

Budget

Choice Hotels (☎ 877-424-6423; www.choicehotels.com)
Days Inn (☎ 800-329-7466; www.daysinn.com)
Motel 6 (☎ 800-466-8356; www.motel6.com)
Red Roof Inn (☎ 800-733-7663; www.redroof.com)
Super 8 (☎ 800-800-8000; www.super8.com)
Travelodge (☎ 800-578-7878; www.travelodge.com)
Vagabond Inn (☎ 800-522-1555; www.vagabondinn.com)

Midrange

Best Western (☎ 800-780-7234; www.bestwestern.com)
Choice Hotels (☎ 877-424-6423; www.choicehotels.com)
Hampton Inn (☎ 800-426-7866; www.hamptoninn.com)
Hilton (☎ 800-445-8667; www.hilton.com)
Holiday Inn (☎ 800-465-4329; www.holiday-inn.com)
Howard Johnson (☎ 800-446-4656; www.hojo.com)
Hyatt (☎ 888-591-1234; www.hyatt.com)
La Quinta (☎ 800-753-3757; www.lq.com)
Marriott (☎ 888-236-2427; www.marriott.com)
Radisson (☎ 888-201-1718; www.radisson.com)
Ramada (☎ 800-272-6232; www.ramada.com)
Sheraton (☎ 800-325-3535; www.sheraton.com)
Westin (☎ 800-937-8461; www.westin.com)

Top End

Four Seasons (☎ 800-819-5053; www.fourseasons.com)
Ritz-Carlton (☎ 800-542-8680; www.ritzcarlton.com)
Starwood (☎ 888-625-5144; www.starwoodhotels.com)
W Hotels (☎ 877-946-8357; www.whotels.com)

.hostelworld.com, which may offer lower rates than the hostels directly. An online resource for traveler reviews is www.hostelz.com.

Motels & Hotels

Motels surround a parking lot and usually have some sort of a lobby. Hotels may provide extra services such as laundry, but these amenities are expensive. If you walk in without reservations, ask to see a room before paying for it, especially at motels.

Rooms are often priced by the size and number of beds, rather than the number of occupants. A room with one double or queen-size bed usually costs the same for one or two people, while a room with a king-size bed or two double beds costs more. There is often a small surcharge for the third and fourth person, but children under a certain age (this varies) may stay free. Cribs or cots usually incur an extra charge.

Many hotels offer suites for people in need of more elbow room. While this should technically get you at least two rooms, one of them a bedroom, this is not always the case, as some properties simply call their larger rooms 'suites' or 'junior suites.' Ask about the layout when booking.

If the rates include breakfast, this may be just a stale donut and wimpy coffee, an all-out gourmet affair with fresh croissants and homemade jam, or anything in between.

ACTIVITIES

For outdoor enthusiasts, California offers the mother lode of possibilities. No matter what kind of adventure you crave, this land of lakes and rivers, ocean and mountains, deserts and forests, has it (for an overview, see p67). Outdoors outfitters and tour operators are listed in the destination chapters.

BUSINESS HOURS

Standard business hours, including for most government offices, are 9am to 5pm Monday to Friday. Banks are usually open 9am to 5pm weekdays; some branches are open Saturday, usually 9am to 2pm. Post offices are open from 8am to 4pm or 5:30pm weekdays, and some are also open Saturday, usually 8am to 2pm.

Restaurants typically serve lunch from 11:30am to 2:30pm and dinner from 5:30pm to 10pm daily. When available, breakfast usually runs from 7am to 1pm. Pubs and bars are typically open from 4pm or 5pm until 2am nightly. Music and dance clubs throw open their doors after 9pm or 10pm, often only on weekends; most close at 2am, but depending on the crowd they may keep going until 4am.

Stores are usually open 10am to 6pm Monday to Saturday and noon to 5pm Sunday. In malls and downtown shopping areas, hours may be extended to 9pm (to 6pm on Sunday). Supermarkets are generally open from 8am until 9pm or even midnight, and most cities have a few 24-hour supermarkets and pharmacies.

Variations on the above are noted in individual reviews.

CHILDREN

California is a tailor-made destination for traveling with kids. For general information, advice and anecdotes, read Lonely Planet's *Travel with Children*. Online resources include www.travelwithyourkids.com and www.flyingwithkids.com.

Practicalities

Children's discounts are widely available for everything from museum admission and movie tickets to bus fares and motel stays. The definition of a 'child' varies – in some places anyone under 18 is eligible, while at others the cut-off is age six.

Airlines usually allow infants (up to age two) to fly for free, while older children requiring a seat of their own qualify for reduced fares. Children receive substantial discounts on Amtrak trains (p738) and Greyhound buses (p733). In cars, any child under age six or weighing less than 60lb must be buckled up in the back seat in a child or infant safety seat. Most car-rental agencies (p735) rent these seats for about $10 per day or $50 per week, but you must book them in advance.

Motels and hotels typically have rooms with two beds or an extra sofa bed, ideal for families. They also have roll-away beds or cots that can be brought in to the room for a surcharge. Some offer 'kids stay free' promotions, although this may apply only if no extra bedding is required. Some B&Bs don't allow children; ask before booking.

Luxury resorts may have on-call babysitting services. At other hotels, the front-desk staff or concierge may help you make arrangements. Be sure to ask whether babysitters are licensed and bonded, what they charge per hour per child, whether there's a minimum fee and if they charge extra for transportation and meals. Tourist-information offices can point you toward local childcare facilities and pediatricians.

It's perfectly fine to bring kids, even toddlers, along to casual restaurants, which often have high chairs. Many diners and family restaurants break out paper placemats and crayons for drawing. Ask about cheaper children's menus too. Baby food, infant formula, soy and cow's milk, disposable diapers (nappies) and other necessities are widely available in drugstores and supermarkets. Most women are discreet about breastfeeding in public. Many public toilets have a baby-changing table (sometimes in men's toilets too), with gender-neutral 'family' facilities available at airports.

Sights & Activities

It's easy to keep kids entertained no matter where you travel in California. Throughout this book, look for family attractions and other fun activities, all marked with the child-friendly icon ( ). If you want to visit Southern California's theme parks during your trip, see our suggested week-long itinerary 'SoCal With Kids' (p33). For our top 10 list of family attractions in California, see p26. At national and state parks, be sure to ask at visitor centers about ranger-led activities and self-guided 'Junior Ranger' programs, in which kids earn themselves a badge after completing an activity booklet that's fun for all ages. Many outdoor activity outfitters and tour operators have specially designed programs for children. In urban areas, see the special 'City for Children' sections in the destination chapters. For more ideas, check out www.visitcalifornia.com and www.thefamilytravelfiles.com/state/california.asp.

CLIMATE CHARTS

The climate charts (opposite) provide a snapshot of California's weather patterns. For advice about the best times to travel in California, see p23.

DANGERS & ANNOYANCES

Despite its seemingly apocalyptic list of dangers – guns, violent crime, riots, earthquakes – California is actually a reasonably safe place to visit. The greatest danger is posed by car accidents (buckle up – it's the law), while the biggest annoyances are city traffic and crowds. Wildlife poses some small threats, and of course

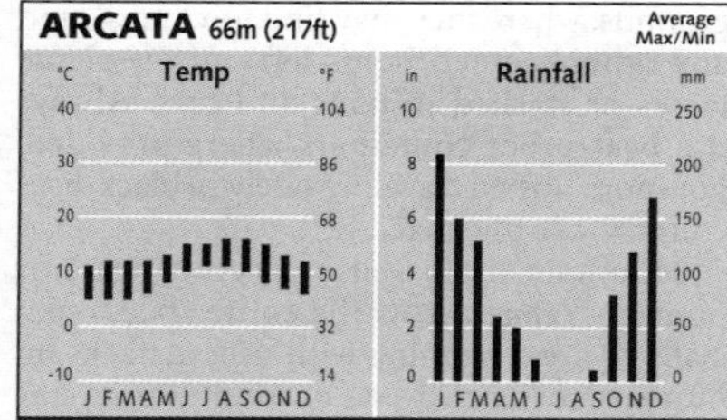

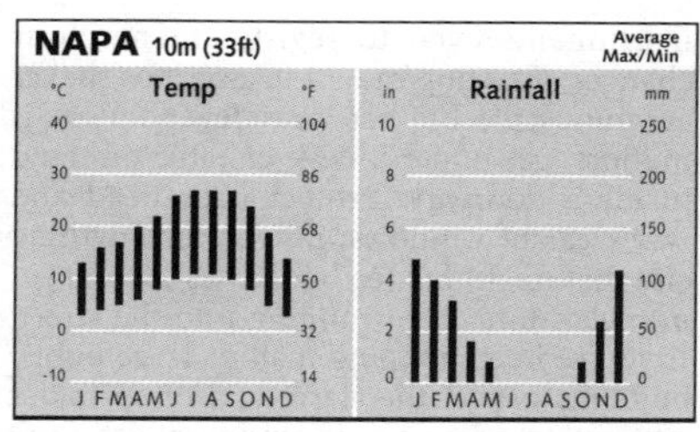

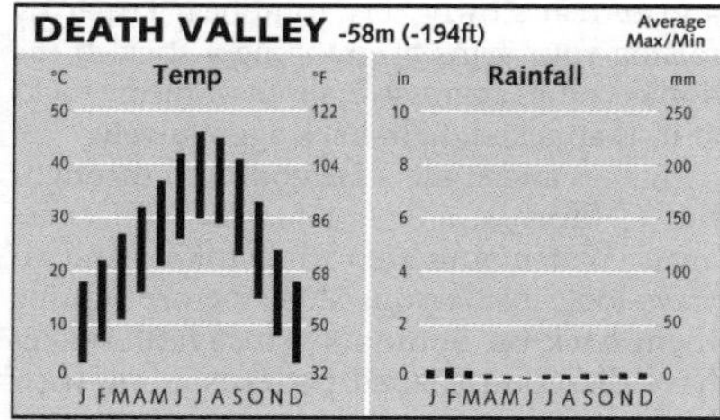

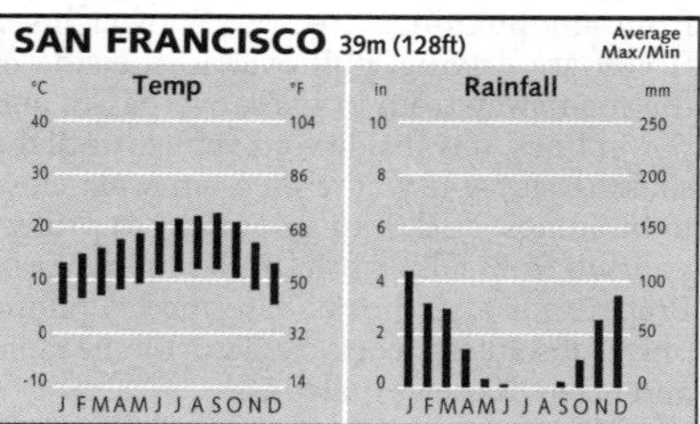

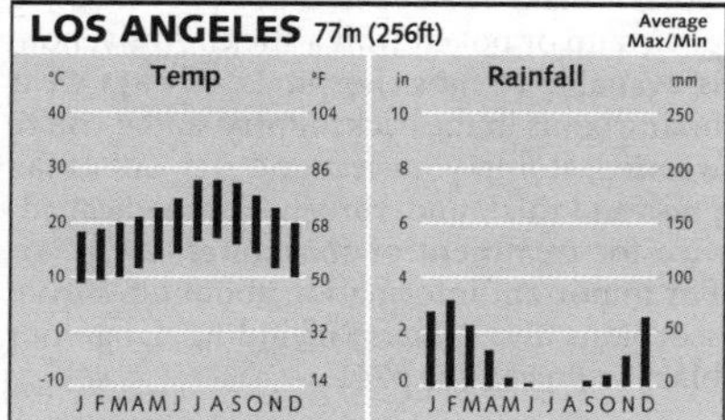

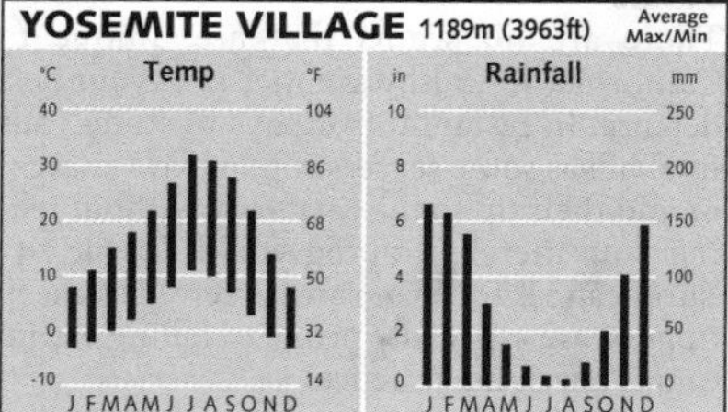

there is the dramatic, albeit unlikely, possibility of a natural disaster, such as an earthquake. Prepare for the worst, but expect the best.

Crime

Tourists will rarely get tricked, conned or attacked simply because they're tourists. Potential violence is a problem for everyone, but don't freak out – just pack your street smarts. Most cities have some 'bad neighborhoods' that should be avoided, particularly after dark. The Dangers & Annoyances sections in the destination chapters provide some details. If you're worried, quiz hotel staff, locals and police about the latest no-go zones.

If you find yourself in a neighborhood where you'd rather not be, look confident. Don't stop every few minutes to check your guidebook or map, and hail a taxi quickly if you can. Try to use ATMs only during the day in well-trafficked areas. Exercise caution in parking lots and garages, especially at night. If your car is bumped from behind by another vehicle in a remote area, try to keep going to a well-lit public place, such as a gas station or even a police station.

If a mugger accosts you, there's no 100% recommended plan of action, but handing over whatever the mugger wants is better than getting attacked. Don't carry valuables or an excess of cash. Don't put all of your money in the same pocket, wallet, handbag or backpack. Keep some money separate, and hand it over fast. Muggers are not happy to find their victims penniless.

That said, don't dwell on crime. Just protect yourself as best you can.

Earthquakes

Earthquakes happen all the time but most are so tiny it takes sensitive seismological instruments even to register them. Your chances of getting caught in a serious shaker are minuscule, but here are a few pointers. If indoors, get under a desk or table or stand inside a doorway. Protect your head and stay clear of windows, mirrors or anything else that might fall (eg bookcases). Don't get into elevators or go running into the street. If you're in a shopping mall or large public building, expect the alarm and/or sprinkler systems to come on. If outdoors, get away from any buildings, trees and power lines. If you are driving, pull over to the side of the road away from bridges, overpasses and power lines; stay inside your vehicle until the shaking stops. If you're on a sidewalk close to buildings, duck into a doorway to protect yourself from falling bricks, glass and debris. Prepare for aftershocks. Use the telephone only if absolutely necessary. Turn on the radio and listen for news bulletins.

Scams

There are no scams that are unique to California. A healthy skepticism is your best defense. In restaurants it pays to study your final bill as some servers slip in extra charges or add their tip to the final tally without telling you, thereby hoping you'll double tip. European visitors, who are perceived as cheap tippers, are especially prone to falling victim to this annoying practice.

Swimming

Popular beaches are patrolled by lifeguards, but even so some of them can be dangerous places to swim. The biggest hazards are riptides and dangerous ocean currents. Obey all posted signs on beaches. If you get caught in a riptide that carries you away from the shore, don't panic and try to swim against the current, or you'll quickly get exhausted and drown. Instead, try to swim parallel to the shoreline and once the current stops pulling you out, swim back to shore.

Wildlife

Never feed or approach wild animals – it causes them to lose their innate fear of humans, which in turn makes them more aggressive, and eventually they may have to be killed to in order to protect people. Feeding or otherwise harassing specially protected wildlife is a crime, subject to enormous fines. Black bears are often attracted to campgrounds, where they may find food, trash and any other scented items left out on picnic tables or stashed in tents and cars. Always use bear-proof containers where provided. For more tips on traveling safely in black-bear country, see the boxed text, p70.

Mountain lions – also called cougars or pumas – range across the entire state, especially in areas teeming with deer. Attacks on humans are rare. If you encounter one, stay calm, pick up small children, face the animal and retreat slowly. Try to appear larger by raising your arms or grabbing a stick. If the lion becomes aggressive, shout or throw rocks at it. If attacked, fight back aggressively.

Snakes and spiders are common throughout California, and not just in wilderness areas. Watch your step while hiking and always look inside your shoes before putting them back on outdoors. Most rattlesnakes have diamond-shaped patterns along their backs. Bites are rare, but occur most often when a snake is stepped on or provoked (eg picked up or poked with a stick). Antivenom is available at most hospitals. Always wear hiking boots in the backcountry, and if you're worried, stomp your feet and stay out of tall grass and thick underbrush. For medical advice for treatment of snakebites, see p741. For important information about bites from scorpions and spiders (including dangerous black widows), see p741.

DISCOUNT CARDS

If SoCal theme parks are the focus of your trip, a **Southern California CityPass** (www.citypass.com) may save you up to 30%. Passes cost $247 for adults ($199 for children aged three to nine), including three-day admission to Disneyland and Disney's California Adventure, one-day admission each to Universal Studios and SeaWorld and another day at either the San Diego Zoo or the San Diego Wild Animal Park. Passes are valid for 14 days from the day of the first use and may be purchased online or at any of the participating attractions. The **Hollywood CityPass** (p509) and **San Francisco CityPass** offer similar schemes. LA also has the **Go Los Angeles Card** (p509).

Members of the **American Automobile Association** (p733) and its international affiliates get small discounts (usually 10%) in many places, including on Amtrak trains. Make it a habit to ask every time you book a room, reserve a car, take a tour or pay an entrance fee at attractions, especially because these discounts are not usually advertised.

Discount coupons can be found at every tourist locale. Some are hardly worth reading, but if you scour tourist agencies and highway welcome centers for brochures, you may find some good ones. Coupons always have restrictions and conditions; read the fine print.

Senior Cards

People over the age of 65 (sometimes 55, 60 or 62) often qualify for the same discounts as students – any ID showing your birth date should suffice as proof of age. US citizens and permanent residents can pay $10 for an 'America the Beautiful' pass (p64), which allows free access to all federal recreational lands, including national parks, and 50% off use fees like camping. Members of the **American Association of Retired Persons** (AARP; ☎ 888-687-2277; www.aarp.org), an advocacy group for those 50 years and older, often qualify for small discounts (usually 10%) on hotels, car rentals and at attractions and entertainment venues. A one-year membership costs $12.50.

Student & Youth Cards

If you're a full-time international student, the **International Student Identity Card** (ISIC; www.isiccard.com) entitles you to discounts on movie and theater tickets, travel insurance and admission to museums and other attractions. For nonstudents under 26, the International Youth Travel Card (IYTC) offers some of the same savings and benefits. If you live in the UK you can apply online. Otherwise, purchase these cards from hosteling organizations or youth-oriented travel agencies such as STA Travel. International and US students can buy the **Student Advantage Card** (☎ 877-256-4672; www.studentadvantage.com) for $22.50 per year to get 15% savings on Amtrak train and Greyhound bus tickets, plus discounts of up to 40% at some hotels, shops and movie theaters.

FESTIVALS & EVENTS

The festivals and events listed below are celebrated statewide, although with much more fanfare and enthusiasm in some places than others. For more details about local celebrations, see the Festivals & Events section of the destination chapters. Also check with local tourism bureaus and chambers of commerce, or contact the **California Tourism Board** (☎ 916-444-4429, 800-862-2543; www.visitcalifornia.com) for upcoming festivals and events.

Chinese New Year Colorful parades, firecrackers and dragon dances in late January or early February. San Francisco's Chinatown is a fantastic place to be.
Valentine's Day Catch the love bug: roses, candy and kisses on February 14.
St Patrick's Day All hail to the patron saint of Ireland – wear green and drink like a fish on March 17.
Cinco de Mayo Viva Mexico! Margaritas, music and merriment celebrate the victory of Mexican forces over the French army at the Battle of Puebla on May 5, 1862. LA and San Diego really do it in style.
Memorial Day Summer is here: flags, patriotism and picnics in late May.
Gay Pride Month Coming out parties and costumed parades with floats happen throughout June. The biggest, bawdiest celebrations are in San Francisco.
Independence Day Red, white & blue: parades, fireworks and barbecues on July 4.
Labor Day The official end of summer, with outdoor barbecues, beach picnics and camping trips over a long weekend in early September.
Halloween On October 31, kids dress up in costumes and go door-to-door trick-or-treating for candy, while adults act out their alter egos after dark. San Francisco's party is the wildest.
Day of the Dead Mexican communities honor deceased relatives with candle-lit memorials on November 2; candy skulls and skeletons are popular.
Thanksgiving On the fourth Thursday of November, family and friends gather for daylong feasts, traditionally involving roasted turkey and watching pro football on TV.
Hanukkah This eight-day Jewish holiday (also called the Festival of Lights) commemorates the victory of the Maccabees over the armies of Syria. Date determined by the Hebrew calendar, but usually begins before Christmas.
Christmas On December 25th, Christ's birth inspires church choir concerts, midnight church services, tree-lighting ceremonies, caroling in the streets and an unseemly consumer binge – culminating, of course, in a visit from Santa.
Kwanzaa (www.officialkwanzaawebsite.org) From December 26 to 31, this African American celebration is a time to give thanks and honor the seven principles.
New Year's Eve Out with the old, in with the new: millions get drunk, resolve to do better, and the next day nurse hangovers while watching college football.

For public and school holidays, see p718.

FOOD

In this book prices for restaurants usually refer to an average main course at dinner; prices do not include drinks, appetizers, desserts, taxes or tips, and the same dish at lunch will usually be cheaper. When price categories are used, 'budget' means mains under $10, 'midrange' means most dinner mains are $10 to $20, and 'top end' means dinner mains starting over $20.

Lunch is generally served between 11:30am and 2:30pm, and dinner between 5:30pm and 10pm daily, though some restaurants close earlier. If breakfast is served, it's usually between 7 and 10am. We've spelled out deviations from these standard opening hours in our reviews.

Like all things Californian, restaurant etiquette tends to be informal. Only a handful of restaurants require more than a dressy shirt, slacks and a decent pair of shoes; most places require far less. Here are more things to keep in mind:

- Tipping 15% to 20% is expected anywhere you receive table service.
- Smoking is illegal indoors; some restaurants have patios or sidewalk tables where lighting up is tolerated.
- You can bring your own wine to most restaurants, but expect to pay a 'corkage' fee of $10 to $30. Lunches rarely include booze these days, though a glass of wine, while uncommon, is usually acceptable.
- It's perfectly fine in California to taste your dining partner's dish. If you ask the waiter to divide a plate between two (or more) people, there may be a small split-plate surcharge.
- Vegetarians and travelers who suffer food allergies or are just plain picky are in luck – most restaurant staff are used to catering to specific food needs.
- If you've got kids in tow, most restaurants will be happy for your business, except high-end establishments (call ahead to check).

GAY & LESBIAN TRAVELERS

California is a magnet for GLBT travelers. The major hot spots are the Castro in San Francisco, West Hollywood (WeHo) and Silver Lake in LA, San Diego's Hillcrest area, the desert oasis of Palm Springs, and Guerneville and Calistoga in the Wine Country. For an overview of the LA scene, see p546; for San Francisco, see p107; for San Diego, see p615; for Palm Springs, see p660; and for Las Vegas, see p701.

Despite widespread tolerance, make no mistake: bigotry still exists. In small towns, especially away from the coast, tolerance often comes down to a 'don't ask, don't tell' policy. The mayor of San Francisco declared same-sex marriage legal in 2004. The next year, the state legislature banned it. In 2008 the Supreme Court of California overturned the ban, however Proposition 8 in the 2008 general election made the same-sex marriage ban permanent.

Damron (www.damron.com) publishes the classic gay travel guides, including *Women's Traveler* and *Men's Travel Guide*, but they're advertiser-driven and sometimes outdated. **OutTraveler** (www.outtraveler.com), **Out & About** (www.gay.com/travel/outandabout) and **PlanetOut** (www.planetout.com/travel) publish downloadable gay travel guides and current articles. **Purple Roofs** (www.purpleroofs.com) lists gay-owned and gay-friendly B&Bs and hotels nationwide. **Travelocity** (www.travelocity.com/gaytravel) also offers gay travel destination guides, hotel listings and vacation deals.

If you find yourself in need of counseling or referrals, call the **Gay, Lesbian, Bisexual & Transgender National Hotline** (☎ 888-843-4564; www.glnh.org; 1-9pm Mon-Fri, 9am-2pm Sat). The **National Gay and Lesbian Task Force** (www.thetaskforce.org) is an advocacy group with a newsy website.

HOLIDAYS

Public Holidays

On the following national holidays, banks, schools and government offices (including post offices) are closed, and transportation, museums and other services operate on a Sunday schedule. Holidays falling on a weekend are usually observed the following Monday.

New Year's Day January 1
Martin Luther King Jr Day Third Monday in January
Presidents' Day Third Monday in February
Easter Sunday March/April
Memorial Day Last Monday in May
Independence Day July 4
Labor Day First Monday in September
Columbus Day Second Monday in October
Veterans' Day November 11
Thanksgiving Day Fourth Thursday in November
Christmas Day December 25

School Holidays

Colleges take a one- or two-week 'spring break' around Easter, sometime in March or April; some hotels raise their rates during this time. School summer vacations run from early

June to late August, making July and August the busiest travel months.

INSURANCE

No matter how long or short your trip, make sure you have adequate travel insurance. At minimum you need coverage for medical emergencies and treatment, including hospital stays and an emergency flight home (see p739). You should also consider coverage for luggage theft or loss and trip cancellation. If you already have a homeowner's policy, see what it will cover and consider getting supplemental insurance to cover the rest. If you have prepaid a large portion of your trip, cancellation insurance may be a worthwhile expense. Finally, if you will be driving it's essential that you have liability insurance (see p734).

Worldwide travel insurance is available at www.lonelyplanet.com/bookings. You can buy, extend and claim online anytime – even if you're already on the road.

INTERNATIONAL VISITORS

Entering the Region

Getting into the USA can be a bureaucratic nightmare, especially as the rules keep changing. For up-to-date information about entry requirements and eligibility, check with a US consulate in your home country or the **US Department of State website** (http://travel.state.gov). For background information, browse the Travel section of the **US Customs & Border Protection website** (www.cbp.gov).

The Department of Homeland Security (DHS) registration program, **US-VISIT** (www.dhs.gov/us-visit), currently includes 285 ports of air, land and sea entry. For most foreign visitors (excluding, for now, most Canadian and some Mexican citizens), registration consists of having a digital photo taken and electronic (inkless) fingerprints made of each index finger; the process takes less than a minute.

No matter what your visa says, US immigration officers have an absolute authority to refuse admission to the USA or to impose conditions. They will ask about your plans and whether you have sufficient funds; it's a good idea to list an itinerary, produce an onward or round-trip ticket and have at least one major credit card. Don't make too much of having friends, relatives or business contacts in the USA – the immigration official may decide this makes you more likely to overstay instead.

PASSPORTS & VISAS

Your passport must be valid for at least six months longer than your intended stay in the USA. All of the following information is highly subject to change. Double-check the ever-changing requirements for passports and visas at http://travel.state.gov/visa.

Under the Visa Waiver Program (VWP), currently citizens of 27 countries (including Australia, Belgium, Denmark, Finland, France, Germany, Iceland, Ireland, Italy, Japan, the Netherlands, New Zealand, Norway, Portugal, Singapore, Spain, Sweden, Switzerland and the UK) currently may enter without a US visa for stays of 90 days or less (no extensions allowed). As of 2009 citizens of VWP countries must register online with the DHS at https://esta.cbp.dhs.gov at least 72 hours before their visit; once travel authorization is approved, your registration is valid for two years.

If your passport does not meet current US standards, you'll be turned back at the border, even if you're from a VWP country and have travel authorization. If your passport was issued before October 26, 2005, it must be 'machine readable' (with two lines of letters, numbers and <<< at the bottom); if it was issued between October 26, 2005, and October 25, 2006, it must be machine-readable and include a digital photo; and if it was issued on or after October 26, 2006, it must be an ePassport containing a digital photo and an integrated RFID chip containing biometric data.

Citizens from all non-VWP countries, as well as those whose passports are not machine-readable or otherwise don't meet the current US standards, will need to wrangle a nonimmigrant visa from a US consulate or embassy abroad. The process costs at minimum a nonrefundable $100, involves a personal interview and can take several weeks, so apply as early as possible.

For now, Canadian citizens arriving from anywhere in the Western hemisphere are technically exempt from both visa and passport requirements, but official proof of citizenship (eg birth certificate, citizenship certificate) and photo ID are still required.

CUSTOMS

You may import duty free 1L of alcohol, if you're over 21; 200 cigarettes (one carton) or 50 cigars (not Cubans), if you're over 18; and $100 worth of gifts ($800 for US citizens). Amounts in excess of $10,000 in cash, traveler's checks, money orders and other cash equivalents must be declared. Unless you're curious about US jails, don't even think about bringing in illegal drugs, drug paraphernalia, firearms or other weapons. For complete information and the latest regulations, contact **US Customs & Border Protection** (☎ 703-526-4200, 877-227-5511; www.cbp.gov).

California is an important agricultural state. To prevent the spread of pests and diseases, certain food items (including meats, fresh fruits and vegetables) may not be brought in to the state. If you drive into California across the border from Mexico or from neighboring states such as Nevada, you may have to stop for a quick inspection and questioning by California Department of Food and Agriculture officials.

Embassies & Consulates

Visas and other travel-related documents are handled by consulates, not embassies. International travelers needing to locate the US consulate in their home country should visit the **US Department of State website** (http://usembassy.state.gov), which has links to all US embassies and consulates abroad.

Most foreign embassies are in Washington DC, but many countries have consular offices in California, usually in LA or San Francisco. For more foreign consulates in California, visit www.sos.ca.gov/business/ibrp/fgncons.htm. To get in touch with your embassy in Washington DC, call that city's directory assistance (☎ 202-555-1212).

Australia Los Angeles (Map pp518-19; ☎ 310-229-2300; 31st fl, Century Plaza Towers, 2049 Century Park E); San Francisco (Map pp88-9; ☎ 415-536-1970; Suite 1800, 575 Market St)

Canada Los Angeles (Map pp512-13; ☎ 213-346-2700; 9th fl, 550 S Hope St)

France Los Angeles (Map pp518-19; ☎ 310-235-3200; Suite 410, 10390 Santa Monica Blvd); San Francisco (Map pp88-9; ☎ 415-397-4330; 540 Bush St)

Germany Los Angeles (Map pp516-17; ☎ 323-930-2703; Suite 500, 6222 Wilshire Blvd); San Francisco (Map pp94-5; ☎ 415-775-1061; 1960 Jackson St)

Ireland San Francisco (Map pp88-9; ☎ 415-392-4214; Suite 3350, 100 Pine St)

Italy Los Angeles (off Map pp518-19; ☎ 310-820-0622; Suite 300, 12400 Wilshire Blvd); San Francisco (Map pp94-5; ☎ 415-931-4924; 2590 Webster St)

Japan Los Angeles (Map pp512-13; ☎ 213-617-6700; Suite 1700, 350 S Grand Ave); San Francisco (Map pp88-9; ☎ 415-777-3533; Suite 2300, 50 Fremont St)

Mexico Los Angeles (Map pp512-13; ☎ 213-351-6800; 2401 W 6th St); San Francisco (Map pp88-9; ☎ 415-354-1700; 532 Folsom St)

Netherlands Los Angeles (Map pp518-19; ☎ 877-388-2443; Suite 1150, 11766 Wilshire Blvd)

New Zealand Los Angeles (Map pp518-19; ☎ 310-566-6555; Suite 600E, 2425 Olympic Blvd)

South Africa Los Angeles (Map pp516-17; ☎ 310-651-5902; 6300 Wilshire Blvd, Suite 600)

Spain Los Angeles (Map pp516-17; ☎ 323-938-0158; 5055 Wilshire Blvd, Suite 860); San Francisco (Map pp88-9; ☎ 415-922-2995; 1405 Sutter St)

UK Los Angeles (off Map pp518-19; ☎ 310-481-0031; Suite 1200, 11766 Wilshire Blvd); San Francisco (Map pp88-9; ☎ 415-617-1300; Suite 850, 1 Sansome St)

Money

The US dollar is divided into 100 cents (¢). Coins come in denominations of 1¢ (penny), 5¢ (nickel), 10¢ (dime), 25¢ (quarter), the seldom-seen 50¢ (half-dollar) and the uncommon $1 coin. Quarters are most commonly used in vending machines and parking meters. Bills come in $1, $2 (rare), $5, $10, $20, $50 and $100 denominations.

Most locals do not carry large amounts of cash for everyday use, relying instead on credit cards, ATMs and debit cards. Some businesses refuse to accept bills over $20. All prices quoted in this book are in US dollars ($) excluding taxes, unless otherwise noted. For currency-exchange rates, see the inside front cover. For more about travel costs in California, see p23.

ATMS

ATMs are available 24/7 at most banks, and in shopping centers, airports, and grocery and convenience stores. Most ATMs charge a service fee of $2 or more per transaction and your own bank may impose additional charges. Withdrawing cash from an ATM using a credit card usually incurs a hefty fee; check with your credit-card company.

CREDIT CARDS

Major credit cards are almost universally accepted. In fact, it's almost impossible to rent a car, book a room or buy tickets over the phone without one. A credit card may also be vital in emergencies. Visa and MasterCard are the most widely accepted.

CURRENCY EXCHANGE

You can exchange money at many banks and at currency-exchange offices such as **American**

Express (☎ 800-297-2977; www.americanexpress.com) and **Travelex** (☎ 888-457-4602; www.travelex.com). Always ask about rates and fees. In rural areas, exchanging money may be a problem, so have plenty of cash or a credit card on hand.

TAXES & TIPPING

There is no value-added tax (VAT) in California. A state sales tax of 7.75% is added to the retail price of most goods and services (gasoline is an exception). Local and city taxes may tack on an additional 1%.

Tipping is *not* optional. Only withhold tips in cases of outrageously bad service. Also see p716.

Airport & hotel porters $2 per bag, minimum per cart $5.
Bartenders 10-15% per round, minimum per drink $1.
Hotel maids $2 to $4 per night, left under the card provided.
Restaurant servers 15-20%, unless a gratuity is already charged on the bill.
Taxi drivers 10-15%, rounded up to the next dollar.
Valet parking attendants At least $2 when handed back the keys.

TRAVELER'S CHECKS

Restaurants, hotels and most shops generally accept US-dollar traveler's checks as they would cash, but small businesses, supermarkets and fast-food chains may refuse them. American Express and Visa are the most widely accepted issuers.

Post

For 24-hour postal information, including post office locations, hours and details about poste-restante/general-delivery mail, contact the **US Postal Service** (USPS; ☎ 800-275-8777; www.usps.com). At press time, standard domestic rates were 42¢ for letters up to 1oz and 27¢ for postcards; international airmail rates were 94¢ (to Canada or Mexico 72¢) for 1oz letters or postcards. For sending important letters or packages overseas, **Federal Express** (FedEx; ☎ 800-463-3339; www.fedex.com) and **UPS** (☎ 800-782-7892; www.ups.com) guarantee on-time delivery.

Telephone

If you're calling from abroad, the international country code for the USA is ☎ 1 (the same as Canada, but international rates apply between the two countries). To make an international call from the USA, dial ☎ 011, then the country code, followed by the area code (usually without the initial '0') and the local number. To reach an international operator, dial ☎ 00.

All phone numbers in California consist of a three-digit area code followed by a seven-digit local number. Typically, if you are calling a number within the same area code, you only have to dial the seven-digit number; however, some places now require you to dial the entire 10-digit number even for a local call. If you are calling long distance, dial ☎ 1 plus the area code plus the phone number.

Toll-free numbers begin with ☎ 800, ☎ 866, ☎ 877 or ☎ 888 and when dialing must be preceded by ☎ 1. Most can be used within the entire USA, although some only work within California, while others only go through when calling from outside California. To find any toll-free number, call ☎ 800-555-1212 (no charge). For free nationwide directory assistance, dial ☎ 800-466-4411 or ☎ 800-373-3411.

CELL PHONES

North American cell phones use GSM 1900/CDMA 800, operating on different frequencies from other systems around the world. The only foreign phones that will work in the USA are tri-band models. You can rent a mobile phone at the Los Angeles and San Francisco airports from **TripTel** (☎ 877-874-7835; www.triptel.com); pricing plans vary, but typically are expensive. It might be cheaper to buy a prepaid SIM card for the USA, which you can insert into your international mobile phone to get a local phone number and voicemail. **Planet Omni** (☎ 877-327-5076; www.planetomni.com) and **Telestial** (☎ 800-707-0031; www.telestial.com) offer this service.

PAY PHONES & PHONECARDS

Public pay phones are mostly coin-operated, although some accept only credit cards (eg in national parks). Local calls generally cost 35¢. **AT&T** (☎ 800-321-0288) and operators (dial ☎ 0) can facilitate long-distance and collect calls, but it's usually cheaper to use a prepaid phonecard, sold at convenience stores, supermarkets and newsstands. Be sure to read the fine print, as many such cards contain hidden charges such as 'activation fees' or a per-call 'connection fee.'

Time

The Pacific time zone is eight hours behind GMT/UTC. Daylight Saving Time (DST), when the clocks move forward one hour, runs from the second Sunday in March to the first Sunday in November.

INTERNET ACCESS

Travelers will have few problems staying connected in tech-savvy California. This book uses an internet icon (💻) when a place has an internet terminal for public use and the word 'wi-fi' when it offers wireless internet access.

Most hotels and some motels have wired or wireless technology (sometimes free, sometimes fee-based) that lets you connect in the comfort of your room if you're traveling with your own laptop or personal digital assistant (PDA). These days you can even connect in the woods: private campgrounds and RV parks (like KOA) increasingly offer wi-fi, as do almost 50 state parks (www.parks.ca.gov), usually near the ranger station or in the campgrounds and picnic areas. Most Starbucks coffee shops and some McDonald's fast-food restaurants are also wi-fi hot spots. Internet access fees at any of these places vary from nothing up to $10 or more per day.

Many independent coffee shops and some airports (including in San Francisco, San Jose, Sacramento, Arcata/Eureka, Redding, Las Vegas and Reno) offer free wi-fi, as do some public libraries. Using internet terminals at libraries is usually free too, but downsides include registration requirements, time limits, queues and slow connections. For pay-as-you-go internet terminals, internet cafés and copy centers such as **FedEx Office** (www.fedex.com) are plentiful, and listed in the Information sections of the destination chapters; expect to pay between $6 and $12 per hour of online time. Full-service internet cafés and copy shops may also let you hook up your own laptop and/or peripherals such as digital cameras to upload, print and burn photos onto CDs (see opposite).

If you're not from the US, remember that you will need an AC adapter and a plug adapter for US sockets – both are available in larger electronics stores. For more information on traveling with a portable computer and the gadgets you might need to help you get online, see www.igo.com or www.teleadapt.com.

See p24 for useful websites when traveling in California.

LEGAL MATTERS

If you are stopped by the police, remain courteous at all times and, if driving, keep your hands where the cop can see them, ie atop the steering wheel. Don't get out of the car unless asked. There is no system of paying fines on the spot. Attempting to pay the fine to the officer is frowned upon at best and may lead to a charge of attempted bribery. For traffic offenses the police officer will explain the options to you. There is usually a 30-day period to pay a fine. Most matters can be handled by mail.

If you are arrested for more serious offenses, you have the right to remain silent. There is no legal reason to speak to a police officer if you don't wish, but never walk away from one until given permission. As a matter of principle under US law, you are presumed innocent until proven guilty. If you are arrested, you are legally allowed to make one phone call. If you can't afford a lawyer, a public defender will be appointed to you free of charge. Foreign travelers who don't have a lawyer, friends or family to help them should call their consulate; the police can provide the number upon request.

When driving in California, you'll need to carry your driver's license (p734) and proof of vehicle registration. Driving under the influence (DUI) of alcohol or drugs is a serious offense, subject to all sorts of nasty consequences (p737). For more information on driving and road rules, see p736.

Bars, clubs and liquor stores often ask for photo identification to prove you are of legal drinking age. Being 'carded' is standard practice; don't take it personally. Consuming alcohol anywhere other than at a residence or a licensed premises is a no-no, which puts parks, beaches and most of the great outdoors off-limits (campgrounds are OK, for now). It is illegal to carry open containers of alcohol inside a vehicle, even if they are empty; if they're not completely full and still sealed, store them in the trunk.

In California, possession of under 1oz of marijuana is a misdemeanor punishable by up to one year in jail, although a fine is more likely for first-time offenders. Possession of any other drug, including cocaine, ecstasy,

THE LEGAL AGE FOR...

- Drinking alcohol: 21
- Driving a car: 16
- Smoking tobacco: 18
- Having consensual sex (heterosexual or homosexual): 18

LSD, heroin, hashish or more than an ounce of pot, is a felony punishable by a lengthy jail sentence, depending on the circumstances. For foreigners, conviction of any drug offense is grounds for deportation.

For police, fire and ambulance emergencies, dial ☎ 911. For nonemergency police assistance, call directory assistance (☎ 411) for the number of the nearest local police station.

MAPS

Most visitors centers distribute free (but often very basic) local maps. Most convenience stores, gas stations and bookstores sell detailed local and regional folding maps (which include street-name indexes) for about $3.50 each. Members of the **American Automobile Association** (AAA; ☎ 877-428-2277; www.aaa.com) and its international affiliates can pick up high-quality road maps for free from any AAA office. For online driving directions and free printable maps, try **Google Maps** (http://maps.google.com), which also lets you download maps directly to your cell phone. For a driving and motorcycling map atlas, the gold standard is Benchmark Press' *California Road & Recreation Atlas* ($24.95), which shows *every* road in the state, along with topographic details, land and water features, campgrounds, trailheads, ski areas and hundreds more points of interest. For information on topographic hiking and wilderness maps, see p72.

PHOTOGRAPHY & VIDEO

Print film is ubiquitous. Drugstores and supermarkets process print film cheaply, about $7 for a 24-exposure roll. One-hour processing services are more expensive, averaging $12.

Digital-camera memory cards and sticks are sold in drugstores, specialty camera stores and chain retailers like Target or Best Buy. Full-service copy centers such as FedEx Office (opposite) often have one-stop digital-photo printing and CD burning stations.

Film can be damaged by excessive heat, so avoid leaving your camera in the car (this goes for digital cameras too). Carry spare batteries to avoid disappointment when your camera dies in the middle of nowhere.

Always ask permission if you want to photograph someone close up. Some Native American reservations prohibit photography and video completely; otherwise, you may be required to purchase a permit, and photo subjects may expect a small tip.

For more picture-taking advice, check out Lonely Planet's *Travel Photography*.

SHOPPING

There's really nothing you can't buy in California, be it high-tech gear or high-fashion couture, flip-flops or funky designer outfits, anime DVDs or sex toys, surf gear or antiques. Antique, secondhand and thrift stores, especially in rural desert and mountain areas, are best for digging up retro Americana and Old West paraphernalia. For hip modern souvenirs, try museum stores, which specialize in unusual items that play off the museum's collection, as well as high-quality original works by California artisans.

Bargain hunters should track down local factory outlets. These are usually malls near a freeway exit on the outskirts of a city where brand-name stores sell their damaged, leftover or out-of-season stock at discounts ranging from modest to practically giveaway. Choices are limited, but the chance of half-price Levi's, Nike shoes or DKNY dresses can be a siren song.

For Native American items, such as rugs, jewelry or artwork, beware that much of the merchandise sold in trading posts is mass-produced. Genuine products usually have a tag or stamp identifying them as 'handmade' while imitations will say something like 'Native American style.' Be conscious of who's doing the selling and ask a lot of questions. Who made the item? What tribe is the artist from? What kinds of materials were used? A reputable dealer will know the answers and be more than happy to tell you all about the item's origin. You can also ask for a certificate of authenticity. Good pieces will be expensive; if they are cheap, they are probably not authentic.

SOLO TRAVELERS

There are no particular problems traveling alone in California. In general, don't advertise where you are staying, or even that you are traveling alone. Americans can be eager to help and even take in solo travelers. However, don't take all offers of help at face value. If someone who seems trustworthy invites you to his or her home, let someone (eg hostel staff) know where you're going. This advice also applies if you go for a long hike by yourself. If something happens and you don't return as expected, you want someone to notice and to know where to begin looking for you. For more advice for women travelers, see opposite.

TOURIST INFORMATION

The **California Division of Tourism** (☎ 916-444-4429, 800-462-2543; www.visitcalifornia.com) operates an excellent website packed with useful pretrip planning information. The office will also mail you a free *Official State Visitors Guide,* but the website has just about all the same information without all the paper.

The state government maintains 13 regional **California Welcome Centers** (www.visitcwc.com). Staff dispense maps and brochures and can help find accommodations. Locations include San Francisco (p84); Oceanside (p647), near San Diego; Auburn (p336), in the Gold Country; Santa Rosa (p219), in the Wine Country; Arcata (p288) on the North Coast; and south of Redding (p302) in the Shasta Cascade.

Almost every city and town has a local visitors center or a chamber of commerce where you can pick up maps, brochures and information. These are listed throughout the destination chapters.

TRAVELERS WITH DISABILITIES

California is an accommodating place for travelers with physical disabilities. The Americans with Disabilities Act (ADA) requires that all public buildings and post-1993 private buildings (eg hotels, restaurants, theaters and museums) be wheelchair accessible. When making a lodging reservation, always make your needs clearly known; for other private venues, call ahead to find out about what access issues to expect.

Telephone companies offer relay operators for the hearing impaired; dial ☎ 711 in California. Many banks provide ATM instructions in Braille.

Most public buses and trains provide wheelchair lifts. You'll find dropped curbs at most intersections, and sometimes audible crossing signals. Major car-rental agencies (p735), notably Budget and Hertz, offer hand-controlled vehicles and vans with wheelchair lifts at no extra charge, but you must reserve them well in advance. **Wheelchair Getaways** (☎ 800-642-2042; www.wheelchairgetaways.com) rents wheelchair-accessible vans throughout California.

All major airlines, Greyhound buses and Amtrak trains can assist travelers with disabilities, although Greyhound and Amtrak usually need at least 48 hours of advance notice. Service animals (eg guide dogs) are allowed to accompany passengers, but bring documentation. Airlines and Greyhound buses accept wheelchairs as checked baggage, while Amtrak allows standard wheelchairs on board trains. On Greyhound, personal care attendants receive 50% off tickets purchased at least one day in advance. On Amtrak, travelers with documented disabilities receive 15% off regular fares.

Many national and state parks and recreation areas have wheelchair-accessible paved, graded dirt or boardwalk nature trails. For free admission to all national parks and federal recreation lands, US citizens and permanent residents with permanent disabilities can get a free 'America the Beautiful' Access Pass (p64). For travelers with limited mobility, *California Parks Access* by Linda and Allen Mitchell contains somewhat dated but still useful information about visiting state and national parks. The **California State Coastal Conservancy** (☎ 510-286-1015; www.scc.ca.gov) offers free downloadable wheelchair riders' guides to the San Francisco, Los Angeles and Orange County coasts.

Organizations that assist travelers with disabilities:

Access-Able Travel Source (☎ 303-232-2979; www.access-able.com) An excellent general travel info website with useful links.

Access Northern California (☎ 510-524-2026; www.accessnca.com) Publishes *Access San Francisco,* available at the San Francisco Visitors Information Center (p84); also has links to more accessible-travel resources, publications and transportation.

Disabled Sports USA Far West (☎ 530-581-4161; www.dsusafw.org) Organizes summer and winter sports and outdoor recreation programs (annual membership from $25).

Flying Wheels Travel (☎ 507-451-5005; www.flyingwheelstravel.com) A full-service travel agency.

Mobility International USA (☎ 541-343-1284; www.miusa.org) Advises travelers on mobility issues and runs educational exchange programs.

Moss Rehabilitation Hospital (☎ 800-225-5667; www.mossresourcenet.org/travel.htm) Extensive contacts for accessible travel.

Society for Accessible Travel & Hospitality (☎ 212-447-7284; www.sath.org) Advocacy group provides general information for travelers with disabilities.

VOLUNTEERING

Volunteer opportunities abound, and they just might provide some of your most memorable experiences: you'll interact with

Californians and the land in ways you never would just passing through. Casual, drop-in volunteer opportunities are common only in cities. You can register online for free with organizations such as **One Brick** (www.onebrick.org), **HandsOn Bay Area** (www.handsonbayarea.org), **LA Works** (www.laworks.com) and **Volunteer San Diego** (www.volunteersandiego.org), then sign up for any volunteer activity that interests you. These nonprofit groups are also a great way to meet locals and socialize. More formal international-exchange programs charge a fee, which usually runs from $200 to $500, depending on the length of the program and what's included (eg housing, meals). None cover travel to the USA.

Recommended volunteer resources and organizations:

California Volunteers (☎ 916-323-7646, 800-567-7278; www.californiavolunteers.org) Official state volunteer directory and matching service, with links to national service days and long-term AmeriCorps programs.

Craigslist.org (www.craiglist.org) Free classified ads for volunteers statewide.

Habitat for Humanity (☎ 229-924-6935; www.habitat.org) Help build homes for impoverished families.

Idealist.org (www.idealist.org) Free online database of short- and long-term volunteer opportunities.

Sierra Club (☎ 415-977-5522; www.sierraclub.org) Volunteer vacations, including for families, focus on restoring wilderness areas (annual membership from $25).

Volunteers for Peace (☎ 802-259-2759; www.vfp.org) Grassroots local volunteer projects emphasize manual labor and international exchange.

Wilderness Volunteers (☎ 928-556-0038; www.wildernessvolunteers.org) Week-long trips help maintain national parks, wildlands and outdoor recreation areas.

WOMEN TRAVELERS

California is generally a safe place for women travelers, even alone and in the cities. Solo women may be more likely to become the target of unwanted attention or harassment, however.

The community website **Journeywoman** (www.journeywoman.com) facilitates women exchanging travel tips and also links to other sites. **Her Own Way** (www.voyage.gc.ca/main/pubs/PDF/her_own_way-en.pdf), a downloadable booklet published by the Canadian government, is filled with good general travel advice, useful for any woman.

Carrying mace or cayenne-pepper spray is legal in California, as long as the spray bottle contains no more than 2.5oz of active product. Federal law prohibits all such sprays from being carried on planes.

If you are assaulted, it may be better to call a rape crisis hotline before (or instead of) calling the **police** (☎ 911). Telephone books have listings of local organizations, or contact the 24-hour **National Sexual Assault Hotline** (☎ 800-656-4673; www.rainn.org). Alternatively, go straight to a hospital emergency room. Police can act insensitively toward sexual-assault survivors, whereas a rape crisis center or hospital will advocate on your behalf and act as a liaison to other community services, including the police.

Planned Parenthood (☎ 800-230-7526; www.plannedparenthood.org) offers referrals to woman-friendly medical clinics throughout the country.

WORK

If you are a foreigner in the USA with a standard nonimmigrant visa, you are forbidden to take paid work in the USA and will be deported if you're caught working illegally. Employers are required to establish the bona fides of their employees or face fines, making it much tougher for a foreigner to get work than it once was.

To work legally, foreigners need to apply for a work visa before leaving home. A J1 visa, for exchange visitors, is issued to young people (age limits vary) for study, student vacation employment, work in summer camps and short-term traineeships with a specific employer. Organizations that can help you obtain such a visa:

American Institute for Foreign Study (☎ 866-906-2437; www.aifs.com)

Council on International Educational Exchange (☎ 800-407-8839; www.ciee.org)

InterExchange (☎ 212-924-0446; www.interexchange.org)

For nonstudent jobs, temporary or permanent, you need to be sponsored by a US employer who will have to arrange an H-category visa. These are not easy to obtain, because the employer has to prove that no US citizen or permanent resident is available to do the job. Seasonal work is possible in some tourist areas, especially ski resorts or through national park concessionaires. Lonely Planet's *Gap Year Book* has more ideas on how to combine work and travel.

For volunteer opportunities, see opposite.

Transportation

CONTENTS

GETTING THERE & AWAY

Flights, tours and train tickets can be booked online at www.lonelyplanet.com/travel_services.

AIR

To get through airport security checkpoints, you need a boarding pass and photo ID. If you beep going through the metal detector, or if x-rays of your carry-on bags look suspicious, you'll undergo a second screening, involving hand-wand and pat-down checks and opening your bags. You can request a private room.

Airport security measures restrict many common items from being carried on planes. These regulations often change. Get information about current restrictions from the **Transportation Security Administration** (TSA; ☎ 866-289-9673; www.tsa.gov), which also provides average security wait times by airport (30 minutes is standard).

At press time, TSA's list of prohibited carry-on items included pocket knives. Also, all liquids and gels must be stored in 3oz or smaller bottles placed inside a quart-sized clear plastic zip-top bag. Exceptions to this rule, which must be declared to checkpoint security officers, include prescription and over-the-counter medications.

All checked luggage is screened for explosives. TSA may open your suitcase for visual confirmation, breaking the lock if necessary. Either leave your bags unlocked or use a TSA-approved lock; see **Travel Sentry** (www.travelsentry.org).

THINGS CHANGE...

The information in this chapter is particularly vulnerable to change. Check directly with the airline or a travel agent to make sure you understand how a fare (and ticket you may buy) works and be aware of the security requirements for international travel. Shop carefully. The details given in this chapter should be regarded as pointers and are not a substitute for your own careful, up-to-date research.

Airports & Airlines

Most international travelers arrive at **Los Angeles International Airport** (LAX; ☎ 310-646-5252; www.lawa.org) or **San Francisco International Airport** (SFO; ☎ 650-821-8211; www.flysfo.com). In the San Francisco Bay area, **Oakland International Airport** (OAK; ☎ 510-563-3300; www.flyoakland.com) and **Mineta San José International Airport** (SJC; ☎ 408-277-4759; www.sjc.org) have limited international services. All of these airports handle domestic arrivals, although flying in to one of the following regional airports may be cheaper and more convenient.

Arcata/Eureka Airport (ACV; ☎ 707-839-5401; www.co.humboldt.ca.us/aviation)

Bob Hope Airport (BUR; ☎ 818-840-8840; www.bobhopeairport.com) In Burbank, Los Angeles County.

Fresno Yosemite International Airport (FYI; ☎ 559-621-4500; www.flyfresno.org)

John Wayne Airport (SNA; ☎ 949-252-5200; www.ocair.com) In Santa Ana, Orange County.

LA/Palmdale Regional Airport (PMD; ☎ 661-266-7600; www.lawa.org/pmd) In north LA County.

Long Beach Airport (LGB; ☎ 562-570-2600; www.longbeach.gov/airport) South of LA.

McCarran International (LAS; ☎ 702-261-5211; www.mccarran.com) In Las Vegas, Nevada.

Monterey Peninsula Airport (MRY; ☎ 831-648-7000; www.montereyairport.com)

Ontario International Airport (ONT; ☎ 909-937-2700; www.lawa.org/ont) In Riverside County, east of LA.

Palm Springs International Airport (PSP; ☎ 760-318-3800; www.palmspringsairport.com)

Redding Municipal Airport (RDD; ☎ 530-224-4320; http://ci.redding.ca.us/transeng/airports/rma.htm)
Reno/Tahoe International Airport (RNO; ☎ 775-328-6870; www.renoairport.com) In Reno, Nevada.
Sacramento International Airport (SMF; ☎ 916-929-5411; www.sacairports.org/int)
San Diego International Airport (SAN; ☎ 619-231-2100; www.san.org)
San Luis Obispo County Regional Airport (SBP; ☎ 805-781-2025; www.sloairport.com)
Santa Barbara Municipal Airport (SBA; ☎ 805-967-7111; www.flysba.com)

AIRLINES FLYING TO/FROM CALIFORNIA

Online, www.seatguru.com has extensive airline information, including seat-by-seat reviews for each aircraft.

Major domestic carriers:

AirTran Airways (FL; ☎ 800-247-8726; www.airtran.com)
Alaska Airlines (AS; ☎ 800-252-7522; www.alaskaair.com)
American Airlines (AA; ☎ 800-433-7300; www.aa.com)
Continental Airlines (CO; ☎ 800-523-3273; www.continental.com)
Delta Air Lines (DL; ☎ 800-221-1212; www.delta.com)
Frontier Air (F9; ☎ 800-432-1359; www.frontierairlines.com)
Hawaiian Airlines (HA; ☎ 800-367-5320; www.hawaiianair.com)
Horizon Air (QX; ☎ 800-547-9308; www.alaskaair.com)
JetBlue Airways (B6; ☎ 800-538-2583; www.jetblue.com)
Midwest Airlines (YX; ☎ 800-452-2022; www.midwestairlines.com)
Northwest Airlines (NW; ☎ 800-225-2525; www.nwa.com)
Southwest Airlines (WN; ☎ 800-435-9792; www.southwest.com)
Spirit Airlines (NK; ☎ 800-772-7117; www.spiritair.com)
United Airlines (UA; ☎ 800-864-8331; www.united.com)
US Airways/America West Airlines (US; ☎ 800-428-4322; www.usairways.com)
Virgin America (VX; ☎ 877-359-8474; www.virginamerica.com)

Major international airlines:

Aer Lingus (EI; ☎ 800-474-7424; www.aerlingus.com)
Aeroméxico (AM; ☎ 800-237-6639; www.aeromexico.com)
Air Canada (AC; ☎ 888-247-2262; www.aircanada.com)
Air France (AF; ☎ 800-237-2747; www.airfrance.com)
Air New Zealand (NZ; ☎ 800-262-1234; www.airnewzealand.com)
Alitalia (AZ; ☎ 800-223-5730; www.alitalia.com)
All Nippon Airways (NH; ☎ 800-235-9262; www.fly-ana.com)
Asiana Airlines (OZ; ☎ 800-227-4262; http://us.flyasiana.com)
British Airways (BA; ☎ 800-247-9297; www.britishairways.com)
British Midland Airways (BD; ☎ 800-788-0555; www.flybmi.com)
Cathay Pacific (CX; ☎ 800-233-2742; www.cathaypacific.com)
EVA Airways (BR; ☎ 800-695-1188; www.evaair.com)
Iberia Airlines (IB; ☎ 800-772-4642; www.iberia.com)
Japan Airlines (JL; ☎ 800-525-3663; www.japanair.com)
Korean Air (KE; ☎ 800-438-5000; www.koreanair.com)
KLM Royal Dutch Airlines (KL; ☎ 800-225-2525; www.klm.com)
Lufthansa Airlines (LH; ☎ 800-399-5838; www.lufthansa.com)
Mexicana (MX; ☎ 800-531-7921; www.mexicana.com)
Philippine Airlines (PR; ☎ 800-435-9725; www.philippineairlines.com)
Qantas Airways (QF; ☎ 800-227-4500; www.qantas.com.au)
Singapore Airlines (SQ; ☎ 800-742-3333; www.singaporeair.com)
Spanair (JK; ☎ 888-545-5757; www.spanair.com)
Thai Airways International (TG; ☎ 800-426-5204; www.thaiairways.com)
Virgin Atlantic Airways (VS; ☎ 800-821-5438; www.virgin-atlantic.com)
WestJet Airlines (WS; ☎ 888-937-8538; www.westjet.com)

Tickets

Getting a cheap airline ticket is a matter of research, reserving early – at least 30 days in advance – and timing. Flying midweek and in the low season (normally fall to spring, excluding holiday periods) is always less expensive, but fare wars crop up anytime. Lower fares may be offered if you stay over a Saturday. You can also get discounts for booking flights and car rental together. Or, you may find domestic US flights are less expensive when added on to your international airfare.

The only way to ensure you've found the cheapest possible ticket for the flight you want is to check every angle, especially by comparing several online travel booking agencies with the airline's own website. Some airlines now guarantee you'll find the lowest fare on their own websites, which advertise promotional fares not available elsewhere on the Web. Learn about bargain fares by signing up for the airlines' free e-newsletters. **Travelzoo** (www.travelzoo.com) selectively gathers and passes along airlines' promotional deals. The *Los*

CLIMATE CHANGE & TRAVEL

Climate change is a serious threat to the ecosystems that humans rely upon, and air travel is the fastest-growing contributor to the problem. Lonely Planet regards travel, overall, as a global benefit, but believes we all have a responsibility to limit our personal impact on global warming.

Flying & Climate Change

Pretty much every form of motor travel generates CO_2 (the main cause of human-induced climate change) but planes are far and away the worst offenders, not just because of the sheer distances they allow us to travel, but because they release greenhouse gases high into the atmosphere. The statistics are frightening: two people taking a return flight between Europe and the US will contribute as much to climate change as an average household's gas and electricity consumption over a whole year.

Carbon Offset Schemes

Climatecare.org and other websites use 'carbon calculators' that allow jetsetters to offset the greenhouse gases they are responsible for with contributions to energy-saving projects and other climate-friendly initiatives in the developing world – including projects in India, Honduras, Kazakhstan and Uganda.

Lonely Planet, together with Rough Guides and other concerned partners in the travel industry, supports the carbon offset scheme run by climatecare.org. Lonely Planet offsets all of its staff and author travel.

For more information check out our website: lonelyplanet.com.

Angeles Times' **Daily Deal Blog** (http://travel.latimes.com/daily-deal-blog) has impartial news about airfare promotions.

The big three online booking websites are **Expedia** (www.expedia.com), **Orbitz** (www.orbitz.com) and **Travelocity** (www.travelocity.com). Similar and worth trying are **Cheap Tickets** (www.cheaptickets.com) and **Lowest Fare** (www.lowestfare.com). Often these sites don't include budget airlines like Southwest.

Metasites are good for price comparisons, as they gather from many sources, but they don't provide direct booking. Try **Kayak** (www.kayak.com), **Mobissimo** (www.mobissimo.com), **Qixo** (www.qixo.com) and **SideStep** (www.sidestep.com).

If you're flexible, you might be able to save a bundle with **Priceline** (www.priceline.com), **Hotwire** (www.hotwire.com) and **Skyauction** (www.skyauction.com). Read all of the fine print carefully. The big downside with Priceline and Hotwire is that the airline and departure times won't be revealed until after you've bought the ticket. For advice about Priceline, which also can be great for car rentals, click to www.biddingfortravel.com.

COURIER FLIGHTS

If you're on a flexible schedule and traveling solo, some companies provide very cheap fares to travelers who act as couriers, accompanying documents or packages. You don't have to handle any shipment personally – just deliver the freight papers to a representative of the courier company at your destination. Your luggage is limited to carry-on and there may also be other restrictions, such as the length of your stay. Courier opportunities are not easy to come by and are only available on international routes. One agency to try is the **Air Courier Association** (☎ 800-383-6814; www.aircourier.org), a US-based clearinghouse that tracks available routes and rates; membership is required, but doesn't guarantee that you'll get a courier flight.

INTERCONTINENTAL (RTW) TICKETS

Round-the-world (RTW) tickets are great if you want to visit other places besides California, otherwise a simple round-trip ticket is usually cheaper. They're of most value for trips that combine the USA with Europe, Asia and/or Australasia.

RTW tickets go by different names depending on their itineraries (such as Pacific Circle, and so on); they use the routes of an airline alliance, such as **Star Alliance** (www.staralliance.com) and **One World** (www.oneworld.com); and they are valid for a fixed period, usually a year. Most RTW fares restrict the number of stops within the USA and Canada. The cheapest fares permit only one stop; others allow more than a dozen. Some airlines 'black out' a few heavily traveled routes (eg Honolulu–Tokyo). After the ticket is purchased, dates can usually be changed without penalty, and tickets can be rewritten to add or delete stops for an extra charge.

For RTW tickets:

Air Brokers International (☎ 800-883-3273; www.airbrokers.com)
Airtreks (☎ 877-247-8735; www.airtreks.com)
Circle the Planet (☎ 800-799-8888; www.circletheplanet.com)
JustFares (☎ 800-766-3601; http://justfares.com)

Asia

Bangkok, Singapore, Kuala Lumpur, Hong Kong, Seoul and Tokyo all have good connections to Los Angeles and San Francisco. Many flights go via Honolulu, but stopovers may cost extra. Bangkok is the discounted fare capital, though its cheapest agents can be unreliable.

Agents serving Asia:

Asia TravelMart (☎ 03-8064-8300; www.asiatravelmart.com) Kuala Lumpur.
Concorde Travel (☎ 852-2526-3391; www.concorde-travel.com) Hong Kong.
No 1 Travel (☎ 03-3205-6073; www.no1-travel.com) Tokyo.
STA Travel Bangkok (☎ 662-236-0262; www.statravel.co.th); Singapore (☎ 6737-7188; www.statravel.com.sg); Tokyo (☎ 03-5391-2922; www.statravel.co.jp)
Traveller Services (☎ 852-2375-2222; www.taketraveller.com) Hong Kong.
Zuji (www.zuji.com)

Australia & New Zealand

The dominant carriers are Qantas and Air New Zealand. United Airlines, US Airways and American Airlines also fly down under. Some flights from Sydney and Melbourne go direct to Los Angeles and San Francisco. Fares from Melbourne, Sydney, Brisbane and sometimes Cairns are often 'common rated' (the same for all cities). Add-on flights to New Zealand cities other than Auckland typically cost US$100 extra.

Agents serving Australia and New Zealand:

Flight Centre Australia (☎ 133-133; www.flightcentre.com.au); New Zealand (☎ 0800-243-544; www.flightcentre.co.nz)
STA Travel Australia (☎ 134-782; www.statravel.com.au); New Zealand (☎ 0800-474-400; www.statravel.co.nz)
Travel.com Australia (☎ 1300-130-482; www.travel.com.au)
Travelocity New Zealand (☎ 0800-451-297; www.travelocity.co.nz)
Zuji (☎ 1300-888-180; www.zuji.com.au)

Canada

Air Canada, Air New Zealand, Alaska Airlines, American Airlines, Northwest Airlines, Qantas Airways, United Airlines and discount carrier WestJet offer regular nonstop service to LAX from major Canadian cities. Air Canada, Air New Zealand and United have flights into San Francisco. WestJet flies to Palm Springs from Calgary, Edmonton and Vancouver. In some cases, it may be cheaper to travel by land to the nearest US city, then take a discounted domestic flight.

Agents serving Canada:

Expedia (☎ 888-397-3342; www.expedia.ca)
Travel Cuts (☎ 866-246-9762; www.travelcuts.com)
Travelocity (☎ 800-457-8010; www.travelocity.ca)

Continental Europe

Many airlines, including Air France, Air New Zealand, Alitalia, American Airlines, British Airways, Continental Airlines, Delta Air Lines, Iberia, KLM/Northwest Airlines, Lufthansa Airlines, Spanair, United Airlines and US Airways have direct flights to LA and San Francisco from major European cities. Discounted fares often involve indirect routes and changing planes. Sometimes an Asian or Middle Eastern carrier will have cheap deals on flights in transit to the USA, but it may be difficult to get a seat.

BELGIUM

Airstop (☎ 070-233-188; www.airstop.be)

FRANCE

Anyway (☎ 0892-302-301; www.anyway.fr)
Easyvols (☎ 0899-700-207; www.easyvols.fr)
Nouvelles Frontières (☎ 0825-000-747; www.nouvelles-frontieres.fr)
Opodo (☎ 0899-653-655; www.opodo.fr)
Voyages Wasteels (☎ 0892-051-155; www.wasteels.fr)
Voyageurs du Monde (☎ 0892-235-656; www.vdm.com)

GERMANY

Expedia (☎ 01805-007-146; www.expedia.de)
Just Travel (☎ 089-747-3330; www.justtravel.de) English-language agency.
Opodo (☎ 01805-676-361; www.opodo.de)

Reiseboerse.com (☎ 030-2800-2800; www.reiseboerse.com)
STA Travel (☎ 069-7430-3292; www.statravel.de)

ITALY
CTS Viaggi (☎ 199-501-150; www.cts.it)
Opodo (☎ 199-404-044; www.opodo.it)

NETHERLANDS & SCANDINAVIA
Airfair (☎ 0900-7-717-717; www.airfair.nl)
ISSTA (☎ 20-589-3000; www.issta.nl)
Kilroy Travels (www.kilroytravels.com) Denmark (☎ 70-15-40-15); Finland (☎ 0203-545-769); Holland (☎ 0900-0400-636); Norway (☎ 47-026-33); Sweden (☎ 0771-545-769)

SPAIN
Barceló Viajes (☎ 902-116-226; www.barceloviajes.com)

Mexico
Aeroméxico and Mexicana are among the airlines with frequent flights to Los Angeles from major Mexican cities. Air New Zealand, Alaska Airlines, American Airlines, Delta Air Lines, Mexicana and Qantas Airways also fly from Mexico City into LAX. San Francisco is primarily served by American, Mexicana and United. Aeroméxico has flights to Ontario and San Diego as well. A flight from Mexico City to Tijuana can cost significantly less than a flight to San Diego, just a few miles north of the US–Mexico border.

Agents serving Mexico:
Despegar (☎ 55-1084-0450; www.mx.despegar.com)
Mundo Joven (☎ 01800-000-0789; www.mundojoven.com)

UK & Ireland
One of the busiest and most competitive air sectors in the world is between the UK and the USA. Air France, Air New Zealand, American Airlines, BMI, British Airways, Continental Airlines, Delta Air Lines, Singapore Airlines, United Airlines, US Airways and Virgin Atlantic Airways all operate direct flights from London to Los Angeles; all but Air France, American and Delta also fly nonstop to San Francisco. From UK regional airports discounted flights may be routed via London, Paris or Amsterdam. Aer Lingus flies nonstop from Dublin to LA, although you'll find more choices and probably cheaper fares via London.

Agents serving the UK and Ireland:
Ebookers (☎ 0871-223-5000; www.ebookers.com)
Flight Centre (☎ 0870-499-0040; www.flightcentre.co.uk)
Opodo (☎ 0871-277-0900; www.opodo.co.uk)
Quest Travel (☎ 0845-263-6963; www.questtravel.com)
STA Travel (☎ 0871-230-0040; www.statravel.co.uk)
Trailfinders (☎ 0845-058-5858; www.trailfinders.co.uk)
Travel Bag (☎ 0800-804-8911; www.travelbag.co.uk)

LAND
Border Crossings
The USA shares land borders with Canada in the north and Mexico in the south. It's relatively easy crossing from the USA into either country; it's crossing into the USA that can pose problems if you haven't brought all of your documents. For passport and visa requirements for foreign travelers, see p719. As of June 2009, US citizens will also be required to produce a passport (or a government-certified equivalent) at overland border crossings with Canada and Mexico; check the ever-changing requirements at http://travel.state.gov. **US Customs & Border Protection** (http://apps.cbp.gov/bwt/) tracks current wait times at every Mexico border crossing. The **Canada Border Services Agency** (www.cbsa-asfc.gc.ca/general/times/menu-e.html) reports border wait times up north. San Ysidro on the US–Mexican border between San Diego and Tijuana is the world's busiest border crossing. For more details on traveling between San Diego and Tijuana, see p641.

BUS
US-based **Greyhound** (☎ 800-231-2222; www.greyhound.com) and **Greyhound México** (☎ 800-710-8819; www.greyhound.com.mx) have cooperative service, with direct buses between main towns in Mexico and California. Northbound buses can take some time to cross the US border, as US immigration may insist on checking every person on board. **Greyhound Canada** (☎ 800-661-8747; www.greyhound.ca) routes between Canada and the US usually require transferring buses at the border.

CAR & MOTORCYCLE
If you're driving into the USA from Canada or Mexico, bring your vehicle's registration papers, liability insurance and driver's license. An international driver's permit is a good supplement. For road rules in California, see p736.

Canadian auto insurance is typically valid in the USA, and vice versa. If your papers are in order, taking your own car across the US–Canada border is usually quick and easy, but occasionally the authorities of either country decide to search a car *thoroughly*. On weekends and holidays, especially in summer, border-crossing traffic can be heavy and waits long.

Unless you're planning an extended stay in Tijuana, taking a car across the Mexican border is more trouble than it's worth. Instead leave your car on the US side and walk or take a shuttle across. Several parking lots (charging $6 to $10 per day) are located off the Camino de la Plaza exit from I-5, south of San Diego. If you do decide to drive across, you must buy Mexican car insurance either beforehand or at the border crossing (see p641). Expect long waits at the border, as security has tightened in recent years.

If you're renting a car or a motorcycle, find out if the agency allows its vehicles to be taken into Mexico or Canada; chances are it doesn't. In that case, don't risk it, because if anything happens to your vehicle, insurance won't cover it and you'll be responsible for all damages or losses.

TRAIN

Amtrak (☎ 800-872-7245; www.amtrak.com) operates a once-daily rail service and several daily Thruway buses from Vancouver, British Columbia in Canada to Seattle, Washington. Customs inspections happen at the border, not upon boarding. From Seattle, Amtrak's *Coast Starlight* (p738) connects south to many destinations in California en route to LA. There is no train service operating between California and Mexico.

Bus

Greyhound (☎ 800-231-2222; www.greyhound.com) is the major long-distance bus company, with routes throughout the USA. Greyhound has recently stopped service to many small towns; routes trace major highways and stop at larger population centers. For more details about Greyhound services, including how to buy tickets, costs, reservations and bus passes, see p732.

Car & Motorcycle

The main freeways connecting California with the rest of the country are I-10 from points east including Albuquerque and Phoenix, I-15 from Las Vegas, I-80 from Reno and Salt Lake City and I-5 from Portland and Seattle. For road conditions and potential hazards, see p736.

Train

Amtrak (☎ 800-872-7245; www.amtrak.com) operates a fairly extensive rail system throughout the USA. Fares vary according to the type of train and seating; on long-distance lines, you can travel in reserved or unreserved coach seats, business class or 1st class, which includes sleeping compartments. Trains are comfortable, if a bit slow, and are equipped with dining and lounge cars on longer journeys (although bringing along your own food and drink is advised – on-board food can be expensive and mediocre; occasionally, it runs out completely).

Long-distance routes to California:

California Zephyr Daily service between Chicago and Emeryville (from $145, 52 hours), near San Francisco, via Salt Lake City and Reno.

Coast Starlight Travels along the West Coast daily from Seattle to LA (from $98, 35 hours) via Portland, Sacramento and Oakland.

Southwest Chief Daily departures between Chicago and LA (from $143, 65 hours) via Albuquerque and Flagstaff.

Sunset Limited Thrice-weekly service between New Orleans and LA (from $133, 46 hours) via Tucson and Palm Springs.

See p738 for details about Amtrak services within California, including costs, reservations, train passes and how to buy tickets.

If California is part of a cross-country itinerary, Amtrak's USA Rail Passes may represent savings. The 15-day National Rail Pass costs $499/$389 per adult during peak/off-peak season, or $599/$469 for a 30-day pass. The 15-day regional West Rail Pass costs $369/329 during peak/off-peak season, or $459/359 for a 30-day pass.

GETTING AROUND

AIR

If your time is limited, consider flying. Besides the major international airports in Los Angeles and San Francisco, flights also depart from smaller regional airports (see p726). Flights between the San Francisco Bay Area and Southern California take off every hour from 6am to 10pm. It's possible to just show up at the airport, buy your ticket and hop on, though you'll have to make time to deal with security lines, and the best fares usually require advance purchase. Flights to smaller destinations tend to be fairly pricey because fewer airlines compete on these routes. See p727 for more on buying tickets – much of the same advice applies for domestic travel.

Several major US carriers fly within California. Flights are often operated by their regional subsidiaries, such as American Eagle, Delta Connection and United Express. Alaska Airlines and its partner airline Horizon Air have perhaps the most extensive intra-California networks. The most popular low-cost airline is Southwest. See p727 for airline contact information.

BICYCLE

Although it's a nonpolluting 'green' way to travel, bicycling California requires focused awareness and a high level of fitness. The distances involved make it hard to cover much ground. Cyclists must follow the same rules of the road as vehicles, but don't expect drivers to always respect your right-of-way. Cars will be your greatest hazard.

Bicycling is permitted on all roads and highways – even along freeways if there's no suitable alternative, such as a frontage road; all mandatory exits are marked. Some cities have designated bicycle lanes. With few exceptions, mountain-biking is prohibited in wilderness areas. In national parks, bicyclists are allowed on all roads that are open to cars, whether paved or dirt, but never on hiking trails. Bikes are allowed on national forest and Bureau of Land Management (BLM) single-track trails. Yield to hikers and stock animals and inquire locally about regulations. The **California Department of Transportation website** (www.dot.ca.gov/hq/tpp/offices/bike) has links to statewide bicycle advocacy groups that have more local information.

Wear a helmet – they're mandatory for anyone under 18. Ensure you have proper lights and reflective gear, especially if you're pedaling at night or in fog. Carry water and a repair kit for flats. Emergency roadside assistance is available from **Better World Club** (☎ 866-238-1137; www.betterworldclub.com). Membership ($40 per year, plus a $12 enrollment fee) entitles you to two free pickups and transportation to the nearest repair shop within a 30-mile radius.

When you tire of pedaling, remember that many local bus companies operate buses equipped with bike racks.

On international and domestic flights, you'll need to disassemble your bike and box it as checked baggage; contact the airline directly before buying your ticket to find out about applicable surcharges (typically $50 to $100, but sometimes more). Greyhound buses will carry boxed bicycles as checked baggage ($20 to $30 surcharge). Most of Amtrak's *Pacific Surfliner* and *Capitol Corridor* trains feature onboard bicycles racks – be sure to book a spot when making ticket reservations (surcharge $5 to $10). On trains without racks, bikes must be put in a box ($15) and checked as luggage ($5). Note that not all stations or trains have checked-baggage service.

Whether it's your own bike or a rental, always use a heavy-duty lock to prevent theft. Look for special bicycle racks in parking garages and areas. If possible, bring your bike inside your hotel room at night.

Purchase

Buying bikes is easy. Specialist cycling shops have the best selection and advice, but sporting-goods stores may have lower prices. Some bicycle stores and rental outfitters also sell used bicycles. To find the best bargains, scour flea markets, garage sales and thrift shops, study the notice boards in hostels and at universities or check the online listings at www.craigslist.org. These will also be the best places to resell your bike before you leave, although stores selling used bikes may also buy from you.

Rental

You can rent bikes by the hour, the day or the week in most cities and major towns. Rentals start around $10 per day for beach cruisers up to $45 for mountain bikes, usually including a helmet and a lock. Most companies require a credit-card security deposit of $200 or more.

BOAT

Boats won't get you around California, although there are a few local services, notably to Catalina Island off the coast of Los Angeles and to the Channel Islands from Ventura or Oxnard, north of LA. On San Francisco Bay, regular ferry routes operate between San Francisco and Sausalito, Larkspur, Tiburon, Angel Island, Oakland, Alameda and Vallejo. Details are given in the destination chapters.

BUS

The cheapest way to get around California is by bus.

Greyhound (☎ 800-231-2222; www.greyhound.com) provides an economical way to travel between major cities and to points along the coast, but won't get you off the beaten path or to national parks. Frequency of service varies from 'rarely' to 'constantly,' but the main routes have service every hour or so, including a few nonstop express buses.

Greyhound is most popular with less-affluent Americans. Generally, buses are fairly comfortable, clean and reliable. Grab a seat toward the front, away from the bathroom. Onboard amenities include slightly reclining seats and freezing air-con; smoking is prohibited. Long-distance buses stop for meal breaks and driver changes.

Bus stations are typically dreary places, often in dodgy areas; if you arrive at night, spend money on a taxi ride into town. In small towns where there is no station, know exactly where and when the bus arrives, be obvious as you flag it down and pay the driver with exact change.

Most baggage has to be checked in: label it clearly to avoid lost luggage. Larger items, including bicycles and skis, can usually be checked for a surcharge ($20 to $30). Travelers with disabilities who need special assistance should call ☎ 800-752-4841 at least 48 hours before traveling.

Bus Passes

If you're planning on making the bus your main method of travel to, from and around California, Greyhound's **Discovery Pass** (☎ 888-454-7277; www.discoverypass.com; $329-750) allows unlimited, unrestricted travel for seven ($329), 15 ($483), 30 ($607) or 60 ($750) consecutive days in the USA and Canada. You can buy passes at select Greyhound terminals up to two hours before departure, or purchase them online in advance, then pick them up using the same credit card with photo ID at least an hour before boarding.

Costs

For lower fares, purchase tickets at least seven days in advance. Round trips are also cheaper. Special promotional fares are often available on the Greyhound website.

Tickets for children ages two to 11 are 40% off. Seniors over 62 qualify for a 5% discount. Students who purchase a Student Advantage Card (p717) save 15% off regular fares; otherwise, students receive 10% off by showing valid student ID.

For specific route and fare information, see the Getting There & Away sections of the destination chapters. Sample routes and fares:

Route	Standard Adult Fare	Duration	Frequency
LA–San Diego	$21	2¼-3½hr	21 daily
San Diego–Anaheim	$22	2-2¼hr	5 daily
San Francisco–LA	$53	7½-12½hr	15 daily
San Francisco–Sacramento	$22	2-2½hr	9 daily
San Francisco–San Luis Obispo	$46	6½-7½hr	4 daily

Reservations

US customers can purchase tickets online or over the phone. If you purchase them 10 days in advance with a major US credit card, tickets will be mailed to your US address. International credit cards are accepted in person at the terminal, or for ordering online in advance for 'Will Call' tickets, which you must pick up at the terminal (bring photo ID). Ticket windows at Greyhound terminals also accept traveler's checks and cash.

On Greyhound, a ticket does not reserve or guarantee a seat on a bus. All seating is normally first come, first served. Greyhound recommends arriving an hour before departure to get a seat; allow extra time on weekends and holidays. Available in some US gateway cities, including Sacramento, San Francisco and LA, a priority-seating reservation ($5) guarantees you a seat and lets you board ahead of other passengers.

CAR & MOTORCYCLE

California's love affair with cars runs so deep it often verges on pathological, and it's here to stay for at least one practical reason: the state is so big, public transportation can't cover it. For flexibility and convenience, you'll want a car. Independence costs you, though, as rental rates and gas prices can eat a good chunk of a travel budget. For recommended maps, see p723.

Automobile Associations

With walk-in offices throughout California, the **American Automobile Association** (AAA; ☎ 877-428-2277; www.aaa.com) offers free maps and trip-planning tools, travel-agency services and discounts on accommodations, auto repair, car and RV rentals, Amtrak tickets, theme parks, sports games and more. AAA's 24-hour **emergency roadside assistance** (☎ 800-400-4222) is also

ROAD DISTANCES (MILES)

Distances are approximate

	Anaheim	Arcata	Bakersfield	Death Valley	Las Vegas	Los Angeles	Monterey	Napa	Palm Springs	Redding	Sacramento	San Diego	San Francisco	San Luis Obispo	Santa Barbara	Sth Lake Tahoe	Yosemite
Anaheim	---																
Arcata	680	---															
Bakersfield	135	555	---														
Death Valley	285	705	235	---													
Las Vegas	265	840	285	140	---												
Los Angeles	25	650	110	290	270	---											
Monterey	370	395	250	495	535	345	---										
Napa	425	265	300	545	590	400	150	---									
Palm Springs	95	760	220	300	280	110	450	505	---								
Redding	570	140	440	565	725	545	315	190	650	---							
Sacramento	410	300	280	435	565	385	185	60	490	160	---						
San Diego	95	770	230	350	330	120	465	520	140	665	505	---					
San Francisco	405	280	285	530	570	380	120	50	490	215	85	500	---				
San Luis Obispo	225	505	120	365	405	200	145	265	310	430	290	320	230	---			
Santa Barbara	120	610	145	350	360	95	250	370	205	535	395	215	335	105	---		
Sth Lake Tahoe	505	400	375	345	460	480	285	160	485	260	100	600	185	390	495	---	
Yosemite	335	465	200	300	415	310	200	190	415	325	160	430	190	230	345	190	---

available to members of international auto-club affiliates, such as CAA in Canada and AA in the UK. The **Better World Club** (☎ 866-238-1137; www.betterworldclub.com) is an ecofriendly alternative that donates 1% of annual revenue to environmental cleanup efforts and mass-transit advocacy. Annual membership in either association costs around $55. AAA offers add-on services for RVs and motorcycles, while Better World Club supports bicyclists (p732).

Bring Your Own Vehicle

If you're driving over the border from Canada or Mexico, see p730. Unless you're moving to the USA, don't even think about shipping your car from overseas.

Driver's Licenses

Foreign visitors can legally drive in California for up to 12 months with their home driver's license. An International Driving Permit (IDP) is not compulsory but could give you greater credibility with traffic police. It sometimes may be required when you are renting a vehicle, especially if your home license is not written in English or doesn't have a photograph. International automobile associations can issue IDPs, valid for one year, for a fee. Always carry your home license together with the IDP.

Fuel & Spare Parts

Gas stations in California, almost all of which are self-service, are easily found everywhere except in sparsely populated areas. Gas (petrol) is sold in gallons (1 US gallon equals 3.78L). At press time, the average price of unleaded gasoline was $3.85 per gallon. Prices are always higher in national parks and other remote mountain and desert regions. Finding spare parts is not a problem, especially in cities and major towns, although actual availability depends on the age and model of your car. Always bring a spare tire and tools in case your car breaks down.

Insurance

Don't put the key into the ignition if you don't have insurance. You risk financial ruin if there's an accident and you aren't covered. If you already have auto insurance (even overseas), or if you buy travel insurance, make sure the policy has enough liability coverage for driving in California. State law requires that all vehicles carry liability insurance, which covers anyone else you injure in an accident. The minimum amount of coverage for bodily injury liability is $15,000 for one person or $30,000 for all injuries in one accident; you must also carry at least $5000 worth of property-damage liability.

Rental-car companies will provide liability insurance, but most charge extra. Rental companies almost never include collision-damage insurance for the vehicle. Instead, they offer an optional Collision Damage Waiver (CDW) or Loss Damage Waiver (LDW), usually with an initial deductible cost of $100 to $500. For an extra premium, you can usually get this deductible covered as well. Paying extra for some or all of this insurance increases the cost of a rental car by at least $15 to $30 a day.

However, the good news is that most credit cards now offer collision-damage coverage for rental cars if you rent for 15 days or fewer and charge the total rental to your card. This is a good way to avoid paying extra fees to the rental company, but if there's an accident you may have to pay the rental-car company first, then seek reimbursement from the credit-card company. Check your credit-card policy carefully.

Parking

Parking is usually plentiful and free in small towns and rural areas, but scarce and expensive in cities. Look for the free-parking icon (P) used in the San Francisco, Los Angeles and San Diego chapters of this book. Otherwise, you can expect to pay as much as $45 for the privilege of leaving your car in a lot or garage overnight. Valet parking at hotels and restaurants is also commonplace in cities. When parking on the street, read all posted regulations and restrictions, such as street-cleaning hours and areas reserved for residents, to avoid being towed. Also, don't park within 15ft of a fire hydrant. Always be aware of painted colored curbs:

Red No parking or stopping anytime.
Yellow Stopping no longer than the posted time to load or unload passengers or freight.
White Stopping only to pick up or drop off passengers or mail.
Green Parking for a limited time, as signposted or painted on the curb.
Blue Parking only for drivers with disabilities (permit required).

Rental

CARS

With advance reservations you should be able to get a mid-size vehicle for about $25 to $45 per day, plus insurance and taxes. Weekend and weekly rates are usually more economical. Airport locations may have cheaper rates but higher fees; city-center offices may do pick-ups and drop-offs. If you belong to an auto club or a frequent-flier program, you may get a discount (or earn frequent-flier miles), so ask. If you get a cheaper fly-drive package, local taxes may be extra when you pick up the car.

Rates generally include unlimited mileage, but expect surcharges for additional drivers and one-way rentals. Some rental companies let you pay for your last tank of gas upfront; this is almost never a good deal. Child or infant safety seats are compulsory (reserve them when booking), costing around $10 per day or $50 per week.

Most rental companies require that that you be at least 25 years old, possess a valid driver's license and have a major credit card, *not* a debit or check card. Some companies may rent to drivers between the ages of 21 and 24 for a surcharge of up to $20 per day.

Major international car-rental companies with branches throughout California:

Alamo (☎ 800-462-5266; www.alamo.com)
Avis (☎ 800-331-1212; www.avis.com)
Budget (☎ 800-527-0700; www.budget.com)
Dollar (☎ 800-800-3665; www.dollar.com)
Enterprise (☎ 800-261-7331; www.enterprise.com)
Fox (☎ 800-225-4369; www.foxrentacar.com)
Hertz (☎ 800-654-3131; www.hertz.com)
National (☎ 800-227-7368; www.nationalcar.com)
Rent-a-Wreck (☎ 800-944-7501; www.rent-a-wreck.com)
Thrifty (☎ 800-847-4389; www.thrifty.com)

You might get a better deal by booking through discount-travel websites like **Priceline** (www.priceline.com) or **Hotwire** (www.hotwire.com), or by using online travel booking agents, such as **Expedia** (www.expedia.com), **Orbitz** (www.orbitz.com) or **Travelocity** (www.travelocity.com). Independent local agencies may offer lower rates; they're also more likely to rent to drivers under 25. **Car Rental Express** (www.carrentalexpress.com) rates and compares independent agencies.

Some major car-rental agencies, including Avis and Hertz, now offer 'green' fleets of hybrid rental cars (eg Toyota Priuses, Honda

Civics, Nissan Altimas, Ford Escape SUVs). **EV Rental Cars** (☎ 877-387-3682; www.evrental.com) rents hybrid cars (from $45 per day) at airports in LA, Orange County, San Diego and the San Francisco Bay Area. In LA, **Simply Hybrid** (☎ 323-653-0011, 888-359-0055; www.simplyhybrid.com) rents environmentally friendly cars from $60 per day.

MOTORCYCLES

Motorcycle rentals and insurance are not cheap, especially if you've got your eye on a Harley-Davidson. Expect to pay at least $90 to $170 per day, plus taxes and fees, depending on the rental location and the size of the motorcycle. Discounts are available for three-day and weekly rentals. Rates usually include helmets, unlimited miles and minimum liability insurance; collision damage waiver (CDW) insurance costs extra. Security deposits range from $1000 to $3000 (credit card required).

Recommended rental agencies:

Dubbelju (☎ 415-495-2774, 866-495-2774; www.dubbelju.com; 698a Bryant St, San Francisco) Rents BMW, Harley-Davidson, Honda and Triumph motorcycles, as well as Yamaha scooters (half/full day $69/99).

Eagle Rider (☎ 888-900-9901; www.eaglerider.com) Nationwide company with 12 branches in California (including LA, San Francisco, San Diego, Lake Tahoe and Palm Springs); also in Las Vegas. One-way rentals cost $175 extra.

Moturis (☎ 800-890-2909; www.moturis.com) National company with outlets in Las Vegas, Long Beach, Los Angeles, Palm Springs, San Diego, San Francisco and San Jose (one-way rental surcharge $191). Also rents recreational vehicles (RVs).

RECREATIONAL VEHICLES

RVs remain popular for travel in California, despite high fuel prices. It's easy to find campgrounds with hookups for electricity and water, but in cities RVs are nothing but a nuisance. They're also cumbersome to drive and waste fuel at a horrifying rate, but they do solve transportation, accommodation and cooking needs in one fell swoop. Even so, there are so many places in national and state parks and in the mountains that RVs can't reach, so if you want to really explore California, forget about RVs.

Book rentals as far in advance as possible. Costs vary by size and model, but you can expect to pay from $60 per day for a small campervan sleeping two adults to at least $100 per day for a 30ft-long RV sleeping up to seven people. Rates often don't include mileage fees (from 30¢ per mile), bedding or kitchen kits (rental fee $40 to $100), vehicle-cleaning fees (at least $75) or taxes.

Recommended rental agencies:

Cruise America (☎ 480-464-7300, 800-671-8042; www.cruiseamerica.com)

El Monte RV (☎ 562-483-4956, 888-337-2214; www.elmonterv.com)

Happy Travel Campers (☎ 310-675-1335, 800-370-1262; www.camperusa.com)

Road Conditions & Hazards

For up-to-date highway conditions in California, including road closures, dial ☎ 800-427-7623 or check www.dot.ca.gov. For Nevada roads, call ☎ 877-687-6237 or check www.nevadadot.com/traveler. Common road hazards include potholes, city commuter traffic, wandering wildlife and, of course, kid-distracted or otherwise enraged drivers.

In places where winter driving is an issue, many cars are fitted with steel-studded snow tires; snow chains may be required in mountain areas. Ideally, carry your own chains and learn how to use them before you hit the road. Otherwise, chains can usually be bought (but not cheaply) in the nearest town. Most car-rental companies don't permit the use of chains. Driving off-road, or on dirt roads, is also prohibited by most rental-car companies, and it can be very dangerous in wet weather.

In rural areas, livestock sometimes graze next to unfenced roads. These areas are typically signed as 'Open Range' with the silhouette of a steer. Where deer and other wild animals frequently appear roadside, you'll see signs with the silhouette of a leaping deer. Take these signs seriously, particularly at night. Also watch out for fallen rocks, which may damage or even disable your car if struck. In coastal areas thick fog may impede driving – slow down, and if it's too soupy get off the road. For desert driving tips, see p671.

Road Rules

In the USA cars drive on the right-hand side of the road. In California, the use of seat belts and infant and child safety seats is required at all times, while motorcyclists must wear helmets. Talking on a cell phone while driving is illegal.

On interstate highways, the speed limit is sometimes raised to 75mph. Unless otherwise posted, the speed limit is 65mph on freeways, 55mph on two-lane undivided highways,

35mph on major city streets and 25mph in business and residential districts and near schools. It's forbidden to pass a school bus when its lights are flashing.

Unless otherwise posted, you may turn right at a red light after coming to a full stop, so long as you don't impede intersecting traffic, which has the right-of-way. You may also turn left on red at two intersecting one-way streets. At four-way stop signs, cars proceed in order of arrival; when two cars arrive simultaneously, the one on the right has the right-of-way. When in doubt, politely wave the other person ahead.

When emergency vehicles approach from either direction, pull over to get out of their way. On freeways, try to pass slower cars on the left. If two cars are trying to get into the same central lane, the one on the right has priority. Carpool lanes marked with a diamond symbol are reserved for cars with multiple occupants; without the minimum number of passengers you risk stiff fines. California has strict antilittering laws. If you are caught throwing anything from a vehicle onto the roadway, you may be fined up to $1000.

Penalties are most severe for 'DUI' – driving under the influence of alcohol and/or drugs. Police can give roadside sobriety checks to assess if you've been drinking or using drugs. If you fail, they'll require you take a breath, urine or blood test to determine the level of alcohol or drugs in your body. Refusal to be tested is treated as if you'd taken the test and failed. The maximum legal blood-alcohol concentration is 0.08%. It's illegal to carry open containers of alcohol inside a vehicle, even if they are empty. Unless containers are full and still sealed, you must store them in the trunk.

The *California Driver Handbook* and *California Motorcycle Handbook* explain everything else you need to know. They're available free from any Department of Motor Vehicles (DMV) office or downloadable from www.dmv.ca.gov.

HITCHHIKING

Hitchhiking in the USA is potentially dangerous and definitely not recommended. Drivers tend to be suspicious of those with their thumbs out. Hitchhiking on freeways is prohibited. You'll see more people hitchhiking (and drivers stopping) in rural areas than in cities, but these places aren't any safer, and with sparse traffic, you may get stranded. A more reliable bet may be to check ride-share boards at hostels or online at www.craigslist.org, www.erideshare.com or www.digihitch.com – use these at your own risk too. In national parks, hitching to and from trailheads is not uncommon.

LOCAL TRANSPORTATION

Except in major cities, public transit is rarely the most convenient option, and coverage to outlying towns and suburbs can be sparse. However, it is usually cheap, safe and reliable. See the Getting Around sections of the destination chapters for details.

Bicycle

Cycling is a feasible way of getting around smaller cities and towns, but it's not much fun in traffic-dense areas such as LA. As rated by the **League of American Bicyclists** (www.bikeleague.org), Arcata, Chico, Davis, Palo Alto, San Francisco, San Jose, San Luis Obispo, Santa Cruz and Santa Barbara are among California's most bike-friendly communities. Bicycles may be carried on some forms of public transportation, but in some places only during restricted hours. Rental shops are listed in the destination chapters.

Boat

Inexpensive water taxis operate in San Diego Bay, Long Beach and Santa Barbara. Small, low-cost ferries shuttle between San Diego and Coronado Island, and between Newport Beach and Balboa Island in Orange County.

Bus, Cable Car, Streetcar & Trolley

Most cities and larger towns have dependable local bus systems, though these are often designed for commuters and provide only limited service in the evening and on weekends. Typical bus fares range from $1 to $3 per ride. San Francisco's Municipal Railway (MUNI) network includes not only buses but also historic streetcars and those famous cable cars. San Diego runs trolleys around downtown and to the Mexican border.

Train

In LA, the Metro is a combined network of subway and light-rail, and Metrolink commuter trains connect LA with surrounding counties. San Diego operates *Coaster* commuter trains along the coast between downtown and Oceanside. To get around San Francisco, the East Bay and the Peninsula, take Bay Area

Rapid Transit (BART) or Caltrain. The Las Vegas Strip has a monorail.

Taxi

Taxis are metered, with flag-fall fees of $2.50 to $3.50 to start, plus $2 to $3 per mile; they charge extra for handling baggage and sometimes for airport pick-ups. Drivers expect a 10% to 15% tip, rounded up to the next dollar. Taxis cruise the busiest areas in large cities, but if you're anywhere else it's easiest to order one by phone.

TRAIN

Amtrak (☎ 800-872-7245; www.amtrak.com) operates comfortable, if somewhat slow and occasionally tardy, trains between major cities and select towns in California. At some stations Thruway buses provide onward connections, but don't worry, they're more civilized than Greyhound.

Routes within California:

Capitol Corridor Links the eastern San Francisco Bay area (including Oakland, Berkeley and Emeryville) and San Jose with Sacramento several times daily. Thruway buses connect west to San Francisco, north to Auburn in the Gold Country and east to Truckee and Reno near Lake Tahoe.

California Zephyr Daily service from Emeryville, near San Francisco, via Sacramento to Truckee and Reno near Lake Tahoe.

Coast Starlight Chugs north–south almost the entire length of the state. Daily stops include LA, Santa Barbara, San Luis Obispo, Paso Robles, Salinas, San Jose, Oakland, Sacramento, Chico, Redding and Dunsmuir.

Pacific Surfliner Over a dozen daily trains ply the San Diego–LA route (via Anaheim, home of Disneyland). Up to five trains continue north to Santa Barbara via Oxnard and Ventura; two trains also connect north to San Luis Obispo. The trip, which hugs the coastline for much of the way, is a scenic treat, with sleek double-decker cars that have panoramic windows.

San Joaquins Several daily departures between Bakersfield and Oakland or Sacramento. Stops include Merced, with onward bus service to Yosemite National Park. From Bakersfield, Thruway buses connect to LA and Las Vegas.

Costs

Tickets can be purchased in person, by telephone or online. Fares depend on the day and month of travel, the route, type of seating and other factors. Special promotions can become available anytime, so be sure to ask or check the website.

Seniors over 62 and students with a Student Advantage Card (p717) or an ISIC card typically receive a 15% discount, while up to two children aged two to 15 who are accompanied by an adult get 50% off. AAA members enjoy 10% off regular fares.

For specific route and fare information, see the Getting There & Away sections of the destination chapters. Sample routes and fares:

Route	Standard Adult Fare	Duration
Emeryville/San Francisco–LA	$52	13hr
Emeryville/San Francisco–San Luis Obispo	$32	6¾hr
Emeryville/San Francisco–Truckee	$42	5½hr
LA–San Luis Obispo	$30	5½hr
LA–Santa Barbara	$21	2¾hr
San Diego–LA	$29	2¾hr

Reservations

Reservations can be made any time from 11 months in advance to the day of departure. Trains can be crowded, especially in summer and around major holidays, so reserve as far in advance as possible. This also gives you the best chance of fare discounts.

Train Passes

Valid for seven days of travel within a 21-day period, Amtrak's good-value California Rail Pass costs $159 ($80 for children ages two to 15). It can be used on the *Capitol Corridor, San Joaquins* and *Pacific Surfliner* trains and most connecting Thruway bus services, as well as on the *Coast Starlight* between LA and Dunsmuir, near Mt Shasta. Purchase passes by phone or in person. You must make separate seat reservations for each leg of travel. For Amtrak's national and interstate passes, see p731.

ALL ABOARD

Napa Valley Wine Train (p197) Traveling in style between Napa and St Helena.

Central Pacific Passenger Depot (p421) Ride along the Sacramento River from Old Sacramento.

Railtown 1897 State Historic Park (p349) A scenic trip through Gold Country from Jamestown.

Roaring Camp Railroads (p451) Narrow-gauge train trips through the redwoods.

Skunk Train (p263) Chugs between Willits and Fort Bragg on the North Coast.

Sugar Pine Railroad (p389) A narrow-gauge woodlands loop just south of Yosemite.

Health Dr David Goldberg

CONTENTS

Generally speaking, California is a healthy place to visit. No prevalent diseases or risks are associated with traveling here, and the USA is well served by hospitals.

BEFORE YOU GO

INSURANCE

Because of the high cost of health care, international travelers should take out comprehensive travel insurance before they leave home. If you have a choice between lower or higher medical expense options, take the higher one for visiting the USA.

Bring any medications you may need in their original containers, clearly labeled. A signed, dated letter from your physician that describes all medical conditions and medications, including generic names, is also a good idea.

If your health insurance does not cover you for medical expenses abroad, consider getting supplemental insurance. Check the **Lonely Planet website** (www.lonelyplanet.com) for more information. Find out in advance whether your insurance plan will make payments directly to health providers or reimburse you later for overseas medical expenditures.

RECOMMENDED VACCINATIONS

No special vaccines are required or recommended for travel to the USA. All travelers should be up-to-date on routine immunizations: tetanus-diphtheria, measles, chicken pox and influenza.

MEDICAL CHECKLIST

Recommended items for a personal medical kit:

- acetaminophen (Tylenol) or aspirin
- anti-inflammatory drugs (eg ibuprofen)
- antihistamines (for hay fever and allergic reactions)
- antibacterial ointment (eg Bactroban) for cuts and abrasions
- steroid cream or cortisone (for poison ivy and other allergic rashes)
- bandages, gauze, gauze rolls
- adhesive or paper tape
- scissors, safety pins, tweezers
- thermometer
- pocket knife
- DEET-containing insect repellent for the skin
- permethrin-containing insect spray for clothing, tents and bed nets
- sunblock

INTERNET RESOURCES

There is a wealth of travel health advice on the internet. The World Health Organization publishes a superb book, called *International Travel and Health,* which is revised annually and is available online at no cost at www.who.int/ith. Another website of general interest is MD Travel Health at www.mdtravelhealth.com, which provides complete travel health recommendations for every country, updated daily, also at no cost.

It's usually a good idea to consult your government's travel health website before departure, if one is available:

Australia (www.smarttraveller.gov.au)
Canada (www.hc-sc.gc.ca/index-eng.php)
UK (www.dh.gov.uk/)
United States (www.cdc.gov/travel)

IN CALIFORNIA

AVAILABILITY & COST OF HEALTH CARE

In general, if you have a medical emergency, your best bet is to find the nearest hospital and go to its emergency room (ER). If the problem isn't urgent, you can call a nearby hospital and ask for a referral to a local physician,

HEALTH

which is usually cheaper than a trip to the emergency room. In a serious emergency, call ☎911 for an ambulance to take you to the nearest ER. Many city hospitals have 'urgent care clinics' designed to deal with walk-in clients with less-than-catastrophic injuries and illnesses. Note that these are for-profit centers and they tend to perform large numbers of expensive tests, even for minor illnesses.

Pharmacies are abundantly supplied, but you may find some medications that are available over the counter in your home country require a prescription in the USA. As always, if you don't have insurance to cover the cost of prescriptions, they can be shockingly expensive.

INFECTIOUS DISEASES

In addition to more common ailments, there are several infectious diseases that may be acquired by mosquito or tick bites.

Giardiasis

This parasitic infection of the small intestine occurs throughout North America and the world. Symptoms may include nausea, bloating, cramps and diarrhea, and may last for weeks. To protect yourself from giardia, you should avoid drinking directly from lakes, ponds, streams and rivers, which may be contaminated by animal or human feces. The infection can also be transmitted from person to person if proper hand washing is not performed. Giardiasis is easily diagnosed by a stool test and readily treated with antibiotics.

HIV/AIDS

As with most parts of the world, HIV infection occurs throughout the USA. You should never assume, on the basis of someone's background or appearance, that they're free of this or any other sexually transmitted disease. Be sure to use a condom for all sexual encounters.

West Nile Virus

This virus was unknown in the USA until a few years ago, but has now been reported in almost all 50 states. The virus is transmitted by culex mosquitoes, which are active in late summer and early fall and generally bite after dusk. Most infections are mild or asymptomatic, but the virus may infect the central nervous system leading to fever, headache, confusion, lethargy, coma and sometimes death. There is no treatment for West Nile virus. For the latest update on the areas affected by West Nile, go to the **US Geological Survey website** (http://westnile maps.usgs.gov).

ENVIRONMENTAL HAZARDS

Altitude Sickness

Visitors from lower elevations undergo rather dramatic physiological changes as they adapt to high altitudes, and while the side effects are usually mild, they can be dangerous if ignored. Some people – age and fitness levels are not predictors of who these will be – will feel the effects of altitude strongly, while others won't even notice.

Symptoms, which tend to manifest during the first day after reaching altitude, may include headache, fatigue, loss of appetite, nausea, sleeplessness, increased urination and hyperventilation due to overexertion. Symptoms normally resolve within 24 to 48 hours. The rule of thumb is, don't ascend until the symptoms descend. More severe cases may display extreme disorientation, ataxia (loss of coordination and balance), breathing problems (especially a persistent cough) and vomiting. These folks should descend immediately and get to a hospital.

To avoid the discomfort characterizing the milder symptoms, drink plenty of water (dehydration exacerbates the symptoms) and take it easy. Schedule a nap if you have a sleepless night and put off serious hiking and biking for a few days, if possible. A mild painkiller like aspirin should take care of the headache.

Bites

ANIMAL BITES

Do not attempt to pet, handle or feed any wild animal, no matter how cuddly it looks; most injuries from animals are directly related to people trying to do just that.

Any bite or scratch by a mammal, including bats, should be promptly and thoroughly cleansed with large amounts of soap and water, followed by application of an antiseptic such as iodine or alcohol. The local health authorities should be contacted immediately for possible post-exposure rabies treatment, whether or not you have been immunized against rabies. It may also be advisable to start an antibiotic, since wounds caused by animal bites and scratches frequently become infected.

MOSQUITO BITES

When mosquitoes are present, keep yourself covered (wear long sleeves, long pants, a hat, and shoes rather than sandals) and apply a good insect repellent, preferably one containing DEET, to exposed skin and clothing. Don't overuse the stuff, though, because neurologic toxicity – though uncommon – has been reported from DEET, especially in children. DEET-containing compounds should not be used at all on kids under age two.

Insect repellents containing certain botanical products, including oil of eucalyptus and soybean oil, are effective but last only 1½ to two hours. Products based on citronella are not effective.

SNAKEBITES

There are several varieties of venomous snakes in the USA, but unlike those in other countries they do not cause instantaneous death and antivenins are available. Rattlesnake bites are fairly common. First aid is to place a light constricting bandage over the bite, keep the wounded part below the level of the heart and move it as little as possible. Stay calm and get to a medical facility as soon as possible. Bring the dead snake for identification if you can, but don't risk being bitten again. Do not use the mythic 'cut an X and suck out the venom' trick, as this causes more damage to snakebite victims than the bites themselves.

Many snakebites result from people picking up the snake, either out of bravado or mistakenly assuming that the animal was dead. Keep a healthy distance away from snakes and watch where you step.

SPIDER & SCORPION BITES

Although there are many species of spiders in California (check out www.calpoison.org for a list of potential biters), one of the most common biting spiders is the black widow. This spider is black or brown in color, measuring about 15mm in body length, with a shiny top, fat body and a distinctive red or orange hourglass figure on its underside. It's usually found in barns, woodpiles, sheds, harvested crops and in the bowls of outdoor toilets.

If bitten by a black widow, you should clean the wound with an antiseptic such as iodine or alcohol and apply ice or cold packs, then go to the nearest emergency room. Complications of a black widow bite may include muscle spasms, breathing difficulties and high blood pressure.

If stung by a scorpion, you should immediately apply ice or a cold pack, immobilize the affected body part and go to the nearest emergency room. To prevent scorpion stings, be sure to inspect and shake out clothing, shoes and sleeping bags before use, and wear gloves and protective clothing when working around piles of wood or leaves.

Poison Control Centers have staff available 24 hours a day and advise about bites, stings and ingested poisons of all kinds. Call ☎ 800-222-1222 anywhere in California for the one nearest you.

TICK BITES

Ticks are parasitic arachnids that may be present in the brush, forest and grasslands, where hikers often get them on their legs or in their boots. Adult ticks suck blood from hosts by burrowing into the skin and can carry infections such as Lyme disease.

Always check your body for ticks after walking through high grass or thickly forested areas. If ticks are found unattached, they can simply be brushed off. If a tick is found attached, press down around the tick's head with tweezers, grab the head and gently pull upwards – do not twist it. (If no tweezers are available, use your fingers, but protect them from contamination with a piece of tissue or paper.) Do not rub oil, alcohol or petroleum jelly on it. If you get sick in the next couple of weeks, consult a doctor. If possible, keep the tick. If you get sick later, it makes treatment a lot easier.

Dehydration

Visitors to the desert may not realize how much water they're losing, as sweat evaporates almost immediately and increased urination (to help the blood process oxygen more efficiently) can go unnoticed. The prudent tourist will make sure to drink more water than usual – think a gallon a day if you're active. Parents can carry fruit and fruit juices to help keep kids hydrated.

Severe dehydration can easily cause disorientation and confusion, and even day hikers have gotten lost and died because they ignored their thirst. So bring plenty of water, even on short hikes...but don't drink *too* much. Hyponatremia occurs when the body becomes overhydrated. The signs of hyponatremia are similar to heat exhaustion, except that lack of thirst is combined with copious clear urine. To treat hyponatremia, rest in a shady place, do not drink any liquids and slowly eat salty foods.

Heat Exhaustion & Heatstroke

Dehydration or salt deficiency can cause heat exhaustion. Take time to acclimatize to high temperatures and make sure you get enough liquids. Salt deficiency is characterized by fatigue, lethargy, headaches, giddiness and muscle cramps. Salt tablets may help. Vomiting or diarrhea can also deplete your liquid and salt levels. Anhydrotic heat exhaustion, caused by the inability to sweat, is quite rare. Unlike other forms of heat exhaustion, it may strike people who have been in a hot climate for some time, rather than newcomers. Always use water bottles on long trips. One gallon of water per person per day is recommended if hiking.

Long, continuous exposure to high temperatures can lead to the sometimes-fatal condition of heatstroke, which occurs when the body's heat-regulating mechanism breaks down and the body temperature rises to dangerous levels. Hospitalization is essential for extreme cases; meanwhile get out of the sun, remove clothing that retains heat (cotton is OK), douse the body with water and fan continuously. Ice or cold packs can be applied to the neck, armpits and groin.

Hypothermia

Skiers and winter hikers will find that temperatures in the mountains or desert can quickly drop below freezing. A sudden soaking or even high winds can lower your body temperature rapidly. Travel with a partner whenever possible.

Seek shelter when bad weather is unavoidable. Woolen clothing and synthetics, which retain warmth even when wet, are superior to cottons. Carry a good-quality sleeping bag and high-energy, easily digestible snacks like chocolate or dried fruit.

The symptoms of hypothermia are exhaustion, numbness, shivering, slurred speech, irrational or violent behavior, lethargy, stumbling, dizzy spells, muscle cramps and violent bursts of energy. Get hypothermia victims out of bad weather and into dry, warm clothing. Give hot liquids (not alcohol or caffeine) and high-calorie, easily digestible food. In advanced stages, place victims in warm sleeping bags cocooned inside a wind- and waterproof outer wrapping. Do not rub victims, who must be handled very gently.

The Authors

SARA BENSON

Coordinating Author, Getting Started, Itineraries, California Camping & Outdoors, Central Coast, The Deserts, Las Vegas, Directory, Transportation

Born in the cornfields outside Chicago, Sara headed to the West Coast after college with just one suitcase and $100 in her pocket. She landed in San Francisco and has bounced around the state ever since, including the Sierra Nevada, Los Angeles and San Luis Obispo County. Sara is also an avid outdoor enthusiast. Her travel writing has featured on popular websites and in magazines and newspapers from coast to coast, including the *Los Angeles Times, San Francisco Chronicle*, *Las Vegas Review-Journal* and *National Geographic Adventure*. The author of 30 travel and nonfiction books, Sara has written Lonely Planet's *Las Vegas* and *Las Vegas Encounter* guides and contributed to *California Trips*.

ALEXIS AVERBUCK

North Coast, Northern Mountains

Alexis Averbuck was born in Oakland but since childhood has been on serial walkabout. Her early jaunts had her road-tripping through Europe and living in Hong Kong, India and Sri Lanka. Soon thereafter she was bitten by the travel-writing bug and covered places as disparate as Guatemala, Italy and Thailand. Now Alexis lives in Hydra, Greece, so for this book she returned to her home state to further explore the back roads of beautiful northern California. Despite having lived in Antarctica for a year and crossed the Pacific by sailboat, Alexis still adores the Mendocino coast. She's also a painter – see her work at www.alexisaverbuck.com.

AMY C BALFOUR

Orange County, San Diego Area

To ensure that readers get the full SoCal experience, Amy has explored the Gaslamp Quarter in the rain, surprised a Wolf's guenon in the San Diego Zoo, worn a cardboard crown at Medieval Times, and spied on guests at the naughty Ivy Hotel from a nearby condo (hey, they left the blinds open). For the last six years she's also had fun hiking, biking and four-wheeling all over the SoCal backcountry. She wrote Lonely Planet's *Los Angeles Encounter* and contributed to *Coastal California*, *Los Angeles & Southern California* and *California Trips*. She's written for *Backpacker*, *Every Day with Rachael Ray*, *Redbook*, *Southern Living*, *Women's Health* and the *Los Angeles Times*.

LONELY PLANET AUTHORS

Why is our travel information the best in the world? It's simple: our authors are passionate, dedicated travelers. They don't take freebies in exchange for positive coverage so you can be sure the advice you're given is impartial. They travel widely to all the popular spots, and off the beaten track. They don't research using just the internet or phone. They discover new places not included in any other guidebook. They personally visit thousands of hotels, restaurants, palaces, trails, galleries, temples and more. They speak with dozens of locals every day to make sure you get the kind of insider knowledge only a local could tell you. They take pride in getting all the details right, and in telling it how it is. Think you can do it? Find out how at **lonelyplanet.com**.

ANDREW BENDER

Los Angeles

Yet another Lonely Planet author with an MBA, this native New Englander first came to Los Angeles after B-school to work in film production, but he ended up leaving the industry to do what every MBA (and production dude) secretly dreams of: traveling and writing about it. These days you can see his writing and photography in the *Los Angeles Times*, *Forbes*, *SilverKris* (Singapore Airlines in-flight magazine), over a dozen Lonely Planet titles including *Los Angeles & Southern California*, and at www.andrewbender.com. When not on the road he can be seen biking the beach in Santa Monica, discovering the next greatest ethnic joint and scheming over ways to spoil his nieces and nephews.

ALISON BING

Destination California, History, Culture, California Flavor, San Francisco

Author, arts commentator and adventurous eater Alison Bing was adopted by California 16 years ago. By now she has done everything you're supposed to do here and a few things you're definitely not, including talking up LA bands in San Francisco bars and falling in love on the 7 Haight bus. Alison holds a graduate degree in international diplomacy, which she regularly undermines with opinionated commentary in magazines, newspapers, on public radio and in more than 20 books.

NATE CAVALIERI

Gold Country, Central Valley

Nate Cavalieri fell hard for Sacramento (what some call the *other* California) the first summer he lived there: it was hotter than hell, the AM station played plenty of Merle Haggard and on a clear day the cool, jagged caps of the Sierras broke up the eastern horizon to suggest the perfect escape plan. His previous titles with Lonely Planet include *Chicago*, *Puerto Rico* and *Volunteer: A Traveler's Guide to Making a Difference Around the World*. He writes about music and travel and lives with his partner and proofreader, Florence.

BETH KOHN

San Francisco Bay Area, Sierra Nevada

A lucky long-time resident of San Francisco, Beth lives to play outside or splash in big puddles of water. For this guide she biked the Bay Area and Lake Tahoe byways, crossed off her first California 14er, dodged pesky statewide wildfires and selflessly soaked in hot springs – for research purposes, of course. Beth is an author of Lonely Planet's *Yosemite, Sequoia & Kings Canyon National Parks* and *USA* guides; you can see more of her work at www.bethkohn.com.

JOHN A VLAHIDES

San Francisco, Wine Country

John Vlahides lives in San Francisco. He's a former luxury-hotel concierge and member of the prestigious Les Clefs d'Or, the international union of the world's elite concierges. He is cofounder of the travel site 71miles.com, and appears regularly on television and radio; watch some of his travel videos on lonelyplanet.tv. John spends his free time singing with the San Francisco Symphony, sunning on the beach beneath the Golden Gate Bridge, skiing the Sierra Nevada and touring California on his motorcycle.

CONTRIBUTING AUTHORS

Dr David Goldberg MD wrote the Health chapter. David completed his training in internal medicine and infectious diseases at Columbia-Presbyterian Medical Center in New York City, where he has also served as voluntary faculty. At present he is an infectious-diseases specialist in Scarsdale, New York State, and the editor-in-chief of the website MDTravelHealth.com.

David Lukas wrote the Environment chapter. A professional naturalist who lives on the edge of Yosemite National Park, David leads natural-history tours around the state and writes about the environment for a wide variety of publications, including over 20 Lonely Planet guides.

Behind the Scenes

THIS BOOK

This 5th edition of California was researched and written by Sara Benson (coordinator), Alexis Averbuck, Amy C Balfour, Andrew Bender, Alison Bing, Nate Cavalieri, Beth Kohn and John A Vlahides. David Lukas wrote the Environment chapter. The Health chapter was adapted from text by Dr David Goldberg. The previous three editions of this book were coordinated and cowritten by Andrea Schulte-Peevers. This guidebook was commissioned in Lonely Planet's Oakland office, and produced by the following:

Commissioning Editor Suki Gear
Coordinating Editor Penelope Goodes
Coordinating Cartographer Sam Sayer
Coordinating Layout Designer David Kemp
Managing Editor Imogen Bannister
Managing Cartographers Shahara Ahmed, Alison Lyall
Managing Layout Designer Celia Wood
Assisting Editors Janet Austin, Shawn Low, Sally O'Brien, Kristin Odijk, Charlotte Orr, Stephanie Pearson, Martine Power
Assisting Cartographers Fatima Basic, Barbara Benson, Andras Bogdanovits, Mick Garrett, Andy Rojas
Cover Designer Pepi Bluck
Project Manager Glenn van der Knijff

Thanks to Jessica Boland, Catherine Craddock, Csanad Csutoros, Rebecca Davey, Owen Eszeki, Brice Gosnell, Naomi Jennings, Michelle Lewis, Wayne Murphy, Raphael Richards, Gerard Walker

THANKS

SARA BENSON

Researching and writing this book would never have been this much fun without my husband, Mike Connolly, who generously acted as my research assistant, photographer, wildlife guide, poker coach and co-conspirator in all kinds of mischief. Many thanks to all of the Californians and Nevadans who helped along my research in the Golden and Silver States, especially those who kindly agreed to be interviewed for this book. Thanks to Suki Gear for trusting me with this ginormous gig and to Alison Lyall, my hero of all things cartographic.

ALEXIS AVERBUCK

Many thanks to Patti and David Averbuck, Aggie Brenneman and Roger Edwards, Douglas Fir and Susan Butler, Rachel Averbuck, Jennifer Hale, Oren Averbuck and Lemont Hale, and Jacob, Lea, Redmond and Eva Averbuck for their generous hospitality and insider knowledge of northern California. Thanks also to Reuben Weinzveg, Padi

THE LONELY PLANET STORY

Fresh from an epic journey across Europe, Asia and Australia in 1972, Tony and Maureen Wheeler sat at their kitchen table stapling together notes. The first Lonely Planet guidebook, *Across Asia on the Cheap,* was born.

Travelers snapped up the guides. Inspired by their success, the Wheelers began publishing books to Southeast Asia, India and beyond. Demand was prodigious, and the Wheelers expanded the business rapidly to keep up. Over the years, Lonely Planet extended its coverage to every country and into the virtual world via lonelyplanet.com and the Thorn Tree message board.

As Lonely Planet became a globally loved brand, Tony and Maureen received several offers for the company. But it wasn't until 2007 that they found a partner whom they trusted to remain true to the company's principles of traveling widely, treading lightly and giving sustainably. In October of that year, BBC Worldwide acquired a 75% share in the company, pledging to uphold Lonely Planet's commitment to independent travel, trustworthy advice and editorial independence.

Today, Lonely Planet has offices in Melbourne, London and Oakland, with over 500 staff members and 300 authors. Tony and Maureen are still actively involved with Lonely Planet. They're traveling more often than ever, and they're devoting their spare time to charitable projects. And the company is still driven by the philosophy of *Across Asia on the Cheap*: 'All you've got to do is decide to go and the hardest part is over. So go!'

Selwyn, Kent Rosenblum, Frank Cardozo, Kristin 'Kale' Bowling and Ned and Maxine Averbuck for their excellent tips. Thanks also to Suki Gear and Sam Benson for their indispensable editorial guidance.

AMY C BALFOUR

Thank you John and Cindy for your Gaslamp Quarter hospitality and to the gang at Klinedinst for up-to-the-minute recs on all things San Diego. Thanks also to Katie, Tyler, Paul and Brian for San Diego guidance, Cheryl for tips on Laguna, and my friends in Tijuana – you know who you are. Thank you Suki for entrusting me with these chapters and your helpful advice, Sam for answering all my questions with patience, and Alison and the cartography gang for making my maps look good!

ANDREW BENDER

Carol Martinez, Robin McClain and Bill Karz at LA Inc, Dan McKernan in Big Bear, Karen and Wayne Olmsted for their hospitality, Suki Gear for the opportunity and smart judgment, and Sam Benson for her consistent good cheer and advice.

ALISON BING

All Californians are entitled to a personal guru, but Alison has two to thank: editor Suki Gear and coordinating author Sam Benson, whose guidance, insight and support make any tricky mental backbend possible. Many thanks and shameless California bear hugs to John Vlahides and Robert Landon for setting giddily high writing standards for this book, to fearless leaders Brice Gosnell and Heather Dickson at Lonely Planet, to the Sanchez Writers' Grotto for steady inspiration, and above all to Marco Flavio Marinucci, whose powerful kindness and bracing espresso make everything possible.

NATE CAVALIERI

Many thanks to Florence, Suki and Sam, without whom this project wouldn't have been nearly as pleasant, and for Sophia, Abram, Darrin and Emily, the world's greatest distractions.

BETH KOHN

A big thanks to Suki Gear for signing me up! As always, Sam Benson is a superstar, helping in more ways than I could ever contemplate. Owen Eszeki and Alison Lyall were fabulous with the mapping, and Felix Thomson gets props for the lowdown on Oaktown. Hugs go to the very patient Jenny G, and as always, my heart goes to Claude Moller, partner in crime.

JOHN A VLAHIDES

Lonely Planet's in-house staffers never get proper credit for all they do. I'm particularly grateful to Suki Gear for her kindness and help; Alison Lyall and Melanie Dankel for their generosity of spirit; Brice Gosnell for demanding I open my big mouth; and Owen Eszeki, Sam Sayer and Penelope Goodes for their fine mapping and editing. Coordinating author Sam Benson is the best I've ever worked with. On the road, Doug White gave me the dirt on Napa, and Sherry Huss exposed Sonoma's underbelly. But I'm most grateful to Gerad Kite for his constant love and support. I dedicate this work to him.

OUR READERS

Many thanks to the travelers who used the last edition and wrote to us with helpful hints, useful advice and interesting anecdotes:

Ida Aarving, Taamila Ahmadov, Emma Barham, Elise Baril, Jeffrey Bell, Marie-Louise Bernal, Mette & Johnathon Stevnhoved Bernsen, Michael Blain, Jenny Bourke, Elizabeth Boyarsky, R Brillantes, Mike Chellman, Marissa Comstock, Racoon Cottage, Jeremy Cutler, Alan Dixon, Judy Dumm, Jan Dumont, Paul Edwards, Pat Eyre, Matthew Fennessy, Anna Fong, Brett Gibbs, Eva Goppoldova, Laura Guidali, Robert Haley, Jahsun Handy, David & Mairin Herman,

SEND US YOUR FEEDBACK

We love to hear from travelers – your comments keep us on our toes and help make our books better. Our well-traveled team reads every word on what you loved or loathed about this book. Although we cannot reply individually to postal submissions, we always guarantee that your feedback goes straight to the appropriate authors, in time for the next edition. Each person who sends us information is thanked in the next edition – and the most useful submissions are rewarded with a free book.

To send us your updates – and find out about Lonely Planet events, newsletters and travel news – visit our award-winning website: **lonelyplanet.com/contact**.

Note: we may edit, reproduce and incorporate your comments in Lonely Planet products such as guidebooks, websites and digital products, so let us know if you don't want your comments reproduced or your name acknowledged. For a copy of our privacy policy visit lonelyplanet.com/privacy.

Trevor Humphreys, Neil Jervis, Andreas Johns, Seghers Jozef, Selma Karcher-Pruess, Gareth Key, Paul Kotz, Lior Levy, Diderik Lund, Ruben Maase, David Maccolue, Gilfredo Marengo, Eugene Mcauley, Joseph Mckenzie, Guy Melvin III, Heather Monell, Mark Morgan, Heinz Mostosi, Laurence Mourou, Christine Northup, Claudia Nowak, Alex Oestreicher, Perry Ohlsson, Gabriele De Paolis, James Passmore, Martin Plant, A N Richmond, Johan Rudqvist, Leila Seppa, Iraz Oyku Soyalp, Julie-Anne Tallon, Joanne Thomson, Nancy Todd, Corinne Turton, Robin Vermoesen, Melanie Visser, Anna Warren, Jakub Welnic, Deb Wyatt, Manuele Zunelli, Koos & Pauline Zwaan

ACKNOWLEDGMENTS

Many thanks to the following for the use of their content:

Globe on title page and map data contained within Geography of California map © Mountain High Maps 1993 Digital Wisdom, Inc.

Cannery Row by John Steinbeck © John Steinbeck, 1945. © renewed Elaine Steinbeck, John Steinbeck IV and Thom Steinbeck, 1973.

Internal photographs: p8 (#2) Chad Ehlers/Photolibrary. All other photographs by Lonely Planet Images, and by Jerry Alexander p6, p13 (#6); John Borthwick p9 (#5); Claver Carroll p13 (#4); Richard Cummins p8 (#3), p14 (#3), p15 (#2); John Elk III p10 (#1), p11 (#5); Lee Foster p7 (#1), p10 (#3), p13 (#2), p15 (#8); Christer Fredriksson p7 (#4); Rick Gerharter p14 (#1); Nicholas Pavloff p16 (#3); Carol Polich p11 (#2); Cheyenne L Rouse p11 (#4); Stephen Saks p9 (#1), p16 (#1, #2); Wes Walker p12 (#3); Brent Winebrenner p12 (#1); Lawrence Worcester p7 (#2).

BEHIND THE SCENES

Index

000 Map pages
000 Photograph pages

000 Map pages
000 Photograph pages

000 Map pages
000 Photograph pages

INDEX

000 Map pages
000 Photograph pages

M

000 Map pages
000 Photograph pages

000 Map pages
000 Photograph pages

GreenDex

It seems like everyone's going 'green' in California these days, but how can you know which businesses are actually ecofriendly and which are simply jumping on the bandwagon?

The following attractions, activities, tour operators, nonprofit centers, educational opportunities, restaurants, shops, lodgings, transportation, and even coffeehouses, brewpubs and vineyards, have been selected by our authors because they demonstrate an active sustainable-tourism policy. Some are involved in conservation or environmental education, others engage with biodynamic agriculture, and many are locally owned and operated, thereby maintaining and preserving local identity, arts and culture.

We want to keep developing our sustainable-tourism content. If you think we've omitted somewhere that should be listed here, or if you disagree with our choices, email us at talk2us@lonelyplanet.com.au and set us straight for next time. For more information about sustainable tourism and Lonely Planet, see www.lonelyplanet.com/responsibletravel.